A PRACTICAL APPROACH TO
CIVIL PROCEDURE

A PRACTICAL APPROACH TO
CIVIL PROCEDURE

TWENTY FIRST EDITION

Professor Stuart Sime, Barrister

BPTC Course Director, The City Law School,
City, University of London

OXFORD
UNIVERSITY PRESS

OXFORD
UNIVERSITY PRESS

Great Clarendon Street, Oxford, OX2 6DP,
United Kingdom

Oxford University Press is a department of the University of Oxford.
It furthers the University's objective of excellence in research, scholarship,
and education by publishing worldwide. Oxford is a registered trade mark of
Oxford University Press in the UK and in certain other countries

Eighteenth edition 2015
Nineteenth edition 2016
Twentieth edition 2017

Impression: 1

Public sector information reproduced under Open Government Licence v3.0
(http://www.nationalarchives.gov.uk/doc/open-government-licence/open-government-licence.htm)

Published in the United States of America by Oxford University Press
198 Madison Avenue, New York, NY 10016, United States of America

British Library Cataloguing in Publication Data
Data available

ISBN 978-0-19-882310-0

Printed in Great Britain by
Bell & Bain Ltd., Glasgow

MH185340961741970

OUTLINE CONTENTS

Preface   xxiii

Abbreviations   xxv

Table of Cases   xxvii

Table of Primary Legislation   liv

Table of Secondary Legislation   lx

Table of Protocols and Guidance   lxxviii

Table of European Legislation   lxxxi

Table of International Treaties and Conventions   lxxxii

1	Introduction	1
2	Funding Litigation	10
3	The Civil Courts	22
4	Overriding Objective and Human Rights	32
5	Pre-Action Protocols	48
6	Issuing and Serving	59
7	Renewal of Process	84
8	Part 8 Claims and Petitions	89
9	Personal Injury Claims under £25,000	99
10	Alternative Dispute Resolution	111
11	Service Outside the Jurisdiction	118
12	Responding to a Claim	132
13	Default Judgment	137
14	Statements of Case	147
15	Track Allocation and Case Management	162
16	Costs Management	183
17	Costs Capping and Protection	191
18	Requests for Further Information	196
19	Parties and Joinder	203
20	Additional Claims under Part 20	221
21	Limitation	231
22	Amendment	249
23	Interim Applications	261
24	Summary Judgment	277
25	Interim Payments	291
26	Security for Costs	297
27	Small Claims Track	306
28	Fast Track	310
29	Multi-Track	317
30	Striking Out, Discontinuance, and Stays	326

31 Disclosure   338

32 Witness Statements, Affidavits, and Depositions   364

33 Hearsay   372

34 Admissions and Documentary Evidence   379

35 Experts   385

36 Offers to Settle   399

37 Sanctions   414

38 Listing and Pre-Trial Reviews   424

39 Trial   429

40 References to the Court of Justice of the European Union   443

41 Judgments and Orders   448

42 Interim Injunctions   458

43 Freezing Injunctions   481

44 Search Orders   493

45 *Norwich Pharmacal* and Related Disclosure Orders   501

46 Costs   511

47 Qualified One-Way Costs Shifting   529

48 Enforcement   534

49 Judicial Review   548

50 Appeals   559

    APPENDIX 1   Additional Chapter   575

Index   577

Access the Online Resource Centre for this title at: www.oxfordtextbooks.co.uk/orc/apacivil21e/.

DETAILED CONTENTS

Preface   xxiii

Abbreviations   xxv

Table of Cases   xxvii

Table of Primary Legislation   liv

Table of Secondary Legislation   lx

Table of Protocols and Guidance   lxxviii

Table of European Legislation   lxxxi

Table of International Treaties and Conventions   lxxxii

---

1 INTRODUCTION   1

  A THE LEGAL PROFESSION   2

  B LAWYERS' DUTIES   2

  C INITIAL INSTRUCTIONS   3

  D CONFIDENTIALITY AND CONFLICT OF INTEREST   5

  E PRE-ACTION CORRESPONDENCE   5

  F MAIN STAGES IN COURT PROCEEDINGS   6

---

2 FUNDING LITIGATION   10

  A DUTY TO ADVISE CLIENTS ON FUNDING   10

  B TRADITIONAL RETAINER   11

  C LEGAL EXPENSES INSURANCE   13

  D AFTER THE EVENT INSURANCE   13

  E CHAMPERTY, THE INDEMNITY PRINCIPLE, AND JACKSON   14

  F CONDITIONAL FEE AGREEMENT   15

  G DAMAGES-BASED AGREEMENT   16

  H THIRD PARTY FUNDING   16

  I LEGAL AID   17

  J IRRECOVERABILITY OF COSTS OF SETTING UP FUNDING   20

    Key points summary   20

---

3 THE CIVIL COURTS   22

  A COURT COMPOSITION AND ADMINISTRATION   22

  B JURISDICTION   25

  C HIGH COURT DIVISIONS   28

D   SPECIALIST COURTS   29
    Key points summary   31

4 OVERRIDING OBJECTIVE AND HUMAN RIGHTS   32

A   SOURCES OF PROCEDURAL LAW   32
B   THE OVERRIDING OBJECTIVE   34
C   ACTIVE CASE MANAGEMENT   35
D   INTERPRETING THE CIVIL PROCEDURE RULES   36
E   APPLICATION OF THE OVERRIDING OBJECTIVE   38
F   HUMAN RIGHTS   40
G   PROCEDURAL ASPECTS ON RAISING HUMAN RIGHTS POINTS   45
    Key points summary   47

5 PRE-ACTION PROTOCOLS   48

A   PRE-ACTION PROTOCOLS   48
B   CASES NOT COVERED BY PRE-ACTION PROTOCOLS   49
C   PROFESSIONAL NEGLIGENCE PRE-ACTION PROTOCOL   49
D   PERSONAL INJURY PROTOCOL   52
E   INSTRUCTION OF EXPERTS   53
F   LIMITATION DIFFICULTIES   55
G   SANCTIONS FOR NON-COMPLIANCE   55
H   ROAD TRAFFIC ACT 1988   56
I   MOTOR INSURERS' BUREAU   56
J   PRE-ACTION PART 36 OFFERS   57
    Key points summary   58

6 ISSUING AND SERVING   59

A   CLAIM FORM   59
B   JURISDICTIONAL ENDORSEMENTS   62
C   PARTICULARS OF CLAIM   62
D   SPECIALIST CLAIMS   62
E   ISSUING A CLAIM FORM   65
F   SERVICE   66
G   SERVICE OF THE CLAIM FORM   67
H   DEEMED DATE OF SERVICE OF THE CLAIM FORM   78
I   SERVICE OF DOCUMENTS OTHER THAN A CLAIM FORM   79
J   DEEMED DATE OF SERVICE (NON-CLAIM FORM DOCUMENTS)   79

K   CERTIFICATE OF SERVICE   80

L   IRREGULAR SERVICE   80

M   FILING   82

    Key points summary   83

---

7   RENEWAL OF PROCESS   84

A   POWER TO RENEW   84

B   CLAIMS IN RESPECT OF CARGO   87

C   MULTIPLE DEFENDANTS   87

D   EFFECT OF STAY   87

E   PROCEDURE ON SEEKING AN EXTENSION   87

F   CHALLENGING AN ORDER GRANTING AN EXTENSION   88

---

8   PART 8 CLAIMS AND PETITIONS   89

A   PART 8 CLAIMS   89

B   PETITIONS   91

C   WINDING-UP PETITIONS   91

---

9   PERSONAL INJURY CLAIMS UNDER £25,000   99

A   CASES COVERED BY THE RTA AND EL/PL PROTOCOLS   100

B   RTA PROTOCOL   100

C   STAGE 1: CLAIM NOTIFICATION   101

D   STAGE 2: MEDICAL EVIDENCE AND NEGOTIATION   104

E   STAGE 3: PART 8 CLAIM TO DETERMINE QUANTUM   106

F   CHILD SETTLEMENT APPLICATIONS   108

G   LIMITATION   109

H   FIXED COSTS UNDER THE RTA AND EL/PL PROTOCOLS   109

I   CASES WHERE PARTIES CAN STOP FOLLOWING THE RTA OR EL/PL PROTOCOLS   109

    Key points summary   110

---

10 ALTERNATIVE DISPUTE RESOLUTION   111

A   ADR PROCESSES   111

B   ADR OR COURT PROCEEDINGS   112

C   COST OF ADR   114

D   REFERENCE TO ADR   114

E   COURT INVOLVEMENT IN ADR   115

    Key points summary   117

11 SERVICE OUTSIDE THE JURISDICTION 118

  A SERVICE ON A FOREIGN DEFENDANT WITHIN THE JURISDICTION 119

  B SUBMISSION TO THE JURISDICTION 119

  C CASES OUTSIDE THE GENERAL RULES 120

  D RECAST JUDGMENTS REGULATION 121

  E ASSUMED JURISDICTION 124

  F SERVICE ABROAD 127

  G PREVENTING CONFLICTS IN JURISDICTION 128

  H INTERIM RELIEF IN SUPPORT OF FOREIGN PROCEEDINGS 130

  I JUDGMENT IN DEFAULT 131

    Key points summary 131

12 RESPONDING TO A CLAIM 132

  A TIME FOR RESPONDING 132

  B ADMISSIONS 132

  C DEFENCES 133

  D ACKNOWLEDGMENT OF SERVICE 133

  E AGREED EXTENSIONS 134

  F DISPUTING SERVICE OR THE COURT'S JURISDICTION 134

  G TRANSFER 135

  H SPECIALIST CLAIMS 136

    Key points summary 136

13 DEFAULT JUDGMENT 137

  A TIME WHEN DEFAULT JUDGMENT MAY BE ENTERED 137

  B EXCLUDED CASES 138

  C ENTERING DEFAULT JUDGMENT 139

  D FINAL JUDGMENT AND JUDGMENT FOR AN AMOUNT TO BE DECIDED 141

  E DECIDING THE AMOUNT OF DAMAGES: DISPOSAL HEARINGS 142

  F SETTING ASIDE DEFAULT JUDGMENTS 143

  G STAY OF UNDEFENDED CASES 146

    Key points summary 146

14 STATEMENTS OF CASE 147

  A FORM OF STATEMENTS OF CASE 148

  B PARTICULARS OF CLAIM 151

C   DEFENCE   154

D   COUNTERCLAIMS AND SET-OFFS   157

E   REPLY AND DEFENCE TO COUNTERCLAIM   159

F   SUBSEQUENT STATEMENTS OF CASE   159

G   DISPENSING WITH STATEMENTS OF CASE   159

H   SCOTT SCHEDULES   160

I   INTERRELATION WITH CASE MANAGEMENT   160

J   USE OF STATEMENTS OF CASE AT TRIAL   161

15 TRACK ALLOCATION AND CASE MANAGEMENT   162

A   PROCEDURAL JUDGES   163

B   DOCKETING   163

C   PROVISIONAL TRACK ALLOCATION   164

D   FILING DIRECTIONS QUESTIONNAIRES   164

E   TRACK ALLOCATION   173

F   ALLOCATION RULES   174

G   NOTICE OF ALLOCATION   176

H   ALLOCATION DIRECTIONS   176

I   ADR AND STAYS TO ALLOW FOR SETTLEMENT   177

J   TRANSFER TO APPROPRIATE COURT   178

K   TRIAL IN THE ROYAL COURTS OF JUSTICE OR ROLLS BUILDING   178

L   CHANGING TRACKS   178

M   SUBSEQUENT CASE MANAGEMENT   179

N   PRE-TRIAL CHECKLISTS   179

O   SHORTER TRIALS AND FLEXIBLE TRIALS SCHEMES   181

    Key points summary   182

16 COSTS MANAGEMENT   183

A   ELEMENTS OF COSTS MANAGEMENT   184

B   CASES GOVERNED BY COSTS MANAGEMENT   184

C   COSTS BUDGETS   185

D   COSTS MANAGEMENT ORDERS   187

E   COSTS BUDGETS AND CASE MANAGEMENT   188

F   JUDICIAL CONTROL OF COSTS BUDGETS   189

G   IMPACT ON COSTS ORDERS   189

    Key points summary   190

17 COSTS CAPPING AND PROTECTION   191

A   COSTS CAPPING ORDERS   191

B   *BEDDOE* ORDERS   192

C   PROTECTIVE COSTS ORDERS   193

D   JUDICIAL REVIEW COSTS CAPPING   194

E   AARHUS CONVENTION CASES   194

F   COSTS LIMITATION ORDERS   195

    Key points summary   195

18 REQUESTS FOR FURTHER INFORMATION   196

A   THE REQUEST FOR FURTHER INFORMATION   197

B   THE RESPONSE   198

C   OBJECTING TO REQUESTS   200

D   ORDERS FOR RESPONSES   200

E   PRINCIPLES   201

F   COLLATERAL USE   202

19 PARTIES AND JOINDER   203

A   DESCRIPTION OF PARTIES   203

B   PARTICULAR CLASSES OF PARTY   203

C   LITIGANTS IN PERSON   213

D   VEXATIOUS LITIGANTS   214

E   JOINDER   214

F   REPRESENTATIVE PROCEEDINGS   215

G   REPRESENTATION OF UNASCERTAINED PERSONS   216

H   INTERVENTION   216

I   CONSOLIDATION   217

J   STAKEHOLDER CLAIMS   217

K   ASSIGNMENT   218

L   GROUP LITIGATION   219

    Key points summary   220

20 ADDITIONAL CLAIMS UNDER PART 20   221

A   NATURE OF ADDITIONAL CLAIMS   221

B   RELATED PROCEDURES   221

C   SCOPE OF PART 20   222

D   STATEMENTS OF CASE IN ADDITIONAL CLAIMS   226

E   CONTRIBUTION NOTICES   228

F   PROCEDURE   228

G   RELATION TO THE MAIN CLAIM   230

   Key points summary   230

21 LIMITATION   231

A   LIMITATION PERIODS   231

B   ACCRUAL OF CAUSE OF ACTION   235

C   CALCULATING THE LIMITATION PERIOD   241

D   DISCRETION   244

E   EQUITABLE REMEDIES, LACHES, AND ACQUIESCENCE   247

   Key points summary   248

22 AMENDMENT   249

A   AMENDMENT BY CONSENT   249

B   AMENDMENT WITHOUT PERMISSION   249

C   PRINCIPLES GOVERNING PERMISSION TO AMEND   250

D   AMENDMENT AFTER THE EXPIRY OF THE LIMITATION PERIOD   254

E   PROCEDURE ON AMENDING   259

   Key points summary   260

23 INTERIM APPLICATIONS   261

A   JURISDICTIONAL RULES   262

B   TIME TO APPLY   262

C   PRE-ACTION INTERIM REMEDIES   263

D   OBLIGATION TO APPLY EARLY   263

E   APPLICATIONS WITHOUT NOTICE   264

F   APPLICATIONS WITH NOTICE   267

G   INTERIM HEARINGS   274

H   SUMMARY DETERMINATION OF INTERIM COSTS   276

I   VARYING OR REVOKING INTERIM ORDERS   276

   Key points summary   276

24 SUMMARY JUDGMENT   277

A   TIME FOR APPLYING FOR SUMMARY JUDGMENT   277

B   DEFENDANT'S APPLICATION: NO DEFAULT JUDGMENT   278

C EXCLUDED PROCEEDINGS   278

D PROCEDURE   279

E ORDERS AVAILABLE   279

F AMENDMENT AT HEARING   289

G SOME OTHER COMPELLING REASON FOR A TRIAL   289

H DIRECTIONS ON SUMMARY JUDGMENT HEARING   290

I SPECIFIC PERFORMANCE, RESCISSION, AND FORFEITURE IN PROPERTY CASES 290

   Key points summary   290

25 INTERIM PAYMENTS   291

A PROCEDURE   291

B GROUNDS   292

C AMOUNT TO BE ORDERED   294

D FURTHER APPLICATIONS   295

E NON-DISCLOSURE   295

F ADJUSTMENT   296

   Key points summary   296

26 SECURITY FOR COSTS   297

A PROCEDURE   297

B THE RESPONDENT   299

C CONDITIONS FOR GRANTING SECURITY FOR COSTS   299

D DISCRETION TO ORDER SECURITY FOR COSTS   302

E AMOUNT   304

F ORDER   305

G SUCCESS BY THE CLAIMANT   305

   Key points summary   305

27 SMALL CLAIMS TRACK   306

A PROVISIONS OF THE CPR THAT DO NOT APPLY   306

B STANDARD DIRECTIONS   307

C SPECIAL DIRECTIONS   307

D DETERMINATION WITHOUT A HEARING   308

E FINAL HEARINGS   308

F COSTS   308

G REHEARINGS   309

28 FAST TRACK — 310

A	ALLOCATION DIRECTIONS	310
B	LISTING DIRECTIONS	313
C	STANDARD FAST TRACK TIMETABLE	313
D	AGREED DIRECTIONS	314
E	VARYING THE DIRECTIONS TIMETABLE	314
F	LISTING FOR TRIAL	314
G	FAST TRACK TRIALS	315
H	COSTS IN FAST TRACK CASES	316
	Key points summary	316

29 MULTI-TRACK — 317

A	AGREED DIRECTIONS	317
B	CASE MANAGEMENT CONFERENCES	319
C	FIXING THE DATE FOR TRIAL	322
D	PRE-TRIAL CHECKLISTS	322
E	LISTING HEARINGS	323
F	PRE-TRIAL REVIEW	323
G	DIRECTIONS GIVEN AT OTHER HEARINGS	324
H	VARIATION OF CASE MANAGEMENT TIMETABLE	325
	Key points summary	325

30 STRIKING OUT, DISCONTINUANCE, AND STAYS — 326

A	THE MAIN RULE	327
B	PROCEDURE ON APPLICATIONS MADE BY PARTIES	327
C	REFERENCES BY COURT OFFICERS	328
D	GENERAL TEST	328
E	NO REASONABLE GROUNDS FOR BRINGING OR DEFENDING THE CLAIM	329
F	ABUSE OF PROCESS	330
G	OBSTRUCTING THE JUST DISPOSAL OF THE PROCEEDINGS	333
H	POWERS AFTER A STRIKING-OUT ORDER IS MADE	334
I	DISCONTINUANCE	334
J	STAYS	336
	Key points summary	337

31 DISCLOSURE   338

  A LAWYERS' RESPONSIBILITIES   341

  B CLIENTS' RESPONSIBILITIES   342

  C STAGE WHEN DISCLOSURE TAKES PLACE   342

  D DISCLOSURE ORDERS   342

  E STANDARD DISCLOSURE   343

  F MENU OPTION DISCLOSURE   345

  G DUTY TO SEARCH   348

  H LIST OF DOCUMENTS   349

  I PRIVILEGE   350

  J INSPECTION   359

  K ORDERS IN SUPPORT OF DISCLOSURE   360

  L DOCUMENTS REFERRED TO IN STATEMENTS OF CASE, ETC.   361

  M ADMISSION OF AUTHENTICITY   362

  N COLLATERAL USE   362

      Key points summary   363

32 WITNESS STATEMENTS, AFFIDAVITS, AND DEPOSITIONS   364

  A TYPES OF WRITTEN EVIDENCE   364

  B WITNESS STATEMENTS   365

  C WITNESS SUMMARIES   369

  D AFFIDAVITS AND AFFIRMATIONS   370

  E DEPOSITIONS   371

33 HEARSAY   372

  A THE HEARSAY RULE   372

  B REAL EVIDENCE   373

  C ADMISSIBILITY OF HEARSAY EVIDENCE   373

  D NOTICE PROCEDURE   375

  E TRIAL   377

      Key points summary   378

34 ADMISSIONS AND DOCUMENTARY EVIDENCE   379

  A NATURE OF ADMISSIONS   379

  B PRE-ACTION ADMISSIONS OF LIABILITY   380

  C PERMISSION TO WITHDRAW AN ADMISSION   380

D   NOTICE TO ADMIT FACTS   381

E   PROVING DOCUMENTS   383

---

35 EXPERTS   385

A   ADMISSIBILITY OF EXPERT EVIDENCE   385

B   CONTROL OF EVIDENCE   388

C   PRIVILEGED NATURE OF EXPERTS' REPORTS   388

D   DISCLOSURE OF EXPERTS' REPORTS   389

E   WRITTEN QUESTIONS TO EXPERTS   393

F   WITHOUT PREJUDICE DISCUSSION   394

G   EXAMINATIONS BY EXPERTS   394

H   TRIAL   396

I   EXPERTS' IMMUNITY FROM SUIT   398

J   USE OF EXPERTS' REPORTS AFTER TRIAL   398

    Key points summary   398

---

36 OFFERS TO SETTLE   399

A   INTRODUCTION   399

B   *CALDERBANK* OFFERS   400

C   OFFERS TO SETTLE   400

D   MAKING A PART 36 OFFER   407

E   ACCEPTANCE OF A PART 36 OFFER   407

F   REJECTIONS, COUNTER-OFFERS, AND SUBSEQUENT OFFERS   409

G   WITHDRAWAL AND CHANGE OF PART 36 OFFERS   409

H   FAILING TO OBTAIN JUDGMENT MORE ADVANTAGEOUS THAN
    A PART 36 OFFER   410

I   ADVISING ON PART 36 OFFERS   412

J   NON-DISCLOSURE TO JUDGE   413

K   PART 36 OFFERS IN APPEALS   413

    Key points summary   413

---

37 SANCTIONS   414

A   NON-COMPLIANCE WITH PRE-ACTION PROTOCOLS   414

B   NON-COMPLIANCE WITH THE CPR   414

C   NON-COMPLIANCE WITH DIRECTIONS   415

D   PRESERVATION OF TRIAL DATE   416

E	APPLICATION FOR SANCTIONS	416
F	UNLESS ORDERS	418
G	NON-COMPLIANCE WITH AN UNLESS ORDER	418
H	EXTENDING TIME AND CORRECTING ERRORS	419
I	RELIEF FROM SANCTIONS AND SETTING ASIDE	420
J	IMPLIED SANCTIONS DOCTRINE	422
	Key points summary	423

38	**LISTING AND PRE-TRIAL REVIEWS**	**424**
A	LISTING FOR TRIAL	424
B	PRE-TRIAL REVIEWS	428
C	LISTING IN THE ROYAL COURTS OF JUSTICE	428
D	ADJOURNMENTS	428

39	**TRIAL**	**429**
A	WITNESSES	429
B	TRIAL DOCUMENTATION	432
C	TRIAL LOCATION	433
D	ALLOCATION TO JUDICIARY	434
E	IMPARTIALITY OF JUDGE	434
F	PUBLIC OR PRIVATE HEARING	435
G	RIGHTS OF AUDIENCE AND THE RIGHT TO CONDUCT LITIGATION	436
H	MCKENZIE FRIENDS	436
I	CONDUCT OF THE TRIAL	437
J	PRELIMINARY ISSUES	440
K	TRIAL BY JURY	441
L	NON-ATTENDANCE AT TRIAL	442
	Key points summary	442

40	**REFERENCES TO THE COURT OF JUSTICE OF THE EUROPEAN UNION**	**443**
A	QUESTIONS WHICH MAY BE REFERRED	443
B	MANDATORY REFERENCES	443
C	DISCRETIONARY REFERENCES	444
D	PROCEDURE IN ENGLAND	446
E	PROCEDURE IN THE COURT OF JUSTICE OF THE EUROPEAN UNION	447
F	COSTS	447

41 JUDGMENTS AND ORDERS 448

A SETTLEMENTS 448

B ORDERS MADE AT HEARINGS 449

C FORM OF JUDGMENTS AND ORDERS 450

D GENERAL RULES RELATING TO DRAWING UP ORDERS AND JUDGMENTS 455

E REGISTER OF JUDGMENTS 457

Key points summary 457

42 INTERIM INJUNCTIONS 458

A JUDGES ABLE TO GRANT INJUNCTIONS 459

B PRE-ACTION APPLICATIONS FOR INTERIM INJUNCTIONS 459

C APPLICATIONS DURING PROCEEDINGS 461

D PRINCIPLES 462

E DEFENCES 474

F THE ORDER 475

G UNDERTAKINGS 477

H INQUIRY AS TO DAMAGES 478

I DISCHARGE 479

J BREACH 479

K EFFECT OF NOT APPLYING FOR INTERIM RELIEF 480

Key points summary 480

43 FREEZING INJUNCTIONS 481

A PROCEDURE 481

B PRINCIPLES 482

C THE ORDER 486

D EFFECT OF THE ORDER 490

E VARIATION OR DISCHARGE OF A FREEZING INJUNCTION 490

F FREEZING INJUNCTIONS AFTER JUDGMENT 491

G PROPRIETARY CLAIMS 492

H WRIT *NE EXEAT REGNO* 492

Key points summary 492

44 SEARCH ORDERS 493

A PROCEDURE 493

B PRINCIPLES 494

C REAL RISK OF DESTRUCTION   495

D FORM OF THE ORDER   496

E PRACTICE ON EXECUTION OF SEARCH ORDERS   496

F PRIVILEGE   498

G DISCHARGE AND VARIATION OF SEARCH ORDERS   499

H AFTER EXECUTION   499

I COLLATERAL USE   500

   Key points summary   500

45 *NORWICH PHARMACAL* AND RELATED DISCLOSURE ORDERS   501

A *NORWICH PHARMACAL* ORDERS   501

B MERE WITNESS RULE   504

C *BANKERS TRUST* ORDERS   504

D DISCLOSURE BEFORE PROCEEDINGS START   505

E DISCLOSURE BY NON-PARTIES   507

F DISCLOSURE OF MEDIATION EVIDENCE   508

G INSPECTION OF PROPERTY DURING PROCEEDINGS   508

H INTERIM DELIVERY-UP OF GOODS   509

   Key points summary   510

46 COSTS   511

A COSTS ORDERS: GENERAL PRINCIPLES   512

B COSTS FOLLOW THE EVENT   514

C RANGE OF POSSIBLE COSTS ORDERS   517

D INTERIM COSTS ORDERS   518

E INFORMING THE CLIENT   520

F INDEMNITY PRINCIPLE   520

G BASIS OF QUANTIFICATION   521

H PROPORTIONALITY   521

I SUMMARY ASSESSMENT   522

J DETAILED ASSESSMENT   523

K FAST TRACK FIXED COSTS   524

L FIXED AND SCALE COSTS   525

M COSTS AND TRACK ALLOCATION   525

N PUBLICLY FUNDED LITIGANTS   525

O *PRO BONO* COSTS ORDERS   526

P COSTS AGAINST NON-PARTIES   526

Q WASTED COSTS ORDERS   526

   Key points summary   528

47 QUALIFIED ONE-WAY COSTS SHIFTING   529

A CASES WHERE QOCS APPLIES   529

B EFFECT OF QOCS   530

C LOSS OF QOCS PROTECTION   531

   Key points summary   533

48 ENFORCEMENT   534

A ENFORCEMENT OF MONEY JUDGMENTS   534

B ENFORCEMENT OF JUDGMENTS FOR THE DELIVERY OF GOODS   543

C ENFORCEMENT OF JUDGMENTS FOR THE POSSESSION OF LAND   543

D RECEIVERS BY WAY OF EQUITABLE EXECUTION   544

E CONTEMPT OF COURT   544

F ENFORCEMENT OF FOREIGN JUDGMENTS   546

   Key points summary   547

49 JUDICIAL REVIEW   548

A PARTIES   548

B *LOCUS STANDI*   549

C PUBLIC LAW   549

D REMEDIES IN JUDICIAL REVIEW   551

E JUDICIAL REVIEW PRE-ACTION PROTOCOL   552

F APPLYING FOR PERMISSION TO PROCEED   553

G SUBSTANTIVE HEARING   555

H CONVERSION TO A COMMON LAW CLAIM   557

I CONSENT ORDERS   558

   Key points summary   558

50 APPEALS   559

A ROUTES OF APPEAL   560

B PERMISSION TO APPEAL   561

C TIME FOR APPEALING   564

D PROCEDURE ON APPEALING   565

E RESPONDENT'S NOTICE   566

F APPLICATIONS WITHIN APPEALS   567

G   STAY   568

H   STRIKING OUT APPEAL NOTICES AND SETTING ASIDE OR
    IMPOSING CONDITIONS   568

I   HEARING OF APPEALS   568

J   APPEAL COURT'S POWERS   571

K   APPEALS BY WAY OF CASE STATED   573

L   APPEALS TO THE SUPREME COURT   573

    Key points summary   574

online
resource
centre

APPENDIX 1 ADDITIONAL CHAPTER   575

    INTRODUCTION: THE JACKSON REFORMS   575

Index   577

PREFACE

Any lawyer practising in the civil courts needs a thorough grasp of practice and procedure. Indeed, knowledge of procedure is probably as important as knowledge of the substantive law. It is not sufficient to have a strong case on the law and facts. It is also important to be able to advance a claim effectively and efficiently from its early stages through to trial (if needs be) in order to ensure the client attains the best result possible given the strengths and weaknesses of the case. Every year a great many cases are won and lost on purely procedural grounds. Further, good use of court procedure can result in a case being materially strengthened. The converse is that poor use of procedure can cause avoidable harm to the client's prospects of success.

Civil procedure can be a very daunting subject. First, there are a number of statutes dealing with the jurisdiction of the civil courts. Secondly, there is a substantial rule book comprising detailed rules of court (the Civil Procedure Rules 1998 (SI 1998/3132)) supplemented by numerous practice directions. The Rules and practice directions are available at <http://www.justice.gov.uk>. They are also printed in full in practitioners' books, such as *Blackstone's Civil Practice* and the *White Book*. There are also official court guides that deal with the practice, sometimes in considerable detail, in the Queen's Bench and Chancery Divisions of the High Court and also the specialist courts, such as the Commercial Court. Statutory provisions, rules, and practice directions can only deal with what should happen in the general run of cases. The courts are, on a day-to-day basis, faced with claims that are unusual, with cases where exceptions should be made to rules worded in a general way or where a more sophisticated approach may be required, and with cases that have not been conducted fully in accordance with the rules. There is therefore a substantial body of relevant case law dealing with procedural issues. Furthermore, there are some areas where procedural and substantive law issues converge.

What the student and newly qualified litigator need is an accessible introduction to the subject. I hope this new edition of this book will continue to perform this function. It seeks to explain the various procedures that either may or must be followed as a claim progresses from its early stages through its interim stages and on to trial, enforcement, and any possible appeal in a straightforward way, but with sufficient detail for the new practitioner to be able to cope with most problems that commonly arise. A number of forms and precedents are included in this book to bring to life the procedures that are discussed. Often they are far shorter than ones that would be met in practice in order to concentrate on what the documents look like, and it should also be borne in mind that there are usually several different approaches used by different lawyers in drafting court documents.

The 21st edition includes all the changes up to those introduced on 6 April 2018. These include a range of statutory instruments and updates to the Civil Procedure Rules and practice directions, up to and including the Civil Procedure (Amendment) Rules 2018 and the 95th Update.

Over the years I have benefitted from the expertise and experience of numerous colleagues at the Treasury Solicitor's Office, chambers, and the City Law School. Liana Green and the staff of Oxford University Press have done an excellent job in the preparation of the new edition. I am especially grateful to my wife Wendy for her encouragement and support during the period when the book was being written.

Stuart Sime
London
April 2018

ABBREVIATIONS

ADR	alternative dispute resolution
app	appendix
AQ	allocation questionnaire
art	article
A/S	acknowledgment of service
ATE	after the event litigation insurance
BCP	*Blackstone's Civil Practice* (Oxford University Press)
BIA	Brunei Investment Agency
Brussels Convention	Convention on jurisdiction and the enforcement of judgments in civil and commercial matters signed at Brussels on 27 September 1968
BTE	before the event litigation insurance (legal expenses insurance)
CA	Court of Appeal
CCA 1984	County Courts Act 1984
CCR	County Court Rules 1981
CEA 1968	Civil Evidence Act 1968
CEA 1972	Civil Evidence Act 1972
CEA 1995	Civil Evidence Act 1995
CFA	conditional fee agreement
ChD	Chancery Division
CJEU	Court of Justice of the European Union (formerly known as the ECJ)
CJJA 1982	Civil Jurisdiction and Judgments Act 1982
CJJA 1991	Civil Jurisdiction and Judgments Act 1991
cl	clause
CLS	Community Legal Service
CLSA 1990	Courts and Legal Services Act 1990
CNF	claims notification form (used in the RTA protocol)
Commercial Court Guide	Admiralty and Commercial Courts Guide
CPFO	Civil Proceedings Fees Order 2008 (SI 2008/1053) as amended
CPR	Civil Procedure Rules 1998 (SI 1998/3132) as amended
CRU	Compensation Recovery Unit, part of the Department for Social Development, and provides certificates of State benefits paid to personal injuries claimants
DBA	damages-based agreement
DX	document exchange
ECHR	European Court of Human Rights
EC Treaty	Treaty Establishing the European Community
EEA	European Economic Area
EEO Regulation	Council Regulation (EC) No 805/2004
EFTA	European Free Trade Association
EL/PL	employers' liability and public liability
EOP (Regulation)	European order for payment; Regulation (EC) No 1896/2006 of 12 December 2006

EU	European Union
EU Treaty	Treaty on the functioning of the European Union
FamD	Family Division
GLO	group litigation order
Hague Convention	Hague Convention on the Service Abroad of Judicial and Extrajudicial Documents in Civil or Commercial Matters (1965)
HL	House of Lords (replaced by the Supreme Court: October 2009)
IA 1986	Insolvency Act 1986
IR 1986	Insolvency Rules 1986 (SI 1986/1925) as amended
Judgments Regulation	Council Regulation (EC) No 44/2001 on jurisdiction and the recognition and enforcement of judgments in civil and commercial matters
Jurisdiction Order 1991	High Court and County Courts Jurisdiction Order 1991 (SI 1991/724)
LA 1980	Limitation Act 1980
LASPO 2012	Legal Aid, Sentencing and Punishment of Offenders Act 2012
LFA	litigation funding agreement
Lugano Convention	Convention on jurisdiction and the enforcement of judgments in civil and commercial matters, 16 September 1988
Member States	Member States of the Jurisdiction Regulation
MF	McKenzie friend
MIB	Motor Insurers' Bureau
MRO	medical reporting organization
ord	order
para	paragraph
PC	Privy Council
PCO	protective costs order
PD	practice direction
PI protocol	Pre-action Protocol for Personal Injury Claims
QBD	Queen's Bench Division
QOCS	qualified one-way costs shifting
r	rule
RCJ	Royal Courts of Justice, Strand, London
reg	regulation
RSC	Rules of the Supreme Court 1965
RTA	road traffic accident
s	section
SC	Supreme Court
SCA 1981	Senior Courts Act 1981
Sch	Schedule
SCR	Supreme Court Rules 2009 (SI 2009/1604)
Service Regulation	Council Regulation (EC) No 1348/2000, reproduced as the annex to PD 6B
SI	statutory instrument
SoGA 1979	Sale of Goods Act 1979
SRA	Solicitors Regulation Authority
TCC	Technology and Construction Court
White Book	*Civil Practice* (Sweet & Maxwell)

TABLE OF CASES

7E Communications Ltd v Vertex
Antennentechnik GmbH [2007] 1 WLR
2175 561
A v C [1981] QB 956. 489
A v C (No 2) [1981] QB 961 488
A v Hoare [2008] 1 AC 844 . . . . 234, 240, 247
A v X and B (2004) LTL 6/4/04 508
A City Council v T [2011] 1 WLR 819 . . . 272
AB v Ministry of Defence [2013] 1 AC 78 . . . 239
AB Bank Ltd v Abu Dhabi Commercial Bank
PJSC [2017] 1 WLR 810 503
ABB Asea Brown Boveri Ltd v Hiscox
Dedicated Corporate Member Ltd [2007]
EWHC 1150 (Comm) 255
Abbey Forwarding Ltd v Hone [2010] EWHC
1532 (Ch) 488
Abbey Forwarding Ltd v Hone (No 3) [2015]
Ch 309; [2014] 3 WLR 1676. 479
Abbey National plc v Frost [1999] 1 WLR
1080 78
Abdulle v Commissioner of Police of the
Metropolis [2016] 1 WLR 898 417
Abela v Baadarani [2013] 1 WLR 2043 78, 127
Abela v Baardarani (No 2) [2018]
1 WLR 89 493
Abela v Hammonds Suddards (2008) LTL
9/12/08 349
Abidin Daver, The [1984] AC 398 129
Abrahams v Lenton [2003] EWHC
1104 (QB) 569
Actavis Ltd v Merck and Co Inc (2007) LTL
7/8/07 512
Adam Phones Ltd v Goldschmidt [1999] 4 All
ER 486 . . . . 497, 498
Adams v Bracknell Forest Borough Council
[2005] 1 AC 76 . . . . 234, 239
Adams v Thomson Holidays Ltd [2009]
EWHC 2559 (QB). 148
Adamson v Halifax plc [2003] 1 WLR 60 . 512
Adan v Securicor Custodial Services Ltd [2005]
PIQR P79 40
Adelson v Associated Newspapers Ltd [2008] 1
WLR 585. . . . . 37, 255
Adoko v Jemal (1999) The Times,
8 July 1999 40
Aer Lingus v Gildacroft Ltd [2006] 1 WLR
1173 240
AES Ust-Kamenogorsk Hydropower Plant LLP
v Ust-Kamenogorsk Hydropower Plant JSC
[2013] 1 WLR 1889. 130

Agyeman v Boadi (1996) 28 HLR 558 158
Aiden Shipping Co Ltd v Interbulk Ltd [1986]
AC 965 526
Aiglon Ltd v Gau Shan Co Ltd [1993] 1
Lloyd's Rep 164. 485
Aims Asset Management v Kazakhstan
Investment Fund Ltd (2002)
LTL 22/5/02. 303
Air Canada v Secretary of State for Trade
[1983] 2 AC 394 359
Aird v Prime Meridian Ltd [2007]
BLR 105 394
AJ Bekhor and Co Ltd v Bilton [1981]
QB 923 481
AK Investment CJSC v Kyrgyz Mobile Tel Ltd
[2011] 4 All ER 1027. 124
Akinleye v East Sussex Hospitals NHS Trust
[2008] LS Law Med 216 282
Akram v Adam [2005] 1 WLR
2762 . . . . 74, 144
Aktas v Adepta [2011] QB 894 . . . . . 247, 327
Akzo Nobel Chemicals Ltd v European
Commission [2010] 5 CMLR 19 355
Al Fayed v Commissioner of Police for the
Metropolis (2002) The Times, 17 June
2002 358
Al-Rawas v Hassan Khan & Co [2017] EWCA
Civ 42 255
Al Rawi v Security Service [2012] 1 AC 531 34,
338
Alawiye v Mahmood [2007] 1 WLR 79 . . . 538
Albon v Naza Motor Trading Sdn Bhd (2007)
LTL 19/11/07. 39
Albon (t/a NA Carriage Co) v Naza Motor
Trading Sdn Bhd (No 2) [2007] 1 WLR
2489 265
Aldi Stores Ltd v Holmes Buildings plc [2005]
PNLR 9. 257
Aldi Stores Ltd v WSP Group plc [2008] 1
WLR 748. 330
Aldridge v Edwards [2000] CPLR 349. 87
Alfred Crompton Amusement Machines Ltd
v Commissioners of Customs and Excise
(No 2) [1974] AC 405 355
Alfred Dunhill Ltd v Sunoptic SA [1979] FSR
337 463
ALG Inc v Uganda Airlines Corporation
(1992) The Times, 31 July 1992. 482
Ali v Courtaulds Textiles Ltd (1999)
The Times, 28 May 1999. 240

Allen v Bloomsbury Publishing plc [2011] FSR 22; (2011) LTL 18/3/11 . . . . 300, 301

Allen v Gulf Oil Refining Ltd [1981] AC 101 440

Allen v Jambo Holdings Ltd [1980] 1 WLR 1252 . . . . 465, 486

Alliance and Leicester Building Society v Ghahremani (1992) 142 NLJ 313 498

Allied Arab Bank Ltd v Hajjar [1988] QB 787 . . . . 484, 492

Allied Dunbar Assurance plc v Ireland (2001) LTL 12/6/01 284

Allison v Horner [2014] EWCA Civ 117 . . 242

Alpha Rocks Solicitors v Alade [2015] 1 WLR 4534 331

Amber Size and Chemical Co Ltd v Menzel [1913] 2 Ch 239 475

Amerada Hess v Rome (2000) The Times, 15 March 2000 . . . . 75, 86

American Cyanamid Co v Ethicon Ltd [1975] AC 396 . . . . 24, 44, 463–73, 483, 492

American Home Products Corporation v Novartis Pharmaceuticals UK Ltd (2001) LTL 13/2/01 507

American Leisure Group Ltd v Garrard [2014] 1 WLR 4102 67

Amoco (UK) Exploration Co v British American Offshore Ltd (2000) LTL 12/12/00 335

Anderton v Clwyd County Council (No 2) [2002] 1 WLR 3174 . . . . 77, 79

Anglo Irish Asset Finance plc v Flood [2011] EWCA Civ 799 572

Anglo Manx Group Ltd v Aitken [2002] BPIR 215 235

Anglo-Eastern Trust Ltd v Kermanshahchi [2002] EWCA Civ 198 289

Ansari v Knowles [2013] EWCA Civ 1448 330

Anton Piller KG v Manufacturing Processes Ltd [1976] Ch 55 . . . . 493–5, 498

Anufrijeva v Southwark London Borough Council [2004] QB 1124 46

Aoun v Bahri [2002] 3 All ER 182 301

Apac Rowena Ltd v Norpol Packaging Ltd [1991] 4 All ER 516 28

Appah v Monseu [1967] 1 WLR 893 300

Arab Monetary Fund v Hashim (No 5) [1992] 2 All ER 911 502

Arbuthnot Latham Bank Ltd v Trafalgar Holdings Ltd [1998] 1 WLR 1426 327

Archbold v Scully (1861) 9 HL Cas 360 . . . 238

Architects of Wine Ltd v Barclays Bank plc [2007] 2 Lloyd's Rep 471 283

Aries Tanker Corporation v Total Transport Ltd [1977] 1 WLR 185 . . . . 87, 287

Arkin v Borchard Lines Ltd (No 2) (2001) LTL 19/6/01 284

Arkin v Borchard Lines Ltd (Nos 2 and 3) [2005] 1 WLR 3055 17

Armes v Godfrey Morgan Solicitors Ltd [2018] 1 WLR 936 255

Arnold v National Westminster Bank plc [1991] 2 AC 93 331

Arrow Trading and Investments Est Ltd v Edwardian Group Ltd [2005] 1 BCLC 696 . . . . 344, 349

Arsenal Football Club plc v Reed [2003] 3 All ER 865 447

Ash v Buxted Poultry Ltd (1989) The Times, 29 November 1989 509

Ashcroft v Bradford & Bingley plc [2010] EWCA Civ 223 244

Ashe v National Westminster Bank plc [2008] 1 WLR 710 235

Ashley v Tesco Stores [2015] 1 WLR 5153 67

Ashmore v British Coal Corporation [1990] 2 QB 338 333

Ashmore v Corporation of Lloyd's [1992] 1 WLR 446 379

Ashton Investments Ltd v Rusal [2007] 1 Lloyd's Rep 311 126

Ashworth Hospital Authority v MGN Ltd [2002] 1 WLR 2033 . . . . 502, 503

Aspin v Metric Group Ltd (2007) LTL 25/9/07 512

Associated British Ports v Transport and General Workers Union [1989] 1 WLR 939 473

Associated Newspapers plc v Insert Media Ltd [1991] 1 WLR 571 466

Astor Chemicals Ltd v Synthetic Technology Ltd [1990] BCLC 1 466

AT & T Istel Ltd v Tully [1993] AC 45 351

Atkinson v Castan (1991) The Times, 17 April 1991 449

Atos Consulting Ltd v Avis Europe plc [2008] Bus LR Digest D20 . . . . 343, 360

Atrium Training Services Ltd, Re [2013] EWHC 2882 (Ch) 348

Attorney-General v Barker [1990] 3 All ER 257 . . . . 472, 474

Attorney-General v British Broadcasting Corporation [2007] EWCA Civ 280 . . 459

Attorney-General v Chaudry [1971] 1 WLR 1614 462

Attorney-General v Guardian Newspapers Ltd (No 2) [1990] 1 AC 109 475

Attorney-General v Leveller Magazine Ltd [1979] AC 440 544

Attorney-General v Punch Ltd [2003] 1 AC
1046 480

Audergon v La Baguette Ltd [2002] CPLR 192
. 146

Austin v Miller Argent (South Wales) Ltd
[2011] Env LR 32 219

Autofocus Ltd v Accident Exchange Ltd [2010]
EWCA Civ. .331

Avinue Ltd v Sunrule Ltd [2004]
1 WLR 634 .308

Awwad v Geraghty and Co [2000] 1 All ER
608 520

Axel Johnson Petroleum AB v MG Mineral
Group AG [1992] 1 WLR 270 158

Ayton v RSM Bentley Jennison [2016] 1 WLR
1281 283

B v Nugent Care Society [2010]
1 WLR 516 . . . . .240, 246

B (A Minor), Re [2000] 1 WLR 790. 397

B (Children), Re (Care Proceedings: Standard
of Proof) [2009] 1 AC 11. 439

B2NET Ltd v HM Treasury (2010) 128 Con
LR 53 466

Babanaft International Co SA v Bassatne
[1990] Ch 13. 484

Baden v Société Générale pour Favoriser
le Développement du Commerce et de
l'Industrie en France SA (27 February
1985, CA, unreported). 381

Baden v Société Générale pour Favoriser
le Développement du Commerce et de
l'Industrie en France SA [1992] 4 All ER
161 381

Baden v Société Générale pour Favoriser
le Développement du Commerce et de
l'Industrie en France SA [1993] 1 WLR
509 383

Bailey v IBC Vehicles Ltd [1998]
3 All ER 570 520

Balabel v Air India [1988] Ch 317 353

Balmoral Group Ltd v Borealis (UK) Ltd
[2006] 2 Lloyd's Rep 629 393

Banco Atlantico SA v British Bank of the
Middle East [1990] 2 Lloyd's Rep
504 129

Banco Nacional de Comercio Exterior SNC v
Empresa de Telecommunicationes de Cuba
SA [2007] 2 All ER (Comm)
1093 . . . . .484, 492

Bandegani v Norwich Union Fire Insurance
Ltd (1999) LTL 20/5/99. 307

Bank für Gemeinwirtschaft AG v City of
London Garages Ltd [1971]
1 WLR 149 .286

Bank Mellat v Nikpour [1985] FSR 87 . . .265

Bank of America National Trust v Chrismas
[1994] 1 All ER 401. . . . . . . .237, 238, 253

Bank of China v NBM LLC [2002] 1 WLR
844 485

Bank of Dubai Ltd v Abbas [1997]
IL Pr 308 122

Bank of England v Riley [1992] Ch 465. . .352

Bank of Ireland v Philip Bank Partnership
[2014] EWHC 284 (TCC) 187, 419

Bank of Tokyo-Mitsubishi UFJ Ltd v Bashan
Gida Sanayi ve Pazarlama AS [2008]
EWHC 659 (Ch) 329

Bank St Petersburg PJSC v Arkhangelsky (No
2) [2016] 1 WLR 1081 436

Bankamerica Finance Ltd v Nock [1988]
AC 1002 . . . . .512, 515

Bankers Trust Co v Shapira [1980] 1 WLR
1274 504

Banque Paribas v Cargill International SA
[1992] 1 Lloyd's Rep 96 126

Banque Saudi Fransi v Lear Siegler Services Inc
[2007] 1 All ER (Comm) 67. 288

Barclay-Johnson v Yuill [1980] 1 WLR 1259
. 485

Barclays Bank Ltd v Tom [1923]
1 KB 221. 225

Barclays Bank plc v Bemister [1989] 1 WLR
128 28

Barclays Bank plc v Eustice [1995] 1 WLR
1238 355

Barings plc v Coopers and Lybrand [2000] 1
WLR 2353. .362

Barings plc v Coopers and Lybrand [2001]
CPLR 451 433

Barings plc v Coopers and Lybrand [2001]
PNLR 22. 387

Barnes v St Helens Metropolitan Borough
Council (Practice Note) [2007]
1 WLR 879 . . . . .241, 328

Barnett v Creggy [2017] Ch 273 244

Barnette v Government of the United States of
America [2004] 1 WLR
2241 40–1

Barnstaple Boat Co Ltd v Jones [2008] 1 All
ER 1124 242

Baron v Lovell [1999] CPLR 630. 320

Barr v Biffa Waste Services Ltd (No 2) [2009]
EWHC 2444 (TCC); [2010] 3 Costs LR
317 192

Barratt Manchester Ltd v Bolton Metropolitan
Borough Council [1998] 1 WLR
1003 479

Barton v Wright Hassall LLP [2018] 1 WLR
1119 . . . . .78, 213–14

Barton Henderson Rasen v Merrett [1993]
 1 Lloyd's Rep 540 330
Basten v Butter (1806) 7 East 479 158
Bates v Croydon London Borough Council
 (2001) LTL 23/1/01 428
Bates v Lord Hailsham of St Marylebone
 [1972] 1 WLR 1373...............459
Bath and North East Somerset District Council
 v Mowlem plc [2004] BLR 153......464
Battley v Faulkner (1820) 3 B & Ald
 288 237
BBC, Re [2015] AC 588..............362
Beaman v ARTS Ltd [1949] 1 KB 550 242
Beddoe, Re [1893] 1 Ch 547 192–3
Bee v Jenson [2007] RTR 9 282
Behbehani v Salem [1989] 1 WLR 723....266
Benham Ltd v Kythira Investments Ltd (2003)
 LTL 15/12/03...................439
Beoco Ltd v Alfa Laval Co Ltd [1995]
 QB 137 ....252, 520
Berkeley Administration Inc v McClelland
 [1990] 2 QB 407 304
Bermuda International Securities Ltd v KPMG
 [2001] CPLR 252 506
Berry v Ashtead Plant Hire Co Ltd [2012]
 PIQR P6 293
Berry Trade Ltd v Moussari (2003) The Times,
 3 June 2003....................356
Best v Charter Medical of England Ltd (2001)
 The Times, 19 November 2001 202
Bestobell Paints Ltd v Bigg [1975]
 FSR 421.......................468
Bhimji v Chatwani [1991] 1 WLR 989....497
Biguzzi v Rank Leisure plc [1999] 1 WLR
 1926 37
Bilkus v Stockler Brunton [2010] 1 WLR
 2526 511
Bilta (UK) Ltd v Nazir [2010] Bus LR
 1634 134
Binks v Securicor Omega Express Ltd [2003] 1
 WLR 2557............150, 151, 251
Bird v Acorn Group Ltd [2017] 1 WLR
 1915 316
Birse Construction Ltd v Haiste Ltd [1996] 1
 WLR 675.......................223
Black v Sumitomo Corporation [2002] 1 WLR
 1562 ....505, 506
Blackham v Entrepose UK [2004] EWCA Civ
 1109 410
Bloomsbury Publishing Group Ltd v News
 Group Newspapers Ltd [2003] 1 WLR
 1633 213
Blore v Ashby (1889) 42 ChD 682.......516
Blunt v Park Lane Hotel Ltd [1942]
 2 KB 253......................350

BMW AG v Commissioners of HM Revenue and
 Customs [2008] EWCA Civ 1028 568
Boehringer Ingelheim Ltd v Vetplus Ltd [2007]
 FSR 29........................469
Bolkiah v KPMG [1999] 2 AC 222 5
Bols Distilleries BV v Superior Yacht Services
 [2007] 1 WLR 12.............125, 275
Bonnard v Perryman [1891] 2 Ch 269 468
Booker McConnell plc v Plascow [1985] RPC
 425 495
Boss Group Ltd v Boss France SA [1997] 1
 WLR 351......................122
Bovale Ltd v Secretary of State for
 Communities and Local Government
 [2009] 1 WLR 2274.................33
Boyce v Wyatt Engineering (2001)
 LTL 1/5/01.....................439
BP Exploration Co (Libya) Ltd v Hunt [1976]
 1 WLR 788 127
Bracegirdle v Oxley [1947] KB 349 573
Bradbury v Enfield London Borough Council
 [1967] 1 WLR 1311...............471
Bradford and Bingley plc v Rashid [2006] 1
 WLR 2066......................356
Brady v Norman [2011] EWCA Civ 107 ..244
Brainbox Digital Ltd v Backbord Media
 GmbH [2018] 1 WLR 1149........478
Brazier v News Group Newspapers Ltd [2016]
 EWCA Civ 79 333
Bremer Vulkan Schiffbau und Maschinenfabrik
 v South India Shipping Corporation Ltd
 [1981] AC 909...................34
Brinkibon Ltd v Stahag Stahl und
 Stahlwarenhandelsgesellschaft mbH [1983]
 2 AC 34.......................126
Brink's Mat Ltd v Elcombe [1988] 1 WLR
 1350 266
Bristol and West plc v Bartlett [2003] 1 WLR
 284 234
Bristol-Myers Squibb Co v Baker Norton
 Pharmaceuticals Inc (No 2) [2001] RPC
 913 457
British Anzani (Felixstowe) Ltd v International
 Marine Management (UK) Ltd [1980] QB
 137 158
British Arab Commercial Bank plc v Alsosaibi
 [2011] EWHC 2444 (Comm) 542
British and Colonial Land Association Ltd v
 Foster (1887) 4 TLR 574..........333
British and Commonwealth Holdings plc v
 Quadrex Holdings Inc [1989]
 QB 842 294
British Gas Trading Ltd v Oak Cash & Carry
 Ltd [2016] EWCA Civ 153; [2016] 1 WLR
 4530 421

British Sky Broadcasting Group plc v Virgin
Media Communications Ltd [2008]
1 WLR 2854 355

British South Africa Co v Companhia de
Moçambique [1893] AC 602 120

British Steel Corporation v Granada Television
Ltd [1981] AC 1096 502

British Waterways Board v Norman (1993) 26
HLR 232 520

Broadley v Guy Clapham and Co [1994] 4 All
ER 439 240

Broadmoor Hospital Authority v Robinson
[2000] QB 775 212

Broderick v Centaur Tipping Services Ltd
(2006) LTL 22/8/06 283

Brooks v AH Brooks & Co [2011] 3 All ER
982 . . . . 74, 134

Brooks v Commissioner of Police for the
Metropolis [2005] 1 WLR 1495 . 284, 329

Brown v Bennett [2002] 2 All ER 273 527

Brown v Innovatorone plc [2009] EWHC 1376
(Comm) 68

Brownlie v Four Seasons Holdings Inc [2018] 1
WLR 192 . . . . 124, 126

Bruce v Odhams Press Ltd [1936]
1 KB 697 149

Buckinghamshire County Council v Moran
[1990] Ch 623 356

Buckland v Palmer [1984] 1 WLR 1109 . . .337

Bullock v London General Omnibus Co [1907]
1 KB 264 515

Bunn v British Broadcasting Corporation
[1998] 3 All ER 552 . . . . 465, 474

Burgess v Stafford Hotel Ltd [1990] 1 WLR
1215 568

Burmah Oil Co Ltd v Bank of England [1980]
AC 1090 359

Burnden Holdings (UK) Ltd v Fielding [2017]
1 WLR 39 233

Burstall v Beyfus (1884) 26 ChD 35 333

Bush v Bank Mandiri (Europe) Ltd (2014) LTL
11/2/14 301

Byrne v Motor Insurers' Bureau [2009]
QB 66 56

C v C (Privilege: Criminal Communications)
[2002] Fam 42 355

C plc v P (Attorney-General intervening)
[2008] Ch 1 .350

Cain v Francis [2009] QB 754 246

Calcraft v Guest [1898] 1 QB 759 357

Calderbank v Calderbank [1976]
Fam 93 . . . . .355, 400

Cambridge Nutrition Ltd v British
Broadcasting Corporation [1990] 3 All ER
523 467

Camdex International Ltd v Bank of Zambia
(No 2) [1997] 1 WLR 632 490

Cameron v Hussain [2018] 1 WLR 657 . . .213

Campbell v Mirror Group Newspapers plc
[2004] 2 AC 457 . . . . 44, 45, 470

Campbell Mussels v Thompson (1984) 81 LS
Gaz 2140 488

Canada Trust Co v Stolzenberg (No 2) [1998]
1 WLR 554 .125

Cantor Index Ltd v Lister (2001)
LTL 22/11/01 . . . . 488, 489

Capital Cameras Ltd v Harold Lines Ltd
[1991] 1 WLR 54 491

Carlson v Townsend [2001] 1 WLR
2415 390

Carnegie v Giessen [2005] 1 WLR 2510 37

Cartledge v E Jopling and Sons Ltd [1963] AC
758 238

Carver v Hammersmith & Queen Charlotte's
Health Authority (2000)
LTL 31/7/00 513

Cassidy v Hawcroft [2000] CPLR 624 362

Castanho v Brown and Root (UK) Ltd [1981]
AC 557 130

Caudle v LD Law Ltd [2008] 1 WLR
1540 209

Cave v Robinson Jarvis & Rolf [2003] 1 AC
384 242

Cayne v Global Natural Resources plc [1984]
1 All ER 225 . . . . 467, 468

CBS United Kingdom Ltd v Lambert [1983]
Ch 37 509

Cebora SNC v SIP (Industrial Products) Ltd
[1976] 1 Lloyd's Rep 271 286

Cecil v Bayat [2011] 1 WLR 3086 . . . . . 78, 86

Central Electricity Board v Halifax
Corporation [1963] AC 785 234

Chandra v Mayor [2017] 1 WLR 729 216

Channel Tunnel Group Ltd v Balfour Beatty
Construction Ltd [1993] AC 334 467

Chaplair Ltd v Kumari [2015] EWCA Civ
798 517

Charles Church Developments Ltd v Stent
Foundations Ltd [2007] 1 WLR 1203;
[2007] CILL 2477 . . . . 55, 258

Charles Church Developments plc v Cronin
[1990] FSR 1 330

Charter plc v City Index Ltd [2008]
Ch 313 223

Chartwell Estate Agents Ltd v Fergies
Properties SA [2014] EWCA Civ 506 . .417

Chatsworth Investments Ltd v Amoco (UK)
Ltd [1968] Ch 665 225

Cheddar Valley Engineering Ltd v
Chaddlewood Homes Ltd [1992] 1 WLR
820 355

Chellaram v Chellaram (No 2) [2002] 3 All
    ER 17 74
Cheltenham and Gloucester Building Society v
    Ricketts [1993] 1 WLR 1545. . . . 483, 490
Cherney v Deripaska [2007] 2 All ER (Comm)
    785 122
Chief Constable of Kent v V [1983]
    QB 34 487
Chief Constable of the North Wales Police v
    Evans [1982] 1 WLR 1155 548
Chiron Corporation v Murex Diagnostics Ltd
    (No 8) [1995] FSR 309 446
Chocoladefabriken Lindt & Sprungli AG v
    Nestlé Co Ltd [1978] RPC 287 355
Choudhary v Bhatter [2010] 2 All ER
    1031 120
Christofi v Barclays Bank plc [2000] 1 WLR
    937 330
Chuku v Chuku [2017] 1 WLR 3137. 301
Ciccone v Associated Newspapers Ltd [2009]
    EWHC 1108 (Ch) 155
Cinpres Gas Injection Ltd v Melea Ltd (2005)
    The Times, 21 December 2005. 264
City and Country Properties Ltd v Kamali
    [2007] 1 WLR 1219. 37
Clancy Consulting Ltd v Derwent Holdings
    Ltd [2010] EWHC 762 (TCC). . . 149, 277
Clarapede and Co v Commercial Union
    Association (1883) 32 WR 262. . . 250, 251
Clark v Ardington Electrical Services (2001)
    LTL 4/4/01. 507
Clarke v Marlborough Fine Art (London) Ltd
    [2002] 1 WLR 1731. 150
Clarke v Slay (2002) LTL 25/1/02 252
Clarke (executor of the Will of Francis
    Bacon, deceased) v Marlborough Fine Art
    (London) Ltd (2001) The Times, 5 July
    2001 233
Clarkson v Gilbert [2000] 2 FLR 839 437
Clayson v Rolls Royce Ltd [1951] 1 KB
    746 228
Clibbery v Allan [2002] Fam 261. . . . . . 42, 43
Clipper Maritime Co Ltd v Mineral
    Import-Export [1981] 1 WLR 1262. . . 488
Cluley v RL Dix Heating (2003) LTL 31/10/03
    258
Clyde and Co LLP v New Look Interiors of
    Marlow Ltd [2009] EWHC 173 (QB) . 149
Co-operative Group Ltd v Carillion JM Ltd
    (2014) LTL 11/2/14 361
Co-operative Retail Services Ltd v Taylor
    Young Partnership Ltd [2002] 1 WLR
    1419 223
Coad v Cornwall and Isles of Scilly Health
    Authority [1997] 1 WLR 189 245

Coastal (Bermuda) Ltd v Esso Petroleum Co
    Ltd [1984] 1 Lloyd's Rep 11 284
Cobbold v London Borough of Greenwich
    (LTL 24/5/01) 250, 251
Cobham v Frett [2001] 1 WLR 1775 571
Coburn v Colledge [1897] 1 QB. 235
Coca-Cola Co v Gilbey [1995] 4 All ER 711
    499
Cocks v Thanet District Council [1983] 2 AC
    286 550
Cohen v Kingsley Napley [2006]
    PNLR 22 238
Collier v Williams [2006] 1 WLR
    1945 . . . . 36, 39, 74, 85, 86, 265
Colliers International Property Consultants v
    Colliers Jordan Lee Jafaar Bhd [2008] 2
    Lloyd's Rep 368. . . . . 270, 417
Collins v Gordon [2008] EWCA Civ 110. . 416
Columbia Picture Industries Inc v Robinson
    [1987] Ch 38. . . . . 496, 498
Colwill v European Heritage Ltd [2014]
    EWCA Civ 238 158
Commercial Bank of the Near East plc v A
    [1989] 2 Lloyd's Rep 319 266
Commissioners of Inland Revenue v Exeter
    City AFC Ltd (2004) LTL 12/5/04 347
Community Care North East v Durham
    County Council [2012] 1 WLR 338. . . 451
Compagnie Financière et Commerciale du
    Pacifique v Peruvian Guano Co (1882) 11
    QBD 55 347
Compagnie Noga d'Importation et
    d'Exportation SA v Abacha [2001] 3 All
    ER 513 456
Compagnie Noga d'Importation et
    d'Exportation SA v Australia and New
    Zealand Banking Group Ltd [2003] 1
    WLR 307. 569
Company (No 004055 of 1991), Re a [1991] 1
    WLR 1003. 526
Comptroller of Customs v Western Lectric Co
    Ltd [1966] AC 367 379
Conlon v Royal Sun Alliance plc [2015] EWCA
    Civ 92 308
Conlon v Simms [2008] 1 WLR 484 332
Connelly v RTZ Corporation plc [1996]
    QB 361 127
Consolidated Contractors International Co
    SAL v Masri [2011] Bus LR D108. . . . 367
Conticorp SA v Central Bank of Ecuador
    [2007] UKPC 40 149
Cooper v Williams [1963] 2 QB 567 336
Coopers Payen Ltd v Southampton Container
    Terminal Ltd [2004] 1 Lloyd's Rep
    331 397

Copeland v Smith [2000] 1 WLR 1371 . . . 240

Corfu Navigation Co v Mobil Shipping Co Ltd [1991] 2 Lloyd's Rep 52 . . . . 300, 301

Cosgrove v Pattison [2001] CPLR 177. . . . 392

Cotton v Rickard Metals Inc [2008] EWHC 824 (QB) 282, 283

Cottrell v Stratton (1872) LR 8 Ch App 295 517

Coulthard v Disco Mix Club Ltd [1999] 2 All ER 457 232

Council of Civil Service Unions v Minister for the Civil Service [1985] AC 374. . . 549–50

Courtenay-Evans v Stuart Passey and Associates [1986] 1 All ER 932 226

Cow v Casey [1949] 1 KB 474. 284

Coward v Phaestos [2014] EWCA Civ 1256 400

Cowl v Plymouth City Council (2001) The Times, 8 January 2001. 115

Cranfield v Bridgegrove Ltd [2003] 1 WLR 2441 . . . . 74, 77, 78, 86

Cream Holdings Ltd v Banerjee [2005] 1 AC 253 . . . . 44, 469

Crédit Agricole Indosuez v Unicof Ltd (2003) LTL 4/2/03. 143

Cressey v E Timm and Son Ltd [2005] 1 WLR 3926 240

Crest Homes plc v Marks [1987] AC 829 . 500

Cretanor Maritime Co Ltd v Irish Marine Management Ltd [1978] 1 WLR 966. 487, 490

Cripps v Heritage Distribution Corporation (1999) The Times, 10 November 1999 304

Cropper v Smith (1884) 26 ChD 700 . . . . 250, 251

Croston v Vaughan [1938] 1 KB 540 228

Customs and Excise Commissioners v Anchor Foods Ltd [1999] 1 WLR 1139 485

Customs and Excise Commissioners v ApS Samex [1983] 1 All ER 1042 . . . . 444, 445

Customs and Excise Commissioners v Barclays Bank plc [2007] 1 AC 181 487

Czarnikow-Rionda Sugar Trading Inc v Standard Bank London Ltd [1999] 1 All ER (Comm) 890 287

D v L [2003] EWCA Civ 1169. 470

D v National Society for the Prevention of Cruelty to Children [1978] AC 171 . . . 355

D (a child), Re [2011] 4 All ER 434 357

D (Minors), Re (Conciliation: Disclosure of Information) [1993] Fam 231 355

Dadourian Group International Inc v Simms [2008] BPIR 508 208

Dadourian Group International Inc v Simms (No 2) [2007] 1 WLR 2967. 484

Daejan Investments Ltd v Park West Club Ltd [2004] BLR 223. 48

Dairy Crest Ltd v Pigott [1989] ICR 92 . . . 472

Dalgety Spillers Foods Ltd v Food Brokers Ltd [1994] FSR 504 466

Dallaway, Re [1982] 1 WLR 756 193

Daly v Sheikh (2004) LTL 13/2/04 569

Daniels v Commissioner of Police for the Metropolis [2005] EWCA Civ 1312 . . . 514

Daniels v Walker [2000] 1 WLR 1382 . . . . 32, 390, 392

Darley Main Colliery v Mitchell (1886) 11 App Cas 127. 238

Darlington Building Society v O'Rourke James Scourfield [1999] PNLR 365 258

Davie v Magistrates of Edinburgh 1953 SC 34. 385

Davy v Pickering [2015] 2 BCLC 116 211

Davy v Spelthorne Borough Council [1984] AC 262 550

Day v William Hill (Park Lane) Ltd [1949] 1 KB 632 333

Dayman v Canyon Holdings Ltd (2006) LTL 11/1/06 361

De Beer v Kanaar & Co [2003] 1 WLR 38 300

De Bry v Fitzgerald [1990] 1 WLR 552 . . . 304

Debtor (No 1 of 1987), Re a [1989] 1 WLR 271 36–7

Debtor (No 50A-SD-95), Re a [1997] Ch 310 243

Den Norske Bank ASA v Antonatos [1999] QB 271 . . . . 350, 489

Denton v TH White Ltd [2014] 1 WLR 3926 . . . . 144, 145, 251, 417, 421–3, 564

Derby and Co Ltd v Weldon (Nos 3 and 4) [1990] Ch 65. 484

Derby and Co Ltd v Weldon (No 9) [1991] 1 WLR 652. 498

Derby and Co Ltd v Weldon (No 10) [1991] 1 WLR 660. 357

Deutsche Bank AG v Vik [2010] EWHC 551 (Comm). 127

Deutsche Bank AG London Branch v Petromena ASA [2015] 1 WLR 4225 135

Deutsche Morgan Grenfell Group plc v Inland Revenue Commissioners [2007] 1 AC 558 . . . . 201, 333

Dietz v Lennig Chemicals Ltd [1969] 1 AC 170. 207

Dimes v Proprietors of Grand Junction Canal (1852) 3 HL Cas 759. 434

Director of the Serious Fraud Offce v Eurasian
    Natural Resources Corpn Ltd [2017] 1
    WLR 4205. 353
Doherty v Allman (1878) 3 App Cas 709. .472
Domicrest Ltd v Swiss Bank Corporation
    [1999] QB 548. 123
Donald v Ntuli [2011] 1 WLR 294 469
Donald Campbell and Co Ltd v Pollock [1927]
    AC 732 512
Donovan v Gwentoys Ltd [1990] 1 WLR
    472 . . . . .231, 246
Dormeuil Fréres SA v Nicolian International
    (Textiles) Ltd [1988] 1 WLR 1362. . . .499
Douglas v Hello! Ltd [2003] 1 All ER 1087;
    (2003) LTL 4/3/03 331
Douihech v Findlay [1990] 1 WLR 269 . . .215
Dover District Council v Sherred (1997) The
    Times, 11 February 1997. 397
DPP v Humphreys [1977] AC 1 331
Drake and Fletcher Ltd v Batchelor (1986) 130
    SJ 285 285
Drinkall v Whitwood [2004] 1 WLR 462. . .207
Dubai Aluminium Co Ltd v Al Alawi [1999]
    1 WLR 1964 355
Dubai Bank Ltd v Galadari (No 3) [1990]
    1 WLR 731 37
Duce v Worcestershire Acute Hospitals NHS
    Trust [2014] EWCA Civ 249 153
Duke of Bedford v Ellis [1901] AC 1 216
Dummer v Brown [1953] 1 QB 710. 284
Dunhill v Burgin (Nos 1 and 2) [2014] 1 WLR
    933 . . . . .205, 207
Dunlop Holdings Ltd v Staravia Ltd [1982]
    Com LR 3 494
Dunn v Glass Systems (UK) Ltd (2007) LTL
    23/7/2007 149
Dunn v Parole Board [2009] 1 WLR 728. .134
Dunnett v Railtrack plc [2002]
    1 WLR 2434 . . . . .161, 513
Dunning v United Liverpool Hospitals' Board
    of Governors [1973] 1 WLR
    586 . . . . .263, 506
Dyson v Attorney-General [1912]
    1 Ch 158 552
Dyson Ltd v Registrar of Trademarks (2003)
    The Times, 23 May 2003. 569

Earl of Malmesbury v Strutt and Parker (2007)
    42 EG 294 (CS) 456
Earl of Malmesbury v Strutt and Parker [2008]
    118 Con LR 68 513
Eastglen Ltd v Grafton [1996] 2 BCLC
    279 526
Easygroup IP Licensing Ltd v Easyjet Airline
    Co Ltd [2009] EWHC 1386 (Ch) 147

Eckman v Midland Bank Ltd [1973]
    QB 519 546
ED & F Man Liquid Products Ltd v Patel
    [2003] CPLR 384 . . . . 144, 282, 283
EDC v United Kingdom [1998] BCC 370. . .42
Edehomo v Edehomo [2011] 1 WLR
    2217 238
Edginton v Clark [1964] 1 QB 367 516
Edmeadcs v Thames Board Mills Ltd [1969] 2
    QB 67 .337, 395
Edward Owen Engineering Ltd v Barclays
    Bank International Ltd [1978]
    QB 159 287
Edwards-Tubb v JD Wetherspoon plc [2011] 1
    WLR 1373. . . . . 53, 388, 391, 396
EE and Brian Smith (1928) Ltd v Hodson
    [2007] EWCA Civ 1210. . . . . . . 475, 571
Eeles v Cobham Hire Services Ltd [2010] 1
    WLR 409. . . . . .294, 295
EF Phillips and Sons Ltd v Clarke [1970] Ch
    322 451
Eilon and Associates Ltd v IP Licensing Ltd
    (2011) LTL 15/4/11 285
Electromagnetic Geoservices ASA v Petroleum
    Geo-Services ASA [2016] 1 WLR
    2353 376
Elliott v Stobart Group Ltd [2015] EWCA Civ
    449 422
Elvanite Full Circle Ltd v AMEC Earth &
    Environmental (UK) Ltd [2013] EWHC
    1643 (TCC). 189
Emerald Supplies Ltd v British Airways plc
    [2010] Ch 48. 212
Emerald Supplies Ltd v British Airways plc
    [2011] Ch 345. 216
Emery v Day (1834) 1 Cr M & R 245. . . .237
EMI Records Ltd v Kudhail [1983] Com LR
    280 216
Energy Venture Partners Ltd v Malabu Oil and
    Gas Ltd [2015] 1 WLR 2309 . . . . 275, 478
Enfield London Borough Council v Mahoney
    [1983] 1 WLR 749. 545
English v Emery Reimbold and Strick Ltd
    [2002] 1 WLR 2409. . . . 42, 513, 516, 571
English and American Insurance Co Ltd v
    Herbert Smith [1988] FSR 232 358
English, Welsh and Scottish Railway Ltd v
    Goodman (2007) LTL 9/5/07. . . . 149, 202
Epping Electrical Co Ltd v Briggs and Forrester
    (Plumbing Services) Ltd, sub nom A v B
    (No 2) [2007] 1 All ER (Comm) 633. . .337
Ernst and Young v Butte Mining plc [1996] 1
    WLR 1605. .335
Ernst and Young v Butte Mining plc (No 2)
    [1997] 1 WLR 1485. 209

Espirit Telecoms UK Ltd v Fashion Gossip Ltd (2000) LTL 27/7/00 284

Essex County Council v R [1994] Fam 167 352–3

Esso Petroleum Co Ltd v Milton [1997] 1 WLR 938. 286

Eurasian Natural Resources Corpn Ltd v Dechert LLP [2016] 1 WLR 5027 435

Euro Brokers Ltd v Rabey [1995] IRLR 206 473

Euroil Ltd v Cameroon Offshore Petroleum SARL [2014] EWHC 215 (Comm) . . . 479

Evans Marshall and Co Ltd v Bertola SA [1973] 1 WLR 349. 464

Evening Standard Co Ltd v Henderson [1987] ICR 588. 472

Excalibur Ventures LLC v Texas Keystone Inc (No 2) [2017] 1 WLR 2221 17

Ezekiel v Orakpo (1994) The Times, 8 November 1994. 540

F and C Alternative Investments (Holdings) Ltd v Barthelemy (No 3) [2013] 1 WLR 548 411

F Hoffmann-La Roche & Co AG v Secretary of State for Trade and Industry [1975] AC 295 478

Fairstar Heavy Transport NV v Adkins [2013] EWCA Civ 886 345

Fakih Brothers v AP Møller (Copenhagen) Ltd [1994] 1 Lloyd's Rep 103 335

Family Housing Association (Manchester) Ltd v Michael Hyde and Partners [1993] 1 WLR 354. 356

Farmizer (Products) Ltd, Re [1997] 1 BCLC 589 234

Favor Easy Management Ltd v Wu [2011] 1 WLR 1803. . . . . 345, 361

Federal Bank of the Middle East Ltd v Hadkinson [2000] 1 WLR 1695 487

Federal Commerce and Navigation Co Ltd v Molena Alpha Inc [1978] 2 QB 927. . . 158

Fellowes and Son v Fisher [1976] QB 122 466

Feltham v Freer Bouskell [2013] EWHC 3086 (Ch). 412

Field v Leeds City Council [2000] 1 EGLR 54 387

Fielding v Rigby [1993] 1 WLR 1355 209

Filmlab Systems International Ltd v Pennington [1995] 1 WLR 673 528

Financial Services Authority v Sinaloa Gold plc [2013] 2 AC 28 486

Finers v Miro [1991] 1 WLR 35. 355

Finlan v Eyton Morris Winfield (A Firm) [2007] 4 All ER 143. 254

Finley v Connell Associates (1999) The Times, 23 June 1999. 330

Fiona Trust Holding Corporation v Privalov (2007) LTL 30/5/07 483

Firm of Solicitors, Re a [1992] QB 959 5

First Gulf Bank v Wachovia Bank National Association (2005) LTL 15/12/05 506

First National Commercial Bank plc v Humberts [1995] 2 All ER 673 238

First Subsea Ltd v Balltec Ltd [2018] Ch 25. 233

Fisher v Brooker [2009] 1 WLR 1764 247

Flightwise Travel Services Ltd v Gill (2003) The Times, 5 December 2003. 482

Foenander v Bond Lewis & Co [2002] 1 WLR 525 564

Folkes v Chadd (1782) 3 Doug KB 157 . . . 385

Football Dataco Ltd v Smoot Enterprises Ltd [2011] 1 WLR 1978. 141

Ford, Re [1900] 2 QB 211 . . . . 146, 288

Forest Heath District Council v ISG Jackson Ltd [2010] EWHC 322 (TCC). 90

Forster v Outred and Co [1982] 1 WLR 86 238

Foseco International Ltd v Fordath Ltd [1975] FSR 507. 464

Foss v Harbottle (1843) 2 Hare 461. 256

Fourie v Le Roux [2007] 1 WLR 320 . . . . 482, 483, 492

Fowler de Pledge v Smith (2003) The Times, 27 May 2003 571

Fox v Foundation Piling Ltd [2011] CP Rep 41 410

Fraser v Evans [1969] 1 QB 349 469

Fred Perry (Holdings) Ltd v Brands Plaza Trading Ltd [2012] FSR 28 418

Friern Barnet Urban District Council v Adams [1927] 2 Ch 25 213

Frost Capital Europe Ltd v Gathering of Developers Inc Ltd (2002) LTL 20/6/02. 301

Fulham Leisure Holdings Ltd v Nicholson Graham and Jones [2006] 2 All ER 599 357

Fuller v Strum [2002] 1 WLR 1097 397

Furniss v Firth Brown Tools Ltd [2008] EWCA Civ 182 240

Fusion Interactive Communication Solutions Ltd v Venture Investment Placement Ltd (No 2) [2005] 2 BCLC 571 209

G v G (Minors: Custody Appeal) [1985] 1 WLR 647. 570

G v Harrow London Borough Council (2004) LTL 20/1/04. .475

Gamlen Chemical Co (UK) Ltd v Rochem Ltd [1979] CA Transcript 777 355

Garbutt v Edwards [2006] 1 WLR 2907 . . .11

Garden Cottage Foods Ltd v Milk Marketing Board [1984] AC 130 466

Garratt v Saxby [2004] 1 WLR 2152. 413

GE Capital Corporate Finance Group v Bankers Trust Co [1995] 1 WLR 172 . . . . .349, 359

Geldoff Metaalconstructie NV v Simon Carves Ltd [2010] BLR 401 . . . . .158, 159

General Accident Fire and Life Assurance Corporation Ltd v Tanter [1984] 1 WLR 100 357

General Mediterranean Holdings SA v Patel [2000] 1 WLR 272. 320

Gentry v Miller [2016] EWCA Civ 141; [2016] 1 WLR 2696 . . . . 144, 145, 422, 423, 442

GFI Group Inc v Eaglestone [1994] IRLR 119. 473

Gibbon v Manchester City Council [2010] 1 WLR 2081. . . . . 399, 406, 409

Giles v Thompson [1994] 1 AC 142. 14

Gillick v West Norfolk and Wisbech Area Health Authority [1986] AC 112. 550

Glicksman v Redbridge Healthcare NHS Trust (2001) LTL 12/7/01 571

Global Torch Ltd v Apex Global Management Ltd (No 2) [2014] 1 WLR 4495. . . 38, 39, 251, 417, 421, 570

Goddard v Nationwide Building Society [1987] QB 670 357

Godin-Mendoza v Ghaidan [2004] 2 AC 557. 41

Godwin v Swindon Borough Council [2002] 1 WLR 997. . . . . 37, 74, 79, 82, 144

Goldtrail Travel Ltd v Onur Air Tasimacilik AS [2017] 1 WLR 3014. . . . . .303, 568

Gomba Holdings (UK) Ltd v Minories Finance Ltd (No 2) [1993] Ch 171 517

Gomez v Gomez-Monche Vives [2009] Ch 245 123

Good Challenger Navengante SA v Metalexportimport SA [2004] 1 Lloyd's Rep 67. 244

Goodale v Ministry of Justice (2009) LTL 9/9/10 348

Goode v Martin [2002] 1 WLR 1828 . . .38, 258

Gover v Propertycare Ltd [2006] ICR 1073 569

Government of Newfoundland v Newfoundland Railway Co (1888) 13 App Cas 199 159

Grant v Easton (1883) 13 QBD 302. 546

Great Atlantic Insurance Co v Home Insurance Co [1981] 1 WLR 529. 357

Great Future International Ltd v Sealand Housing Corporation [2001] CPLR 293 489

Green v Rozen [1955] 1 WLR 741. 448

Greene v Associated Newspapers Ltd [2005] QB 972 .44, 468

Greening v Williams (1999) The Times, 10 December 1999 406

Grender v Dresden [2009] EWHC 500 (Ch). 516

Grobbelaar v Sun Newspapers Ltd (1999) The Times, 12 August 1999 177

Grovewood Holdings plc v James Capel and Co Ltd [1995] Ch 80. 337

Grovit v De Nederlandsche Bank NV [2008] 1 WLR 51. 121

Guardian News and Media Ltd, Re [2010] 2 AC 697 435

Guerrero v Monterrico Metals plc [2010] EWHC 3228 (QB). 177

Guinness Peat Properties Ltd v Fitzroy Robinson Partnership [1987] 1 WLR 1027 . . . . .357, 358

Gulati v MGN Ltd [2017] QB 149. 44

Gulf International Bank v Al Ittefaq Steel Products [2010] EWHC 2601 (QB). . .133

Gunn v Taygroup Ltd [2010] EWHC 665 (TCC) 381

Gupta v Partridge [2018] 1 WLR 1 543

Gurtner v Circuit [1968] 2 QB 587 . . .78, 217

Gwembe Valley Development Co Ltd v Koshy (No 3) [2004] 1 BCLC 131 233

H v News Group Newspapers Ltd [2011] 1 WLR 1645. . . . . .43, 470

H v Schering Chemicals Ltd [1983] 1 WLR 143 396

H (Minors), Re (Sexual Abuse: Standard of Proof) [1996] AC 563 . . . . .275, 439

H Clark (Doncaster) Ltd v Wilkinson [1965] Ch 694. 381

Hadmor Productions Ltd v Hamilton [1983] 1 AC 191 570

Hagen, The [1908] P 189. 125

Hague Plant Ltd v Hague [2014] EWCA Civ 1609 . . . . 38, 39, 571

Hall v Stone (2007) The Times, 1 February 2008 512

Hallam Estates Ltd v Baker [2014] EWCA Civ 661 . . . . .415, 419

Hallam-Eames v Merrett (1995) The Times, 25 January 1995. 243

Halle v Trax BW Ltd [2000] BCC 1020 193

Halsey v Milton Keynes General NHS Trust [2004] 1 WLR 3002. . . . . . . 115, 116, 514

Hamilton v Al Fayed (No 2) [2003] QB 1175 . . . . 43, 303, 526

Hancock Shipping Co Ltd v Kawasaki Heavy Industries Ltd [1992] 1 WLR 1025 . . . 258

Haq v Singh [2001] 1 WLR 1594. 256

Harakas v Baltic Mercantile and Shipping Exchange Ltd [1982] 1 WLR 958 469

Harcourt v FEF Griffin [2007] PIQR Q177. 196

Harland and Wolff Pension Trustees Ltd v Aon Consulting Financial Services Ltd [2010] ICR 121. 257

Harrington v Polytechnic of North London [1984] 1 WLR 1293. 504

Harrison v Bottenheim (1878) 26 WR 362 290

Harrison v Tew [1990] 2 AC 523. 34

Harrison v University Hospitals Coventry & Warwickshire NHS Trust [2017] 1 WLR 4456 190

Hart v Emelkirk Ltd [1983] 1 WLR 1289 . 544

Hart v Rogers [1916] 1 KB 646 158

Hart Investments Ltd v Fidler [2007] BLR 30 145

Hart Investments Ltd v Larchpark Ltd [2008] 1 BCLC 589. 304

Hartley v Birmingham City District Council [1992] 1 WLR 968. 246

Hashtroodi v Hancock [2004] 1 WLR 3206 85

Hassan Khan & Co v Al-Rawas [2017] 1 WLR 2301 257

Hateley v Morris [2004] 1 BCLC 582 417

Haward v Fawcetts [2006] 1 WLR 682 . . . 243

Hawkins v Black (1898) 14 TLR 398. 212

Heaton v AXA Equity & Law Life Assurance Society plc [2002] 2 AC 329 332

Heaven v Road and Rail Wagons Ltd [1965] 2 QB 355 84

Hegglin v Person(s) Unknown [2014] EWHC 3793 (QB) 187

Henderson v Foxworth Investments Ltd [2014] 1 WLR 2600 570

Henderson v Henderson (1843) 3 Hare 100 . . . . 331, 332

Henderson v Jaoun [2002] 1 WLR 2971 123

Hendy v Milton Keynes Health Authority (1991) 3 Med LR 114 240

Henley v Bloom [2010] 1 WLR 1770 . . . 39, 333

Henry v British Broadcasting Corporation [2006] 1 All ER 154. 192

Henry v News Group Newspapers Ltd [2013] EWCA Civ 19 39

Henry Boot Construction Ltd v Alstom Combined Cycles Ltd [2005] 1 WLR 3850 . . . . 237, 574

Hepworth Plastics Ltd v Naylor Bros (Clayware) Ltd [1979] FSR 521 475

Heron v TNT (UK) Ltd [2014] 1 WLR 1277 526

Hertfordshire Investments Ltd v Bubb [2000] 1 WLR 2318. 572

Hertsmere Primary Care Trust v Administrators of Balasubramanium's Estate [2005] 3 All ER 274 . . . . . . 40, 406

Highgrade Traders Ltd, Re [1984] BCLC 151 354

Hills Contractors & Construction Ltd v Struth [2014] 1 WLR 1. 68

Hirschon v Evans [1938] 2 KB 801 539

Hoddinott v Persimmon Homes (Wessex) Ltd [2008] 1 WLR 806. 134

Hodgson v Imperial Tobacco Ltd [1998] 1 WLR 1056. 15

Hofer v Stawson [1999] 2 BCLC 336. 286

Holley v Smyth [1998] QB 726 468

Hollington v F Hewthorn & Co Ltd [1943] 1 KB 587 332

Holtby v Hodgson (1889) 24 QBD 103 . . . 448

Holyoake v Candy [2017] 3 WLR 1131 490

Home Office v Dorgan [2002] 1 WLR 3174 78

Homebase Ltd v LSS Services Ltd (2004) LTL 28/6/04 288

Hong Kong and Shanghai Banking Corporation v Kloeckner & Co AG [1990] 2 QB 514. 159

Horne-Roberts v SmithKline Beecham plc [2002] 1 WLR 1662. 255

Horton v Sadler [2007] 1 AC 307 247

Howard E Perry and Co Ltd v British Railways Board [1980] 1 WLR 1375 464

Howe v David Brown Tractors (Retail) Ltd [1991] 4 All ER 30. 257

Howe v Motor Insurers' Bureau (No 2) [2018] 1 WLR 923 529

Howglen Ltd, Re [2001] 1 All ER 376 508

Howlett v Davis [2018] 1 WLR 948. 532

HP Bulmer Ltd v J Bollinger SA [1974] Ch 401. 444, 445

HRH Prince of Wales v Associated Newspapers Ltd [2008] Ch 57. . . . . 283, 469, 470

Hubbard v Pitt [1976] QB 142. 466

Hubbard v Vosper [1972] 2 QB 84 475

Hughes v Jones [1996] PIQR P380 247

Hughes v Kingston upon Hull City Council [1999] QB 1193. 520

Hunter v Chief Constable of the West Midlands
Police [1982] AC 529 . . . . .330, 331
Huscroft v P&O Ferries [2011] 1 WLR
939 300
Hussain v Birmingham City Council [2005]
EWCA Civ 1570 145
Hutchison Telephone (UK) Ltd v Ultimate
Response Ltd [1993] BCLC 307 299
Hyams v Plender [2001]
1 WLR 32 . . . . 42, 564
Hydropol Hot Tubs Ltd v Roberjot [2011]
EWHC 121 (Ch) 371
Hytrac Conveyors Ltd v Conveyors
International Ltd [1983] 1 WLR 44. . .500

Incasep Ltd v Jones (2001) LTL 26/1/01. . .474
Independiente Ltd v Music Trading On-Line
(HK) Ltd [2008] 1 WLR 608. 478
Indicil Salus Ltd v Chandrasekaran (2006) LTL
16/2/06 499
Infabrics Ltd v Jaytex Ltd (No 2) [1985] FSR
75 360
Inland Revenue Commissioners v National
Federation of Self-Employed and Small
Businesses Ltd [1982] AC
617 . . . . .549, 555
Innovare Displays plc v Corporate Broking
Services Ltd [1991] BCC 174. . . . 303, 305
Inquiry under the Company Securities (Insider
Dealing) Act 1985, Re an [1988]
AC 660 503
Intense Investments Ltd v Development
Ventures Ltd [2005] BLR 478 143
International Bulk Shipping and Services Ltd v
Minerals and Metals Trading Corporation
of India [1996] 1 All ER 1017. 255
International Finance Corporation v Utexafrica
Sprl (2001) LTL 9/5/01 244
Interoil Trading SA v Watford Petroleum Ltd
(2003) LTL 16/7/03 304
Iraqi Ministry of Defence v Arcepey Shipping
Co SA [1981] QB 65 488
Irwin v Lynch [2011] 1 WLR 1364 256
Irwin Mitchell Solicitors v Patel (2003) LTL
15/4/03 264
IXIS Corporate and Investment Bank v WestLB
AG [2007] EWHC 1748 (Comm) 217

J v Oyston [2002] CPLR 563. 526
JA Pye (Oxford) Ltd v Graham [2003] 1 AC
419 235
Jablochkoff Co v McMurdo [1884]
WN 84. 516
Jackson v Marley Davenport Ltd [2004] 1
WLR 2926. 389

Jackson v Ministry of Defence [2006] EWCA
Civ 46 356
Jaggard v Sawyer [1995] 1 WLR 269. 480
Jameel v Dow Jones Co Inc [2005]
QB 946 330
Jameson v Central Electricity Generating Board
[1998] QB 323; [2000] 1 AC
455 . . . . .223, 332
Jani-King (GB) Ltd v Prodger (2007) LTL
10/4/07 418
Janov v Morris [1981] 3 All ER 780 327
Jefferson v National Freight Carriers plc
[2001] 2 Costs LR 313 192
Jet Airways (India) Ltd v Barlowworld Handling
Ltd [2014] EWCA Civ 1311 505
Jeyaretnam v Mahmood (1992) The Times, 21
May 1992 130
Jirehouse Capital v Beller [2009]
1 WLR 751 301
JN Dairies Ltd v Johal Dairies Ltd [2010]
EWCA Civ 348 . . . . .149, 369
Johnson v Gore Wood & Co [2002]
2 AC 1. .328, 332
Johnson v Gore Wood (No 2) (2004) The
Times, 17 February 2004. 413
Johnson v Taylor Bros and Co [1920]
AC 144 125
Johnson v Wyatt (1863) De GJ & S 18 . . .474
Jones v Gurney [1913] WN 72. 301
Jones v Jones [1970] 2 QB 576 87
Jones v Kaney [2011] 2 AC
398 . . . . 386, 387, 391, 393, 398
Jones v National Coal Board [1957]
2 QB 55. 439
Jones v Stones [1999] 1 WLR 1739 247
Jones v University of Warwick [2003] 1 WLR
954 . . . . .44, 322
JP Morgan Chase Bank v Springwell
Navigation Corp [2007] 1 All ER (Comm)
549 . . . . .388, 390
JSC BTA Bank v Ablyazov [2010] 1 WLR
976 352
JSC BTA Bank v Ablyazov (No 15) [2017] 1
WLR 603. 331
JW Spear & Sons Ltd v Zynga Inc [2013]
EWHC 1640 (Ch) 250
JX MX v Dartford & Gravesham NHS Trust
[2015] EWCA Civ 96. 208

Kadhim v Brent London Borough Council
(2001) The Times, 27 March 2001. 38
Kearsley v Klarfeld [2006] 2 All ER
303 176
Keays v Murdoch Magazines (UK) Ltd [1991]
1 WLR 1184 .441

Keefe v Mapfre Mutalidad Cia De Seguros Y
    Reasaguros SA [2016] 1 WLR 905 . . . 204
Keen Phillips v Field [2007] 1 WLR
    686 419
Kennedy v Cordia (Services) LLP [2016] 1
    WLR 597. 387
Kenneth Allison Ltd v AE Limehouse Ltd
    [1992] 2 AC 105 77
Kennett v Brown [1988] 1 WLR 582 257
Kensington International Ltd v Congo [2008]
    1 WLR 1144 130
Ketteman v Hansel Properties Ltd [1987] AC
    189 . . . . 251, 253
Kevythalli Design v ICE Associates [2010]
    EWCA Civ 379 302
Kew v Bettamix Ltd [2007] PIQR P210 . . . 240
Khan v R M Falvey & Co [2002]
    PNLR 28 238
Khiaban v Beard [2003] 1 WLR 1626 62
Khorasandjian v Bush [1993] QB 727 475
Kiam v MGN Ltd (No 2) [2002] 1 WLR
    2810 518
Kimathi v Foreign and Commonwealth Office
    (No 2) [2017] 1 WLR 1081 209
King v Daltray [2003] EWCA Civ 808 568
King v Telegraph Group Ltd [2005] 1 WLR
    2282 40
Kinnear v Falconfilms NV [1996]
    1 WLR 920 124
Kirk v Walton [2009] EWHC 703 (QB) . . . 151
Kirklees Metropolitan Borough Council v
    Wickes Building Supplies Ltd [1993] AC
    227 478
Kirkman v EuroExide Corporation (CMP
    Batteries Ltd) [2007] All ER (D) 209 . . . 386
Kirkup v British Rail Engineering Ltd [1983] 1
    WLR 1165. . . . . 202, 390
Kitcat v Sharp (1882) 48 LT 64 356
KJM Superbikes Ltd v Hinton [2009] 1 WLR
    2406 151
Kleinwort Benson Ltd v Lincoln City Council
    [1999] 2 AC 349 243
Knauf UK GmbH v British Gypsum Ltd [2002]
    1 WLR 907; [2002] 2 Lloyd's Rep
    416 . . . . 78, 124, 228
Knight v Rochdale Healthcare NHS Trust
    [2004] 1 WLR 371. 241
Knight v Sage Group plc (1999)
    LTL 28/4/99. 336
Kojima v HSBC Bank plc [2012] 1 All ER
    1392 381
Kolden Holdings Ltd v Rodette Commerce Ltd
    [2008] Bus LR 1051 128
Koo Golden East Mongolia v Bank of Nova
    Scotia [2008] QB 717 502

Korea National Insurance Corporation v
    Allianz Global Corporate and Specialty AG
    [2007] 2 CLC 748 279
Korner v H Korner and Co Ltd [1951]
    Ch 10. 515
Kotonou v National Westminster Bank plc
    [2011] 1 All ER (Comm) 1164. 331
KR v Bryn Alyn Community (Holdings) Ltd
    [2003] QB 1441. 245
Krysia Maritime Inc v Intership Ltd [2009] 1
    All ER (Comm) 292. 512
Kuenyehia v International Hospitals Group
    Ltd (2006) The Times, 17 February
    2006 . . . . 77, 78
Kuwait Airways Corporation v Iraqi Airways
    Co [1995] 1 WLR 1147. 211
Kuwait Airways Corporation v Iraqi Airways
    Co (No 6) [2005] 1 WLR 2734 355
Kuwait Oil Co (KSC) v Idemitsu Tankers KK
    [1981] 2 Lloyd's Rep 510 129

La Chemise Lacoste SA v Sketchers USA Ltd
    (2006) LTL 24/5/06 252
Ladd v Marshall [1954] 1 WLR
    1489 . . . . 440, 572, 574
Lahey v Pirelli Tyres Ltd [2007]
    1 WLR 998 407
Lakatamia Shipping Co Ltd v Su [2015] 1
    WLR 291. 487
Lakhani v Mahmud [2017] 1 WLR
    3482 421
Lancashire County Council v Taylor [2005] 1
    WLR 2668. 40
Land and Property Trust Co plc, Re [1991] 1
    WLR 601. 526
Langley v North West Water Authority [1991]
    1 WLR 697 34
Langston v Amalgamated Union of Engineering
    Workers (No 2) [1974] ICR 510 473
Lansing Linde Ltd v Kerr [1991] 1 WLR
    251 468
Larby v Thurgood [1993] ICR 66 386
Lauritzencool AB v Lady Navigation Inc
    [2005] 1 WLR 3686. 475
Lavelle v Lavelle (2004) The Times, 9 March
    2004 42
Lavelle v Noble [2011] EWCA Civ 441 . . . 389
Law Debenture Trust Corporation (Channel
    Islands) Ltd v Lexington Insurance Co
    (2001) LTL 12/11/01 217
Lawrence v Fen Tigers [2014] AC
    822 . . . . 466, 475
Lawrence v Poorah [2008] UKPC 21 161
Lawrence David Ltd v Ashton [1991] 1 All ER
    385 472

Leeds City Council v Price [2005] 1 WLR
1825 41
Leicester Circuits Ltd v Coates Industries plc
[2003] EWCA Civ 333. 513
Leicester Wholesale Fruit Market Ltd v
Grundy [1990] 1 WLR 107 254
Leisure Data v Bell [1988] FSR 367 474
Lennon v Birmingham City Council (2001)
LTL 27/3/01. 331
Les Laboratories Servier v Apotex Inc [2007]
EWHC 591 (Pat) 381
Letang v Cooper [1965] 1 QB 232 233
Lewis v Commissioner of Inland Revenue
[2001] 3 All ER 499. 193
Lewis and Peat (Produce) Ltd v Almatu
Properties Ltd (1992) The Times, 14 May
1992 487
Leyvand v Barasch (2000) The Times, 23
March 2000. 304
Liddell v Middleton [1996] PIQR P36 386
Lidl UK GmbH v Davies [2008] EWCA Civ
976 252
Lighting and Lamps UK Ltd v Clarke (2016)
LTL 4/3/2016. 567
Lillicrap v Nalder and Son [1993]
1 WLR 94 357
Lilly Icos Ltd v Pfizer Ltd [2002] 1 WLR
2253 362
Linda, The [1988] 1 Lloyd's Rep 175 129
Lipkin Gorman v Karpnale Ltd [1989] 1 WLR
1340 . . . . 161, 383
Little Olympian Each Ways Ltd, Re [1995] 1
WLR 560. 300
Lloyds Bowmaker Ltd v Britannia Arrow
Holdings plc [1988] 1 WLR
1337 . . . . 265, 266, 491
Locabail International Finance Ltd v
Agroexport [1986] 1 WLR 657 474
Locabail (UK) Ltd v Bayfield Properties Ltd
[2000] QB 451. 434
Lock International plc v Beswick [1989] 1
WLR 1268. 495–6
Loftus, Re [2005] 1 WLR 1890 235
Lombard North Central plc v Automobile World
(UK) Ltd [2010] EWCA Civ 20 161
London Regional Transport v Mayor of
London [2003] EMLR 4 469
Long v Tolchard and Sons Ltd (1999) The
Times, 5 January 2000. 245–7
Longstaff International Ltd v Baker and
McKenzie [2004] 1 WLR
2917 . . . . 303, 304
Lonrho Ltd v Shell Petroleum Co Ltd [1980]
QB 358; [1980] 1 WLR 627 345
Loose v Williamson [1978] 1 WLR 639 . . . 503

Lord Bethell v SABENA [1983] 3
CMLR 1 444
Loutchansky v Times Newspapers (No 1)
[2002] QB 321. 349
Lovell v Lovell [1970] 1 WLR 1451. 202
Loveridge v Healey [2004] EWCA Civ
173 289
Lowsley v Forbes [1999] 1 AC 329 243
Lucas v Barking, Havering and Redbridge
Hospitals NHS Trust [2004] 1 WLR
220 361
Lucasfilm Ltd v Ainsworth [2010] Ch
503 . . . . 120, 445
Lunnun v Singh [1999] CPLR 587 143
Lynch v James Lynch and Sons (Transport) Ltd
(2000) LTL 8/3/00 248
Lysaght v Commissioners of Inland Revenue
[1928] AC 234. 300

M (A Minor), Re (1989) 88 LGR 841 358
M & R (Minors), Re (Sexual Abuse: Expert
Evidence) [1996] 4 All ER 239. 386
MA Holdings Ltd v R (George Wimpey UK
Ltd) [2008] NPC 6. 37
Mac Hotels Ltd v Rider Levett Bucknall UK
Ltd [2010] EWHC 767 (TCC). 357
McCafferty v Metropolitan Police District
Receiver [1977] 1 WLR 1073 246
McCall v Poulton [2009] PIQR P8. 445
McCauley v Vine [1999] 1 WLR 1997 284
McCheane v Gyles (No 2) [1902]
1 Ch 915 217
McDonald v Horn (1994) The Times, 10
August 1994 193
McDonald's Corporation v Steel [1995] 3 All
ER 615 330
McDonald's Hamburgers Ltd v Burgerking UK
Ltd [1987] FSR 112. 479
McDonnell v Walker [2010] PIQR P5 246
McE v Prison Service of Northern Ireland
[2009] 1 AC 908 . . . . 353, 359
McFaddens Solicitors v Chandrasekaran
[2007] EWCA Civ 220. 569
McFarlane v EE Caledonia Ltd (No 2) [1995]
1 WLR 366 526
McKennitt v Ash [2008] QB 73 . . . . . . 44, 470
McKenzie v McKenzie [1971] P 33 436
Maclaine Watson and Co Ltd v International
Tin Council [1988] Ch 1 544
Macleish v Littlestone [2016] 1 WLR
3289 410
Macmillan Inc v Bishopsgate Investment Trust
plc [1993] 1 WLR 1372. 431
McPhilemy v Times Newspapers Ltd [1999] 3
All ER 775. 201

McPhilemy v Times Newspapers Ltd [2000] CPLR 335 438

McTaggart v McTaggart [1949] P 94 355

Machkevitch v Kirill Ace Stein [2016] EWHC 1210 (Comm) 362

Maguire v Molin [2003] 1 WLR 644 179

Maharanee Seethaderi Gaekwar of Baroda v Wildenstein [1972] 2 QB 283 119

Mahkutai, The [1996] AC 650 126

Malekout v Medical Sickness Annuity and Life Assurance Society Ltd (2003) LTL 20/10/03 417

Malgar Ltd v ER Leach (Engineering) Ltd [2000] FSR 393 371

Maltez v Lewis (1999) The Times, 4 May 1999 42

Mann v Chetty [2001] CP Rep 24 389

Manor Electronics Ltd v Dickson [1988] RPC 618 496

Manta Line Inc v Sofianites [1984] 1 Lloyd's Rep 14 135

Maple Leaf Macro Volatility Master Fund v Rouvroy [2009] 2 All ER (Comm) 287; aff'd [2009] EWCA Civ 1334 134

Marc Rich & Co AG v Società Italiana Impianti PA (No 2) [1992] 1 Lloyd's Rep 624 135

Marcan Shipping (London) Ltd v Kefalas [2007] 1 WLR 1864. 419

Marcus v Medway Primary Care Trust [2011] EWCA Civ 750 513

Mareva Compania Naviera SA v International Bulkcarriers SA [1980] 1 All ER 213 481

Marlton v Tektronix UK Holdings Ltd (2003) LTL 10/2/03. 344

Maronier v Larmer [2003] QB 620 547

Marren v Dawson Bentley and Co Ltd [1961] 2 QB 135. 241

Marsh v Sofaer [2004] PNLR 24 353

Martin v Kaisary [2006] PIQR P5 254

Martin v Randall [2007] EWCA Civ 1155 . . . . 400, 411

Martin v Triggs Turner Barton (2008) The Times, 5 February 2008. 344

Mason v First Leisure Corporation plc (2003) LTL 30/7/03. 86

Masri v Consolidated Contractors International UK Ltd (No 2) [2008] 1 All ER (Comm) 305; [2009] QB 450. 484

Masri v Consolidated Contractors International (UK) Ltd (No 4) [2009] Bus LR 246; [2010] 1 AC 90 . . . . 121, 535

Masri v Consolidated International Co SAL (No 3) [2012] 1 WLR 223. 561

Masterman-Lister v Brutton and Co (Nos 1 and 2) [2003] 1 WLR 1511 205

Matthews v Kuwait Bechtel Corporation [1959] 2 QB 57 125

Matthews v Metal Improvements Co Inc [2007] CP Rep 27 399

Mayne Pharma (USA) Inc v Teva UK Ltd (2004) LTL 3/12/04. 459

Mead General Building Ltd v Dartmoor Properties Ltd [2009] BCC 510 289

Meadow v General Medical Council [2007] QB 462 398

Medcalf v Mardell [2003] 1 AC 120 527

Medicaments and Related Classes of Goods (No 4), Re [2002] 1 WLR 269. 435

Mediterranean Shipping Co v OMG International Ltd [2008] EWHC 2150 (Comm). 484

Medway Oil and Storage Co Ltd v Continental Contractors Ltd [1929] AC 88. 516

Megarity v DJ Ryan and Sons Ltd [1980] 1 WLR 1237. 396

Memory Corporation plc v Sidhu (No 2) [2000] 1 WLR 1443. . . . . 266, 482

Mercury Communications Ltd v Director General of Telecommunications [1996] 1 WLR 48. 550

Merrett v Babb [2001] QB 1174 256

Metall und Rohstoff AG v Donaldson Lufkin and Jenrette Inc [1990] 1 QB 391 . . . . 125, 126

Miles v Bull [1969] 1 QB 258 290

Miles v ITV Networks Ltd (2003) LTL 8/12/03 284

Miller v Cawley (2002) The Times, 6 September 2002. 439

Miller v Garton Shires [2007] RTR 24. . . . 283

Millharbour Management Ltd v Weston Homes Ltd [2011] 3 All ER 1027 216

Millhouse Capital UK Ltd v Sibir Energy plc [2009] 1 BCLC 298. 265

Mionis v Democratic Press SA [2018] 2 WLR 565 44

Mireskandari v Associated Newspapers Ltd [2010] EWHC 967 (QB) 327

Mitchell v News Group Newspapers Ltd [2013] EWCA Civ 1537; [2014] 1 WLR 795 . . . . 38, 187, 325, 418

Mitchelstown Co-operative Society Ltd v Société des Produits Nestlé SA [1989] FSR 345 464

Mitsui and Co Ltd v Nexen Petroleum UK Ltd [2005] 3 All ER 511. 502

Moat Housing Group-South Ltd v Harris [2006] QB 606. 459

Mobil Cerro Negro Ltd v Petroleos de Venezuela
SA [2008] 1 Lloyd's Rep 684 484
Mohun-Smith v TBO Investments Ltd [2016] 1
WLR 2919. . . . . .428, 442
Molins plc v GD SpA [2000] 1 WLR 1741. . 76
Mölnlycke AB v Procter and Gamble Ltd
[1992] 1 WLR 1112. 123
Monroe v Hopkins (No 2) [2017] 1 WLR
358 562
Monsanto v Tilly (1999) The Times, 30
November 1999. 326
Montecchi v Shimco (UK) Ltd [1979] 1 WLR
1180 485
Montpellier Estates Ltd v Leeds City Council
[2012] EWHC 1343 (QB) 345, 348
Morgan v Spirit Group Ltd [2011]
PIQR P9 523
Morgan, Re (1887) 35 ChD 492 334
Morgan Crucible Co plc v Hill Samuel and Co
Ltd [1991] Ch 295. 329
Morgans v Needham (1999) The Times, 5
November 1999. 361
Morley v Inglis (1837) 4 Bing NC 58. 158
Morning Star Co-operative Society Ltd v
Express Newspapers Ltd [1979]
FSR 113. . . . . .463, 465
Morris v Bank of America National Trust
[2000] 1 All ER 954. . . . . .36, 149
Morris v Stratford-on-Avon Rural District
Council [1973] 1 WLR 1059 374
Mortimer v Bailey (2004) LTL 29/10/04 . .480
Morton v Portal Ltd [2010] EWHC 1804
(QB). 513
Mothercare Ltd v Robson Books Ltd [1979]
FSR 466. 463
Motorola Credit Corporation v Uzan [2002] 2
All ER (Comm) 945. 489
Motorola Credit Corporation v Uzan (No 2)
[2004] 1 WLR 113. 131
Motto v Trafigura Ltd [2012] 1 WLR 657. . .20
Mouchel Ltd v Van Oord (UK) Ltd [2011] BLR
492 223
Mouna, The [1991] 2 Lloyd's Rep
221 . . . . .86, 570
Moy v Pettman Smith [2005] 1 WLR
581 413
Mucelli v Government of Albania [2009] 1
WLR 276. . . . . .66, 80
Mueller Europe Ltd v Central Roofing (South
Wales) Ltd [2013] CILL 3293 . . .345, 348
Mulkerrins v PricewaterhouseCoopers [2003]
1 WLR 1937 331
Multinational Gas and Petrochemical Co v
Multinational Gas and Petrochemical
Services Ltd [1983] Ch 258 126

Murray v Express Newspapers plc [2009] Ch
481 469
Mutch v Allen [2001] CPLR 200 394
MV Yorke Motors v Edwards [1982] 1 WLR
444 . . . . .146, 288
N (A Child), Re (McKenzie Friend: Rights of
Audience) [2008] 1 WLR 2743 437
N (A Minor), Re (Sexual Abuse: Video
Evidence) [1997] 1 WLR 153. 386
N (Infants), Re [1967] Ch 512 68
Nanglegan v Royal Free Hampstead NHS
Trust [2002] 1 WLR 1043 82
Nash v Eli Lilly and Co [1993] 1 WLR
782 . . . . .245, 246
Nasser v United Bank of Kuwait [2002] 1
WLR 1868. . . . . .37, 43, 297, 302
Nata Lee Ltd v Abid [2015]
2 P & CR 3 .213
National Bank of Sharjah v Dellborg (1992)
The Times, 24 December 1992. 265
National Commercial Bank Jamaica Ltd v
Olint Corporation Ltd [2009] 1 WLR
1405 . . . . .463, 465, 474
National Justice Compania Naviera SA v
Prudential Assurance Co Ltd [1993] 2
Lloyd's Rep 68. . . . . .393, 396
National Mortgage and Agency Co of New
Zealand Ltd v Gosselin (1922) 38 TLR
832 126
National Westminster Bank plc v Aaronson
(2004) LTL 9/3/04 428
National Westminster Bank plc v Daniel
[1993] 1 WLR 1. 275
National Westminster Bank plc v King [2008]
Ch 385. 178
National Westminster Bank plc v Rushmer
[2010] 2 FLR 362 . . . . .39, 542, 571
Nationwide Building Society v Various
Solicitors [1999] PNLR 53. 353
Navitaire Inc v Easyjet Airline Co Ltd [2006]
RPC 4 440
Ndole Assets Ltd v Designer M & E Services
UK Ltd [2017] 1 WLR 4367 77
Neck v Taylor [1893] 1 QB 560. 299
Negocios Del Mar SA v Doric Shipping
Corporation SA [1979] 1 Lloyd's Rep
331 491
Nelson v Clearsprings (Management) Ltd
[2007] 1 WLR 962. 82
Nelson v Rye [1996] 1 WLR 1378 232–4
Neufville v Papamichael (1999) LTL
23/11/99 442
Newland v Boardwell [1983] 1 WLR
1453 155

Nichia Corporation v Argos Ltd [2007] Bus LR 1753 349

Nigel Witham Ltd v Smith [2008] CILL 2557 117

Ninemia Maritime Corporation v Trave Schiffahrtsgesellschaft mbH & Co KG [1983] 1 WLR 1412; [1983] 2 Lloyd's Rep 660; aff'd [1983] 2 Lloyd's Rep 660 483–5

Nomura International plc v Granada Group Ltd [2007] 2 All ER (Comm) 878 . . . . . 37, 330

Norbrook Laboratories Ltd v Carr [2010] EWCA Civ 1108 321

Nordstern Allgemeine Versicherungs AG v Internav Ltd [1999] 2 Lloyd's Rep 139 526

Northampton Coal, Iron and Waggon Co v Midland Waggon Co (1878) 7 ChD 500 301

Norwich Pharmacal Co v Customs and Excise Commissioners [1974] AC 133 501–4

Nottingham Building Society v Peter Bennett and Co (1997) The Times, 26 February 1997 76

Nottingham County Council v Bottomley [2010] Med LR 407 205

Nouri v Marvi [2011] PNLR 7 238

Nova (Jersey) Knit Ltd v Kammgarn Spinnerei GmbH [1977] 1 WLR 713 285

NP Engineering and Security Products Ltd, In re [1998] 1 BCLC 208 209

NWL Ltd v Woods [1979] 1 WLR 1294 . . . . 467–9, 471

O2 (UK) Ltd v Dimension Data Network Services Ltd (2007) LTL 8/11/07 294

Oaktree Financial Services Ltd v Higham (2004) LTL 11/5/04 481

Oates v Harte Reade and Co [1999] PIQR P120 234

OBG Ltd v Allan [2008] 1 AC 1 469

Oceanbulk Shipping and Trading SA v TMT Asia Ltd [2011] 1 AC 662 356

Oceanica Castelana Armadora SA v Mineral-importexport [1983] 1 WLR 1294 487

O'Connor v Bar Standards Board [2017] 1 WLR 4833 40

OCS Group Ltd v Wells [2009] 1 WLR 1895 . . . . 344, 506

Office Overload Ltd v Gunn [1977] FSR 39 472

Official Custodian for Charities v Mackey [1985] Ch 168 473

Ofulue v Bossert [2009] 1 AC 990 . . . 244, 355

Oil & Mineral Development Corporation Ltd v Sajjad (2001) LTL 3/12/01 252

Olatawura v Abiloye [2003] 1 WLR 275 . . . 300

Omar v Omar [1995] 1 WLR 1428 504

Omega SA v Omega Engineering Inc [2011] EWCA Civ 645 284

OMV Petrom SA v Glencore International AG [2017] 1 WLR 3465 411

Ord v Upton [2000] Ch 352 208

O'Reilly v Mackman [1983] 2 AC 237 . . . 328, 549, 550, 556

Orford v Rasmi Electronics Ltd (2004) LTL 4/8/04 569

Orwell Steel (Erection and Fabrication) Ltd v Asphalt and Tarmac (UK) Ltd [1984] 1 WLR 1097 491

Owen v Grimsby and Cleethorpes Transport [1992] PIQR Q27 249

Oxley v Penwarden [2001] CPLR 1 391

Oystertec plc v Davidson (2004) LTL 7/4/04 489

P v Home Office [2017] 1 WLR 3189 550

P&O Nedlloyd BV v Arab Metals Co [2007] 1 WLR 2483 257

P&O Nedlloyd BV v Arab Metals Co (No 2) [2007] 1 WLR 2288 . . . . 247, 279

P & S Amusements Ltd v Valley House Leisure Ltd [2006] EWHC 1510 (Ch) 283

Packman Lucas Ltd v Mentmore Towers Ltd [2010] BLR 465 542

Paddick v Associated Newspapers Ltd (2003) LTL 10/12/03 343

Panayiotou v Sony Music Entertainment (UK) Ltd [1994] Ch 142 . . . . 431, 432

Pannone LLP v Aardvark Digital Ltd [2011] 1 WLR 2275 450

Paragon Finance plc v DB Thakerer and Co [1999] 1 All ER 400 233

Parkinson v Myer Wolff (23 April 1985, unreported) 300

Parr's Banking Co v Yates [1898] 2 QB 460 237

Patel v Air India Ltd [2010] EWCA Civ 443 527

Patel v Patel [2000] QB 551 135

Patel v WH Smith (Eziot) Ltd [1987] 1 WLR 853 473

Patterson v Ministry of Defence [1987] CLY 1194 453

Payabi v Armstel Shipping Corporation [1992] QB 907 . . . . 87, 254

PCW (Underwriting Agencies) Ltd v Dixon [1983] 2 All ER 158 488

Pearce v Ove Arup Partnership Ltd (2001) LTL 2/11/01 387

Pearson v Naydler [1977] 1 WLR 899 304

Peco Arts Inc v Hazlitt Gallery Ltd [1983] 1
   WLR 1315. 242–3
Peet v Mid-Kent Healthcare Trust [2002] 1
   WLR 210. . . . . 391, 392, 396–7
Penningtons v Abedi (1999) LTL 13/8/99. . 283
Pepin v Watts [2001] CPLR 9. 523
Pepper v Hart [1993] AC 593 272
Perotti v Collyer-Bristow [2004] 2 All ER 189;
   [2004] 4 All ER 53. . . . . 17, 565
Personal Management Solutions Ltd v Gee 7
   Group Ltd [2016] 1 WLR 2132. 505
PGF II SA v OMFS Co 1 Ltd [2014] 1 WLR
   1386 116
Philipps v Philipps (1878) 4 QBD 127 333
Phillips v News Group Newspapers Ltd [2013]
   1 AC 1. 352
Phillips v Symes (No 2) [2005] 1 WLR
   2043 398
Phillips v Symes (No 3) [2008] 1 WLR 180,
   HL. 78, 82, 420
Phoenix Finance Ltd v Fédération
   Internationale de l'Automobile (2002) The
   Times, 27 June 2002 49
Phonographic Performance Ltd v Department
   of Trade and Industry [2004] 1 WLR
   2893 238
Phonographic Performance Ltd v Planet Ice
   (Peterborough) Ltd (2003) LTL
   2/2/04 289
Pinson v Lloyds and National Provincial
   Foreign Bank Ltd [1941] 2 KB 72 155
Pirelli General Cable Works Ltd v Oscar Faber
   and Partners [1983] 2
   AC 1 . . . . 238, 243
PJS v News Group Newspapers Ltd [2016] AC
   1081 44
Play It Ltd v Digital Bridges Ltd [2005] EWHC
   1001 (Ch) 466
Plevin v Paragon Personal fnance Ltd (No 2)
   [2017] 1 WLR 1249. 15
Polanski v Condé Nast Publications Ltd [2005]
   1 WLR 637 432
Polaroid Corporation v Eastman Kodak Co
   [1977] RPC 379. 463
Polivitte Ltd v Commercial Union Assurance
   Co plc [1987] 1 Lloyd's Rep 379 396
Polly Peck International plc v Nadir (No 2)
   [1992] 4 All ER 769. 492
Polydor Ltd v Harlequin Record Shops Ltd
   [1982] CMLR 413. 444
Poole Borough Council v Hambridge [2007]
   EWCA Civ 990 561
Porter v Magill [2002] 2 AC 357 . . . . . 43, 434
Porter v National Union of Journalists [980]
   IRLR 40. 463
Porzelack KG v Porzelack (UK) Ltd [1987] 1
   WLR 420. 302
Potters-Ballotini Ltd v Weston-Baker [1977]
   RPC 202 466
Powell v Brent London Borough Council
   [1988] ICR 176 464
Power Curber International Ltd v National
   Bank of Kuwait SAK [1981] 1 WLR
   1233 287
Practice Direction (Administrative Court:
   Uncontested Proceedings) [2008] 1 WLR
   1377 558
Practice Direction (Citation of Authorities)
   [2001] 1 WLR 1001. 271
Practice Direction (Citation of Authorities)
   [2012] 1 WLR 780. 272
Practice Direction (Court of Appeal:
   Procedure) [1995] 1 WLR 1191. 572
Practice Direction (Hansard: Citations) [1995]
   1 WLR 192 272
Practice Direction (Juries: Length of Trial)
   [1981] 1 WLR 1129. 441
Practice Direction (RCJ: Reading Lists and
   Time Estimates) [2000] 1 WLR
   208 433
Practice Guidance (Interim Non-disclosure
   Orders) [2012] 1 WLR 1003 470
Practice Note [1927] WN 290 451
Practice Note (McKenzie Friends: Civil and
   Family Courts) [2010] 1 WLR 1881 . . . 436
Practice Statement (House of Lords: Judicial
   Precedent) [1966] 1 WLR 1234 234
Practice Statement (Trust Proceedings:
   Prospective Costs Orders) [2001] 1 WLR
   1082 193
Prescott v Bulldog Tools Ltd [1981] 3 All ER
   869 395
Prince Radu of Hohenzollern v Houston
   [2009] EWHC 398 (QB) 333
Pritam Kaur v S Russell and Sons Ltd [1973]
   QB 337 241
Procon (Great Britain) Ltd v Provincial
   Building Co Ltd [1984] 1 WLR 557. . . 304
Professional Information Technology
   Consultants Ltd v Jones (2001) LTL
   7/12/01 252
Project Development Co Ltd SA v KMK
   Securities Ltd [1982] 1 WLR 1470. . . . 490
Property Alliance Group Ltd v Royal Bank of
   Scotland plc [2016] EWHC
   207 (Ch) 31
Property Alliance Group Ltd v Royal Bank of
   Scotland plc [2016] 1 WLR 361. 356
Property Alliance Group Ltd v Royal Bank of
   Scotland plc [2016] 1 WLR 992. 353

Property Alliance Group Ltd v Royal Bank
of Scotland plc [2015] EWHC 3341
(Ch) 354, 358
Prudential Assurance Co Ltd v Fountain Page
Ltd [1991] 1 WLR 756 398
PSM International plc v Whitehouse [1992]
IRLR 279. 479
Public Trustee v Williams (2000) LTL
10/2/00 283
Pugh v Cantor Fitzgerald International [2001]
CPLR 271 143
Purcell v FC Trigell Ltd [1971] 1 QB 358. . 450

Quest Advisors Ltd v McFeely [2011] EWCA
Civ 1517 292

R v Advertising Standards Authority Ltd, ex p
Vernons Organisation Ltd [1992] 1 WLR
1289 552
R v Barnet London Borough Council, ex p
Shah [1983] 2 AC 309 300
R v Board of Visitors of Hull Prison,
ex p St Germain (No 2) [1979] 1 WLR
1401 556
R v Bow Street Metropolitan Stipendiary
Magistrate, ex p Pinochet Ugarte (No 2)
[2000] 1 AC 119 434
R v Boyes (1861) 1 B & S 311 351
R v Broadcasting Complaints Commission,
ex p Owen [1985] QB 1153. 557
R v Broadcasting Standards Commission, ex p
British Broadcasting Corporation [2001]
QB 885 43
R v Criminal Injuries Compensation Board, ex
p Lain [1967] 2 QB 864. 548
R v Dairy Produce Quota Tribunal for England
and Wales, ex p Caswell [1989] 1 WLR
1089 553
R v Davies [1962] 1 WLR 1111. 388
R v Dodson (1984) 79 Cr App R 220 373
R v Electricity Commissioners, ex p London
Electricity Joint Committee Co (1920) Ltd
[1924] 1 KB 171 551
R v General Medical Council, ex p Gee [1987]
1 WLR 564 548
R v Gough [1993] AC 646 42
R v Henn [1981] AC 850 445
R v HM Treasury, ex p British
Telecommunications plc [1994] 1 CMLR
621 471
R v Horsham District Council, ex p Wenman
[1995] 1 WLR 680. 527
R v Independent Television Commission, ex p
TSW Broadcasting Ltd (1992) The Times,
30 March 1992 556

R v Independent Television Commission, ex p
TV NI Ltd (1991) The Times, 30 December
1991 553
R v Inner London Crown Court, ex p Baines
and Baines [1988] QB 579. 353
R v Inspectorate of Pollution, ex p Greenpeace
Ltd [1994] 1 WLR 570 549
R v Kearley [1992] 2 AC 228 372
R v Kensington Income Tax Commissioners,
ex p Princess Edmond de Polignac [1917]
1 KB 486 265
R v Lanfear [1968] 2 QB 77. 397
R v Lord Chancellor, ex p Child Poverty Action
Group [1999] 1 WLR 347 195
R v Ministry of Agriculture, Fisheries and
Food, ex p Monsanto plc [1999] QB
1161 471
R v Poplar Borough Council, ex p London
County Council (No 2) [1922]
1 KB 95 551
R v Powell (1841) 1 QB 352 551
R v Secretary of State for Employment, ex p
Equal Opportunities Commission [1995] 1
AC 1 549 550
R v Secretary of State for the Environment, ex
p Hackney LBC [1983] 1 WLR
524 331
R v Secretary of State for the Environment, ex
p Powis [1981] 1 WLR 584 557
R v Secretary of State for Health, ex p
Furneaux [1994] 2 All ER 652. 553
R v Secretary of State for Health, ex p Imperial
Tobacco Ltd [2001] 1 WLR 127 444
R v Secretary of State for the Home
Department, ex p Quaquah [2000] HRLR
325 42
R v Secretary of State for the Home
Department, ex parte Simms [2000] 2 AC
115 353
R v Secretary of State for Transport, ex p
Factortame Ltd (No 7) [2001] 1 WLR
942 235
R v Sharp [1988] 1 WLR 7 372
R v Stratford-on-Avon District Council, ex p
Jackson [1985] 1 WLR 1319 553
R v Wandsworth County Court, ex p
Wandsworth London Borough Council
[1975] 1 WLR 1314. 543
R v Wood (1982) 76 Cr App R 23 373
R (Alconbury Developments Ltd) v Secretary
of State for the Environment, Transport
and the Regions [2003] 2 AC 295 42
R (B) v Secretary of State for Foreign and
Commonwealth Affairs [2005]
QB 643 41

R (Ben-Abdelaziz) v Haringey London
Borough Council [2001] 1 WLR
1485 548

R (Buglife) v Medway Council [2011]
Env LR 27 553

R (Burkett) v Hammersmith and Fulham
London Borough Council [2002] 1 WLR
1593 553

R (Campaign for Nuclear Disarmament) v
Prime Minister of the United Kingdom
[2002] EWHC 2712 (Admin) 195

R (Compton) v Wiltshire Primary Care Trust
[2009] 1 WLR 1436. 194

R (Corner House Research) v Director of the
Serious Fraud Office [2008] EWHC 246
(Admin) 36, 147

R (Corner House Research) v Secretary of
State for Trade and Industry [2005] 1
WLR 2600. 194

R (Edwards) v Environment Agency [2008] 1
WLR 1587. 572

R (Garner) v Elmbridge Borough Council
[2010] EWCA Civ 1006. 194–5

R (Gerber) v Wiltshire Council [2016] 1 WLR
2593 553

R (Horvath) v Secretary of State for the
Environment, Food and Rural Affairs
[2007] NPC 83 447

R (Hysaj) v Secretary of State for the Home
Department [2015] 1 WLR
2472 . . . . 213, 422

R (KB) v South London and West Region
Mental Health Tribunal [2004]
QB 936 46

R (Kehoe) v Secretary of State for Work and
Pensions [2004] 1 WLR 2757 . . . . . 41, 42

R (Lawer) v Restormel Borough Council
[2008] HLR 20 265

R (Macrae) v Hertfordshire District Council
(2012) LTL 9/3/12 553

R (McVey) v Secretary of State for Health
[2010] EWHC 437 (Admin) 557

R (McVey) v Secretary of State for Health
[2010] EWHC 1225 (Admin) 553

R (Mohamed) v Secretary of State for Foreign
and Commonwealth Affairs [2011] QB
218; on appeal [2009] 1 WLR 2579 . . . 502

R (Morgan Grenfell and Co Ltd) v Special
Commissioner of Income Tax [2003] 1 AC
563 352

R (O) v Secretary of State for the Home
Department [2016] UKSC 19. 555

R (Omar) v Secretary of State for Foreign and
Commonwealth Affairs [2014] QB
112 502

R (O'Shea) v Coventry Magistrates' Court
[2004] Crim LR 948 373

R (Pelling) v Bow County Court [2001]
UKHRR 165 42

R (Prudential plc) v Special Commissioners of
Income Tax [2011] QB 669 352

R (S) v Chief Constable of South Yorkshire
[2004] 1 WLR 2196. 41

R (Simmons) v Bolton Metropolitan Borough
Council [2011] EWHC 2729
(Admin) 261

R (Sivasubramaniam) v Wandsworth County
Court [2003] 1 WLR 475 549

R (Ullah) v Special Adjudicator [2004] 2 AC
323 41

R (Wilkinson) v Responsible Medical Officer
Broadmoor Hospital [2002] 1 WLR
419 557

Radiocomms Systems Ltd v Radio
Communications Systems Ltd [2010]
EWHC 149 (Ch) 282

Rahamim v Reich (2009) LTL
10/2/09 . . . . 417, 418

Raja v Van Hoogstraten (No 9) [2009] 1 WLR
1143 . . . . 34, 144

Rajval Construction Ltd v Bestville Properties
Ltd [2011] CILL 2994 145

Rall v Hume [2001] 3 All ER 248 . . . . 44, 322

Rank Film Distributors Ltd v Video Information
Centre [1982] AC 380 . . . . 350, 351

Ras al Khaimah Investment Authority v
Bestfort Development LLP [2018] 1 WLR
1099 484

Rasool v West Midlands Passenger Transport
Executive [1974] 3 All ER 638. 378

Rassam v Budge [1893] 1 QB 571 333

Rasu Maritima SA v Perusahaan Pertambangan
Minyak Dan Gas Bumi Negara [1978] QB
644 485

Ratten v UBS AG [2014] EWHC 665
(Comm) 40

Rawlinson & Hunter Trustees SA v Director of
the Serious Fraud Office (No 2) [2015] 1
WLR 797. 358

RBG Resources plc v Rastogi (2002) LTL
31/5/02 478

RBS Rights Issue Litigation, Re [2017] 1 WLR
3539; [2017] 1 WLR 4635. 17

RC Residuals Ltd v Linton Fuel Oils Ltd
[2002] 1 WLR 2782. 77

RE Jones Ltd v Waring and Gillow Ltd [1926]
AC 670 286

Re-Source America International Ltd v Platt
Site Services Ltd (2004) 95 Con
LR 1 223

Reader v Molesworths Bright Clegg [2007] 1
WLR 1082. 238

Redevco Properties v Mount Cook Land Ltd
(2002) LTL 30/7/02 284

Reed Executive plc v Reed Business
Information Ltd [2004] 1 WLR
3026 356

Reeves v Butcher [1891] 2 QB 509. . .235, 237

Regione Piemonte v Dexia Crediop SpA [2014]
EWCA Civ 1298 145

Reid Minty v Taylor [2002] 1 WLR
2800 518

Relational LLC v Hodges [2011] EWCA Civ
774 304

Relfo Ltd v Varsani [2011] 1 WLR 1402 . . .74

Restick v Crickmore [1994] 1 WLR 420 . . .28

Rewia, The [1991] 2 Lloyd's Rep 325 123

Ricci v Chow [1987] 1 WLR 1658. 504

Riddick v Thames Board Mills Ltd [1977] QB
881 362

Ridehalgh v Horsefield [1994] Ch 205. . . .527

Riniker v University College London [2001] 1
WLR 13. 564

Riverpath Properties Ltd v Brammall (2002)
The Times, 16 February 2002 275

Robert v Momentum Services Ltd [2003] 1
WLR 1577. 419

Roberts v Gill and Co [2011] 1 AC
240 .209, 257, 574

Roberts Petroleum Ltd v Bernard Kenny Ltd
[1983] 2 AC 192 539

Roche v Sherrington [1982] 1 WLR 599 . . .256

Rockwell Machine Tool Co Ltd v EP Barrus
(Concessionaires) Ltd [1968] 1 WLR
693 341

Rofa Sport Management AG v DHL
International (UK) Ltd [1989] 1 WLR
902 . . . . .336, 449

Rogers v East Kent Hospitals NHS Trust
[2009] LS Law Med 153 39

Rogers v Hoyle [2015] QB 265 388

Rolf v De Guerin [2011] CP Rep 24. 412

Romain v Scuba TV Ltd [1997] QB 887 . . .234

Ronex Properties Ltd v John Laing
Construction Ltd [1983] QB 398. 330

Rose v Lynx Express Ltd [2004] 1 BCLC
455 505

Rotherham v Priest (1879) 41 LT 558 285

Rothwell v Chemical and Insulating Co Ltd
[2008] 1 AC 28 240

Rottenberg v Monjack [1993] BCLC
374 463

Roundstone Nurseries Ltd v Stephenson
Holdings Ltd [2009] 5 Costs LR
787 . . . . .138, 145

Roussel Uclaf v GD Searle and Co Ltd [1977]
FSR 125. 466

Rowley v Liverpool City Council (1989) The
Times, 26 October 1989 344

Roy v Kensington and Chelsea and
Westminster Family Practitioner
Committee [1992] 1 AC 624 551

Royal Brompton Hospital NHS Trust v
Hammond [2001] BLR 297. . . . .282, 283

Royal Brompton Hospital NHS Trust v
Hammond (No 3) [2002] 1 WLR
1397 223

Rubin v Expandable Ltd [2008] 1 WLR
1099 . . . . .37, 357

Rush and Tompkins Ltd v Greater London
Council [1989] AC 1280 356

Russian Commercial and Industrial Bank v
British Bank for Foreign Trade Ltd [1921]
2 AC 438. 552

S v Beach [2015] 1 WLR 2701. 146

S (Minors) (Care Order: Implementation of
Care Plan), Re [2002] 2 AC 291 46

SAFA v Banque du Caïre [2000] 2 All ER
(Comm) 567 . . . . .286, 287

St Edmundsbury and Ipswich Diocesan Board
of Finance v Clark [1973] Ch 323 432

St Merryn Meat Ltd v Hawkins (2001) LTL
2/7/01 266

Salekipour v Parmar [2016] QB 987 34

Salford Estates (No 2) Ltd v Altomart Ltd
[2015] 1 WLR 1825. 422

Sanderson v Blyth Theatre Co [1903] 2 KB
533 . . . . .515, 516

Sardinia Sulcis, The [1991] 1 Lloyd's Rep
201 255

Sarwar v Alam [2002] 1 WLR 125. 13

Savings and Investment Bank Ltd v Fincken
[2004] 1 WLR 667. 356

Sawyer v Atari Interactive Inc [2005] EWHC
2351 (QB) 134

Sayers v Clarke Walker [2002] 1 WLR
3095 422

Sayers v Hunt [2013] 1 WLR 1695 246

Sayers v SmithKline Beecham plc [2005] PIQR
P8 334

SCF Finance Co Ltd v Masri [1985] 1 WLR
876 487

Schmidt v Wong [2006] 1 WLR 561. 494

Schneider v Batt (1881) 8 QBD 701, CA . . .226

Schott Kem Ltd v Bentley [1991]
1 QB 61. 295

Seaconsar Far East Ltd v Bank Markazi
Jomhouri Islami Iran [1994] 1 AC
438 124

Seals v Williams [2015] EWHC 1829
(Ch) 116

Secretary of State for Defence v Guardian
Newspapers Ltd [1985] AC 339 503

Secretary of State for the Environment, Food
and Rural Affairs v Meier [2009] 1 WLR
2780 273

Secretary of State for the Home Department v
AHK [2009] 1 WLR 2049 436

Secretary of State for Trade and Industry v
Bairstow [2004] Ch 1 332

Secretary of State for Trade and Industry v
Lewis (2001) The Times, 16 August 2001
. . . . 569

Seele Austria GmbH and Co KG v Tokio
Marine Europe Insurance Ltd [2009] BLR
481 257

Series 5 Software Ltd v Clarke [1996] 1 All ER
853 467

Serious Organised Crime Agency v Namli
[2011] EWCA Civ 1411. 343

SES Contracting Ltd v UK Coal plc (2007) 33
EG 90 (CS) 507

Sewell v Electrolux Ltd (1997) The Times, 7
November 1997. 397

Seyfang v GD Searle and Co [1973] QB 148
. . . . 393

Shah v HSBC Private Bank (UK) Ltd [2011]
EWCA Civ 1154 . . . . 343, 344

Shanning International Ltd v George Wimpey
International Ltd [1989] 1 WLR
981 294

Sharab v Prince Al-Waleed bin Talal bin Abdal-
Aziz-Al-Saud [2009] 2 Lloyd's Rep
160 125–7

Sharland v Sharland [2015] 3 WLR
1070 451

Sharp v Leeds City Council [2017] EWCA Civ
33 109

Shell Chemicals UK Ltd v Vinamul Ltd (1991)
The Times, 7 March 1991, CA. 156

Shepherd Homes Ltd v Sandham [1971] Ch
340 474

Shepherd Neame Ltd v EDF Energy Networks
(SPN) plc [2008] Bus LR Digest D43 . . . 396

Shepherds Investments Ltd v Walters [2007]
EWCA Civ 292 519

Sheppard and Cooper Ltd v TSB Bank plc
[1996] 2 All ER 654. 473

Shlaimoun v Mining Technologies
International Inc [2012] EWCA Civ 772
. . . . 300

Shovelar v Lane [2012] 1 WLR 637. 516

Shyam Jewellers Ltd v Cheesman (2001) LTL
29/11/01 275

Sibthorpe v Southwark London Borough
Council [2011] 1 WLR 2111 14

Siebe Gorman and Co Ltd v Pneupac Ltd
[1982] 1 WLR 185. 450

Simmons v Castle [2013] 1 WLR 1239 14

Sinclair v Chief Constable of West Yorkshire
(2000) LTL 12/12/00 282

Sinclair Investment Holdings SA v Versailles
Trade Finance Ltd [2006] 1 BCLC
60 149

Singh v Observer Ltd [1989] 2 All ER
751 526

Sions v Price The Independent, 19 December
1988 486

Sir Lindsay Parkinson & Co v Triplan Ltd
[1973] QB 609. 302

Siskina, The [1979] AC 210 . . . . 130, 462, 483

Slater v Buckinghamshire County Council
[2004] EWCA Civ 1478. 161

Slazengers Ltd v Seaspeed Ferries International
Ltd [1987] 1 WLR 1197; [1988] 1 WLR
221 301

SMAY Investments Ltd v Sachdev [2003] 1
WLR 1973. 135

Smith v Cardiff Corporation [1954]
1 QB 210. 216

Smith v Chief Constable of Sussex [2008]
PIQR P12 329

Smith v Henniker-Major [2003] Ch 182 . . . 257

Smith v Inner London Education Authority
[1978] 1 All ER 411. 471

Smith v Probyn (2000) The Times, 29 March
2000 . . . . 67, 86

Smith v Secretary of State for Energy and
Climate Change [2014] 1 WLR
2283 . . . . 505, 506

Smith v White Knight Laundry Ltd [2001] 1
WLR 616. 235

SmithKline Beecham plc v Apotex Europe Ltd
[2006] 1 WLR 872. 457

SmithKline and French Laboratories Ltd v RD
Harbottle (Mercantile) Ltd [1980] RPC
363 503

Sociedade Nacional de Combustíveis de
Angola UEE v Lundqvist [1991] 2 QB
310 351

Société Commerciale de Réassurance v ERAS
(International) Ltd [1992]
2 All ER 82 243

Société Eram Shipping Co Ltd v Compagnie
Internationale de Navigation [2004] 1 AC
260 539

Société Nationale Industrielle Aérospatiale v
Lee Kui Jak [1987] AC
871 . . . . 130, 473

Solo Industries v Canara Bank [2001] 2 All ER (Comm) 217; [2001] 1 WLR 1800 . . . . 286, 287

Solomon v Cromwell Group plc [2012] 1 WLR 1048 407

Somerset-Leeke v Kay Trustees [2004] 3 All ER 406 303

Sony/ATV Music Publishing LLC v WPMC Ltd [2017] EWHC 456 (Ch) 411

South Cambridgeshire District Council v Persons Unknown (2004) The Times, 11 November 2004 213

South Carolina Insurance Co v Assurantie Maatschappij 'De Zeven Provincien' NV [1987] AC 24 462

Southern & District Finance plc v Turner (2003) LTL 7/11/03 560

Sowerby v Charlton [2006] 1 WLR 568 . . . 380

Speed Up Holdings Ltd v Gough and Co (Handly) Ltd [1986] FSR 330 305

Spice Girls Ltd v Aprilia World Service BV (No 3) (2000) The Times, 12 September 2000 456

Spiliada Maritime Codaverrporation v Cansulex Ltd [1987] AC 460 . . . . 126, 127, 129

Spillman v Bradfield Riding Centre [2007] EWHC 89 (QB) 294

Spoor v Green (1874) LR 9 Ex 99 238

Sports Network Ltd v Calzaghe [2008] EWHC 2566 (QB) 417

SSL International plc v TTK Lig Ltd [2012] 1 Lloyd's Rep 107 76

Stabilad Ltd v Stephens and Carter Ltd [1999] 1 WLR 1201 305

Staines v Walsh (2003) The Times, 1 August 2003 266

Stallwood v David [2007] 1 All ER 206 . . . 393

Standard Bank plc v Agrinvest International Inc [2010] 2 CLC 886 145

Standard Steamship Owners' Protection and Indemnity Association (Bermuda) Ltd v Gann [1992] 2 Lloyd's Rep 528 129

Starr v National Coal Board [1977] 1 WLR 63 395

State Trading Corporation of India v Doyle Carriers Inc [1991] 2 Lloyd's Rep 55 . . . 290

Statue of Liberty, The [1968] 1 WLR 739 . . . 373

Steadman-Byrne v Amjad [2007] 1 WLR 2484 435

Steele v Mooney [2005] 2 All ER 256 86

Steele v Steele (2001) The Times, 5 June 2001 441

Stephen v Riverside Health Authority (1989) The Times, 29 November 1989 240

Stephenson (SBJ) Ltd v Mandy (1999) The Times, 21 July 1999 40

Stevens v Gullis [2000] 1 All ER 527 387

Stevens v School of Oriental and African Studies (2000) The Times, 2 February 2001 42

Stewart Gill Ltd v Horatio Myer and Co Ltd [1992] QB 600 159

Stewart v Engel [2000] 1 WLR 2268 . . . . 289, 456

Stockler v Fourways Estates Ltd [1984] 1 WLR 25 488

Stott v West Yorkshire Road Car Co Ltd [1971] 2 QB 651 230

Straker v Tudor Rose [2007] EWCA Civ 368 . . . . 55, 513

Strickson v Preston County Court [2007] EWCA Civ 1132 549

Stringman v McArdle [1994] 1 WLR 1653 295

Stubbings v Webb [1993] 2 AC 498 234

Sullivan v West Yorkshire Passenger Transport Executive [1985] 2 All ER 134 396

Sumitomo Corpn v Crédit Lyonnais Rouse Ltd [2002] 1 WLR 479 354

Summers v Fairclough Homes Ltd [2012] 1 WLR 2004 . . . . 37, 331, 532

Swain v Hillman [2001] 1 All ER 91 . . . . 282, 563

Swain-Mason v Mills & Reeve [2011] 1 WLR 2735 251

Swansea City Council v Glass [1992] QB 844 236

Swindale v Forder [2007] 1 FLR 1905 457

Symphony Group plc v Hodgson [1994] QB 179 . . . . 472, 526

Taly NDC International NV v Terra Nova Insurance Co Ltd [1985] 1 WLR 1359 299

Tanfern Ltd v Cameron-MacDonald [2000] 1 WLR 1311 571

Tasyurdu v Immigration Appeal Tribunal [2003] CPLR 343 569

Tate Access Floors Inc v Boswell [1991] Ch 512 499

Taylor v Inntrepreneur Estates (CPC) Ltd (2001) LTL 31/1/01 329–30

Taylor v Lawrence [2003] QB 528 . . . 434, 572

Taylor v Ribby Hall Leisure Ltd [1998] 1 WLR 400 232

Tchenguiz v Director of the Serious Fraud Office [2015] 1 WLR 838 271

Tchenguiz v Grant Thornton UK LLP [2017] EWHC 310 (Comm) 362

Tchenguiz v Grant Thornton UK LLP [2015]
  EWHC 405 (Comm) 148
TDK Tape Distributor (UK) Ltd v Videochoice
  Ltd [1986] 1 WLR 141 . . . . 488, 490
Technocrats International Inc v Fredic Ltd
  [2005] 1 BCLC 467 491
Tecnion Investments Ltd, Re [1985]
  BCLC 434 345
Test claimants in the FII Group Litigation v
  Revenue and Customs Commissioners
  [2012] 1 WLR 2375 293
Texaco Ltd v Arco Technology Inc (1989) The
  Times, 13 October 1989 513
Texuna International Ltd v Cairn Energy Ltd
  [2005] 1 BCLC 579 303
TG Can Ltd v Crown Packaging UK plc [2007]
  EWHC 1271 (QB) 252
Thane Investments Ltd v Tomlinson (No 1)
  [2003] EWCA Civ 1272 485
Thevarajah v Riordan [2016] 1 WLR
  76 . . . . 276, 422
Third Chandris Shipping Corporation v
  Unimarine SA [1979] QB 645 485
Thomas v Home Office [2007] 1 WLR
  230 84
Thompson v Brown [1981] 1 WLR 744 . . 241,
  245, 246
Thomson v Lord Clanmorris [1900] 1 Ch
  718 235
Thoni GmbH & Co KG v RTP Equipment Ltd
  [1979] 2 Lloyd's Rep 282 287
Thorn plc v MacDonald [1999] CPLR
  660 144
Thorne v Heard [1894] 1 Ch 599 233
Thorne v Lass Salt Garvin [2009] EWHC 100
  (QB) 569
Thorp v Holdsworth (1876) 3 ChD
  637 155
Three Rivers District Council v Bank of
  England (No 3) [2003]
  2 AC 1 . . . . 43, 283, 326, 328, 329
Three Rivers District Council v Governor and
  Company of the Bank of England (No 6)
  [2005] 1 AC 610 353
Thurrock Borough Council v Secretary of State
  for the Environment, Transport and the
  Regions (2000) The Times, 20 December
  2000 80
Tibbles v SIG plc [2012] 1 WLR
  2591 . . . . 179, 276
Tinsley v Sarker (2004) LTL 23/7/04 295
TIP Communications LLC v Motorola Ltd
  [2009] EWHC 212 (Pat) 39
TIP Communications LLC v Motorola Ltd
  [2009] EWHC 1486 (Pat) 348

TJ Brent Ltd v Black and Veatch Consulting
  Ltd [2008] EWHC 1497 (TCC) 49, 55
Totalise plc v Motley Fool Ltd (2001) The
  Times, 15 March 2001 503
Totty v Snowden [2002] 1 WLR 1384 37
Tower Hamlets London Borough Council v
  Begum [2003] 2 AC 430 42
Towler v Wills [2010] EWHC 1209 (Comm)
  149
Trader Publishing Ltd v Autotrader.Com Inc
  [2010] EWHC 142 (Ch) 149, 196
Travelers Insurance Co Ltd v Countryside
  Surveyors Ltd [2011] 1 All ER (Comm)
  631 505
Trident International Freight Services Ltd v
  Manchester Ship Canal Co [1990] BCLC
  263 . . . . 302, 303
Triplex Safety Glass Co Ltd v Lancegaye Safety
  Glass (1934) Ltd [1939] 2 KB 395 . . . 350–1
Trustees of Stokes Pension Fund v Western
  Power Distribution (South West) plc
  [2005] 1 WLR 3595 410
TSB Private Bank International SA v Chabra
  [1992] 1 WLR 231 484
Tudor Accumulator Co Ltd v China Mutual
  Steam Navigation Co Ltd [1930] WN 200
  509
Turner, Re [1907] 2 Ch 126 193
Tweed v Parades Commission [2007] 1 AC 650
  . . . . 367, 556
Tyburn Productions Ltd v Conan Doyle [1991]
  Ch 75 121

Umm Qarn Management Co Ltd v Bunting
  [2001] CPLR 21 325
Unilever plc v Procter and Gamble Co [2000] 1
  WLR 2436 356
Unique Pub Properties Ltd v Licensed
  Wholesale Co Ltd (2003) LTL
  13/10/03 475
Unisoft Group Ltd (No 1), Re [1993]
  BCLC 1292 299
Unisoft Group Ltd (No 2), Re [1993]
  BCLC 532 304
Unisoft Group Ltd (No 3), Re [1994]
  1 BCLC 609 . . . . 150, 200
United Bank Ltd v Asif (2000) LTL
  11/2/00, CA 283
United Mizrahi Bank Ltd v Doherty [1998]
  1 WLR 435 488
United States Securities and Exchange
  Commission v Manterfield [2010]
  1 WLR 172 478
United Trading Corp SA v Allied Arab Bank
  Ltd [1985] 2 Lloyd's Rep 554n 287

Universal Thermosensors Ltd v Hibben [1992]
1 WLR 840 496

Utilise TDS Ltd v Davies *See* Denton v TH
White Ltd

Van Aken v Camden London Borough Council
[2003] 1 WLR 684. 83

Van Hoorn v Law Society [1985] QB 106 . . .19

VDU Installations Ltd v Integrated Computer
Systems and Cybernetics Ltd [1989]
FSR 378. 497

Vedatech Corporation v Seagate Software
Information (2001) LTL
29/11/01 .37, 302

Ventouris v Mountain [1991] 1 WLR
607 353

Ventouris v Mountain (No 2) [1992] 1 WLR
887 377

Veracruz Transportation Inc v VC Shipping Co
Inc [1992] 1 Lloyd's Rep 353. 483

Vinos v Marks & Spencer plc [2001] 3 All ER
784 . . . . .37, 82

Virk v Gan Life Holdings plc (1999) 52 BMLR
207 237

Viscount Chelsea v Muscatt [1990]
2 EGLR 48 473

Vitpol Building Service v Samen [2009]
Bus LR D65. . . . . .33, 90

VTB Capital plc v Nutritek International Corp
[2013] 2 AC 337 . . . . 126, 262, 368

W (Children), Re (Permission to Appeal)
[2007] Fam Law 897 563

W & H Trade Marks (Jersey) Ltd v W and H
Trade Marks (Jersey) Ltd [1986]
AC 368 329

Wade v Turfrey (2007) LS Law Medical
352 295

Wagenaar v Weekend Travel Ltd [2015] 1
WLR 1968. . . . . .33, 530

Wake Forest University Health Sciences v
Smith and Nephew plc [2009] EWHC 45
(Pat). 466

Wakefield v Duke of Buccleugh (1865) 12 LT
628 464

Walker v Walker (2005) LTL 27/1/05. 335

Walker v Wilsher (1889) 23 QBD
335 356

Walker Construction (UK) Ltd v Quayside
Homes Ltd [2014]
EWCA Civ 93 . . . . 400, 406, 522

Walkley v Precision Forgings Ltd [1979] 1
WLR 606. 247

Wallersteiner v Moir (No 2) [1975]
QB 373 193

Walley v Stoke-on-Trent City Council [2007] 1
WLR 352. 380

Walsham Chalet Park Ltd v Tallington Lakes
Ltd [2014] EWCA Civ 1607 417

Walton v Allman [2016] 1 WLR 2053 542

Wandsworth London Borough Council v
Winder [1985] AC 461 551

Wardle Fabrics Ltd v G Myristis Ltd [1984]
FSR 263. 497

Warren v Mendy [1989] 1 WLR 853 475

Warren v Uttlesford District Council [1996]
COD 262. 37

Warren v Warren [1997] QB 488 431

Watkins v Jones Maidment Wilson [2008]
PNLR 23 238

Watts v Oakley [2006] EWCA Civ 1905 . .389

Waugh v British Railways Board [1980] AC
521 . . . . .350, 354

Weait v Jayanbee Joinery Ltd [1963] 1 QB
239 258

Webb v Liverpool Women's NHS Foundation
Trust [2016] 1 WLR 3899 412

Webster v Ridgeway Foundation School
Governors [2009] ELR 439 359

Wedstock Realizations Ltd, Re [1988] BCLC
354 193

Weld v Petre [1929] 1 Ch 33 247

Weller v Associated Newspapers Ltd [2016] 1
WLR 1541. 469

Welsh Development Agency v Redpath
Dorman Long Ltd [1994] 1 WLR
1409 253

Wenlock v Moloney [1965] 1 WLR 1238 . . .329

Wentworth v Bullen (1840) 9 B & C 840 . . .450

West Bromwich Building Society v Wilkinson
[2005] 1 WLR 2303. 236

West Country Renovations Ltd v McDowell
[2013] 1 WLR 416. 29

West of England Steamship Owners' Protection
and Indemnity Association Ltd v John
Holman and Sons [1957]
1 WLR 1164 .126

West London Pipeline and Storage Ltd v Total
UK Ltd [2008] 1 CLC 935. 196

West London Pipeline and Storage Ltd v Total
UK Ltd [2008] 2 CLC 258. 349

Westcott v Westcott [2009] QB 407 43

Westinghouse Electric Corporation Uranium
Contract Litigation, Re [1978]
AC 547 217

Wheeler v Chief Constable of Gloucestershire
Constabulary [2013] EWCA Civ
1791 523

Wheeler v Le Marchant (1881) 17 ChD
675 . . . . .355, 359

White v White (2001) LTL 21/6/01 571

White and Co v Credit Reform Association and Credit Index Ltd [1905] 1 KB 653 202

Whitehead v Avon County Council (1995) The Times, 3 May 1995 396

Whitehouse v Jordan [1981] 1 WLR 246 . . . . 387, 393

William Hill Organisation Ltd v Tucker [1999] ICR 291. 473

Williams v Beesley [1973] 1 WLR 1295 441

Williams v Central Bank of Nigeria [2014] AC 1189 233

Williams v Lishman, Sidwell, Campbell & Price Ltd [2009] PNLR 34. 243

Williams v Lishman, Sidwell, Campbell & Price Ltd [2010] PNLR 25. 242

Willis v MRJ Rundell & Associates Ltd [2013] EWHC 2923 (TCC). 188, 190, 522

Willis v Nicholson [2007] PIQR P22 192

Willson v Ministry of Defence [1991] 1 All ER 638 453

Wilson v First County Trust (No 2) [2004] 1 AC 816. . . . . .41, 272

Wiltshire County Council v Frazer (No 2) [1986] 1 WLR 109. 544

Winter v Winter (2000) LTL 10/11/00 513

Winthorp v Royal Exchange Assurance Co (1755) 1 Dick 282 301

Woodley v Woodley (1993) The Times, 15 March 1993. 543

Woods v Duncan [1946] AC 401 336

Woollard v Fowler (24 May 2006, unreported) 99

Workvale Ltd, Re [1992] 1 WLR 416. 211

Worldwide Corporation Ltd v GPT Ltd [1998] EWCA Civ 1894 251

Worrall v Reich [1955] 1 QB 296 388

WPP Holdings Italy SRL v Benatti [2007] 1 WLR 2316. .275

X Ltd v Morgan-Grampian (Publishers) Ltd [1991] 1 AC 1 . . . . 502, 503

YD (Turkey) v Secretary of State for the Home Department [2006] 1 WLR 1646. 36

Yeo v Times Newspapers Ltd (No 2) [2015] 1 WLR 3031. . . . . 185, 189

Young v JR Smart (Builders) Ltd (No 2) (2000) LTL 7/2/00. .252

Yousif v Salama [1980] 1 WLR 1540. 494

Z Ltd v A-Z and AA-LL [1982] QB 558 . . . . 480, 487, 490

Zockoll Group Ltd v Mercury Communications Ltd [1998] FSR 354. 474

Court of Justice of the European Union Cases

Corman-Collins SA v La Maison du Whiskey SA (Case C-9/12) [2014] QB 431. 121

Effer SpA v Kantner (38/81) [1982] E CR 825 122

Elchinov v Natsionalna zdravnoosiguritelna kasa (Case C-173/09) [2011] PTSR 1308 445

Elefanten Schuh GmbH v Jacqmain (150/80) [1981] ECR 1671 (ECJ). 135

Etablissements A de Bloos Sprl v SCA Bouyer (14/76) [1976] ECR 1497 122

Foto-Frost v Hauptzollamt Lübeck-Ost (314/85) [1987] ECR 4199 445

Garland v British Rail Engineering Ltd [1983] 2 AC 751. 444

Handelskwekerij GJ Bier BV v Mines de Potasse d'Alsace SA (21/76) [1978] QB 708 123

Jégo-Quéré et Cie SA v Commission of the European Communities (T-177/01) [2003] QB 854 447

Kalfelis v Bankhaus Schröder, Münchmeyer, Hengst & Co (189/87) [1988] ECR 5565 . . . . 122, 124

Kernkraftwerke Lippe-Ems GmbH v Hauptzollamt Osnabrück (Case C-5/14) [2016] 2 WLR 369. 444

Kleinwort Benson Ltd v Glasgow City Council (Case C-346/93) [1996] QB 57 443

Marinari v Lloyds Bank plc (Case C-364/93) [1996] QB 217. 123

Netherlands v Rüffer (814/79) [1980] ECR 3807 123

O'Byrne v Aventis Pasteur MSD Ltd (Case C-358/08) [2010] 1 WLR 1412 254

Overseas Union Insurance Ltd v New Hampshire Insurance Co (Case C-351/89) [1992] QB 434. 128

Plaumann & Co v Commission of the European Economic Community (Case C-25/62) [1963] ECR 95 447

R v Secretary of State for Transport, ex p Factortame Ltd (No 2) (Case C-213/89) [1991] 1 AC 603 . . . . 471, 552

Shenavai v Kreischer (266/85) [1987] ECR 239 122

Srl Cilfit v Ministry of Health (Case 283/81) [1982] ECR 3415 444

Turner v Grovit (Case C-159/02) [2005] AC 101 130

Union de Pequeños Agricultores v Council
    of the European Union (Case C-50/00P)
    [2003] QB 893 447
West Tankers Inc v Riunione Adriatica Di
    Sicurita SpA (Case C-185/07) [2009] 1 AC
    1138 130
Zuckerfabrik Süderdithmarschen AG v
    Hauptzollamt Itzehoe (Case C-143/88 &
    C-92/89) [1991] ECR I-415 446

European Court of Human Rights Cases

Fayed v United Kingdom (Case No
    18/1993/423/502) (1994) 18 EHRR
    383 41
Halford v United Kingdom (1997) 24 EHRR
    523 43
Hannover v Germany (App No 59320/00)
    (2005) 40 EHRR 1 469

Hoare v United Kingdom (2011) 53 EHRR
    SE1 511
JA Pye (Oxford) Ltd v United Kingdom (App
    No 44302/02) (2007) 23 BHRC
    405 231
Marckx v Belgium (1979) 2 EHRR
    330 43
Muyldermans v Belgium (1991) 15 EHRR
    204 42
Perez de Rada Cavanilles v Spain (1998) 29
    EHRR 109 43
Ringeisen v Austria (No 1) (1971) 1 EHRR
    455 41–2
Schalk & Kopf v Austria (Application No
    3014/04) 43
Stubbings v United Kingdom (1997) 23 EHRR
    213 43
Werner v Austria (1997) 26 EHRR
    310 42

TABLE OF PRIMARY LEGISLATION

Table of UK Statutes

Access to Health Records Act 1990 345
Access to Justice Act 1999
    s 29 14
    s 30 14
    s 54(4) 563, 564
    s 57(1) 561
Administration of Estates Act 1925
    s 38 26
    s 41 26
    s 43 26
Administration of Justice Act 1920 546
Administration of Justice Act 1969
    s 12 561
    s 13 561
    s 15 561
Administration of Justice Act 1970
    s 11 543
Arbitration Act 1996 115
    s 9 . . . . 115, 134, 337
Attachment of Earnings Act 1971
    s 1 535
    s 3(3) 539
    s 6(1) 539
    s 8(2)(b) 540
    s 15 540
    s 23 540
    s 24 540
Bankers' Books Evidence Act 1879 504
Banking Act 1987
    s 42 352
Bill of Rights 1689
    art 9 470
Bills of Exchange Act 1882 286
    s 3(1) 285
    s 10(2) 237
    s 14(3) 237
    s 27 286
    s 29 286
    s 29(3) 286
    s 30(2) 286
    s 38 286
    s 47(2) 237
    s 57 64
Carriage by Air Act 1961
    Sch 1 232
Charging Orders Act 1979 26
    s 1(1) 540
    s 1(2) 535
    s 1(5) 542

    s 2 541
    s 2(1) 541
    s 2(2) 541
    s 2(3) 541
    s 3(4) 540
Child Support Act 1991 41
Children Act 1989
    Pt IV (ss 31–42) 352
    Pt V (ss 43–52) 352
    s 25 562
    s 96 375
    s 98 352
Civil Evidence Act 1968
    s 14(1) 350
Civil Evidence Act 1972
    s 2 389
    s 3(2) 388
    s 3(3) 388
Civil Evidence Act 1995 (CEA)
    s 1(1) 373, 374, 378
    s 1(2)(a) 372
    s 1(2)(b) 374
    s 2 375
    s 2(1)(a) 375, 376
    s 2(1)(b) 375
    s 2(4) 376
    s 3 376
    s 4(1) 378
    s 4(2) 378
    s 5(1) 375
    s 5(2) 377
    s 6(2) 374
    s 6(3) 374
    s 7(2) 375
    s 7(3) 375
    s 8 377
    s 8(2) 383
    s 9 377
    s 9(1) 377
    s 9(2) 377
    s 9(2)(a) 377
    s 11 373
    s 13 372
    s 14(1) 374
Civil Jurisdiction and Judgments
  Act 1982 (CJJA)
    s 1(3) 299
    s 25 . . . . 130, 131, 462, 483
    s 25(1) 125, 130
    s 25(2) 131

s 43(2) 120
s 45(3) 123
s 49 129
Sch 4 118
Civil Liability (Contribution) Act 1978
s 1 228
s 1(1) 223
s 2 228
s 4 514
s 6(1) 223
Civil Procedure Act 1997 34
s 1(3) 33
s 2 33
s 5 33
s 5(1) 33
s 5(2) 33
s 7 493
s 9(1) 33
Companies Act 1985 94
s 727 75
Companies Act 2006 . . . . .30, 66
s 994 . . . . .299, 344, 474
s 1029 211
s 1030(2) 211
s 1030(3) .211, 235
s 1030(4) 211
s 1032(3) 211
s 1139 75
s 1139(2) 211
Sch 4, para 4 75
para 8 75
Company Directors Disqualification
Act 1986 30
Constitutional Reform Act 2005
s 59(1) 23
Consumer Credit Act 1974 . . . . .139, 534
s 141 25
Consumer Protection Act 1987 . 231, 241, 254
Contempt of Court Act 1981
s 10 . . . . .502, 503
s 14(1) 545
County Courts Act 1984 (CCA) 32
s 15 26
s 15(2)(a) 27
s 15(2)(b) 27
s 21 26
s 23 27
s 23(c) 534
s 25 26
s 38 462
s 38(3) 27, 548
s 40 136
s 40(1)(b) 28
s 42 136
s 42(1)(b) 28

s 51 452
s 52 . . . . .263, 505, 530
s 53(2) 507
s 60 436
s 66 441
s 69 . . . . .72, 152, 153, 411
s 76 33
s 111(1) 543
s 112 538
s 139 26
Courts Act 1971
s 24 23
Courts Act 2003
s 98 457
s 100 454
Courts and Legal Services Act 1990 (CLSA) . 14
s 1 25
s 58 15
s 58AA 16
s 58C 13
Crime and Courts Act 2013
s 17 23
Crime (International Co-operation)
Act 2003 502
Criminal Justice Act 2003 373
ss 75–97 351
Criminal Justice and Courts Act 2015
s 57 . . . . .331, 454, 532
s 57(2) 454
s 57(3) 455
s 57(4) 455
s 57(5) 455
ss 63–66 561
s 84 557
s 85 554
s 86 554
s 87 556
s 88(2) 194
s 88(6) 194
s 89(2) 194
Criminal Law Act 1967 14
s 14(2) 14
Criminal Procedure Act 1865
s 3 374
s 4 374
s 5 374
s 8 394
Crown Proceedings Act 1947
s 17 212
s 21(2) 552
Damages Act 1996
s 2 454
s 2(3) 454
Data Protection Act 1984 355
Debtors Act 1869

s 5 543
Defamation Act 1996
    s 5 244
Defamation Act 2013 469
    s 2 . . . . 44, 469
    s 3 469
    s 4 469
    s 11 441
Defective Premises Act 1972
    s 1(5) 232
Diplomatic Privileges Act 1964 212
Domicile and Matrimonial Proceedings
    Act 1973
    s 5 121
Employment Rights Act 1996
    s 111(2) 232
Equality Act 2010
    s 114 25
European Communities Act 1972 350
Extradition Act 2003 80
Fatal Accidents Act 1976 . . 126, 231, 240, 292,
    409, 529
    s 1 238
Foreign Judgments (Reciprocal Enforcement)
    Act 1933 546
Foreign Limitation Periods Act 1984 235
Fraud Act 2006
    s 13 352
Housing Act 1957
    s 10(3) 236
Housing Act 1985
    Pt IV 26
    Pt V 26
    s 110 26
    s 181 26
Housing Act 1988 278
    Pt I (ss 1–45) 26
    s 40(4) 26
Human Rights Act 1998
    s 2 . . . . 41, 46, 272
    s 2(1) 32
    s 3 258
    s 3(1) 32, 38
    s 4 . . . . 40, 45, 554
    s 4(4) 46
    s 4(5) 46
    s 4(6) 46
    s 5 45
    s 6 468
    s 6(1) 40
    s 7 . . . . 40, 46
    s 7(1) 45, 548
    s 7(1)(a) 27, 45
    s 7(5) 40, 45, 232
    s 8(1) 40, 46

s 8(3) 40, 46
s 9 554
s 9(3) 45
s 9(5) 45
s 12(2) 469
s 12(3) 44, 45, 468
s 12(4) 469
s 22(4) 548
Inheritance (Provision for Family and
    Dependants) Act 1975 185
    s 2 26
Insolvency Act 1986 30
    s 117 93
    s 122 94
    s 122(1) 91
    s 123 91
    s 123(1)(a) 92
    s 125 97
    s 127 96
    s 130(2) 211
    s 202 97
    s 285(3) 208
    s 305(4) 208
    s 306 208
Insurance Companies Act 1982 30
Interpretation Act 1978 36
    s 7 83
Judgments Act 1838 518
Justice and Security Act 2013 435
    s 6 139
    s 6(11) 358
Land Registration Act 2002 236
    s 32 541
    s 34 541
    Sch 6 236
    Sch 12 236
Landlord and Tenant Act 1954
    Pt II (ss 23–46) 26
    s 63 26
Late Payment of Commercial Debts (Interest)
    Act 1998 153
Latent Damage Act 1986 243
Law of Property Act 1925 26
    s 49 26
    s 76(1)(D) 224
    Sch 2, Pt IV 224
Law Reform (Miscellaneous Provisions)
    Act 1934 . . . . 238, 241
    s 1(1) 529
Legal Aid, Sentencing and Punishment of
    Offenders Act 2012 (LASPO) 20
    s 9(1) 18
    s 25 . . . . 19, 525
    s 26 . . . . 20, 525
    s 26(1) 20, 522

s 26(6)(d) 20
s 45 16
s 46 13
s 46(2) 13
Legal Services Act 2007 . . . . .2, 99
s 12 436
s 13 436
s 176 436
s 176(1) 436
s 188(2) 436
s 190 355
s 194 526
Sch 2 436
Sch 3, para 1(2) .436
    para 1(6) .436
Sch 4 436
Limitation Act 1980 (LA 1980) 43, 231
s 2 . . . . .232, 234
s 3(1) 239
s 3(2) 239
s 4 239
s 4(1) 239
s 4A 232
s 5 232
s 6 237
s 8 234
s 8(1) 232
s 9 234
s 9(1) 232
s 10(1) 232
s 10(3) 241
s 10(4) 241
s 11 245
s 11(1) 234
s 11(4) 232, 234, 239
s 11(5) 241
s 11A 232, 244, 245
s 11A(3) 254
s 11A(4) 241
s 12 . . . . .241, 245
s 12(2) 232
s 14 . . . . .150, 234, 239, 243, 245, 441
s 14(1) 239, 240
s 14(1)(a) 240
s 14(1)(b) 240
s 14(3) 239, 240
s 14A 243
s 14A(1) 243
s 14A(4) 243
s 14A(10) 243
s 14B 243
s 15(1) 232
s 19 232
s 20(1) 232
s 20(5) 234

s 21(1) 233
s 21(1)(a) .232, 233
s 21(1)(b) 233
s 21(3) 232, 233
s 22(a) 235
s 24 243
s 24(1) 232, 243
s 24(2) 244
s 28 242
s 29 . . . . .202, 244
s 29(6) 244
s 30 244
s 32(1)(a) 242
s 32(1)(b) 242
s 32(1)(c) 243
s 32A 244
s 33 . . . . . . .150, 211, 234, 244, 247, 257
s 33(3) 245, 246
s 33(3)(a) 245
s 33(3)(b) .245, 246
s 33(3)(d) 245
s 33A 244
s 35 255
s 35(1) 254
s 35(1)(a) .228, 241
s 35(2) 254
s 35(3) 254, 257
s 35(4) 255 256
s 35(5)(a) 257
s 35(5)(b) 254
s 35(6) 256
s 35(6)(a) 255
s 35(6)(b) 255 256
s 36 232
s 36(1) 247
s 36(2) 247
Sch 1 235
Local Government Act 1972
s 2 211
Local Land Charges Act 1975 26
London Government Act 1963
s 1 211
Magistrates' Courts Act 1980
s 111 573
s 111(5) 573
Maritime Conventions Act 1911 232
Mental Capacity Act 2005 205
s 3 205
Merchant Shipping Act 1995
s 190(3) 232
s 190(4) 232
Sch 6, Pt I, art 16 232
Oaths Act 1978 . . . . .365, 438
Offences Against the Person Act 1861
s 16 355

Partnership Act 1890
    s 1(1) 209
    s 5 209
    s 6 209
    s 9 ....209, 256
    s 10 209
    s 12 209
    s 15 379
Patents Act 1977
    s 103 355
Prevention of Terrorism Act 2005 435
Regulation of Investigatory Powers
    Act 2000 353
Rent Act 1977 278
    s 141 26
Rent (Agriculture) Act 1976
    s 26 26
Representation of the People Acts 91
Road Traffic Act 1988 56
    s 39 52
    s 145 ....56, 205
    s 151 293
Sale of Goods Act 1979 237
    s 12(1) 237
    s 28 237
    s 49(1) 237
    s 49(2) 237
    s 53(1) 158
Senior Courts Act 1981 (Supreme Court
    Act 1981) (SCA) 32, 34
    ss 20–24 30
    s 31(2A) 557
    s 31(2B) 557
    s 31(3) 549
    s 31(3)(b) 554
    s 31(5)(a) 551
    s 31(5)(b) 551
    s 31(5A) 551
    s 31(6) 553
    s 32A 452
    s 33 ....263, 531
    s 33(2) 342, 505, 507, 510
    s 34(2) 342, 507, 510
    s 35A 64, 153, 227, 411
    s 37 552
    s 37(1) 462, 482, 484, 544
    s 37(2) 486
    s 37(3) 485
    s 42 213
    s 49(2) 214, 253
    s 49(3) 336
    s 51 ....512, 526
    s 51(1) 512
    s 51(6) 526
    s 51(7) 527

    s 51(7A) 528
    s 51(8) 28, 514
    s 51(9) 28
    s 51(13) 527
    s 54 568
    s 61 28
    s 69 441
    s 72 ....351–2, 499
    s 72(5) 351
    Sch 1 28
Settled Land Act 1925
    s 113 26
Slander of Women Act 1891 514
Social Security (Recovery of Benefits)
    Act 1997 ....15, 27, 292
    s 1A 452
Solicitors Act 1974
    s 50(1) 2
    s 69(1) 235
    s 87(1) 511
State Immunity Act 1978 212
Telecommunications Act 1984
    s 43(1)(a) 355
Theft Act 1968
    s 31 352
Torts (Interference with Goods) Act 1977   140,
    509
    s 3 543
    s 4 510
    s 4(2) 509
Trade Union and Labour Relations
    (Consolidation) Act 1992
    s 10 211
    s 219 471
    s 220 471
    s 221(2) 471
Tribunals, Courts and Enforcement
    Act 2007 22
    s 62(1) 536
    s 63 534
    s 64 534
    s 70(1) 534
    Sch 10 23
    Sch 12
        para 6(3)(a) 537
        para 9(a) 537
        para 10 537
        para 11 537
        para 12 536
        para 13 537
        para 13(4) 537
        paras 14–19A 536
        para 14(6) 537
        para 16 537
        para 34 537

para 35 537
para 36 537
para 37 537
para 40 537
para 41 537
para 50 537
para 51 537
para 60 218

para 60(4) 218
Trustee Act 1925
    s 63A 26
Trusts of Land and Appointment of Trustees
    Act 1996 185
    s 14 542
Unfair Contract Terms Act 1977 159

TABLE OF SECONDARY LEGISLATION

UK Statutory Instruments

Access to Justice Act 1999 (Destination of
    Appeals) Order 2016 (SI 2016/917)
    (the 'Destination of Appeals Order')
    art 6 560
Certification of Enforcement Agents
    Regulations 2014 (SI 2014/421) 534
Civil Jurisdiction and Judgments Act 1982
    (Interim Relief) Order 1997 (SI 1997/302)
    . . . . 130, 483
Civil Jurisdiction and Judgments Order 2001
    (SI 2001/3929)
    Sch 1, para 9(2) 121
    ch 1, para 9(6) 122
Civil Legal Aid (Costs) Regulations 2013 (SI
    2013/611)
    regs 5–8 20
    regs 9–20 20
    reg 21 525
Civil Legal Aid (Merits Criteria) Regulations
    2013 (SI 2013/104) 17
    reg 5 18
    reg 43 19
Civil Legal Aid (Procedure) Regulations 2012
    (SI 2012/3098)
    reg 40 20
Civil Legal Aid (Remuneration) Regulations
    2013 (SI 2013/422) 523
Civil Proceedings Fees Order 2008
    (SI 2008/1053) 312
Civil Procedure (Amendment) Rules 2013
    (SI 2013/262) 575
Civil Procedure Rules 1998 (CPR) (SI
    1998/3132)
    Pt 1
        r 1.1 34–5
        r 1.1(1) 36, 38
        r 1.1(2) 34, 162
        r 1.1(2)(a) 34
        r 1.1(2)(b) 34
        r 1.1(2)(c) 34, 310
        r 1.1(2)(d) 35, 263
        r 1.1(2)(e) 35
        r 1.1(2)(f) 35, 145, 314, 420
        r 1.2 32
        r 1.2(b) 37
        r 1.3 32
        r 1.4 . . . . 32, 157
        r 1.4(1) 35
        r 1.4(2) 35

r 1.4(2)(a) 35, 415, 513
r 1.4(2)(b) 35, 513
r 1.4(2)(c) 35, 278, 326
r 1.4(2)(d) 35
r 1.4(2)(e) 35, 115, 177
r 1.4(2)(f) 35, 177
r 1.4(2)(g) 35
r 1.4(2)(h) 35, 202, 389
r 1.4(2)(j) 35, 273
r 1.4(2)(k) 35, 273
r 1.4(2)(l) 35
Pt 2
    r 2.3(1) 66, 83, 250
    r 2.4 163
    r 2.8 . . . . 79, 273
    r 2.8(5) 67
    r 2.9 417
    r 2.9(1) 450
    r 2.11 . . . . 84, 415
    PD 2B 24, 163, 317, 459
        para 2 24
        para 6.1 163
        para 6.2 25
        para 7 489
        para 7A 24, 45
        para 8.1 24
        para 8.1(b) 25
        para 11.1 . . . . 24, 434
    PD 2C
        para 2 65
        para 3.1(3) 65
    PD 2D 36
    PD 2E 24
Pt 3 191
    r 3.1 82
    r 3.1(2) 321
    r 3.1(2)(a) . . . 271, 314, 400, 419, 423,
        553, 564
    r 3.1(2)(b) 428
    r 3.1(2)(d) 273
    r 3.1(2)(f) 300, 336
    r 3.1(2)(g) 217
    r 3.1(2)(i) 40, 215
    r 3.1(2)(k) 177
    r 3.1(2)(ll) 184
    r 3.1(2)(m) 82, 116, 274
    r 3.1(3) 145, 450
    r 3.1(5) 56
    r 3.1(7) 179, 276, 451
    r 3.1(8) 36

r 3.1A 213
r 3.1A(3) .213
r 3.1A(5) .213
r 3.2 328
r 3.3 419
r 3.3(1) 274
r 3.3(2) 274
r 3.3(3) 274, 319
r 3.3(5)(a) 273
r 3.3(5)(b) 274
r 3.3(6) 274
r 3.3(7) 214
r 3.4 . . . 139, 157, 326, 328, 329, 532
r 3.4(1) 327
r 3.4(2) 327
r 3.4(2)(a) 327, 329, 532
r 3.4(2)(b) 327, 330, 333, 532
r 3.4(2)(c) 327, 417
r 3.4(3) 334
r 3.4(4) 327
r 3.4(5) 327
r 3.4(6) 214
r 3.5 .418–20
r 3.5(2)(a) 419
r 3.5(2)(b) 419
r 3.5(3) 419
r 3.5(4) 419
r 3.5A 135
r 3.6 420
r 3.6(4) 420
r 3.7 . . . . 173, 180, 312, 323, 414
r 3.7(7) 180
r 3.7A 414
r 3.7A(1)(a) 181
r 3.7A(1)(b) 180
r 3.7A1 . . . . .180, 414
r 3.7A1(4) 180
r 3.7A1(11) 180
r 3.7AA 180, 414
r 3.8(1) 418–20
r 3.8(2) 418
r 3.8(3) 415
r 3.8(4) 314, 325, 415
r 3.9 . . . . 82, 146, 180, 187, 564
r 3.9(1)(a) 145, 421
r 3.9(1)(b) 421
r 3.10 .80, 82
r 3.10(b) 419, 420
r 3.11 214
r 3.12 184
r 3.12(1) .184
r 3.12(1)(e) 184
r 3.12(1A) 184
r 3.12(2) .320
r 3.13 169

r 3.13(1) 185, 214
r 3.13(2) .187
r 3.14 . . . . .187, 414, 420
r 3.15(1) .187
r 3.15(2) 187, 188
r 3.15(3) .189
r 3.15(4) .188
r 3.16(1) .189
r 3.16(2) .189
r 3.17 320
r 3.17(1) 177, 188
r 3.17(2) .188
r 3.18 . . . . .190, 422
r 3.19(1) .191
r 3.19(2) .191
r 3.19(5) 191, 192
r 3.19(6) .192
r 3.19(7) .192
r 3.20(1) .191
r 3.20(2) .191
r 3.20(3) .192
PD 3A 329
  para 1.5. 333
  para 1.7. 277
  para 1.9. 418
  para 2.1. 328
  para 2.3. 328
  para 2.4. 328
  para 4.2. 334
  para 5.1. 328
  para 5.2. 327
  para 7.9. 214
PD 3B 180
PD 3C 214
PD 3D
  para 2 294
  para 6.7. 294
PD 3E
  para 2(b). 184
  para 2.3. 320
  para 3 184–5
  para 5 185
  para 6(a) 185
  para 6(c) 185
  para 6A .187
  para 7.2. 189
  para 7.3. 188
  para 7.4. 188
  para 7.5. 189
  para 7.6. 189
  para 7.7. 188
  para 7.8. 185
  para 7.10. 188
  Annex, Precedent H 185
PD 3F

para 1.1 192
para 1.2 191
para 2 191
para 5.5 191
Pt 5
  PD 5A
    para 2.1 150
    para 2.2 148
  PD 5B, para 2.3 83
  PD 5B, para 4.2(a) 83
Pt 6 . . . . .67, 75
Section IV (rr 6.30–6.47) 66
  r 6.1 66
  r 6.1(a) 66
  r 6.2(b) 79
  r 6.2(c) 66, 67
  rr 6.3–6.9 210
  rr 6.3–6.13 68
  r 6.3(1) 68
  r 6.3(1)(b) 76
  r 6.3(2) 75
  r 6.3(3) 75
  r 6.4 77
  r 6.4(1)(b) 77
  r 6.5 . . . . .67–9, 74
  r 6.5(1) 68
  r 6.5(2) 68, 69
  r 6.5(3) 67
  r 6.5(3)(b) 76
  r 6.5(3)(c) 76
  r 6.6 207
  r 6.6(1) 74, 75, 77
  r 6.6(2) 74
  r 6.7 . . . . .68, 69, 74, 76, 86
  r 6.7(1) 73
  r 6.7(2) 69
  r 6.7(3) 69
  r 6.8 . . . . .68, 74, 76
  r 6.9 . . . . .68, 74, 75, 76
  r 6.9(2) 210
  r 6.9(3) 74
  r 6.9(4)(a) 74
  r 6.10 . . . . .68, 76
  r 6.11 . . . . .74, 77
  r 6.11(2) 77
  r 6.12 .74
  r 6.13 .74
  r 6.14 . . . . .77–80, 144
  r 6.15 . . . . .68, 75, 77
  r 6.15(1) 77, 78
  r 6.15(2) 77
  r 6.16(1) 78
  r 6.16(2) 78
  r 6.17(1) 140
  r 6.17(2) 80

r 6.17(2)(b) 140
rr 6.20–6.29 79
r 6.20 .79
r 6.21 .79
r 6.21(1) 261, 272
r 6.21(2) 455
r 6.22 .79
r 6.23(1) 228
r 6.23(b) 86
r 6.23(2) 79, 228
r 6.23(2)(c) 79
r 6.23(3) 79
r 6.23(5) 77
r 6.23(6) 77
r 6.24 .79
r 6.26 . . . . .77, 79, 80
r 6.27 .79
r 6.28 .79
r 6.33 .122
r 6.33(2B) 119
r 6.34 .124
r 6.34(1)(b) 124
r 6.35 .128
r 6.36 . . . . .118, 124
r 6.37 .124
r 6.37(1) 127
r 6.37(1)(b) 124
r 6.37(5) 128
rr 6.42–6.46 127
PD 6A .68
  para 2.1 76
  para 3.1 76
  para 4.1 76
  para 4.1(2) 76
  para 4.1(2)(b) 77
  para 4.1(2)(c) 76
  para 4.2 77
  para 4.3 77
  para 6.2 76
  para 6.2(2) 211
  para 8.1 77
  para 10.7 79
PD 6B .128
  para 2.1 124
  para 3 126
  para 3.1 . . . . .124, 125, 127
  para 3.1(3) 125, 127
  para 3.1(6)(b) 126
  para 3.1(6)(c) 126
  para 3.1(6)(d) 126
  para 3.1(9) 126
  Annex 145
Pt 7 . . . . .89, 137, 138, 147, 557
  r 7.3 .215
  r 7.4 .132

r 7.4(1) 62
r 7.4(2) 62
r 7.5 . . . . 67, 78, 84
r 7.5(1) 67, 68, 119
r 7.5(2) 67, 119
r 7.6 . . . . 82, 84–5
r 7.6(1) 84
r 7.6(2) 85
r 7.6(2)(a) 85
r 7.6(2)(b) 85
r 7.6(3) 86
r 7.6(3)(a) 86
r 7.6(3)(b) 85, 86
r 7.6(4) 85, 264
r 7.6(4)(a) 85
r 7.6(4)(b) 85
r 7.11 45
PD 7A
    para 2.5. 29
    para 3.6. . . . . 28, 62
    para 4A.1 65
    para 5.1. 241
    para 5.2. 241
    para 5.3. 241
    para 5.4. 241
    para 5A.3 209
    paras 5B.1–5B.3 . . . . 210, 337
PD 7E
    para 4 66
    para 5.7. 66
    para 7.1. 66
    para 11 66
    para 12.1. 66
    para 12.2. 66
Pt 8 . . . . 89–98, 546
    r 8.1(2)(a) 89
    r 8.2 90
    r 8.2A 106
    r 8.3 106
    r 8.3(1) 90
    r 8.5 106
    r 8.5(1) 90
    r 8.5(2) 90
    r 8.5(5) 90
    r 8.5(6) 90
    r 8.6 106
    r 8.7 106
    r 8.8 106
    r 8.9(c) 90
PD 8A
    para 3.4. 90
    para 3.5. 90
    para 6.1. 90
    para 6.2. 90
    para 6.4. 90

para 7.2. 90
para 8.2. 90
para 9.4. 90
PD 8B 104
    para 1.1(2) 108
    para 2.2. 106
    para 4.1. 108
    para 6.1. 106
    para 6.1A 107
    para 6.3. 107
    para 6.5. 108
    para 7.2(1) 108
    para 7.2(2) 108
    para 8.1. 107
    para 8.2. 107
    para 9.1. 108
    para 10.1. 108
    para 11.1. 108
    para 12.5. 109
    para 17.1. 108
Pt 9
    r 9.1(2) 132
    r 9.2 132
Pt 10
    r 10.3 137
    r 10.3(1) 132
    r 10.4 134
PD 10
    para 4.4. 210
    para 5.3. 134
Pt 11 120
    r 11(1). 134
    r 11(2). 134
    r 11(4). 134, 135
    r 11(6). 134
    r 11(7)(b). 135
Pt 12 . . . . 131, 229
    r 12.2 139
    r 12.2(b) 138
    r 12.3 138
    r 12.3(3) 139, 328
    r 12.3(3)(a) 278
    r 12.5 141
    r 12.5A 135
    r 12.7 142
    r 12.7(2)(b) 173
    r 12.9 140
    r 12.10(a)(i). 140
    r 12.10(a)(ii). 140
    r 12.10(b) 140
    r 12.10(b)(i). 131
    r 12.11(2) 141
PD 12
    para 1.2. 139
    para 1.3. 139

para 4.1. 140
para 4.2. 140
para 4.3. 140
para 4.5. 140
para 4.6. 141
para 5.1. 141
Pt 13
r 13.2 143
r 13.3 . . . . 143, 144, 146
r 13.3(1)(a) 143
r 13.3(1)(b) 144
r 13.3(2) 144, 145
r 13.4 136
r 13.4(1A) 135
Pt 14
r 14.1(2) 379
r 14.1(5) 380
r 14.1A(1) 380
r 14.1A(2)(a) 380
r 14.1A(2)(b) 380
r 14.1A(3)(a) 380
r 14.1A(3)(b) 380
r 14.1B 380
r 14.1B(2)(a) 105
r 14.1B(2)(b) 108
r 14.2(1) 132
r 14.4 139
r 14.7 139
r 14.7A 135
r 14.8 174
r 14.12(2A) 135
r 14.13(3A) 135
PD 14
para 1.1(2) 380
para 7.2. 380
Pt 15
r 15.2 154
r 15.4 . . . . 132, 138
r 15.4(1)(b) 133
r 15.5 138
r 15.5(1) 134
r 15.6 154
r 15.8 159
r 15.11 146
PD 15
para 1.3. 133
para 3.2A 159
para 3.4. 146
Pt 16 39
r 16.2(1)(a) 148
r 16.4(1)(a) 201, 326
r 16.5(1) 155
r 16.5(2) 155
r 16.5(2)(a) 326
r 16.5(3) 155

r 16.5(5) 155
r 16.5(6) 155
r 16.8 159
PD 16 151
para 1.4. 148
para 4.1. 153
para 4.2. 153
para 4.3. 153
para 4.3A 153
para 7.3. . . . . 150, 151, 199
para 7.4. 151
para 8.2. 149
para 10.7. 134
para 13.1. 231
para 13.3(1) 149
para 13.3(2) 149
para 13.3(3) 150
para 15 553
para 15.1. . . . . 41, 45, 565
para 15.1(2) 554
Pt 17
r 17.1(1) 249
r 17.1(2)(a) 249
r 17.1(2)(b) 250
r 17.1(3) 250
r 17.2 250
r 17.2(2) 250
r 17.4 257
r 17.4(2) 258
r 17.4(3) 255
r 17.4(4) 256
PD 17
para 1.2(2) 259
para 1.4. 259
para 2.2. 259
para 2.2(2) 259
Pt 18 . . . . 197, 198, 199
r 18.1 196
r 18.2 202
PD 18 197
para 1.2. . . . . 197, 201
para 1.3. 197
para 1.5. 197
para 1.6. 197
para 1.6(2)(c) 197
para 1.7. 197
para 2.3. 198
para 2.4. 200
para 5.2. 200
para 5.3. 201
para 5.4. 201
para 5.5. 201
Pt 19 300
r 19.1 215
r 19.2 253

r 19.2(2)–(4) 253
r 19.2(2) 208, 209, 216
r 19.2(2)(b) 222, 225
r 19.2(3) 253
r 19.2(4) 218, 253, 254
r 19.3 215
r 19.3(2) .253
r 19.4(1) 219, 250
r 19.4(2) .259
r 19.4(3) 219, 259
r 19.4(4) 219, 253
r 19.4(5) 219, 259
r 19.4(6) 219, 260
r 19.4A(1) 45
r 19.4A(2) 45
r 19.4A(3) 45
r 19.4A(4) 45
r 19.5(2)(b) 256
r 19.5(3)(a) 255
r 19.5(3)(b) 256
r 19.5(3)(c) 254
r 19.5(4)(a) 257
r 19.5(4)(b) 257
r 19.6(1) 215
r 19.6(4) 216
r 19.7 216
r 19.7A(1) 208
r 19.7A(2) 208
r 19.8 209
r 19.8(1)(a) 209
r 19.8(2)(b)(ii) 209
r 19.8(3)(b) 209
r 19.8(5) 209
r 19.10 .219
r 19.11 .219
r 19.12(1)(a) 219
r 19.12(1)(b) 219
r 19.12(4) 219
PD 19A .520
para 3.2 .260
para 5.2 .218
para 6.2 .45
Annex 211
PD 19B, para 3.3 219
PD 19C, para 2(2) 193
Pt 20 . . . . 124, 147, 179, 221–39, 530
r 20.2 . . . . 222, 225
r 20.2(1)(b) 224
r 20.3(3) 229
r 20.4(2)(a) 158
r 20.5 222
r 20.6 . . . . 228, 229
r 20.6(2) 228
r 20.7(2) 228, 241
r 20.7(3)(a) 229

r 20.7(5) 229, 264
r 20.8(1)(a) 158
r 20.8(1)(b) 229
r 20.8(2) 228
r 20.8(3) 229
r 20.9 . . . . 224, 229
r 20.9(2) 225
r 20.9(2)(c) 225
r 20.10 .229
r 20.11 .229
r 20.11(1)(a)(ii) 229
r 20.11(2)(b) 229
r 20.11(3) 229
r 20.12 . . . . 226, 229
r 20.13 .229
r 20.13(2) 229
PD 20
para 1.2 .222
para 2.1 .229
para 5.1 .229
para 5.3 .230
para 7.2 .226
para 7.3 .226
para 7.4 .226
para 7.4(c) 222
para 7.5 .226
para 7.9 .226
para 7.11 226
Pt 21 205
r 21.1(2)(c) 205
r 21.1(2)(d) 205
r 21.2 205
r 21.2(3) 205
r 21.3(2)(b) 205
r 21.4(2) 205
r 21.4(3) 205
r 21.4(3)(c) 205, 516
r 21.5 205
r 21.5(2) 205
r 21.5(3) 205
r 21.5(4) 205
r 21.6 205
r 21.9 207
r 21.9(2) 207
r 21.10 . . . . 207, 409
r 21.10(1) 207
r 21.10(2) 89, 108
r 21.11 .208
r 21.12 .516
PD 21
paras 6.3–6.9 454
para 6.4 .208
para 9.2 .208
para 9.7 .208
para 9.8 .208

para 11 516
Pt 22
r 22.1(1)(a) 150
r 22.1(2) 150
r 22.1(3) 267
r 22.1(4) 267
r 22.1(6) 151, 265
r 22.2(2) 325
PD 22
para 2.1. 267
para 2.2A 185
para 4.2. 151
Pt 23 . . . . . . 108, 187, 194, 200, 218, 327,
409, 419, 479, 490
r 23.2(1) 262
r 23.2(2) 262
r 23.2(3) 262
r 23.2(4) 262, 460
r 23.2(4A) 262
r 23.2(5) 262
r 23.3(1) 264, 267
r 23.3(2)(b) 460
r 23.4(1) 264
r 23.4(2) 264
r 23.6 . . . . .264, 267
r 23.7(1) 272
r 23.7(1)(b) 299
r 23.7(2) 367
r 23.7(3) 270, 367
r 23.7(5) 267, 272
r 23.8 273
r 23.9 . . . . .87, 328
r 23.9(2) 266
r 23.9(3) 266
r 23.10 . . . . .87, 144, 328
r 23.11(1) 275
r 23.12 214
PD 23A 172
para 2.1. . . . . .264, 267, 460
para 2.3. 267
para 2.7. . . . . .262, 278, 328
para 2.9. 274
para 2.10. 264
para 4.1A 273
para 4.2. 264
para 5A.1 262
para 6.1. 273
para 6.9. 274
para 6.10(4) 274
para 6.10(5) 274
para 6.11. 273
para 6.12. 273
para 6.13. 273
para 8 274
para 9.1. 267

para 9.2. 367
para 9.4. . . . . .270, 367
para 9.6. . . . . .270, 367
para 10.2. 456
para 10.3. 456
para 11A.1 337
para 11A.3 337
para 12 272
para 12.1. 272
Pt 24 . . . . .139, 164, 280, 326
r 24.2 . . . . .282, 284, 422
r 24.2(b) 289
r 24.3(1) 279
r 24.3(2) 278
r 24.4(1) 263, 277
r 24.4(2) 278
r 24.4(3) 278, 279
r 24.4(4) 279
r 24.5(1) 279
r 24.5(2) 279
r 24.5(3) 279
r 24.6 290
PD 24
para 2(5) 279
para 2(6) 277
para 4 288
para 5.1. 279
para 5.2. 288
para 7 290
para 10 290
Pt 25 .34
r 25.1 509
r 25.1(1)(c) 314
r 25.1(1)(c)(i). 492
r 25.1(1)(d) 314
r 25.1(1)(f) 481, 492
r 25.1(1)(g) 489
r 25.1(1)(h) 493
r 25.1(1)(k) 291
r 25.1(4) 458
r 25.2(1) 459
r 25.2(1)(b) 263
r 25.2(2) 262, 459
r 25.2(2)(b) 263
r 25.2(2)(c) 277
r 25.2(3) 263, 335, 461, 505
r 25.2(4) 263, 505
r 25.3(2) 267, 279
r 25.3(3) 264, 461
r 25.6(1) 263, 291
r 25.6(2) 295
r 25.6(4) 292
r 25.6(5) 292
r 25.6(7) 295
r 25.7 292

r 25.7(1) .292
r 25.7(1)(a) 292
r 25.7(1)(b) 292
r 25.7(1)(c) 292–4
r 25.7(1)(d) 292, 293
r 25.7(1)(e) 292, 293
r 25.7(4) .294
r 25.7(5) 293, 294
r 25.8 296
r 25.9 295
r 25.10 .479
r 25.11 . . . . .180, 479
r 25.12 .300
r 25.12(1) 299
r 25.13 . . . . .300, 302
r 25.13(1)(a) 302
r 25.13(2) 299–300
r 25.13(2)(a) 300, 302
r 25.13(2)(a)(ii) 300
r 25.13(2)(c) 301, 303
r 25.13(2)(g) 301
r 25.14 . . . . .17, 299
r 25.14(1)(a) 302
r 25.15 . . . . .299, 301
PD 25A 450, 489, 496
    paras 1.1–1.4 459
    para 2.1. 460
    para 2.3. 461
    para 2.4. . . . . .460, 489
    para 3.1. . . . . .482, 494
    para 3.3. 461
    para 3.4. 461
    para 4.2. 460
    para 4.3(1) 482
    para 4.3(3) 367
    para 4.4(2) 461
    para 4.5(5) 460
    para 5.1. 478
    para 5.1(1) 478
    para 5.1(4) 460
    para 5.2. . . . . .464, 478
    para 5.3. 478
    para 5.4. 475
    para 5.5. 475
    para 7.2. 494
    para 7.3. 494
    para 7.3(2) 495
    para 7.4(1) 496
    para 7.4(2) 496
    para 7.4(5) 497
    para 7.4(6) 496
    para 7.5(2) 497
    para 7.5(3) 497
    para 7.5(4) 498
    para 7.5(5) 498

para 7.5(6) 497
para 7.5(7) 497
para 7.5(8)–(10) 497
para 7.5(11) 498
para 7.5(12) 498
para 7.5(13) 498
para 7.6. 494
Annex 489, 496
PD 25B
    para 1.2. 291
    para 2.1. 291
    para 2.1(2) 294
    para 3 295
    paras 4.1–4.4 295
    para 5 296
Pt 26
    r 26.2 136
    r 26.2A(3) 65
    r 26.2A(4) 135
    r 26.2A(5A). 66
    r 26.2A(6) 136
    r 26.3(1) 164
    r 26.3(1)(a) 164
    r 26.3(2) 159
    r 26.3(6) 159
    r 26.3(6A) 164, 314, 415
    r 26.3(7A)(a) 172, 415
    r 26.3(7A)(b) 172, 173, 415
    r 26.3(8) 173
    r 26.3(8)(d) 173
    r 26.3(10) 173
    r 26.4 .86
    r 26.4(2) 177
    r 26.4(2A) 177
    r 26.4(3) 177
    r 26.4(4) 177
    r 26.4(5) 177
    r 26.4A 116, 307
    r 26.5(1) 173
    r 26.5(2) 173, 177
    r 26.5(2A) 116
    r 26.5(4) 173
    r 26.6(1)–(4) 175
    r 26.6(1)(a) 175
    r 26.6(1)(b) 175
    r 26.6(2) 175
    r 26.6(3) 174
    r 26.6(5) 175, 311
    r 26.6(6) 175
    r 26.7(2) 176
    r 26.7(4) 175
    r 26.8 . . . . .174, 176
    r 26.8(2) 174
    r 26.9 176
    r 26.10 178

r 26.11(1) 441
PD 26
    para 2.2(3) 263
    para 2.2(3)(a) 328
    para 2.3(1) 164
    para 2.3(2) 164
    para 2.4. . . . . 164, 288, 332
    para 3.1(1) 177
    para 5.3(1) 263, 278, 328
    para 5.3(2) 278, 328
    para 5.3(3) 278, 328
    para 5.3(4) 278, 328
    para 5.4. 278
    para 7.4. 174
    para 7.5. 176
    para 7.7. 176
    para 8.1(1)(d) 175
    para 8.1(2) 175
    para 9.1(3)(c) 175
    para 10.2(5) 178
    para 10.2(6) 178
    para 10.2(8) 178
    para 10.2(10) 178
    para 11.1. 179
    para 11.1(1) 179
    para 11.2. 179
    para 12 142
    para 12.1. 293
    para 12.2(2) 143
    para 12.3(1) 142
    para 12.4(2) 142
    para 12.4(3) 142
    para 12.4(4) 142
    para 12.6. 143
Pt 27
    r 27.2(1) 307, 458
    r 27.2(3) 306
    r 27.5 . . . . 175, 306
    r 27.8 308
    r 27.10 308
    r 27.11(3) 309
    r 27.14 522
    r 27.14(2)(g) 309
    r 27.14(3) 309
    r 27.15 . . . . 179, 523
PD 27
    para 2.5. 307
    para 3.2(2) 308
    para 3.2(4) 308
Pt 28
    r 28.2(1) 310
    r 28.2(2)–(4) 312
    r 28.2(2) 311
    r 28.2(4) 312
    r 28.3 311

r 28.3(2) 311
r 28.4 415
r 28.4(1) 314
r 28.4(2) 314
r 28.5 424
r 28.5(2) 312
r 28.6(1) 314
r 28.6(1)(b) 315
PD 28 . . . . 314, 416
    para 2.3. 311
    para 2.5. 310
    para 2.8. 311
    para 3 . . . . 311, 314
    para 3.3. 310
    para 3.8. 456
    para 3.9(4) 311
    para 3.11. 310
    para 3.12. 311
    para 3.13. 312
    para 4.2(2) 274
    para 4.5(1) 314
    para 5.4. . . . . 416, 428
    para 5.4(6) 314
    para 6.3. 315
    para 6.5. 315
    para 7.2(1) 315
    para 8.1. 434
    para 8.2. 437
    para 8.3. 316
    para 8.6. 316
    App. 316
Pt 29
    r 29.1(2) 164, 318, 319
    r 29.2(2) 321, 322, 424
    r 29.2(3) 322
    r 29.3(2) 319
    r 29.4 317
    r 29.5 415
    r 29.5(1) 325
    r 29.6 . . . . 322, 424
    r 29.6(1) 322
    r 29.6(3) 323
    r 29.6(4) 323
    r 29.7 323
PD 29 416
    para 2 317
    para 2.6A 29
    para 3.1. 317
    para 3.2(2) 317
    para 3.4. 324
    para 3.5. . . . . 317, 325
    para 3.6. 325
    para 3.7. 319
    para 3.8. . . . . 261, 325
    para 3.10. 163

para 4.6. 317
para 4.7. 317
para 4.12(2) 319
para 4.13. 319
para 5.1. 320
para 5.2(3) 320
para 5.3. 320
para 5.4. 320
para 5.6. 320
para 5.7. 320
para 5.8. 263
para 5.9. 321
para 6 .324
para 6.2. 263
para 6.2(2) 274
para 6.5(1) 325
para 7.4. . . . . .416, 428
para 8.1(2) 322
para 8.3(1) 323
para 8.3(2) 323
para 9.2. 324
para 9.3. 324
para 10.1. . . . . .324, 434
para 10.2. 437
Pt 30 136
r 30.2(2) 178
r 30.3(2) 178
r 30.3(2)(g) 45
r 30.5 28
Pt 31 . . . . . . 167, 322, 339, 361, 362, 383
r 31.2 350
r 31.3(2) 360
r 31.4 .344
r 31.5 .177
r 31.5(1) 342, 343
r 31.5(2) 345
r 31.5(3)–(8) 343
r 31.5(3) 319, 345
r 31.5(4) 345
r 31.5(5) 319, 347
r 31.5(6) 345–7
r 31.5(7) 345–7
r 31.5(7)(d) 347
r 31.5(7)(f) 347
r 31.5(8) 347–8
r 31.5(9) 345
r 31.6 . . . . 339, 340, 343, 505
r 31.6(a) 343
r 31.6(b) 340
r 31.6(b)(i). 343
r 31.6(b)(ii) 343
r 31.6(b)(iii). 343–4
r 31.6(c) 340, 344
r 31.7 .348
r 31.7(3) 349
r 31.8(1) 344

r 31.8(2) 345
r 31.10 349
r 31.10(2) 343
r 31.10(3) 343
r 31.10(4)(b) 350
r 31.10(6) 349
r 31.10(7) 349
r 31.10(8) 345
r 31.11(1) 342
r 31.11(2) 342
r 31.12 360
r 31.14 . . . . .37, 357, 361
r 31.14(1) 361
r 31.14(2) 361
r 31.15(a) 359
r 31.15(b) 359
r 31.15(c) 360
r 31.16 506
r 31.16(3) 505
r 31.16(3)(a) 505
r 31.16(3)(b) 505
r 31.16(3)(c) 505
r 31.16(3)(d) 505, 506
r 31.16(4) 506
r 31.16(5) 506
r 31.17(2) 508
r 31.17(3)(a) 507
r 31.17(3)(b) 507
r 31.17(4) 508
r 31.17(5) 508
r 31.19 360
r 31.19(2) 360
r 31.19(3) 350
r 31.19(4) 360
r 31.20 358
r 31.21 . . . . .343, 360, 415
r 31.22 362
r 31.22(1) 362
r 31.22(2) 362
r 31.22(3) 362
PD 31A
para 2 349
para 4.3. 349
para 4.7. 349
para 5.4. 361
PD 31B 167, 344, 345
para 7 341
para 8 344
paras 14–19 344
para 30(2). 360
para 33 360
Pt 32
r 32.1 . . . . .177, 322, 388, 499
r 32.1(1) 322
r 32.1(2) 177, 322
r 32.1(3) 322

r 32.2 177
r 32.2(1) 267
r 32.2(3) 368
r 32.3 432
r 32.4(1) 365
r 32.4(2) 368
r 32.4(3)(a) 368
r 32.4(3)(b) 368
r 32.5(2) 369, 438
r 32.5(3) 369, 438
r 32.5(4) 369, 438
r 32.5(5) 438
r 32.6 142
r 32.6(1) 267
r 32.6(2)(a) 267
r 32.6(2)(b) 267
r 32.7 275
r 32.7(1) 367
r 32.7(2) 367
r 32.9(1) 369
r 32.10 . . . . 314, 325, 368, 415
r 32.11 369
r 32.12 369
r 32.14 . . . . 151, 369
r 32.15(2) 267
r 32.16 370
r 32.18 381
r 32.18(3) 381
r 32.19 383
r 32.19(1) 362
r 32.19(2) 362
PD 32 . . . . 365, 370
      para 1.7. 267
      paras 2–16 370
      para 3.2. 370
      para 4.1. 370
      para 5 370
      para 6.1(1) 370
      para 6.1(2) 370
      para 6.1(4) 370
      para 7.1(1) 370
      para 7.1(2) 370
      para 7.1(3) 371
      para 7.2. 371
      para 8.1. 370
      para 9 370
      para 13.1. 381
      para 16 370
      para 27.1. 384
      para 27.2. . . . . 315, 384
      Annex 1 371
      Annex 3 432
Pt 33
r 33.2 . . . . 375, 376, 432
r 33.2(3) 376

r 33.2(4) 376
r 33.3 376
r 33.4 376
r 33.5 377
r 33.6 432
r 33.6(4) 321
r 33.9 46
Pt 34
r 34.2(4)(b) 431
r 34.3(4) 431
r 34.5 431
r 34.7 431
r 34.8 . . . . 371, 431
r 34.8(1) 365, 371
r 34.8(3) 371
r 34.8(4) 371
r 34.8(6) 371
r 34.8(7) 371
r 34.9(1) 371
r 34.9(2) 371
r 34.9(4) 371
r 34.9(5) 371
r 34.9(6) 371
r 34.11 . . . . 371, 431
r 34.11(1) 371
r 34.11(4) 371
rr 34.13–34.24 431
Pt 35 . . . . 388, 389, 398
r 35.1 . . . . 388, 389, 396
r 35.2(1) 388
r 35.3 387
r 35.4 177
r 35.4(1) 388
r 35.4(2) 390
r 35.4(3) 390
r 35.4(3A) 390
r 35.4(3B) 390
r 35.5(2) 307, 311, 390
r 35.6 . . . . 312, 393
r 35.7 . . . . 311, 396
r 35.7(1) 391
r 35.8 391
r 35.10 392
r 35.10(4) 361, 392
r 35.11 396
r 35.12 . . . . 394, 397
r 35.13 . . . . 314, 325, 393, 415
r 35.22 406
PD 35 . . . . 388, 392
      para 2.1. 387
      para 2.5. 393
      para 3.1. 392
      para 3.2. 392
      para 3.2(2) 393
      para 5 392

para 7 391
para 8 389
para 9.1. 394
para 9.2. 394
para 11.1. 397
para 11.2. 397
para 11.3. 397
para 11.4(1) 397
para 11.4(2) 397
para 11.4(3) 397
Pt 36 . . . . . 4, 14, 40, 49, 51, 57, 336, 521
r 36.1(1) .399
r 36.2(2) .400
r 36.2(3) .404
r 36.3(c) .408
r 36.3(d) .408
r 36.3(e) .408
r 36.3(g) .531
r 36.3(g)(ii) 400
r 36.4 . . . . 400, 404
r 36.4(1) .413
r 36.4(2) .413
r 36.5 406
r 36.5(1)(a) 400
r 36.5(1)(b) 57, 400
r 36.5(1)(c) 57, 400
r 36.5(1)(d) 57, 400
r 36.5(1)(e) 57, 400
r 36.5(2) 57, 400
r 36.5(4) 57
r 36.6(1) 57, 406
r 36.6(2) 400, 406
r 36.7(1) 400, 407
r 36.8(1) .407
r 36.8(2) .407
r 36.8(3) .407
r 36.9 408
r 36.9(1) .407
r 36.9(2) .409
r 36.9(3) .409
r 36.9(4)(a) 409
r 36.9(4)(b) 409
r 36.10(2)(a) 409
r 36.10(2)(b) 409
r 36.10(3) 409
r 36.11 405
r 36.11(1) 407
r 36.11(2) 408
r 36.11(3)(a) 408
r 36.11(3)(b) 409
r 36.11(3)(c) 409
r 36.11(3)(d) 408, 409
r 36.12(2) 408
r 36.12(3) 408
r 36.13 57
r 36.13(1) 407

r 36.13(2) 405, 408
r 36.13(2)(b) 408
r 36.13(3) 407
r 36.13(4)(b) 408
r 36.13(6) 408
r 36.14(1) 407
r 36.14(2) 407
r 36.14(3) 408
r 36.14(5) 407
r 36.14(6)(a) 407
r 36.14(8) 410
r 36.15 405
r 36.15(4) 408
r 36.16(2) 413
r 36.16(3)(a) 407
r 36.16(3)(c) 413
r 36.16(3)(d) 413
r 36.16(4) 413
r 36.17 . . . . 410, 412
r 36.17(1) 410
r 36.17(2) 410
r 36.17(3) 58, 531
r 36.17(3)(a) 411
r 36.17(3)(b) 411
r 36.17(4) .58
r 36.17(4)(d) 411, 412
r 36.17(5) 412
r 36.17(5)(a) 412
r 36.17(6) 411
r 36.17(7)(a) 410
r 36.18 406
r 36.19 406
r 36.20 . . . . .57, 400
r 36.22(6)(c) 410
r 36.23 412
r 36.28(1) 107
r 36.29 109
PD 36A
para 1.1. .57
para 1.2. 407
para 2.2. 409
para 3.1. 407
para 3.2. 408
para 3.3. 409
Pt 37
r 37.2 406
r 37.2(1) .283
r 37.3 407
Pt 38
r 38.1(1) .334
r 38.2(1) .334
r 38.2(2)(a) 334
r 38.2(2)(b) 334
r 38.2(2)(c) 334
r 38.2(3) .334
r 38.3(2) .335

r 38.3(3) 335
r 38.3(4) 335
r 38.4 335
r 38.6 532
r 38.6(1) 335
r 38.6(2) 335
r 38.6(3) 335
r 38.7 335
r 38.8 335
Pt 39 33
r 39.2 . . . . 42, 264, 462
r 39.2(1) 435
r 39.2(3) 435
r 39.2(3)(c) 435
r 39.3(1) 442
r 39.3(2) 442
r 39.3(3) 442
r 39.3(4) 442
r 39.3(5) 422, 442
r 39.4 315
r 39.5 172
r 39.5(2) 432
r 39.6 436
PD 39A 33
para 1.10 274
para 3 432
para 3.3 384
para 4.2 449
para 5 437
para 5.2 210
para 5.3 436
para 6.1 440
para 7 438
para 8.1 . . . . 46, 272
PD 39B 33
Pt 40
r 40.2(1) 455, 456, 457
r 40.2(2) 455
r 40.2(4) 450
r 40.3(1) 455
r 40.3(3) 455
r 40.4(1) 455
r 40.4(2) 455
r 40.5 455
r 40.6 455
r 40.6(2)(b) 455
r 40.6(5) 456
r 40.6(6) 456
r 40.6(7)(b) 451
r 40.7(1) 448, 564
r 40.8A 535
r 40.9A 535
r 40.11 452
r 40.13(2) 452
r 40.13(3) 452

PD 40B
para 3.4 451
para 3.5 . . . . 451, 456
para 4.3 457
para 4.4 457
para 5.1 452
para 5.1A 452
para 8.2 418
para 12 452
PD 40E 572
Pt 41
r 41.2(1)(a) 453
r 41.3(6) 454
r 41.3A 409
r 41.8(1) 454
r 41.8(2)–(4) 454
PD 41A 453
PD 41B, para 2 454
Pt 44 165
r 44.2 . . . . 383, 518, 528
r 44.2(1) 512
r 44.2(1)(c) 518
r 44.2(2) 512
r 44.2(2)(a) 411
r 44.2(4) 512
r 44.2(4)(c) 400, 410, 411
r 44.2(5) 512
r 44.2(6) 517
r 44.2(6)(g) 518
r 44.2(7) 518
r 44.2(8) 524
r 44.3(1) 521
r 44.3(2) 13
r 44.3(3) 521
r 44.3(5) 39, 522
r 44.4(3)(h) 190
r 44.5 517
r 44.7 518
r 44.7(1)(a) 523
r 44.7(1)(c) 523
r 44.8 520
r 44.9(1)(a) 180
r 44.10(1) 518
r 44.10(2) 518
r 44.10(4) 517
r 44.11 422
r 44.12 . . . . 515, 517, 531
r 44.13(1) 529
r 44.13(2) 530
r 44.14 530
r 44.14(1) 530–2
r 44.14(2) 531
r 44.14(3) 531
r 44.15 530–2
r 44.16 530

r 44.16(1) 532
r 44.16(2) 532
r 44.16(3) 533
r 44.17 530
PD 44
　para 4.2. . . . . .252, 519
　para 5.1. 520
　paras 7.1–7.3 517
　para 8.2. 520
　para 9.2. 276
　para 9.2(b) 573
　para 9.4. 522
　para 9.5. 276
　para 9.6. 523
　para 9.7. 519
　para 9.8. . . . . .522, 523
　para 9.9(1) 522
　para 9.9(2) 522
　para 10.1. 520
　para 10.3. 520
　para 12.2. 532
　para 12.3. 533
　para 12.4(a) 532
　para 12.4(b) 532
　para 12.4(c). 532
　para 12.5. 533
Pt 45 . . . . 133, 184, 522–4
Section II (rr 45.9–45.15) 407
Section IIIA (rr 45.29A–45.29L) . .407
Section VI (rr 45.30–45.32). 524
rr 45.1–45.8 525
r 45.1(1) 525
rr 45.16–45.27 109
r 45.18 . . . . 105, 106
r 45.19 . . . . 105, 106
r 45.19(2A) 104
r 45.24(2A) 101
rr 45.29A–45.29L 316
r 45.29A(1) 109
r 45.29A(2) 109
rr 45.29B–45.29L 109
r 45.29B 109
r 45.29C 109
r 45.29E 316
r 45.29F(4) 109
r 45.29I(2A) 104
rr 45.30–45.36 184
rr 45.37–45.40 316
r 45.38(3) 524
r 45.38(4) 525
r 45.38(6) 524
r 45.39(2) 525
r 45.39(7) 525
r 45.39(8) 525
r 45.40 525

rr 45.41–45.44 195
r 45.42(1) 195
r 45.42(2) 195
r 45.43 195
r 45.44 195
r 45.45(2) 195
PD 45 .524
Section IV (paras 3.1–3.3) 525
　para 4.2. 524
　para 5.1. 195
　para 5.2. 195
Pt 46
r 46.1(2) 507
r 46.1(3) 507
r 46.3 .193
r 46.4 . . . . .516, 523
r 46.5 .213
r 46.6 .219
r 46.7 .526
r 46.8(2) 528
r 46.11(2) 525
r 46.13(1) 525
r 46.13(2) 178, 179
r 46.13(3) 525
r 46.17(1) 194
rr 46.61–46.64 315
PD 46
　para 2.1. 516
　para 3.4. 213
　para 5.2. 528
　para 5.3. 528
　para 5.4. 528
　para 5.5. 528
　para 5.6. 528
　para 5.7. 528
　para 5.9. 528
Pt 47
r 47.6(1) 524
r 47.7 .524
r 47.9 .524
r 47.9(4) 524
r 47.11 524
r 47.13 524
r 47.15 524
r 47.20 404
r 47.21 562
PD 47, para 13.2(i) 521
Pt 48, r 48.2. 530
Pt 49
PD 49A .30
PD 51A, para 19(3)(b). 336
PD 51N. 181
　para 2.58. 184
PD 51O. 83
　para 8.2. 83

para 10.2. 83
para 13.1. 83
PD 51Q 24
PD 51R 66
PD 51S 65
Pt 52
r 52.1(2) 562
r 52.1(3)(f) 567
r 52.3(1) 561
r 52.3(1)(a) 562
r 52.3(2) 562
r 52.3(2)(b) 562
r 52.3(3) 562
r 52.4(1) 562
r 52.4(2) 562
r 52.4(6) 562
r 52.5(1) 562
r 52.5(2) 562
r 52.5(3) 562
r 52.5(4)(a) 562
r 52.5(4)(b) 563
r 52.6(1) 563
r 52.6(2) 563
r 52.7(1) 563
r 52.7(2) 563
r 52.12(2) 565
r 52.12(2)(a) 564
r 52.12(2)(b) 564
r 52.12(3) 565, 566
r 52.13(1) 566
r 52.13(2) 566
r 52.13(3) 567
r 52.13(4) 567
r 52.13(5) 567
r 52.13(6) 567
r 52.15(1) 555, 564
r 52.15(2) 555, 564
r 52.16 568
r 52.17 567
r 52.18(1) 568
r 52.18(2) 568
r 52.18(3) 568
r 52.20(1) 571
r 52.20(2) 571
r 52.20(2)(e) 573
r 52.20(3) 571
r 52.20(6) 214
r 52.21(1) 569
r 52.21(2) 572
r 52.21(3) 569, 571
r 52.21(4) 570
r 52.21(5) 565
r 52.22 573
r 52.23(1) 561
r 52.30 572
r 52.30(1) 572

r 52.30(3) 572
PD 52A–52E 562
PD 52A
para 4.6. 563
para 5.3. 573
para 7.1. 572
Table 1 560
Table 3 560
PD 52B
para 2.1. 561
para 3.2. 564
para 4.3. . . . . .565, 567
para 5.1. 566
para 6.2. 565
para 6.4. 565
para 8.1. 566
para 8.3. 565
Table A 561
Table B 561
PD 52C 566
para 2 566
para 3 565
para 4 564
para 4(3)(b). 564
para 5(1) 565
para 7.1A 565
para 8(2). 567
para 8(3). 567
para 9 . . . . .565, 567
para 13 565
para 16(1) 563
para 16(2) 563
para 18 563
para 19(1). 563, 566
para 20 566
para 27 565
para 29 271
para 30(3). 568
para 31 271
PD 52E
para 2.3. 573
para 2.4. 573
Pt 54 .66
r 54.3(2) 552
r 54.5 . . . . .232, 552
r 54.5(1) 553
r 54.5(2) 553
r 54.5(5) 553
r 54.6 553
r 54.6(2) 554
r 54.7 554
r 54.7A 549
r 54.7A(3) 549
r 54.8 194
r 54.8(2)(a) 555
r 54.8(2)(b) 555

r 54.8(4) 555
r 54.9(1) 555
r 54.10 555
r 54.10(2) 551
r 54.11 555
r 54.11A 555
r 54.12(3) 555
r 54.13 556
r 54.14 556
r 54.17 556
r 54.20 557
rr 54.21–54.24 . . . . .30, 548
PD 54A 553
    para 2.1. .30
    para 5.1. 553
    para 5.6. 554
    para 5.7. 554
    para 5.9. 554
    para 8.2. 556
    para 8.5. 555
    para 10.1. 556
    para 12.1. 556
    para 13.2. 556
    para 15.1. 556
    para 15.2. 556
    para 16.1. 557
    para 17 .558
Pt 55
r 55.3(1) 65
r 55.6 213
PD 55A
paras 2.1–2.7. 153
Pt 58 29
r 58.5(1)(a) 65
r 58.5(1)(c) 65
r 58.5(2) 62
r 58.5(3) 62
r 58.6 136
r 58.6(1) 138
r 58.8 136
r 58.13(1) 173
r 58.13(3) 174
PD 58
    para 1.2. .25
    para 2.3. .62
    para 9 77
    para 10.2. 174
    para 11.3. 324
    para 11.4. 324
    para 13.1. 270
    para 13.2. 270
Pt 59
r 59.5(1) 138
r 59.7 138
r 59.11 174
PD 59

para 1.2. .30
Pt 60
r 60.3 136
r 60.6 . . . . .29, 173
PD 60
    para 3.2. .62
    para 8(1). 136
    para 8.2. 174
    App A 174
    App B 174
Pt 61
r 61.3(3) 65
r 61.3(4) 136
r 61.3(5) 65
r 61.9(1) 136
PD 61, para 2 174
Pt 62
r 62.7(1) 174
Pt 63 30
r 63.1(2)(f) 30
r 63.1(2)(g) 30
r 63.1(2)(h) 30
r 63.8 174
r 63.17A 30
Pt 63A 31
Pt 64
PD 64B, para 4.4. 212
Pt 66 211
PD 66, Annex 212
Pt 68
r 68.2(1) 446
r 68.2(4) 446
r 68.3 446
r 68.4(2) 446
r 68.5 447
PD 68
    para 1.1. 446
    para 1.5. . . . . .446, 446
    para 2.2. 447
Pt 69
r 69.3 544
r 69.4 544
r 69.5 544
r 69.8 544
r 69.10 544
PD 69
    para 4 544
    para 5 544
    para 7 544
    para 10 .544
Pt 70
r 70.2(2)(b) 534
r 70.2A 479
PD 70
    para 6A.1 210
    paras 6A.2–6A.4. 210

para 9.1. 535
Pt 71 535
    r 71.2 535
    r 71.3 535
    r 71.4 535
    r 71.5 536
    r 71.8 534
    PD 71 536
        para 1.2. 535
        para 2.2. 535
        para 3 535
        para 4.2. 536
        para 5.1. 536
        para 7.1. 536
Pt 72
    r 72.3 . . . . .534, 538
    r 72.4(1) 538
    r 72.4(3) 539
    r 72.4(4) 538
    r 72.5(1)(a) 538
    r 72.5(1)(b) 538
    r 72.5(2) 538
    r 72.6 538
    r 72.6(1) 538
    r 72.6(2) 538
    r 72.6(4) 538
    r 72.7 539
    r 72.8 539
    r 72.8(5) 539
    r 72.8(6) 539
    r 72.9(2) 539
    PD 72
        para 1.2. 538
        para 1.3. 538
        para 3.1. 538
        para 3.2. 538
Pt 73
    r 73.3(2) 535
    r 73.3(5) 541
    r 73.6(3) 541
    r 73.7(5) 542
    r 73.7(6) 542
    r 73.8 542
    r 73.10A(2) 542
    r 73.10A(3) 542
    r 73.10C 542
    PD 73
        para 1.2. 541
        para 4.3. 542
        para 4.5. 542
Pt 74 546
    rr 74.27–74.33 547
    PD 74B 547
Pt 76

r 76.22 .435
r 76.23 .436
r 76.28 .436
Pt 78 306
    r 78.26 508
Pt 81
    r 81.5 545
    r 81.6 545
    r 81.8 545
    r 81.9 545
    r 81.14 545
    r 81.14(3) 545
    r 81.14(5) 545
    r 81.17 . . . . .151, 369
    r 81.18 . . . . .151, 369, 545
    r 81.18(3) 151
    rr 81.19–81.27 546
    r 81.28(1) 545
    r 81.28(2) 545
    PD 81
        para 10(2). 545
        para 12(4). 545
        para 13.2(4) 545
        Annex 3 545
Pt 82 . . . . .139, 358, 436
    r 82.9–82.15 436
Pt 83
    r 83.2 535
    r 83.2A 543
    r 83.4(5) 536
    r 83.7 535
    r 83.9 536
    r 83.13(2) 543
    r 83.13(3) 543
    r 83.15 536
    r 83.15(10) 536
    r 83.23 543
    r 83.24 543
    r 83.26(8) 543
Pt 85
    r 85.4 218
    r 85.4(6) 218
    r 85.5(2) 218
    r 85.5(6) 218
    r 85.5(7) 218
    r 85.10 218
    r 85.11 218
Pt 86
    r 86.2(2) 218
    r 86.2(6) 218
    r 86.3 218
Pt 89
    r 89.3 535
r 89.7(1) 540

Conditional Fee Agreements (Miscellaneous Amendments) Regulations 2003 (SI 2003/1240)................14
Conditional Fee Agreements Order 2013 (SI 2013/689)
art 2...........................15
Conditional Fee Agreements (Revocation) Regulations 2005 (SI 2005/2305) 15
Consumer Credit (Increase of Monetary Limits) (Amendment) Order 1998 (SI 1998/996).....................25
County Court Jurisdiction Order 2014 (SI 2014/503)....................27
art 3....................534, 535
County Court Remedies Regulations 1991 (SI 1991/1222) 481
County Court Remedies Regulations 2014 (SI 2014/982) 260, 481, 493
reg 5 500
County Court Rules 1981 (SI 1981/1687) ..37
Ord 28, r 1.....................535
Cross-Border Mediation (EU Directive) Regulations 2011 (SI 2011/1133)...................244
Damages (Variation of Periodical Payments) Order 2005 (SI 2005/841) 454
Damages-Based Agreements Regulations 2013 (SI 2013/609).....................16
reg 3 16
reg 4 16
European Communities (Rights against Insurers) Regulations 2002 (SI 2002/3061) 204
reg 2(1) 204, 205
reg 2(3) 205
reg 3 204
reg 3(2) 204
Family Procedure Rules 2010 (SI 2010/2995) 91
PD 30A 560
High Court and County Courts Jurisdiction Order 1991 (SI 1991/724)...........25
art 4A 28
art 5...........................27
art 6...........................27
art 8(1)(a) 534
art 8(1)(b) 534
Insolvency (England and Wales) Rules 2016 (SI 2016/1024) (IR 2016) 91, 286
r 1.35..........................94
r 7.5...........................94
r 7.6..........................147
r 7.10(4) 96

r 7.12..........................96
r 7.15(3) 96
r 12.1(2) 174
r 12.59........................560
Sch 4, para 2 95
Lay Representatives (Rights of Audience) Order 1999 (SI 1999/1225) 308
Money Laundering Regulations 2007 (SI 2007/2157)
reg 3 3
reg 5 3
reg 7 3
Offers to Settle in Civil Proceedings Order 2013 (SI 2013/93) 411
Overseas Companies Regulations 2009 (SI 2009/1801)................210–11
Recovery of Costs Insurance Premiums in Clinical Negligence Proceedings (No 2) Regulations 2013 (SI 2013/739).....................13
Rules of the Supreme Court 1965 (SI 1965/1776)..................37, 85
Ord 15, r 6(6) 256
Ord 20, r 5......................255
Ord 62, r 6(7) 383
Social Security (Recovery of Benefits) Regulations 1997 (SI 1997/2205) 295
Supreme Court Rules 2009 (SI 2009/1603) 574
r 7 574
r 10(1).........................574
r 11(1).........................574
r 12 574
r 16(1).........................574
r 18(1).........................574
r 18(1)(c) 574
r 18(2).........................574
r 28 574
Taking Control of Goods Regulations 2013 (SI 2013/1894)
reg 4 537
re g 5 537
reg 6 536
reg 8 536
reg 9 536
reg 10 536
reg 12 536
reg 13 536
reg 14 537
reg 15 537
reg 20 536
regs 23–27......................537
reg 43 537

TABLE OF PROTOCOLS AND GUIDANCE

Chancery Guide
    Chapter 16. 25
    para 3.23. 322
    para 14.7. 24
    para 14.8. 24
    para 15.34. 270
    paras 16.36–16.39. 456
    para 17.27. 323
    para 20.4. 324
    paras 21.6–21.8. 428
Commercial Court Guide
    para D2. 163
    para D4.1 163
    para D5.1 174
    para D6.1 174
    para D7.1 174
    para D14. 323
    para D16.1 424
    para D8.5 174
    para F1.3. 460
    para F5.4. 270
    para F5.5. 271
    para F6.4. 270
    para F6.5. 271
    para F8 271
    para F11 270
    para F13.1. 271
    app 2. 323
    app 10, para 1 297
    app 10, para 3 298
Guidance for the Instruction of Experts in Civil
    Claims 2014 392
    para 38 391
Practice Direction—Directors Disqualification
    Proceedings
    para 2.1. 174
Practice Direction—Insolvency Proceedings . 30
Practice Direction—Pre-Action Conduct . . . 48
    para 4 55
    para 4.6(5). 518
    para 6(a) 49
    para 6(b) 49
    para 7 49
    para 11 49
    para 13 55
    para 15 55
    para 16 55
    para 17 55

    Annex A, para 4.2 49
Pre-Action Protocol for Claims for Damages
    in Relation to the Physical State of
    Commercial Property at Termination of a
    Tenancy. 48
Pre-Action Protocol for Construction and
    Engineering Disputes 48
    para 5.5 389
Pre-Action Protocol for Defamation. 48
Pre-Action Protocol for Disease and Illness
    Claims 48, 378
Pre-Action Protocol for Housing Disrepair. . 48
Pre-Action Protocol for Judicial Review 48, 552
    para 14 552
    para 20 552
    para 21 552
    para 22 552
    para 23 552
    Annex A. 552
    Annex B. 552
Pre-Action Protocol for Low Value Personal
    Injury Claims in Road Traffic Accidents
    (RTA Protocol) 48, 49, 52, 380
    para 1.1(1). 103
    para 1.1(A1) 104
    para 1.1(10A) 104
    para 1.1(16). 104
    para 1.2(1). 100
    para 4.1(2). 100
    para 4.1(4). 100
    para 4.2. 100
    para 4.3. 109
    para 4.4. 100
    para 4.5. 100
    para 4.5(1). 100
    para 4.6. 104
    para 5.1. 101
    para 5.7. 109
    para 5.8. 109
    para 5.10. 104
    para 5.11. 110
    para 5.67. 106
    para 5.68. 106
    para 6.2. 103
    para 6.3. 103
    para 6.3A. 101
    para 6.4. 103
    para 6.6. 103

para 6.7 103
para 6.8 109
para 6.8(2) 101
para 6.10 103
para 6.12 103
para 6.15 103
para 6.15(1) 109
para 6.15(2) 110
para 6.15(3) 110
para 6.15(4)(a) 109
para 6.15(4)(b) 110
para 6.16 103
para 6.17 110
para 6.18 . . . . 103, 110
para 6.19 110
para 6.19A 103
para 7.1 104
para 7.2 104
para 7.3 104
para 7.5 104
para 7.6 104
para 7.8A 104
para 7.12 104
para 7.13 294
para 7.28 110
para 7.29 110
para 7.33 105
para 7.35 105
para 7.37 105
para 7.38 105
para 7.39 110
para 7.39(a) 110
para 7.39(b) 110
para 7.40 110
para 7.41 105
para 7.42 105
para 7.44 105
para 7.46 110
para 7.47 106
para 7.49 105
para 7.50 105
paras 7.51–7.62 102
para 7.63 105
para 7.64 106
para 7.66 106
para 7.75 110
para 7.76 110
Pre-Action Protocol for Low Value Personal
  Injury (Employers' Liability and Public
  Liability) Claims (EL/PL) . . 48, 49, 52, 100
  para 4.1(3) 100
  para 4.1(4) 100
  para 4.3 100

para 7.12 294
Pre-Action Protocol for Personal Injury Claims
  (PI Protocol) 48, 51, 390
  para 1.1.1 52
  para 1.1.2 52
  para 1.2 52
  para 1.4.2 52
  para 3.1 52
  para 3.3 52
  para 4.1 53
  para 5.1 52
  para 5.3 52
  para 5.5 52
  para 6.2 53
  para 6.3 53
  para 6.5 53
  para 7.1.1 53
  para 7.1.3 53
  para 7.1.4 53
  para 7.2 53
  para 7.4 54
  para 7.6 53
  para 7.7 53
  para 8.1.1(b) 53
  para 9 53
  para 11.1 53
Pre-Action Protocol for Possession claims
  based on Mortgage or Home Purchase
  Plan Arrears in Respect of Residential
  Property 48
Pre-Action Protocol for Possession Claims
  based on Rent Arrears 48
Pre-Action Protocol for Professional
  Negligence 49
  para 1.4 49
  para 2.3 50
  para 5.1 49
  para 5.2 49
  para 5.4 49
  para 6.1 50
  para 6.2 50
  para 6.3 50
  para 7.1 50
  para 8.2 50
  para 8.4 50
  para 9.2.1 51
  para 9.3 51
  para 9.4.1 51
  para 9.4.2 51
  para 9.4.3(b) 51
  para 10.1 50
  para 11.1 50
  para 11.2 50

para 11.3 50
para 12.1 50
para 12.3 50
para 14.3 51
Pre-Action Protocol for the Resolution of
Clinical Disputes 380

Queen's Bench Guide
para 7.10.8 270
para 7.10.9 270
para 7.10.10 270
para 7.11.3 272
paras 9.4.5–9.4.8 428

TABLE OF EUROPEAN LEGISLATION

EU Primary Legislation

Treaty on the Functioning of the European
    Union. 445
    art 263. 447
    art 267. . . . . 443, 444

EU Secondary Legislation
Directives

Directive 85/374/EEC
    art 11. 254
Directive 2006/123/EC. 69
Directive 2008/52/EC (Mediation Directive)
    113
    art 2. 508
Directive 2011/92/EU
    art 10a. 194

Regulations

Regulation 44/2001/EC (Judgments
    Regulation) 300, 303, 485, 546
    art 31. 484
    art 34. 546
    art 34(1) 547
    art 35. 546
    art 36. 547
Regulation 805/2004/EC (EEO Regulation)547
Regulation 861/2007/EC (Small Claims
    Procedure) 306
Regulation 1206/2001 432
Regulation 1215/2012/EU (recast Judgments
    Regulation) 118–24
    art 1. . . . . 121, 131
    art 4. 131
    art 4(1) 121
    art 5(2) 119
    arts 7–26 122
    art 7. . . . . 122, 131
    art 7(1) 122, 123

art 7(1)(a) 122
art 7(1)(b) 122
art 7(2) 123
art 7(3) 120
art 7(6) 126
art 8. 131
art 8(1) 123
art 8(2) 124
art 8(3) 124
art 24. . . . . 120, 122, 135
art 24(1) 120
art 24(2)–(5) 120
art 25. 122
art 25(1) 122
art 26. 135
art 27. 120
art 29. . . . . 128, 337
art 29(1) 128
art 29(3) 128
art 30. . . . . 129, 337
art 30(1)–(3) 129
art 63. 122
Regulation 1346/2000/EC (Insolvency
    Proceedings). 97
    art 1.2 94
    art 3. . . . . 94, 98
Regulation 1393/2007/EC (Service Regulation)
    . . . . 127, 140
    art 7(2) 128
    art 19. 140
    art 19.4 145
Regulation 2201/2003/EC 121

European Court Rules

European Court Procedure Rules 2012
    art 91. 447
    art 94. 446
    art 95. 446
    arts 105–118 446

TABLE OF INTERNATIONAL TREATIES AND CONVENTIONS

Aarhus Convention 194–5, 478
Brussels Convention 1968 . . . . 124, 130
Convention on Choice of Court Agreements
    2005 (Hague Convention 2005) . .118–19,
    299
European Convention on Human Rights
    (ECHR) 32
    art 5 46
    art 6 . . . . 41, 42
    art 6(1) . . . 41–3, 144, 208, 274, 297, 308,
       435, 526, 547
    art 8 . . . . . 43, 44, 322, 359, 469, 470, 542
    art 8(1) 43
    art 8(2) 43
    art 10 . . . . 44, 469, 470
    art 10(1) 44, 45, 469
    art 10(2) 44, 45, 470
    Protocol 1, art 1 . . . . 231, 511, 542
Hague Convention 2005 *See* Convention on
    Choice of Court Agreements 2005 (Hague
    Convention 2005)
Hague Convention on the Service Abroad of
    Judicial and Extra-Judicial Documents in
    Civil or Commercial Matters 1965 . . . 127
Hague–Visby Rules
    art III, r 6 . . . . 87, 254
Lugano Convention 1988 . . . . 118, 130
Modified Convention 118, 124, 140
New York Convention 1958 113

1

INTRODUCTION

A THE LEGAL PROFESSION 1.06
B LAWYERS' DUTIES. 1.09
C INITIAL INSTRUCTIONS. 1.10
D CONFIDENTIALITY AND CONFLICT OF
   INTEREST 1.18
E PRE-ACTION CORRESPONDENCE. 1.21
F MAIN STAGES IN COURT
   PROCEEDINGS .1.22

This book deals with the mechanics of how legal and equitable rights are asserted, deter-   **1.01**
mined, and enforced through the civil courts. The civil courts perform the important function of resolving disputes that cannot be resolved by agreement between the parties.

It is axiomatic that the courts exist to do justice between the parties who come to them.   **1.02**
Justice is not simply a matter of achieving the right result. It has long been recognized that
where justice is delayed justice may be denied. In recent times there has been a growing
concern that for many people access to justice might also be denied unless litigation can be
conducted at proportionate cost. However, the law is often far from straightforward, and
frequently the factual background to a dispute needs considerable investigation before it
can be resolved by negotiation or at trial.

Litigants are often unable to cope with the complexities of the law on their own, and have   **1.03**
to seek assistance from the legal profession. Litigation can be very expensive, and the
important topic of funding will be considered further in Chapter 2.

The cost and delays inherent in litigation, together with the stress and time often involved,   **1.04**
mean that it is invariably best if matters can be resolved amicably without resorting to
court proceedings. Pre-action protocols on reasonable conduct to resolve matters before
starting proceedings are discussed in Chapter 5, and alternative dispute resolution ('ADR')
procedures are discussed in Chapter 10. However, some people simply refuse to negotiate,
or ignore correspondence, or make unrealistic offers, or insist on continuing with conduct
infringing another's rights. In such cases the injured party may have little option but to
commence proceedings.

Court proceedings fall into two categories. Proceedings are most frequently used for   **1.05**
resolving civil disputes. For example, it may be necessary to go to court to enforce payment
under a contract, or to seek compensation for personal injuries where a reasonable offer is
not forthcoming, or to seek an injunction to restrain tortious conduct which the defendant
threatens to continue. In the second category, it is necessary to apply to the court for an
order before certain conduct can be safely undertaken. For example, executors may seek
the court's directions if the terms of a testator's will are unclear, or the court's approval
may be sought where parties have agreed a settlement of a dispute where the claimant is
a child.

A THE LEGAL PROFESSION

1.06 In England and Wales there is a split legal profession, with solicitors and barristers (the latter are also known as counsel). In general, solicitors provide the direct point of contact with clients, and provide from within their firms most legal services for clients. Barristers provide a referral service of specialist advisory, drafting, and advocacy services as and when instructed by solicitors. A solicitor will, therefore, have general day-to-day management of a case, conducting the correspondence and negotiations, and gathering the evidence, but may instruct a barrister for specific tasks in the course of the litigation, such as drafting the statements of case and representing the client at hearings.

1.07 Solicitors may be in practice on their own (sole practitioners), but it is rather more common for solicitors to work in partnerships or limited liability partnerships ('LLPs'). Multidisciplinary practices and alternative business structures are permitted by the Legal Services Act 2007. These allow legal businesses to offer a range of professional services, such as accountancy, tax and insurance services, as well as legal services, and also allow outside ownership (so that a business providing legal services may be owned by non-lawyers). A traditional solicitors' firm will typically have a number of fully qualified solicitors as partners, and other fully qualified solicitors as employed assistant solicitors. The firm may have non-solicitor fee earners, such as legal executives (who have qualifications granted by the Institute of Legal Executives), and non-qualified fee earners, such as litigation managers and clerks. The firm may also have some trainees and para-legals (who assist the lawyers, but are not necessarily legally qualified), and will have a number of administrative employees.

1.08 Barristers have traditionally been sole practitioners, and are usually tenants in sets of chambers having a number of members. Alternatively, barristers may be employed by central and local government agencies or businesses, and may also operate in alternative business structures. At the top of the profession are Queen's Counsel ('silks'), with the bulk of the profession made up of 'juniors'. Barristers completing their training are called pupils. The point of contact between solicitors and barristers is the barristers' clerk.

B LAWYERS' DUTIES

1.09 Solicitors are officers of the court (Solicitors Act 1974, s 50(1)), and consequently have duties not only to do their best for their clients, but also never to deceive or knowingly or recklessly mislead the court (see the Solicitors Regulation Authority ('SRA') Code of Conduct 2011, Outcome 5.1 (<http://www.sra.org.uk/solicitors/handbook/welcome.page>)). Counsel are under similar obligations (see the Code of Conduct of the Bar of England and Wales, CD1 and 2, and rC3 (<http://www.barstandardsboard.org.uk/regulatory/>)), which provide that while barristers must act in the best interests of each client, they must observe their duty to the court in the administration of justice, and must not deceive or knowingly or recklessly mislead the court. Both solicitors and barristers have professional duties to ensure clients are informed in writing of the terms on which they are instructed, the persons who will be providing the legal services, how those services are regulated, and the relevant complaints procedures. Solicitors' client care letters are discussed at 2.04, and for barristers, see the Code of Conduct of the Bar at oC18, rC22, oC25, and rC99.

C INITIAL INSTRUCTIONS

The first interview with the client

When a member of the public goes to a solicitor's office for the first time, the solicitor will **1.10** ask about the nature of the problem and what it is that the potential client is seeking to achieve. So far as possible, clients are encouraged to relate the facts of the case in their own words, so that the true problem can be identified. This will enable the solicitor to decide whether to accept instructions from the client. It will also form the basis of the client's written statement that will be used if proceedings are issued, which will usually be drawn up by the solicitor and signed by the client.

Where the matter involves a financial or real property transaction, the solicitor must apply **1.11** customer due diligence measures when establishing a business relationship with the client (Money Laundering Regulations 2007 (SI 2007/2157), regs 3, 5, and 7). There is a similar obligation when an occasional transaction is to be entered into with a value of €15,000 or more. Customer due diligence means identifying the customer and verifying the customer's identity on the basis of documents, data, or information obtained from a reliable and independent source, such as a passport, or photo-card driving licence, or birth certificate, and keeping a record of the identification evidence. Most statutory instruments can be found at <http://www.legislation.gov.uk>.

If the solicitor decides to take the case, a plan of action should be agreed with the client in **1.12** relation to any further inquiries that need to be made. The client will usually be asked to provide details of any witnesses to the events in question, and the solicitor will arrange for signed statements to be taken from them. The solicitor will advise whether it will be necessary to obtain expert advice on any aspects of the case, and must advise the client on the duty to the court to preserve all relevant documents (including documents adverse to the client's case). Arrangements should also be made to preserve any real evidence, such as the goods bought, or equipment relevant to an accident, or samples for forensic analysis. The solicitor will usually ask to be provided with copies of all relevant documents at an early stage. The client will be advised to keep a note of all relevant developments if the dispute is of a continuing nature, such as a nuisance. Where the client is suffering continuing losses, the client will be advised to keep a record of those losses. This arises, for example, if a commercial client has an ongoing loss of profits, and in many personal injuries claims, where the claimant may need further medical treatment and might incur expenditure on prescriptions, medical appliances, and travel, etc. Where the client is seeking to bring a claim, it is common for inquiries to be made about the financial standing of the proposed defendants to ensure that they are worth suing. During the early stages of preparation, the parties' investigations and correspondence for the purposes of litigation are protected from disclosure by legal professional privilege.

The question of payment for the solicitor's services should be discussed at the first interview. **1.13** This is considered more fully in Chapter 2. Under a traditional retainer the client agrees to pay the solicitor's charges and disbursements, usually with an initial payment on account and monthly or quarterly billing thereafter. Hourly rates are based on the seniority of the fee earner and the charge-out rates of the firm (which are connected with the geographical location of the firm). Disbursements cover expenses such as court fees and fees for counsel and any experts. Solicitors have a professional obligation to ensure the fee agreement with their client is legal, suitable, and in the client's best interest (SRA Code of Conduct, Outcome 1.6). It is necessary therefore to consider with the client other forms of fee arrangement. Options include:

(a) public funding under the legal aid scheme;

(b) conditional fee agreement ('CFA'), which is commonly called a 'no win, no fee' agreement;

(c) damages-based agreement ('DBA'), which is a type of contingency fee agreement under which the lawyer is paid by a percentage of the amount recovered in the proceedings;

(d) before the event litigation expenses insurance ('BTE'), which the client may have for example under a motor or household insurance policy;

(e) after the event litigation expenses insurance ('ATE'), which is an insurance policy taken out after a dispute arises, typically to cover the risk of paying the other side's costs;

(f) third party funding, under which an outside investor pays the solicitor's charges for a share in any sum recovered in the proceedings; and

(g) funding by an organization connected with the client, such as their employer or trade union.

1.14 The solicitor may be able to advise the client about the merits of the case and its financial and other implications at the first interview. If it is not possible to give full advice at that stage, advice will be given when the necessary inquiries have been completed. In many cases solicitors will instruct counsel to give specialist advice on the merits and remedies available, such advice being given either orally in conference or in writing in the form of counsel's opinion. The initial advice on costs, which will include advising on the risk of having to pay the costs of the other side if the case is unsuccessful, and other matters, such as the identity of the fee earner conducting the case and information about complaints procedures, must be confirmed in a client care letter (see figure 2.1).

1.15 The solicitor should also agree with the client the scope of the solicitor's authority in relation to the dispute. In particular, it should be agreed whether the solicitor should correspond with the other side, and whether proceedings should be instituted. The solicitor should keep the client informed of developments and of any changes in the risks of litigation.

1.16 A solicitor retained by a defendant has similar duties regarding preserving and preparing evidence, and advising on costs, funding, and the merits. It is of particular importance to advise a defendant of the possibilities of settling on reasonable terms, and of making a Part 36 offer to protect the defendant's position on costs. A Part 36 offer is a formal offer to settle the dispute on stated terms. These offers provide for an acceptance period of at least 21 days. If they are not accepted, the usual position is that, if the claimant wins the case but fails to do better than the offer, the claimant will be awarded costs only up to the 21st day after the offer was made, but will be ordered to pay the defendant's costs thereafter. Making a shrewd Part 36 offer very soon after being notified of a dispute is an extremely effective way of disposing of many claims. If the offer is not accepted, the claimant is left with double the usual pressure: not only must they win, but they must also obtain a judgment which is more advantageous than the offer if they are to recover all their costs. Pre-action offers under Part 36 are considered at 5.30ff, with the main discussion in Chapter 36.

Written instructions

1.17 Solicitors receive instructions in documentary form most frequently from established clients. Such clients may well be very familiar with the litigation process, as where a hire-purchase company has a large number of customers who fall into arrears on their instalments. In an ideal world all the necessary information and documentary evidence for the solicitor to conduct the case through its initial stages will be enclosed with the written instructions. However, written instructions are not always complete, and the solicitor may need to clarify certain matters, ensure there are no further relevant documents in the client's possession, take statements from witnesses, ensure evidence is preserved, etc.

D CONFIDENTIALITY AND CONFLICT OF INTEREST

A solicitor or barrister owes a duty of confidentiality to his or her clients. Consequently, a **1.18**
solicitor or barrister must not disclose documents or talk about a client's case with anyone
not connected with the case without the client's instructions. This duty is buttressed by the
fact that documents and information in the hands of the solicitor or barrister are protected
by legal professional privilege. It sometimes happens that a solicitor is approached by a
prospective client in relation to a dispute with someone who is an existing client of the
solicitor's firm. Where this happens, or where it subsequently appears that joint clients in
fact have conflicting interests, the solicitor will, in general, have to refuse to act for one or
both parties. It may be that, after receiving full advice on the potential conflict, both parties
agree to the solicitor acting for them both.

A solicitor who is possessed of relevant confidential information will be restrained from **1.19**
acting against the former client (*Re a Firm of Solicitors* [1992] QB 959). In the case of a
firm previously retained by a client, the partners and employees who are in possession of
confidential information may be restrained from acting against the former client, and this
continues even if they change firms. Members and employees of the firm who never had
possession of relevant confidential information are in a rather more complex position.
While they remain with the firm they will, generally, be precluded from acting against the
former client of the firm, but it is possible they may be allowed to act if there is no real (as
opposed to fanciful) risk that relevant confidential information might have been communicated to them (*Re a Firm of Solicitors* [1992] QB 959).

In *Bolkiah v KPMG* [1999] 2 AC 222 the claimant had retained the defendant firm of **1.20**
accountants in his private capacity to provide extensive litigation support services of a
kind commonly provided by solicitors in relation to proceedings he was involved in. In
the course of this retainer the defendants became privy to detailed information relating
to the claimant's financial affairs, and no fewer than 168 of the defendants' employees
were involved. Some months after the conclusion of the claimant's action, the defendants
were retained by the claimant's former employer (the Brunei Investment Agency ('BIA')) to
investigate the location of substantial funds that had been transferred during his period of
employment. Aware of a possible conflict of interest, the defendants erected an information
barrier (also known as a 'Chinese wall') around the department conducting the BIA investigation. The defendants did not, however, ask for the claimant's consent to them acting for
the BIA. It was held that the claimant was entitled to an injunction restraining the defendants from continuing to act in the BIA investigation. Such injunctions will be granted unless
the firm produces clear and convincing evidence that effective measures have been taken
to ensure that no disclosure of the former client's affairs will be made to the department
acting for the new client, and that there is no risk of the former client's information reaching the department acting for the new client. Although, in some cases, Chinese walls may
be sufficient protection, there is a very heavy burden on the firm to prove this, and it will
be very difficult for the firm to do so unless those measures were an established part of the
firm's organizational structure.

E PRE-ACTION CORRESPONDENCE

After taking instructions from a client, a solicitor will usually enter into correspondence **1.21**
with the other side to the dispute. It is usual in most cases to have a period of negotiations
before court proceedings are commenced. Sometimes receipt of a solicitor's letter by the
other side will indicate that the client is taking the dispute seriously and will encourage

them to make a reasonable offer in settlement of the dispute without the need to resort to proceedings. There is detailed guidance on the content of pre-action correspondence: see Chapter 5. This includes providing full details of the claim to the other side, and giving serious consideration to the use of alternative dispute resolution processes before issuing proceedings: see Chapter 10.

F MAIN STAGES IN COURT PROCEEDINGS

1.22 When commencing proceedings, decisions have to be made about the appropriate court and type of proceedings to use. Generally, as discussed at 3.18ff and especially 3.22, the claimant has a complete choice between commencing proceedings in either the High Court or the County Court. Broadly, however, the High Court should be used only for the most important cases and those worth more than £100,000. Personal injuries cases must be commenced in the County Court unless the amount claimed exceeds £50,000 (see 3.27). As a guide, the main stages in a common law claim, whether it is proceeding in the County Court or the High Court, are shown in figure 1.1.

Issue of a claim form

1.23 Court proceedings are commenced by issuing a claim form. This involves drawing up the document on the appropriate form (usually form N1), taking (or sending by post) copies to the court office, paying a fee, and having the claim form stamped with the court's official seal. There are specialist claim forms for use in certain types of proceedings (eg the Admiralty and Commercial Courts), and an alternative 'Part 8' claim form for proceedings pursuant to statute and for questions of construction (see Chapter 8).

1.24 Time stops running for limitation purposes on the date proceedings are brought. Generally, a defendant has a complete defence if the relevant limitation period has expired before proceedings are brought, although in some cases the court has a discretion to allow proceedings to continue despite the expiry of the primary limitation period. Limitation is discussed in some detail in Chapter 21.

Service of process

1.25 As a general rule, the defendant must be served with the claim form together with a 'response pack' within four months after issue. In non-specialist cases service may be by the claimant or the court. Usually, the court will serve by first-class post. Where service is effected by the claimant, a number of methods of service are permitted, but the most common are by first-class post, insertion through the letter box at the defendant's address, and personal service, which involves handing the documents to the defendant in person. In general litigation a defendant is required to file a formal response to the claim within 14 days after service of the particulars of claim. In the Commercial Court the defendant must respond within 14 days of service of the claim form. This is done by returning a form of acknowledgment of service (which should have been part of the response pack) to the court office, by using the forms of admission and defence and counterclaim enclosed with the response pack, or by filing a formal defence.

Statements of case

1.26 In common law claims, the factual contentions advanced by both parties must be reduced into writing in formal documents known as statements of case. These are discussed further

Figure 1.1 General sequence of events in claims under the CPR

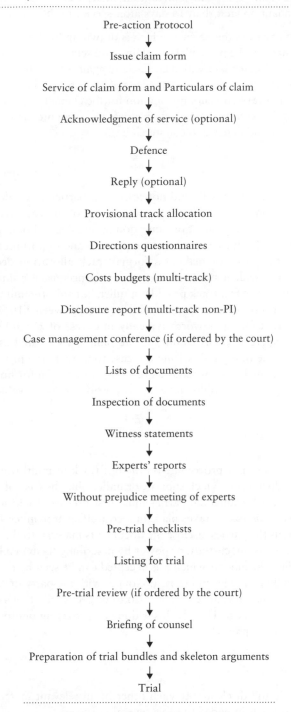

Pre-action Protocol
↓
Issue claim form
↓
Service of claim form and Particulars of claim
↓
Acknowledgment of service (optional)
↓
Defence
↓
Reply (optional)
↓
Provisional track allocation
↓
Directions questionnaires
↓
Costs budgets (multi-track)
↓
Disclosure report (multi-track non-PI)
↓
Case management conference (if ordered by the court)
↓
Lists of documents
↓
Inspection of documents
↓
Witness statements
↓
Experts' reports
↓
Without prejudice meeting of experts
↓
Pre-trial checklists
↓
Listing for trial
↓
Pre-trial review (if ordered by the court)
↓
Briefing of counsel
↓
Preparation of trial bundles and skeleton arguments
↓
Trial

in Chapter 14. The claimant's case is contained in the particulars of claim. This sets out the facts in a structured way, and is designed to show how the legal requirements of the claimant's causes of action against the defendant are satisfied. Particulars of claim are sometimes incorporated in the claim form, and sometimes kept separate. If separate, they should be served on the defendant no later than 14 days after service of the claim form.

1.27 The next statement of case is the defence, which is drawn up by the defendant. It responds to the allegations made in the particulars of claim, and sets up any specific defences available to the defendant. A defendant with a cross-claim against the claimant may add a counterclaim to the defence. Often, the only statements of case are the claim form, particulars of claim, and defence. However, it is not uncommon for the claimant to respond with a reply, and, if the defendant has counterclaimed, with a defence to counterclaim (a claimant doing both will serve a reply and defence to counterclaim).

Track allocation

1.28 In general litigation, the court will send notices to the parties when defences have been filed making a provisional allocation of the case to one of the case management tracks, and giving a deadline for filing directions questionnaires. These should provide the court with information to enable it to assess how complicated and important the claim is likely to be, and provide the basis for making a formal track allocation decision. The small claims track aims to provide a swift and inexpensive procedure for simple claims worth no more than £10,000. The fast track provides a fuller, but still streamlined, procedure for somewhat more important cases, typically with a value between £10,000 and £25,000. The multi-track is used for cases worth typically in excess of £25,000. Some specialist claims, such as Commercial Court claims, are automatically treated as allocated to the multi-track. At the same time as allocating the case to a track, the procedural judge will give directions for the further steps required to prepare the claim for final determination, with the level of preparation laid down being proportionate to the value and complexity of the case.

Disclosure

1.29 After track allocation, in cases proceeding on the fast track or multi-track, the parties are required to disclose documents which support or undermine the case of the party holding them. In most multi-track claims the parties must first prepare disclosure reports, which are designed to ensure disclosure takes place in a cost-efficient manner. In most fast track and multi-track claims the parties disclose the documents material to the case which are or have been in their possession, custody, or power by describing them in a list of documents. The list is divided into documents which it is accepted can be seen by the other side, those which are protected by privilege, and those no longer with the party making the list. After lists have been exchanged, the parties are entitled to inspect each other's documents, other than those covered by privilege. Usually this is done by providing photocopies. Disclosure is discussed further in Chapter 31.

Exchange of evidence

1.30 The parties must give full disclosure to each other of all relevant material in advance of trial. Advance disclosure is intended to serve several purposes:

(a) to allow the parties to assess the true strengths of their cases in advance of trial;
(b) to promote settlements;
(c) to prevent the parties being taken by surprise at trial; and
(d) to prevent unnecessary adjournments.

Thus, in addition to disclosing material documents, directions invariably require the par- **1.31**
ties to exchange the written reports of experts and the statements of factual witnesses
they intend to call at trial. Where a party intends to adduce hearsay evidence at trial,
adequate notice identifying the hearsay evidence must be served on the other side, usually
at the same time as witness statements are exchanged. Exchange of evidence is discussed
in Chapters 32 to 35.

Listing for trial

The courts try to list cases for final determination as soon as possible. In small claims track **1.32**
cases this is done at track allocation. In fast track cases the trial should be no later than
30 weeks after allocation. There is no set time limit for multi-track cases. In fast track and
multi-track cases the court may give a fixed hearing date (a 'fixture'), or a 'trial window'.
Most Commercial Court cases are given fixed trial dates. To assist the listing process, and
to ensure the claim is in fact ready for trial, the court may send pre-trial checklists to the
parties, and may hold listing hearings and pre-trial reviews.

Trial

At trial, witnesses will be called to give oral testimony on the facts left in contention by **1.33**
the statements of case, and the court will consider the contemporaneous documentation
and any other relevant and admissible evidence adduced by either side. Trials are normally
conducted by a judge sitting alone. After hearing the evidence and submissions by counsel,
the judge will give final judgment on the issues between the parties: see Chapter 39.

Assessment of costs

After giving judgment, the judge will hear submissions on the question of costs. Normally **1.34**
costs follow the event, which means that the party winning at trial recovers its costs from
the other side: see Chapter 46. The party awarded its costs then needs to have them quantified into a sum of money. In the absence of agreement, this is done through the process of
assessment, described at 46.46–46.64.

2

FUNDING LITIGATION

A DUTY TO ADVISE CLIENTS ON
   FUNDING. 2.03
B TRADITIONAL RETAINER 2.04
C LEGAL EXPENSES INSURANCE. 2.07
D AFTER THE EVENT INSURANCE. 2.08
E CHAMPERTY, THE INDEMNITY
   PRINCIPLE, AND JACKSON 2.10

F CONDITIONAL FEE AGREEMENT 2.14
G DAMAGES-BASED AGREEMENT 2.19
H THIRD PARTY FUNDING. 2.22
I LEGAL AID. 2.25
J IRRECOVERABILITY OF COSTS OF
   SETTING UP FUNDING 2.48
   Key points summary 2.49

2.01 It is a practical fact that litigation can be expensive, and often takes a considerable time to bring to a conclusion. Solicitors acting for a potential litigant are under a professional duty to advise the client on the likely cost of bringing the matter to court, and also to advise on the possible costs liability to the other side. This is important, because the usual rule is that an unsuccessful party will be ordered to pay the costs of the successful party. People contemplating going to court therefore have to take into account the fact that if the claim is unsuccessful they will potentially have to pay not only their own lawyers' fees and expenses, but also those of the other side. If a claim is successful, the other side will normally be ordered to pay costs, but (even if they have the financial means to pay) there is often a difference between what must be paid to one's own solicitors (because these costs are assessed on the indemnity basis: see 46.46), and what is recoverable from the other side, which is usually assessed on the less generous standard basis.

2.02 Lawyers acting for a party are entitled to seek payment on account as the claim progresses, and are not always expected to wait until the conclusion of the case before asking for payment. A client making payments on account is also not so likely to be taken by surprise by a very large bill. An important consideration for many clients is whether their lawyers will take a case through to trial, if needs be, without demanding any money, or no more than relatively small amounts of money, on account of costs until after the case is completed. If their lawyers are unwilling to act on this basis, clients who are unable to afford to pay either have to abandon their claims, or seek funding from an outside source for their claims.

A DUTY TO ADVISE CLIENTS ON FUNDING

2.03 Initial interviews with clients were discussed in Chapter 1. Solicitors are under a professional duty to ensure their clients know the options on funding, and understand their main features. Part of the discussion will be devoted to advising the client on the most appropriate way of funding the solicitor's own charges, and part will focus on the possible costs liabilities between the parties. Solicitors are only allowed to enter into funding arrangements that are legal and which are suitable to meet the client's needs, and must give their clients the best possible information about the overall cost of their case (SRA Code of

Conduct 2011, Outcomes 1.6 and 1.13). This is usually done by providing the client with a detailed client care letter at the outset of the retainer. This should give the name and status of the person with day-to-day conduct of the case, and the person the fee earner reports to. A breach of the costs provisions of the SRA Code of Conduct does not render the retainer illegal, but can be taken into account in assessing the amount of costs payable (*Garbutt v Edwards* [2006] 1 WLR 2907).

B TRADITIONAL RETAINER

Under a traditional retainer the client is obliged to pay the solicitor's costs of conducting **2.04** a case at an agreed hourly rate. To ensure compliance with the SRA Code of Conduct, the solicitor should send a client care letter to the client confirming the details of charging rates, estimating the costs that will be incurred, and the arrangements for billing the client. An example is shown in figure 2.1.

Figure 2.1 Client care letter

Smallwood & Co., Solicitors
Mrs Jane Goddard
Europa Games Importers (Morton) Ltd
Snow Hill Industrial Estate
Morton
Gloucestershire

Dear Mrs Goddard

Claim against Commodities & Freight Carriers Ltd

I am writing to confirm our discussion in which you confirmed the board of Europa Games Importers (Morton) Ltd wish to instruct this firm to pursue a claim for damages for breach of contract against Commodities & Freight Carriers Ltd. I am Paul Grainer, and I will be dealing with the company's claim. I am an assistant solicitor in this firm.

Board Resolution
At our meeting you agreed to provide me with a copy of the relevant board resolution resolving to pursue this claim and instruct this firm. You also agreed to provide me with copies of the company's last two sets of filed accounts.

Estimated Costs
At this stage I can give no more than a general estimate of the cost of this claim, as one of the most important factors in determining the legal costs in pursuing a claim is the extent to which the defendant will oppose the claim. In some cases a satisfactory settlement can be negotiated without the need for proceedings, but in others proceedings have to be issued in order to focus the defendant's mind on the claim and to convince him that he must treat the claim seriously. In other cases proceedings have to be taken to trial in order to get the court's ruling on the claim. I ought to mention that the majority of claims are settled without a trial taking place.

Although it is impossible to give a precise estimate for the overall costs, the rate charged by this firm for my work is based on an hourly expense rate with an element of profit. The hourly rate for your claim will be £152.00. As a general guide, most letters and telephone conversations are charged on a unit basis, with each unit being 6 minutes or 1/10 of an hour. Meetings with you and witnesses, preparing documents and long letters, and attending court will be charged based on the time spent, or, if estimated, at the rate of 10 minutes per page. My estimate is that this claim will involve approximately 120 hours of time, which would mean this firm's charges before VAT would amount to £18,240, to which there must

Figure 2.1   *continued*

be added the cost of disbursements (see below). This estimate will need to be revised if the claim is heavily defended, or if the defendant is willing to negotiate an early settlement. You will be informed if there is any alteration in this estimate as the claim develops.

Responsibility for Disbursements

Court fees, expert's reports, experts attending trial, and barristers' fees are known as 'disbursements', and have to be paid in addition to this firm's expense rate costs. Disbursements are likely to be in the region of £5,000.

Steps in the Claim

I expect that the following steps will be necessary for the purposes of your claim: preparation of your written statement; detailed letter of claim to the defendant; correspondence with the defendant's insurers and solicitors throughout the claim; obtaining an expert's report; obtaining details of your financial losses; issuing court proceedings; preparing statements of case; considering documents served by the defendant's solicitors in the proceedings; disclosing all relevant documentation to the defendant; completing various court documents; tracing and taking statements from other witnesses; possible attendance at court for a case management conference; arranging for a barrister to represent your company at trial; preparing papers for trial; attending trial; dealing with recovery of damages and costs, which may include preparation of a detailed bill.

The Company's Responsibility for Costs

In this case I expect to recover damages from the defendant and a contribution towards your company's costs. Regardless of the outcome of the case, you will be fully liable for this firm's costs and disbursements. If costs are recovered from the defendant these are likely to cover the bulk of the costs incurred by this firm, but I have to warn you that it is not uncommon for there to be a shortfall between the costs recovered from the other side and the costs of this firm, which the company will remain liable to pay.

I must advise you that if the company brings proceedings and the claim fails, it is most likely that the court will order the company to pay the defendant's costs.

Other Methods of Funding

There are legal expenses insurance policies which may be taken out to cover both the company's legal costs and those of the other side, which we discussed when we met. At this stage you do not wish to take this further, but as the claim progresses this may need to be reconsidered. We also discussed conditional fee, or 'no win, no fee', arrangements, and damages-based agreements (contingency fee agreements), which you also decided against at this stage. Again, this may need to be reconsidered, particularly if proceedings are to be issued. We discussed legal aid, but, as I advised, this is not available for claims brought by companies.

Next Steps

Every effort will be made to deal with your claim efficiently and quickly. However, if any problems arise which we cannot resolve between ourselves, there is a complaints procedure in operation in this firm. The initial point of contact is Miss Rosemary Williams, who is a partner in the firm, and you should contact her in the event of a complaint. Mr Smallwood, the senior partner, has final responsibility for all complaints. I can provide a copy of our complaints procedure on request.

When you have had a chance to consider this letter, please sign one of the copies provided and return it to me. The other copy is for your records. If there is anything in this letter or about the company's claim that you wish to discuss, please feel free to telephone or arrange an appointment.

Yours sincerely

Charge-out rates are based on the salaries of the staff and fee earners working at the solici- **2.05** tor's office together with an element representing the firm's profits. The modern approach is to fix a single hourly rate for each fee earner in the firm (or grade of fee earner) taking these factors into account. A variation on this approach is to adopt regional rates for different grades of fee earner based on guideline rates published by the Senior Courts Costs Office. These can be seen in BCP, Chapter 71, tables 71.2 to 71.4. Grade A covers solicitors with over eight years' post-qualification experience in litigation. Grade B covers more junior solicitors and senior legal executives with over four years' litigation experience. Grade C covers legal executives and fee earners of equivalent experience. Grade D covers trainees and para-legals. An alternative method has been to quote a lower hourly rate, but to add a mark-up of a variable percentage (say 50 per cent for ordinary litigation). Clients tend to find being quoted a simple hourly rate easier to understand.

In addition, the client will be expected to pay for disbursements. These are sums paid by the **2.06** firm during the course of litigation in respect of court fees, experts' and counsel's fees, the cost of making copies of photographs, and similar expenditure. It is normal for solicitors to ask for sums on account of costs when they are first retained, and periodically during the course of litigation.

C LEGAL EXPENSES INSURANCE

Some clients have the benefit of legal expenses insurance, often as part of their motor or **2.07** home insurance policies (BTE insurance). In these cases the costs incurred on behalf of the client will be met by the legal expenses insurer. In the ordinary course of events the BTE insurer should be used in preference to other methods of funding (*Sarwar v Alam* [2002] 1 WLR 125). Checking whether there is BTE cover should be one of the first tasks of a solicitor taking on new instructions. Often these insurers require the client's lawyers to provide advice on the merits of the claim from time to time so they can assess whether continuing the litigation can be justified under the terms of the insurance.

D AFTER THE EVENT INSURANCE

A client will often be justifiably concerned about meeting the potential liability for the **2.08** other side's costs if the case is unsuccessful. The usual rule is that the unsuccessful party in proceedings is ordered to pay the successful party's costs (CPR, r 44.3(2)). The other side's costs generally have to be paid out of the losing party's personal resources. It may be possible for the client to arrange ATE insurance to cover the other side's costs. Unless the prospects of success are very high, such insurance is quite expensive, with the premium being related to the likely level of the other side's costs and the risk of losing. Before the Jackson Reforms of 1 April 2013, ATE premiums were recoverable against an unsuccessful party, but recoverability was revoked by the Legal Aid, Sentencing and Punishment of Offenders Act 2012 ('LASPO 2012'), s 46(2).

An exception applies to ATE premiums for expert reports on liability and causation in **2.09** clinical disputes (Courts and Legal Services Act 1990 ('CLSA 1990'), s 58C, inserted by LASPO 2012, s 46). Provided the claim has a financial value exceeding £1,000, a costs order in a clinical negligence claim may include provision for payment by the unsuccessful party of the premium or part of the ATE premium relating to the cost of obtaining expert reports on liability or causation (Recovery of Costs Insurance Premiums in Clinical Negligence Proceedings (No 2) Regulations 2013 (SI 2013/739)).

E CHAMPERTY, THE INDEMNITY PRINCIPLE, AND JACKSON

2.10 A solicitor wishing to assist a client who cannot afford the costs of litigation may be prepared to take up the case on terms that payment for the work done on the client's behalf will be sought only if the claim is successful. Agreements of this sort have traditionally been regarded as illegal and unenforceable, because they savour of champerty and maintenance. 'Maintenance' describes supporting or intermeddling in litigation without just cause. 'Champerty' is an aggravated form of maintenance under which the person intermeddling with the litigation seeks to obtain a share in the proceeds of the suit (*Giles v Thompson* [1994] 1 AC 142). Despite the fact that maintenance and champerty are no longer crimes or torts (since the Criminal Law Act 1967), contracts savouring of maintenance or champerty remain contrary to public policy and are, in contract terms, illegal (s 14(2)). Any illegality in the funding arrangement of a successful party has the consequence that they cannot recover costs from the losing party, by reason of the so-called 'indemnity principle' (see 46.43).

2.11 The law in this area has been developing. Legal aid was substantially reformed on 1 April 2000, and one of the effects was that far less money was available for public funding of civil proceedings. To compensate for this, and to preserve meaningful rights to access to justice for those who were no longer entitled to legal aid (and also to assist middle-income members of the public), the CLSA 1990 and the Access to Justice Act 1999 were passed to encourage the use of conditional fee agreements ('CFAs') (see 2.14). Since 2 June 2003, it has been possible to enter into a special type of CFA under which the client is liable to pay his legal representative's costs only to the extent that they are recovered from the other side (Conditional Fee Agreements (Miscellaneous Amendments) Regulations 2003 (SI 2003/1240)), abrogating the indemnity principle for this type of CFA. In *Sibthorpe v Southwark London Borough Council* [2011] 1 WLR 2111 it was held that an indemnity given to a client by a solicitor against liability for the other side's costs (because ATE insurance was either not available or too expensive for the client) was not champertous.

2.12 Although the *Jackson Review of Civil Litigation Costs* (2009, Ministry of Justice) ('the Jackson Review') included a recommendation for the abolition of the indemnity principle, this has not been enacted, and the indemnity principle remains. Two of the central recommendations of the Jackson Review were the abolition of the recoverability of success fees from unsuccessful parties, and the legalization of contingency fees. Evidence gathered by the Jackson Review showed that recoverability of CFA success fees resulted in substantial inefficiencies in the legal system. The Jackson Review also concluded that recoverability produced an unfair imbalance between CFA funded litigants and their opponents, with the CFA funded party enjoying the benefits of litigation without financial risk at the expense of the other side.

2.13 Removing the right to recover CFA success fees (and other additional liabilities in respect of ATE insurance premiums and membership organizations under the Access to Justice Act 1999, ss 29 and 30) was recognized by the Jackson Review as moving the balance too far in the other direction. Accordingly, further simultaneous reforms took effect on 1 April 2013 as follows:

(a) including a cap on the success fee that the legal representatives can recover from their client in personal injuries claims at 25 per cent of damages excluding damages in respect of future loss;

(b) increasing general damages for personal injuries and suffering by 10 per cent. This was put into effect by *Simmons v Castle* [2013] 1 WLR 1239. The increase applies to a wide range of causes of action, and is not limited to pain, suffering, and loss of amenity in personal injuries claims;

(c) enhancing damages by a further 10 per cent as a reward for effective claimant's Part 36 offers (see 36.33);

(d) banning referral fees; and

(e) introducing costs protection for claimants in personal injuries claims in the form of qualified one-way costs shifting ('QOCS', see Chapter 47).

F CONDITIONAL FEE AGREEMENT

Nature of CFAs

A CFA is a 'no win, no fee' agreement. Being a contract, in principle a CFA can be assigned **2.14** from one firm of solicitors to another *(Plevin v Paragon Personal finance Ltd (No 2)* [2017] 1 WLR 1249). Under a CFA a solicitor may agree that the client will be liable to pay the firm's costs only if the claim is successful, but if it is successful, the solicitor will be entitled to charge at his or her usual rate (the 'base costs') plus a 'success fee' calculated as a percentage uplift on those usual costs. The success fee will be a percentage of the costs otherwise chargeable to the client, and should be related to the risks involved in the litigation. It cannot be more than 100 per cent of the solicitor's usual fees. If the claim is unsuccessful, the costs of the other side will usually be payable by the client, although ATE insurance may be obtained to cover this risk.

Statutory authorization for CFAs was conferred by the CLSA 1990, s 58. Any concern that **2.15** a CFA complying with the statutory requirements might be attacked by the opposite side as savouring of maintenance or champerty was removed by *Hodgson v Imperial Tobacco Ltd* [1998] 1 WLR 1056. Most of the technical rules on the format of CFAs were revoked with effect from 1 November 2005 (Conditional Fee Agreements (Revocation) Regulations 2005 (SI 2005/2305)). The only continuing requirements for non-personal injuries CFAs are that they must:

(a) be in writing;

(b) relate to a type of case where CFAs are permitted (all civil proceedings other than family cases, Conditional Fee Agreements Order 2013 (SI 2013/689), art 2; and

(c) specify the success fee, if any, which must not exceed 100 per cent.

A success fee cannot, in any type of case, exceed 100 per cent of the legal representative's **2.16** base costs (art 3). In personal injuries claims there is a further restriction for proceedings at first instance (arts 4 and 5). In these cases the success fee must not exceed 25 per cent of the damages recovered for pain, suffering, and loss of amenity and the damages for past pecuniary loss, net of sums recoverable by the Compensation Recovery Unit ('CRU') under the Social Security (Recovery of Benefits) Act 1997.

No win, no fee relates to the legal representative's own charges. This does not cover disburse- **2.17** ments, so the CFA will usually make express provision for who (the solicitor or the client) is liable for these. In cases where counsel is instructed there will usually be a CFA between the client and the solicitor and a second CFA between the solicitor and counsel. Model forms of CFAs have been drafted in consultation between the Law Society and the Bar Council.

Level of the success fee

The maximum success fee is 100 per cent of the legal representatives' base costs. Theoreti- **2.18** cally, a 100 per cent success fee is appropriate for a claim with a 50:50 chance of success. This is because, if the lawyers have two such cases, they will get double their fees on the successful claim, and nothing for the unsuccessful claim. If the merits are better than 50:50 the success fee should be lower than 100 per cent. For example, if the prospects of success are 75 per cent, the success fee should be 33 per cent.

G DAMAGES-BASED AGREEMENT

2.19 Like the CFA, a damages-based agreement ('DBA') is a 'no win, no fee' agreement. The difference is that in a successful DBA case the legal representative receives a percentage of the damages recovered by the client, whereas in a CFA case the success fee element is simply a percentage uplift of the base costs for the work done by the legal representative. DBAs became legal for general civil litigation on 1 April 2013 (CLSA, s 58AA as amended by LASPO 2012, s 45).

2.20 A DBA will be enforceable if it complies with the following requirements (Damages-Based Agreements Regulations 2013 (SI 2013/609)):

(a) it is in writing;

(b) it does not relate to proceedings which cannot be the subject of an enforceable CFA (which are available for all types of civil proceedings other than family cases, see 2.15), or to proceedings of a description prescribed by the Lord Chancellor (at present there are none);

(c) it does not provide for a payment above the prescribed amount (see 2.21);

(d) its terms and conditions comply with any prescribed requirements. These terms must specify (reg 3):

  (i)   the claim or proceedings or parts of them to which the DBA relates;

  (ii) the circumstances in which the representative's payment, expenses and costs, or part of them, are payable; and

  (iii) the reason for setting the amount of the payment at the level agreed; and

(e) the person providing services under the DBA has complied with any prescribed requirements concerning the provision of information (there are none for non-employment law DBAs).

2.21 Prescribed limits on the amount of DBA payments are set out in reg 4. They only apply to first instance matters, which fall into two categories in non-employment proceedings:

(a) in respect of non-personal injuries claims, a DBA must not require an amount to be paid by the client other than costs and expenses which are net of any costs and expenses which have been paid by another party to the proceedings. The amount to be paid by the client must not exceed 50 per cent of the sums ultimately recovered by the client. These costs and expenses may include disbursements in respect of counsel's fees as well as other types of disbursements; and

(b) in a claim for personal injuries a DBA must not provide for a payment exceeding 25 per cent of the combined sums in sub-paras (i) and (ii) which are ultimately recovered by the client. These sums are:

  (i)   general damages for pain, suffering, and loss of amenity; and

  (ii) damages for past pecuniary loss,

  net of any recoverable CRU payments.

H THIRD PARTY FUNDING

2.22 Third party funding is also known as 'litigation funding', and the funding agreement that may be entered into between the party and the funder is called a litigation funding agreement ('LFA'). Under a LFA, a funder invests funds to finance litigation to enable a litigant to meet the costs of resolving a dispute by litigation or arbitration. Usually the LFA will provide that the funder will receive a share of the proceeds of the claim if the litigation is successful.

There is a Code of Conduct for Litigation Funders, which provides that funders should not **2.23** seek any payment from the litigant in excess of the proceeds of the dispute being funded, unless the litigant is in material breach of the terms of the LFA. The LFA should state to what extent the funder is liable to the litigant to meet the liability for any adverse costs orders, to meet any ATE premium, provide security for costs, or meet any other financial liability. It should also state the extent to which the funder may provide input to the litigant's decisions in relation to settlement, and whether the funder may terminate the LFA, for example if the funder reasonably believes the dispute is no longer commercially viable.

At present LFAs are not regulated by statute, largely because they are not widely used. Their **2.24** validity is said to have been confirmed by *Arkin v Borchard Lines Ltd (Nos 2 and 3)* [2005] 1 WLR 3055. Where the claim fails, the third party funder may be ordered to pay a contribution towards the winner's costs (*Excalibur Ventures LLC v Texas Keystone Inc (No 2)* [2017] 1 WLR 2221). A third party funder can be ordered to provide security for costs (CPR, r 25.14, see Chapter 26), and a party can be ordered to disclose the identity of their third party funder (*In re RBS Rights Issue Litigation* [2017] 1 WLR 3539; [2017] 1 WLR 4635).

I LEGAL AID

Since 1 April 2013, public funding of litigation through legal aid has been administered **2.25** by the Legal Aid Agency. The courts have no power to provide litigants with such funding (*Perotti v Collyer-Bristow* [2004] 2 All ER 189). Legal aid encompasses advice, assistance, and representation by lawyers, and also other types of services including those provided by the not-for-profit sector. Legal aid firms are required to enter into standard-form contracts with the Legal Aid Agency. Among the contractual documentation is a specification, which sets out rules governing the day-to-day running of the contract work the firm can do for legally aided clients. This will specify the types of work that will be covered by legal aid, details of how the work must be performed, and the rates of payment.

Forms of service

There are various 'forms of civil legal service' available through legal aid (Civil Legal Aid (Merits Criteria) Regulations 2013 (SI 2013/104)). The idea is that the amount of public funding **2.26** given to a case should be commensurate with its needs, so that limited funding will be given if that is all that is needed, but that full public funding will be given to the most deserving cases.

Legal help

This is the lowest level of service, and includes providing advice and legal assistance on **2.27** things like how the law applies to a particular case. It is intended for people on low incomes who need initial advice and to assist with the early investigation of claims, and is intended to provide a limited amount of legal help at a modest cost to the taxpayer.

Help at court

This authorizes legal representation for the purposes of a particular hearing, without the **2.28** lawyer becoming the client's legal representative in the proceedings. Again, the intention is that limited legal assistance will be given, covering no more than is necessary, so as to keep the cost to the taxpayer to the minimum.

Legal representation

This covers individuals contemplating legal proceedings or who are parties to particular proceedings. This will fund 'investigative representation' or 'full representation'. Investigative **2.29** representation is limited to investigating the strength of contemplated proceedings, issuing proceedings, and conducting proceedings broadly up to obtaining information relevant to advising on the prospects of success. Full representation means legal representation other than investigative representation.

Family help

2.30 Family help may be provided in relation to family disputes, and may include assistance in resolving a dispute through negotiation or otherwise. It does not cover representation at a contested final hearing or appeal. It encompasses two levels of service. Family help (lower) is limited to all steps up to issue of proceedings. Family help (higher) can be used to issue proceedings and for representation in such proceedings other than at a contested final hearing.

Specific directions

2.31 Other services are not strictly forms of service covered by the main legal aid scheme, but there is some public funding of other cases if a specific order or direction is made. This may happen in important test cases and possibly also in group litigation.

Excluded categories

2.32 Public funding under the Community Legal Service is not available in claims for damages for personal injuries or death. Conveyancing, making wills, defamation claims, matters relating to company or partnership law, and various other categories of work are excluded from the scheme.

Financial eligibility

2.33 Legal aid is available to clients who are unable to afford to litigate. The financial limits are set at very low levels, although they are subject to annual uprating. Those who satisfy the eligibility rules fall into two categories. Those who are least well off receive funding entirely financed by the State. Those over certain stated limits have to pay contributions towards the cost of the legal services provided either through one-off payments or by instalments.

Individual

2.34 Legal aid is available only to individuals (LASPO 2012, s 9(1)). Consequently, it is not available to limited liability companies, although it may be available to partnerships, though not on matters of partnership law or relating to the carrying-on of the firm's business.

Criteria for funding

2.35 There are detailed rules setting out the criteria for granting the different forms of civil legal services. These are intended to reflect the requirements of the different levels of service, and also to ensure that public money is targeted at the cases that deserve or need it.

Merits of the case

2.36 The prospects of success criterion is divided into the following categories (Civil Legal Aid (Merits Criteria) Regulations 2013, reg 5):

(a) 'very good', meaning 80 per cent or more;
(b) 'good', meaning 60 per cent to 80 per cent;
(c) 'moderate', meaning 50 per cent to 60 per cent;

(d) 'borderline', meaning that, because of disputes of fact, law, or expert evidence, it is not possible to say that the prospects of success are better than 50 per cent, but the case is not 'unclear';

(e) 'poor', meaning 20 per cent to 50 per cent;

(f) 'very poor' meaning less than 20 per cent;

(g) 'unclear' meaning there are identifiable investigations that could be carried out, after which a reliable estimate of prospects should be possible.

The merits criterion is usually only met if the prospects are very good, good, or moderate **2.37** (reg 43). In borderline or poor cases, the merits criterion will be treated as met if this is necessary to prevent a breach of the individual's Convention/EU rights.

Statutory charge

By virtue of LASPO 2012, s 25, the legal aid monies spent in providing the civil legal **2.38** services to the client constitute a first charge on any property recovered or preserved in the proceedings or by any settlement or compromise of the dispute. This means that any money, costs, or other property recovered in a publicly funded claim automatically becomes the subject of an unwanted charge in favour of the State, which can use the damages recovered to reimburse itself for the costs incurred on behalf of the publicly funded client.

The underlying principle is to place a publicly funded party in a similar position to a party **2.39** privately funding litigation, whose primary responsibility at the end of proceedings is to pay the costs incurred by his or her own solicitors in bringing or defending the claim.

The charge applies only if there is a net liability to the Legal Aid Agency. This means that it **2.40** is first necessary to calculate the total costs incurred on behalf of the publicly funded client, then deduct any contributions paid by the publicly funded client, and also deduct any costs paid by the other side. The statutory charge will be for the amount, if any, of the balance. The charge attaches to any property recovered or preserved in the claim. This includes, in the case of proceedings concluded by a court order, any property or money which was the subject matter of the proceedings, and in the case of proceedings concluded by a settlement, any property or money received under the settlement, even if it was not claimed in the proceedings (*Van Hoorn v Law Society* [1985] QB 106). Property is 'recovered' if the publicly funded client gains ownership or possession of it through the proceedings. It is 'preserved' if another's claim to ownership or possession is defeated.

Whenever property is recovered or preserved for a publicly funded person, it is the duty of **2.41** that person's solicitor to inform the Legal Aid Agency immediately so that the charge can be registered and enforced. It can be enforced in the same way as other charges. Enforcement can be postponed if immediate repayment would be unreasonable and if the charge relates to property to be used as a home for the client or his dependants, or, where the relevant proceedings are family proceedings, it relates to money to pay for such a home.

Solicitors have professional duties to advise clients who apply for public funding of the **2.42** effects of the statutory charge. This should be done both personally and in writing.

Payment to Legal Aid Agency of sums received

By reason of the fact that costs and damages recovered by a publicly funded party are subject to the first charge in favour of the Legal Aid Agency, only the publicly funded party's solicitor or the Legal Aid Agency can give a valid discharge for the amount paid. In no circumstances should damages or costs be paid to the publicly funded party directly. **2.43**

Revocation and discharge

2.44 Public funding may be revoked or discharged on a number of grounds. Decisions to revoke are made on the ground of misconduct by the publicly funded client, whereas discharge may occur for perfectly innocent reasons, such as the death of the client, completion of the work, or where the client's circumstances change so he or she is no longer eligible.

Duties to the Legal Aid Agency

2.45 Publicly funded clients and their legal representatives are under continuing duties to comply with the provisions of LASPO 2012 and the relevant regulations. These duties are directed at ensuring that public funding is granted and continued only in justifiable cases. Legal aid providers have duties to report various matters, such as any refusal to accept an offer to settle or an offer to use ADR, or any information which might affect the client's continued qualification for civil legal services (Civil Legal Aid (Procedure) Regulations 2012 (SI 2012/3098), reg 40).

Protection against costs and costs against the Lord Chancellor

2.46 Publicly funded litigants are generally protected against having to pay the costs of the other side if they are unsuccessful, by virtue of LASPO 2012, s 26(1), and the Civil Legal Aid (Costs) Regulations 2013 (SI 2013/611), regs 5–8. Section 26 provides that the costs ordered against an individual in relevant civil proceedings must not exceed the amount (if any) which it is reasonable for the individual to pay having regard to all the circumstances, including:

(a) the financial resources of all of the parties to the proceedings; and
(b) their conduct in connection with the dispute to which the proceedings relate.

2.47 It is possible for a non-legally aided party who wins a case against a legally aided party to obtain a costs order against the Lord Chancellor (LASPO 2012, s 26(6)(d), and the Civil Legal Aid (Costs) Regulations 2013, regs 9–20). There are severe restrictions on these orders, which include requirements that they are only available if the court is satisfied that:

(a) the non-legally aided party will suffer financial hardship unless the order is made; and
(b) it is just and equitable that costs should be paid out of public funds.

J IRRECOVERABILITY OF COSTS OF SETTING UP FUNDING

2.48 Legal costs for representing a client are incurred from the point a person becomes the lawyer's client. Work done by the lawyer in setting up the funding arrangements, such as obtaining public funding, or entering into a CFA or DBA, is for the purpose of securing a client. It therefore forms part of the lawyer's overheads, and is not chargeable as such to the client, and is not recoverable from the losing side on a party and party costs order (*Motto v Trafigura Ltd* [2012] 1 WLR 657 at [107]–[114]).

KEY POINTS SUMMARY

2.49 • Solicitors are under a professional duty to advise clients on the options for funding litigation.

- The advice, and agreed funding method, should be confirmed in writing in a 'client care letter'.

- Most commercial clients simply pay their lawyers under the traditional retainer, normally with an agreed hourly rate.

- CFAs, or 'no win, no fee' agreements, are increasingly common. They allow a lawyer to agree not to charge the client if the proceedings are unsuccessful, but to charge an uplift or 'success fee' of up to 100 per cent over the solicitor's usual costs if the proceedings are successful.

- DBAs are a form of contingency fee agreement under which the lawyer is paid out of the sums recovered in the proceedings.

- Public funding is rarely met in commercial litigation. It is restricted to individuals with modest income and capital, and there are wide exclusions from the scheme. Even where the scheme applies, there are exacting requirements to be met before public funding becomes available.

3

THE CIVIL COURTS

A COURT COMPOSITION AND
  ADMINISTRATION 3.04

B JURISDICTION 3.16

C HIGH COURT DIVISIONS 3.32

D SPECIALIST COURTS 3.34

Key points summary 3.43

3.01 Civil proceedings in England and Wales may be conducted in magistrates' courts, the County Court, and the High Court. Annually about 1.4 million claims are started in the County Court, with about 20,000 claims being started in the Queen's Bench Division and about 30,000 in the Chancery Division. The great majority of these are little more than debt recovery cases. Only about 13 per cent of issued claims are defended, and only about 3.5 per cent progress through to trial (Ministry of Justice figures). Civil procedure concentrates on defended claims.

3.02 Appeals are usually taken to the next more senior tier of the judicial system (eg an appeal from a District Judge is taken to the Circuit Judge), with further appeals to the Court of Appeal and the Supreme Court. Appeals are considered in Chapter 50. This chapter deals first with the composition and administration of the civil courts, and then with matters relating to jurisdiction and the allocation of business.

3.03 In addition, a wide range of civil disputes are determined in various tribunals, including employment tribunals and social security tribunals. The composition of and procedure followed by tribunals are regulated by the Tribunals, Courts and Enforcement Act 2007 and by different sets of rules laid down by statutory instruments for each type of tribunal. Tribunals will only be considered further in this book where their procedures impact on the traditional courts system.

A COURT COMPOSITION AND ADMINISTRATION

Magistrates' courts

3.04 England and Wales are divided into local justice areas, each served by a magistrates' court. There are about 300 District Judges and Deputy District Judges sitting in the magistrates' courts, and approximately 30,000 lay magistrates in England and Wales. The administration of each magistrates' court is run by a magistrates' clerk, who may be assisted by a number of assistants. Assistants must be legally qualified, and clerks must be barristers, solicitors, or assistants of at least five years' standing. Cases are usually heard by benches of three magistrates. The chairman of the bench is addressed as 'Sir' or 'Madam'. Courts hearing family proceedings are known as family proceedings courts, and must not comprise more than three justices, all of whom must be members of a family panel. A family proceedings court must, so far as practicable, include both a man and a woman.

County Court

The bulk of civil claims, particularly lower value claims and claims which do not involve **3.05** complex issues or specialist law, are brought in the County Court. There is a single County Court with jurisdiction across the whole of England and Wales (Crime and Courts Act 2013, s 17), but that sits in a number of County Court hearing centres across the country. Most of the administration work connected with the County Court is done locally at hearing centres. However, County Court claims where the only remedy sought is money must be commenced by sending the papers to the County Court Money Claims Centre in Salford, and to cater for bulk users of the courts, such as hire-purchase, mail order, and public utility companies, proceedings in debt recovery claims may be issued at the County Court Business Centre in Northampton. Claimants using the County Court Business Centre deliver their draft claim forms in computer-readable form, and the Centre produces computer-printed claim forms which are dispatched using automatic mailing equipment.

Each County Court hearing centre is presided over by a Circuit Judge, who is a profes- **3.06** sional lawyer with a seven-year judicial appointment qualification (Tribunals, Courts and Enforcement Act 2007, Sch 10). Circuit Judges sit in the Crown Court as well as the County Court, the intention being to give them a broad spectrum of judicial experience. County Court trials are mainly conducted by Circuit Judges and by recorders sitting alone. Recorders are part-time judges. They are barristers or solicitors who are still in private practice and who are appointed to sit in the Crown Court and the County Court for a number of weeks each year. If through pressure of work it becomes expedient to do so, it is possible to appoint deputy circuit judges and assistant recorders as a temporary measure under the Courts Act 1971, s 24. The correct mode of address for Circuit Judges, recorders, and their deputies is 'Your Honour'.

Each County Court hearing centre also has one or more District Judges, who must have **3.07** a five-year general qualification. District Judges conduct most of the interim proceedings in the County Court. They also conduct most small claims hearings (see Chapter 27) and possession claims, and have power to conduct trials where the amount claimed does not exceed £25,000. District Judges are addressed as 'Sir' or 'Madam'.

The administrative staff of the County Court are civil servants employed by the Ministry **3.08** of Justice. They are headed by the court manager, and most correspondence with the court should be addressed to that official. Some quasi-judicial functions connected with enforcing judgments are fulfilled by the administrative staff, but they are mainly involved in drawing up, issuing, and serving court documents and maintaining court records. Enforcement agents, who were formerly known as bailiffs, have responsibility for physically enforcing judgments, and sometimes serve documents. They are civil servants employed by the Ministry of Justice.

High Court

The High Court, Crown Court, and Court of Appeal together comprise the Senior Courts **3.09** of England and Wales (Constitutional Reform Act 2005, s 59(1)). The High Court consists of three Divisions, namely the Queen's Bench Division ('QBD'), Chancery Division ('ChD'), and Family Division ('FamD'). Each Division has its own judiciary and its own administrative offices for issuing process, arranging interim hearings and trials, and for enforcement, etc. Specialist courts exist within the QBD and ChD to deal with particular classes of cases. The ChD and specialist courts like the Commercial Court, the Admiralty Court, the Technology and Construction Court, and the Companies Court are organized into the Business and Property Courts of England and Wales to facilitate the deployment of specialist judges where these are required. Public law cases, particularly applications for judicial review, are dealt with separately in the Administrative Court of the QBD.

3.10 The main administrative offices and court facilities of the QBD and the Court of Appeal are located at the Royal Courts of Justice ('RCJ'), Strand, London. Specialist Lists and the Chancery Division are located in the Rolls Building in Fetter Lane, and the Family Division is in First Avenue House, Holborn. In addition, most large towns and cities have District Registries of the High Court with jurisdiction to deal with High Court claims, including Business and Property claims, with a regional connection.

3.11 Interim applications in the High Court are mainly dealt with by Masters in London and by District Judges in the District Registries. Trials tend to be heard by the justices of the High Court, also known as 'puisne judges'. The correct mode of address for the justices of the High Court and for deputy judges sitting as High Court judges is 'My Lord' or 'My Lady', and 'Your Lordship' or 'Your Ladyship'. Masters are addressed 'Master', and District Judges are addressed 'Sir' or 'Madam'. As in the County Court, the administrative work of the High Court is performed by civil servants employed by the Ministry of Justice. However, enforcement is conducted by enforcement officers, who, unlike enforcement agents, their County Court equivalents, are not civil servants.

Technical distribution of business between judiciary

3.12 While in practical terms Masters and District Judges tend to hear interim applications whereas Circuit Judges and High Court judges (here referred to as 'judges') tend to deal with trials, technically in most situations both levels of judiciary have first instance jurisdiction. The main exceptions are that:

(a) search orders, freezing orders, and ancillary orders to these orders can only be made by a judge (PD 2B, para 2);
(b) human rights claims involving claims in respect of a judicial act or claims for declarations of incompatibility can only be heard by a judge (para 7A); and
(c) various low-level decisions in the County Court Claims Centre (see 6.11) and the County Court Business Centre (see 6.12) can be made without a hearing by 'legal advisers', who are legally qualified civil servants (PD 51Q).

3.13 There are various other restrictions and exceptions set out in PD 2B. It means that Masters and District Judges technically can hear trials. Guidance given in the ChD is to the effect that trials by Masters are exceptional because of the pressure of work in their main area of responsibility, interim applications. Masters are only likely to try simpler cases, and where the time estimate does not exceed five days (*Chancery Guide*, para 14.7). In the County Court, District Judges typically are trial judges for claims on the small claims and fast tracks (PD 2B, para 11.1), whereas Circuit Judges tend to try multi-track claims.

3.14 Technically, Masters and District Judges can hear applications for interim injunctions that are not search or freezing orders. However, *American Cyanamid* injunctions are also invariably listed before judges rather than Masters (*Chancery Guide,* para 14.8). Non-injunction applications should be listed before a Master, but a request can exceptionally be made to the Master to release an application to be dealt with by a judge (para 14.3). A similar approach is taken in the High Court and the County Court (PD 2B, para 8.1), but in the County Court there is a list of injunctive applications which are typically dealt with by District Judges. These include injunctions in proceedings where the value of the claim does not exceed £25,000 (para 8.1(b)). In the specialist lists it is more common for a claim to be 'docketed' to a particular judge, who deals with both interim applications and the trial.

In the Chancery and Queen's Bench Divisions there are arrangements for assigning claims **3.15** to individual Masters. Once assigned a claim may be transferred to another Master, and the fact that a claim has been assigned does not prevent it being dealt with by another Master (PD 2B, para 6.2). However, the usual rule is that once a claim is assigned all applications in that claim will be dealt with by the assigned Master. Interim applications to the judge in the Chancery Division (judge's applications) are made to the Chancery Applications Judge (*Chancery Guide*, Chapter 16). Interim applications in the Commercial Court are dealt with by a Commercial Judge (PD 58, para 1.2).

B JURISDICTION

Magistrates' courts

Obviously, most of the work conducted in the magistrates' courts relates to criminal pros- **3.16** ecutions. However, they also have jurisdiction over a number of civil matters, and deal with about 120,000 such cases each year. Civil jurisdiction is given by various statutes. Often, magistrates are given the task of dealing with cases in the grey area between the civil and criminal law. It is sometimes difficult to determine whether an application under a particular statute is civil or criminal, but, generally, if liability under a statute results in the possible imposition of a penalty, it probably creates a criminal offence. Procedurally, the distinction is whether the applicant needs to request the issue of a summons by complaint or by information. Civil matters are commenced by filing complaints, criminal matters by filing informations.

Magistrates' jurisdiction includes family law matters, and making orders against those **3.17** defaulting in the payment of their local government taxes. Many statutes allow civil applications to be made to the magistrates, mostly on technical regulatory matters.

Division of business between the County Court and High Court

The County Court and the High Court have concurrent jurisdiction over most categories **3.18** of cases: see Courts and Legal Services Act 1990 ('CLSA 1990'), s 1, and the High Court and County Courts Jurisdiction Order 1991 (SI 1991/724) ('Jurisdiction Order 1991'). Although the general rule is that the claimant is free to choose whether to issue proceedings in the County Court or the High Court, special provision is made for a number of categories of cases, and the rules relating to these categories will be considered later. Also, even where the claimant has a choice between the County Court and the High Court, there are further rules on trial venue which should be taken into account, as the future need to transfer the claim may result in delay and wasted costs.

Cases allocated exclusively to the County Court

The County Court has exclusive jurisdiction over a number of cases. Examples are: **3.19**

(a) claims to enforce regulated agreements and linked transactions under the Consumer Credit Act 1974 (Consumer Credit Act, s 141; SI 1998/996);
(b) claims to redress unlawful discrimination (eg under the Equality Act 2010, s 114).

Claims which should be brought in the County Court

3.20   There are a number of statutes which, while not precluding applications pursuant to
their provisions being brought in the High Court, provide that if the proceedings are
brought in the High Court the applicant will not be entitled to recover any costs. The
effect is to channel almost all applications under such statutes into the County Court.
Examples are:

(a) applications under the right-to-buy legislation in Part V of the Housing Act 1985
   (s 181);
(b) applications in respect of secure tenancies in Part IV of the Housing Act 1985 (s 110);
(c) applications by tenants and landlords under the Rent Act 1977 (s 141);
(d) applications under the Rent (Agriculture) Act 1976 (s 26).

3.21   Another device to encourage use of the County Court is adopted by the Housing Act 1988,
Part I, which deals with assured tenancies and assured shorthold tenancies. Section 40(4) of
the Act provides that, if an application under Part I is made to the High Court rather than
the County Court, the applicant will not be entitled to recover more in the way of costs than
if the application had been taken in the County Court.

Concurrent jurisdiction

3.22   The bulk of civil proceedings can be brought either in the High Court or the County Court
at the claimant's option. These include:

(a) claims in contract and in tort (CCA 1984, s 15);
(b) claims for the recovery of land (CCA 1984, s 21);
(c) applications for orders under the Inheritance (Provision for Family and Dependants)
   Act 1975, s 2 (CCA 1984, s 25);
(d) applications for relief from forfeiture (CCA 1984, s 139);
(e) applications under the Landlord and Tenant Act 1954, Part II, in relation to the security
   of tenure of business tenants (Landlord and Tenant Act 1954, s 63).

Cases where there is limited County Court jurisdiction

3.23   In a number of classes of cases the High Court and the County Court have concurrent
jurisdiction if the value of the case falls below a statutory limit, but if its value exceeds that
limit, the case can only be brought in the High Court. There are two main types of limit.
The first is a limitation of £5,000 on the amount claimed. The other is a limitation on the
value of the estate, trust, or property subject to the proceedings.

3.24   Cases subject to a £5,000 limit for County Court proceedings are unusual, but include
applications for compensation for defective search certificates under the Local Land
Charges Act 1975 and charging orders under the Charging Orders Act 1979.

3.25   Instances of cases where the jurisdiction of the County Court is limited by the value of the
estate, trust, or property are:

(a) proceedings under various provisions of the Law of Property Act 1925, such as applying for requisitions in conveyancing under s 49, the Settled Land Act 1925, s 113, the
   Trustee Act 1925, s 63A, and the Administration of Estates Act 1925, ss 38, 41, and 43,
   are limited to £30,000;

(b) general County Court equitable jurisdiction in relation to the administration of estates, execution of trusts, and proceedings for specific performance (CCA 1984, s 23) is limited to £350,000 (County Court Jurisdiction Order 2014 (SI 2014/503)).

Cases allocated exclusively to the High Court

The following categories of cases can only be brought in the High Court: **3.26**

(a) applications for judicial review (CCA 1984, s 38(3));
(b) claims for libel or slander (CCA 1984, s 15(2)(b));
(c) claims in which the title to any toll, fair, market, or franchise is in question (CCA 1984, s 15(2)(a));
(d) applications concerning decisions of local authority auditors (Jurisdiction Order 1991, art 6);
(e) claims under the Human Rights Act 1998, s 7(1)(a) in respect of a judicial act.

Personal injuries cases

Special provision is made for personal injuries cases by the Jurisdiction Order 1991, art 5, **3.27** which provides that, where the claimant does not reasonably expect to recover more than £50,000, the claim must be commenced in the County Court. The term 'personal injuries' includes disease, impairment of physical or mental condition, and death. The value of the claim is determined as at the date the claim is commenced, and is calculated by adding together:

(a) general damages for pain, suffering, and loss of amenity relating to the injury itself;
(b) special damages for actual financial losses incurred to date; and
(c) future losses, such as loss of earnings and the cost of future medical care. Future losses are calculated by finding the claimant's annual loss and multiplying it by a number of years' purchase, and applying a modifier based on the claimant's educational background and any disability. The multiplier is dependent on factors such as the claimant's age and likely retirement age, and takes into account the benefit to the claimant of getting the money in advance. The modifier reflects factors, other than death, which affect the claimant's future income-earning capacity (claimants with better educational qualifications tend to have greater job security, and those who are more disabled less job security). Details can be found in the Ogden tables.

In making this calculation the following rules are applied: **3.28**

(a) any sums which are required to be paid to the Secretary of State by virtue of the recoupment of benefits provisions under the Social Security (Recovery of Benefits) Act 1997 are taken to be part of the claim;
(b) claims for interest and costs are disregarded;
(c) no account is taken of a possible finding of contributory negligence; and
(d) if provisional damages are claimed, no account is taken of the possibility of a future application for further damages.

The great majority of personal injuries claims are for less than £50,000, and so will **3.29** usually be commenced in the County Court. It is very rare for general damages alone to exceed £50,000, but where the claimant has suffered a significant permanent injury which has resulted in ongoing loss of earnings or a permanent need for medical care, future losses can far exceed £50,000. If High Court proceedings are justified, the claimant must endorse the claim form with a statement that the value of the claim exceeds £50,000 (PD 7A, para 3.6).

Money claims

3.30 Non-personal injuries money claims in which the County Court has jurisdiction may only be commenced in the High Court if the value of the claim is more than £100,000 (Jurisdiction Order 1991, art 4A).

Commencing in the wrong court

3.31 Generally, when proceedings are commenced in the wrong court they will be transferred to the correct court, and the claimant will usually be penalized by being made to pay the costs of the application to transfer the claim and, if ultimately successful, may have any award of costs reduced by up to 25 per cent (Senior Courts Act 1981 ('SCA 1981'), s 51(8) and (9)). However, if the court is satisfied that the claimant knew or ought to have known that the proceedings were being commenced in the wrong court, the court has a discretion whether to order a transfer or to strike out the proceedings (CCA 1984, ss 40(1)(b) and 42(1)(b)). According to *Restick v Crickmore* [1994] 1 WLR 420, striking out is inappropriate for bona fide mistakes, but would be a proper response to instances where starting in the wrong court was a deliberate attempt to harass a defendant, or a deliberate attempt to run up unnecessary costs, or was done in defiance of a warning from the defendant about the proper venue for the proceedings.

C HIGH COURT DIVISIONS

3.32 Business is allocated between the three High Court Divisions in accordance with the SCA 1981, s 61 and Sch 1. The broad effect is that:

(a) the QBD deals with all judicial review, admiralty, and commercial matters. In addition, it is usually the most appropriate division for dealing with claims seeking common law remedies (debt, damages, recovery of land, recovery of goods), which include most claims in contract and tort;

(b) the ChD has been assigned all cases involving the sale, exchange, or partition of land; mortgages; execution of trusts; administration of estates; bankruptcy; taking of partnership accounts; rectification, etc. of deeds; probate; intellectual property; and company matters. It can also deal with other areas, such as claims in contract and tort, which are not assigned specifically to either of the other Divisions; and

(c) the FamD has been assigned all matrimonial and related matters.

3.33 It is possible to transfer claims between Divisions, and to and from specialist lists, under CPR, r 30.5. This will be appropriate where a claim is proceeding in one Division but raises specialist points which would be within the expertise and knowledge of judges in another Division or specialist list. However, a case will not usually be transferred merely because it would be dealt with more speedily or efficiently elsewhere: see *Barclays Bank plc v Bemister* [1989] 1 WLR 128. If a case is assigned by the SCA 1981 to one Division but is inadvertently commenced in the wrong Division, it will usually be transferred with very little argument, as there is a danger that judges dealing with unfamiliar cases may make mistakes, as happened in *Apac Rowena Ltd v Norpol Packaging Ltd* [1991] 4 All ER 516.

D SPECIALIST COURTS

Business and Property Courts

High Court cases in the ChD, the Commercial Court, the Technology and Construction **3.34** Court, the Circuit Commercial Court, and the Admiralty Court come under the umbrella of the Business and Property Courts (PD Business and Property Courts, para 1.1). These include most specialist cases, including company, insolvency, probate, intellectual property, and arbitration claims (para 1.5(2)), each of which has its own 'list' with specialist judges with expertise in the area. High Court claim forms in these cases need to be marked as 'Business and Property Courts' in the top right hand corner (PD 7A, para 2.5). Designated District Registries including Birmingham, Cardiff, Manchester, and Newcastle upon Tyne, also deal with Business and Property cases. Parties should use these regional courts if their dispute arose in a region outside London. They are required to explain in detail in their directions questionnaires why they have commenced such a claim in London if there is an available regional specialist court (PD 29, para 2.6A). Lower value specialist claims may be issued in one of nine designated County Court hearing centres, and need to be marked as 'Business and Property work' (PD Business and Property Courts, paras 4.1 and 4.3).

Technology and Construction Court

Cases in the QBD, ChD, or County Court may be dealt with in the Technology and Con- **3.35** struction Court ('TCC') if they involve prolonged examination of documents or accounts, or technical, scientific, or local investigations. Typically, the TCC deals with civil engineering and building disputes, professional negligence cases involving architects, surveyors, and accountants, and information technology cases. Cases may be commenced in the TCC, or may be transferred there at a later stage. Claims with a value up to £250,000 should usually be commenced in the County Court, or will be transferred there if they are commenced in the High Court (*West Country Renovations Ltd v McDowell* [2013] 1 WLR 416). Once in the TCC all statements of case are marked 'Technology and Construction Court' in the top right corner below the entry for the parent court classified as either 'HCJ' (the most heavy and complex cases, which will be tried by a High Court judge) or 'SCJ' (all other TCC claims, which will be tried by a senior circuit judge, who is addressed as 'Your Honour'). The case is then allocated to a named TCC judge. The TCC judges keep close control over the cases assigned to them, dealing with all interim applications as well as the trial. All TCC cases are allocated to the multi-track (CPR, r 60.6). Trials before TCC judges are conducted as nearly as possible in the same way as other High Court trials.

Commercial Court

Claims of a commercial nature in the QBD of the High Court may be commenced in or trans- **3.36** ferred to the Commercial Court. Statements of case are marked 'Commercial Court' after the entries relating to the division and Business and Property Courts. The cases covered include those involving shipping, international carriage of goods, insurance, banking, international credit, mercantile contractual disputes, and commercial arbitrations. Commercial cases are governed by CPR, Part 58. They are often very weighty pieces of litigation, and despite the requirement that commercial statements of case must be in point form and must be as brief as possible, statements of case in the Commercial Court are often characterized by length and complexity.

Circuit Commercial Court

3.37 Commercial claims in the provinces are dealt with by the Circuit Commercial Court in the Birmingham, Bristol, Cardiff, Leeds, Liverpool, Manchester, and Newcastle upon Tyne District Registries (PD 59, para 1.2). There is also a Circuit Commercial Court in London. Circuit Commercial Court claims are governed by CPR, Part 59. Similar provision has been made for County Court claims of a commercial nature, which may be issued in one of the designated Business and Property Courts hearing centres.

Admiralty Court

3.38 Admiralty jurisdiction is exercised by the QBD of the High Court (see SCA 1981, ss 20–24). Admiralty cases include claims to the possession or ownership of ships, for damage received or done by a ship, for personal injuries involving ships, for damage to goods carried by ship, and for salvage or towage. Admiralty claims may be either *in rem* or *in personam*. A claim *in rem* is usually against a ship, although it may be against cargo or freight. It allows the claimant to arrest the *res*, which provides security for the claimant and is obviously useful if the true defendant is resident abroad. A claim *in personam* is similar to general actions against named defendants. The Admiralty Court largely follows the practice in the Commercial Court.

Administrative Court

3.39 Judicial review claims are dealt with by the Administrative Court, which is a specialist court within the QBD (PD 54A, para 2.1). Judicial reviews of planning decisions are dealt with by the Planning Court (CPR, rr 54.21–54.24). Judicial review is considered in more detail in Chapter 49.

Companies Court

3.40 The Companies Court is a part of the ChD and deals with applications under the Companies Act 2006, the Insurance Companies Act 1982, the Insolvency Act 1986, and the Company Directors Disqualification Act 1986. It has its own special practice direction, PD 49A, and, in relation to insolvency matters, PD Insolvency Proceedings.

Patents Court and Intellectual Property Enterprise Court

3.41 Proceedings involving the validity, revocation, amendment, and alleged infringement of patents, registered designs, registered trade marks, and other intellectual property claims are brought in the Patents Court, which is part of the ChD (CPR, r 63.1(2)(f)). Where the value of the claim does not exceed £500,000 the claim may be brought in the Intellectual Property Enterprise Court (r 63.17A), which is a specialised list within the ChD (r 63.1(2)(g)). Judges in the Intellectual Property Enterprise Court are called enterprise judges (r 63.1(2)(h)). Procedure in these claims is governed by CPR, Part 63, and the court has its own court guide.

Financial List

3.42 Sophisticated banking claims and claims requiring specialist knowledge of financial markets, typically with a value exceeding £50 million, should be commenced in the Financial

List (CPR, Part 63A). This is a specialist list straddling the Commercial Court and the Chancery Division. It is most suitable for cases raising issues of market significance, as opposed to those raising factual issues relevant only to the parties (*Property Alliance Group Ltd v Royal Bank of Scotland plc* [2016] EWHC 207 (Ch)).

KEY POINTS SUMMARY

- For most civil claims the claimant has a free choice between the High Court and the County **3.43** Court.
- Broadly, the High Court should be used for the more important and complex claims.
- Broadly, common law claims are suitable for the QBD, whereas equity claims are more suitable for the ChD.
- The Commercial Court deals with QBD claims involving international and domestic trade, banking, and insurance. Equivalent lower value claims are dealt with in designated County Court hearing centres as Business and Property work.
- Masters deal with most interim applications in the QBD and ChD. In the Commercial Court they are dealt with by Commercial Court judges. In the County Court and District Registries of the High Court they are dealt with by District Judges.
- Multi-track trials are generally dealt with by judges in the High Court, and Circuit Judges in the County Court. Fast track trials and small claims hearings are usually heard by District Judges.

4

OVERRIDING OBJECTIVE AND HUMAN RIGHTS

A SOURCES OF PROCEDURAL LAW 4.04

B THE OVERRIDING OBJECTIVE 4.13

C ACTIVE CASE MANAGEMENT 4.14

D INTERPRETING THE CIVIL
PROCEDURE RULES 4.18

E APPLICATION OF THE OVERRIDING
OBJECTIVE 4.25

F HUMAN RIGHTS 4.33

G PROCEDURAL ASPECTS ON RAISING
HUMAN RIGHTS POINTS..............4.55

Key points summary 4.66

4.01 One of the fundamental concepts of the CPR is that they contain, as the very first rule, a statement of the overall purpose behind the civil justice system. This is known as the 'overriding objective', which is to deal with cases justly and at proportionate cost. By CPR, r 1.2, the court has to give effect to the overriding objective when making decisions and when interpreting the rules. The parties are, by r 1.3, required to help the court to further the overriding objective. By r 1.4 the court must further the overriding objective by actively managing cases. It is therefore a pervading concept that must always be kept in mind at all stages in civil proceedings.

4.02 Of similar importance is the Human Rights Act 1998. By s 3(1), so far as it is possible to do so, primary legislation and subordinate legislation (which includes the CPR) must be read and given effect to in a way which is compatible with the rights set out in the European Convention on Human Rights. Section 2(1) provides that a court determining a question which arises in connection with a Convention right must take into account any judgment, decision, declaration, or advisory opinion of the European Court of Human Rights. Although lawyers have to take a responsible attitude in raising human rights points (*Daniels v Walker* [2000] 1 WLR 1382), such points do arise on occasion when courts are considering procedural applications, and the CPR and practice directions have been drafted with a view to being compatible with the Convention.

4.03 This chapter will consider the sources of procedural law, the general principles relevant to civil procedure established by the overriding objective, and the European Convention on Human Rights, and also some rules on how the courts approach construing the CPR. Where human rights points arise in relation to specific areas of civil procedure, they will also be discussed in the relevant chapters of this book.

A SOURCES OF PROCEDURAL LAW

Statutory sources

4.04 The primary source of law governing procedure in the High Court and Court of Appeal is the Senior Courts Act 1981. The SCA 1981 used to be known as the Supreme Court Act 1981, but had to be re-named when the Supreme Court replaced the House of Lords in October 2009. The equivalent source for the County Court is the County

Courts Act 1984. Both statutes are often expressed in very wide terms, leaving the detailed mechanics of many of the procedures used in the courts to be set out in rules of court.

By the Civil Procedure Act 1997, s 2, a body known as the Civil Procedure Rule **4.05** Committee is empowered to make rules governing the practice and procedure to be followed in the civil courts. By s 1(3) the rules must be both simple and simply expressed. The principal rules made by the Committee are the Civil Procedure Rules 1998 (SI 1998/3132) ('CPR'). The CPR are divided into Parts, each divided into a number of rules. Amendments are made to the CPR (also by statutory instrument) several times each year. These usually have transitional provisions, but the underlying principle is that amendments to the CPR have immediate effect even on existing litigation, so the presumption against retrospection does not apply (*Wagenaar v Weekend Travel Ltd* [2015] 1 WLR 1968). Most of the Parts of the CPR are supplemented by one or more detailed practice directions ('PD'). Thus, PD 39A and PD 39B supplement CPR, Part 39. Electronic versions of the SCA 1981, CCA 1984, CPR, and PDs can be found:

(a) for statutes, at **<http://www.legislation.gov.uk>**;
(b) for the CPR, PDs, court forms, court guides, etc., at **<http://www.justice.gov.uk>**.

Practice directions and court guides

Practice directions may be made by the Lord Chief Justice, or his nominee, with the agreement **4.06** of the Lord Chancellor (Civil Procedure Act 1997, s 5(1) as amended), or with the approval of the Lord Chancellor and Lord Chief Justice (s 5(2)). 'Practice directions' for this purpose covers both practice directions expressly supplementing the CPR and general practice directions which in the past were made by the courts from time to time (s 9(1)). A purported practice direction that did not comply with the procedures in s 5 will be *ultra vires* (*Bovale Ltd v Secretary of State for Communities and Local Government* [2009] 1 WLR 2274). In contrast, a judge is permitted to lay down guidance suggesting procedures that should be followed without infringing s 5, provided the guidance is consistent with the CPR and main practice directions (*Bovale Ltd v Secretary of State for Communities and Local Government*).

Detailed court guides dealing with the mechanics for starting and conducting proceedings **4.07** have been published for the QBD and ChD, and also for most of the specialist courts such as the TCC and Admiralty and Commercial Courts. Technically, the court guides have no formal status, and provide no more than guidance (*Bovale Ltd v Secretary of State for Communities and Local Government* [2009] 1 WLR 2274). They cannot define the courts' jurisdiction, and they cannot override provisions in the CPR or PDs (*Vitpol Building Service v Samen* [2009] Bus LR D65).

Judicial sources

Although the CPR and practice directions are of quite considerable length, very often they **4.08** state the principles to be applied on the various procedures available in general terms, leaving details to be worked out by the courts on a case-by-case basis.

Lacunae in the County Court Rules

The CPR provide a single set of rules covering both the High Court and the County Court. **4.09** There should be identical coverage for both courts, but out of an excess of caution the CCA 1984, s 76, provides that:

> In any case not expressly provided for by or in pursuance of this Act, the general principles of practice in the High Court may be adopted and applied to proceedings in the County Court.

Inherent jurisdiction

Inherent jurisdiction of the High Court

4.10 Being the successor to the old common law courts, the High Court has inherent jurisdiction to control its procedure to ensure its proceedings are not used to achieve injustice. Perhaps the most important statement on this subject is that of Lord Diplock in *Bremer Vulkan Schiffbau und Maschinenfabrik v South India Shipping Corporation Ltd* [1981] AC 909 at 977, where his Lordship said the High Court has:

> ... a general power to control its own procedure so as to prevent its being used to achieve injustice. Such a power is inherent in its constitutional function as a court of justice. Every civilised system of government requires that the State should make available to all its citizens a means for the just and peaceful settlement of disputes between them as to their respective legal rights. The means provided are courts of justice to which every citizen has a constitutional right of access in the role of plaintiff to obtain the remedy to which he claims to be entitled in consequence of an alleged breach of his legal or equitable rights by some other citizen, the defendant. Whether or not to avail himself of this right of access to the court lies exclusively within the plaintiff's choice; if he chooses to do so, the defendant has no option in the matter; his subjection to the jurisdiction of the court is compulsory. So, it would stultify the constitutional role of the High Court as a court of justice if it were not armed with power to prevent its process being misused in such a way as to diminish its capability of arriving at a just decision of the dispute.

4.11 Thus, where a party in a High Court claim makes an application for an order which is not contemplated by the SCA 1981 or the CPR or seeks an order in circumstances not envisaged by those provisions, it is possible for the court to grant relief by resorting to its inherent jurisdiction. A cautious approach is adopted to attempts to expand the reach of the courts through use of the inherent jurisdiction (*Al Rawi v Security Service* [2012] 1 AC 531). Nevertheless, procedures such as freezing injunctions (see Chapter 43) and search orders (see Chapter 44) were initially developed by means of the exercise of the High Court's inherent jurisdiction. As an area develops there comes a point when it might be codified by statutory provisions (eg by the Civil Procedure Act 1997 and CPR, Part 25 for freezing injunctions and search orders). At that stage the better view is that the inherent jurisdiction no longer applies as the source of the jurisdiction, having been replaced in that area by the provisions in the statute or CPR (*Harrison v Tew* [1990] 2 AC 523; *Raja v Van Hoogstraten (No 9)* [2009] 1 WLR 1143).

Inherent jurisdiction of the County Court

4.12 Being a creature of statute, the better view is that the County Court has no inherent jurisdiction (*Salekipour v Parmar* [2016] QB 987). *Langley v North West Water Authority* [1991] 1 WLR 697 is a rather surprising decision to the effect that the County Court does have an inherent jurisdiction, but is almost certainly wrong.

B THE OVERRIDING OBJECTIVE

4.13 Rule 1.1 of the CPR provides:

(1) These rules are a new procedural code with the overriding objective of enabling the court to deal with cases justly and at proportionate cost.
(2) Dealing with a case justly includes, so far as is practicable—
    (a) ensuring that the parties are on an equal footing;
    (b) saving expense;
    (c) dealing with the case in ways which are proportionate—
        (i) to the amount of money involved;
        (ii) to the importance of the case;

(iii) to the complexity of the issues; and

(iv) to the financial position of each party;

(d) ensuring that it is dealt with expeditiously and fairly;

(e) allotting to it an appropriate share of the court's resources, while taking into account the need to allot resources to other cases; and

(f) enforcing compliance with rules, practice directions and orders.

C ACTIVE CASE MANAGEMENT

Rule 1.4(1) of the CPR provides that the court must further the overriding objective by actively managing cases. By r 1.4(2), active case management includes: **4.14**

(a) encouraging the parties to cooperate with each other in the conduct of the proceedings;

(b) identifying the issues at an early stage;

(c) deciding promptly which issues need full investigation and trial and accordingly disposing summarily of the others;

(d) deciding the order in which issues are to be resolved;

(e) encouraging the parties to use an alternative dispute resolution procedure if the court considers that appropriate and facilitating the use of such procedure;

(f) helping the parties to settle the whole or part of the case;

(g) fixing timetables or otherwise controlling the progress of the case;

(h) considering whether the likely benefits of taking a particular step justify the cost of taking it;

(i) dealing with as many aspects of the case as it can on the same occasion;

(j) dealing with the case without the parties needing to attend at court;

(k) making use of technology; and

(l) giving directions to ensure that the trial of a case proceeds quickly and efficiently.

General case management

In the general run of cases there will be active judicial case management at the following stages: **4.15**

(a) At the allocation stage, where not only will the court allocate the case to one of the case management tracks, but it will also give directions setting a timetable for the future steps to be taken in the case. Judges take a particularly active part in case management conferences and other procedural hearings, where they seek to identify and limit the issues between the parties, and ensure the necessary preparatory work for the trial is done within the shortest reasonable time. Judges may contact the parties directly to monitor compliance with directions. See Chapter 15.

(b) When the court gives directions on the evidence it will permit to be adduced at trial. This particularly applies to expert evidence, which the court may say is totally unnecessary; or it may say that there should be a single, jointly instructed, expert; or that expert evidence will be restricted to written reports. See Chapter 35.

(c) Regarding listing for trial. The court will be concerned to ensure the trial takes place with as little delay as possible, will make such orders as may be necessary to ensure avoidable delays do not occur, and will make directions to ensure the parties realize they are working towards a trial date or trial window which will only be moved as a last resort. Parties guilty of delay will be penalized by the imposition of sanctions. See Chapter 37.

(d) At the trial itself, where the court has wide powers to control the sequence of events and to impose time limits on the presentation of evidence and on speeches. See Chapter 39.

(e) Regarding costs, where the proportionality concept may be applied to reduce costs which are out of proportion to the value and complexity of the case, and where parties who have not abided by the ethos encapsulated by the overriding objective may find that they are penalized in costs. See Chapter 46.

Consequences of active case management

4.16 In addition to the examples mentioned at 4.15, active case management is also important in ensuring interim applications are dealt with in a proportionate manner (see Chapter 23). The court can take the initiative by making directions and even by striking-out proceedings which disclose no reasonable grounds for bringing the claim (see Chapter 30). It can list a summary judgment hearing where it appears a claim or defence has no real prospect of success (see Chapter 24). It may require a party to provide further information about the issues or evidence in the case, or about the progress made in the case (see Chapter 18). Direct monitoring of compliance with directions (CPR, r 3.1(8)), and a strict approach to compliance with directions (see Chapter 37), have tended to shift control of litigation from the parties to the judiciary. Although litigation has traditionally been conducted in an adversarial manner, this is being slowly eroded into a more inquisitorial process.

Making use of technology

4.17 The courts are increasingly aware of the savings that can be made by the use of developing technology. Judges may contact solicitors by telephone or e-mail in order to monitor compliance with directions (CPR, r 3.1(8)). There is provision in the rules for holding interim hearings by telephone (see Chapter 23). Some documents, particularly draft orders (which are often revised before being approved by the judge), must be submitted to the court by e-mail or on a digital storage device to facilitate production of the formal order. On occasion, the court will allow evidence to be given by video-conferencing, or will order that substantial parts of the documentation be provided in electronic form, supported by hypertext or other links to enable the judge to move rapidly from one document to another. Use of technology to this extent is far more likely in particularly heavy litigation. In *Morris v Bank of America National Trust* [2000] 1 All ER 954, the Court of Appeal stressed that use of technology is acceptable only if it will save time or money, and if it will not unfairly prejudice any of the parties.

D INTERPRETING THE CIVIL PROCEDURE RULES

General approach to interpretation

4.18 Courts sometimes say they apply a purposive approach to the interpretation of the CPR (*YD (Turkey) v Secretary of State for the Home Department* [2006] 1 WLR 1646, *R (Corner House Research) v Director of the Serious Fraud Office* [2008] EWHC 246 (Admin)). Without expressly saying so, most appellate decisions on the CPR apply traditional legalistic, literal, interpretative techniques. The fact there is a practice direction on the meaning of 'will' and 'must' (PD 2D) underlines the point. As the CPR is a statutory instrument, the Interpretation Act 1978 applies as an aid to interpretation (*Collier v Williams* [2006] 1 WLR 1945).

New procedural code

4.19 By virtue of r 1.1(1), the CPR are declared to be 'a new procedural code'. Making the CPR a new procedural code means that a new start was made (*Re a Debtor (No 1 of*

1987) [1989] 1 WLR 271), so that cases decided under the previous rules of court are not binding authorities on the meaning of the CPR. The CPR are not merely a more modern restatement of the old rules (the RSC and CCR), but a complete replacement of those rules. Leading cases adopting this approach include *Biguzzi v Rank Leisure plc* [1999] 1 WLR 1926 on sanctions (see 37.18) and *Nasser v United Bank of Kuwait* [2002] 1 WLR 1868 on security for costs (see 26.21).

The courts have found it increasingly difficult to maintain this approach, and there are **4.20** many examples where old cases (and sometimes the wording of the old rules) have been applied as a guide to the interpretation of the CPR. Where the CPR completely fail to deal with a topic, the court can adopt provisions from the pre-CPR rules or practice (*Carnegie v Giessen* [2005] 1 WLR 2510). Examples where the courts have resorted to pre-CPR cases as a guide to current practice include: *Nomura International plc v Granada Group Ltd* [2007] 2 All ER (Comm) 878 on a technical point in relation to striking out; *Adelson v Associated Newspapers Ltd* [2008] 1 WLR 585 on substituting parties after limitation (see 22.29); *City and Country Properties Ltd v Kamali* [2007] 1 WLR 1219 in relation to the address for service of a defendant while temporarily out of the jurisdiction (see 6.25); and *Vedatech Corporation v Seagate Software Information* (2001) LTL 29/11/01 on security for costs (see 26.22). *Dubai Bank Ltd v Galadari (No 3)* [1990] 1 WLR 731 was applied by *Rubin v Expandable Ltd* [2008] 1 WLR 1099, in interpreting the meaning of 'mentioned' in CPR, r 31.14, and *MA Holdings Ltd v R (George Wimpey UK Ltd)* [2008] NPC 6 applied *Warren v Uttlesford District Council* [1996] COD 262 on non-parties seeking permission to appeal. The Supreme Court has a tendency to review case law of some antiquity when deciding important points of principle (an example is *Summers v Fairclough Homes Ltd* [2012] 1 WLR 2004 on striking out of fraudulent claims). It could be objected that all these cases are unsound as they fail to apply the principle that the CPR is a new procedural code. They are probably better considered as practical law-making in circumstances where the courts are faced with situations not expressly covered by the CPR.

Overriding objective as a guide to interpretation

Where there are no express words in the CPR dealing with a situation, the court is bound **4.21** to consider which interpretation best reflects the overriding objective when construing the rules (CPR, r 1.2(b); *Totty v Snowden* [2002] 1 WLR 1384 at [34]). Use of the overriding objective is considered more fully at 4.25ff.

Natural meaning when interpreting the CPR

The CPR have been deliberately drafted in a plain English style in order to make them intel- **4.22** ligible to lay people using the courts. When construing the rules the courts primarily seek to find the natural meaning of the words used. Although CPR, r 1.2(b), says that the court must seek to give effect to the overriding objective when it interprets any rule, the Court of Appeal has said this does not apply when the words of a rule are clear. In *Vinos v Marks & Spencer plc* [2001] 3 All ER 784 (approved in *Godwin v Swindon Borough Council* [2002] 1 WLR 997), May LJ said that interpretation to achieve the overriding objective does not enable the court to say that provisions which are quite plain mean what they do not mean, nor that the plain meaning of the rules should be ignored. The court cannot, therefore, assume a discretion in order to assist a deserving case where there is no jurisdiction to make an order, even by resorting to the overriding objective (*Godwin v Swindon Borough Council* [2002] 1 WLR 997 at [45]).

Human rights as a guide to interpretation

4.23 *Goode v Martin* [2002] 1 WLR 1828 held that what would have been the plain meaning of a provision of the CPR applying traditional rules of construction could be avoided in a case where that meaning would have infringed a party's rights under the European Convention on Human Rights. Section 3(1) of the Human Rights Act 1998 provides that 'so far as it is possible to do so, primary legislation and subordinate legislation must be read and given effect in a way which is compatible with the Convention rights'. To do this, the court was prepared to read additional words into a rule. Further discussion of the impact of the Human Rights Act 1998 on civil procedure can be found at 4.33ff.

Rules of precedent

4.24 Where a provision of the CPR has been construed by a previous decision of a higher court, subsequent cases have to apply the provision in the same way as the previous, binding, decision. The basic rules of precedent are that, although the Supreme Court (until October 2009, the House of Lords) can sometimes depart from its previous rulings, decisions (as opposed to *obiter dicta*) of the Supreme Court, House of Lords, and Court of Appeal are binding on the Court of Appeal and all lower courts. Previous decisions from the County Court and High Court are no more than persuasive. Exceptions to the rules of precedent are applied with great care. Where the point in the previous authority was assumed without argument, even where the point was essential to the earlier decision, a later court can depart from that assumption after hearing full argument (*Kadhim v Brent London Borough Council* (2001) *The Times*, 27 March 2001).

E APPLICATION OF THE OVERRIDING OBJECTIVE

4.25 Placing the overriding objective as the first rule in the CPR was deliberately designed to emphasize a change in culture. Litigation must be conducted in an efficient, cooperative way, avoiding expense and delay. Originally the overriding objective was to conduct litigation justly, but this was changed by the Civil Justice Reforms 2013 to include 'and at proportionate cost'. Another change made in 2013 was to include the need to enforce compliance with rules and court orders as part of dealing with cases justly and at proportionate cost. One of the important aims of the Jackson Reforms was to ensure that procedural orders reflect not only the interests of the case in hand, but also promote the interests of the administration of justice more generally (*Global Torch Ltd v Apex Global Management Ltd (No 2)* [2014] 1 WLR 4495 at [25]). In modern times it is recognized that court resources are finite, so the court is entitled to take into account that an individual case must not take an unfair amount of judicial resources away from other claims (*Hague Plant Ltd v Hague* [2014] EWCA Civ 1609 at [25]). Devoting court resources in this way means that while justice is done in the majority of cases, procedural justice might mean that justice on the merits is not available in some cases (*Mitchell v News Group Newspapers Ltd* [2014] 1 WLR 795 at [17]).

Dealing with cases justly

4.26 The main concept in CPR, r 1.1(1), means that the primary concern of the court is doing justice. This involves dealing with the real case of both sides to the dispute, and wherever possible deciding the case on the merits. This is tempered by the second element of r 1.1(1) that justice must be achieved at proportionate cost. There will therefore be cases which are dismissed for procedural default, because the courts are not there to provide justice at any price. Parties have to cooperate with the courts in achieving the overriding objective. For example, standing witnesses down in advance of an application to adjourn a trial was regarded as failing to act justly in *Albon v Naza Motor Trading Sdn Bhd* (2007) LTL 19/11/07, because it prevented the court from determining the application on its merits.

Equal footing

Ensuring the parties are on an equal footing is primarily concerned with the unfair **4.27** exploitation of superior resources, rather than issues such as a failure to provide information (*Henry v News Group Newspapers Ltd* [2013] EWCA Civ 19). However, not providing the opposite party with a letter sent to the judge, and thereby failing to give the other side an opportunity to respond to it, is a serious procedural irregularity (*National Westminster Bank plc v Rushmer* [2010] 2 FLR 362). The fact one party is better informed or better advised, or has stronger evidence, than the other does not mean there is an inequality of arms unless the inequality is very substantial and very prejudicial (*Henley v Bloom* [2010] 1 WLR 1770).

Proportionality

Proportionality lies at the heart of much of the CPR. The existence of the three case man- **4.28** agement tracks (see Chapters 27 to 29) is designed to ensure that procedures for preparing cases for trial are in line with the importance and value of each case. Controlling costs may be achieved directly through costs management (see Chapter 16) and restricting recoverable costs to proportionate amounts (see 46.49, and r 44.3(5)), and indirectly by controlling disclosure (see Chapter 31), and restricting the numbers of witnesses and experts parties can use (see Chapters 32 and 35). Applications, even if they have some merit, but are on minor matters which the court might regard as tactical posturing, may be dismissed on grounds of proportionality (*TIP Communications LLC v Motorola Ltd* [2009] EWHC 212 (Pat)). Statements of case that are excessively long and which fail to comply with the requirements in CPR, Part 16 may be disallowed because they will generate disproportionate costs (*Hague Plant Ltd v Hague* [2014] EWCA Civ 1609).

Proportionality is also important in relation to the imposition of sanctions (see Chapter 37). **4.29** Taking a point that particulars of claim were served one minute late was regarded as unmeritorious in the absence of prejudice in *Rogers v East Kent Hospitals NHS Trust* [2009] LS Law Med 153. In relation to sanctions, proportionality is, perhaps surprisingly, not essentially about making the punishment fit the crime. A sanction of entering judgment for US$6 million for failing to sign personally a disclosure statement was held by the Supreme Court in *Global Torch Ltd v Apex Global Management Ltd (No 2)* [2014] 1 WLR 4495 not to have been disproportionate, even in circumstances where the claimant had a weak case that it was owed the money. This was because of the self-evident importance of compliance with court orders, the need to ensure continuing respect for the authority of the court, and because the breach had been persisted in despite several opportunities to comply.

Dealing with cases expeditiously and fairly, and saving expense

Procedures should be adopted to keep litigation as inexpensive as possible. This means, for **4.30** example, that routine case management decisions and uncontentious applications should be disposed of on the papers without hearings (*Collier v Williams* [2006] 1 WLR 1945).

In *Adan v Securicor Custodial Services Ltd* [2005] PIQR P79 the claimant asked the court to use CPR, r 3.1(2)(i), which gives the court a power to order separate trials, so that his claim for damages could be decided when he was discharged from long-term hospitalization. The application was refused as contrary to the overriding objective. It would have exposed the defendant's insurers to an uncertain liability for an indefinite period, which was oppressive and undesirable.

Allotting an appropriate share of the court's resources

4.31 In *Stephenson (SBJ) Ltd v Mandy* (1999) *The Times*, 21 July 1999, the Court of Appeal refused to consider the merits of an interim appeal because there was only a short time to trial so the appeal was not a good use of the court's resources. An appeal was also dismissed in *Adoko v Jemal* (1999) *The Times*, 8 July 1999, on the ground of allotting to it no more than an appropriate share of the court's resources. In this case the appellant had failed to correct the appellant's notice despite a warning from the respondent that it was seriously defective, and had failed to comply with the directions relating to appeal bundles. The Court of Appeal spent over an hour trying to sort out the papers, and then decided it was inappropriate that any further share of the court's resources should be allocated to the appeal.

Cooperating

4.32 Solicitors were criticized in *King v Telegraph Group Ltd* [2005] 1 WLR 2282, for sending a letter of claim in vituperative language which the court felt was designed to raise hostility and increase costs. Taking a point that correspondence agreeing that costs budgets would be exchanged 'by 28 February' and 'on 28 February' meant that service on 28 February was a day late was regarded as both wrong and undermining the duty of cooperation in *Ratten v UBS AG* [2014] EWHC 665 (Comm). There was a breach of the duty to cooperate in *Hertsmere Primary Care Trust v Administrators of Balasubramanium's Estate* [2005] 3 All ER 274, where a party refused to tell the other side the nature of a technical error in a Part 36 offer.

F HUMAN RIGHTS

4.33 The European Convention on Human Rights was brought into effect in the UK by the Human Rights Act 1998. The text of the Act and the Convention can be found in *Blackstone's Civil Practice* ('BCP'), app 4.

4.34 A court finding that a statute conflicts with the Convention may make a declaration of incompatibility under s 4, though such a declaration should only be granted to a claimant who is or could be personally adversely affected by the impugned legislation (*Lancashire County Council v Taylor* [2005] 1 WLR 2668). It is unlawful for a public authority to act in a way which is incompatible with a Convention right (s 6(1)). A person who is a victim of any such unlawful act may rely on their Convention rights in any court proceedings, and may bring proceedings under the Act against the public authority (s 7). Proceedings must be brought within one year or such longer period as the court considers equitable in all the circumstances (s 7(5) and *O'Connor v Bar Standards Board* [2017] 1 WLR 4833). If the court finds that the public authority has acted unlawfully (or proposes to do so), it may grant such relief or remedy as it considers appropriate (s 8(1)). Damages, however, can only be granted if the court is satisfied that such an award is necessary to afford just satisfaction to the claimant (s 8(3), and see 4.64). The Convention generally only applies to breaches occurring within the territory of a contracting State, and it is only in cases of extreme unfairness that the court will give indirect effect to the Convention (*Barnette v*

Government of the United States of America [2004] 1 WLR 2241). However, the actions of British consular officials abroad can be subject to the Convention (*R (B) v Secretary of State for Foreign and Commonwealth Affairs* [2005] QB 643).

Where a party seeks to rely in civil proceedings on any provision or right, or seeks a remedy **4.35** available, under the Human Rights Act 1998, this must be stated in their statement of case with precise details of the rights relied upon and remedies sought (PD 16, para 15.1). This is why claim forms ask the question (under the heading) whether the claim raises any issues under the Act (see form 6.1). Giving notice to the Crown, and intervention by the appropriate minister, are considered at 4.58–4.59.

A court or tribunal determining a question which has arisen in connection with a Conven- **4.36** tion right must take into account judgments, etc., of the European Court of Human Rights ('ECHR') (Human Rights Act 1998, s 2). One consequence of this has been a move away from a literalistic approach to interpretation towards a purposive approach concentrating on achieving the aims of the Convention right under consideration (*Godin-Mendoza v Ghaidan* [2004] 2 AC 557). The wording of s 2 means that decisions of the ECHR are not binding, but provide authoritative guidance in domestic courts (*R (S) v Chief Constable of South Yorkshire* [2004] 1 WLR 2196). Where there is clear and consistent ECHR case law on a point, a domestic court will need a strong reason before departing from it (*R (Ullah) v Special Adjudicator* [2004] 2 AC 323). However, where there is a Supreme Court decision on a point, a domestic court below the Supreme Court must follow the Supreme Court decision even if there is a subsequent conflicting ECHR decision (*Leeds City Council v Price* [2005] 1 WLR 1825).

Right to a fair hearing

Principles relating to a fair hearing

Article 6(1) of the European Convention on Human Rights provides: **4.37**

> In the determination of his civil rights and obligations or of any criminal charge against him, everyone is entitled to a fair and public hearing within a reasonable time by an independent and impartial tribunal established by law. Judgment shall be pronounced publicly but the press and public may be excluded from all or part of the trial in the interest of morals, public order or national security in a democratic society, where the interests of juveniles or the protection of the private life of the parties so require, or to the extent strictly necessary in the opinion of the court in special circumstances where publicity would prejudice the interests of justice.

The basic principle underlying art 6(1) is that civil claims must be capable of being sub- **4.38** mitted to a judge for adjudication (*Fayed v United Kingdom* (Case No 18/1993/423/502) (1994) 18 EHRR 383). It typically applies where the only forum for deciding a dispute is not an independent and impartial tribunal, or where there are procedural bars on bringing a claim, or where procedural bars prevent a claim being decided on its merits. Article 6(1) is not engaged where the complaint is about how the law is framed, and it cannot be used as a means of creating a substantive right having no basis in national law (*Wilson v First County Trust (No 2)* [2004] 1 AC 816).

Where it is alleged that art 6 is infringed by a statute which replaces a right to litigate with **4.39** an administrative system (such as the Child Support Act 1991), or by a tribunal system with limited rights of recourse to the courts, *R (Kehoe) v Secretary of State for Work and Pensions* [2004] 1 WLR 2757 shows there are three questions to be answered:

(a) whether the case involved a determination of the claimant's 'civil rights and obligations'. These are not limited to rights protected by private as opposed to public law. A public law decision can come within the meaning of the expression in art 6 if it has an effect on the claimant's private law rights (*Ringeisen v Austria (No 1)* (1971) 1 EHRR

455; *R (Alconbury Developments Ltd) v Secretary of State for the Environment, Transport and the Regions* [2003] 2 AC 295);

(b) whether the administrative determination of the claimant's rights was subject to control by a court having full jurisdiction to deal with the case as the nature of the case required (*R (Alconbury Developments Ltd) v Secretary of State for the Environment, Transport and the Regions*). The right to resort to judicial review of administrative decisions should satisfy art 6 provided there is no substantial factual investigation required: see *Tower Hamlets London Borough Council v Begum* [2003] 2 AC 430; and

(c) where the claimant's right of access to a court is restricted, whether the restrictions satisfied the test of proportionality. This requires a balance between the legitimate objectives of the administrative scheme and the means used to achieve them (*R (Kehoe) v Secretary of State for Work and Pensions*).

Rights established by art 6

4.40 Under art 6(1) litigants are entitled to a fair hearing before an impartial tribunal. It is for this reason that most, but not all, hearings in civil cases, whether they be trials or interim applications, are in public (CPR, r 39.2; *Werner v Austria* (1997) 26 EHRR 310, and *Clibbery v Allan* [2002] Fam 261). Rule 39.2 of the CPR was challenged as *ultra vires* in *R (Pelling) v Bow County Court* [2001] UKHRR 165 on the ground that it allows some hearings to be conducted in private, but the challenge was unsuccessful. Although generally art 6(1) requires hearings to be conducted in the presence of the parties, this is only necessary in civil cases where the court has to make a decision relating to a party's personal character (*Muyldermans v Belgium* (1991) 15 EHRR 204).

4.41 In order to be fair the parties should be afforded equality of arms. While this means that parties should be given adequate time and facilities to pursue their case (*R v Secretary of State for the Home Department, ex p Quaquah* [2000] HRLR 325), it does not mean that a party should be prevented from being represented by a Queen's Counsel on the ground that the other side cannot afford to pay the fees commanded by a QC (*Maltez v Lewis* (1999) *The Times*, 4 May 1999).

4.42 All the circumstances of the case will be considered in deciding whether a hearing is held within a reasonable time, including the importance and difficulties of the case and the conduct of the parties (*EDC v United Kingdom* [1998] BCC 370). A stay pending payment of the costs of an earlier claim does not conflict with the European Convention on Human Rights, art 6(1). Such a stay can be imposed even where the parties were not entirely the same, provided the second claim arose out of substantially the same facts as the previous claim (*Stevens v School of Oriental and African Studies* (2000) *The Times*, 2 February 2001).

4.43 Compliance with art 6 requires reasons to be given for a court's decisions. The detail required by art 6 does not exceed that required by domestic law (*English v Emery Reimbold and Strick Ltd* [2002] 1 WLR 2409), but must be sufficient for an appeal court to understand the basis for the decision should there be an appeal. Just because reasons are short does not mean they infringe art 6(1) (*Hyams v Plender* [2001] 1 WLR 32 at [17]). Reasons, even if short and even if for costs orders, must be clear, and cannot be left to inference (*Lavelle v Lavelle* (2004) *The Times*, 9 March 2004).

Application of art 6 to civil litigation

4.44 Before implementation of the Convention, the House of Lords held that a judge should not sit at a hearing if there was a real danger of bias (*R v Gough* [1993] AC 646). European Convention jurisprudence has established that there will be a breach of art 6 if there is an objectively justified reason or fear of a lack of impartiality on the part of the judge dealing with a case. Accordingly, English judges should excuse themselves from sitting, not where there is a real danger of bias, but where a fair-minded and informed observer would conclude there was a real possibility of bias (*Porter v Magill* [2002] 2 AC 357).

Time limits and limitation periods may infringe art 6(1) if they are disproportionately short **4.45** (*Perez de Rada Cavanilles v Spain* (1998) 29 EHRR 109, where a three-day time limit was held to infringe art 6(1)). The periods laid down by the Limitation Act 1980 are unlikely to be seen as infringing art 6(1) (*Stubbings v United Kingdom* (1997) 23 EHRR 213).

Applications for summary judgment have been said to be consistent with the need to have **4.46** a fair trial under art 6(1) (*Three Rivers District Council v Bank of England (No 3)* [2003] 2 AC 1). Likewise, an order for security for costs does not infringe art 6(1), although the right of access to the courts has to be taken into account (*Nasser v United Bank of Kuwait* [2002] 1 WLR 1868). The essential policy when considering matters such as security for costs, CFAs, and costs orders against non-parties, is that the need to protect the successful party by granting an effective costs order has to yield to the right of access to the courts to litigate the dispute in the first place (*Hamilton v Al Fayed (No 2)* [2003] QB 1175 applying art 6(1)).

Right to respect for private and family life

Article 8 of the European Convention on Human Rights provides: **4.47**

1. Everyone has the right to respect for his private and family life, his home and his correspondence.
2. There shall be no interference by a public authority with the exercise of this right except such as is in accordance with the law and is necessary in a democratic society in the interests of national security, public safety or the economic wellbeing of the country, for the prevention of disorder or crime, for the protection of health or morals, or for the protection of the rights and freedoms of others.

Article 8 provides a qualified (see art 8(2)) protection for private and family life. Family life **4.48** includes the relationships between spouses, parents and children, unmarried couples and their children, grandparents and grandchildren (*Marckx v Belgium* (1979) 2 EHRR 330), and cohabiting same-sex couples in stable *de facto* partnerships (*Schalk & Kopf v Austria* (Application No 3014/04), although the 'right to marry' is within the margin of appreciation of Member States). The article probably does not protect corporations (*R v Broadcasting Standards Commission, ex p British Broadcasting Corporation* [2001] QB 885). Substantive rules, such as the immunity from suit in respect of out-of-court statements relating to the investigation of crime, often need to be reassessed to determine whether they comply with Convention rights (*Westcott v Westcott* [2009] QB 407, where the established law was held to comply with art 8(2)).

Article 8(1) may be invoked to protect personal and private details about individuals, infor- **4.49** mation about children, private correspondence, and telephone conversations (see *Halford v United Kingdom* (1997) 24 EHRR 523, which involved telephone conversations from a private office at work). A balance sometimes has to be struck between the protection in art 8(1) and the need for a fair and public trial in art 6(1). In *Clibbery v Allan* [2002] Fam 261 at [82], it was held that this balance is usually struck in favour of confidentiality where a family law hearing involves children, but in *H v News Group Newspapers Ltd* [2011] 1 WLR 1645 the Court of Appeal made the point that parties cannot simply consent to their case being subject to anonymity orders and reporting restrictions: these are matters for the court to decide.

4.50   Article 8 may have an impact on the use of videos in civil proceedings. They are some-times used by defendants in personal injuries claims in cross-examining the claimant by playing certain parts of a covertly shot video of the claimant going to the shops, hospi-tal, at work, or in the garden in order to undermine the claimant. Such use will usually be legitimate, but a direction is likely to be made limiting the footage to be shown (in *Rall v Hume* [2001] 3 All ER 248 the footage to be shown was limited to 20 minutes). Although the court will wish to uphold art 8, a video shot inside the claimant's home in clear breach of art 8 was allowed in evidence in *Jones v University of Warwick* [2003] 1 WLR 954.

4.51   The existence of art 8 has assisted the courts in developing the scope of the actions for breach of confidence based on the misuse of private information (*Campbell v Mirror Group Newspapers Ltd* [2004] 2 AC 457 and *McKennitt v Ash* [2008] QB 73). The posi-tion has been reached where the Supreme Court has recognized the existence of a tort of invasion of privacy (*PJS v News Group Newspapers Ltd* [2016] AC 1081), and principles have been laid down for calculating damages for misuse of private information (*Gulati v MGN Ltd* [2017] QB 149).

Freedom of expression

4.52   Article 10 of the European Convention on Human Rights provides:

1.   Everyone has the right to freedom of expression. This right shall include freedom to hold opinions and to receive and impart information and ideas without interference by public authority and regardless of frontiers. This Article shall not prevent States from requiring the licensing of broadcasting, television or cinema enterprises.
2.   The exercise of these freedoms, since it carries with it duties and responsibilities, may be subject to such formalities, conditions, restrictions or penalties as are prescribed by law and are necessary in a democratic society, in the interests of national security, territorial integ-rity or public safety, for the prevention of disorder or crime, for the protection of health or morals, for the protection of the reputation or rights of others, for preventing the disclosure of information received in confidence, or for maintaining the authority and impartiality of the judiciary.

4.53   Article 10(1) provides that everyone has the right to freedom of expression. This right is subject to safeguards in art 10(2), which include restrictions for the protection of the reputation or rights of others. These include any rights of others under validly concluded contracts, such as restrictions on further publication set out in a Tomlin order (*Mionis v Democratic Press SA* [2018] 2 WLR 565). The Human Rights Act 1998, s 12(3), provides that no relief to restrain publication before trial which might affect the art 10(1) right is to be allowed 'unless the court is satisfied that the applicant is likely to establish that the publication should not be allowed'. This has altered the common law test (as set out in *American Cyanamid Co v Ethicon Ltd* [1975] AC 396: see 42.64) in applications for inter-im injunctions where art 10 rights are in issue. While s 12(3) has an important impact in breach of confidence claims, it does not affect the position in defamation claims where the defendant relies on the defence of truth (now in the Defamation Act 2013, s 2, see *Greene v Associated Newspapers Ltd* [2005] QB 972).

4.54   Interim injunctions in claims for breach of confidence should normally be governed by *American Cyanamid*, as adapted by the Human Rights Act 1998, s 12(3). Instead of merely showing a serious issue to be tried, in most cases the applicant must establish a case which will probably ('more likely than not') succeed at trial. The court will then exercise its dis-cretion, taking into account the jurisprudence on art 10 and any other relevant matters. In *Cream Holdings v Banerjee* [2005] 1 AC 253, the House of Lords said the court must adopt a flexible approach to s 12(3). If demanding a case that will probably succeed does not achieve the legislative intention behind s 12(3), or fails to give effect to countervailing Convention rights, a lesser degree of likelihood will suffice to satisfy the test. A balance has to be struck between the competing interests in protecting private and family life under art 8(1), freedom of expression under art 10(1), and the protection of the reputation and rights of others under art 10(2): see *Campbell v Mirror Group Newspapers plc* [2004] 2 AC 457. For more detailed discussion see 42.61.

G PROCEDURAL ASPECTS ON RAISING HUMAN RIGHTS POINTS

Jurisdiction

Claims under the Human Rights Act 1998, s 7(1)(a) in respect of a judicial act must be **4.55** brought in the High Court (CPR, r 7.11) and within a year of the act complained of (s 7(5)). Other civil claims under the Human Rights Act 1998 can be brought in the County Court or the High Court. Deputy High Court judges, Masters, and District Judges cannot try claims under the Human Rights Act 1998, s 7(1)(a), in respect of a judicial act, nor claims for declarations of incompatibility under s 4 (PD 2B, para 7A).

Statement of case

Claim forms and appeal notices have boxes on the printed forms for indicating whether the **4.56** case or appeal raises any point under the Human Rights Act 1998. In addition, the statement of case must set out full details of the human rights point, including the Convention right relied upon, the alleged infringement, and the relief sought (PD 16, para 15.1).

In claims for damages in respect of a judicial act the claim must be stated in the statement **4.57** of case, notice given to the Crown (usually the Lord Chancellor), and the appropriate minister may be joined either on application by the minister or by direction of the court (r 19.4A(3), (4)).

Intervention in human rights claims

The court may not make a declaration of incompatibility under the Human Rights Act **4.58** 1998, s 4 (for which see 4.63), unless 21 days' notice has been given to the Crown (Human Rights Act 1998, s 5 and CPR, r 19.4A(1)). Directions requiring notice to be given will usually be made at a case management conference (PD 19A, para 6.2). In these cases a minister, or other person permitted by the Human Rights Act 1998, is entitled to be joined as a party on giving notice to the court (r 19.4A(2)).

Where claims are made for damages under the Human Rights Act 1998, s 7(1) or 9(3), in **4.59** respect of a judicial act, notice must be given to the Crown (r 19.4A(3)). Where the appropriate person (defined in s 9(5) as the minister responsible for the relevant court) does not apply to be joined to such a claim within 21 days or such other period as the court directs, the court may itself join the appropriate minister as a party (r 19.4A(4)).

Transfer

If there is a real prospect of the court making a declaration of incompatibility under the **4.60** Human Rights Act 1998, s 4, that is a factor to be taken into account in considering whether to transfer the claim to the High Court (CPR, r 30.3(2)(g)).

Previous findings

4.61 In claims for remedies under the Human Rights Act 1998, s 7, in respect of judicial acts alleged to have infringed rights under the European Convention, art 5 (to liberty and security of person), the court hearing the claim may, but is not required to, proceed on the basis of the finding of another court or tribunal that the claimant's rights have been infringed (CPR, r 33.9).

Authorities

4.62 Lists of authorities relied upon for interpretation under the Human Rights Act 1998, s 2, must be given to the court and the other parties not less than three days before the hearing (PD 39A, para 8.1).

Remedies under the Human Rights Act 1998

4.63 Under the Human Rights Act 1998, s 8(1), the court may grant such relief or remedy, or make such order, within its powers as it considers just and appropriate. The restriction to granting relief within its powers means that quashing orders, mandatory orders, and prohibitory orders cannot be granted in County Court proceedings (because of CCA 1984, s 38(3)). Where the court is satisfied that a legislative provision is incompatible with a Convention right it has a discretion to make a declaration of incompatibility under the Human Rights Act 1998, s 4. Declarations of incompatibility cannot be made by the County Court, s 4(5), and there are restrictions on the making of such declarations in respect of secondary legislation (s 4(4)). Declarations of incompatibility cannot be made where statutes simply fail to protect Convention rights: they are restricted to situations where actual provisions are incompatible (*Re S (Minors) (Care Order: Implementation of Care Plan)* [2002] 2 AC 291 at 322). A declaration of incompatibility does not annul the infringing statutory provision, and is not even binding on the parties to the proceedings in which it is made (s 4(6)). Its main purpose is to alert the legislature to the problem, and enable amending legislation to be passed through a fast track procedure.

4.64 Damages for breach of Convention rights should be awarded only where this is 'necessary' to afford just satisfaction to the victim: Human Rights Act 1998, s 8(3). Where a breach has clearly caused significant pecuniary loss, damages may be awarded to place the claimant in the position they would have been in without the breach (*Anufrijeva v Southwark London Borough Council* [2004] QB 1124 at [59]). In other cases, where a breach may result in distress, anxiety, and possibly psychiatric trauma, the primary remedy is to grant a declaration, with damages seen as a last resort. The seriousness of the breach, and resource implications, are important factors (*Anufrijeva v Southwark London Borough Council* [2004] QB 1124). Where damages are appropriate, they should be no lower than in comparable torts, and should so far as possible reflect the English level of damages (*R (KB) v South London and West Region Mental Health Tribunal* [2004] QB 936).

Determining claims for damages for breach of human rights

4.65 There is concern that the costs of bringing claims for compensation for breach of human rights can be disproportionate to the amount of compensation awarded. Normally, these claims must be brought by judicial review, but if damages is the only remedy sought they have to be brought by ordinary claim. Such claims are brought in the Administrative Court (*Anufrijeva v Southwark London Borough Council* [2004] QB 1124). This case made the point that alternatives to litigation, such as making a complaint to an ombudsman, should be considered, and that damages claims should be determined in a summary manner, with no more than three cases being cited, and hearings lasting no more than half a day.

KEY POINTS SUMMARY

- The CPR and PDs are the procedural rules governing civil proceedings. They are a 'new procedural code', so for most purposes pre-1999 cases are redundant.   **4.66**

- Gaps in the CPR may be filled by resorting to the court's inherent jurisdiction or, very exceptionally, old procedural rules.

- The most important rule is the 'overriding objective' of dealing with claims justly and at proportionate cost.

- The courts seek to give effect to the overriding objective by active case management.

- It is unlawful for a public authority to act in a way which is incompatible with a Convention right.

- In civil litigation, the most important Convention rights are the right to a fair trial (art 6), the right to respect for private and family life (art 8), and the right to freedom of expression (art 10).

- Where the court is invited to make a declaration of incompatibility, the relevant minister has to be notified and may intervene.

5

PRE-ACTION PROTOCOLS

A PRE-ACTION PROTOCOLS 5.02

B CASES NOT COVERED BY PRE-ACTION
PROTOCOLS 5.04

C PROFESSIONAL NEGLIGENCE
PRE-ACTION PROTOCOL 5.06

D PERSONAL INJURY PROTOCOL 5.10

E INSTRUCTION OF EXPERTS 5.16

F LIMITATION DIFFICULTIES 5.20

G SANCTIONS FOR NON-COMPLIANCE 5.21

H ROAD TRAFFIC ACT 1988 . . . . .5.25

I MOTOR INSURERS' BUREAU 5.26

J PRE-ACTION PART 36 OFFERS 5.30
Key points summary 5.37

5.01 In almost every case, before proceedings are issued, it is expected that the claimant will enter into correspondence to give the intended defendant a chance to negotiate a compromise to the dispute. If this is successful, both sides will save a great deal in legal costs and the effort required in conducting litigation. There are exceptions. Where a limitation period is about to expire, or if the claimant needs to apply for a freezing or search order, pre-action correspondence may be extremely unwise (see, eg, 43.04). For most cases, however, the courts expect the parties to make clear to each other their allegations and answers on the main issues in the dispute, and to cooperate with each other in making pre-action investigations into the evidence (particularly investigations involving experts). Doing so will put the parties in a position where they can make offers to settle on an informed basis at an early stage without needing to have recourse to proceedings.

A PRE-ACTION PROTOCOLS

5.02 To promote consistency in the approach to pre-action correspondence and investigations the Ministry of Justice has published 15 pre-action protocols, covering personal injury, low-value road traffic accidents ('RTAs'), low-value employers' liability and public liability ('EL/PL'), clinical negligence, disease and illness, debt recovery, housing disrepair, possession claims by social landlords, mortgage possession, commercial property dilapidations, construction and engineering, professional negligence, defamation, and judicial review cases. Compliance with an applicable protocol is regarded as the normal, reasonable approach to pre-action conduct, and any departure may have to be explained to a court if litigation ensues, and may be met with sanctions imposed by the court (see 5.23). They apply to third party proceedings (see Chapter 20) as well as to normal proceedings between claimants and defendants (*Daejan Investments Ltd v Park West Club Ltd* [2004] BLR 223).

5.03 The published protocols do not cover commercial and contractual damages claims, or many other types of litigation. Such cases are governed by general pre-action guidance set out in PD Pre-action conduct, described at 5.04–5.05. This chapter will then describe the important features of the professional negligence and personal injuries protocols. It then discusses pre-action notification of defendants in road traffic cases and claims against the Motor Insurers'

Bureau. It ends by considering pre-action offers to settle. The RTA protocol (and the similar EL/PL protocol), together with their related rules within the CPR, are described in Chapter 9.

B CASES NOT COVERED BY PRE-ACTION PROTOCOLS

In cases not covered by an approved protocol, the court will expect the parties, in accord- **5.04** ance with the overriding objective, to act reasonably in exchanging information and documents relevant to the claim and generally in trying to avoid the necessity for the start of proceedings. This means that the parties should follow a reasonable procedure, suitable to the particular circumstances. Normally this will involve the claimant writing a detailed letter before claim complying with the requirements of PD Pre-action conduct, para 6(a). These include setting out the facts and the basis of the claim, what the claimant wants from the defendant, and should enclose the key documents relied upon in support of the claim. The letter should include the principal matters relied upon, rather than needing to set out every detail (*TJ Brent Ltd v Black and Veatch Consulting Ltd* [2008] EWHC 1497 (TCC)). If a claimant brings and loses a claim not governed by any pre-action protocol without having sent a letter before claim, the court may make an order for indemnity basis costs (*Phoenix Finance Ltd v Fédération Internationale de l'Automobile* (2002) *The Times*, 27 June 2002 and see 46.46).

The defendant should be given a reasonable time to reply, based on the nature of the **5.05** case. In simple debt cases this may be 14 days, rising to 90 days in complex matters (PD Pre-action conduct, para 6(b)). A full response should say whether liability is accepted in full, or in part, or denied. If liability is denied the response must give detailed reasons and enclose the key documents relied upon (Annex A, para 4.2). Both parties should consider whether the claim could be settled by using mediation or some other form of alternative dispute resolution ('ADR') (see Chapter 10). Although parties are never obliged to use ADR, the courts increasingly see litigation as the last resort, and parties may be required to provide evidence that they considered ADR before issuing proceedings (para 11). Both sides should attempt to resolve the dispute by making realistic Part 36 offers (see 5.30–5.36) before proceedings are commenced. If expert evidence is required, the parties should consider how best to minimize expense, such as through instructing a single joint expert (para 7, and see 5.16).

C PROFESSIONAL NEGLIGENCE PRE-ACTION PROTOCOL

The professional negligence protocol applies to claims against professionals in tort and **5.06** for breach of the contractual duty to act with reasonable skill and care, and also to claims for breach of fiduciary duty. It does not govern claims against architects, engineers, and quantity surveyors (which are governed by the construction and engineering dispute protocol) or claims in medical negligence (which are governed by the clinical disputes protocol) (para 1.4).

Under the protocol, as soon as the claimant decides there is a reasonable chance he will be **5.07** suing, he is encouraged to notify the professional by sending a preliminary notice (para 5.1). This should give a brief outline of the grievance, and if possible, an indication of the value of the claim (para 5.2). The professional should acknowledge this notice within 21 days (para 5.4). The parties are required to consider whether some form of ADR would be more suitable than litigation (para 12.1). Both sides may be required to provide the court with evidence that ADR was considered. A party's refusal to engage with, or silence in response to, an invitation to participate in ADR might be considered unreasonable by the court, and could lead to the court ordering that party to pay additional costs (para 12.3). If ADR fails to resolve the dispute, the procedures under the protocol may need to be adapted as appropriate (para 2.3).

5.08 A claimant with grounds for a claim should write a detailed letter before claim to the professional (paras 6.1 and 6.2, and see figure 5.1). Letters before claim do not have the same formal status as statements of case (see Chapter 14), and can be departed from as investigations produce a fuller picture of the circumstances (para 6.3). The professional should acknowledge receipt of the letter of claim within 21 days (para 7.1), and has three months from the date of the acknowledgment to investigate the case (para 8.2). During this stage the parties should supply promptly whatever information or documentation is reasonably requested from the other side and which will assist in clarifying or resolving the issues in the dispute (paras 8.4 and 10.1). It is recognized that in professional negligence disputes the parties need some flexibility in their approach to obtaining expert evidence (para 11.2), and that separate expert reports may be needed on breach of duty, causation, and/or quantum (para 11.1). Parties are reminded that experts' reports obtained before proceedings will only be permitted in proceedings with the express permission of the court (para 11.3).

Figure 5.1 Letter before claim

Smallwood & Co., Solicitors
4 Market Place, Corby, Northamptonshire NN17 6AL

Messrs Clifford & Stephens
38 High Street
Corby
Northants

Dear Sir

Valuation of Shares in Wilson Joinery Company Limited

We are instructed by Mr Graham Johnson to claim damages for breach of contract and negligence in respect of your valuation of the 20,000 ordinary shares ('the shares') in Wilson Joinery Company Limited ('the Company') purchased by our client.

We have also written to Mrs Elizabeth Crouch, the vendor of the shares, in a related dispute concerning alleged misrepresentations and breach of contract in relation to the sale of the shares. A copy of that letter is enclosed.

Background Facts
As you are aware, your firm was retained by our client to value the shares following the procedure set out in the Articles of Association of the Company for the purchase of shares at a fair valuation. Copies of the Articles, the letter of instruction, your letter confirming your appointment, and your letter setting out your valuation of the shares, are enclosed. You valued the shares at £240,000, and our client bought the shares for that sum (copy letters and transfer enclosed).

Recent management accounts (copies of which are also enclosed) that have come into our client's possession show that the Company is and has throughout been insolvent.

Legal Basis of Claim
Our client alleges you are in breach of contract and negligent in that your firm:

(a) failed to conduct the valuation exercise competently or with reasonable skill and care;

Figure 5.1 *continued*

(b) used historic cost valuations for assets which were no longer owned by the Company or which had suffered serious depreciation at the time of your valuation;

(c) failed to take into account prospective liabilities adequately or at all;

(d) failed to make proper provision for bad debts.

Consequences of Breach

As a result of these breaches, you valued the shares in the Company at £240,000, whereas in fact the Company was insolvent at that time and the shares were worthless. At that time the Company was likely to be wound up or struck off the register in the near future, and there was no prospect of a legal distribution to the shareholders. Acting on your firm's advice, and as a result of your failure to exercise reasonable skill and care and other breaches, our client paid £240,000 for the shares. If our client had been given correct advice by your firm he would have been advised against buying the shares, he would not have bought them, and he would not have lost the purchase price he in fact paid.

Our client holds your firm responsible for this loss, and seeks damages in the sum of £240,000 together with interest at the rate of 8 per cent per annum from the date of the share purchase.

Experts

No expert has been appointed at this stage. Our view is that a valuation expert will be needed to report on the approach to valuing the shares adopted by your firm, and on the financial position of the Company and the value of the shares at the time your firm advised our client. Please let us know in your response to this letter whether you agree to the joint instruction of an expert for these purposes. If you agree, we will provide you with a list of names from which we hope we can select an agreed jointly instructed expert.

Response

The Professional Negligence Pre-action protocol applies to this claim. Please forward a copy of this letter to your insurers immediately. Under the Protocol you are required to acknowledge this letter within 21 days of receiving it. The Protocol allows you three months from the date of acknowledgment to investigate this claim and send a letter of response or letter of settlement.

Yours faithfully,

Smallwood & Co.

When his investigations are completed the professional should send the claimant a letter of **5.09** response and/or a letter of settlement. A letter of response should be an open letter (which the claimant can disclose to the court) giving a reasoned response to the letter before claim. It must make clear what, if anything, is admitted, and give specific comments on the allegations made by the claimant if liability is denied (para 9.2.1). A professional may also or alternatively send a letter of settlement (para 9.3). This may be an open letter, or without prejudice, or without prejudice save as to costs, or a Part 36 offer. It should set out the professional's views on the issues (if there is no letter of response), and makes a settlement proposal or asks for further information to enable the professional to formulate settlement proposals. If liability is denied without any proposals for settlement, the claimant is free to issue proceedings (para 9.4.1). Otherwise, the parties should enter into negotiations, aiming to conclude matters within six months of the date of the acknowledgment to the letter of claim (para 9.4.2). Before commencing proceedings the claimant should give the professional 14 days' notice (para 14.3), and the parties should attempt to identify the issues still in dispute (para 9.4.3(b)).

D PERSONAL INJURY PROTOCOL

5.10 The Pre-action Protocol for Personal Injury Claims ('PI protocol') is designed primarily for personal injuries claims worth up to £25,000 or, in other words, cases likely to be allocated to the fast track if proceedings are commenced (para 1.1.1). The spirit of the protocol should be followed in larger cases (para 1.1.2). Low-value (between £1,000 and £25,000) RTA and EL/PL claims are covered by the RTA and EL/PL protocols, which are discussed in Chapter 9, but will proceed under the general PI protocol if they exit the RTA or EL/PL protocols (para 1.2). The parties can depart from the detail in the PI protocol, but the court will want an explanation of the reasons for departing from it if proceedings are subsequently issued (para 1.4.2). The protocol lays down a number of steps that should be taken before proceedings are issued, and also provides templates for the more important letters that ought to be written.

5.11 In the early stages, the claimant may choose to send an informal letter of notification to the defendant or the defendant's insurer intimating the claim (para 3.1). Doing so will not start the protocol timetable, but should be acknowledged within 14 days of receipt (para 3.3). It provides an informal means of opening the channels of communication, and notifies the defendant that a claim is going to be made, enabling the defendant's insurer to contact and interview witnesses at an early stage while the events should be reasonably fresh in their memories.

5.12 The formal protocol procedure is commenced by sending two copies of a letter of claim to the defendant (para 5.1). One copy is for the defendant and the other for his insurer. The letter should contain a clear summary of the facts, the nature of the injuries, and details of the financial losses claimed (para 5.3). If a case ceases to be covered by the RTA or EL/PL protocol (see Chapter 9), the claim notification form ('CNF') (see 9.11) may be used as the letter before claim (PI protocol, para 5.5). If possible the letter of claim should indicate which documents should be disclosed by the defendant at this stage. Detailed lists of the types of documents that should be disclosed for different types of personal injuries cases are set out in annexes to the protocol. By way of example, the list for RTA cases is set out as figure 5.2. There

Figure 5.2 Standard disclosure list for road traffic accident cases

SECTION A
In all cases where liability is at issue:
(i) Documents identifying the nature, extent and location of damage to defendant's vehicle where there is any dispute about point of impact.
(ii) MOT certificate where relevant.
(iii) Maintenance records where vehicle defect is alleged or it is alleged by defendant that there was an unforeseen defect which caused or contributed to the accident.

SECTION B
Accident involving commercial vehicle as potential defendant:
(i) Tachograph charts or entry from individual control book.
(ii) Maintenance and repair records required for operators' licence where vehicle defect is alleged or it is alleged by defendants that there was an unforeseen defect which caused or contributed to the accident.

SECTION C
Cases against local authorities where highway design defect is alleged:
(i) Documents produced to comply with s 39 of the Road Traffic Act 1988 in respect of the duty designed to promote road safety to include studies into road accidents in the relevant area and documents relating to measures recommended to prevent accidents in the relevant area.

are even more detailed lists for accidents at work, especially in cases where specific statutory provisions apply.

The defendant must reply in 21 days naming any insurer (para 6.2). A failure to reply with- **5.13** in this time justifies the issue of proceedings without further compliance with the protocol. The defendant, or the defendant's insurer, has a maximum of three months from acknowledging the letter of claim to investigate the claim and state whether liability is denied, and, if so, on what grounds (para 6.3). Both parties are required to consider whether early rehabilitative treatment will be of benefit to the claimant (para 4.1). Both parties are also obliged to consider whether mediation or other ADR procedures should be used, and may be penalized in costs if this is ignored (para 9).

In cases where the defendant disputes liability the defendant should enclose with the letter **5.14** of response documents in their possession which are material to the issues between the parties (para 6.5). The aim of early disclosure is to help in clarifying or resolving issues in dispute (para 7.1.1). If liability is admitted, disclosure will be limited to quantum (para 7.1.3), and the claimant will need to provide a schedule of past and future expenses, even if this is provisional (para 8.1.1(b)). Parties should also preserve documents and relevant evidence, such as CCTV recordings (para 7.1.4). The next step will be to obtain medical evidence dealing with the client's injuries. The protocol encourages the use of a jointly selected medical expert, which is discussed more fully at 5.16ff.

Once these steps have been taken the parties are encouraged to consider negotiating and **5.15** using ADR procedures before starting proceedings. At this stage the parties should have reasonable evidence on both liability and quantum, and should be able to make informed Part 36 offers (see 5.30ff) in an attempt to settle without the need for proceedings. Before issuing proceedings it might be sensible for the parties jointly to review the issues in dispute and the evidence likely to be required. If proceedings are imminent, any insurer acting for the defendant should be invited to nominate solicitors within 7–14 days of the intended date of issue (para 11.1).

E INSTRUCTION OF EXPERTS

Different protocols have different approaches to the appointment of experts. Complex dis- **5.16** putes often justify each side instructing their own experts. In such cases each side chooses who they will instruct, based largely on who their lawyers think will be most convincing in court. Several of the protocols encourage joint instruction of experts. This involves the parties agreeing on an expert, and both parties giving instructions to the expert (ideally by an agreed letter of instruction, but otherwise by separate letters of instruction). A variation is the joint selection of experts, a procedure encouraged by the PI protocol (para 7.2). The expectation is that the selection and instruction of experts will be largely completed before proceedings are issued (*Edwards-Tubb v JD Wetherspoon plc* [2011] 1 WLR 1373).

Under joint selection, the claimant (or any other party) should give the other party a list **5.17** of the name(s) of one or more experts in the relevant specialty who are considered to be suitable to instruct. Within 14 days the defendant may indicate an objection to one or more of the listed experts (this period becomes 35 days if the expert is nominated in the letter of claim, being 21 days for the reply to the letter of claim, plus 14 days to object to the expert, see para 7.6). Provided the defendant does not object to all the proposed experts, the claimant should then instruct a mutually acceptable expert from those remaining from the original list. If the defendant objects to all the listed experts, the parties may instruct experts of their own choice (para 7.7). It would be for the court to decide subsequently, if proceedings are issued, whether either party had acted unreasonably.

5.18 Some solicitors choose to obtain medical reports through medical agencies, rather than directly from a specific doctor or hospital. The defendant's prior consent to this being done should be sought, and if the defendant so requests, the agency should be asked to provide in advance the names of the doctor(s) whom they are considering instructing (para 7.4).

5.19 A model form of letter of instruction can be seen in figure 5.3. This is adapted slightly from the model letter contained in the personal injury pre-action protocol.

Figure 5.3 Model letter of instruction to medical expert

Dear Sir or Madam

Our client: Phillippa May Myers
Our client's address: 47 Forest Road, Corby, Northants
Our client's DoB: 14 July 1981
Telephone No: 01536 764 9933
Date of accident: 19 July 2017

We are acting for Phillippa Myers in connection with injuries received in a road traffic accident on 19 July 2017. The main injuries appear to have been fractures to her right leg, a whiplash injury to her cervical spine, and a nervous reaction involving disturbance of sleep, flashbacks, and panic attacks, particularly when travelling by car.

Examination and Report
We should be obliged if you would examine our client and let us have a full and detailed report dealing with any relevant pre-accident medical history, the injuries sustained, treatment received and present condition, dealing in particular with the capacity for work and giving a prognosis.

It is central to our assessment of the extent of our client's injuries to establish the extent and duration of any continuing disability. Accordingly, in the prognosis section we would ask you specifically to comment on any areas of continuing complaint or disability or impact on daily living. If there is such continuing disability you should comment upon the level of suffering or inconvenience caused and, if you are able, give your view as to when or if the complaint or disability is likely to resolve.

Appointment with Client and Fees
Please send our client an appointment direct for this purpose. Should you be able to offer a cancellation appointment please contact our client direct. We confirm we will be responsible for your reasonable fees.

We are obtaining the notes and records from our client's GP and hospitals attended, and will forward them to you when they are to hand.

Format of Report
In order to comply with Court Rules we would be grateful if you would address your report to 'The Court'. The report must refer to this letter and to any other written or oral instructions given, it must give details of your qualifications and of any literature or other materials used in compiling the report, and where there is a range of opinion it must summarize the range of opinion and give reasons for your opinion. At the end of the report you will need to include a statement that you understand your duty to the Court and have complied with it. Above your signature please include a statement in the following terms: 'I confirm that insofar as the facts stated in my report are within my own knowledge I have made clear which they are and I believe them to be true, and that the opinions I have expressed represent my true and complete professional opinion.'

Figure 5.3 *continued*

In order to avoid further correspondence we can confirm that on the evidence we have there is no reason to suspect we may be pursuing a claim against the hospital or its staff.

Time for Report
We look forward to receiving your report within six weeks. If you will not be able to prepare your report within this period please telephone us upon receipt of these instructions.

When acknowledging these instructions it would assist if you could give an estimate as to the likely timescale for the provision of your report and also an indication as to your fee.

Yours faithfully

Smallwood & Co.

F LIMITATION DIFFICULTIES

Compliance with the pre-action protocols provides no excuse for failing to issue proceed- **5.20**
ings before expiry of any period of limitation (PD Pre-action conduct, para 17). If proceedings are issued before the parties have complied with the steps required by any relevant protocol, the parties should apply for a stay of proceedings pending completion of the steps required by the protocol.

G SANCTIONS FOR NON-COMPLIANCE

Compliance with the protocols must not be used as a tactical device to secure an **5.21**
unfair advantage (PD Pre-action conduct, para 4). However, where a failure to comply arises through slackness or deliberate flouting, a claimant may be justified in commencing proceedings without going through the rest of the procedures laid down in the protocol, and either party may find they are penalized by the court at a later stage.

Charles Church Developments Ltd v Stent Foundations Ltd [2007] CILL 2477 expressed **5.22**
the view that the court should consider any costs penalty for non-compliance with a pre-action protocol at an early stage. In practice, this is often left until the end of the case. Sanctions should not be imposed if there has been substantial compliance with the relevant protocol (*TJ Brent Ltd v Black and Veatch Consulting Ltd* [2008] EWHC 1497 (TCC)) and the court will not be concerned with minor or technical shortcomings (PD Pre-action conduct, para 13).

If, taking into account the overall effect of any non-compliance, the court decides to impose **5.23**
a sanction, it may by PD Pre-action conduct, paras 15 and 16:

(a) order a stay of the proceedings to allow compliance with the protocol;
(b) order the party at fault to pay all or part of the costs of the proceedings. The order should be proportionate to the breach. A failure to negotiate was reflected by a 10–15 per cent reduction in costs in *Straker v Tudor Rose* [2007] EWCA Civ 368;
(c) order the party at fault to pay those costs on an indemnity basis;
(d) if the party at fault is a claimant in whose favour an order for the payment of damages or some specified sum is subsequently made, deprive that party of interest on such sum and in respect of such period as may be specified, and/or award interest at a lower rate than that at which interest would otherwise have been awarded;

(e) if the party at fault is a defendant and an order for the payment of damages or some specified sum is subsequently made in favour of the claimant, award interest on such sum and in respect of such period as may be specified at a higher rate, not exceeding 10 per cent above base rate, rather than the rate at which interest would otherwise have been awarded.

5.24 Further, the court may make an order that the defaulting party should pay a sum of money into court if the default was without good reason (CPR, r 3.1(5)).

H ROAD TRAFFIC ACT 1988

5.25 The Road Traffic Act 1988 provides for the compulsory insurance of drivers of road vehicles against liability in respect of death or bodily injury of any person, or in respect of damage to property caused by the use of a vehicle on a road (s 145). Provided the claimant gives the defendant's insurer notice of the proceedings before or within seven days after they are commenced, the insurer is obliged to satisfy any judgment that may be obtained.

I MOTOR INSURERS' BUREAU

5.26 Compulsory insurance will not provide an insurer who will pay an injured claimant's damages if the motorist responsible for the injury fails to stop at the scene of the accident, or if the motorist was uninsured. To cover these situations the Secretary of State has entered into two agreements with the Motor Insurers' Bureau providing for compensation to be payable in these circumstances. The Motor Insurers' Bureau ('MIB') is a company registered under the Companies Acts, and effectively represents the motor insurance companies.

5.27 One of the agreements is the Motor Insurers' Bureau (Compensation of Victims of Untraced Drivers) Agreement 2003. It applies to cases where someone is killed or injured by an untraced motorist and where, on the balance of probabilities, the untraced driver would have been liable to the victim. The accident has to be reported to the police within 14 days, or as soon as is reasonable, and the applicant must have cooperated with the police. An application for compensation must be made to the MIB within three years of the accident. Time does not run against a child until they reach 18 (*Byrne v Motor Insurers' Bureau* [2009] QB 66). The application is then investigated by the MIB, which may reject the application, or make an award in a similar manner to that used by the court. The agreement also contains detailed provisions for appeals.

5.28 The other agreement is the Motor Insurers' Bureau (Compensation of Victims of Uninsured Drivers) Agreement 1999. By cl 7 of the agreement, the MIB will incur no liability unless an application is made in the prescribed form, and unless certain information and documents are provided to the MIB relating to the proceedings against the uninsured driver and other matters. Proper notice of the bringing of proceedings must be given within 14 days of commencement (cl 9(1)). 'Proper notice' means notice that proceedings have been commenced, provision of the sealed claim form or another official document evidencing issue of the proceedings, and copies of:

(a) any insurance policy providing benefits in the event of the victim's death or injury;
(b) all relevant correspondence;
(c) the particulars of claim; and

(d) documents served with the particulars of claim (ie medical report and schedule of special damages).

The particulars of claim, medical report, and schedule of special damages may be served on **5.29**
the MIB no later than seven days after service on the defendant. Provided these, and certain
other, requirements are satisfied, the MIB will pay the amount of any unsatisfied judgment
to the claimant (cl 5(1)).

J PRE-ACTION PART 36 OFFERS

As mentioned in the introduction to Chapter 2, the usual rule in litigation is that the winner **5.30**
will recover its costs from the losing party. A person receiving a letter before claim may, on
investigating the matter, come to the view there is some merit in the claim. Possibilities are:

(a) that the claim is bound to succeed for the full amount claimed. In this type of case there
    may be little alternative but to pay in full, or make proposals to pay by instalments;
(b) that the claim is bound to succeed, but the sum claimed is excessive, unclear, or arguably more than might be awarded by the court;
(c) that the claim has some prospects of success on the merits, with quantum accepted in
    full subject to liability; or
(d) that the claim has some prospects of success, and quantum is disputed.

In each of these situations the proposed defendant is likely to be best advised to make an **5.31**
offer to settle. The terms offered will depend on the legal advice given on the prospects of
success on liability and the range of likely awards on quantum. An offer to settle may take
one of several forms. It may be made in a face-to-face meeting, by telephone, electronically,
or by letter, and can be made:

(a) in an 'open' communication. This has the disadvantage that, if the offer is not accepted,
    it may be used by the other side as an admission on liability and quantum. If the offer
    is refused, it can be used on the question of costs. Open offers tend to be used by parties
    who are confident of their position;
(b) in a 'without prejudice' communication (see 31.57–31.61). This has the advantage that
    the offer cannot be referred to in court for any purpose, but the disadvantage is that it
    also cannot be used on the question of costs; or
(c) in a communication (usually a letter) treated as 'without prejudice save as to costs'.
    This can take the form of a Part 36 offer or that of a *Calderbank* offer. Such an offer
    cannot be used by either side on the questions of liability and quantum, but can be
    referred to on the question of costs.

A Part 36 offer must be in writing, either in a letter or by using form N242A (PD 36A, para **5.32**
1.1), make clear it is made pursuant to Part 36 (CPR, r 36.5(1)(b)), and specify a period of
not less than 21 days within which the defendant will be liable for the claimant's costs in
accordance with r 36.13 or 36.20 if the offer is accepted (rr 36.5(1)(c) and 36.5(2)). This
21-day period is called the 'relevant period'. The offer must be clear on whether it relates
to the whole or part of the claim or to an issue (r 36.5(1)(d)), and whether it takes into
account any counterclaim (r 36.5(1)(e)). In money claims a single sum of money must be
offered (r 36.6(1)), which is treated as inclusive of interest to the end of the relevant period (r 36.5(4)). There are further required formalities in personal injury claims regarding
the deduction of State benefits, claims for future pecuniary loss, and provisional damages
claims (see 36.09).

5.33 If the Part 36 offer is accepted, it takes effect in accordance with its terms.

5.34 The practical reason for making a Part 36 offer is that, if it is not accepted, the issue regarding costs in the proceedings is whether the judgment in the proceedings is for a sum exceeding the amount of the offer (taking interest into account). If the judgment does not exceed the amount of the offer, the theory is that the claimant should have accepted the offer, so that the claimant is responsible for both sides' costs from the expiry of the relevant period. In such a case, at trial the judge will usually, unless it is thought unjust to do so:

(a) award the claimant its costs up to the expiry of the relevant period; and
(b) award the defendant its costs thereafter (r 36.17(3)).

5.35 A proposed defendant who makes a Part 36 offer shortly after receiving a letter before claim can potentially throw the entire costs risk of the litigation onto the proposed claimant, even if the claimant wins on liability, provided the offer is at least as good as the final award. Proposed claimants therefore have to be very cautious about ignoring or rejecting these offers.

5.36 Proposed claimants can also make Part 36 offers. Such an offer from a claimant is a proposal to accept a specified sum (or other terms) in settlement of the claim. If a claimant's Part 36 offer is not accepted, and if the claimant does at least as well as the offer when the claim is finally disposed of, the court may award an additional 10 per cent on the damages award, indemnity basis costs (see 46.46–46.48) and enhanced rates of interest (r 36.17(4)) (see 36.33).

KEY POINTS SUMMARY

5.37 • Pre-action protocols give guidance on the exchange of information and evidence before proceedings are commenced.

• Litigation is seen as a last resort. Parties are expected to have at least considered ADR (see Chapter 10) before issuing proceedings.

• There are 14 published protocols.

• In cases not covered by a published protocol, parties must comply with the ethos of the protocols and the guidance given in PD Pre-action conduct.

6

ISSUING AND SERVING

A CLAIM FORM 6.02

B JURISDICTIONAL ENDORSEMENTS 6.05

C PARTICULARS OF CLAIM 6.06

D SPECIALIST CLAIMS 6.07

E ISSUING A CLAIM FORM 6.09

F SERVICE 6.14

G SERVICE OF THE CLAIM FORM 6.15

H DEEMED DATE OF SERVICE OF THE
CLAIM FORM 6.46

I SERVICE OF DOCUMENTS OTHER
THAN A CLAIM FORM 6.47

J DEEMED DATE OF SERVICE
(NON-CLAIM FORM DOCUMENTS) 6.50

K CERTIFICATE OF SERVICE 6.55

L IRREGULAR SERVICE 6.56

M FILING 6.58

Key points summary 6.62

The usual way to commence civil proceedings is by issuing a claim form. There is a prescribed **6.01** form for the claim form, N1. There are some other methods of commencing proceedings, and they will be considered in Chapter 8. Issuing a claim involves the court sealing the claim form with its official seal. This is not quite the same thing as 'bringing' a claim for the purposes of stopping time running for limitation purposes (see 21.38), although often the two events will happen on the same day. Service is about notifying the other side about steps taken in proceedings. Generally, a claim form must be served within four months of being issued. In certain circumstances the four-month period may be extended, which is a subject considered in Chapter 7. The main topics that will be considered in this chapter will be issuing and serving proceedings. There are slightly different rules governing service of documents other than the claim form, and these will be considered towards the end of the chapter.

A CLAIM FORM

It is the responsibility of the claimant's solicitors to prepare the claim form before issue. For **6.02** most proceedings there is a general-purpose claim form (form N1: see form 6.1) that can be used. A completed claim form will:

(a) set out the names and addresses of the respective parties;
(b) give a concise statement of the nature of the claim;
(c) state the remedy sought; and
(d) contain a statement of value where the claim is for money.

The statement of value will give the amount sought if the claim can be specified, including **6.03** a statement of accrued interest. This is particularly aimed at debt claims, but many District Judges are of the view that a claimant can specify the amount sought in a damages claim by putting a figure on the amount of damages claimed. In cases where damages are to be decided by the court, the statement of value must state whether it is expected that the amount that will be recovered is no more than £10,000; between £10,000 and £25,000; or more than £25,000. As will be seen in Chapter 15, these are the bands used for case

Form 6.1 Form N1 Claim form

Claim Form

In the	HIGH COURT OF JUSTICE, QBD
Fee Account no.	
Help with Fees - Ref no. (if applicable)	H W F - -

You may be able to issue your claim online which may save time and money. Go to www.moneyclaim.gov.uk to find out more.

	For court use only
Claim no.	
Issue date	

SEAL

Claimant(s) name(s) and address(es) including postcode

STEPHENSON HYPERLINKS PLC
18-24 HARDWICK STREET
LEICESTER
LE5 8DA

Defendant(s) name and address(es) including postcode

LOMAX FISHING EQUIPMENT LIMITED
20 MORTON STREET
NOTTINGHAM NG3 4TF

Brief details of claim

The price due and payable under an oral contract made on 16 February 2016 between the Claimant and the Defendant for designing and supplying computer equipment and software together with compensation and interest pursuant to the Late Payment of Commercial Debts (Interest) Act 1998.

Value

£162,447.00 plus compensation for late payment of £100 and accrued interest (1 year 20 days) at 8.25% per annum amounting to £14,136.22.

You must indicate your preferred County Court Hearing Centre for hearings here *(see notes for guidance)*

Defendant's name and address for service including postcode	LOMAX FISHING EQUIPMENT LIMITED 20 MORTON STREET NOTTINGHAM NG3 4TF		£
		Amount claimed	176,683.20
		Court fee	8,834.16
		Legal representative's costs	TBA
		Total amount	**£185,517.36**

For further details of the courts www.gov.uk/find-court-tribunal.
When corresponding with the Court, please address forms or letters to the Manager and always quote the claim number.

Form 6.1 *continued*

	Claim No.	

Does, or will, your claim include any issues under the Human Rights Act 1998? ☐ Yes ☑ No

Particulars of Claim (attached)(to follow)

1. At all material times the Claimant has been in business designing bespoke computer systems for other businesses, and the Defendant has been in business selling angling equipment.

2. By an oral contract ('the Contract') made at the Defendant's offices by Mrs Lisa Stephenson acting on behalf of the Claimant and Mr James Lomax acting on behalf of the Defendant on 16 February 2016 and evidenced in writing by letters (true copies of which are served with these Particulars of Claim) from the Claimant to the Defendant dated 4 March 2016 and from the Defendant to the Claimant dated 18 March 2016, the Claimant agreed to design and supply certain computer equipment and software to the Defendant being a bespoke computer order processing system for the Defendant's business (together referred to as 'the computer system').

3. There were express terms of the Contract that:

(a) the equipment and services provided under the Contract would be paid for by the Defendant at rates set out in the Claimant's price list dated 5 January 2016, plus VAT; and

(b) payment would be made within 30 days of being invoiced.

4. It was an implied term of the Contract that the Defendant would pay interest on late payments under the Contract pursuant to the Late Payment of Commercial Debts (Interest) Act 1998.

5. The Claimant's claim is for £135,372.50 plus VAT being the price of the computer system provided to the Defendant. Full particulars are given in the invoices detailed below, true copies of which are served with these Particulars of Claim.

PARTICULARS

4 May 2016	To Invoice No: 3510	£80,000.00
12 June 2016	To Invoice No: 3831	£17,494.75
20 July 2016	To Invoice No: 4023	£28,800.00
3 August 2016	To Invoice No: 4169	£9,077.75
Sub-total		£135,372.50
VAT at 20%		£27,074.50
Total		£162,447.00

6. The Claimant further seeks compensation for late payment of £100 and interest at 8.25% per annum on the sum of £162,447.00 from 2 September 2016 to 25 September 2017 amounting to £14,136.22 and continuing at the daily rate of £36.71 pursuant to the Late Payment of Commercial Debts (Interest) Act 1998.

Statement of Truth

*(I believe)(The Claimant believes) that the facts stated in these particulars of claim are true.

* I am duly authorised by the claimant to sign this statement

Full name Catherine Wilson

Name of claimant's legal representative's firm Smallwoods LLP

signed _____ position or office held Assistant Solicitor

*(Claimant)(Litigation friend) (if signing on behalf of firm or company)

(Claimant's legal representative) *delete as appropriate

SMALLWOODS LLP
4 MARKET PLACE
LEICESTER
LE2 4CP

Claimant's or claimant's legal representative's address to which documents or payments should be sent if different from overleaf including (if appropriate) details of DX, fax or e-mail.

management track allocation. In some cases all that can be said is that the amount cannot be stated. Non-personal injuries damages claims in the High Court must state that the claimant expects to recover more than £100,000 (PD 7A, para 3.6, the High Court threshold). In personal injuries claims the statement of value must say whether the general damages expected for pain, suffering, and loss of amenity are below or above £1,000 (which is a threshold used for allocation to the fast track), and if the claim is issued in the High Court, that the claimant expects to recover more than £50,000.

6.04 A fee is payable based on the stated value of the claim and accrued interest. There are detailed rules on fee remission for litigants who would otherwise be unable to afford access to justice. There is nothing to prevent a claimant stating a value below the full potential loss, even though the effect may be that a smaller fee will be payable (*Khiaban v Beard* [2003] 1 WLR 1626).

B JURISDICTIONAL ENDORSEMENTS

6.05 In claims in the High Court, the claim form must, unless the claim is for a specified amount, be endorsed with either:

(a) a statement that the claimant expects to recover more than £100,000 (or more than £50,000 in personal injuries claims); or

(b) a statement that a named enactment provides that the claim may be commenced only in the High Court; or

(c) a statement that the claim is for a named specialist High Court list, or the claim form must comply with the requirements laid down in a practice direction for one of the specialist lists.

C PARTICULARS OF CLAIM

6.06 Particulars of claim is the term used to describe the formal written statement setting out the nature of the claimant's case together with the nature of the relief or remedy sought from the defendant. Further information regarding the contents of particulars of claim can be found in Chapter 14. It can be included in the claim form (on the reverse of the form), or be set out in a separate document. If the particulars of claim are to be set out in a separate document, the claim form must state that the particulars are either attached or will follow. Where they are to follow, the particulars of claim must be served within 14 days after service of the claim form (CPR, r 7.4(1)), and in any event within the period of validity of the claim form (usually four months from issue: see CPR, r 7.4(2)). If the particulars of claim are served late, an application should be made for relief from sanctions (see Chapter 37).

D SPECIALIST CLAIMS

6.07 There are certain specialized claim forms, such as the N1(CC) (see form 6.2) and arbitration claims claim forms (N8) used in the Commercial Court, and forms N5, N5A, and N5B are used in possession claims. There are three different Admiralty Court claim forms (for Admiralty claims *in rem*, Admiralty limitation claims, and other Admiralty claims). A claim form in the Commercial Court (form N1(CC)) should be marked 'Queen's Bench Division, Commercial Court' in the top right-hand corner (PD 58, para 2.3). Claims brought in the TCC must be marked 'Technology and Construction Court' in the second line in the top right-hand corner (PD 60, para 3.2). A statement of value is not required in the Commercial Court (r 58.5(2)), but claims for interest must be set out both on the claim form and the particulars of claim (r 58.5(3)). If the particulars of claim are not contained in or served

Form 6.2 Form N1(CC) Commercial Court claim form

<table>
<tr>
<td rowspan="3">
Claim Form
</td>
<td colspan="2">
In the High Court of Justice
Queen's Bench Division
Commercial Court
Royal Courts of Justice
</td>
</tr>
<tr>
<td colspan="2" align="right">*for court use only*</td>
</tr>
<tr>
<td>Claim No.
Issue date</td>
<td></td>
</tr>
</table>

Claimant(s)

SECURE BANK PLC

SEAL

Defendant(s)

LANDMARK TRADERS GRIMSTEAD LIMITED

Name and address of Defendant receiving this claim form

LANDMARK TRADERS GRIMSTEAD LIMITED
Unit 6 Biscay Trading Estate
Epsom
Surrey
KT3 8DN

Amount claimed	£394,450.95
Court fee	£1,670
Solicitor's costs	TBA
Total amount	

The court office at the Admiralty and Commercial Registry, Royal Courts of Justice, Strand, London WC2A 2LL is open between 10 am and 4.30 pm Monday to Friday. When corresponding with the court, please address forms or letters to the Court Manager and quote the claim number.

N1(CC) Claim form (CPR Part 7) (03.02)

	Claim No.	

Brief details of claim

The claim is for £394,450.95 being the amount payable under a bill of exchange of £385,000 drawn by the Defendant on Carstairs Bank Plc in favour of Heathmarket Import and Export Limited and payable on [date] ("the bill of exchange") plus interest on that sum at 8% per annum for 112 days amounting to £9,450.95 by way of damages under the Bills of Exchange Act 1882, section 57 or as interest pursuant to the Senior Courts Act 1981, section 35A to the date of issue of this claim and continuing at the daily rate of £84.38. The bill of exchange was delivered to and paid by the Claimant, but was dishonoured when the Claimant presented it at Carstairs Bank Plc after payment had been countermanded by Heathmarket Import and Export Limited. In the circumstances the Claimant is the entitled to the sums claimed as the holder in due course of the bill of exchange.

Particulars of claim (*attached)(*will follow if an acknowledgment of service is filed that indicates an intention to defend the claim)

Statement of Truth

*(I believe)(The Claimant believes) that the facts stated in this claim form *(and the particulars of the claim attached to this claim form) are true.

* I am duly authorised by the claimant to sign this statement

Full name _____

Name of *(claimant)('s solicitor's firm) Messrs Pamsons _____

signed_____ position or office held _____
*(Claimant)('s solicitor)   (if signing on behalf of firm, co£mpany or corporation)

*delete as appropriate

	Claimant's or solicitor's address to which documents or payments should be sent if different from overleaf including (if appropriate) details of DX, fax or e-mail.
Messrs Pamsons, 18 High Street, London EC1A 6FB	

with the claim form, the N1(CC) must state that if an acknowledgment of service is filed indicating an intention to defend, particulars of claim will follow (r 58.5(1)(a)).

In some of the specialist lists there are also special rules on service. For example, the particulars **6.08** of claim for Admiralty claims *in rem* must be contained in the claim form or served within 75 days of the claim form (r 61.3(3)), the claim form must be served within 12 months of issue (r 61.3(5)). In the Commercial Court, particulars of claim which are not served with the claim form must be served within 28 days of filing of the acknowledgment of service (r 58.5(1)(c)).

E ISSUING A CLAIM FORM

Procedure on issuing a claim

The claimant's solicitors will make sufficient copies of the claim form for themselves, the **6.09** court, and each defendant. They retain one, and send the others to the court office, together with the prescribed fee, under cover of a letter asking for the claim to be issued. Alternatively, the claimant's solicitors may attend personally at the court office to ensure the claim is issued, which may be sensible if time is short. If the documents are sent by post, the court office stamps the covering letter when it is received. The court issues the claim by sealing the claim forms, and enters details of the claim in its records. On issuing the claim the court will allocate a claim number to the case, which it endorses on the claim forms. The court then sends a form called a notice of issue (forms N205A to N205C) to the claimant's solicitors. This form tells the claimant the claim number, the date of issue, confirms receipt of the issue fee, and, if service is effected by the court, also confirms the date of service.

Which court office

In the High Court, the QBD, ChD, specialist courts, and district registries all have their own **6.10** court offices. In the County Court, non-money claims and Part 8 claims can be issued at any County Court hearing centre (PD 2C, para 2). There is not complete freedom of choice. For example, probate, technology and construction, intellectual property, and insolvency proceedings have to be commenced in a designated County Court hearing centre (PD 2C, para 3.1(3)). A slightly different approach is taken by CPR, r 55.3(1), which provides that claims for the recovery of land will be sent to the County Court hearing centre serving the address of the land if the claim was not issued there. County Court money claims are issued at the County Court Money Claims Centre if issued in hard copy, or at the County Court Business Centre if issued electronically (see 6.11 and 6.12).

County Court money claims

County Court claims where the only remedy sought is an amount of money, whether speci- **6.11** fied or unspecified, are started by sending the claim form by post for issue to the County Court Money Claims Centre in Salford (PD 7A, para 4A.1). There is a pilot scheme for filing claims at the County Court Money Claims Centre online (PD 51S). The claimant must specify their 'preferred hearing centre' in the claim form. Undefended money claims are often sent to the claimant's preferred hearing centre (there are a number of technical rules dealing with the situations where this happens, but broadly cover situations where the court has to assess the amount payable or the rate of payment). A defended claim for a specified sum of money against a defendant who is an individual is sent to the defendant's home court or the hearing centre specified in the defendant's directions questionnaire (r 26.2A(3)). If there is more than one defendant, the claim is sent to the home court of the defendant who first files their defence. The defendant's home court is the County Court hearing centre serving the address where the defendant resides or carries on business (r 2.3(1)). This will be the County Court at Central London if the claim is provisionally allocated to the multi-track and the defendant resides in London (r 26.2A(5A)). This usually happens when all parties have filed their directions questionnaires, or when any stay to attempt settlement has expired.

Money Claim Online

6.12 Money claims with a value up to £100,000 where neither party is a child or protected party, and where certain other conditions set out in PD 7E, para 4 are satisfied, can be issued electronically using a scheme known as 'Money Claim Online', using **<http://www. moneyclaim.gov.uk>**. These claims are issued in the County Court Business Centre by sending the court service an online claim form and paying the issue fee electronically. The particulars of claim may be filed and served separately from the claim form, but, if endorsed on the claim form, must not exceed 1,080 characters. Service of the claim form is effected by the court, and is deemed to be effected on the fifth day after issue irrespective of whether that day is a business day or not (para 5.7). Defendants can respond either electronically or by using hard copies (para 7.1). If no response is obtained, judgment can be entered in default by filing an electronic request (para 11). Where the defendant is an individual the claim will be sent to the defendant's home court on various events, including the filing of a defence (para 12(1)). Where the defendant is not an individual, the claim will be sent to the County Court hearing centre that serves the claimant's address as stated in the claim form (para 12(2)).

Online Court

6.13 PD 51R is a pilot scheme setting up an 'Online Court' for selected claims up to £10,000 that would otherwise have been issued through Money Claim Online. The term is rather misleading, because the Online Court only deals with issue, service, response, possible stay for settlement (see 15.35), and judgment in default (slightly adjusting the procedure described in chapter 13). Once these steps have been completed (and for various other reasons) the claim leaves the pilot scheme, from which point the rest of the CPR apply to the claim.

F SERVICE

6.14 The most important purpose of service is to inform the defendant of the contents of the claim form and the nature of the claimant's case (*Abela v Baadarani* [2013] 1 WLR 2043). There are two slightly different systems dealing with service within the jurisdiction. One deals with service of originating process (primarily this is the claim form), but also petitions (for which see Chapter 8; CPR, r 6.2(c)), and the other deals with service of all other types of document used during the course of proceedings (eg statements of case, lists of documents, and application notices). There is a third system relating to service at the registered office of a company or LLP under the Companies Act 2006 (see 6.28). A fourth system deals with service outside the jurisdiction (see Chapter 11). Part 6 does not apply where other rules (eg those in Part 54 on judicial review, see Chapter 49) contain specific provisions on service (r 6.1). Nor does Part 6 apply where a statute makes express provision about service (r 6.1(a) and *Mucelli v Government of Albania* [2009] 1 WLR 276, and see 6.54). It is worth noting that 'service' deals with providing documents to the other side, and the related concept of 'filing' deals with providing documents to the court.

G SERVICE OF THE CLAIM FORM

Period of validity

Periods of validity of claim forms are set out in CPR, r 7.5:   **6.15**

    (a) Where the claim form is served within the jurisdiction, the claimant must complete the step required in the following table [see table 6.1] in relation to the particular method of service chosen, before 12.00 midnight on the calendar day four months after the date of issue of the claim form.

    (b) Where the claim form is to be served out of the jurisdiction, the claim form must be served in accordance with Section IV of Part 6 within six months of the date of issue.

Service of a claim form in England and Wales must be effected within four months after the   **6.16** date of issue. Although a claim form may be served on the day it is issued, the effect of r 7.5(1) is to disregard that day for the purpose of calculating the period of validity. Strictly, this means a claim form is valid for four months and a day (*Smith v Probyn* (2000) *The Times*, 29 March 2000), so that a claim form issued on 8 May would still be valid on 8 September.

The period of validity for service is six months if the defendant is served outside the juris-   **6.17** diction (CPR, r 7.5(2)). This applies whether or not permission is required for service abroad (see Chapter 11). The six-month period of validity applies where service is effected in Scotland (*Ashley v Tesco Stores Ltd* [2015] 1 WLR 5153). Where a defendant is outside the jurisdiction, but is in fact served within the jurisdiction (eg where the defendant agrees to service at their solicitor's office in England), the period of validity is four months (*American Leisure Group Ltd v Garrard* [2014] 1 WLR 4102).

No specific provision is made for petitions (the extended definition of 'claim' in r 6.2(c)   **6.18** only applies to Part 6). This is because the rules lay down a seven-day minimum period before the hearing for service of a petition, and the date of the hearing should be fixed when the petition is presented.

Expiry of period of validity

Where a claim form is served within the jurisdiction, by CPR, r 7.5(1), the claimant must   **6.19** complete the step required for the method of service the claimant chooses to use by 12.00 midnight on the calendar day four months after the date of issue of the claim form. All the claimant has to do is to take the relevant step. Whether the deemed date of service (see 6.46) takes place later, or the claim form never arrives, or is delayed in transmission, is irrelevant. Table 6.1 sets out the step the claimant is required to take for each method of service.

By r 2.8(5), when a period of time specified by the CPR for doing any act 'at the court   **6.20** office' ends on a day when that office is closed, the act is deemed to have been done in time

Table 6.1 Step required for service under CPR, r 7.5(1)

Method of service	Step required
First-class post, DX, or other delivery service which provides for delivery on the next business day	Posting, leaving with, delivering to, or collection by the relevant service provider
Delivery of the document to or leaving it at the relevant place	Delivering to or leaving the document at the relevant place
Personal service under r 6.5	Completing the relevant step required by r 6.5(3)
Fax	Completing the transmission of the fax
Other electronic method	Sending the e-mail or other electronic transmission

if done on the next day on which the court office is open. This does not apply to service, because this has to be effected on the defendant, rather than at the court office (*Re N (Infants)* [1967] Ch 512). This ought not to cause any difficulties, because all the claimant needs to do under r 7.5(1) is to take steps that are under the claimant's control (eg posting, or completing the transmission of a fax) by midnight on the final day. It does not matter when the document actually arrives.

Documents to be served

6.21   The documents to be served comprise the sealed claim form, the particulars of claim (although these may follow), and a 'response pack'. The response pack consists of forms of acknowledgment of service, admission, defence, and counterclaim. Form N9 (see form 6.3) is a combined cover sheet for the response pack and tear-off acknowledgment of service form. There is also a combined form of defence and counterclaim. There are two types of admission form and also two types of defence and counterclaim form. Forms N9A and N9B are for use in claims for specified amounts of money. Forms N9C and N9D are for use in claims for unspecified sums of money and in non-money claims. An example of form N9C is shown in form 6.4 and an example of form N9D in form 6.5. In personal injuries claims the particulars of claim will have to be accompanied by a medical report and schedule of past and future expenses and losses, and these must be served with the claim form if the particulars of claim are served at the same time.

Methods of service

6.22   Permissible methods of service are set out in CPR, r 6.3(1), which provides:

A claim form may . . . be served by any of the following methods—

(a) personal service in accordance with rule 6.5;
(b) first class post, document exchange or other service which provides for delivery on the next business day, in accordance with [PD 6A];
(c) leaving it at a place specified in rule 6.7, 6.8, 6.9 or 6.10 [the address at which the defendant may be served];
(d) by fax or other means of electronic communication in accordance with [PD 6A]; or
(e) any method authorised by the court under rule 6.15 [alternative service].

6.23   It is not open to a party to devise their own methods of bringing claims to the attention of the defendant (*Brown v Innovatorone plc* [2009] EWHC 1376 (Comm)). In this case the defendant's solicitor merely entered into correspondence on behalf of the defendant. This was not the same as the situation set out at 6.24(b) below, which meant that sending the claim form to the solicitor was not effective service on the defendant. Apart from service by fax or e-mail, it is the original, sealed, copy of the claim form that must be served. Posting a photocopy is not service (*Hills Contractors & Construction Ltd v Struth* [2014] 1 WLR 1).

Hierarchy of modes of service of claim forms

6.24   There is a hierarchy of methods and places of service for claim forms which is set out in CPR, rr 6.3–6.13. The prescribed hierarchy is:

(a) if an enactment, a provision of the CPR or any PD or court order requires personal service, that method must be used (r 6.5(1)). Otherwise,
(b) if the defendant notifies the claimant in writing of the defendant's solicitor's address for service, or the defendant's solicitor notifies the claimant in writing that the solicitor is instructed by the defendant to accept service, the claim form must be served at the business address of the defendant's solicitor (r 6.7(1)). A similar requirement to serve at the business address of a solicitor in Scotland or Northern Ireland, or a European lawyer

Form 6.3 Form N9, including acknowledgment of service

Response pack

You should read the 'notes for defendant' attached to the claim form which will tell you when and where to send the forms.

Included in this pack are:

- either **Admission Form N9A** (if the claim is for a specified amount)
- or **Admission Form N9C** (if the claim is for an unspecified amount or is not a claim for money)

- either **Defence and Counterclaim Form N9B** (if the claim is for a specified amount)
- or **Defence and Counterclaim Form N9D** (if the claim is for an unspecified amount or is not a claim for money)

- **Acknowledgment of service** (see below)

		Complete
If you admit the claim or the amount claimed and/or you want time to pay	⇨	the admission form
If you admit part of the claim	⇨	the admission form and the defence form
If you dispute the whole claim or wish to make a claim (a counterclaim) against the claimant	⇨	the defence form
If you need 28 days (rather than 14) from the date of service to prepare your defence, or wish to contest the court's jurisdiction	⇨	the acknowledgment of service
If you do nothing, judgment may be entered against you		

Acknowledgment of service

Defendant's full name if different from the name given on the claim form

In the	
Claim No.	
Claimant (including ref.)	
Defendant	

Address to which documents about this claim should be sent (including reference if appropriate)

	If applicable
Telephone no.	
Fax no.	
DX no.	
Postcode ☐☐☐☐ ☐☐☐☐ **Your ref.**	

E-mail

Tick the appropriate box

1. I intend to defend all of this claim ☐
2. I intend to defend part of this claim ☐
3. I intend to contest jurisdiction ☐

(My) (Defendant's) date of birth is

☐☐ / ☐☐ / ☐☐☐☐

If you file an acknowledgment of service but do not file a defence within 28 days of the date of service of the claim form, or particulars of claim if served separately, judgment may be entered against you.

If you do not file an application to dispute the jurisdiction of the court within 14 days of the date of filing this acknowledgment of service, it will be assumed that you accept the court's jurisdiction and judgment may be entered against you.

If served outside the jurisdiction see CPR rule 6.35 and 6.37(5).

Signed

(Defendant) (Defendant's legal representative) (Litigation friend)

Position or office held (if signing on behalf of firm or company)

Date ☐☐ / ☐☐ / ☐☐☐☐

For further details of the courts www.gov.uk/find-court-tribunal. When corresponding with the Court, please address forms or letters to the Manager and always quote the claim number.

N9 Response pack (04.14) © Crown copyright 2014

located in any European Economic Area ('EEA') State, applies where the defendant or the lawyer gives written notice that service may be effected at the lawyer's business address (r 6.7(2), (3) and EC Directive 2006/123/EC);

(c) if mandatory personal service (r 6.5) or mandatory service on the defendant's solicitor (r 6.7) do not apply, the claimant has the choice of serving a claim form either:

(i) by personal service (r 6.5(2)); or

Form 6.4 Form N9C Admission (unspecified amount non-money and return of good claims)

Admission (unspecified amount, non-money and return of goods claims)

- Before completing this form please read the notes for guidance attached to the claim form. If necessary provide details on a separate sheet, add the claim number and attach it to this form.
- If you are not an individual, you should ensure that you provide sufficient details about the assets and liabilities of your firm, company or corporation to support any offer of payment made.

In the	County Court
Claim No.	4YK 73619
Claimant (including ref.)	Mr William Lake
Defendant	Mrs Helen Russell

In non-money claims only

☐ I admit liability for the whole claim
(Complete section 11)

In return of goods cases only

Are the goods still in your possession?

☐ Yes　　☐ No

Part A Response to claim *(tick one box only)*

☐ I admit liability for the whole claim but want the court to decide the amount I should pay / value of the goods

OR

☑ I admit liability for the claim and offer to pay £3,500.00 in satisfaction of the claim
(Complete part B and sections 1 - 11)

Part B How are you going to pay the amount you have admitted? *(tick one box only)*

☐ I offer to pay on (date)

OR

☑ I cannot pay the amount immediately because *(state reason)*

I cannot afford to pay

AND

I offer to pay by instalments of £ 50.00 per month
per (week)(month)

starting *(date)* in 4 weeks

1 Personal details

Surname	Russell
Forename	Helen

☐Mr　☑Mrs　☐Miss　☐Ms

☑Married　☐Single　☐Other *(specify)*

Date of birth: 2 2 0 7 1 9 7 0

Address: 47 Outram Road, Oldham

Postcode OL8 3WJ

Tel. no. 0161 290 9924

2 Dependants *(people you look after financially)*

Number of children in each age group

under 11 **2**　11-15 ☐　16-17 ☐　18 & over ☐

Other dependants *(give details)*

3 Employment

☐ **I am employed as a** Administrative Assistant
My employer is Blackburn District Council
Jobs other than main job *(give details)* None

☐ **I am self employed as a**
Annual turnover is.......................... £

☐ **I am not** in arrears with my national insurance contributions, income tax and VAT

☐ **I am** in arrears and I owe........... £

Give details of:
(a) contracts and other work in hand
(b) any sums due for work done

☐ **I have been unemployed for** 　years　months

☐ **I am a pensioner**

4 Bank account and savings

☑ **I have a bank account**

　☐ The account is in credit by........ £

　☑ The account is overdrawn by.... £ 2,780.00

☐ **I have a savings or building society account**

　The amount in the account is.......... £

5 Residence

I live in　☐ my own property　☐ lodgings
☐ jointly owned house　☑ rented property
☐ council accommodation

Form 6.4 *continued*

6 Income

My usual take home pay *(including overtime, commission, bonuses etc)*	£	1,250	per m
Income support	£	nil	per m
Child benefit(s)	£	120	per m
Other state benefit(s)	£	nil	per
My pension(s)	£	nil	per
Others living in my home give me	£	nil	per
Other income *(give details below)*			
	£		per
	£		per
	£		per
Total income	£	1,370	per

8 Priority debts *(This section is for arrears only. Do not include regular expenses listed in section 7)*

Rent arrears	£	80	per m
Mortgage arrears	£		per
Council tax/Community Charge arrears	£		per
Water charges arrears	£		per
Fuel debts: Gas	£		per
Electricity	£	10	per m
Other	£		per
Maintenance arrears	£		per
Others *(give details below)*			
	£		per
	£		per
Total priority debts	£	90	per m

7 Expenses

(Do not include any payments made by other members of the household out of their own income)

I have regular expenses as follows:

Mortgate *(including second mortgage)*	£		per
Rent	£	560	per m
Council tax	£	65	per m
Gas	£	40	per m
Electricity	£	45	per m
Water charges	£	26	per m
TV rental and licence	£	20	per m
HP repayments	£	120	per m
Mail order	£	40	per m
Housekeeping, food, school meals	£	520	per m
Travelling expenses	£	40	per m
Children's clothing	£	50	per m
Maintenance payments	£		per
Others *(not court orders or credit debts listed in sections 9 and 10)*			
	£		per
	£		per
	£		per
Total expenses	£	1,526	per m

9 Court orders

Court	Claim No.	£	per
Total court order instalments		£	per

Of the payments above, I am behind with payments to *(please list)*

10 Credit debts

Loans and credit card debts *(please list)*

	£	56	per m
	£		per
	£		per

Of the payments above, I am behind with payments to *(please list)*

11 Declaration   I declare that the details I have given above are true to the best of my knowledge

Signed	**Position or office held**
Date	*(if signing on behalf of firm or company)*

Form 6.5 Form N9D Defence and Counterclaim (unspecified amount non-money and return of good claims)

Defence and Counterclaim
(unspecified amount, non-money and return of goods claims)

Name of court COUNTY COURT	
Claim No.	4YK 982645
Claimant (including ref.)	Miss PHILLIPPA MAY MYERS
Defendant	Mr NIGEL JAMES STANIFORTH

- Fill in this form if you wish to dispute all or part of the claim and/or make a claim against the claimant (a counterclaim)
- You have a limited number of days to complete and return this form to the court.
- Before completing this form, please read the notes for guidance attached to the claim form.
- Please ensure that all the boxes at the top right of this form are completed. You can obtain the correct names and number from the claim form. The court cannot trace your case without this information.

How to fill in this form
- Set out your defence in section 1. If necessary continue on a separate piece of paper making sure that the claim number is clearly shown on it. In your defence you must state which allegations in the particulars of claim you deny and your reasons for doing so. If you fail to deny an allegation it may be taken that you admit it.
- If you dispute only some of the allegations you must
  - specify which you admit and which you deny; and
  - give your own version of events if different from the claimant's.
- If the claim is for money and you dispute the claimant's statement of value, you must say why and if possible give your own statement of value.

- If you wish to make a claim against the claimant (a counterclaim) complete section 2.
- Complete and sign section 3 before returning this form.

Where to send this form
- send or take this form immediately to the court at the address given on the claim form.
- Keep a copy of the claim form and the defence form.

Need help with your legal problems?
Community legal advice is a free confidential service, funded by legal aid. They can help you find the information and advice you need by putting you in touch with relevant agencies, helplines or local advice services. And if you are eligible for legal aid, the service can offer specialist legal advice over the telephone in cases involving: debt; housing; employment; benefits; and education

Call **0845 345 4 345** or **www.communitylegaladvice.org.uk**

1. Defence

1. Paragraph 1 of the Particulars of Claim is admitted.

2. Paragraph 2 of the Particulars of Claim is denied. The collision occurred as the Claimant was passing some parked cars on the nearside. The Claimant approached the Defendant who was driving in the opposite direction. The Claimant was driving too fast and failed to give way to the Defendant. The collision occurred because the Claimant drove her car partly on the wrong side of the road, having failed to wait in a safe place, and thereby collided with the Defendant's car.

3. It is denied that the Defendant was negligent or that any negligence on the part of the Defendant that may be proved caused the collision, whether as alleged in paragraph 3 of the Particulars of Claim or at all, for the reasons set out in paragraphs 2 and 4 of this Defence.

4. Further or alternatively, the collision was caused either wholly or in part by the negligence of the Claimant.

PARTICULARS OF NEGLIGENCE

The Claimant was negligent in that she:

(a) Drove too fast;

(b) Failed to give way to the Defendant's car;

(c) Failed to wait in a gap in the parked cars on the Claimant's side of the road where the Defendant's car would have passed safely;

(d) Failed to keep any or any proper look out;

(e) Drove too far over into the oncoming lane; and/or

(f) Failed to brake sufficiently, in time or at all.

5. The Claimant is required to prove the alleged or any personal injuries, loss and damage and the amounts claimed.

6. Paragraph 6 of the Particulars of Claim is admitted.

(continue over the page)

N9D Defence and Counterclaim (unspecified amount, non-money and return of goods claims) (04.08)   © Crown copyright 2008

Form 6.5 *continued*

Claim No.	4YK 982645

Defence (continued)

2. If you wish to make a claim against the claimant (a counterclaim)

- To start your counterclaim, you will have to pay a fee. Court staff can tell you how much you have to pay.
- You may not be able to make a counterclaim where the claimant is the Crown (e.g. a Government Department). Ask at your local county court office for further information.

If your claim is for a specific sum of money, how much are you claiming?

£

I enclose the counterclaim fee of

£95.00

My claim is for *(please specify nature of claim)*

7. Damages for negligence being the cost of repairs to the Defendant's car, amounting to £2,100, and interest on the amount awarded at 8% per annum under the County Courts Act 1984, s. 69.

What are your reasons for making the counterclaim?
If you need to continue on a separate sheet put the claim number in the top right hand corner.

8. The Defendant repeats paragraphs 1 to 5 of the Defence.
9. By reason of the negligence of the Claimant as set out in paragraph 4 of the Defence, the Defendant has suffered loss and damage, being the cost of repairs to his car, registration number JH09 KJP, amounting to £2,100.
10. The Defendant claims interest at 8% per annum on the amount found due pursuant to the County Courts Act 1984,

3. Signed - To be signed by you or by your solicitor or litigation friend.

*(I believe) (The defendant believes) that the facts stated in this form are true.
*I am duly authorised by the defendant to sign this statement.

delete as appropriate

Position or office held
(If signing on behalf of firm or company)

Date 2 2 / 0 9 / 2 0 1 4

Defendant's date of birth, if an individual 1 4 / 0 5 / 1 9 8 1

Give an address to which notices about this case can be sent to you

	If applicable	
Fox and Headley, 52 Higham Road, Kettering, Northants.		
	Telephone no.	01562 891744
	Fax no.	01562 891767
Postcode N N 1 6 2 C H	DX no.	9945 Kettering 2

E-mail	

(ii) at an address at which the defendant resides or carries on business within the UK or any other EEA state which the defendant has given for the purpose of service of the proceedings (r 6.8); or

(iii) by a contractually agreed method of service (r 6.11); or

(iv) where they apply, under the special rules dealing with service on the Crown (r 6.10), or in accordance with r 6.12 on an agent of a principal who is outside the jurisdiction, or in accordance with r 6.13 if the defendant is a child or protected party;

(d) if mandatory personal service (r 6.5) or mandatory service on the defendant's solicitor (r 6.7) do not apply, and the defendant has not given an address for service (r 6.8), the claim form may be served at the defendant's usual or last known address under r 6.9 [see 6.25–6.27].

Address where a defendant may be served

6.25 Rule 6.9 of the CPR sets out in tabular form the appropriate places of service for different types of party: see table 6.2. An address for service must include a full postcode or its equivalent in any relevant EEA State, unless the court otherwise orders (r 6.6(2)). For individuals it is their usual or last known residence. For limited liability companies it is their principal office or any place of business having a real connection with the dispute. Subject to the right to serve on an EEA, etc. lawyer, the address used for service has to be within the jurisdiction (r 6.6(1)).

Defendant's residence

6.26 A defendant's residence is where they live based on their pattern of life (*Relfo Ltd v Varsani* [2011] 1 WLR 1402). Consequently, it is possible for a defendant to have more than one 'usual residence' for the purposes of CPR, r 6.9 (*Relfo Ltd v Varsani*). The address for a defendant who is a tenant of a room is the house address, not that of the room (*Akram v Adam* [2005] 1 WLR 2762). An address owned by someone else, but used occasionally by the defendant and other members of his family when they visited England, is not his residence for the purpose of r 6.9 (*Chellaram v Chellaram (No 2)* [2002] 3 All ER 17). Where the defendant has a usual or last known residence within the jurisdiction, service at that address will be effective even if the defendant was temporarily abroad on the date of service (*City and Country Properties Ltd v Kamali* [2007] 1 WLR 1219).

Last known address

6.27 As can be seen from table 6.2, a defendant may be served at a 'last known' residence or place of business. Provided the address used was at one time the defendant's residence (*Collier v Williams* [2006] 1 WLR 1945), and provided it is the last address known to the claimant as such, it follows from *Godwin v Swindon Borough Council* [2002] 1 WLR 997 and *Cranfield v Bridgegrove Ltd* [2003] 1 WLR 2441 that once it is proved that documents were sent or left there in accordance with one of the permitted methods of service (see 6.22), they will be deemed to have been served, and evidence will not be admissible to prove they were not received by the defendant (see 6.46 and 6.51). If the claimant has reason to believe the last known address is no longer one where the defendant resides or carries on business, the claimant must take reasonable steps to find the defendant's current address (CPR, r 6.9(3)). In a claim against a partnership, knowing that a partner has left the partnership is enough to trigger the duty to make reasonable inquiries (*Brooks v AH Brooks & Co* [2011] 3 All ER 982). Where, having made reasonable inquiries, the claimant discovers the defendant's current address, the claim form must be served at that address (r 6.9(4)(a)). If those inquiries point to some other address or method by which service could be effected, the claimant must make an application for alternative service

Table 6.2 Addresses for service on different types of party

Nature of defendant to be served	Place of service
Individual	Usual or last known residence
Individual being sued in the name of a business	Usual or last known residence of the individual; or principal or last known place of business
Individual who is suing or being sued in the name of a partnership	Usual or last known residence of the individual; or principal or last known place of business of the partnership
Limited liability partnership	Principal office of the partnership; or any place of business of the partnership within the jurisdiction which has a real connection with the claim
Corporation (other than a company) incorporated in England and Wales	Principal office of the corporation; or any place within the jurisdiction where the corporation carries on its activities and which has a real connection with the claim
Company registered in England and Wales	Principal office of the company; or any place of business of the company within the jurisdiction which has a real connection with the claim
Any other company or corporation	Any place within the jurisdiction where the corporation carries on its activities; or any place of business of the company within the jurisdiction

under r 6.15 (see 6.40). It is only where these alternatives are not available that service may be effected at an address where the defendant no longer resides. If, on making reasonable inquiries, the defendant is found to be living abroad, the claimant cannot comply with rr 6.6(1) and 6.9, and instead will have to attempt service outside the jurisdiction in accordance with the rules discussed in Chapter 11.

Service on companies and LLPs

Instead of serving a company under the CPR at its principal office or place of business having **6.28** a real connection with the dispute, a company may be served personally (see 6.30) or at its registered office (Companies Act 2006, s 1139) or other address agreed by the company (Sch 4, para 4). Company addresses can be found at <http://www.companieshouse.gov.uk>. Service under s 1139 must be at the company's registered office. Consequently, leaving the documents with a receptionist or security guard at the reception area of a managed building is not enough (*Amerada Hess v Rome* (2000) *The Times*, 15 March 2000) unless the company agrees to some such method of service (Companies Act 2006, Sch 4, para 8). Service under s 1139 is sanctioned under the CPR, r 6.3(2), as is the similar service on limited liability partnerships provision in the Companies Act 1985, s 727, by r 6.3(3). The effect is that r 6.3(2) and (3) bring service at the registered office, etc. under the Companies Acts within the scheme of CPR, Part 6, which should mean the deemed date of service and other provisions in Part 6 apply in these situations (*Ashley v Tesco Stores Ltd* [2015] 1 WLR 5153, Arden LJ at [14]).

Effecting service

Personal service

Personal service is effected by leaving the documents that have to be served with the **6.29** defendant. Where the defendant is uncooperative, it is sufficient to mention the nature of the documents and to leave them reasonably near the defendant. It is also sufficient to hand them to the defendant, provided the defendant has them long enough to see what they are, even if the defendant then hands them back to the process server saying they are not being accepted (*Nottingham Building Society v Peter Bennett and Co* (1997) *The Times*, 26 February 1997).

6.30 Personal service on a company is effected by leaving the documents with a person in a senior position (CPR, r 6.5(3)(b)), which in turn means a director, treasurer, secretary, chief executive, manager, or other officer (PD 6A, para 6.2). Personal service on a company is only permissible if the company is within the jurisdiction: the fact a director happens to be within the jurisdiction is not enough (*SSL International plc v TTK Lig Ltd* [2012] 1 Lloyd's Rep 107). Personal service on a partnership where partners are sued in the name of the partnership is effected by leaving the claim form with a partner or a person having the control or management of the partnership business at its principal place of business (CPR, r 6.5(3)(c)).

Post

6.31 It is to be noticed that under CPR, r 6.3(1)(b), service may be effected by first-class post or any other postal delivery method that involves next-business-day delivery. Royal Mail and other commercial operators may be used provided the method used involves next-business-day delivery. Documents sent by slower delivery methods, such as second-class post, are not served in accordance with the rules. Such service would be irregular, though it is possible (but not certain) that it would be validated under r 3.10. Postal service is effected by placing the document in a post box, or leaving it with or having it collected by the relevant service provider (PD 6A, para 3.1).

Leaving the documents at the defendant's address

6.32 This may be done by inserting the documents through the letter box at the defendant's address or that of the defendant's solicitor (in accordance with r 6.7, 6.8, 6.9, or 6.10), or otherwise leaving the documents at that address (eg by entering an office and leaving the documents on the reception desk).

Document exchange (DX)

6.33 This is a system used by the great majority of solicitors and chambers, and a number of other businesses, for transporting documents between their offices. It only works between offices using the system. Members pay periodic lump sums for the service. Generally documents put into the document exchange system arrive the next business day, although there are occasional delays. It is a permissible method of service only if the defendant's address where they are to be served includes a DX number, or where the writing paper of the defendant or its solicitor includes a DX number, and they have not stated they are unwilling to be served by DX (PD 6A, para 2.1).

Electronic methods of service

6.34 Where a document is to be served electronically (including fax and e-mail), the party to be served, or its solicitor, must have previously indicated in writing that it is willing to accept service by this method (PD 6A, para 4.1).

6.35 Where electronic means are to be used for serving on a party (as opposed to a solicitor), the willingness to accept electronic service must be expressly given for this purpose, although including a fax or e-mail address on a statement of case will be taken as a sufficient indication (para 4.1(2)(c)). Including a fax number on the litigant's letterhead is not enough (*Molins plc v GD SpA* [2000] 1 WLR 1741). For electronic service on a solicitor, express agreement, including an electronic address on a statement of case, or including a fax number on the solicitor's writing paper constitute sufficient indications (para 4.1(2)). Including an e-mail address on a solicitor's writing paper only amounts to an agreement to service by this method if it is also stated that the e-mail address may be used for service (para 4.1(2)(b)). Where a party seeks to serve electronically, he should first inquire whether the recipient has any limitations on matters such as on the format of transmitted documents or the size of attachments (para 4.2). A party who, in an emergency facing an opponent, refuses to agree to electronic service is likely to have difficulty resisting an application for relief from sanctions (*RC Residuals Ltd v Linton Fuel Oils Ltd* [2002] 1 WLR 2782). On the other hand, dispatching documents by fax without obtaining the defendant's prior agreement is more than a minor departure from the rules (*Kuenyehia v International Hospitals Group Ltd* (2006) *The Times*, 17 February 2006).

6.36 In order to comply with the requirement in CPR, r 6.6(1), that addresses used for service must be within the jurisdiction (or EEA, etc. lawyer's address), any fax number given for the purpose of service must be at the address for service (r 6.23(5)), and e-mail and other electronic identifications are deemed to be at the address for service (r 6.23(6)). There is no need to serve an additional hard copy after using fax or electronic methods of service (PD 6A, para 4.3), because rr 6.14 and 6.26 give rise to an irrebuttable presumption of due service (see 6.46).

Contractual method of service

6.37 Where a contract contains a term providing that proceedings may be served in a particular way, and the claim form is limited to claims arising from that contract, service will be valid if effected in accordance with the contractual term (CPR, r 6.11). Standard-form contracts often contain such provisions, as do contracts involving international trade. If a contractual provision involves serving a party outside the jurisdiction, the rules on service outside the jurisdiction (see Chapter 11) must also be complied with (r 6.11(2)).

Ad hoc agreement on service

6.38 It was held in *Anderton v Clwyd County Council (No 2)* [2002] 1 WLR 3174 that the only legitimate methods of service are those laid down by CPR, Part 6 (and the Companies Act 2006). *Cranfield v Bridgegrove Ltd* [2003] 1 WLR 2441 at [81], [85], however, approved *Kenneth Allison Ltd v AE Limehouse Ltd* [1992] 2 AC 105, which held that an *ad hoc* agreement between the parties about the method of service is also effective.

Usual method of service

6.39 Generally, service will be by the court (CPR, r 6.4), which will serve by first class post (PD 6A, para 8.1). In the Commercial Court the claim form is served by the claimant (PD 58, para 9). In general litigation, a party can take responsibility for effecting service by giving notice to the court (r 6.4(1)(b)). They will then either serve the document themselves, or it will be served on their behalf by a solicitor or an unqualified process server (agent) (*Ndole Assets Ltd v Designer M & E Services UK Ltd* [2017] 1 WLR 4367).

Alternative service

6.40 Sometimes it is not possible to effect service using the various methods set out earlier, or the reasonable steps taken to find the defendant where the claimant has only a 'last known' address discloses some other means that could be used to bring the claim to the defendant's attention. The defendant may be evading service, or prove difficult to find. In such cases the court may allow service by an alternative method or at an alternative place under CPR, r 6.15, provided there is a good reason for making the order. Such orders can be made prospectively (r 6.15(1)), or retrospectively to approve steps already taken in attempting to effect service (r 6.15(2)).

6.41 The wording of r 6.15(1) indicates there should be a two-stage test (with a condition that there must be a 'good reason', followed by a discretion, indicated by the word 'may'). Despite this, the Supreme Court has held it is a one-stage test, with the court being required to undertake an factual evaluation of whether there is a good reason, and if there is, a requirement to make the order (*Barton v Wright Hassall LLP* [2018] 1 WLR 1119). In making this evaluation the court will take into account all the circumstances of the case, including whether:

(a) the contents of the claim form were brought to the attention of the defendant before it expired, which is regarded as a critical factor (*Abela v Baadarani* [2013] 1 WLR 2043);

(b) the claimant has taken reasonable steps to effect service in accordance with the rules; and

(c) there is any prejudice to the defendant if the order is made, given what the defendant knew about its contents.

6.42 An application for an alternative service order needs to be supported by written evidence which must:

(a) state the reason alternative service is sought;

(b) state the proposed alternative method or place of service; and

(c) explain why it is believed service will be effective if the alternative method or place is used.

6.43 Examples of possible methods of alternative service are by advertisement in a newspaper; service by text message; and service on the defendant at the address of his or her insurer (*Gurtner v Circuit* [1968] 2 QB 587). In *Abbey National plc v Frost* [1999] 1 WLR 1080, which involved a claim against a solicitor, it was held that an order to effect alternative service of proceedings upon the Solicitors' Indemnity Fund would be allowed. An order for alternative service at an address within the jurisdiction will not be made if its purpose is to evade the restrictions on serving defendants outside the jurisdiction (for which, see Chapter 11) (*Knauf UK GmbH v British Gypsum Ltd* [2002] 1 WLR 907). Alternative service of English proceedings in an overseas jurisdiction is an interference with the sovereignty of that State, and will not be ordered other than in special circumstances (*Cecil v Bayat* [2011] 1 WLR 3086).

Dispensing with service of the claim form

6.44 The court may dispense with service of the claim form if there are exceptional circumstances (CPR, r 6.16(1)). An application under this rule may be made at any time, may be made without notice, and must be supported by evidence (r 6.16(2)).

6.45 There may be an exceptional case where there has been a minor departure from the rules on service (*Cranfield v Bridgegrove Ltd* [2003] 1 WLR 2441). An example is *Home Office v Dorgan* (one of the cases reported at [2002] 1 WLR 3174), where a service deadline by fax was missed by three minutes. This power may be used where one of the translations of the claim form is omitted in a case where service has to be effected outside the jurisdiction (*Phillips v Symes (No 3)* [2008] 1 WLR 180, HL). Common errors, such as serving by fax when the defendant has not consented to such service, are not sufficiently exceptional (*Kuenyehia v International Hospitals Group Ltd* (2006) *The Times*, 17 February 2006). Where a draft, unsealed, claim form was sent to the defendant's insurers during the period of validity, but service was not duly effected on the defendant, it could not be said that the circumstances were exceptional so as to justify dispensing with service (*Cranfield v Bridgegrove Ltd*).

H DEEMED DATE OF SERVICE OF THE CLAIM FORM

6.46 A claim form served within the UK in accordance with these rules is deemed to be served on the second business day after completion of the step required by CPR, r 7.5 (r 6.14). A 'business day' is any day except Saturday, Sunday, a bank holiday, Good Friday, and Christmas Day (r 6.2(b)). Rule 6.14 creates an irrebuttable presumption of law, which means evidence to contradict the deemed date of service is inadmissible. See 6.51.

I SERVICE OF DOCUMENTS OTHER THAN A CLAIM FORM

Service of documents other than the claim form within the jurisdiction is governed by CPR, **6.47**
rr 6.20–6.29. The normal rule is that the party has to serve the other side if it prepared the relevant document, and the court will do so if it prepared the document (r 6.21). In either case the court can order otherwise.

The available methods of service are the same as for claim forms (r 6.20, and see 6.22). **6.48**
While personal service must be used if this is prescribed (r 6.22, eg, for orders with penal notices, applications to commit), generally documents other than claim forms are served at the address the party gives as the address where they may be served. Claimants do this by stating their address on the claim form, and defendants do likewise by stating their address on the acknowledgment of service or defence. Where the party has a solicitor or EEA lawyer acting for them, the address is that of their solicitor or EEA lawyer (r 6.23(2)). A litigant in person has to provide an address for service which must be within the jurisdiction or within the EEA (r 6.23(2)(c), (3)). Any change to these addresses has to be notified to the court and other parties as soon as it takes place (r 6.24).

The court also has powers to order service of documents other than the claim form by **6.49**
alternative methods or at alternative places (r 6.27), and to dispense with service of such documents (r 6.28). See 6.40–6.45.

J DEEMED DATE OF SERVICE (NON-CLAIM FORM DOCUMENTS)

Where documents other than the claim form are served within the UK, by CPR, r 6.26, they **6.50**
are deemed to be served on the day shown in table 6.3.

The deemed dates of service set out in table 6.3 take effect on proving one of the prescribed methods **6.51**
of service, and cannot be displaced by evidence tending to prove some other date of actual receipt (*Godwin v Swindon Borough Council* [2002] 1 WLR 997; *Anderton v Clwyd County Council (No 2)* [2002] 1 WLR 3174). It will be noticed that the deemed dates of service set out in table 6.3 sometimes refer to 'days' and sometimes refer to 'business days'. 'Business days' are defined by r 6.2(b) as excluding Saturdays, Sundays, bank holidays, Christmas Day, and Good Friday. References in table 6.2 to 'days' are to calendar days (*Anderton v Clwyd County Council (No 2)*), so include weekends and public holidays. *Anderton v Clwyd County Council (No 2)* makes it clear that r 2.8, which excludes weekends and public holidays when calculating periods of less than five days, does not apply. This is because r 2.8 applies when calculating the time 'for doing any act'. Nothing is 'done' when calculating a deemed date: it is simply a fictitious date.

Most of the entries in table 6.3 are self-explanatory. It will be noticed, however, that there is no **6.52**
reference in table 6.3 providing for different treatment of documents posted after the last collection on a day. This means, for example, that a document sent by first-class post on a Friday at 10 p.m. is deemed to be served on the Monday. It does not matter that this is after the last post on the Friday. The second day after Friday is the Sunday. As this is not a business day, service is deemed to occur on Monday, the next business day after the Sunday. A document posted on a bank holiday Monday (it does not matter that this is not a business day) is deemed to be served on the second day thereafter, which is Wednesday, which is a business day (PD 6A, para 10.7). These results cannot be rebutted by evidence to the contrary, even evidence that there is no postal collection after 10 p.m. (*Anderton v Clwyd County Council (No 2)*.)

Table 6.3 Deemed dates of service

Method of service	Deemed day of service
First-class post (or other service which provides for delivery on the next business day)	The second day after it was posted, left with, delivered to, or collected by the relevant service provider provided that day is a business day; or if not, the next business day after that day
Document exchange	The second day after it was left with, delivered to, or collected by, the relevant service provider provided that day is a business day; or if not, the next business day after that day
Delivering the document to or leaving it at a permitted address	If it was delivered to or left at the permitted address on a business day before 4.30 p.m., on that day; or in any other case, on the next business day after that day
Fax	If the transmission of the fax is completed on a business day before 4.30 p.m., on that day; or in any other case, on the next business day after the day on which it was transmitted
Other electronic method	If the e-mail or other electronic transmission is sent on a business day before 4.30 p.m., on that day; or in any other case, on the business day after the day on which it was sent
Personal service	If the document is served personally before 4.30 p.m. on a business day, on that day; or in any other case, on the next business day after that day

6.53 Service by fax is deemed to take effect the same day if the transmission is completed before 4.30 p.m. on a business day. Faxes sent after 4.30 p.m. or on non-business days are deemed to be served on the next business day. Evidence of the date of actual receipt is inadmissible.

6.54 The deeming provisions in rr 6.14 and 6.26 only apply where service is effected under Part 6. They do not apply where a document is served under a statute rather than under Part 6. For example, in *Mucelli v Government of Albania* [2009] 1 WLR 276 a notice of appeal under the Extradition Act 2003 was sent by fax a few minutes after (what would now be 4.30 p.m.) on the final day for service, but was held to have been served in time because under the statute, service could be effected at any time up to midnight on the final day.

K CERTIFICATE OF SERVICE

6.55 A party effecting service is often required to file a certificate of service. For example, a claimant who serves the claim form is required to file a certificate of service within 21 days of service of the particulars of claim, unless all the defendants file acknowledgments of service within that time (CPR, r 6.17(2)). An example is shown in form 6.6.

L IRREGULAR SERVICE

6.56 A party who starts a claim using the wrong form, or relying on the wrong statutory provision, is likely to be granted permission to amend in order to deal with the claim justly (particularly if the defendants are not misled by the mistakes) (*Thurrock Borough Council v Secretary of State for the Environment, Transport and the Regions* (2000) *The Times*, 20 December 2000). Where service is attempted, but executed incorrectly, an application may be made under CPR, r 3.10 to remedy the error in the procedure. On such an application

Form 6.6 Certificate of service

Certificate of service

Name of court	Claim No.
COUNTY COURT AT COVENTRY	7YK 74281

Name of Claimant
Mrs JANE WATKINS

Name of Defendant
Miss ELEANOR DANIELS

On what day did you serve? `2 1 / 0 8 / 2 0 1 7`

The date of service is `2 3 / 0 8 / 2 0 1 7`

What documents did you serve?
Please attach copies of the documents you have not already filed with the court.

Claim Form, Particulars of Claim, Medical Report and Schedule of Past and Future Loss and Expense

On whom did you serve?
(If appropriate include their position e.g. partner, director).

The Defendant

How did you serve the documents?
(please tick the appropriate box)

- [✓] by first class post or other service which provides for delivery on the next business day
- [ ] by delivering to or leaving at a permitted place
- [ ] by personally handing it to or leaving it with (................time left, where document is other than a claim form) *(please specify)*

  [ ]

- [ ] by other means permitted by the court *(please specify)*

  [ ]

- [ ] by Document Exchange
- [ ] by fax machine (................time sent, where document is other than a claim form) *(you may want to enclose a copy of the transmission sheet)*
- [ ] by other electronic means (................time sent, where document is other than a claim form) *(please specify)*

  [ ]

Give the address where service effected, include fax or DX number, e-mail address or other electronic identification

27 Waterfall Road,
Coventry,
CV5 9GA

Being the
- [ ] claimant's
- [✓] defendant's
- [ ] solicitor's
- [ ] litigation friend

- [✓] usual residence
- [ ] last known residence
- [ ] place of business
- [ ] principal place of business
- [ ] last known place of business
- [ ] last known principal place of business
- [ ] principal office of the partnership
- [ ] principal office of the corporation
- [ ] principal office of the company
- [ ] place of business of the partnership/company/corporation within the jurisdiction with a connection to claim
- [ ] other *(please specify)*

  [ ]

I believe that the facts stated in this certificate are true.

Full name	Lena Carol Hughes

Signed		Position or office held	Trainee Solicitor

(Claimant) (Defendant) ('s solicitor) ('s litigation friend)　　　(If signing on behalf of firm or company)

Date `2 3 / 0 8 / 2 0 1 7`

N215 Certificate of service (09.11)　　　© Crown copyright 2011

Form 6.6 *continued*

Rules relating to the service of documents are contained in Part 6 of the Civil Procedure Rules (www.justice.gov.uk) and you should refer to the rules for information.

Calculation of deemed day of service of a claim

A claim form served within the UK in accordance with Part 6 of the Civil Procedure rules is deemed to be served on the second business day after the claimant has completed the steps required by CPR 7.5(1).

Calculation of the deemed day of service of documents other than the claim form (CPR 6.26)

Method of service	Deemed day of service
First class post or other service which provides for delivery on the next business day	The second day after it was posted, left with, delivered to or collected by the relevant service provider provided that day is a business day; or if not, the next business day after that day
Document exchange	The second day after it was left with, delivered to or collected by the relevant service provider provided that day is a business day; or if not, the next business day after that day
Delivering the document to or leaving it at a permitted address	If it is delivered to or left at the permitted address on a business day before 4.30pm, on that day; or in any other case, on the next business day after that day
Fax	If the transmission of the fax is completed on a business day before 4.30pm, on that day; or in any other case, on the next business day after the day on which it was transmitted
Other electronic method	If the email or other electronic transmission is sent on a business day before 4.30pm, on that day; or in any other case, on the next business day after the day on which it was sent
Personal service	If the document is served personally before 4.30pm on a business day, it is served on that day; or in any other case, on the next business day after that day

In this context 'business day' means any day except Saturday, Sunday or a bank holiday; (under the Banking and Financial Dealings Act 1971 in the part of the UK where service is to take place) includes Good Friday and Christmas Day.

the court will consider whether the claimant has taken all reasonable steps to put the matter right once the problem was discovered (*Nanglegan v Royal Free Hampstead NHS Trust* [2002] 1 WLR 1043). Attempting to serve at the wrong address is an error of procedure which may be remedied by an order under either r 3.10 or the general power to make orders for furthering the overriding objective in r 3.1(2)(m) (*Nelson v Clearsprings (Management) Ltd* [2007] 1 WLR 962, at [48]). In *Phillips v Symes (No 3)* [2008] 1 WLR 180 the House of Lords said that an order under r 3.10 was probably appropriate where the package sent to the defendant (who was in Switzerland) in error failed to include the English-language version of the claim form.

6.57 The position is different where the real problem is that the claimant has missed the four- (or six-) month period of validity for the claim form. The general position is that such cases have to be approached applying CPR, r 7.6. This rule, which is discussed in Chapter 7, is regarded as providing a complete code on extending the period of validity of claim forms (*Vinos v Marks & Spencer plc* [2001] 3 All ER 784 and *Godwin v Swindon Borough Council* [2002] 1 WLR 997). As a result, attempts made by claimants to use general powers in the CPR to rectify late or defective service (rr 3.1 extending time, 3.9 seeking relief from sanctions, and 3.10 correcting errors of procedure) have usually been rejected. If there are exceptional circumstances the court may, however, make an order for alternative service (see 6.40–6.43) or dispense with service (see 6.44).

M FILING

6.58 Most of the important documents used in litigation, such as the claim form, statements of case, and witness statements, have to be filed at court. The courts maintain their own files on every case that is issued, placing on the court file additional documents such as correspondence, notices of hearings, and court orders. Filing is a matter of delivering (not merely posting) the relevant documents to the court office (CPR, r 2.3(1)).

Traditionally, filing is by lodging hard copies of the relevant documents at the court office. It **6.59** is possible to file documents electronically, provided the court has an e-mail address listed at the Courts and Tribunals Finder website (**<http://courttribunalfinder.service.gov.uk/courts/>**): see PD 5B. In the High Court the facility is only available if no fee is payable for the step in question, but there are fee payment facilities for the County Court (PD 5B, para 2.3). There are technical requirements for the format of attachments, and things like statements of truth.

There is a rather more sophisticated Electronic Working Pilot Scheme operating in the **6.60** Rolls Building for ChD and specialist claims (PD 51O). This involves replacing paper based court claim files with electronic case files in PDF format. Under PD 51O claims are issued and sealed electronically, fees are paid online, and documents are filed as the claim progresses in PDF format. There are some relics from the past. For example, service still has to be effected by the parties using CPR Part 6 (PD 51O, para 8.2), and bundles of documents used for hearings have to be filed in hard copy form (paras 10.2 and 13.1), although an additional copy in PDF format may also be lodged.

Filing is not the same thing as service, so the deemed service rules (see 6.46 and 6.50–6.54) **6.61** do not apply. Filing takes effect immediately if documents are lodged at court during business hours, or even if they are delivered through the court's letter box at a time when the court is closed (*Van Aken v Camden London Borough Council* [2003] 1 WLR 684). Documents that are posted to the court are deemed to be filed when the package would have been delivered in the ordinary course of posting, unless the contrary is proved (Interpretation Act 1978, s 7). An email received by the court between 4.00 p.m. and 11.59 p.m. is deemed to be filed on the next day the court is open (PD 5B, para 4.2(a)).

KEY POINTS SUMMARY

- Civil proceedings are commenced by issuing a claim form. **6.62**

- Issue takes place when the claim form is sealed by the court.

- Details of the cause of action and remedies sought are contained in the particulars of claim. This may be endorsed on the claim form, attached to the claim form, or served separately.

- Service must be effected in accordance with the hierarchy of methods of service set out in Part 6 (personal service—service on the defendant's solicitor—service at the address given by the defendant—service at the defendant's usual address—service at the last known address).

- Domestic claim forms are valid for four months for the purpose of service. Where service is to be effected outside the jurisdiction, the period of validity is six months.

- The deemed dates of service create irrebuttable presumptions of due service on the dates set out in CPR, rr 6.14 and 6.26. This means evidence is not admissible to prove the document did not in fact arrive, or that it arrived on some other date.

- Where there are problems in effecting service, consideration should be given to seeking an order for service by an alternative method, or at an alternative place, or to dispense with service.

7

RENEWAL OF PROCESS

A POWER TO RENEW 7.03

B CLAIMS IN RESPECT OF CARGO 7.13

C MULTIPLE DEFENDANTS 7.14

D EFFECT OF STAY 7.15

E PROCEDURE ON SEEKING
AN EXTENSION 7.16

F CHALLENGING AN ORDER
GRANTING AN EXTENSION 7.18

7.01 As was seen in Chapter 6, after proceedings have been commenced by issuing a claim form or other originating process, they must be brought to the attention of the defendants or respondents by service. Generally, originating process remains valid for the purpose of service for a period of four months (see 6.14–6.19). A party bringing proceedings is entitled to make full use of the limitation period before issuing process, and, in addition, is entitled to wait until the final day of the period of validity before effecting service. Thus, it is possible for a defendant to be first informed of a claim by service of proceedings some months after the expiry of the limitation period. Of course, whether it is wise to delay service is another question. Service of proceedings marks a watershed in the litigation process. It is at this point that the defendant is put on formal notice that legal proceedings have been brought, and the time limit on service of proceedings is one which is relaxed with extreme caution.

7.02 If there are good reasons for not effecting service of the claim form during its period of validity, an extension may be granted either by consent or on making a without-notice application to the court. Consent for an extension is only effective if given by the written agreement of the parties (CPR, r 2.11, and *Thomas v Home Office* [2007] 1 WLR 230). A court asked to give permission to extend the period of validity of a claim form will always bear in mind that it is contrary to general principle to allow stale claims to proceed. As Megaw J said in *Heaven v Road and Rail Wagons Ltd* [1965] 2 QB 355 at 366:

> It is unfair to defendants, and it makes the administration of justice more uncertain, if litigation is delayed so that witnesses die or cannot be traced; or memories fade; and defendants are entitled to know definitely, at the expiry of some defined time, whether or not they are to be pursued in the courts.

Accordingly, the discretion to extend the period of validity of originating process is sparingly used.

A POWER TO RENEW

7.03 It is provided by CPR, r 7.6, that:

(1) The claimant may apply for an order extending the period for compliance with rule 7.5.

(2) The general rule is that an application to extend the time for compliance with rule 7.5 must be made—

(a) within the period specified by rule 7.5; or

(b) where an order has been made under this rule, within the period for service specified by that order.

(3) If the claimant applies for an order to extend the time for service of the claim form after the end of the period specified by rule 7.5 or by an order made under this rule, the court may make such an order only if—

(a) the court has failed to serve the claim form; or

(b) the claimant has taken all reasonable steps to comply with rule 7.5 but has been unable to do so; and

(c) in either case, the claimant has acted promptly in making the application.

(4) An application for an order extending the time for compliance with rule 7.5—

(a) must be supported by evidence; and

(b) may be made without notice.

The form of CPR, r 7.6, shows that a different approach will be taken depending on whether **7.04** or not the application to extend the period of validity of the claim form is made while the claim form is still valid. Rule 7.6 is intended to form a self-contained code on extending the validity of claim forms, and other powers in the CPR will either not be applied, or will be applied only in exceptional circumstances, to evade the restrictions in r 7.6. See the discussion at 6.39–6.43 and 6.54–6.55.

Applications made during the period of validity

No criteria are laid down in r 7.6 itself indicating how the discretion to extend should **7.05** be exercised where an extension to the period of validity is sought while the originating process is still valid. In *Hashtroodi v Hancock* [2004] 1 WLR 3206, the court felt it appropriate to give only general guidance on the principles to be applied under r 7.6(2), namely:

(a) the discretion to extend the period of validity of a claim form should be exercised in accordance with the overriding objective; and

(b) the reason for the failure to serve within the specified period is a highly material factor. If there is a very good reason for the failure to serve, an extension will usually be granted. If there is no more than a weak reason, the court is very unlikely to grant an extension (*Collier v Williams* [2006] 1 WLR 1945).

Rix LJ in *Cecil v Bayat* [2011] 1 WLR 3086 at [109] adopted the principles that had been **7.06** developed under the RSC, namely:

(a) an extension under r 7.6(2) can only be granted if there is a good reason for granting more time to serve the claim form; and

(b) if there is a good reason, the court must consider the balance of hardship between the parties in either granting or refusing the extension of time.

Reverting to the pre-CPR principles is controversial. However, where an extension to the **7.07** period of validity of a claim form is sought that will or may have the effect of depriving the defendant of a limitation defence (see Chapter 21), those principles underpin a defendant's fundamental right to be sued, if at all, no later than the limitation period plus the initial period of validity of the claim form (Zuckerman, *Civil Procedure* (3rd edn, Sweet & Maxwell, 2013), para 5.92).

Seeking an extension following the negligence or incompetence of the claimant's solicitors **7.08** in failing to serve the claim form in time will inevitably be regarded as a bad reason (*Hashtroodi v Hancock*). The following are also regarded as inadequate reasons:

(a) deliberately not serving in order to avoid prejudicing ongoing negotiations. This was the result in *The Mouna* [1991] 2 Lloyd's Rep 221, and would certainly be the same under the CPR, given r 26.4, which allows the court to grant a stay of the proceedings to allow for settlement of the case by ADR;

(b) awaiting an expert's report for the purposes of drafting the particulars of claim. This is a reason for obtaining an extension for service of the particulars of claim, not for an extension of time for the claim form (*Collier v Williams*). A claimant in this situation should serve the claim form, and seek an extension of the particulars of claim;

(c) seeking time to prepare the particulars of claim, schedule of loss and damage, and medical evidence, which is similar to (b) (*Mason v First Leisure Corporation plc* (2003) LTL 30/7/03); and

(d) seeking an extension while arranging funding for the litigation. Very limited costs are involved in putting a claim form in the post. This situation should be addressed by seeking a stay of the claim while funding is arranged (*Cecil v Bayat*).

7.09 Good reasons are almost always based on difficulties in effecting service of the claim form, such as problems in tracing the defendant for the purpose of service, and situations where the defendant is evading service. Another situation is where the claimant could not have known about the claim until the last moment (*Cecil v Bayat* at [108]). The only apparent exception in the reported cases is *Steele v Mooney* [2005] 2 All ER 256. An extension was granted to allow the claimant to formulate its particulars of claim following delays in obtaining medical records from the defendant. The question of discretion whether to grant an extension was conceded. The case was explained by Rix LJ in *Cecil v Bayat* as one where the defendant knew of the impending claim and had himself materially contributed to the delay by deliberately not providing documents he was obliged to provide.

7.10 When considering the balance of hardship the most important factor is whether the limitation period has or might have expired. Even if the claim is a strong one, where the defendant might be deprived of a limitation defence, an extension will only be granted in exceptional circumstances (*Cecil v Bayat*, Stanley Brunton LJ at [55]).

Applications made after the expiry of the period of validity

7.11 For applications after the claim form has expired, fairly exacting criteria have been laid down by r 7.6(3). A case where the court fails to serve because it completely overlooks the claim form comes within r 7.6(3)(a) just as much as a case where the court tries unsuccessfully to effect service (*Cranfield v Bridgegrove Ltd* [2003] 1 WLR 2441). In this situation the court will usually grant an extension. Under r 7.6(3)(b) it will be seen that there should have been efforts to serve, and that there must be no unexplained delay in making the application (albeit the application is made after the expiry of the period of validity). In *Smith v Probyn* (2000) *The Times*, 29 March 2000, the claimant served proceedings on the defendant's solicitors in the mistaken belief that they were authorized to accept service, but having failed to obtain written confirmation that they were authorized as required at the time (see r 6.7, discussed at 6.23(b)). An extension was then sought, but was refused because there had been nothing to prevent personal service.

7.12 It is not all that likely that a claimant who has been making efforts to serve will simultaneously forget about the period of validity. However, r 7.6 will assist a claimant who tries to effect service, but who later discovers that the method used was ineffective (*Amerada Hess v Rome* (2000) *The Times*, 15 March 2000, discussed at 6.27). The rule is most likely to assist a claimant who believes the court is effecting service, and later discovers this is not the case.

B CLAIMS IN RESPECT OF CARGO

Claims in respect of cargo carried by sea are governed by the special one-year limitation **7.13** period in the Hague–Visby Rules, art III, r 6. Once the year has elapsed, the claim is extinguished if proceedings have not been commenced (*Aries Tanker Corporation v Total Transport Ltd* [1977] 1 WLR 185). The effect is that there is no power to extend validity more than one year after accrual of the cause of action: *Payabi v Armstel Shipping Corporation* [1992] QB 907.

C MULTIPLE DEFENDANTS

It was argued in *Jones v Jones* [1970] 2 QB 576 that where there are several defendants it is **7.14** necessary to serve only one of them within the period of validity of the originating process, and that the others could be served at leisure at some later time. If the argument had been accepted, it would have meant that a second defendant could have been validly served several years after issue provided the first defendant had been served during the initial period of validity. The Court of Appeal held that the rule (as it then stood) was not capable of bearing such a construction, with the result that every defendant on whom it is intended to serve proceedings must be served during the period of validity.

D EFFECT OF STAY

While a stay is in operation no steps may be taken in the claim other than an application to **7.15** remove the stay. However, time continues to run for the purposes of the period of validity of the claim form (*Aldridge v Edwards* [2000] CPLR 349).

E PROCEDURE ON SEEKING AN EXTENSION

Applications for renewal are of necessity made before the defendant is on the record, so **7.16** must be made without notice, and the practice is that they are made without an oral hearing. The application notice must be supported by written evidence which should set out all the relevant circumstances. As the application is made without notice, the claimant must give full and frank disclosure of all material facts, including those going against the granting of the order. The written evidence should include the following details:

(a) the date of accrual of the cause of action and, if it has passed, the date of expiry of the primary limitation period;
(b) the date of issue of the originating process;
(c) a full explanation of the reasons for not having served process;
(d) the period of the extension sought and the reasons for it;
(e) the dates and periods of any previous renewals; and
(f) if the application is made after the expiry of the period of validity of the originating process, a full explanation of the circumstances excusing the late application.

Once the order has been made, the application notice and evidence in support must be **7.17** served with the order on the party against whom the order was sought, unless the court otherwise orders (CPR, r 23.9). The order will contain a notice informing the defendant of the right to apply to set aside the order granting the extension, and any application to set aside must be made within seven days of service of the order (r 23.10).

F CHALLENGING AN ORDER GRANTING AN EXTENSION

7.18 A defendant will learn that an extension has been granted when the claim form is served. The order granting the extension may be challenged, but the defendant will first have to acknowledge service of the proceedings, stating an intention to defend, and must then issue an application notice supported by written evidence asking for an order setting aside the order granting the extension. See 12.13.

8

PART 8 CLAIMS AND PETITIONS

A PART 8 CLAIMS.....................8.04   **C** WINDING-UP PETITIONS..............8.15

B PETITIONS........................8.12

Part 8 claims and petitions are forms of originating process. They can be used only for **8.01** commencing certain specific types of proceedings as expressly provided by the statute, procedural rules imposed by statutory instrument, or rules of court governing the type of proceedings in question.

Often, the provisions requiring a certain type of application to be made by Part 8 claim **8.02** form or petition will lay down additional procedural requirements. These additional procedural requirements usually specify whether there must be written evidence in support, and may also lay down various matters that must be included in that evidence. Sometimes detailed codes of procedure are laid down for specific types of proceedings. A highly modified Part 8 procedure is laid down for Stage 3 of the RTA and EL/PL protocols for determining the amount of damages in low-value personal injuries cases (see Chapter 9).

Most types of proceedings which have to be brought by either Part 8 claim form or petition **8.03** are very narrow and specialized, but some are of great importance. The most important types of proceedings which must be commenced by petition are those for divorce, judicial separation, bankruptcy, and the winding-up of companies. Detailed rules apply to these forms of petition. Petitions for winding-up of companies are considered at 8.15ff by way of illustration.

A PART 8 CLAIMS

The main type of originating process under the CPR is the Part 7 claim form previously **8.04** discussed in Chapter 6. That type of claim form is used for almost all types of proceedings where there is likely to be a dispute of fact. The issues raised in such claims are defined in written statements of case that have to be served and filed by each party (see Chapter 14).

An alternative procedure for bringing a claim is that laid down in CPR, Part 8. A claim **8.05** brought under Part 8 has its own 'Part 8 claim form' (form N208). Part 8 claims are for use where there is no substantial dispute of fact (CPR, r 8.1(2)(a)). One example is a claim brought by a trustee or executor seeking the court's ruling on the true meaning of a clause in a trust deed or will. In such a case the court is simply being asked to construe a document, and there should be no dispute of fact. A Part 8 claim can be used for some applications pursuant to statute or statutory instrument. For example, Part 8 claims are used for approval of children's settlements where proceedings have not been commenced (r 21.10(2)). A detailed list of applications under various statutes which must be commenced using the Part 8 procedure, can be found in the table following PD 8A, para 9.4.

8.06 The courts will entertain a 'hybrid Part 8' claim that involves a short hearing with oral evidence to resolve a limited factual dispute in a Part 8 claim (*Vitpol Building Service v Samen* [2009] Bus LR D65). The emphasis is on the limited nature of such a factual dispute. Where the dispute has any substance the claim has to be brought in the usual way with a Part 7 claim so the dispute can be defined using statements of case (*Forest Heath District Council v ISG Jackson Ltd* [2010] EWHC 322 (TCC)).

Issue and service

8.07 A Part 8 claim form must be in form N208 (form N208(CC) in the Commercial Court). It must state that Part 8 applies, and must set out the question the claimant wants the court to decide or the remedy sought. If the claim is brought pursuant to statute the relevant statute must be stated (CPR, r 8.2). Otherwise, a Part 8 claim form looks very much like an ordinary claim form.

8.08 Where it appears to a court officer that a claim has been inappropriately issued using the Part 8 procedure, the claim may be referred to a judge to decide how the case should be dealt with (PD 8A, para 3.4). A procedural judge may at any stage order the claim to continue as a Part 7 claim, and where this happens the court will issue directions and allocate the claim to a track (para 3.5).

8.09 The normal rules relating to service apply to Part 8 claims: see Chapter 6.

Evidence in support and reply

8.10 Any evidence the claimant relies upon must be filed and served with the claim form (CPR, r 8.5(1) and (2)). This can be in the form of witness statements or affidavits (PD 8A, para 7.2). After the claim form has been issued and served, any defendants have 14 days to acknowledge service (r 8.3(1)). An acknowledgment of service should be on the prescribed form (form N210). Defendants must file their evidence when they acknowledge service. The claimant may file and serve evidence in reply within 14 days thereafter (r 8.5(5) and (6)).

Case management

8.11 Part 8 claims are treated as allocated to the multi-track (CPR, r 8.9(c)), although the court may override this and allocate the claim to a track (PD 8A, para 8.2). The court may give directions for managing the claim either immediately on being issued or later, and on an application by a party or of its own initiative (PD 8A, para 6.1). In claims where there is no dispute, such as child and protected party settlements, and in other cases where it is convenient (eg mortgage possession claims), the court will usually fix a hearing date when the claim is issued. Where the court does not fix a date for the hearing, it will give directions for the disposal of the claim as soon as practicable after the defendant has acknowledged service, or after the period for acknowledging service has expired (PD 8A, para 6.2). If the case merits it, the court will convene a directions hearing (para 6.4).

B PETITIONS

As mentioned earlier in this chapter, typical examples of petitions are those for divorce, **8.12** judicial separation, bankruptcy of individuals, and winding-up of companies. Matrimonial petitions are governed by the Family Procedure Rules 2010 (SI 2010/2995). Insolvency petitions are governed by the Insolvency (England and Wales) Rules 2016 (SI 2016/1024) ('IR 2016'). Petitions are almost unknown, especially in the County Court, outside these areas. The procedure to be followed on general-form petitions, such as election petitions under the Representation of the People Acts, is considered in this section.

Form of petitions

Petitions must be in form N200. A replica of the royal arms must be printed or embossed **8.13** at the head of the first page. The title identifies the court in which the petition is to proceed. The next line says the petition is brought 'In the matter of' the Act which gives the court power to entertain the proceedings. It may also state it is brought 'In the matter of [an identified trust, settlement, company or property]'. Like a statement of case, the body of the petition states, usually in several numbered paragraphs, the grounds on which the petitioner claims to be entitled to an order from the court. It then includes a concise statement of the relief or remedy claimed. It will conclude with a statement of the names of the persons, if any, who are intended to be served with the petition, and the addresses of the petitioner and the petitioner's solicitors. A High Court petition may be commenced either in London or in one of the Chancery district registries.

Subsequent steps

On issuing a petition the proper officer of the court will fix a date for the hearing. This **8.14** may be the final hearing or a directions hearing. Evidence at the hearing is usually taken by witness statement or affidavit.

C WINDING-UP PETITIONS

Proceedings for the compulsory winding-up of companies are governed by the Insol- **8.15** vency Act 1986 ('IA 1986') and the IR 2016. The IA 1986, s 122(1), sets out the grounds for making an order for the compulsory winding-up of a company, the one most commonly invoked being that the company is unable to pay its debts as they fall due. A company is deemed, by virtue of the IA 1986, s 123, to be unable to pay its debts if, *inter alia*:

(a) it has been served with a statutory demand for a debt exceeding £750 and it has failed to pay or compound for it within 21 days after service. An example of a statutory demand is shown in figure 8.1;

(b) judgment has been entered against it and execution has been returned unsatisfied in whole or in part.

Figure 8.1 Statutory demand

STATUTORY DEMAND UNDER SECTION 123(1)(a) OF THE INSOLVENCY ACT 1986

WARNING

- This is an IMPORTANT document.
- This demand must be dealt with WITHIN 21 DAYS after its service upon the company or a winding-up order could be made in respect of the company.
- Please read the demand and notes carefully.

DEMAND

TO FOTHERGILL (GR) & CO. LIMITED, registered number 98567891

Registered office: 31 Jebson Avenue, Swindon, Wiltshire SN1 5ES

This demand is made under section 123(1)(a) of the Insolvency Act 1986, and is served on you by the creditor:

Name: Roberts (HKT) Machine Tools Limited, registered number 54321987

Address: 64 Victoria Street, Birmingham B8 9JY

The creditor claims that the company owes the sum of £87,557.01, full particulars of which are set out on page 2.

The creditor demands that the company do pay the above debt or secure or compound for it to the creditor's satisfaction. The company must pay the debt claimed in the demand within 21 days of service of the demand on the company after which the creditor may present a winding up petition unless the company offers security for the debt and the creditor agrees to accept security or the company compounds the debt with the creditor's agreement.

Signature of individual

Name   HOWARD KENNETH THOMAS ROBERTS

            (BLOCK LETTERS)

Date: 08 May 2018

Position with or relationship to creditor: Director

I am duly authorized to make this demand on the creditor's behalf.

Address: 7 Burnham Grove, Birmingham B5 7DP

NB THE PERSON MAKING THIS DEMAND MUST COMPLETE THE WHOLE OF THIS PAGE, PAGE 2 AND PARTS A AND B (AS APPLICABLE) ON PAGE 3.

PARTICULARS OF DEBT

15.2.2018 Machine tools. Invoice RB 45782

            3 of lathes model GH Mk 456/2;

            1 of guillotine model Mk VI;

            2 of burners model 3429193.

	£72,964.17
VAT at 20%	£14,592.84
	Total £87,557.01

Figure 8.1 *continued*

PART A

The individual with whom a officer or representative of the company may communicate with a view to securing or compounding the debt to the creditor's satisfaction is:

Name HOWARD KENNETH THOMAS ROBERTS

         (BLOCK LETTERS)

Address: 7 Burnham Grove, Birmingham B5 7DP

Telephone no. 0121 853 9483

Reference RB 45782

PART B

For completion if the creditor is entitled to the debt by way of assignment

	Name	Date of Assignment
Original Creditor		
Assignees		

HOW TO COMPLY WITH A STATUTORY DEMAND

If the company wishes to avoid a winding-up petition being presented it must pay the debt shown on page 1, particulars of which are set out on page 2 of this notice, within the period of 21 DAYS AFTER its service upon the company. Alternatively, the company can attempt to come to a settlement with the creditor. To do this the company should:

- inform the individual named in Part A above immediately that it is willing and able to offer security for the debt to the creditor's satisfaction; or

- inform the individual named in Part A above immediately that it is willing and able to compound for the debt to the creditor's satisfaction.

If the company disputes the demand in whole or in part it should contact the individual named in Part A immediately.

REMEMBER! THE COMPANY HAS ONLY 21 DAYS AFTER THE DATE OF SERVICE ON IT OF THIS DOCUMENT BEFORE THE CREDITOR MAY PRESENT A WINDING-UP PETITION.

NOTE: the company has the right to make an application to the court for an injunction restraining the creditor from presenting or advertising a petition for the winding-up of the company.

The court to which an application should be made is the court having jurisdiction to wind up the company under section 117 of the Insolvency Act 1986.

A number of persons have *locus standi* to petition for the winding-up of a company. These **8.16** include the company itself, its directors, or the Secretary of State, but most petitions are brought by unpaid creditors. The petition must be brought in the High Court if the company has paid-up share capital in excess of £120,000, otherwise there is concurrent jurisdiction between the High Court and the County Court (IA 1986, s 117). Certain County Court hearing centres have been nominated to deal with insolvency matters. High Court petitions are presented in the Companies Court of the ChD.

Commencement

8.17   Before presenting a petition the petitioner must conduct a search of the Central Registry of Winding-Up Petitions to check there is no outstanding petition against the company. This is a computerized register that can be searched by a personal attendance at the Companies Court General Office. A petition is commenced by filing the petition in court and paying a court fee and lodging a deposit to cover the official receiver's fees. The petition must include details prescribed by IR 2016, rr 1.35 and 7.5. A petition based on the statutory demand in figure 8.1 is illustrated in figure 8.2. An additional copy must be provided for service on the company. The court seals the petition and endorses it with the hearing date.

Figure 8.2 Winding-up petition

IN THE HIGH COURT OF JUSTICE   No 9452 of 2018

CHANCERY DIVISION

COMPANIES COURT

IN THE MATTER of G R Fothergill & Co. Limited, registered number 98567891

THE APPLICATION IS MADE UNDER the Insolvency Act 1986, section 122

To Her Majesty's High Court of Justice

The petition of HKT Roberts Machine Tools Limited, registered number 54321987, whose registered office is 64 Victoria Street, Birmingham B8 9JY.

1 G R Fothergill & Co. Limited, Registered No: 98567891 (hereinafter called 'the Company') was incorporated on 4 November 1988 under the Companies Act 1985 as a company limited by shares.

2 The registered office of the Company is at 31 Jebson Avenue, Swindon, Wiltshire SN1 5ES.

3 The nominal capital of the Company is £500,000 divided into 500,000 shares of £1 each. The amount of the capital paid up or credited as paid up is £300,000.

4 The Company was established to carry on business as motor component manufacturers.

5 The Company is indebted to the Petitioner in the sum of £87,557.01 in respect of machine tools sold and delivered by the Petitioner to the Company on 15 February 2017.

6 A statutory demand was served on the Company by leaving it at the Company's registered office on 8 May 2018 the Petitioner served on the Company by leaving it at the company's registered office a demand requiring the company to pay the said sum, which demand was in the prescribed form.

7 Over 21 days have now elapsed since service of the statutory demand, but the Company has neglected to pay or satisfy the above sum or any part of it, or to make any offer to the Petitioner to secure or compound the same.

8 The Company is not an insurance undertaking; a credit institution; collective investment undertaking or an investment undertaking providing services involving the holding of funds or securities for third parties as referred to in Article 1.2 of the EC Regulation.

9 For the reasons set out in the statement of Howard Roberts supported by a statement of truth filed with this Petition, it is considered that the EC Regulation on Insolvency Proceedings apply and these proceedings will be main proceedings as defined in Article 3 of the EC Regulation.

10 The Company is insolvent and unable to pay its debts.

11 In the circumstances it is just and equitable that the Company should be wound up.

Figure 8.2 *continued*

The Petitioner therefore prays as follows:

(1) that R Fothergill & Co. Limited, Registered No: 98567891 may be wound up by the Court under the provisions of the Insolvency Act 1986; or
(2) that such other order may be made as the Court thinks just.

Note: It is intended to serve this petition on G R Fothergill & Co. Limited.

Statement of Truth

I believe that the facts stated in this petition are true.

I am duly authorized by the petitioner to sign this statement.

Signed: Howard Roberts

Office held: Director of HKT Roberts Machine Tools Limited

(if signing on behalf of a company)

Dated: 10 July 2018

ENDORSEMENT

This petition having been presented to the Court on 10 July 2018 will be heard at the 7 Rolls Building, Fetter Lane, London EC4A INL on:

Date: 17 October 2018

Time: 10.30 hours (or as soon thereafter as the petition can be heard).

The solicitor to the Petitioner is:

Messrs Collins, Brown and Heath, of 7 Ingrave Road, Birmingham B5 8EP.

Telephone: 0121 215 8349

Reference: RB 45782

Service

Service of the petition must be effected at the company's registered office. Under the IR 2016, Sch 4, para 2, service is effected either by: **8.18**

(a) handing the documents to a person who acknowledges himself to be, or who is to the best of the server's knowledge and belief, a director, officer, or employee of the company; or
(b) handing the documents to a person who acknowledges being authorized to accept service on the company's behalf; or
(c) (where no such person as mentioned is available) depositing the documents at or about the registered office in such a way that they are likely to come to the notice of a person attending the office.

If none of these methods is practicable, service may be effected at the company's last known **8.19** principal place of business, or on its secretary, a director or principal officer, wherever that person may be found. Otherwise, an order for substituted service may be sought.

8.20 After service the petitioner is required to file a certificate of service, which must specify the manner in which service was effected.

Advertisement

8.21 A petitioning creditor does not petition for his or her personal benefit only, but as a member of the class of creditors. Advertising the petition (technically called giving 'notice of the petition') notifies other creditors that a petition has been presented, and gives them an opportunity to appear at the hearing to support or oppose the making of a winding-up order.

It also notifies persons who may have dealings with the company. By virtue of the IA 1986, s 127, if a winding-up order is eventually made any dispositions of the company's property after the date of presentation of the petition are avoided unless validated by the court. For this reason, banks and other traders may refuse to do further business with the company after becoming aware that a petition has been presented. Consequently, advertisement is regarded as a serious step.

8.22 The advertisement must contain details of the company and the hearing date, and invites creditors to give notice of their intention to appear at the hearing to the petitioner's solicitor by 4 p.m. on the business day before the hearing. It must appear in the *Gazette* at least seven business days after service of the petition on the company, and at least seven business days before the hearing (IR 2016, r 7.10(4)).

Certificate of compliance

8.23 No later than five business days before the hearing the petitioner must file in court a certificate of compliance (IR 2016, r 7.12). This gives the dates of presenting the petition, service, advertisement, and hearing. A copy of the advertisement and the certificate of service must be filed with the certificate of compliance.

Disputes by the company

8.24 There are three courses open to a company which disputes the debt which founds a petition:

(a) apply for an injunction to restrain the petition (and/or advertisement) (for which, see 42.79); or

(b) apply to strike out the petition as an abuse of process (for which, see 30.21); or

(c) file a witness statement in opposition to the petition not less than five business days before the hearing showing at least an arguable dispute that the debt is presently owing.

A genuine dispute over a debt must be resolved by an ordinary civil claim. If it is not clear that the alleged debt is presently owing, the winding-up petition will be dismissed.

Supporting and opposing creditors

8.25 Supporting and opposing creditors who intend to appear at the hearing should give notice to that effect to the petitioner's solicitors by 4 p.m. on the day before the hearing. Thereafter, the petitioner's solicitors will compile a list of appearances giving details of all creditors who duly gave notice. The list has to be handed in to the court before the hearing commences (IR 2016, r 7.15(3)).

Hearing

High Court winding-up petitions are heard by an Insolvency and Companies Court Judge **8.26** on Mondays in open court. At the hearing the court has power to dismiss the petition, adjourn the hearing conditionally or unconditionally, or make interim orders or any other order it thinks fit (IA 1986, s 125). If all the necessary steps have been taken and all the paperwork is in order, an undefended hearing will take a matter of seconds and the winding-up order is made as of right. A typical submission made by counsel for the petitioner is:

> Sir, this is a trade creditor's petition in the sum of £87,557 odd. So far as I am aware the company does not appear and the lists are negative. My application is for the usual compulsory order, main proceedings.

This submission indicates the nature of the petition, that the company is not represented in **8.27** court to dispute the debt (see 8.24), that no creditors have given notice of their intention to appear, and that therefore there are no entries on the list of appearances (see 8.25), and asks the court to make a winding-up order in the usual terms (see figure 8.3). The reference to 'main proceedings' is to Council Regulation (EC) No 1346/2000, which provides that the main insolvency proceedings in relation to a debtor in the EU should be presented in the EU State where the centre for the debtor's main interests is situated. Paragraphs 8 and 9 of the petition (see figure 8.2) deal with the same Regulation.

Defects in the procedure or paperwork fall into three categories. Minor defects may be **8.28** waived by the court and a winding-up order will still be made. Whether a defect is sufficiently minor to be waived is a question of degree, with much turning on whether the company or other creditors could have been prejudiced or misled. For example, a non-misleading typing error might be waived, but a failure to state the method of service in the certificate of service is likely to lead to an adjournment. If there is a defect which is not capable of remedy, the petition will be dismissed. An example would be advertising the petition before service on the company.

Liquidation

If a winding-up order is made, the court notifies the official receiver who becomes the **8.29** liquidator of the company. If the company has insufficient assets to cover the costs of winding up, the official receiver may apply for an early dissolution under the IA 1986, s 202. Otherwise, the liquidator's task is to get in the assets of the company and to pay its creditors in accordance with their respective priorities. When this has been done, the liquidator files a report with the registrar of companies, and the company is dissolved three months later.

Figure 8.3 Winding-up order

IN THE HIGH COURT OF JUSTICE   No 9452 of 2018

CHANCERY DIVISION

COMPANIES COURT

Insolvency and Companies Court Judge Young

Monday 17 October 2018

IN THE MATTER of G R Fothergill & Co. Limited, registered number 98567891

Figure 8.3 *continued*

AND IN THE MATTER of the Insolvency Act 1986

Upon the petition of a creditor of the company presented to this court on 10 July 2018

And upon hearing counsel for the Petitioner and no one appearing for and on behalf of the said Respondent company

And upon reading the evidence

It is ordered that G R Fothergill & Co. Limited be wound up by this court under the provisions of the Insolvency Act 1986.

And the court being satisfied on the evidence that the EC Regulation does apply and that these proceedings are main proceedings as defined in Article 3 of the EC Regulation.

And it is ordered that the costs of HKT Roberts Machine Tools Limited of the said petition be paid out of the assets of the company.

Dated 17 October 2018

Note: One of the official receivers attached to the court is by virtue of this order liquidator of the company.

9

PERSONAL INJURY CLAIMS UNDER £25,000

A CASES COVERED BY THE RTA
   AND EL/PL PROTOCOLS 9.04

B RTA PROTOCOL 9.06

C STAGE 1: CLAIM NOTIFICATION 9.09

D STAGE 2: MEDICAL EVIDENCE AND
   NEGOTIATION 9.17

E STAGE 3: PART 8 CLAIM TO
   DETERMINE QUANTUM 9.30

F CHILD SETTLEMENT APPLICATIONS 9.39

G LIMITATION 9.42

H FIXED COSTS UNDER THE RTA
   AND EL/PL PROTOCOLS 9.43

I CASES WHERE PARTIES CAN STOP
   FOLLOWING THE RTA OR EL/PL
   PROTOCOLS 9.45

   Key points summary 9.47

There are approximately 950,000 personal injuries claims each year (*Ministry of Justice* **9.01** *Impact Assessment* IA No: MoJ 190, 2013). Of these, about 750,000 cases arise from road traffic accidents ('RTAs'), 90,000 are employers' liability cases ('EL'), and 100,000 are public liability cases ('PL'). About 90 per cent of these are cases where the damages are estimated at between £1,000 and £25,000. Claimant solicitors and defendant insurers and solicitors increasingly deal with these cases on a commoditized basis, a process which is encouraged by the reforms introduced by the Legal Services Act 2007. 'Commoditization' is not an exact term, but describes the move away from each client having a personal relationship with their solicitor and receiving a personalized service, to clients being introduced to solicitors through referral agencies with legal services being conducted in a cost-efficient way, often for a fixed fee. Referral agencies include BTE insurers, claims management companies (who often advertise for customers on television etc.), and trade unions.

Two particular features of the commoditized approach to personal injury claims are the **9.02** use of medical reporting organizations ('MROs') and computerized systems for assessing damages for pain, suffering, and loss of amenity. MROs are medical agencies that provide medical experts who write reports and appear as expert witnesses in personal injuries claims. A MRO will charge fees for its services, which are recoverable from the unsuccessful party as disbursements when costs are assessed (see Chapter 46 and *Woollard v Fowler* (24 May 2006, unreported)). There are complaints that commonly only 35–50 per cent of the fees charged by MROs are paid to the medical experts providing the expert evidence (*Jackson Review of Civil Litigation Costs*, para 22.3.21). There are two main software systems which are used primarily by defendants' insurers in quantifying damages for pain, suffering, and loss of amenity. Problems discussed in the *Jackson Review of Civil Litigation Costs*, ch 21, included unthinking settlement of cases on the figure provided by the computer, evidence that in all cases that went to a hearing (literally 100 per cent of such cases) awards by the courts exceeded the figure provided by the software, and limited authority given by insurance companies to claims negotiators to exceed the computer-based figure.

9.03 It is in this context that the Ministry of Justice has promulgated two protocols and a number of related provisions in the CPR to deal with most personal injuries claims valued at between £1,000 and £25,000. They are designed to provide a streamlined and swift process for settling by agreement personal injuries claims where liability is admitted. They provide a highly regulated system for dealing with these claims, with short, fixed periods for most of the necessary steps, prescribed interim payments, and a regime of fixed costs. Unlike the other protocols, the RTA and EL/PL protocols are in reality an alternative to litigation, rather than a precursor to court proceedings. It has been recognized that using these two protocols tends to result in significant savings in time and costs.

A CASES COVERED BY THE RTA AND EL/PL PROTOCOLS

9.04 A claim will be covered by the RTA protocol if:

(a) the claim is for damages arising from a road traffic accident (RTA protocol, para 4.2);
(b) the defendant was a road user (para 4.5(1));
(c) the claim includes damages in respect of personal injury (para 4.1(2));
(d) the claimant values the claim between £1,000 and £25,000 on a full liability basis (para 4.1(3), (4)); and
(e) the claim does not fall into any of the excluded categories (para 4.5) (see 9.08).

9.05 A claim will be covered by the EL/PL protocol if:
(a) the claim includes damages in respect of personal injury;
(b) the claimant values the claim between £1,000 and £25,000 on a full liability basis (para 4.1(3), (4)); and
(c) the claim does not fall into any of the excluded categories set out in para 4.3.

B RTA PROTOCOL

9.06 This chapter will consider the provisions of the RTA protocol. The EL/PL protocol is in very similar terms. The process under the RTA protocol is divided into three stages, which are shown in figure 9.1.

Valuing the claim

9.07 A claim will not be covered by the RTA protocol if the small claims track (for which see 15.24–15.26) would be the normal track for the claim (RTA protocol, para 4.1(4)). This means that claims where the damages for pain, suffering, and loss of amenity will be less than £1,000 are outside the RTA protocol. These claims are excluded because there is a no-costs rule in small claims track cases (see 27.14), which is inconsistent with the fixed costs regime under the RTA protocol. In deciding whether the claim exceeds £25,000 the claimant should:

(a) include pecuniary losses;
(b) exclude the value of vehicle-related damage (para 4.4); and
(c) exclude interest (para 1.2(1)).

Excluded cases

9.08 The following situations are outside the RTA Protocol, para 4.5, namely cases:

(1) made to the MIB pursuant to the Untraced Drivers' Agreement 2003 (see 5.27);
(2) where the claimant or defendant is deceased;

Figure 9.1 RTA protocol: the three stages

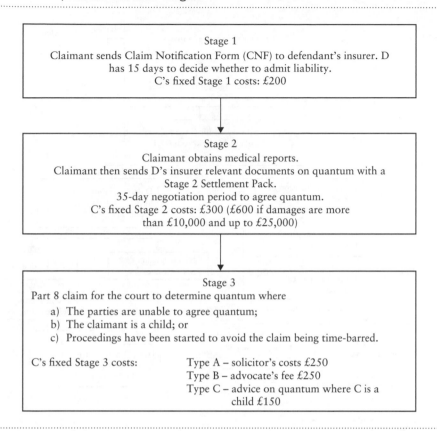

Stage 1
Claimant sends Claim Notification Form (CNF) to defendant's insurer. D
has 15 days to decide whether to admit liability.
C's fixed Stage 1 costs: £200

Stage 2
Claimant obtains medical reports.
Claimant then sends D's insurer relevant documents on quantum with a
Stage 2 Settlement Pack.
35-day negotiation period to agree quantum.
C's fixed Stage 2 costs: £300 (£600 if damages are more
than £10,000 and up to £25,000)

Stage 3
Part 8 claim for the court to determine quantum where

a) The parties are unable to agree quantum;
b) The claimant is a child; or
c) Proceedings have been started to avoid the claim being time-barred.

C's fixed Stage 3 costs: Type A – solicitor's costs £250
Type B – advocate's fee £250
Type C – advice on quantum where C is a
child £150

(3) where the claimant or defendant is a protected party (see 19.07);
(4) where the claimant is bankrupt; or
(5) where the defendant's vehicle is registered outside the UK.

C STAGE 1: CLAIM NOTIFICATION

9.09 Figure 9.2 is a flow diagram showing the steps that have to be followed in Stages 1 and 2 of the RTA protocol. With the exception of the defendant only claim notification form (see 9.12), all communications under the RTA protocol must be sent electronically (RTA protocol, para 5.1).

Starting the RTA protocol process

9.10 The first step is to conduct a search using the <http://www.askCUEPI.com> website, which will generate a unique reference number for the claim (RTA protocol, para 6.3A). This website is run by the Claims and Underwriting Exchange, and is a means of checking whether the claimant has made a previous claim. Failing to use this reference number on the claim documents means that no costs will be allowed unless there are exceptional circumstances (CPR, r 45.24(2A)), but is not a valid reason for taking the claim out of the RTA protocol (para 6.8(2)).

Figure 9.2 Flow diagram of Stages 1 and 2 under the RTA protocol

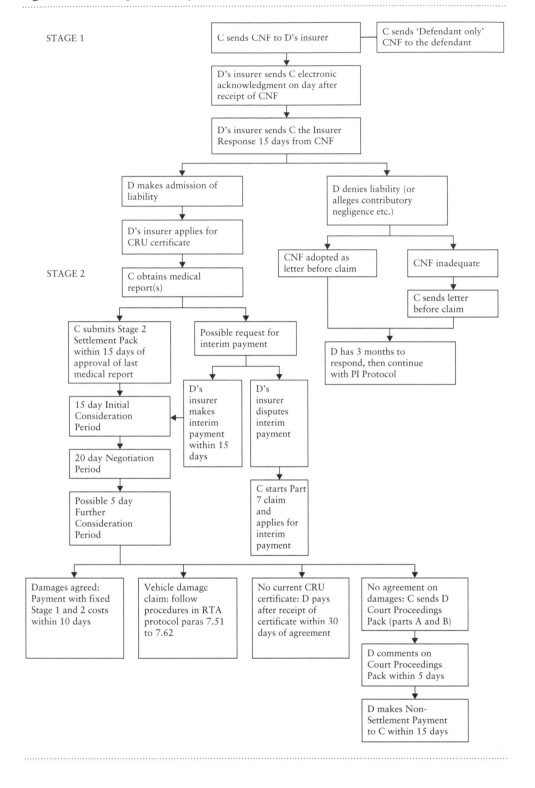

A claimant should then complete a claim notification form ('CNF', which is available on **9.11** the HM Courts and Tribunals Service website as form RTA 1). All boxes in the CNF that are marked as mandatory must be completed, together with the ask CUEPI reference number and electronic contact details. The claimant must make a reasonable attempt to complete those boxes that are not marked as mandatory (RTA protocol, para 6.3). Details of rehabilitation, following the principles in the Rehabilitation Code in the PI protocol (see 5.13), must be included in the CNF (para 6.7). There is an obligation to state whether any vehicle damage claim is being dealt with separately by third parties, or, if not, to include details of the vehicle damage claim together with relevant invoices and receipts (para 6.4). The CNF must be verified by a statement of truth. On the electronically completed form, this requirement is satisfied by entering the name of the person verifying the form in the signature box (para 6.6).

The CNF must be sent electronically to the defendant's insurer. The relevant address should **9.12** be available on the RTA PI Claims Process website at **<http://www.claimsportal.org.uk>**. To make use of this website it is necessary to register online. At the same time as the CNF is sent to the insurer, or as soon as practicable thereafter, a 'Defendant Only CNF' (form RTA 2) must be sent to the defendant by first-class post (para 6.2).

Response by defendant's insurer

An electronic acknowledgment must be sent by the defendant's insurer on the next busi- **9.13** ness day after receipt of the CNF (RTA protocol, para 6.10). The insurer has 15 days to investigate liability, and must complete the 'Insurer Response' section of the CNF ('the CNF response') and send it to the claimant within 15 business days of receipt of the CNF. The principal question for the insurer is whether liability will be admitted. Secondary questions are whether there will be an allegation of contributory negligence (para 6.15), or an allegation that a low-speed impact could not have caused the alleged injuries (para 6.19A). If liability is denied, brief reasons for that denial must be set out in the CNF response (para 6.16). An admission of liability for the purposes of the RTA protocol is by para 1.1(1) an admission that:

(a) the accident occurred;
(b) the accident was caused by the defendant's breach of duty;
(c) the defendant caused some loss to the claimant, the nature and extent of which is not admitted; and
(d) the defendant has no accrued defence under the Limitation Act 1980.

CRU certificate

The defendant must, before the end of Stage 1, apply for a CRU certificate of recoverable **9.14** benefits (RTA protocol, para 6.12). This is needed for negotiation purposes, and sets out the amount that the defendant has to pay to the government in reimbursement of State benefits paid to the claimant as a result of the relevant injury.

Stage 1 fixed costs

Except where the claimant is a child, the defendant must pay the Stage 1 fixed costs in **9.15** cases where liability is admitted or liability is admitted with an allegation of contributory negligence restricted to the claimant's admitted failure to wear a seat belt (RTA protocol, para 6.18). These costs must be paid within ten days after sending the CNF response to the claimant.

Litigants in person

9.16 Claimants who act in person have to comply with the RTA protocol. There is a decided measure of unreality about how litigants in person are expected to find out all that is needed, from identifying the various sources (the protocol, various provisions within the CPR, and PD 8B), to registering online with RTA PI Claims Process, submitting an electronic CNF to the appropriate insurer, and attaching scanned supporting documents. After a claimant acting in person has sent the CNF, the defendant's insurer is required to explain the period within which a response must be sent and that the claimant may obtain independent legal advice, and the defendant must undertake the ask CUEPI search (RTA protocol, para 5.10). The fixed costs in RTA protocol cases only apply where a claimant has a legal representative (para 4.6), so litigants in person are entitled to normal costs at litigant in person rates.

D STAGE 2: MEDICAL EVIDENCE AND NEGOTIATION

Medical evidence

9.17 On completion of Stage 1, the claimant should obtain a medical report, if one has not already been obtained (RTA protocol, para 7.1). Medical experts may, but do not have to, use the medical report standard form (RTA 3). It is expected that most claimants will obtain a medical report from one expert (para 7.2). In soft tissue injury claims the usual position is that the claimant must obtain a fixed cost medical report from an accredited medical expert selected using the MedCo Portal at **<http://www.medco.org.uk>** (para 7.8A). This applies to claims brought by occupants of motor vehicles where the significant injury caused is a soft tissue injury, and includes cases where there is a minor psychological injury of secondary importance (para 1.1(16)). MedCo Registration Solutions is a not-for-profit organization that runs an internet portal for sourcing medical experts. The expert chosen must have no involvement (even through an associate) in treating the claimant (paras 1.1(A1) and 1.1(10A)). Fairly modest fixed costs are recoverable for these reports (CPR rr 45.19(2A), 45.29I(2A)).

9.18 In claims not exceeding £10,000 it is expected that the medical expert will not need to see any medical records (para 7.5). Further experts may be instructed where the injuries require reports from more than one medical discipline. The claimant must check the factual accuracy of any medical report before it is sent to the defendant. There will be no further opportunity for the claimant to challenge the factual accuracy of a medical report after it has been sent to the defendant (para 7.3). Updating reports may be needed where, for example, the claimant is receiving continuing treatment (para 7.6), and this may justify an agreed extension to the protocol timeline (para 7.12).

Interim payment

9.19 Where there is a stay for updating reports, the claimant can request an interim payment of £1,000, which generally the defendant's insurer must pay within ten days (RTA protocol, paras 7.13–7.18). A claimant may make a request for an interim payment exceeding £1,000, in which case the defendant's insurer has 15 days to consider the matter. If the defendant fails to make the interim payment, or if the claimant is not satisfied with the defendant's response to the request, the claimant has ten days to give notice that the claim will no longer be governed by the RTA protocol.

Stage 2 settlement pack

After obtaining the necessary medical reports, the claimant must send the defendant's **9.20** insurers a Stage 2 settlement pack within 15 days of the claimant approving the final medical report and agreeing to rely on the prognosis in that report (RTA protocol, para 7.33). This pack consists of:

(a) the Stage 2 settlement pack form (form RTA 5). This includes space for the claimant to make an offer of what they will accept in settlement of the claim. Where the defendant alleges contributory negligence because of the claimant's failure to wear a seat belt, the form must give the claimant's suggested percentage reduction (which may be 0 per cent);
(b) medical reports (which in soft tissue injury claims must be fixed cost medical reports);
(c) evidence of pecuniary losses;
(d) evidence of disbursements (eg the cost of any medical report);
(e) any non-medical expert report;
(f) any medical records or photographs served with the medical reports; and
(g) any witness statements.

Consideration of claim and negotiation

There is a 35-day period (which can be extended by agreement) for consideration of the **9.21** Stage 2 settlement pack by the defendant ('the total consideration period', RTA protocol, para 7.35). This includes an initial period of up to 15 days for the defendant to consider the documents and make an offer. Within this period the defendant must either accept the offer made by the claimant on the Stage 2 settlement pack form or make a counter-offer using that form (para 7.38). When making a counter-offer the defendant must propose an amount for each head of damage. Where the defendant has obtained a CRU certificate the counter-offer must state the name and amount of any deductible amount (para 7.42). If there is no current CRU certificate, a fresh certificate will be needed (paras 7.49, 7.50, and 7.63). The defendant must also explain in the counter-offer why a particular head of damage is less than the amount claimed by the claimant. The explanation will assist the claimant when negotiating a settlement and will allow both parties to focus on those areas of the claim that remain in dispute (para 7.41).

Once the initial consideration period has elapsed, the defendant can only withdraw the **9.22** admission of liability with the claimant's consent (CPR, r 14.1B(2)(a)).

The remaining 20 days is for any further negotiation between the parties ('the negotiation **9.23** period'). If there is an offer within five days of the end of the 35-day period, there is an automatic five-day extension to give time for the other side to consider whether to accept the offer (para 7.37).

Terms of offers

Any offer to settle made at any stage by either party will automatically include, and cannot **9.24** exclude (RTA protocol, para 7.44):

(a) the Stage 1 and Stage 2 fixed costs in CPR, r 45.18, and Type C fixed costs of any additional advice on quantum;
(b) an agreement in principle to pay relevant disbursements under r 45.19; and
(c) in a soft tissue injury claim, the cost of obtaining a fixed cost medical report.

Payment after acceptance of offer

9.25 Where the claimant is an adult and the claim is settled during Stage 2, the defendant must pay:

(a) the agreed damages less any deductible amount which is payable to the CRU and any interim payment;

(b) any unpaid Stage 1 and the Stage 2 fixed costs in CPR, r 45.18, and Type C fixed costs of any additional advice on quantum; and

(c) the relevant disbursements under r 45.19.

9.26 These sums must be paid within ten days of agreeing the settlement (RTA protocol, para 7.47).

Failure to compromise

9.27 If the parties do not reach agreement in the total consideration period, the claimant is required by RTA protocol, para 7.64, to send the defendant's insurer the court proceedings pack (parts A and B) (forms RTA 6 and RTA 7), which must contain:

(a) the final schedule of the claimant's losses and the defendant's responses, together with supporting comments and evidence from both parties on the disputed heads of damage (part A); and

(b) the final offer and counter-offer from the Stage 2 settlement pack (part B).

9.28 The court proceedings pack (part A) must not raise anything that has not been raised in the Stage 2 settlement pack form (para 7.66). The defendant has five days to make any comments on this pack (para 5.67), and can nominate a legal representative to accept service of court proceedings (para 5.68).

Stage 2 payment

9.29 Where the claimant is an adult, the defendant must within 15 days of receipt of the court proceedings pack make a payment to the claimant of:

(a) the final offer of damages made by the defendant in the court proceedings pack, less any deductible amount which is payable to the CRU and any interim payment;

(b) any unpaid Stage 1 and the Stage 2 fixed costs; and

(c) any agreed disbursements.

E STAGE 3: PART 8 CLAIM TO DETERMINE QUANTUM

9.30 Figure 9.3 is a flow diagram showing the steps that have to be followed in Stage 3 in cases governed by the RTA protocol. Similar procedures apply to cases governed by the EL/PL protocol. Stage 3 involves a Part 8 claim to assess damages where the claim has not been settled in Stage 1 or 2. The procedure followed under PD 8B is a substantially modified version of the normal Part 8 procedure described in Chapter 8. Most of the provisions of CPR, Part 8 are disapplied (rr 8.2A, 8.3, 8.5, 8.6, 8.7, 8.8, and 8.9(c) are disapplied, see PD 8B, para 2.2).

Filing and service

9.31 By PD 8B, para 6.1, the claimant must file with the claim form and serve on the defendant:

(a) the court proceedings pack (part A);

(b) the court proceedings pack (part B) (the claimant and defendant's final offers) in a sealed envelope. These are treated as modified Part 36 offers (a subject dealt with in

Figure 9.3 Flow diagram of Stage 3 under the RTA protocol

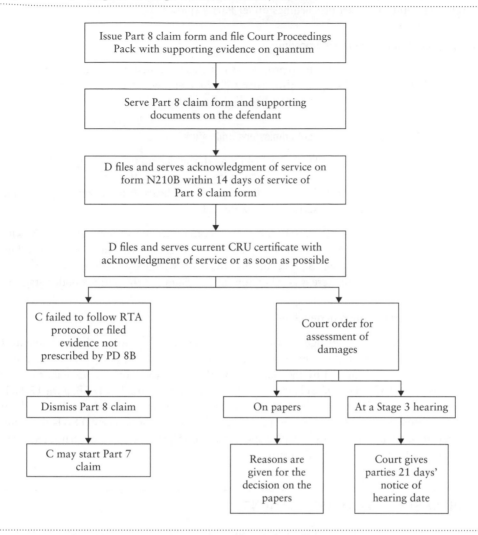

Chapter 36), and must not be communicated to the court until the claim is determined (CPR, r 36.28(1));

(c) copies of medical reports (which, with a minor exception, must be fixed cost medical reports in soft tissue injury claims (PD 8B, para 6.1A);

(d) evidence of special damages; and

(e) evidence of disbursements.

The claimant can only use documents that have already been sent to the defendant under **9.32** the relevant protocol (para 6.3).

Acknowledgment of service

The defendant must file and serve an acknowledgment of service in form N210B not more **9.33** than 14 days after service of the claim form (PD 8B, para 8.1). At the same time the defendant must file a current CRU certificate (para 8.2).

Where the defendant opposes the claim because the claimant has either not followed the **9.34** relevant protocol or has filed and served additional or new evidence with the claim form that had not been provided under the relevant protocol, the court will dismiss the claim and the claimant may start proceedings under Part 7 (para 9.1).

Changing to or from the PD 8B procedure

9.35 The court can order a Part 7 claim to proceed as if it was governed by the Stage 3 procedure in PD 8B (PD 8B, para 4.1). It may also order a PD 8B claim which is unsuitable for the PD 8B procedure to continue as if it were a Part 7 claim (para 7.2(2)).

Withdrawal of RTA or EL/PL protocol admissions and offers

9.36 Once the Part 8 claim under PD 8B has been issued, the defendant can only withdraw an admission made under the relevant protocol with the consent of all the other parties or with the court's permission (CPR, r 14.1B(2)(b)). An application for permission is made using the Part 23 procedure described in Chapter 23.

9.37 A party may only withdraw a RTA or EL/PL protocol offer after proceedings have started with the court's permission (PD 8B, para 10.1). Where the court gives permission the claim will no longer continue under the Stage 3 procedure and the court will give directions. The court will only give permission where there is good reason for the claim not to continue under Stage 3.

Directions for determination of quantum

9.38 After the defendant acknowledges service, the court will decide whether the assessment of damages will be conducted on the papers or at a hearing (PD 8B, para 11.1). There will be a hearing if it is requested by the claimant on the claim form or the defendant on the acknowledgment of service. The claim will not be allocated to a track (PD 8B, para 17.1). If the court concludes that further evidence is required, it will be converted to a Part 7 claim and will not proceed under PD 8B (para 7.2(1)). A determination under PD 8B is therefore a matter of the court assessing the value of the claim on the basis of the evidence gathered under Stages 1 and 2 of the relevant protocol.

F CHILD SETTLEMENT APPLICATIONS

9.39 Where the claimant is a child the prudent course is to obtain court approval of any settlement (CPR, r 21.10(2)). It is for this reason that the automatic payment provisions in Stage 2 of the RTA and EL/PL protocols only apply where the claimant is not a child.

9.40 Court approval of a settlement in a claim by a child which is governed by a relevant protocol has to be sought under PD 8B (PD 8B, para 1.1(2)). In these cases, PD 8B, para 6.5 provides that the claimant must provide to the court the following documents when the Part 8 claim is issued in addition to the standard documents required under PD 8B:

(a) a draft consent order;
(b) the advice by counsel, solicitor, or other legal representative on the amount of damages; and
(c) a statement verified by a statement of truth signed by the litigation friend which confirms whether the child has recovered in accordance with the prognosis and whether there are any continuing symptoms.

9.41 This statement at sub-para (c) enables the court to decide whether to order the child to attend the settlement hearing. At the hearing the court will decide whether the proposed settlement terms are fair compensation for the benefit of the child. Where the settlement is not approved the claim will no longer continue under the Stage 3 procedure and the court will give directions (para 12.5).

G LIMITATION

Where compliance with the RTA or EL/PL protocol is not possible before the expiry of the **9.42** limitation period, the claimant may start proceedings and apply to the court for an order to stay (ie suspend) the proceedings while the parties take steps to follow the protocol (eg RTA protocol, para 5.7 and see 30.50). Such proceedings should be commenced under Part 8 and follow the procedure in PD 8B. If the parties are unable to reach a settlement while the claim is stayed by the end of Stage 2 of the protocol, the claimant must, in order to proceed to Stage 3, apply to lift the stay and request directions in the existing proceedings (para 5.8).

H FIXED COSTS UNDER THE RTA AND EL/PL PROTOCOLS

There is a detailed system of fixed costs in RTA and EL/PL protocol claims which apply **9.43** while the claim is proceeding under the relevant protocol. The basic amounts laid down by the RTA protocol are included in figure 9.1. The detailed rules are in CPR, rr 45.16–45.27, and the effect of the parties' final offers (which are revealed to the judge once the claim is determined) is as set out in r 36.29.

A second system of fixed costs applies when a claim leaves either the RTA or EL/PL protocol **9.44** (r 45.29A(1)), which effectively lays down a fixed costs system for fast track personal injuries claims. The fixed costs are the only costs recoverable in these cases. This means there is no jurisdiction to make a separate costs order for things like pre-action disclosure applications (*Sharp v Leeds City Council* [2017] EWCA Civ 33). Disease cases are excluded from the fixed costs regime (r 45.29A(2)), and so are claims leaving either the RTA or EL/PL protocols during any period they are allocated to the multi-track (r 45.29B). There are detailed rules on how much will be allowed by way of fixed costs (rr 45.29B–45.29L). Broadly:

(a) fixed costs are higher for claims with a greater value. The main categories are claims valued between £1,000 and £5,000, claims over £5,000 up to £10,000, and claims over £10,000. For claimants this is the amount of the agreed settlement or the amount found at trial (r 45.29C). For defendants it is the sum specified in the claim form (r 45.29F(4));
(b) fixed costs are higher the further the case proceeds. The staging points are settlement before issuing a Part 7 claim, settlement after issue but before trial, and disposal at trial; and
(c) higher amounts are provided for EL and PL claims than RTA claims.

I CASES WHERE PARTIES CAN STOP FOLLOWING THE RTA OR EL/PL PROTOCOLS

The relevant protocol ceases to apply in the following situations (references are to the RTA **9.45** protocol):

(a) where, at any stage, the claimant notifies the defendant that the claim has now been revalued at more than £25,000 (para 4.3);
(b) where the defendant notifies the claimant that it considers that inadequate mandatory information has been provided in the CNF (paras 6.8 and 6.15(4)(a));
(c) where the defendant alleges contributory negligence (other than in relation to the claimant's admitted failure to wear a seat belt) (para 6.15(1));

(d) where the defendant does not admit liability within the 15 days allowed for sending the CNF response (para 6.15(3));

(e) where the defendant does not complete and send the CNF response within the 15 days allowed (para 6.15(2));

(f) where the defendant notifies the claimant that the defendant considers that if proceedings were issued the small claims track would be the normal track for that claim (para 6.15(4)(b));

(g) where the defendant fails to pay the Stage 1 fixed costs within the ten-day period specified in para 6.18, and the claimant gives written notice that the claim will no longer continue under the protocol to the defendant within ten days thereafter (para 6.19);

(h) where the claimant is not satisfied with the defendant's response to a request for an interim payment in Stage 2 (paras 7.28 and 7.29);

(i) where the defendant gives notice to the claimant within the initial 15-day consideration period after receiving the Stage 2 settlement pack that the defendant considers that the small claims track would be the normal track for the claim (para 7.39(a)); or

(j) where the defendant gives notice to the claimant within the initial 15-day consideration period after receiving the Stage 2 settlement pack withdrawing the admission of causation (para 7.39(b));

(k) where the defendant does not respond within the initial 15-day consideration period (para 7.40);

(l) where a party withdraws an offer made in the Stage 2 settlement pack form after the total consideration period (para 7.46);

(m) where the defendant fails to make the Stage 2 payment (para 7.75); and

(n) where the claimant gives notice to the defendant that the claim is unsuitable for the protocol (eg because there are complex issues of fact or law in relation to the vehicle-related damages) (para 7.76).

9.46   Where a claim drops out of the RTA protocol in Stage 1, pre-action conduct should continue under the PI protocol where appropriate (para 6.17). Generally, the CNF will stand as the letter before claim for the purposes of the PI protocol, unless the CNF is regarded as inadequate. Where a case drops out of the RTA protocol in Stage 2, further progress is often through starting a Part 7 claim (paras 7.28, 7.29, 7.39, 7.40, and 7.75). Claims which are discontinued under the protocol cannot subsequently re-enter the process (para 5.11).

KEY POINTS SUMMARY

9.47
- The RTA protocol is for road traffic accident personal injury claims between £1,000 and £25,000 where the defendant admits liability.

- A similar protocol applies to employers' liability and public liability claims, again with values between £1,000 and £25,000.

- Stage 1 covers the commencement of the protocol by sending the CNF, with a response by the defendant's insurer.

- Stage 2 covers obtaining medical reports followed by a 35-day period of consideration and negotiation.

- The expectation is that many cases will be settled at Stage 2, together with fixed costs.

- If the case is not settled, Stage 2 ends with the claimant sending the defendant's insurer a court proceedings pack (parts A and B), and the defendant making a part payment consisting of the minimum amounts that will become payable after Stage 3.

- Stage 3 is a Part 8 claim leading to an assessment of damages by the court, with fixed costs.

10

ALTERNATIVE DISPUTE RESOLUTION

A ADR PROCESSES 10.02
B ADR OR COURT PROCEEDINGS 10.04
C COST OF ADR 10.10
D REFERENCE TO ADR 10.11
E COURT INVOLVEMENT IN ADR 10.12
Key points summary 10.17

Sir Rupert Jackson has said that alternative dispute resolution ('ADR'), particularly media- **10.01** tion, has a vital role to play in reducing the costs of civil disputes by fomenting the early settlement of cases. In the preface to the *White Book* (Sweet & Maxwell, 2014) Sir Rupert said: 'The aim is that, in general, no case should come to trial without the parties at least having seriously considered some form of ADR to seek to settle their dispute.' ADR takes many forms, from simple negotiations, through to the complexity of commercial arbitrations. The full range of possibilities are discussed in S Blake, J Browne, and S Sime, *The Jackson ADR Handbook* (2nd edn, Oxford University Press, 2016). As a result there should be a form of ADR appropriate to assist in resolving most disputes and differences.

A ADR PROCESSES

ADR broadly falls into adjudicative and non-adjudicative processes, depending on whether **10.02** the process results in a decision made by a third party neutral (adjudicative), or whether the process is aimed at enabling the parties to reach an agreed settlement (non-adjudicative). The main types of ADR process are:

(a) negotiation, either between the parties directly, or through their legal representatives;
(b) mediation, where a third party neutral facilitates the parties in seeking a settlement;
(c) conciliation, which is similar to mediation, but may have a statutory framework, such as conciliation services provided by the Advisory, Conciliation and Arbitration Service ('ACAS') in employment disputes;
(d) early neutral evaluation ('ENE'), in which a third party neutral is appointed to evaluate all or part of a dispute and to provide an opinion on the merits;
(e) expert determination ('ED'), under which an expert is appointed by the parties to decide all or part of a dispute;
(f) complaints and ombudsman schemes, which are frequently used to deal with problems raised by customers or users of public services;
(g) adjudication, which is used to provide a speedy decision in construction industry disputes; and
(h) arbitration, which is in effect a private form of litigation.

Table 10.1 sets out the key features of four types of ADR process. The various commercial **10.03** dispute resolution providers have put together a number of different dispute resolution models, together with published rules, which allows parties to choose the one which is best suited for resolving their dispute. Arbitration is intended to be a direct replacement for litigation, with an arbitrator making a decision which is binding on the parties. Other ADR procedures provide a means of finding a solution, but leave litigation open if the parties do not reach a compromise. For example, mediation can assist the parties in focusing on the issues that are causing the problem, which in turn can help them in reaching an agreement either of the whole dispute, or in relation to aspects of the dispute. If they do not reach an overall compromise, litigation is available to decide the unresolved matters.

Table 10.1 ADR procedures

Type	Main features	Suitable cases
Commercial arbitration	Determination by professional arbitrator. Complex and potentially expensive procedure. Avoids court and avoids appeals.	Commercial cases Building disputes Contracts with arbitration clauses
Adjudication in construction disputes	Speedy independent adjudication of disputes involving builders. Enables contractors to get paid without delay. Not final.	Non-payment for building work
Mediation (formal)	Mediator facilitates negotiation, but does not make decisions. Aims at negotiated settlement or narrowing of issues. Mediator often a senior professional.	Personal injuries Clinical disputes Professional negligence General litigation
Community mediation	Mediator acts as a facilitator. Usually adopts a more informal approach than in formal mediation. Mediator often respected member of the community.	Neighbour disputes Antisocial behaviour

B ADR OR COURT PROCEEDINGS

Advantages and disadvantages of ADR and litigation

10.04 Advantages claimed for ADR include:

(a) ADR procedures are more flexible than litigation;

(b) ADR procedures are usually simpler than litigation, with less demanding preparation required, and the strict rules of evidence not applying;

(c) ADR procedures can be arranged to suit the convenience of the parties, in a suitable location, resulting in minimum of disruption to their businesses;

(d) ADR is often speedier than litigation;

(e) trials in litigation are generally in public, whereas ADR takes place in private;

(f) ADR is usually less stressful than litigation;

(g) ADR can produce solutions going beyond the strict parameters of the original dispute. A court only has jurisdiction to make orders within the confines of the issues raised by the statements of case;

(h) ADR is less confrontational, which means it provides a better prospect of enabling parties to maintain long-term relationships (eg between businesses or neighbours; there are situations, eg, where there is a distribution contract, or a commercial lease, where the parties are tied into a long-term relationship in any event);

(i) ADR is felt to be less expensive than litigation;

(j) arbitration awards are generally final, so usually avoid the risk of the parties facing an appeal;

(k) arbitration works well in international disputes, where arbitration awards can be easily enforced across different jurisdictions, provided the country in question is one of the more than 150 countries that are signatories to the New York Convention 1958 (<http://www.uncitral.org>); and

(l) while there is more limited international recognition of mediation agreements, cross-border mediation settlements within the EU can be enforced using a mediation settlement enforcement order under the Mediation Directive (Directive 2008/52/EC).

Disadvantages involved in ADR procedures can include the following: **10.05**

(a) ADR procedures agreed before a dispute arose may be inappropriate for resolving the actual dispute that has arisen;

(b) where parties agree to ADR after a dispute has arisen, the parties may find it difficult to agree the details of the procedure to be followed (eg the identity of the arbitrator or mediator, payment of fees, rules to govern the ADR);

(c) in ADR procedures where the parties have to pay fees to the arbitrator or mediator, the fees may make the process more expensive than litigation;

(d) ADR can on occasion be an expensive, time-consuming diversion, particularly if one of the parties is not genuine about their participation in the procedure;

(e) a party with a strong case on the law and evidence may have to abandon their actual rights if the ADR procedure is to achieve anything;

(f) litigation may become inevitable if an arbitrator or an expert in ED makes an error of law or jurisdiction, thereby substantially increasing the costs and delay;

(g) ADR procedures sometimes become unworkable if there are multiple parties; and

(h) enforcement of the amount determined (by agreement or by the tribunal) is easier in litigation, when compared to non-arbitration ADR procedures.

Where the balance lies in any individual case depends on the circumstances. If a party **10.06** needs a remedy that only a court can provide, there is no real option. If both sides to a dispute realize that each has strengths and weaknesses, mediation or conciliation can save them both from becoming embroiled in protracted litigation. Parties faced with a two-week trial may well find a day spent in mediation will save them a great deal of time and costs. Parties with a sensitive business dispute may prefer to arbitrate in order to ensure there is no public trial. Sometimes a party with a very strong case (but not sufficiently strong to seek summary judgment) will achieve a great deal by using ADR. For example, the services of a mediator might make it plain to the other side that there are substantial problems with their case, and they should be more realistic about settling the claim.

The choice between using ADR or going to court may also turn on what the client is seek- **10.07** ing to achieve. It may be that one mode of dispute resolution is better at delivering the required result than the other. By using ADR, any of the following may be achieved:

(a) a change in the way the other party behaves, or measures to prevent a similar problem arising again;

(b) putting right a mistake;

(c) a promise that the other party will not do something;

(d) the repair or replacement of an item purchased;

(e) an apology, or an explanation; or

(f) compensation.

10.08　Court proceedings may result in:

(a) a prohibitory injunction (eg to stop tortious conduct);
(b) specific performance of a contractual obligation;
(c) rectification of a document, or rescission of a contract;
(d) the return of property (land or goods);
(e) compensation; or
(f) a declaration from the court about the respective rights of the parties.

10.09　A client whose main interest is to obtain compensation may achieve that goal by using mediation or resorting to litigation. On the other hand, a client who is more interested in preventing the same thing happening to other people, or in getting an apology, may be best advised to use a complaints procedure followed up by a reference to the relevant ombudsman. Some matters are very urgent and important, and going to court may be the only way to safeguard the client's interests. Examples are where there is an imminent threat to the client's property, or where publication of a libel is likely to happen in the next edition of a newspaper. Further, there are some cases where court approval is essential, for example cases involving unclear provisions in wills, and approval of compromises for clients who lack legal capacity. If limitation is about to expire, it may be necessary to issue court proceedings in order to preserve the client's rights.

C COST OF ADR

10.10　While ADR is generally regarded as being cheaper than litigation, it can still be expensive. Much depends on the type of ADR used, and the value and complexity of the dispute. For example:

(a) community mediation is usually free. Parties may incur travel and other expenses;
(b) ombudsman schemes are free to the person complaining;
(c) family mediation services often charge an hourly rate. Some have a scale of fees, based on the financial circumstances of the client. Family mediation may be funded through legal aid;
(d) commercial mediation service providers charge according to the complexity and value of the claim. Mediation fees are calculated on the basis of an instruction fee per party (typically in the region of £250) plus an hourly mediation rate ranging from £200 per hour for junior mediators to £600 per hour for senior mediators. There may also be room hire costs and fees for other services. It is possible that legal aid will pay the cost of mediation for a party who is financially eligible;
(e) consumer arbitration schemes typically cost between £10 and £100, but some are free; and
(f) commercial arbitration providers may charge a registration fee, and/or a deposit (both of which could be £2,000 or £3,000, through to fees up to £500,000 in large commercial cases), and/or daily or hourly fees for the arbitrator or arbitrators. Some arbitrations use panels of three arbitrators. Fees and room charges are usually similar to the amounts payable for commercial mediation.

D REFERENCE TO ADR

10.11　Use of ADR is almost always voluntary, so usually rests on an agreement between the parties. The parties can agree to use ADR either before or after a dispute arises. Contracting parties who anticipate possible problems ahead may insert an ADR clause into their contract, sometimes as part of the contract's standard terms and conditions. See table 10.2 for typical clauses. Such a clause has to be adhered to. If legal proceedings are commenced in breach of an agreement to use ADR, particularly arbitration (for which, see the Arbitration Act 1996, s 9), the court is likely to grant a stay of the proceedings or even an anti-suit injunction, and award costs on the indemnity basis (see 30.52 and 46.47).

Table 10.2 ADR Contract Clauses

Type of clause	Wording
Reference to arbitration	Any dispute or difference arising out of or in connection with this contract shall be determined by the appointment of a single arbitrator to be agreed between the parties, or failing agreement within 14 days after either party has given to the other a written request to concur in the appointment of an arbitrator, by an arbitrator to be appointed by the President or a Vice President of the Chartered Institute of Arbitrators. The seat of the arbitration shall be England and Wales.
Rules for the arbitration	The arbitration shall be governed by both the Arbitration Act 1996 and the Controlled Cost Rules of the Chartered Institute of Arbitrators ('the Rules'), or any amendments to those provisions. The Rules are deemed to be incorporated by reference into this clause.
Mediation	Any dispute arising out of or in connection with this contract shall, at first instance, be referred to a mediator for resolution. The parties shall attempt to agree upon the appointment of a mediator, upon receipt, by either of them, of a written notice to concur in such appointment. Should the parties fail to agree within 14 days, either party, upon giving written notice, may apply to the President or the Deputy President, for the time being, of the Chartered Institute of Arbitrators, for the appointment of a mediator.

E COURT INVOLVEMENT IN ADR

Active case management includes encouraging the parties to use ADR if the court consid- **10.12**
ers that appropriate, and facilitates its use (CPR, r 1.4(2)(e)). The position taken by the courts, particularly *Halsey v Milton Keynes General NHS Trust* [2004] 1 WLR 3002 and the pre-action protocols (see Chapter 5), has been that the parties are required to consider ADR, but with the courts stopping short of ordering them to engage in ADR. Lawyers on both sides are obliged to consider alternatives to litigation, such as mediation, and to resort to proceedings only where this is really unavoidable (*Cowl v Plymouth City Council* (2001) *The Times*, 8 January 2002). The courts encourage the use of ADR by:

(a) holding parties to pre-dispute agreements to use ADR by granting stays to proceedings commenced in breach of an ADR clause;
(b) making orders declaring the rights of the parties under ADR clauses, or providing machinery for implementing ADR clauses;
(c) staying court proceedings, typically for a month, at the case management conference stage for the purpose of using ADR;
(d) ensuring the parties have addressed, or will address, whether ADR might be useful as a means of resolving their dispute, typically at case management conferences;
(e) making orders that make it plain that the court expects serious consideration to be given to the use of ADR (see figure 10.1). The model directions on the Ministry of Justice website contain similar provisions, such as para 2 of the basic multi-track directions (see figure 15.2);
(f) imposing costs sanctions on parties who act unreasonably in relation to ADR.

Figure 10.1 Commercial Court ADR Order

1. On or before [date] the parties shall exchange lists of three neutral individuals who are available to conduct ADR procedures in this case prior to [date]. Each party may [in addition] [in the alternative] provide a list identifying the constitution of one or more panels of neutral individuals who are available to conduct ADR procedures in this case prior to [date].

2. On or before [date] the parties shall in good faith endeavour to agree a neutral individual or panel from the lists so exchanged and provided.

3. Failing such agreement by [date] the Case Management Conference will be restored to enable the Court to facilitate agreement on a neutral individual or panel.

4. The parties shall take such serious steps as they may be advised to resolve their disputes by ADR procedures before the neutral individual or panel so chosen by no later than [date].

5. If the case is not finally settled, the parties shall inform the Court by letter prior to [disclosure of documents/exchange of witness statements/exchange of experts' reports] what steps towards ADR have been taken and (without prejudice to matters of privilege) why such steps have failed. If the parties have failed to initiate ADR procedures the Case Management Conference is to be restored for further consideration of the case.

6. [Costs].

Note: The term 'ADR procedures' is deliberately used in the draft ADR order. This is in order to emphasize that (save where otherwise provided) the parties are free to use the ADR procedure that they regard as most suitable, be it mediation, early neutral evaluation, non-binding arbitration, etc.

10.13 There is a Small Claims Mediation Service operated by Her Majesty's Courts and Tribunals Service that applies to claims that would normally be allocated to the small claims track, other than RTA, personal injury, and housing disrepair claims (CPR, r 26.4A). When all parties indicate on their directions questionnaires that they agree to mediation, the claim will be referred to the Mediation Service. If this results in the claim being settled, the proceedings will be stayed with permission to apply for judgment for the unpaid balance of the settlement agreement or for the claim to be restored for hearing of the full amount claimed. If the claim is not settled, it will be allocated to a track no later than four weeks after the last directions questionnaire was filed (r 26.5(2A)).

10.14 Case management powers available to the court include conducting an ENE with the aim of helping the parties settle their litigation (CPR, r 3.1(2)(m)). This rule gives effect to *Seals v Williams* [2015] EWHC 1829 (Ch). ENE can be particularly useful where the parties have differing views of the issues in dispute and the strength of their respective cases. Norris J said conducting an ENE, and expressing provisional, non-binding, views on a particular hypothesis or upon the judge's overall impression of the case was an inherent part of the judicial function. An ENE order requires careful directions, with the settlement judge having no further involvement with the case after the ENE.

10.15 Costs sanctions may be imposed if a party unreasonably refuses an offer to use ADR (*Halsey v Milton Keynes General NHS Trust* [2004] 1 WLR 3002). As a general rule, failing to respond to an invitation to participate in ADR will in itself be unreasonable (*PGF II SA v OMFS Co 1 Ltd* [2014] 1 WLR 1386). Assuming a party states their grounds for refusing ADR at the time, according to *Halsey v Milton Keynes General NHS Trust* reasonableness has to be considered taking into account all the circumstances of the case, but in particular:

(a) the nature of the dispute. Most cases are suitable for ADR, but there are some, such as fraud cases, and where injunctive relief is required, which are not;

(b) the merits of the case: it may not be unreasonable to refuse ADR if the party has a very strong case;

(c) the extent to which other ADR methods have been attempted;

(d) whether ADR costs would be disproportionately large;

(e) whether any delay in arranging ADR would be prejudicial;

(f) whether ADR had a reasonable prospect of success; and

(g) whether the court has made an ADR order.

A related problem is in deciding the best time to attempt some form of ADR. Premature **10.16** attempts at mediation can waste costs. Delaying making a reference to ADR can mean that a case passes the point where costs already expended by both sides make a negotiated settlement almost impossible. See *Nigel Witham Ltd v Smith* [2008] CILL 2557.

KEY POINTS SUMMARY

- Adjudicative ADR results in the third party neutral deciding the dispute or difference between **10.17** the parties.

- Non-adjudicative ADR processes involve moving the parties towards reaching a compromise agreement between themselves.

- Rules of court require parties to consider using ADR.

- Sanctions may be imposed on parties who act unreasonably.

11

SERVICE OUTSIDE THE JURISDICTION

A SERVICE ON A FOREIGN DEFENDANT
    WITHIN THE JURISDICTION..........11.04
B SUBMISSION TO THE JURISDICTION ...11.07
C CASES OUTSIDE THE GENERAL RULES..11.10
D RECAST JUDGMENTS REGULATION 11.15
E ASSUMED JURISDICTION...........11.36
F SERVICE ABROAD.................11.47

G PREVENTING CONFLICTS IN
    JURISDICTION....................11.52
H INTERIM RELIEF IN SUPPORT
    OF FOREIGN PROCEEDINGS.........11.62
I JUDGMENT IN DEFAULT 11.64
    Key points summary 11.65

11.01 Litigation of an international character potentially raises problems over which legal system should deal with a particular case. This may arise where the litigants are in different countries, or where the problem giving rise to the litigation took place in a different country, or where the subject matter of the dispute (such as a dispute over land, or about shares in a company) is situated in a different country. For this purpose the jurisdiction is England and Wales. Different solutions have been devised for different situations. In what may be described as claims *in rem*, such as claims involving title to land, jurisdiction is given to the country where the property is located (see 11.10ff). Sometimes, particularly in commercial contracts, the parties agree to a 'jurisdiction clause' to confer jurisdiction on the courts of a named country, a position that is usually upheld by the courts. In other cases the defendant will 'submit to the jurisdiction' by not objecting to service (see 11.07). Even in the absence of an agreement, the courts in England and Wales (and they are not alone in this) will, in suitable cases, 'assume' jurisdiction over certain cases despite their international nature (see 11.36). In other cases jurisdiction between competing jurisdictions may be resolved by international conventions.

11.02 The inter-relation between assumed jurisdiction and the jurisdiction conventions is broadly that:

(a) where the defendant is outside Europe and one or two other countries, service outside the jurisdiction is only allowed with the court's permission under CPR, r 6.36;

(b) Regulation (EU) No 1215/2012 of the European Parliament and Council (the 'recast Judgments Regulation') covers cases where the parties are domiciled in Member States of the EU. The primary rule is that defendants must be sued where they are domiciled, but there are wide exceptions which, if they apply, result in the claimant being able to serve proceedings outside the jurisdiction without the court's permission (see 11.15ff);

(c) similar arrangements also apply to Iceland, Norway, and Switzerland (under the Lugano Convention), and different 'parts' of the UK (England and Wales, Scotland, and Northern Ireland, under what is called the Modified Convention, set out in the CJJA 1982, Sch 4); and

(d) claims brought under exclusive choice of court agreements under the Convention on Choice of Court Agreements (the Hague Convention 2005). At present the Hague

Convention 2005 has been ratified only by the EU and Mexico. These claims can also be served outside the jurisdiction without court permission (CPR, r 6.33(2B)).

The courts are also concerned that the same dispute should not be litigated in several coun- **11.03** tries at the same time, with the risk of irreconcilable judgments and difficulties regarding the recognition of judgments for enforcement purposes. These problems are addressed by rules in the recast Judgments Regulation requiring courts other than the one first seized of the case either to decline jurisdiction or stay their proceedings (see 11.52–11.54), and (in relation to assumed jurisdiction) by the courts' powers to stay English proceedings on the ground of *forum non conveniens* (see 11.55ff) and to grant injunctions to restrain foreign proceedings (see 11.60). Determining the system of law to be applied to resolve legal proceedings where one or more of the parties is in an overseas jurisdiction is a matter of private international law. As such it is outside the scope of this book, and specialist works should be consulted.

A SERVICE ON A FOREIGN DEFENDANT WITHIN THE JURISDICTION

Under the assumed jurisdiction rules, a foreign defendant is amenable to the jurisdiction **11.04** of the courts in this country if process is served upon the defendant within the jurisdic- tion. Applying this rule, jurisdiction was established in *Maharanee Seethaderi Gaekwar of Baroda v Wildenstein* [1972] 2 QB 283, where the proceedings were served on the defendant while on a temporary visit to this country to attend the Ascot Races. This rule has been abolished for cases governed by the recast Judgments Regulation, which by art 5(2) provides that jurisdiction against EU defendants cannot be founded on national rules.

It is possible to issue a claim form against a foreign defendant marked 'Not to be served **11.05** out of the jurisdiction'. The intention when this is done is usually either to effect service on the defendant during a temporary visit to this country (unless the defendant lives in the EU) or to secure the defendant's agreement to service within the jurisdiction (often on English solicitors). The period of validity of an originating process intended to be served within the jurisdiction is four months, not six (CPR, r 7.5(1) and (2)).

If a domestic claim form has been issued, and it is later discovered that the defendant is **11.06** outside the jurisdiction, or if a claim form marked 'Not to be served out of the jurisdiction' cannot be served within the jurisdiction for any reason, the proper procedure is to apply for permission to issue a concurrent claim form for service outside the jurisdiction (a matter of practice not expressly covered by the CPR).

B SUBMISSION TO THE JURISDICTION

Regardless of whether the court would otherwise have jurisdiction, a defendant may submit to **11.07** the jurisdiction of the courts of this country. It may be that a defendant recognizes the advan- tages of litigating in England, and will agree to English proceedings being served at the offices of a solicitor in England. Alternatively, a domestic claim form may be sent to a defendant out- side the jurisdiction in breach of the rules requiring permission to serve (see 11.36ff), and the defendant proceeds to contest the claim on its merits without objecting to the defects in service. In the absence of any express agreement to submit to the jurisdiction, it is a question whether the defendant's conduct, when viewed objectively in the context of all the circumstances of the case, is inconsistent with maintaining an objection to the jurisdiction of the court.

A defendant who is served with proceedings in breach of the rules on service outside the **11.08** jurisdiction and who intends to dispute jurisdiction should acknowledge service and make an application under CPR, Part 11, disputing the jurisdiction of the court within 14 days of acknowledging. If an application is made within this time, conduct will be treated as a submission to the jurisdiction only if it is wholly unequivocal (see 12.13–12.18).

11.09 A claimant who has commenced proceedings gives the court jurisdiction to hear a counter-claim even if it covers issues that took place outside the jurisdiction.

C CASES OUTSIDE THE GENERAL RULES

11.10 Certain types of proceedings affect rights *in rem*. Both under the common law rules and under the recast Judgments Regulation special rules govern where many of these types of proceedings must be litigated. The main policy consideration justifying these special rules is that rights *in rem* are often protected by detailed national laws, and the courts of the country in question are in the best position to apply them.

Exclusive jurisdiction under the recast Judgments Regulation

11.11 Article 24 of the recast Judgments Regulation allocates exclusive jurisdiction, regardless of the domicile of the parties, over five categories of cases. The courts of the contracting States are required, of their own motion, to declare they have no jurisdiction in these cases (art 27).

11.12 'Regardless of the domicile', the phrase used in art 24, applies as between the courts of Member States (*Choudhary v Bhatter* [2010] 2 All ER 1031). It does not create an 'extra-EU jurisdiction' or 'universal international jurisdiction' (*Lucasfilm Ltd v Ainsworth* [2010] Ch 503 at [129], [183]).

11.13 Exclusive jurisdiction under the recast Judgments Regulation is given in:

(a) proceedings which have as their object rights *in rem* in immovable property or tenancies of immovable property to the courts of the contracting State in which the property is situated (art 24(1));

(b) proceedings having as their object the validity of the constitution, nullity, or dissolution of companies or associations of natural or legal persons, or of their organs, to the courts in the country where the relevant body has its 'seat' (art 24(2)). This is the country where the company or association was incorporated or formed, or where its central management and control are exercised (CJJA 1982, s 43(2));

(c) proceedings concerning the validity of entries in a public register to the courts of the State where the register is kept (art 24(3));

(d) proceedings concerning the registration or validity of patents, trade marks, designs, and similar rights to the courts of the State where the property in question has been registered or where registration has been applied for (art 24(4)). This does not extend to claims for infringement of patents, which are claims in tort and may be brought in accordance with art 7(3) (see 11.27); and

(e) enforcement proceedings to the courts of the State in which the judgment is to be enforced (art 24(5)).

Under the assumed jurisdiction rules

11.14 There is a similar list of special cases under the rules governing assumed jurisdiction:

(a) claims founded on a dispute as to the title to, or possession of, land must be brought in the courts of the country where the land is situated (*British South Africa Co v Companhia de Moçambique* [1893] AC 602);

(b) claims founded on the validity or infringement of foreign copyrights, trade marks, and patents have to be brought in the country where they are registered (*Tyburn Productions Ltd v Conan Doyle* [1991] Ch 75); and

(c) family law cases are governed by the Domicile and Matrimonial Proceedings Act 1973, s 5 and Council Regulation (EC) No 2201/2003.

D RECAST JUDGMENTS REGULATION

The recast Judgments Regulation is designed to determine the international jurisdiction of the courts of the Member States, to facilitate recognition, and to introduce a simple procedure for securing the international enforcement of judgments. Where it applies, the recast Judgments Regulation prevails over any national rules on jurisdiction (*Corman-Collins SA v La Maison du Whiskey SA* (Case C-9/12) [2014] QB 431). The main rule is that a claim must be brought in the courts of the country where the defendant is domiciled. However, there are many exceptions. Where the recast Judgments Regulation applies to a defendant outside the jurisdiction, English proceedings may be issued and served without permission. **11.15**

It is important that the recast Judgments Regulation is interpreted in the same way in all the Member States. Obviously, there are many differences in the domestic laws applied in the various Member States, particularly between the civil and common law systems. The Court of Justice of the European Union ('CJEU') has therefore regularly decided that legal concepts used in what is now the recast Judgments Regulation must be given a 'Community meaning'. This involves attempting to discover shared principles, a far from simple task. **11.16**

Scope of the recast Judgments Regulation

By art 1 the recast Judgments Regulation applies to civil and commercial proceedings whatever the nature of the court or tribunal. It does not apply to revenue, customs, social security, insolvency, arbitration (because this is covered by the New York Convention, 1958), or administrative matters, nor to proceedings relating to the status or legal capacity of natural persons, rights in property arising out of a matrimonial relationship (which are governed by Council Regulation (EC) No 2201/2003), wills, or succession. Consequently, it does not apply to a claim by or against a public law body concerning the exercise of its public powers (*Grovit v De Nederlandsche Bank NV* [2008] 1 WLR 51). **11.17**

It is substantive jurisdiction that is determined by the jurisdictional provisions of the Judgments Regulation. This stems from the word 'sued' in art 4(1) (see 11.19). It means that a court with jurisdiction over the substantive claim also has jurisdiction to grant interim or ancillary orders in the claim (*Masri v Consolidated Contractors International (UK) Ltd (No 4)* [2010] 1 AC 90). **11.18**

Domicile

The general rule

The general rule laid down by the recast Judgments Regulation, art 4(1) is that a person must be sued in the courts of the Member State where the defendant is domiciled. Domicile of individuals is governed by the Civil Jurisdiction and Judgments Order 2001 (SI 2001/3929), Sch 1, para 9(2), which says an individual is domiciled in the UK if: **11.19**

(a) he is resident in the UK; and

(b) the nature and circumstances of his residence indicate that he has a substantial connection with the UK.

11.20   By para 9(6), unless the contrary is proved, an individual is presumed to have a substantial connection with the UK after being resident in the UK for three months. Being a resident is not the same as having a residence in the jurisdiction (*Cherney v Deripaska* [2007] 2 All ER (Comm) 785 at [16]). An individual is resident for this purpose if he has a settled or usual place of abode within the jurisdiction. This requires some degree of permanence or continuity (*Bank of Dubai Ltd v Abbas* [1997] IL Pr 308).

11.21   By the recast Judgments Regulation, art 63, a corporation is domiciled where it has its 'statutory seat', central administration, or principal place of business. A company's statutory seat is its registered office or, if it does not have one, the place where it was incorporated. A company's 'principal place of business' is the place at the heart of its operations, or where it is controlled and managed.

Exceptions to the rule that jurisdiction is based on domicile

11.22   Although the primary rule is that jurisdiction under the recast Judgments Regulation is based on domicile, there are wide exceptions in arts 7–26. The basic scheme under the exceptions, as confirmed by CPR, r 6.33, is that the courts of England and Wales will have jurisdiction to hear and determine a claim under the recast Judgments Regulation if:

(a) the case falls within one of the provisions set out in arts 7–26;
(b) there are no proceedings pending involving the same claim in another Member State; and
(c) the defendant is domiciled in a Member State.

11.23   However, the requirement of having a defendant domiciled in a Member State is dispensed with in some consumer and employment cases, and in cases falling within art 24 (exclusive jurisdiction: see 11.13) and art 25 cases (jurisdiction clauses).

Contract

11.24   Article 7(1)(a) provides in part that a person domiciled in one Member State may alternatively 'be sued in matters relating to a contract, in the courts for the place of performance of the obligation in question'. In *Kalfelis v Bankhaus Schröder, Münchmeyer, Hengst & Co* (Case 189/87) [1988] ECR 5565 the European Court of Justice ('ECJ') laid down the general principle that the special jurisdiction given by art 7 must be interpreted restrictively as it derogates from the principle that jurisdiction is vested in the courts of the country where the defendant is domiciled. Nevertheless, in *Effer SpA v Kantner* (Case 38/81) [1982] ECR 825 the ECJ held that art 7(1) applies even where the existence of the contract on which the claim is based is disputed by the defendant. What is required is a 'good arguable case' that the place of performance of the obligation was in England (*Boss Group Ltd v Boss France SA* [1997] 1 WLR 351).

11.25   In *Etablissements A de Bloos Sprl v SCA Bouyer* (Case 14/76) [1976] ECR 1497 the ECJ held that the 'obligation' in art 7(1) refers to the contractual obligation forming the basis of the legal proceedings. Where a claimant brings a claim concerning a number of obligations under a single contract, it is the principal obligation that determines jurisdiction under art 7(1) (*Shenavai v Kreischer* (Case 266/85) [1987] ECR 239). In contracts for the sale of goods the place of performance is where the goods were or should have been delivered, and in contracts for the provision of services it is where the services were or should have been provided (art 7(1)(b)).

11.26   Article 25(1) applies to contracts with jurisdiction clauses regardless of the domicile of the parties. In such a case the jurisdiction clause will confer exclusive jurisdiction on the courts of the designated Member State, provided the clause is in writing or evidenced in writing, or if the clause is in a form that accords with the practices either of the parties or widely known usage in international trade or commerce.

Tort

A claim in tort may be brought in the country either where the defendant is domiciled **11.27** or where the harmful event occurred or may occur (art 7(2)). It was held by the ECJ in *Handelskwekerij GJ Bier BV v Mines de Potasse d'Alsace SA* (Case 21/76) [1978] QB 708 that this gives the claimant the option of commencing proceedings either in the country where the wrongful act or omission took place, or in the country where the damage occurred.

In personal injuries claims the wrongful act will be the original accident (*Henderson v* **11.28** *Jaoun* [2002] 1 WLR 2971). In negligent misstatement cases it will be the place where the statement was made rather than where it was received (*Domicrest Ltd v Swiss Bank Corporation* [1999] QB 548).

The place where the damage occurred is not the place where the damage was quantified **11.29** or where steps were taken to mitigate the effects of the wrongful conduct of the defendant (*Netherlands v Rüffer* (Case 814/79) [1980] ECR 3807). Further, the 'place where the damage occurred' cannot be construed as encompassing any place where adverse consequences of an event which have already caused actual damage elsewhere could be felt (*Marinari v Lloyds Bank plc* (Case C–364/93) [1996] QB 217). It therefore does not include a place where a claimant claimed to have suffered loss consequential on initial damage suffered in another contracting State.

Along the same lines as contract cases under art 7(1), the Court of Appeal in *Mölnlycke AB* **11.30** *v Procter and Gamble Ltd* [1992] 1 WLR 1112 held that the court has power to filter off frivolous or vexatious use of the jurisdiction given by art 7(2) by insisting that the claimant must establish a good arguable case on the merits.

Trusts

A claim against a settlor, trustee, or beneficiary of a trust created by the operation of a statute, **11.31** or by a written instrument, or created orally and evidenced in writing, may be brought in the courts of the country where the trust is domiciled (art 7(6)). This form of wording excludes implied and constructive trusts, and a person with power to appoint who will take assets under a trust is not a 'trustee' for this purpose unless expressly named as a trustee (*Gomez v Gomez-Monche Vives* [2009] Ch 245). A trust is domiciled in England if English law is the system of law with which the trust has its closest and most real connection (CJJA 1982, s 45(3)).

Co-defendants

It is provided by art 8(1), that: **11.32**

> a person domiciled in a Member State may also be sued, where he is one of a number of defendants, in the courts for the place where any one of them is domiciled provided the claims are so closely connected that it is expedient to hear and determine them together to avoid the risk of irreconcilable judgments resulting from separate proceedings.

The first precondition is that there must be a valid claim against the defendant domi- **11.33** ciled within the jurisdiction (*The Rewia* [1991] 2 Lloyd's Rep 325). It is then necessary to consider whether the joinder is valid. According to the ECJ, the proper use of art 8(1) is to avoid the risk of irreconcilable judgments and to prevent related claims proceeding in different contracting States (*Kalfelis v Bankhaus Schröder, Münchmeyer, Hengst & Co* (Case 189/87) [1988] ECR 5565).

Counterclaims and additional claims under Part 20

11.34 By art 8(2) and (3), counterclaims arising from the same facts as those founding the claim and additional claims under Part 20 may be brought in the court in which the claimant's claim is pending. In *Kinnear v Falconfilms NV* [1996] 1 WLR 920 a claim was commenced in England by the administrators of an actor's estate against a film company claiming damages arising out of a riding accident during the shooting of a film in Spain. The film company issued an additional claim seeking an indemnity or a contribution against the Spanish hospital that treated the actor, claiming that the actor's death was caused by the negligence of the hospital. It was held that the hospital could be brought in as a third party in the English proceedings, because the nexus required for bringing claims against third parties under CPR, Part 20 (see Chapter 20), was in practical terms sufficient to satisfy the requirements of the special jurisdiction conferred by art 8(2). Contribution notices are not claim forms and therefore cannot be served outside the jurisdiction (*Knauf UK GmbH v British Gypsum Ltd* [2002] 2 Lloyd's Rep 416).

Procedure on commencing proceedings pursuant to the recast Judgments Regulation

11.35 Where proceedings can be served outside the jurisdiction pursuant to the provisions of the recast Judgments Regulation, service may be effected without the permission of the court (CPR, r 6.33). The claimant is required to file a notice in form N510 with the claim form containing a statement of the grounds on which the claimant is entitled to serve the claim form outside the jurisdiction (r 6.34 and PD 6B, para 2.1). The N510 has to be served with the claim form (r 6.34(1)(b)).

E ASSUMED JURISDICTION

11.36 The rules discussed in this section deal with the situation where it is desired to serve English proceedings on a defendant living in a country outside the scope of the Brussels, Lugano, or Modified Convention, or the original or recast Judgments Regulation. If service is to be effected out of the jurisdiction in such a country, permission must first be obtained from the English court. Unless permission is obtained, and if the defendant's address is outside the jurisdiction, when the claim form is issued it will be stamped 'Not for service out of the jurisdiction'.

Basic principles governing applications for permission

11.37 The requirements that need to be satisfied if the English courts are to grant permission to serve proceedings outside the jurisdiction under the court's assumed jurisdiction are those laid down by the House of Lords in *Seaconsar Far East Ltd v Bank Markazi Jomhouri Islami Iran* [1994] 1 AC 438 as altered by what is now CPR, r 6.37. The intending claimant must establish that:

(a) there is a good arguable case that the court has jurisdiction within one of the 20 grounds set out in PD 6B, para 3.1 (r 6.36);

(b) the claim has a reasonable prospect of success (r 6.37(1)(b)). This is the same as the test applied for summary judgment and setting aside default judgments (*AK Investment CJSC v Kyrgyz Mobile Tel Ltd* [2011] 4 All ER 1027 at [71]; *Brownlie v Four Seasons Holdings Inc* [2018] 1 WLR 192 at [7]); and

(c) the case is a proper one for service outside the jurisdiction.

Grounds for granting permission to serve outside the jurisdiction

More than 20 grounds on which permission may be granted for service outside the jurisdic- **11.38** tion are set out in PD 6B, para 3.1. They include cases where:
(a) a claim is made for a remedy against a person domiciled within the jurisdiction;
(b) a claim is made for an injunction ordering the defendant to do or refrain from doing an act within the jurisdiction;
(c) a claim is made against a defendant on whom the claim form has been or will be served and there is between the claimant and the defendant a real issue which it is reasonable for the court to try, and the claimant wishes to serve the claim form on another person who is a necessary or proper party to that claim; . . .
(d) a claim is made for an interim remedy under CJJA 1982, s 25(1);
(e) a claim is made in respect of a contract where the contract:
 (i) was made within the jurisdiction;
 (ii) was made by or through an agent trading or residing within the jurisdiction;
 (iii) is governed by English law; or
 (iv) contains a term to the effect that the court shall have jurisdiction to determine any claim in respect of the contract;
(f) a claim is made in respect of a breach of contract committed within the jurisdiction;
(g) a claim is made in tort where:
 (i) damage was sustained, or will be sustained, within the jurisdiction; or
 (ii) damage which has been or will be sustained results from an act committed, or likely to be committed, within the jurisdiction.

General interpretation

As these provisions allow the court to exercise an exorbitant jurisdiction, they are to be **11.39** strictly construed in favour of the overseas party (*The Hagen* [1908] P 189). Although the claimant can choose which ground or grounds to rely on (*Matthews v Kuwait Bechtel Corporation* [1959] 2 QB 57), the claimant must specifically state those grounds in the evidence in support of the application, and will not be permitted to raise alternative grounds on a defendant's application to discharge the order granting permission (*Metall und Rohstoff AG v Donaldson Lufkin and Jenrette Inc* [1990] 1 QB 391). While some cases, such as *Johnson v Taylor Bros and Co* [1920] AC 144, say that the case must fall within the overall purposes of the relevant ground, not merely its strict letter, there are other cases, such as *Sharab v Prince Al-Waleed bin Talal bin Abdal-Aziz-Al-Saud* [2009] 2 Lloyd's Rep 160, which say there is no need to come within the spirit of the relevant sub-paragraph as well as its letter.

As mentioned at 11.37, the applicant is required to have a good arguable case for establish- **11.40** ing one of the grounds in para 3.1. This means that the applicant needs to have a much better argument on the material available than the respondent (*Canada Trust Co v Stolzenberg (No 2)* [1998] 1 WLR 547, 554; *Bols Distilleries BV v Superior Yacht Services* [2007] 1 WLR 12 at [26]–[28]).

Necessary or proper party

Where PD 6B, para 3.1(3) is relied upon, the claimant's evidence must set out the grounds for **11.41** believing that there is a real issue which the court may reasonably be asked to try between the claimant and the defendant who has already been served. Once this has been established, the claimant must further show that the second defendant is a necessary or proper party to the claim. There is particular reluctance to allow service under this paragraph given its anomaly (in relation to the other grounds) in not being founded upon any territorial connection between the claim and the jurisdiction of the English courts (*Multinational Gas and Petrochemical Co v Multinational Gas and Petrochemical Services Ltd* [1983] Ch 258). An example of where it might be used is where a partnership has been served in England, and it is sought to serve a foreign partner (*West of England Steamship Owners' Protection and Indemnity Association Ltd v John Holman and Sons* [1957] 1 WLR 1164).

Contract

11.42   Whether a contract was made within the jurisdiction depends on general contractual principles (*Brinkibon Ltd v Stahag Stahl und Stahlwarenhandelsgesellschaft mbH* [1983] 2 AC 34). Paragraph 3.1(6)(b) of PD 6B is given a wide interpretation, and even includes a case where the defendant's London agent merely sent the claimant the defendant's price list and forwarded the claimant's order to the defendant (*National Mortgage and Agency Co of New Zealand Ltd v Gosselin* (1922) 38 TLR 832). An express term that the contract is governed by English law should bring the case within PD 6B, para 3.1(6)(c). An implication that a contract is governed by English law may arise by course of dealings where earlier transactions between the parties were governed by English law (*Banque Paribas v Cargill International SA* [1992] 1 Lloyd's Rep 96). An express jurisdiction clause (PD 6B, para 3.1(6)(d)) will almost always be given effect by the courts, but there are sometimes questions whether the claimant is a party entitled to rely on the clause in cases where there are interlocking contracts (see, eg, *The Mahkutai* [1996] AC 650).

Tort

11.43   Jurisdiction in tort under PD 6B, para 3.1(9), is in the same terms as the recast Judgments Regulation, art 7(2) (see 11.27). Jurisdiction may be founded either through the tortious act being committed in England or on the basis of damage being suffered in England. 'Damage' means actionable harm caused by the defendant's wrongful act (*Brownlie v Four Seasons Holdings Inc* [2018] 1 WLR 192). In *Ashton Investments Ltd v Rusal* [2007] 1 Lloyd's Rep 311 the defendant was alleged to have hacked into a computer server in London from outside the jurisdiction. It was held the damage was sustained and the relevant act was committed within the jurisdiction. If separate acts constituting a single tort are committed here and abroad, the question is whether the tort was in substance committed within the jurisdiction (*Metall und Rohstoff AG v Donaldson Lufkin and Jenrette Inc* [1990] 1 QB 391).

Forum non conveniens

11.44   Permission to serve out of the jurisdiction should only be granted where the court is satisfied that England is the proper place in which to bring the claim (*VTB Capital plc v Nutritek International Corporation* [2013] 2 AC 337). The leading case is *Spiliada Maritime Corporation v Cansulex Ltd* [1987] AC 460. Lord Goff of Chieveley laid down the general principle that the court has to identify the forum in which the case can be most suitably tried in the interests of all the parties and for the ends of justice. The burden of proof rests on the claimant to show that England is clearly the most appropriate place for the trial of the claim.

11.45   Matters to be considered include the availability of witnesses, the governing law, the residence and/or places of business of the parties, and the ground in PD 6B, para 3, relied upon. Other factors include the languages used by the witnesses and courts, and the relative ease of enforcement of any judgment both in this and the proposed jurisdiction (*Sharab v Prince*

Al-Waleed bin Talal bin Abdal-Aziz-Al-Saud [2009] 2 Lloyd's Rep 160). The availability of public funding is, however, irrelevant: see *Connelly v RTZ Corporation plc* [1996] QB 361. The weight to be attached to the relevant factors depends on all the circumstances of the case. As Lord Goff said in *The Spiliada*, the importance to be attached to any particular ground invoked by the claimant may vary from case to case. For example, the fact that English law is the putative law of the contract may be of very great importance (as in *BP Exploration Co (Libya) Ltd v Hunt* [1976] 1 WLR 788), but it may be of little importance when seen in the context of the whole case.

Procedure on seeking permission

As there is no defendant on the record, an application for permission to serve a claim form **11.46** out of the jurisdiction should be made without notice. There will be no hearing. The evidence must state, according to CPR, r 6.37(1):

(a) the grounds on which the application is made and the paragraphs of PD 6B, para 3.1 relied upon;
(b) that in the witness's belief, the claimant has a reasonable prospect of success. Simply stating such a belief is not enough, given the need to establish a claim with a reasonable prospect of success. The witness statement needs to cover all the elements of the cause of action (*Deutsche Bank AG v Vik* [2010] EWHC 551 (Comm));
(c) the defendant's address or, if unknown, in what place or country the defendant is or can probably be found; and
(d) where the application is made under para 3.1(3) (that the defendant is a necessary or proper party), the grounds for believing that there is a real issue between the claimant and the existing defendant which it is reasonable for the court to try.

F SERVICE ABROAD

Effecting service abroad

Under modern conditions, effecting service abroad is generally a pragmatic problem **11.47** resolved by adopting the most efficient means of conducting the litigation (*Abela v Bardarani* [2013] 1 WLR 2043). The general rule is that service abroad must be effected in accordance with the law of the country where it is sought to effect service. In practice, service out of the jurisdiction may be effected either under the EU Service Regulation (Regulation (EU) No 1393/2007), through diplomatic channels, or, where permitted under local law, informally by the claimant.

Service through diplomatic channels under the Hague Convention

A large number of countries, including the UK, are parties to the Hague Convention on the **11.48** Service Abroad of Judicial and Extra-judicial Documents in Civil or Commercial Matters (1965) ('Hague Convention'). The Hague Convention, however, gives way to the EU Service Regulation (see 11.49). Each contracting State has designated a central authority to receive and transmit requests for service from other contracting States. A claim form may be served in another contracting State either through the central authority in the State in question, or, if permitted by the law of that country, through the judicial authorities of that country or the British consular authority in that country. There are detailed requirements in CPR, rr 6.42–6.46 on the documents that need to be filed at the Foreign Service Department at the RCJ.

Service under the Service Regulation

11.49 The Service Regulation applies to all EU Member States apart from Denmark, and supersedes all previous service treaties for its members. The Foreign Process Department at the RCJ is the transmitting and receiving agency for England and Wales under the Service Regulation. Claimants serving process in Member States need to file the claim form and translations at the Foreign Process Department, which will transmit the documents to the receiving agency of the country in question. The receiving agency then serves the documents on the defendants. The intention is that the whole process should take no more than a month (art 7(2)).

Other methods of service out of the jurisdiction

11.50 There are a number of countries, mainly in Europe, with which the UK has bilateral civil procedure conventions. Process may be served in these countries through their judicial authorities, or through the British consular authority in that country, subject to local laws, in much the same way as described in 11.48. If there is no bilateral convention with the country where service has to be effected, it is still possible to use British consular authorities or seek the assistance of the government of the country in question, but there is a greater risk that these methods will be contrary to local law. In practice, lawyers in the country in question are usually appointed as agents to advise and effect service.

Responding to a claim served out of the jurisdiction

11.51 Enhanced periods for responding to claims served out of the jurisdiction are provided by CPR, rr 6.35 and 6.37(5). If the defendant is in an EU Member State, the time for acknowledging service or filing the defence is 21 days from the date of service of the particulars of claim. Such a defendant who acknowledges service first has a total of 35 days from the date of service of the particulars of claim in which to file the defence. Defendants who are in countries or territories outside the Member States have even longer periods in which to respond, with different periods being laid down in PD 6B for different countries depending on how remote they are.

G PREVENTING CONFLICTS IN JURISDICTION

Judgments Regulation cases

Lis pendens

11.52 Article 29(1) of the recast Judgments Regulation provides:

> . . . where proceedings involving the same cause of action and between the same parties are brought in the courts of different Member States, any court other than the court first seised shall of its own motion stay its proceedings until such time as the jurisdiction of the court first seised is established.

By art 29(3), where the jurisdiction of the court first seised is established, any court other than the court first seised shall decline jurisdiction in favour of that court.

11.53 This article is designed to prevent parallel proceedings before the courts of different contracting States, and to avoid the conflicts that might otherwise result. It is to be interpreted broadly, and covers all situations of *lis pendens*, irrespective of the parties' domicile (*Overseas Union Insurance Ltd v New Hampshire Insurance Co* (Case C–351/89) [1992] QB 434). Priority under art 29 is given to the court 'first seised'. This occurs when documents capable of being served are lodged with the court to institute proceedings (*Kolden Holdings Ltd v Rodette Commerce Ltd* [2008] Bus LR 1051).

Related actions

Article 30 deals with cases where a second claim is similar to, or related to, an earlier claim, **11.54** but is not the same. In these cases the second court may stay its proceedings (art 30(1)), and may decide to decline jurisdiction if both cases are proceeding at first instance (art 30(2)). Claims are deemed to be related where they are so closely connected that it is expedient to hear and determine them together to avoid the risk of irreconcilable judgments resulting from separate proceedings (art 30(3)). Once it is held that proceedings are related, the court has a discretion whether to grant a stay, but it will be unusual for the stay to be refused (*The Linda* [1988] 1 Lloyd's Rep 175).

Stays on the ground of *forum non conveniens*

Under the assumed jurisdiction rules, in order to prevent completely unsuitable claims pro- **11.55** ceeding, the courts have a discretion to stay English proceedings on the principle of *forum non conveniens*. In cases involving jurisdiction between EU Member States, the CJJA 1982, s 49, provides that nothing in the Act shall prevent the court from staying proceedings on the ground of *forum non conveniens* or otherwise, where to do so is not inconsistent with what is now the recast Judgments Regulation. This means that there is no power to order a stay where that is inconsistent with the recast Judgments Regulation.

Appropriate forum

In *Spiliada Maritime Corporation v Cansulex Ltd* [1987] AC 460 Lord Goff of Chieveley said: **11.56**

> The basic principle is that a stay will only be granted on the ground of *forum non conveniens* where the court is satisfied that there is some other available forum, having competent jurisdiction, which is the appropriate forum for the trial of the action, i.e. in which the case may be tried more suitably for the interests of all the parties and the ends of justice.

The burden of proof rests on the defendant to show there is some other clearly more appropri- **11.57** ate forum. If there is no other more suitable forum, the stay should usually be refused. In considering whether there is an alternative forum, the court will look for the country 'with which the claim has the most real and substantial connection' (*The Abidin Daver* [1984] AC 398 *per* Lord Keith of Kinkel). Where the defendant has an established place of business within the jurisdiction, very clear and weighty grounds must be shown for refusing to exercise jurisdiction (*Banco Atlantico SA v British Bank of the Middle East* [1990] 2 Lloyd's Rep 504). The court will also consider the availability of factual and expert witnesses, the law governing the dispute, and whether the parties have conferred jurisdiction on any particular court. Usually, it is best for proceedings to be continued in the country whose law governs the dispute (*Standard Steamship Owners' Protection and Indemnity Association (Bermuda) Ltd v Gann* [1992] 2 Lloyd's Rep 528). An alternative forum which simply applies its own laws irrespective of the generally accepted rules on the conflict of laws is unlikely to be regarded as a suitable alternative (*Banco Atlantico SA v British Bank of the Middle East*). Convincing reasons must usually be shown before the court will go behind an express agreement between the parties as to jurisdiction (*Kuwait Oil Co (KSC) v Idemitsu Tankers KK* [1981] 2 Lloyd's Rep 510).

Reasons of justice

If there is some more appropriate forum, the court may refuse a stay if, in all the circum- **11.58** stances of the case, justice requires that a stay should not be granted (*Spiliada Maritime Corporation v Cansulex Ltd* [1987] AC 460). The burden of proof regarding showing some reason for not granting a stay despite there being some more suitable forum is on the claimant. A stay may be refused, for example where the claimant has cogent evidence that justice will not be done in the foreign jurisdiction (*The Abidin Daver* [1984] AC 398). However, a fear that justice will not be done in the claimant's own country, if that is the appropriate forum, is irrelevant (*Jeyaretnam v Mahmood* (1992) *The Times*, 21 May 1992).

Legitimate personal or juridical advantage

11.59   There are many cases where a claimant can secure some advantage by commencing proceedings in one jurisdiction rather than another, which will be taken into account. Examples include the measure of damages, the vigour of the procedures on disclosure, the power to award interest, and the length of the limitation period.

Injunctions to restrain foreign proceedings

11.60   An English court may grant an injunction restraining the institution or continuance of foreign proceedings. Such an injunction is granted only when it is required for the ends of justice (*Castanho v Brown and Root (UK) Ltd* [1981] AC 557). It was put slightly differently in *Société Nationale Industrielle Aérospatiale v Lee Kui Jak* [1987] AC 871, where it was held that an anti-suit injunction will be granted only if pursuit of the foreign proceedings would be vexatious and oppressive.

11.61   In *Turner v Grovit* (Case C-159/02) [2005] AC 101, the ECJ held that it is inconsistent with what is now the recast Judgments Regulation for the courts in England to restrain defendants from commencing or continuing proceedings in another Member State even when those defendants are acting in bad faith with the purpose of frustrating proceedings properly before the English courts. In the same way it is contrary to the recast Judgments Regulation for the court in a second Member State to grant an injunction to restrain proceedings in a first Member State on the ground that those proceedings would be contrary to an arbitration agreement (*West Tankers Inc v Riunione Adriarica Di Sicurita SpA* (Case C-185/07) [2009] 1 AC 1138). *West Tankers Inc v Riunione Adriatica Di Sicurita SpA* governs cases where the competing jurisdiction is in another Member State. Where the competing jurisdiction is elsewhere, the High Court continues to have jurisdiction to grant anti-suit injunctions to restrain litigation that would be in repudiatory breach of an arbitration agreement (*AES Ust-Karmengorsk Hydropower Plant LLP v Ust-Karmengorsk Hydropower Plant JSC* [2013] 1 WLR 1889).

H INTERIM RELIEF IN SUPPORT OF FOREIGN PROCEEDINGS

11.62   Section 25(1) of the CJJA 1982 confers on the High Court in England power to grant interim relief in the absence of substantive proceedings, where proceedings have been or will be commenced in another State. The principle underpinning s 25 is that the court should assist the courts of other jurisdictions by providing such interim relief as would be available if it were itself seised of the substantive proceedings (*Kensington International Ltd v Congo* [2008] 1 WLR 1144). The power to grant interim relief extends to any proceedings in any State, whether it is in Europe or elsewhere (Civil Jurisdiction and Judgments Act 1982 (Interim Relief) Order 1997 (SI 1997/302)). This solves the difficulty encountered in *The Siskina* [1979] AC 210 (see 42.27 and 43.10), where the House of Lords held that the English courts had no power to grant a freezing injunction over assets within the jurisdiction in the absence of a cause of action justiciable here, because a freezing injunction is a form of relief, not a substantive cause of action.

11.63   Two key restrictions in the original s 25 (that the overseas jurisdiction had to be a Brussels or Lugano Convention contracting State, and that the substantive proceedings had to come within the scope of what is now the Judgments Regulation, art 1) were removed by the 1997 Order. The only remaining limitation is under s 25(2), that the court may refuse relief if, in its opinion, the fact that the court has no jurisdiction apart from s 25 makes it inexpedient for it to grant the interim relief that is sought. In deciding whether interim relief is 'inexpedient' under s 25(2), according to *Motorola Credit Corporation v Uzan (No 2)* [2004] 1 WLR 113, the following factors should be considered:

(a) whether making the order will interfere with the management of the case in the primary court;

(b) whether it is the policy in the primary jurisdiction to refuse to grant interim relief in the form being sought;

(c) whether there is a danger that the order will give rise to disharmony or confusion, or the risk of conflicting, inconsistent, or overlapping orders in other jurisdictions; and

(d) whether the interim relief can be enforced. Enforcement against each defendant has to be considered separately.

I JUDGMENT IN DEFAULT

No special rule applies in cases of assumed jurisdiction regarding entering judgment in default other than the need for waiting for the enhanced period laid down for responding to the claim. Where service outside the jurisdiction has been effected without permission under the recast Judgments Regulation, judgment in default can be entered only by application under CPR, Part 12 (CPR, r 12.10(b)(i), and see 13.17 for the procedure). **11.64**

KEY POINTS SUMMARY

- Generally proceedings have to be served within the jurisdiction. There always has to be a sound basis before proceedings can be served outside the jurisdiction. **11.65**

- Where the defendant is domiciled in the EU, the general rule is that they must be sued in the country where they are domiciled.

- If jurisdiction can be established against an EU defendant (such as under art 7 or 8 of the recast Judgments Regulation):

  (a) the claimant can choose whether to sue in England (under art 7 or 8) or in the defendant's country of domicile (under art 4); and

  (b) English proceedings may be served without permission.

- If jurisdiction can be established against a defendant who is outside the EU under CPR, r 6.36 and PD 6B, para 3.1, proceedings can be served outside the jurisdiction only with the permission of the court.

- The times for responding to claims served outside the jurisdiction are extended (to take into account the realities of postal delivery).

- If a defendant outside the jurisdiction does not respond to the claim, judgment in default can be entered in the usual way if permission to serve outside the jurisdiction was obtained (because the defendant is outside the EU), but permission to enter judgment in default must be sought if the defendant was served without permission under the recast Judgments Regulation.

12

RESPONDING TO A CLAIM

A TIME FOR RESPONDING.............12.02

B ADMISSIONS 12.04

C DEFENCES 12.08

D ACKNOWLEDGMENT OF SERVICE......12.09

E AGREED EXTENSIONS..............12.12

F DISPUTING SERVICE OR THE COURT'S JURISDICTION....................12.13

G TRANSFER.......................12.19

H SPECIALIST CLAIMS................12.21

Key points summary 12.24

12.01 A defendant who intends to contest proceedings must respond to the claim by filing an acknowledgment of service and/or by filing a defence. Defended claims become subject to the court's case management system, with the court making provisional track allocation decisions, followed by the parties filing directions questionnaires. A procedural judge then makes case management directions and confirms the allocation of the claim to a case management track (see Chapter 15). If a defendant fails to make any response to a claim the usual result is that a default judgment will be entered within a relatively short period after service (see Chapter 13). There are cases where the defendant has no real answer to a claim, but may want time to pay. This is considered at 12.04–12.06. There are other cases where the defendant objects to the jurisdiction of the court. These cases are considered at 12.13–12.18.

A TIME FOR RESPONDING

12.02 For claims governed by the main provisions of the CPR, the event that starts time running against the defendant for the purpose of responding to the claim is service of the particulars of claim (CPR, r 9.1(2)). The defendant has 14 days from the deemed date of service of the particulars of claim (r 10.3(1), r 14.2(1), and r 15.4) to do one of the following:

(a) file or serve an admission; or
(b) file a defence (which may be combined with making a counterclaim); or
(c) file an acknowledgment of service (r 9.2).

12.03 This means that the defendant is under no immediate obligation to respond to proceedings if the claim form is served with particulars of claim to follow (CPR, r 9.1(2)). A claim form may be served on which are set out the particulars of claim (as in figure 14.1), or the particulars of claim may form a separate document which may be served either with the claim form or later. Where the claim form and the particulars of claim are separate documents, the particulars should be served within 14 days of the claim form and in any event during the period of validity of the claim form (r 7.4).

B ADMISSIONS

12.04 A defendant who admits the claim is normally best advised to complete the admission form included in the response pack. As mentioned at 6.20, there are two types of admission form. N9A is used in claims for specified sums of money, and N9C is for use in claims for unspecified amounts of money, non-money claims, and claims for the return of goods. An example of form N9C was illustrated in form 6.4. The form allows the defendant to admit either the whole claim or just a part. If the whole claim is admitted, the defendant needs to decide about payment. If the whole sum is paid within 14 days of service of the claim form, the defendant's liability for the claimant's costs will be limited to certain fixed sums laid down in CPR, Part 45. This assists the defendant, because fixed costs are considerably lower than the sums recoverable in contested litigation.

If the defendant needs time to pay, the admission form allows him to make an offer to pay **12.05** by instalments. If this is done, the defendant must also complete a large number of questions set out in the form dealing with the defendant's personal and financial circumstances. The form will be sent to the claimant. The claimant will then consider the offer, and, if it is acceptable, will notify the court and a judgment will be entered for payment by the instalments offered by the defendant. Claimants often agree on purely pragmatic grounds, in that it is better to get the money by instalments than not at all. If the claimant does not agree to the offer to pay by instalments, the rules make provision for the rate of payment to be determined by the court. The courts work on the principle that mere inability to pay does not normally justify postponement of the claimant's entitlement to payment (*Gulf International Bank v Al Ittefaq Steel Products* [2010] EWHC 2601 (QB)).

A defendant can also use the admission form to make a partial admission, denying the rest **12.06** of the claim. The part that is denied has to be dealt with in a defence, which should be filed at court with the admission form. Again, if this happens the claimant is asked whether the partial admission is acceptable, and if so a judgment will be entered in that sum.

Formal and informal admissions are considered further at 34.02–34.04. **12.07**

C DEFENCES

A defendant disputing a claim must file a defence. One of the forms in the response pack **12.08** is a form of defence and counterclaim, there being different forms for claims for specified amounts (form N9B) and for unspecified and non-money claims (form N9D). An example of form N9D was given at form 6.5. It has spaces where the defendant can set out the reasons why the claim is disputed, and also for details of any counterclaim. Alternatively, the defendant can draft a defence using ordinary paper, see figure 14.3. This is recognized by PD 15, para 1.3, which provides merely that a defence 'may' be set out in the response pack form. This alternative is often used by lawyers acting for clients, because well-drafted defences tend to set out the facts in some detail, and the space on the form is quite limited. Consideration of what needs to go into defences and counterclaims is given in Chapter 14.

D ACKNOWLEDGMENT OF SERVICE

Acknowledgments of service are used if the defendant is unable to file a defence in the time **12.09** limited, or if the defendant intends to dispute the court's jurisdiction. By acknowledging service a defendant is given an extra 14 days for filing the defence, so that the defence need not be served until 28 days after service of the particulars of claim (CPR, r 15.4(1)(b)).

The acknowledgment of service form is combined with the cover sheet of the response pack **12.10** (form N9): see form 6.3. The intention is that the defendant will cut the form along the line one-third of the way down the page, and return the lower two-thirds to the court. It has a heading setting out the court, claim number, and the parties. If the defendant has been misnamed, the correct name should be inserted in the space provided. A defendant who is an individual must state his date of birth (PD 16, para 10.7). The defendant's address for service, which must be within the jurisdiction, must be provided. If the defendant is acting by a solicitor, the address for service will be the solicitor's address. The defendant must tick a box indicating whether the whole of the claim is to be defended or just a part, or whether the court's jurisdiction will be contested. The form is then signed, dated, and returned to the court. Two or more defendants acting through the same solicitors need file only a single acknowledgment of service (PD 10, para 5.3).

12.11   Once the acknowledgment of service has been filed, the court must notify the claimant in writing (CPR, r 10.4). This is normally done by sending a copy of the form to the claimant's solicitor.

E AGREED EXTENSIONS

12.12   The parties may agree to extend the time for serving a defence, but any agreement can be for only a maximum of a further 28 days (CPR, r 15.5(1)). The defendant has to notify the court in writing of the agreed extension. The restricted period for agreed extensions is to ensure the court retains control over proceedings in accordance with its case management functions.

F DISPUTING SERVICE OR THE COURT'S JURISDICTION

12.13   As indicated at 12.10, a defendant disputing service or the court's jurisdiction must return the acknowledgment of service form to the court within 14 days after service of the particulars of claim indicating that jurisdiction is being challenged by ticking the relevant box on the form (CPR, r 11(2)). Part 11 is not limited to disputes over the court's territorial jurisdiction (see Chapter 11), but also applies where the defendant disputes the court's power or authority to try the claim (*Hoddinott v Persimmon Homes (Wessex) Ltd* [2008] 1 WLR 806). Examples are where the defendant alleges that purported service was ineffective or disputes an order extending the period of validity of a claim form (see Chapter 7). Failing to tick the dispute jurisdiction box on the acknowledgment of service in these situations waives any defects in service (*Brooks v AH Brooks & Co* [2011] 3 All ER 982). Conversely, a dispute that amounts to a procedural defence, such as the expiry of limitation (see Chapter 21), or that the claim has no real prospect of success (see Chapter 24), do not engage Part 11 (*Dunn v Parole Board* [2009] 1 WLR 728). Nor do applications to stay court proceedings under the Arbitration Act 1996, s 9 (*Bilta (UK) Ltd v Nazir* [2010] Bus LR 1634).

12.14   Within the next 14 days after acknowledging service, the defendant must issue an application notice seeking an order declaring that the court has no jurisdiction or should not exercise any jurisdiction it might have (r 11(1) and (4)). The court has a discretion to extend this 14-day period (*Sawyer v Atari Interactive Inc* [2005] EWHC 2351 (QB)), but a failure to apply within the time limit may be taken as a submission to the jurisdiction (*Maple Leaf Macro Volatility Master Fund v Rouvroy* [2009] 2 All ER (Comm) 287 at [187], unaffected by the appeal at [2009] EWCA Civ 1334). If the defendant disputes the court's jurisdiction, there is no need to serve a defence until after the application is determined. If the application is successful the court may make consequential directions setting aside the claim form, or service, or discharging prior orders, or staying the proceedings (r 11(6)). If the application fails, the defendant is given 14 days from the date of the hearing to file a second acknowledgment of service (r 11(7)(b)), after which the claim proceeds in the usual way, but with the court giving directions for filing and serving the defence, followed by track allocation or judgment in default. Filing the second acknowledgment of service amounts to submitting to the jurisdiction (*Deutsche Bank AG London Branch v Petromena ASA* [2015] 1 WLR 4225, and see 11.07).

Applications disputing the court's jurisdiction are sometimes met by arguments that the **12.15** defendant has submitted to the court's jurisdiction, or has waived any irregularity in service. As mentioned at 11.07, in the absence of any express agreement to submit to the jurisdiction, it is a question whether the defendant's conduct, when viewed objectively in the context of all the circumstances of the case, is inconsistent with maintaining an objection to the jurisdiction of the court. If an application disputing the court's jurisdiction is made within the 14 days allowed by r 11(4), conduct will be treated as a submission to the jurisdiction only if it is wholly unequivocal.

For example, a defendant who has applied to dispute jurisdiction who attends before a **12.16** judge to challenge a freezing injunction obtained without notice has not thereby unequivocally submitted to the jurisdiction, unless he also agrees to an order regulating his position pending trial (*SMAY Investments Ltd v Sachdev* [2003] 1 WLR 1973). Making an application for 'directions' is also equivocal, because the directions could have been for a stay of the proceedings (*Patel v Patel* [2000] QB 551).

If an application disputing jurisdiction is not made within the 14-day period, a defendant **12.17** may be held to have submitted to the jurisdiction by:

(a) instructing a solicitor to accept service in the jurisdiction (*Manta Line Inc v Sofianites* [1984] 1 Lloyd's Rep 14); or

(b) appearing to contest the merits. An example is *Marc Rich & Co AG v Società Italiana Impianti PA (No 2)* [1992] 1 Lloyd's Rep 624, where the defendant was held to have submitted to the jurisdiction of the courts in Italy by delivering a statement of case disputing the merits of the claim.

A similar principle applies in recast Judgments Regulation cases, where art 26 provides **12.18** that the courts of a Member State have jurisdiction where the defendant 'enters an appearance' unless the appearance is entered to contest jurisdiction. The reference to entering an appearance is to acknowledging service or filing a defence. From *Elefanten Schuh GmbH v Jacqmain* (Case 150/80) [1981] ECR 1671 (ECJ), it appears that a defence contesting jurisdiction and the merits in the alternative does not constitute a submission to the jurisdiction. However, it is not possible to submit to the jurisdiction of a court where the courts of another country have exclusive jurisdiction under art 24.

G TRANSFER

County Court money claims are started in the County Court Money Claims Centre (if **12.19** issued in hard copy) or the County Court Business Centre (if issued electronically) (see 6.11 and 6.12). These claims will need to be sent to a County Court hearing centre if a hearing is required, or if the claim is defended. Likewise, it is felt to be fair to transfer defended High Court specified money claims to the defendant's home court. There is therefore a system for automatically:

(a) sending County Court money claims to the claimant's preferred hearing centre where the claim is undefended and the court needs to either assess the amount payable or the rate of payment (CPR, rr 3.5A, 12.5A, 13.4(1A), 14.7A, 14.12(2A), 14.13(3A), and 26.2A(4));

(b) sending County Court claims for specified sums of money to the defendant's home court where the defendant is an individual. This happens at the 'relevant time', which is when all parties have filed their directions questionnaires, or when a stay to attempt mediation has expired, or if an application is made to set aside a default judgment (rr 13.4, 26.2A(3), (6)). Where there is more than one defendant, the case is sent to the home court of the defendant who first files a defence; and

(c) transferring High Court claims for specified sums of money to the defendant's home court where the defendant is an individual. These claims are transferred to the defendant's home court if a defence is filed or if an application is made to set aside a default judgment (rr 13.4, 26.2).

12.20 Transfers in other cases are governed by CCA 1984, ss 40 and 42 and by CPR, Part 30. Non-automatic transfers are usually dealt with in case management directions at the allocation stage, so will be considered at 15.37–15.40.

H SPECIALIST CLAIMS

12.21 Different rules apply in relation to responding to claims in specialist proceedings. In the TCC defendants must respond after service of the particulars of claim in the usual way by acknowledging service and filing a defence (CPR, r 60.3). However, once an acknowledgment of service or defence is filed the court will fix a case management conference (PD 60, para 8.1), after which the court exerts even greater control of the litigation than in usual multi-track claims.

12.22 The Admiralty Court has its own form for acknowledging service (form ADM2) including special acknowledgment of service forms, which must be filed within 14 days of service of the claim form (rather than the particulars of claim) (r 61.3(4)). This means that judgment in default can be obtained in claims *in rem* in default of either an acknowledgment of service or a defence (r 61.9(1)).

12.23 There are also specialist acknowledgment of service forms for use in the Commercial Court (N9(CC), N210(CC), and N213(CC)). An acknowledgment of service is required within 14 days of service of the claim form, even where the claim form is served without particulars of claim (r 58.6). Default judgment may be obtained without filing particulars of claim if the defendant fails to acknowledge service (r 58.8).

KEY POINTS SUMMARY

12.24
- In non-specialist Part 7 claims (typical litigation), the defendant must respond by acknowledging service or filing a defence within 14 days of service of the particulars of claim.
- Filing an acknowledgment of service extends the period for responding to 28 days.
- These periods can be extended by agreement or court order.
- In Commercial Court claims the defendant is required to acknowledge service of the claim form, even where this does not include particulars of claim.
- There are different boxes on the acknowledgment of service form (see form 6.3) for defending on the merits and for contesting jurisdiction.

13

DEFAULT JUDGMENT

A TIME WHEN DEFAULT JUDGMENT
   MAY BE ENTERED 13.04

B EXCLUDED CASES 13.10

C ENTERING DEFAULT JUDGMENT 13.13

D FINAL JUDGMENT AND JUDGMENT
   FOR AN AMOUNT TO BE DECIDED 13.20

E DECIDING THE AMOUNT OF DAMAGES:
   DISPOSAL HEARINGS 13.23

F SETTING ASIDE DEFAULT
   JUDGMENTS 13.29

G STAY OF UNDEFENDED CASES 13.42
   Key points summary 13.44

Judgment in default may be entered where the defendant fails to defend a claim. It produces **13.01** a judgment in favour of a claimant without holding a trial. The procedure is designed to prevent unnecessary expenditure of time, money, and court resources in protracted litigation over undefended claims. It is appropriate where the defendant is not defending on the merits.

A large proportion of the claims brought in the civil courts are little more than debt recov- **13.02** ery actions. Often, there is no dispute that the defendant has purchased goods or agreed to pay for services provided by the claimant, and has not paid for them. In fact there are hundreds of thousands of cases each year where proceedings are issued and served, and then are simply ignored by the defendants. Once the time for responding to the claim has elapsed, the claimant will think about entering judgment in default.

Actually entering a judgment in default is usually a purely administrative matter, and **13.03** involves no consideration by the court of the merits of the claim. All the claimant usually has to do, once the time for responding to the claim has elapsed, is to return a request form to the court asking for judgment to be entered. This will then be acted upon by the administrative staff at the court, and a judgment will be entered. Such a judgment binds the defendant just as much as if it had been entered after a contested trial, and may be enforced in the normal way. However, it may be set aside if the defendant can show a real prospect of defending the claim (see 13.32).

A TIME WHEN DEFAULT JUDGMENT MAY BE ENTERED

Part 7 claims

A defendant to a Part 7 claim (ie an ordinary non-specialist claim) who has been served **13.04** with the particulars of claim has 14 days from the effective date of service to make a response (CPR, r 10.3). Slightly longer periods are allowed where proceedings are served outside the jurisdiction. A response may be entered by filing an acknowledgment of service or a defence. The 14 days are calculated using the ordinary rules on calculating the effective date for service, for which see Chapter 6. Consequently, a defendant cannot be in default until that time has elapsed. For non-specialist Part 7 claims, a defendant cannot be in default if a claim form is served without particulars of claim until the particulars of claim are actually served. In such cases, time starts running for default judgment purposes only from the effective date of service of the particulars of claim.

13.05 A defendant who has taken the precaution of acknowledging service has a total of 28 days from the effective date of service of the particulars of claim in which to serve a defence and prevent judgment being entered in default (CPR, r 15.4).

13.06 For ordinary claims r 12.3 allows a claimant to enter a default judgment in the following circumstances:

(a) if the defendant has not filed an acknowledgment of service or a defence to the claim (or any part of the claim), and 14 days have expired since service of the particulars of claim; or

(b) if the defendant has filed an acknowledgment of service but has not filed a defence, and 28 days have expired since service of the particulars of claim.

13.07 These periods can be extended, either by agreement (for a further period of up to 28 days: r 15.5) or by order of the court. Extensions of time are granted quite readily in complicated cases or where there are genuine reasons for not being able to file a defence within the time limited by the rules. Obviously, where an extension has been granted, default judgment may be entered only once the extended period has expired (r 12.3). Similarly, time does not run during the period of any stay of the proceedings (see 30.47ff and *Roundstone Nurseries Ltd v Stephenson Holdings Ltd* [2009] 5 Costs LR 787).

Commercial and Circuit Commercial Court claims

13.08 In every claim proceeding in the Commercial Court and the Circuit Commercial Court, after service of the claim form (whether with or without particulars of claim) the defendant must file an acknowledgment of service (CPR, rr 58.6(1) and 59.5(1)). This means that default judgments can be obtained in these courts:

(a) if the defendant fails to acknowledge service within 14 days of service of the claim form; or

(b) if the defendant fails to file and serve a defence within 14 days of service of the particulars of claim.

13.09 In the Commercial Court the procedure for entering default judgment is the same as the normal rules described at 13.13ff. In the Circuit Commercial Court, judgment in default of an acknowledgment of service can only be entered on making an application (without notice) to the court (r 59.7).

B EXCLUDED CASES

Part 8 claims and petitions

13.10 Judgment in default is not available in Part 8 claims (CPR, r 12.2(b)). The procedure relating to petitions does not include acknowledging service or serving defences, so default judgments are not available in this form of litigation either.

Excluded Part 7 claims

13.11 Default judgments are not available in a number of Part 7 claims even if the defendant fails to respond to the claim. Excluded cases where the nature of the proceedings is a bar to obtaining a default judgment are set out in CPR, r 12.2 and PD 12, paras 1.2 and 1.3, as follows:

(a) claims for the delivery of goods subject to an agreement regulated by the Consumer Credit Act 1974;
(b) claims for provisional damages;
(c) claims governed by certain specialized procedures which do not include a requirement to file a defence or acknowledgment of service, or which provide special rules for obtaining default judgments. Cases falling into this subcategory are:
  (i) admiralty proceedings;
  (ii) arbitration proceedings;
  (iii) possession claims; and
  (iv) contentious probate proceedings.

Claims excluded by reason of steps taken

In certain circumstances, some step taken by the defendant will prevent the claimant entering judgment in default. Cases in this category are set out in CPR, r 12.3(3), which says that a claimant may not obtain a default judgment if: **13.12**

(a) the defendant has applied for summary judgment under Part 24, or to strike out the claim under r 3.4, and that application has not been disposed of;
(b) the defendant has satisfied the whole claim (including any claim for costs) on which the claimant is seeking judgment;
(c) (i) the claimant is seeking judgment on a claim for money; and
  (ii) the defendant has filed or served on the claimant an admission under r 14.4 or 14.7 (admission of liability to pay all of the money claimed) together with a request for time to pay; or
(d) notice has been given of an intention to make an application for a declaration under the Justice and Security Act 2013, s 6 and CPR, Part 82, and that application has not been disposed of. This deals with closed material applications in relation to sensitive material which, if disclosed, would be injurious to national security.

C ENTERING DEFAULT JUDGMENT

Money claims and claims for delivery of goods

In claims seeking to recover money and/or the delivery of goods (provided the defendant has the alternative of paying the value of the goods), which are by far the most common types of cases, default judgments are available simply by filing a standard-form request. The claimant entering the judgment sends the form to the court office and a member of the court staff will enter the judgment. There is no hearing and no question of trying to persuade the court to enter judgment. **13.13**

When proceedings are issued the court will send the claimant a notice of issue. There are three different forms of notice of issue: one for specified money claims, another for unspecified money claims, and the third for non-money claims. The two money claim notices (forms N205A and N205B) include a tear-off section for the request for judgment. In the top part of the form the court staff enter the claim number, the date of issue, and the dates when the claim form was posted to the defendant, the deemed date of service, and the date by which the defendant has to respond. All the claimant has to do is wait until the time for responding has elapsed, then, if the claim is for a specified sum of money, tick a box saying **13.14** the defendant has failed to respond, enter the defendant's date of birth (if known) and details of the judgment sought. This involves calculating the amount owed together with interest and fixed costs (as set out in the CPR), and deciding whether to ask for the whole sum to be paid immediately or by stated instalments. The request form is then signed, dated, and returned to the court.

13.15 If the particulars of claim were served by the claimant, judgment in default cannot be obtained unless a certificate of service (see form 6.6) has been filed: CPR, r 6.17(2)(b) and PD 12, para 4.1. There is no need for such a certificate if service is effected by the court (r 6.17(1)).

Non-money claims

13.16 Default judgments in non-money and non-recovery of goods claims (principally these will be cases where some form of equitable relief is sought, such as injunctions) have to be applied for (see 13.18). In other words, where equitable relief is sought and the defendant does not defend the claim, a judgment can be obtained only at a hearing before a Master, District Judge, or judge who will decide whether to exercise the court's discretion to grant the relief sought.

Money and goods claims where permission is required

13.17 Within the context of claims seeking money or recovery of goods, there are a number of exceptional cases where default judgments cannot be entered by filing a request, but only by obtaining permission after making an application. These are:

(a) Where the claim form was served out of the jurisdiction without permission (pursuant to the recast Judgments Regulation, the Lugano Convention, the Hague Convention 2005, or the Modified Convention) (CPR, r 12.10(b)). Service outside the jurisdiction was considered in Chapter 11. Where service is effected outside the jurisdiction under the Service Regulation (see 11.49), judgment in default cannot be given until it is established that service was effected by a method prescribed by the internal law of the receiving State or that the documents were actually delivered to the defendant or to his residence by another method provided by the Service Regulation (Service Regulation, art 19). The claimant's evidence in support of the application for judgment must establish that the claim is one that the English court has power to hear and decide, that no other court has exclusive jurisdiction, and that the claim form has been properly served in accordance with the relevant Convention or Regulation (PD 12, para 4.3). The evidence in this particular case must be on affidavit (rather than the usual witness statement format) (PD 12, para 4.5).

(b) Where the defendant is a child or protected party (CPR, r 12.10(a)(i)). Before applying for judgment the claimant must apply for the appointment of a litigation friend to represent the person under disability. On the application for judgment the evidence must satisfy the court that the claimant is entitled to the judgment sought (PD 12, para 4.2).

(c) Where the claim is for or includes costs other than fixed costs (CPR, r 12.9).

(d) Where the claim is brought by one spouse against the other on a claim in tort (CPR, r 12.10(a)(ii)).

(e) Where the claim seeks delivery-up of goods where the defendant is not to be allowed the alternative of paying their value. Relief in this form, unlike other types of delivery-up orders which may be asked for in claims relating to goods, is discretionary (see the Torts (Interference with Goods) Act 1977), which is why an application must be made.

The evidence in support must identify the goods and say where the goods are believed to be kept and why the claimant says an order for specific delivery-up should be granted (PD 12, para 4.6). Usually this will have to be because of the rare or irreplaceable nature of the goods concerned.

Applications for permission to enter default judgment

Chapter 23 describes how to make applications. The application will be made by issuing an application notice, which must state the defendant's date of birth (if known), and must be supported by written evidence. The evidence should include a certificate of service if the particulars of claim were served by the claimant. There is no need to serve the evidence in support on any defendant who did not acknowledge service (CPR, r 12.11(2)). This means that a defendant who acknowledged service but failed to file a defence has to be served with the evidence in support. Although the evidence in support in many cases does not need to be served on the defendant, the defendant should in all cases (other than service outside the jurisdiction, see 13.17 sub-para (a)) be given notice of the application itself by being served with the application notice (PD 12, para 5.1). **13.18**

The purpose behind requiring permission before default judgments are entered in the cases described at 13.16 and 13.17 is to enable the court to grant relief appropriate to the circumstances of the case or to scrutinize the application in a number of situations where care is needed before judgment is entered. They impose obligations to ensure procedural fairness. They do not amount to entering judgment on the merits (*Football Dataco Ltd v Smoot Enterprises Ltd* [2011] 1 WLR 1978). A defendant may seek to prevent judgment being entered in default by filing or seeking to file an acknowledgment of service or a defence on or just before the return day for the claimant's application. Where this happens the defendant should issue a cross-application for an extension of time. Whether permission will be granted is a matter for the court's discretion. **13.19**

D FINAL JUDGMENT AND JUDGMENT FOR AN AMOUNT TO BE DECIDED

There are two main types of judgment obtainable in money claims. The best type is a final judgment, which will require the defendant to pay a set amount of money usually within 14 days. Apart from giving the defendant a limited amount of time to raise the money, this type of judgment allows the claimant to recover the whole sum straight away or to apply to enforce if the defendant does not pay. **13.20**

The other type is a judgment for damages to be decided by the court. There are variations on this form of judgment, such as judgments for the value of goods to be decided by the court and judgment for the amount of interest to be decided by the court. This type of judgment is sometimes called an 'interlocutory judgment', and the rules occasionally refer to this type of judgment as a 'relevant order'. This second type of judgment means that liability has been established and will not be considered any further, but all questions relating to the amount of damages or interest payable, or the value of the goods, have yet to be determined. **13.21**

Final judgment will be entered in claims for specified sums (CPR, r 12.5), whereas judgment for damages to be decided will be entered in claims for unspecified amounts. There is some doubt as to what is meant by 'specified'. It could mean simply that the claim form has set out a specified sum sought by the claimant. Alternatively, it could mean the same thing as a liquidated demand. Liquidated demands are claims such as for the **13.22** repayment of a loan or bank overdraft, or for the price of goods or services, or for rent. For each of these the amount claimed is fixed by the underlying agreement between the parties. This is so even though the amount may need to be calculated, such as the interest payable on the overdraft, or the rent payable over a period of time. Liquidated demands are usually contrasted with claims for unliquidated damages, such as for personal injuries or for the unsatisfactory quality of goods sold. Valuing an unliquidated claim requires an exercise of judicial judgment. Consequently, one school of thought takes the view that all damages claims are unspecified, and so default judgments in these cases should be for damages to be decided. However, the other school of thought takes the view that if the claimant spells out in the particulars of claim the amount of damages claimed the claim becomes one for a specified amount, so that a final judgment can be obtained.

E DECIDING THE AMOUNT OF DAMAGES: DISPOSAL HEARINGS

13.23 When the court enters a default judgment of the second type for damages or interest to be decided, or for the value of goods to be decided by the court, it will give any directions it considers appropriate. Further, if it thinks it appropriate, it will also allocate the claim to a case management track (CPR, r 12.7). Alternatively, the court may list the matter for a disposal hearing, or will stay the action while the parties try to settle the case using ADR or other means.

13.24 The orders being considered here are described as 'relevant orders' by PD 26, para 12. In addition to being one of the possibilities on obtaining a default judgment, they may also be made on entry of judgment on an admission; on the striking out of a statement of case; on a summary judgment application; on the determination of a preliminary issue or on a split trial as to liability; or even by consent or at trial.

Disposal hearings

13.25 At a disposal hearing the court will either give directions or decide the amount payable (PD 26, para 12.4(2)). Relevant orders made by entry of default judgment without a hearing are usually dealt with in this way.

13.26 If the case is listed for a disposal hearing and the claim is worth less than £10,000, the court will usually allocate it to the small claims track (for costs purposes) and decide the amount payable there and then (PD 26, paras 12.3(1), 12.4(3)). If the financial value of the claim is more than £10,000 the court may still determine the amount payable at the disposal hearing, but in these cases the ordinary costs rules will apply. In cases determined at disposal hearings evidence may, unless the court otherwise directs, be adduced under CPR, r 32.6 (PD 26, para 12.4(4)). This means that reliance may be placed on the matters set out in the particulars of claim (provided it is verified by a statement of truth) or by witness statement. The evidence relied upon must be served on the defendant at least three clear days before the disposal hearing.

Allocating relevant order cases to tracks

13.27 Allocating a case to the fast track or multi-track after a relevant order has been made should happen only if the amount payable is genuinely disputed on grounds that appear to be substantial (PD 26, para 12.4(3)). Track allocation is considered further in Chapter 15.

Hearing to assess damages

Generally, hearings to assess damages will be listed before Masters and District Judges irre- **13.28** spective of the amount in issue (PD 26, para 12.6), but the court may give directions specifying the level or type of judge who is to deal with the case (PD 26, para 12.2(2)). Other directions made will include a timetable for disclosure of documents, the exchange of witness statements, and for the admission of expert evidence and disclosure of reports from experts. Hearings to assess damages are trials, and so trial bundles and formal evidence are required. On an assessment of damages the defendant can raise any point which goes to quantification of the damage, provided that it is not inconsistent with any issue settled by the judgment (*Lunnun v Singh* [1999] CPLR 587). Where judgment for damages to be assessed was entered after the court rejected a defence that the claimant was guilty of gross misconduct disentitling him to any damages, it was still open for the defence to raise mitigation of damages on the assessment (*Pugh v Cantor Fitzgerald International* [2001] CPLR 271).

F SETTING ASIDE DEFAULT JUDGMENTS

The CPR, rr 13.2 and 13.3, provide grounds on which the court either may or must set **13.29** aside or vary judgments entered in default. The court may exercise these powers either on an application made by the defendant or on its own initiative. Litigation is not a game of 'snap', and it has long been recognized that the court needs to have the power to set aside judgments entered without a full consideration of the merits of the claim.

Setting aside as of right

In limited circumstances the court *must* set aside a default judgment. This is restricted to **13.30** certain cases where the default judgment was wrongly entered (CPR, r 13.2). There is a restrictive definition for this, limited to:

(a) situations where the essential conditions about failing to acknowledge service or defend, or the relevant time having elapsed, are not satisfied; or
(b) the claim was satisfied before judgment was entered; or
(c) the defendant had already applied for summary judgment or to strike out the claim; or
(d) the defendant had already filed an admission requesting time to pay.

Judgment was set aside as of right under para (a) in *Crédit Agricole Indosuez v Unicof Ltd* **13.31** (2003) LTL 4/2/03. The claimant purported to serve the claim form by leaving it with the defendant's company secretary in Kenya, whereas service in Kenya had to be by leaving the claim form at the company's registered office. As the claim form had not been served, the defendant was entitled to have the judgment set aside. Judgment was also set aside as of right in *Intense Investments Ltd v Development Ventures Ltd* [2005] BLR 478, because it had been entered by the request method (see 13.13–13.15) in circumstances where the application method (see 13.16–13.19) should have been used.

Discretion to set aside

In other cases, the court has a discretion whether to set aside or vary a default judgment. **13.32** The requirements are:

(a) the defendant must have a real prospect of successfully defending the claim (CPR, r 13.3(1)(a)); or

(b) whether there is some other good reason why the judgment should be set aside or varied, or for the defendant to be allowed to defend the claim (CPR, r 13.3(1)(b)); and

(c) in either case, taking into account a range of factors, including whether the application to set aside has been made promptly (CPR, r 13.3(2)).

13.33 On an application to set aside under r 13.3 it is necessary to consider first the express requirements of r 13.3, and secondly to consider the relief from sanctions principles laid down in *Denton v TH White Ltd* [2014] 1 WLR 3926 (see 37.22ff and *Gentry v Miller* [2016] 1 WLR 2696). In *Thorn plc v MacDonald* [1999] CPLR 660, the Court of Appeal approved the following principles under r 13.3:

(a) while the length of any delay in making the application must be taken into account, any pre-action delay is irrelevant;

(b) any failure by the defendant to provide a good explanation for the delay is a factor to be taken into account, but is not always a reason to refuse to set aside;

(c) the primary considerations are whether there is a defence with a real prospect of success, and that justice should be done. The question whether there is a defence with a real prospect of success is the same as on applications for summary judgment (*ED & F Man Liquid Products Ltd v Patel* [2003] CPLR 384), and is discussed in detail at 24.15–24.42;

(d) prejudice (or the absence of it) to the claimant also has to be taken into account.

13.34 *Gentry v Miller* decided that:

(a) the first *Denton* principle, consideration of whether the breach was serious or significant, applies to the delay in acknowledging service or filing a defence, which is the original breach that resulted in the default judgment being entered; and

(b) while promptness is part of the r 13.3 test, it also has to be considered as part of all the circumstances of the case, which is the third *Denton* principle.

Some other good reason

Defendant unaware of the proceedings

13.35 Once it is proved (eg by a certificate of service) that proceedings have been served by one of the methods prescribed by the CPR, service is deemed to take effect on the date laid down by r 6.14 (see 6.40), and evidence to prove the contrary is not admissible (see 6.45). This is so even if the documents are returned undelivered provided they were sent to the correct address for service. Where a default judgment has been entered after the expiry of 14 days from the deemed date of service in a case where the defendant did not in fact receive the proceedings, setting aside is subject to the court's discretion rather than as of right (*Godwin v Swindon Borough Council* [2002] 1 WLR 997). Such a defendant will either have to show a defence with a real prospect of success, or rely on non-service as 'some other good reason' for setting aside the judgment. According to May LJ this may arise where a defendant would have paid instead of having an embarrassing judgment entered, and it may give grounds for departing from the usual rule of the defendant being ordered to pay the costs thrown away (see 13.40). Requiring a defendant who is deemed to have been served to show a defence with a real prospect of success or some other good reason before setting aside does not infringe the European Convention on Human Rights, art 6(1) (*Akram v Adam* [2005] 1 WLR 2762). It would be wrong to give too much weight to the comment of Mummery LJ in *Raja v Van Hoogstraten (No 9)* [2009] 1 WLR 1143 at [84] that in cases where the defendant is unaware of the proceedings any default judgment should be set aside unless there are exceptional circumstances, as the case was about a different provision in the CPR (r 23.10).

Failure to include the response pack

In *Rajval Construction Ltd v Bestville Properties Ltd* [2011] CILL 2994 the claimant failed **13.36** to enclose a response pack when serving the claim form and particulars of claim. Whether this amounts to a 'good reason' for setting aside a default judgment depends on the circumstances. In this case the defendant was in effect a litigant in person, so the lack of the response pack justified setting aside the default judgment without conditions.

Claimant's conduct amounting to a good reason

It can be relevant for the court to consider the conduct of the parties in deciding whether **13.37** there is some other good reason for setting aside a default judgment (*Hart Investments Ltd v Fidler* [2007] BLR 30). There may be a good reason for setting aside where the conduct in entering the judgment is regarded as unreasonable, such as where the claimant takes advantage of a mutual failing to extend a stay (*Roundstone Nurseries Ltd v Stephenson Holdings Ltd* [2009] 5 Costs LR 787).

Promptness, general discretion, and relief from sanctions

As mentioned at 13.32, the court will take into account whether an application to set **13.38** aside a default judgment has been made promptly. In *Regione Piemonte v Dexia Crediop SpA* [2014] EWCA Civ 1298 Christopher Clarke LJ at [40] said that the considerations in r 3.9 and the approach in *Denton* must be taken into account under r 13.3(2), which makes clear by the use of the word 'include' that there may be a number of factors the court should take into account. These include enforcing compliance with rules, practice directions, and court orders as required by r 1.1(2)(f), as well as the need to apply promptly as expressly stated by r 13.3(2). *Gentry v Miller* [2016] 1 WLR 2696 points out that r 3.9(1)(a) (the need for litigation to be conducted efficiently and proportionately) also needs to be given particular weight. On the facts of *Regione Piemonte* a seven-month delay was held to be serious and significant, which meant the application to set aside had not been made promptly, and there were no other factors to justify setting aside. Where there is undue delay, it is clear that an application to set aside a default judgment can fail purely on this ground, even if there is a defence with a real prospect of success (*Standard Bank plc v Agrinvest International Inc* [2010] 2 CLC 886).

Discretion where defendant outside jurisdiction

Where service was effected outside the jurisdiction under the Service Regulation (see annex **13.39** to PD 6B), the court has power under the Service Regulation, art 19(4), to relieve the defendant from the effect of any judgment entered in default if:

(a) the defendant, without any fault on his part, did not have knowledge of the documents served in sufficient time to defend; and
(b) the defendant discloses a *prima facie* defence to the claim on its merits.

Setting aside on conditions

If the court sets aside a default judgment, it may do so on terms (CPR, r 3.1(3)). Conditions **13.40** imposed on setting aside a default judgment are not intended to punish the defendant, but to ensure that justice is achieved between the parties (*Hussain v Birmingham City Council* [2005] EWCA Civ 1570). In most cases the defaulting defendant will be ordered to pay the claimant's costs thrown away. In addition, the court may consider imposing a condition that the defendant must pay a specified sum of money into court to await the final disposal of the claim. Typically this is the full amount of the claim, but it must not be a figure the defendant will find it impossible to pay, because that would be tantamount to refusing to set aside (*MV Yorke Motors v Edwards* [1982] 1 WLR 444). The sum paid into court makes it easy for the claimant to recover any sum found due at trial, and also operates as a secured fund if the defendant becomes insolvent (*Re Ford* [1900] 2 QB 211).

Consequential orders

13.41 On setting aside a default judgment the court may need to make consequential orders dealing with any steps, such as enforcement action, taken by the claimant relying on the default judgment. A final injunction (or other final equitable relief) granted by a judge (see 13.16) based on the defendant's failure to defend may be set aside applying the principles under r 13.3 on an application to set aside the underlying default judgment on liability (*S v Beach* [2015] 1 WLR 2701).

G STAY OF UNDEFENDED CASES

13.42 If none of the defendants to a claim file admissions or defences, the claimant should generally enter judgment in default shortly after the time for filing has elapsed, but in any event within six months of the period for filing the defence. Once the six months have elapsed, the claim is automatically stayed by virtue of CPR, r 15.11.

13.43 Any party may apply to lift the stay. This is done by making an application in accordance with the procedure discussed in Chapter 23, giving the reason for the delay in proceeding with or responding to the claim (PD 15, para 3.4). In considering whether to lift the stay the court will apply the criteria for granting relief from sanctions in r 3.9, which are discussed in Chapter 37: see *Audergon v La Baguette Ltd* [2002] CPLR 192.

KEY POINTS SUMMARY

13.44 • Judgment in default may be entered once the period for responding to a claim has elapsed.

  • In money claims, default judgment is usually entered simply by filing a certificate of service and a request for judgment.

  • In non-money claims (mostly claims for equitable relief) and certain exceptional cases (eg where the defendant is a child or patient), a formal application must be made for default judgment.

  • Final judgment will be entered in money claims for specified amounts.

  • In money claims where the amount sought is unspecified, any default judgment will be for damages to be decided by the court.

  • A default judgment which is entered irregularly (eg prematurely) will be set aside as of right.

  • A regular default judgment will only be set aside if there is a defence with a real prospect of success or some other good reason for allowing the defendant to defend the claim.

  • Conditions as to costs and paying money into court may be imposed if a default judgment is set aside.

14

STATEMENTS OF CASE

A FORM OF STATEMENTS OF CASE 14.05
B PARTICULARS OF CLAIM 14.20
C DEFENCE 14.27
D COUNTERCLAIMS AND SET-OFFS 14.32
E REPLY AND DEFENCE TO
    COUNTERCLAIM 14.39
F SUBSEQUENT STATEMENTS OF CASE .. 14.41
G DISPENSING WITH STATEMENTS
    OF CASE 14.42
H SCOTT SCHEDULES 14.43
I INTERRELATION WITH CASE
    MANAGEMENT 14.44
J USE OF STATEMENTS OF CASE
    AT TRIAL 14.45

14.01 The early stages of a common law action commenced by ordinary claim form are dominated by the exchange of statements of case by the respective parties. Statements of case are formal documents used in litigation to define what each party says about the case. They have a number of functions, including:

(a) Informing the other parties of the case they will have to meet. This helps to ensure neither party is taken by surprise at trial.
(b) Defining the issues that need to be decided. This helps to save costs by limiting the investigations that need to be made and the evidence that needs to be prepared for the trial, and also helps to reduce the length of trials.
(c) Providing the judges dealing with the case (both for case management purposes and at trial) with a concise statement of what the case is about.

14.02 'Statements of case' include all the following documents:

(a) the claim form;
(b) particulars of claim where this document is not included in a claim form;
(c) defence;
(d) counterclaim;
(e) additional claims under Part 20 (which will be considered further in Chapter 20);
(f) reply to defence;
(g) Scott schedules (*Easygroup IP Licensing Ltd v Easyjet Airline Co Ltd* [2009] EWHC 1386 (Ch)); and
(h) any further information given in relation to these documents whether voluntarily or by court order (see Chapter 18).

14.03 The equivalent documents used in judicial review proceedings are statements of case (*R (Corner House Research) v Director of the Serious Fraud Office* [2008] EWHC 246 (Admin)). Winding-up petitions have to be verified by a statement of truth (IR 2016, r 7.6), so they should also be regarded as statements of case.

14.04 Statements of case in Part 7 claims are served in sequence, with the claimant serving particulars of claim first, followed by a defence from the defendant, then possibly a reply from the claimant. They are often the first documents read by a judge, and obviously it is wise to give a good impression by ensuring they are well drafted. Also, a party may be prejudiced on the substantive issues in the claim if they are not adequately set out in the statements of case, particularly if the court refuses permission to amend (a topic considered in Chapter 22).

A FORM OF STATEMENTS OF CASE

Physical form

14.05 A statement of case, like all other court documents, should be on A4 paper (unless the form of the document makes this impractical), of durable quality, and with a margin of at least 35 mm (PD 5A, para 2.2). It must be fully legible, and should normally be typed. It should be securely bound together in a manner that will not hamper filing (if this is not possible, each page should include the claim number). A statement of case exceeding 25 pages must be accompanied by a short summary (PD 16, para 1.4). Exceeding 25 pages without first seeking permission may result in adverse costs orders (*Tchenguiz v Grant Thornton UK LLP* [2015] EWHC 405 (Comm)).

Heading

14.06 A statement of case starts with a heading. This will include the name of the court in which the claim is proceeding, such as by the words 'IN THE COUNTY COURT' or 'IN THE HIGH COURT OF JUSTICE'. In High Court cases this is followed by the Division (QBD, ChD, or FamD). Claims in a specialist court then identify that court. Traditionally this information is set out in the top left-hand corner. Traditionally, the claim reference number will appear in the top right-hand corner. This is the number allocated to the claim by the court when it is issued.

14.07 There then follows the title of the proceedings. The word 'BETWEEN' appears on the left-hand side underneath the name of the court. This is followed by the names of the parties down the centre of the page, with the claimants' names first, and the word 'Claimants' on the right-hand side of the page, followed by the names of the defendants, and the word 'Defendants' on the right-hand side of the page. The defendants are separated from the claimants by the word 'and'. Multiple claimants or defendants are usually numbered '(1)', '(2)', etc. to the left of their names. Rules on how to name different types of party can be found in 19.04ff.

14.08 After setting out the names of the parties the heading will state the form of statement of case, such as 'PARTICULARS OF CLAIM', 'DEFENCE', or 'REPLY', usually in the centre of the page and between horizontal straight lines.

Contents

14.09 A claim form need only contain a concise statement of the nature of the claim (CPR, r 16.2(1)(a)). This imposes an obligation to inform the defendant in the simplest terms of the case the defendant has to meet (*Adams v Thomson Holidays Ltd* [2009] EWHC 2559 (QB)). Other statements of case should set out sufficient details of the facts relied upon for the other parties to know the case that is being advanced and for the court to be able to see what the issues are. Pages should be numbered consecutively, and the text should be divided into numbered paragraphs. All numbers and dates must be expressed as figures (PD 5A, para 2.2). The allegations should be stated in a summary form, and as briefly as the nature of the case permits. This means that all the elements necessary for establishing a cause of action or defence must be set out in the statement of case, and if even a single essential allegation is omitted, the statement of case will be amenable to being struck out (see Chapter 30, and *Bruce v Odhams Press Ltd* [1936] 1 KB 697). Further, sufficient background facts should be included so that a judge reading the statement of case for the first time will be able to understand the essential factual basis of the claim or defence.

The main rules in drafting statements of case are that they should set out the facts relied **14.10** upon, not the law and not the evidence. Despite this some leeway is given by the CPR. A party may refer to any point of law on which the claim or defence is based (PD 16, para 13.3(1)). This does not oblige a party to particularize or explain its legal arguments in its statement of case: that is the function of skeleton arguments (*Trader Publishing Ltd v Autotrader.Com Inc* [2010] EWHC 142 (Ch)). A statement of case may (not must) give the name of any witness intended to be called (para 13.3(2)). Any allegation that a witness or party has stolen evidence from the other side, or that an attempt has been made to bribe a witness, must be set out in the statement of case (*JN Dairies Ltd v Johal Dairies Ltd* [2010] EWCA Civ 348).

General allegations have to be supported by particulars. Commonly occurring examples **14.11** are particulars of negligence, of breach of statutory duty, of breach of contract, and of loss and damage. More specific examples include particulars of fraud, illegality, misrepresentation, breach of trust, knowledge, notice of a fact, unsoundness of mind, undue influence, wilful default, and mitigation of damage (PD 16, para 8.2). An allegation of 'systematic overcharging' has to be supported by particulars of the supposed system (*Clyde and Co LLP v New Look Interiors of Marlow Ltd* [2009] EWHC 173 (QB)). The extent of the particulars required depends on the nature of the allegation. Clear and detailed particulars will be required to support an allegation of fraud. Failing to plead losses flowing from specific transactions in a claim against a company director based on a conflict of interests was held to be defective in *Towler v Wills* [2010] EWHC 1209 (Comm)). Simply pleading the number of hours worked multiplied by the applicable hourly rates is sufficient for a claim for unpaid building work (*Clancy Consulting Ltd v Derwent Holdings Ltd* [2010] EWHC 762 (TCC)).

Material documents should in general simply be referred to, but with sufficient detail to **14.12** enable them to be identified. Quoting from documents is necessary in libel and misrepresentation claims to identify the words complained of. Quoting can also be useful in other cases (*Morris v Bank of America National Trust* [2000] 1 All ER 954), but can be counter to the overriding objective, particularly where the quotations are lengthy or numerous.

The ultimate purpose of statements of case is to inform the other party of the case against **14.13** him (*Conticorp SA v Central Bank of Ecuador* [2007] UKPC 40). The pleading in this case was regarded as being sufficient even though the issues were convoluted, because they were not in doubt, partly because of further information (see Chapter 18) which had been provided. An issue may also be sufficiently pleaded without express allegations provided the allegations which are pleaded raise the issue by clear implication (*Sinclair Investment Holdings SA v Versailles Trade Finance Ltd* [2006] 1 BCLC 60). On the other hand, a claim making broad, unfocused, and unparticularized allegations was struck out in *English, Welsh and Scottish Railway Ltd v Goodman* (2007) LTL 9/5/07. A 221-page particulars of claim was struck out in *Dunn v Glass Systems (UK) Ltd* (2007) LTL 23/7/07 because it was excessively long, contained details which were irrelevant to the cause of action, and contained a large number of incomprehensible terms.

There is no need to anticipate the other side's statement of case, so a claimant generally **14.14** should not answer possible lines of defence in the particulars of claim (this is the function of the reply). One well-settled exception to this relates to personal injuries claims issued more than three years after the relevant accident, where it is usual in the particulars of claim to give the grounds for alleging that the claimant can take the benefit of the Limitation Act 1980, s 14 or 33 (see 21.28 and 21.55ff). Facts presumed by law to be true need not be set out in the statement of case of the party relying on the presumption.

14.15 There is no objection to a claimant advancing alternative claims, provided the alternative sets of facts are clearly stated. In such cases the claimant can sign the statement of truth, which has the effect of stating the claimant's honest belief that on either one set of facts or the other his claim is made out. What is not permitted is a unified claim with contradictory facts, because in such a case the claimant cannot honestly sign a statement of truth (*Clarke v Marlborough Fine Art (London) Ltd* [2002] 1 WLR 1731). The dividing line between these two concepts has to be drawn applying the overriding objective. An alternative claim that is wholly speculative will not be allowed. On the other hand, a claimant will be allowed to plead different versions of how an incident happened where he has no personal knowledge of the material events, and has to rely on independent witnesses who give different versions of the facts. Another example is where the claimant, perhaps through having honestly convinced himself of the truth of his version of events as set out in the particulars of claim, gives evidence, but a different version of events emerges from the body of evidence at the trial. Permission is often given in such cases to plead the version that has emerged at trial. See *Binks v Securicor Omega Express Ltd* [2003] 1 WLR 2557. It is improper to set out facts in a statement of case which are contrary to the known and uncontested documentary evidence (*Re Unisoft Group Ltd (No 3)* [1994] 1 BCLC 609 at 618).

Supporting documentation

14.16 The parties are permitted to attach or serve with their statements of case copies of any documents which are considered necessary for the claim or defence (PD 16, para 13.3(3)). Documents served with a statement of claim may include experts' reports. In contract claims based on written agreements copies of the agreement or documents constituting the agreement must be attached to or served with the particulars of claim (para 7.3).

Final endorsements

14.17 A statement of case must bear the signature of the legal representative who drafted it. The engrossed version of a draft settled by counsel usually has counsel's name in capitals at the end of the draft, and is signed by the solicitor who has conduct of the case. A solicitor or employee of a firm of solicitors should sign in the firm's name (PD 5A, para 2.1). Litigants in person sign their own statements of case. Particulars of claim and defences should give an address for service, which should be within the jurisdiction or within the EEA, in order to comply with CPR, r 6.23(2).

Statement of truth

14.18 Every statement of case should be verified by a statement of truth (CPR, r 22.1(1)(a)). This states that the facts set out in the statement of case are believed to be true. The purpose of the statement of truth is to eliminate claims in which a party had no honest belief and to discourage claims unsupported by evidence which are put forward in the hope that something may turn up on disclosure or at trial (*Clarke v Marlborough Fine Art (London) Ltd* [2002] 1 WLR 1731). When a statement of case is amended, the court may dispense with reverification (r 22.1(2)). This power may be exercised where a party relies, in the alternative, on facts asserted by the other side which are inconsistent with the facts he relies on for his primary case (*Binks v Securicor Omega Express Ltd* [2003] 1 WLR 2557). The statement of truth must generally be signed by the party on whose behalf the statement of case has been drafted, or by that party's legal representative (r 22.1(6)). Any failure to include a statement of truth may result in an application for an unless order, with striking out as the sanction (PD 22, para 4.2).

Any person who makes, or causes to be made, a false statement in a document verified by **14.19** a statement of truth without an honest belief in its truth may be punished for contempt of court (CPR, r 32.14). However, proceedings for contempt under this rule may be brought only by the Attorney-General or with the permission of the court (rr 81.17, 81.18). In County Court cases, permission needs to be sought from a single judge of the High Court (r 81.18(3)). A party intending to make such an application should give advance warning to the maker of the statement, but such warning should not be given until after that person has given evidence (*KJM Superbikes Ltd v Hinton* [2009] 1 WLR 2406). The question on an application for permission is whether the matter is sufficiently serious that committal proceedings will be in the public interest (*KJM Superbikes Ltd v Hinton*). At the committal hearing the falsity and lack of honest belief have to be proved beyond reasonable doubt (*Kirk v Walton* [2009] EWHC 703 (QB)).

B PARTICULARS OF CLAIM

Contents

The particulars of claim will set out the claimant's causes of action and the relief or remedy **14.20** claimed. As mentioned at 14.09, the particulars of claim must set out the essential elements of the causes of action asserted. The particulars must also set out the facts giving rise to the dispute, and must cover the facts which are the essential elements, as a matter of law, of the cause of action on which the case is based. For certain categories of claim (eg personal injuries claims, fatal accidents, hire-purchase claims, claims raising human rights issues, and claims for the recovery of land) PD 16 sets out details that need to be included in the particulars of claim. An example of particulars of claim in a personal injuries claim can be seen in figure 14.1. An example of particulars of claim incorporated into a claim form in a breach of contract claim can be seen in form 6.1. In contractual claims the particulars of claim should state whether the agreement was written or oral, its date, and who acted for each side in forming the contract. Written contracts must be attached to or served with the particulars of claim, and in oral contracts the particulars must include the contractual words used, who said them, to whom, when, and where (PD 16, paras 7.3, 7.4).

Figure 14.1 Particulars of Claim

IN THE COUNTY COURTBETWEEN:—   Claim No 8YK982645

Mrs PHILLIPPA MAY MYERS   Claimant

and

Mr NIGEL JAMES STANIFORTH   Defendant

PARTICULARS OF CLAIM

Figure 14.1 *continued*

1 On 19 July 2017 the Defendant was driving a car registration number CY09 733 JLF west along the A427 near Weldon, Northamptonshire, and the Claimant was driving her car registration number PD61 KWM east along the A427 travelling towards the Defendant's car.

2 As the Defendant approached the Claimant's car he was in the process of overtaking a line of vehicles. At this location the A427 is a single lane carriageway, and the Defendant was therefore driving in the oncoming lane.

3 The Defendant failed to return to his own lane, and collided with the Claimant's car ('the collision').

4 The collision was caused by the negligence of the Defendant.

PARTICULARS OF NEGLIGENCE

The Defendant was negligent in:

    (a) failing to keep any or any proper look-out;

    (b) failing to see the Claimant's car, or to notice or take account of the presence or approach of the Claimant's car;

    (c) driving on the wrong side of the road when it was unsafe to do so;

    (d) overtaking when it was unsafe to do so;

    (e) driving too fast in the circumstances;

    (f) failing to give precedence to the Claimant's vehicle; and/or

    (g) failing to stop, slow down, or steer so as to avoid the collision.

5 As a result of the matters set out above the Claimant has suffered personal injuries, pain, suffering, loss, and damage.

PARTICULARS OF INJURY

The Claimant, who was born on 14 July 1981 and was aged 36 years at the date of the collision, suffered:

    (a) fractured right fibula and tibia;

    (b) whiplash injuries to her cervical spine;

    (c) multiple cuts, abrasions, and bruises;

    (d) nervous reaction involving flashbacks, disturbance of sleep, and panic attacks.

Further particulars of the Claimant's injuries are given in the medical report of Mr S Long served with these particulars of claim.

PARTICULARS OF LOSS AND DAMAGE

The Claimant's losses are set out in the Schedule of Past and Future Loss and Expense served with these particulars of claim.

6 Further, the Claimant is entitled to interest pursuant to the County Courts Act 1984, section 69:

    (a) upon special damages at the full relevant special account rates from the date of accrual of each item of non-recurring special damage and at half the relevant special account rates for the period of each item of recurring special damage; and

    (b) upon general damages at the rate of 2 per cent per annum from the date of service of the claim form, until the date of judgment or earlier payment.

Figure 14.1 *continued*

AND the Claimant seeks:
  (1) Damages;
  (2) Interest pursuant to the County Courts Act 1984, section 69.

Statement of Truth

(I believe) (The Claimant believes) that the facts stated in these particulars of claim are true.

I am duly authorized by the Claimant to sign this statement.

In addition to setting out the cause of action relied upon, particulars of claim must include **14.21** details of the remedies being claimed. Thus particulars of claim must contain details of any claim for aggravated or exemplary damages, any claim for provisional damages, and any other remedy sought. Particulars of claim must also give full details of any interest claimed, including the rate, period covered, and the authority for claiming it. Interest claims are most often based on the CCA 1984, s 69, the SCA 1981, s 35A, or the Late Payment of Commercial Debts (Interest) Act 1998. See BCP, Chapter 64.

The form for the statement of truth required for particulars of claim is: **14.22**

  I believe [The Claimant believes] that the facts stated in these particulars of claim are true.

Personal injuries claims

Particulars of claim in personal injuries claims must, in addition to stating the basis of **14.23** the claim, state the claimant's date of birth and give brief details of the injuries sustained (PD 16, para 4.1).

Further, the claimant must attach a schedule of details of any past and future expenses and **14.24** losses that are claimed (para 4.2), which must also be verified by a statement of truth. A simple example is given in figure 14.2. A medical report should be attached to or served with the particulars of claim dealing with the injuries sustained (para 4.3). This report should deal with condition and prognosis, but does not need to extend to breach of duty and causation, even in a clinical dispute case (*Duce v Worcestershire Acute Hospitals NHS Trust* [2014] EWCA Civ 249). In soft tissue injury claims (see 9.17) the claimant may not proceed unless the report used is a fixed cost medical report from an accredited medical expert (PD 16, para 4.3A).

Recovery of land

In claims for the recovery of land the particulars of claim must identify the land sought to be **14.25** recovered, state whether the claim relates to residential premises, give details of any tenancy agreement, information about any mortgage, and various other details as set out in PD 55A, paras 2.1–2.7. There are prescribed forms for particulars of claim in several types of claim for the recovery of land, such as N119, which is the prescribed form of particulars of claim for possession claims for rented property. This document is three pages long, and divided into ten paragraphs with boxes to be completed with information about the tenancy and the tenant.

Human rights points

Where a party seeks to raise a human rights point, the particulars of claim (and any other **14.26** type of statement of claim or appeal notice filed on behalf of that party) must set out precise details of the Convention right relied upon. It must also give details of the alleged infringement and it must state the relief sought (PD 16, para 15.1).

Figure 14.2 Schedule of special damages

IN THE COUNTY COURT   Claim No 8YK982645

BETWEEN:—

Mrs PHILLIPPA MAY MYERS   Claimant

and

                                                         Defendant
Mr NIGEL JAMES STANIFORTH

SCHEDULE OF PAST AND FUTURE
LOSS AND EXPENSE AT 23 MAY 2018

                                                         AMOUNT
ITEM

1 Before the accident on 19 July 2017 the Claimant was   £35,806.75
employed as a data analyst with a salary of £1,813 per month
net. The Claimant has been unable to return to work, and
her contract of employment was terminated with effect from
1 September 2017. She has been unable to find employment and
has been unemployed for 1 year, 7 months, 21 days.

2 Continuing loss of earnings at the rate of £1,813 net per
month.

3 The Claimant's salary in her former employment as a data
analyst was subject to upwards annual review on 1 January
each year. She accordingly has a continuing loss in the net
amount of each annual review, full particulars of which will be
given on disclosure of documents.

4 Damaged clothing comprising:

Dress	£45.99
Cardigan	£29.99
Shoes	£27.49
Watch	£54.00
Sub-total	£157.47

5 Travel to hospital outpatients department   £35.00

6 Prescriptions: 4 at £8.60   £34.40

Statement of Truth

I believe that the facts stated in this schedule of past and future loss and expense are true.

Signed:

Dated:

C DEFENCE

General

14.27 The defence is intended to answer the allegations made in the particulars of claim. Like all
other statements of case, a defence must contain a statement of truth. The defence must
be filed at court (CPR, r 15.2) and served on every other party (r 15.6) within 14 days of

service of the particulars of claim, or 28 days if the defendant has acknowledged service. Several defendants with the same interest in a claim may serve identical defences, in which case they must act by the same solicitors and instruct the same counsel at trial. Defendants who serve different defences may instruct the same or different lawyers.

Answering the particulars of claim

By CPR, r 16.5(1), a defence must state: **14.28**

(a) which allegations in the particulars of claim are denied. Denials are used for any facts which, if they had occurred, would have been within the defendant's knowledge. This covers cases where the defendant has an alternative version of the events, and also cases where the defendant deduces that the particulars of claim must be wrong because if they were correct the defendant would know about the matter;
(b) which allegations the defendant is unable to admit or deny, but which he requires the claimant to prove. It is inappropriate to make a non-admission on a matter on which the defendant must have personal knowledge. Such a matter must either be admitted or denied with reasons (*Ciccone v Associated Newspapers Ltd* [2009] EWHC 1108 (Ch)); and
(c) which allegations are admitted. Facts which are admitted are no longer in issue, and evidence on them will not be received at trial. It is an abuse not to admit facts demonstrably known to be true to the defendant (*Newland v Boardwell* [1983] 1 WLR 1453).

Any specific allegation that is not answered will be taken to be put in issue if the general **14.29** nature of the defence on the issue appears from what is said in the defence. Otherwise the issue is deemed to be admitted (CPR, r 16.5(3) and (5)). Where a paragraph in the particulars of claim sets up a contention followed by a number of sub-paragraphs, each containing allegations of fact, a general response to the main allegation without responding to the individual sub-paragraphs may be inadequate, depending on the circumstances and how important the allegations are (*Ciccone v Associated Newspapers Ltd*, where further particulars were required). The amount of any money claim is deemed to be in dispute unless expressly admitted. If the claimant's statement of value is disputed, the defendant must say why and, if able to, give a counter-estimate (r 16.5(6)).

Any denial of an allegation in the particulars of claim must be backed up by reasons in the **14.30** defence. A defendant who intends to put forward a different version of events from the one advanced by the claimant has to state the alternative version in the defence (r 16.5(2)). A denial must go to the root of the allegation in the particulars of claim, and must not be evasive. An equivocal denial may be taken by the court to be an admission. For example, stating that 'the terms of the arrangement were never definitely agreed upon as alleged' was held to be evasive and to be an admission that an arrangement was made in *Thorp v Holdsworth* (1876) 3 ChD 637. A denial that follows the wording of the particulars of claim too closely may result in a pregnant negative—a denial pregnant with an unstated affirmative case. For example, in *Pinson v Lloyds and National Provincial Foreign Bank Ltd* [1941] 2 KB 72 the claimant stated that the defendants had 'effected purchases and sales without having been authorised to do so'. The defendants denied that 'they effected purchases or sales without having been authorised by the [claimant] to do so'. This was embarrassing, because it could have been a denial that the defendants entered into the transactions at all, or it could have been a denial of lack of authority pregnant with an affirmative case that they had the claimant's authority.

Any affirmative case and any defences must be expressly set out. Each defence should be **14.31** set out in a separate paragraph. The defence must specifically set out any matter, such as performance, release, expiry of limitation, fraud, or illegality, which is a defence to the claim, or which might take the claimant by surprise, or which raises issues of fact not included in the particulars of claim. Failing to set out such matters may debar the defendant from raising them at trial (*Shell Chemicals UK Ltd v Vinamul Ltd* (1991) *The Times*, 7 March 1991, CA). Similarly, any matters in mitigation, limitation, or reduction of damages must be expressly stated. Where the defendant is an individual, his date of birth must be stated in the defence (PD 16, para 10.7). A precedent defence is illustrated at figure 14.3.

Figure 14.3 Defence

IN THE HIGH COURT OF JUSTICE   Claim No. HQ18 87105
QUEEN'S BENCH DIVISION
BETWEEN:—

STEPHENSON HYPERLINKS PLC

Claimant

—and—

LOMAX FISHING EQUIPMENT LIMITED

Defendant

DEFENCE

1 Paragraph 1 of the Particulars of Claim is admitted.

2 Save that it is denied that there was a contract concluded between the parties, paragraph 2 of the Particulars of Claim is admitted. The conversation on 16 February 2016 and the letters dated 5 March 2016 and 19 March 2016 were only negotiations between the parties, and there was no final agreement either on these occasions or at all.

3 By reason of the matters set out in paragraph 2 above, paragraph 3 of the Particulars of Claim is denied.

4 Save that it is admitted that the Claimant sent the invoices listed in paragraph 4 of the Particulars of Claim to the Defendant, paragraph 4 of the Particulars of Claim is denied for the reasons set out in paragraph 2 above.

5 In a telephone conversation on 14 August 2017 the Defendant acting through Mr Lomax informed the Claimant that its invoices had been wrongly raised because there was no contract between the parties.

6 Further or alternatively, if, which is denied, it is found that there was a contract between the Claimant and the Defendant for the supply of a computer system, the Defendant relies on the facts and matters set out in paragraphs 7 to 13 of this Defence. Reference to 'the Agreement' are to such contract as may be found to have been entered into between the Claimant and the Defendant for the supply by the Claimant of a computer order processing system.

7 At all material times the Claimant was acting in the course of its business as a computer software development company.

8 There were express terms of the Agreement that:

   (a) the Claimant would supply a computer order processing system that was compatible with the existing software used by the Defendant; and

   (b) the price would be payable 30 days after invoice following completion of the installation of a fully working computer order processing system for the Defendant's angling equipment business.

Figure 14.3 *continued*

9 It was an implied term of the Agreement that the Claimant would carry out the supply of the computer order processing system with reasonable skill and care.

10 On 12 June 2017 technical staff from the Claimant attended at the premises of the Defendant, and connected certain computer equipment to the Defendant's existing computer system, and sought to run certain software.

11 The Claimant is in breach of the express and implied terms set out in paragraphs 8(a) and 9 above.

PARTICULARS OF BREACH

(a) The Claimant supplied software that was incompatible with the existing software used by the Defendant.

(b) The Claimant failed to carry out the supply of the computer order processing system with reasonable skill and care, in that the software supplied failed to operate and caused the Defendant's existing computer system to crash.

12 As a result of the breaches set out in paragraph 11 above and the Claimant's continuing failure to supply a computer order processing system that works and/or that is compatible with the Defendant's existing software, the Claimant has shown it is unable or unwilling to perform its obligations under the Agreement, and the Defendant is entitled to treat itself as discharged from its obligations under the Agreement.

13 Further or alternatively, the Claimant has failed to supply a working, compatible, computer order processing system to the Defendant, and consequently the time for payment of the price for the Claimant services under the Agreement as set out in paragraph 8(b) above the Claimant has not yet arisen.

D. COUNSEL

Statement of Truth

[I believe] [The Defendant believes] that the facts stated in the defence are true.

Signed

Dated

Fox and Headley, of 52 Higham Road, Kettering, Northants, NN16 2CH, Solicitors for the Defendant.

D COUNTERCLAIMS AND SET-OFFS

Counterclaims

A defendant with a cause of action against the claimant can raise it either by bringing separate proceedings or by counterclaiming in the present proceedings. The subject matter of a counterclaim need not be of the same nature as the original claim, or even analogous to it. The only limitation is that the parties to the counterclaim have to sue and be sued in the same capacities as they appear in the main claim. A counterclaim is in substance a separate claim. Safeguards against misuse of the right to counterclaim are provided by the court's case management powers in CPR, rr 1.4 and 3.4, either to strike out the counterclaim, or to order it to be tried separately. A counterclaim must comply with the **14.32** rules relating to particulars of claim. It can be made using one of the forms included in the response pack.

14.33 Assuming there is also a defence, the combined statement of case is known as a defence and counterclaim. It must be verified by a statement of truth. A counterclaim may be made without permission if filed with the defence (CPR, r 20.4(2)(a)). An issue fee based on the full value of the counterclaim is payable, and a copy of the additional claim form must be served on every other party when the defence is served (r 20.8(1)(a)).

Set-offs

14.34 Cross-claims that are closely connected with the claim may operate as set-offs. A set-off can be used as a full or partial defence to the claim. As such it can be pleaded in the defence, and, if established, will reduce or remove the amount otherwise owed by the defendant. A set-off that is worth more than the claim can also be raised as a counterclaim. Where the defendant decides to plead a set-off only as a defence, it is not open to the court at trial to give judgment to the defendant on the excess if at trial the court finds that the set-off is larger than the claim: this can only be done if the set-off is pleaded as a counterclaim (*Colwill v European Heritage Ltd* [2014] EWCA Civ 238).

14.35 Established set-off situations are:

(a) Mutual debts. By virtue of the 18th-century Statutes of Set-off, mutual debts owed between the claimant and the defendant can be set off against each other. There is no need for the transactions giving rise to the debts to be connected other than through the parties. They need not be debts, strictly so called, but may sound in damages provided they are capable of being ascertained with precision at the time of the application (*Morley v Inglis* (1837) 4 Bing NC 58, applied in *Axel Johnson Petroleum AB v MG Mineral Group AG* [1992] 1 WLR 270).

(b) Sale of goods. By virtue of the Sale of Goods Act 1979, s 53(1), a buyer may set off counterclaims for breach of the statutory implied conditions about satisfactory quality, fitness for purpose, and correspondence to description against a claim by the seller for the price.

(c) On a claim for the price of services, for example where a builder is suing for the price of building work done, the defendant can set off a counterclaim for damages for poor workmanship in respect of the contract the claimant is suing on (*Basten v Butter* (1806) 7 East 479).

(d) Arrears of rent. Where a landlord brings an action claiming arrears of rent, the tenant is allowed to set off a counterclaim for damages against the landlord for breach of a covenant in the lease in respect of which the landlord is claiming (*British Anzani (Felixstowe) Ltd v International Marine Management (UK) Ltd* [1980] QB 137, not following *Hart v Rogers* [1916] 1 KB 646, confirmed by *Agyeman v Boadi* (1996) 28 HLR 558).

(e) Equitable set-off.

14.36 An equitable set-off arises where a cross-claim is so closely connected with the claim that it would be manifestly unjust to allow the claimant to enforce payment on the claim without taking into account the cross-claim (*Federal Commerce and Navigation Co Ltd v Molena Alpha Inc* [1978] 2 QB 927 as interpreted by *Geldoff Metaalconstructie NV v Simon Carves Ltd* [2010] BLR 401). In applying this test there are two elements:

(a) a formal requirement of a close connection between the claim and cross-claim;

(b) a functional requirement that it would be manifestly unjust to enforce the claim without taking into account the cross-claim.

While there are these two elements, it is a single test, and not a two-stage test. It will usu- **14.37**
ally be satisfied where the cross-claim arises out of the self-same contract as the claim.
However, there is no universal rule that cross-claims arising out of the same contract as
the claim are always equitable set-offs (*Government of Newfoundland v Newfoundland
Railway Co* (1888) 13 App Cas 199), and there are cases where equitable set-offs have
been found in two-contract cases (this was the result in *Geldoff Metaalconstructie NV v
Simon Carves Ltd*).

It is open to the parties to a contract to exclude any right to set-off by an express term to **14.38**
that effect (*Hong Kong and Shanghai Banking Corporation v Kloeckner & Co AG* [1990]
2 QB 514), but it is possible that such a term may be unreasonable and rendered ineffective by virtue of the Unfair Contract Terms Act 1977, as happened in *Stewart Gill Ltd v
Horatio Myer and Co Ltd* [1992] QB 600. It is also possible for the parties to include the
opposite type of clause providing that any cross-claim will constitute a set-off (*Geldoff
Metaalconstructie NV v Simon Carves Ltd*).

E REPLY AND DEFENCE TO COUNTERCLAIM

A reply may be used to narrow the issues by making admissions, or to assert an affirmative **14.39**
case in answer to the defence. However, it cannot make any allegations inconsistent with
the particulars of claim (which should be raised by amending the particulars of claim). Like
other statements of case the reply must be verified by a statement of truth. A reply must
be filed and served on the other parties with the claimant's directions questionnaire (CPR,
r 15.8). This deadline is stated in the provisional allocation notice, which the court sends to
the parties shortly after filing of defences (r 26.3(2)). The deadline must be no shorter than
14 days after service of the provisional allocation notice (small claims track) or 28 days for
fast track and multi-track claims (r 26.3(6)).

Where the defendant has made a counterclaim the claimant must serve a defence to coun- **14.40**
terclaim, which must comply with the rules relating to defences. This means it must be
filed and served within 14 days of service of the counterclaim. If combined with a reply
the statement of case is called a reply and defence to counterclaim. The deadline for filing a defence to counterclaim will often expire before the deadline for filing a reply (see
14.39). In this situation the court will normally order the defence to counterclaim to be
filed by the same date as the reply. If the court does not make such an order, the claimant
may need to file the reply and the defence to counterclaim as separate documents (PD 15,
para 3.2A).

F SUBSEQUENT STATEMENTS OF CASE

Statements of case after the reply are exceptionally rare. The statement of case after a reply **14.41**
is a rejoinder, followed by a surrejoinder and a rebutter.

G DISPENSING WITH STATEMENTS OF CASE

The court has a power to order a claim to continue without any further statements of case **14.42**
(CPR, r 16.8). This may be appropriate in cases involving points of law or construction
which do not raise issues of fact.

H SCOTT SCHEDULES

14.43 A Scott schedule is often used in building disputes. It is usually drawn up by the claimant, and sets out the detailed allegations against the defendant in tabular form. Commonly, there will be columns setting out the alleged defects, their cause, any remedial works, and the sum claimed, with further columns for the defendant's answers and the court's award.

I INTERRELATION WITH CASE MANAGEMENT

14.44 Filing of the defence triggers the start of standard case management intervention by the court. The court will provisionally allocate the claim to a case management track. This is followed by the parties completing directions questionnaires, which is followed by the court making case management directions. These topics will be considered further in Chapter 15. The overall scheme is shown in figure 14.4.

Figure 14.4 Diagram illustrating early stages in litigation

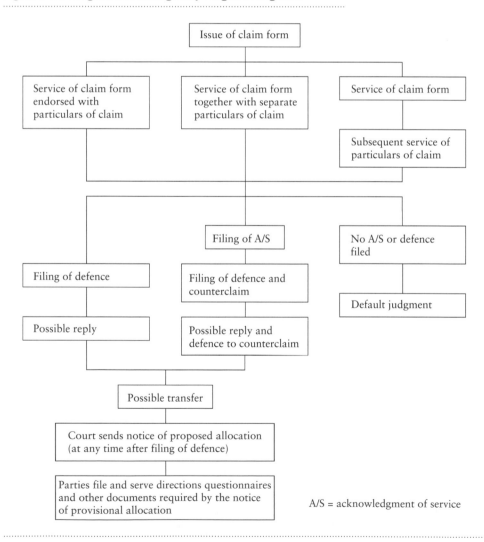

J USE OF STATEMENTS OF CASE AT TRIAL

As part of the purpose of statements of case is to define the issues in the claim, a party **14.45** is quite justified in omitting to prove matters which could be relevant to the case for the other side, but are not in the party's own statements of case. Indeed, strictly, evidence on matters that have not been included in statements of case should not be adduced, and the judge must not give judgment relying on issues that are not in the statements of case (*Lipkin -Gorman v Karpnale Ltd* [1989] 1 WLR 1340). Unpleaded points also cannot be used as the basis of an appeal (*Dunnett v Railtrack plc* [2002] 1 WLR 2434). In deciding whether an allegation is unpleaded, the court must give a fair reading to the statement of case (*Lawrence v Poorah* [2008] UKPC 21), and some indulgence is also given if the facts supporting the unpleaded allegations are adequately set out in the evidence exchanged before trial so the other side are not taken by surprise (*Slater v Buckinghamshire County Council* [2004] EWCA Civ 1478).

If it appears that the statements of case do not adequately set out the case for either or **14.46** both parties, the onus is on the party seeking to rely on the allegation to seek permission to amend, even during the trial (*Lombard North Central plc v Automobile World (UK) Ltd* [2010] EWCA Civ 20). However, as will be seen in Chapter 22, certain types of amendment cannot be made after the relevant limitation period has expired, and, even if the court has a discretion to allow an amendment, there are circumstances in which late amendments will not be allowed.

15

TRACK ALLOCATION AND CASE MANAGEMENT

A PROCEDURAL JUDGES 15.05

B DOCKETING. 15.06

C PROVISIONAL TRACK ALLOCATION 15.09

D FILING DIRECTIONS
  QUESTIONNAIRES. 15.10

E TRACK ALLOCATION 15.17

F ALLOCATION RULES 15.21

G NOTICE OF ALLOCATION 15.32

H ALLOCATION DIRECTIONS 15.33

I ADR AND STAYS TO ALLOW FOR
  SETTLEMENT. .15.35

J TRANSFER TO APPROPRIATE
  COURT. 15.37

K TRIAL IN THE ROYAL COURTS
  OF JUSTICE OR ROLLS BUILDING 15.41

L CHANGING TRACKS 15.42

M SUBSEQUENT CASE MANAGEMENT 15.46

N PRE-TRIAL CHECKLISTS 15.47

O SHORTER TRIALS AND
  FLEXIBLE TRIALS SCHEMES. 15.51

  Key points summary 15.54

15.01 Judicial case management of civil litigation is one of the central planks of the CPR. In exercising their powers to manage cases, the courts will be seeking to secure the overriding objective of the CPR of ensuring that cases are dealt with justly and at proportionate cost. Rule 1.1(2) provides that dealing with cases justly and at proportionate cost includes ensuring that they are dealt with expeditiously and fairly, allotting to them an appropriate share of the court's resources, and ensuring they are dealt with proportionately, bearing in mind factors such as the importance and complexities of the issues and the value of the claim. This will include identifying the issues in the case, summarily disposing of some issues and deciding the order in which other issues are to be resolved, fixing timetables for the procedural steps in preparing cases for trial, and limiting evidence, particularly documentary and expert evidence.

15.02 To assist with this process defended claims are assigned to one of three 'tracks'. The smallest and simplest cases are assigned to the 'small claims track'. Cases expected to last one day or less and with a value in the range of £10,000 to £25,000 are usually allocated to the 'fast track' with standard directions and tight timetables of up to 30 weeks for completion of the interim stages before trial. Larger and more important cases are assigned to the 'multi-track'. Cases on the multi-track have widely differing values and complexity, and the courts are given a great deal of flexibility in the way they can manage these cases commensurate with the particular features of each case. Multi-track cases are dealt with mainly at civil trial centres, and are usually transferred to such locations at an early stage. There are proposals, not yet implemented, for a fourth 'intermediate track' for certain claims up to £100,000.

15.03 To ensure that case management is proportionate, there is active judicial intervention only to the extent cases require it. Basic management, with a fixed timetable and standard procedure, is used wherever possible, on the multi-track as well as on the fast track. Directions may be given without hearings and by consent. The CPR give the courts powers to hold five types of procedural hearing:

(a) allocation hearings;
(b) case management conferences;

(c) hearings at the pre-trial checklist stage (sometimes known as 'listing hearings');

(d) pre-trial reviews; and

(e) costs management conferences (for which see Chapter 16).

The majority of defended cases will proceed between the filing of a defence and trial with **15.04** directions in a more or less standard form, but tailored to the needs of the particular case, without the need for the parties to attend court for a directions hearing, with case management hearings restricted to the more difficult and important cases.

A PROCEDURAL JUDGES

Case management decisions may, by CPR, r 2.4, be taken by any judicial officer, whether **15.05** a District Judge, Master, Registrar in Bankruptcy, or judge, subject to any specific contrary provision in any enactment, rule, or practice direction. However, PD 29, para 3.10, says (in relation to multi-track cases) that Masters will in general perform case management functions in the Royal Courts of Justice, District Judges in district registry cases, and either District Judges or Circuit Judges in County Court cases. Practice Direction 2B enables Masters and District Judges to deal with all types of application, but with express exceptions set out in the practice direction. Exceptions include search orders and applications affecting the liberty of the subject, which must be dealt with by a judge.

B DOCKETING

Cases in the Chancery and Queen's Bench Divisions are assigned to individual Masters (PD **15.06** 2B, para 6.1), although from time to time hearings may be dealt with by other Masters or deputies as the circumstances may require, and cases may be transferred from one Master to another. In the Commercial Court an applicant must give the name of any judge who previously dealt with the case, so that if reasonably practicable further applications can be dealt with by the same judge (*Commercial Court Guide*, para D 4.4).

A more formal docketing system has been introduced with the Jackson Reforms of 1 April **15.07** 2013. This is a system of assigning a case to one judge from issue up to and including trial. Its purpose is to ensure judicial continuity, which is felt to improve efficiency and the ability of the court to manage cases actively. As it covers trial as well as the interim stages, it is wider than the system of assigning Masters in the QBD and ChD. Normally, small claims and fast track cases will not be suitable for docketing. It is likely that in these cases having a single managing judge would increase costs. Docketing is not even right for every multi-track claim. Straightforward multi-track cases are unlikely to benefit from docketing. Generally, it will be the more complex and specialist claims which will be the most suitable for docketing. Factors regarded as relevant for the appointment of a designated judge in the Commercial Court include the importance and complexity of the case, and whether there are likely to be multiple interim applications (*Commercial Court Guide*, para D 4.1).

A party seeking the appointment of a designated judge should apply in writing to the **15.08** judge in charge of the list at the time of fixing the case management conference. Once appointed, the designated judge will preside at all subsequent pre-trial case management conferences and other hearings, other than applications for an interim payment, and will also be the trial judge.

C PROVISIONAL TRACK ALLOCATION

15.09 Every defended claim has to be allocated to one of the three tracks (small claims track, fast track, multi-track). When a defendant files a defence, by CPR, r 26.3(1)(a) a court officer will provisionally decide the track which appears to be most suitable for the claim, and serve on each party a notice of proposed allocation. The notice of proposed allocation will:

(a) specify any matter to be complied with by the date specified in the notice;
(b) require the parties to file a completed directions questionnaire and serve copies on all other parties;
(c) state the address of the court or the court office to which the directions questionnaire must be returned;
(d) inform the parties how to obtain the directions questionnaire; and
(e) if a case appears suitable for allocation to the fast track or multi-track, require the parties to file proposed directions by the date specified in the notice.

D FILING DIRECTIONS QUESTIONNAIRES

15.10 The date for filing and serving directions questionnaires and other documents specified by the court will be given in the notice of proposed allocation served by the court under CPR, r 26.3(1). This date will be at least 14 days after deemed service of the notice for small claims track cases, and 28 days for fast track and multi-track claims. The parties are not permitted to vary this date (r 26.3(6A)). In addition to directions questionnaires, the court may require the parties to file other documents at the same time. This might include:

(a) draft proposed directions;
(b) in multi-track claims, costs budgets, and budget discussion reports (see Chapter 16); and
(c) in multi-track claims, disclosure reports (see Chapter 31).

15.11 The parties should consult one another and cooperate in completing the directions questionnaires and giving other information to the court (PD 26, para 2.3(1)). An example of a directions questionnaire is shown in form 15.1. The parties must try to agree the case management directions (para 2.3(2)), and proposed directions should be filed with the questionnaires. Specimen directions for multi-track claims are available on the Ministry of Justice website at **<http://www.justice.gov.uk/courts/procedure-rules/civil>** which should be taken as the starting point when drafting proposed directions (r 29.1(2)). Standard multi-track directions are shown in figure 15.1.

15.12 Where a court hearing takes place (eg on an application for an interim injunction or for summary judgment under CPR, Part 24) before the claim is allocated to a track, the court may at that hearing dispense with directions questionnaires, treat the hearing as an allocation hearing, make an order for allocation, and give directions for case management (PD 26, para 2.4).

Failure to comply with directions notice

15.13 Where a party fails to comply with a directions notice (typically by not filing the directions questionnaire) by the date specified by the court, the likelihood is that a sanction will

Form 15.1 Form N181, directions questionnaire (fast track and multi-track)

Directions questionnaire (Fast track and Multi-track)

In the	Claim No.
HIGH COURT OF JUSTICE	HQ15 87105

To be completed by, or on behalf of,

STEPHENSON HYPERLINKS PLC

who is [1ˢᵗ][2ⁿᵈ][3ʳᵈ][   ][Claimant][Defendant][Part 20 claimant] in this claim

You should note the date by which this questionnaire must be returned and the name of the court it should be returned to since this may be different from the court where the proceedings were issued.

If you have settled this claim (or if you settle it on a future date) and do not need to have it heard or tried, you must let the court know immediately.

If the claim is not settled, a judge will allocate it to an appropriate case management track. To help the judge choose the most just and cost-effective track, you must now complete the directions questionnaire.

You should write the claim number on any other documents you send with your directions questionnaire. Please ensure they are firmly attached to it.

A Settlement

Notes

Under the Civil Procedure Rules parties should make every effort to settle their case before the hearing. This could be by discussion or negotiation (such as a roundtable meeting or settlement conference) or by a more formal process such as mediation. The court will want to know what steps have been taken. Settling the case early can save costs, including court hearing fees.

For legal representatives only

I confirm that I have explained to my client the need to try to settle; the options available; and the possibility of costs sanctions if they refuse to try to settle.

[✓] I confirm

For all

Your answers to these questions may be considered by the court when it deals with the questions of costs: see Civil Procedure Rules Part 44.

1. Given that the rules require you to try to settle the claim before the hearing, do you want to attempt to settle at this stage?

   [✓] Yes   [ ] No

2. If Yes, do you want a one month stay?

   [✓] Yes   [ ] No

3. If you answered 'No' to question 1, please state below the reasons why you consider it inappropriate to try to settle the claim at this stage.

Reasons:

The court may order a stay, whether or not all the other parties to the claim agree. Even if you are requesting a stay, you must still complete the rest of the questionnaire.

More information about mediation, the fees charged and a directory of mediation providers is available online from www.civilmediation.justice.gov.uk This service provides members of the public and businesses with contact details for national civil and commercial mediation providers, all of whom are accredited by the Civil Mediation Council.

Form 15.1 *continued*

B | Court

B1. (High Court only)

The claim has been issued in the High Court. Do you consider it should remain there?   ☑ Yes   ☐ No

If Yes, in which Division/List?

QUEEN'S BENCH DIVISION

If No, in which County Court hearing centre would you prefer the case to be heard?

High Court cases are usually heard at the Royal Courts of Justice or certain Civil Trial Centres. Fast or multi-track trials may be dealt with at a Civil Trial Centre or at the court where the claim is proceeding.

B2. Trial (all cases)

Is there any reason why your claim needs to be heard at a court or hearing centre?   ☐ Yes   ☑ No

If Yes, say which court and why?

C | Pre-action protocols

You are expected to comply fully with the relevant pre-action protocol.

Have you done so?   ☑ Yes   ☐ No

If you have not complied, or have only partially complied, please explain why.

Before any claim is started, the court expects you to have complied with the relevant pre-action protocol, and to have exchanged information and documents relevant to the claim to assist in settling it. To find out which protocol is relevant to your claim see: www.justice.gov. uk/guidance/courts-and-tribunals/courts/procedure-rules/civil/menus/protocol.htm

D | Case management information

D1. Applications

Have you made any application(s) in this claim?   ☐ Yes   ☑ No

If Yes, what for? (e.g. summary judgment, add another party).

For hearing on ☐☐ / ☐☐ / ☐☐☐☐

D1. Applications

It is important for the court to know if you have already made any applications in the claim (or are about to issue one), what they are for and when they will be heard. The outcome of the applications may affect the case management directions the court gives.

D2. Track

If you have indicated in the proposed directions a track attached which would not be the normal track for the claim, please give brief reasons below for your choice.

D2. Track

The basic guide by which claims are normally allocated to a track is the amount in dispute, although other factors such as the complexity of the case will also be considered. Leaflet *EX305 – The Fast Track and the Multi-track*, explains this in greater detail.

Form 15.1 *continued*

D   **Case management information** (continued)   Notes

D3. Disclosure of electronic documents (multi-track cases only)

If you are proposing that the claim be allocated to the multi-track:

1. Have you reached agreement, either using the Electronic Documents   ☐ Yes   ☑ No
   Questionnaire in Practice Direction 31B or otherwise, about the scope
   and extent of disclosure of electronic documents on each side?

2. If No, is such agreement likely?   ☑ Yes   ☐ No

3. If there is no agreement and no agreement is likely, what are
   the issues about disclosure of electronic documents which the
   court needs to address, and should they be dealt with at the Case
   Management Conference or at a separate hearing?

>

D4. Disclosure of non-electronic documents (all cases)

What directions are proposed for disclosure?

> 1. Standard disclosure of non-electronic documents by lists, to be
> exchanged by 4pm 28 days after directions.
> 2. Inspection by 4pm 14 days thereafter.
> 3. Electronic Documents Questionnaires to be exchanged by 4pm
> 28 days after directions; disclosure in native format by agreement.

For all multi-track cases, except personal injury.

Have you filed and served a disclosure report (Form N263)   ☑ Yes   ☐ No
(see Civil Procedure Rules Part 31).

Have you agreed a proposal in relation to disclosure that meets the   ☑ Yes   ☐ No
overriding objective?

If Yes, please ensure this is contained within the proposed directions
attached and specify the draft order number.

> 4

E   **Experts**

Do you wish to use expert evidence at the trial or final hearing?   ☑ Yes   ☐ No   There is no presumption that expert evidence is necessary,
  or that each party will be entitled to their own expert(s).
Have you already copied any experts' report(s) to the other party(ies)?   ☑ None yet obtained   Therefore, the court requires a short explanation of your
               ☐ Yes   ☐ No   proposals with regard to expert evidence.

Do you consider the case suitable for a single joint expert in any field?   ☑ Yes   ☐ No

Form 15.1 *continued*

E   **Experts** (continued)   Notes

Please list any single joint experts you propose to use and any other experts you wish to rely on. Identify single joint experts with the initials 'SJ' after their name(s). Please provide justification of your proposal and an estimate of costs.

Expert's name	Field of expertise (e.g. orthopaedic surgeon, surveyor, engineer)	Justification for expert and estimate of costs
Mr Jonathan Cousins	Computer software design	There are disputes between the parties over the capabilities and functions of the software supplied to the Defendant, which are technical issues that cannot be resolved without the assistance of an expert. Estimated costs: £6,000.

F   **Witnesses**

Which witnesses of fact do you intend to call at the trial or final hearing including, if appropriate, yourself?

Witness name	Witness to which facts
Mrs Lisa Stephenson	The contract and contractual specification
Mr Peter Giles	Software design and capabilities
Miss Kelly Hammond	Software installation and events at the Defendant's premises relating to commissioning

G   **Trial or Final Hearing**

How long do you estimate the trial or final hearing will take?

☐ less than one day   ☐ one day   ☑ more than one day

☐ Hrs   2 State number of days

Give the best estimate you can of the time that the court will need to decide this case. If, later you have any reason to shorten or lengthen this estimate you should let the court know immediately.

Are there any days within the next 12 months when you, an expert or an essential witness will not be able to attend court for trial or final hearing?

You should only enter those dates when you, your expert(s) or essential witnesses will not be available to attend court because of holiday or other commitments.

If Yes, please give details

Name	Dates not available
Mr Jonathan Cousins	See attached list

You should notify the court immediately if any of these dates change.

4

Form 15.1 *continued*

H **Costs**   Notes

Do not complete this section if:

    1) you do not have a legal representative acting for you

    2) the case is subject to fixed costs

If your claim is likely to be allocated to the Multi-Track form Precedent H
must be filed at in accordance with CPR 3.13.

                    I confirm Precedent H is attached. ☑

I **Other information**

Do you intend to make any applications in the future?   ☐ Yes   ☑ No

If Yes, what for?

In the space below, set out any other information you consider will help the judge to manage the claim.

We are seeking to agree with the Defendant the appointment of Mr Jonathan Cousins as a jointly instructed computer systems design expert.

Although documents were exchanged pursuant to Practice Direction Pre-Action Conduct before proceedings were commenced, and some contractual documents were delivered with the Particulars of Claim, we consider that full standard disclosure, together with disclosure of electronic documents including the use of electronic documents questionnaires, is necessary for the just disposal of this claim.

Form 15.1 *continued*

J Directions

You must attempt to agree proposed directions with all other parties. **Whether agreed or not a draft of the order for directions which you seek must accompany this form.**

All proposed directions for multi-track cases must be based on the directions at www.justice.gov.uk/courts/procedure-rules/civil

All proposed directions for fast track cases must be based on CPR Part 28.

Signature

Date
☐☐ / ☐☐ / ☐☐☐☐

[Legal Representative for the][1ˢᵗ][2ⁿᵈ][3ʳᵈ][   ]
[Claimant][Defendant][Part 20 claimant]

Please enter your name, reference number and full postal address including details of telephone, DX, fax or e-mail

Catherine Wilson, Smallwoods LLP, 4 Market Place, Leicester	If applicable	
	Telephone no.	0116 8334518
	Fax no.	
	DX no.	1733 Leicester 1
Postcode L E 2 4 C P	Your ref.	L8725/CW

E-mail	CWilson@smallwoods.com

Figure 15.1 Standard Directions: multi-track

ORDER	In the County Court District Judge Xxxxx	Case number: XXxxxx
Parties	X	Claimant
	Y	Defendant

Warning: you must comply with the terms imposed upon you by this order otherwise your case is liable to be struck out or some other sanction imposed. If you cannot comply you are expected to make formal application to the court before any deadline imposed upon you expires.

On xxxx

District Judge Xxxxx sitting at Xxxxx, considered the papers in the case and

ordered that:

(1) The Claim is allocated to the Multi-Track and is assigned to His Her Honour District Judge Xxxxx for case management.

(2) At all stages the parties must consider settling this litigation by any means of Alternative Dispute Resolution (including Mediation); any party not engaging in any such means proposed by another must serve a witness statement giving reasons within 21 days of that proposal; such witness statement must not be shown to the trial judge until questions of costs arise.

(3) Disclosure of documents will be dealt with as follows:
   (a) by 4pm on xxxx the parties must give to each other standard disclosure of documents by list and category.
   (b) by 4pm on xxxx any request must be made to inspect the original of, or to provide a copy of, a disclosable document.
   (c) any such request unless objected to must be complied with within 14 days of the request.
   (d) by 4pm on xxxx each party must serve and file with the Court a list of issues relevant to the search for and disclosure of electronically stored documents, or must confirm there are no such issues, following Practice Direction 31B.

(4) Evidence of fact will be dealt with as follows:
   (a) by 4pm on xxxx all parties must serve on each other copies of the signed statements of themselves and of all witnesses on whom they intend to rely and all notices relating to evidence.
   (b) Oral evidence will not be permitted at trial from a witness whose statement has not been served in accordance with this order or has been served late, except with permission from the Court.
   (c) Evidence of fact is limited to xx witnesses on behalf of each party.
   (d) Witness statements must not exceed xx pages of A4 in length.

(5) No expert evidence is necessary.

(6) Schedules of Loss must be updated as follows:
   (a) by 4pm on xxxx the Claimant must send an up to date schedule of loss to each other party.
   (b) by 4pm on xxxx a Defendant, in the event of challenge, must send an up to date counter-schedule of loss to the Claimant.

Figure 15.1 *continued*

(7) The trial will be listed as follows.
  - (a) The trial window is between xxxx and xxxx inclusive.
  - (b) The estimated length of trial is xx days.
  - (c) By 4pm on xxxx the parties must file with the court their availability for trial, preferably agreed and with a nominated single point of contact. They will be notified of the time and place of trial.
  - (d) By 4pm on xxxx pre-trial check lists must be sent to the court.

(8) Pre-trial directions are as follows:
  - (a) There will be a pre-trial review 4 weeks before the trial window starts with a time estimate of 30 minutes.
  - (b) The pre-trial review may be conducted by telephone if the parties so agree, unless the court orders otherwise. The Claimant must make the relevant arrangements in accordance with Practice Direction 23A Civil Procedure Rules.
  - (c) At least 3 clear days before the pre-trial review the Claimant must file and send to the other party or parties preferably agreed and by e-mail:
    - (i) draft directions
    - (ii) a chronology
    - (iii) a case summary.

(9) The trial directions are as follows:
  - (a) Not more than 7 nor less than 3 clear days before the trial, the Claimant must file at court and serve an indexed and paginated bundle of documents, which complies with the requirements of Rule 39.5 Civil Procedure Rules and Practice Direction 39A. The parties must endeavour to agree the contents of the bundle before it is filed. The bundle will include:
    - (i) a chronology.
    - (ii) a trial timetable.
  - (b) the parties must file with the court and exchange skeleton arguments at least 3 days before the trial by e-mail.

(10) Because this Order has been made without a hearing, the parties have the right to apply to have the Order set aside, varied or stayed. A party making such an application must send or deliver the application to the court (together with any appropriate fee) to arrive within 7 days of service of this Order.

(11) The parties may, by prior agreement in writing, extend the time for directions, in the Order dated xxxx, by up to 28 days and without the need to apply to Court. Beyond that 28 day period, any agreed extension of time must be submitted to the Court by e-mail including a brief explanation of the reasons, confirmation that it will not prejudice any hearing date and with a draft Consent Order in Word format. The Court will then consider whether a formal Application and Hearing is necessary.

be imposed. There are different consequences for County Court money claims and High Court claims for a specified amount of money.

15.14 In County Court money claims, on a default in complying with a directions notice the court will serve a further notice on the defaulting party requiring compliance within a further seven days (CPR, r 26.3(7A)(a)). Non-compliance with this further notice results in the automatic striking out of the defaulting party's statement of case without any further order from the court (r 26.3(7A)(b)).

In High Court claims for a specified amount of money, on a failure to comply with a directions **15.15** notice the court will make such order as it considers appropriate (CPR, r 26.3(8)), including:

(a) an order for directions;
(b) an order striking out the claim;
(c) an order striking out the defence and entering judgment; or
(d) listing the case for a case management conference.

Where an order has been made under r 26.3(7A)(b) or (8), the party in default will not **15.16** normally be entitled to the costs of any application to set aside or vary that order, nor for attending any case management conference under r 26.3(8)(d), and will be ordered to pay the costs caused by the default to any party who was not in default (r 26.3(10)).

E TRACK ALLOCATION

Time when allocation takes place

Under CPR, r 26.5(1), the court will allocate the claim to a track when all parties have **15.17** filed their directions questionnaires, or when giving directions under r 26.3(8) (see 15.15). The court may hold an allocation hearing if it thinks it is necessary (r 26.5(4)), but will frequently deal with track allocation and directions without a hearing.

Allocation in particular situations

In a number of cases events in the case mean that provisional track allocation and direc- **15.18** tions do not take place in the normal sequence:

(a) In cases where there is a stay for settlement (see 15.35) or small claims mediation (see 10.13), allocation is dealt with at the end of the period of the stay or mediation period (CPR, r 26.5(2), (2A)).
(b) In cases which are automatically transferred or sent to a County Court hearing centre, allocation decisions are made by a procedural judge of the destination court.
(c) In cases which could be allocated either to the fast track or to the multi-track, allocation decisions are usually taken in the court where the proceedings are commenced, but occasionally they will be transferred to the appropriate civil trial centre for allocation and directions.
(d) Where a claimant enters a default judgment for an amount of money to be decided by the court or for the value of goods or the amount of interest to be decided by the court, the case will not be 'defended', in that a defence will not have been filed. These cases therefore are not governed by the standard track allocation provisions. Instead, when judgment is entered the court will give any necessary directions and will, if appropriate, allocate the case to one of the three tracks (r 12.7(2)(b)). These cases are considered further at 13.23ff.
(e) When judgment is entered for damages to be decided on an admission by the defendant in a claim for money that has not been specified, then, as in sub-para (d), the court will give any necessary directions and, if appropriate, allocate the case to one of the three tracks (r 14.8). These cases are also considered at 13.23ff.

Initial case management in specialist claims

Most types of specialist proceedings are treated as allocated to the multi-track. This includes **15.19** claims allocated to the Technology and Construction Court (r 60.6), proceedings in the Commercial List in the Queen's Bench Division (r 58.13(1)), patent and registered designs claims (the effect of r 63.8), admiralty proceedings (PD 61, para 2), Circuit Commercial Court claims (r 59.11), arbitration claims (r 62.7(1)), directors disqualification proceedings (PD Directors Disqualification Proceedings, para 2.1), and insolvency proceedings (Insolvency (England and Wales) Rules 2016 (SI 2016/1024), r 12.1(2)). A four-track system is used in the Chancery Division based on different levels of judicial involvement in case management (*New Case Management Tracks in Chancery*, 2015).

15.20 Directions questionnaires are not, in general, used in specialist cases automatically allocated to the multi-track. Each specialist court has its own procedure dealing with case management at the allocation stage. In the TCC, the court will send the parties a case management questionnaire and a case management directions form (PD 60, para 8.2 and apps A and B). In the Commercial Court, after service of the defence, the legal representatives for each party must liaise for the purpose of preparing a short case memorandum and a list of common ground and issues, and the claimant's solicitors must prepare a case management bundle (*Commercial Court Guide*, paras D5.1, D6.1, and D7.1). The claimant must apply for a case management conference within 14 days after service of the last defence to ensure this takes place as soon as practicable (r 58.13(3); PD 58, para 10.2). Seven days before the case management conference each party must file a completed case management information sheet, in the form set out in the *Commercial Court Guide* and it is this form that takes the place of the directions questionnaire (para D8.5, and see form 15.1). On the other hand, directions questionnaires are used in Chancery Division cases despite the fact these cases are automatically allocated to the multi-track.

F ALLOCATION RULES

15.21 The primary rules for track allocation are based on the financial value of the claim. This is the monetary value of the claim disregarding any amount not in dispute, any claim for interest or costs, and also disregarding any allegation of contributory negligence (CPR, r 26.8(2)). It is for the court to assess the value of the claim, though it will take into account the way in which the claim is formulated in the particulars of claim and any information given in the directions questionnaires. Any sum for which the defendant does not admit liability is in dispute, but the court will not regard the following as in dispute (PD 26, para 7.4):

(a) sums for which summary judgment on a part of a claim has been entered;
(b) any distinct items in the claim for which the defendant has admitted liability; and
(c) any distinct items in the claim which have been agreed between the parties.

15.22 Generally claims are allocated in accordance with their financial value, but a claim may be allocated to a track which is not the one normally appropriate to its value if the procedural judge decides that it can be dealt with more justly on that other track, taking into account a number of factors set out in CPR, r 26.8 (see 15.30). The court has the power to allocate a case to a track lower than that indicated by its financial value without needing to obtain the consent of the parties.

Small claims track

15.23 The small claims track is intended to provide a proportionate procedure for the most straightforward types of cases, such as consumer disputes, small accident claims, disputes about the ownership of goods, and certain landlord and tenant cases. This is the normal track for defended claims with a value not exceeding £10,000 (CPR, r 26.6(3)).

Although most claims under £10,000 will be allocated to the small claims track, the following **15.24** types of claim will not normally be allocated there even if they have a value under £10,000:

(a) personal injuries cases where the value of the claim for pain, suffering, and loss of amenity exceeds £1,000 (r 26.6(1)(a) and (2));
(b) claims by tenants of residential premises seeking orders that their landlords should carry out repairs or other works to the premises where the value of the claim exceeds £1,000 (r 26.6(1)(b));
(c) claims by residential tenants seeking damages against their landlords for harassment or unlawful eviction (r 26.7(4)); and
(d) claims involving a disputed allegation of dishonesty (PD 26, para 8.1(1)(d)).

Even if the claim is worth less than £10,000 there may be other reasons why it should not **15.25** be allocated to the small claims track. One relates to expert evidence, which is not allowed in small claims track cases, either by calling an expert at the hearing or simply relying on an expert's report, unless the court gives permission (CPR, r 27.5). Another is the length of the hearing. The court will not normally allow more than one day for a hearing of a small claims track case (PD 26, para 8.1(2)).

Fast track

The fast track is the normal track for cases broadly falling into the £10,000 to £25,000 **15.26** bracket, and which can be disposed of by a trial which will not exceed a day. There are therefore two factors for deciding whether the fast track is the normal track for defended cases that are not allocated to the small claims track. The first factor, value (CPR, r 26.6(1)–(4)), is to the effect that the following cases will normally be allocated to the fast track:

(a) personal injuries cases with a financial value between £10,000 and £25,000;
(b) personal injuries cases with an overall value under £10,000, but where the damages for pain, suffering, and loss of amenity are likely to exceed £1,000;
(c) claims by residential tenants for orders requiring their landlords to carry out repairs or other work to the premises where the value of the claim is between £1,000 and £25,000;
(d) claims by residential tenants for damages against their landlords for harassment or unlawful eviction where the value of the claim does not exceed £25,000; and
(e) other categories of cases where the value of the claim is between £10,000 and £25,000.

The second factor, disposal at trial (r 26.6(5)), is to the effect that cases falling within the **15.27** normal limits for allocation to the fast track must also be likely to be disposed of by a trial lasting no more than a day, and with oral expert evidence limited to experts in no more than two expert fields and to one expert per field of expertise. The possibility that the trial might last longer than a day (which in this context means five hours) is not necessarily a conclusive reason for allocating a case to the multi-track (PD 26, para 9.1(3)(c)), though in practice such cases are almost always so allocated.

Multi-track

The multi-track is the normal track for claims not falling within the rules for allocation to **15.28** either the small claims or fast track (CPR, r 26.6(6)). Typically these will be cases involving claims exceeding £25,000, and cases worth less than that sum where the trial is likely to exceed a day. Part 8 claims (r 8.9(c)) and specialist proceedings (see 15.19) are usually treated as allocated to the multi-track. Stage 3 RTA and EL/PL protocol cases (see Chapter 9), despite being Part 8 claims, are treated as not allocated to any track (PD 8B, para 17.1).

Claims with no financial value

15.29 Claims with no financial value will be allocated to the track which the procedural judge considers to be most suitable to enable it to be dealt with justly, taking into account the factors discussed at 15.30 (CPR, r 26.7(2)).

Discretionary factors

15.30 In addition to the financial value of the claim (if it has one), when deciding which track to allocate it to the court is required to have regard to the following factors (CPR, r 26.8):

(a) the nature of the remedy sought;

(b) the likely complexity of the facts, law, or evidence. Low-value claims in emerging areas may be suitable for the multi-track (*Kearsley v Klarfeld* [2006] 2 All ER 303);

(c) the number of parties or likely parties;

(d) the value of any counterclaim or other additional claim and the complexity of any matters relating to those claims (the court will not aggregate the sums claimed in the claim, counterclaim, and so on, but will generally simply look at the value of the largest of the cross-claims: PD 26, para 7.7);

(e) the amount of oral evidence which may be required;

(f) the importance of the claim to persons who are not parties to the proceedings;

(g) the views expressed by the parties, which will be regarded as important, though not binding on the court (PD 26, para 7.5); and

(h) the circumstances of the parties.

15.31 Applying these factors, the following types of cases will usually be allocated to the multi-track even if the amount at stake is within the normal financial value for allocation to the fast track:

(a) cases involving issues of public importance;

(b) test cases;

(c) medical negligence cases; and

(d) cases where there is a right to trial by jury, including deceit cases.

G NOTICE OF ALLOCATION

15.32 After the court has decided on the track to which a case is allocated, it will send a notice of allocation to the parties (CPR, r 26.9). Several forms of notice of allocation have been devised for different circumstances. There are four different forms for cases allocated to the small claims track (N157 to N160), one for the fast track (N154), and one for the multi-track (N155). Each has a space for allocation directions and for the judge's reasons for the allocation decision.

H ALLOCATION DIRECTIONS

15.33 The type of directions the court will make at the allocation stage depends on which track the case is allocated to, and the circumstances of the case. Typically the court will make standard directions in small claims track cases (see Chapter 27). In fast track and multi-track cases there are more highly developed standard directions. In both fast track and multi-track cases the court will consider making directions covering disclosure of documents, exchange of witness statements, disclosure of experts' reports and narrowing the expert evidence issues, and listing the claim for trial. In multi-track cases the court will also consider whether to convene a case management conference (see 29.06), a costs management conference (see 16.26), or a pre-trial review (see 29.26). In ChD and specialist claims in the Rolls Building the court may consider applying the cut-down procedures laid down in PD 51N under the Shorter and Flexible Trials Pilot Schemes, see 15.51.

When making directions the court will be astute to apply the overriding objective (CPR, r 1.1) **15.34** and will have regard to any available costs budgets (r 3.17(1), for which see Chapter 16). It will seek to ensure that the case is prepared properly so that the claim can be determined justly, but it will also seek to avoid unnecessary expense. Where appropriate it will use its powers under CPR, rr 3.1(2)(k), 31.5, 32.1, 32.2, and 35.4. Rule 3.1(2)(k) allows the court to exclude an issue from consideration. This may be used where an issue is not of significant probative value, and where the costs involved in investigating it will be disproportionate to its value (*Guerrero v Monterrico Metals plc* [2010] EWHC 3228 (QB)). Rule 31.5 allows the court to limit or dispense with standard disclosure. Rule 32.1 gives the court a wide-ranging power to give directions about the issues on which it requires evidence, the nature of the evidence which it requires to decide those issues, and the way in which the evidence is to be placed before the court. The power under the rule may be used to exclude evidence that would otherwise be admissible (r 32.1(2); *Grobbelaar v Sun Newspapers Ltd* (1999) *The Times*, 12 August 1999). Rule 32.2 allows the court to limit the length or format of witness statements, and r 35.4 gives the court a power to restrict expert evidence. These powers may be used in combination to ensure cases are progressed at proportionate cost.

I ADR AND STAYS TO ALLOW FOR SETTLEMENT

One of the court's case management functions is to help the parties to settle the whole or **15.35** part of the case (CPR, r 1.4(2)(f)), and another is to encourage the parties to use alternative dispute resolution ('ADR') procedures if appropriate and to facilitate the use of such procedures (r 1.4(2)(e), and see Chapter 10). The pre-action protocols (see Chapter 5) require all potential litigants to at least consider possible ADR methods of achieving a settlement before commencing proceedings. It may be that ADR has not been attempted before a case reaches the track allocation stage of litigation. Where there is a chance that ADR or further negotiation may result in a settlement, the CPR give the court the power to order a stay of proceedings for the possible settlement of the case.

The directions questionnaire allows a party to include a request for the proceedings to be **15.36** stayed while the parties try to settle the case. If all the parties make such a request a direction will be made staying the proceedings for one month (rr 26.4(2) and 26.4A). The court has power on its own initiative to direct that the proceedings be stayed for one month, or such specified period as the court thinks appropriate (r 26.4(2A)). A judge may extend the stay for such specified period as is thought appropriate (r 26.4(3)), which will generally be granted on receipt of a letter from either party confirming that the extension is sought with the agreement of all the parties and explaining the steps being taken and the identity of the mediator or expert assisting with the process (PD 26, para 3.1(1)). Extensions will not usually exceed four weeks at a time unless there are clear reasons to justify a longer time. During the period of such a stay the claimant is under a duty to inform the court if a settlement is reached (CPR, r 26.4(4)). If, by the end of the defined period of the stay, the claimant has not told the court that the case has been settled, the court will give such directions for the management of the case as it considers appropriate, including allocating it to an appropriate track (rr 26.4(5) and 26.5(2)). The periods of stays under these rules are carefully restricted so as to prevent the procedure being used to secure protracted 'authorized' delays after proceedings are commenced, under the guise of attempting to settle.

J TRANSFER TO APPROPRIATE COURT

15.37   Subject to the rules relating to commencing proceedings in the High Court, a claimant has a free choice of which court to use when commencing proceedings (see Chapter 3). Sending money claims to the claimant's preferred court or to the defendant's home court was considered at 12.19.

15.38   If automatic transfer does not apply, the court may in its discretion transfer the case to the most appropriate court. If a case has been started in the wrong court, the court may order it to be transferred to the correct court, may allow it to continue where it is, or may strike it out (CPR, r 30.2(2), and see 3.32).

15.39   Cases started in the correct court, which are not covered by the automatic transfer rules may be transferred to the High Court or County Court, between County Court hearing centres or district registries, and between Divisions, and to and from specialist courts, at the court's discretion. A case may be transferred to the County Court even though its value exceeds the relevant County Court limit (*National Westminster Bank plc v King* [2008] Ch 385). Criteria for deciding whether to transfer are set out in the Jurisdiction Order of 1991 and in r 30.3(2). These criteria include the value of the claim, the simplicity or complexity of the facts and issues, the importance of the case, whether it would be more convenient to try the case in another court, the facilities in the proposed court, and the availability of specialist judges.

15.40   Cases commenced in courts that are not civil trial centres (such courts are described as 'feeder courts') are considered by a procedural judge when defences are filed. If it appears that the case is suitable for allocation to the multi-track, the District Judge will normally make an order allocating the case to the multi-track, will give case management directions, and transfer the claim to a civil trial centre (PD 26, para 10.2(5)). Exceptionally, a case may be allocated to the multi-track and be retained in a feeder court. This will happen where it is envisaged that there may need to be more than one case management conference and the parties or their legal advisers are located inconveniently far from the designated civil trial centre (PD 26, para 10.2(10)) or where pressure of work in the trial centre has led to the designated civil judge approving retention of the case by the feeder court. If it is not possible to decide whether a case should be allocated to the fast or multi-track, the procedural judge will either hold an allocation hearing at the feeder court, or transfer the case to a civil trial centre for the allocation decision to be made there (paras 10.2(6) and (8)).

K TRIAL IN THE ROYAL COURTS OF JUSTICE OR ROLLS BUILDING

15.41   In principle only the most important cases should be managed and tried in the Royal Courts of Justice or Rolls Building (see 3.10) as opposed to another civil trial centre. Thus, in general, cases with an estimated value of less than £100,000 will be transferred to the County Court.

L CHANGING TRACKS

15.42   After a claim has been allocated to a track the court may make a subsequent order reallocating it to a different track (CPR, r 26.10). When a claim is reallocated, the costs rules of the first track apply up to the date of reallocation, and the costs rules of the second track apply thereafter (r 46.13(2)). This means that where a claim was initially allocated to the small claims track, and is later reallocated to another track, the small claims costs restrictions cease to apply from the date of reallocation (r 27.15). Rule 46.13(2) is subject to the court otherwise ordering. Any alternative order should be made at the time of reallocation. In *Tibbles v SIG plc* [2012] 1 WLR 2591 the parties and the court overlooked what is now r 46.13(2) until the claimant realized about 11 months after the claim had been reallocated to the fast track from the small claims track that its costs prior to reallocation would not be recoverable. It was held that by that time it was too late to vary the original order under r 3.1(7).

A party who is dissatisfied with an allocation decision may challenge the decision either **15.43** by appealing up to the next higher court or by making an application back to the judge who made the initial decision (PD 26, para 11.1(1)). Applications should be used where the decision was made without any hearing of which the party was given due notice or if there has been a material change of circumstances. If the party was present, represented, or given due notice of the hearing where the decision was made, the only appropriate route is by way of appeal (PD 26, paras 11.1 and 11.2).

If an additional claim under Part 20 is issued, it may be necessary to redetermine the most **15.44** suitable track for the proceedings. Mere issue of an additional claim will not have this effect, but where a defence to an additional claim has been filed the proceedings will be reconsidered by the procedural judge to determine whether the claim should remain on its existing track (particularly in cases on the small claims and fast tracks) and whether there needs to be any adjustment to the timetable. At the same time the procedural judge will consider whether the additional claim should be dealt with separately from the main claim.

If the value of a claim is substantially increased on an amendment to the statement of case **15.45** the claim will usually be reallocated. However, permission to amend may be refused if reallocating will involve aborting a trial where a fast track claim is being tried by a District Judge, and the amendment will bring the claim into the multi-track (*Maguire v Molin* [2003] 1 WLR 644).

M SUBSEQUENT CASE MANAGEMENT

Chapters 27 to 29 deal in more detail with the further progress of cases on each of the **15.46** three case management tracks following allocation. Figure 15.2 shows the routes which cases may take from either a defence being filed or a 'relevant order' being made up to the decision to allocate the case to a case management track. Figure 15.3 shows in broad terms what happens to cases on the three case management tracks from the time they are allocated to a track until trial.

N PRE-TRIAL CHECKLISTS

On the small claims track the usual position is that directions including fixing the date for **15.47** the hearing are made when the claim is allocated to the small claims track. For claims on the fast track (see 28.17) and multi-track (see 29.21) it is usual for directions to include a requirement to file pre-trial checklists after the exchange of witness statements and experts' reports, and before the hearing of any pre-trial review (for which, see 29.26). A hearing fee is payable when the pre-trial checklist is filed or, if pre-trial checklists are not used, when the court fixes the trial date or trial window (CPFO, fee 2.1).

Figure 15.2 Routes to making track allocation decision

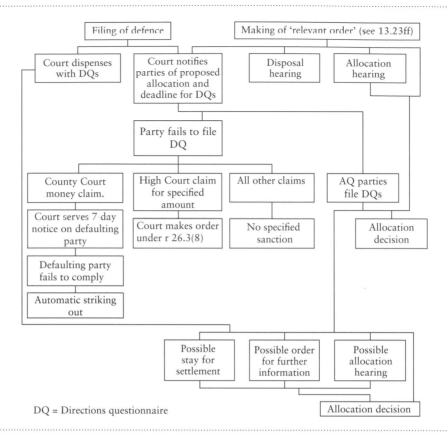

DQ = Directions questionnaire

Non-payment of the hearing fee

15.48   For claims on all three case management tracks, CPR, rr 3.7 and 3.7A1, provide that the claim will be struck out automatically if the hearing fee is not paid after due warning. A fee notice sent by the court may be in the same document as the notice of the trial date, or may be in a separate document (r 3.7A1(4)). Practice Direction 3B says that if a claim is struck out, the court will send the defendant a notice which will explain the effect of r 25.11, which provides that any interim injunction will cease to have any effect after 14 days unless the claimant applies to reinstate the claim. On the claim being struck out the defendant is entitled to its costs on the standard basis (r 44.9(1)(a)).

15.49   Once the claim has been struck out the court retains a power to reinstate it (r 3.7(7)), and on such an application the court will apply the criteria set out in r 3.9 relating to applications for relief from sanctions (see Chapter 37). However, any order for reinstatement will be made conditional on the fee being paid within two days of the order if the claimant is present at the hearing, otherwise within seven days of service of the order.

15.50   If there is a claim and also a counterclaim, non-payment by the claimant of the hearing fee only results in the striking out of the claim, and the counterclaim stands (r 3.7A1(11)). If the action is proceeding only on the counterclaim the hearing fee is payable by the defendant (notes to CPFO, fee 2.1), so in that case the automatic striking out for non-payment of the hearing fee applies to the counterclaim (rr 3.7A(1)(b) and 3.7AA). There is a separate

Figure 15.3 The case management tracks

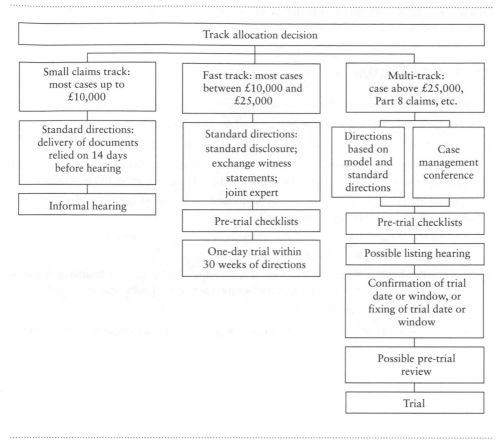

automatic striking out provision relating to non-payment of the issue fee for a counter-claim in r 3.7A(1)(a).

---

0 SHORTER TRIALS AND FLEXIBLE TRIALS SCHEMES

There are two pilot schemes running for three years in the Rolls Building courts (the Chancery Division, Commercial Court, London Mercantile Court, and TCC) which are designed to reduce the costs of simpler claims in these specialised courts. Where they apply the usual case management provisions in the CPR are replaced by the provisions of PD 51N. **15.51**

A claimant will put a case on the shorter trials scheme before issuing the claim form, which is suitable for cases where the trial will not exceed four days. Practice Direction 51N provides for simplified pre-action conduct, followed by statements of case not exceeding 20 pages, the agreement of the issues before the first case management conference, restriction of disclosure to documents relied upon, and trial witness statements limited to 25 pages. Trial judges case manage these claims, with the aim of ensuring trial estimates are adhered to. **15.52**

On the other hand, a case might join the flexible trials scheme by making an application to do so at the first case management conference. This is likely to be suitable for slightly more complicated specialist claims. The normal rules on pre-action conduct and statements of case apply. Standard disclosure is usually ordered, but with adverse documents being **15.53** limited to those known about without making a search. Lay and expert evidence will be limited to identified witnesses or issues as set out in directions. Submissions at trial will be made in writing, with oral submissions and cross-examination subject to time limits.

KEY POINTS SUMMARY

15.54
- Claims not exceeding £10,000 are usually allocated to the small claims track.
- Claims between £10,000 and £25,000 are usually allocated to the fast track.
- Claims over £25,000 and specialist court cases are usually allocated to the multi-track.
- Strictly, the allocation procedure applies in defended cases. Claims where there is default judgment for damages to be assessed may be, but often are not, allocated to a track.
- In general litigation, provisional allocation is followed by directions questionnaires and then formal track allocation by a procedural judge.
- In Commercial Court claims a case management information sheet is used instead of the directions questionnaire.
- At the track allocation stage, the court will give directions laying down a timetable of steps to be taken to prepare the case for trial and for the exchange of evidence.
- Directions may be given without a hearing.
- Particularly in multi-track cases, directions may be given at a case management conference.

16

COSTS MANAGEMENT

A ELEMENTS OF COSTS
   MANAGEMENT 16.06
B CASES GOVERNED BY COSTS
   MANAGEMENT 16.07
C COSTS BUDGETS 16.10
D COSTS MANAGEMENT ORDERS 16.17

E COSTS BUDGETS AND CASE
   MANAGEMENT 16.24
F JUDICIAL CONTROL OF COSTS
   BUDGETS 16.25
G IMPACT ON COSTS ORDERS.........16.31
   Key points summary 16.33

Costs management describes the procedures used by the courts to manage the steps to **16.01** be taken in civil proceedings while also managing the costs to be incurred by the parties in taking those steps to ensure that litigation is conducted at proportionate cost. It was introduced on 1 April 2013, and the rules have been revised several times. Costs management is undertaken with the assistance of detailed costs budgets prepared by the parties, which need to be agreed between the parties or approved by the court. These budgets are then used as the basis for making decisions on the proportionate steps the parties will be ordered to take to prepare the case for trial.

Costs management serves a number of purposes. As described by the *Jackson Report* at **16.02** ch 40, litigation can be seen in commercial terms as a potentially expensive project. It is sound business sense to ensure the client and others involved in such a project have a clear budget at an early stage so they can see what the potential financial consequences will be, and to assist in keeping the sums spent on the litigation to the budget as the case progresses. Solicitors have professional obligations to their clients to ensure they have the information they need to make informed decisions about whether and how to pursue their legal remedies (SRA Code of Conduct 2011, Outcomes 1.12 and 1.13, and Indicative Behaviour 1.14). Costs budgeting and costs management go further, because this information has to be shared with the other parties, and is subject to scrutiny and approval by the court.

One peculiarity of litigation is that at the time when costs are being incurred, no one knows **16.03** who will be paying the bill because of the rule that costs normally follow the event. There is sometimes the feeling that the more a party spends, the more likely it is that the other side will end up paying the bill. As Sir Rupert Jackson said, this gives rise to a sort of 'arms race'. Another feature of litigation costs is that, without costs management by the court, neither party has any effective control over the (potentially recoverable) costs which the other side is running up.

Introducing costs management was not without its risks. There were two significant nega- **16.04** tive factors identified by the *Jackson Report*, ch 40, para 7.1:

(a) costs management generates additional costs. It is only worth incurring these additional costs if there are net savings through the better management of the case as a result of the process; and

(b) costs management imposes additional demands on the limited resources of the court.

16.05 These risks mean that full costs management is not suitable for all cases. Low- and medium-value cases, typically those on the small claims and fast tracks, are unlikely to provide sufficient costs savings to make full costs management cost-effective. It was also concluded by the Jackson Review that certain high-value claims should not be subject to the general rules on costs management. As a result, costs management is primarily aimed at multi-track claims other than the most complex types of claim.

A ELEMENTS OF COSTS MANAGEMENT

16.06 The essential elements of costs management are that:

(a) the parties prepare and exchange litigation budgets;

(b) the parties discuss and potentially agree each other's budgets;

(c) the court states the extent to future budgeted costs are approved, and may comment on past incurred costs;

(d) so far as possible, the court manages the case so that it proceeds within the approved budgets;

(e) as the case proceeds the parties may file amended budgets, subject to court approval; and

(f) at the end of the litigation, the recoverable costs of the winning party are assessed in accordance with the approved future budgeted costs.

B CASES GOVERNED BY COSTS MANAGEMENT

16.07 For claims commenced on or after 6 April 2016, costs management applies by virtue of CPR, r 3.12(1) to all Part 7 multi-track cases except:

(a) where the amount of money claimed as stated in the claim form is £10 million or more;

(b) where the claim is for a monetary remedy that is not quantified or not fully quantified, or is for non-monetary relief, but the claim form contains a statement that the claim is valued at £10 million or more;

(c) where the claim is made by or on behalf of a child;

(d) where the claim is subject to fixed costs or scale costs (for which see 46.65);

(e) where the court otherwise orders (r 3.12(1)(e));

(f) where the claim is proceeding under the Shorter Trials Pilot Scheme (PD 51N, para 2.58);

(g) 'ordinarily' costs management is disapplied in claims where the claimant has severely impaired life expectation (five years or less) (PD 3E, para 2(b)).

16.08 Fixed costs are laid down by CPR, Part 45, and scale costs apply to cases in the Intellectual Property Enterprise Court (rr 45.30–45.36). The words 'where the court otherwise orders' in r 3.12(1)(e) mean that the court may make a specific order disapplying costs management from a multi-track case that would otherwise come within r 3.12.

16.09 It is provided in r 3.12(1A) that costs management will also apply to any other proceedings (including applications) where the court so orders. Further, r 3.1(2)(ll) gives the court the power to order any party to file and exchange a costs budget. This means the court can apply costs management to fast track claims and Part 8 claims if it so decides. In cases not normally subject to costs management, there is an obligation on the parties at an early stage to consider and, where practicable, to discuss whether to apply for an order for the provision of costs budgets with a view to a costs management order being made (PD 3E, para 3). This is particularly appropriate in unfair prejudice petitions, director disqualification proceedings, claims under the Trusts of Land and Appointment of Trustees Act 1996 and the Inheritance (Provision for Family and Dependants) Act 1975, and in Part 8 claims involving substantial disputes of fact (PD 3E, para 5). Costs management may also be appropriate in personal injury claims and clinical disputes worth more than £10 million (para 5).

C COSTS BUDGETS

In cases governed by costs management, unless the court otherwise orders, all parties except **16.10** litigants in person must file and exchange costs budgets with their directions questionnaires if the value of the claim is less than £50,000, otherwise not later than 21 days before the first case management conference (CPR, r 3.13(1)). A litigant in person, even though not required to prepare a budget, must nevertheless be provided with a copy of the budget of any other party (PD 3E, para 7.8).

Format of costs budgets

By PD 3E, para 6(a), unless the court otherwise orders, a costs budget must be in the form **16.11** of Precedent H annexed to PD 3E, see form 16.1. It must be in landscape format with an easily legible typeface. It requires each side to provide information on time costs and disbursements for the following stages in the litigation:

(a) pre-action costs;
(b) issue and statements of case;
(c) case management conference;
(d) disclosure;
(e) witness statements;
(f) expert reports;
(g) pre-trial review;
(h) trial preparation;
(i) trial;
(j) settlement; and
(k) contingencies, which are anticipated costs not falling into the main categories, such as mediation, applications to amend, and applications for disclosure from non-parties. Contingencies should only be included if they are foreseen as more likely than not to be required (*Yeo v Times Newspapers Ltd (No 2)* [2015] 1 WLR 3031 at [71]).

Costs to be included in the budget should include the time costs for attendance of the **16.12** client, correspondence with the other side, and general project and strategy management for each stage. Anticipating possible events that will impact on costs estimates, such as unwanted interim applications by the other side, and including them in the original costs budget under 'contingencies', may avoid the need to return to court with revised costs budgets. In substantial cases, the court may direct that budgets be limited initially to only part of the proceedings and subsequently extended to cover the whole proceedings. In cases where a party's budgeted costs do not exceed £25,000 or the value of the claim does not exceed £50,000, the parties must only use the first page of Precedent H (PD 3E, para 6(c)).

A costs budget must be dated and verified by a statement of truth signed by a senior legal **16.13** representative of the party (PD 3E, para 6(a) and PD 22, para 2.2A). A solicitor who signed a costs budget without the words of the statement of truth was regarded as having

Form 16.1 Costs budget

Costs budget of [Claimant / Defendant] dated [   ]

In the:

Parties: xxx
        yyy

Claim number: zzz

Work done / to be done	Incurred		Estimated		Total (£)
	Disbs (£)	Time costs (£)	Disbs (£)	Time costs (£)	
Pre-action costs	£0.00	£0.00			£0.00
Issue / statements of case	£0.00	£0.00	£0.00	£0.00	£0.00
CMC	£0.00	£0.00	£0.00	£0.00	£0.00
Disclosure	£0.00	£0.00	£0.00	£0.00	£0.00
Witness statements	£0.00	£0.00	£0.00	£0.00	£0.00
Expert reports	£0.00	£0.00	£0.00	£0.00	£0.00
PTR			£0.00	£0.00	£0.00
Trial preparation			£0.00	£0.00	£0.00
Trial			£0.00	£0.00	£0.00
ADR / Settlement discussions	£0.00	£0.00	£0.00	£0.00	£0.00
Contingent cost A:			£0.00	£0.00	£0.00
Contingent cost B:			£0.00	£0.00	£0.00
GRAND TOTAL (including both incurred costs and estimated costs)	£0.00	£0.00	£0.00	£0.00	£0.00

This estimate excludes VAT (if applicable), success fees and ATE insurance premiums (if applicable), costs of detailed assessment, costs of any appeals, costs of enforcing any judgment and [complete as appropriate]

Approved budget		£	-	-
Budget drafting	1% of approved budget or £1,000	£	-	-
Budget process	2%	£	-	-

Statement of Truth

This budget is a fair and accurate statement of incurred and estimated costs which it would be reasonable and proportionate for my client to incur in this litigation.

Signed

Position

version 24/02/2016 Appendix A

committed an error of form rather than substance in *Bank of Ireland v Philip Bank Partnership* [2014] EWHC 284 (TCC). The statement of truth is as follows:

> This budget is a fair and accurate statement of incurred and estimated costs which it would be reasonable and proportionate for my client to incur in this litigation.

Failure to file a costs budget

Unless the court otherwise orders, any party who fails to file a costs budget despite being **16.14** required to do so will be treated as having filed a budget comprising only the applicable court fees (CPR, r 3.14). This is intended to be a draconian sanction. Failing to file costs budgets is regarded as a serious breach of the CPR, because a court cannot manage the litigation and the costs to be incurred unless costs budgets are filed in good time before the first case management conference (*Mitchell v News Group Newspapers Ltd* [2014] 1 WLR 795 at [30]).

A party who is in default of the requirement to file a costs budget will need to apply under **16.15** r 3.9 for relief from the sanction prescribed by r 3.14, see Chapter 37. This is done by making an application in accordance with Part 23 supported by evidence. If relief is granted it is also necessary to consider the terms to be imposed. These might include disallowing all or part of the costs, apart from court fees, from the approved costs budget of the defaulting party for the period of the default. The normal sanction is adjusted to the loss of 50 per cent of the defaulting party's costs if the defaulting party makes a successful Part 36 offer (see 36.39).

Budget discussion reports

After receipt of costs budgets the parties (other than litigants in person) must discuss each **16.16** others' budgets and compile a budget discussion report in Precedent R (PD 3E, para 6A). This sets out agreed figures for each phase; identifies figures for phases that are not agreed; and contains a brief summary of the grounds of dispute. An agreed budget discussion report must be filed at court no later than seven days before the first case management conference (CPR, r 3.13(2)).

D COSTS MANAGEMENT ORDERS

Nature of costs management orders

In addition to exercising its other powers, the court may manage the costs to be incurred **16.17** ('budgeted costs') by any party in any proceedings (CPR, r 3.15(1)). Costs management is mainly a forward-looking process which deals with the anticipated future costs of the proceedings. Costs incurred in the proceedings before the court deals with costs management are called 'incurred costs'. The court may manage costs by making a 'costs management order' (r 3.15(2)). By such order the court will:

(a) record the extent to which the budgeted costs are agreed between the parties; or
(b) in respect of budgeted costs which are not agreed, record the court's approval after making appropriate revisions; and
(c) record the extent (if any) to which incurred costs are agreed.

Where costs budgets have been filed and exchanged the court will make a costs management **16.18** order unless it is satisfied that the litigation can be conducted justly and at proportionate cost in accordance with the overriding objective without such an order being made (r 3.15(2)). A court has to make a costs management order where it is not satisfied that the litigation is being conducted at proportionate cost (*Hegglin v Person(s) Unknown* [2014] EWHC 3793 (QB)).

Approval of costs budgets

16.19   The primary position is that costs budgets should be agreed by the parties. If the budgeted costs or incurred costs are agreed between all parties, the court will record the extent of such agreement (PD 3E, para 7.3). In so far as the budgeted costs are not agreed, the court will review them and, after making any appropriate revisions, record its approval of the budgeted costs (para 7.3). A court considering disputed costs budgets will look at both the total costs and have regard to the costs of each stage of the proceedings. The question for the court is whether the total budgeted costs of each stage falls within the range of reasonable and proportionate costs for the case. As part of this process the court will consider hourly rates and estimated hours in the budget, but it is not the role of the court to fix or approve the hourly rates claimed (para 7.10).

16.20   When considering a costs budget the court will apply the proportionality test in r 44.3(5) (see 46.50). The judge carrying out costs management will not only scrutinize the reasonableness of each party's budget, but also stand back and consider whether the total sums on each side are proportionate in accordance with the definition of proportionality in r 44.3(5).

16.21   While the court will not revise the incurred costs, the court may record its comments on the incurred costs and should take the incurred costs into account when considering the reasonableness and proportionality of all subsequent budgeted costs (PD 3E, para 7.4). Indeed, the court may record its comments on incurred costs whether or not it makes a costs management order (r 3.15(4)).

16.22   If the court refuses to approve the budgeted costs, it cannot go on to make a costs management order (*Willis v MRJ Rundell & Associates Ltd* [2013] EWHC 2923 (TCC) at [25]), because r 3.15(2) requires agreed or approved budgeted costs as a precondition for a costs management order.

16.23   After its budgeted costs have been approved or agreed, each party is required to re-file its costs budget in the form approved with recast figures, which has to be annexed to the order approving it (PD 3E, para 7.7). Thereafter, a party who chooses to spend more than the approved budget will be litigating in part at their own expense, unless the conduct of the paying party results in a more generous assessment of costs.

E COSTS BUDGETS AND CASE MANAGEMENT

16.24   Costs budgeting is intended to provide a measure of certainty over the costs exposure of the parties. It is also intended to provide an effective case management tool for judges when considering the directions that are best suited to the case in hand. When making any case management decision, the court will have regard to any available costs budgets of the parties and will take into account the costs involved in each procedural step (CPR, r 3.17(1)). This is so whether or not a costs budgeting order has been made (r 3.17(2)). This means that in deciding what directions to make, the court will have to consider the costs impact of those steps. Examples given by Ramsey J in the 16th Implementation Lecture included:

(a) whether full electronic disclosure will result in disproportionate costs;

(b) whether it is proportionate to have standard disclosure, or whether the costs of more limited disclosure would be more proportionate; and

(c) the impact on costs of expert evidence and witness statements.

F JUDICIAL CONTROL OF COSTS BUDGETS

If a costs management order has been made, the court will thereafter control the parties' **16.25** budgets in respect of recoverable costs (CPR, r 3.15(3)). The court may set a timetable or give other directions for future reviews of budgets (PD 3E, para 7.5).

Costs management conferences

The court may convene a hearing which is solely for the purpose of costs management (eg **16.26** to approve a revised costs budget). Such a hearing is referred to as a 'costs management conference' (CPR, r 3.16(1)). Where practicable, costs management conferences should be conducted by telephone or in writing (r 3.16(2)), and with points made in correspondence taking the place of formal skeleton arguments (*Yeo v Times Newspapers Ltd (No 2)* [2015] 1 WLR 3031 at [58]).

Reviews of costs budgets

Each party is required to revise its costs budget in respect of future costs upwards or **16.27** downwards, if significant developments in the litigation warrant such revisions (PD 3E, para 7.6). This must be done in advance of the conclusion of the claim. An application to revise a costs budget at the end of a trial is too late (*Elvanite Full Circle Ltd v AMEC Earth & Environmental (UK) Ltd* [2013] EWHC 1643 (TCC)). The onus is on the parties to put forward revised budgets if significant developments in the litigation make this desirable. Such amended budgets must be submitted to the other parties for agreement. In default of agreement, the amended budgets have to be submitted to the court, together with a note of:

(a) the changes made and the reasons for those changes; and
(b) the objections of any other party.

The court may approve, vary, or disapprove the revisions, having regard to any significant **16.28** developments which have occurred since the date when the previous budget was approved or agreed. It may be necessary to hold a costs management conference for this purpose.

Costs relating to costs management

Ensuring that the costs involved in the process do not themselves add to the problem of **16.29** excessive litigation costs has always been a concern. Save in exceptional circumstances, PD 3E, para 7.2 says:

(a) the recoverable costs of initially completing Precedent H shall not exceed the higher of £1,000 or 1 per cent of the total of the incurred costs and budgeted costs; and
(b) all other recoverable costs of the budgeting and costs management process shall not exceed 2 per cent of the total of the incurred costs and budgeted costs.

In so far as such costs exceed these limits they will have to be borne by the client or be **16.30** absorbed in the firm's overheads.

G IMPACT ON COSTS ORDERS

A two-speed approach seems to be contemplated when it comes to costs management and **16.31** the costs of the proceedings:

(a) Cases where a costs management order has been made. In these cases, CPR, r 3.18, provides that when assessing costs on the standard basis, the court will:

    (i) have regard to the receiving party's last approved or agreed budgeted costs for each phase of the proceedings;

    (ii) not depart from such approved or agreed budgeted costs unless satisfied that there is good reason to do so; and

    (iii) take into account any comments recorded on the face of any court order about incurred costs.

(b) Cases where costs budgets have been used, but there has been no costs management order. In these cases, one of the factors the court will have regard to is the receiving party's last approved budget (r 44.4(3)(h)). This applies to all assessments, but in the absence of a costs management order, a 20 per cent increase in costs over the budget may be taken as evidence the costs are unreasonable or disproportionate. Cases where the court refuses to approve costs budgets fall into this category (*Willis v MRJ Rundell & Associates Ltd* [2013] EWHC 2923 (TCC)).

16.32 In cases where there is a costs management order, the need to show a good reason for departing from the budget applies only to budgeted costs. It does not apply to already incurred costs, which are subject to detailed assessment in the usual way (*Harrison v University Hospitals Coventry & Warwickshire NHS Trust* [2017] 1 WLR 4456). This case also holds that a good reason is required whether the suggestion is to depart from the last budget either upwards or downwards, and makes the point that r 3.18 is a significant fetter on the court's ability to depart from the last approved budget, and so the court should not adopt a lax or over-indulgent approach to finding a good reason. Where costs budgets have been approved by the court and revised at regular intervals, the receiving party is unlikely to persuade the court that costs incurred in excess of the budget are reasonable and proportionate (*Henry v News Group Newspapers Ltd* [2013] EWCA Civ 19 at [28]).

KEY POINTS SUMMARY

16.33 • Costs management involves the court managing a case to ensure the procedural steps taken by the parties are conducted at proportionate cost.

• Costs management primarily applies to multi-track claims.

• Where it applies, the parties must produce and seek to agree costs budgets.

• Where the parties cannot agree, the court will consider, amend, and approve the parties' costs budgets.

• The court may make a costs management order, following which the court will control the parties' costs budgets.

• Costs allowed at the end of the case are likely to be limited to the amounts in any approved budgets.

17

COSTS CAPPING AND PROTECTION

A COSTS CAPPING ORDERS 17.02
B *BEDDOE* ORDERS 17.10
C PROTECTIVE COSTS ORDERS 17.15
D JUDICIAL REVIEW COSTS CAPPING 17.19

E AARHUS CONVENTION CASES 17.21
F COSTS LIMITATION ORDERS 17.23
   Key points summary 17.24

Costs capping orders, as the name suggests, limit the amount of costs a party may be **17.01** ordered to pay to its opponent. This chapter will first consider the general rules governing costs capping in CPR, Part 3. It will then consider a number of more specialized costs protection orders, namely:

(a) *Beddoe* orders;
(b) protective costs orders;
(c) judicial review costs capping orders;
(d) Aarhus Convention cases; and
(e) costs limitation orders.

Qualified one-way costs shifting, which also has the effect of limiting the costs a party may be required to pay, is considered in Chapter 47.

A COSTS CAPPING ORDERS

Nature of costs capping orders

A costs capping order is an order limiting the amount of future costs (including disbursements) **17.02** which a party may recover pursuant to an order for costs subsequently made (CPR, r 3.19(1)). For this purpose 'future costs' are those incurred in respect of work done after the date of the costs capping order, but excluding the amount of any additional liability (r 3.19(2)).

Procedure for applying for a costs capping order

An application for a costs capping order may be made at any stage of the proceedings **17.03** (CPR, r 3.19(5)), although it should be made as soon as possible and preferably before the first case management hearing (PD 3F, para 1.2). Where a costs capping order is sought in relation to trust funds, notice of the intention to apply for the order must be filed with the first statement of case or (in relation to Part 8 claims) with the evidence (para 5.5).

The application is made using the procedure in CPR, Part 23 (CPR, r 3.20(1)). The application notice must set out whether the order is sought in respect of the costs of the whole proceedings or on a particular issue which is ordered to be tried separately. It must be accompanied by a costs budget (see 16.10) supported by a statement of truth setting out the costs incurred by the applicant to date and the likely future costs (r 3.20(2); PD 3F, para 2). **17.04**

Directions may be made for dealing with the application, which may include filing schedules of costs, time estimates, and whether the judge should sit with an assessor (r 3.20(3)).

Requirements for making a costs capping order

17.05 By CPR, r 3.19(5), a costs capping order can only be made if:

(a) it is in the interests of justice to make the order;
(b) there is a substantial risk that without the order costs will be disproportionately incurred; and
(c) the risk of disproportionate costs cannot be adequately controlled by case management directions and orders or by the detailed assessment of costs.

17.06 If these conditions are made out, the court has a discretion whether to make the order which it exercises taking into account all the circumstances of the case, but in particular r 3.19(6):

(a) whether there is a substantial imbalance between the financial positions of the parties;
(b) whether the costs of determining the amount of the cap are likely to be proportionate to the overall costs of the litigation;
(c) the stage which the proceedings have reached; and
(d) the costs which have been incurred to date and the future costs.

17.07 The criteria for making costs capping orders demand a restrictive approach, and will be satisfied only in an exceptional case (PD 3F, para 1.1; *Barr v Biffa Waste Services Ltd (No 2)* [2009] EWHC 2444 (TCC), [2010] 3 Costs LR 317). In *Henry v British Broadcasting Corporation* [2006] 1 All ER 154 a costs capping order was refused because the application was made at a very late stage close to the trial. One of the reasons given in *Willis v Nicholson* [2007] PIQR P22 for refusing a cap beyond limiting the claimant to his latest estimate, rather than by a costs capping order, was a concern about the time and costs that would have been involved in having a costs judge decide what the costs cap should be.

17.08 Nevertheless, there will be cases where '... it would be very much better for the court to exercise control over costs in advance, rather than to wait reactively until after the case is over and the costs are being assessed' (*King v Telegraph Group Ltd* [2005] 1 WLR 2282, at [92] *per* Brooke LJ). The object of the order is to encourage the parties to plan the case in advance so as to ensure that costs are proportionate (*Jefferson v National Freight Carriers plc* [2001] 2 Costs LR 313).

Form of cost capping orders

17.09 Costs capping orders are usually drafted to avoid an inflexible cap, while enabling the court to retain control over the amount of costs at any time. Either party may apply to vary the order, which may be allowed only if there has been a material change of circumstances or if there is some other compelling reason why a variation should be allowed (CPR, r 3.19(7)).

B *BEDDOE* ORDERS

17.10 A *Beddoe* order may be sought by trustees and similar persons and orders that they be indemnified against the costs of and incidental to civil proceedings, which are paid out of the trust or other fund. These orders take their name from *Re Beddoe* [1893] 1 Ch 547. It is often called a pre-emptive costs order. Its purpose is to protect trustees who have nothing to gain personally from proceedings, but are under a duty to preserve the funds under their care.

Persons who can apply

Beddoe orders may be available in favour of: **17.11**

(a) trustees, executors, and personal representatives (these are the traditional categories);

(b) a receiver of a company in liquidation (*Re Wedstock Realizations Ltd* [1988] BCLC 354);

(c) employees engaged in hostile litigation against their pension fund trustees (*McDonald v Horn* (1994) *The Times*, 10 August 1994);

(d) a liquidator considering bringing proceedings for wrongful trading, preferences, or in respect of transactions at an undervalue (*Lewis v Commissioner of Inland Revenue* [2001] 3 All ER 499); and

(e) a shareholder making a derivative claim on behalf of a company, or other body capable of suing in its own name (*Wallersteiner v Moir (No 2)* [1975] QB 373. This form of *Beddoe* order is sometimes called *Wallersteiner* order).

Procedure for seeking a *Beddoe* order

The fact that a pre-emptive costs order is sought must be stated in the claim form (PD 19C, **17.12** para 2(2)). If an indemnity is also sought for the costs of the application for permission to continue the claim, that must be stated in the permission application (PD 19C, para 2(2)).

Where trustees properly exercise a power vested in them to agree the costs of another party in relation to the administration of a trust there is no need for a court order, and the assessment of the costs can be dealt with under CPR, r 46.3. Where the trustees have no such power, or decide against exercising it, an application will be necessary if a *Beddoe* order is to be made, and *Practice Statement (Trust Proceedings: Prospective Costs Orders)* [2001] 1 WLR 1082 applies. This sets out a model form of *Beddoe* order, and provides that in the absence of a dispute as to whether such an order is appropriate most such applications will be dealt with on the papers.

Discretion to make a *Beddoe* order

Each application depends on its own facts and is essentially a matter for the discretion of **17.13** the Master or judge who hears it. The court will take into consideration the effect the order would have on the defendant's interests in the fund or company. For example, it may be unfair that a successful defendant who is not required to pay the unsuccessful claimant's costs should nevertheless have to bear a substantial loss in the value of his share in the fund or shares in the company given the effect of the order is to require the fund or company to pays the costs (*Halle v Trax BW Ltd* [2000] BCC 1020).

In exercising that discretion the court will take into account the following considerations: **17.14**

(a) the importance of affording full and proper protection for the costs and expenses of trustees and personal representatives acting properly to protect the fund against adverse claims (*Re Turner* [1907] 2 Ch 126);

(b) the prospects of success in the underlying action (*Re Dallaway* [1982] 1 WLR 756);

(c) whether there is a real possibility of the order operating unjustly; and

(d) the importance of the litigation to the trust or company.

C PROTECTIVE COSTS ORDERS

A protective costs order ('PCO') is similar to a *Beddoe* order, but: **17.15**

(a) under a *Beddoe* order the applicant is given an indemnity for his costs by the company or out of the fund which he is seeking to protect;

(b) under a PCO the applicant is given an immunity against paying the costs of the defendant. Typically, PCOs are made in judicial review proceedings where the claimant will gain no personal benefit from a successful result.

Procedure for seeking a PCO

17.16　The procedure for seeking a PCO, according to *R (Corner House Research) v Secretary of State for Trade and Industry* [2005] 1 WLR 2600, is that:

(a) the claim form should on its face include the claim for the PCO;
(b) if the defendant intends to resist the application, reasons should be set out in the acknowledgment of service under CPR, r 54.8; and
(c) a judge will consider the application on the papers.

17.17　If the order is refused, the applicant can ask for a hearing, which should not exceed one hour. If the order is granted, the defendant has the right to apply to have the order set aside, but has to show compelling reasons to alter the order (*R (Compton) v Wiltshire Primary Care Trust* [2009] 1 WLR 1436). A PCO usually also results in a costs capping order being imposed (see 17.02), unless the applicant's lawyers are acting *pro bono*.

Requirements for making a PCO

17.18　Following *R (Corner House Research) v Secretary of State for Trade and Industry* [2005] 1 WLR 2600, the following requirements must be met before a PCO can be made:

(a) the issues raised in the claim must be of general public importance;
(b) the public interest must require the resolution of those issues;
(c) the applicant must have no private interest in the outcome of the case; and
(d) having regard to the financial resources of the applicant and respondent, and to the amount of costs likely to be involved, it must be fair and just to make the order.

D　JUDICIAL REVIEW COSTS CAPPING

17.19　A judicial review costs capping order is an order limiting or removing the liability of a party to judicial review proceedings to pay another party's costs in connection with any stage of the proceedings (Criminal Justice and Courts Act 2015, s 88(2)). An application for such an order must be made on notice in accordance with CPR, Part 23 (r 46.17(1)), and must normally be made in or accompany the claim form (PD 46, para 10.2). By s 88(6), the court may make a judicial review costs capping order only if:

(a) the proceedings are public interest proceedings;
(b) without an order the applicant would cease to participate in the proceedings; and
(c) it would be reasonable for the applicant to withdraw or cease to participate.

17.20　An order that limits or removes the costs liability of the claimant if relief is not granted in the judicial review proceedings must also limit or remove the costs liability of the other party to pay the claimant's costs (s 89(2)).

E　AARHUS CONVENTION CASES

17.21　Directive 2011/92/EU (the Aarhus Convention) provides that proceedings about the effects of certain public and private projects on the environment must be dealt with by procedures that are fair, equitable, timely, and not prohibitively expensive (art 10a and *R (Garner) v*

Elmbridge Borough Council [2010] EWCA Civ 1006). To give effect to the Aarhus Convention, the usual position in judicial review environmental claims brought by members of the public against public bodies laid down by CPR, r 45.43 is that party and party costs orders are limited to:

(a) £5,000 against a claimant where the claimant is claiming only as an individual and not as, or on behalf of, a business or other legal person;
(b) £10,000 against a claimant in all other cases; and
(c) £35,000 against a defendant.

The court may vary these amounts, or may remove the limits altogether, where to do so will **17.22** not make the costs prohibitively expensive for the claimant (r 45.44). To take advantage of these provisions the claimant is required to state in the claim form that the claim is an Aarhus Convention claim, and must file a schedule of the claimant's financial resources (r 45.42(1)). A defendant may object by denying the claim is an Aarhus Convention claim in the acknowledgment of service, setting out the grounds for such denial, after which the court will determine whether the claim is an Aarhus Convention claim at the earliest opportunity (r 45.45(5)(c)). It is also open for the claimant to opt out of the protection given by the Aarhus Convention, such as by simply not stating in the claim form that it is an Aarhus Convention claim (r 45.42).

F COSTS LIMITATION ORDERS

There is jurisdiction to make a pre-emptive order limiting the costs an applicant might be **17.23** ordered to pay the other side if the litigation is unsuccessful (*R v Lord Chancellor, ex p Child Poverty Action Group* [1999] 1 WLR 347). A party seeking such an order should say so in the claim form (*R (Campaign for Nuclear Disarmament) v Prime Minister of the United Kingdom* [2002] EWHC 2712 (Admin)). The discretion to make such an order should be exercised only in the most exceptional cases, and where the court is satisfied:

(a) that the issues raised are truly ones of general importance;
(b) that it has sufficient appreciation of the merits of the claim to conclude it is in the public interest to make an order; and
(c) that the respondent has a clearly superior capacity to bear the costs of the proceedings than the applicant.

KEY POINTS SUMMARY

- A costs capping order imposes a limit on the future costs a party may recover under a future **17.24** costs order. They are of general application.

- *Beddoe* orders are often called pre-emptive costs orders. They are typically sought by trustees, receivers, or shareholders, and order the trust or company to pay the applicant's costs regardless of the ultimate result.

- A PCO gives the applicant immunity from paying the other side's costs.

- A judicial review costs capping order limits or removes the costs liability of a party to judicial review proceedings, usually on a reciprocal basis.

- CPR, rr 45.41–45.45 impose limits on the costs that may be ordered in environmental law claims to give effect to the Aarhus Convention.

- Costs limitation orders impose a limit on the amount of costs the applicant can ultimately be ordered to pay the other side if unsuccessful.

18

REQUESTS FOR FURTHER INFORMATION

A THE REQUEST FOR FURTHER
INFORMATION.....................18.04
B THE RESPONSE....................18.09
C OBJECTING TO REQUESTS 18.12

D ORDERS FOR RESPONSES...........18.14
E PRINCIPLES 18.17
F COLLATERAL USE 18.23

18.01 Sometimes a party will take the view that the statement of case provided by the other side is not as clear as it should be, or fails to set out the other side's case with the precision that would be expected. In such cases a request may be made for further information about the facts on which the other side's case is based. Generally it is to be expected that such requests should be made shortly after the relevant statement of case is served.

18.02 The situation described in the previous paragraph is in fact just one of the situations in which it may be appropriate for a request to be made for further information, and is not limited to deficiencies in the other side's statement of case. Further information can also be sought to clarify any matter in dispute, or to seek information about any such matter, even though the point in question is not contained in or referred to in a statement of case (CPR, r 18.1). The procedure can therefore be used to try to find out about facts that might be expected to be contained in the witness statements (in which case the application would normally be expected to be made after the exchange of witness statements).

18.03 The procedure can also be used by the court of its own initiative for a variety of purposes, including court-led inquiries into the facts relied upon by a party and requests aimed at finding out information for case management purposes. The request procedure cannot be used to seek information on the nature and extent of the insurance cover available to meet a claim, even in cases where it would be irrational to devote a great deal of costs on investigating quantum if the resources available to the defendant are limited (*West London Pipeline and Storage Ltd v Total UK Ltd* [2008] 1 CLC 935, disapproving *Harcourt v FEF Griffin* [2007] PIQR Q177). Nor, according to *Trader Publishing Ltd v Autotrader.Com Inc* [2010] EWHC 142 (Ch), should it be used for:

(a) tactical reasons;
(b) obtaining further explanation of matters clearly put in issue on the existing statements of case;
(c) seeking explanations of the other side's legal case; or
(d) obtaining information for reasons unconnected with the present litigation.

A THE REQUEST FOR FURTHER INFORMATION

Format of the request

A party seeking clarification or information is, in PD 18, called the first party, and the party **18.04** from whom the clarification or information is sought is called the second party. The first party should serve the second party with a written request for the clarification or information sought, stating a date by which the response to the request should be served. If practicable the request should be served by e-mail (PD 18, para 1.7). The date must allow the second party a reasonable time to respond. Such a request is known as a preliminary request, and is served without the need for a prior court order or direction.

A request should be concise and strictly confined to matters which are reasonably neces- **18.05** sary and proportionate to enable the first party to prepare its own case or to understand the case that has to be met (PD 18, para 1.2). A request may be made by letter if the text of the request is brief and the reply is likely to be brief. If a request is made by letter, it must contain a clear statement that it contains a request under CPR, Part 18, and the letter must be limited to dealing with the request under Part 18 (PD 18, para 1.5).

More complex requests resemble statements of case: see figure 18.1. Technically, requests **18.06** are not statements of case but merely lists of questions, so are not verified by statements of truth. Most requests leave no space for answers, which appear in a separate response document. Alternatively, a request may be prepared in such a way that the response may be given on the same document. In a request in this form the text of the request appears as the left-hand half of each sheet, so that the text of each response can then be inserted on the right. A party serving a request in this form must serve two copies on the second party (PD 18, para 1.6(2)(c)).

Requests must, so far as possible, be made in a single comprehensive document, and not **18.07** made piecemeal (PD 18, para 1.3).

Contents of the request

A request for information, whether made by letter or separate document, must, by PD 18, **18.08** para 1.6:

(a) be headed with the name of the court, the title of the claim, and the claim number;
(b) state in its heading that it is a request made under Part 18;
(c) state the date on which it is made;
(d) where the request relates to a document (eg a statement of case or witness statement), identify that document and, if relevant, the paragraph or words to which it relates;
(e) set out in separate numbered paragraphs each request for information or clarification; and
(f) state the date by which the first party expects a response to the request.

Figure 18.1 Request for further information

....

IN THE HIGH COURT OF JUSTICE   Claim No 18BM 47644
BUSINESS AND PROPERTY COURTS IN BIRMINGHAM
CIRCUIT COMMERCIAL COURT (QBD)

Figure 18.1 *continued*

BETWEEN

GREMMEL ENGINEERING LIMITED   <u>Claimant</u>

and

MARKWARD IMPORTS LIMITED   <u>Defendant</u>

REQUEST FOR FURTHER INFORMATION OF THE
PARTICULARS OF CLAIM AND CLARIFICATION
UNDER PART 18

Made on behalf of Markward Imports Limited (the first party) to Gremmel Engineering Limited (the second party) dated 22 August 2018.

<u>Under paragraph 2</u>

Of: '… by an agreement made on 14 November 2016 the Defendant agreed with the Claimant to sell and supply 4,000 metric tonnes of steel rods …'

<u>Requests</u>
1. Was the alleged agreement written or oral?
2. If it was written, please identify the document or documents in which it was made, and provide copies in accordance with Practice Direction 16, paragraph 7.3.
3. If it was oral, please state:

     (a) where the agreement was made; and

     (b) as precisely as possible the words used.

<u>Clarification of the Claimant's case</u>

<u>Request</u>
4. Is it alleged that the agreement alleged in paragraph 2 of the Particulars of Claim was made under the framework agreement as set out in paragraphs 5 and 6 of the Defence?

Take notice that these requests are to be answered no later than 4.00 p.m. on 12 September 2018.

Dated 22 August 2018 by Messrs Whitely & Hilt of 34 St Andrews Road, Birmingham, B1 9FP, solicitors for the Defendant.

B THE RESPONSE

18.09 If the request is in the format having the requests on the left of the page with the responses to be entered on the right-hand side, the second party may use the document supplied for the purpose for the response. Otherwise, a response must, by PD 18, para 2.3:

(a) be headed with the name of the court and the title and number of the claim;

(b) in its heading identify itself as a response to that request;

(c) repeat the text of each separate paragraph of the request and set out under each paragraph the response to it; and

(d) have attached to it a copy of any document not already in the possession of the first party which forms part of the response.

An example of a response is given at figure 18.2.

Figure 18.2 Response to request for further information

IN THE HIGH COURT OF JUSTICE   Claim No 18BM 47644
BUSINESS AND PROPERTY COURTS IN BIRMINGHAM
CIRCUIT COMMERCIAL COURT (QBD)
BETWEEN

GREMMEL ENGINEERING LIMITED   Claimant

and

MARKWARD IMPORTS LIMITED   Defendant

FURTHER INFORMATION OF THE PARTICULARS OF
CLAIM AND CLARIFICATION UNDER PART 18

This further information of the Particulars of Claim and clarification is given by the
Claimant to the Defendant pursuant to the Request dated 22 August 2018 made by the
Defendant.

Under paragraph 2
Of: '…by an agreement made on 14 November 2016 the Defendant agreed with the
Claimant to sell and supply 4,000 metric tonnes of steel rods…'

Request
1. Was the alleged agreement written or oral?

Response
Written.

Request
2. If it was written, please identify the document or documents in which it was made, and
   provide copies in accordance with Practice Direction 16, paragraph 7.3.

Response
The Claimant's purchase order dated 24 October 2016 and an e-mail from the Defendant
to the Claimant dated 14 November 2016, copies of which are attached to this Response.

Request
3. If it was oral, please state:
   (a) where the agreement was made; and
   (b) as precisely as possible the words used.

Response
Not applicable.

Clarification of the Claimant's case

Request
4. Is it alleged that the agreement alleged in paragraph 2 of the Particulars of Claim
   was made under the framework agreement as set out in paragraphs 5 and 6 of the
   Defence?

Response
No.

Figure 18.2 *continued*

Statement of truth
- (I believe) (The Claimant believes) that the facts stated in this response to a request for further information are true.
- I am duly authorized by the Claimant to sign this statement.

Full name:

Name of Claimant's solicitor's firm: Messrs Young & Thompson

Signed: Position or office held:

- (Claimant) (Litigation Friend) (if signing on behalf of firm or company) (Claimant's solicitor)
- *delete as appropriate*

Dated 5 September 2018, by Messrs Young & Thompson, of 40 High Street, Barnet EN10 4SL, solicitors for the Claimant.

18.10 Under the old rules, and presumably this holds good under the CPR, it was regarded as improper for the response to a request to set out matters in answer that departed from the second party's earlier statement of case (*Re Unisoft Group Ltd (No 3)* [1994] 1 BCLC 609).

18.11 The second party must serve the response on the first party, and must file at court and serve on every other party a copy of the request and of the response (PD 18, para 2.4). Unlike requests, responses are statements of case and should be verified by a statement of truth (para 3).

C OBJECTING TO REQUESTS

18.12 If the second party objects to answering a request, or if the second party considers the time given by the first party to be too short, the second party should inform the first party of the objection promptly and within the time stated for the response given by the first party (PD 18, para 4.1). Objections could include the disproportionate nature of the request, or that it infringes privilege or otherwise infringes the overriding objective.

18.13 Objections to providing further information must be made in writing, and must state the reasons for making the objection. Where the complaint is that the time given by the first party is too short, the objection must give a date by which the second party expects to have responded.

D ORDERS FOR RESPONSES

18.14 If a request for further information is not responded to, the first party is entitled to apply to the court for an order requiring the second party to reply in a stated period of time. Applications are made in the usual way under CPR, Part 23 (see Chapter 23). The first party will issue an application notice, which must generally be served on the second party at least three clear days before the return day. The application notice will either set out or have attached to it the text of the order sought. This must set out the matters in respect of which further information is sought (PD 18, para 5.2), and this can usually best be done by reference to the request previously served upon the second party.

Both parties should consider whether they will serve evidence in support or in opposition to the application (PD 18, para 5.4). If the first party has not served a preliminary request on the second party, the reasons for not doing so should be dealt with in the written application or evidence in support. If a preliminary request was made, the notice or evidence in support should describe the response, if any, received from the second party (para 5.3). **18.15**

There is no need to inform the second party of the application for such an order if the second party failed to make any response at all to the preliminary request within the time stated by the first party, and provided at least 14 days have passed since the request was served (PD 18, para 5.5). **18.16**

E PRINCIPLES

As previously mentioned at 18.05, a request for further information should be concise and strictly confined to matters which are reasonably necessary and proportionate to enable the first party to prepare its own case or to understand the case that must be met. **18.17**

Applying the overriding objective and as PD 18, para 1.2 makes clear, any requests made for information should be reasonably necessary and proportionate. A request for further information may be the proportionate method for dealing with a statement of case which does not provide full information, rather than the more drastic approach of applying to strike out (*Deutsche Morgan Grenfell Group plc v Inland Revenue Commissioners* [2007] 1 AC 558). **18.18**

Requests related to statements of case

Particulars of claim and other statements of case should contain a *concise* statement of the facts relied upon (CPR, r 16.4(1)(a); *McPhilemy v Times Newspapers Ltd* [1999] 3 All ER 775). The statements of case should therefore set out the parameters of the case that is being advanced by each party. They identify the issues and the extent of the dispute between the parties, and should make clear the general nature of the case of the pleader. **18.19**

In *McPhilemy v Times Newspapers Ltd*, Lord Woolf MR pointed out that excessive detail in the statements of case can obscure the issues rather than providing clarification. Further, after disclosure of documents and the exchange of witness statements the statements of case frequently become of only historical interest. Unless there is some obvious purpose to be served by fighting over the precise terms of a statement of case, contests over its terms are to be discouraged. **18.20**

Clarification requests

Requests for further information about statements of case (see 18.19–18.20) are met far more frequently than general requests for clarification (see request 4 in figure 18.1). Requests of this second type are aimed at clarification of the facts relating to the issues in the case without being tied to the wording of the other side's statement of case. They can be useful, but can be time-consuming and expensive diversions from sensible preparation of the case. This type of request therefore tends to be carefully policed by the courts. **18.21**

There are a number of well-established reasons for disallowing requests for clarification: **18.22**

(a) 'Fishing' requests. A request is fishing if the party making it does not have evidence supporting the cause of action or defence being put forward, but hopes something may turn up in response to the request (*Best v Charter Medical of England Ltd* (2001) *The Times*, 19 November 2001).

(b) Requests put for an unfair purpose. An example was *Lovell v Lovell* [1970] 1 WLR 1451, where the purpose behind asking a particular request was to obtain a written acknowledgment of a debt for the purpose of the Limitation Act 1980, s 29 (see 21.50).

(c) Oppressive requests. These ask for information going beyond the level of detail that can reasonably be expected (*White and Co v Credit Reform Association and Credit Index Ltd* [1905] 1 KB 653).

(d) Requests that are not precisely formulated (*Kirkup v British Rail Engineering Ltd* [1983] 1 WLR 1165).

(e) Where the request is not necessary for saving costs (CPR, r 1.4(2)(h)). A common example is where the information sought is likely to be included under standard disclosure (see Chapter 31) or in exchanged witness statements (see Chapter 32), so the request duplicates steps that will be taken later in the proceedings. Whether this will be an effective answer depends on the circumstances of the case (*English, Welsh and Scottish Railway Ltd v Goodman* (2007) LTL 9/5/07).

F COLLATERAL USE

18.23 Rule 18.2 of the CPR says that the court may direct that information provided either voluntarily or after an order must not be used for any purpose other than for the proceedings in which it is given. Consideration should be given to asking for such a direction whenever sensitive information is to be given in answer to a request for information. See also the discussion in relation to disclosure at 31.88–31.90.

19

PARTIES AND JOINDER

A DESCRIPTION OF PARTIES 19.03
B PARTICULAR CLASSES OF PARTY 19.04
C LITIGANTS IN PERSON 19.44
D VEXATIOUS LITIGANTS 19.47
E JOINDER 19.49
F REPRESENTATIVE PROCEEDINGS 19.56
G REPRESENTATION OF
   UNASCERTAINED PERSONS 19.60

H INTERVENTION 19.61
I CONSOLIDATION 19.63
J STAKEHOLDER CLAIMS 19.66
K ASSIGNMENT .19.71
L GROUP LITIGATION 19.73
   Key points summary 19.76

As the remedies granted by the courts are generally effective only as between the parties, **19.01** it is important to take care when drafting proceedings that no mistakes are made over the parties to be brought in. Although it is possible to correct most mistakes by amendment at a later stage, the passing of a limitation period may prevent this, and, in any event, avoidable amendments will be penalized in costs and may weaken the credibility of the case at trial.

This chapter will first look at the rules relating to different classes of party, and will then **19.02** consider the rules governing multi-party litigation.

A DESCRIPTION OF PARTIES

The descriptions of the parties according to the nature of the court proceedings are set out **19.03** in table 19.1.

Table 19.1 Descriptions of parties

Type of proceedings	Issuing party	Party served
Claim form	Claimant	Defendant
Interim application	Applicant	Respondent
Additional claim under Part 20	Defendant	Third (or Fourth, etc.) Party
Petition	Petitioner	Respondent
Bankruptcy	Petitioner	Debtor
Notice of appeal	Appellant	Respondent
Enforcement	Judgment creditor	Judgment debtor

B PARTICULAR CLASSES OF PARTY

Table 19.2 sets out the form of words to be used to describe different types of parties in the **19.04** heading of statements of case and other court documents. Paragraphs 19.05–19.46 comment on the various rules.

Table 19.2 Names of parties in court documents

Class of party	Examples of forms of words
Individuals	Mr HUGH TREVOR GROVES
change of name	Mrs JANE HALL (formerly Ms JANE OLD)
Children	Miss JANE OLD (a child, by Mrs CAROL OLD her litigation friend)
Child reaching full age	Miss JANE OLD (formerly a child but now of full age)
Protected party	Mr HENRY RIMMER by Ms MARY JONES his litigation friend
Partnership	HUNT & MURRAY (a firm)
Sole trader	Mr MARK ALAN WATSON, trading as FOREST SHOES
Corporation sole	MICHAEL, Bishop of Lincoln
Companies	
limited	CLARKE'S LINEN IMPORTS LIMITED
status unclear from name	CLARKE'S PROVIDENT (a company limited by guarantee)
in liquidation	BEN CLOVE LIMITED (in liquidation)
Bankrupts	The trustee of the estate of Mr HUGH TREVOR GROVES, a bankrupt
Deceased party	Mrs MARY JONES (executrix of the estate of Mr CLIVE DEAN deceased)
Deceased defendant, no grant of probate or administration	The personal representatives of Mr CLIVE DEAN deceased
Relator proceedings	The Attorney-General at the relation of Mr GAVIN WILSON
Representative proceedings	Mr HUGH TREVOR GROVES and Mr CLIVE DEAN on behalf of themselves and all other persons carrying on trade as fishermen in the parish of Holcombe
Intervention	(Miss MARY JONES intervening)

Individuals

19.05 Individuals should be given their full names and titles in all court documents. Initials may be used if these are all that is known, and it is also possible to commence proceedings using only the defendant's surname. A litigant who changes their name, for example on marriage, must file a notice of the change at the court office and serve it on the other parties.

Direct claims against insurers

19.06 Normally a claimant can only bring a claim against a tortfeasor, which means there is generally no direct claim against a defendant's insurer. Legal systems in other jurisdictions sometimes allow direct claims against insurers (such as in personal injuries claims in Spain, see *Keefe v Mapfre Mutalidad Cia De Seguros Y Reasaguros SA* [2016] 1 WLR 905). In England and Wales the only exception is provided by the European Communities (Rights against Insurers) Regulations 2002 (SI 2002/3061), which allow claimants to bring proceedings in tort arising out of road accidents against the insurer of the vehicle alleged to be responsible for the accident (reg 3). This is in addition to the existing right of action against the driver (reg 3(2)). An 'accident' for the purposes of the Regulations means an accident on a road or other public place in the UK caused by, or arising out of, the use of any insured vehicle (reg 2(1)). A 'vehicle' is any land-based vehicle other than a train which is normally based in the UK (reg 2(1)). A vehicle is 'insured' if there is a policy of insurance in force fulfilling the requirements of the Road Traffic Act 1988, s 145 (reg 2(3)).

Persons under disability

There are two categories of persons under disability: children and protected parties. Persons under 18 years of age are children. A protected party is a party, or intended party, who lacks capacity within the meaning of the Mental Capacity Act 2005 to conduct proceedings (CPR, r 21.1(2)(c), (d)). There is a presumption of full mental capacity, which is displaced where an individual has an impairment of their mind or brain which prevents them from being able to make relevant decisions (*Masterman-Lister v Brutton and Co (Nos 1 and 2)* [2003] 1 WLR 1511, Mental Capacity Act 2005, s 3). For the purposes of CPR, Part 21, this is the capacity to conduct the claim or cause of action the claimant in fact has (*Dunhill v Burgin (Nos 1 and 2)* [2014] 1 WLR 933 at [18]). **19.07**

Litigation friends

A person under disability must sue and be sued by a litigation friend (CPR, r 21.2), although the court may grant permission for a child to conduct proceedings without a litigation friend (r 21.2(3)). A child's litigation friend is normally a relative with no interest in the litigation adverse to that of the child. In *Nottingham County Council v Bottomley* [2010] Med LR 407 the local authority's director of social care could not act as the child's litigation friend because the local authority had a financial interest in a periodical payments order that conflicted with the interests of the child. A deputy appointed by the Court of Protection under the Mental Capacity Act 2005 with power to conduct proceedings on the protected party's behalf is entitled to be their litigation friend in the relevant proceedings (r 21.4(2)). **19.08**

A person may become a litigation friend without needing a court order by following the procedure in CPR, r 21.5. A deputy intending to act as a litigation friend for a protected party must file an official copy of the order of the Court of Protection when the claim form is issued or (if acting for a defendant) when he first takes a step in the proceedings (r 21.5(2)). In the absence of such a deputy, r 21.4(3) permits a person who can fairly and competently conduct proceedings on the protected party's behalf, who has no adverse interest, and who (if acting for a claimant) undertakes to pay any costs the protected party may be ordered to pay, to act as the protected party's litigation friend. Such a person needs to file and serve a certificate of suitability (r 21.5(3), (4)). Likewise, a person acting as a litigation friend for a child must file a certificate of suitability. An example of such a certificate is shown in form 19.1. In addition, a litigation friend willing to act on behalf of a claimant has to undertake to pay any costs which the child or protected party may be ordered to pay in relation to the proceedings, subject to any right he may have to be repaid from the assets of the child or protected party (r 21.4(3)(c)). Undertakings are not required from litigation friends acting on behalf of defendants. **19.09**

Where a party under a disability does not have a litigation friend, the court may appoint one on an application made by the person wishing to be the litigation friend or by a party (CPR, r 21.6). This may be necessary, for example, where the person under a disability is the defendant, because until a litigation friend is appointed no steps can be taken in the proceedings other than issuing and serving the claim form, and applying for the appointment of a litigation friend (r 21.3(2)(b)). **19.10**

A child acting by a litigation friend should be referred to in the title to the proceedings as 'Master JOHN SMITH (a child by Mrs HELEN SMITH his litigation friend)'. A child acting without a litigation friend is referred to as 'Master JOHN SMITH (a child)'. **19.11**

Form 19.1 Certificate of suitability of litigation friend

Certificate of suitability of litigation friend

If you are acting
- **for a child,** you must serve a copy of the completed form on a parent or guardian of the child, or if there is no parent or guardian, the carer or the person with whom the child lives
- **for a protected party,** you must serve a copy of the completed form on one of the following persons with authority in relation to the protected party as: (1) the attorney under a registered enduring power of attorney (2) the donee of the lasting power of attorney; (3) the deputy appointed by the Court of Protection; or if there is no such person, an adult with whom the protected party resides or in whose care the protected party is. You must also complete a certificate of service (obtainable from the court office)

You should send the completed form to the court with the claim form (if acting for the claimant) or when you take the first step on the defendant's behalf in the claim together with the certificate of service (if applicable).

Name of court	
COUNTY COURT AT BARNET	
Claim No.	
Claimant (including ref.)	Miss JOCELYN GRIEBART (a child by Mrs LYNNE GRIEBART)
Defendant (including ref.)	Mr HOWARD MORRIS

You do not need to complete this form if you are a deputy appointed by the Court of Protection with power to conduct proceedings on behalf of the protected party.

I consent to act as litigation friend for <u>JOCELYN GRIEBART</u>
(claimant)(defendant)

I believe that the above named person is a

☑ child ☐ protected party *(give your reasons overleaf and attach a copy of any medical evidence in support)*

I am able to conduct proceedings on behalf of the above named person competently and fairly and I have no interests adverse to those of the above named person.

delete if you are acting for the defendant

*I undertake to pay any costs which the above named claimant may be ordered to pay in these proceedings subject to any right I may have to be repaid from the assets of the claimant.

Please write your name in capital letters

☐ Mr ☑ Mrs ☐ Miss Surname <u>GRIEBART</u>

☐ Ms ☐ Other _____ Forenames <u>LYNNE</u>

Address to which documents in this case are to be sent.

Whitely & Hilt 34 Brimsdown Road, Barnet, EN7 8RW	**I certify that the information given in this form is correct** Signed _____ Date _____

The court office at Kigmaker House, 19-21 Station Road, New Barnet, Herts., EN5 1PF

is open between 10 am and 4 pm Monday to Friday. When corresponding with the court, please address forms or letters to the Court Manager and quote the claim number.

N235 Certificate of suitability of litigation friend (10.07) ©Crown copyright 2007

Child attaining 18 years

A child who is a party to proceedings and who reaches full age must serve on the other parties **19.12** and file at court a notice stating that he or she is now over 18 and that the litigation friend's appointment has ceased (CPR, r 21.9). The notice must also give an address for service and state whether or not he or she intends to carry on being a party. Such a party who carries on will be described as 'Mr JOHN SMITH (formerly a child but now of full age)'. If the child (now of full age) fails to serve such a notice, the litigation friend can serve a notice to the effect that the child has reached full age and the appointment as litigation friend has ceased. A child claimant's litigation friend's liability in costs continues until notice is given to the other parties.

Protected party recovering

When a protected party regains or acquires capacity, the litigation friend's appointment **19.13** continues until it is ended by a court order (CPR, r 21.9(2)). The application for such an order may be made by the former protected party, the litigation friend, or any party.

Service on person under disability

Originating process must be served on a child's parent or guardian or, if there is none, the **19.14** person with whom the child resides or in whose care he or she is. In the case of a protected party, process must be served on the person with authority in relation to the protected party (the attorney under a registered enduring power of attorney, the donee under a lasting power of attorney, or the deputy appointed by the Court of Protection), failing which, on the adult with whom the protected party resides or in whose care he or she is (CPR, r 6.6).

Limitation

Periods of limitation do not run against persons under disability at the time the cause of **19.15** action accrued: see 21.40.

Approval of settlements

Under CPR, r 21.10 there are two regimes for seeking court approval of settlements of **19.16** claims by or against persons under disability. Under both regimes, until a proposed settlement is approved by the court there is no binding contract, and either party may back out of it (*Dietz v Lennig Chemicals Ltd* [1969] 1 AC 170; *Drinkall v Whitwood* [2004] 1 WLR 462). Seeking approval of a consent judgment (see 41.02) is not the same as a proper application under r 21.10. This is because the underlying policy of r 21.10 is to protect persons under a disability from themselves and from their legal advisers, who through lack of skill or experience might otherwise settle their claims for far less than they are worth (*Dunhill v Burgin (Nos 1 and 2)* [2014] 1 WLR 933 at [18]).

Where the settlement is agreed before proceedings are commenced the rules are permis- **19.17** sive. Although this is the position in theory, in practice approval is always sought in order to give the defendant a valid discharge for the money paid and to ensure there can be no question of unfairness to the person under disability. Approval is sought by issuing a Part 8 claim form (CPR, r 21.10(2)). The second regime is mandatory. A settlement reached after proceedings have been commenced must be approved by the court if it is to be valid. Approval is sought by issuing an ordinary application notice (CPR, r 21.10(1)).

If a Part 8 claim is used, the claim form must set out details of the claim and also the terms **19.18** of the settlement or compromise, or must have attached to it a draft consent order. Both types of application must be supported by written evidence. Information to be provided includes whether and to what extent the defendant admits liability, the age and any occupation of the child, the litigation friend's approval of the proposed settlement, and details of any relevant prosecution. In personal injuries claims the evidence must deal with the circumstances of the accident, and in many cases the police report must be obtained. Medical reports, quantum precedents, and a statement of past and future loss and expense must be made available to the court. In all except very clear cases a copy of an opinion from counsel on the merits of the settlement, together with the instructions (unless sufficiently set out in the opinion) must also be supplied to the court (PD 21, para 6.4).

19.19 Most applications for approval are heard by Masters and District Judges sitting in private. When considering the proposed settlement, the court has to weigh the claimant's prospects of success against the likely level of damages on full liability, and decide whether the proposed settlement is in the interests of the person under disability. If the court decides the settlement is not in the interests of the person under disability, the application is adjourned for the parties to negotiate new terms. An anonymity order will usually be made to protect the privacy of the child (*JX MX v Dartford & Gravesham NHS Trust* [2015] EWCA Civ 96), but the decision will be pronounced in public in accordance with the European Convention on Human Rights, art 6(1).

Investment of funds

19.20 If approval is given, directions are given as to how the money shall be dealt with (CPR, r 21.11). Investment decisions for the money are made by the Court Funds Office (PD 21, para 9.2). If the money to be invested is very small, the court may order it to be paid to the litigation friend to be put into a building society account for the child's use (para 9.7). The underlying principle is that such funds should be applied for the purpose for which the damages were awarded. For example, the court will be careful to avoid the money being applied for the general benefit of a child's family. On reaching 18 an application can be made for payment out to the child (para 9.8).

Trusts and estates

19.21 Trustees, executors, and administrators should act jointly, and all should be named in any proceedings (as defendants if they will not consent to act as claimants). Regarding beneficiaries, it is provided by CPR, r 19.7A(1), that a claim may be brought by or against trustees, executors, or administrators without the need to join the beneficiaries. This is invariably the most convenient way of bringing proceedings, and where this is done any judgment or order in the claim is binding on the beneficiaries unless the court orders otherwise (r 19.7A(2)).

Bankruptcy

19.22 A bankrupt's estate vests in the trustee in bankruptcy on the appointment of the trustee (Insolvency Act 1986, s 306), who becomes the person who should be named in litigation involving the bankrupt's estate. A bankrupt has no standing to make applications in litigation even in the period between the making of a bankruptcy order and the appointment of a trustee (*Dadourian Group International Inc v Simms* [2008] BPIR 508). By way of exception, claims for personal injuries and defamation remain vested in the bankrupt (*Ord v Upton* [2000] Ch 352).

19.23 The heading in a claim involving a trustee in bankruptcy does not individually identify the trustee, but refers to the trustee simply by his office (see table 19.2 and the IA 1986, s 305(4)). Where a party becomes bankrupt during the currency of proceedings, the trustee in bankruptcy may be ordered to be substituted for the bankrupt (CPR, r 19.2(2)). Proceedings against a bankrupt may only be commenced with the court's permission (IA 1986, s 285(3)). Proceedings commenced without such permission are a nullity, and cannot be retrieved by granting retrospective permission (*Fusion Interactive Communication Solutions Ltd v Venture Investment Placement Ltd (No 2)* [2005] 2 BCLC 571).

Deceased parties

Generally, causes of action other than for defamation survive a claimant's death, and vest **19.24** in the deceased's personal representatives, who should be named as parties in any litigation. Problems arise in the period between someone's death and the grant of letters of administration or probate ('the grant'), some of which, but not all, are addressed by CPR, r 19.8. As a question of substantive law, a claim commenced in the name of a claimant who died before the claim was issued, and before the grant, is a nullity and will be struck out (*In re NP Engineering and Security Products Ltd* [1998] 1 BCLC 208; *Kimathi v Foreign and Commonwealth Office (No 2)* [2017] 1 WLR 1081). If the deceased is to be the defendant, a claim can be brought before the grant, and it will be treated as if it was brought against the estate of the deceased (r 19.8(3)(b)), and the claimant will need to apply to the court for an order appointing a person to represent the deceased (r 19.8(2)(b)(ii)).

Where a party dies after the claim form is issued the position is different. The claim as issued **19.25** is not a nullity. It is not a nullity even if the claimant dies in the period between issue and service of the claim form (*Fielding v Rigby* [1993] 1 WLR 1355). Any of the parties may apply to the court for an order that the claim may proceed in the absence of a person to represent the estate of the deceased (r 19.8(1)(a)). If such an order is made, any judgment or order made in the claim will still bind the estate of the deceased (r 19.8(5)). Before the grant there is a limited power for a person to take essential steps to preserve and protect the deceased's estate, but unless an application is necessary, the court will refuse to make an order without a grant (*Caudle v LD Law Ltd* [2008] 1 WLR 1540). After a grant has been obtained, the personal representatives may be ordered to be made parties by substitution (r 19.2(2)). Substitution of personal representatives in proceedings commenced before the expiry of limitation does not infringe the Limitation Act 1980, whether the death occurs before or after the expiry of limitation (*Roberts v Gill and Co* [2011] 1 AC 240 at [103]).

Partnerships

A partnership exists where a number of people carry on a business in common with a view **19.26** of profit (Partnership Act 1890, s 1(1)). Every partner is an agent for the firm (s 5). In most situations a partnership will be bound by acts done on behalf of the firm (ss 6 and 10), and the individual partners will also be personally liable, either jointly or jointly and severally (ss 9 and 12). The partners who will be liable are those who were partners at the time of the relevant event.

Partnerships typically trade under a firm name. This often consists of the surnames of **19.27** each of the partners, but many partnerships use a brand name, or words to describe their main business activities. By PD 7A, para 5A.3, where a partnership has a name, unless it is inappropriate to do so, claims must be brought in or against the name under which the partnership carried on business at the time the cause of action accrued. This is done by adding the words '(a firm)' after its name in the title to the proceedings. Use of the partnership name is simply the shorthand method of specifically naming as defendants (or claimants) each of the persons who were partners when the cause of action accrued (*Ernst and Young v Butte Mining plc (No 2)* [1997] 1 WLR 1485 *per* Lightman J). Consequently, naming individual partners as well as the partnership in the firm name is an irregularity because the partners are effectively being sued twice (*Brown v Innovatorone plc* [2009] EWHC 1376 (Comm)).

19.28 A document may be served on partners by the usual methods: personal service, first-class post, by leaving it at the defendant's address, and, subject to certain conditions, through the document exchange, or by fax or other means of electronic communication (CPR, rr 6.3–6.9). For individuals suing or being sued in the name of a partnership, the place of service is their usual or last known residence, or the principal or last known place of business of the partnership (r 6.9(2)). Personal service on a partnership was considered at 6.24.

Acknowledgment of service

19.29 Paragraph 4.4 of PD 10 provides that where a claim is brought against a partnership:

(a) service must be acknowledged in the name of the partnership on behalf of all persons who were partners at the time when the cause of action accrued; and

(b) the acknowledgment of service may be signed by any of those partners, or by any person authorized by any of those partners to sign it.

Disclosure of partners' names

19.30 Any party to a claim may make a request to the firm, stating the date when the relevant cause of action accrued, seeking details of the partners at that time. The partners are obliged to provide a 'partnership membership statement' within 14 days of receipt of such a request. This is a written statement of the names and last known places of residence of all the persons who were partners at the time the cause of action accrued (PD 7A, paras 5B.1–5B.3).

Enforcement

19.31 A judgment obtained against a partnership may be enforced against any partnership property within the jurisdiction (PD 70, para 6A.1). Depending on the circumstances, it may also be enforced against a partner who acknowledged service as a partner, or a person who is found by the court to have been a partner at the relevant time (PD 70, paras 6A.2–6A.4).

Companies

19.32 A registered company must be named using the full registered name. Where its legal status is not apparent from its name, for example a company limited by guarantee or in liquidation, this must be included in the heading. Service on companies was considered at 6.22 and 6.24.

Representation of companies

19.33 Companies are artificial bodies, so need to act through directors or other duly authorized individuals. Where a director or some other individual appears for a company at a hearing, a written statement must be completed giving the company's full name, its registered number, the status of the representative within the company (eg being a director), and the date and form by which the representative was authorized to act for the company. For example: '17 September 2018: Board resolution dated 17 September 2018'. See PD 39A, para 5.2.

Overseas companies

19.34 A company incorporated outside Great Britain which establishes a place of business in Great Britain must register certain documents and particulars with the registrar of companies. Among these is a list of the names and addresses of persons resident in Great Britain authorized to accept service of process on the company's behalf (see the Overseas

Companies Regulations 2009 (SI 2009/1801)). Documents may be served on an overseas company by leaving them at, or sending them by post to, the registered address of a person authorized to accept service. If there is no such person, or if service cannot be effected, the documents may instead be left at or sent to any place of business of the company within the UK (Companies Act 2006, s 1139(2)).

Companies in liquidation

The Insolvency Act 1986, s 130(2), provides that, when a winding-up order has been made **19.35** or a provisional liquidator appointed, no proceedings shall be continued against the company or its property except by permission of the court and subject to such terms as the court may impose.

Once the liquidation is complete, the company involved will be dissolved. Although disso- **19.36** lution puts an end to the company's corporate existence, it may still be possible to bring a claim against it by applying to the court for an order for the restoration of the company to the register under the Companies Act 2006, s 1029. Such applications are made from time to time by claimants claiming damages for personal injuries against dissolved companies which were insured at the time of the accident. Section 1030(2) provides that no order shall be made if it appears 'that the proceedings would fail by virtue of any enactment as to the time within which proceedings must be brought'. In *Re Workvale Ltd* [1992] 1 WLR 416 a company was restored despite the fact that the primary limitation period had expired. The Court of Appeal held it was sufficient that the claimant had an arguable case for the exercise of the court's discretion to 'disapply' the usual three-year limitation period under the Limitation Act 1980, s 33 (discussed further at 21.55ff).

Outside the field of personal injuries claims, companies can be restored up to six years after **19.37** the date of dissolution (s 1030(4)). On restoring a company to the register, the court may make consequential directions under s 1032(3) for the purpose of placing the company and all other persons as nearly as possible into the position they would have been in had the company not been dissolved. These can include directions that the period the company was dissolved shall not count for limitation purposes (s 1030(3) and *Davy v Pickering* [2015] 2 BCLC 116).

Bodies suing in their own names

The following bodies may sue and be sued in their own names: **19.38**

(a) Corporations other than registered companies. Service may be effected on the mayor, chairman, or president, or the town clerk, or other similar officer (PD 6A, para 6.2(2)). It was held in *Kuwait Airways Corporation v Iraqi Airways Co* [1995] 1 WLR 1147 that a junior employee left in charge of the defendant's UK office was a 'similar officer' within the meaning of the predecessor to this provision.

(b) Trade unions and unincorporated employers' associations (Trade Union and Labour Relations (Consolidation) Act 1992, s 10).

(c) London boroughs (London Government Act 1963, s 1), metropolitan districts, and non-metropolitan counties and districts (Local Government Act 1972, s 2).

(d) Most central government departments: see the list published by the Minister for the Civil Service in the Annex to PD 19A. Proceedings involving the Crown are governed by the special code in CPR, Part 66 which gives the Crown a number of procedural privileges not enjoyed by other litigants.

(e) There are numerous quasi-governmental public bodies which are not formal departments of State. These bodies will usually have an implicit power to bring proceedings to protect their special interests in the performance of their functions (*Broadmoor Hospital Authority v Robinson* [2000] QB 775).

Her Majesty's Attorney-General

19.39 In the following situations proceedings are brought in the name of or against the Attorney-General:

(a) where a central government department is not mentioned on the Crown Proceedings Act 1947, s 17, list (see the Annex to PD 66);

(b) claims to enforce public rights in the absence of persons who have sustained special damage, such as to abate a public nuisance, or to compel the performance of a public duty, are the prerogative of the Attorney-General and are brought by relator proceedings in the name of the Attorney-General (*Emerald Supplies Ltd v British Airways plc* [2010] Ch 48 at [30], at first instance);

(c) in Chancery claims including the administration of a charity (PD 64B, para 4.4) or where a bequest could be construed as being charitable, but is not in favour of a registered charity, the Attorney-General is named to protect the charitable interest; and

(d) applications for vexatious litigant orders (see 19.46–19.47) are made by the Attorney-General.

Foreign parties

19.40 Proceedings, including additional claims under Part 20, cannot be brought by a person voluntarily resident in an enemy country. Foreign sovereigns, ambassadors, high commissioners and their staffs, and certain other diplomatic staff cannot be sued in this country (State Immunity Act 1978; Diplomatic Privileges Act 1964, etc.). Where proceedings involving foreign parties do not contravene these rules, it may be necessary to obtain permission to issue and serve proceedings: see Chapter 11. If English proceedings are commenced in a case with a foreign element, it is possible that they may be stayed under the doctrine of *forum non conveniens*: see 11.55.

Unincorporated associations

19.41 Social and sporting clubs, social societies, and other unincorporated associations have no separate legal personality and cannot be parties to proceedings in their own right. Where proceedings are necessary there are two main options. These are:

(a) Proceedings in the name of or against an individual member or members. This depends on a member or members being found with personal rights or liabilities which are reasonably similar to those asserted by or against the unincorporated association. The result is that members who are not made parties will have no direct interest in the proceedings.

(b) Representative proceedings (see 19.56–19.59). Such proceedings are usually brought in the name or names of one or more committee members of the association 'on behalf of [themselves] and all other members of the [name of the association]'.

19.42 Where the latter option is used when bringing proceedings, it is permissible for the claimants to state the association's principal address in the originating process rather than the named parties' home addresses (see *Hawkins v Black* (1898) 14 TLR 398, where claimants suing as representatives of the Honourable Society of the Middle Temple were allowed to give the 'Treasury, Middle Temple Lane' as their address).

Persons unknown

Under the pre-CPR rules it was an almost invariable rule that proceedings and orders could **19.43** only be granted against named parties (*Friern Barnet Urban District Council v Adams* [1927] 2 Ch 25). For some years there has been an exception for claims against trespassers (CPR, r 55.6). A more general exception has developed under the CPR. PD 7A, para 4.1(3) says the claim form 'should' state the full name of each party, which was interpreted by *Bloomsbury Publishing Group Ltd v News Group Newspapers Ltd* [2003] 1 WLR 1633 (affirmed by *South Cambridgeshire District Council v Persons Unknown* [2004] EWCA Civ 1280), to mean there is no absolute requirement that a defendant must be named. In the first of these cases the claimant was allowed to join 'person or persons unknown' as second defendants to a claim where an interim injunction was granted restraining disclosure of the contents of or information from a book prior to its publication date. These cases glide over PD 16, para 2.6, which says the claim form 'must' include the full name of each party. They were extended by *Cameron v Hussain* [2018] 1 WLR 657 to allow proceedings seeking damages arising out of a road traffic accident against 'the person unknown driving vehicle registration number Y598 SPS who collided with vehicle registration number KG03 ZIZ on 26 Mat 2013'. The registered keeper of the car in question was a person who was not himself insured to drive it, and who was not the driver at the time of the collision. The car was insured in the name of Nissar Bahadur, a fictitious identity. When deciding to allow a claim to proceed against a person unknown, the crucial questions are:

(a) that the description used must be sufficiently certain so as to identify both those who are included and those who are not;

(b) proceeding in this way must be both necessary and efficacious. In *Cameron v Hussain* it allowed the claimant to secure a judgment which could be enforced against the insurance company under the Road Traffic Act 1988, s 151; and

(c) on the facts of the case it needs to be in accordance with the overriding objective.

C LITIGANTS IN PERSON

Many litigants cannot afford legal representation, or choose to represent themselves. **19.44** Guidelines for lawyers dealing with opponents who are litigants in person were published by the Law Society, CILEX, and BSB in June 2015. These recommend adopting a professional, co-operative and courteous approach, with care being taken to avoid legal jargon in correspondence with a litigant in person. They also suggest recommending to the litigant in person that they should seek independent legal advice. Lawyers must not take unfair advantage of a litigant in person, but are under no obligation to help a litigant in person run their case, or to take any action on their behalf, unless ordered by the court to do so, or if the lawyer considers doing so is required by their duty to the court. Some litigants in person are assisted by McKenzie friends, see 39.32.

Broadly, the rules of procedure apply equally to represented and unrepresented parties, **19.45** but with some exceptions. Being a litigant in person with no experience of legal proceedings is not a good reason for not complying with the CPR or court orders (*R (Hysaj) v Secretary of State for the Home Department* [2015] 1 WLR 2472). Basic fairness dictates that no special indulgence should be shown to a litigant in person. One person's advantage is another's disadvantage (*Barton v Wright Hassall LLP* [2018] 1 WLR 1119 at [18]). However, being a litigant in person may make a difference 'at the margin' (*Nata Lee Ltd v Abid* [2015] 2 P & CR 3 at [53]), which Lord Sumption JSC has interpreted to mean that it may increase the weight to be given to some other, more directly relevant, factor (*Barton v*

Wright Hassall LLP at [18]). Unless the rules are particularly inaccessible or obscure, Lord Sumption has said it is reasonable to expect a litigant in person to familiarize themselves with them.

19.46 When exercising its case management powers the court must have regard to whether any of the parties are acting in person (CPR, r 3.1A). In cases with litigants in person, the starting point for case management directions are the standard directions available on the Ministry of Justice website (r 3.1A(3)). Litigants in person are not required to provide costs budgets (r 3.13(1)), but may claim costs at a special litigants in person rate of £19 per hour (r 46.5 and PD 46, para 3.4). At hearings the court must adopt procedures designed to further the overriding objective. This may include the judge ascertaining from the litigant in person the areas on which witnesses may give evidence-in-chief or which should be covered in cross-examination, and the judge putting such questions as the judge considers proper to witnesses (r 3.1A(5)).

D VEXATIOUS LITIGANTS

19.47 A small minority of litigants misuse the freedom of access to the courts by launching large numbers of unmeritorious actions or numerous interim applications, causing a great deal of anxiety and trouble to their victims, and usually with little prospect of costs being recovered. Where it is proved that a litigant 'has habitually and persistently and without reasonable cause' instituted vexatious proceedings or applications, the High Court is given power by SCA 1981, s 42, on the application of the Attorney-General, to make a civil proceedings order. A person subject to such an order is prevented from continuing or commencing or making applications in civil proceedings without the permission of the High Court. If permission is granted, the defendant to the new proceedings may apply to set aside the permission (PD 3A, para 7.9).

19.48 In slightly less serious cases the court may make a civil restraint order under CPR, r 3.11. These come in three different forms (limited, extended, and general: see r 2.3(1)), and restrain a person from issuing claims or making applications in proceedings or courts defined in the order. They are used in particular where a litigant has a history of issuing claims or making applications which are totally without merit (PD 3C). Where a court strikes out a statement of case, or deals with an application or appeal, which it considers to be totally without merit, that fact must be recorded in the order it makes, and the court must consider whether it should make a civil restraint order (rr 3.3(7), 3.4(6), 23.12, 52.20(6)).

E JOINDER

19.49 As a general principle, SCA 1981, s 49(2), provides that every court exercising civil jurisdiction in England and Wales:

> shall so exercise its jurisdiction in every cause or matter before it as to secure that, as far as possible, all matters in dispute between the parties are completely and finally determined, and all multiplicity of legal proceedings with respect to any of those matters is avoided.

Deciding whether to join parties or causes of action

19.50 Generally it is for the claimant to decide which causes of action to pursue in a claim and which parties to claim against. A claim is sufficiently constituted if it asserts a single cause of action by a single claimant against a single defendant. If the claimant has more than one cause of action, it is possible to bring a separate claim for each. This will mean paying separate issue fees for each claim, is likely to be more expensive in costs if the factual issues are similar, runs the risk of irreconcilable judgments, and may give rise to problems of *res judicata*. It is obvious that if an accident gives rise to claims in negligence and breach of statutory duty then they should be brought by a single claim. Regarding parties, where rights are vested in persons jointly they must all be joined as claimants (or added as defendants if they will not consent to acting as claimants: CPR, r 19.3). Similarly, where liability is joint but not several everyone jointly liable must be made a defendant. Examples are trustees and personal representatives, joint tenants, and joint contractors. Where liability is several, or where a claimant has related causes of action against different persons, it may be possible to deal with all the causes in a single claim: see 19.51ff. Whether it is prudent to do so depends on a number of factors. For example, some of the possible defendants may be impecunious, or the evidence against some of the possible defendants may be weaker than against others.

Joinder of causes of action

Pursuing more than one cause of action in the same proceedings is permitted by CPR, r 7.3, **19.51** which provides:

> The claimant may use a single claim form to start all claims which can be conveniently disposed of in the same proceedings.

Joinder of parties

It is provided in CPR, r 19.1, that: **19.52**

> any number of claimants or defendants may be joined as parties to a claim.

Apart from the operation of the overriding objective, the only restriction against joinder of **19.53** parties appears to be that there must be a cause of action against each of the parties joined. There is no jurisdiction under the rule to join people purely for the purpose of obtaining disclosure against them (*Douihech v Findlay* [1990] 1 WLR 269). Contrast the situation where there is a cause of action against the defendant, but the primary purpose in joining him is to obtain disclosure, and the special cases of *Norwich Pharmacal* and *Bankers Trust* orders (see 45.02ff and 45.14ff).

Joint claimants (but not co-defendants) must not have conflicting interests in the litigation, **19.54** and must act by the same solicitors and counsel.

Discretion to order separate trials

Even if joinder is technically permissible within these rules, the court has a discretionary **19.55** power to order separate trials in order to ensure that the case proceeds quickly and efficiently (CPR, r 3.1(2)(i)).

F REPRESENTATIVE PROCEEDINGS

It is provided in CPR, r 19.6(1), that: **19.56**

> where more than one person has the same interest in a claim—
>
> (a) the claim may be begun; or
> (b) the court may order that the claim be continued,
>
> by or against one or more of the persons who have the same interest as representatives of any other persons who have that interest.

19.57   By CPR, r 19.6(4), unless the court otherwise directs, any judgment or order made in representative proceedings is binding on all persons represented in the claim, but may be enforced by or against such a person only with the permission of the court. Permission should be granted unless there are special circumstances (*Chandra v Mayor* [2017] 1 WLR 729).

19.58   According to *Duke of Bedford v Ellis* [1901] AC 1 and *Emerald Supplies Ltd v British Airways plc* [2011] Ch 345 persons will have the 'same interest' if:

(a) they have a common interest; and

(b) they have a common grievance;

(c) the relief sought is in its nature beneficial to all whom the claimant proposes to represent; and

(d) the criteria for inclusion in the class must not depend on the outcome of the claim itself, because in such a case the members of the class cannot be identified as having the same interest when the claim is begun.

19.59   In *Duke of Bedford v Ellis* it was held that six fruitgrowers were entitled to represent all other fruitgrowers claiming rights over stands at the defendant's market. Likewise in *Millharbour Management Ltd v Weston Homes Ltd* [2011] 3 All ER 1027 a number of tenants in a mansion block were allowed to represent all the tenants in proceedings against the landlord for disrepairs. However, if on analysis it appears that members of the class in fact have competing interests it will not be appropriate to allow representative proceedings (*Smith v Cardiff Corporation* [1954] 1 QB 210). Representative defendants may be used, for example, in cases where numerous persons are alleged to be infringing the claimant's copyright (*EMI Records Ltd v Kudhail* [1983] Com LR 280).

G REPRESENTATION OF UNASCERTAINED PERSONS

19.60   In Part 8 claims to construe wills and trusts, and in proceedings involving the estates of deceased persons or trust property, where any person is an unborn person or cannot be easily ascertained or found, or there is a class of persons, some of whom are not yet born, or cannot easily be found or ascertained, or it would further the overriding objective (eg by saving costs) to make the order, the court may appoint one or more persons to represent those persons (CPR, r 19.7). Applications for representation orders are normally stated on the Part 8 claim form and orders are usually made on the hearing, although it is possible to apply earlier. If an order is made, any judgment is binding on the persons represented.

H INTERVENTION

19.61   Under CPR, r 19.2(2), a non-party may intervene and be added as a party on the ground either:

(a) that the presence of the intervener before the court is desirable to ensure that all matters in dispute can be resolved; or

(b) that there exists a question or issue between the intervener and an existing party which it would be desirable to determine at the same time as the existing claim.

19.62   Examples of where the court may exercise its discretion to allow a person to intervene include:

(a) Cases where the intervener's legal, property, or financial rights will be directly affected. Thus, the Motor Insurers' Bureau may be allowed to intervene where a defendant in a personal injuries case arising out of a motor accident is untraced or uninsured, because the Bureau will be required to pay any damages awarded (*Gurtner v Circuit* [1968] 2 QB 587).

(b) Where a private claim affects the prerogatives of the Crown or involves questions of public policy the Attorney-General may intervene. An example is *Re Westinghouse Electric Corporation Uranium Contract Litigation* [1978] AC 547, where the question was whether the extraterritorial effect of the US antitrust legislation was an infringement on the sovereignty of the UK.

(c) Where a member of a class which the claimant claims to represent disputes the claimant's entitlement to represent the class (*McCheane v Gyles (No 2)* [1902] 1 Ch 915).

I CONSOLIDATION

Closely connected claims may be ordered to be consolidated (CPR, r 3.1(2)(g)). This means that they will continue and be tried as if they were a single claim. Consolidation is likely to be convenient only where there is a strong overlap between two claims, or where there is a risk of irreconcilable judgments. Where there is minimal overlap, consolidation is inappropriate (*Law Debenture Trust Corporation (Channel Islands) Ltd v Lexington Insurance Co* (2001) LTL 12/11/01). In *IXIS Corporate and Investment Bank v WestLB AG* [2007] EWHC 1748 (Comm) the applicant was the claimant in one claim, and the defendant in another claim. The other parties in the two claims were different. Although there was a degree of overlap between the two cases, a trial date had been fixed in one case whereas the other had not reached the defence stage. It was therefore neither fair nor just to order consolidation. **19.63**

A consolidation order can be made only if all the claims are before the court at the same time. Therefore applications will need to be made in each of the claims returnable at the same time, or a single application must be issued fully stating the titles of all the claims. If the order is made, one of the claims will be nominated as the lead claim, and consequential directions will be given for the future conduct of the other claims. **19.64**

Alternatives to consolidating mentioned in the rules include ordering the claims to be tried by the same judge one after the other, and staying all but one of the claims until after the determination of that one. **19.65**

J STAKEHOLDER CLAIMS

Stakeholder claims and applications, and claims on controlled goods, are related procedures for determining competing claims where the person in possession of goods does not claim a beneficial interest in the goods. In essence, these procedures enable the person in possession of the goods to bring the competing claimants before the court so that the issue as to ownership can be determined as between the competing claimants. **19.66**

Stakeholder claims and applications

Stakeholder claims and applications arise where a person holding goods or money, or liable on a debt, is or expects to be sued by two or more persons making adverse claims to the property in question. For example, Nigel leaves a car with a garage for minor repairs. Before the work is completed, the garage receives a claim to the car from Janice who claims to be its true owner. The garage may not know who to deliver the car to, so may protect **19.67** itself by using stakeholder proceedings. The claim is made using the Part 8 procedure, unless it is made in existing proceedings, in which case an application is made using the Part 23 procedure (CPR, r 86.2(2)). It must be supported by a witness statement stating that the stakeholder claims no interest in the subject matter of the dispute other than for charges or costs, is not colluding with any of the claimants, and is willing to pay or transfer the subject matter of the dispute into court or to dispose of it as directed by the court.

19.68 The papers must be served on all competing claimants. They then have 14 days to file and serve witness statements specifying the money or property claimed, and setting out the grounds of their claim to the subject matter of the dispute (r 86.2(6)). There will then be a hearing at which the court may by r 86.3:

(a) order that any stakeholder or claimant to the subject matter of the dispute be made a defendant;
(b) order that an issue between the parties be stated and tried;
(c) determine the stakeholder application summarily;
(d) give directions for the summary determination of the application; or
(e) give directions for the retention, sale, or disposal of the subject matter of the dispute, and for the payment of any proceeds of sale.

Claims on controlled goods and executed goods

19.69 A similar procedure applies where goods are taken by an enforcement officer or enforcement agent pursuant to a writ or warrant of control (see Chapter 48), and a claim is made by a non-party that goods taken control of are his and not the debtor's (Tribunals, Courts and Enforcement Act 2007, Sch 12, para 60). Before any court application is made, the person claiming the goods must (within seven days of the goods being taken by the enforcement officer or enforcement agent) give notice in writing to the enforcement officer or agent identifying the goods and stating the grounds of their claim (CPR, r 85.4). This is then conveyed to the judgment creditor within the next three days, who then has seven days to state whether the competing claim is admitted or disputed. If the creditor admits the competing claim, the enforcement power ceases to be exercisable (r 85.4(6)).

19.70 Where the non-party's claim is disputed, the non-party must make a Part 23 application supported by a witness statement describing the claimed goods and setting out the grounds of the claim. Supporting documents must be exhibited to the witness statement (r 85.5(2)). The non-party is normally required to pay an amount equal to the value of the disputed goods into court (Tribunals, Courts and Enforcement Act 2007, Sch 12, para 60(4) and CPR, r 85.5(6)). On receipt of the application the court may give directions, list the application for a hearing, determine the amount of the payment to be made by the non-party, and make directions for the retention, sale, or disposal of the goods (r 85.5(7)). At the hearing the court may determine the application summarily or give directions for the trial of any issue raised by the application (rr 85.10, 85.11).

K ASSIGNMENT

19.71 It is provided in CPR, r 19.2(4), that:

the court may order a new party to be substituted for an existing one if—

(a) the existing party's interest or liability has passed to the new party; and
(b) it is desirable to substitute the new party so that the court can resolve the matters in dispute in the proceedings.

Permission from the court is required if the substitution is sought after the proceedings **19.72** have been served (r 19.4(1)). An application for a substitution order may be made without notice, but must be supported by evidence (r 19.4(3)). The evidence must show the stage the claim has reached, and set out the details of how the interest or liability was transferred (PD 19A, para 5.2). Where substitution of a claimant is sought, the signed consent of the proposed new claimant must be filed with the court (CPR, r 19.4(4)). If the order is granted, it must be served on all the existing parties and anyone else whom it affects (r 19.4(5)). The court may also make consequential directions regarding service of statements of case and other documents, and for the management of the claim (r 19.4(6)).

L GROUP LITIGATION

Where a number of claims give rise to common or related issues of fact or law, the court **19.73** may make a group litigation order ('GLO'): see CPR, rr 19.10 and 19.11. Although there is no minimum number of claims for a GLO, they must be sufficiently numerous to justify taking this course (*Austin v Miller Argent (South Wales) Ltd* [2011] Env LR 32). A GLO can be made only with the consent of a senior judge (President of the QBD, Chancellor of the High Court for ChD claims, and Head of Civil Justice for the County Court): PD 19B, para 3.3. These orders are most likely to be made where a number of claims are made arising out of a disaster (eg a serious public transport accident) or where a number of claims are made against a manufacturer having a common cause (eg claims arising out of the side effects of a medication). If a GLO is made it will:

(a) contain directions about maintaining a group register of the claims governed by the GLO;
(b) specify the GLO issues to be dealt with under the group litigation and identify the claims which can be managed under the GLO; and
(c) specify the court that will manage the group litigation.

Further directions made under a GLO include directing that group claims must be trans- **19.74** ferred to the management court; that certain details must be included in particulars of claim to show that the criteria for entry of the claim on that group register have been met; that future claims raising GLO issues must be commenced in the management court; that one or more of the claims shall proceed as test cases; and that the others shall be stayed until further order. Documents disclosed (see Chapter 31) in a GLO claim are treated as disclosed to all the parties on the group register (CPR, r 19.12(4)), unless the court otherwise orders. Any judgment or order made in a claim on the group register is binding on the parties to all the other claims, unless the court otherwise orders (r 19.12(1)(a)). The court may give directions as to the extent that an order or judgment shall bind the parties to claims added to the group register after the order or judgment was made or given (r 19.12(1)(b)).

Regarding costs, the usual rule in CPR, r 46.6, is that where a group litigant is the pay- **19.75** ing party, he will, in addition to any costs he is liable to pay to the receiving party, be liable for:

(a) the individual costs of his own claim; and
(b) an equal proportion, together with the other group litigants, of the common costs, which are the costs incurred in relation to the GLO issues, costs incurred in a test claim, and costs incurred by the lead solicitor in administering the group litigation.

KEY POINTS SUMMARY

19.76
- There are technical rules for how litigants must be named. The key is being accurate, so there is no doubt as to who is named.

- Special care must be taken with companies, etc. This may simply be a case of ensuring it is correctly identified as 'Limited', 'plc', 'LLP', etc. Note also that every registered company has a name which is unique to itself, and that many companies have very similar names.

- Initially it is for the claimant to decide who should be parties to a claim, and on which causes of action to raise. Defendants can object if the choice results in inconvenience. Defendants can add parties by making additional claims (see Chapter 20), and outsiders can apply to intervene.

- Certain parties have protections not enjoyed by other litigants. Primary examples are children and protected parties, and to a lesser extent, the Crown.

- Special rules apply to other types of party, such as bankrupts, partnerships, companies, and trusts.

20

ADDITIONAL CLAIMS UNDER PART 20

A NATURE OF ADDITIONAL CLAIMS......20.01

B RELATED PROCEDURES 20.03

C SCOPE OF PART 20 ....20.04

D STATEMENTS OF CASE IN
    ADDITIONAL CLAIMS 20.24

E CONTRIBUTION NOTICES 20.30

F PROCEDURE 20.32

G RELATION TO THE MAIN CLAIM........20.39
    Key points summary 20.40

A NATURE OF ADDITIONAL CLAIMS

A defendant to an existing claim is permitted, within certain limits, to bring a claim against **20.01** a third party. Usually, the Part 20 procedure is invoked to pass the defendant's liability on to the third party. A defendant with a cause of action against a third party has the alternative option of commencing separate proceedings. However, it will often be more convenient to bring what is called an 'additional claim' under Part 20, because this tends to keep costs to a minimum, avoids multiple proceedings, and avoids the danger of inconsistent judgments.

Like an ordinary claim, an additional claim is brought by issuing a claim form in the court **20.02** office, but a special form has to be used (see figure 20.1). Once served, the third party becomes a party to the claim with the same rights to defend as if duly sued in the ordinary way by the defendant. Although related to the main action between the claimant and the defendant, to a large extent additional claims have a life of their own independent of the main claim.

B RELATED PROCEDURES

A defendant who blames or has a claim against another person needs to decide on the most **20.03** appropriate way of proceeding. The following situations should be distinguished from each other and from additional claims under Part 20:

(a) When the defendant blames someone else and claims to have no personal responsibility for the claimant's damage, the matter should be pleaded in the defence, and an additional claim is inappropriate. Examples are: where a defendant is sued in respect of a road traffic accident and alleges the accident was wholly the responsibility of someone else (claimant, co-defendant, or non-party); where a defendant is sued for breach of contract and alleges he was acting, as known by the claimant, as agent for his principal; and where a defendant is sued for breach of contract and relies on an exclusion clause absolving him from liability in respect of a breach caused by the fault of a subcontractor.

(b) A defendant with a cross-claim against the claimant may either counterclaim in the present proceedings or commence separate proceedings. Counterclaiming usually has the advantage in costs. Counterclaims are discussed at 14.32–14.38. Rather confusingly, the rules governing counterclaims are also found in CPR, Part 20.

(c) A defendant with a cross-claim against the claimant and a non-party either jointly or severally may bring that claim by counterclaim, the non-party being brought in as a third party, a situation considered at 20.05–20.06.

(d) A defendant who blames or has a claim against another party (invariably a co-defendant) may issue a type of additional claim which is unofficially referred to as a contribution notice: see 20.30–20.31. For example, one of several co-defendants sued in respect of a road traffic accident may deny liability, but accept there is a possibility that the court might find him partly to blame for the claimant's injuries. In such circumstances it may be appropriate for the defendant to seek a contribution towards any damages that he may be ordered to pay from some or all of the co-defendants by serving contribution notices.

(e) A defendant who wishes to have some legal or factual question that arises in the existing proceedings brought by the claimant resolved also between him and some non-party has the option of commencing separate proceedings or seeking an order that the non-party be joined to the existing claim under CPR, r 19.2(2)(b) (see 20.18).

C SCOPE OF PART 20

20.04 The situations in which a defendant may bring an additional claim are set out in CPR, r 20.2. There are three types of such claims:

(a) counterclaims brought by the defendant against the claimant (as discussed at 14.32–14.33), and counterclaims against the claimant and a third party (discussed at 20.05–20.06);

(b) claims brought by the defendant seeking a contribution (see 20.07–20.09), or an indemnity (see 20.10–20.13), or some other remedy (see 20.14–20.15), either from an existing party (also known as a contribution notice), or against a non-party (a true third party claim); and

(c) claims brought by third parties against other persons (whether parties or not), which are referred to as fourth party (etc.) proceedings.

Counterclaims against the claimant and another person

20.05 The rules on counterclaims are to be found in CPR, Part 20, but they are treated very differently from true third party claims. The straightforward situation of a defendant counterclaiming against a claimant has already been mentioned. A rather more complex situation is where the defendant wants to make a counterclaim against the claimant and someone else. Before making such a counterclaim the defendant must obtain an order from the court adding the new party to the proceedings as an additional party (CPR, r 20.5). An application for such an order may be made without notice, and a draft of the proposed statement of case must be filed with the application notice (PD 20, para 1.2). The evidence in support of the application has to set out the stage reached in the main claim, the nature of the claim against the new party, and a summary of the facts on which that claim is based.

20.06 If an order is made adding the new party (who is referred to as the 'third party'—see PD 20, para 7.4(c)—although their role is as a defendant to the counterclaim), the court will also give directions for managing the case. These are likely to include provision for service of all statements of case on the third party together with a response pack and a time for responding to the counterclaim, the role the third party can play at trial, as well as the usual matters such as disclosure of documents, witness statements, etc. In the title to the proceedings the various parties are described as follows:

Miss CAROL CARTER	<u>Claimant</u>
and	
Mr DAVID DEAN	<u>Defendant</u>
and	
Mr NORMAN PARR	<u>Third Party</u>

As with other counterclaims, a counterclaim against a third party needs to be issued and an issue fee must be paid (together with a fee for adding the third party).

Contribution

Typically, a right to a contribution arises in situations where there are joint tortfeasors, **20.07** joint contractors, joint sureties, joint debtors, or joint trustees. Further, by the Civil Liability (Contribution) Act 1978, s 1(1): '. . . any person liable in respect of any damage suffered by another person may recover contribution from any other person liable in respect of the same damage (whether jointly liable with him or otherwise)'. The 'damage' referred to is damage suffered by the claimant. It is the wrong causing the injury: it is not referring to the injury itself (*Jameson v Central Electricity Generating Board* [1998] QB 323). Note also that the word used is 'damage' rather than 'damages' (*Birse Construction Ltd v Haiste Ltd* [1996] 1 WLR 675). The 1978 Act extends the reach of the contribution principle to cover cases whatever the legal basis of the liability, whether in tort, breach of contract, breach of trust, or otherwise (s 6(1)). It can also cover a contribution towards costs (*Mouchel Ltd v Van Oord (UK) Ltd* [2011] BLR 492).

In deciding whether the defendant and the third party are 'liable for the same damage', the **20.08** words from s 1(1) must be given their natural and ordinary meaning, without any restrictive or expansive gloss (*Royal Brompton Hospital NHS Trust v Hammond (No 3)* [2002] 1 WLR 1397). The words do not cover damage which is merely substantially or materially similar (*per* Lord Steyn). In *Charter plc v City Index Ltd* [2008] Ch 313 it was held that, while a contribution could be claimed for breach of trust to make good the claimant's loss, a claim for an account of profits arising from a breach of trust falls outside s 1(1). If the third party has no liability to the claimant, such as through a term in a contract absolving the third party from liability, the defendant cannot claim contribution from the third party (*Co-operative Retail Services Ltd v Taylor Young Partnership Ltd* [2002] 1 WLR 1419).

The extent of the contribution that may be claimed depends on the nature of the case. In **20.09** equity, the usual principle is one of equality. In the case of joint tortfeasors contributions are assessed on the basis of causation and blameworthiness. Usually the court attributes a percentage of blame to each party, but in a suitable case can order a party to make a 100 per cent contribution (*Re-Source America International Ltd v Platt Site Services Ltd* (2004) 95 Con LR 1).

Indemnity

Whereas a right to a contribution has the effect of sharing the responsibility for the liability **20.10** to the claimant, the effect of an indemnity is that the defendant can recover the entirety of his liability to the claimant from the third party. Entitlement to an indemnity may arise by contract, under statute, or by virtue of the relationship between the parties.

20.11 A common instance of indemnities arising by contract is the contract of insurance. A defendant sued in respect of an insured risk could issue an additional claim seeking an indemnity against the insurer, although this will be unnecessary if the insurer accepts liability. More generally, whether in any individual case there is a contractual indemnity depends on the express terms of the contract.

20.12 An example of a statutory indemnity is provided by the Law of Property Act 1925, s 76(1)(D) and Sch 2, Part IV. This relates to a conveyance by way of mortgage of freehold property subject to a rent or of leasehold property. In such a conveyance the statute implies a covenant to indemnify the mortgagee against all claims, damages, and costs incurred by reason of any non-payment of the rent or non-observance of any provision in the lease.

20.13 Indemnities arising by virtue of the relationship between the parties depend on the substantive law. Thus, a principal is required to indemnify an agent in respect of liabilities incurred by the agent when acting within authority. Similarly, a surety who is sued may claim an indemnity from the principal debtor. Where one of several trustees has misapplied trust funds for personal use it is possible for all the trustees to be liable for breach of trust, but the trustee guilty of misapplying the funds may be required to indemnify the others.

Some other remedy

20.14 Rule 20.2(1)(b) of the CPR also allows additional claims to be made against third parties seeking 'some other remedy' beyond a contribution or indemnity. On the face of them these are wide words, and clearly some limitation has to be applied, otherwise they would allow the defendant to make an additional claim against anyone for any type of remedy whether connected to the original claim or not. Restrictions are to be found in r 20.9, which sets out the factors the court should take into account when considering whether to dismiss an additional claim, or to order it to be dealt with as a separate claim (see 20.20–20.23). These factors include the degree of connection between the original claim and the additional claim, and also whether the remedy sought in the additional claim is substantially the same as the remedy sought in the original claim. Without a substantial connection between the two claims, it will usually be inconvenient for them to be dealt with at the same time.

20.15 One everyday situation is where a claimant seeks damages for personal injuries against the defendant arising out of a road traffic accident. The defendant claims the accident was at least partly the fault of the third party, another driver. In addition to seeking a contribution in respect of the claim against him (see 20.07–20.09), the defendant could also claim damages for his or her own personal injuries as related relief against the third party.

Related question

20.16 As mentioned at 20.03, sub-para (e), there are situations where a defendant wishes to have an issue that arises between him and the claimant decided also as between him and a non-party. One of the reasons for this being desirable is that, unless the issue is decided in proceedings to which all those affected by the decision are parties, those who are not parties to the first claim that goes to final determination will not be bound by the result. They may therefore seek to persuade another court that the issue should be decided differently. A defendant caught in the middle may find that the issue is decided against him, with opposite results, in two sets of proceedings. To avoid this happening it is desirable that all those affected are made parties to the first claim.

20.17 An example of where this may arise is a claim for breach of a construction contract where the defendant is the main contractor. If the defence is that the contract has been frustrated, it may be appropriate for the frustration question to be determined also as between the defendant and any subcontractors. Another example is where a defendant is sued for the delivery-up of goods which the claimant alleges have been stolen. If the defence is that one of the exceptions to the *nemo dat* rule applies, the defendant may want that issue determined also as between the defendant and the third party from whom the goods were bought.

One way of avoiding the risk of irreconcilable judgments is by joining the other persons affected by the issue to the original claim under CPR, r 19.2(2)(b). This allows parties to be joined to existing proceedings on the ground that there is an issue between the defendant and the new party which is connected to the matters in dispute and it is desirable to add the new party to resolve that issue. **20.18**

A strict reading of the rules suggests that this is the only procedural method for dealing with related questions, other than by commencing separate claims. Under the old rules, however, related questions were often dealt with by raising them in third party claims, and many practitioners continue using additional claims for this purpose. Some support for this use of additional claims can be found in r 20.9(2)(c) (see 20.22), but this arises only when the court is considering whether an additional claim should be allowed to continue. It should not be regarded as increasing the scope of Part 20 (see r 20.2, where the determination of related questions is not mentioned). **20.19**

Discretion

Even if a claim falls within the grounds set out in CPR, r 20.2, the court retains a discretion whether to allow the additional claim to continue. An objection to the continuation of third party proceedings should normally be taken when the court considers the future conduct of the case following the filing of the defence to the additional claim. **20.20**

In *Chatsworth Investments Ltd v Amoco (UK) Ltd* [1968] Ch 665, Russell LJ said that the court has to take a wide approach, and must ask whether the additional claim in question accords with the general functions of third party proceedings. These functions were set out by Scrutton LJ in *Barclays Bank Ltd v Tom* [1923] 1 KB 221 at 224, as follows: **20.21**

(a) to safeguard against differing results, and to ensure the third party is bound by the decision between the claimant and the defendant. If instead separate proceedings are taken, the court hearing the second action is not bound by the decision in the first action;
(b) to ensure the question between the defendant and the third party is decided as soon as possible after the decision between the claimant and the defendant; and
(c) to save the expense of two trials. A party commencing separate proceedings unnecessarily where an additional claim could have been used may be penalized in costs.

These ideas are largely reflected in CPR, r 20.9(2), which provides that, in deciding whether to grant permission to allow an additional claim to be made (where permission is needed: see 20.34), or to dismiss an additional claim at a later stage, the matters the court will take into account include: **20.22**

(a) the degree of connection between the additional claim and the main claim;
(b) whether the defendant is seeking substantially the same remedy as is being claimed by the claimant; and
(c) whether the additional claim raises any question connected with the subject matter of the main claim.

Examples under the old rules include *Chatsworth Investments Ltd v Amoco (UK) Ltd,* where the additional claim was dismissed because the disputes in the original claim and **20.23** the additional claim were in reality independent of each other. Additional claims have also been dismissed where all the matters arising between the various parties could not be resolved in one trial (*Schneider v Batt* (1881) 8 QBD 701, CA) and where the third party faced difficulties in investigating the alleged facts and a fixed trial date would have had to be vacated (*Courtenay-Evans v Stuart Passey and Associates* [1986] 1 All ER 932).

D STATEMENTS OF CASE IN ADDITIONAL CLAIMS

Claim form in additional claims

20.24   There are prescribed forms for use in additional claims. Form N211 is used in general litigation, and form N211CC is the equivalent claim form for use in the Commercial Court.

Particulars of additional claim

20.25   The title to an additional claim includes details of the court and claim number. It then has a list of all the parties, giving each party a separate description (PD 20, para 7.2). Claimants and defendants in the original claim are called 'claimants' and 'defendants' in the additional claim, a position that does not change even if they acquire an additional procedural status (para 7.3). The first additional party is called the 'third party'. Subsequently added parties are the 'fourth party', 'fifth party', etc., in the order in which they are joined to the proceedings (para 7.4). If an additional claim is brought against more than one party jointly, they are known as the 'first-named third party' and 'second-named third party', etc. (para 7.5). If an additional party ceases to be a party, all the remaining parties retain their existing nominal status (para 7.9).

20.26   The name of the statement of case, which is traditionally set out in tramlines beneath the parties in the title, must reflect the nature of the document and its relation to the parties. For example, a 'defendant's additional claim against third party' is an additional claim brought by the defendant against a single additional party, the third party.

20.27   It is established drafting practice to set out in the opening paragraphs of the particulars of an additional claim summaries of the original and any existing additional claims. These paragraphs also state that copies of the previous statements of case are being served with the present statement of case (in compliance with r 20.12), and (usually) deny the claim made against the drafting party. This provides a context for the rest of the statement of case against the additional party, and also allows certain terms to be defined for use in the rest of the draft.

Subsequent statements of case

20.28   A third party seeking to defend against an additional claim will file and serve a 'third party's defence to defendant's additional claim'. It should be drafted in accordance with the principles discussed for normal defences at 14.27ff.

20.29   In proceedings where there are fourth or subsequent parties, they should be referred to in the text of statements of case, witness statements, etc., by name, suitably abbreviated if appropriate (para 7.11). If parties have similar names, suitable distinguishing abbreviations should be used. An example can be seen in figure 20.1.

Figure 20.1 Third party's additional claim against fourth party

IN THE HIGH COURT OF JUSTICE   Claim No. HQ18 96789

QUEEN'S BENCH DIVISION

BETWEEN:—

CHEDISTON WHOLESALE LIMITED	Claimant
—and—	
LINSTEAD FRUITGROWERS LIMITED	Defendant
—and—	
METFIELD WHOLESALERS LIMITED	Third Party
—and—	
HARVEY & Co (a Firm)	Fourth Party

THIRD PARTY'S ADDITIONAL CLAIM AGAINST FOURTH PARTY

1 In its claim against the Defendant the Claimant claims damages and interest pursuant to the Senior Courts Act 1981, section 35A, for alleged breach of a contract in writing dated 20 June 2016 ('the third contract') for the sale of 500 tonnes of Metfield dessert pears ('the goods'). Copies of the third contract, Claim Form, and Particulars of Claim are served with these particulars of additional claim.

2 The Defendant denies it is liable to the Claimant on the grounds set out in the Defence, a copy of which is served with these particulars of additional claim.

3 In its additional claim against the Third Party, the Defendant claims damages and interest pursuant to the Senior Courts Act 1981, section 35A, for alleged breach of a contract in writing dated 9 June 2016 ('the second contract') for the goods. Copies of the second contract, Additional Claim Form, and Defendant's Additional Claim against Third Party are served with these particulars of additional claim.

4 The Third Party denies it is liable to the Defendant on the grounds set out in the Third Party's Defence to Defendant's Additional Claim, a copy of which is served with these particulars of additional claim. If, contrary to the Third Party's Defence to Defendant's Additional Claim, the Third Party is held liable in whole or in part to the Defendant, the Third Party claims against the Fourth Party ('Harvey &Co')[to be indemnified against] [alternatively, a contribution towards] [its liability, if any, to the Defendant][damages and interest pursuant to the Senior Courts Act 1981, section 35A, for alleged breach of a contract in writing dated 23 May 2016 ('the first contract') for the goods] for the reasons set out below.

5 [Continue with details of the claim against the Fourth Party as in normal particulars of claim.]

Statement of Truth

(I believe) (The Third Party believes) that the facts stated in this Third Party's additional claim against Fourth Party are true.

I am duly authorized by the Third Party to sign this statement.

Full name

Figure 20.1 *continued*

Name of Third Party's solicitor's firm   Boardman, Phipps & Co.

Signed

Dated

E CONTRIBUTION NOTICES

20.30 A defendant who has an additional claim against another defendant may issue a contribution notice under CPR, r 20.6. A defendant must, by r 20.6(2), obtain permission to file and serve a contribution notice unless this is done either:

(a) with that defendant's defence; or
(b) if the claim for the contribution or indemnity is against a defendant added to the claim after the original defence was filed, within 28 days after the new defendant filed its defence.

A contribution notice follows the same general form as described earlier.

20.31 Issuing a contribution notice inevitably involves incurring costs. If the defendant claims a contribution (and no other relief) under the Civil Liability (Contribution) Act 1978, s 1, against a co-defendant who is jointly liable for the damage sustained by the claimant, the trial judge has power under s 2 of the same Act to apportion liability between them and to order them to contribute between each other even in the absence of a contribution notice. Accordingly, in these circumstances the practice is not to issue a contribution notice, but simply to write to the co-defendant warning of the intention to ask for such an order. Indeed, in such cases, costs will usually be disallowed if a contribution notice is issued: see *Croston v Vaughan* [1938] 1 KB 540. However, if a defendant seeking contribution from a co-defendant in addition wishes to obtain disclosure of documents or to seek further information under Part 18 from the co-defendant, a contribution notice should be served (*Clayson v Rolls Royce Ltd* [1951] 1 KB 746).

F PROCEDURE

Limitation

20.32 For limitation purposes an additional claim is commenced when the claim form in the additional claim is issued by the court. See the Limitation Act 1980, s 35(1)(a), CPR, r 20.7(2), and the discussion at 21.39.

Contribution notices

20.33 These may be issued at any time (CPR, r 20.8(2)). They must be served, using the usual rules on service, on the other defendant (r 20.6). Contribution notices are not claim forms, so permission cannot be sought to serve one outside the jurisdiction (see 11.34 and *Knauf UK GmbH v British Gypsum Ltd* [2002] 2 Lloyd's Rep 416). A defendant who acknowledges service is required by r 6.23(1), (2), to provide an address for service within the UK or the EEA, and it is this address which is used for serving contribution notices.

Additional claims against non-parties

Permission to issue

Permission to issue an additional claim form against a non-party is not required if it **20.34** is issued before or at the same time as the defence to the original claim is filed (CPR, r 20.7(3)(a)). Once the defence has been filed, permission must be sought. Permission is usually sought without giving notice to any of the existing parties or anyone else (r 20.7(5)). The application notice has to be supported by evidence setting out the stage the main claim has reached together with a timetable of the claim to date; the nature of the additional claim; the facts on which it is based; and the name and address of the proposed third party (PD 20, para 2.1). Where delay has been a factor an explanation for the delay should be included. The discretionary factors discussed at 20.20–20.23 will be applied on the application for permission (r 20.9). If the court grants permission, it will at the same time give directions as to service of the additional claim form (r 20.8(3)).

Service

The additional claim form must be served within 14 days of being issued (CPR, r 20.8(1)(b)). **20.35** An additional claim form must be served with a response pack of forms for acknowledging service, admitting, and defending the claim. It must also be served with copies of all the statements of case already served in the proceedings (r 20.12). A copy of the additional claim form must also be served on all other existing parties.

The third party becomes a party to the proceedings once served with the additional claim **20.36** form (r 20.10).

Default judgment

There are three different ways in which default judgments take effect in different types **20.37** of Part 20 claims. First, failing to respond to a counterclaim may result in a default judgment being entered, because CPR, Part 12 expressly applies to counterclaims (r 20.3(3)). Secondly, there is no default judgment process for contribution notices under r 20.6 (see 20.30), because Part 12 does not apply (r 20.3(3)), and nor does the special process in r 20.11 (r 20.11(1)(a)(ii)). Thirdly, all other types of third party claims are governed by the special process in r 20.11. Under r 20.11, if the defendant in the third party claim fails to file a defence or acknowledge service within the 14-day response period, the Part 20 defendant is deemed to admit the additional claim, and is bound by any judgment in the main proceedings. If default judgment is entered in the main proceedings, the Part 20 claimant is in turn able to enter a default judgment in the Part 20 claim simply by filing a request in the relevant practice form (r 20.11(2)(b)). However, permission to enter the default judgment in the Part 20 claim is required if either the claimant has not satisfied the default judgment entered in the main proceedings, or if the Part 20 claim seeks a remedy other than a contribution or an indemnity (r 20.11(3)).

Case management

Where a defence is filed to an additional claim, the court will consider the future conduct **20.38** of the proceedings and give appropriate directions (CPR, r 20.13). In doing so, the court will ensure that, as far as possible, the claim and additional claim are managed together (r 20.13(2)). Usually a case management hearing will be convened (PD 20, para 5.1), with notice being given to all affected parties. The court may use this hearing as a forum for summarily dismissing the additional claim, or for entering summary judgment (para 5.3). More usually it will give directions:

(a) as to the way in which the claims, issues, and questions raised in the additional claim should be dealt with;

(b) as to the part, if any, that the third party will take at the trial of the original claim;

(c) as to the extent to which the third party will be bound by any judgment or decision made in the original claim; and

(d) as to further case management matters, such as disclosure of documents, exchange of witness statements, experts, trial estimates, and the trial date or window.

G RELATION TO THE MAIN CLAIM

20.39 Although it is procedurally connected with the main claim, an additional claim is in many respects a separate claim. Settlement, dismissal, or striking out of the main claim will not usually terminate third party proceedings (*Stott v West Yorkshire Road Car Co Ltd* [1971] 2 QB 651). Whether there is any point in continuing an additional claim after the termination of the main claim depends on the nature of the third party relief claimed. If the defendant claims an indemnity or contribution from the third party and the main claim is dismissed or struck out, the additional claim will end as its basis has gone. However, if the main claim is settled, the question whether the third party must contribute or indemnify remains alive, so the additional claim will continue. Further, if the defendant is claiming related relief, or is seeking the determination of a related question, again the additional claim will continue for that to be resolved.

KEY POINTS SUMMARY

20.40 • An additional claim typically will seek to pass any liability established against the defendant to a third party.

• This is achieved by seeking indemnities, contributions, or related remedies against the third party.

• A third party may in turn seek to pass on its liability to a fourth party, and so on.

• Permission to issue an additional claim is not required if the additional claim is issued before or at the same time as the defendant files its defence.

• An additional claim operates as a separate claim within the original claim. It is commenced by issuing an additional claim form, the defendant's case against the third party must be set out in a statement of case, the third party must be served with a response pack (and must file a defence to the additional claim), and the court will case-manage the additional claim.

21

LIMITATION

A LIMITATION PERIODS 21.04
B ACCRUAL OF CAUSE OF ACTION 21.13
C CALCULATING THE LIMITATION
   PERIOD 21.38
D DISCRETION 21.53
E EQUITABLE REMEDIES, LACHES,
   AND ACQUIESCENCE 21.65
   Key points summary 21.68

Expiry of a limitation period provides a defendant with a complete defence to a claim. Lord **21.01**
Griffiths in *Donovan v Gwentoys Ltd* [1990] 1 WLR 472 said, 'the primary purpose of the
limitation period is to protect a defendant from the injustice of having to face a stale claim,
that is a claim with which he never expected to have to deal'. If a claim is brought a long
time after the events in question, the likelihood is that evidence which may have been available earlier may have been lost, and the memories of witnesses who may still be available
will inevitably have faded or become confused. Further, it is contrary to general policy to
keep people perpetually at risk.

Limitation is a procedural defence. It will not be taken by the court of its own motion, but **21.02**
must be specifically set out in the defence (PD 16, para 13.1). Time-barred cases rarely go
to trial. If the claimant is unwilling to discontinue the claim, it is usually possible for the
defendant to apply successfully for the claim to be struck out (see Chapter 30) as an abuse
of the court's process.

Normally, the only consequence of the expiry of a limitation period is that the defendant **21.03**
acquires a technical defence to the claim. The claimant still has a cause of action, but one
that cannot be enforced. In cases of adverse possession of land and conversion, expiry of
the limitation period has the additional consequence of extinguishing the party's title to
the land or goods. Extinguishing title does not infringe the First Protocol of the European
Convention on Human Rights, art 1 (*JA Pye (Oxford) Ltd v United Kingdom* (Application
No 44302.02) (2007) 23 BHRC 405).

A LIMITATION PERIODS

Most limitation periods are laid down in the Limitation Act 1980 ('LA 1980') as amended. **21.04**
Several other statutes lay down limitation periods, and some procedural rules impose time
limits which act rather like limitation periods. There has been a move in recent legislation
towards flexible limitation periods for some types of cases, which will be considered at
21.53ff. However, the usual rule is that no objection can be taken to a claim started on the
last day of the limitation period, but there is a complete defence if proceedings are issued
one day late. Table 21.1 sets out the limitation periods for the most important classes of
cases.

Table 21.1 Limitation periods

Class of claim	Limitation period
1 Fraudulent breach of trust	None (LA 1980, s 21(1)(a))
2 Recovery of land	12 years (LA 1980, s 15(1))
3 Recovery of money secured by mortgage	12 years (LA 1980, s 20(1))
4 Specialty	12 years (LA 1980, s 8(1))
5 Recovery of a sum due under statute	6 years (LA 1980, s 9(1))
6 Enforcement of a judgment	6 years (LA 1980, s 24(1))
7 Contract	6 years (LA 1980, s 5)
8 Recovery of trust property and breach of trust	6 years (LA 1980, s 21(3))
9 Recovery of arrears of rent	6 years (LA 1980, s 19)
10 Tort (except those listed subsequently)	6 years (LA 1980, s 2)
11 Defective Premises Act 1972 claims	Defective Premises Act 1972, s 1(5))
12 Personal injuries claims	3 years (LA 1980, s 11(4))
13 Fatal Accidents Act 1976 claims	3 years (LA 1980, s 12(2))
14 Personal injuries or damage to property claims under the Consumer Protection Act 1987	3 years (LA 1980, s 11A)
15 Carriage by Air Act 1961 claims	2 years (Carriage by Air Act 1961, Sch 1)
16 Claims for personal injuries or damage to vessel, cargo, or property, or personal injuries to passengers at sea	2 years (Merchant Shipping Act 1995, s 190(3) and Sch 6, Part I, art 16)
17 Contribution under the Civil Liability (Contribution) Act 1978	2 years (LA 1980, s 10(1))
18 Contribution under the Maritime Conventions Act 1911	1 year (Merchant Shipping Act 1995, s 190(4))
19 Defamation and malicious falsehood	1 year (LA 1980, s 4A)
20 Claims under the Human Rights Act 1998, s 7(1)(a)	1 year (Human Rights Act 1998, s 7(5))
21 Applications for judicial review	3 months (CPR, r 54.5)
22 Unfair dismissal under the Employment Rights Act 1996	3 months (Employment Rights Act 1996, s 111(2))

Cases outside the Limitation Act

21.05   A claim which is outside the provisions of the LA 1980 is not subject to a strict period of limitation (*Nelson v Rye* [1996] 1 WLR 1378). It may, however, be subject to a time limit by analogy to the LA 1980 (LA 1980, s 36 and *Coulthard v Disco Mix Club Ltd* [1999] 2 All ER 457), or it may be subject to the defences of laches and acquiescence (as in *Nelson v Rye*, but see the discussion at 21.07). Further, if there is no limitation period, the court may still strike out the proceedings as an abuse of process. In *Taylor v Ribby Hall Leisure Ltd* [1998] 1 WLR 400 an application to commit was delayed by about five years. It was struck out, the court taking into account factors such as the prospects of the court exercising its supervisory powers at the hearing, and the public interest in the efficient administration of justice and the compliance with court orders and undertakings.

Categorization problems in trusts and equity claims

In trusts cases the main rules are the six-year limitation period in claims for breach of trust **21.06** and to recover trust property (LA 1980, s 21(3)), and the unlimited period for bringing claims in respect of any fraud or fraudulent breach of trust to which the trustee was party or privy (s 21(1)(a)) and for claims to recover from a trustee trust property in the possession of the trustee or which was previously received by the trustee and converted to the trustee's use (s 21(1)(b)). A trustee who had negligently left trust money with a solicitor who then embezzled it, but who was not a party to nor privy to the solicitor's fraud was held in *Thorne v Heard* [1894] 1 Ch 599 to be entitled to rely on a limitation defence after six years (class 8 in table 21.1). On the other hand, a claim for an account of profits against a director following a deliberate non-disclosure of an interest was held in *Gwembe Valley Development Co Ltd v Koshy (No 3)* [2004] 1 BCLC 131 to be a fraudulent breach of trust within s 21(1) (a), with the result that there was no period of limitation. It was held that a breach of trust was fraudulent if it was dishonest. Section 21(1)(b) applies not only to cases where a trustee misapplies trust property that was in the trustee's personal possession, but also to cases where the transfer of trust property was effected through an agent or through companies directly or indirectly controlled by the trustee (*Burnden Holdings (UK) Ltd v Fielding* [2017] 1 WLR 39 at [34] and [37], with the result there is no limitation period). In *Clarke (executor of the Will of Francis Bacon, deceased) v Marlborough Fine Art (London) Ltd* (2001) *The Times*, 5 July 2001, it was said that it is probable that in undue influence claims the only time-related defences available were laches and acquiescence (and presumably, affirmation).

In *Nelson v Rye* [1996] 1 WLR 1378 it was held that a claim for breach of fiduciary duty **21.07** *simpliciter* is outside the provisions of the LA 1980, and so is not subject to any limitation period. This case has been called into question by subsequent decisions, particularly *Paragon Finance plc v DB Thakerer and Co* [1999] 1 All ER 400. In *Nelson v Rye* the claimant was a musician and sought accounts from his former manager stretching back 11 years before proceedings were issued. Millett LJ in *Paragon Finance plc v DB Thakerer and Co* pointed out that every agent owes fiduciary duties to his principal, and without something more the claim would have been subject to the usual six-year limitation period. The defendant in *Nelson v Rye* was no more than an accounting party who had failed to account. To have been entitled to a longer limitation period, the claimant would have had to show, among other things, that the defendant owed fiduciary duties in relation to the money.

Millett LJ in *Paragon Finance plc v DB Thakerer and Co* (approved by the Supreme Court **21.08** in *Williams v Central Bank of Nigeria* [2014] AC 1189) further pointed out that there is a distinction between two categories of constructive trust claim:

(a) Where the constructive trustee, although not expressly appointed as a trustee, has assumed the duties of a trustee before the events which are alleged to constitute the breach of trust. This includes company directors, because they are entrusted with stewardship of the company's property (*Burnden Holdings (UK) Ltd v Fielding* [2018] 2 WLR 885), and this first category potentially applies to all types of breach of fiduciary duty by directors (*First Subsea Ltd v Balltec Ltd* [2018] Ch 25). In this category the defendant is a real trustee, and the provisions of the LA 1980, s 21(1), may apply if the other conditions of the subsection are satisfied, with the result that there may be an unlimited period for bringing proceedings.

(b) Where the constructive trust is merely the creation of the court as a remedy to meet the alleged wrongdoing. This covers cases of ancillary liability, and includes claims of knowing receipt and dishonest assistance in the fraudulent breach of trust of another (*Williams v Central Bank of Nigeria* [2014] AC 1189). In this category there is no real trust, and usually no prospect of a proprietary remedy. The defendant is merely said to be liable to account as a constructive trustee. In this category the other provisions of the LA 1980 apply, with the result that the period will usually be six years from accrual.

Categorization problems in personal injuries claims

21.09 Claims for personal injuries (class 12 in table 21.1) comprise all claims in negligence, nuisance, and breach of duty (including contractual and statutory duties) where the claim to relief consists of or includes damages in respect of personal injuries to the claimant or any other person (LA 1980, s 11(1)). Under LA 1980, s 11(4), the basic limitation period for such claims is three years. An attempt was made to avoid this limitation period in *Letang v Cooper* [1965] 1 QB 232. The claimant was injured when the defendant drove his car over her legs while she was sunbathing on the grass in the car park of a hotel. Proceedings were issued four years afterwards, but the cause of action was pleaded both in negligence and in trespass to the person. The Court of Appeal overruled the trial judge and held the claim was time-barred. Two reasons were advanced. One was that where an injury is inflicted negligently rather than intentionally, the only cause of action is in negligence, so the claimant is unable to rely on the six-year limitation period in trespass (class 10). The second reason was that the phrase 'breach of duty' in what is now LA 1980, s 11(1), covered a breach of any duty under the law of tort. Between 1993 and 2008 (*Stubbings v Webb* [1993] 2 AC 498 and *A v Hoare* [2008] 1 AC 844), the courts applied a false distinction between intentional and unintentional trespasses to the person. Intentional cases were said to be governed by the six-year limitation period for general tort claims in LA 1980, s 2. However, this meant that the date of knowledge (LA 1980, s 14) and discretion (LA 1980, s 33) provisions did not apply, generating unjust results. For example, the perpetrator of child abuse had a cast-iron limitation defence six years after limitation started to run, whereas a secondary party (eg the child's mother, or the proprietors of a care home) could be perpetually at risk of being sued because of the effect of ss 14 and 33. *A v Hoare* departed from *Stubbings v Webb*, applying *Practice Statement (House of Lords: Judicial Precedent)* [1966] 1 WLR 1234, with the result that all personal injury claims are governed by the three-year limitation period and ss 14 and 33.

21.10 A negligent failure by an education authority to improve the consequences of the claimant's dyslexia by appropriate teaching, or a negligent failure to treat a physical injury, are both claims for personal injuries (*Adams v Bracknell Forest Borough Council* [2005] 1 AC 76), and are governed by the usual three-year limitation period. Further, a claim in professional negligence against a solicitor arising out of the firm's handling of a divorce ancillary relief claim, which included a claim for anxiety and stress arising out of the firm's alleged mishandling of her claim, became, for that reason, a claim in respect of personal injuries and subject to a three-year limitation period rather than the usual six-year period for claims in tort and breach of contract (*Oates v Harte Reade and Co* [1999] PIQR P120).

Other categories

21.11 Claims to recover the principal due under a mortgage, even after the mortgaged property is sold, are governed by the 12-year limitation period in class 3, whereas claims for interest are limited to six years by s 20(5) (*Bristol and West plc v Bartlett* [2003] 1 WLR 284). A claim to recover rent due under a lease under seal is governed by the six-year limitation period in class 9, not the 12 years in class 4 (*Romain v Scuba TV Ltd* [1997] QB 887). Although statutes are specialties, money claims pursuant to statute are governed by the six-year period in s 9 (class 5) (*Central Electricity Board v Halifax Corporation* [1963] AC 785 and *Re Farmizer (Products) Ltd* [1997] 1 BCLC 589), whereas claims for other remedies pursuant to statute will be governed by the 12-year period in s 8 (class 4). A claim for damages for infringement of a right conferred by Community law amounts to a breach of statutory duty, and so is subject to a six-year limitation period in tort (class 10) (*R v Secretary of State for Transport, ex p Factortame Ltd (No 7)* [2001] 1 WLR 942).

Foreign limitation periods

Where, in accordance with the rules of private international law, the law of any other country is to be taken into account in any claim in England and Wales, the law of that other country relating to limitation must be applied, unless this conflicts with public policy or if it would cause undue hardship (Foreign Limitation Periods Act 1984). **21.12**

B ACCRUAL OF CAUSE OF ACTION

The rules on accrual fix the date from which time begins to run for limitation purposes. **21.13** Lindley LJ in *Reeves v Butcher* [1891] 2 QB 509 stated the general rule which is '… that the statute runs from the earliest time at which an action could be brought'. In other words, time runs from the point when facts exist establishing all the essential elements of the cause of action. A distinction is drawn between the substantive elements and mere procedural requirements. Thus, a solicitor can commence a claim to recover costs from a client only if at least a month has elapsed since a bill for those costs has been delivered to the client (Solicitors Act 1974, s 69(1)). In *Coburn v Colledge* [1897] 1 QB 702 it was held that the requirement to furnish a bill was only a procedural matter, and time ran from completion of the work as opposed to delivery of the bill. Sometimes this can be a difficult distinction to draw. For example, *Re Loftus* [2005] 1 WLR 1890 held that time runs in a claim to the personal estate of a deceased person under the LA 1980, s 22(a) from the end of the executor's year.

In addition to the elements of the cause of action being present, there must be a party **21.14** capable of suing and a party liable to be sued. So, if goods are converted after the owner has died intestate, time runs only from the date letters of administration are taken out (*Thomson v Lord Clanmorris* [1900] 1 Ch 718 *per* Vaughan Williams LJ). On the other hand, time continues running during a period in which the defendant is an undischarged bankrupt (*Anglo Manx Group Ltd v Aitken* [2002] BPIR 215). If it is necessary to restore a company against which a claim is to be made to the register, the date of accrual remains based on the date of the breach (or other element of the cause of action), not on the date of restoration (*Smith v White Knight Laundry Ltd* [2001] 1 WLR 616). Although the court has power under the Companies Act 2006, s 1030(3), to direct that the period between dissolution and restoration shall not count for the purposes of limitation, a direction under this provision should not normally be made unless notice of the application had been served on all parties who could be expected to oppose it.

Accrual in claims for the recovery of land

Detailed rules dealing with accrual in recovery of land cases are set out in LA 1980, Sch **21.15** 1. Broadly, time runs from the taking of adverse possession where the person bringing the claim has a present interest in the land but will be delayed until the determination of the preceding interest in the case of future interests. The rules on 'adverse possession' were restated in *JA Pye (Oxford) Ltd v Graham* [2003] 1 AC 419, and apply in all claims for the recovery of land (*Ashe v National Westminster Bank plc* [2008] 1 WLR 710). The question is whether the defendant squatter had dispossessed the paper owner by going into ordinary possession of the land for the requisite 12 years without the consent of the owner. There are two elements, factual possession, which requires an appropriate degree of physical control, and an intention to possess, which is an intention to exclude the world at large, including the paper owner, so far as that is reasonably practicable and so far as the processes of the law will allow.

21.16 Adverse possession of registered land is governed by the Land Registration Act 2002, Schs 6 and 12. These provisions support the principle under the 2002 Act that the register is to be a complete and accurate record of the state of the title to registered land at any given time, so that it is possible to investigate title to land online, and with the absolute minimum of additional inquiries and inspections. Under the 2002 Act a person claiming adverse possession of registered land for at least ten years is allowed to apply for registration. The usual evidence of adverse possession is required. The registered owner and any chargees and other interested persons are then served with notice of the application, and they may serve counter-notice. If they fail to do so, the applicant will be registered as the registered proprietor in place of the former proprietor, and free from former charges. If counter-notice is served the application is dismissed unless one of three grounds is established. These are that it would be unfair to dispossess the applicant because of an equity by estoppel; that the applicant has an independent right that suggests he ought to be registered as the owner; or that there has been a reasonable mistake as to boundaries. If an exception applies the applicant will be registered in place of the registered proprietor, and this happens notwithstanding objections from registered chargees. However, charges will continue to apply unless as a matter of general law the applicant's rights have priority over the charge. Where prior charges continue to apply the applicant can apply for an apportionment of the charges between the land acquired by adverse possession and the remainder of the original title.

21.17 If an application under the 2002 Act is dismissed the registered owner then has two years in which to take action to evict the person claiming adverse possession or otherwise regularize the position. If they fail to do so, once the two years have elapsed the person claiming adverse possession may re-apply for registration, and, if still in possession, will be automatically registered in place of the existing registered owner. If this happens, the applicant is registered with a new, separate title, and takes free of any former registered charge.

Shortfall on mortgage

21.18 A claim to recover the shortfall of money advanced by a building society secured by a traditionally worded mortgage accrues when the principal money becomes payable. This will usually be the date of first default (*West Bromwich Building Society v Wilkinson* [2005] 1 WLR 2303).

Money due under statute

21.19 In *Swansea City Council v Glass* [1992] QB 844 the council brought a claim to recover the cost of repairing a house owned by the defendant and let to a tenant where the defendant had failed to effect necessary repairs. The claim was brought under the Housing Act 1957, s 10(3), and was commenced over six years after the work was done, but less than six years after a demand for payment. It was held that time ran from completion of the work, so the claim was statute-barred.

Contract

21.20 Time runs from the breach of contract. When this is depends on the nature of the obligation sued on and the terms of the contract, and also on whether a repudiatory breach is accepted by the claimant. Applying the general rule, causes of action in breach of contract will accrue as follows:

(a) In claims for breach of the implied terms as to satisfactory quality, etc., in the Sale of Goods Act 1979 ('SoGA 1979'), time normally starts running on delivery of the goods (*Battley v Faulkner* (1820) 3 B & Ald 288).

(b) In claims for late delivery of goods, time runs from the contractual date for delivery.

(c) In claims based on the implied term as to title to goods sold, time runs from the date of the contract, or, in the case of an agreement to sell, from the date title was to pass (see SoGA 1979, s 12(1)).

(d) Claims for the price of goods sold accrue on the contractual date for payment (SoGA 1979, s 49(2)), failing which on the date property in the goods passes to the buyer (s 49(1)) or the date the buyer is informed that the seller is ready and willing to deliver (s 28).

(e) In claims based on defective building work, time usually starts running on practical or substantial completion.

(f) Claims for the price of entire contracts for work and services accrue on completion of the work (*Emery v Day* (1834) 1 Cr M & R 245).

(g) In a construction contract where the price is payable by instalments due on stated dates, time runs in respect of each instalment from the due date (*Henry Boot Construction Ltd v Alstom Combined Cycles Ltd* [2005] 1 WLR 3850).

(h) Claims by banks to recover overdrafts from customers normally accrue on service of a demand in writing (LA 1980, s 6). There is an exception in s 6 relating to loans where the debtor also enters into a collateral obligation to pay, such as by delivering a promissory note, but most bank overdrafts fall into the main category.

(i) Claims against sureties and guarantors usually accrue on default by the principal debtor (*Parr's Banking Co v Yates* [1898] 2 QB 460).

(j) Accrual in the case of negotiable instruments is somewhat complicated. Claims against acceptors and makers based on non-payment accrue on the maturity of the instrument, unless it is a bill of exchange which is accepted after maturity, in which case time runs from the date of acceptance (Bills of Exchange Act 1882, s 10(2)). Bills of exchange often mature on fixed dates, but if they mature (say) a fixed period of time after sight, time starts running on the expiry of that fixed period after acceptance (or after noting or protesting if it is not accepted) (s 14(3)). A claim against a drawer or endorser after dishonour by non-payment accrues when the bill is duly presented for payment and payment is refused or cannot be obtained, or, if presentment is excused, when the bill is overdue and unpaid (s 47(2)).

(k) Accrual in claims against insurers depends on the terms of the policy. The general rule is that time starts running at the date of the loss. For example, claims for constructive total loss accrue on the date of the casualty (*Bank of America National Trust v Chrismas* [1994] 1 All ER 401). However, it is open to the parties to displace the general rule by creating conditions precedent to the insured's right to payment. For example, in *Virk v Gan Life Holdings plc* (1999) 52 BMLR 207 critical illness benefit became payable under a policy if the insured survived 30 days after suffering a stroke. It was held that time started running 30 days after the stroke.

In cases where the claimant has accepted an anticipatory breach as a repudiation, time **21.21** starts running from the date of acceptance rather than the contractual date for performance of the obligation in question (*Reeves v Butcher* [1891] 2 QB 509). Claims for consequential losses, such as salvage charges arising out of a claim based on the loss of a ship, against an insurer are not separate causes of action, so accrual turns on the date of the underlying cause of action (the casualty), not on the date the consequential loss was incurred (*Bank of America National Trust v Chrismas* [1994] 1 All ER 401). There are several types of contractual obligation that give rise to continuing or repeated breaches. An example of a continuing breach is a failure to comply with a covenant to keep in repair (*Spoor v Green* (1874) LR 9 Ex 99 at 111), and an example of a repeated breach is a failure to pay rent (*Archbold v Scully* (1861) 9 HL Cas 360). In these cases the claimant will be able to succeed in respect of the consequences of breach over the six-year period (12 years for claims on a specialty) before the claim form is issued.

General claims in tort

21.22 The general rule is that, in addition to proving that the defendant is guilty of some wrongful conduct, liability in tort can only be established on proof of damage. Usually, damage is the final matter to come into existence, so the usual rule is that time runs in tort from the date when damage is sustained. The important date is the date damage was sustained, not the date on which the claimant discovered the damage (*Cartledge v E Jopling and Sons Ltd* [1963] AC 758). In *Pirelli General Cable Works Ltd v Oscar Faber and Partners* [1983] 2 AC 1 it was held that a cause of action for negligent design of a chimney arose when cracking in the structure first developed, and not when the damage could have been or was in fact discovered.

21.23 In a claim against a solicitor for negligent advice, actual damage is suffered when the advice is acted upon, such as by executing a document (*Forster v Outred and Co* [1982] 1 WLR 86) or completion of a conveyancing transaction (*Nouri v Marvi* [2011] PNLR 7, although sometimes the relevant point in time is exchange of contracts, see *Edehomo v Edehomo* [2011] 1 WLR 2217). In *Watkins v Jones Maidment Wilson* [2008] PNLR 23, negligent advice resulted in an immediate measurable loss because the claimant lost the chance of negotiating a better agreement. Where a claimant seeks to sue a solicitor for negligently allowing a claim to be struck out (as a sanction for breach of directions or the requirements of the CPR), time runs from the date when the claimant had no arguable basis for avoiding the claim being struck out, not from the date on which it was actually struck out (*Khan v RM Falvey & Co* [2002] PNLR 28; but see also *Cohen v Kingsley Napley* [2006] PNLR 22). Where the claim is in respect of a transaction entered into through a breach of duty owed by the defendant to the claimant (eg a loan agreement entered into in reliance on a negligent property valuation), time will run from the date the transaction was entered into if the claimant suffered a loss there and then. If there was no immediate loss, such as where the security for a loan was worth more than the loan when it was first advanced (albeit not as much as the defendant's valuation), time will start running only when the value of the security falls below the amount of the loan (see the discussion in *First National Commercial Bank plc v Humberts* [1995] 2 All ER 673).

21.24 If a person injured in an accident later dies as a result of those injuries, the cause of action vesting in the injured person's estate under the Law Reform (Miscellaneous Provisions) Act 1934 accrued at the date of the accident. However, the related cause of action for the benefit of the injured person's dependants under the Fatal Accidents Act 1976, s 1, accrues on the date of death, with the result there are two limitation periods (*Reader v Molesworths Bright Clegg* [2007] 1 WLR 1082).

21.25 The decision in *Darley Main Colliery v Mitchell* (1886) 11 App Cas 127 on continuing torts giving a fresh cause of action each time damage is suffered applies to subsidence claims and trespass claims based on leaving things on the claimant's land. The same principle was applied in *Phonographic Performance Ltd v Department of Trade and Industry*

[2004] 1 WLR 2893, a claim for breach of statutory duty against the Crown for failing to implement an EU Directive.

Trespass and libel

These are actionable *per se*, so time runs from the wrongful act since there is no require- **21.26**
ment to prove damage.

Conversion

Time runs from the date the goods were converted. A number of special rules apply: **21.27**

(a) where goods are converted more than once, the original six-year period continues to run and is not renewed (LA 1980, s 3(1));
(b) at the end of the original six-year period the true owner's title is extinguished (LA 1980, s 3(2));
(c) subject to (d), there is no time limit where goods are stolen (LA 1980, s 4);
(d) where goods are converted (but not stolen) and are then stolen at a later date, proceedings in respect of the theft are barred once the true owner's title is extinguished under s 3(2) by virtue of the original conversion (LA 1980, s 4(1)).

Personal injuries claims: date of knowledge

Time runs in personal injuries claims from the date the cause of action accrued or, if later, **21.28**
the date of the claimant's date of knowledge (LA 1980, s 11(4)). Date of knowledge is defined by s 14(1) as:

> ... the date on which [the claimant] first had knowledge of the following facts—
> (a) that the injury in question was significant; and
> (b) that the injury was attributable in whole or in part to the act or omission which is alleged to constitute negligence, nuisance or breach of duty; and
> (c) the identity of the defendant; and
> (d) if it is alleged that the act or omission was that of a person other than the defendant, the identity of that person and the additional facts supporting the bringing of an action against the defendant.

The subsection concludes by providing that knowledge that any acts or omissions did or **21.29**
did not, as a matter of law, involve negligence, nuisance, or breach of duty is irrelevant.

The claimant is taken to know facts observable or ascertainable by him or her, and also **21.30**
facts ascertainable with the help of expert advice which it would have been reasonable to obtain (LA 1980, s 14(3)). A substantially objective test was said to apply to s 14(3) in *Adams v Bracknell Forest Borough Council* [2005] 1 AC 76. It is to be expected that claimants who have suffered significant injuries will seek professional advice on the cause of their problems, even if they have serious difficulties with reading and writing as a result of unaddressed dyslexia (*Adams v Bracknell Forest Borough Council*). However, in *AB v Ministry of Defence* [2013] 1 AC 78 the Supreme Court held that time will start running against a claimant who believes their injury is attributable to the relevant act or omission 'with sufficient confidence to justify embarking on the preliminaries to the issue of a claim form, such as submitting a claim to a proposed defendant, taking legal and other advice, and collecting evidence'. While suspicion is not knowledge within the meaning of s 14, reasonable belief will normally suffice.

21.31 In *Ali v Courtaulds Textiles Ltd* (1999) *The Times*, 28 May 1999, the Court of Appeal held that the claimant in an industrial deafness case could not be said to know his deafness was attributable to his working conditions, as opposed to being age-induced, until after he had been advised by his doctors. In *Copeland v Smith* [2000] 1 WLR 1371, the claimant's solicitor was dilatory in obtaining a police road accident report, which would have included the details of the defendant's identity. It was held that the proviso to s 14(3) was not intended to give an extended period to a person whose solicitor acted in a dilatory manner in obtaining information which is obtainable without particular expertise, and the claimant was fixed with constructive knowledge which the claimant's solicitors ought to have acquired.

21.32 An injury is 'significant' for the purposes of LA 1980, s 14(1)(a), if the claimant would reasonably have considered it sufficiently serious to justify proceedings against a defendant who does not dispute liability and is able to satisfy any judgment. The court has to find what the claimant knew (and should have known under s 14(3)) about his injuries, and then decide whether a reasonable person with that knowledge would have considered the injuries sufficiently serious to justify commencing proceedings (*A v Hoare* [2008] 1 AC 844). It is not a question of whether the claimant, with the claimant's level of intelligence, was reasonable in considering the injury was not sufficiently serious (*B v Nugent Care Society* [2010] 1 WLR 516). The burden of proof on whether the claimant knew an injury was significant is on the defendant (*Furniss v Firth Brown Tools Ltd* [2008] EWCA Civ 182). It was held in *Stephen v Riverside Health Authority* (1989) *The Times*, 29 November 1989, that the early symptoms of cancer arising from excessive radiation received from a medical X-ray did not amount to a significant injury. The presence of pleural plaques as a result of exposure to asbestos was held to be no injury at all in *Rothwell v Chemical and Insulating Co Ltd* [2008] 1 AC 28, because the evidence was that pleural plaques cause no symptoms and do not increase susceptibility to asbestos-related diseases.

21.33 As to s 14(1)(b), it is clear that knowledge detailed enough to enable the claimant's advisers to draft particulars of claim is not required before time starts to run, and there is no requirement that the claimant must be aware that the defendant's conduct is actionable. To hold that this is the case would be contrary to the final words of s 14(1) that knowledge that any acts or omissions do or do not constitute negligence as a matter of law is irrelevant. Time runs under this element when the claimant (or the claimant's doctor) concluded there was a real possibility that the defendant's activities caused the claimant's injury, such that a reasonable person would then investigate the link further (*Kew v Bettamix Ltd* [2007] PIQR P210). In *Broadley v Guy Clapham and Co* [1994] 4 All ER 439 the claimant had gone into hospital for a knee operation, and left suffering from a condition known as foot drop. It was held that time started to run when the claimant had both a 'broad knowledge' that the operation had caused an injury to her foot, and specific knowledge that the operation had been carried out in such a way as to damage a nerve in her leg (the cause of her foot-drop condition). She had the requisite broad knowledge shortly after the operation, and should have had the specific knowledge within a few months after the operation if she had taken the appropriate expert advice. Whether the relevant facts could be known only after obtaining an expert's report depends on the complexity of the case (*Hendy v Milton Keynes Health Authority* (1991) 3 Med LR 114).

21.34 Time was postponed in *Cressey v E Timm and Son Ltd* [2005] 1 WLR 3926 on the ground that the claimant did not know the precise legal identity of his employer, because his pay slips were issued by one company, but he was employed by a different, but related, company.

Fatal accidents and death: date of knowledge

21.35 Time runs in claims brought by dependants under the Fatal Accidents Act 1976 from the date of death or the 'date of knowledge' (as set out in 21.28) of the person for whose benefit the proceedings are brought (LA 1980, s 12). In proceedings brought for the benefit of the deceased's estate under the Law Reform (Miscellaneous Provisions) Act 1934 time runs from the date of death or the personal representative's 'date of knowledge' (LA 1980, s 11(5)).

Defective products

Claims under the Consumer Protection Act 1987 in respect of personal injuries or damage **21.36** to property must be brought within ten years and accrue on the date of damage or the 'date of knowledge' (LA 1980, s 11A(4)).

Accrual in contribution claims

Contribution claims accrue on the date the amount of the underlying liability is fixed, disre- **21.37** garding any possible appeal. If determined by the court, time runs from judgment; if fixed by agreement, time runs from the date of settlement (LA 1980, s 10(3) and (4)). Time runs from agreement or judgment for the final amount, not from an interim payment (*Jellett v Brooke* [2017] 1 WLR 1177). In the case of split trials, time runs from the judgment on quantum (*Aer Lingus v Gildacroft Ltd* [2006] 1 WLR 1173). Where a firm agreement to settle the primary claim is made, time starts running immediately under s 10(4), and does not start again if the agreement is subsequently recorded in a consent order. However, if the agreement contains a term requiring a consent order before it takes effect, time will run from the order not the agreement. See *Knight v Rochdale Healthcare NHS Trust* [2004] 1 WLR 371.

C CALCULATING THE LIMITATION PERIOD

Time runs from the day following the day on which the cause of action arose, as parts of **21.38** a day are ignored (*Marren v Dawson Bentley and Co Ltd* [1961] 2 QB 135). It runs until the claim is brought, as opposed to issued (*Barnes v St Helens Metropolitan Borough Council (Practice Note)* [2007] 1 WLR 879) or served (*per* Lord Diplock in *Thompson v Brown* [1981] 1 WLR 744). As claim forms are date-stamped when they are issued, the date of issue is often the best evidence of when the claim is brought. A claimant may send a claim form to the court office for issue. Letters requesting the issue of claim forms will be date-stamped on receipt, and the date of receipt will stop time running for limitation purposes if the court does not issue the claim form on the same day (PD 7A, paras 5.1 and 5.2). An inquiry as to the date on which a claim form was received by the court should be directed to a court officer (para 5.3). Ultimately, however, a claim is brought when the claimant delivers all the relevant documents to the court office for issue (even if the office is closed at that time: see *Barnes v St Helens Metropolitan Borough Council (Practice Note)*). If the court office is closed on the final day of the limitation period, proceedings are deemed to be in time if they are issued on the next day the court office is open (*Pritam Kaur v S Russell and Sons Ltd* [1973] QB 337). Paragraph 5.4 goes on to say that parties should recognize the importance of establishing the date of receipt if a limitation period is approaching, and should take steps to record the date of receipt. In cases where limitation might be a problem, it is usually best to make a personal attendance at court to issue the proceedings.

Additional claims under Part 20 are commenced for limitation purposes on the date the **21.39** claim form under Part 20 is issued (LA 1980, s 35(1)(a)). This is because s 35(1)(a) uses the word 'commenced' rather than 'brought', a point confirmed in relation to third party proceedings by CPR, r 20.7(2).

Disability

21.40 There are two categories of persons under disability: children and persons of unsound mind. By virtue of LA 1980, s 28, time does not run against a child until that person's 18th birthday. Also by virtue of s 28, time does not run against a person of unsound mind if that person was under disability at the date the cause of action accrued. Thus, an adult who is immediately rendered of unsound mind by an accident is not subject to limitation until he or she recovers. The same applies to a child who has a cause of action while of sound mind, but who becomes of unsound mind before reaching the age of majority. However, time will continue to run during a period of mental disorder where a cause of action accrues to an adult who was of sound mind at the date of accrual.

Fraud

21.41 In claims based on fraud, the limitation period does not begin to run until the claimant discovers the fraud or could with reasonable diligence have discovered it (LA 1980, s 32(1)(a)). Time does not run while the claimant merely suspects dishonesty (*Barnstaple Boat Co Ltd v Jones* [2008] 1 All ER 1124), but only from when the precise fraud as pleaded was or could have been discovered (*Allison v Horner* [2014] EWCA Civ 117). This provision applies only where fraud is the essence of the claim. A claim in conversion where the defendant has incidentally been guilty of fraud or dishonesty does not bring the provision into effect (*Beaman v ARTS Ltd* [1949] 1 KB 550).

Concealment

21.42 Time does not run where any fact relevant to the claim has been deliberately concealed by the defendant until the concealment is discovered or with reasonable diligence could have been discovered (LA 1980, s 32(1)(b)). A fact is 'relevant' if it ought to be pleaded in the particulars of claim (*Williams v Lishman, Sidwell, Campbell & Price Ltd* [2010] PNLR 25). In *Cave v Robinson Jarvis & Rolf* [2003] 1 AC 384 the House of Lords held that s 32(1)(b) deprives a defendant of a limitation defence:

(a) where the defendant has taken active steps to conceal his breach of duty after he has become aware of it; and

(b) where the defendant is guilty of deliberate wrongdoing and conceals or fails to disclose it in circumstances where the wrongdoing is unlikely to be discovered for some time.

21.43 However, the mere fact that the defendant intended to do the act complained of does not mean that s 32(1)(b) applies to prevent time running. If the defendant is unaware of his alleged error or that he may have failed to take proper care, there is nothing for the defendant to disclose, and time is not prevented from running by s 32(1)(b). Consequently, time will run where a surgeon negligently leaves a swab inside a patient; and where an anaesthetist negligently administers the wrong drug; and where a solicitor gives a client negligent advice. Time will not run if the surgeon deliberately left the swab inside the patient, or if the lawyer after giving negligent advice fails to disclose other facts which he is under a duty to disclose to the client which would have alerted the client to the negligent nature of the advice.

Mistake

21.44 Where the claim is for relief from the consequences of a mistake, time does not run until the mistake is, or could with reasonable diligence have been, discovered (LA 1980, s 32(1)(c)). What amounts to 'reasonable diligence' is a question of fact. In *Peco Arts Inc v Hazlitt*

Gallery Ltd [1983] 1 WLR 1315, a case involving an alleged mistake over whether a 19th-century drawing was an original signed by the artist, it was held that the term meant doing what an ordinary prudent buyer of a valuable work of art would do. In *Kleinwort Benson Ltd v Lincoln City Council* [1999] 2 AC 349, the House of Lords held that the LA 1980, s 32(1)(c) applies to all mistakes, whether of fact or of law, so that it could apply where the claimant had paid money to the defendant under a mistake of law.

Latent damage

It follows from the decision in *Pirelli General Cable Works Ltd v Oscar Faber and Partners* **21.45** [1983] 2 AC 1, noted at 21.22, that it is possible for a claim in tort to be statute-barred before the claimant knows that damage has been sustained, because time runs from the date of damage rather than discovery. To mitigate this position the Latent Damage Act 1986 inserted ss 14A and 14B into the LA 1980. These provisions apply to actions for negligence other than for personal injuries (s 14A(1)). They are restricted to claims in tort, and do not extend to claims for 'contractual negligence' (*Société Commerciale de Réassurance v ERAS (International) Ltd* [1992] 2 All ER 82).

Two alternative periods of limitation are provided by LA 1980, s 14A(4), namely, six years **21.46** from accrual and three years from the 'starting date'. The first of these periods is simply the usual period for actions in tort. The 'starting date' is the earliest date the claimant knew:

(a) that the relevant damage was sufficiently serious to justify proceedings; and
(b) that the damage was attributable to the alleged negligence; and
(c) the defendant's identity.

A claimant is also fixed with constructive knowledge from facts observable or ascertainable by himself or with the help of an appropriate expert (s 14A(10)). This is a reference to advice from an independent expert rather than the potential defendant (*Williams v Lishman, Sidwell, Campbell and Price Ltd* [2009] PNLR 34).

These concepts are very similar to those in s 14 (see 21.28) and it was accepted in *Hallam-* **21.47** *Eames v Merrett* (1995) *The Times*, 25 January 1995 that the authorities on s 14 apply to applications under s 14A. 'Knowledge' in s 14A means knowing with sufficient confidence to justify embarking on the preliminaries to issuing proceedings. Under condition (b), it is clear the claimant does not need to know that the defendant's conduct could be characterized as negligent. Instead, it is enough for the claimant to have broad knowledge of the facts on which the complaint is based, combined with knowing as a real possibility that the alleged acts or omissions caused the damage under condition (a) (*Haward v Fawcetts* [2006] 1 WLR 682).

In order to give some protection to defendants who might otherwise be perpetually at risk, **21.48** s 14B provides a longstop or overriding time limit for bringing proceedings of 15 years from the act or omission alleged to constitute the negligence causing the claimant's damage.

Judgments

By the LA 1980, s 24(1), an action may not be brought upon any judgment after the expiry **21.49** of six years from the date on which the judgment became enforceable. In *Re a Debtor (No 50A–SD–95)* [1997] Ch 310 a judgment creditor served a statutory demand based on a judgment entered eight years previously. It was held that bankruptcy proceedings based on the statutory demand constituted an 'action' on the judgment, and would be time-barred under s 24. However, bringing an 'action' on a judgment is limited to a fresh action, and does not include proceedings by way of execution (*Lowsley v Forbes* [1999] 1 AC 329). If enforcement proceedings are brought more than six years after judgment, the LA 1980, s 24(2), will limit the interest that can be claimed on the judgment debt to that accrued over six years.

Acknowledgments and part-payments

21.50　Under the LA 1980, s 29, acknowledging title to land, acknowledging a debt or other liquidated pecuniary claim (for which, see *Barnett v Creggy* [2017] Ch 273), and making part payments have the effect of renewing the limitation period from the date of acknowledgment or payment. Acknowledgments and part-payments are separate concepts. Under s 30 any acknowledgment must be in writing and signed by the person liable or his agent. A typed signature on a telex is enough (*Good Challenger Navengante SA v Metalexportimport SA* [2004] 1 Lloyd's Rep 67). An acknowledgment in a pleading takes effect on its date, and is not a continuing acknowledgment (*Ofulue v Bossert* [2009] 1 AC 990). However, an acknowledgment in a privileged communication cannot be used under s 29 (*Ofulue v Bossert*).

21.51　Whether a part payment is 'in respect of' the sum owed is a question of fact, but once it is established that only one debt is owed by the defendant it is readily inferred that any part payment is in respect of that debt (*Ashcroft v Bradford & Bingley plc* [2010] EWCA Civ 223). The part-payment of rent or interest due at any time does not extend the time for claiming the balance (s 29(6)), but a payment made outside a repayment schedule has the effect of renewing the limitation period (*International Finance Corporation v Utexafrica Sprl* (2001) LTL 9/5/01).

Cross-border mediation

21.52　Under the LA 1980, s 33A, where the limitation period would expire between the start and eight weeks after the end of a cross-border mediation, the limitation period will instead expire eight weeks after the mediation ends. See the Cross-Border Mediation (EU Directive) Regulations 2011 (SI 2011/1133) and S Blake, J Browne, and S Sime, *A Practical Approach to ADR* (5th edn, Oxford University Press, 2018), ch 19).

D DISCRETION

Judicial review

21.53　The three-month time limit for bringing judicial review proceedings can be extended if good reasons are shown: see 49.26–49.28.

Defamation

21.54　Where defamation or malicious falsehood proceedings are not commenced within the one-year time limit, the court may direct that the limitation period shall not apply if it appears equitable to allow the action to proceed, having regard to the balance of prejudice between the claimant and the defendant (LA 1980, s 32A, as substituted by the Defamation Act 1996, s 5). This section is similar to s 33 (see 21.55ff), but it is applied more restrictively given the short one-year limitation period in defamation (*Brady v Norman* [2011] EWCA Civ 107).

Personal injuries claims

21.55　A wide discretion is given to override the usual three-year limitation period in personal injuries claims by LA 1980, s 33, which in part provides:

If it appears to the court that it would be equitable to allow an action to proceed having regard to the degree to which—

(a) the provisions of section 11 or 11A or 12 of this Act prejudice the plaintiff or any person whom he represents; and
(b) any decision of the court under this subsection would prejudice the defendant or any person whom he represents;

the court may direct that those provisions shall not apply to the action, or shall not apply to any specified cause of action to which the action relates.

...

In acting under this section the court shall have regard to all the circumstances of the case and in particular to—

(a) the length of, and the reasons for, the delay on the part of the plaintiff;
(b) the extent to which, having regard to the delay, the evidence adduced or likely to be adduced by the plaintiff or the defendant is or is likely to be less cogent than if the action had been brought within the time allowed by section 11, by section 11A or (as the case may be) by section 12;
(c) the conduct of the defendant after the cause of action arose, including the extent (if any) to which he responded to requests reasonably made by the plaintiff for information or inspection for the purpose of ascertaining facts which were or might be relevant to the plaintiff's cause of action against the defendant;
(d) the duration of any disability of the plaintiff arising after the date of the accrual of the cause of action;
(e) the extent to which the plaintiff acted promptly and reasonably once he knew whether or not the act or omission of the defendant, to which the injury was attributable, might be capable at that time of giving rise to an action for damages;
(f) the steps, if any, taken by the plaintiff to obtain medical, legal, or other expert advice and the nature of any such advice he may have received.

The circumstances set out in s 33(3) are those which experience had indicated were **21.56** of real importance in considering where the balance of prejudice was likely to lie. The delay referred to in para (a) is the same as that referred to in para (b), namely, the delay after the expiry of the primary limitation period as extended, if appropriate, by the claimant's date of knowledge under s 14 (*Long v Tolchard and Sons Ltd* (1999) *The Times*, 5 January 2000), although only limited weight will be given to reasons for delay after the date of knowledge in cases where s 14 extends the normal limitation period (*KR v Bryn Alyn Community (Holdings) Ltd* [2003] QB 1441). The reasons for the delay to be considered are those of the claimant: it is a subjective test (*Coad v Cornwall and Isles of Scilly Health Authority* [1997] 1 WLR 189). Having found what the reason is for the delay, the court must then decide whether the reason is good or bad. The question of cogency in para (b) is concerned only with the loss or adverse effect on evidence through the passage of time. A court is not entitled in an application under s 33 to find prejudice to the defendant by assuming that omissions or contradictions in the claimant's evidence may be excused by the trial judge (*Nash v Eli Lilly and Co* [1993] 1 WLR 782).

The period of disability referred to in para (d) is one of mental disability arising after the **21.57** accrual of the cause of action, and hence one which does not prevent time running (see 21.40).

The leading authority on s 33 is *Thompson v Brown* [1981] 1 WLR 744, in which the **21.58** House of Lords held that the court has a discretion unfettered by any rules of practice, that the court must consider all the circumstances of the case, and is not restricted to the matters specifically set out in s 33(3). The court must balance all the relevant circumstances, whether specifically mentioned in s 33(3) or not, and must not in effect make its decision based on only one or some of those circumstances (*B v Nugent Care Society* [2010] 1 WLR 516). How difficult it is for the claimant to persuade the court to exercise the discretion depends on the facts of the particular case (*Sayers v Hunt* [2013] 1 WLR 1695).

21.59 Lord Diplock said in *Thompson v Brown* that a direction under s 33 is always prejudicial to the defendant, but the extent of the prejudice is related to the strength or otherwise of the claim or defence. Parker LJ in *Hartley v Birmingham City District Council* [1992] 1 WLR 968 expressed the view that the merits of the claimant's case are of little importance, on the ground that the stronger the merits the greater the prejudice to both the claimant and the defendant of the decision under s 33 going against them. This is contrary to Lord Diplock's view in *Thompson v Brown*, and contrary to subsequent cases. These include *Nash v Eli Lilly and Co* [1993] 1 WLR 782, where a finding that the claims were weak was regarded as an important factor in refusing to make orders under s 33, and *Long v Tolchard and Sons Ltd* (1999) *The Times*, 5 January 2000, where it was said that, if the claimant has a strong, or even a cast-iron, case against the original tortfeasor, that is an important factor to place into the balance that has to be struck.

21.60 Another circumstance not mentioned in s 33(3), but regarded as of considerable importance in *Thompson v Brown*, is whether the claimant has an alternative claim in negligence against his or her solicitor for failing to issue proceedings in time. This factor is reduced if there is real doubt about the strength of the claim against the solicitor, and in any event the claimant will suffer some prejudice through further delay, instructing unknown solicitors to pursue the new claim, the old solicitors knowing the weaknesses of the original claim, and possible restrictions in obtaining disclosure against the original defendants.

21.61 Also important is the period of delay between the accident and the defendant being informed of the claim. A defendant who is informed of the potential claim at an early stage has the opportunity to investigate the facts while the events are still fresh in witnesses' memories, even if proceedings are issued rather late, and hence cannot complain of significant prejudice under s 33(3)(b). This seems to have been a significant factor in *Thompson v Brown* and also in *Hartley v Birmingham City District Council* [1992] 1 WLR 968. In *Cain v Francis* [2009] QB 754 it was held that in early notification cases, financial prejudice to the defendant should not be taken into account. Conversely, in *Donovan v Gwentoys Ltd* [1990] 1 WLR 472 there was a delay in excess of six years before the defendants were given full details of the claim. In fact proceedings were issued only six months late, as the claimant was a child at the date of the accident. She instructed solicitors 19 days before her 18th birthday, so she had an alternative claim against her solicitors. It was held that the delay in notifying the defendants was an extremely important consideration, that it would be inequitable to require the defendants to meet such a stale claim, and the claimant would suffer only the slightest prejudice in being required to sue her solicitors. Permission was refused. The different results in the cases in this paragraph turn on whether there is forensic prejudice as a result of the delay (*McDonnell v Walker* [2010] PIQR P5).

21.62 Many reasons for not bringing a claim, such as a reluctance to sue one's present employer, can be important factors under s 33. So, in *McCafferty v Metropolitan Police District Receiver* [1977] 1 WLR 1073 Lawton LJ said, '… the court should be understanding of men who, after taking an overall view of their situation, come to the conclusion that they would prefer to go on working rather than become involved in litigation'. Likewise, deciding not to sue a defendant at a time when the defendant had no money to pay any judgment may justify a period of delay (*A v Hoare* [2008] 1 AC 844).

Applications under s 33 should generally be made to a judge, although in the County Court **21.63** they can be made to a District Judge if the value of the claim does not exceed £25,000 (the trial jurisdiction for District Judges): *Hughes v Jones* [1996] PIQR P380. It is incumbent on the claimant to disclose all relevant circumstances at the hearing of the application and, if this is breached, the decision may be set aside (*Long v Tolchard and Sons Ltd* (1999) *The Times*, 5 January 2000).

Issuing a second claim

It sometimes happens that the claimant issues a personal injuries claim within the primary **21.64** limitation period, but allows the claim to lapse, for example by not serving the claim form within the four-month period of validity. *Horton v Sadler* [2007] 1 AC 307 (departing from the earlier House of Lords' decision in *Walkley v Precision Forgings Ltd* [1979] 1 WLR 606) held that if the claimant then issued a second claim form after the expiry of limitation the court has a discretion under s 33 to disapply the limitation period in the second claim, with the fact that it is a second claim case being a factor to be taken into account in deciding where the balance of prejudice lies. It was further held in *Aktas v Adepta* [2011] QB 894 that issuing a second claim in these circumstances is not an abuse of process.

E EQUITABLE REMEDIES, LACHES, AND ACQUIESCENCE

By LA 1980, s 36(1), the usual time limits in the Act do 'not apply to any claim for specific **21.65** performance of a contract or for an injunction or for other equitable relief, except in so far as any such time limit may be applied by the court by analogy'. The court refused to apply any limitation period (other than laches and acquiescence) to a claim for specific performance in *P&O Nedlloyd BV v Arab Metals Co (No 2)* [2007] 1 WLR 2288.

The defences of laches and acquiescence are preserved by s 36(2). Laches operates to bar **21.66** equitable relief (only), and applies where the defendant has detrimentally relied on delay in bringing a claim (*Fisher v Brooker* [2009] 1 WLR 1764). The period of delay, the events during that period, and the balance of justice are taken into account in deciding whether a claim is barred by laches. The defence of acquiescence applies where there has been an encouragement or allowance of a party to believe something to his detriment (*Jones v Stones* [1999] 1 WLR 1739). There is probably no difference between these formulations of laches and acquiescence, a point noted in *Fisher v Brooker*. The first question is whether one party, by its action or inaction, has encouraged the other party to believe a certain state of affairs. The second question is whether there was reliance on that encouragement. Thirdly, whether in all the circumstances of the case it would be unconscionable for the first party to then insist on its legal rights. It is incorrect to concentrate on the period of delay as being enough of itself.

The period of delay likely to give rise to these equitable defences depends on the nature **21.67** of the relief claimed and the facts of the case. Delay in the context of interim injunctions is considered in 42.83. In the case of actions to redeem mortgages, a period of 20 years was said to be a convenient guide in *Weld v Petre* [1929] 1 Ch 33. Laches was held to be a defence where a shareholder failed to assert his rights for 24 years in *Lynch v James Lynch and Sons (Transport) Ltd* (2000) LTL 8/3/00.

KEY POINTS SUMMARY

21.68
- Limitation runs from accrual, which is when all the necessary elements for the cause of action are in existence.
- Technically, time runs from the day after the accident or breach (parts of days are disregarded), and stops running when the claim is brought. This is when the claimant has done everything they can to issue the claim form.
- Time does not run if the claimant is under disability, and in cases of fraud, mistake, and concealment.
- In personal injury and latent damage claims time will not start running until the claimant has the requisite 'knowledge'.
- In personal injury and defamation claims the court has a discretion to 'disapply' the primary limitation period.
- If a claim is time-barred, the defendant should plead limitation in the defence, and should consider applying to strike out the claim as an abuse of process (see Chapter 30).

22

AMENDMENT

A AMENDMENT BY CONSENT. 22.04

B AMENDMENT WITHOUT PERMISSION. . .22.05

C PRINCIPLES GOVERNING
PERMISSION TO AMEND. 22.08

D AMENDMENT AFTER THE EXPIRY
OF THE LIMITATION PERIOD. 22.23

E PROCEDURE ON AMENDING. 22.44

Key points summary 22.50

Changes in the parties' knowledge of a case as it progresses and straightforward drafting **22.01**
errors make it necessary on occasion to make amendments to their statements of case. The
underlying principle is that all amendments should be made which are necessary to ensure
that the real question in controversy between the parties is determined, provided such
amendments can be made without causing injustice to any other party.

Amendments are allowed either: **22.02**

(a) with the consent of the other parties (see 22.04); or
(b) in the absence of consent and without the need for permission from the court, provided
the amendment is made before the statement of case is served (see 22.05–22.07); or
(c) with the permission of the court. Usually permission is granted, but on terms as to the
payment of the costs occasioned by the amendment (see 22.16). However, there may
be problems in making an application to amend in the later stages of proceedings (see
22.10) or after the expiry of the limitation period (see 22.23–22.43).

Not every minor development needs to be reflected in an amendment to the statements of **22.03**
case. So, for example, in personal injuries cases it is not necessary to amend each time the
claimant's medical condition changes or updated medical reports are obtained (*Owen v
Grimsby and Cleethorpes Transport* [1992] PIQR Q27).

A AMENDMENT BY CONSENT

A statement of case can be amended at any stage of the proceedings with the written con- **22.04**
sent of all the parties (CPR, r 17.1(2)(a)). By way of exception, amendments to add, remove,
or substitute parties always require the permission of the court (see 22.19).

B AMENDMENT WITHOUT PERMISSION

Amendments that can be made without permission

By CPR, r 17.1(1), a party is allowed to amend a statement of case at any time before it **22.05**
has been served on any other party. As we have seen at the beginning of Chapter 14, the
term 'statements of case' is defined as the claim form, particulars of claim, the defence,
reply, additional claims under Part 20, and any further information given in relation to

them (r 2.3(1)). Once it has been served, a statement of case can be amended only with the consent of the other parties or the permission of the court. The right to amend without permission is therefore largely restricted to amendments to the claim form and particulars of claim in the period between issue and service, which could be as long as four months. Other statements of case could be amended without permission in the period between filing and service, but in most cases this will be a very short period of time.

22.06 Amendments made before service can be as wide-ranging as may be desired, including adding, removing, or substituting parties (CPR, r 19.4(1)), and even deleting and replacing the whole of the original text, and still will not require the court's permission (r 17.1(3)). However, amendments to the particulars of claim of this nature before service of the particulars of claim may require consent or permission if the claim form has already been served, because (eg) amendments to the parties in the particulars of claim will involve consequential amendments to the claim form and, if the claim form has been served, consent or permission will be required for the amendment to the claim form.

Objecting to amendments made without permission

22.07 A party served with a statement of case amended without permission can object to the amendment by issuing an application notice seeking an order disallowing the amendment pursuant to CPR, r 17.2. Such an application should be made within 14 days of service of the amended statement of case (r 17.2(2)). The general approach is to disallow amendments made without permission if permission would not have been granted had an application needed to be made (for which, see 22.08–22.22).

C PRINCIPLES GOVERNING PERMISSION TO AMEND

22.08 The courts have power under CPR, r 17.1(2)(b), to allow the amendment of a statement of case. The rule simply says that amendments may be made with the permission of the court, without saying how the discretion will be exercised. A court asked to grant permission to amend will therefore base its decision on the overriding objective (*JW Spear & Sons Ltd v Zynga Inc* [2013] EWHC 1640 (Ch)). One view is that disposing of a case justly will mean that amendments should be allowed to enable the real matters in controversy between the parties to be determined. In *Cropper v Smith* (1884) 26 ChD 700 Bowen LJ said he knew of '… no kind of error or mistake which, if not fraudulent or intended to overreach, the court ought not to correct, if it can be done without injustice to the other party'. In *Clarapede and Co v Commercial Union Association* (1883) 32 WR 262 Brett MR went so far as to say:

> However negligent or careless may have been the first omission, and however late the proposed amendment, the amendment should be allowed if it can be made without injustice to the other side. There is no injustice if the other side can be compensated in costs.

22.09 A modern reformulation of this principle can be found in *Cobbold v London Borough of Greenwich* (LTL 24/5/01), where Gibson LJ said an application to amend should be considered applying the overriding objective, which includes ensuring the case is dealt with expeditiously and fairly. In achieving this Gibson LJ said:

> Amendments in general ought to be allowed so that the real dispute between the parties can be adjudicated upon provided that any prejudice to the other party or parties caused by the amendment can be compensated in costs, and the public interest in the efficient administration of justice is not significantly harmed.… There is always prejudice when a party is not allowed to put forward his real case, provided it is properly arguable.

The quotation from *Cropper v Smith* was relied on by counsel before the Supreme Court in **22.10** *Global Torch Ltd v Apex Global Management Ltd (No 2)* [2014] 1 WLR 4495, and summarily rejected by Lord Neuberger of Abbotsbury PSC at [27] as having been overtaken by the CPR. In *Ketteman v Hansel Properties Ltd* [1987] AC 189 one of the defendants, who had previously been defending the claim on its merits, applied at trial during the closing speeches to amend its defence to plead that the claim was time-barred under the Limitation Act. Lord Griffiths, commenting on the decision in *Clarapede and Co v Commercial Union Association* (1883) 32 WR 262, said:

> ... whatever may have been the rule of conduct a hundred years ago, today it is not the practice invariably to allow a defence which is wholly different from that pleaded to be raised by amendment at the end of the trial even on terms that an adjournment is granted and that the defendant pays all the costs thrown away. There is a clear difference between allowing amendments to clarify the issues in dispute and those that permit a distinct defence to be raised for the first time.

It follows from *Ketteman v Hansel Properties Ltd* that there will be reluctance to allow **22.11** 'late amendments', although it may be perfectly proper to allow a late amendment for the purpose of clarifying the issues between the parties. Where this is done to reflect a version of the facts that only emerges with the evidence at the trial, an amendment is generally permitted as this accords with the overriding objective (*Binks v Securicor Omega Express Ltd* [2003] 1 WLR 2557).

In *Worldwide Corporation Ltd v GPT Ltd* [1998] EWCA Civ 1894 counsel for the claim- **22.12** ant realized the claimant could not win on the pleaded case, and so a radically amended particulars of claim was sent to the defendant 11 days before trial. Permission to amend was refused based on the court weighing various factors, following the approach laid down in *Ketteman v Hansel Properties Ltd*. These authorities were approved by the Court of Appeal in *Swain-Mason v Mills & Reeve* [2011] 1 WLR 2735, where permission was refused for an amendment sought on the second day of the trial, even though the amendments were not as far-reaching as those in *Ketteman v Hansel Properties Ltd* and *Worldwide Corporation Ltd v GPT Ltd*. In *Swain-Mason v Mills & Reeve* it was held that adopting the approach in *Cobbold v London Borough of Greenwich* is wrong in law. It is not entirely clear whether the Court of Appeal intended to say it is wrong in law in all cases, or only if permission to amend is sought at a late stage.

It is submitted that the distinction between the two approaches depends on how con- **22.13** tentious the amendment is in objective terms. The open approach indicated by the 19th-century cases has been consigned to history. Consistently with the approach on whether it is reasonable to oppose an application for relief from sanctions (see 37.32 and *Denton v TH White Ltd* [2014] 1 WLR 3926), where it is obvious that permission to amend will be granted, the other side should consent, and in such cases if consent is not forthcoming the court should not waste much time in considering whether to grant permission. Minor amendments, tidying up amendments, and amendments made in the early stages of the litigation should fall into this category.

Cases where it is not obvious that the amendment should be allowed include cases where **22.14** there is an argument that the amended case does not have a real prospect of success, where the amendment is made late in the proceedings, where allowing a wide-ranging amendment will result in a lot of work done on the case going to waste, and where the proposed amendment will have a tendency to overreach the other side. If so, the court will have to balance a number of factors along the lines laid down by *Ketteman v Hansel Properties plc*. These include the exact stage reached in the proceedings, how great a change is made by the proposed amendments, whether there is a real prospect of success, whether the other side is taken by surprise (or whether the new case has been foreshadowed in the earlier statements of case or other documents), whether an adjournment to the trial will be necessary, whether there is any prejudice to the other side, and the effects on other litigants and the administration of justice.

Merits of the amended case

22.15 A proposed amendment will be refused where the amended case has no real prospect of success (*Oil & Mineral Development Corporation Ltd v Sajjad* (2001) LTL 3/12/01; *Clarke v Slay* (2002) LTL 25/1/02). Amendments were refused in *TG Can Ltd v Crown Packaging UK plc* [2007] EWHC 1271 (QB) where the claimant sought to add implied terms to the particulars of claim. The court held that there was no basis, such as to give business efficacy to the contract, for implying the proposed terms. As with many other interim applications, the evidence on the merits of the substantive claim will usually be incomplete and untested by cross-examination. It will be inappropriate to refuse an amendment on the merits if, for example, one of the main issues turns on a disputed oral conversation, because that is a matter to be determined at trial (*Young v JR Smart (Builders) Ltd (No 2)* (2000) LTL 7/2/00).

Costs of amendment

22.16 The usual rule is that where an amendment is allowed, the party seeking to amend must pay the other side the costs of and occasioned by the amendment (*Lidl UK GmbH v Davies* [2008] EWCA Civ 976). These costs will comprise the correspondence relating to the application to amend, preparation for and attendance at the application, and the costs relating to any consequential amendment of subsequent statements of case (PD 44, para 4.2). Generally, consent (see 22.04) should be given for any amendment sought by the other side in order to save costs unless there are substantial grounds for objecting. An unreasonable refusal to consent may result in the loss of the usual costs order against the party applying to amend (*La Chemise Lacoste SA v Sketchers USA Ltd* (2006) LTL 24/5/06).

22.17 A very late amendment may be allowed with an appropriately onerous order as to costs. In *Beoco Ltd v Alfa Laval Co Ltd* [1995] QB 137 the claimant was allowed to make a fifth amendment to its statement of case on the sixth day of the trial. The proposed amendment pleaded an alternative claim against the first defendant which could not be brought by separate proceedings. Disallowing the amendment would therefore have caused real prejudice to the claimant. However, the previously pleaded case against the first defendant was weak (and in the event failed at trial), and the first defendant had decided against protecting itself by making a payment into court (for which, see Chapter 36). To avoid injustice to the first defendant, the claimant (who won on the amended claim) was ordered to pay the first defendant's costs up to the date of the amendment and 85 per cent of its costs thereafter. Such a penal approach is not always correct. In *Professional Information Technology Consultants Ltd v Jones* (2001) LTL 7/12/01, the claim succeeded on the basis of a late amendment, but this was reflected by simply reducing the costs of the claim recovered by the claimant by one-third.

Addition, removal, and substitution of parties

22.18 One of the most fundamental types of amendment is where it is proposed to make a change in the parties to the claim. Sometimes this is little more than a technicality, such as where the amendment seeks to correct a mistake in the name of one of the parties if no one has been misled by the way that party was originally named (this is not uncommon when suing businesses, which sometimes trade through limited liability companies with similar names, and which sometimes appear to be partnerships when in fact they are companies). At the other end of the scale are cases where, late in the litigation process, the claimant realizes that a completely new party needs to be added to the claim, in which event all the stages in the claim will have to be repeated with the new party.

The main test of whether a change involving the addition or substitution of a party may be **22.19** made is whether the amendment is 'desirable': see CPR, r 19.2(2)–(4). Nobody, however, may be added as a claimant unless he or she consents in writing and the consent is filed at court (r 19.4(4)). A person who refuses to consent to being added as a claimant may be added as a defendant, unless the court orders otherwise (r 19.3(2)). Further, the court's permission is always required to remove, add, or substitute a party, unless the claim form has not been served (r 19.4(1)).

Rule 19.2 of the CPR provides, so far as is material: **22.20**

> (2) The court may order a person to be added as a new party if—
>   (a) it is desirable to add the new party so that the court can resolve all matters in dispute in the proceedings; or
>   (b) there is an issue involving the new party and an existing party which is connected to the matters in dispute in the proceedings, and it is desirable to add the new party so that the court can resolve that issue.
> (3) The court may order any person to cease to be a party if it is not desirable for that person to be a party to the proceedings.
> (4) The court may order a new party to be substituted for an existing one if—
>   (a) the existing party's interest or liability has passed to the new party; and
>   (b) it is desirable to substitute the new party so that the court can resolve the matters in dispute in the proceedings.

The rule is designed to prevent claims being defeated on technical grounds relating to the **22.21** parties which have or should have been joined. This is in accordance with the statutory objective in the SCA 1981, s 49(2), of ensuring that all matters in dispute between the parties are completely and finally determined, and of avoiding all multiplicity of proceedings. The discretion granted under the rule is applied in accordance with the overriding objective along similar lines to those discussed at 22.08–22.15. As with other amendments, permission is usually granted on terms that the amending party must pay the costs of and arising from the amendment.

Adding defendants close to the expiry of limitation

A person added as a defendant by amendment becomes a party for the first time when **22.22** the amended proceedings are served (*Ketteman v Hansel Properties Ltd* [1987] AC 189). This is important in cases where amendments are sought close to the expiry of a limitation period, because if service is to be effected after limitation expires, the additional requirements discussed at 22.23–22.43 will also need to be fulfilled if permission to amend is to be granted (*Bank of America National Trust and Savings Association v Chrismas* [1994] 1 All ER 401). Consequently, if an order to add a new party is made close to the expiry of limitation where the conditions for amendments after the expiry of limitation do not apply, the order granting permission to amend should impose a condition that service on the additional defendants must be effected before the expiry of the limitation period. If the application is heard after the limitation period has expired, the court is obliged to apply the more exacting after-expiry of limitation requirements (*Welsh Development Agency v Redpath Dorman Long Ltd* [1994] 1 WLR 1409).

D AMENDMENT AFTER THE EXPIRY OF THE LIMITATION PERIOD

22.23 An amendment to add or substitute a new party or a new cause of action is deemed to be a separate claim and to have been commenced on the same date as the original proceedings (LA 1980, s 35(1) and (2)). Consequently, if the original proceedings were commenced within the relevant limitation period, and an amendment is allowed adding a party or cause of action after the expiry of the limitation period, the defendant will be deprived of the limitation defence, and will usually suffer injustice not compensable by an order for costs. The usual rule, therefore, is that such amendments are not permitted (LA 1980, s 35(3)). There are, however, a number of exceptions which are considered later. It seems that if there is a dispute about whether a limitation period has expired, the test is whether the claim is unarguably time-barred (*Leicester Wholesale Fruit Market Ltd v Grundy* [1990] 1 WLR 107).

22.24 The statutory relation back in the LA 1980, s 35(1), applies only to the procedural time bars in the LA 1980. It does not apply to contractual or substantive time limits, like that in the Hague–Visby Rules, art III, rule 6, which have the effect that on expiry of the period laid down the claimant's cause of action ceases to exist (*Payabi v Armstel Shipping Corporation* [1992] QB 907). Likewise, defective product claims against the producer under the Consumer Protection Act 1987 are extinguished on the expiry of the ten-year limitation period in the LA 1980, s 11A(3) (giving effect to Directive 85/374, art 11). This means that generally the producer cannot be substituted as a defendant after this period has expired (*O'Byrne v Aventis Pasteur MSD Ltd* (Case C-358/08) [2010] 1 WLR 1412).

Amendment of parties after the limitation period

22.25 The addition or substitution of new parties after the expiry of any limitation period is permitted only if it is necessary for the determination of the original claim (LA 1980, s 35(5)(b)). An amendment to add an alternative claim against a new party is not 'necessary' for this purpose (*Martin v Kaisary* [2006] PIQR P5). There are a number of circumstances, which are discussed at 22.26–22.41, where amendments to the parties may be allowed despite the expiry of the limitation period. Unless the case falls into one of these categories, an amendment to the parties after the expiry of the limitation period cannot be allowed even if it is 'necessary' in the colloquial meaning of that word.

Assignment or transmission of interest

22.26 Rule 19.2(4) of the CPR provides that the court may make an order for a new party to be substituted for an existing party if:

(a) the existing party's interest or liability has passed to the new party; and
(b) it is desirable to substitute the new party so that the court can resolve the matters in dispute in the proceedings.

22.27 This rule allows claims in which the interest of a party has been assigned, transmitted, or devolved on another to be carried on by the person now having an interest in the dispute. This may occur, for example, if the original party dies so that his or her interest passes to executors or administrators, or where the original party's interest is assigned to another person. Once limitation has passed, substitution of the new party may be allowed if the original party's interest has passed to the new party on the original party's death or bankruptcy (CPR, r 19.5(3)(c)). In *Finlan v Eyton Morris Winfield (A Firm)* [2007] 4 All ER 143, an amendment was allowed after the expiry of limitation to substitute an assignment of the cause of action which was executed after the claim form was issued.

Correcting a genuine mistake

One of the grounds on which the addition or substitution of a new party after the expiry **22.28** of limitation will be regarded as 'necessary' within the meaning of the LA 1980, s 35, is where the new party is substituted for a party whose name was given in mistake for the new party's name (s 35(6)(a)). Rules of court can be made for allowing such an amendment, which may impose further restrictions (s 35(4)). There are two provisions in the CPR dealing with this situation, which have to be read together, namely:

(a) Rule 19.5(3)(a) of the CPR which provides that the addition or substitution of a party will be necessary (for the purposes of LA 1980, s 35) if the new party is to be substituted for a party who was named in the claim form in mistake for the new party; and

(b) Rule 17.4(3) of the CPR which provides that the court may allow an amendment to correct a mistake as to the name of a party, but only where the mistake was genuine and not one which would cause reasonable doubt as to the identity of the party in question. This applies where the amendment does not involve substituting a new party, but is limited to correcting the name of the original party.

Courts dealing with applications under r 19.5(3)(a) apply the same principles as those gov- **22.29** erning the now repealed RSC, ord 20, r 5 (*Adelson v Associated Newspapers Ltd* [2008] 1 WLR 585). Accordingly, in these applications:

(a) the court must be satisfied that the person who made the mistake, directly or through an agent, was the person responsible for issuing the claim form (r 19.5(3)(a));

(b) the applicant has to show that, had the mistake not been made, the new party would have been named in the claim form;

(c) the mistake has to be as to the name of the party rather than as to the identity of the party (*The Sardinia Sulcis* [1991] 1 Lloyd's Rep 201);

(d) no injustice should be caused if the application is granted. Often there will be a connection between the party named in the claim form and the party to be substituted (although this is not a requirement), and often the party intended to be substituted will have been aware of the proceedings (again this is not a formal requirement). If the party to be substituted was unaware of the claim, the court is likely to exercise its discretion against granting the application (*Horne-Roberts v SmithKline Beecham plc* [2002] 1 WLR 1662); and

(e) all that is permitted is a substitution of parties, not the addition of an extra party (*Armes v Godfrey Morgan Solicitors Ltd* [2018] 1 WLR 936).

Under CPR, r 17.4(3), whether a mistake would cause reasonable doubt as to the identity **22.30** of the party intending to sue has to be determined objectively having regard to what is said in the claim form in the light of what was known by the defendant and the context in which the claim was made (*ABB Asea Brown Boveri Ltd v Hiscox Dedicated Corporate Member Ltd* [2007] EWHC 1150 (Comm)). A description of the role played by the claimant in the particulars of claim attached to the claim form may be sufficiently clear to avoid such doubt (*International Bulk Shipping and Services Ltd v Minerals and Metals Trading Corporation of India* [1996] 1 All ER 1017).

Claim cannot properly be carried on without the new party

Once a limitation period has expired, the addition or substitution of a new party may also **22.31** be regarded as 'necessary' within the meaning of the LA 1980, s 35, where the original claim cannot be maintained by or against an existing party unless the new party is joined or substituted as a claimant or defendant (s 35(6)(b)). This provision may also be subject to further restrictions imposed by rules of court (s 35(4)).

22.32 The relevant rule is CPR, r 19.5(3)(b), which provides that amendments under s 35(6)(b) may be made when claims cannot 'properly be carried' on without the amendment. Some commentators have said that the rule gives a general discretion to the court to consider whether evading the provisions of the LA 1980 by amendment would be 'proper'. However, this cannot be correct, because rules of court made under the LA 1980, s 35(4), can impose further restrictions going beyond s 35(6), but cannot relax the basic requirements of that subsection. The phrase 'cannot properly be carried on' in r 19.5(3)(b) therefore cannot be any wider than the phrase 'cannot be maintained' in s 35(6).

22.33 Situations within r 19.5(3)(b) are probably similar to those set out in the pre-1999 RSC, ord 15, r 6(6). This set out five categories of cases where errors in naming parties gave rise to a legal bar to obtaining a remedy, and it was only in these five categories where it was considered 'necessary' (the same word used in the present rules in r 19.5(2)(b) in this context) to add a party once limitation had expired (a view which is strongly supported by *Merrett v Babb* [2001] QB 1174). The old categories were where:

(a) the new party was a necessary party to the claim in that property is vested in him at law or in equity and the claimant's proceedings asserting an equitable interest in that property were liable to be defeated unless the new party was joined; or

(b) the relevant cause of action was vested in the new party and the claimant jointly but not severally; or

(c) the new party was the Attorney-General and the proceedings should have been brought by relator proceedings in his name; or

(d) the new party was a company in which the claimant was a shareholder and on whose behalf the claimant was suing to enforce a right vested in the company; or

(e) the new party was sued jointly with the defendant and was not also liable severally with him and failure to join the new party might render the claim unenforceable.

22.34 It will be appreciated that these categories were rather restricted. A right or liability would be vested in persons jointly but not severally (grounds (b) and (e) at 22.33) where, for example, a contract by its terms was made jointly between numerous persons (see, eg, *Roche v Sherrington* [1982] 1 WLR 599). Another example was the joint liability of partners in respect of contracts entered into on behalf of the partnership under the Partnership Act 1890, s 9. An example under (c) was an action in respect of public nuisance, which had to be brought on the relation of the Attorney-General. Paragraph (d) was intended to assist in cases falling foul of the rule in *Foss v Harbottle* (1843) 2 Hare 461. A similar situation arose in *Irwin v Lynch* [2011] 1 WLR 1364, where an amendment was allowed substituting a company as the claimant in place of its administrator in a misfeasance claim against the company's directors, which could only be brought by the company.

Alteration of capacity

22.35 An amendment may be allowed after the expiry of the limitation period to alter the capacity in which a party claims. This applies whether the new capacity is one which that party had at the date the proceedings were commenced or is one acquired thereafter (CPR, r 17.4(4)). 'Capacity' in this rule is used in the sense of legal competence or status to bring or defend a claim. It could not be used where a claimant wrongly issued proceedings in her own right (because the cause of action had vested in her trustee in bankruptcy), and thereafter took an assignment from the trustee, and asked for permission to amend to plead the assignment. This was because both before and after the proposed amendment the claimant was purporting to sue in her personal capacity, so there was no 'alteration of capacity' (*Haq v Singh* [2001] 1 WLR 1594). The final words of r 17.4(4) ('or has since acquired') allow amendments in the case of administrators of estates, who only acquire their capacity as such from the date of the grant of letters of administration (*Roberts v Gill and Co* [2011] 1 AC 240 at [34]).

Personal injuries cases

The LA 1980, s 35(3), provides that an amendment may be allowed after the expiry of the **22.36** primary limitation period in a personal injuries case, provided the court makes a direction under the LA 1980, s 33 (for which see 21.55–21.64). This provision is incorporated into the CPR in r 19.5(4)(a). In *Howe v David Brown Tractors (Retail) Ltd* [1991] 4 All ER 30 the Court of Appeal held that an amendment to add a party under what is now r 19.5(4)(a) could be made only if an application to disapply the usual three-year limitation period under the LA 1980, s 33, had already been made and granted, or if a s 33 application was made at the same time as the application to amend. This has been reversed by r 19.5(4)(b), which provides that an amendment may be allowed if a s 33 issue is directed to be determined at trial.

Amendment of causes of action after the expiry of the limitation period

Amendments to add causes of action are generally not allowed once limitation has expired. **22.37** In deciding whether an amendment amounts to a new cause of action it is necessary to compare the essential factual elements of the existing and proposed causes of action (*Aldi Stores Ltd v Holmes Buildings plc* [2005] PNLR 9). An amendment to plead consequential loss in a professional negligence claim was interpreted as simply adding a new head of damage, so was not a new cause of action in *Harland and Wolff Pension Trustees Ltd v Aon Consulting Financial Services Ltd* [2010] ICR 121. However, making an amendment to justify a claim on a different factual basis amounts to making a new claim even if the sum claimed remains unchanged (*Seele Austria GmbH and Co KG v Tokio Marine Europe Insurance Ltd* [2009] BLR 481).

Exceptions where a new cause of action may be added to an existing claim after the rel- **22.38** evant period of limitation has expired are:

(a) where the claim is in respect of personal injuries and the court makes a direction under the LA 1980, s 33, that the usual limitation period shall not apply (LA 1980, s 35(3));
(b) where the new cause of action is an original set-off or counterclaim (LA 1980, s 35(3)). An original set-off or counterclaim is one made by an original defendant who has not previously pleaded a counterclaim, and the counterclaim must be made against the original claimant (see *Kennett v Brown* [1988] 1 WLR 582, which is still good law on this point). An original set-off or counterclaim can be brought under LA 1980, s 35(3), only if it was not time-barred on the date the claimant brought the main claim (*Hassan Khan & Co v Al-Rawas* [2017] 1 WLR 2301); and
(c) where the new cause of action arises out of the same facts or substantially the same facts as are already in issue in the original claim (LA 1980, s 35(5)(a) and CPR, r 17.4).

Same or substantially the same facts

Whether amendments involve the same or substantially the same facts as those already in **22.39** issue is largely a matter of impression. In deciding whether the new cause of action arises out of substantially the same facts as those originally pleaded it is necessary to identify '... the bare minimum of essential facts abstracted from the original pleading [and to compare that] with the minimum as it would be constituted under the amended pleading' (*P&O Nedlloyd BV v Arab Metals Co* [2007] 1 WLR 2483 at [14], applying the similar test from *Smith v Henniker-Major* [2003] Ch 182). An amendment adding a new duty or obligation usually raises a new cause of action, whereas pleading additional facts, or better particulars, allegedly constituting a breach of the duty already pleaded, usually will not (*Darlington Building Society v O'Rourke James Scourfield* [1999] PNLR 365). If the new plea introduces an essentially distinct allegation, it will be a new cause of action. Where the only difference is the addition of a new remedy, there is no addition of a new cause of action.

22.40 In *Goode v Martin* [2002] 1 WLR 1828, the claimant sought permission to amend her claim after the expiry of limitation to plead that on the alternative version of the facts pleaded in the defence, the defendant would still be liable to her. The judge held that there was no power to allow the amendment, because r 17.4(2) allows such amendments if the new claim arises out of the same or substantially the same facts 'as a claim in respect of which [the claimant] has already claimed', and the facts relied upon were pleaded by the defendant. The Court of Appeal held that the Human Rights Act 1998, s 3, allowed it to read the words 'are already in issue on' into this rule, with the effect that the court had power to allow the amendment as it was based on facts put in issue by the defence. It also allows a claimant to adopt facts after the expiry of limitation which had been pleaded by one defendant by amending the particulars of claim against another defendant (*Charles Church Developments Ltd v Stent Foundations Ltd* [2007] 1 WLR 1203).

22.41 In *Hancock Shipping Co Ltd v Kawasaki Heavy Industries Ltd* [1992] 1 WLR 1025 permission to amend the particulars of claim was sought three years after service of the original statement of case, and after the limitation period had expired. In considering whether it is just to allow an amendment in such circumstances, the court held that it had to take into account that granting permission will deprive the defendant of an accrued limitation defence, but could exercise its discretion to allow the amendment in the light of all the relevant factors. An important factor is the degree to which the defendant is prejudiced in being unable to investigate the facts of the new claim through the disappearance of evidence. The Court of Appeal in *Hancock Shipping Co Ltd v Kawasaki Heavy Industries Ltd* disallowed certain of the proposed amendments on the ground that the defendant would be prejudiced through the loss of evidence, but allowed certain other amendments which were closely related to the claim already made as there was likely to be little prejudice through the loss of evidence.

Amendments after the limitation period affecting accrued rights

22.42 A defendant will not be given permission to amend where the effect of the proposed amendment is to transfer responsibility for the claim on to a non-party who cannot be sued by the claimant as a result of the expiry of the relevant limitation period. An example is *Cluley v RL Dix Heating* (2003) LTL 31/10/03, where the claimant sued for breach of contract. After the expiry of the limitation period, the defendant sought to amend its defence, which had admitted the contract but denied breach, to plead that there was no contract with the claimant and that the claimant should have sued other parties. Suing the other parties was no longer viable because of the expiry of limitation. Permission to amend was refused, because even an order for costs could not put the claimant into the same position as if the proposed defence had been pleaded at the proper time.

22.43 Much depends on whether the defendant has been at fault in not pleading the proposed defence at the proper time. So, in *Weait v Jayanbee Joinery Ltd* [1963] 1 QB 239 through no fault of their own, the defendants discovered after the expiry of the limitation period that the claimant's injuries were probably worse than they should have been through the intervening negligence of the doctor who treated the claimant. An amendment to the defence to plead the doctor's negligence was allowed, despite the fact that the claimant could not make a claim against the doctor as that claim was time-barred. Further, an amendment blaming a non-party may be allowed if it alleges facts within the knowledge of the claimant, since in such a case the claimant is prejudiced by his or her own failure to sue the non-party in time, rather than by some line of defence being made known at a late stage.

E PROCEDURE ON AMENDING

Making the amendment

Words added to a document are written or typed in red ink, and words deleted are struck **22.44** through in the same colour. Reamendments are made in green ink, and subsequent amendments in violet, then yellow. If the amendments cannot be conveniently incorporated into the original document, a fresh document should be prepared. However, there are two other options:

(a) using a monochrome typeface, but with a numeric code indicating the amendments (PD 17, para 2.2(2)); or
(b) simply retyping the document incorporating the changes and omitting deleted text (PD 17, para 2.2).

The court may, if it thinks it desirable, direct that the amendments be shown in one or other of the ways described.

If there is a substantial change the document should be reverified by a statement of truth **22.45** (PD 17, para 1.4). The amended statement of case should be endorsed 'Amended [Particulars of Claim] by Order of District Judge [name of judge] dated [date]'.

Applying for permission

A party seeking permission to amend must issue an application notice. An application **22.46** may be made by an existing party or by a person who wishes to become a party (CPR, r 19.4(2)). There is an express provision requiring evidence in support of an application under r 19.2(4) for the substitution of a new party where an existing party's interest has passed (eg on death), and that type of application can be made without notice (r 19.4(3)). Any other type of application for addition or substitution does not strictly have to be supported by written evidence, though the circumstances may make this desirable. This is particularly so in applications where the expiry of the limitation period is relevant. The proposed amended statement of case must be filed with the application (PD 17, para 1.2(2)).

Applications for permission to amend are usually made on notice to all other parties. As **22.47** indicated earlier in this chapter, applications in the later stages of litigation can be made to the trial judge. Otherwise they tend to be dealt with by District Judges and Masters as part of the case management functions of the court.

Procedure after permission is granted

If permission to amend is granted by the court, the order will be drawn up and served in the **22.48** usual way on the parties. If the order provides for the addition, removal, or substitution of a party, the order must also be served on the party affected by the order (CPR, r 19.4(5)). Court fees are also payable when new parties are brought in.

22.49 Any order granting permission to make an amendment may include consequential directions, particularly regarding amendments to other statements of case, and perhaps altering any existing directions timetable. Where an amendment involves the addition, removal, or substitution of a party, CPR, r 19.4(6) and PD 19A, para 3.2 provide that consequential directions may also deal with:

(a) filing and serving of the amended claim form and particulars of claim on any new defendant, usually within 14 days;
(b) serving other relevant documents on the new party;
(c) providing the new defendant with a response pack for the purpose of admitting, defending, or counterclaiming;
(d) serving the order on all parties and any other person affected by it; and
(e) the management of the proceedings.

KEY POINTS SUMMARY

22.50 • Permission to amend is required if the statement of case has been served.

• Normally, consent from the other parties is an alternative to seeking the court's permission to amend.

• Normally, permission is granted on condition that the party amending pays the costs of and occasioned by the amendments.

• Late amendments are sometimes disallowed.

• The statutory relation back in the Limitation Act 1980, s 35, means that there are restrictions on amending after limitation has expired.

• Amendments after the expiry of limitation to change parties are usually allowed only if there was a mistake.

• Amendments after limitation to change causes of action are usually restricted to cases where the new case arises out of facts which are the same or substantially the same as those already in issue.

23

INTERIM APPLICATIONS

A JURISDICTIONAL RULES 23.06
B TIME TO APPLY 23.09
C PRE-ACTION INTERIM REMEDIES 23.10
D OBLIGATION TO APPLY EARLY 23.13
E APPLICATIONS WITHOUT NOTICE 23.18
F APPLICATIONS WITH NOTICE 23.28

G INTERIM HEARINGS 23.57
H SUMMARY DETERMINATION OF
  INTERIM COSTS 23.63
I VARYING OR REVOKING
  INTERIM ORDERS 23.64
  Key points summary 23.66

It is often necessary or desirable to seek orders and directions from the court in advance **23.01** of the final, substantive, hearing of a case. Directions are made in most defended cases at the track allocation stage, which is usually a few weeks after proceedings are served (see Chapter 15). Directions are formal requirements laid down by the court, usually a District Judge or Master, dealing with matters such as the times by when evidence must be exchanged between the parties and setting a timetable for preparing the case for trial.

Orders are usually made by District Judges and Masters, although several types of order **23.02** can be granted only by judges. An order is a formal decision by the court granting a remedy or relief to a party, usually in the stages before the final determination of a case. Interim orders are also sometimes made after the substantive hearing of a claim, and sometimes the relief granted at trial includes various types of orders. Interim orders, for example, include remedies such as interim injunctions (see Chapter 42) and security for costs (see Chapter 26); they may impose a sanction on a party who fails to keep to the timetable laid down by a previous order giving directions (see Chapter 37) or may grant permission to renew the claim form (see Chapter 7) or to amend a statement of case (see Chapter 22). Once an interim order has been obtained, it must be drawn up, a topic discussed at 41.37ff.

Orders are usually sought on an application made by one of the parties, and are usually **23.03** made 'on notice', giving the other side an opportunity to argue against the order being made. However, orders can be made by the court of its own initiative, or on an application listed by the court of its own initiative, and in certain circumstances an application can be made 'without notice' to the other parties.

Parties seeking interim orders or directions on notice have to issue an application notice in **23.04** form N244, pay a court fee, and often have to provide written evidence in support. Unless there is some specific permission to the contrary, applications have to be made using the official form rather than informally by letter (*R (Simmons) v Bolton Metropolitan Borough Council* [2011] EWHC 2729 (Admin)). In general the documentation must be served on the other parties at least three clear days before the return date (when the application will be heard). Generally, service must be effected by the applicant, although the court may order otherwise (CPR, r 6.21(1)).

23.05 There is always a danger of hearings on interim applications being blown out of proportion. Lawyers quite understandably seek to do everything they can to advance their client's case. *VTB Capital plc v Nutritek International Corporation* [2013] 2 AC 337 was a complex interim application to set aside permission to serve outside the jurisdiction and to amend the particulars of claim. There were 27 bundles of documentary evidence and 14 bundles of authorities for the hearing before the judge, who had to do two days of pre-reading before the interim hearing which lasted six days. In the Supreme Court Lord Neuberger of Abbotsbury PSC said at [89] that the Woolf and Jackson Reforms allow judges to invoke their case management powers to curtail the evidence that is submitted, refuse to hear argument on excessive numbers of authorities, and do whatever reading is necessary away from the courtroom, to ensure applications are kept within proportionate bounds.

A JURISDICTIONAL RULES

Court

23.06 In general an application must be made to the court where the claim is presently being dealt with. This will normally be the court where the proceedings were commenced (CPR, r 23.2(1)). In County Court money claims, applications are made to the County Court Money Claims Centre until the claim is sent to a County Court hearing centre (PD 23A, para 5A.1). The normal rules are departed from where:

(a) the claim has been transferred (r 23.2(2));
(b) the claim has been listed for trial at another court, in which event the application should be made to the trial court (r 23.2(3)); or
(c) the application is made after judgment, in which event the application may need to be made to the court dealing with enforcement (r 23.2(5)).

23.07 An application for pre-action remedies should be made to the court where the substantive proceedings are likely to be brought, unless there is a good reason for applying to another court (CPR, r 23.2(4)). Pre-action remedies in County Court money claims can be made at any County Court hearing centre, unless any enactment, rule, or practice direction provides otherwise (r 23.2(4A)). For example, search orders must (except in limited circumstances) be applied for in the High Court (County Court Remedies Regulations 2014 (SI 2014/982)).

Judge

23.08 The division of work between High Court and Circuit Judges on the one hand, and Masters and District Judges on the other, is considered at 3.12 to 3.15. Most interim applications are dealt with by Masters and District Judges, but search orders have to be dealt with by judges, and most interim injunction applications are in practice dealt with by judges.

B TIME TO APPLY

23.09 The basic rules are that an interim application should be made as soon as it becomes apparent it is necessary or desirable (PD 23A, para 2.7), but after the party making the application has come on to the court record. For a claimant this is after proceedings are issued, and for a defendant it is after service is acknowledged or a defence is filed (CPR, r 25.2(2)).

C PRE-ACTION INTERIM REMEDIES

A claimant may exceptionally make an application for an interim order before the commencement of proceedings (CPR, r 25.2(2)(b)) if either: **23.10**

(a) the matter is urgent; or
(b) it is otherwise desirable to grant the interim remedy before the claim is brought in the interests of justice.

The courts may thus entertain pre-commencement applications for urgent interim injunctions (eg some libel cases where publication is threatened within hours of the applicant finding out about the matter) and some applications for freezing injunctions and search orders.   **23.11**

If a pre-action interim remedy is granted, the court should give directions requiring a claim to be commenced (r 25.2(3)). Rule 25.2(4) points out that such directions need not be given where an order is made for pre-action disclosure or inspection under the SCA 1981, s 33, or the CCA 1984, s 52 (see Chapter 45). This is because such an order may result in the applicant deciding not to bring substantive proceedings at all, as recognized in *Dunning v United Liverpool Hospitals' Board of Governors* [1973] 1 WLR 586. Normally directions for bringing substantive proceedings are made in other types of pre-action order.   **23.12**

D OBLIGATION TO APPLY EARLY

The obligation to apply early for an interim remedy stems from the overriding objective, which includes ensuring that cases are dealt with expeditiously (CPR, r 1.1(2)(d)).   **23.13**

Parties should normally notify the court of any intention to apply for interim relief which may dispose of the case or reduce the issues or amount in dispute, when they file their directions questionnaires (PD 26, para 2.2(3)).   **23.14**

In multi-track cases the appropriate time to consider most forms of interim relief, if possible, is the first case management conference. A party that wishes to invite the court to make directions or orders of types not usually dealt with in case management conferences, and which are likely to be opposed, is required by PD 29, para 5.8, to issue and serve an application returnable at the same time as that set for the case management conference (with a time estimate if it is clear that the time originally allowed for the case management conference will be insufficient, so a fresh date can be fixed). Paragraph 3.8 expressly says that applications in multi-track cases must be made as early as possible so as to minimize the need to change the directions timetable, and an application to vary a directions timetable laid down by the court (perhaps on its own initiative) must ordinarily be made within 14 days of service of the directions (para 6.2).   **23.15**

There are some express restrictions in the CPR about when some types of application can be made. Examples include summary judgment, which can be applied for only after the defendant has acknowledged service or entered a defence (r 24.4(1)), and interim payments, where a similar restriction applies (r 25.6(1)). Nevertheless, summary judgment (and striking-out) applications should normally be made on or before filing of directions questionnaires (PD 26, para 5.3(1)).   **23.16**

Of course the need for an interim remedy may not become apparent until some later stage. Rule 25.2(1)(b) of the CPR provides that applications can be made even after final judgment has been given. Where it becomes necessary to make an application shortly before   **23.17** trial, it should be dealt with on the pre-trial review if there will be one (there is a pre-trial review about eight to ten weeks before the trial in some multi-track cases: see 29.26). If this is not possible, another option is to make the application at the start of the trial itself.

E APPLICATIONS WITHOUT NOTICE

Procedure on without-notice applications

23.18 The general rule is that all applications must be made on notice to the other parties (CPR, r 23.4(1)). It is wrong, for example, to apply for an 'unless order' (see 37.15ff) without notice (*Irwin Mitchell Solicitors v Patel* (2003) LTL 15/4/03). Applications can be made without notice only where permitted by a provision in the CPR, a practice direction, or a court order (r 23.4(2)). For example, applications to extend the time for serving a claim form (renewal of process) are permitted without notice (r 7.6(4)), as are applications for permission to issue additional claims after filing of the defence (r 20.7(5)). These are both examples of applications where the opposite party will not be on the court record when the application is made. Other situations where applications may be made without giving notice to the other parties are:

(a) Where the application arises in urgent circumstances, so there is no practical possibility of giving the required minimum of three clear days' notice to the other side. In cases of this sort informal notification should be given to the other parties unless the circumstances require secrecy (PD 23A, para 4.2).

(b) Where a party decides to make an application at a hearing that has already been fixed, but there is insufficient time to serve an application notice. In cases of this sort the applicant should inform the other parties and the court (preferably in writing) as soon as possible of the nature of the application, the reason for it, and then make the application orally at the hearing (PD 23A, para 2.10).

(c) Where the application depends on secrecy for its efficacy, such as most applications for freezing injunctions and search orders.

23.19 Like applications on notice, applications without notice should normally be made by filing an application notice (CPR, r 23.3(1)) in form N244, which must state the order being sought and the reasons for seeking the order (r 23.6). The application notice must also be signed, and include the title of the claim, its reference number, and the full name of the applicant. If the applicant is not already a party it should also give the applicant's address for service. If the applicant wants a hearing, that too must be stated (PD 23A, para 2.1). The application should normally be supported by evidence, which should, in addition to setting out the evidence in support of the relief sought, state the reasons why notice was not given (CPR, r 25.3(3)). Where electronic filing is used in the Business and Property Courts (see 6.59), all the documents that the judge needs to read must be sent in a single filing, with each document clearly labelled, together with all relevant previous orders. Non-compliant applications are simply rejected (PD Commercial Court, 1 February 2018).

Hearing of without-notice applications

23.20 It follows from PD 23A, para 2.1 that an application without notice can be adjudicated upon with or without a hearing. Hearings of without-notice applications are technically in public (r 39.2), but usually take place in the judge's private room. Advocates have a duty to take a full note on any without-notice hearing, which should be provided to other persons affected by the order (*Cinpres Gas Injection Ltd v Melea Ltd* (2005) *The Times*, 21 December 2005). If the applicant is disappointed with an order made without a hearing, the application can be renewed to a judge at the same level as the one who dealt with the application on the papers (*Collier v Williams* [2006] 1 WLR 1945). The renewed application is dealt with at a hearing.

Duty of full and frank disclosure

There is a duty of full and frank disclosure in applications made without notice. It extends **23.21** both to facts within the actual knowledge of the claimant and to facts which would have been known on the making of reasonable inquiries. The duty is to disclose facts material to the matter being decided on the application. What is material depends on the nature of the application. Facts going to granting permission to serve outside the jurisdiction are not relevant on an application for permission to serve by an alternative method (*Albon (t/a NA Carriage Co) v Naza Motor Trading Sdn Bhd (No 2)* [2007] 1 WLR 2489 at [47]). Proper disclosure requires advocates to identify all relevant documents for the judge, taking the judge to the particular passages in those documents, and ensuring the judge is aware of the legal significance of the material (*R (Lawer) v Restormel Borough Council* [2008] HLR 20).

If the applicant is found to be guilty of material non-disclosure, the order will ordinar- **23.22** ily be discharged regardless of the merits on the full facts: *R v Kensington Income Tax Commissioners, ex p Princess Edmond de Polignac* [1917] 1 KB 486. While court has jurisdiction to continue or re-grant the order, the jurisdiction to do so should be exercised sparingly, taking into account the degree and extent of the culpability in making the non-disclosure (*Millhouse Capital UK Ltd v Sibir Energy plc* [2009] 1 BCLC 298). Innocent non-disclosures are more likely to be forgiven than deliberate ones, but the court also has to take into account how important the undisclosed matters were to the application, the merits of the claim, and the need to uphold the principle of full and frank disclosure.

Full and frank disclosure in freezing injunction applications

Freezing injunction applications are considered in Chapter 43, and are invariably made **23.23** without notice. To determine whether there has been a material non-disclosure on such an application, it is first necessary to consider the affidavit in support to see whether any adverse facts which the applicant either knew or could have discovered have been omitted. All material facts must appear in the affidavit itself, not in documents exhibited to it (*National Bank of Sharjah v Dellborg* (1992) *The Times*, 24 December 1992). Secondly, it is necessary to consider whether anything omitted was 'material' in the sense that it would have affected the judgment of a reasonable tribunal when deciding whether to grant the freezing injunction in question: *Lloyds Bowmaker Ltd v Britannia Arrow Holdings plc* [1988] 1 WLR 1337.

Facts are material if they are necessary to enable the court to exercise its discretion on a **23.24** proper basis, bearing in mind the need to act fairly between the parties, the fact that the defendant has not been heard, and the inherent hardship and inconvenience caused by a freezing injunction. There is obviously a distinction between what are material facts and documents for the purposes of the application for the injunction and those which will be relevant at the trial of the claim, and a claimant should not feel it is necessary to exhibit more than a few key documents to the affidavit in support of the application without notice: *National Bank of Sharjah v Dellborg*. Instances where facts have been held to be material include:

(a) mistakes in framing the cause of action: *Bank Mellat v Nikpour* [1985] FSR 87;

(b) failing to disclose the existence of proceedings in another country: *Behbehani v Salem* [1989] 1 WLR 723;

(c) failing to disclose weaknesses in the claimant's financial position, which are relevant to the value of the claimant's undertaking in damages and to the undertaking to indemnify third parties; and

(d) misstating the source of information included in the affidavits in support of the without-notice application (*St Merryn Meat Ltd v Hawkins* (2001) LTL 2/7/01, where it was said that the information was obtained using a bugged telephone in the claimants' offices, whereas in fact it was obtained using an interception device at the defendant's home).

23.25 The duty to make full and frank disclosure is a continuing one, so the applicant has a duty to bring to the attention of the court any material changes in the circumstances after a freezing injunction has been granted: *Commercial Bank of the Near East plc v A* [1989] 2 Lloyd's Rep 319. The duty continues to the first hearing on notice on most matters, but continues until the final disposal of the claim on the question of the applicant's financial circumstances (*Staines v Walsh* (2003) *The Times*, 1 August 2003).

23.26 As mentioned at 23.22, a *locus poenitentiae* may sometimes be afforded. In deciding what should be the consequences of any breach of duty, it is necessary to take into account all the relevant circumstances, including the gravity of the breach, the excuse or explanation offered, the severity and duration of any prejudice occasioned, and whether the consequences of the breach were remediable and had been remedied. The court must also apply the overriding objective and the need for proportionality: *Memory Corporation plc v Sidhu (No 2)* [2000] 1 WLR 1443. It is important that the rule against material non-disclosure does not itself become an instrument of injustice: *Brink's Mat Ltd v Elcombe* [1988] 1 WLR 1350. The court has a discretion to continue the order or to make a new order on terms (such as on costs or payment of damages) 'if the original non-disclosure was innocent and if an injunction could properly be granted even had the facts been disclosed' (*per* Glidewell LJ in *Lloyds Bowmaker Ltd v Britannia Arrow Holdings plc*). 'Innocence' in this connection depends on whether the omission was made intentionally, but, of course, there are degrees of culpability. Much depends on the quality of the facts that have not been disclosed. Some facts are so important that the court will readily infer that the non-disclosure was deliberate. Others, being material but not central to the application, will be more readily forgiven. See the judgment of Woolf LJ in *Behbehani v Salem*.

Orders made without notice

23.27 Where an order is made against a person without notice, CPR, r 23.9(2), provides that the order must be served on that person together (unless the court orders otherwise) with the application notice and any evidence in support. The order must, by virtue of r 23.9(3), contain a statement to the effect that the person against whom it is made has a right to apply to set aside or vary the order within seven clear days of service of the order. Applications to set aside or vary are normally made back to the judge who made the original order.

F APPLICATIONS WITH NOTICE

Documentation

An interim application should normally be made by filing an application notice stating the **23.28** order being sought and the reasons for seeking it (CPR, rr 23.3(1) and 23.6). The application notice must be signed, and should include the title of the claim, its reference number, and the full name of the applicant. If the applicant is not already a party it should also give the applicant's address for service. If the applicant wants a hearing, that too must be stated (PD 23A, para 2.1). The application should normally be supported by written evidence setting out the facts justifying the relief sought (CPR, r 25.3(2)). The notice must be filed at court together with the prescribed fee, and served as soon as possible thereafter (see 23.47). The standard form of application notice is form N244: see form 23.1.

On receipt of the application notice the court may either notify the parties of the time and **23.29** date of the hearing, or notify them that it proposes to consider the application without a hearing (PD 23A, para 2.3).

Evidence in support

The general rule is that applications for interim remedies must be supported by evidence **23.30** (CPR, r 25.3(2)), but evidence in support is not required when applying for case management directions. Some judgment is required from lawyers when deciding whether they need evidence for their applications. Paragraph 9.1 of PD 23A specifically mentions that, as a practical matter, the court will often need to be satisfied by evidence of the facts that are relied on in support of, or for opposing, an application.

Four options are available to the applicant regarding the format of the evidence to be used **23.31** in support of an interim application. They are:

(a) To provide sufficiently full factual information in support of the application in the body of the application notice itself (CPR, rr 22.1(3) and 32.6(2)(b)), and include a statement of truth in the notice. This is a signed statement that the applicant believes that any facts stated in the application are true (r 22.1(4) and (6); PD 22, para 2.1).
(b) To rely on the facts stated in a statement of case filed in the proceedings, provided it contains a statement of truth (CPR, r 32.6(2)(a)). This will usually have been previously served and filed, and if so there is no need to reserve or refile (r 23.7(5)).
(c) To rely on witness statements, each with statements of truth signed by the witnesses (rr 22.1(4) and 32.6(1)). The witness statements used may be ones drafted specifically for the interim application, or it may be possible to rely on the main witness statements that have been disclosed on the substantive issues in the case. The general rule is that any fact that needs to be proved at any hearing other than the trial should be proved by the evidence of witnesses in writing (r 32.2(1)), and it is further provided by r 32.6(1) that at hearings other than the trial evidence is to be by witness statement unless the court, a practice direction, or any other enactment requires otherwise. Consequently, evidence by witness statement is the primary means of adducing evidence at interim hearings. The format of witness statements is considered in Chapter 32.
(d) To rely on affidavit evidence. Rule 32.15(2) allows a witness to give evidence by affidavit at any hearing other than a trial if he or she chooses to do so. This also allows the use of affirmations (PD 32, para 1.7). However, using affidavits may result in the loss of the additional costs over and above the cost of using an ordinary witness

Form 23.1 Form N244 Application notice

N244

Application notice

For help in completing this form please read the
notes for guidance form N244Notes.

Name of court COUNTY COURT		Claim no.
Fee account no. (if applicable)	**Help with Fees – Ref. no.** (if applicable)	
	H W F – ☐☐☐ – ☐☐☐	
Warrant no. (if applicable)		
Claimant's name (including ref.) Mrs JANE WATKINS		
Defendant's name (including ref.) Miss ELEANOR DANIELS		
Date		

1. What is your name or, if you are a legal representative, the name of your firm?

   Headley & Co

2. Are you a   ☐ Claimant   ☐ Defendant   ☑ Legal Representative

   ☐ Other *(please specify)*

   If you are a legal representative whom do you represent?   Defendant

3. What order are you asking the court to make and why?

   1. That judgment in default be set aside under CPR, r 13.3; and
   2. That the costs of this application be provided for,
   because the Defendant has a real prospect of successfully defending the claim.

4. Have you attached a draft of the order you are applying for?   ☐ Yes   ☑ No

5. How do you want to have this application dealt with?   ☑ at a hearing   ☐ without a hearing

   ☐ at a telephone hearing

6. How long do you think the hearing will last?   ☐ Hours   45 Minutes

   Is this time estimate agreed by all parties?   ☐ Yes   ☑ No

7. Give details of any fixed trial date or period   None

8. What level of Judge does your hearing need?   District Judge

9. Who should be served with this application?   Claimant

9a. Please give the service address, (other than details of the
   claimant or defendant) of any party named in question 9.

Form 23.1 *continued*

10. What information will you be relying on, in support of your application?

☑ the attached witness statement

☐ the statement of case

☐ the evidence set out in the box below

If necessary, please continue on a separate sheet.

Statement of Truth

(I believe) (The applicant believes) that the facts stated in this section (and any continuation sheets) are true.

Signed _____ Dated _____

Applicant('s legal representative)('s litigation friend)

Full name _____

Name of applicant's legal representative's firm _____

Position or office held _____
(if signing on behalf of firm or company)

11. Signature and address details

Signed _____ Dated _____

Applicant('s legal representative's)('s litigation friend)

Position or office held   Assistant Solicitor
(if signing on behalf of firm or company)

Applicant's address to which documents about this application should be sent

Headley & Co 52 Higham Road Kettering Northants Postcode N N 1 6 2 C H	If applicable	
	Phone no.	01562 891744
	Fax no.	
	DX no.	9945 Kettering 2
	Ref no.	43332/PDL

E-mail address	

statement. There are situations where affidavit evidence is required either by specific court order, or by virtue of a practice direction or other enactment. Affidavits are required, for example, in support of applications for search orders, freezing injunctions, orders to require an occupier to permit another to enter land, and applications for permission to make a committal application. The format of affidavits is considered in Chapter 32.

23.32 The evidence in support must be filed at court, although the exhibits should not be filed unless the court otherwise directs (PD 23A, para 9.6). The evidence (including exhibits) in support must be served with the application (CPR, r 23.7(3)). If the evidence in support does not contain a statement of truth the usual order is to allow a limited period to refile the document duly verified. Setting aside an order based on unverified evidence was regarded as disproportionate in *Colliers International Property Consultants v Colliers Jordan Sdn Bhd* [2008] 2 Lloyd's Rep 368.

23.33 Any evidence which a respondent wishes to rely upon must be served as soon as possible, and in any event in accordance with any directions the court may have given (PD 23A, para 9.4). The court will not take kindly to respondents who serve evidence in response at the last minute, particularly if this results in a wasted hearing and a need to adjourn.

23.34 In the Commercial Court, evidence in answer to an application must be filed and served within 14 days after service of the application notice and evidence in support (PD 58, para 13.1). Any evidence in reply must be filed and served seven days thereafter. If the hearing of the application is likely to last more than half a day, these periods are extended to 28 and 14 days respectively (para 13.2).

Bundles of documents

23.35 Sometimes it is appropriate to prepare bundles of documents for interim applications. Often it is sufficient to rely on the application notice, written evidence, and exhibits without the need to go to the expense of compiling formal bundles. Sometimes the statements of case and evidence on the substantive issues should be included, and sometimes previous orders and correspondence. Bundles should be prepared for applications whenever more than 25 pages are involved (*Queen's Bench Guide*, para 7.10.8) although it must be said that even in straightforward applications it is easy to exceed this. Copies of authorities should be included in the bundles (*Queen's Bench Guide*, para 7.10.10). In the Commercial Court, an application bundle must be filed by 1 p.m. one clear day before the hearing (two clear days for 'heavy' applications lasting more than half a day). The case management bundle must also be available at the hearing (*Commercial Court Guide*, paras F5.4, F6.4, F11).

23.36 All parties should cooperate in agreeing bundles, and should make clear whether they are simply agreeing which documents should be included in the bundles, or whether they are also agreeing that the included documents are to be treated as evidence of the facts stated in them and/or that the documents to be included are agreed to be authentic.

23.37 For Chancery applications, the applicant should ensure that one copy of the bundle is lodged at court at least two and not more than seven clear working days before the hearing (*Chancery Guide*, para 15.34), whereas Queen's Bench Masters are usually given their bundles at the hearing (*Queen's Bench Guide*, para 7.10.9). All parties and the court must be provided with identical bundles.

Skeleton arguments

Skeleton arguments, chronologies, and bundles of authorities are used by advocates at **23.38** interim hearings, trials, and appeals in support of their oral submissions. They will not be required for the more straightforward types of interim hearings, but are usually required for hearings before High Court judges and are often used for hearings before Circuit Judges. They are not insisted on if the application is likely to be short or if it is so urgent that preparation of a skeleton argument is impracticable. For substantial applications skeletons should be delivered to the court two clear days before the hearing. For shorter applications, or urgent applications, they may be delivered the day before the hearing or at the hearing.

In the Commercial Court, for ordinary applications lasting up to half a day, skeleton argu- **23.39** ments must be filed by 1 p.m. on the day before the hearing. For heavy applications, the applicant must file and serve its skeleton argument and any *dramatis personae* two clear days before the hearing, and the respondent one clear day before the hearing (*Commercial Court Guide*, paras F5.5, F6.5). A chronology is often also useful. Copies of authorities must be provided with the skeleton arguments (para F13.1). Each party must provide the court with a reading list by 1 p.m. on the day before the hearing (para F8).

Skeleton arguments are intended to assist the court in dealing with its business in a timely **23.40** and efficient manner (*Tchenguiz v Director of the Serious Fraud Office* [2015] 1 WLR 838). A skeleton argument should provide a concise summary of the party's submissions on the issues raised by the application, and should be as brief as the nature of the case allows. It should both define and confine the areas of controversy, and should avoid extensive quotations. There are different maximum page lengths in different courts, but even in the Court of Appeal there is a ceiling of 25 pages (PD 52C, para 31). A skeleton argument needs to be persuasive, but is not a substitute for oral argument. It should cite the main authorities relied upon, be divided into numbered paragraphs, be paginated, make use of abbreviations (such as 'C' for claimant, 'A/345' for page 345 of bundle A) and give dates in the form '23.4.2018'. In more substantial applications it should have a reading list for the judge of the core documents.

Authorities

As a matter of professional etiquette, authorities relied upon must be provided to the other **23.41** side in good time before the hearing. There is no need to provide authorities for propositions not in dispute. In the County Court it is usually necessary to have photocopies of reports available at the hearing. In the High Court, lists of authorities should be provided to the head usher by 5.30 p.m. on the working day before the hearing. For Court of Appeal hearings, once the parties have been notified of the date fixed for hearing, the appellant's advocate must file a bundle containing photocopies of the principal authorities each side will be relying upon seven days before the hearing (PD 52C, para 29). Obviously, this can be done only after conferring with the advocate for the respondent. Normally, even for appeal hearings the bundle should contain no more than ten authorities. Any bundle or list of authorities must contain a certificate by the advocate that the following requirements have been complied with.

Practice Direction (Citation of Authorities) [2001] 1 WLR 1001 provides that the follow- **23.42** ing types of authorities should not be cited unless they establish a new principle or extend the law:

(a) law reports of applications attended by one party only;
(b) applications for permission to appeal;

(c) applications that only decide the application is arguable; and

(d) County Court cases (other than to illustrate damages in personal injuries claims or to illustrate current authority where no higher authorities are available).

23.43 The same practice direction says that skeleton arguments will have to justify reliance on decisions that merely apply decided law to the facts, and also decisions from other jurisdictions. Decisions of the Court of Justice of the European Union ('CJEU') and organs of the European Convention on Human Rights are treated as domestic authorities for this purpose. For each authority cited, the skeleton must state the proposition of law the case demonstrates, and identify the relevant paragraph numbers from the judgments in support. *Practice Direction (Citation of Authorities)* [2012] 1 WLR 780 provides that it is permissible to cite judgments by means of copies reproduced from electronic sources, but neutral citation reports should only be used when no recognized reports are available (*A City Council v T* [2011] 1 WLR 819). Electronic copies should preferably be in 12-point font (although ten- or 11-point fonts are acceptable), and the advocate presenting the report must be satisfied that it has not been reproduced in a garbled form.

23.44 If it is necessary to rely on an authority referred to in the Human Rights Act 1998, s 2, the authority cited should be an authoritative and complete report, and copies must be served and filed not less than three days before the hearing (PD 39A, para 8.1). If an extract from *Hansard* is to be used in accordance with the principles in *Pepper v Hart* [1993] AC 593 as refined by *Wilson v First County Trust (No 2)* [2004] 1 AC 816, copies should be served on the other parties and the court, together with a brief summary of the argument based on the extract, five working days before the hearing: *Practice Direction (Hansard: Citations)* [1995] 1 WLR 192.

Chronologies and lists of persons

23.45 Skeleton arguments are often accompanied by chronologies and lists of relevant persons. Good chronologies have short entries for the material events, phrased in a non-contentious way to promote agreement with the other parties.

Draft orders

23.46 Paragraph 12 of PD 23A says that except in the most simple applications the applicant should bring to the hearing a draft of the order sought. The hard copy brought to court should be double spaced (*Queen's Bench Guide*, para 7.11.3). If the order is unusually long or complex, the draft should be supplied on disk as well as on hard copy (PD 23A, para 12.1). Preparing draft orders is particularly important in all types of interim injunction applications, and whenever the order is at all complicated or unusual. Draft orders are also useful if a detailed directions timetable needs to be laid down. For almost all other types of application the short particulars of the orders sought normally inserted in the N244 will be sufficient.

Service

23.47 The normal rule is that the applicant will serve the application notice, any draft order and evidence in support, although the court may decide to deal with service (CPR, r 6.21(1)). There is no requirement to refile or reserve documents which have already been filed or served at an earlier stage (CPR, r 23.7(5)).

23.48 Service must be effected as soon as possible after the application is issued, and in any event not less than three days before it is to be heard (r 23.7(1)). In accordance with the general rules on computing time in r 2.8, this means clear days (excluding the date of effective service and the date of the hearing), and, because the period is less than five days, also excluding weekends, bank holidays, Christmas, and Good Friday. Thus, take, for example, a hearing which is listed for Wednesday 10 October 2018. Assume the solicitor for the applicant decides to serve the application and evidence in support by document exchange. The three clear days before the hearing are Friday 5, Monday 8, and Tuesday 9 October 2018. The documents must therefore be deemed to be served no later than Thursday 4 October. As this is a business day, and given the provision in r 6.26 that documents transmitted by DX are deemed to be served on the second day after being left at the document exchange, the latest the documents could be left at the document exchange would be Tuesday 2 October 2018.

Where it is not possible to serve within this time limit the circumstances may justify an **23.49** application without notice (see 23.18), or an application may be made to abridge time under r 3.1(2)(a). Abridging time may be appropriate where a respondent is repeating behaviour previously adjudicated upon (*Secretary of State for the Environment, Food and Rural Affairs v Meier* [2009] 1 WLR 2780 at [82]).

Disposal without a hearing

Rule 23.8 of the CPR provides that the court may deal with an interim application without **23.50** a hearing if either:

(a) the parties agree that the court should dispose of the application without a hearing (the applicant's view on whether there should be a hearing should be stated in the application notice); or
(b) the court does not consider that a hearing would be appropriate.

A party dissatisfied with any order or direction made without a hearing is able to apply to **23.51** have it set aside, varied, or stayed (r 3.3(5)(a)). Such an application must be made within seven days after service of the order, and the right to make such an application must be stated in the order (r 3.3(5)(b) and (6)).

Hearings by telephone

Active case management in accordance with the overriding objective includes dealing with **23.52** cases without the parties needing to attend court, and by making use of technology (CPR, r 1.4(2)(j) and (k)). Both may be achieved by dealing with some applications by telephone conference calls, which is specifically provided for by r 3.1(2)(d). The rule enables the court to hold a hearing by telephone or any other method of direct oral communication, so other means of electronic communication may be used as technology develops. A telephone hearing is most commonly used in a 'telephone conference-enabled court', and is most frequently used for case management hearings and interim hearings estimated to take no more than an hour.

If an application is to be heard by telephone, the application notice must be served at least **23.53** five clear days before the hearing (PD 23A, para 4.1A). The 'designated legal representative', who is usually the solicitor for the applicant (para 6.1), is responsible for setting up the telephone hearing. In multi-track claims, and in other cases if the court so directs, the designated legal representative is required to file and serve a case summary and draft order by 4 p.m. at least two days before the hearing (paras 6.11 and 6.12). Any other documents relied upon must be filed and served by the party relying on them within the same time limit (para 6.13). The conference call for the hearing should be fully connected at least ten minutes before the time for the hearing (para 6.10(5)), with the call being set up with the designated legal representative (and counsel) being called first, then the other parties and their counsel, and finally the judge (para 6.10(4)). No party or representative may attend in person unless every other party agrees (para 6.9).

Orders made on the court's own initiative

23.54 Rule 3.3(1) of the CPR gives the court a power to make orders of its own initiative. This power is intended to be exercised for the purpose of managing the case and furthering the overriding objective (r 3.1(2)(m)). Orders made in this way must, by virtue of r 3.3(5)(b) and (6), include a statement that parties who are affected may apply within seven days (or such other period as the court may specify) after service for the order to be set aside, varied, or stayed. Failing to make an application to vary or set aside is likely to result in the court assuming the orders or directions made were correct in the circumstances then existing (PD 28, para 4.2(2), for fast track cases; PD 29, para 6.2(2), for multi-track cases).

23.55 There is a related power enabling the court to make orders on its own initiative after giving the parties an opportunity of making representations on the matter. Where the court proposes to make such an order it will specify a time within which the representations must be made (CPR, r 3.3(2)).

Hearings convened on the court's own initiative

23.56 In addition, the court has a power to fix a hearing for the purpose of deciding whether to make any order it might propose to make of its own initiative. For example, in order to reduce the issues in a case it might convene a summary judgment hearing. Unless some other period is specified in the rules regarding notice, any application convened by the court must be notified to parties likely to be affected by the proposed order at least three clear days in advance (CPR, r 3.3(3)).

G INTERIM HEARINGS

Procedure at hearings

23.57 The general rule is that interim hearings will be in public (CPR, r 39.2; European Convention on Human Rights, art 6(1)). In practice the public do not attend most hearings before Masters and District Judges, even if notionally they are heard in public, because most interim applications are conducted in chambers, with limited facilities for accommodating the public. If a large number of people wish to attend, the judge may adjourn to a larger room or court (PD 39A, para 1.10).

23.58 In addition to dealing with the specific application that has been made, the court may wish to review the conduct of the case as a whole and give any necessary case management directions. The parties will therefore have to be prepared for this and be able to answer any questions the court may ask (PD 23A, para 2.9). The procedural judge will keep, by way either of a note or a tape recording, brief details of all proceedings, including a short statement of the decision taken at each hearing (PD 23A, para 8).

23.59 In most courts applications are given specific hearing times, and are called in one at a time. The main exceptions are judge's applications in the Chancery Division. For these the judge sitting has a discretion as to the order in which applications are heard. However, urgent applications and applications affecting the liberty of the subject are given priority, followed by ineffective applications (those which are to be adjourned or have settled), then effective applications usually in order of their time estimates, with the shortest applications being heard earliest. Applications estimated for more than two hours are usually made applications by order.

Resolving disputes on the written evidence

The general rule is that at interim hearings the procedural judge has to accept the veracity **23.60** of the written evidence filed by the parties. Where there is a conflict between the written evidence relied upon by opposing sides, there are four alternative approaches that may be adopted by the court:

(a) leave the resolution of the conflict until trial. As stated in *Shyam Jewellers Ltd v Cheesman* (2001) LTL 29/11/01, choosing between witnesses is the function of the trial judge. This means that the dispute is usually resolved in favour of the claim going to trial, or in favour of refusing relief that depends on disputed facts, or in favour of preserving the status quo;

(b) order the cross-examination of the disputed witnesses at the interim hearing under CPR, r 32.7. This power is rarely used because it involves delay and additional expense;

(c) go behind a disputed witness statement. This is done where there is some inherent improbability being asserted or where there is extraneous evidence contradicting it. It has also been held that it is permissible for the judge to disregard the written evidence if it is incredible (*National Westminster Bank plc v Daniel* [1993] 1 WLR 1); or

(d) determine the disputed issue (without rejecting the evidence as incredible) applying the standard of proof laid down for the specific procedure, or the fall-back position of a 'good arguable case' (*Re H Minors (Sexual Abuse): Standard of Proof* [1996] AC 563; *Bols Distilleries v Superior Yacht Services Ltd* [2007] 1 WLR 12). The good arguable case standard of proof is a lower test than the trial standard of proof, which is on the balance of probabilities. It is intended to reflect the limitations in deciding between competing versions inherent in an interim hearing with written evidence, and the need to avoid applications degenerating into mini-trials (*WPP Holdings Italy SRL v Benatti* [2007] 1 WLR 2316). It is completely contrary to principle to require proof on the balance of probabilities on an interim application (*Energy Venture Partners Ltd v Malabu Oil and Gas Ltd* [2015] 1 WLR 2309, Tomlinson LJ at [53]).

In choosing between these options the court will apply the overriding objective. In this context **23.61** this includes avoiding interim applications becoming mini-trials, and finding the best way of resolving the dispute commensurate with its importance and not prejudicing either side.

Non-attendance

The court may proceed in the absence of any party to an application (CPR, r 23.11(1)). **23.62** When this happens the court has a general discretion to relist the application, which is exercised by taking into account factors such as the reasons for the absence, the interests of justice, any undue delay since the missed hearing, whether either party has acted on the order, and whether there is a real prospect of the court changing the order (*Riverpath Properties Ltd v Brammall* (2002) *The Times*, 16 February 2002).

H SUMMARY DETERMINATION OF INTERIM COSTS

23.63 Where an interim application is disposed of in less than a day (which will cover the vast majority of such applications), the court will normally make a summary assessment of the costs of the application immediately after making its order (PD 44, para 9.2). This is considered in more detail at 46.52. To assist the judge in summarily assessing costs the parties are required by PD 44, para 9.5, to file and serve not less than 24 hours before the interim hearing signed statements of their costs for the interim hearing in form N260.

I VARYING OR REVOKING INTERIM ORDERS

23.64 A power under the CPR to make an order includes a power to vary or revoke the order (r 3.1(7)). Upholding the finality of decisions, avoiding giving litigants a second bite of the cherry, and supporting the appeals system all point towards a restrictive approach to applications under r 3.1(7). *Tibbles v SIG plc* [2012] 1 WLR 2591 therefore held that a court will normally only vary or revoke an earlier order if the application is made promptly and either:

(a) there has been a material change of circumstances; or
(b) the facts on which the original order was made were misstated; or
(c) there was a manifest mistake on the part of the judge in formulating the original order.

23.65 *Tibbles v SIG plc* was approved by the Supreme Court in *Thevarajah v Riordan* [2016] 1 WLR 76, where it was held that late compliance with an unless order (for which see 37.15) after the deadline had expired was not a material change of circumstances. *Thevarajah v Riordan* also decided at [18] that the *Tibbles v SIG plc* criteria apply both to express applications to vary or revoke an earlier order, and to applications which effectively require an earlier order to be varied or rescinded.

KEY POINTS SUMMARY

23.66
- Interim applications without notice are exceptional, and are broadly restricted to urgent applications and applications made before a defendant has been served with the main proceedings.

- Applications are made by issuing an application notice (N244), and have to be supported by written evidence.

- If an application is made without notice, the applicant has a duty of full and frank disclosure.

- A respondent (or non-party) who is unhappy with an order made without notice can apply to the judge who made the order to set aside or vary the terms of the order.

- In the High Court, and particularly in the Chancery Division and Commercial Court, there are obligations to provide application bundles, skeleton arguments, chronologies, and reading lists.

- Summary assessment of costs is normally undertaken in interim applications lasting up to one day.

24

SUMMARY JUDGMENT

A TIME FOR APPLYING FOR SUMMARY
JUDGMENT 24.03

B DEFENDANT'S APPLICATION:
NO DEFAULT JUDGMENT. 24.08

C EXCLUDED PROCEEDINGS 24.09

D PROCEDURE .24.10

E ORDERS AVAILABLE 24.14

F AMENDMENT AT HEARING 24.49

G SOME OTHER COMPELLING
REASON FOR A TRIAL. 24.50

H DIRECTIONS ON SUMMARY
JUDGMENT HEARING 24.51

I SPECIFIC PERFORMANCE,
RESCISSION, AND FORFEITURE IN
PROPERTY CASES. 24.52
Key points summary 24.53

In cases where the defendant fails to defend it is usually possible to enter a default judg-   **24.01**
ment (see Chapter 13). Where there is no real defence, a defendant may go through the
motions of defending in order to delay the time when judgment may be entered. It is possible for defendants to put up the pretence of having a real defence to such an extent that
some cases run all the way through to trial before judgment can be entered. The CPR provide several ways of preventing this happening. The court can use its power to strike out
(see Chapter 30) to knock out hopeless defences, such as those that simply do not amount
to a legal defence to a claim. Entering summary judgment is a related procedure, and is
used where a purported defence can be shown to have no real prospect of success and there
is no other compelling reason why the case should be disposed of at trial. Indeed, PD 3A,
para 1.7, recognizes that there will be cases where applications for summary judgment and
striking out may be sought in the alternative. In *Clancy Consulting Ltd v Derwent Holdings Ltd* [2010] EWHC 762 (TCC) the court struck out certain paragraphs in a defence
that consisted of bare denials, and granted summary judgment on the parts struck out.

The procedure for entering summary judgment is not limited to use by claimants against   **24.02**
defendants. Defendants may apply for summary judgment to attack weak claims brought
by claimants. Further, summary judgment can be used by the court of its own initiative to
perform the important function of stopping weak cases from proceeding. The procedure
can also be used for the purpose of obtaining a summary determination of some of the
issues in a case, thereby reducing the complexity of the trial.

A TIME FOR APPLYING FOR SUMMARY JUDGMENT

A claimant may apply for summary judgment only after the defendant has filed either an   **24.03**
acknowledgment of service or a defence (CPR, r 24.4(1)). By analogy with r 25.2(2)(c), a
defendant likewise can apply for summary judgment only after either filing an acknowledgment of service or a defence. Where the claimant has failed to comply with a relevant
pre-action protocol, an application for summary judgment will only be entertained after
the period for filing a defence has expired (PD 24, para 2(6)).

24.04 Applications for summary judgment should normally be made in the period between acknowledgment of service and filing of the applicant's directions questionnaire (PD 26, para 5.3(1)). This is normally the appropriate time, because, if the other side has no realistic prospects of success, entering summary judgment early prevents unnecessary costs being incurred. Question D1 in the directions questionnaire (see form 15.1) specifically asks whether an application for summary judgment is pending. If for any reason the application is not made before allocation, there is still a general obligation to apply as soon as it becomes apparent that it is desirable to do so (PD 23A, para 2.7).

Before filing the defence

24.05 If the application is made after filing an acknowledgment of service, but before filing of the defence, there is no need to file a defence before the hearing (CPR, r 24.4(2)). At that stage the court will give directions, which will include providing a date for filing the defence.

Before allocation to a track

24.06 Paragraph 5.3(2) of PD 26 provides that where a party makes an application for summary judgment before the claim has been allocated to a track the court will not allocate the claim before hearing the application. If a party files a directions questionnaire stating an intention to apply for summary judgment but has not yet made an application, the judge will usually direct the listing of an allocation hearing (para 5.3(3) and (4)). The summary judgment application may be heard at the allocation hearing if the application notice has been issued and served in sufficient time.

Hearings fixed by the court of its own initiative

24.07 The rules specifically mention that the court may fix a summary judgment hearing of its own initiative (CPR, r 24.4(3)), and doing so may further the overriding objective, which includes deciding promptly which issues need full investigation and trial, and accordingly disposing summarily of the others (r 1.4(2)(c)). If the court is minded to make use of this power, it is most likely to do so on the initial scrutiny at the track allocation stage shortly after filing of the defence. If the court uses the power, it will not allocate the case to a track, but instead it will fix a hearing, giving the parties 14 days' notice and informing them of the issues it proposes to decide (PD 26, para 5.4).

B DEFENDANT'S APPLICATION: NO DEFAULT JUDGMENT

24.08 Where a defendant has applied for summary judgment against a claimant, the claimant cannot obtain a default judgment until the summary judgment application has been disposed of (CPR, r 12.3(3)(a)).

C EXCLUDED PROCEEDINGS

24.09 Under CPR, r 24.3(2), an application for summary judgment cannot be brought against the defendant in:

(a) residential possession proceedings against a mortgagor or a tenant or person holding over whose occupancy is protected by the Rent Act 1977 or the Housing Act 1988; or

(b) admiralty claims *in rem*.

In applications against claimants there are no excluded types of proceedings (CPR, r 24.3(1)).

D PROCEDURE

The general rules on making interim applications (see Chapter 23) apply on making an application for summary judgment, with certain refinements. The application is made by application notice (see form 24.1), which must be supported by evidence (CPR, r 25.3(2)). The evidence in support is most likely to be contained either on page 2 of the application notice, or in a separate witness statement. It is a risky course to rely on facts set out in a statement of case without more detailed witness statement evidence, particularly in support of an alleged oral agreement (*Korea National Insurance Corporation v Allianz Global Corporate and Specialty AG* [2007] 2 CLC 748). The evidence in support of an application by a claimant will have to state a belief that there is no defence with a reasonable prospect of success and should give details of the background facts and exhibit relevant documentation. On an application by the defendant there may or may not be a filed defence. If not, clearly the evidence will have to explain why the claim is unlikely to succeed, and will probably have to go into the background in some detail. **24.10**

Instead of the usual notice period of three clear days which applies to most types of interim application, the notice period in applications for summary judgment is 14 clear days (r 24.4(3)). The respondent must file and serve any evidence in reply at least seven clear days before the hearing (r 24.5(1)). The application notice must inform the respondent of this time limit (PD 24, para 2(5)). If the applicant wishes to respond to the respondent's evidence, the further evidence must be served and filed at least three clear days before the hearing of the application (r 24.5(2)). The 14-day period of notice may be varied by practice directions (r 24.4(4)) and has been shortened for specific-performance claims (see 24.52). **24.11**

In cases where the hearing is fixed by the court on its own initiative, all parties must file and serve their evidence at least seven clear days before the return day, and if they want to respond to their opponents' evidence, that must be done at least three clear days before the return day (r 24.5(3)). **24.12**

On an application by a claimant for summary judgment, the court cannot in effect reverse the tables on the claimant and dismiss the claim under PD 24, para 5.1, without the claimant being put on notice (usually through a cross-application) and being given an opportunity to address the court and place before it any relevant material (*P&O Nedlloyd BV v Arab Metals Co (No 2)* [2007] 1 WLR 2288). **24.13**

E ORDERS AVAILABLE

Range of orders

Orders available on a summary judgment application include: **24.14**

(a) giving judgment on the claim;
(b) striking out or dismissal of the claim;
(c) dismissal of the application;
(d) making a conditional order; and
(e) granting summary judgment subject to a stay of execution.

Form 24.1 Application for Summary Judgment

N244

Application notice

For help in completing this form please read the notes for guidance form N244Notes.

Name of court HIGH COURT, QBD	Claim no.
Fee account no. (if applicable)	**Help with Fees – Ref. no.** (if applicable)
	H W F – ☐☐☐ – ☐☐☐
Warrant no. (if applicable)	
Claimant's name (including ref.) SECURE BANK PLC	
Defendant's name (including ref.) LANDMARK TRADERS GRIMSTEAD LIMITED	
Date	

1. What is your name or, if you are a legal representative, the name of your firm?

   Messrs Pamsons

2. Are you a   ☐ Claimant   ☐ Defendant   ☑ Legal Representative

   ☐ Other *(please specify)*

   If you are a legal representative whom do you represent?   Claimant

3. What order are you asking the court to make and why?

   Summary Judgment in favour of the Claimant under CPR, Part 24, for £394,450.95 and interest and costs. Because the Claimant believes the Defendant has no real prospect of successfully defending this claim and the Claimant knows of no other compelling reason why the case should be disposed of at a trial.

4. Have you attached a draft of the order you are applying for?   ☐ Yes   ☑ No

5. How do you want to have this application dealt with?   ☑ at a hearing   ☐ without a hearing

   ☐ at a telephone hearing

6. How long do you think the hearing will last?   1 Hours   00 Minutes

   Is this time estimate agreed by all parties?   ☑ Yes   ☐ No

7. Give details of any fixed trial date or period   None

8. What level of Judge does your hearing need?   Master

9. Who should be served with this application?   Defendant

9a. Please give the service address, (other than details of the claimant or defendant) of any party named in question 9.

Form 24.1 *continued*

10. What information will you be relying on, in support of your application?

     ☑ the attached witness statement

     ☐ the statement of case

     ☐ the evidence set out in the box below

If necessary, please continue on a separate sheet.

TAKE NOTICE that if the Defendant wishes to rely on written evidence, it must file the written evidence at court and serve copies on the Claimant's solicitors at least 7 days before the summary judgment hearing.

Statement of Truth

(I believe) (The applicant believes) that the facts stated in this section (and any continuation sheets) are true.

Signed _____   Dated _____
     Applicant('s legal representative)('s litigation friend)

Full name _____

Name of applicant's legal representative's firm _____

Position or office held _____
(if signing on behalf of firm or company)

---

11. Signature and address details

Signed _____   Dated _____
     Applicant('s legal representative's)(~~'s litigation friend~~)

Position or office held   Partner _____
(if signing on behalf of firm or company)

Applicant's address to which documents about this application should be sent

Messrs Pamsons 18 High Street London	If applicable	
	Phone no.	0207 566 9010
	Fax no.	0207 566 9446
	DX no.	436456 City 2
Postcode E C 1 A 6 F B	Ref no.	47466/LJB

E-mail address	ljbaker@pamsons.com

Test for entering summary judgment

24.15   Rule 24.2 of the CPR provides:

> The court may give summary judgment against a claimant or defendant on the whole of a claim or on a particular issue if—
>
> (a) it considers that—
>
>> (i)   that claimant has no real prospect of succeeding on the claim or issue; or
>> (ii) that defendant has no real prospect of successfully defending the claim or issue; and
>
> (b) there is no other compelling reason why the case or issue should be disposed of at a trial.

Burden of proof

24.16   Although CPR, r 24.2 is not explicit about the burden of proof on an application for summary judgment, it appears to be settled by *ED and F Man Liquid Products Ltd v Patel* [2003] CPLR 384, that the burden rests on the applicant to prove that the respondent's case has no real prospects of success.

Standard for entering summary judgment

24.17   An application for summary judgment is decided applying the test of whether the respondent has a case with a real prospect of success, which is considered having regard to the overriding objective of dealing with the case justly. The question whether there is a real prospect of success is not approached by applying the balance of probabilities standard of proof required at trial (*Royal Brompton Hospital NHS Trust v Hammond* [2001] BLR 297). At the other end of the range, applying a test of whether the claim is arguable will also give grounds for appeal because this is too lax (*Sinclair v Chief Constable of West Yorkshire* (2000) LTL 12/12/00). In order to have a real prospect of success a case has to carry some degree of conviction, and has to be better than merely arguable (*Bee v Jenson* [2007] RTR 9).

24.18   In *Swain v Hillman* [2001] 1 All ER 91, Lord Woolf MR said that the words 'no real prospect of succeeding' did not need any amplification as they spoke for themselves. The word 'real' directed the court to the need to see whether there was a realistic, as opposed to a fanciful, prospect of success. The phrase does not mean 'real and substantial' prospect of success. Nor does it mean that summary judgment will be granted only if the claim or defence is 'bound to be dismissed at trial'. If the defendant's evidence, taken at its highest, shows a distinctly improbable defence, it is right to enter summary judgment (*Akinleye v East Sussex Hospitals NHS Trust* [2008] LS Law Med 216). Lord Woolf MR went on to say in *Swain v Hillman* that summary judgment applications have to be kept within their proper role. They are not meant to dispense with the need for a trial where there are issues which should be considered at trial. Nor is summary judgment suitable for cases that depend on second- or third-hand evidence (*Radiocomms Systems Ltd v Radio Communications Systems Ltd* [2010] EWHC 149 (Ch)). If the respondent's case has some prospects of success, summary judgment should be refused (*Cotton v Rickard Metals Inc* [2008] EWHC 824 (QB)).

Defence on the merits

24.19   On an application for summary judgment by a claimant, the defendant may seek to show a defence with a real prospect of success by setting up one or more of the following:

(a) a substantive defence, for example *volenti non fit injuria*, frustration, illegality, etc.;
(b) a point of law destroying the claimant's cause of action;
(c) a denial of the facts supporting the claimant's cause of action;

(d) tender before action (for which, see CPR, r 37.2(1), and *Ayton v RSM Bentley Jennison* [2016] 1 WLR 1281), or payment of the amount claimed; or

(e) further facts answering the claimant's cause of action, for example an exclusion clause, or that the defendant was an agent rather than a principal.

Weak defences

Most summary judgment applications are decided on the basis of the facts which are **24.20** not disputed by the respondent, together with the respondent's version of the disputed facts (*HRH Prince of Wales v Associated Newspapers Ltd* [2008] Ch 57). This does not mean that filing a witness statement will prevent summary judgment being entered. This is because there are, as discussed at 23.60, cases where the court will go behind written evidence which is incredible, and the court will also disregard fanciful claims and defences. A claim or defence may be fanciful where it is entirely without substance, or where it is clear beyond question that the statement of case is contradicted by all the documents or other material on which it is based (*Three Rivers District Council v Bank of England (No 3)* [2003] 2 AC 1). There is no rule of practice that summary judgment cannot be given if a case is weak despite there being some documentary evidence in support (*Miller v Garton Shires* [2007] RTR 24). The judge should take into account the filed witness statements and also consider whether the case is capable of being supplemented by evidence at trial (*Royal Brompton Hospital NHS Trust v Hammond* [2001] BLR 297).

In *United Bank Ltd v Asif* (2000) LTL 11/2/00, CA, the court considered the defence put **24.21** forward, and decided it was fanciful and no more than a sham, and so summary judgment was entered. This might be the case where there are no primary facts to support the alleged defence (*P & S Amusements Ltd v Valley House Leisure Ltd* [2006] EWHC 1510 (Ch)). There may be no real prospect of success if the defence consists entirely of admissions and bare denials (*Broderick v Centaur Tipping Services Ltd* (2006) LTL 22/8/06). In *Penningtons v Abedi* (1999) LTL 13/8/99 there had been ongoing litigation in which the defendant had advanced a series of defences which had each been shown to be false. An application was made for summary judgment, and it was held that the defendant's conduct of the litigation was such that there was no realistic prospect of her successfully defending the claim. In *ED and F Man Liquid Products Ltd v Patel* [2003] CPLR 384, a defence which might have had a real prospect of success was destroyed by clear, written admissions made by the defendant.

In *Public Trustee v Williams* (2000) LTL 10/2/00 the claimant, as executor of a deceased's **24.22** estate, sought to recover the sum of £74,000 which was received by one of the defendants and used by her to buy a house. The evidence of the recipient filed in response to an application for summary judgment was at its best unclear and at its worst confusing about where she thought the money had come from. However, there was no clear evidence that the money had come from the estate, and it was held that it was not a suitable case for summary judgment. A stronger case was *Architects of Wine Ltd v Barclays Bank plc* [2007] 2 Lloyd's Rep 471. In this case the key issue was a matter of banking practice, and the burden of proof as a matter of substantive law on that issue rested on the defendant bank. It was held that, where the only evidence on a summary judgment application on that issue was the bank's own evidence of its practices, it was impossible to say that the bank had no real prospect of success in its defence, so summary judgment was refused.

Mini-trials

Summary judgment hearings should not be allowed to degenerate into mini-trials of dis- **24.23** puted facts (*Cotton v Rickard Metals Inc* [2008] EWHC 824 (QB)). They are simply summary hearings to dispose of cases where there is no prospect of success. Without allowing the application to become a mini-trial, there are occasions when the court has to consider fairly voluminous evidence before it can understand whether there is a real prospect of success (*Miles v ITV Networks Ltd* (2003) LTL 8/12/03), provided this will not require prolonged argument (*Three Rivers District Council v Bank of England (No 3)* [2003] 2 AC 1, see 24.26).

Negligence claims

24.24 Although there is nothing in principle preventing a claimant from applying for summary judgment in claims seeking damages for negligence, such cases invariably involve disputed factual issues, so it is rare for a court to find there is no real defence once liability is denied. An exception was *Dummer v Brown* [1953] 1 QB 710, where summary judgment was given against the defendant, a coach driver, who had previously pleaded guilty to dangerous driving in respect of the accident giving rise to the claim. Even if there is a conviction summary judgment may be refused if there are good reasons for believing that the conviction was erroneous (*McCauley v Vine* [1999] 1 WLR 1997).

Claims involving reprehensible conduct

24.25 Summary judgment will almost always be inappropriate where there are allegations of deceitful, dishonest, or unlawful conduct (*Espirit Telecoms UK Ltd v Fashion Gossip Ltd* (2000) LTL 27/7/00). The critical attention to the evidence required at trial in fraud claims means that it will be difficult to succeed on a summary judgment application in such a case (*Allied Dunbar Assurance plc v Ireland* (2001) LTL 12/6/01).

Contract claims, complex claims, and points of law

24.26 Complex claims, cases relying on complex inferences of fact, and cases with issues involving mixed questions of law and fact where the law is complex, are likely to be inappropriate for summary judgment (*Three Rivers District Council v Bank of England (No 3)* [2003] 2 AC 1; *Arkin v Borchard Lines Ltd (No 2)* (2001) LTL 19/6/01). Summary disposal is also inappropriate if the case is in a developing field of law (*Brooks v Commissioner of Police of the Metropolis* [2005] 1 WLR 1495 at [3]). The simpler the case, the easier it is for the court to find the claim or defence to be fanciful or contradicted by the documentary evidence.

24.27 Where a clear-cut issue of law is raised by way of defence in an application for summary judgment, the court should decide it immediately. This is so even if the question is, at first blush, of some complexity and therefore will take some time to argue fully (see Lord Greene MR in *Cow v Casey* [1949] 1 KB 474). Not deciding a case once full argument has been addressed to the court on the issue will result in the case going to trial where the argument will be rehearsed again, with consequent delay and unnecessary expense. Likewise, where the point at issue is one of the construction of contractual documents, the court will decide the point on the summary judgment application, provided it is relatively straightforward (*Coastal (Bermuda) Ltd v Esso Petroleum Co Ltd* [1984] 1 Lloyd's Rep 11).

24.28 A short point on whether a term can be implied into a contract may also be suitable for summary judgment (*Omega SA v Omega Engineering Inc* [2011] EWCA Civ 645). Although CPR, r 24.2, expressly says that the court can give summary judgment on particular issues, the court may consider that where there are connected issues, some of which should go to trial, summary judgment should be refused on the others as well (*Redevco Properties v Mount Cook Land Ltd* (2002) LTL 30/7/02).

Partial defence

Where the defendant has a defence to only part of the claim the most natural order is to **24.29** grant judgment for the part of the claim against which there is no defence, and to dismiss the application as to the balance.

Cross-claims

Cross-claims fall into three categories. Where the only answer to the claim is a cross-claim, **24.30** the nature and effect of the three types are as follows:

(a) Cross-claims unconnected with the claim. Here, summary judgment should be entered. An example is *Rotherham v Priest* (1879) 41 LT 558, where the claimant claimed arrears of rent, and the defendant counterclaimed in libel. It was held that the counterclaim was totally foreign to the claim, so summary judgment was given to the claimant. The result would be the same under the CPR.

(b) Counterclaims linked to the claim. The appropriate order is to enter judgment subject to a stay of execution pending trial of the counterclaim. In *Drake and Fletcher Ltd v Batchelor* (1986) 130 SJ 285, Sir Neil Lawson said that in considering whether to grant a stay of execution, 'the question is whether the two contracts are so closely linked that it would be fair and equitable to deprive the [claimant] of the fruits of its judgment until resolution of the counterclaim'. The judge said there were three matters which needed to be considered:

  (i) The degree of connection between the claim and the counterclaim.

  (ii) The strength of the counterclaim. The weaker it was, the weaker the case for granting a stay.

  (iii) The claimant's ability to satisfy any judgment on the counterclaim. Any doubt on this matter strengthened the case for granting a stay.

(c) Set-offs. Where a counterclaim amounts to a set-off it is a defence to the claim and any summary judgment application should be dismissed, provided the value of the set-off is at least equal to the value of the claim. Where a set-off is not worth as much as the claim, the appropriate order is for summary judgment for the undisputed balance. An unquantified set-off is no defence (*Eilon and Associates Ltd v IP Licensing Ltd* (2011) LTL 15/4/11). The nature of set-offs is considered in Chapter 14.

The cheque rule

Cheques are one form of bill of exchange. Where goods or services are paid for by cheque, **24.31** two contracts are entered into by the parties. The first contract is the underlying contract for the sale of goods or for the provision of services. The second contract is contained in the cheque, whereby the drawer of the cheque undertakes to pay the payee the sum stated. If a cheque is dishonoured, the seller has the option of suing on the underlying contract or on the cheque. If the seller sues on the underlying contract, the buyer is entitled to rely on any set-off that may be available in respect of that contract by way of defence to an application for summary judgment. However, if the seller sues on the cheque, the buyer is permitted to raise only limited defences on an application for summary judgment. The reason probably stems from the unconditional nature of a bill of exchange, as provided by the Bills of Exchange Act 1882, s 3(1). As Lord Wilberforce said in *Nova (Jersey) Knit Ltd v Kammgarn Spinnerei GmbH* [1977] 1 WLR 713, bills of exchange 'are taken as equivalent to deferred instalments of cash'. Therefore English law does not allow unliquidated crossclaims or defences to be made. The rule is regarded as being of considerable importance to the business community, and the courts will not 'whittle away [the] rule of practice by introducing unnecessary exceptions to it under influence of sympathy-evoking stories' (*per* Sachs LJ in *Cebora SNC v SIP (Industrial Products) Ltd* [1976] 1 Lloyd's Rep 271). The cheque rule applies to:

(a) cheques and bills of exchange;
(b) direct debits (*Esso Petroleum Co Ltd v Milton* [1997] 1 WLR 938);
(c) letters of credit (*SAFA v Banque du Caïre* [2000] 2 All ER (Comm) 567); and
(d) performance bonds (*Solo Industries v Canara Bank* [2001] 2 All ER (Comm) 217).

24.32 The cheque rule does not prevent a defendant raising a liquidated cross-claim as a defence. Nor does it apply in the context of statutory demands (*Hofer v Stawson* [1999] 2 BCLC 336, for which see the Insolvency (England and Wales) Rules 2016 (SI 2016/1024)).

24.33 There are some exceptional cases where summary judgment will not be given where the defendant raises an unliquidated cross-claim and certain defences (see 24.36–24.41). Before looking at these it is necessary to consider the nature of the claimant's title to the bill of exchange.

Types of holder of a bill of exchange

24.34 Under the Bills of Exchange Act 1882 there are four types of holder of a bill of exchange. A mere holder is a person in possession of the bill. Although a mere holder can sue on the bill and give a valid discharge (s 38), any claim is prone to be defeated for want of consideration. A holder for value is a person in possession of a bill who has given consideration sufficient to support a simple contract, or who derives title directly or indirectly from a previous holder who gave value for the bill (s 27). A holder for value cannot be defeated on the ground of want of consideration. A holder in due course is broadly a holder of a complete and regular bill who gave value for it in good faith without notice of any defect in the title of the person who negotiated it (s 29). A holder in due course obtains title to the bill free from equities and defects in the title of the transferor. The fourth type of holder is one who derives title through a holder in due course, and who broadly has all the rights of a holder in due course (s 29(3)).

24.35 An application for summary judgment by a mere holder will always be defeated by a plea of want of consideration, whereas an application by a holder in due course should always succeed as such a holder takes free of equities. If the claimant's title as a holder in due course is challenged by the defendant, judgment will be given for the claimant only if the claim to be a bona fide holder for value is supported by unchallenged or unchallengeable contemporary documents (*Bank für Gemeinwirtschaft AG v City of London Garages Ltd* [1971] 1 WLR 149). Holders for value are the most problematic category. They are also the most numerous, given that an immediate party to a bill cannot be a holder in due course (*RE Jones Ltd v Waring and Gillow Ltd* [1926] AC 670).

Fraud, duress, and illegality

24.36 To amount to a defence against a holder for value, an allegation of fraud, duress, or illegality must be supported by evidence. A mere allegation in the defendant's written evidence is insufficient (*Bank für Gemeinwirtschaft AG v City of London Garages Ltd* [1971] 1 WLR 149). Such a defence will not, however, avail against a holder in due course (see the Bills of Exchange Act 1882, s 30(2)).

No consideration

24.37 As explained earlier, there will be a defence where the claimant is a mere holder who has given no consideration for the bill sued on. A total failure of consideration arises where a buyer lawfully rejects goods sold, the buyer being entitled to recover the price from the seller. Again summary judgment should be refused. Likewise, a liquidated partial failure of consideration is a defence *pro tanto* (*Thoni GmbH & Co KG v RTP Equipment Ltd* [1979] 2 Lloyd's Rep 282).

Misrepresentation

A misrepresentation made to induce the defendant to give a cheque will be a defence to a **24.38** claim on the cheque, but an allegation that the claimant made a misrepresentation about the quality of the subject matter of the underlying contract (eg the goods in a sale of goods) will not be a defence to a claim on a cheque. Following *SAFA v Banque du Caïre* [2000] 2 All ER (Comm) 567 and *Solo Industries v Canara Bank* [2001] 2 All ER (Comm) 217, a distinction needs to be drawn between:

(a) cases where there is a misrepresentation by a beneficiary which was made directly to induce the execution of the bill of exchange (or other payment obligation covered by the cheque rule). Provided there is a real prospect of establishing the misrepresentation, summary judgment on the cheque (or other payment obligation) should be refused; and

(b) cases where an allegation of misrepresentation is in reality an allegation relating to the underlying contract of services or sale on which the payment obligation is based. In these cases summary judgment should be entered on the cheque (or other payment obligation), with no stay of execution. The courts need to be particularly astute in ensuring the cheque rule is not diluted by treating cases in this category as ones affecting the cheque or other payment obligation covered by the cheque rule.

International trade

Irrevocable letters of credit are treated as cash and must be honoured. If the bank **24.39** refuses to honour such a transaction, the court will grant summary judgment to the claimant (*Power Curber International Ltd v National Bank of Kuwait SAK* [1981] 1 WLR 1233). Summary judgment will also be given on a claim for freight even if there is a cross-claim relating to the cargo (*Aries Tanker Corporation v Total Transport Ltd* [1977] 1 WLR 185).

Performance bonds

A bank which gives a performance bond must honour that obligation according to its **24.40** terms. The bank cannot rely on issues relating to the relations between the supplier and the customer, nor whether the supplier has performed its obligations, nor with any question of whether the supplier is in default. The bank must pay according to its guarantee, on demand if so stipulated, without proof or conditions. The only exception is where there is clear fraud of which the bank has notice at the date when payment was due (*Edward Owen Engineering Ltd v Barclays Bank International Ltd* [1978] QB 159 at 171).

The fraud exception applies where there is clear evidence both of the fraud and the **24.41** bank's knowledge. There must be a real prospect on the material available that the only realistic inference is that the beneficiary could not have honestly believed in the validity of its demand on its performance bond (*United Trading Corporation SA v Allied Arab Bank Ltd* [1985] 2 Lloyd's Rep 554n as interpreted by *Solo Industries UK Ltd v Canara Bank* [2001] 1 WLR 1800 at [32]). In applying this test the court must be careful not to upset what is in effect a strong presumption in favour of fulfilment of the bank's obligation under a performance guarantee (*Czarnikow-Rionda Sugar Trading Inc v Standard Bank London Ltd* [1999] 1 All ER (Comm) 890 at 913). The effect is that there is a

heightened test in relation to the fraud exception in an application for summary judgment against a bank (*Banque Saudi Fransi v Lear Siegler Services Inc* [2007] 1 All ER
(Comm) 67 at [16]). Conversely, in an application for summary judgment by a bank
which has honoured a performance bond against a person who has given the bank
a counter-indemnity, the normal 'real prospect of success' test applies (*Banque Saudi
Fransi v Lear Siegler Services Inc* at [18]).

Summary judgment on admissions

24.42 Admissions made by the other side may be relied upon in support of an application
for summary judgment. Obviously, if a claim, or an important issue in a claim, is
admitted there may be no real prospect of success in any filed defence. The nature of
admissions, and the circumstances in which they may be retracted, are considered at
34.02–34.09.

Conditional orders

24.43 Paragraph 4 of PD 24 provides that, where it appears to the court possible that a claim or
defence may succeed but improbable that it will do so, the court may make a conditional
order. Paragraph 5.2 provides that a conditional order is an order which requires a party:

(a) to pay a sum of money into court; or
(b) to take a specified step in relation to his claim or defence, as the case may be, and which
provides that that party's claim will be dismissed or his statement of case will be struck
out if he does not comply.

Where money is paid into court in compliance with a conditional order, the claimant is
a secured creditor for that amount in the event of the defendant's bankruptcy (*Re Ford*
[1900] 2 QB 211).

24.44 Conditional orders are appropriate for cases in the grey area between granting judgment and dismissing the application. For example, in *Homebase Ltd v LSS Services
Ltd* (2004) LTL 28/6/04, the claimant made a claim against the defendant seeking five
months' licence fees for occupying a site. The defendant filed a witness statement to the
effect that the claimant had orally agreed that the defendant need pay nothing until
the claimant had obtained consent from its landlord to assign the land to the defendant. The claimant denied there was any such agreement. A conditional order was made
because, although the defendant's story was not incredible (which would have resulted
in judgment for the claimant), its story was unlikely and was not supported by any contemporaneous documents.

24.45 If the court decides to make the respondent to the application pay money into court under
a conditional order, it must decide how much should be paid in. The starting point has
traditionally been the full amount of the claim. However, the court has a discretion, which
it will exercise in accordance with the overriding objective. Obviously, the more uncertain the defence, the more likely it is that the court will order the full amount to be paid
in. Another factor is the defendant's ability to pay. Lord Diplock in *MV Yorke Motors v
Edwards* [1982] 1 WLR 444 endorsed the following principles:

(a) Defendants seeking to limit a financial condition must make full and frank disclosure of their finances. This is done on affidavit or witness statement. It is common for
defendants who realize that a conditional order may be made to produce such written
evidence in advance of the summary judgment hearing, and to disclose it to the claimant on the claimant undertaking not to refer to it unless a conditional order is made.

(b) Reliance on a public funding certificate as evidence of impecuniosity is not enough.

(c) The test is whether it will be impossible for the defendant to comply with the financial condition, as opposed to merely finding it difficult. An impossible condition is tantamount to entering judgment.

MV Yorke Motors were suing Mr Edwards for breach of warranty of title in relation to a **24.46** contract for the sale of a car for £23,520. An order equivalent to a conditional order was made, because the court was sceptical about his defence that he was acting only as the agent for a foreign buyer. By the time of the hearing Mr Edwards was unemployed, living with his father, and in receipt of legal aid with a nil contribution. The House of Lords substituted a condition of bringing £3,000 into court.

The defendant should be given an opportunity to produce evidence as to means. A claimant **24.47** may need to give advance notice that such an order is to be sought if summary judgment is not ordered, or an adjournment may be necessary (*Anglo-Eastern Trust Ltd v Kermanshahchi* [2002] EWCA Civ 198).

Summary judgment subject to a stay of execution

Summary judgment subject to a stay of execution has the effect that the claimant has won **24.48** the case, but will not be paid until some other event, such as the trial of a counterclaim, when the stay will be lifted. It may be ordered where there is a counterclaim (not amounting to a set-off) which is linked to the claim (see 24.30(b)). More generally, such an order may be appropriate where there is some unresolved matter which may mean it is unjust for payment to be required immediately. This may arise where the party required to make the payment may not be able to recover its money, for example where there is a substantial risk of the claimant becoming insolvent (*Mead General Building Ltd v Dartmoor Properties Ltd* [2009] BCC 510).

F AMENDMENT AT HEARING

There are many cases where the defective nature of one side's statement of case becomes **24.49** clear at the hearing of an application for summary judgment. If the defect is one of how the case is put rather than of substance, the court has a wide power to allow an amendment to correct the problem, which can be exercised at the hearing (*Stewart v Engel* [2000] 1 WLR 2268). A defendant seeking to avoid summary judgment being entered on an admission has to issue an application for permission to amend, otherwise the court is entitled to enter judgment on the unamended statement of case (*Loveridge v Healey* [2004] EWCA Civ 173).

G SOME OTHER COMPELLING REASON FOR A TRIAL

Summary judgment will be refused if there is some other compelling reason why the case **24.50** should be disposed of at a trial (CPR, r 24.2(b)). Seeking an adjournment to negotiate with the claimant was not regarded as compelling in *Phonographic Performance Ltd v Planet Ice (Peterborough) Ltd* (2003) LTL 2/2/04. Reasons for going to trial include:

(a) The respondent is unable to contact a material witness who may provide material for a defence.

(b) The case is highly complicated such that judgment should be given only after mature consideration at trial.

(c) The facts are wholly within the applicant's hands. In such a case it may be unjust to enter judgment without giving the respondent an opportunity of establishing a defence in the light of disclosure or after serving a request for further information (*Harrison v Bottenheim* (1878) 26 WR 362). However, summary judgment will not necessarily be refused in cases where the evidence for any possible defence could only lie with the applicant if there is nothing devious or artificial in the claim (*State Trading Corporation of India v Doyle Carriers Inc* [1991] 2 Lloyd's Rep 55).

(d) The applicant has acted harshly or unconscionably, or the facts disclose a suspicion of dishonesty or deviousness on the part of the applicant, such that judgment should be obtained only in the light of publicity at trial. An example is *Miles v Bull* [1969] 1 QB 258, where possession proceedings had the appearance of a device to evict the defendant.

H DIRECTIONS ON SUMMARY JUDGMENT HEARING

24.51 If a summary judgment application is dismissed or otherwise fails finally to dispose of the claim, the court will give case management directions for the future conduct of the case (PD 24, para 10), which may include directions for filing and service of a defence (CPR, r 24.6), and may dispense with directions questionnaires and allocate the case to a case management track (PD 26, para 2.4).

I SPECIFIC PERFORMANCE, RESCISSION, AND FORFEITURE IN PROPERTY CASES

24.52 An even speedier process for obtaining summary judgment is available by virtue of PD 24, para 7, in claims for specific performance and similar claims arising out of mortgage and tenancy agreements. Summary judgment in these cases can be sought at any time after the claim is served, rather than having to wait until after acknowledgment or defence, and the application can be made even in the absence of particulars of claim. The application notice, evidence in support, and a draft order must be served no less than four clear days before the hearing.

KEY POINTS SUMMARY

24.53
- Summary judgment applications can be made by either party or by the court.
- The test is whether the respondent has a case with a real prospect of success, or if there is some compelling reason for having a trial.
- Default judgment is for cases where the defendant does not respond. Summary judgment is for cases where the defendant does respond, and one side believes there is not much merit in the other side's case.
- Summary judgment applications are dealt with on the basis of written evidence, and, if successful, result in judgment without a trial, which is why the test is so stringent.

25

INTERIM PAYMENTS

A PROCEDURE 25.04
B GROUNDS 25.07
C AMOUNT TO BE ORDERED 25.17
D FURTHER APPLICATIONS. 25.23

E NON-DISCLOSURE 25.24
F ADJUSTMENT .25.25
Key points summary 25.26

An order for interim payment is defined in CPR, r 25.1(1)(k) as an order for payment of a sum **25.01** of money by a defendant on account of any damages, debt, or other sum (except costs) which the court may hold the defendant liable to pay. Such orders are likely to be made in claims where it appears that the claimant will achieve at least some success, and where it would be unjust to delay, until after the trial, payment of the money to which the claimant appears to be entitled. The purpose behind this procedure is to alleviate the hardship that may otherwise be suffered by claimants who may have to wait substantial periods of time before they recover any damages in respect of wrongs they may have suffered. In addition to providing resources to the claimant, making an interim payment will sometimes enable the claimant to pay for treatment, or to save assets which would otherwise be lost, or to have an asset repaired earlier than might otherwise be the case, and may thereby reduce the amount of the claim. Further, making an early interim payment will reduce the defendant's liability to pay interest.

Cases on the small claims track are unlikely to be large enough to justify the expense of **25.02** applications for interim payments, and small claims and fast track cases, unless delayed, are likely to proceed to final hearing with such speed that there will be little point in making an application, unless the hearing results in a judgment for damages to be assessed. Most applications for interim payments are therefore likely to be made in multi-track cases (or cases likely to be allocated to the multi-track when track allocation is considered).

There is nothing to prevent the parties agreeing to a voluntary interim payment, and these are **25.03** quite common in cases where liability is not in dispute but where quantum is still being investigated. However, the permission of the court must be obtained if a voluntary interim payment is being considered where the claimant is a person under disability (PD 25B, para 1.2).

A PROCEDURE

An application for an order for an interim payment cannot be made until the period for filing **25.04** an acknowledgment of service has expired (CPR, r 25.6(1)). Applications are made on notice, and must be served at least 14 clear days before the hearing of the application. Applications must be supported by evidence which must be served with the application. Paragraph 2.1 of PD 25B provides that the evidence in support should set out all relevant matters including:

(a) the amount sought by way of interim payment;
(b) what the money will be used for;

(c) the likely amount of money that will be awarded;

(d) the reasons for believing the relevant ground (see 25.07ff) is satisfied;

(e) in a personal injuries claim, details of special damages and past and future loss; and

(f) in a claim under the Fatal Accidents Act 1976, details of the persons on whose behalf the claim is made and the nature of the claim.

25.05 All relevant documents in support should be exhibited. In personal injuries claims these will include the medical reports.

25.06 Respondents who wish to rely on witness statements in reply must file and serve their evidence at least seven clear days before the hearing. In personal injuries claims the respondent will need to obtain a certificate of recoverable benefits from the Secretary of State under the Social Security (Recovery of Benefits) Act 1997, which is needed for the purposes of framing the order. If the applicant wants to respond to the respondent's evidence, any further evidence must be filed and served at least three clear days before the return day (CPR, r 25.6(4) and (5)).

B GROUNDS

General conditions

25.07 The conditions which must be satisfied before an interim payment order can be made are set out in CPR, r 25.7. Under r 25.7(1), an interim payment may be ordered only if:

(a) the defendant has admitted liability to pay damages or some other sum of money to the claimant (r 25.7(1)(a)); or

(b) the claimant has obtained judgment against the defendant for damages or some other sum (other than costs) to be assessed (r 25.7(1)(b)); or

(c) the court is satisfied that, if the claim went to trial, the claimant would obtain judgment against the defendant from whom the interim payment is sought for a substantial amount of money (other than costs) (r 25.7(1)(c)); or

(d) the claimant is seeking possession of land, and the court is satisfied that if the case went to trial the defendant would be held liable to pay the claimant a sum of money for use and occupation of the land while the claim is pending (r 25.7(1)(d)); or

(e) the claim is brought against more than one defendant, and the further conditions set out in 25.08–25.10 are satisfied (r 25.7(1)(e)).

These categories are comprehensive, and there is no other basis on which an interim payment can be ordered (*Quest Advisors Ltd v McFeely* [2011] EWCA Civ 1517).

Multiple defendants

25.08 Applications for interim payments where there is more than one defendant, but it is clear the claimant has a very strong case against one identified defendant, are usually dealt with under r 25.7(1)(c). Provided there is a sufficiently strong case on the merits against an identified defendant, it does not matter under r 25.7(1)(c) that there are other defendants named in the proceedings.

25.09 Rather more frequently, particularly where defendants are sued in the alternative, a claimant may be able to persuade a court on an application for an interim payment that a claim against multiple defendants will succeed, but cannot identify which of the defendants will lose. In such a case the claimant can rely on r 25.7(1)(e). This allows a court to make an interim payment order where:

(a) there are two or more defendants;

(b) the court is satisfied that if the claim went to trial the claimant would obtain judgment for a substantial sum of money (other than costs) against at least one of the defendants against whom the interim payment is sought (*Berry v Ashtead Plant Hire Co Ltd* [2012] PIQR P6);

(c) the court cannot determine under r 25.7(1)(c) which of the defendants will lose; and

(d) all the defendants are either insured, public bodies, or are defendants whose liability will be met by an insurer under the Road Traffic Act 1988, s 151, or an insurer acting under the Motor Insurers' Bureau Agreement or by the Motor Insurers' Bureau itself.

The requirement under r 25.7(1)(e) that all the defendants must be insured, etc., means that **25.10** if it transpires that an interim payment has been ordered against a defendant who later avoids liability at trial, it should be possible to make effective adjustments (see 25.25) so that the defendants who are found liable (or their insurers) will reimburse those ordered to make the interim payment.

Standard of proof

On an application under CPR, r 25.7(1)(c), (d), or (e) (see 25.07), the court has to be **25.11** satisfied on the balance of probabilities that the claimant 'would' obtain judgment, and for a substantial amount of money (*Test claimants in the FII Group Litigation v Revenue and Customs Commissioners* [2012] 1 WLR 2375). Being likely to succeed at trial is not enough. A 'substantial amount of money' means substantial as opposed to negligible, and has to be considered in the context of the claim.

Relationship with summary judgment

It is quite common to combine applications for summary judgment with applications for **25.12** interim payments. Summary judgment is available where the defence has no real prospect of success, and interim payments are available where the claimant can show that liability will be established. Obviously these are similar concepts. Further, on the summary judgment application the court may make a 'relevant order' (PD 26, para 12.1) entering judgment for damages to be assessed, which would itself provide grounds for making an order for an interim payment. Another possibility is that the court may make a conditional order on the summary judgment application, with the condition being compliance with an interim payment order.

It is questionable whether it is possible to make an interim payment order if a summary **25.13** judgment application is unsuccessful. As summary judgment will be given unless the defence has a real prospect of success, there can be no doubt that if summary judgment is refused it would be inconsistent for the court then to decide that the claimant 'would' succeed so as to give grounds for an interim payment. There is even a little doubt about whether making an interim payment order can be consistent with making a conditional order, because if the defence is on the border of having a real prospect of success (the situation where conditional orders are appropriate), it is difficult to see how the court can simultaneously find that the claimant will win for the purposes of making an interim payment order.

Effect of counterclaims and defences

When deciding on an order for interim payment the court 'must take into account' any **25.14** relevant set-off or counterclaim and any contributory negligence (CPR, r 25.7(5)). From the context of this provision it clearly applies at the second stage of an interim payment application when the court is considering the amount to be ordered by way of an interim payment. Counterclaims and allegations of contributory negligence with reasonable prospects of success obviously affect the likely amount of the final judgment. Rule 25.7(5), however, has no express restriction to quantum. Unlike unconnected cross-claims, set-offs are also defences. Consequently, the existence of a set-off with a reasonable prospect of success should also be taken into account at the first stage when the court is considering the grounds for granting an interim payment, and may prevent the court being satisfied that the claimant will obtain judgment for the purposes of r 25.7(1)(c). See *Shanning International Ltd v George Wimpey International Ltd* [1989] 1 WLR 981.

25.15 Where there is a counterclaim worth less than the claim an interim payment may be appropriate. In *O2 (UK) Ltd v Dimension Data Network Services Ltd* (2007) LTL 8/11/07 summary judgment on a claim for unpaid telephone services was refused as there was a real prospect that a defence of overcharging and a counterclaim might succeed. However, the court found that the defendant was bound to have to pay something for the services provided by the claimant, and an interim payment was made on that basis.

Discretion

25.16 Even if the claimant establishes a ground for making an interim payment, the court retains a discretion whether to make an order. In one of the old cases (*British and Commonwealth Holdings plc v Quadrex Holdings Inc* [1989] QB 842) it was said that the court may take into account the respondent's lack of means either in refusing to make an order or in fixing its amount.

C AMOUNT TO BE ORDERED

Reasonable proportion of total award

25.17 The court is not permitted to order an interim payment of more than a reasonable proportion of the likely amount of any final judgment, taking into account any contributory negligence and any relevant set-off or counterclaim (CPR, r 25.7(4) and (5)). The correct approach is to find the likely overall award, then apply a discount for any contributory negligence (or counterclaim), and then reduce the amount again to arrive at a suitable 'reasonable proportion'. The judge is obliged to make an actual assessment, and is not permitted to take short-cuts such as basing the interim payment on offers made by the defendant (*Eeles v Cobham Hire Services Ltd* [2010] 1 WLR 409). A reasonable proportion may well be a high proportion, provided the assessment of the likely final award is conservative. The objective is to avoid making an overpayment. In *Spillman v Bradfield Riding Centre* [2007] EWHC 89 (QB) the judge deducted 25 per cent as the 'reasonable proportion' from the overall likely award in order on the facts of the case.

25.18 There is a standard interim payment of £1,000 under both the RTA protocol (para 7.13) and the EL/PL protocol (para 7.12), and of £50,000 in mesothelioma cases where the defendant fails to show cause on all issues (PD 3D, paras 2 and 6.7).

Need for the interim payment

25.19 Paragraph 2.1(2) of PD 25B, which says the evidence in support of the application must deal with the items or matters in respect of which the interim payment is sought, could be misinterpreted as meaning that interim payments should be made only for purchases the claimant needs to make. This idea was rejected under the old rules for commercial claims

(*Schott Kem Ltd v Bentley* [1991] 1 QB 61), personal injury claims (*Stringman v McArdle* [1994] 1 WLR 1653), and under the CPR by *Wade v Turfrey* (2007) LS Law Medical 352. Where the interim payment is limited to an advance payment out of the damages alleged to have been suffered to the date of the application the judge should not be influenced by how the claimant may intend to spend any interim payment (*Eeles v Cobham Hire Services Ltd* [2010] 1 WLR 409).

Information on what the claimant intends to use the money for may assist the court on **25.20** why the money is needed urgently, or in deciding how much to order. However, the court is not concerned with how a claimant of full capacity spends a final award in damages, and should not try to prescribe what an interim payment is spent on either. Despite the general principle, the rule in *Stringman v McArdle* must not be applied in a mechanistic way. There are cases where the intended use of the money may be relevant because the payment may prejudice the trial or the position of the defendant in the proceedings or prejudge an issue to be determined at the trial (*Tinsley v Sarker* (2004) LTL 23/7/04). Where the interim payment is sought in order to pay for future expenses, it is essential to establish a real need for the money, and an award will be made only if the judge can confidently predict that the trial judge will wish to award a capital sum greater than past special damages and damages for pain, suffering, and loss of amenity (*Eeles v Cobham Hire Services Ltd*).

Certificate of State benefits

In personal injuries claims the defendant will need to obtain a certificate of recoverable **25.21** benefits from the Secretary of State under the Social Security (Recovery of Benefits) Act 1997. A copy of the certificate should be filed at the hearing, and any order made must set out the amount by which the payment to be made to the claimant has been reduced in accordance with the Act and the Social Security (Recovery of Benefits) Regulations 1997 (SI 1997/2205) (PD 25B, paras 4.1–4.4).

Payment by instalments

Rule 25.6(7) of the CPR allows an interim payment order to require payment by instal- **25.22** ments. Where this happens, the order should set out the total amount of the interim payment, the amount of each instalment, the number of instalments and the date they are to be paid, and to whom the payments should be made (PD 25B, para 3).

D FURTHER APPLICATIONS

The claimant is permitted to make more than a single application for an interim payment **25.23** (CPR, r 25.6(2)). In practice, a second or subsequent application will have to be justified by a change in circumstances or other cause being shown, such as an increase in the special damages claim through additional loss of income or expenses being incurred, or through unforeseen delays in determining the claim.

E NON-DISCLOSURE

The fact that a defendant has made an interim payment must not be disclosed to the trial **25.24** judge until all questions of liability and quantum have been determined (CPR, r 25.9), unless the defendant agrees. This is important, as the trial judge may (unwittingly) be influenced by knowing that the court has previously decided that the claimant will win, and that the claim is worth more than the amount of the interim payment. In advance of trial a request should be made to the court office to remove all references to interim payments from the court file to avoid accidental disclosure to the trial judge. Where a claimant (usually through ignorance) does disclose this information prematurely, the judge may abort the trial and consider making a wasted costs order against the lawyer responsible.

F ADJUSTMENT

25.25 The court has powers to order all or part of an interim payment to be repaid, to vary or discharge an interim payment order, and to order a co-defendant to reimburse a defendant who has made an interim payment (provided the defendant who made the interim payment has claimed a contribution, indemnity, or other remedy against the co-defendant being ordered to reimburse) (CPR, r 25.8). Interest may be ordered in favour of the defendant on any overpaid interim payment. These powers are usually exercised, if at all, at trial. Paragraph 5 of PD 25B contains detailed rules on recording the effect of interim payments and any order for adjustment on the final award for damages.

KEY POINTS SUMMARY

25.26
- An interim payment provides the claimant with money on account of the likely award at trial.
- Different grounds for applying for interim payments are set out at 25.07.
- The amount ordered must not exceed a reasonable proportion of the likely final award taking into account any counterclaim and contributory negligence.

26

SECURITY FOR COSTS

A PROCEDURE 26.04

B THE RESPONDENT 26.06

C CONDITIONS FOR GRANTING
 SECURITY FOR COSTS 26.09

D DISCRETION TO ORDER SECURITY
 FOR COSTS. 26.20

E AMOUNT 26.31

F ORDER 26.33

G SUCCESS BY THE CLAIMANT 26.35
 Key points summary 26.36

Generally, the question of who pays for the costs of a claim is not determined until the claim **26.01** is finally disposed of, whether by consent, interim process, or trial. This is because the usual rule is that the successful party recovers costs from the loser and the outcome on the merits is known only when judgment is obtained. It is for this reason that the parties are not generally allowed to anticipate the eventual costs order by asking for interim orders that their opponents provide funds as security to pay for the costs of the claim. Despite this, it is accepted that there have to be exceptions for cases where there is a significant risk of defendants suffering the injustice of having to defend proceedings with no real prospect of being able to recover costs if they are ultimately successful. An order for security for costs does not infringe the European Convention on Human Rights, art 6(1), although the right of access to the courts has to be taken into account: *Nasser v United Bank of Kuwait* [2002] 1 WLR 1868.

An order for security for costs can be made only against a party in the position of a claimant. **26.02** Once security is given it may be retained, subject to the court's discretion, pending an appeal. An order for security for costs usually requires the claimant to pay money into court as security for the payment of any costs order that may eventually be made in favour of the defendant, and staying the claim until the security is provided. On the application three matters arise:

(a) whether one of the conditions for ordering security for costs is satisfied;
(b) if so, whether, having regard to all the circumstances of the case, it would be just to exercise the court's discretion in favour of making the order; and
(c) if so, how much security should be provided.

Each of these three matters will be considered after first looking at the procedure for mak- **26.03** ing the application and the capacity of the respondent to the application.

A PROCEDURE

The first application for security should normally be made at the first case management **26.04** conference (see *Commercial Court Guide*, app 10, para 1). It is made using the usual Part 23 procedure of issuing an application notice (see form 26.1) supported by written evidence. The written evidence should deal with the grounds on which security is sought, and with any factors relevant to the exercise of the court's discretion. These include the location of the claimant's assets, and any practical difficulties in enforcing any order for costs (see

Form 26.1 Application for Security for Costs

N244

Application notice

For help in completing this form please read the notes for guidance form N244Notes.

Name of court HIGH COURT, QBD		Claim no.
Fee account no. (if applicable)	Help with Fees – Ref. no. (if applicable)	
	H W F – ☐☐☐ – ☐☐☐	
Warrant no. (if applicable)		
Claimant's name (including ref.) CASPKEELER PRODUCTS LIMITED		
Defendant's name (including ref.) LOAMER TECHTRONICS LIMITED		
Date		

1. What is your name or, if you are a legal representative, the name of your firm?

   Messrs Pamsons

2. Are you a ☐ Claimant ☐ Defendant ☑ Legal Representative

   ☐ Other *(please specify)*

   If you are a legal representative whom do you represent? Defendant

3. What order are you asking the court to make and why?

   1 Claimant do give security for the Defendant's costs because the Claimant is a company and there is reason to believe it will be unable to pay the Defendant's costs if ordered to do so
   2 The claim to be stayed pending provision of such security. 3 Claimant to pay the Defendant's costs.

4. Have you attached a draft of the order you are applying for? ☐ Yes ☑ No

5. How do you want to have this application dealt with? ☑ at a hearing ☐ without a hearing

   ☐ at a telephone hearing

6. How long do you think the hearing will last? 2 Hours 30 Minutes

   Is this time estimate agreed by all parties? ☑ Yes ☐ No

7. Give details of any fixed trial date or period — None

8. What level of Judge does your hearing need? — Master

9. Who should be served with this application? — Claimant

9a. Please give the service address, (other than details of the claimant or defendant) of any party named in question 9.

Commercial Court Guide, app 10, para 3). It also needs to include an estimate of the defendant's likely costs of defending the claim, which should usually be given in the same form of statement of costs as is used for summary assessments and exhibited to the written evidence.

Invariably the application should be made on notice to the claimant, and should be served **26.05** on the claimant at least three clear days before the day appointed for hearing the application (CPR, r 23.7(1)(b)). Applications for security for costs will be inappropriate in cases on the small claims track because of the restrictions on the recovery of costs in these claims. Applications for further security or to vary the terms on which security is given may be made as circumstances change during the course of a claim.

B THE RESPONDENT

An order for security for costs can be made only against a party acting as a claimant (CPR, **26.06** r 25.12(1)). This means that security for costs can be ordered against a defendant who counterclaims against a claimant. However, with regard to counterclaims, a distinction needs to be drawn between simple counterclaims, where it is possible to obtain orders for security against defendants (*Hutchison Telephone (UK) Ltd v Ultimate Response Ltd* [1993] BCLC 307), and set-offs, where it has been held that security will not usually be ordered: *Neck v Taylor* [1893] 1 QB 560. The reason for this distinction is that a set-off, if established, amounts to a defence to the claim, so a defendant raising a set-off is for this purpose regarded as simply defending and not as advancing a claim.

A defendant who issues an additional claim form stands in the position of a claimant with **26.07** regard to the third party, so may be ordered to provide security for the third party's costs. However, the original claimant does not stand in the position of a claimant with regard to a third party brought in by the original defendant, unless, as a result of directions given in the additional claim, the third party is ordered to defend jointly with the original defendant (*Taly NDC International NV v Terra Nova Insurance Co Ltd* [1985] 1 WLR 1359 *per* Parker LJ). The question is one of capacity in the main action. There is therefore no jurisdiction to order a defendant to provide security for the costs of any interim application it may make: *Taly NDC International NV v Terra Nova Insurance Co Ltd*.

Security for costs may be ordered against any party in the position of a claimant, even if **26.08** not strictly a 'claimant'. An example is a petitioner on an unfair prejudice petition under the Companies Act 2006, s 994: *Re Unisoft Group Ltd (No 1)* [1993] BCLC 1292. Another example is an appellant to an appeal (or a respondent who cross-appeals): see CPR, r 25.15. By r 25.14, an order for security for costs may also be made against someone other than a claimant if the court is satisfied that the person against whom the order is sought either:

(a) assigned the claim to the claimant with a view to avoiding the possibility of being ordered to pay costs; or
(b) has contributed or agreed to contribute to the claimant's costs in return for a share of any money or property which the claimant may recover in the proceedings.

C CONDITIONS FOR GRANTING SECURITY FOR COSTS

Security for costs can be ordered only if one of the conditions set out in CPR, r 25.13(2), **26.09** is satisfied. The conditions are:

(a) the claimant is—
   (i) resident out of the jurisdiction; but
   (ii) not resident in a Brussels Contracting State, a state bound by the Lugano Convention, a state bound by the 2005 Hague Convention, or a Regulation State, as defined in section 1(3) of the Civil Jurisdiction and Judgments Act 1982 . . .

(c) the claimant is a company or other body (whether incorporated inside or outside Great Britain) and there is reason to believe that it will be unable to pay the defendant's costs if ordered to do so;

(d) the claimant has changed his address since the claim was commenced with a view to evading the consequences of the litigation;

(e) the claimant failed to give his address in the claim form, or gave an incorrect address in that form;

(f) the claimant is acting as a nominal claimant, other than as a representative claimant under Part 19, and there is reason to believe that he will be unable to pay the defendant's costs if ordered to do so;

(g) the claimant has taken steps in relation to his assets that would make it difficult to enforce an order for costs against him.

26.10 By a combination of CPR, r 3.1(2)(f) and (3)(a) the court has a power to make an order equivalent to providing security for costs in a number of situations. These include granting security for costs as a sanction for breach of directions (*Olatawura v Abiloye* [2003] 1 WLR 275 and see Chapter 37); or as a conditional order on an application for summary judgment (*Allen v Bloomsbury Publishing plc* [2011] FSR 22; and see 24.43); or as a condition on setting aside a default judgment (see 13.40); or in relation to an appeal (*Shlaimoun v Mining Technologies International Inc* [2012] EWCA Civ 772). None of these situations should be regarded as a less onerous route to obtaining an order for security for costs, and the court must still bear in mind the principles in rr 25.12 and 25.13 before making such an order (*Huscroft v P&O Ferries* [2011] 1 WLR 939).

Resident outside the jurisdiction

26.11 Residence is determined by the claimant's habitual or normal residence, as opposed to any temporary or occasional residence (see *Lysaght v Commissioners of Inland Revenue* [1928] AC 234, a tax case, and *R v Barnet London Borough Council, ex p Shah* [1983] 2 AC 309, a case on entitlement to a grant for education, as applied in *Parkinson v Myer Wolff* (23 April 1985, unreported), a case on security for costs). The question is one of fact and degree, and the burden of proof is on the defendant. An English merchant seaman should not be regarded as ordinarily resident abroad, nor should someone who intends to emigrate until he or she has left the country: *Appah v Monseu* [1967] 1 WLR 893. A foreign business person who makes regular visits to England would probably be regarded as resident abroad, but there will come a point, through the length of time spent in this country and other factors, such as owning a house here, when ordinary residence will be established.

26.12 Although most companies reside in the country where they are incorporated, strictly they reside where their central control and management are. This is a question of fact. In *Re Little Olympian Each Ways Ltd* [1995] 1 WLR 560 Lindsay J identified the following as matters to be considered: the contents of the company's objects clause, its place of incorporation, where its real trade or business is carried on, where its books are kept, where its administrative work is done, where its directors meet or reside, where it 'keeps house', where its chief office is situated, and where its secretary resides.

26.13 The wording of CPR, r 25.13(2)(a)(ii) was altered to take into account *De Beer v Kanaar & Co* [2003] 1 WLR 38 and it means that security for costs can be ordered where the claimant is resident in a jurisdiction outside the scope of the Judgments Regulation and the Lugano Convention, even if the claimant has assets within a Convention State.

26.14 Security for costs may be ordered where there are joint claimants, some of whom are resident outside the jurisdiction. According to Lord Donaldson of Lymington MR in *Corfu Navigation Co v Mobil Shipping Co Ltd* [1991] 2 Lloyd's Rep 52 the basic principle underlying CPR, r 25.13(2)(a), is that it is *prima facie* unjust for a foreign claimant, who is in practical terms almost immune from the enforcement of any costs order that may be made, to be allowed to proceed with a claim without making funds available within the jurisdiction against which such an order can be enforced. It would, however, be appropriate to refuse to order security where it is probable that each of the joint claimants will be held to be liable for all the defendant's costs if the action is unsuccessful, provided the English claimants are likely to be able to pay those costs (*Winthorp v Royal Exchange Assurance Co* (1755) 1 Dick 282 as explained in *Slazengers Ltd v Seaspeed Ferries International Ltd* [1987] 1 WLR 1197 and in the light of *Corfu Navigation Co v Mobil Shipping Co Ltd*). Conversely, security may well be ordered where the English claimants are joined for the purpose of defeating an application for security (*Jones v Gurney* [1913] WN 72), or where it is impossible to predict the likely outcome on costs, or where each claimant is likely to be liable for only a portion of the defendant's costs: *Slazengers Ltd v Seaspeed Ferries International Ltd* [1987] 1 WLR 1197; [1988] 1 WLR 221.

Impecunious company

Impecuniosity is no ground for ordering security for costs against an individual claimant, **26.15** the principle being that individuals should not be prevented from seeking justice through want of means. Companies, being artificial persons, need no such protection. Ground (c) applies to limited companies registered under the Companies Acts, and also unlimited companies, companies with a single member (*Jirehouse Capital v Beller* [2009] 1 WLR 751), and other corporations.

The defendant has the burden of proving that a claimant company will be unable to pay **26.16** any costs that ultimately may be awarded in the defendant's favour. Proof that the company is in liquidation is *prima facie* evidence that it will be unable to pay any costs order: *Northampton Coal, Iron and Waggon Co v Midland Waggon Co* (1878) 7 ChD 500. Otherwise, what is now CPR, r 25.13(2)(c) requires credible testimony of the company's inability to pay. This obviously requires a comparison between the company's assets and the likely costs. Inability to pay may be inferred from evidence that the claimant has declared unusually large dividends after the dispute arose: *Frost Capital Europe Ltd v Gathering of Developers Inc Ltd* (2002) LTL 20/6/02.

Nominal claimant

Typical attributes of a nominal claimant include having no personal connection with the **26.17** claim (other than legal title to bring the proceedings), no role in raising the funds to finance the litigation, and no interest in the final outcome (*Allen v Bloomsbury Publishing plc* (2011) LTL 18/3/11). An element of duplicity is normally required. Being a trustee, executor, or personal representative (even without also being a beneficiary) does not make the claimant nominal (*Chuku v Chuku* [2017] 1 WLR 3137).

Taking steps to avoid enforcement

Under CPR, r 25.13(2)(g), security for costs may be ordered where the claimant has taken **26.18** steps in relation to his assets to make it more difficult to enforce an order for costs. There is no need under this paragraph to show that steps were taken with a view to making enforcement more difficult: the test is objective, and motive is irrelevant (*Bush v Bank Mandiri (Europe) Ltd* (2014) LTL 11/2/14). Thus, in *Aoun v Bahri* [2002] 3 All ER 182 security for costs was ordered because the claimant had sold his home in Australia, which made it objectively more difficult to enforce a costs order against him, even though there was no evidence that this was done with a view to avoiding paying costs.

Security for costs of appeals

By virtue of CPR, r 25.15, the court may order security for costs against an appellant in **26.19** respect of the costs of the appeal on the same grounds as security may be ordered against a claimant under r 25.13. The rule only applies once permission to appeal (see 50.18) has been granted (*Kevythalli Design v ICE Associates* [2010] EWCA Civ 379). Likewise, a respondent who cross-appeals may be ordered to provide security for the costs of the cross-appeal.

D DISCRETION TO ORDER SECURITY FOR COSTS

26.20 Once it has been established that the case comes within one of the conditions set out in 26.09, the court has a general discretion whether to grant an order for security. In exercising this discretion the court will have regard to all the circumstances of the case, and consider whether it would be just to make the order (CPR, rr 25.13(1)(a) and 25.14(1)(a)).

Pre-CPR principles

26.21 There is a conflict in the Court of Appeal authorities on the extent to which it is appropriate to consider the pre-CPR cases on the exercise of the discretion to award security for costs. This reflects the wider conflict on whether the introduction of the CPR has achieved its objective of making a new start based on the fact it was a new procedural code (see 4.19 and 4.20). One view, exemplified by *Nasser v United Bank of Kuwait* [2002] 1 WLR 1868, is that the substantial body of pre-CPR case law is consigned to history. On this basis, the discretion has to be exercised applying the overriding objective, and by affording a proportionate protection against the difficulty identified by the ground relied upon as justifying security for costs in the case in question.

26.22 Other cases, such as *Vedatech Corporation v Seagate Software Information* (2001) LTL 29/11/01, expressly apply pre-CPR principles, particularly those laid down in *Sir Lindsay Parkinson & Co v Triplan Ltd* [1973] QB 609. In that case Lord Denning MR said the following factors are relevant when the court is exercising its discretion whether to order security for costs:

(a) Whether the claim is bona fide and not a sham. Factors to be taken into account on this are:
  (i) whether the claimant has reasonably good prospects of success;
  (ii) whether the defendant has made any admissions in its statement of case or elsewhere; and
  (iii) whether there has been a substantial offer to settle (as opposed to a small offer to get rid of a nuisance claim).
(b) Whether the defendant is using the application for security oppressively so as to stifle a genuine claim.
(c) Delay in making the application.

Prospects of success

26.23 There is no doubt that the prospect of success at trial is one of the matters that may sometimes be taken into account on the application. If this is taken too far, an application for security may be blown up to an investigation similar to a trial. In a passage approved by the Court of Appeal in *Trident International Freight Services Ltd v Manchester Ship Canal Co* [1990] BCLC 263, Browne-Wilkinson V-C in *Porzelack KG v Porzelack (UK) Ltd* [1987] 1 WLR 420 said at 423:

> Undoubtedly, if it can clearly be demonstrated that the [claimant] is likely to succeed, in the sense that there is a very high probability of success, then that is a matter that can properly be weighed in the balance. Similarly, if it can be shown that there is a very high probability that the defendant will succeed, that is a matter that can be weighed. But for myself I deplore

the attempt to go into the merits of the case, unless it can clearly be demonstrated one way or another that there is a high degree of probability of success or failure.

If there is no defence to the claim, it will almost certainly be unjust to order security. In such **26.24** a case the defendant is highly unlikely to recover costs in any event, and ordering security often has the practical effect of preventing the claimant from proceeding with the claim.

Stifling a genuine claim

The question of stifling a genuine claim is a corollary to the question whether the claim- **26.25** ant's claim is a sham. The essential policy is that the need to protect the defendant has to yield to the claimant's right of access to the courts to litigate the dispute if it is a genuine claim: *Hamilton v Al Fayed (No 2)* [2003] QB 1175, a case on costs orders against non-parties, where the importance of the European Convention on Human Rights, art 6(1), was stressed. Where the claimant's claim has a good chance of success (there being no need for anything higher), the court will hesitate before making an order which will have the practical effect of preventing the claimant from proceeding. If the case is one where the court feels that security should be ordered, it can fix the amount of the security at a level which will not stifle the claimant in proceeding further: *Innovare Displays plc v Corporate Broking Services Ltd* [1991] BCC 174. It is for the company to establish, on the balance of probabilities, that the funds to pay the security will not be made available to it, whether by a major shareholder or some other closely related person, taking into account the separate legal personality of a company (*Goldtrail Travel Ltd v Onur Air Tasimacilik AS* [2017] 1 WLR 3014). For this purpose, the court does not have to take at face value protestations by the company that no funds will be made available, particularly where a wealthy owner has in the past provided funds when required.

Delay in applying

Applications for security for costs should be made at an early stage in the proceedings. **26.26** Lateness may of itself be a reason for refusing an order. There have been cases where security has been refused because the application was made just a few days or even a few hours before the trial. An example is *Innovare Displays plc v Corporate Broking Services Ltd* [1991] BCC 174 where a reduced order was made on account of delay.

Resident outside the jurisdiction

Where security is sought against a claimant outside the Brussels and Lugano Convention **26.27** and Judgments Regulation States, the order should reflect the obstacles in the way of, or the costs of, enforcing an English judgment for costs against the particular claimant or in the particular country concerned: *Nasser v United Bank of Kuwait* [2002] 1 WLR 1868. It is the difficulty of enforcing in the place where the assets are likely to be, rather than enforcement in the country where the respondent happens to live, that has to be considered: *Aims Asset Management v Kazakhstan Investment Fund Ltd* (2002) LTL 22/5/02. Orders have been refused on account of the ease of enforcement in Monaco (*Somerset-Leeke v Kay Trustees* [2004] 3 All ER 406) and the British Virgin Islands (*Longstaff International Ltd v Baker and McKenzie* [2004] 1 WLR 2917). Having considered the evidence, according to *Texuna International Ltd v Cairn Energy Ltd* [2005] 1 BCLC 579, the court has to decide whether the claimant's country is:

(a) one where the obstacles to enforcement are so great that the claimant should be required to give security for the whole costs of the claim; or

(b) one where enforcement is simply more expensive than in England and Wales. In these cases the security should reflect the likely additional expense.

26.28 Since the effectiveness of enforcement is the most important consideration, the following factors need to be taken into account if present:

(a) Whether the claimant has substantial assets within the jurisdiction. If so this is a weighty factor against ordering security: *De Bry v Fitzgerald* [1990] 1 WLR 552. Assets within the jurisdiction include damages which the claimant hopes to recover in other proceedings: *Cripps v Heritage Distribution Corporation* (1999) *The Times*, 10 November 1999.

(b) The degree of permanence of those assets, and whether the claimant has a substantial connection with this country: *Leyvand v Barasch* (2000) *The Times*, 23 March 2000.

(c) The ability of the claimant to transfer assets around the world, as in *Berkeley Administration Inc v McClelland* [1990] 2 QB 407.

Impecunious company

26.29 The rationale behind ordering security against an impecunious company is to safeguard the defendant against the prospect of encountering real difficulty in enforcing any order for the costs of the claim. Megarry V-C in *Pearson v Naydler* [1977] 1 WLR 899 said, at 906:

> It is inherent in the whole concept of [CPR, r 25.13(2)(c)] that the court is to have power to order the company to do what it is likely to find difficulty in doing, namely to provide security for the costs which *ex hypothesi* it is likely to be unable to pay. At the same time, the court must not allow the [rule] to be used as an instrument of oppression, as by shutting out a small company from making a genuine claim against a large company.

26.30 The critical question is whether the company will be able to meet the costs order at the time when the order has to be paid (*Re Unisoft Group Ltd (No 2)* [1993] BCLC 532 at 534). The court must consider the nature and liquidity of the company's assets (*Longstaff International Ltd v Baker and McKenzie* [2004] 1 WLR 2917). It will also take into account whether the company's want of means has been brought about by any conduct by the defendant, such as, in a claim for breach of contract, delay in payment or the defendant's delay in performing its part of the contract (*Interoil Trading SA v Watford Petroleum Ltd* (2003) LTL 16/7/03).

E AMOUNT

26.31 *Procon (Great Britain) Ltd v Provincial Building Co Ltd* [1984] 1 WLR 557 establishes the principle that any security should be such as the court thinks just in all the circumstances. The amount should be neither illusory nor oppressive (*Hart Investments Ltd v Larchpark Ltd* [2008] 1 BCLC 589). In applications under r 25.13(2)(a) the amount is usually based on the additional costs of enforcing any judgment for costs in the overseas jurisdiction (*Relational LLC v Hodges* [2011] EWCA Civ 774). Applications based on the other grounds may result in security based on the total costs of defending the claim. It is usual to exhibit a summary statement of costs to the defendant's evidence in support. There is no rule of practice that the court will always reduce the defendant's estimate by a third (*Procon (Great Britain) Ltd v Provincial Building Co Ltd*), but it is usual to make a deduction from the defendant's costs estimate to take into account any likely reduction on assessment of costs, and also to make an arbitrary discount in respect of future costs to take account of the chances of settling.

As was mentioned at 26.25 and 26.26, relevant factors going to the court's discretion which **26.32** are in the claimant's favour, but which are not strong enough to deprive the defendant of an order for security, may be taken into account when deciding the amount of security to order. Thus, in *Innovare Displays plc v Corporate Broking Services Ltd* [1991] BCC 174, which was discussed at 26.25, the lateness of the application and the difficulty faced by the claimants in providing security were taken into account by ordering the claimants to provide security in the sum of £10,000 when the defendant's estimated costs were £147,000.

F ORDER

Orders for security for costs should follow form PF 44. It is usual to require security to **26.33** be given by payment into court, although bonds and guarantees are alternatives, as are solicitors' undertakings. Until security is given the claim will be stayed. If the claimant fails to provide security in compliance with the order, the defendant can apply for the claim to be struck out: *Speed Up Holdings Ltd v Gough and Co (Handly) Ltd* [1986] FSR 330. If security is provided the claim continues. After trial, the defendant, if successful, will have a secured fund from which its costs can be paid.

In the Commercial Court defendants are sometimes required to give undertakings in dam- **26.34** ages if security is ordered, and instead of ordering a stay it is more usual to give a time for providing the security with liberty to apply for dismissal of the claim in the event of default.

G SUCCESS BY THE CLAIMANT

In cases where the claimant is successful, normally the trial judge will accede to an applica- **26.35** tion on the claimant's behalf for the security money in court to be repaid to the claimant, or for the release of any other security. If the defendant wishes to appeal, however, the court has a discretion whether to impose a stay on the release of the security so as to provide continued security for the costs up to trial in the event that the defendant's appeal succeeds: *Stabilad Ltd v Stephens and Carter Ltd* [1999] 1 WLR 1201. In considering whether to impose such a stay, Auld LJ said that the fact that the claimant had succeeded at first instance was irrelevant. Factors to be considered were the risks of the claimant being unable to pay the costs to trial if the security was released, the claimant's need for the money provided as security for fighting the appeal, and the prospects of the appeal succeeding.

KEY POINTS SUMMARY

- An order for security for costs requires a claimant to provide a fund which can be used by the **26.36** defendant to pay its costs if it defeats the claim.
- Security for costs is only available against claimants and parties in the position of claimants.
- The main grounds for seeking security for costs are that the claimant is resident outside the EU; that it is a company in financial difficulties; or that the claimant has taken steps to avoid enforcement.
- If a ground is made out, the court retains a discretion to refuse security for costs.
- The court also has a wide discretion on the amount of security to be provided.

27

SMALL CLAIMS TRACK

A PROVISIONS OF THE CPR THAT
  DO NOT APPLY .27.03

B STANDARD DIRECTIONS 27.04

C SPECIAL DIRECTIONS 27.05

D DETERMINATION WITHOUT A HEARING 27.09

E FINAL HEARINGS 27.10

F COSTS 27.14

G REHEARINGS 27.16

27.01 In accordance with the principles set out in the overriding objective that cases should be dealt with proportionately to the amount at stake and to the importance of the case, the CPR provide for the allocation of claims with a limited financial value to what is known as the small claims track. This is intended to provide a streamlined procedure with limited pre-trial preparation, with very restricted rules on the recovery of costs from the losing party, and without the strict rules of evidence. It is appropriate for the most straightforward types of cases, such as consumer disputes, accident claims where the injuries suffered are not very serious, disputes about the ownership of goods, and landlord and tenant cases other than claims for possession. As discussed at 15.24, broadly, claims allocated to this track will be those with a value not exceeding £10,000.

27.02 Regulation (EC) No 861/2007 of 11 July 2007 established a European Small Claims Procedure. The Regulation (as amended) applies to cross-border cases in civil and commercial matters where the value of the claim does not exceed €5,000. Procedural rules for European Small Claims can be found in CPR, Part 78.

A PROVISIONS OF THE CPR THAT DO NOT APPLY

27.03 The idea behind having a small claims track is to provide a relatively inexpensive means of resolving disputes having a limited financial value. Some of the more sophisticated procedures available for larger claims are therefore inappropriate for cases on the small claims track, and do not apply (or do not apply in full) once a case has been allocated to the small claims track. These include:

(a) most interim remedies, except interim injunctions;

(b) standard disclosure of documents (a more limited form of disclosure applies: see 27.04);

(c) most of the rules on experts, in particular, no expert may give evidence, whether orally or in writing, in a small claims track case without the permission of the court (CPR, r 27.5);

(d) requests for further information can only be made by the court (r 27.2(3)); and

(e) Part 36 offers (because this would interfere with the no costs rule: see 27.14–27.15).

B STANDARD DIRECTIONS

A claim that would normally be allocated to the small claims track may instead be referred **27.04** for small claims mediation under CPR, r 26.4A, see 10.13. Once a case has been allocated to the small claims track the court will give directions, which are usually set out in the notice telling the parties that the case has been allocated to this track. A number of options are available to the court, but it is most likely that the court will give what are described as standard directions. Different forms of standard directions apply to different categories of small claims. However, the general form of standard directions provides for:

(a) the parties to serve on the other side copies of the documents they intend to rely upon no later than 14 days before the hearing;
(b) the original documents to be brought to the hearing;
(c) notice of the hearing date and the length of the hearing (a hearing fee is payable within 14 days of the notice);
(d) the parties to contact each other with a view to settling the dispute or narrowing the issues, with an obligation to inform the court if the dispute is settled; and
(e) informing the parties that expert evidence is not allowed without the court's express permission.

C SPECIAL DIRECTIONS

A District Judge allocating a claim to the small claims track may decide that standard direc- **27.05** tions will not ensure that the case is properly prepared, and may instead formulate special directions specifically for the case in hand. At the same time the District Judge may fix the date for the final hearing, or may list the matter for further directions. Alternatively, if the District Judge takes the view that it will be necessary to have a hearing with the parties present in court to ensure that they understand what they must do to prepare the case, or if the District Judge is minded to consider whether the claim should be struck out or summarily disposed of, the case will be listed for a preliminary hearing where these matters can be dealt with.

Special directions may include the exchange of witness statements. Criteria for deciding **27.06** whether to make such a direction are found in PD 27, para 2.5, which include the nature of the dispute, the amount claimed, and the policy of giving parties in small claims cases access to justice without undue formality.

The general rule in small claims track cases is that no expert evidence is allowed, **27.07** whether oral or in the form of a report. In return, the court will not always insist on the production of expert evidence, whereas it might be required for a similar case on one of the other tracks (*Bandegani v Norwich Union Fire Insurance Ltd* (1999) LTL 20/5/99, where the claimant did not produce expert evidence for the value of a car which had been damaged in an accident). If a party regards expert evidence as necessary, a special direction will be required, and this should be mentioned in the directions questionnaire.

Where witness statements or expert reports are used in small claims cases, they do not have **27.08** to comply with the strict rules on format discussed in Chapters 32 (witness statements) and 35 (experts), because the relevant provisions of the CPR are excluded from small claims cases by r 27.2(1). Expert evidence will be limited to the use of the expert's report unless calling the expert at the hearing is in the interests of justice (r 35.5(2)).

D DETERMINATION WITHOUT A HEARING

27.09　If all the parties agree, a small claim can be determined by the District Judge on the papers without a hearing (CPR, r 27.10). Consent is essential, because otherwise determination on the papers would infringe the European Convention on Human Rights, art 6(1), which lays down a right to a public hearing.

E FINAL HEARINGS

27.10　Final hearings in small claims track cases are usually dealt with by District Judges. Hearings are generally conducted in the judge's room rather than in one of the courtrooms.

27.11　The general intention is that parties should be able to represent themselves in small claims track cases. Corporate bodies may be represented by any of their officers or employees (PD 27, para 3.2(4)). There is nothing to stop a party being represented by a lawyer, and this is quite common in cases where one or both of the parties has the benefit of insurance. A party (including a company, see *Avinue Ltd v Sunrule Ltd* [2004] 1 WLR 634) may have a lay representative at the hearing, but generally only if the client also attends (Lay Representatives (Rights of Audience) Order 1999 (SI 1999/1225); PD 27, para 3.2(2)).

27.12　Small claims hearings are informal, and the strict rules of evidence do not apply (CPR, r 27.8). The District Judge may proceed in any way that is considered fair. The District Judge may ask the witnesses questions before allowing the parties to do so, may refuse to allow cross-examination until all the witnesses have given evidence-in-chief, and may impose limits on the scope of cross-examination. Unless the District Judge intervenes in one of these ways, the usual sequence of events is for the claimant's representative to make a short opening (just a few sentences) and then to call the claimant's evidence. Everyone will be sitting around the District Judge's table, so no one leaves his or her seat when this is being done. Each witness is questioned first on behalf of the claimant, then on behalf of the defendant. The District Judge makes a note of the evidence as it is given, and will ask questions as appropriate. There may be scope for some re-examination. Once all the claimant's evidence has been introduced, the claimant's representative says that is the case for the claimant. It is then the defendant's opportunity to call evidence. Once the defendant's evidence has been introduced, the defendant's representative will make some closing remarks. The claimant's representative's closing submissions come last.

27.13　The District Judge will usually give a short reasoned judgment there and then. The judgment is likely to be as short and simple as the nature of the case will allow. After giving judgment, the District Judge will consider the form of the order to be made and costs are considered.

F COSTS

27.14　Claims allocated to the small claims track are subject to severe costs restrictions. The restrictions apply both up to the original hearing and on any subsequent appeal (*Conlon v Royal Sun Alliance plc* [2015] EWCA Civ 92). On the small claims track no costs will be ordered between the parties except:

(a) the fixed costs relating to issuing the claim;
(b) in cases involving a claim for an injunction or specific performance, the cost of legal advice and assistance up to £260;

(c) court fees. These are likely to include the issue fee, an allocation fee if the claim is worth more than £1,500, and a hearing fee;

(d) witnesses' expenses reasonably incurred for travel and subsistence;

(e) loss of earnings or leave up to £95 per day;

(f) experts' fees, up to £750 per expert;

(g) costs resulting from unreasonable behaviour;

(h) Stage 1 and Stage 2 fixed costs under the RTA or EL/PL protocols (see Chapter 9) where the claimant reasonably believed the claim had a value exceeding the small claims limit and the defendant has not paid these fixed costs; and

(i) in an appeal, the cost of an approved transcript.

27.15 The effect of these restrictions is that usually in small claims track cases the costs awarded to the successful party are restricted to disbursements and out-of-pocket expenses. In most small claims the winner is not awarded anything for the cost of employing a legal representative. There is, however, an exception if the court finds that one of the parties has behaved unreasonably (CPR, r 27.14(2)(g)). In a suitable case the court can treat a refusal of a Part 36 offer as 'unreasonable behaviour', and if so the offer would be taken into account on costs (r 27.14(3)). Where the court finds there has been unreasonable behaviour, the court may make a summary assessment of costs in favour of the innocent party.

G REHEARINGS

27.16 A party who did not attend the final hearing may apply to set aside the order made in his or her absence and for an order that the claim be reheard. An application for a rehearing must be made within 14 days of the absent party being notified of the judgment. A rehearing will be allowed only if there is a good reason for the absence and if the absent party has a reasonable prospect of success at a reconvened hearing (CPR, r 27.11(3)).

28

FAST TRACK

A ALLOCATION DIRECTIONS 28.03
B LISTING DIRECTIONS 28.12
C STANDARD FAST TRACK TIMETABLE 28.13
D AGREED DIRECTIONS 28.14
E VARYING THE DIRECTIONS TIMETABLE. .28.15

F LISTING FOR TRIAL 28.17
G FAST TRACK TRIALS 28.23
H COSTS IN FAST TRACK
  CASES. 28.24
  Key points summary 28.25

28.01 The fast track is intended to cover the majority of defended claims within the £10,000 to £25,000 monetary band. It will also deal with non-monetary claims such as injunctions, declarations, and claims for specific performance which are unsuitable for the small claims track and do not require the more complex treatment of the multi-track. The fast track provides a 'no-frills' procedure for medium-sized cases that do not justify the detailed and meticulous preparation appropriate for complex and important cases. Instead, a case allocated to this track will be progressed to trial within a short timescale after the filing of a defence. Rule 1.1(2)(c) of the CPR provides that part of the overriding objective is that cases should be dealt with proportionately, and it is this idea that underlies the whole concept of having a fast track.

28.02 When claims are allocated to the fast track, directions will be given setting out the time-table to be followed, with a fixed trial date or trial period no more than 30 weeks later. It is intended that the timetable will be long enough for the parties to undertake the work necessary for preparing the case for trial, but sufficiently tight to discourage elaboration. The court will enforce the timetable it sets so as to ensure that fast track cases proceed to a speedy resolution by trial if they are not settled beforehand. It is for this reason that, as will be seen in this chapter, although some scope is given for the parties to alter some of the dates in the timetable set by the court, changing the date of the trial is only a matter of last resort.

A ALLOCATION DIRECTIONS

28.03 When it allocates a case to the fast track, the court will at the same time give case manage-ment directions and set a timetable for the steps to be taken from that point through to trial (CPR, r 28.2(1)). The directions given will be designed to ensure that the issues are identi-fied and the necessary evidence is prepared and disclosed (PD 28, para 3.3). Usually the court will give standard directions of its own initiative without a hearing, but will take into account the respective statements of case, the directions questionnaires, and any further information provided by the parties. Occasionally it may hold a directions hearing, such as when it is proposing to make an unusual order, for example to appoint an assessor (PD 28, para 3.11). It is the duty of the parties to ask for all directions that might be needed on any hearing that may be fixed (para 2.5). If any direction or order is required that has not been provided for, it is the duty of the parties to make an application as soon as possible so as to avoid undue interference with the overall timetable (para 2.8). If a directions hearing becomes necessary because of the default of any of the parties, the court will usually impose a sanction (para 2.3).

Typically, by CPR, rr 28.2(2) and 28.3, the matters to be dealt with in directions given on allocation to the fast track will include: **28.04**

(a) disclosure of documents;
(b) service of witness statements;
(c) expert evidence; and
(d) fixing a date for the trial, or a period in which the trial is to take place.

Disclosure

Disclosure is discussed fully in Chapter 31. In most cases, disclosure in some form should **28.05** have taken place before proceedings were issued. Information about this should have been given with the directions questionnaire. Based on the respective statements of case and these questionnaires, the procedural judge may direct the parties to give standard disclosure as one of the directions made at this stage, or may direct that no disclosure need take place, or may specify the documents or classes of documents which the parties must disclose (CPR, r 28.3(2); PD 28, para 3). The standard directions will provide for disclosure to be given by service of lists of documents, which must be delivered by a specified calendar date. It is also possible for disclosure to be given more informally without a list and with or without a disclosure statement. Disclosure is likely to be ordered for 28 days after service of the notice of allocation (PD 28, para 3.12).

Witness statements

The exchange of witness statements is considered further in Chapter 32. Standard direc- **28.06** tions will usually provide for simultaneous exchange by a specified calendar date of statements from all the factual witnesses on whose evidence each party intends to rely. Exchange is likely to be required between seven and ten weeks from the order for directions (PD 28, para 3.12).

Expert evidence

Under the CPR cases will not normally be on the fast track unless oral expert evidence **28.07** at trial is limited to one expert per party in each expert field, and to two fields of expertise (CPR, r 26.6(5)). It is difficult to see how any more experts could give evidence within the time limit for a fast track hearing. In order to keep down costs and to reduce the length of fast track trials, it will be usual for the court to make directions for the instruction of a single joint expert unless there is good reason for doing something else (r 35.7 and PD 28, para 3.9(4)). In addition, in fast track cases the court will not direct an expert to attend at trial unless it is necessary to do so in the interests of justice (r 35.5(2)).

Normally expert evidence should be prepared and/or exchanged about 14 weeks after the **28.08** order giving directions (PD 28, para 3.12). The standard fast track directions have several different options regarding expert evidence, as alternatives to the instruction of single joint experts. Options provided within the standard directions are:

(a) Sequential service of experts' reports. Normally it will be the claimant who will serve first.

(b) Simultaneous exchange of reports on some issues, with sequential service on the others.

(c) Holding of a discussion between experts in cases where the other side's reports cannot be agreed within a short time (usually 14 days) after service. This form of direction provides for a specified calendar date by which the discussion must take place, and the filing of a joint statement of the agreed issues and those in dispute (with reasons for the lack of agreement) by another specified date (which will often be close to the date for filing pre-trial checklists).

(d) That expert evidence is not necessary and no party has permission to call or rely on expert evidence at the trial.

(e) That the parties may rely on experts' reports at trial, but cannot call oral expert evidence.

(f) That the parties may rely on experts' reports, and the court will reconsider whether there is any need for experts to be called when the claim is listed for trial.

Questions to experts

28.09 The standard directions also make provision pursuant to the power given by CPR, r 35.6, for written questions to be put to the other side's experts for the purpose of clarifying their reports. Questions can be sent direct to the expert, but copies should be sent to the other side's solicitors.

Filing pre-trial checklists

28.10 Standard fast track directions will provide for all parties to file completed pre-trial checklists in form N170 no later than specific dates set out in the directions, unless the court considers the claim can be listed for trial without the need for these checklists. When they are used, pre-trial checklists must be returned within the time specified by the court, which will be no later than eight weeks before the trial date or the beginning of the trial period (CPR, r 28.5(2)). A hearing fee is payable by the claimant whether or not pre-trial checklists are used (Civil Proceedings Fees Order 2008 (SI 2008/1053) ('CPFO'), fee 2.1). If this fee is not paid the court will send a notice to pay in form N173, and failing payment within the time stated in the notice, the claim will be struck out (r 3.7).

Fixing the date for trial

28.11 When giving directions the court will fix the trial date or a period, not exceeding three weeks, in which the trial is to take place, and which will be specified in the notice of allocation (CPR, r 28.2(2)–(4)). Rule 28.2(4) provides that the 'standard' period between the giving of directions and the trial will be not more than 30 weeks. It is therefore open for procedural judges to lay down even tighter timetables, which may happen if the court decides that some or all of the usual steps can be omitted, or if it is informed that a pre-action protocol has been complied with or that the steps it was contemplating have already been taken (PD 28, para 3.13). There is also scope, if the procedural judge can be persuaded that it is necessary, for the timetable to be longer than the standard period.

B LISTING DIRECTIONS

The court may hold a listing hearing, after which it will confirm the trial date and may give **28.12** further directions. However, in most cases it will not feel the need to have a listing hearing, and will simply confirm or alter the trial date as appropriate, and may make further directions.

C STANDARD FAST TRACK TIMETABLE

Table 28.1 charts the progress of a fast track case from issue, through allocation to the **28.13** fast track, up to trial. The case illustrated takes 39 weeks, or about nine months, from issue to trial. The various stages will vary from case to case (eg where there is a stay for negotiation or if the claimant effects service rather than the court) and, as mentioned in 28.11, even the 30-week period between directions and trial may be considerably reduced in some cases. It will be obvious that the parties will have to be in a high state of preparedness before proceedings are issued in all but the very simplest of cases if they are to have any real prospect of adhering to such tight timetables without being forced on the mercy of the courts.

Table 28.1 Progress of fast track case to trial

Week	Step in the proceedings	Time limit
1	Issue of proceedings. Service takes effect on second day after posting	Usual limitation period 4 months from issue (6 months if outside the jurisdiction)
3	Acknowledgment of service or filing of defence	14 days after deemed service of the particulars of claim
(Say) 3	Provisional track allocation	On filing defence
(Say) 3	Possible transfer to defendant's home court	On filing defence
7	Return of directions questionnaires	Not less than 28 days after service of provisional track allocation notice
(Say) 9	Allocation decision and directions given by the procedural judge	After return of directions questionnaires
13	Disclosure of documents	Usually 4 weeks after allocation
19	Exchange of witness statements	Usually 10 weeks after allocation
19	Service of hearsay notices	With exchanged witness statements
23	Experts' reports	Usually 14 weeks after allocation
29	Service of pre-trial checklists (may be dispensed with)	Usually 20 weeks after allocation
31	Return of pre-trial checklists	Usually 22 weeks after allocation
(Say) 33	Any directions arising out of the pre-trial checklists	Optional
(33)	Hearing if pre-trial checklists not returned	Only if parties in default
36	Confirmation of trial date	3 weeks before trial
36	Service of notice to admit	3 weeks before trial
38	Lodging trial bundle	3 to 7 days before trial
39	Service and filing of statements of costs	Not less than 2 days before the hearing
39	Trial	30 weeks after allocation

D AGREED DIRECTIONS

28.14 The parties are encouraged to seek to agree suitable directions to be submitted to the court with their directions questionnaires. If this is done, the court will at least take them into account when giving directions, and if they are suitable, will simply approve them. To be approved the directions should essentially follow these rules (PD 28, para 3), which means they must deal with disclosure, witness statements, and expert evidence, lay down a timetable by calendar dates, and provide for a trial or trial period no more than 30 weeks after the start of the timetable.

E VARYING THE DIRECTIONS TIMETABLE

28.15 It is a fundamental rule that parties must comply with rules, practice directions, and court orders (CPR, r 1.1(2)(f)). Many of the timetabling requirements set out in the CPR and in court directions have stated consequences for non-compliance, even in the absence of an unless order (for which, see 37.15). For example, non-compliance with an order for the exchange of witness statements debars the defaulting party from calling those witnesses at trial without the court's permission (r 32.10), and non-compliance with a direction for the disclosure of an expert's report has a similar effect (r 35.13). In these situations the parties can only agree to a maximum 28-day extension, and must comply with the requirements of r 3.8(4) (see 37.06). There are other types of directions where no consequence is laid down for non-compliance, and in these situations r 3.8 does not apply. Examples are directions relating to access and inspection of property under r 25.1(1)(c) and (d), and directions for further information under Part 18. In these cases, an agreed extension that does not impinge on a hearing date or a date for filing pre-trial checklists needs to be made in writing, but can be of any length (provided it does not interfere with any hearting date), and does not need to be filed in court (PD 28, para 4.5(1)). In any of the situations mentioned in this paragraph, where the parties cannot agree to an extension, an application can be made to the court for the extension of time under r 3.1(2)(a).

28.16 A party that wishes to vary the date fixed for returning directions questionnaires or pre-trial checklists or for the trial must apply to the court (CPR, rr 26.3(6A) and 28.4(1)). Any other date set by the court also cannot be varied by the parties if the variation would make it necessary to vary the dates for either filing pre-trial checklists or trial (r 28.4(2)). It is made very clear by PD 28, para 5.4(6), that a variation involving loss of the trial date on account of any failure to comply with case management directions is a matter of last resort. However, there will be cases where it will become necessary to vary the timetabled date for trial. Examples include cases where there are significant problems with the evidence, where there is a change of solicitor, where proceedings are issued at the very end of the limitation period, and in personal injuries cases where the prognosis is uncertain. If there is no option but to postpone the trial, the postponement will be for the shortest possible time, and the court will give directions for taking the necessary steps as rapidly as possible.

F LISTING FOR TRIAL

28.17 On receipt of the pre-trial checklists, under CPR, r 28.6(1), the court will:

(a) Fix the date for the trial (or, if it has already done so, confirm the date).
(b) Give any further directions for the trial as may seem necessary, including setting a trial timetable. Standard directions for this stage are set out in the appendix to PD 28.
(c) Specify any further steps that need to be taken before trial.

If none of the pre-trial checklists is returned within the stated time, the court will normally **28.18** make an order that, if no pre-trial checklists are filed within seven days from service of the order, the claim and any counterclaim will be struck out. If only some of the parties are in default, the court will give listing directions based on the checklists that are returned (PD 28, para 6.5).

The parties should seek to agree directions at the pre-trial checklists stage, and they may **28.19** submit a proposed order (PD 28, para 7.2(1)). Usually directions will be made by the court without a hearing, but it may decide to hold a listing hearing, giving the parties three clear days' notice (PD 28, para 6.3). Notice of a listing hearing will be in form N153.

Trial timetable

The court may, if it considers that it is appropriate to do so, set a timetable for the trial. **28.20** Setting a timetable is discretionary (CPR, r 28.6(1)(b)). If it decides to set a timetable, the court must consult with the parties (r 39.4). A trial timetable defines how much time the court will allow at trial for the various stages of the trial itself. A simple direction may limit the time to be spent by each party in calling its evidence and in addressing the court in closing submissions. More sophisticated timetables will define how much time will be allowed for each witness, or even for cross-examination and re-examination.

Trial bundles

Standard directions made after receipt of pre-trial checklists will provide that an indexed, **28.21** paginated bundle of documents contained in a ring-binder must be lodged with the court not more than seven days or less than three days before the trial. The parties must seek to agree the contents of the trial bundle a reasonable time in advance, which in practical terms means no later than 14 days before the trial. All documents contained in agreed bundles are admissible at the hearing as evidence of their contents unless the court orders otherwise, or a party gives written notice objecting to the admissibility of particular documents (PD 32, para 27.2). The claimant is responsible for lodging the bundle. Bundles must be lodged at court so that the trial judge can read the case papers in advance of the trial. Identical bundles will be needed for each of the parties, with an additional bundle for the witness box.

Case summary

Standard listing directions give the procedural judge the option of directing that a case **28.22** summary should be included in the trial bundle. This document is intended to be non-partisan, and to be agreed if possible. It should be no more than 250 words long, and should outline the matters in issue, referring where appropriate to the relevant documents in the trial bundle. Again, responsibility for this rests with the claimant.

G FAST TRACK TRIALS

The trial of a fast track claim will usually take place in the County Court hearing centre **28.23** where it is proceeding, but may take place in a civil trial centre or any other hearing centre if it is appropriate because of listing difficulties, the needs of the parties, or for other reasons. The judge may be a District Judge or a Circuit Judge. The trial judge will generally have read the trial bundle and will usually dispense with opening speeches. Unless the trial judge otherwise directs, the trial will be conducted in accordance with any order previously made (see 28.20), although the judge is free to set a fresh trial timetable (PD 28, para 8.3). Given the time constraints and the need for proportionality, the trial judge will almost invariably order witness statements to stand as the evidence-in-chief and otherwise control the evidence to be presented. If a trial is not concluded on the day it is listed, the judge will normally sit on the following day to complete it (PD 28, para 8.6). In such an event no further costs will be allowed to the parties.

H COSTS IN FAST TRACK CASES

28.24 In fast track cases:

(a) there is a system of fixed costs in CPR, rr 45.29A–45.29L, for personal injuries claims covered by either the RTA protocol or the EL/PL protocol (see Chapter 9, and the fixed costs rules described at 9.44). Road traffic, employers' liability, and public liability cover the great majority of personal injuries claims, and these protocols cover claims with values between £1,000 and £25,000, so match the usual ambit of the fast track. Effectively, therefore, there is a fixed costs regime covering the whole of the work done by legal representatives in the case for almost all personal injuries claims on the fast track;

(b) trial costs for all fast track claims are fixed. 'Trial' for this purpose includes a disposal hearing (see 13.23) to assess damages (*Bird v Acorn Group Ltd* [2017] 1 WLR 1915). This covers only the costs of the trial itself. In personal injury claims the fixed amounts are part of the overall fixed costs scheme, and are set out in rr 45.29C and 45.29E. For non-personal injury cases the amounts are set out in rr 45.37–45.40, with the amount allowed depending on the amount recovered, with a small uplift if counsel is attended by a solicitor (see 46.61–46.64);

(c) the general rule is that at the end of a fast track trial the court will make a summary assessment of the costs of the whole claim immediately after giving judgment (PD 44, para 9.2). To assist the judge in assessing costs, the parties are required to file and serve, not less than two days before the trial, signed statements of their costs in form N260.

KEY POINTS SUMMARY

28.25   • Most cases on the fast track have a monetary value between £10,000 and £25,000.

• It is a 'fast' track because standard directions allow 30 weeks for completion of all the steps required to get the case ready for trial, and for the trial date or period.

• Fast track trials are proper trials, like multi-track trials (but unlike small claims track hearings).

• On the fast track the parties are usually required to use single joint experts, and directions usually permit expert evidence to be given simply by adducing the expert's report, rather than with the expert in attendance.

• Fast track trials usually last up to one day, and costs are usually dealt with on a summary assessment at the end of the trial.

29

MULTI-TRACK

A AGREED DIRECTIONS 29.04
B CASE MANAGEMENT
  CONFERENCES .29.06
C FIXING THE DATE FOR TRIAL 29.19
D PRE-TRIAL CHECKLISTS 29.21
E LISTING HEARINGS 29.25

F PRE-TRIAL REVIEW 29.26
G DIRECTIONS GIVEN AT OTHER
  HEARINGS 29.34
H VARIATION OF CASE MANAGEMENT
  TIMETABLE 29.35
  Key points summary 29.37

The multi-track is intended for the most important cases. However, a vast range of cases **29.01** are dealt with on this track, from simple contractual disputes involving little more than £25,000, to complex commercial cases involving difficult issues of fact and law with values of several million pounds, to cases where perhaps no money is at stake but which raise points of real public importance. Case management on the multi-track is intended to reflect this. Simpler cases are given standard directions without the need for hearings, and the parties are expected to comply with those directions without complicating or delaying matters. At the other end of the scale, the courts adopt a far more active approach, possibly with several directions hearings in the form of case management conferences and pre-trial reviews. The courts adopt a flexible approach to ensure that each case receives the right amount of case management input from the court (PD 29, para 3.2(2)). Straightforward multi-track cases may be given tight timetables from defence to trial that are similar to those on the fast track.

Cases on the multi-track will generally be dealt with either in the Royal Courts of Justice, **29.02** the Rolls Building, or other civil trial centre (PD 29, paras 2 and 3.1). The procedural judge may need to order a transfer on first consideration or at an allocation hearing: see 15.39–15.41. Case management will generally be dealt with by Masters and District Judges (PD 2B), unless the case has been selected for docketing (see 15.06). It is the duty of the parties at all hearings to consider whether any directions should be made, as this can avoid the need for additional case management hearings later on (PD 29, para 3.5).

Once a case is allocated to the multi-track the court will give directions and hold such **29.03** procedural hearings as may be appropriate in order to progress the case to trial or resolution by other means. Figure 29.1 illustrates the main stages in the progress of a multi-track case to trial.

A AGREED DIRECTIONS

The parties in a multi-track case must endeavour to agree appropriate directions (CPR, **29.04** r 29.4). If they reach agreement, they should submit their proposals to the court at least seven days before any case management conference. The court may simply approve the proposed directions without the need for a directions hearing (PD 29, paras 4.6 and 4.7).

Figure 29.1 The multi-track

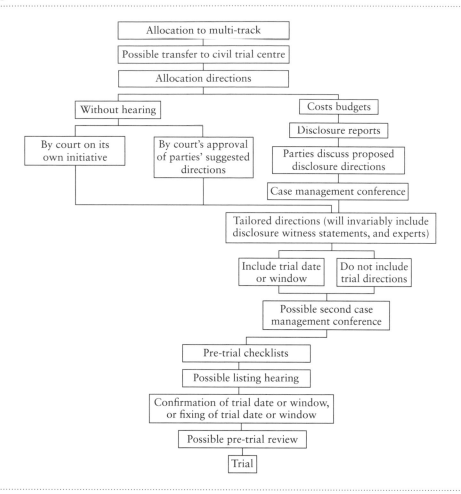

This is encouraged, as it obviously saves costs and court time. In order to obtain the court's approval the agreed directions should be based on the standard directions available on the Ministry of Justice website (CPR, r 29.1(2), see Chapter 15 and figure 15.1), and must:

(a) if appropriate, include a direction regarding the filing of a reply;
(b) if appropriate, provide for amending any statement of case;
(c) include provision about the disclosure of documents;
(d) include provision about both factual and expert evidence (the provision about expert evidence may be to the effect that no expert evidence is required);
(e) if appropriate, include dates for service of requests for further information and/or questions to experts, and when they should be answered;
(f) include a date or a period when it is proposed the trial will take place; and
(g) if appropriate, a date for a case management conference.

29.05 It will be seen that only items (c), (d), and (f) are obligatory in all cases, although the others will frequently arise in practice. Proposed agreed directions must lay down a timetable by reference to calendar dates. The court will scrutinize the timetable carefully, with particular attention to the proposals for the trial and case management conference, and will be astute to ensure these are no later than is reasonably necessary. Ultimate responsibility for case management remains at all times with the court, and it cannot be assumed that even agreed directions will always be approved.

B CASE MANAGEMENT CONFERENCES

Case management conferences are not simply directions hearings, but are intended to ensure **29.06** that the real issues between the parties are identified. Side issues will be dispensed with either by agreement between the parties with due encouragement from the judge, or by means of summary judgment or striking-out determinations at an early stage. Case management conferences may be held immediately after a case is allocated to the multi-track or at any time thereafter through to the listing stage. They can be used as the vehicle for laying down directions at the allocation stage, or may be used later in order to assess how the case is progressing when the initial directions on allocation should have been completed. Normally the court has a discretion whether to call a case management conference. However, where it is contemplated that an order may be made either for the evidence on a particular issue to be given by a single expert, or that an assessor should be appointed, PD 29, para 4.13, provides that a case management conference must be held unless the parties have consented to the order in writing.

Procedure before the case management conference

There is a commitment towards having case management conferences listed as promptly **29.07** as possible (PD 29, para 4.12(2)). The minimum period of notice the court will give to the parties of the date for the case management conference is three clear days (CPR, r 3.3(3); PD 29, para 3.7). In practice the parties need to anticipate the possibility of there being a case management conference some weeks in advance.

There are six items that need to be addressed in advance of the first case management con- **29.08** ference in multi-track claims:

(a) not less than 14 days before the first case management conference each party must file and serve a disclosure report complying with r 31.5(3), see Chapter 31. Personal injuries claims are excepted from this requirement; and
(b) the parties must seek to agree directions. This includes (in non-personal injuries claims) an obligation on the parties to meet or speak on the telephone at least seven days before the case management conference to seek to agree a proportionate proposal for disclosure of documents (r 31.5(5)). In all multi-track claims there is a more general obligation to endeavour to agree all the appropriate directions for the case (r 29.1(2));
(c) a costs budget and budget discussion report (see Chapter 16), unless the case is excluded from costs management (see 16.07);
(d) attempts to agree costs budgets if costs management applies;
(e) a case management bundle for use at the case management conference; and
(f) possibly, a case summary (see 29.12).

Attendance at case management conferences

If a case management conference is to be attended by a legal representative on behalf **29.09** of a party, the representative must be someone familiar with the case (CPR, r 29.3(2)). They must be able to field the questions that are likely to be covered at the hearing, and have the authority to agree and/or make representations on the matters reasonably to be expected to arise. Where the inadequacy of the person attending or his or her instructions leads to the adjournment of the hearing, it will be normal for a wasted costs order to be made (PD 29, para 5.2(3)), or even an order for indemnity-basis costs and interest on damages at a higher rate than usual (*Baron v Lovell* [1999] CPLR 630).

Business at case management conferences

29.10 At a case management conference the court will, as stated by CPR, rr 3.12(2) and 3.17, PD 3E, para 2.3, and PD 29, para 5.1:

(a) make a thorough review of the steps the parties have taken to date in preparing the case for trial;

(b) consider the extent to which they have complied with any previous orders and directions;

(c) review any costs budgets that have not been agreed between all the parties, make any appropriate revisions, and approve revised budgets;

(d) decide on the directions needed to progress the claim in accordance with the overriding objective and taking into account the costs budgets;

(e) ensure that reasonable agreements are made between the parties about the matters in issue and the future conduct of the claim; and

(f) record all such agreements.

29.11 To assist the court the legal representatives for all parties should ensure that all documents (and in particular witness statements and expert reports) the court is likely to ask to see are brought to court. They should also consider whether the parties themselves should attend. If the witness statements and experts' reports have not been exchanged at the time of the case management conference, it should follow from *General Mediterranean Holdings SA v Patel* [2000] 1 WLR 272 that the only reports and statements that can legitimately be called for are those that have been disclosed or that may be voluntarily disclosed at the hearing.

Case summary

29.12 By PD 29, para 5.6, the parties must consider whether the court may be assisted by a written case summary. This should be a short document not exceeding 500 words which is designed to assist the court in understanding and dealing with the issues raised in the case (PD 29, para 5.7). It should give a brief chronology of the claim, and state the factual issues that are agreed and those in dispute, and the nature of the evidence needed to decide them. Responsibility for preparing the document rests with the claimant, and if possible it should be agreed by the other parties.

Usual directions

29.13 In all cases the court will set a timetable at the case management conference for the steps it decides are necessary for preparing the case for trial (PD 29, paras 5.3 and 5.4). Typically the court will consider giving directions on the following matters:

(a) Whether orders for amendment and/or for further information may be appropriate if the statements of case are insufficiently clear for the other side to understand the case that has to be met.

(b) The scope of disclosure of documents required.

(c) The nature of the expert evidence required, and how and when it should be obtained. The court will not give permission for the use of expert evidence unless it can identify each expert by name or field of expertise, and say whether each expert's evidence should be given orally or by use of a report. Further matters that may be considered are whether the evidence on a particular issue should be given by a single expert, and whether there should be discussions between the experts.

(d) Disclosure of witness statements and summaries.

(e) Whether further information should be provided on matters other than statements of case, such as witness statements.

(f) Arrangements for questions that may be put to experts.

(g) Whether there should be split trials on liability and quantum, or whether there should be the trial of one or more preliminary issues.

(h) Whether there should be another case management conference or a pre-trial review.

(i) Whether it is possible to fix a date for the trial, or to give a trial 'window'. The court will be anxious to comply with the rule that the trial should be fixed as soon as practicable (CPR, r 29.2(2)).

(j) Whether the trial should be dealt with by a High Court judge, or by a specialist judge. If so, the court will also consider transferring the case to the appropriate court (PD 29, para 5.9).

Unusual directions and orders

It is the duty of the parties to ensure that all interim matters are dealt with at the case **29.14** management conference. If they want an order dealing with a matter that is not normally dealt with at a case management conference, such as an order for an interim payment or for specific disclosure, and they know the application is likely to be opposed, they should issue and serve an application notice in time for it to be heard at the conference. The more unusual the proposed order or direction, the greater the need to give proper notice to the other parties. It is not open to a judge to dismiss the claim on a hearing for directions without giving the parties advance notice so they can make effective representations (*Norbrook Laboratories Ltd v Carr* [2010] EWCA Civ 1108).

Other directions from those provided for by CPR, r 3.1(2), that may be considered in **29.15** appropriate cases include:

(a) directing that part of the proceedings, such as a counterclaim, be dealt with as separate proceedings;

(b) staying the whole or part of the proceedings either generally or until a specified date or event;

(c) consolidating proceedings;

(d) trying two or more claims at the same time;

(e) deciding the order in which issues are to be tried;

(f) excluding an issue from consideration; and

(g) requiring proceedings in the High Court to be heard by a Divisional Court rather than by a single judge.

Plans, photographs, and models

Where a party intends to use photographs, plans, models, and similar items as evidence at **29.16** trial, then generally notice should be given to the other parties by the date for disclosing witness statements (CPR, r 33.6(4)).

Video evidence

Provided it is relevant, video evidence is generally admissible. A party may wish to use **29.17** video evidence to illustrate a manufacturing process, or the scene of an accident (although photographs will usually be sufficient, and are far simpler to handle in court). Rather more striking are surveillance recordings used from time to time in personal injuries claims to test whether the claimant is as badly injured as is claimed. As audio-visual recordings fall into the wide definition of 'documents' for the purposes of CPR, Part 31, the usual rules on disclosure and inspection apply (see Chapter 31). Furthermore, there is an obligation to inform the court at the first opportunity that such evidence will be relied upon, as arrangements need to be made to ensure compatible equipment is available at trial, and extra time will be required for the trial for showing the evidence (*Rall v Hume* [2001] 3 All ER 248).

Controlling evidence

29.18 Under CPR, r 32.1(1), the court has a general power to control evidence by making directions as to the issues on which it requires evidence, the nature of that evidence, and how it is to be placed before the court. This power may be exercised to exclude otherwise admissible evidence (r 32.1(2)), and may be used to limit cross-examination (r 32.1(3)). The power under r 32.1 could be used to exclude evidence obtained by unlawful means, but covert surveillance evidence obtained in breach of the European Convention on Human Rights, art 8 and by trespassing inside the claimant's home was admitted in *Jones v University of Warwick* [2003] 1 WLR 954. The court was influenced by the fact that experts retained by both sides had already seen and commented on the surveillance evidence, and by its power to impose other sanctions, such as in costs.

C FIXING THE DATE FOR TRIAL

29.19 The court will fix the trial date or the period in which the trial is to take place as soon as practicable (CPR, r 29.2(2)). This may be possible when it gives allocation directions, but in complex cases (and also, perhaps, badly prepared cases and cases where the facts are developing, such as many personal injuries claims) this may have to be delayed, perhaps for a considerable period of time. Where fixing the trial date is postponed, it may be revisited either at a later case management conference, or on the application of the parties, or after further scrutiny by the court.

29.20 When the court fixes the date for trial (or lays down a trial period or 'window'), it will give written notice to the parties, and will also specify a date by which the parties must file pre-trial checklists (r 29.2(3)). The court may alternatively make an order for an early trial on a fixed date and dispense with pre-trial checklists (PD 29, para 8.1(2)), or may simply list the case for trial (CPR, r 29.6(1)).

D PRE-TRIAL CHECKLISTS

29.21 Pre-trial checklists in form N170 will (unless dispensed with) be sent out to the parties by the court for completion and return by the date specified in the directions given when the court fixed the date or period for trial (CPR, r 29.6). The forms should be served by the court at least 14 days before they must be returned. Each party is under an obligation to return a completed checklist before the specified date, and the claimant is required to pay a hearing fee (CPFO, fee 2.1). If pre-trial checklists are dispensed with, this fee is payable within 14 days of dispatch of the notice of the trial date or period. In cases which are proceeding on a counterclaim alone the fee is payable by the defendant. There is a possible sanction of automatic striking out for non-payment after a reminder from the court (CPR, r 3.7).

In the Commercial Court, pre-trial checklists must be in the form set out in the *Commercial* **29.22**
Court Guide, app 2. They must be returned to the court at least three weeks before the
trial (para D14).

Purpose of pre-trial checklists

Pre-trial checklists are used to check that earlier orders and directions have been com- **29.23**
plied with, and to provide up-to-date information to assist the court with deciding
when to hold the trial and how long it will take, and in making trial timetable directions. Once all the checklists have been received, or the time limit has expired, the file
will be placed before the procedural judge, who will make directions for trial along the
same lines as those set out in 29.32, or direct that there should be a listing hearing or
pre-trial review.

Failure to file pre-trial checklists

If no one returns a pre-trial checklist by the specified date, the court will usually make an **29.24**
order that the parties must do so within seven days of service of the order, failing which the
claim and any counterclaim will be struck out (PD 29, para 8.3(1)). Where only some of
the parties file pre-trial checklists, the court will fix a listing hearing. It will also fix a listing
hearing if any of the checklists do not provide the necessary information, or if the court
considers that such a hearing is necessary to decide what further directions should be given
to complete the preparations for trial (CPR, r 29.6(3)).

E LISTING HEARINGS

Listing hearings (technically, these are called 'hearings under r 29.6(4)') serve a similar **29.25**
purpose to pre-trial reviews, but concentrate on making the decisions relevant to fixing
the date of the trial. They are fixed for dates as early as possible, and the parties are given
at least three clear days' notice of the date. Even if a listing hearing is fixed because some
of the parties did not file their pre-trial checklists, the court will normally fix or confirm the trial date and make orders about the steps to prepare the case for trial (PD 29,
para 8.3(2)).

F PRE-TRIAL REVIEW

If a pre-trial review is listed, it is likely to take place about four to ten weeks before trial. **29.26**
Pre-trial reviews are not held in all cases. In the Chancery Division they are used in cases
where the trial is estimated at five days or more (*Chancery Guide*, para 17.27). The intention is that they should be conducted by the eventual trial judge.

Before the pre-trial review

In some cases a pre-trial review may be required by directions made by the court at an **29.27**
earlier stage, such as on allocation or at a case management conference. In other cases the
court may decide to hold a pre-trial review of its own initiative, such as when it considers
the pre-trial checklists. In this event it will give the parties at least seven clear days' notice
of the hearing of a pre-trial review (CPR, r 29.7).

29.28 In the Chancery Division the claimant should, seven days before the pre-trial review, circulate a list of matters to be considered at the pre-trial review, including suggestions for how the case should be tried. Other parties must respond at least two days before the hearing (*Chancery Guide*, para 20.04). The claimant's solicitors should deliver to the Listing Office (or Master if the pre-trial review is to be conducted by a Master) by 10 a.m. on the day before the hearing a bundle containing all the pre-trial checklists, the list of matters to be considered, the proposed trial timetable, statements of case, interim orders, trial witness statements, and experts' reports, but no more than 100 pages (para 20.05).

29.29 In the Commercial Court, before the pre-trial review the parties must discuss and attempt to agree a draft trial timetable, which should be filed at least two days before the hearing (PD 58, paras 11.3 and 11.4). Any difference of view should be clearly identified.

Attendance

29.30 The same rules about a fully informed representative being present apply to pre-trial reviews as apply to case management conferences (see 29.09) and in the specialist courts in particular they should be attended by the trial advocates.

Pre-trial review directions

29.31 At a pre-trial review the court will not readily change earlier directions, and will assume the parties were content with the original directions if they failed to apply within 14 days for variation of case management directions (PD 29, paras 6 and 9.3).

29.32 Perhaps the most important task on a pre-trial review is to determine the timetable for the trial itself. This can lay down time limits for examination and cross-examination of witnesses, and for speeches. Doing this is intended to force advocates to focus their preparation, and to produce well-managed trials. Other matters to be dealt with are:

(a) Evidence, particularly expert evidence. At this stage there should have been full disclosure and perhaps also discussions between the experts. It may be possible to make more rigorous directions about which experts really do need to be called at the trial, and which experts (or which parts of the expert evidence) can be taken from the experts' reports.

(b) The extent to which information technology will be used at the trial.

(c) A time estimate for the trial.

(d) Preparation and organization of trial bundles.

(e) Fixing a trial date or week.

(f) Fixing the place of trial. This will normally be the court where the case is being managed, but it may be transferred depending on the convenience of the parties and the availability of court resources (PD 29, para 10.1).

Agreed pre-trial review directions

29.33 The parties are required to seek to agree the directions to be made on the pre-trial review, and may file an agreed order (PD 29, para 9.2). The court may then make an order in the terms agreed, or make some other order, or reject the proposals and continue with the pre-trial review.

G DIRECTIONS GIVEN AT OTHER HEARINGS

29.34 The court is not restricted to making case management directions on the occasions described earlier, but can do so on any occasion on which the case comes before the court (PD 29, para 3.4). In fact, whenever there is a hearing it is the duty of the parties to consider whether any directions should be made, and to make any appropriate application on that occasion (PD 29, para 3.5). Further, the court may hold a directions hearing on its own initiative on three clear days' notice whenever it appears necessary to do so. This can include situations where progress is delayed because one or other of the parties is in default of directions previously made (PD 29, para 3.6). It can also occur because a party needs a direction not already in place, perhaps because a need to amend, or to ask for further information, has arisen since the last case management hearing. In such cases the application must be made as soon as possible so as to minimize the disruption to the original timetable (PD 29, para 3.8).

H VARIATION OF CASE MANAGEMENT TIMETABLE

Case management directions in multi-track claims fall into three categories: **29.35**

(a) Those that can be varied only by an order made by the court on an application by a party seeking a variation (CPR, r 29.5(1)). These 'key dates' are:
  (i)   dates for returning directions questionnaires;
  (ii) dates fixed for holding a case management conference;
  (iii) dates fixed for holding a pre-trial review;
  (iv) dates specified for the return of pre-trial checklists; and
  (v)   dates fixed for trial (including a trial 'window').
(b) Rules, practice directions, and court orders which specify the consequence of failure to comply. These include directions for the exchange of witness statements and disclosure of experts' reports (the sanctions for non-compliance are in rr 32.10 and 35.13), as well as express 'unless' orders (for which, see 37.15). These can be varied by agreement for a maximum of 28 days, and only if the requirements in r 3.8(4) are complied with (see 37.06).
(c) All other types of case management direction. These may be varied by the parties by consent, provided the variation does not affect any of the 'key dates', without needing to file anything with the court (PD 29, para 6.5(1)).

If there has been a real change in circumstances there is usually no objection to the court **29.36** varying or revoking previous directions using the power given by r 3.1(7) (for which, see 23.64). Where there are no changed circumstances, any review of directions made on notice has to be made by way of appeal (*Umm Qarn Management Co Ltd v Bunting* [2001] CPLR 21). If there is no appeal, the court will work on the basis that the directions in the case were reasonable when made (*Mitchell v News Group Newspapers Ltd* [2014] 1 WLR 795).

KEY POINTS SUMMARY

- The multi-track caters for cases over £25,000 and a wide range of specialist court claims. **29.37**

- Simple multi-track cases are dealt with in ways similar to cases proceeding on the fast track.

- More complex cases have case management which is tailored to the case in hand.

- Case management by the court can take place as 'file-work', based on directions questionnaires, pre-trial checklists, and proposed directions filed by the parties.

- Alternatively, the court may require the parties to attend case management conferences, listing hearings, and/or pre-trial reviews for the purpose of setting directions and agreeing trial timetables.

- Although the court may direct the joint instruction of experts in multi-track cases, the greater importance and complexity of these cases often means the court will permit the parties to instruct their own experts, who are often called as witnesses at trial.

30

STRIKING OUT, DISCONTINUANCE, AND STAYS

A THE MAIN RULE 30.04
B PROCEDURE ON APPLICATIONS
   MADE BY PARTIES 30.09
C REFERENCES BY COURT OFFICERS 30.12
D GENERAL TEST 30.13
E NO REASONABLE GROUNDS FOR BRINGING
   OR DEFENDING THE CLAIM 30.16
F ABUSE OF PROCESS 30.21

G OBSTRUCTING THE JUST DISPOSAL
   OF THE PROCEEDINGS 30.32
H POWERS AFTER A STRIKING-OUT
   ORDER IS MADE..................30.37
I DISCONTINUANCE.................30.38
J STAYS 30.47
   Key points summary 30.53

30.01 By CPR, r 3.4, the court has the power to order the whole or any part of a statement of case to be struck out. This power may be resorted to on an application by a party seeking to attack the statement of case drafted by the other side. It may also be used by the court of its own initiative, with (and sometimes without) the involvement of the 'innocent' party. This may be because of failure to comply with the requirement to give a concise statement of the facts on which the claimant relies (r 16.4(1)(a)) or the requirement to give the reasons for any denial in a defence (r 16.5(2)(a)). A related use of the power is where it is alleged that a statement of case, even if its contents are assumed to be true, does not amount to a sustainable claim or defence as a matter of law. Striking out is also used to prevent the misuse of the right to issue proceedings, on the ground that proceedings are an abuse of process. These facets of the jurisdiction to strike out will be considered in this chapter.

30.02 An alternative use of striking out is as a means of enforcing compliance with the general provisions of the CPR, practice directions, and court orders and directions as part of the court's case management functions. This aspect of striking out will be considered in Chapter 37 as part of the discussion on non-compliance and sanctions.

30.03 It is recognized in several places in the CPR and practice directions that striking out under r 3.4 is closely related to the jurisdiction to enter summary judgment under Part 24, discussed in Chapter 24. Both powers are used to achieve the active case management aim of summarily disposing of issues that do not need full investigation at trial (r 1.4(2)(c)). In *Three Rivers District Council v Bank of England (No 3)* [2003] 2 AC 1, Lord Hope at [91] said that, under r 3.4, the court generally is only concerned with the statement of case which it is alleged discloses no reasonable grounds for bringing or defending the claim. In *Monsanto v Tilly* (1999) *The Times*, 30 November 1999, Stuart Smith LJ said that Part 24 gives a wider scope for dismissing a claim or defence than striking out. The court should look to see what will happen at the trial and, if the case is so weak that it has no reasonable prospects of success, summary judgment should be entered.

A THE MAIN RULE

Rule 3.4(2) of the CPR provides: **30.04**

The court may strike out a statement of case if it appears to the court—

(a) that the statement of case discloses no reasonable grounds for bringing or defending the claim;

(b) that the statement of case is an abuse of the court's process or is otherwise likely to obstruct the just disposal of the proceedings; or

(c) that there has been a failure to comply with a rule, practice direction or court order.

A striking-out order may apply to all or part of a statement of case (r 3.4(1)). Rule 3.4(5) **30.05** provides that r 3.4(2) does not limit any other power of the court to strike out a statement of case. An example is r 22.2(2), which allows the court to strike out a statement of case which is not verified by a statement of truth.

After striking out

If the entire claim is struck out there is no platform for making subsequent interim applica- **30.06** tions (*Mireskandari v Associated Newspapers Ltd* [2010] EWHC 967 (QB)). All that can be done thereafter is to appeal, assess damages, assess costs, or enforce judgment.

Starting a second claim after striking out

Rule 3.4(4) of the CPR provides that where a claim is struck out and the claimant is ordered **30.07** to pay the defendant's costs, if the claimant commences a second claim arising out of substantially the same facts as those forming the basis of the struck-out claim, the defendant may apply for a stay of the second claim until the costs of the first claim have been paid.

Starting a second claim after an earlier claim has been struck out may itself be an abuse of **30.08** process within the meaning of r 3.4(2)(b). In *Janov v Morris* [1981] 3 All ER 780 (which is still good law, *Aktas v Adepta* [2011] QB 894), a second claim was commenced after a first claim based on the same cause of action had been struck out for failing to comply with an unless order. No explanation was advanced by the claimant for the failure to comply with the order in the earlier proceedings, so the second claim was struck out as an abuse of process. As explained by Dunn LJ, a second claim may be an abuse where there had been inordinate and inexcusable delay, or where there had been intentional and contumelious default, for example disobedience of a peremptory order. Intentional and contumelious default can also be established where there has been a wholesale disregard of court orders (*Arbuthnot Latham Bank Ltd v Trafalgar Holdings Ltd* [1998] 1 WLR 1426).

B PROCEDURE ON APPLICATIONS MADE BY PARTIES

An application to strike out made by a party should be brought by issuing an application **30.09** notice in accordance with the procedure in CPR, Part 23 (see Chapter 23). Paragraph 5.2 of PD 3A says that, while many applications to strike out can be made without evidence in support (the poor drafting of the statement of case may be self-evident, or the point may be one of law on which no evidence would be required), the applicant should always consider whether facts need to be proved. If so, evidence in support should usually be filed and served, unless the facts relied upon have already been adequately evidenced in, say, a statement of case which included a statement of truth. The court has the power to treat an application to strike out as one for summary judgment in order to dispose of issues or claims that do not deserve full investigation at trial (*Three Rivers District Council v Bank of England (No 3)* [2003] 2 AC 1 at [88]).

30.10   In accordance with PD 23A, para 2.7, any application to strike out should be made as soon as it becomes apparent that it is desirable to make it. Applications to strike out should normally be made in the period between acknowledgment of service and filing of directions questionnaires (PD 26, para 5.3(1), and see also PD 3A, para 5.1). A defendant who files a defence and defends on the merits will be taken to have acquiesced, and thereafter it is too late to apply to strike out as an abuse of process if the abuse is founded on the bringing of the claim (*Johnson v Gore Wood and Co* [2002] 2 AC 1). If a striking-out application is issued before the defence is filed, default judgment cannot be entered until the striking-out application has been disposed of (CPR, r 12.3(3)). If a striking-out application is contemplated, but has not been dealt with by the time directions questionnaires have to be returned, the intention to make the application should be included as extra information provided when the questionnaire is returned (PD 26, para 2.2(3)(a)).

30.11   Paragraph 5.3(2) of PD 26 provides that where a party makes an application to strike out before the claim has been allocated to a track the court will not allocate the claim before hearing the application. By PD 26, para 5.3(3) and (4), where a party files a directions questionnaire and states an intention to strike out but has not yet done so, the judge will usually direct that an allocation hearing is listed. The striking-out application may be heard at the allocation hearing if the application notice has been issued and served in sufficient time.

C REFERENCES BY COURT OFFICERS

30.12   A claim form that has been lodged for issuing may be referred by a court official to the judge (CPR, r 3.2), and this power may be exercised where it is felt that the claim form (which in context means the particulars of claim) is amenable to being struck out under r 3.4 (PD 3A, para 2.1) or if it is totally devoid of merit. The court staff who receive a claim form, fee etc. for the purpose of issue are not performing any judicial function, and have no power to reject the documents (*Barnes v St Helens Metropolitan Borough Council (Practice Note)* [2007] 1 WLR 879 at [19]; PD 3A, para 2.1). If the claim form is very defective, such as through not naming any parties, or not including any details of the claim, it may be rejected on the basis that it is not a claim form at all (*per* Tuckey LJ). Where a claim form is referred to the judge, an order may be made which is designed to ensure the claim is disposed of, or proceeds, in a way that accords with the rules. For example, the judge may stay the claim until amended particulars of claim complying with the rules is filed (PD 3A, para 2.4). The judge has a discretion whether to hear the claimant before making such an order (para 2.3). If an order is made without giving notice to the claimant, CPR, rr 23.9 and 23.10 apply, so that the order has to include a statement that the claimant has the right within seven days after service of the order to apply to vary or set it aside.

D GENERAL TEST

30.13   The jurisdiction to strike out is to be used sparingly, because striking out deprives a party of its right to a trial, and of its ability to strengthen its case through the process of disclosure and other court procedures such as requests for further information. Further, examination and cross-examination of witnesses often changes the complexion of a case. The result is that striking out is limited to plain and obvious cases where there is no point in having a trial.

The principles from *W & H Trade Marks (Jersey) Ltd v W and H Trade Marks (Jersey) Ltd*   **30.14**
[1986] AC 368, the leading case under the old rules, were approved in *Three Rivers District
Council v Bank of England (No 3)* [2003] 2 AC 1 at [96]–[97]. The claimant's application
to strike out the defence took seven days to argue before the judge, six days in the Court
of Appeal, and four days in the House of Lords. The case reiterated the point that striking
out was appropriate only in plain and obvious cases. Sometimes, a case would only become
clear after protracted argument. Lord Templeman said that:

> . . . if an application to strike out involves a prolonged and serious argument the judge should,
> as a general rule, decline to proceed with the argument unless he not only harbours doubts
> about the soundness of the pleading but, in addition, is satisfied that striking out will obviate
> the necessity for a trial or will substantially reduce the burden of preparing for trial or the
> burden of the trial itself.

Where several of the grounds stated in CPR, r 3.4 are relied on in a single application, the   **30.15**
court will often take a broad-brush approach and simply ask whether the case is a plain
and obvious one for striking out, rather than considering each of the grounds in detail. The
'plain and obvious' test will not be adjusted where one of the parties is suffering from an
inequality of arms (*Bank of Tokyo-Mitsubishi UFJ Ltd v Bashan Gida Sanayi ve Pazarlama
AS* [2008] EWHC 659 (Ch)).

E NO REASONABLE GROUNDS FOR BRINGING OR DEFENDING THE CLAIM

Applications under CPR, r 3.4(2)(a), may be made on the basis that the statement of case   **30.16**
under attack fails on its face to disclose a claim or defence which is sustainable as a matter
of law. On hearing such an application it will be assumed that the facts alleged are true
(*Morgan Crucible Co plc v Hill Samuel and Co Ltd* [1991] Ch 295 *per* Slade LJ). For pur-
ists it ought to be unnecessary to seek to undermine the claim or defence under r 3.4(2)(a)
with evidence in support. The rules do not, however, contain any express ban on adducing
evidence in support: see 30.09.

A number of examples of statements of case open to attack under CPR, r 3.4(2)(a), are   **30.17**
given by PD 3A. A claim may be struck out if it sets out no facts indicating what the claim
is about (eg a claim simply saying it is for 'Money owed £5,000'), or if it is incoherent and
makes no sense, or if the facts it states, even if true, do not disclose a legally recognizable
claim against the defendant. A defence may be struck out if it consists of a bare denial or
otherwise fails to set out a coherent statement of facts, or if the facts it sets out, even if true,
do not amount in law to a defence to the claim.

A cause of action that is unknown to the law will be struck out; as will, subject to the court   **30.18**
giving permission to amend, a statement of case that omits some material element of the
claim or defence. A statement of case ought also to be struck out if the facts set out do not
constitute the cause of action or defence alleged, or if the relief sought would not be ordered
by the court. A defence may be struck out if it does not answer the claim being made.

Striking out may be refused in developing areas of law (*Brooks v Commissioner of Police*   **30.19**
for the Metropolis [2005] 1 WLR 1495), and will be refused if the application requires
minute and protracted examination of documents (*Wenlock v Moloney* [1965] 1 WLR
1238; *Three Rivers District Council v Bank of England (No 3)* [2003] 2 AC 1). Judges
often apply the test of whether the claim is bound to fail, so that even a case 'fraught with
difficulty' will not be struck out (*Smith v Chief Constable of Sussex* [2008] PIQR P12). On
the other hand, the documents may make it plain there is no case. In *Taylor v Inntrepreneur*

Estates (CPC) Ltd (2001) LTL 31/1/01, the claimant brought a claim seeking a declaration that a lease agreement had come into force, damages for breach of the lease, and damages for misrepresentation resulting from having entered into the alleged lease. On the documents it was clear that throughout the parties had negotiated on a 'subject to contract' basis. It was held that as no written agreement had been signed, no lease had been entered into. It followed that there were no reasonable grounds for bringing the claim.

30.20 The court may allow a party to amend rather than strike out, but the power to amend will be exercised in accordance with the overriding objective (see *Finley v Connell Associates* (1999) *The Times*, 23 June 1999, where permission to amend was granted, and *Christofi v Barclays Bank plc* [2000] 1 WLR 937, where permission was refused). An amendment should be permitted as an alternative to striking out only if there is a real prospect of establishing the amended case (*Charles Church Developments plc v Cronin* [1990] FSR 1).

F ABUSE OF PROCESS

30.21 The first half of CPR, r 3.4(2)(b), gives the court power to strike out a statement of case which is an abuse of the court's process. This is a power 'which any court of justice must possess to prevent misuse of its procedure in a way which, although not inconsistent with the literal application of its procedural rules, would nevertheless be manifestly unfair to a party to litigation before it, or would otherwise bring the administration of justice into disrepute among right-thinking people' (*per* Lord Diplock in *Hunter v Chief Constable of the West Midlands Police* [1982] AC 529 at 536). While in almost all cases there will be many factors that have to be weighed, whether there is an abuse of process is a question of judgment to which there is only one answer, and is not a matter of discretion (*Aldi Stores Ltd v WSP Group plc* [2008] 1 WLR 748).

General examples of abuse of process

30.22 A claim that is issued after the expiry of limitation may be struck out as an abuse of process (*Ronex Properties Ltd v John Laing Construction Ltd* [1983] QB 398). Seeking redress for a public authority's infringement of the claimant's public law rights by issuing an ordinary claim rather than by judicial review may be an abuse of process (*O'Reilly v Mackman* [1983] 2 AC 237, see 49.09).

30.23 In *Barton Henderson Rasen v Merrett* [1993] 1 Lloyd's Rep 540 Saville J said that it is an abuse of the court's process to issue proceedings with no intention of taking the case any further. In contentious matters the courts exist for the purpose of determining claims. Therefore, starting a claim with no intention of pursuing it is not using the court's processes for the purposes for which they were designed. It is also an abuse of process to issue a claim form at a time when the claimant lacks knowledge of any basis for bringing the claim, even if by the time of the striking-out application the claimant has sufficient facts to plead a claim (*Nomura International plc v Granada Group Ltd* [2007] 2 All ER (Comm) 878).

30.24 A claim may be struck out as an abuse of process where there has been no real or substantial wrongdoing, even if the defendant's conduct technically amounts to a cause of action (*Jameel v Dow Jones Co Inc* [2005] QB 946). This may be the case where the claimant has already obtained all he is ever going to by way of redress, so that further litigation will be futile (*Ansari v Knowles* [2013] EWCA Civ 1448). According to *McDonald's Corporation v Steel* [1995] 3 All ER 615, it is an abuse of process where the statement of case is incurably incapable of proof.

Destruction of evidence before proceedings are commenced in an attempt to pervert **30.25** the course of justice may result in a claim or defence being struck out. Destruction of evidence after proceedings are issued may be visited by striking out if a fair trial is no longer achievable (*Douglas v Hello! Ltd* [2003] 1 All ER 1087). Striking out is also possible where evidence has been forged, or if a party or its witnesses engage in dishonest conduct relating to the proceedings, or if there has been other misconduct which is so serious that it would be an affront to the court to permit the claim to continue. Such cases can result in striking out as an abuse of process if a fair trial is no longer possible (*Summers v Fairclough Homes Ltd* [2012] 1 WLR 2004), or with the whole claim being dismissed at trial under the Criminal Justice and Courts Act 2015, s 57 (see 41.36). Some caution should be exercised before striking out a claim on the basis of alleged fraud on an interim application without cross-examination of witnesses (*Alpha Rocks Solicitors v Alade* [2015] 1 WLR 4534).

Collateral attack abuse of process

It is an abuse of process to use a civil claim to mount a collateral attack on a factual issue **30.26** previously decided in another court of competent jurisdiction (*Hunter v Chief Constable of the West Midlands Police* [1982] AC 529). Typically, the collateral attack doctrine applies where the issue is identical, the current claimant had a full opportunity to contest the issue in the earlier case, and the later claim is a misuse of the court's procedure. The doctrine can apply to a person who was not a party to the earlier proceedings, but not having been a party means the factors that have to be weighed may well point against the subsequent claim being an abuse of process (*JSC BTA Bank v Ablyazov (No 15)* [2017] 1 WLR 603).

Relitigation amounting to an abuse of process

There have been several cases dealing with whether a claim which is inconsistent with **30.27** an earlier claim or evidence given by the claimant in earlier proceedings (eg an affidavit used in an application to discharge a freezing injunction) should be struck out as an abuse of process. As stated by Morgan J in *Kotonou v National Westminster Bank plc* [2011] 1 All ER (Comm) 1164 the cases fall into two categories:

(a) cases where the litigant in the second claim is making a collateral attack on the decision in earlier proceedings (the principle in *Hunter v Chief Constable of the West Midlands Police* [1982] AC 529); and

(b) cases where the litigant in the second claim wishes to make a claim which was not made in the earlier proceedings, but which the court finds he could and should have made in the earlier proceedings (the principle in *Henderson v Henderson* (1843) 3 Hare 100).

The *Henderson v Henderson* principle goes beyond the doctrine of estoppel *per rem judicat-* **30.28** *am. Res judicata* applies where there has been an earlier final decision on exactly the same cause of action between the same parties (cause of action estoppel) and where the issues raised in an earlier claim are identical to the issues raised in a later claim (issue estoppel), see *Arnold v National Westminster Bank plc* [1991] 2 AC 93. Issue estoppel applies where a final order is made in a civil case, and it does not matter whether the order was made by consent or after argument (*Lennon v Birmingham City Council* (2001) LTL 27/3/01). It does not apply to issues decided in prior criminal proceedings (*DPP v Humphreys* [1977] AC 1) or to findings in judicial review proceedings (*R v Secretary of State for the Environment, ex p Hackney LBC* [1983] 1 WLR 524). Nor does it apply to interim civil orders, because these are not designed to be conclusive (*Autofocus Ltd v Accident Exchange Ltd* [2010] EWCA Civ 788). Where the parties in the two claims are not the same, issue estoppel does not apply (*Mulkerrins v PricewaterhouseCoopers* [2003] 1 WLR 1937).

30.29 Under the *Henderson v Henderson* principle, it is only an abuse of process to challenge the findings in the earlier claim if it would be manifestly unfair to a party in the later claim for the issues to be relitigated, or if relitigating will bring the administration of justice into disrepute (*Secretary of State for Trade and Industry v Bairstow* [2004] Ch 1). The underlying public interest is that there should be finality in litigation, and that a party should not be vexed twice. In considering whether the second claim is an abuse it is necessary to decide not merely that the second claim could have been brought in the earlier claim, but whether it should have been brought in the first claim. The effect of the rule from the law of evidence in *Hollington v F Hewthorn & Co Ltd* [1943] 1 KB 587 is that previous findings from cases involving different parties are inadmissible as evidence of the facts on which those findings were based. What *Secretary of State for Trade and Industry v Bairstow* does is to provide a means of circumventing that rule on the theory that, if an abuse of process is established, the party against whom the previous finding was made is prevented from asserting facts contrary to the previous finding (*Conlon v Simms* [2008] 1 WLR 484 at [177], *per* Ward LJ).

30.30 In applying the *Secretary of State for Trade and Industry v Bairstow* principle, the court has to make a broad, merits-based judgment taking account of all the public and private interests involved, and all the facts. The court must focus on the crucial question whether, in all the circumstances, the claimant is misusing or abusing the process of the court (*Johnson v Gore Wood & Co* [2002] 2 AC 1). In this case, Mr Johnson was a shareholder in a company which had sued the defendant solicitors. That first claim was settled, with the compromise agreement containing a clause seeking to limit the defendant's liability to Mr Johnson personally. Mr Johnson then sued the solicitors in his personal capacity, and the defendant applied to strike out his personal claim as an abuse. Certain heads of claim were struck out, as they merely reflected losses suffered by his company, but others were arguably recoverable in his own right, and it was held that, even though his personal claim could have been joined with the first claim by the company, it was not on the facts an abuse to have brought the personal claim by separate proceedings.

Settlement acting as a bar to later proceedings

30.31 Settling a claim can act as a bar to later proceedings. In *Jameson v Central Electricity Generating Board* [2000] 1 AC 455, in the original claim the deceased accepted £80,000 from his former employer in 'full and final settlement and satisfaction of all the causes of action' set out in his statement of claim against his employer in respect of asbestos-related disease. After his death his widow brought the present claim against the Board as the owner of premises where the deceased had been exposed to asbestos. The claim against the Board was struck out. The reasoning, as interpreted by the House of Lords in *Heaton v AXA Equity & Law Life Assurance Society plc* [2002] 2 AC 329 and subsequent cases, was that:

(a) a claim for unliquidated damages, whether in contract or tort, is capable of being fixed in a specific sum of money either on judgment or by agreement;

(b) whether a compromise fixes the full measure of the claimant's loss depends on the proper construction of the compromise agreement. Lord Bingham in *Heaton v AXA Equity & Law Life Assurance Society plc* said that in construing a compromise agreement for this purpose one significant factor is whether the claimant has expressly reserved the right to sue other persons, although the absence of such a reservation is by no means conclusive in favour of an argument that other claims are extinguished;

(c) whether a compromise extinguishes other claims between the parties also depends on the proper construction of the agreement. Use of the phrase 'in full and final settlement' tends towards the conclusion that other claims are extinguished, and if worded widely might even be treated as including claims of which the party was unaware (*Brazier v News Group Newspapers Ltd* [2016] EWCA Civ 79). This can be avoided by including an express reservation, or by the use of other restrictive words. In *Henley v Bloom* [2010] 1 WLR 1770 a compromise in full and final settlement of any claim in respect of improvements the claimant had made to a leased flat was held to apply only to improvements made by the tenant, and did not prevent the claimant making a subsequent claim for damages against the landlord for disrepairs; and

(d) if a compromise, on its proper construction, fixes the full measure of the claimant's loss, the compromise extinguishes the claim so that other claims for the same damage cannot be pursued against other persons, whether in contract or tort.

G OBSTRUCTING THE JUST DISPOSAL OF THE PROCEEDINGS

The second half of CPR, r 3.4(2)(b), allows the court to strike out a statement of case which **30.32** obstructs the just disposal of the proceedings. This is expanded upon by PD 3A, para 1.5, which provides that a claim may come within r 3.4(2)(b) if it is vexatious, scurrilous, or obviously ill-founded. Poorly drafted statements of case may be struck out on this ground, such as where the pleading is unclear and not readily cured by amendment, or where it seeks to reverse the burden of proof (*Prince Radu of Hohenzollern v Houston* [2009] EWHC 398 (QB)). An overly pedantic approach to the niceties of pleading may, however, be contrary to the overriding objective (*Deutsche Morgan Grenfell Group plc v Commissioners of Inland Revenue* [2007] 1 AC 558).

Whether a statement of case is vexatious depends 'on all the circumstances of the case: **30.33** the categories are not closed and the considerations of public policy and the interests of justice may be very material' (*per* Stuart-Smith LJ in *Ashmore v British Coal Corporation* [1990] 2 QB 338). The applicant in *Ashmore v British Coal Corporation* was one of 1,500 women claiming they were employed on less favourable terms than certain male comparators. Fourteen cases were selected for determination, and the eventual finding was in favour of the employer. The applicant then sought to proceed with her claim. Although the previous determination was not strictly binding, the applicant's claim was struck out as being frivolous and vexatious. Pleadings under the old system have also been struck out on this ground where a party has been joined merely to obtain disclosure of documents or costs (*Burstall v Beyfus* (1884) 26 ChD 35) or where a claim is a disguised action for gaming debts (*Day v William Hill (Park Lane) Ltd* [1949] 1 KB 632).

Rassam v Budge [1893] 1 QB 571 concerned a claim for damages for slander. Instead of **30.34** pleading to the words alleged by the claimant, the defence set out the defendant's rather different version of what he had said, and pleaded the words he alleged he had spoken were true. These allegations were struck out as tending to prejudice the fair trial of the claim, because they left it unclear whether the issue was whether the words complained of by the claimant were spoken and published, or whether those words were true.

In *Philipps v Philipps* (1878) 4 QBD 127 Cotton LJ said, at 139: **30.35**

> . . . in my opinion it is absolutely essential that the pleading, not to be embarrassing to the defendants, should state those facts which will put the defendants on their guard and tell them what they have to meet when the case comes on for trial.

A defence will be struck out if it does not make clear how much of the claim is admitted **30.36** and how much is denied (*British and Colonial Land Association Ltd v Foster* (1887) 4 TLR 574). Mere prolixity or setting out of inconsistent claims or defences would be unlikely to result in striking out (see, eg, *Re Morgan* (1887) 35 ChD 492), although costs sanctions may be imposed if the case is protracted as a result.

H POWERS AFTER A STRIKING-OUT ORDER IS MADE

30.37 When a court strikes out a statement of case it may enter such judgment as the successful party appears entitled to (PD 3A, para 4.2) and make any consequential order it considers appropriate (CPR, r 3.4(3)). If a claim survives a striking-out application, the court may dispense with the need to file directions questionnaires, allocate the claim to a track, and make case management directions (PD 26, para 2.4).

I DISCONTINUANCE

30.38 From time to time a claimant may think better of having commenced proceedings, and will want to pull out of them without incurring all the costs of litigating to trial. A claimant who wishes to discontinue proceedings must file a notice of discontinuance. The general rule is that once a claim is discontinued, the claimant has to pay the defendant's costs of the claim.

What may be discontinued

30.39 A claimant may discontinue:

(a) the whole claim (CPR, r 38.1(1)); or
(b) part of the claim (ie some of the causes of action pleaded: r 38.1(1)); and
(c) against all of the defendants (r 38.2(3)); or
(d) against some of the defendants (r 38.2(3)).

Permission to discontinue

30.40 Generally, a claimant has the right to discontinue without seeking permission first (CPR, r 38.2(1)). However, in some circumstances permission is required. These are:

(a) If an interim injunction has been granted in relation to the claim being discontinued, permission has to be sought from the court (r 38.2(2)(a)).
(b) If any party has given an undertaking to the court in relation to the claim being discontinued, permission has to be sought from the court (r 38.2(2)(a)).
(c) If the claimant has received an interim payment (whether by agreement or pursuant to a court order) in relation to the claim being discontinued, permission must be sought from the court or consent must be given in writing by the defendant (r 38.2(2)(b)).
(d) Where there is more than one claimant, the claimant wishing to discontinue must either obtain permission to discontinue from the court, or obtain consent in writing from all the other claimants (r 38.2(2)(c)).
(e) Where a claim is brought by a person under a disability, approval by the court is required if a discontinuance amounts to a settlement or compromise of the claim (*Sayers v SmithKline Beecham plc* [2005] PIQR P8).

30.41 If consent is required, the signed consent(s) must be obtained before the claimant files the notice of discontinuance. If the court's permission has to be sought, a separate application for permission must be issued, and the claimant is only allowed to file the notice of discontinuance after the order granting permission is made.

Procedure for discontinuing

A claimant discontinues all or part of the claim by filing a notice of discontinuance (form **30.42**
N279) with the court, and serving a copy on all other parties. Regarding contents:

(a) The notice of discontinuance that is filed at court must state that copies have been
    served on all other parties (CPR, r 38.3(2)).
(b) In cases where the consent of another party is required, all copies of the notice of dis-
    continuance must have copies of the consent annexed (r 38.3(3)).
(c) In cases where there is more than one defendant, the notice of discontinuance must
    identify the defendants against whom the claim is being discontinued (r 38.3(4)).

Setting aside notice of discontinuance

A defendant may apply for an order setting aside a notice of discontinuance served without **30.43**
consent or permission, provided the application is made within 28 days of the notice (CPR,
r 38.4). A notice of discontinuance was set aside in *Fakih Brothers v AP Møller (Copenhagen) Ltd* [1994] 1 Lloyd's Rep 103, where it was served to avoid the imposition of an
onerous term in a consent order, and in *Ernst and Young v Butte Mining plc* [1996] 1 WLR
1605, where it was served in order to pre-empt the effective service of a counterclaim.

Effect of discontinuance

Notice of discontinuance takes effect, and brings the proceedings to an end as against each **30.44**
defendant, on the date it is served upon that defendant. Unless the court orders otherwise,
the claimant is liable for the defendant's costs up to the date of service of the notice of discontinuance (r 38.6(1)). However, there are no costs consequences regarding discontinued
small claims track cases (r 38.6(3)). The court can reverse the usual costs rule on a discontinuance where the claimant has in effect obtained all the relief sought in the proceedings
(*Amoco (UK) Exploration Co v British American Offshore Ltd* (2000) LTL 12/12/00), or
where there has been a change of circumstances making it uneconomic to continue (*Walker
v Walker* (2005) LTL 27/1/05).

If only part of the claim is discontinued, the claimant's liability is limited to the costs of **30.45**
the part of the claim that has been discontinued. Usually the claimant does not have to pay
the defendant's costs following a partial discontinuance until the conclusion of the claim.
However, the court may in its discretion order these costs to be paid immediately, either
after they have been agreed between the parties or after they have been assessed by the
court (r 38.6(2)). Where the claimant is required to pay the costs of the discontinued part
of the claim straight away, the liability to do so arises 14 days after the relevant costs are
agreed or assessed by the court. Failure to pay gives grounds for the court imposing a stay
on the remainder of the proceedings until the costs are paid (r 38.8).

Subsequent proceedings

A claimant who discontinues after a defence has been filed is not allowed to commence **30.46**
new proceedings against the same defendant arising out of the same or substantially the
same facts as the original claim, unless the court first gives permission for the second claim
to be issued (CPR, r 38.7). If permission is granted, the court will normally give directions
regarding issuing the substantive second claim (r 25.2(3)).

J STAYS

30.47 By CPR, r 3.1(2)(f), the court has a general case management power to stay the whole or any part of any proceedings or judgment either generally or until a specified date or event. This rule derives from the SCA 1981, s 49(3), which provides that nothing in the Act affects the power of the High Court and Court of Appeal to stay proceedings where the court thinks fit to do so, either of its own initiative or on the application of any person, whether or not a party to the proceedings. While a stay is in place the proceedings remain alive, but no further steps may be taken to progress the claim other than applying to lift the stay. A stay on a judgment prevents any steps being taken to enforce it, until the stay is lifted. Note that a stay may apply to only part of the proceedings, and where this applies obviously the remaining parts of the proceedings will continue. A stay may be lifted on proper grounds being shown (*Cooper v Williams* [1963] 2 QB 567).

Stay on settlement

30.48 Proceedings are stayed when a Part 36 offer is accepted (see Chapter 36).

30.49 Ordinary consent orders following a compromise of a claim frequently provide for the stay of the proceedings (*Rofa Sport Management AG v DHL International (UK) Ltd* [1989] 1 WLR 902). Similarly, a Tomlin order (see 41.18–41.21) provides for the stay of the proceedings on the terms set out in a schedule to the order, with permission to apply for the purpose of carrying out the terms of the agreement.

Stays in pending proceedings

30.50 There may be reasons relating to the efficient progress of the proceedings which make granting a stay desirable. Examples are:

(a) Where there is no issue on liability in a personal injury case, but a clear prognosis will not be possible for some time. This possibility is referred to in PD 51A, para 19(3)(b), where the machinery referred to is an adjournment to determine prognosis.

(b) Where a claim is issued without complying with the relevant pre-action protocol because the solicitor acting for the claimant is instructed shortly before the expiry of the limitation period. A stay may be granted in the early stages of the proceedings to enable the steps of the protocol to be completed.

(c) Where a personal injuries claim is issued close to the expiry of limitation without sufficient medical evidence substantiating the claimant's injuries because of difficulties in obtaining the necessary evidence. This arose in *Knight v Sage Group plc* (1999) LTL 28/4/99, where the court gave the claimant three months to obtain and disclose the necessary evidence.

(d) Where a claim is commenced, and subsequent events show that there is a possibility that the proceedings will not serve a useful purpose. For example, a claim may be brought in professional negligence seeking an indemnity in respect of the claimant's potential liability to a stranger to the proceedings. If it transpires that there is a possibility that the stranger to the litigation may never make a claim against the claimant, it may be appropriate to order a stay until the stranger's claim becomes time-barred.

(e) The court may order a stay at the allocation stage to allow for the possibility of settlement under CPR, r 26.4 (see 15.36).

(f) The usual stay ordered as part of an order making a reference to the Court of Justice of the European Union (see Chapter 40).

(g) Stays imposed pending the resolution of a test case (*Woods v Duncan* [1946] AC 401).

Stays to enforce compliance with orders

Sometimes the court imposes stays as a means of enforcing compliance with its orders. This **30.51** is going to be effective only against a claimant or a party in the position of a claimant, such as a defendant making a counterclaim. Examples are:

(a) Stays which are normally imposed pending the provision of security for costs (see Chapter 26).

(b) A stay imposed where the claimant in a personal injuries claim refuses a reasonable request for a medical examination (*Edmeades v Thames Board Mills Ltd* [1969] 2 QB 67 and Chapter 35).

(c) A stay pending a satisfactory undertaking as to costs or otherwise connected with the way in which a claim is funded (*Grovewood Holdings plc v James Capel and Co Ltd* [1995] Ch 80).

(d) A second claim may be stayed pending payment of the costs of an earlier discontinued claim (see 30.45) or the costs of an earlier claim that was struck out (see 30.07).

(e) Where partners fail to comply with a demand for their names and addresses under PD 7A, paras 5B.1–5B.3.

Stays to protect concurrent claims

There is a general public interest in avoiding a multiplicity of claims. Sometimes it is simply **30.52** an abuse of process to bring duplicate sets of proceedings, with the result that the later proceedings will be struck out (*Buckland v Palmer* [1984] 1 WLR 1109). The following examples stop a little way short of being suitable for striking out, but stays may be imposed instead:

(a) Where the dispute should be dealt with by arbitration rather than by litigation (Arbitration Act 1996, s 9). Costs after a stay (or anti-suit injunction) granted to prevent a breach of an arbitration clause are likely to be awarded on the indemnity basis (*Epping Electrical Co Ltd v Briggs and Forrester (Plumbing Services) Ltd, sub nom A v B (No 2)* [2007] 1 All ER (Comm) 633).

(b) Where the dispute should be dealt with in the administration of an insolvent person's estate.

(c) Stays on the ground of *forum non conveniens* (see 11.55).

(d) Stays under the recast Judgments Regulation (see arts 29 and 30 at 11.52–11.54).

(e) Stays until the resolution of connected pending criminal proceedings. Applications for such stays may be made by any party to the civil claim, or the prosecutor or any defendant to the criminal proceedings (PD 23A, para 11A.1). The evidence in support of the application must contain an estimate of the expected duration of the stay, and must identify the respects in which continuing the civil claim may prejudice the criminal trial (para 11A.3).

KEY POINTS SUMMARY

- Striking-out applications are often combined with applications for summary judgment. **30.53**

- Striking out is aimed at the way in which a claim or defence is formulated in the statement of case, or if it is otherwise an abuse of process. Summary judgment is aimed at weakness on the merits.

- A party who realizes their case is doomed is often best advised to discontinue to prevent further costs building up, but usually has to pay the costs of the other parties to date.

- Stays are temporary halts in proceedings, and can be granted for a range of reasons. A stay is normally lifted once the reason no longer applies.

31

DISCLOSURE

A LAWYERS' RESPONSIBILITIES 31.04

B CLIENTS' RESPONSIBILITIES 31.05

C STAGE WHEN DISCLOSURE
TAKES PLACE 31.06

D DISCLOSURE ORDERS 31.09

E STANDARD DISCLOSURE 31.13

F MENU OPTION DISCLOSURE 31.22

G DUTY TO SEARCH 31.30

H LIST OF DOCUMENTS 31.32

I PRIVILEGE........................31.37

J INSPECTION 31.73

K ORDERS IN SUPPORT OF
DISCLOSURE 31.77

L DOCUMENTS REFERRED TO IN
STATEMENTS OF CASE, ETC. 31.84

M ADMISSION OF AUTHENTICITY 31.87

N COLLATERAL USE 31.88

Key points summary 31.91

31.01 In almost all types of civil disputes there will be documentary evidence relating to the matters in issue. In a contractual claim, for example, there are likely to be documents evidencing or comprising the negotiations leading up to the contract being entered into, there are likely to be contractual documents, including things like quotations, orders, delivery notes, invoices, and standard terms of trading, documents recording any work done or materials bought for the purposes of the contract, and subsequent correspondence dealing with any complaints about performance. Even in claims which appear to be mainly concerned with oral evidence, such as accident claims, it is likely there will be accident report forms, accident book entries, documents made in compliance with the health and safety legislation, medical records about the treatment given, and financial documentation dealing with things like the claimant's salary (wages slips, P60s, and employers' salary records) and out-of-pocket expenses (for which there should be receipts).

31.02 In most claims while there may be a significant number of documents, they can often be included in one or two lever arch files. There are however cases where there are vast amounts of documentation dealing with the issues raised. An extreme case was *Al Rawi v Security Service* [2012] 1 AC 531 where the defendants had approximately 250,000 relevant documents, and where its lawyers estimated that conducting a public interest immunity exercise (see 31.70) would take three years. Controlling the costs of disclosure in complex cases is a major problem.

31.03 The parties obviously need to retain and marshal the documentation in their own possession for the purposes of assisting their own cases. Beyond this, however, the CPR require the parties to give advance notice to their opponents of all the material documentation in their control, and this duty extends not only to favourable documentation, but also to documents that might assist the other side. This is done in two stages. Typically at the first stage the parties send each other lists of documents (see form 31.1), a process called 'disclosure'. The second stage is 'inspection', which is the process by which the other side can request copies of documents appearing in the list of documents, typically with photocopies being provided by the disclosing party.

List of documents: standard disclosure

In the	
HIGH COURT OF JUSTICE	
QUEEN'S BENCH DIVISION	
Claim No.	HQ15X 96789
Claimant (including ref)	CHEDISTON WHOLESALERS LIMITED
Defendant (including ref)	LINSTEAD FRUITGROWERS LIMITED
Date	15.10.2015

Notes

- The rules relating to standard disclosure are contained in Part 31 of the Civil Procedure Rules.
- Documents to be included under standard disclosure are contained in Rule 31.6
- A document has or will have been in your control if you have or have had possession, or a right of possession, of it **or** a right to inspect or take copies of it.

Disclosure Statement

I, the above named

☑ Claimant ☐ Defendant

☐ Party (if party making disclosure is a company, firm or other organisation identify here who the person making the disclosure statement is and why he is the appropriate person to make it)

state that I have carried out a reasonable and proportionate search to locate all the documents which I am required to disclose under the order made by the court on (date of order) 14.09.2015

☑ I did not search for documents:-

☑ pre-dating 01.01.2012

☑ located elsewhere than

The Claimant's offices and the Claimant's solicitor's offices.

☑ in categories other than

Those relevant to the issues in this claim.

☐ for electronic documents

☑ I carried out a search for electronic documents contained on or created by the following: (list what was searched and extent of search)

Documents on the Claimant's office server, PCs, laptops and notebooks, including word processed documents, spreadsheets, emails and attachments to emails.

Form 31.1 *continued*

☑ I did not search for the following:-

☑ documents created before

01.01.2012

documents contained on or created by the ☑ Claimant ☐ Defendant

☐ PCs   ☑ portable data storage media

☐ databases   ☐ servers

☑ back-up tapes   ☑ off-site storage

☑ mobile phones   ☐ laptops

☐ notebooks   ☑ handheld devices

☑ PDA devices

documents contained on or created by the ☑ Claimant ☐ Defendant

☐ mail files   ☐ document files

☐ calendar files   ☑ web-based applications

☐ spreadsheet files   ☑ graphic and presentation files

documents other than by reference to the following keyword(s)/concepts
(delete if your search was not confined to specific keywords or concepts)

I certify that I understand the duty of disclosure and to the best of my knowledge I have carried out that duty. I further certify that the list of documents set out in or attached to this form, is a complete list of all documents which are or have been in my control and which I am obliged under the order to disclose.

I understand that I must inform the court and the other parties immediately if any further document required to be disclosed by Rule 31.6 comes into my control at any time before the conclusion of the case.

☐ I have not permitted inspection of documents within the category or class of documents (as set out below) required to be disclosed under Rule 31(6)(b)or (c) on the grounds that to do so would be disproportionate to the issues in the case.

Signed   **Date**   15.10.2015

(Claimant)(Defendant)('s litigation friend)

Form 31.1 *continued*

List and number here, in a convenient order, the documents (or bundles of documents if of the same nature, e.g. invoices) in your control, which you do not object to being inspected. Give a short description of each document or bundle so that it can be identified, and say if it is kept elsewhere i.e. with a bank or solicitor	I have control of the documents numbered and listed here. I do not object to you inspecting them/producing copies.

1 Copy letters from Claimant to Defendant (12 items)	6.1.2012-1-7.2014
2 Letters from Defendant to Claimant	18.1.2012-1.7.2014
3 Emails between Claimant and Defendant (30 items)	20.1.2012-1.7.2014
4 Sale contract	26.5.2012
5 Resale contract	16.6.2012
6 Emails between Claimant and sub-purchasers	16.6.2012-1.7.2012
7 Copy letters Claimant's solicitors to Defendant	various
8 Copy letters Claimant's solicitors to Defendant's solicitors	various
9 Letters Defendant's solicitors to Claimant's solicitors	various
10 Statements of case common to both parties	various

List and number here, as above, the documents in your control which you object to being inspected. (Rule 31.19)	I have control of the documents numbered and listed here, but I object to you inspecting them: 1 Communications between the Claimant and its solicitors in their professional capacity for the purpose of giving and receiving legal advice. 2 Instructions to, opinion of, and drafts settled by counsel. 3 Communications between the Claimant's officers and employees when litigation was pending or contemplated for the purpose of obtaining information or evidence for use in this claim.

Say what your objections are	I object to you inspecting these documents because: They are, as appears from their nature, protected from production by legal professional privilege being documents which came into being for and in contemplation of this claim.

List and number here, the documents you once had in your control, but which you no longer have. For each document listed, say when it was last in your control and where it is now.	I have had the documents numbered and listed below, but they are no longer in my control. The originals of the documents numbered 1, 7 and 8 in the first part of this list, which are assumed to be in the control of their respective recipients.

A LAWYERS' RESPONSIBILITIES

As soon as litigation is contemplated, the parties' legal representatives must inform their **31.04** clients of the need to preserve disclosable documents (PD 31B, para 7), so that all original documents are preserved and made available at the disclosure stage (*Rockwell Machine Tool Co Ltd v EP Barrus (Concessionaires) Ltd* [1968] 1 WLR 693). This extends to electronic documents that might otherwise be deleted in accordance with the client's usual document retention policy, and to real evidence, such as pathology samples. Counsel cannot continue to act for a client who refuses to accept counsel's advice to disclose material documents (Code of Conduct of the Bar of England and Wales, guidance gC13).

B CLIENTS' RESPONSIBILITIES

31.05   The primary obligation to make full disclosure of material documents rests with the client. As will be seen, 'standard disclosure' in the course of fast track and multi-track claims involves the client conducting a reasonable search for disclosable documents, and then personally signing a 'disclosure statement' to the effect that the nature of the duty to disclose is understood and has been complied with. The obligation is a continuing one and includes documents that come within a party's control at any stage until the proceedings are concluded (CPR, r 31.11(1)). If documents come to a party's notice after lists have been exchanged, the party is under an immediate obligation to notify every other party (r 31.11(2)).

C STAGE WHEN DISCLOSURE TAKES PLACE

31.06   The main obligation to disclose documents arises in fast track and multi-track claims as a result of directions made at the allocation stage, or at the first case management conference. Generally, these directions will include provision for disclosure and inspection of documents. The direction will state whether lists of documents should be provided, and whether a disclosure statement is required (see later). It will also give a calendar date for the last day for compliance. Allocation takes place within a few weeks of the filing of defences and disclosure is normally ordered for a few weeks thereafter. The result is that disclosure is often required about two months after the defence is filed. As we saw in Chapter 27, the same does not apply in small claims track cases, where there is no obligation to serve lists of documents and disclosure is usually limited to disclosing the documents each party intends to rely upon.

31.07   As discussed in Chapter 5, a wide range of documents that might be disclosed during proceedings will be disclosed beforehand in compliance with the pre-action protocols. Key documents, such as medical reports in personal injuries claims, and written contracts in contract claims, have to be served with the particulars of claim (see Chapter 14). If full disclosure has already taken place, the court should be informed with the directions questionnaires so that the directions made on allocation reflect the correct position.

31.08   There are also a number of somewhat specialized disclosure procedures which are resorted to only in cases where there is a real litigation reason for incurring the additional expense that they entail. These additional procedures are:

(a) *Norwich Pharmacal* orders (see 45.02–45.12), which are used to obtain information (which can include documentation) designed to assist in identifying a tortfeasor;
(b) pre-commencement disclosure orders under the SCA 1981, s 33(2): see 45.18;
(c) disclosure orders against persons who are not parties to the substantive litigation, under the SCA 1981, s 34(2): see 45.27;
(d) search orders, which allow a claimant, through a supervising solicitor, to take disclosable documents from the premises of a defendant who is likely to destroy the evidence rather than voluntarily providing it under an ordinary disclosure order: see Chapter 44.

D DISCLOSURE ORDERS

31.09   To ensure disclosure takes place in a proportionate manner, disclosure in fast track and multi-track cases can take one of two paths:

(a) in fast track claims, multi-track personal injuries claims, and other multi-track claims where the court makes a specific direction to this effect, disclosure is governed by CPR, r 31.5(1); and

(b) in all other multi-track claims disclosure is governed by r 31.5(3)–(8).

In fast track and other claims in category (a), by virtue of r 31.5(1): **31.10**

(a) the court may make an order for 'disclosure', which means an order to give standard disclosure (see 31.13) unless the court directs otherwise; or
(b) the court may dispense with or limit standard disclosure; or
(c) the parties may agree in writing to dispense with or to limit standard disclosure.

In multi-track claims not within category (a) at 31.09 disclosure follows what is called the 'menu' option, see 31.22. **31.11**

A party who fails to disclose or to permit inspection of documents in breach of a disclosure order may not rely on the undisclosed documents unless the court gives permission (r 31.21). A party aggrieved by the other side's failure to disclose documents may apply for any of the orders discussed at 31.77–31.83 to enforce compliance. **31.12**

E STANDARD DISCLOSURE

Standard disclosure typically applies to fast track claims, and is one of the menu options in multi-track cases. It involves each party making a reasonable search for material documents (see 31.30), and then making and serving on every other party a list of documents (see form 31.1) identifying the documents being disclosed in a concise, convenient form (r 31.10(2) and (3)). **31.13**

Documents to be disclosed under standard disclosure

The nature of the documents that must be disclosed under standard disclosure is described by CPR, r 31.6, which provides: **31.14**

Standard disclosure requires a party to disclose only—
(a) the documents on which he relies; and
(b) the documents which—
    (i) adversely affect his own case;
    (ii) adversely affect another party's case; or
    (iii) support another party's case; and
(c) the documents which he is required to disclose by a relevant practice direction.

These categories come close to requiring disclosure of relevant documents (in the sense of being relevant evidence in the case), but technically they are slightly differently worded and not quite the same as relevance (*Shah v HSBC Private Bank (UK) Ltd* [2011] EWCA Civ 1154). They do not cover documents relevant only to credibility (*Favor Easy Management Ltd v Wu* [2011] 1 WLR 1803). Documents that are not relevant to the issues in the case will not come into any of the categories (*Atos Consulting Ltd v Avis Europe plc* [2008] Bus LR Digest D20). Determining whether a document falls into any of these categories is to be judged against the statements of case, and is not enlarged by reference to matters raised elsewhere, even in exchanged witness statements (*Paddick v Associated Newspapers Ltd* (2003) LTL 10/12/03).

Rule 31.6(a) covers documents that a party intends to rely on in support of their affirmative case (*Shah v HSBC Private Bank (UK) Ltd*). Damaging documents have to be disclosed under r 31.6(b)(i). Rule 31.6(b)(ii) is probably intended to cover documents in the control of party A in a multi-party claim which adversely affect the case of party B against party C (*Serious Organised Crime Agency v Namli* [2011] EWCA Civ 1411). Rule 31.6(b)(ii) and **31.15**

(iii) assume that the other party has an affirmative case that can be adversely affected or supported: where this is not so, there is nothing for these provisions to bite upon (*Shah v HSBC Private Bank (UK) Ltd*). Rule 31.6(c) includes documents that need to be disclosed under PD Pre-action conduct and PD 31B, which deals with disclosure of electronic documents.

31.16　Standard disclosure will require an employer in a personal injuries claim to disclose documents relating to other accidents involving the same machinery. Employers must also disclose the earnings of comparative employees (*Rowley v Liverpool City Council* (1989) *The Times*, 26 October 1989). Claimants in personal injuries claims must disclose their medical records, even back to birth, so the defendant's medical advisers can see whether the claimant had any medical history relevant to the extent or effect of the alleged injuries (*OCS Group Ltd v Wells* [2009] 1 WLR 1895). In professional negligence claims against solicitors the entirety of the solicitor's original file is almost invariably covered by standard disclosure (*Martin v Triggs Turner Barton* (2008) *The Times*, 5 February 2008). In an unfair prejudice case under the Companies Act 2006, s 994, where it was alleged the directors were receiving excessive remuneration, standard disclosure included financial documents such as accounts and budgets (*Arrow Trading and Investments Est Ltd v Edwardian Group Ltd* [2005] 1 BCLC 696). However, the courts will not allow disclosure to be used to 'fish' for a case. A party which does not have the materials for even an arguable claim, but hopes to find evidence from the other side, is said to be fishing.

'Document'

31.17　For the purposes of disclosure, the word 'document' means anything on which information of any description is recorded (CPR, r 31.4). It is not restricted to writing, nor to paper documents. It will cover e-mails, text messages on mobile telephones, and relevant information stored on a computer hard drive or digital storage device. The latter includes documents which have been 'deleted' and technical information known as 'metadata'. It also covers photographs, sound, and audio-visual recordings.

Electronic documents

31.18　Increasingly, a great deal of the most important documentation in a case will have been sent electronically, and there may be a wide range of different electronic devices that contain records of relevant information. Where there was a dispute as to whether a contractual document was sent by e-mail, disclosure was ordered of the relevant hard disks, backups, and server (*Marlton v Tektronix UK Holdings Ltd* (2003) LTL 10/2/03). Practice Direction 31B seeks to ensure that the parties comply with their obligations to give standard disclosure of electronic documents, while adhering to the overriding objective and avoiding unnecessary costs being incurred through taking the process too far. The parties are required to discuss the use of technology for the purposes of managing disclosure of electronic documents (para 8), and are encouraged to seek appropriate directions for disclosure at the first case management conference (paras 14–19). They may use electronic documents questionnaires (which have to be verified by a statement of truth) to exchange information on their electronic documents so that suitable directions can be devised. Directions for the disclosure of electronic documents that may be made are considered at 31.29.

'Control'

31.19　Disclosure must be made of documents which are, or have been, in a party's control (CPR, r 31.8(1)). 'Control' is defined as covering documents which are or have been in a party's physical possession, and also where a party had a right to possession or to inspect or take copies (r 31.8(2)). There is control over documents if there is a prior or current practice of a party having access and inspection rights over documents in the possession of someone else (*Montpellier Estates Ltd v Leeds City Council* [2012] EWHC 1343 (QB) at [33]).

An employer or principal has a right to possession of documents in the hands of an employ- **31.20**
ee in the course of the employee's employment or an agent in the course of the agency (*Fairstar Heavy Transport NV v Adkins* [2013] EWCA Civ 886). A company's documents may be under the control of a majority shareholder who has complete control over the company's affairs (*Re Tecnion Investments Ltd* [1985] BCLC 434), and it is possible for a subsidiary company's documents to be in the control of its parent company (*Lonrho Ltd v Shell Petroleum Co Ltd* [1980] QB 358; [1980] 1 WLR 627). Insurance claims documents in the possession of an insurer are in the control of the insured (*Mueller Europe Ltd v Central Roofing (South Wales) Ltd* [2013] CILL 3293). While UK patients have control of their medical records by virtue of the Access to Health Records Act 1990, this depends on local legislation, so patients may not have control over medical records in other jurisdictions (*Favor Easy Management Ltd v Wu* [2011] 1 WLR 1803).

Limiting standard disclosure

Even in fast track claims and other cases not governed by menu option disclosure, the court **31.21**
may dispense with or limit standard disclosure. Further, the parties may agree in writing to dispense with or to limit standard disclosure. The court may make directions requiring disclosure but dispensing with lists, or for disclosure to take place in stages, and the parties may agree to disclosure taking place in a similar informal, or staged, manner. For example, it is provided in CPR, r 31.10(8), that the parties may agree in writing:

(a) to disclose documents without making a list; and
(b) to disclose documents without the disclosing party making a disclosure statement.

F MENU OPTION DISCLOSURE

In non-personal injuries multi-track claims, menu option disclosure applies unless the court **31.22**
otherwise orders (CPR, r 31.5(2)). To the extent that the documents to be disclosed are electronic, the provisions of PD 31B (see 31.18) apply in addition to the menu option provisions (r 31.5(9)). Menu option disclosure takes place in three stages.

Stage 1: Disclosure report

Not less than 14 days before the first case management conference ('CMC') each party must **31.23**
file and serve a disclosure report in form N263 (CPR, r 31.5(3), see form 31.2) together with their electronic documents questionnaires if these have been exchanged under PD 31B (r 31.5(4)). A disclosure report must be verified by a statement of truth (r 31.5(3), and must:

(a) describe briefly what documents exist or may exist that are or may be relevant to the matters in issue in the case;
(b) describe where and with whom those documents are or may be located;
(c) in the case of electronic documents, describe how those documents are stored;
(d) estimate the broad range of costs that could be involved in giving standard disclosure in the case, including the costs of searching for and disclosing any electronically stored documents. This ties in with costs budgeting, see 16.10; and
(e) state which of the directions under r 31.5(6) or (7) are to be sought.

Form 31.2 Disclosure report

Disclosure report

Name of court	Claim No.

To be completed by, or on behalf of,

who is [1ˢᵗ][2ⁿᵈ][3ʳᵈ][   ][Claimant][Defendant]
[Part 20 claimant] in this claim

1. Please describe in the table below (or in a separate document filed with this report), using the number 1, 2 etc., all documents which exist or may exist and which may be relevant to the issues in the case and in respect of each such document, where and with whom it may be found, and in the case of electronic documents how the same are stored.

No.	Document description	Where it may be found	(if an electronic document) how it is stored

Note: If an Electronic documents questionnaire (Form N264) has been exchanged, it must be filed with this report.

2. Please state in the box below the broad range of costs that could be involved in giving standard disclosure in this case, including the costs of searching for and disclosing any electronically stored documents.

3. To the extent that this is not already dealt with in Section D4 of your Directions Questionnaire, please state in the boxes below your proposed directions for disclosure to include what particular scope and form of disclosure and related directions you propose for yourself and the other parties by reference to CPR 31.5 (6) and (7) and if not standard the broad range of costs for disclosure.

If not standard, broad range of costs	Form of disclosure (CPR 31.5 (6))

Other disclosure directions (CPR 31.5 (7))

I believe that the facts stated in this Disclosure Report are true.

Signature	Your name and full postal address		
			If applicable
		Telephone no.	
[Legal Representative for the][1ˢᵗ][2ⁿᵈ][3ʳᵈ][ ]		Fax no.	
[Claimant][Defendant][Part 20 claimant]		DX no.	
Date	Postcode	Your ref.	
	E-mail		

Stage 2: Agreeing proposal for disclosure

Not less than seven days before the first CMC the parties must, at a meeting or by tel- **31.24**
ephone, discuss and seek to agree a proposal in relation to disclosure that meets the overriding objective (CPR, r 31.5(5)). A similar discussion must also be held on any other
occasion as the court may direct (r 31.5(5)). Any agreed proposal should be filed at court.
By r 31.5(6), if the parties agree proposals for the scope of disclosure which the court
considers are appropriate in all the circumstances, the court may approve them without a
hearing and give directions in the terms proposed.

Stage 3: CMC menu disclosure

If disclosure directions have not been made without a hearing under CPR, r 31.5(6), at **31.25**
the first or any subsequent CMC the court will decide on the appropriate orders to make
about disclosure. It will do so having regard to the overriding objective, the available costs
budgets, and the need to limit disclosure to that which is necessary to deal with the case
justly (r 31.5(7)). The menu available under r 31.5(7) comprises orders:

(a) dispensing with disclosure;
(b) that a party disclose the documents on which it relies (see 31.15), and at the same time
    request any specific disclosure it requires from any other party;
(c) directing, where practicable, the disclosure to be given by each party on an issue by
    issue basis;
(d) that each party disclose any documents which it is reasonable to suppose may contain
    information which enables that party to advance its own case or to damage that of any
    other party, or which leads to an enquiry which has either of those consequences;
(e) for standard disclosure;
(f) in whatever form the court considers appropriate.

Train of inquiry documents

Rule 31.5(7)(d) of the CPR allows the court to make an order for disclosure of train of inquiry **31.26**
documents. These are documents which are not themselves relevant, but which could provide
information that could lead to a train of inquiry resulting in finding relevant documents
(*Compagnie Financière et Commerciale du Pacifique v Peruvian Guano Co* (1882) 11 QBD
55). Orders for disclosure of train of inquiry documents are rare (albeit not unknown: see
Commissioners of Inland Revenue v Exeter City AFC Ltd (2004) LTL 12/5/04), because they
increase costs and are unlikely to be justified on proportionality grounds.

Key of the warehouse order

Rule 31.5(7)(f) of the CPR allows the court to make any other order in relation to disclo- **31.27**
sure that the court considers appropriate. It allows the court, for example, to make a 'key
of the warehouse' order. Such an order requires each party to hand over all its documents
after removing any privileged documents, and the other side can then choose which documents it wishes to use in the litigation.

Disclosure directions

By CPR, r 31.5(8) the court may at any point give directions as to how disclosure is to be **31.28**
given, and in particular may direct:

(a) what searches are to be undertaken, of where, for what, in respect of which time peri-
    ods and by whom, and the extent of any search for electronically stored documents;

(b) whether lists of documents are required;

(c) how and when the disclosure statement is to be given;

(d) in what format documents are to be disclosed (and whether any identification is required);

(e) what is required in relation to documents that once existed but no longer exist; and

(f) whether disclosure shall take place in stages.

Directions for disclosure of electronic documents

31.29 Keeping down the costs of disclosure of electronic documents is a major problem in commercial litigation. Part of the concern is directed to the costs of searching for electronic documents, and part to the 'downstream' cost of dealing with the documents once they have been identified (*TIP Communications LLC v Motorola Ltd* [2009] EWHC 1486 (Pat)). Intelligent use of the menu options is intended to assist in ensuring electronic disclosure does not become disproportionately expensive while also ensuring that proper disclosure is made. Depending on the circumstances of the case, some of the following directions may be made to deal with disclosure of electronic documents:

(a) arrangements for harvesting electronic documents. This involves identifying the individuals whose electronic documents should be brought into the disclosure exercise, which of their electronic devices (PCs, laptops, PDAs, mobile telephones, etc.) should be included, the dates of the documents to be covered by the exercise, and whether the exercise includes deleted files and files from back-up storage devices;

(b) providing the other side with the total number of documents harvested. Large numbers of documents usually mean that sophisticated search directions will be required;

(c) whether harvested documents should be loaded onto an appropriate system (*Montpellier Estates Ltd v Leeds City Council* [2012] EWHC 1343 (QB));

(d) arrangements for conducting a proportionate search of the harvested material. A discussion between the legal representatives of the parties may be ordered to seek agreement on how the search should be conducted;

(e) applying keyword searches to identify relevant documents from those harvested. Parties should usually agree a list of keywords;

(f) whether software should be used to decouple duplicates to reduce the number of documents to be disclosed (*Goodale v Ministry of Justice* (2009) LTL 9/9/10);

(g) whether a suitably qualified information technology consultant who is experienced in electronic disclosure should be retained to conduct the technical aspects of the search.

G DUTY TO SEARCH

31.30 When giving standard disclosure, a party is required to make a reasonable search for documents falling within the meaning of standard disclosure (CPR, r 31.7). The rule sets out factors relevant in deciding on the reasonableness of a search, which include:

(a) the number of documents involved;

(b) the nature and complexity of the proceedings;

(c) the ease and expense of retrieval of any particular document; and

(d) the significance of any document which is likely to be located during the search.

31.31 It is implicit in the obligation in r 31.7 that the search should be meaningful and effective (*Mueller Europe Ltd v Central Roofing (South Wales) Ltd* [2013] CILL 3293). A search not carried out in good faith will not be reasonable (*Re Atrium Training Services Ltd* [2013] EWHC 2882 (Ch)). The rule does not demand that no stone be left unturned

(*Abela v Hammonds Suddards* (2008) LTL 9/12/08). It may be reasonable, for example, to decide not to search for documents coming into existence before some particular date, or to limit the search to certain specific places, or to documents falling into particular categories (PD 31A, para 2). A more limited search would be appropriate for secondary as opposed to primary evidence (*Nichia Corporation v Argos Ltd* [2007] Bus LR 1753). Secondary evidence is merely an aid in assessing the primary evidence in a case.

H LIST OF DOCUMENTS

The list

Disclosure will usually be made by serving lists of documents (see the example in form 31.1). **31.32** As the name suggests, a list of documents simply lists the documents that a party has relating to the case. It must identify the documents in a convenient order and as concisely as possible. It must indicate which documents are said to be privileged (see 31.37), and which documents are no longer available and what has happened to them. Further, the list must contain a disclosure statement (see 31.33) unless this has been dispensed with (by the court or by agreement in writing between the parties).

Disclosure statement

A list of documents must contain a 'disclosure statement' setting out the extent of the search **31.33** that has been made and certifying that the party understands the duty to disclose and that to the best of the disclosing party's knowledge the duty has been carried out. Where a party has not searched for a category or class of document on the ground that to do so would be unreasonable (see 31.30), this must be stated in the disclosure statement and the categories or classes of document not searched for must be identified (CPR, r 31.7(3)). Any such limitation on the search can be challenged by applying to the court (*Nichia Corporation v Argos Ltd* [2007] Bus LR 1753). The list of documents in form 31.1 includes a disclosure statement. Making a false disclosure statement, without an honest belief in its truth, may be punished as a contempt of court (CPR, r 31.23).

A disclosure statement is not a mere technicality. Its purpose is to impose a positive duty on **31.34** each party to give full standard disclosure. It has to be signed by the party in person, not by their solicitor (r 31.10(6)). If there are several claimants or defendants in a case, each should sign a disclosure statement. Providing a single composite list of documents does not satisfy r 31.10 (*Arrow Trading and Investments Est Ltd v Edwardian Group Ltd* [2005] 1 BCLC 696). Where the party making the disclosure statement is a company, firm, or association, the statement must identify the person making the statement and explain why he or she is a suitable person to make it (CPR, r 31.10(7)). The statement will have to give that person's name and address, as well as the office or position he or she holds within the organization (PD 31A, para 4.3). An insurer is allowed to sign a disclosure statement on behalf of the insured (para 4.7), which is helpful because sometimes the insured has no real interest in the litigation, and leaves everything to the insurer under its right of subrogation.

A party's statement as to the relevance of documents for the purposes of standard disclo- **31.35** sure is usually conclusive (*Loutchansky v Times Newspapers (No 1)* [2002] QB 321; *GE Capital Corporate Finance Group v Bankers Trust Co* [1995] 1 WLR 172) to avoid court time being wasted on satellite issues. Ultimately, the court may investigate the matter to avoid a party being the judge in his own cause (*West London Pipeline and Storage Ltd v Total UK Ltd* [2008] 2 CLC 258).

Lost and destroyed documents

31.36 Documents that are no longer available, because they have been lost, destroyed, or sent to someone else, must still be 'disclosed' by identifying them in the list of documents (CPR, r 31.2). The third section of the list is specifically designed for documents in this category. All that is required is that such documents be identified, together with the reason why they are no longer available (r 31.10(4)(b)). Obviously, there is no requirement to give inspection.

I PRIVILEGE

31.37 Privileged documents must be disclosed, but need not be made available for inspection by the other side. This means they must be identified in the second section of the list of documents, and the party asserting the right or duty to withhold inspection must state in the list the grounds on which that assertion is based (CPR, r 31.19(3)). The three heads of privilege will be considered in this section (where there is a right to withhold disclosure), together with public interest immunity (where there is a duty to withhold disclosure). When considering these different heads of privilege, it is worth bearing in mind the comment made by Lord Edmund-Davies in *Waugh v British Railways Board* [1980] AC 521 at 543:

> . . . we should start from the basis that the public interest is, on balance, best served by rigidly confining within narrow limits the cases where material relevant to litigation may be lawfully withheld. Justice is better served by candour than by suppression.

Privilege against self-incrimination

The common law rule

31.38 In *Blunt v Park Lane Hotel Ltd* [1942] 2 KB 253, Goddard LJ said:

> . . . the rule is that no one is bound to answer any question [or produce any document] if the answer thereto would, in the opinion of the judge, have a tendency to expose [him or her] to any criminal charge, penalty, or forfeiture which the judge regards as reasonably likely to be preferred or sued for.

31.39 The opening words show that it is only 'compelled' evidence that is protected. Pre-existing evidence found on the defendant's computer during the execution of a search order is not protected (*C plc v P (Attorney-General intervening)* [2008] Ch 1). Exposure to the risk of a penalty under EU legislation forming part of the law of the UK by virtue of the European Communities Act 1972 is a penalty for these purposes.

31.40 If there is no realistic chance of a prosecution, the privilege is not engaged (*Blunt v Park Lane Hotel Ltd* [1942] 2 KB 253). In *Rank Film Distributors Ltd v Video Information Centre* [1982] AC 380 it was held that the privilege could be relied on where a criminal charge was more than a contrived, fanciful, or remote possibility. The privilege may arise, not only when answering might increase the risk of being prosecuted, but also where the prosecution may make use of the answer in deciding whether to prosecute, and where the prosecution may seek to rely on the answer in establishing guilt (*Den Norske Bank ASA v Antonatos* [1998] QB 271). Merely asserting there is a risk is not enough: the risk must be real and appreciable (*Rank Film Distributors Ltd v Video Information Centre*).

31.41 The privilege extends to providing documents or answers that tend to expose the spouse or civil partner of the person asserting the privilege to criminal proceedings or proceedings for the recovery of a penalty (Civil Evidence Act 1968, s 14(1)). As a corporation has legal personality it can claim the privilege (*Triplex Safety Glass Co Ltd v Lancegaye Safety Glass*

(1934) Ltd [1939] 2 KB 395). In such cases it may be necessary to distinguish between the corporation and its officers and employees, and to consider whether all or only some of them may be at risk of criminal proceedings (*Sociedade Nacional de Combustiveis de Angola UEE v Lundqvist* [1991] 2 QB 310).

The privilege may be lost by the turn of events. Once the party has been prosecuted, whether **31.42** resulting in a conviction or an acquittal, he cannot be prosecuted again except in the limited circumstances provided by the Criminal Justice Act 2003, ss 75–97. In some cases the party may be given a pardon, which again eliminates the risk of prosecution (*R v Boyes* (1861) 1 B & S 311). If the Crown Prosecution Service indicates in writing that it will not make use of the information sought for the purposes of any criminal proceedings against the party or his wife, and if a clause stating that no disclosure made in compliance with the order will be used in evidence in the prosecution of any offence committed by the party or his wife is included in the order, the court may conclude there is no realistic risk of use by the prosecution, and hold the privilege does not apply (*AT & T Istel Ltd v Tully* [1993] AC 45).

Statutory limitations on the rule

One of the strange consequences of these rules is that the risk of documents being used **31.43** against the party for the purposes of criminal proceedings is obviously greater in cases where the defendant is alleged to have been particularly dishonest, and the worse the conduct alleged the greater the prospect of a successful claim to the privilege. After *Rank Film Distributors Ltd v Video Information Centre* [1982] AC 380 there were fears that the privilege would operate to frustrate the use of search orders in intellectual property piracy claims, and Parliament intervened by enacting the SCA 1981, s 72. This provides in part:

(1) In any proceedings to which this subsection applies a person shall not be excused, by reason that to do so would tend to expose that person, or his or her spouse, to proceedings for a related offence or for the recovery of a related penalty—
   (a) from answering any question put to that person in the first-mentioned proceedings; or
   (b) from complying with any order made in those proceedings.
(2) Subsection (1) applies to the following civil proceedings in the High Court, namely—
   (a) proceedings for infringement of rights pertaining to any intellectual property or for passing off;
   (b) proceedings brought to obtain disclosure of information relating to any infringement of such rights or to any passing off; and
   (c) proceedings brought to prevent any apprehended infringement of such rights or any apprehended passing off.
(3) Subject to subsection (4), no statement or admission made by a person—
   (a) in answering a question put to him in any such proceedings to which subsection (1) applies; or
   (b) in complying with any order made in such proceedings, shall, in proceedings for any related offence or for the recovery of any related penalty, be admissible in evidence against that person or (unless they married after the making of the statement or admission) against the spouse of that person.
(4) Nothing in subsection (3) shall render any statement or admission made by a person as there mentioned inadmissible in evidence against that person in proceedings for perjury or contempt of court.
(5) In this section—
   'intellectual property' means any patent, trade mark, copyright, design right, registered design, technical or commercial information or other intellectual property;

'related offence', in relation to any proceedings to which subsection (1) applies, means—

(a) in the case of proceedings within subsection (2)(a) or (b)—
  (i) any offence committed by or in the course of the infringement or passing off to which those proceedings relate; or
  (ii) any offence not within sub-paragraph (i) committed in connection with that infringement or passing off, being an offence involving fraud or dishonesty;
(b) in the case of proceedings within subsection (2)(c), any offence revealed by the facts on which the [claimant] relies in those proceedings.

31.44 It will be seen that the effect of the section is to remove the privilege against self-incrimination in relation to claims involving the infringement of intellectual property rights and passing off, but also to provide that the answers given shall not be used in any related criminal prosecution. Intellectual property has a wide meaning as set out in s 72(5). Purely personal information will not come within s 72(5), but voice mail messages which contain a mix of personal and commercially confidential material will come within s 72(5) if the commercially confidential messages form a substantial proportion of the total (*Phillips v News Group Newspapers Ltd* [2013] 1 AC 1).

31.45 In addition to intellectual property claims covered by the SCA 1981, s 72, the privilege against self-incrimination has been removed:

(a) in civil proceedings for the recovery or administration of any property, for the execution of any trust or for an account of any property or dealings with property in relation to offences under the Theft Act 1968 (see Theft Act 1968, s 31);
(b) in civil proceedings for the recovery or administration of any property, for the execution of any trust or for an account of any property or dealings with property in relation to offences under the Fraud Act 2006 (see Fraud Act 2006, s 13). In *Kensington International Ltd v Congo* [2008] 1 WLR 1144, it was held that while certain corruption offences identified by the respondents were not offences under the Fraud Act 2006, they were 'related offences' for the purposes of s 13, as they involved 'fraudulent conduct or purpose'. Money laundering offences also come within s 13 (*JSC BTA Bank v Ablyazov* [2010] 1 WLR 976). The result is that the Fraud Act exception to the privilege is fairly wide-ranging;
(c) in proceedings under Parts IV and V of the Children Act 1989 (see Children Act 1989, s 98); and
(d) certain proceedings under the Banking Act 1987 (this was held to be an implied result of the Banking Act 1987, s 42, by *Bank of England v Riley* [1992] Ch 465).

While there has been no universal removal of the privilege against self-incrimination in civil cases, the patchwork of removals covers most of the common situations.

Legal professional privilege

31.46 Legal professional privilege protects the right of a person to obtain skilled advice about the law without the fear that what is discussed may be used against them at a later stage. The privilege belongs to the client, not to the solicitor, though the solicitor is under a duty to the client to assert it unless it is waived by the client. It is restricted to the legal profession, and does not extend to tax law advice given by an accountant (*R (Prudential plc) v Special Commissioners of Income Tax* [2011] QB 669). The privilege is a fundamental human right long established at common law, buttressed by the European Convention on Human Rights, art 8 and forms part of Community law (*R (Morgan Grenfell and Co Ltd) v Special Commissioner of Income Tax* [2003] 1 AC 563). There are long-established exceptions relating to iniquity (see 31.55), and the welfare of children (*Essex County*

Council v R [1994] Fam 167). With proper safeguards, a statute (eg the Regulation of Investigatory Powers Act 2000, dealing with covert surveillance) may remove the privilege either expressly or by necessary implication (*R v Secretary of State for the Home Department, ex parte Simms* [2000] 2 AC 115).

There are two classes of legal professional privilege: that arising out of the relationship of **31.47** solicitor and client even if no litigation is contemplated; and communications connected with contemplated or pending litigation. Documents which came into existence otherwise than for the purposes of the present litigation, but which have been obtained for a party's solicitor for the purpose of use in the present litigation, are not privileged and must be produced to the other side for inspection (*Ventouris v Mountain* [1991] 1 WLR 607).

Legal advice privilege

Confidential communications between a solicitor and client made for the purpose of giv- **31.48** ing or receiving of legal advice are protected by legal professional privilege. The principle is that a client should be able to get legal advice in confidence. In *Three Rivers District Council v Governor and Company of the Bank of England (No 6)* [2005] 1 AC 610 at [50] Lord Rodger of Earlsferry said it does not matter whether the communication is directly between the client and the legal adviser, or if it is made through an intermediate agent. Where the client is a company, the usual position is that it is only the board of directors who are authorized to obtain legal advice on the company's behalf (*Director of the Serious Fraud Office v Eurasian Natural Resources Corpn Ltd* [2017] 1 WLR 4205).

'Legal advice' covers telling a client the law, and also includes advice as to what should **31.49** prudently and sensibly be done in the relevant legal context (*Balabel v Air India* [1988] Ch 317). Information passed between a solicitor and a client as part of the continuum aimed at keeping both informed so that advice may be given are privileged (Taylor LJ at 330). This is so even if there is no express reference to seeking advice (*Property Alliance Group Ltd v Royal Bank of Scotland plc* [2016] 1 WLR 992). To be protected the advice must be sought or given in a relevant legal context (*Three Rivers District Council v Governor and Company of the Bank of England (No 6)* [2005] 1 AC 610) and for a permissible (non-dishonest) purpose (*McE v Prison Service of Northern Ireland* [2009] 1 AC 908 at [117]). In doubtful cases, according to Lord Scott of Foscote in *Three Rivers* at [38], there are two questions. First, did the advice sought relate to the rights, liabilities, obligations, or remedies of the client under private law or under public law? Secondly, if so, did the occasion on which the communication took place and its purpose make it reasonable to expect that the privilege would apply? Putting it a different way, according to Lord Rodger of Earlsferry at [58], the important question is whether the lawyer is being asked in his capacity as a lawyer to provide legal advice. This means:

(a) Communications for the primary object of actual or contemplated civil or criminal proceedings will be privileged.
(b) Conclusions reached by a solicitor from such communications are also privileged (*Marsh v Sofaer* [2004] PNLR 24).
(c) Privilege attaches to advising on matters such as the conveyance of property or drawing up of a will (*Three Rivers District Council (No 6)* at [55]).
(d) Privilege does not apply to the actual conveyancing documents (*R v Inner London Crown Court, ex p Baines and Baines* [1988] QB 579) because they are not communications.
(e) Privilege applies to a solicitor advising on the best way to present evidence to a private, non-statutory inquiry, coroner's inquest, or statutory inquiry (*Three Rivers District Council (No 6)* at [44]).

(f) Privilege does not apply to client ledger accounts (*Nationwide Building Society v Various Solicitors* [1999] PNLR 53) because they are internal records, not communications dealing with advice.

(g) Privilege does not cover investment advice, nor advice as a patent or estate agent, nor when a solicitor is acting as a business adviser, because there is no relevant legal context.

Communications connected to litigation

31.50 Confidential communications between a solicitor or a client and a third party where the dominant purpose in creating the document is to use it or its contents in order to obtain legal advice or to help in the conduct of litigation which was at that time reasonably in prospect are privileged. This head of privilege is sometimes called litigation privilege. The rule is relatively straightforward in relation to solicitors' communications, and covers letters to and statements from witnesses, and letters to and reports from experts. In relation to clients' communications the rule has a more narrow effect.

31.51 In *Waugh v British Railways Board* [1980] AC 521 the claimants' representative sought disclosure of an internal inquiry report prepared by two of the Board's officers two days after the accident. The report was headed 'For the information of the Board's solicitor', but the written evidence on the application for disclosure made it clear that there were two purposes in providing the report, namely, to establish the cause of the accident so that safety measures could be introduced, and for legal advice in the event of any claim. The Board regarded both purposes as of equal importance. It was held that the report had to be disclosed. It would have been protected by legal professional privilege only if the legal advice aspect had been the dominant purpose. According to Lord Edmund-Davies, a dominant purpose is one with a 'clear paramountcy'.

31.52 Just because a report is compiled shortly after the relevant event does not mean that it cannot be privileged (*Re Highgrade Traders Ltd* [1984] BCLC 151, a fire investigation report in a suspected insurance arson case). This case is also authority for the proposition that the dominant purpose must be that of the person commissioning the report, not necessarily that of the author.

31.53 Secretly recorded conversations were considered in *Property Alliance Group Ltd v Royal Bank of Scotland plc* [2015] EWHC 3341 (Ch). The claimant's managing director arranged to meet two of the defendant's former employees telling them it was to discuss future business, but his real purpose was to record the conversation for possible use in the litigation. It was held there were two competing purposes, but given the deception the court should consider the dominant purpose from the point of view of the former employees. Their purpose was not connected to litigation, so the recording was not privileged.

Copies of documents

31.54 Copies and translations of privileged documents are themselves privileged. However, copies and translations of non-privileged documents are generally not protected by privilege. By way of exception, a compilation of copies or translations of documents obtained from third parties may be protected by legal professional privilege if disclosing them may betray the trend of advice given by the solicitor to the client. This exception does not apply, however, where the original documents came from the client (*Sumitomo Corpn v Crédit Lyonnais Rouse Ltd* [2002] 1 WLR 479).

Crime and iniquity

31.55 The privilege does not apply where the purpose behind seeking legal advice is 'iniquitous', such as to devise a structure for a transaction to prejudice the interests of the client's creditors

(*Barclays Bank plc v Eustice* [1995] 1 WLR 1238). The privilege was lost on this ground in a case where a search order was obtained using information which had been gathered in breach of the Data Protection Act 1984 (*Dubai Aluminium Co Ltd v Al Alawi* [1999] 1 WLR 1964). Communications in furtherance of a fraud or crime are not protected by privilege (*Finers v Miro* [1991] 1 WLR 35). An affidavit setting out the details of an abusive telephone call (which was an offence contrary to the Telecommunications Act 1984, s 43(1)(a)), and a threat to rip someone's throat out (which was a threat to kill contrary to the Offences Against the Person Act 1861, s 16) was held not to be privileged in *C v C (Privilege: Criminal Communications)* [2002] Fam 42. It does not matter whether or not the solicitor was aware of the client's intent (*Gamlen Chemical Co (UK) Ltd v Rochem Ltd* [1979] CA Transcript 777). The principle applies whether or not the claim is founded on the particular fraud in question (*Kuwait Airways Corporation v Iraqi Airways Co (No 6)* [2005] 1 WLR 2734).

Other confidential relationships

The general position in domestic law is that legal professional privilege covers communications with in-house lawyers in the same way as communications with independent lawyers (*Alfred Crompton Amusement Machines Ltd v Commissioners of Customs and Excise (No 2)* [1974] AC 405). In relation to investigations into anti-competitive practices under EU law, legal professional privilege does not apply to in-house counsel because they lack independence (*Akzo Nobel Chemicals Ltd v European Commission* [2010] 5 CMLR 19). The privilege also extends to communications with barristers, and to other persons authorized to provide advocacy, litigation, conveyancing, and probate services (Legal Services Act 2007, s 190), and to certain patent proceedings (Patents Act 1977, s 103). There is no duty of confidentiality between opposing lawyers in litigation (*British Sky Broadcasting Group plc v Virgin Media Communications Ltd* [2008] 1 WLR 2854). Privilege does not extend to doctors, priests, or others entrusted with confidences (*Wheeler v Le Marchant* (1881) 17 ChD 675). However, a third party, whether official or unofficial, who receives information in confidence with a view to matrimonial conciliation will not be compelled by the courts to disclose what was said without the parties' agreement (*McTaggart v McTaggart* [1949] P 94; *D v National Society for the Prevention of Cruelty to Children* [1978] AC 171). This privilege, which is based on the sanctity of marriage, also extends to proceedings under the Children Act 1989 (*Re D (Minors) (Conciliation: Disclosure of Information)* [1993] Fam 231). **31.56**

Without prejudice communications

'Without prejudice' communications, whether oral or in writing, which are made with the genuine intention of seeking a settlement of litigation are privileged from disclosure (*Ofulue v Bossert* [2009] 1 AC 990). A variant is an offer made 'without prejudice save as to costs', commonly called a *Calderbank* offer (see 36.04). The policy is to encourage negotiations by removing the potential embarrassment of concessions made in the course of negotiations being used at trial against the party who made them. The privilege applies even if the words 'without prejudice' are not used, provided the purpose was to seek a settlement (*Chocoladefabriken Lindt & Sprungli AG v Nestlé Co Ltd* [1978] RPC 287). Where the parties enter into 'without prejudice' negotiations, ongoing negotiations will continue to be privileged until one party brings it home to the other party that the 'without prejudice' basis of the negotiations is at an end. Thus, in *Cheddar Valley Engineering Ltd v Chaddlewood Homes Ltd* [1992] 1 WLR 820 it was held that prefacing one telephone offer with the word 'open' was insufficient to bring home the change in basis when further telephone negotiations and a letter did not repeat the word 'open'. **31.57**

Including the words 'without prejudice' will not attach privilege to communications intended to prejudice the recipient or which are no more than an assertion of one party's **31.58** rights (*Buckinghamshire County Council v Moran* [1990] Ch 623), nor to letters seeking time to pay an admitted liability (*Bradford and Bingley plc v Rashid* [2006] 1 WLR 2066). The privilege has a wide scope, and applies for example, to:

(a) joint settlement meetings, except to the extent they are stated to be without prejudice save as to costs (*Jackson v Ministry of Defence* [2006] EWCA Civ 46);

(b) without prejudice communications relied on to establish whether a party had unreasonably refused a proposal for ADR (*Reed Executive plc v Reed Business Information Ltd* [2004] 1 WLR 3026);

(c) genuine settlement discussions between a bank and a regulator in relation to a regulatory investigation (*Property Alliance Group Ltd v Royal Bank of Scotland plc* [2016] 1 WLR 361).

31.59 Once a document is protected by 'without prejudice' privilege, it will always (subject to the following paragraph), be privileged. Thus an admission made in 'without prejudice' communications by one party will not be admissible in other proceedings against that party (*Rush and Tompkins Ltd v Greater London Council* [1989] AC 1280).

31.60 'Without prejudice' negotiations which result in a settlement are, however, admissible to prove the terms of the settlement (*Walker v Wilsher* (1889) 23 QBD 335) or, where relevant under the normal rules governing the interpretation of contracts, to show the true meaning of the agreement (*Oceanbulk Shipping and Trading SA v TMT Asia Ltd* [2011] 1 AC 662). Marking a letter 'without prejudice' will not protect the evidence of a threat as to what will happen if an offer is not accepted (*Kitcat v Sharp* (1882) 48 LT 64). Further, 'without prejudice' correspondence is often used in interim applications, particularly applications seeking sanctions for default or relief from sanctions (*Family Housing Association (Manchester) Ltd v Michael Hyde and Partners* [1993] 1 WLR 354). The privilege will not attach if it is being abused, but it will only be lost in truly exceptional circumstances. A mere inconsistency between an admission made on a without prejudice occasion and the pleaded case or the facts stated in a witness statement of the party making the admission will not result in the privilege being lost (*Savings and Investment Bank Ltd v Fincken* [2004] 1 WLR 667). This is so even if persistence in the inconsistent position might lead to perjury.

31.61 Not only are without prejudice documents privileged from use in the instant proceedings, they should not be used to found subsequent proceedings. If they are, the subsequent proceedings will be struck out as an abuse of process, unless the claimant in the subsequent proceedings can show that the statements relied upon were made improperly, or that there is some other public interest reason in favour of their subsequent use (*Unilever plc v Procter and Gamble Co* [2000] 1 WLR 2436). This exception applies only if there is a very clear abuse of a privileged occasion (*Berry Trade Ltd v Moussari* (2003) *The Times*, 3 June 2003).

Waiver of privilege

31.62 Legal professional privilege belongs to, and can be waived by, the client. The privilege in 'without prejudice' communications belongs to both sides jointly, and can be waived only if both sides consent (*Rush and Tompkins Ltd v Greater London Council* [1989] AC 1280). Adverse inferences will not be drawn from a refusal to waive privilege (*Reed Executive plc v Reed Business Information Ltd* [2004] 1 WLR 3026).

31.63 Waiver of privilege may be given expressly, or implicitly by disclosing a privileged document to the other side. Examples include disclosure by service of a hearsay notice; by inclusion as an exhibit to a witness statement; by using the document to refresh the memory of a witness while giving evidence; and use of documents in re-examination to rebut an allegation of recent fabrication. However, there is no waiver of privilege simply by referring to a document in a witness statement, despite r 31.14 (for which, see 31.84; *Rubin v Expandable Ltd* [2008] 1 WLR 1099). Privilege is only waived if there is both a clear reference to the document, and if it is relied on for the purpose of making a particular point (*Mac Hotels Ltd v Rider Levett Bucknall UK Ltd* [2010] EWHC 767 (TCC)). If there is a clear reference to privileged material for making a particular point, the privilege is waived even if the client and their legal representatives did not appreciate they would be waiving privilege (*Re D (a child)* [2011] 4 All ER 434). A party waives privilege for trial purposes by using materials in an interim application (*Derby and Co Ltd v Weldon (No 10)* [1991] 1 WLR 660).

In *Great Atlantic Insurance Co v Home Insurance Co* [1981] 1 WLR 529 the Court of **31.64** Appeal held that, where part of a document was used in counsel's opening, privilege was waived as to the whole of the document unless it was a clearly separable document with different parts dealing with completely different subjects. Once privilege on a subject has been waived, the waiver will be taken to extend to any associated material (*Derby and Co Ltd v Weldon (No 10)*), but the court will seek to define the subject matter of the waiver quite restrictively (*General Accident Fire and Life Assurance Corporation Ltd v Tanter* [1984] 1 WLR 100). The question in such cases is one of defining the 'transaction', because the waiver only extends to documents which are part of the transaction (*Fulham Leisure Holdings Ltd v Nicholson Graham and Jones* [2006] 2 All ER 599).

A person who has been a client of a solicitor and who institutes legal proceedings against **31.65** that solicitor impliedly waives privilege over all documents concerned with the claim to the extent necessary to enable the court to adjudicate the dispute fully and fairly. In *Lillicrap v Nalder and Son* [1993] 1 WLR 94, property developers sued their solicitors for negligently failing to advise them about a right of way over some land they purchased. The claimants had used the solicitors on a number of other transactions, and the solicitors said their files on those other transactions showed the claimants habitually ignored their warnings, so would have bought the land even if they had been properly advised. The Court of Appeal held that the previous transactions were relevant to an issue in the present proceedings, so the implied waiver extended to them as well as to the transaction in question.

Secondary evidence

It was held in *Calcraft v Guest* [1898] 1 QB 759 that secondary evidence, such as a copy, **31.66** of otherwise privileged material is admissible at trial. In *Goddard v Nationwide Building Society* [1987] QB 670, Nourse LJ said that it makes no difference how the privileged material was obtained. Even if confidential documents have been obtained by theft they will be admissible. However, the party who would otherwise be able to claim privilege may apply for an injunction to restrain use of such material if it has not yet been used in the litigation (*Goddard v Nationwide Building Society*). However, the manner in which the documents came into that party's possession is important, because the party claiming privilege may be held to have waived the privilege. In *Guinness Peat Properties Ltd v Fitzroy Robinson Partnership* [1987] 1 WLR 1027 the defendant allowed the claimant to inspect certain files before serving a list of documents. By accident, a privileged letter was left in one of the files, and the claimant took a copy of it. The document later appeared in the defendant's list of documents, without a claim for privilege, and the claimant was again allowed to inspect it at the defendant's solicitors' office, but was not given a copy. Slade LJ said at 1044:

> Care must be taken by parties to litigation in the preparation of their lists of documents and no less great care must be taken in offering inspection of the documents disclosed. Ordinarily, in my judgment, a party to litigation who sees a particular document referred to in the other side's list, without

privilege being claimed, and is subsequently permitted inspection of that document, is fully entitled to assume that any privilege which might otherwise have been claimed for it has been waived.

31.67 As Slade LJ said, this is ordinarily the position. It is subject to two exceptions:

(a) where a party or its solicitor procures inspection of the relevant document by fraud; and
(b) where a party or its solicitor realizes on inspection that the document has been revealed as a result of an obvious mistake.

Obvious mistake

31.68 It is provided by CPR, r 31.20, that where a party inadvertently allows a privileged document to be inspected, the party who has inspected the document may only use it or its contents with the permission of the court. The need for permission under r 31.20 and the jurisdiction to grant injunctions to prevent use co-exist with r 31.20 being used by recipients of privileged documents, and injunctions being sought by parties who mistakenly allow access to their privileged documents. In both situations the question is whether there has been an obvious mistake. *Guinness Peat Properties Ltd v Fitzroy Robinson Partnership* was an example of an obvious mistake, as, being a trained lawyer, the claimant's solicitor must have realized the privileged nature of the letter as soon as he read it. In *English and American Insurance Co Ltd v Herbert Smith* [1988] FSR 232 counsel's clerk allowed counsel's instructions and papers (including witness statements and counsel's written opinion) to be sent to the other side's solicitors. An injunction was granted restraining use being made of any of the information in the papers. Compare *Al Fayed v Commissioner of Police for the Metropolis* (2002) *The Times,* 17 June 2002, where the injunction was refused because the recipient solicitors genuinely thought the other side's counsel's opinions had been disclosed on purpose.

31.69 A distinction was drawn in *Rawlinson & Hunter Trustees SA v Director of the Serious Fraud Office (No 2)* [2015] 1 WLR 797 between documents covered by legal professional privilege (where permission to use the documents was granted under r 31.20) and documents protected by public interest immunity (where permission was refused because of the duty to withhold such documents). Making use of an inadvertently disclosed document before seeking permission under r 31.20 may result in a sanction being imposed (see Chapter 37 and *Property Alliance Group Ltd v Royal Bank of Scotland plc* [2015] EWHC 3341 (Ch)).

Public interest immunity

General principles

31.70 Certain documents must be withheld from production on the ground that disclosure would be injurious to the public interest. Such documents fall into two categories: those which form part of a 'class' of documents which needs to be protected, and those which need to be protected due to the sensitivity of their particular 'contents'. Contents immunity attaches, for example, to diplomatic dispatches and documents relating to national security. There is a wide variation in the 'classes' of documents protected, from Cabinet minutes to more routine documents like local authority social work records: *Re M (A Minor)* (1989) 88 LGR 841. There is a special closed material procedure in CPR, Part 82, dealing with material which would be damaging to the interests of national security (Justice and Security Act 2013, s 6(11)).

Ministerial certificates

31.71 The responsible minister may provide a certificate stating the grounds of the objection and identifying the class (if any) to which the document in question belongs. Such certificates are usually only issued on solid grounds, and are usually taken as determining the question whether the 'class' of documents specified is protected by public interest immunity. However, such certificates are not, as a matter of law, conclusive (*Burmah Oil Co Ltd v Bank of England* [1980] AC 1090). If a strong case (there are in fact several formulations of the standard applicable: see *Burmah Oil Co Ltd v Bank of England*) is made out that the contents of the documents are material to the issues in the claim, and if there are grounds to doubt whether the balance of the public interest is against disclosure, the court has a discretion to review the claim to immunity. If these conditions are satisfied, the court will weigh (a) the public interest in the due administration of justice against (b) the public interest established by the claim to immunity. It is for the party seeking disclosure to establish clearly that the balance falls decisively in favour of (a) (*Air Canada v Secretary of State for Trade* [1983] 2 AC 394). The weight on either side depends on the importance of the 'class' and the probable evidential value of the document—see Lord Fraser of Tullybelton in the *Air Canada* case—and the court may need to inspect the document.

Other confidential information

Privilege based on a confidential relationship is restricted to the legal profession, and does **31.72** not extend to doctors, priests, social workers, etc. (*Wheeler v Le Marchant* (1881) 17 ChD 675). Interviews with medical advisers are nevertheless often treated as being in a similar position to legal advice. This is partly because they may be covered by litigation privilege, and partly because they are an aspect of the right to respect for private life which is protected by the European Convention on Human Rights, art 8 (*McE v Prison Service of Northern Ireland* [2009] 1 AC 908). Article 8 may also protect non-medical information, for example some school records, on the basis that disclosure may interfere with the private lives of those discussed in the records (*Webster v Ridgeway Foundation School Governors* [2009] ELR 439).

J INSPECTION

Personal inspection

A party which has served a list of documents must allow the other parties to inspect the **31.73** documents listed which are in its control, other than those for which a claim is made to withhold inspection on the grounds of privilege. A party wishing to inspect must send a written notice to that effect to the other side, and the other side must give its permission within the next seven days (CPR, r 31.15(a) and (b)).

Redacted copies

Normally the whole of a document can be inspected, but there is scope for blanking out **31.74** irrelevant passages (*GE Capital Corporate Finance Group Ltd v Bankers Trust Co* [1995] 1 WLR 172) or passages with sensitive information (*Webster v Ridgeway Foundation School Governors* [2009] ELR 439).

Provision of copies

Alternatively, the inspecting party can conduct the inspecting process at arm's length by **31.75** sending a notice to the other party requiring the supply of copies of the documents in the first part of the list, and undertaking to pay reasonable copying charges. Such a request must be complied with within seven days (CPR, r 31.15(c)).

Inspection of electronic documents

31.76 Inspection of electronic documents may be given in electronic format (PD 31B, para 30(2)). Unless otherwise agreed or ordered, electronic documents must be disclosed in their native form, preserving any metadata (para 33).

K ORDERS IN SUPPORT OF DISCLOSURE

Failure to disclose or give inspection

31.77 Where a party fails to serve a list of documents in accordance with the court's directions, or fails to give inspection, an application can be made for an order compelling performance. Before issuing the application the innocent party should write to the defaulting party inviting them to remedy the default within a stated reasonable period. If the default has not been remedied by the time the application is heard, the court will usually make an 'unless order' requiring the matter to be put right within a stated period, and specifying some sanction in default. Sanctions can include striking out the defaulting party's statement of case.

31.78 Documents that are not disclosed before trial can only be relied upon by the defaulting party with the court's permission (CPR, r 31.21). It is also open to the court to make adverse inferences against the defaulting party (*Infabrics Ltd v Jaytex Ltd (No 2)* [1985] FSR 75).

Objections to disclosure or inspection

31.79 Procedures for determining disputed claims to withhold disclosure and inspection are provided in CPR, r 31.19. Claims for protection are usually made in the list of documents served by a party (r 31.19(4)). Alternatively, an order may be sought from the court for withholding disclosure (public interest immunity) or inspection (other claims to privilege or based on alleged irrelevance). On a hearing under r 31.19, *Atos Consulting Ltd v Avis Europe plc* [2008] Bus LR Digest D20 it was stated that the court must:

(a) consider the evidence produced on the application;
(b) uphold the right to withhold inspection if this is established on the evidence and no sufficient grounds are put forward for challenging that right;
(c) order inspection if the evidence does not establish a right to withhold the documents;
(d) order further evidence to be produced if insufficient grounds have been shown for challenging the alleged right to withhold, or for the court to inspect the documents if there is no other means of deciding the matter; and
(e) invite representations after any inspection.

31.80 In relation to claims to withhold disclosure on the ground of public interest immunity, r 31.19(2) provides that, unless the court otherwise orders, any order made under r 31.19 must not be served on any other person, and must not be open to inspection by any other person.

Specific disclosure and specific inspection

Jurisdiction

31.81 It is provided in CPR, r 31.12, that:

(1) The court may make an order for specific disclosure or specific inspection.

(2) An order for specific disclosure is an order that a party must do one or more of the following things—
  (a) disclose documents or classes of documents specified in the order;
  (b) carry out a search to the extent stated in the order;
  (c) disclose any documents located as a result of that search.
(3) An order for specific inspection is an order that a party permit inspection of a document referred to in r 31.3(2).

Specific disclosure applications are typically made in three situations. First, they provide **31.82** a mechanism for getting the court to adjudicate on whether the other side have given full standard disclosure. If it is established that the other side has not given standard disclosure, specific disclosure will usually be ordered (PD 31A, para 5.4). Secondly, this procedure may be used if a party wants, for example, train of inquiry documents (see 31.26), or the disclosure of documents relating to credibility (*Favor Easy Management Ltd v Wu* [2011] 1 WLR 1803 at [20]). On such applications the court will be particularly astute to apply the overriding objective (PD 31A, para 5.4). Thirdly, the procedure can be used before standard disclosure, for example where the defendant needs disclosure in order to plead a proper defence (*Dayman v Canyon Holdings Ltd* (2006) LTL 11/1/06).

Procedure

Applications for specific disclosure are made by application notice supported by written evi- **31.83** dence, and are made on at least three clear days' notice to the other side. The application must specify the order asked for. It is usual to describe the various categories of documents sought in a schedule to the application. Descriptions must, however, be sufficiently precise for the other side to know what is required. An application for disclosure of 'all documents relating to [the other side's] financial and tax affairs which are necessary to prove quantum' was held to be too imprecise in *Morgans v Needham* (1999) *The Times*, 5 November 1999. The evidence in support must state a belief that the other side has or had certain specific documents relating to the claim in his or her control, and that each class of documents sought is disclosable under standard disclosure, or should otherwise be disclosed in accordance with the overriding objective.

L DOCUMENTS REFERRED TO IN STATEMENTS OF CASE, ETC.

By CPR, r 31.14(1), a party is entitled to inspect any documents mentioned in a statement **31.84** of case, witness statement, witness summary, or affidavit. A document is 'mentioned' for the purposes of r 31.14 if there is a 'direct allusion' to it (*Rubin v Expandable Ltd* [2008] 1 WLR 1099). In this case a witness statement which said 'he wrote to me' made a direct allusion to the covering letter, even though the letter was not relied upon in the witness statement. The question of whether an incautious reference to a privileged document in a witness statement waives privilege is considered at 31.63.

The party wishing to inspect needs to serve a notice requiring documents to be made avail- **31.85** able for inspection. The other party then has seven days to permit inspection. Normally the document has to be provided, unless there is a good reason for not doing so (*Co-operative Group Ltd v Carillion JM Ltd* (2014) LTL 11/2/14).

A party may also make an application for an order for inspection of a document mentioned **31.86** in an expert's report (r 31.14(2)), but where the document mentioned is part of the expert's instructions, such an order will only be made if there are reasonable grounds for believing that the expert's report does not provide a complete and accurate statement of those instructions (r 35.10(4)). Provided the expert sets out the material parts of documents used in compiling the report, the court will not order the inspection of those documents (*Lucas v Barking, Havering and Redbridge Hospitals NHS Trust* [2004] 1 WLR 220).

M ADMISSION OF AUTHENTICITY

31.87 By CPR, r 32.19(1), a party is deemed to admit the authenticity of documents disclosed by the other side under Part 31, unless the party serves a notice requiring the document to be proved at trial. Such a notice must be served by the latest date for serving witness statements (or seven days after disclosure if this is later) (r 32.19(2)). Notice to prove should be in form N268.

N COLLATERAL USE

31.88 A party which receives documents disclosed under Part 31 may use those documents only for purposes connected with the proper conduct of the present litigation (CPR, r 31.22(1)). 'Use' covers everything from revealing the other side's documents to a newspaper through to reviewing them for relevance as part of the receiving party's disclosure obligations in another case (*Tchenguiz v Grant Thornton UK LLP* [2017] 1 WLR 2809). Any misuse of the documents may be restrained by injunction, or punished as a contempt of court, or by striking out subsequent proceedings based on documents disclosed in the course of earlier proceedings (*Riddick v Thames Board Mills Ltd* [1977] QB 881). The protection against subsequent use of disclosed documents is not, however, absolute. Rule 31.22 provides:

  (1) A party to whom a document has been disclosed may use the document only for the purpose of the proceedings in which it is disclosed, except where—
   (a) the document has been read to or by the court, or referred to, at a hearing which has been held in public;
   (b) the court gives permission; or
   (c) the party who disclosed the document and the person to whom the document belongs agree.
  (2) The court may make an order restricting or prohibiting the use of a document which has been disclosed, even where the document has been read to or by the court, or referred to, at a hearing which has been held in public.
  (3) An application for such an order may be made—
   (a) by a party; or
   (b) by any person to whom the document belongs.

31.89 From *Barings plc v Coopers and Lybrand* [2000] 1 WLR 2353, it seems that documents read by the judge, whether in or out of court, should be regarded as in the public domain. Further, where documents have been put before the court for the purpose of being read in evidence, the burden of proof is on the person contending that they were not read by the judge. Once documents have been used in open court, an order restricting or prohibiting subsequent use will be made only if there are very good reasons for departing from the usual rule of publicity (*Lilly Icos Ltd v Pfizer Ltd* [2002] 1 WLR 2253). The starting point is the principle of open justice (*Re BBC* [2015] AC 588). Confidentiality of the documents is not necessarily enough to justify reimposing a restriction on use, but private banking details are usually protected (*Machkevitch v Kirill Ace Stein* [2016] EWHC 1210 (Comm)).

31.90 The prohibition against using material for collateral purposes does not apply to documents referred to in affidavits and witness statements, as these are regarded as having been voluntarily disclosed: *Cassidy v Hawcroft* [2000] CPLR 624.

KEY POINTS SUMMARY

- In fast track claims the court typically makes a direction that the parties should give stand- **31.91** ard disclosure of documents about a month after the order for directions.

- Standard disclosure requires parties to disclose documents which support their own case, and also documents which adversely affect them, adversely affect another party, or which support another party's case.

- Menu option disclosure applies to most multi-track claims.

- A document for this purpose is anything on which information is recorded, and extends to computer documents, metadata, sound, and moving picture recordings.

- Parties typically give disclosure by serving lists of documents.

- Privileged documents appear in the second section of the list, and do not have to be made available for inspection.

- Inspection is the second stage of the disclosure process, and usually takes place by sending copies to the other side, although personal inspection is also possible.

- Orders for specific disclosure may be sought if it is felt that the other side have not complied with their disclosure obligations.

32

WITNESS STATEMENTS, AFFIDAVITS, AND DEPOSITIONS

A TYPES OF WRITTEN EVIDENCE 32.02
B WITNESS STATEMENTS 32.08
C WITNESS SUMMARIES 32.26

D AFFIDAVITS AND AFFIRMATIONS 32.28
E DEPOSITIONS .32.33

32.01 This chapter is concerned with the rules relating to the use of written evidence in civil proceedings. Under the CPR, evidence given in civil trials is given primarily from the witness box, but with witness statements exchanged well before trial standing as the evidence-in-chief of the witnesses. The purpose behind requiring the parties to exchange their witnesses' statements is to save time and costs at trial, and to enable the parties to evaluate the merits of their dispute with a view to settlement. Written evidence in support of interim applications can be given by a variety of different methods, but the principal means is by way of signed witness statements. Affidavits are sworn written statements: see 32.04.

A TYPES OF WRITTEN EVIDENCE

32.02 There are seven main types of written evidence used in civil proceedings: witness statements, witness summaries, affidavits, affirmations, statements of case, the second page of an application notice, and depositions.

Witness statements and witness summaries

32.03 Witness statements are formal documents setting out in writing the facts that a witness is able to talk about. A witness statement must be signed by the witness, and must contain a statement of truth, which usually appears at the end. Witness statements are a means of adducing evidence on interim applications, and are also used for giving advance notice of the evidence that will be given by the lay witnesses at trial. The current practice is usually for exchanged witness statements to stand as the evidence-in-chief of the witnesses at trial. Witness summaries are used where there is a problem in obtaining signed witness statements, see 32.26.

Affidavits and affirmations

32.04 Affidavits take a form almost identical to that of witness statements, but have a 'commencement' at the beginning, and end with a 'jurat' rather than a statement of truth (see 32.28). An affidavit must be sworn by the deponent before a solicitor or someone else authorized to take oaths, and the fact they are sworn statements is the main difference between them and witness statements. Fees are payable when affidavits are sworn, which also marks them off from the more informal witness statements. There are a limited number of situations where affidavits must be used. These include applications for freezing injunctions and search orders, and on applications to commit for contempt of court. They can, generally, be used as an alternative to witness statements for other interim applications, but this rarely happens because the additional cost of using this form of evidence will be disallowed. Affirmations are almost identical to affidavits, but the maker of an affirmation will affirm to the truth of its contents, rather than swearing to its truth, as permitted by the Oaths Act 1978.

Statements of case

As seen in Chapter 14, statements of case have to be verified by a statement of truth. They **32.05** can therefore be used as the evidence in support of interim applications (provided they cover the material relevant to the application). In practice the contents of a party's statement of case almost always have to be supplemented, even for the simplest forms of interim application.

Application notice

The prescribed form of application notice, form N244, contains a section (para 10 on the **32.06** second page) where the applicant can set out the facts in support of the application. It is completed by a signed statement of truth. This is perhaps the least formal means of adducing evidence at an interim application, and also probably the most common. An example of an application notice is illustrated as form 23.1.

Depositions

A party may apply for an order for a potential witness to be examined before the hearing **32.07** takes place (CPR, r 34.8(1)). The witness is examined in much the same way as at trial, and their testimony is recorded in a document called a deposition, which can be used at trial. Such orders are typically made where the witness is likely to be unavailable or too infirm to attend the trial.

B WITNESS STATEMENTS

Format

By CPR, r 32.4(1), a witness statement is a written statement signed by a person which **32.08** contains the evidence which that person would be allowed to give orally. Detailed requirements are set out in PD 32. An example is illustrated in figure 32.1.

It will contain a formal heading with the title of the proceedings. In the top right-hand **32.09** corner it should state the party on whose behalf it is made; the initials and surname of the witness; whether it is the first, second, etc., statement of the witness; the references of the exhibits included; and the date it is made. The opening paragraph should give details of the witness's occupation or description, and, if relevant, state the position he holds and the name of his employer, and should also state if he is a party in the proceedings or employed by a party.

The text of the statement must, if practicable, be in the witness's own words. It should be **32.10** expressed in the first person. It is usually convenient to follow the chronological sequence of events. Each paragraph should, so far as possible, be confined to a distinct portion of the subject. The statement should indicate sections of its content that are made only

Figure 32.1 Witness statement

Made on behalf of: Claimant
Witness: C. Holmes
Statement number: 1
Exhibits: CH 1–CH 3
Date made: 26.6.2018
Claim No 18BD 98858

IN THE COUNTY COURT AT BRADFORD
BETWEEN:—

COLIN HOLMES   <u>Claimant</u>
and
GILLIAN DUTTON   <u>Defendant</u>

WITNESS STATEMENT OF COLIN HOLMES

1 I am COLIN HOLMES, a Financial Services Adviser of 17 Conniston Road, Bradford BD8 3PR. I am the Claimant, and I make this witness statement in support of my application for an interim injunction against the Defendant.

2 17 Conniston Road is the house where my wife and I have made our home and raised our family since 1994. There is now shown to me marked '**CH 1**' a bundle containing true copies of relevant Land Registry office copy entries, and the entries, including Land Registry plan, for number 17 are at pages 1 to 3. It will be seen that I am the sole registered proprietor.

3 When we bought our house in 1994 we also bought a piece of land ('the garden'), formerly owned by the railway company, that lies at the rear of the gardens of the odd-numbered houses in Conniston Road. The garden is about 0.5 of an acre in area, and we use it as a garden to grow fruit and vegetables. True copies of the relevant Land Registry office copy entries are at pages 4 to 6 of exhibit '**CH 1**'. Again, I am the sole registered proprietor.

4 It will also be seen from page 4 of exhibit '**CH 1**' that the garden has the benefit of a right of way along the passage ('the drive') running between the houses at numbers 25 and 27 Conniston Road. The drive is located on land forming part of the title to number 27. It is about 30 metres long, about 3 metres wide, and its surface is of compacted gravel.

5 Number 27 is owned by the Defendant, and true copies of the Office Copy entries relating to this property can be found at pages 7 to 9 of exhibit '**CH 1**'. It will be seen on page 7 that the drive is subject to rights of way.

6 In March 2018 the Defendant fitted a gate across the drive together with a lock and bolt. This can be identified from my sketch drawing on page 1 of exhibit '**CH 2**', which is now shown to me, which comprises two drawings that I have made which are relevant to this dispute. The Defendant stated that she had fixed the gate, lock and bolt in a letter to me and my wife dated 21 March 2018, which is at page 2 of exhibit '**CH 3**', which is a bundle containing true copies of relevant correspondence.

[*Continue with further narrative*]

Statement of truth

I believe that the facts stated in this witness statement are true.

Signed

COLIN HOLMES

Date 26 June 2018

I believe that the facts stated in this witness statement are true.

from knowledge and belief as opposed to matters within the witness's own knowledge, and should state the sources of any matters of information and belief. If the source is a person, they should be named (*Consolidated Contractors International Co SAL v Masri* [2011] Bus LR D108). Documents referred to in the statement should be formally exhibited (*Tweed v Parades Commission for Northern Ireland* [2007] 1 AC 650). The statement must include a signed statement that the witness believes the facts it contains are true. False statements may be punished as contempt of court. The form of statement of truth is:

I believe that the facts stated in this witness statement are true.

All numbers, including dates, should be expressed in figures. Witness statements must be produced on durable A4 paper with a 35 mm margin typed on one side of the paper only. Wherever possible they should be securely bound in a manner that will not hamper filing. If they are not securely bound, each page should bear the claim number and initials of the witness. **32.11**

Disclosure of written evidence in interim applications

Witness statements for use in support of interim applications on notice should, where service is to be effected by the court, be filed with the application notice (CPR, r 23.7(2)). At para 10 of the standard form of application notice (N244: see form 23.1) the applicant has to indicate the nature of the written evidence relied upon, which should be attached to the notice. If the applicant is to effect service, the written evidence must be served with the application notice (r 23.7(3)). The evidence (but not the exhibits) must be filed at court (PD 23A, para 9.6), but the copies served on the other parties should include the exhibits. **32.12**

A court will sometimes give directions as to when any further written evidence should be served and filed (PD 23A, para 9.2), this being particularly relevant for the evidence relied upon by the respondents. Respondents must comply with any such directions, and should, in any event, serve and file their written evidence as soon as possible (para 9.4). This is important, because if a respondent serves its evidence shortly before the hearing (or even at the door of the court), the probability is that the hearing will have to be adjourned, with the costs of the adjournment usually being paid by the party responsible for the late service of the evidence. **32.13**

Interim applications without notice fall into two categories. First, there are those, such as applications for freezing injunctions, where it is essential that no prior notification is given to the respondents in order to ensure the interim relief is effective. In this category, the evidence in support of the application is not served on the respondents until after the without-notice application has been dealt with. In the second category it is simply a lack of time that makes it necessary to apply without giving the usual three clear days' notice. In these cases the applicant should take steps to give informal notice of the hearing to the respondents (PD 25A, para 4.3(3)), and this may include service of the written evidence in support. **32.14**

Cross-examination of witnesses in interim applications

The usual position is that evidence in interim applications is placed before the court in written form, and no 'live' evidence is called. However, there are occasions where the facts adduced in a witness statement (or affidavit) are seriously challenged, and the court may be persuaded to make an order granting permission to cross-examine the person who signed the witness statement or swore the affidavit (CPR, r 32.7(1)). These orders are made only if there are good reasons to justify the additional delay and expense. If such an order is made, the challenged evidence may be used only if the witness attends in compliance with the order, unless the court gives permission (r 32.7(2)). **32.15**

Exchange of trial witness statements

32.16 The main rule relating to the use of witness statements is to be found in r 32.4(2) of the CPR, which provides:

> The court will order a party to serve on the other parties any witness statement of the oral evidence which the party serving the statement intends to rely on in relation to any issues of fact to be decided at the trial.

32.17 Witness statements are not usually exchanged in small claims track cases, so the following discussion is largely limited to fast track and multi-track cases. When directions are made on allocating a case to the fast track or multi-track, or at a case management conference, the court will make provision for the date by when witness statements must be exchanged. It is to be noted that the rule uses the word 'will', with the clear intention that disclosure directions are to be made in every fast track and multi-track case.

32.18 Normally mutual exchange is required, and it usually takes place a few weeks after disclosure and inspection of documents. Part of the reason why witness statements are exchanged after disclosure of documents is that the witnesses may need to comment on some of the documentation in their statements. The court retains a discretion to order sequential disclosure of witness statements (r 32.4(3)(a)) and has a discretion whether to require the disclosed statements to be filed (r 32.4(3)(b)).

Limiting witness statements

32.19 There are occasions when the courts have to use their case management powers to control the volume of written evidence parties intend to use at trial. Judicial case management is intended to secure the fair and efficient progress of the trial, and there have been instances when parties have sought to use an excessive number of witness statements, or excessively long witness statements. For example, one of the witnesses in *VTB Capital plc v Nutritek International Corporation* [2013] 2 AC 337 made no less than 12 witness statements in support of an interim application. Courts can control this by making directions under CPR, r 32.2(3):

(a) identifying or limiting the issues to which factual evidence may be directed;
(b) identifying witnesses to be called or whose statements should be read; and
(c) limiting the length or format of witness statements.

Privilege

32.20 Until a witness statement is disclosed, it is clearly protected by legal professional privilege. All that is required by CPR, r 32.4(2) is for the statements of witnesses who are intended to be called to be disclosed. Therefore, any statements taken from harmful witnesses can be left on the solicitor's file, and need not be disclosed to the other side. If, however, a witness is to be called at trial, his or her witness statement will have to be disclosed in accordance with the court's directions. Service waives the privilege.

Failure to comply with directions

32.21 If a witness statement is not served within the time specified in the directions, the witness may be called to give oral evidence only with permission (CPR, r 32.10). Non-compliance with directions is considered generally in Chapter 37.

Evidence-in-chief at trial

Exchanged witness statements stand as the witnesses' evidence-in-chief unless the court **32.22** otherwise orders (CPR, r 32.5(2)). A direction to the contrary may be appropriate where there are allegations of serious misconduct (*JN Dairies Ltd v Johal Dairies Ltd* [2010] EWCA Civ 348, where there were allegations of bribery and of stealing confidential documents). A witness may, and provided the court considers there is good reason not to confine the witness to the contents of the disclosed statement, amplify his or her witness statement and give evidence in relation to new matters that have arisen since the statement was served (r 32.5(3) and (4)).

Cross-examination at trial

Cross-examination in civil trials can range over any relevant matter that the witness can **32.23** deal with, both as to the issues and as to credibility. It need not be confined to the matters addressed in the witness's statement. One of the tools of the cross-examiner is to pick out previous inconsistent statements made by the witness. In this connection, r 32.11 of the CPR provides:

> Where a witness is called to give evidence at trial, he may be cross-examined on his witness statement whether or not the statement or any part of it was referred to during the witness's evidence in chief.

Collateral use

After a statement has been exchanged, CPR, r 32.12 provides that it may only be used for **32.24** the purposes of the present proceedings, unless and to the extent that:

(a) the witness gives consent in writing; or
(b) the court grants permission; or
(c) the statement has been put in evidence at a hearing in public.

False witness statements

By CPR, r 32.14, proceedings for contempt of court may be brought against any person **32.25** who makes a false statement in a document verified by a statement of truth without an honest belief in its truth. Such proceedings can be brought only by the Attorney-General or with the permission of the court (rr 81.17 and 81.18).

C WITNESS SUMMARIES

A party who is unable to obtain signed statements before the time prescribed for exchange **32.26** may apply for permission to serve witness summaries instead of witness statements. The application is made without notice (CPR, r 32.9(1)). Such orders can be granted only if the party is unable to obtain the relevant witness statement. Unless the court orders otherwise, a witness summary must be served within the period in which a witness statement would have had to be served.

Witness summaries are simply summaries of the evidence that would have been included in **32.27** a witness statement. They could be unsigned draft statements, or even just an indication of the issues it is hoped the witness could deal with.

D AFFIDAVITS AND AFFIRMATIONS

Form of affidavits

32.28 Rule 32.16 of the CPR provides that affidavits must be in the form set out in PD 32, paras 2–16. The form of an affidavit is broadly similar to that of a witness statement, described at 32.08–32.11:

(a) An affidavit must be typed on one side only of consecutively numbered sheets of durable A4 paper with a 35 mm margin (PD 32, para 6.1(1), (2), and (4)).

(b) It must have the same corner markings as witness statements (PD 32, para 3.2).

(c) It must be headed in the same way as witness statements.

(d) After the heading and before the body of the affidavit there should appear a commencement (PD 32, para 4.1). This should read:

I [full name] of [address, which can be a business address if sworn in the deponent's professional, business, or occupational capacity] state on oath:

(e) Text and exhibits are dealt with in the same way as witness statements.

(f) Alterations need to be initialled by both the deponent and the person taking the affidavit (PD 32, para 8.1).

(g) Instead of a statement of truth, an affidavit ends with a jurat. The jurat must follow on from the body of the affidavit, and must not appear on a separate page. After giving the oath the affidavit has to be signed by all deponents (exceptionally an affidavit may be sworn by more than one person) and be completed by the person taking the affidavit. The person taking the affidavit must insert his or her full address, sign the jurat, and print his or her name and qualification under the signature (PD 32, para 5).

Qualification of person taking an affidavit

32.29 A person who takes an affidavit must be duly qualified (solicitors, commissioners for oaths, magistrates, certain court officials and judges, British consuls, and others authorized by statute, eg barristers), and independent of the parties and their representatives (PD 32, para 9).

Affirmations

32.30 Affirmations are similar to affidavits, but the deponent will affirm rather than swear when executing the document. They can be used whenever an affidavit may or must be used. All the provisions in PD 32 relating to affidavits apply also to affirmations (PD 32, para 16). For affirmations the commencement should read:

I [full name] of [address] do solemnly and sincerely affirm:

In an affirmation, the word 'sworn' in the jurat is replaced by the word 'affirmed'.

Inability of deponent to read or sign an affidavit

32.31 Where an affidavit is sworn by a person who is unable to read or sign it, the person before whom it is sworn must certify in the jurat that he or she has read the affidavit to the deponent and that the deponent appeared to understand it (PD 32, para 7.1(1) and (2)). The person who took the affidavit must also certify that, in his or her presence, the deponent signed it or made his or her mark (para 7.1(3)). Two versions of the form of the certificate appear in annex 1 to PD 32. If such a certificate is not included in the jurat, the affidavit may not be used unless the court is satisfied that it was read to the deponent and he or she appeared to understand it (para 7.2).

False affidavits

A false affidavit or affirmation may be punished as a contempt of court. There will be a **32.32** contempt if the maker of the affidavit knew it was false and that it was likely to interfere with the course of justice (*Malgar Ltd v ER Leach (Engineering) Ltd* [2000] FSR 393). The maker may also be prosecuted for perjury if it is knowingly false, because the jurat makes an affidavit the equivalent of testimony on oath (*Hydropol Hot Tubs Ltd v Roberjot* [2011] EWHC 121 (Ch) at [59]).

E DEPOSITIONS

A party seeking to rely on evidence in a deposition must first apply for an order for the wit- **32.33** ness to be examined before the hearing takes place (CPR, r 34.8(1)). When the court makes an order for a deposition to be taken, it may also order the party who obtained the order to serve a witness statement or witness summary in relation to the evidence to be given by the person to be examined (r 34.8(7)). Once the order is obtained it has to be served on the witness, together with conduct money (a sum reasonably sufficient to cover travel costs and loss of earnings, r 34.8(6)).

Subject to any directions contained in the order for examination, the examination must **32.34** be conducted in the same way as if the witness were giving evidence at a trial (r 34.9(1)). Depositions can be taken before a judge or an examiner of the court (r 34.8(3)), who must ensure the evidence given by the witness is recorded in full (r 34.9(4)). The order may require the witness to attend for the purpose of recording their oral testimony, but it can also require the witness to produce documents that are considered necessary for the purpose of the examination (r 34.8(4)). If all the parties are present, the examiner may conduct the examination of a person not named in the order for examination if all the parties and the person to be examined consent (r 34.9(2)).

After the deposition has been taken the examiner must send a copy to the person who **32.35** obtained the order for the examination of the witness and to the court (r 34.9(5)). It is the responsibility of the party who obtained the order to serve the other parties (r 34.9(6)). A party intending to put a deposition in as evidence at a hearing must serve notice of his intention to do so on every other party at least 21 days before the day fixed for the hearing (r 34.11). A deposition ordered under r 34.8 may be given in evidence at a hearing unless the court orders otherwise (r 34.11(1)). However, the court retains a discretion to require a deponent to attend the hearing and give evidence orally (r 34.11(4)).

33

HEARSAY

A THE HEARSAY RULE 33.02

B REAL EVIDENCE 33.07

C ADMISSIBILITY OF HEARSAY EVIDENCE 33.09

D NOTICE PROCEDURE. 33.16

E TRIAL. 33.26

Key points summary 33.29

33.01 This chapter considers the admissibility of and procedural matters relating to hearsay evidence in civil cases. Evidence is no longer excluded in civil cases solely on the ground that it is hearsay. Judicial suspicion of hearsay evidence continues, however, and a number of procedural requirements attach to the adduction of hearsay evidence. It therefore continues to be important to be able to identify hearsay evidence when it arises. Some general principles of evidence are dealt with in 33.02–33.08 before the main provisions of the Civil Evidence Act 1995 ('CEA 1995') are considered at 33.09ff. A party intending to rely on a hearsay statement must generally serve notice of that intention on the other parties, a matter considered at 33.16ff. Use of hearsay statements at trial is discussed at 33.26ff and 39.43–39.46.

A THE HEARSAY RULE

33.02 At common law, subject to a number of exceptions, hearsay evidence was inadmissible. The exact boundaries of the hearsay rule have never been easy to state. Broadly, a question of hearsay arises where a statement, whether of fact or opinion, no matter how it is made, is made otherwise than by a person while giving oral testimony in court and is relied on as evidence of the truth of its contents (see, eg, the speech of Lord Havers in *R v Sharp* [1988] 1 WLR 7, and the CEA 1995, ss 1(2)(a) and 13). There were two aspects of the hearsay rule, namely, the rule against narrative and the strict hearsay rule.

33.03 The rule against narrative arose when a witness who had sworn to the relevant facts in the witness box was asked whether he or she had told the same story on an earlier occasion. This was not allowed (subject to exceptions eg to rebut an allegation of recent fabrication) on the obvious basis that witnesses should not be allowed to manufacture corroboration for their evidence simply by repeating the story on several occasions before the trial.

33.04 The strict hearsay rule arose where an assertion on an earlier occasion was sought to be proved either by calling to give evidence a witness who heard the assertion being made or who saw some conduct which was alleged to convey a particular meaning (eg sign language), or by adducing a document containing the assertion. Hearsay also arose where a witness was called to prove conduct which impliedly contained an assertion, such as where a police officer gave evidence of telephone calls inquiring about drugs from unidentified members of the public to a particular address to prove that those premises were being used to supply drugs: *R v Kearley* [1992] 2 AC 228.

It will be noted that the formulation of the hearsay rule in the first paragraph of this section **33.05** extends the rule to cover expressions of opinion (including opinion expressed in experts' reports) as well as statements of fact by lay persons, to which the rule is traditionally applied.

Conversely, a previous statement has never been hearsay when it is proved, not to establish **33.06** the truth of its contents, but to prove that it was made. An example is where the claimant in a libel claim seeks to prove that the words complained of were published. In such a case the claimant does not assert the truth of the words (and in fact will contend that they are false), but needs to prove they were published to establish one of the elements of the cause of action.

B REAL EVIDENCE

There is a distinction at common law between hearsay and real evidence. Unlike hearsay, **33.07** real evidence is admissible at common law. Sometimes evidence which superficially resembles hearsay will in fact be regarded as real evidence. Generally, real evidence consists of physical objects that are produced for inspection by the court. For example, in an action for personal injuries against an employer, the machine which caused the injury may be produced to show how the accident happened, or in an action against a shop for breach of the statutory implied terms a radio may be produced to show it does not work. However, the distinction between hearsay and real evidence becomes rather fine when the court is asked to consider printouts and recordings made by various machines. In *The Statue of Liberty* [1968] 1 WLR 739 the disputed evidence consisted of a cinematograph film of the radar echoes, recorded mechanically without human intervention, of vessels involved in a collision at sea. Sir Jocelyn Simon P held the recording was admissible as real evidence, despite the fact that the purpose in adducing it was to prove that the recorded movements of the ships were true. This principle has been applied in criminal cases to a computer used to calculate the chemical composition of samples of metal (*R v Wood* (1982) 76 Cr App R 23); computer records showing details of access gained and attempts to gain access to certain web pages (*R (O'Shea) v Coventry Magistrates' Court* [2004] Crim LR 948); and photographs taken by a security camera in a building society office (*R v Dodson* (1984) 79 Cr App R 220).

If information is produced by a machine in similar circumstances to those just described, **33.08** it is probable that a civil court would also decide that it was not hearsay, but admissible as real evidence. Some doubt must remain whether this is certainly so, because it is widely accepted that the cases referred to were decided before the position was liberated by statutory intervention (particularly the CEA 1968, the CEA 1995, and the Criminal Justice Act 2003), and were motivated by a desire to evade the hearsay rule in respect of otherwise highly persuasive evidence. Adducing mechanical recordings, computer printouts, and the like as real evidence may be seen as an evasion of the notice procedure under the CEA 1995.

C ADMISSIBILITY OF HEARSAY EVIDENCE

Under the CEA 1995

Hearsay, as an exclusionary rule, was abolished for all civil proceedings by the CEA 1995, **33.09** s 1(1), which provides: 'in civil proceedings evidence shall not be excluded on the ground that it is hearsay'. By s 11 'civil proceedings' is defined as meaning civil proceedings before any civil tribunal in relation to which the strict rules of evidence apply, whether as a matter of law or by agreement of the parties.

33.10 Section 1(2)(b) extends the scope of admissible hearsay to include hearsay of whatever degree. This means that multiple hearsay (hearsay on hearsay) is generally admissible in civil proceedings. For example, Alan witnessed a road traffic accident, and saw one of the motor cars going through a red traffic light. If Alan told Bert, or wrote down his account of the accident in his notebook, proof either by calling Bert or by producing the notebook would amount to ordinary, first-hand, hearsay. Proof by calling Carol, who was told about the accident by Bert recounting what Alan had told him, or by calling Diane, who had read Alan's notebook, would amount to second-hand (multiple) hearsay. All of this is potentially admissible under s 1(1).

33.11 However, to prevent abuse by witnesses manufacturing supporting evidence along the lines of the old rule against narrative, CEA 1995, s 6(2), provides that a party which has called or intends to call a person as a witness in civil proceedings (Alan in the example given) in general may not also adduce previous statements made by that witness. There are three exceptions to this exclusion:

(a) Where the court grants permission for the adduction of the previous statement. Generally it is to be expected that permission will not be granted. It may be, however, that, due to the passage of time since witnessing the relevant events, the witness is, by the time of trial, unable to give a coherent account from the witness box. If this is simply through temporary forgetfulness, it can normally be remedied by the device of allowing the witness to see an earlier statement for the purpose of refreshing the memory. If the problem is more deep-rooted, however, such as where through the onset of some illness or the passage of a great deal of time, or because the only earlier statements were not made sufficiently contemporaneously with the events to be used as memory-refreshing documents, the court may well grant permission for the earlier statements to be adduced. Something rather similar occurred in the CEA 1968 case of *Morris v Stratford-on-Avon Rural District Council* [1973] 1 WLR 1059, where one of the drivers had made a written statement of the events at an accident to an insurance company about nine months after the accident. His evidence at trial was unexpectedly confused and inconsistent. The statement to the insurance company was too old to be used as a memory-refreshing document, but permission was granted for its admission under the CEA 1968. It is likely that permission would be granted in similar circumstances under the CEA 1995.

(b) Where it is sought to adduce the earlier statement to rebut a suggestion made in cross-examination that the witness's evidence has been fabricated. It is fairly unusual for suggestions to be made to witnesses to the effect 'When did you first make up this story?' However, when it does happen, the party calling the witness is entitled to adduce an earlier statement from the witness proving the witness has been telling a consistent story for some time.

(c) There is express provision in s 6(2) that the prohibition does not extend to precluding the practice of witnesses adopting their exchanged statements as their evidence-in-chief.

33.12 By s 14(1), nothing in the CEA 1995 affects the exclusion of evidence on grounds other than it being hearsay. The CEA 1995 therefore does not render admissible evidence which would otherwise be excluded by virtue of any other enactment, any rule of law, or for failure to comply with rules of court or an order of the court. Hearsay evidence may, therefore, be excluded, for example, because it is irrelevant, non-expert opinion, or because the court refuses permission to call the witness who was to be called to prove it on a failure to exchange the witness's signed statement in accordance with the rules of court. Section 6(3) provides that the Act does not expand the circumstances in which previous inconsistent statements may be put in cross-examination, or the degree to which a party may seek to cross-examine hostile witnesses (which remain governed by the Criminal Procedure Act 1865, ss 3, 4, and 5).

Further, the CEA 1995, s 5(1), provides that hearsay evidence shall not be admitted in civil proceedings if and to the extent that either:

(a) it consists of a statement of a person who would not be a competent witness; or
(b) it is to be proved by a person who is not a competent witness.

Incompetence of witnesses is based on an inability to understand the nature of the oath. It can **33.13** extend to very young children (children who can give unsworn evidence under the provisions of the Children Act 1989, s 96, if they understand the duty to tell the truth and have sufficient understanding to justify their evidence being given, are not incompetent for this purpose) and adults suffering from certain mental or physical infirmities affecting their understanding.

The effect of the CEA 1995 is in accordance with the present general policy that, particu- **33.14** larly in cases tried by judges sitting alone, so far as possible all evidence should be admissible with the only question being one of weight. The general policy also dictates that the parties to litigation should prepare for trial in an open manner with as much prior disclosure as possible. Usually, notice of an intention to rely on hearsay evidence must be given at the same time as witness statements are exchanged (in accordance with directions from the court). Open preparation has the merit that it allows the parties to assess the merits of their respective cases with greater certainty. This should promote the prospects of an early settlement of an action, thereby avoiding the need for a trial.

Former common law exceptions to the hearsay rule

Six former common law exceptions to the hearsay rule are preserved and converted into **33.15** statutory exceptions by CEA 1995, s 7(2) and (3). The exceptions concerned are:

(a) published works on matters of a public nature;
(b) public documents, such as official registers;
(c) records of certain courts, treaties, pardons, etc.;
(d) reputation adduced to establish good or bad character;
(e) reputation or family tradition on a question of pedigree; and
(f) reputation or family tradition on the existence of a public or general right, or to identify a person or thing.

D NOTICE PROCEDURE

Advance notice

A party intending to rely on hearsay evidence at trial is required to serve notice of that **33.16** intention on the other side in advance of the trial (CEA 1995, s 2). This section provides that rules of court may be made specifying the situations in which advance notice must be given where a party intends to rely on hearsay evidence. The CPR, r 33.2, provides:

(1) Where a party intends to rely on hearsay evidence at trial and either—
　(a) that evidence is to be given by a witness giving oral evidence; or
　(b) that evidence is contained in a witness statement of a person who is not being called to give oral evidence;
　that party complies with section 2(1)(a) of the Civil Evidence Act 1995 by serving a witness statement on the other parties in accordance with the court's order.
(2) Where paragraph (1)(b) applies, the party intending to rely on the hearsay evidence must, when he serves the witness statement—
　(a) inform the other parties that the witness is not being called to give oral evidence; and

   (b) give the reason why the witness will not be called.

  (3) In all other cases where a party intends to rely on hearsay evidence at trial, that party complies with section 2(1)(a) of the Civil Evidence Act 1995 by serving a [hearsay] notice on the other parties . . .

33.17 However, by r 33.3 there is no need to serve a hearsay notice in relation to:

  (a) evidence at hearings other than trials;

  (aa) an affidavit or witness statement which is to be used at trial but which does not contain hearsay evidence; or . . .

  (c) where the requirement is excluded by a practice direction.

33.18 Hearsay evidence is often given by witnesses who repeat what they were told on a previous occasion, and, as witness statements are supposed to set out the evidence each witness is expected to say in chief, hearsay evidence will usually be set out in the exchanged witness statements. The effect of rr 33.2 and 33.3 is that hearsay notices are not often required because any hearsay relied upon ought to be included in the exchanged witness statements.

Form of hearsay notices

33.19 By CPR, r 33.2(3), a hearsay notice must:

  (a) identify the hearsay evidence;

  (b) state that the party serving the notice proposes to rely on the hearsay evidence at trial; and

  (c) give the reason why the witness will not be called.

33.20 By r 33.2(4), the party proposing to rely on the hearsay evidence must:

  (a) serve the notice no later than the latest date for serving witness statements; and

  (b) if the hearsay evidence is to be in a document, supply a copy to any party who requests one.

A single hearsay notice may deal with the hearsay evidence of more than one witness.

Failure to serve hearsay notice

33.21 By CEA 1995, s 2(4), failure to serve a hearsay notice whether in time or at all does not affect the admissibility of the hearsay evidence, but may be taken into account by the court:

  (a) in exercising its discretionary powers, particularly on costs; and

  (b) as adversely affecting the weight of the evidence.

Power to call witness for cross-examination on hearsay evidence

33.22 The CEA 1995, s 3, envisages parties in receipt of hearsay notices being able to summon the makers of hearsay statements for cross-examination. If this is to be done, an application for permission to call the maker of the statement must be issued no later than 14 days after the day on which a notice of intention to rely on the hearsay evidence was served on the applicant (CPR, r 33.4). The power in r 33.4 to order the maker of a hearsay statement to attend for cross-examination is limited to cross-examining that person on the contents of their hearsay statement, and does not permit cross-examination on any wider basis (*Electromagnetic Geoservices ASA v Petroleum Geo-Services ASA* [2016] 1 WLR 2353).

The application must be made by issuing an application notice. Consideration should be **33.23** given to supporting the application with evidence in writing, although there is no strict requirement for this.

Credibility notices

By CPR, r 33.5, a party intending to adduce evidence (for which, see 33.27) to attack the **33.24** credibility of the maker of the statement must serve a notice on the party intending to rely on the hearsay evidence of the intention of mounting such an attack within 14 days after service of the hearsay notice.

Business document certificates

By the CEA 1995, s 9(1), business (which is defined as including any activity regularly **33.25** carried on over a period of time, whether for profit or not) and public authority (which includes any public or statutory undertaking or government department) records may be received in evidence without further proof. A document will, by s 9(2), be taken as being such a record if a certificate signed by an officer of the business or authority is produced to the court. A document purporting to be such a certificate is deemed by s 9(2)(a) to have been duly given by an appropriate officer and signed by him or her. These provisions are designed to facilitate the ease of proof of records without the need to call anyone from the records department of the business concerned. In practice, in addition to the certificate, a hearsay notice will also be required in order to satisfy the requirements of the rules of court.

E TRIAL

Adducing the evidence in court

(a) Where the hearsay statement is contained in a business record, it will be enough to **33.26** adduce the record and a certificate complying with the CEA 1995, s 9.
(b) Where the hearsay statement is contained in a document, by the CEA 1995, s 8, it may be proved either:
  (i) by the production of that document; or
  (ii) by the production of a copy of that document (it being immaterial whether the original is still in existence or the number of removes between the original and the copy adduced in court), authenticated in such manner as the court may approve. The words in parenthesis, which come from s 8(2), abolish the ancient best evidence rule in civil claims. The authentification needed is that the copy adduced is a true copy of the original. Normally it would be expected that a witness will be called to the witness box in order to testify to the authenticity of the document. As Staughton LJ said in *Ventouris v Mountain (No 2)* [1992] 1 WLR 887, a document is not produced to the court simply by counsel handing it to the court. Rather, it should be produced by a witness who is qualified to do so in accordance with the rules of evidence, and saying what the document is.
(c) Oral hearsay will need to be proved by calling a witness who heard the hearsay statement.

Credibility

By the CEA 1995, s 5(2), evidence is admissible to attack or support the credibility of hear- **33.27** say statements adduced at trial, unless under the rules of evidence a denial by the witness would have been final. This means that evidence relevant to collateral issues cannot be adduced. What is allowed is evidence that the maker of the statement has been convicted of a crime, evidence of any bias of the maker of the statement in favour of the party adducing the statement, and evidence that the maker of the statement has made any previous statement inconsistent with the statement relied upon. As already discussed, prior notice of the intention to attack the hearsay statement in any of these ways must be given within 14 days of service of the hearsay notice.

Weight

33.28 In assessing the weight (if any) to be given to hearsay evidence the court is required, by the CEA 1995, s 4(1), to have regard to any circumstances from which inferences can reasonably be drawn as to the reliability or otherwise of the evidence. Section 4(2) lists a number of particular factors, namely:

(a) whether it would have been reasonable and practicable for the party by whom the evidence was adduced to have produced the maker of the statement as a witness. It was stated by Finer J in *Rasool v West Midlands Passenger Transport Executive* [1974] 3 All ER 638 that if the whereabouts abroad of an important witness in a substantial case can be easily ascertained, but a party chooses to rely on hearsay evidence rather than calling the maker of the statement to give evidence, there is no doubt that little weight would be attached to the evidence;

(b) whether the original statement was made contemporaneously with the occurrence or existence of the matters stated;

(c) whether the evidence is multiple hearsay;

(d) whether any person involved had any motive to conceal or misrepresent the facts;

(e) whether the original statement was an edited account, or was made in collaboration with another or for a particular purpose;

(f) whether the circumstances in which the evidence is adduced as hearsay are such as to suggest an attempt to prevent proper evaluation of its weight; and

(g) any failure to give due notice of the adduction of the hearsay evidence.

KEY POINTS SUMMARY

33.29
- Hearsay evidence is where a witness gives evidence of facts they have not personally experienced for the purpose of proving the truth of those facts.

- Hearsay may be written or oral, and may be first-hand, second-hand, etc.

- In civil cases, evidence is not inadmissible purely on the ground that it is hearsay (CEA 1995, s 1(1)), even if it is multiple hearsay.

- Hearsay notices must be served at the same time as witness statements are exchanged when a party intends to rely on hearsay at trial.

- Hearsay notices are not required in respect of interim hearings. In most other situations service of a witness statement avoids the need for a hearsay notice.

- Where one party intends to rely on hearsay evidence, the other side can apply for an order that the maker of the statement attend trial for cross-examination.

- In practice, trial judges give limited weight to hearsay evidence.

34

ADMISSIONS AND DOCUMENTARY EVIDENCE

A NATURE OF ADMISSIONS............34.02

B PRE-ACTION ADMISSIONS
   OF LIABILITY.....................34.05

C PERMISSION TO WITHDRAW
   AN ADMISSION...................34.08

D NOTICE TO ADMIT FACTS 34.10

E PROVING DOCUMENTS..............34.16

This chapter is concerned with the rules relating to the proof of admissions and documents **34.01** at trial.

A NATURE OF ADMISSIONS

Admissions may be formal or informal. Formal admissions have the effect of establishing **34.02** the facts admitted. As the matter will no longer be in issue, neither side is permitted to adduce evidence on it. Informal admissions, such as oral out-of-court statements made by a party against their own interests, are merely items of evidence. While an informal admission may be a compelling item of evidence (if it was not true, why say it?), being an item of evidence it can be disproved by other evidence in the case. Adverse statements made in the following situations are examples of formal admissions:

- admissions in acknowledgments of service;
- admissions made on filing admission forms from the response pack (forms N9A and N9C);
- admissions in statements of case, which include replies to requests for further information;
- admissions of the whole or part of another's case made by letter after proceedings have been commenced (CPR, r 14.1(2));
- admissions made and recorded at case management hearings;
- admissions made in reply to notices to admit (see 34.10–34.15);
- admissions made by counsel at trial.

Under the general law of evidence, binding admissions can sometimes be made by persons **34.03** connected with a party. Typical examples are admissions made by partners (see the Partnership Act 1890, s 15), predecessors in title, and referees.

An 'admission' made without knowledge of the facts said to have been admitted has **34.04** little if any evidential value (*Comptroller of Customs v Western Lectric Co Ltd* [1966] AC 367). Also, the 'admission' must be one of fact, not law. In *Ashmore v Corporation of Lloyd's* [1992] 1 WLR 446 the House of Lords held that statements made by members of the Committee of Lloyd's, said to be admissions that the defendants owed a duty of care to 'Names' (members of underwriting syndicates), concerned a question of law and so the statements were neither relevant nor admissible.

B PRE-ACTION ADMISSIONS OF LIABILITY

34.05 One of the purposes of the pre-action protocols (see Chapter 5) is to enable defendants to assess the strength of the claim they are facing, and to decide whether to admit liability at an early stage. Usually, defendants keep to such pre-action admissions, but sometimes defendants change their minds once proceedings are issued. At common law there is no restriction on a defendant withdrawing a pre-action admission (*Sowerby v Charlton* [2006] 1 WLR 568), as an admission made in correspondence is an informal admission. A withdrawn admission has still been made, so it remains an item of evidence, but has to be read together with the withdrawal when assessing its weight. For non-personal injuries claims, withdrawn pre-action admissions may be relied upon in a summary judgment application if, with the other facts in the case, any defence has no real prospects of success. It may also be possible to strike out the defence of a defendant who makes and then withdraws an admission if the withdrawal was made in bad faith (*Walley v Stoke-on-Trent City Council* [2007] 1 WLR 352).

34.06 Personal injuries claims divide into those within and outside the RTA and EL/PL protocols (see Chapter 9). Admissions in cases within these protocols can be withdrawn during the initial consideration period, but thereafter they can be withdrawn only with the consent of the claimant (and once proceedings have started, either with consent or court permission) (CPR, r 14.1B). In other personal injuries claims, provided the conditions set out in 34.07 are satisfied, a pre-commencement admission may be withdrawn in the period before a claim is issued only with the consent of the claimant (r 14.1A(3)(a)). After proceedings are issued, a pre-action admission may only be withdrawn if all the parties consent or if the court gives permission (r 14.1A(3)(b)).

34.07 The conditions are that the pre-action admission was made:

(a) by a notice in writing (r 14.1A(1));
(b) in a claim governed by either the Pre-action Protocol for Personal Injury Claims; the Pre-action Protocol for the Resolution of Clinical Disputes; or the Pre-action Protocol for Disease and Illness Claims (PD 14, para 1.1(2)); and
(c) either after the defendant received a letter of claim written in accordance with the relevant pre-action protocol (r 14.1A(2)(a)) or if the admission is stated to be made under Part 14 (r 14.1A(2)(b)).

C PERMISSION TO WITHDRAW AN ADMISSION

34.08 Permission is required to amend or withdraw an admission if:

(a) it was a pre-action admission in a personal injury claim, proceedings have now started, and the other party will not consent to the admission being withdrawn (CPR, rr 14.1A(3)(b) and 14.1B(2)(b)); or
(b) it was made after proceedings were commenced (r 14.1(5)). It may also be necessary to amend the relevant statement of case or notice to admit.

34.09 In deciding whether to give permission, the court is required by PD 14, para 7.2, to have regard to all the circumstances of the case, including seven factors (which are set out below).

This entrusts the judge with making a multi-factorial value judgment which will be difficult to set aside on an appeal (*Kojima v HSBC Bank plc* [2012] 1 All ER 1392). The factors are:

(a) the grounds upon which the applicant seeks to withdraw the admission, including whether or not new evidence has come to light which was not available at the time the admission was made. In *Les Laboratories Servier v Apotex Inc* [2007] EWHC 591 (Pat) the threshold was said to be whether there were plausible grounds for supposing that the admission made was in fact false;

(b) the conduct of the parties, including any conduct which led the applicant into making the admission;

(c) any prejudice that may be caused to any person if the admission is withdrawn. Permission to amend may be refused where the circumstances in which the admission was made give rise to an estoppel (*H Clark (Doncaster) Ltd v Wilkinson* [1965] Ch 694), for which there has to be some evidence of detrimental reliance on the admission (*Gunn v Taygroup Ltd* [2010] EWHC 665 (TCC));

(d) the prejudice that may be caused to any person if the application is refused;

(e) the stage in the proceedings at which the application to withdraw is made, and in particular in relation to the trial date or window;

(f) the prospects of success (if the admission is withdrawn) of the claim or part of the claim in relation to which the admission was made; and

(g) the interests of the administration of justice.

D NOTICE TO ADMIT FACTS

In order to ensure that the court's time at trial is not wasted in having to determine facts **34.10** and issues that could reasonably be admitted, a party may serve the other side with a notice to admit facts (CPR, r 32.18). A notice to admit facts must be served no later than 21 days before the trial. An example is shown in form 34.1.

Notices to admit are looked on favourably by the courts, because they narrow the issues **34.11** to be decided at trial and therefore tend to save costs and reduce delays. In *Baden v Société Générale pour Favoriser le Développement du Commerce et de l'Industrie en France SA* (27 February 1985, CA, unreported) Lawton LJ said that notices to admit were of the greatest importance in the administration of justice and ought to be more frequently used. In the same case at first instance, reported 11 years after the event at [1992] 4 All ER 161, Peter Gibson J at 277 said the commonly accepted basis for the proper use of the procedure is to procure admissions on matters not really in dispute as distinct from matters the subject of real controversy which the party served may reasonably refuse to admit.

Use of admissions

Admissions made in response to a notice to admit are formal admissions as between the **34.12** parties who served and were served with the notice, but only for the purposes of the case in hand. Other parties to the present action are not entitled to make use of such admissions, although they may be entitled to serve their own notice to admit (CPR, r 32.18(3)).

Costs consequences

Under the rules of court in force before the introduction of the CPR, a party which **34.13** refused or neglected to make an admission after being served with a notice to admit facts would usually be ordered to pay the costs of proving those facts at trial, and the costs

Notice to admit facts

In the HIGH COURT OF JUSTICE QUEEN'S BENCH DIVISION	
Claim No.	HQ14 87105
Claimant (include Ref.)	STEPHENSON HYPERLINKS PLC
Defendant (include Ref.)	LOMAX FISHING EQUIPMENT LIMITED

I (We) give notice that you are requested to admit the following facts or part of case in this claim:

1. Under cover of an email dated 9 April 2012 the Claimant sent to the Defendant a copy of its price list dated 10 January 2012.
2. On 12 June 2012 Mrs Lisa Stephenson and Mr Alexander Parker attended the Defendant's premises for a full working day.
3. The purpose of the visit on 12 June 2012 was to commission the software developed by the Claimant for the Defendant pursuant to the Contract.

I (We) confirm that any admission of fact(s) or part of case will only be used in this claim.

Signed

(Claimant)(Defendant)('s Solicitor)

Position or office held Solicitor
(If signing on behalf of firm or company)

Date

- -

Admission of facts

I (We) admit the facts or part of case (set out above)(in the attached schedule) for the purposes of this claim only and on the basis that the admission will not be used on any other occasion or by any other person.

Signed

(Claimant)(Defendant)('s Solicitor)

Position or office held
(If signing on behalf of firm or company)

Date

The court office at Royal Courts of Justice, Strand, London WC2A 2LL

is open between 10 am and 4 pm Monday to Friday. Address all communication to the Court Manager quoting the claim number

N266 - w3 Notice to admit facts (4.99)   *Printed on behalf of The Court Service* occasioned by and thrown away as a result. There is no express equivalent of RSC, ord 62, r 6(7) in the CPR. However, the court's discretion on costs under r 44.2 is wide enough to achieve the same result.

The effect is that if the party refusing to make the admissions wins at trial, instead of hav- **34.14** ing an expectation of recovering the entire costs of the proceedings under the principle that costs usually follow the event (for which, see 46.04ff), it will most likely have to pay the costs (including related costs) of proving the facts not admitted, and will only recover the balance of the costs of the claim.

The trial judge always has a discretion whether to impose this costs sanction. According **34.15** to the Court of Appeal in *Lipkin Gorman v Karpnale Ltd* [1989] 1 WLR 1340, the judge should ask whether in the circumstances of the case the facts ought to have been admitted, and whether it would be just to require the winner at trial to pay the costs involved in proving the facts not admitted. It is open to the court to find that it was reasonable to contest some of the facts stated in a notice to admit, but not others, and to operate the costs rule over the facts which should reasonably have been admitted, as in *Baden v Société Générale pour Favoriser le Développement du Commerce et de l'Industrie en France SA* [1993] 1 WLR 509. The question whether the facts subject to a notice to admit are controversial in the context of the case is one of degree. Simply because the existence of a fact may not be capable of being finally established until it is found at trial does not mean that the court will refuse to penalize a party refusing to admit it (the *Baden* case).

E PROVING DOCUMENTS

Best evidence rule

At common law there was a general rule that a party relying on the contents of a document **34.16** at trial had to prove those contents by producing the original. This was an aspect of the best evidence rule, but was abolished for civil cases by the CEA 1995, s 8(2) (see 33.26).

Exhibits to witness statements and affidavits

Exhibits in witness statements and affidavits are usually photocopies. The originals must be **34.17** brought to court for inspection by the judge at the hearing (PD 32, para 13.1).

Documents in the possession of a witness

Where a document is in the possession of a non-party, that person is a witness and may **34.18** be compelled under a witness summons to attend court at the trial with the document (see 39.03). Generally, if a witness fails to produce a document in answer to a witness summons the only remedy is to punish the witness for disobeying the summons and to claim damages.

Authenticity of disclosed documents

Parties are deemed to admit the authenticity of documents disclosed to them under CPR, **34.19** Part 31 (generally, the documents disclosed under a list of documents), unless they serve a notice to prove in form N268. This must specify the documents being challenged, and must be served by the latest date for serving witness statements, or within seven days of disclosure, whichever is the later (r 32.19).

Trial bundles

34.20 Trial bundles are considered at 39.12. By PD 32, para 27.1, the court may give directions requiring the parties to use their best endeavours to agree the bundles of documents to be used at any hearing. Once this has been done, all the documents in the agreed bundles are admissible as evidence of their contents unless the court otherwise orders, or a party has given written notice of their objection to the admissibility of specified documents (para 27.2). The originals of the documents in the trial bundles should be made available at trial (PD 39A, para 3.3).

35

EXPERTS

A ADMISSIBILITY OF EXPERT EVIDENCE . . 35.02

B CONTROL OF EVIDENCE 35.16

C PRIVILEGED NATURE OF EXPERTS'
REPORTS 35.18

D DISCLOSURE OF EXPERTS'
REPORTS 35.21

E WRITTEN QUESTIONS TO EXPERTS 35.42

F WITHOUT PREJUDICE DISCUSSION 35.43

G EXAMINATIONS BY EXPERTS 35.45

H TRIAL 35.53

I EXPERTS' IMMUNITY FROM SUIT 35.63

J USE OF EXPERTS' REPORTS AFTER
TRIAL 35.65

Key points summary 35.66

At trial, questions of fact are decided by the tribunal of fact (in civil litigation usually **35.01** the judge) based on the oral evidence of witnesses, documentary and real evidence, and any inferences which may fairly be drawn from that evidence. Increasingly, however, civil claims raise scientific and technical issues which a judge could not reasonably be expected to decide without the assistance of expert opinion from practitioners from the field in question. This chapter is concerned with the principles governing the use of expert evidence in civil claims.

A ADMISSIBILITY OF EXPERT EVIDENCE

Issues of an artistic, scientific, or technical nature must be decided on the basis of expert **35.02** evidence. Thus, the opinion of an eminent engineer was admitted in *Folkes v Chadd* (1782) 3 Doug KB 157 on the effect of an artificial bank on the silting of a harbour. In the absence of expert evidence, such an issue must be decided against the party having the burden of proof. Expert evidence is subject to considerations of weight, and, even if uncontradicted, is not bound to be accepted by the court. As Lord President Cooper said in *Davie v Magistrates of Edinburgh* 1953 SC 34:

> Their duty is to furnish the judge . . . with the necessary scientific criteria for testing the accuracy of their conclusions, so as to enable the judge . . . to form [his or her] own independent judgment by the application of these criteria to the facts proved in evidence. The scientific opinion evidence, if intelligible, convincing and tested, becomes a factor (and often an important factor) for consideration along with the whole other evidence in the case, but the decision is for the judge.

There are five preconditions for the admission of expert evidence: **35.03**

(a) the issue must call for expertise;
(b) the area must be an established field of expertise;
(c) the witness must be suitably qualified;
(d) the expert must be independent and impartial; and
(e) permission to adduce the expert evidence must be obtained from the court.

Issue requiring expertise

35.04 Experts, like other witnesses, may give evidence of primary facts within their own knowledge. Thus, an expert surveyor called to give evidence in rent review proceedings may give factual evidence of the dimensions of the premises in question if those facts are known to the witness. However, the real purpose in calling the surveyor is to express an expert opinion on the rental value of the premises and how it compares with other properties in the area. An expert is permitted to do this only if the matter calls for expertise. This means that the matter must be outside the knowledge and experience of the tribunal of fact. Typical examples are:

(a) medical evidence on the extent and prognosis of personal injuries;
(b) surveying evidence as to the state of an allegedly defective building;
(c) handwriting evidence as to the authorship of disputed writing; and
(d) accountancy evidence to establish an alleged loss of profits.

35.05 Conversely, if the matter is one within the experience of most members of the public, an expert's opinion on the matter is not admissible. For example, questions of credibility, even of children, are for the judge, and expert evidence on whether a child is to be believed is strictly inadmissible (*Re N (A Minor) (Sexual Abuse: Video Evidence)* [1997] 1 WLR 153). A more indulgent approach, however, was taken in *Re M and R (Minors) (Sexual Abuse: Expert Evidence)* [1996] 4 All ER 239, where Butler-Sloss LJ felt that expert evidence on children's credibility should be admitted, the proper control mechanism being in assessing its weight. Another example is *Larby v Thurgood* [1993] ICR 66 where it was held that the claimant's motivation to find better-paid employment was a matter within ordinary experience and that 'expert' evidence from an employment consultant on the matter was inadmissible. However, an employment consultant would be able to give expert opinion evidence concerning the employment situation in a particular area and the prospects for a person in the claimant's position of finding work.

35.06 In *Liddell v Middleton* [1996] PIQR P36 Stuart-Smith LJ gave guidance aimed at limiting the use of accident reconstruction experts in road traffic personal injuries claims. His Lordship accepted that such witnesses are necessary and useful in cases where there are no witnesses capable of describing what has happened, and where the expert is able scientifically to deduce pre-accident speeds and movements of vehicles from their positions after the accident, marks and debris on the road, and damage to the vehicles. What such an expert is not allowed to do is to analyse the witness statements and from them to draw conclusions about when the motorists should have seen each other, what avoiding action they should have taken, and whether any of the drivers should be criticized for what they did or did not do. Those are all matters for the judge, who does not require expert guidance on them.

35.07 It is also possible that an expert may be called to give factual evidence about facts known to the expert. Examples are the treating doctor, or the architect on a building project. In such a case the individual is called as a factual witness, not an expert (*Kirkman v Euro-Exide Corporation (CMP Batteries Ltd)* [2007] All ER (D) 209), although they are also frequently asked for their professional opinion (*Jones v Kaney* [2011] 2 AC 398).

Established field of expertise

35.08 In most cases this will be obvious, but in developing areas the court must be satisfied by the party seeking to call the evidence that there is a body of expertise governed by recognized standards or rules of conduct capable of influencing the court's decision on any of the issues which it has to decide, and that the witness has sufficient familiarity with and knowledge of the area of expertise to be of value to the court (*Barings plc v Coopers and Lybrand* [2001] PNLR 22).

Qualifications

A person is an 'expert' if he or she is skilled in the field in question through qualifications **35.09** or experience. A car mechanic may be an expert simply through experience in working with cars. A person with paper qualifications, but little experience, should be instructed as an expert with great caution, because even if accepted by the court as an expert, his or her opinion is unlikely to carry much weight. Furthermore, experts are permitted to express an opinion only within their field of expertise. So, a consultant orthopaedic surgeon would not be allowed to express an opinion on a psychiatric matter, nor would a surveyor be allowed to express an opinion on an architectural question.

Independence and impartiality

The CPR place a lot of emphasis on the importance of experts remaining independent of **35.10** the parties and state that the expert's primary duty is to the court rather than the party paying his or her fees. Rule 35.3 provides:

(1) It is the duty of experts to help the court on the matters within their expertise.
(2) This duty overrides any obligation to the person from whom experts have received instructions or by whom they are paid.

It is now established that '. . . the requirement of independence and impartiality is ... one of **35.11** admissibility rather than merely the weight of the evidence ...' *per* Lord Reed in *Kennedy v Cordia (Services) LLP* [2016] 1 WLR 597 at [51]. While this is desirable in higher value claims, it is inefficient and expensive in lower value claims, where before *Kennedy v Cordia (Services) LLP* it was common for professionally qualified employees of parties to be called as experts provided they understood their primary duty was to the court (*Field v Leeds City Council* [2000] 1 EGLR 54).

It is important that expert evidence should be, and should be seen to be, the independent **35.12** product of the expert uninfluenced by the exigencies of the litigation (*Whitehouse v Jordan* [1981] 1 WLR 246 and PD 35, para 2.1). An expert must give his evidence honestly, even if this involves concessions that are contrary to his client's interests (*Jones v Kaney* [2011] 2 AC 398 at [50]). Where an expert adopts a biased or irrational approach, it may be appropriate for the judge to refer the witness's conduct to the relevant professional body, after giving the witness a suitable period of time to make representations: *Pearce v Ove Arup Partnership Ltd* (2001) LTL 2/11/01.

In *Stevens v Gullis* [2000] 1 All ER 527 an expert instructed by one of the parties demon- **35.13** strated by his conduct that he had no conception of the requirements imposed on experts by the CPR. He failed to state in his report that he understood his duty to the court, failed to set out his instructions, and also failed to cooperate with the other experts in signing an agreed memorandum following a without prejudice meeting of experts. It was held that in the circumstances he should be debarred from giving evidence in the case.

Ultimate issue rule

At common law an expert was not allowed to express an opinion directly on one of the **35.14** issues in a case, on the ground that doing so would usurp the function of the tribunal of fact. Thus, a handwriting expert was said to be allowed to express views about the similarities between two pieces of writing, but could not express an opinion that they were written by the same person. This anachronistic rule was abolished for civil cases by the Civil Evidence Act 1972 ('CEA 1972'), s 3(3). However, it is not for experts to attempt to make findings of fact. Instead, they should express their opinions on the basis of assumed facts which should be clearly identified and stated in their reports (*JP Morgan Chase Bank v Springwell Navigation Corporation* [2007] 1 All ER (Comm) 549 at [21]).

Non-expert opinion evidence

35.15 Generally, witnesses who are not qualified as experts can only give evidence as to facts. The reason is that inferences to be drawn from the facts are matters for the tribunal of fact. Exceptionally, lay witnesses may express opinions as a way of conveying facts they have perceived if describing those events in detail would be unduly difficult and artificial. For example, a lay witness is permitted to give an estimate of a person's age rather than describing the details of the person's appearance. Other examples include estimates of speed and distance, the state of the weather ('it was cold for that time of year'), and whether a person appeared to be drunk. Authority for the last of these propositions is *R v Davies* [1962] 1 WLR 1111. In this case three soldiers, who were witnesses to a road accident, were allowed to give evidence that they had formed the impression that the defendant had taken drink. Lord Parker CJ said the witness 'must describe of course the facts upon which he relies, but it seems to this court that he is perfectly entitled to give his impression as to whether drink had been taken or not'. Statutory confirmation of the general rule is given by the CEA 1972, s 3(2). However, a non-expert witness is not permitted to express an opinion on a matter calling for expertise.

B CONTROL OF EVIDENCE

35.16 It is provided in CPR, r 32.1, that the court may control the evidence to be adduced in the course of proceedings, which may involve excluding evidence that would otherwise be admissible. This is supplemented by r 35.1, which says the expert evidence must be restricted to that which is reasonably required to resolve the proceedings, and by r 35.4(1), which imposes a requirement that expert evidence is only admissible with the court's permission.

35.17 Part 35 of the CPR and PD 35 contain detailed requirements and restrictions on the use of expert evidence. However, they only apply to an expert witness, who is 'a person who has been instructed to give or prepare expert evidence for the purposes of proceedings' (r 35.2(1)). This means that a document prepared by a person who is qualified to be an expert is not caught by Part 35 at all if the document was not prepared on instructions for the purposes of court proceedings. Consequently, a report into an aeroplane accident by an expert aviation inspector prepared for the relevant government ministry was held in *Rogers v Hoyle* [2015] QB 265 to be admissible, and did not have to comply with Part 35.

C PRIVILEGED NATURE OF EXPERTS' REPORTS

35.18 An expert who is instructed to give an opinion in relation to proposed or actual proceedings will invariably do so initially in the form of a written report. Such a report is protected by legal professional privilege, and need not be disclosed to the other side. It has been held (subject to joint instruction and *Edwards-Tubb* orders, for which see 35.28), that an order compelling the exchange of experts' reports offends this privilege and will not be made (*Worrall v Reich* [1955] 1 QB 296).

Consequently, a party who does not like the opinion expressed by one expert is permitted **35.19** to seek another opinion in the hope that it will be more favourable, and may rely at trial solely on the expert holding the most favourable view.

Privilege attaches to a report until it is disclosed, usually pursuant to directions (see 35.23). **35.20** Disclosing the final version of an expert's report does not waive privilege in earlier drafts of the report (*Jackson v Marley Davenport Ltd* [2004] 1 WLR 2926). A directions order which provides that a party 'shall file and serve' a report must be read as subject to an implied 'if relied upon' clause, otherwise it would amount to a direction to waive privilege in the report (*Watts v Oakley* [2006] EWCA Civ 1905).

D DISCLOSURE OF EXPERTS' REPORTS

Rules of court have been made under the CEA 1972, s 2, providing for the disclosure of **35.21** reports of experts intended to be called at trial. This includes expert evidence originally obtained for other proceedings (*Lavelle v Noble* [2011] EWCA Civ 441: DNA evidence originally obtained for criminal proceedings had to comply with the requirements of CPR, Part 35 if it was to be used in civil proceedings). These rules do not alter the substantive rules on the admissibility of expert evidence and do not abrogate legal professional privilege. A party is still permitted to seek another expert if the first expert's advice is unpalatable. However, the rules do generally require prior disclosure as a condition precedent to the admissibility of expert evidence at trial. They support the policy of open preparation for trial, with the object of avoiding trial by ambush and the promotion of early settlements.

Pre-action disclosure of reports

In several of the pre-action protocols it is contemplated that there should be pre-action dis- **35.22** closure of experts' reports. In some, for example, the personal injuries protocol, this is seen as inevitable for the purpose of assessing the extent of the claimant's injuries. In others, such as the construction and engineering disputes protocol (para 5.5) it is clear that seeking expert evidence is almost a last resort prior to commencing proceedings. The personal injuries protocol favours the joint selection of experts (see 35.28), whereas the professional negligence and the construction disputes protocols favour joint instruction.

Directions

Directions dealing with expert evidence will usually be made when the case is allocated **35.23** to the fast track or multi-track, or on the case management conference. The primary rule is that no party may call an expert or put in evidence an expert's report without the court's permission (CPR, r 35.4(1)). In the absence of a direction, therefore, expert evidence is inadmissible. In deciding whether to grant permission, and if so to what extent, the court will seek to restrict expert evidence to that which is reasonably required to resolve the proceedings (r 35.1). It will also consider whether there is a cogent need for the evidence and how helpful the evidence would be (*Mann v Chetty* [2001] CP Rep 24), and whether these benefits justify the costs involved (r 1.4(2)(h)). Where directions require an act to be done by an expert, or otherwise affect an expert, the party instructing the expert must serve a copy of the order on the expert (PD 35, para 8).

Limiting expert evidence

The court can use its power to control evidence to prevent the parties calling unnecessary **35.24** expert evidence at trial. This is particularly important, because professional experts are entitled to charge fees at commercial rates for the time they are engaged on a case, and these are often well in excess of £1,000 per day. When the parties apply for permission they must provide an estimate of the costs of the proposed experts (CPR, r 35.4(2)). In soft tissue injury claims (see 9.17) any permission is likely to be limited to a fixed cost medical report by an accredited medical expert (r 35.4(3B)). If the court decides that the parties may call expert evidence, it should generally give permission only for expert evidence from named experts in named fields, and the order may specify the issues which the expert evidence should address (r 35.4(3)). It is wrong in principle to allow a party to call more than one expert in a particular field of expertise, without very good reasons (*JP Morgan Chase Bank v Springwell Navigation Corporation* [2007] 1 All ER (Comm) 549).

35.25   The court also has to decide whether to allow the expert evidence to be adduced simply by reference to experts' reports, or whether to allow the experts to be called to give oral evidence at the trial. Particularly in cases on the small claims and fast tracks, the court will allow an expert to give oral evidence only if it is necessary in the interests of justice to do so (r 35.5(2)), but even in multi-track claims oral expert evidence is regarded as a last resort: *Daniels v Walker* [2000] 1 WLR 1382.

Exchange of reports

35.26   If the court allows both parties to adduce expert evidence, it usually makes directions (usually at allocation or on a case management conference) for the mutual exchange of reports by a stated date.

Sequential disclosure

35.27   In exceptional circumstances, directions may provide for sequential disclosure of reports. Such a direction may be justified on costs grounds where it is likely that the claimant's report will be agreed. Another example is *Kirkup v British Rail Engineering Ltd* [1983] 1 WLR 1165, where a total of 8,661 claims were made by the defendants' employees for damages for industrial deafness. The statements of case in many of the cases were in very general terms. Mutual disclosure of experts' reports would have required the defendants to have compiled wide-ranging experts' reports on noise levels in all their engineering workshops. Sequential disclosure was ordered to enable the defendants to produce expert evidence relevant to each claim.

Single joint experts and joint selection of experts

35.28   Directions permitting each party to instruct its own expert often result in conflicting expert evidence, which can lead to escalating costs. Whether this is worthwhile depends on the importance and complexity of the case, so such directions are more commonly met in multi-track cases. It is different in cases on the small claims and fast tracks, where the normal direction is for permission to be given for expert evidence from only one expert (CPR, r 35.4(3A)). A distinction has to be made between a single joint expert and a jointly selected expert. The former is instructed to prepare a report for the court on behalf of two or more parties (including the claimant), and as each side contributes to the expert's fees, each is entitled to a copy of the expert's report. The latter is instructed by one party, who is liable to pay the expert's fees, and who alone is entitled to see the report (*Carlson v Townsend* [2001] 1 WLR 2415). The joint selection of an expert under the Personal Injuries Pre-Action Protocol is of the latter type. In most cases the claimant will rely on the jointly selected expert's report in support of the injuries alleged in the claim, and will waive privilege by serving the report with the particulars of claim. According to *Edwards-Tubb v JD Wetherspoon plc* [2011] 1 WLR 1373 if the claimant decides not to use the jointly instructed expert, and instructs another expert, the court should usually order the original report to be disclosed to the defendant as a condition for being given permission to rely on the new expert's report (an *Edwards-Tubb* order). This was seen as justified as a means of restraining expert shopping by claimants.

Letters of instruction

Best practice to be followed by experts and those instructing them is given in the *Guid-* **35.29** *ance for the Instruction of Experts in Civil Claims 2014*, which is available at <http:// www.judiciary.gov.uk>. The main obligation is to explain the purpose of the report, describe what needs to be investigated, and to explain the issues in the case. All the necessary background information should also be provided. The terms of the expert's retainer should state that the expert will perform the functions specified in the CPR, so that the expert's duties to the court do not conflict with his duties to the client (*Jones v Kaney* [2011] 2 AC 398 at [49]). Where there is a joint instruction of an expert, the parties should try to agree the joint instructions, and to agree on the documents to be provided to the expert (para 38). If the parties cannot agree, ultimately they can both send instructions to the expert, sending a copy to the other side (r 35.8). An example of a letter of instruction is shown in figure 5.3.

Directions for a single joint expert

Where two or more parties wish to submit expert evidence on a particular issue, the court **35.30** may direct that the evidence on that issue is to be given by a single joint expert (CPR, r 35.7(1)). In deciding whether to make directions for separate experts or a single joint expert PD 35, para 7, provides that the court will take into account all the circumstances, and in particular whether:

(a) it is proportionate to have separate experts for each party on a particular issue with reference to:
   (i)   the amount in dispute;
   (ii) the importance to the parties; and
   (iii) the complexity of the issue;
(b) the instruction of a single joint expert is likely to assist the parties and the court to resolve the issue more speedily and in a more cost-effective way than separately instructed experts;
(c) expert evidence is to be given on the issue of liability, causation, or quantum;
(d) the expert evidence falls within a substantially established area of knowledge which is unlikely to be in dispute or there is likely to be a range of expert opinion;
(e) a party has already instructed an expert on the issue in question and whether or not that was done in compliance with any practice direction or relevant pre-action protocol;
(f) questions put to the expert (see 35.42) are likely to remove the need for the other party to instruct an expert if one party has already instructed an expert;
(g) questions put to a single joint expert may not conclusively deal with all issues that may require testing prior to trial;
(h) a conference may be required with the legal representatives, experts, and other witnesses which may make instruction of a single joint expert impractical; and
(i) a claim to privilege makes the instruction of any expert as a single joint expert inappropriate.

In substantial claims it is rare for the court to insist on a single joint expert. This is par- **35.31** ticularly so if there is more than one school of thought on the central issues (*Oxley v Penwarden* [2001] CPLR 1). In clinical disputes, it was suggested in *Peet v Mid-Kent Healthcare Trust* [2002] 1 WLR 210 that the balance between proportionality and expense could be achieved by allowing the parties to call their own experts on the medical issues, but to direct the instruction of a joint expert on the non-medical issues.

35.32 If the court makes such a direction, unless the parties agree on the expert to be instructed, the court may select an expert from a list submitted by the parties, or direct how the expert should be selected. Once selected, each instructing party may give instructions to the expert, sending a copy to the other instructing parties. The normal direction provides that the fees of the expert are to be met equally by the instructing parties.

35.33 A party will not be permitted to invite a jointly instructed expert to a conference without the written consent of the other parties: *Peet v Mid-Kent Healthcare Trust*.

Disagreement with joint report

35.34 According to Lord Woolf MR in *Daniels v Walker* [2000] 1 WLR 1382, obtaining a joint report should be regarded as a first step in obtaining expert evidence on the relevant issue. Normally, it is hoped it will also be the last step. However, if on receipt of the joint report one of the parties, for reasons that are not fanciful, decides to challenge the expert's conclusions, that party may be allowed to obtain evidence from another expert to test the conclusions in the joint report. Factors to be taken into account in exercising the discretion to allow a second expert to report include the nature of the case, the amount at stake, the effect of allowing another expert to report, any delay, and any impact on keeping the trial date (*Cosgrove v Pattison* [2001] CPLR 177). Once a second report is available, the court should reconsider the matter, perhaps after directing questions to the experts and discussion between them (for which, see 35.42 and 35.43). If there are unresolved issues after this process, the court may give permission for both experts to give oral evidence at the trial.

Form of experts' reports

35.35 By virtue of CPR, r 35.10, and PD 35, paras 3.1 and 3.2, an expert's report must:

(a) be addressed to the court;
(b) give details of the expert's qualifications;
(c) give details of any literature or other materials the expert has relied on in making the report;
(d) contain a statement setting out the substance of all facts and instructions given to the expert that are material to the report. By CPR, r 35.10(4) and PD 35, para 5, the instructions referred to will not be protected by privilege, but cross-examination of experts on the contents of their instructions will not be allowed without consent of the party who gave the instructions or unless the court permits it;
(e) make clear which facts stated in the report are within the expert's own knowledge;
(f) say who carried out any examination, measurement, test, or experiment which the expert has used in the report, give the qualifications of that person, and say whether the tests, etc., were carried out under the expert's supervision;
(g) where there is a range of opinion on the matters dealt with in the report, summarize the range of opinion and give reasons for the expert's own opinion;
(h) contain a summary of the conclusions reached;
(i) if the expert is unable to give an opinion without qualification, state the qualification;
(j) contain a statement that the expert understands their duty to the court, has complied with that duty, and is aware of the requirements of Part 35, PD 35 and the *Guidance for the Instruction of Experts in Civil Claims 2014*.

35.36 An expert's report should be as concise as the nature of the case allows, and should avoid a convoluted approach such as by requiring a reader to track an argument from the main text and back and forth through various schedules. It must state clearly and prominently any key points of disagreement with the other side, and include reference to any facts known to the expert which may have a significant bearing on the issues in the case, even if unfavourable to his client (*Balmoral Group Ltd v Borealis (UK) Ltd* [2006] 2 Lloyd's Rep 629).

An expert's report must be verified by a statement of truth in the following form: **35.37**

> I confirm that insofar as the facts stated in my report are within my own knowledge I have made clear which they are and I believe them to be true, and that the opinions I have expressed represent my true and complete professional opinion.

Can an expert's report be settled by counsel? In *Whitehouse v Jordan* [1981] 1 WLR 246,   **35.38**
Lord Wilberforce commented at 256–7 that:

> while some degree of consultation between experts and legal advisers is entirely proper, it is necessary that expert evidence presented to the court should be, and should be seen to be, the independent product of the expert, uninfluenced as to form or content by the exigencies of litigation. To the extent that it is not, the evidence is likely to be not only incorrect but self-defeating.

If an expert changes his or her mind on a material matter after the exchange of reports, that   **35.39**
change of view should be communicated to the other parties (and to the court if reports have been lodged at court): PD 35, para 2.5. A frank concession of the change of view is regarded as performance of the expert's duty to the court, rather than a basis for suing the expert for negligence (*Jones v Kaney* [2011] 2 AC 398 at [56]).

Supporting documents

Published and unpublished information forming part of the general corpus of knowledge   **35.40**
in a particular field may be relied on by an expert in reaching an opinion: *Seyfang v GD Searle and Co* [1973] QB 148. Experts also often back up their opinions by referring to photographs, plans, survey reports, and other factual materials. Details of any material relied upon should be given in the report (PD 35, para 3.2(2)), and copies of factual documentation should be served on the other parties together with the report: *National Justice Compania Naviera SA v Prudential Assurance Co Ltd* [1993] 2 Lloyd's Rep 68. Important scientific papers relevant to the issues should be included in the report, and not simply produced at the trial (*Balmoral Group Ltd v Borealis (UK) Ltd* [2006] 2 Lloyd's Rep 629).

Failure to disclose report

By CPR, r 35.13, a party which fails to disclose an expert's report may not use the report at   **35.41**
the trial or call the expert to give evidence orally unless the court gives permission. Similar principles apply on such an application as on any other application for relief from sanctions (see Chapter 37).

E WRITTEN QUESTIONS TO EXPERTS

A party may put to an expert instructed by another party, or to a single joint expert, written   **35.42**
questions about the expert's report for the purpose of clarifying the report (CPR, r 35.6). This does not, of course, prevent a party putting written questions to his own expert (*Stallwood v David* [2007] 1 All ER 206 at [30]). Directions dealing with expert evidence will usually provide a date by when questions should be put to the experts. The expert's answers to such questions are treated as part of the expert's report. Questions must be proportionate and purely for clarification if they are put to the expert without permission,

but it is possible to ask about matters not in the expert's report (as long as they are within the expert's expertise) with the consent of the other side or the court's permission: *Mutch v Allen* [2001] CPLR 200.

F WITHOUT PREJUDICE DISCUSSION

35.43 There are occasions where wide divergences of view between the experts on the two sides are more apparent than real. An off-the-record discussion (either face to face or by telephone or other means of communication) can often narrow the areas of dispute. To assist this, the court has power, under CPR, r 35.12, at any stage to direct a discussion between experts, and the parties must consider with their experts, at an early stage, whether there is likely to be any useful purpose in holding an experts' discussion and if so when (PD 35, para 9.1). The purpose of discussions between experts is to agree and narrow issues, and is not for the purpose of the experts seeking to settle the case (para 9.2). A court direction for an experts' discussion will normally also provide that, following the discussion, the experts must prepare a statement within seven days of the discussion setting out:

(a) the issues on which they agree; and
(b) the issues on which they disagree with a summary of their reasons for disagreeing.

35.44 In *Aird v Prime Meridian Ltd* [2007] BLR 105 directions were given for mediation, with a joint statement to be prepared by the parties' experts. A draft joint statement was headed 'without prejudice', but the final version had these words removed. The mediation failed to settle the case. It was held that the joint statement did not acquire without prejudice status by being used in the mediation, so was admissible in the proceedings.

G EXAMINATIONS BY EXPERTS

35.45 It will be rare for an expert to be able to give a valuable opinion without first examining the subject matter relevant to that opinion. Where that subject matter is under the control of the party instructing the expert, there should be no problem. Where it is in the possession of the other side or of a non-party, it is necessary to seek either its consent or a court order for inspection by the expert. The powers available to the court are considered at 45.35–45.38. Some more specific issues will be considered here.

Comparison of handwriting

35.46 A party seeking to prove or disprove the authenticity or authorship of a piece of writing may adduce evidence of the three following kinds:

(a) Factual testimony from witnesses who saw the document being written, or who can say the alleged author did not write it. These witnesses may be the actual person concerned, or persons present at the time (eg attesting witnesses to a will).
(b) Opinion evidence from a person familiar with the handwriting of the alleged author. For example, a secretary may be an 'expert' on an employer's signature, having seen the employer regularly sign letters over a period of several years. Such a secretary would, of course, be allowed to give an opinion only on whether a disputed signature was that of the employer in question, and would not be an expert on signatures generally.
(c) Evidence from a handwriting expert comparing the disputed writing with a control sample from the alleged author under the Criminal Procedure Act 1865, s 8.

Medical examinations of the claimant

In personal injuries cases, unless the defendant is prepared to agree the claimant's expert's **35.47** report, the defendant's medical experts will need to examine the claimant if they are to be able to give meaningful advice. However, any form of medical examination will infringe the fundamental human right to personal liberty, so it has always been held that there is no power to order a claimant to submit to a medical examination (given the sanction of committal to prison should the claimant fail to comply). As it is the sanction for non-compliance that is objectionable, the courts have been able to avoid the injustice of defendants being disadvantaged by the indirect method of ordering a stay of the claim if a claimant refuses a reasonable request for a medical examination on behalf of a defendant: *Edmeades v Thames Board Mills Ltd* [1969] 2 QB 67. In effect, the claimant is given a choice. Either the claimant consents to submit to the medical examination by the defendant's medical expert, or the claimant refuses and the action is stayed. A stayed claim remains in being, but no further steps may be taken (with the effect of preventing the claimant going to trial).

In *Edmeades v Thames Board Mills Ltd* it was held that a stay would be granted if it was **35.48** just and reasonable in the circumstances. As interpreted by Scarman LJ in *Starr v National Coal Board* [1977] 1 WLR 63, there are two elements:

(a) the defendant's request for the medical examination must be reasonable; and
(b) the claimant's refusal to consent to the examination, or agreement subject to conditions, must be such as to prevent the just determination of the claim.

In the usual run of cases, it will always be reasonable for the defendant to ask for at **35.49** least one medical examination of the claimant to ensure that the defendant is not put at a disadvantage. If the claim takes a long time to get to trial, such that the claimant's condition may have materially altered since the defendant's initial medical examination, it will be reasonable for the defendant to be given a second examination. If the claimant's injuries cross the boundaries of several medical specializations, the claimant will be required to submit to examinations by several experts on behalf of the defendant. It may be that, having conducted a general examination of the claimant, an expert acting for the defendant comes to the view that the true extent of the claimant's injuries can only be discovered by some unusual procedure, or even by an exploratory operation. Whether the claim would be stayed if the claimant refused to undergo such a procedure depends on the balance between the need for the procedure for the proper preparation of the defendant's case and the reasonableness of the claimant's refusal on the grounds of pain, inconvenience, and risk to health (*Prescott v Bulldog Tools Ltd* [1981] 3 All ER 869).

An objection to being medically examined by even a single named doctor is usually unrea- **35.50** sonable. The reason for this is that the claimant can choose any expert, and the defendant should be given the same opportunity: *Starr v National Coal Board*.

A claimant is entitled to insist on a number of minor conditions before consenting to a **35.51** medical examination on the defendant's behalf, without risking the claim being stayed. These include:

(a) that the defendant pays any loss of earnings incurred by the claimant in attending the examination;
(b) that the defendant pays any out-of-pocket expenses incurred by the claimant in attending;
(c) that the doctor will not discuss the accident with the claimant save in so far as this is necessary for the purpose of the examination; and

(d) that a friend, relative, or legal representative attends with the claimant for moral support unless the friend will interfere with the examination, such as where the expert is a psychiatrist: *Whitehead v Avon County Council* (1995) *The Times*, 3 May 1995.

35.52 It has been held that it is never reasonable to insist that the defendant must disclose the report compiled after the examination as a condition of consenting to an examination: *Megarity v DJ Ryan and Sons Ltd* [1980] 1 WLR 1237. This is because the report is protected by legal professional privilege, and would give the claimant an advantage not enjoyed by the defendant.

H TRIAL

General position of experts

35.53 Directions for disclosure of experts' reports are merely procedural. Questions of admissibility remain in the province of the trial judge: *Sullivan v West Yorkshire Passenger Transport Executive* [1985] 2 All ER 134.

35.54 Experts often sit in court throughout proceedings to listen to the evidence and to advise counsel for the party instructing them. Traditionally, expert witnesses are called as part of the evidence of a particular party, with the claimant's experts being called as part of the claimant's case, and the defendant's experts being called some time later as part of the defendant's case. However, the court may direct that experts in like disciplines give their evidence on an issue-by-issue basis (PD 35, para 11.2), or the court may make an order for concurrent expert evidence (see 35.58). When experts are called to give evidence, their reports are usually put in evidence at the commencement of their examination-in-chief. They will often explain any technical matters in their reports, and may comment on the evidence already given. They may seek to support their conclusions with published and unpublished materials. Although facts contained in such materials are not strictly proved, they are of some probative value and may be used by the court as supporting any inferences which can fairly be drawn from them: *H v Schering Chemicals Ltd* [1983] 1 WLR 143. An expert may be asked for an opinion on hypothetical facts (on the basis that those facts will be proved by subsequent evidence).

35.55 An expert should give the court independent assistance by way of objective, unbiased opinion regarding matters within the expertise of the expert: *Polivitte Ltd v Commercial Union Assurance Co plc* [1987] 1 Lloyd's Rep 379 *per* Garland J. Experts called to give evidence in both the High Court and the County Court should never assume the role of the advocate: *National Justice Compania Naviera SA v Prudential Assurance Co Ltd* [1993] 2 Lloyd's Rep 68.

35.56 By CPR, r 35.11, any party may put in evidence any report disclosed by the other side. This rule provides an absolute right to rely on experts' reports disclosed by other parties, unrestricted by any discretion whether in rr 35.1 or 35.7 or otherwise (*Shepherd Neame Ltd v EDF Energy Networks (SPN) plc* [2008] Bus LR Digest D43; doubted by *Edwards-Tubb v JD Wetherspoon plc* [2011] 1 WLR 1373).

Jointly instructed expert at trial

35.57 In the normal course of things, a jointly instructed expert's report should be the evidence in the case on the issues covered by that report. Normally there should be no need for such a report to be amplified or tested by cross-examination (*Peet v Mid-Kent Healthcare Trust* [2002] 1 WLR 210). It might be appropriate to order attendance for cross-examination where a single joint expert delivers his report shortly before the trial, or where the expert has not considered all the written questions put to him (*Coopers Payen Ltd v Southampton Container Terminal Ltd* [2004] 1 Lloyd's Rep 331). If, exceptionally, the expert is called at trial, any cross-examination should be restricted as far as possible: *Peet v Mid-Kent Healthcare Trust*. If there is no other direct evidence, the evidence given by a single joint expert is likely to be compelling (*Coopers Payen Ltd v Southampton Container Terminal Ltd*). A judge may depart from it only in exceptional circumstances and after fully explaining the reasons.

Concurrent evidence ('hot-tubbing')

Directions may be made at any time, but typically at the first case management conference, **35.58** providing that some or all of the experts from like disciplines must give their evidence concurrently (PD 35, para 11.1). This means that at the trial instead of going into the witness box on their own and being examined-in-chief, cross-examined, and re-examined like other witnesses, the experts in a discipline will all give evidence together from the witness box or witness table.

Where a direction for concurrent evidence has been made the court may direct that the **35.59** parties agree an agenda of points to be discussed by the experts at trial (para 11.3). This is usually based upon the areas of disagreement identified in the experts' joint statement made pursuant to r 35.12 (see 35.43).

At the trial, when the time comes for the experts to give their evidence, each of the relevant **35.60** experts will take the oath or affirm (para 11.4). Subject to the judge's discretion to modify the procedure, the judge will initiate the discussion by asking the experts, in turn, for their views on the items on the agenda (para 11.4(1)). Once an expert has expressed a view the judge may ask questions about it. At one or more appropriate stages when questioning a particular expert, the judge may invite the other expert to comment or to ask that expert's own questions of the first expert.

The parties' representatives may then question the experts (para 11.4(2)). Such questioning **35.61** may be designed to test the correctness of an expert's view, or seek clarification of it, or to elicit evidence which has been omitted in the judge-led questioning. After questioning by counsel, the judge may summarize the experts' different positions on the issue and ask them to confirm or correct that summary (para 11.4(3)).

Conflicts between experts and other evidence

It is a common occurrence that the parties will adduce conflicting expert evidence. When **35.62** this happens the duty of the judge is to make findings of fact and resolve the conflict: *Sewell v Electrolux Ltd* (1997) *The Times*, 7 November 1997. Where there is a conflict between an expert and lay witnesses, generally the judge should refuse to accept the lay evidence in preference to uncontradicted expert evidence: *Re B (A Minor)* [2000] 1 WLR 790. However, the judge is not obliged to accept expert evidence if there are sufficient grounds for rejecting it, such as where it does not speak to a relevant issue (*R v Lanfear* [1968] 2 QB 77), or where the judge does not believe the expert or is otherwise unconvinced by it (*Dover District Council v Sherred* (1997) *The Times*, 11 February 1997). Also, there are cases where lay evidence may be preferred to expert evidence, such as where attesting witnesses are preferred to a handwriting expert over a contested will: *Fuller v Strum* [2002] 1 WLR 1097.

I EXPERTS' IMMUNITY FROM SUIT

35.63 Professional people called to give factual evidence (see 35.07) are treated as lay witnesses for the purposes of witness immunity, which means they cannot be sued in defamation or negligence for anything they say or do relating to being a witness. This includes preparation of witness statements as much as giving evidence in court. Expert witnesses within the meaning of CPR, Part 35 (those selected, instructed, and paid for by a party), while they enjoy immunity from suit in defamation, do not have any immunity for negligence or breach of contract (*Jones v Kaney* [2011] 2 AC 398).

35.64 An expert who has caused significant expense to be incurred through flagrant, reckless disregard of his duties to the court may be ordered to pay any wasted costs (*Phillips v Symes (No 2)* [2005] 1 WLR 2043). An expert's conduct in litigation may also be the subject of disciplinary procedures by his professional regulator (*Meadow v General Medical Council* [2007] QB 462).

J USE OF EXPERTS' REPORTS AFTER TRIAL

35.65 Unlike disclosed documents and exchanged witness statements, experts' reports disclosed to the other side are not subject to any implied undertaking not to use them for collateral purposes unconnected with the present litigation. See *Prudential Assurance Co Ltd v Fountain Page Ltd* [1991] 1 WLR 756.

KEY POINTS SUMMARY

35.66
- Where a matter arising at trial is outside the reasonable experience of the judge, usually because it is a technical matter relating to art, science, or professional (non-legal) judgment:
  - expert evidence on the matter is admissible; and
  - the judge is not competent to decide the matter without expert evidence.
- Expert evidence is not allowed except with the permission of the court. It is therefore essential both to obtain directions dealing with expert evidence and to comply with them.
- There is a vast range of possible directions that could be made relating to expert evidence. They include joint selection, joint instruction, separate instruction, disclosure of reports, putting written questions to experts, without prejudice discussions between experts, permission to rely on reports only at trial, permission to call experts as witnesses at trial, and concurrent evidence.
- An expert's primary duty is to the court, not to the party paying the fees.
- Experts are required to give their independent opinion on the issues within their area of expertise.
- There are detailed requirements on the format of experts' reports, which must include a statement of truth.

36

OFFERS TO SETTLE

A INTRODUCTION .36.01

B *CALDERBANK* OFFERS 36.04

C OFFERS TO SETTLE 36.05

D MAKING A PART 36 OFFER 36.13

E ACCEPTANCE OF A
PART 36 OFFER 36.14

F REJECTIONS, COUNTER-OFFERS,
AND SUBSEQUENT OFFERS 36.24

G WITHDRAWAL AND CHANGE
OF PART 36 OFFERS 36.25

H FAILING TO OBTAIN JUDGMENT
MORE ADVANTAGEOUS THAN A
PART 36 OFFER 36.28

I ADVISING ON PART 36 OFFERS 36.40

J NON-DISCLOSURE TO JUDGE 36.41

K PART 36 OFFERS IN APPEALS 36.44
Key points summary 36.45

A INTRODUCTION

Litigation is essentially about resolving disputes. Ultimately, this can be achieved by a **36.01** judgment delivered at trial, but it has long been recognized that this has to be a last resort, and that there are better ways of bringing disputes to an end. There are various alternative dispute mechanisms that can assist in this process (for full details see S Blake, J Browne, and S Sime, *A Practical Approach to ADR* (5th edn, Oxford University Press, 2018). Part of this is direct negotiation between the parties or their advisers. Negotiation can take place informally, for example over the telephone, or at formal meetings, but probably most commonly through written correspondence. To ensure unfair advantage is not taken of comments made in negotiations if the case cannot be settled, communications between the parties for the purpose of seeking to settle a dispute are protected by without prejudice privilege (see 31.57–31.61). Most communications attempting to move towards settlement of a dispute are of this nature, and cannot be disclosed to the court (other than as evidence to prove that the claim has been settled, if one of the parties later resiles from the agreement). If this was the entire story, there would be no means available to a party who feels the other side have been unreasonably difficult in negotiations to bring that conduct to the court's attention for the purpose of it being reflected in the order for costs.

What CPR, Part 36 does is to provide a means for a party to make a formal offer in settle- **36.02** ment of the claim which will be treated as without prejudice for the purposes of liability and remedies, but which can be disclosed to the court on the question of costs. This is done by making a written offer complying with certain formalities, which has an initial 'relevant' period for considering whether to accept of at least 21 days. Its function is to place the other side on risk as to costs if it is not accepted and the offeree then fails to achieve a result in the litigation which is more advantageous than the terms of the offer (*Matthews v Metal Improvements Co Inc* [2007] CP Rep 27). A party who receives a realistic formal offer is therefore best advised to accept it, thereby settling the claim.

According to CPR, r 36.1(1) and *Gibbon v Manchester City Council* [2010] 1 WLR 2081, **36.03** Part 36 is a self-contained procedural code that has to be understood in its own terms, and without importing other rules from the law of contract except where this is clearly intended. This rather controversial approach has produced the result that sometimes Part 36 operates in the same way as the law of contract, but not always. For example, a Part 36 offer that is accepted within the 21-day relevant period produces a contract settling the claim in the terms of the offer. Conversely, rejecting a Part 36 offer, or making a counter-offer, does not prevent the offeree later changing their mind and accepting the original offer, providing it has not been expressly withdrawn.

B *CALDERBANK* OFFERS

36.04 A '*Calderbank offer*' is a written offer to settle stated to be 'without prejudice save as to costs' (see *Calderbank v Calderbank* [1976] Fam 93). Provided it is made in a genuine attempt to settle a dispute such an offer will be protected from disclosure to the court without the joint consent of both parties until all questions on liability and remedies have been decided. Being without prejudice 'save as to costs' means that the communication can then be relied upon on the question of costs. This is confirmed by CPR, r 44.2(4)(c), which says that in deciding what order if any to make about costs, one of the circumstances that must be taken into account is any admissible offer to settle which is not a Part 36 offer. *Calderbank* offers operate on a quite distinct basis from Part 36 offers. Although there is a wide discretion (*Coward v Phaestos Ltd* [2014] EWCA 1256), failing to beat a *Calderbank* offer may result in the winner having to pay some or even all the offeror's costs from the date the winner should have responded to the *Calderbank* offer (*Walker Construction (UK) Ltd v Quayside Homes Ltd* [2014] EWCA 93).

C OFFERS TO SETTLE

36.05 An offer to settle within the meaning of CPR, Part 36 (a 'Part 36 offer'), may be made at any time, including before the commencement of proceedings (r 36.7(1), see 5.30–5.36) or in appeal proceedings (r 36.4). Parties are not obliged to use the Part 36 format when making an offer to settle, but if they do not, the consequences in CPR, Part 36, do not apply (r 36.2(2)).

Formalities

36.06 A Part 36 offer must:

(a) be made in writing (CPR, r 36.5(1)(a)). Although a Part 36 offer may be made in a letter, it is better to use form N242A (see form 36.1 and PD 36A, para 1.1);

(b) make clear that it is made pursuant to Part 36 (r 36.5(1)(b));

(c) if made at least 21 days before trial, specify a period of not less than 21 days within which the defendant will be liable for the claimant's costs in accordance with r 36.13 or 36.20 if the offer is accepted (rr 36.5(1)(c) and 36.5(2)). This 21-day period is called the 'relevant period' in Part 36. An offeree who needs more time to investigate should ask the offeror to consent to extend the relevant period, failing which an application to extend the time for acceptance should be made under r 3.1(2)(a) (*Martin v Randall* [2007] EWCA Civ 1155). In cases where an offer is made less than 21 days before the start of the trial, the relevant period is the period up to the end of the trial (r 36.3(g)(ii));

(d) state whether it relates to the whole of the claim, or part of it, or to an issue that arises in the claim, and if so, which part or issue (r 36.5(1)(d)); and

(e) state whether it takes into account any counterclaim (r 36.5(1)(e)).

Form 36.1 Notice of offer to settle—Part 36

....

| Click here to reset form | Click here to print form |

Offer to settle
(Section I – Part 36)

This form may be used to settle the whole or part of, or any issue that arises in, a claim, counterclaim, other additional claim, appeal or cross-appeal. It may also be used to settle detailed costs assessment proceedings.

A **Notice of acceptance** form is attached to this form should the offeree wish to use it.

In the (If proceedings have started)
HIGH COURT OF JUSTICE, QBD
Claim No. (or other ref.)
HQ16 96789
Name of Claimant (including ref.)
CHEDISTON WHOLESALERS LIMITED
Name of Defendant (including ref.)
LINSTEAD FRUITGROWERS LIMITED

**Before completing this form or responding to the offer
please read the notes on pages 4 and 5**

To the Offeree ('s legal representative) (Insert name and address)

Wilcox Solicitors,
36 Princes Avenue,
Cheltenham,
Gloucestershire,
GL50 2SP

Take notice that (insert name of party making the offer)

Defendant

makes this offer to settle pursuant to Part 36 of the Civil Procedure Rules 1998.

This offer is intended to be a ☑ defendant's ☐ claimant's Part 36 offer.

If the offer is accepted within 21 days of service of this notice, the defendant will be liable for the claimant's costs in accordance with rule 36.13.

Note: Specify a period which, subject to rule 36.5(2), must be at least 21 days

The offer is to settle: *(tick as appropriate)*

☑ the whole of ☐ part of ☐ a certain issue or issues in
(give details over the page) (give details over the page)

the
☑ claim ☐ counterclaim ☐ other additional claim
☐ appeal ☐ cross-appeal ☐ detailed costs assessment proceedings

N242A Offer to settle (Section I - Part 36) (06.15)

Form 36.1 *continued*

Please give details below of the offer you are making (If necessary continue on a separate sheet ensuring the claim number, if proceedings have started, is shown clearly)

£175,000, inclusive of interest to 21 days after service of this notice, in full and final settlement of this claim.

The offer ☐ does ☑ does not take into account ☑ all ☐ part of the following counterclaim (or other adverse claim):

There is no counterclaim.

Form 36.1 *continued*

Is this a personal injury claim?   ☐ Yes, please **complete section 2,**
section 3 if applicable and **section 4**

☑ No, please go to **Section 4**

SECTION 2

PERSONAL INJURY CLAIMS   **Note:** See rule 36.19

Is there a claim for provisional damages?   ☐ Yes, complete **either** part **A** or **B** below

☐ No, please go to **Section 3**

A The offer is made in satisfaction of the claim on the assumption that the claimant will not:

☐ develop
(state the disease)

OR

☐ suffer
(state type of
deterioration)

But if this does occur, the claimant will be entitled to claim
further damages at any time before

Day   Month   Year

B

☐ This offer does not include an offer in respect of the claim for provisional
damages.

SECTION 3
To be completed only by DEFENDANTS in PERSONAL INJURY claims   **Note:** See rule 36.22

A ☐ This offer is made without regard to any liability for recoverable benefits under
the Social Security (Recovery of Benefits Act) 1997.

OR

B ☐ This offer is intended to include any relevant deductible benefits for which the
defendant is liable under the Social Security (Recovery of Benefits Act) 1997.

The amount of £   is offered by way of gross compensation.

If you have ticked **B**, complete this section

☐ The defendant has not yet received a certificate of recoverable benefits.

OR

☐ The following amounts in respect of the following benefits are to be
deducted. Please give details below.

Type of benefit	Amount

The net amount offered is therefore   £

page 3

Form 36.1 *continued*

....

SECTION 4

Complete in ALL cases

Details of the party making the offer

Full name	Linstead Fruitgrowers Limited
Name of firm (if applicable)	Wilcox Solicitors

Signed

	Position held Partner
	(If signing on behalf of a firm or company)

Offeror('s legal representative)

Date

[ ] [ ] [ ] [ ] [ ] [ ]
Day   Month   Year

IMPORTANT NOTES:

1. This form may be used to settle the whole or part of, or any issue that arises in, a claim, counterclaim, other additional claim, appeal or cross-appeal. It may also be used to settle detailed costs assessment proceedings.

2. When used to make a Part 36 offer in respect of an appeal, an appellant seeking to settle their appeal should make a claimant's offer while a respondent should make a defendant's offer. [See rule 36.4.]

3. When used to make a Part 36 offer in respect of a counterclaim or other additional claim or a cross-appeal in certain appeal proceedings:

   - the party bringing the counterclaim, additional claim or cross-appeal can make (a) a claimant's offer on such counterclaim, additional claim or cross-appeal; or (b) a defendant's offer on the claim or appeal; and

   - the party bringing the original claim or appeal can make (a) a claimant's offer on such claim or appeal; or (b) a defendant's offer on the counterclaim or cross-appeal.

   In any case the offeror should make plain whether the offer takes into account any adverse claim. For example, when making an offer on a claim, state whether it takes into account the counterclaim. Equally when making an offer on a counterclaim, state whether it takes into account the claim. [See rules 36.2(3), 20.2 & 20.3 in respect of counterclaims and other additional claims. See rules 36.2(3) and 36.4 in respect of cross-appeals.]

4. When this form is used to make a Part 36 offer in detailed costs assessment proceedings, the receiving party in the assessment should make a claimant's offer while the paying party should make a defendant's offer. [See rule 47.20.]

5. In summary, Part 36 provides that:

   - A party making a defendant's offer is offering something to settle their opponent's claim, counterclaim, additional claim, appeal, cross-appeal or costs assessment proceedings and to accept a liability to pay costs.

   - A party making a claimant's offer is offering to accept something to settle their own claim, counterclaim, additional claim, appeal, cross-appeal or costs assessment proceedings on terms that their opponent pays their costs.

6. Part 6 of the Civil Procedure Rules makes detailed provision for the service of court documents.

Form 36.1 *continued*

NOTICE OF ACCEPTANCE

NOTES:

1. This form is suitable for the simple acceptance of the offer.

2. Where an offer relates only to part of the proceedings and the offeree wishes to abandon the balance of the claim then this should be made clear when accepting the offer.
   [See rule 36.13(2).]

3. See rule 36.15 where the offer was made by one or more but not all of the defendants.

In the (If proceedings have started)	HIGH COURT OF JUSTICE, QBD
Claim No. (or other ref.)	HQ15X 96789
Name of Claimant (including ref.)	CHEDISTON WHOLESALERS LIMITED
Name of Defendant (including ref.)	LINSTEAD FRUITGROWERS LIMITED

To the Offeror/legal representative

Take notice that (insert name of party accepting the offer)

accepts this offer to settle pursuant to rule 36.11 of the Civil Procedure Rules 1998.

Details of the party accepting the offer

Full name

Name of firm (if applicable)

Signed

Offeree('s legal representative)

Position held (If signing on behalf of a firm or company)

Date

Day Month Year

Terms of the offer

36.07 A Part 36 offer needs to state the terms of the proposed compromise, which should be sufficiently precise and certain for an effective contract to be formed if the offer is accepted. It is important to be clear on whether the offer is in full and final settlement of all matters in dispute between the parties, or defined matters between the parties, and whether the offer takes into account matters such as any cross-claim or previous interim payment. The terms of the offer must include the costs consequences of acceptance: see 36.06, sub-para (c), namely that the defendant will be liable for the claimant's costs if the offer is accepted. In practical terms this can make it impossible for a defendant to make a workable Part 36 offer once the costs in the case have built up (*Walker Construction (UK) Ltd v Quayside Homes Ltd* [2014] EWCA Civ 93, where the costs eventually came to £345,000 in a case where judgment was given for £10,000).

Additional formalities for money claims

36.08 Part 36 offers made by defendants in claims for money must offer to pay a single sum of money (CPR, r 36.6(1)). An offer to pay all or part of a sum of money at a date later than 14 days following the date of any acceptance is not treated as a Part 36 offer unless the offeree accepts the offer (r 36.6(2)). The single sum offered is treated as inclusive of all interest to the end of the relevant period (r 36.5(4)).

Additional requirements in personal injuries claims

36.09 When making a Part 36 offer in a claim for damages for personal injuries, the offer must:

(a) comply with the requirements in CPR, r 35.22, relating to the recovery of State benefits under the Social Security (Recovery of Benefits) Act 1997;

(b) in cases where there is a claim for future pecuniary loss, deal with the additional requirements set out in r 36.18; and

(c) in cases where there is a claim for provisional damages, deal with the additional requirements set out in r 36.19.

Technical defects in offers to settle

36.10 Significant departures from the five formalities laid down by CPR, r 36.5 (see 36.06) will mean that an offer is not a Part 36 offer at all (*Gibbon v Manchester City Council* [2010] 1 WLR 2081). Part 36 was replaced on 6 April 2015, and slight changes to r 36.5 on the formalities required for Part 36 offers were intended to avoid some of the problems that had previously been raised over compliance. Minor defects in Part 36 offers are likely to be corrected under CPR, r 3.10, which gives the court a discretion to correct errors in procedure (*Hertsmere Primary Care Trust v Administrators of Balasubramanium's Estate* [2005] 3 All ER 274).

Defence of tender before claim

36.11 A defendant who wishes to rely on a defence of tender before claim must make a payment into court of the amount said to have been tendered (CPR, r 37.2). The payment should be made at the time of filing the defence (*Greening v Williams* (1999) *The Times*, 10 December 1999). Money paid into court in support of a defence of tender before claim may not be paid out without the court's permission, except where it is accepted without needing permission and the defendant agrees that the sum in court can be used to satisfy the offer (r 37.3). The rule (see 36.41) that Part 36 offers must not be communicated to the trial judge does not apply to tenders before claim (r 36.16(3)(a)).

Clarification

If the terms of a Part 36 offer are unclear, the offeree may ask the offeror to clarify the offer **36.12** (CPR, r 36.8(1)). The request should be made within seven days of service of the offer, and the offeror should respond within seven days of receiving the request (r 36.8(1) and (2)). If the offeror fails to provide the requested clarification, the offeree is entitled to apply for an order that it be provided. Such an order will also specify the date when the Part 36 offer is to be treated as having been made (r 36.8(3)).

D MAKING A PART 36 OFFER

A Part 36 offer is made when it is served on the offeree (CPR, r 36.7(1)). One of the **36.13** prescribed methods of service in r 6.20 should be used, see 6.21 and 6.46. Where the offeree is legally represented, the offer must be served on the legal representative (PD 36A, para 1.2).

E ACCEPTANCE OF A PART 36 OFFER

Notice of acceptance

Accepting a Part 36 offer covering the whole of a claim compromises the entire claim. After **36.14** acceptance the offeror cannot seek to change or withdraw the offer (CPR, r 36.9(1)). An offer is accepted by serving written notice of acceptance (there is no prescribed form, so a letter will suffice) on the offeror (CPR, r 36.11(1)). It is also necessary to file the notice of acceptance with the court (PD 36A, para 3.1). In most cases the offeror should serve the notice of acceptance during the relevant period. When this happens the defendant must pay the claimant's standard-basis costs up to the date of notice of acceptance (r 36.13(1), (3)). The claimant is entitled to 100 per cent of their assessed costs, and the court has no jurisdiction to order payment of only a proportion of those costs (*Lahey v Pirelli Tyres Ltd* [2007] 1 WLR 998). By way of exception, the claimant is only entitled to fixed costs after accepting a Part 36 offer in RTA and EL/PL personal injury claims worth less than £25,000. This is because these cases have a special fixed costs regimes as provided by CPR, Part 45 Sections II and IIIA (r 36.13(3) and *Solomon v Cromwell Group plc* [2012] 1 WLR 1048).

Stay on acceptance

If a Part 36 offer is accepted, the claim will be stayed (CPR, r 36.14(1)) on the terms of the **36.15** offer (r 36.14(2)). A stay under r 36.14(1) does not affect the power of the court to enforce the terms of the Part 36 offer within the existing proceedings, nor to deal with any question of costs or interest on costs relating to the proceedings (r 36.14(5) and (8)).

Time for payment

Unless the parties agree otherwise in writing, where a Part 36 offer to pay money is accept- **36.16** ed, payment must be made within 14 days of the acceptance (CPR, r 36.14(6)(a)).

Late acceptance

36.17 Notice of acceptance may be served at any time, including after the relevant period (CPR, r 36.11(2)), provided the offer has not been withdrawn in accordance with r 36.9. Where a Part 36 offer is accepted after the relevant period, liability for costs must be determined by the court unless the parties reach agreement on costs (r 36.13(4)(b)). Unless it considers it unjust to do so, the court must order that:

(a) the claimant is entitled to costs up to the expiry of the relevant period; and

(b) the offeree do pay the offeror's costs for the period from the expiry of the relevant period to the date of acceptance.

36.18 In considering whether it would be unjust to make the usual costs order, the court must take into account all the circumstances of the case, including the terms of any Part 36 offers, the stage the relevant Part 36 offer was made, the information available to the parties when the Part 36 offer was made, the conduct of the parties in providing information, and whether the offer was a genuine attempt to settle the proceedings (r 36.13(6)).

Acceptance during trial, and split trials

36.19 A notice of acceptance served while a trial is in progress will only be effective if the court's permission is given (r 36.11(3)(d)). For this purpose 'a trial' means any trial in a case, including, for example, split trials of liability and quantum (r 36.3(c)). A trial is 'in progress' from the time when it starts until the time judgment is given or handed down (r 36.3(d)). To avoid the trial judge being informed about the Part 36 offer (see 36.41), unless the parties agree otherwise, the application for permission must be dealt with by a different judge (PD 36A, para 3.2). An offer cannot be accepted after the case has been 'decided', which is when all the issues in the case have been determined (r 36.3(e)).

36.20 Where there is a split trial, any Part 36 offer relating only to the issues that have been decided cannot be accepted after judgment has been given on the split trial (r 36.12(2)). Where there is a Part 36 offer that goes wider than the issues decided in a split trial, the Part 36 offer cannot be accepted (unless the parties agree) for a period of seven clear days following the split trial (r 36.12(3)). This is to give the offeror a short period to re-assess the situation in the light of the judgment on the split trial, and to change or withdraw the offer without being on risk that the offeree will take advantage of the situation and immediately accept what may now be a very generous offer.

Acceptance relating to part of the claim

36.21 An acceptance of a Part 36 offer relating to only part of the claim results in a settlement of the claim only if the claimant abandons the balance of the claim (CPR, r 36.13(2)(b)). In this situation the claimant is only entitled to the costs relating to the part of the claim covered by the offer, unless the court orders otherwise (r 36.13(2)).

36.22 Alternatively, the offeree may accept a Part 36 offer on part of the claim without abandoning the rest of the claim. In this situation the part of the claim covered by the offer will be stayed on the terms of the offer (r 36.14(3)), the rest will proceed towards trial, and the court has a discretion on the costs of the compromised part of the claim.

Permission to accept

36.23 The court's permission is required for an acceptance of a Part 36 offer where:

(a) the Part 36 offer is made by some, but not all, of a number of defendants (CPR, rr 36.11(3)(a) and 36.15(4));

(b) the claim is for damages for personal injuries, the offer is intended to include any deductible amounts under the Social Security (Recovery of Benefits) Act 1997, and further deductible benefits or a deductible lump sum have been paid to the claimant since the date of the offer (r 36.11(3)(b)). In this situation the application must state the net amount offered in the Part 36 offer, the deductible amounts accrued at the date of the offer, and those that have subsequently accrued. The application must be accompanied by a copy of the current certificate of recoverable amounts (PD 36A, para 3.3);

(c) an apportionment is required under r 41.3A (Fatal Accidents Act claims) (r 36.11(3)c));

(d) a trial is in progress (r 36.11(3)(d)); or

(e) any of the parties is a child or protected party (r 21.10).

F REJECTIONS, COUNTER-OFFERS, AND SUBSEQUENT OFFERS

There is no need for the offeree to give an express rejection of a Part 36 offer. An express **36.24** rejection by the offeree has no effect, and making a counter-offer does not prevent the offeree later accepting the original offer. This is because Part 36 offers can only be terminated before acceptance by action taken by the offeror (*Gibbon v Manchester City Council* [2010] 1 WLR 2081). It follows from *Gibbon v Manchester City Council* that making a revised offer will often result in there being two live offers. This can be avoided by making the first offer time limited, so that it expires on a date stated in the offer itself, as permitted by r 36.9(4)(b). Having two or more live Part 36 offers from one party can also be avoided by changing or withdrawing earlier offers by a notice of change or notice of withdrawal under r 36.9(2).

G WITHDRAWAL AND CHANGE OF PART 36 OFFERS

Before the expiry of the relevant period

An offeror is entitled to serve a notice of change or a notice of withdrawal of a Part 36 **36.25** offer even before the expiry of the relevant period, provided the offer has not been accepted at that point in time. In such a case the notice takes effect at the expiry of the relevant period if the offeree does not serve a notice of acceptance within the relevant period (CPR, r 36.10(2)(a)). If the offeree serves a notice of acceptance within the relevant period, that acceptance takes effect unless the offeror applies for permission to change or withdraw the offer within seven days of the offeree's notice of acceptance (r 36.10(2)(b)). Permission is sought by making an application in accordance with Part 23 to a judge other than the trial judge (PD 36A, para 2.2). Permission may be granted if there has been a change of circumstances since making the original offer, provided it is in the interests of justice to give permission (r 36.10(3)).

After the expiry of the relevant period

After expiry of the relevant period and provided the offeree has not previously served **36.26** notice of acceptance, the offeror may withdraw the offer or change its terms to be less advantageous to the offeree without the permission of the court (CPR, r 36.9(4)(a)). This is done by serving written notice on the offeree (r 36.9(2)). A change in the terms of a Part 36 offer (whether it is an improved offer or one which is less advantageous to the offeree) takes effect when written notice of the change is served on the offeree (r 36.9(3)).

Effect of a withdrawn Part 36 offer

36.27 A withdrawn Part 36 offer ceases to have the effect on costs and interest of a subsisting Part 36 offer (CPR, r 36.17(7)(a)). However, r 44.2(4)(c) requires the court to consider any admissible offer to settle which does not have the costs consequences set out in Part 36 in deciding what order to make about costs. Without prejudice offers (see 31.57) are not admissible, whereas open offers and offers made without prejudice save as to costs are admissible on the question of costs. This gives the court a wide discretion, to be exercised applying the overriding objective. In a suitable case the court can even treat a withdrawn Part 36 offer as having the same costs consequences as if it had not been withdrawn (*Trustees of Stokes Pension Fund v Western Power Distribution (South West) plc* [2005] 1 WLR 3595).

H FAILING TO OBTAIN JUDGMENT MORE ADVANTAGEOUS THAN A PART 36 OFFER

36.28 There are potential damages, costs, and interest consequences (CPR, r 36.17(1)) for not accepting a Part 36 offer. These apply where:

(a) the claimant fails to obtain a judgment more advantageous than a Part 36 offer made by the defendant; or

(b) judgment is entered against the defendant which is at least as advantageous to the claimant as the proposals set out in a Part 36 offer made by the claimant.

36.29 In deciding whether a judgment in a money claim is more advantageous than a Part 36 offer, the judgment simply needs to be better in money terms than the offer by any amount, however small (r 36.17(2)). It is necessary to compare the judgment with the terms of the offer. Any admission of part of the claim made otherwise than in the Part 36 offer, such as in the defence, is ignored (*Macleish v Littlestone* [2016] 1 WLR 3289). Where the offer includes interest, the court must recalculate the interest included in the judgment to find the sum in interest that would have been awarded on the relevant date (*Blackham v Entrepose UK* [2004] EWCA Civ 1109, and see 36.08). Where there are deductible State benefits the question is whether the claimant has failed to recover, after deduction of recoverable amounts, a sum greater than the net sum stated in the Part 36 offer in compliance with r 36.22(6)(c).

36.30 Rule 36.17(2) is intended to provide a clear-cut dividing line. If the judgment exceeds a defendant's Part 36 offer even by a small amount the claimant should normally be awarded its whole costs. In personal injuries claims this is so even if the judgment is significantly less than the amount claimed. Even if the court takes the view the original claim was exaggerated, the claimant should normally be awarded its costs if the judgment exceeds the defendant's offer, unless the court decides the claimant has been dishonest (*Fox v Foundation Piling Ltd* [2011] CP Rep 41).

36.31 The consequences in r 36.17 do not apply:

(a) where the court considers it would be unjust to apply the usual consequences laid down in r 36.17 (see 36.35);

(b) where the Part 36 offer has been withdrawn, or changed to terms less advantageous to the offeree than the judgment (see 36.27);

(c) where an admissible offer does not comply with the technical requirements of Part 36. It is wrong in principle to apply the intentionally draconian consequences set out in r 36.17 to offers that do not comply with Part 36. In these cases the offer is simply taken into account in deciding on the order for costs under r 44.2(4)(c) (*F and C Alternative Investments (Holdings) Ltd v Barthelemy (No 3)* [2013] 1 WLR 548);

(d) if the Part 36 offer was made less than 21 days before the trial (unless the court abridges time);

(e) where qualified one way costs shifting applies, where the effects are modified (see 47.10); or

(f) where the offeror is treated as having filed a costs budget limited to court fees for failing to file a costs budget on time, the effects are also modified (see 36.39).

Offers made by defendants

Where the judgment is not more advantageous than a Part 36 offer made by a defendant, **36.32** unless the court considers it unjust to do so, the court will order:

(a) the defendant to pay the claimant's costs up to the expiry of the relevant period applying the usual principle that costs follow the event (CPR, r 44.2(2)(a)). This is an almost invariable rule, and an order running from the date of the offer rather than the expiry of the relevant period will be corrected on appeal (*Martin v Randall* [2007] EWCA Civ 1155);

(b) the claimant to pay the defendant's costs, including any recoverable pre-action costs, from the expiry of the relevant period (r 36.17(3)(a)); and

(c) the claimant to pay interest on the defendant's costs (r 36.17(3)(b)).

Offers made by claimants

Where the judgment is at least as advantageous as a Part 36 offer made by a claimant, **36.33** unless the court considers it unjust to do so, the court will order:

(a) interest on the judgment (excluding interest) awarded at a rate not exceeding 10 per cent above base rate for some or all of the period since the expiry of the relevant period. Where interest is also awarded under the CCA 1984, s 69, or the SCA 1981, s 35A, the total rate of interest may not exceed 10 per cent above base rate (CPR, r 36.17(6)). Enhanced interest is partly compensatory, reflecting the cost of money (for which a rate of 3 per cent above base rate is typical, *Sony/ATV Music Publishing LLC v WPMC Ltd* [2017] EWHC 456 (Ch)), but also partly penal. When combined with unreasonable behaviour, the full 10 per cent above base rate may be appropriate (*OMV Petrom SA v Glencore International AG* [2017] 1 WLR 3465);

(b) the defendant to pay the claimant's costs, including any recoverable pre-action costs, after the expiry of the relevant period on the indemnity basis;

(c) interest on those indemnity-basis costs at a rate not exceeding 10 per cent above base rate; and

(d) an additional amount not exceeding £75,000 calculated in accordance with the following paragraph.

The 'additional amount' was introduced on 1 April 2013 as part of the Jackson Reforms. **36.34** It is in effect an addition to the damages awarded, and is intended to provide a reward with real value to a claimant who makes a successful claimant's Part 36 offer. By the Offers to Settle in Civil Proceedings Order 2013 (SI 2013/93), and CPR, r 36.17(4)(d), slightly different approaches are taken in money and non-money claims:

(a) in money claims the additional amount is 10 per cent on the first £500,000 of the damages or other money award, plus 5 per cent on any sum awarded above £500,000 and up to £1,000,000. Using these figures, the maximum additional amount is £75,000; and

(b) in non-money claims the additional amount is calculated at 10 per cent for the first £500,000 and 5 per cent on the next £500,000 of the costs awarded to the claimant.

Unjust to make usual costs and interest orders

36.35 It is far from easy to persuade a judge that it would be unjust (see 36.32) to apply the usual rule that the claimant must pay the defendant's costs from the expiry of the relevant period. In cases where the offeror loses on an important issue at trial the discretion under CPR, r 36.17(5), allows the court to make an issue-based costs order or a percentage costs order on the ground that partial success is part of all the circumstances of the case (r 36.17(5)(a)), but only if the usual r 36.17 costs orders would be unjust. The burden is on the offeree to show it would be unjust, and the burden is a formidable one (*Webb v Liverpool Women's NHS Foundation Trust* [2016] 1 WLR 3899).

36.36 The additional amount awarded to claimants who make successful Part 36 offers in r 36.17(4)(d) was seen by Sir Rupert Jackson as being an integral part of the reforms that included abolishing the recoverability of CFA success fees and other additional liabilities (see Chapter 2). Abolition of success fees, increasing damages by 10 per cent, and the ability of claimants to augment their damages by a further 10 per cent by making an effective Part 36 offer, are parts of a balanced package. The balance in the package of reforms will only be maintained if the courts are ready to award the additional amount where the claimant has made a successful claimant's Part 36 offer. Payment of the additional amount was refused in *Feltham v Freer Bouskell* [2013] EWHC 3086 (Ch) because the principal ground on which the claimant won was only raised during opening speeches, combined with late disclosure of documents and the fact the Part 36 offer was made only slightly more than 21 days before the trial.

36.37 In considering whether it would be unjust to make an order under CPR, r 36.17(3), or (4) on costs or interest, the court will, by r 36.17(5), take into account all the circumstances of the case, including:

(a) the terms of the Part 36 offer;
(b) the stage in the proceedings when the Part 36 offer was made, and in particular the period between the offer and the start of the trial;
(c) the information available to the parties at the time when the Part 36 offer was made; and
(d) the conduct of the parties with regard to giving or refusing to give information for the purposes of enabling the offer to be made or evaluated; and
(e) whether the offer was a genuine attempt to settle the proceedings.

36.38 It is a fundamental error to penalize a party in costs for failing to achieve a better result than its own Part 36 offer (*Rolf v De Guerin* [2011] CP Rep 24).

Costs limited through failing to file costs budget

36.39 In cases where costs budgeting applies, failure to file a costs budget on time results in being treated as having filed a costs budget limited to court fees (see 16.15) unless relief from sanctions is granted. A party in this position would have very little incentive to make a Part 36 offer. To ameliorate the situation CPR, r 36.23 provides that such a party will be awarded half its costs for periods when otherwise it would have been awarded its costs in relation to late acceptance of Part 36 offers or if it has made a successful Part 36 offer for the purposes of r 36.17.

I ADVISING ON PART 36 OFFERS

36.40 There is a heavy responsibility on legal representatives advising their clients on whether offers should be made or accepted. Clients must be fully informed of the costs implications of an offer. This will include the amount that will be deducted by the adviser's firm in respect of costs, how that sum is calculated, and the client's right to the assessment of the firm's costs (SRA Code of Conduct 2011, Outcomes 1.13 and 1.14). Frequently, lawyers find themselves advising clients on these matters at the door of the court. When this happens they should concentrate on giving clear advice that can be readily understood by the client. They are not required to catalogue every factor that may have a bearing on whether an offer should be made or accepted (*Moy v Pettman Smith* [2005] 1 WLR 581).

J NON-DISCLOSURE TO JUDGE

The fact there has been a Part 36 offer (except in the case of a tender before claim) must not be disclosed to the court at trial until the case has been decided (CPR, r 36.16(2)). This embargo applies to trials, including split trials, but not to interim applications. In advance of trial a request should be made to the court office to remove all references to any offers to settle from the court file to avoid accidental disclosure to the trial judge. If all the parties agree in writing, this embargo can be lifted (r 36.16(3)(c)). At the end of a split trial the trial judge can be informed in full of Part 36 offers relating only to the issues decided in that hearing, and of the existence, but not the terms, of any offers going beyond the issues decided in that hearing (r 36.16(3)(d) and (4)). **36.41**

If the fact there has been a Part 36 offer is disclosed in error to the judge, the judge has a discretion whether to continue with the trial or to withdraw. The judge is entitled to continue if satisfied there will be no prejudice to either side: *Garratt v Saxby* [2004] 1 WLR 2152. A judge should not be too ready to withdraw, and if satisfied that no injustice will be done, may continue with the trial. Matters to consider include the overriding objective, saving expense, and dealing with claims justly and proportionately. **36.42**

The embargo on disclosing Part 36 offers to the judge applies to all questions relating to liability and remedies. A Part 36 offer cannot be referred to for the purpose of assessing damages or the amount of interest payable on a money claim (*Johnson v Gore Wood (No 2)* (2004) *The Times*, 17 February 2004). **36.43**

K PART 36 OFFERS IN APPEALS

A Part 36 offer which is made before trial has effect in relation to the costs of the proceedings up to the final disposal of the proceedings at first instance (CPR, r 36.4(1)). Costs protection for appeal proceedings may be obtained by making a separate Part 36 offer in the appeal proceedings (r 36.4(2)). **36.44**

KEY POINTS SUMMARY

- Part 36 offers are formal offers to settle having costs consequences if they are not accepted. **36.45**

- Before trial, a Part 36 offer remains open for acceptance until it is withdrawn, either by being time limited or by service of a written notice of withdrawal.

- If a Part 36 offer is accepted, the case is settled, usually on terms that the defendant will also pay the claimant's costs (because in effect the claimant has won).

- If Part 36 offers are not accepted, the important question on costs is whether the eventual judgment is more advantageous than the offer, rather than the usual question of which party has won.

- Part 36 offers are made without prejudice save as to costs, and must not be mentioned to the trial judge until all questions on liability and quantum are finally determined.

37

SANCTIONS

A NON-COMPLIANCE WITH PRE-ACTION
   PROTOCOLS 37.02

B NON-COMPLIANCE WITH THE CPR 37.03

C NON-COMPLIANCE WITH DIRECTIONS . .37.04

D PRESERVATION OF TRIAL DATE. 37.08

E APPLICATION FOR SANCTIONS. 37.09

F UNLESS ORDERS 37.15

G NON-COMPLIANCE WITH AN UNLESS
   ORDER 37.17

H EXTENDING TIME AND CORRECTING
   ERRORS 37.20

I RELIEF FROM SANCTIONS AND
   SETTING ASIDE. 37.22

J IMPLIED SANCTIONS DOCTRINE 37.33
   Key points summary 37.37

37.01 So that the court can ensure that its case management directions and orders are complied with, and to retain control over the conduct of litigation, it needs to be armed with suitable coercive powers. These are provided in the CPR in the form of sanctions. These range from adverse interim costs orders through to striking out the whole or part of the defaulting party's statement of case. In imposing a sanction the court will have two purposes in mind. It will primarily be concerned with ensuring its orders and directions are complied with, so that both parties can prepare properly for the trial, and that the trial can take place fairly and without undue delay. This may be achieved by making an 'unless' order giving the defaulting party a last chance to comply, failing which some draconian sanction will take effect, or by refusing to give relief from sanctions imposed by the CPR. Its secondary purpose is to punish the defaulting party for the past default. The balance between these two concepts will vary from case to case.

A NON-COMPLIANCE WITH PRE-ACTION PROTOCOLS

37.02 Various sanctions may be imposed where there has been non-compliance with a relevant pre-action protocol: see 5.21–5.24.

B NON-COMPLIANCE WITH THE CPR

37.03 There are various provisions in the CPR and practice directions that impose sanctions in default of due compliance. The most well-known examples are:

(a) non-payment of the hearing fee after the time set by a notice of non-payment, following which the claim (CPR, rr 3.7 and 3.7A1) or counterclaim (rr 3.7A and 3.7AA) is automatically struck out;

(b) failing to file a costs budget, which results in recoverable costs being limited to court fees, unless the court otherwise orders (r 3.14);

(c) failing to file a directions questionnaire in a County Court money claim after the court sends a seven-day notice under r 26.3(7A)(a), which results in the defaulting party's statement of case being struck out (r 26.3(7A)(b));

(d) failing to disclose or give inspection of documents relied upon. The sanction is not being allowed to use the documents at trial unless the court gives permission (r 31.21);

(e) failing to serve a witness statement as ordered by the court, with the sanction that the witness cannot be called at trial unless the court gives permission (r 32.10); and

(f) failing to disclose an expert's report, which means the defaulting party may not use the report at the trial or call the expert to give evidence orally, unless the court gives permission (r 35.13).

C NON-COMPLIANCE WITH DIRECTIONS

Agreeing new deadlines

It is to be expected that from time to time one or other of the parties to proceedings will **37.04** be unable to keep to the directions timetable imposed by the court. Since the Civil Justice Reforms of 2013 the courts have been less tolerant than previously of unjustified delays and breaches of court orders (*Hallam Estates Ltd v Baker* [2014] EWCA Civ 661 at [29]). However, if the non-compliance is through events outside the control of the defaulting party or is otherwise not deliberate, the parties should cooperate, in compliance with CPR, r 1.4(2)(a), and resolve the difficulty by agreeing a new timetable. The time specified by any provision of the CPR or by the court for doing any act may be varied by the written agreement of the parties, unless there is an express prohibition on variation in the rules (r 2.11).

Prohibitions on parties agreeing between themselves fall into two categories. First, 'key' **37.05** dates, namely those relating to filing directions questionnaires, case management conferences, pre-trial reviews, filing pre-trial checklists, and trial (rr 26.3(6A), 28.4, and 29.5) cannot be changed without a court order. Secondly, where a rule, practice direction, or court order requires a party to do something within a specified time and also specifies the consequence of failure to comply, the time for compliance cannot be extended by consent, and requires a court order (r 3.8(3)). As is clear from 37.03, there are many provisions in the CPR that specify the consequences of non-compliance, so r 3.8(3) has a wide ambit.

In an attempt to avoid the courts being flooded with applications to extend time, an excep- **37.06** tion is provided by r 3.8(4), which allows the parties to agree an extension of time of an order with specified consequences for breach provided:

(a) the court does not make an order preventing the parties agreeing an extension;
(b) the time for complying with the order has not expired;
(c) the extension is agreed in writing;
(d) the extension does not exceed 28 days; and
(e) the extension does not put at risk any hearing date.

If the parties need more than 28 days, they must submit a draft consent order with an application to extend time, together with the reasons for the extension, and confirmation that it will not impact on any hearing date.

Warning other side

A party not in default faced with an opponent who has not complied with the court's direc- **37.07** tions is not entitled to try to make matters worse for the defaulting party by sitting back and allowing further time to go by. Nor is the party not in default entitled to jump the gun by making an immediate application for an order with sanctions. Instead, the correct procedure is for the innocent party to write to the defaulting party referring to the default, asking for it to be rectified within a short reasonable period (usually seven or 14 days), and giving warning of an intention to apply for an order if the default is not remedied. If there is continued default, the innocent party may apply for an order to enforce compliance or for a sanction to be imposed or both. Any application for such an order must be made without delay. If the innocent party does delay in making the application, the court may take the delay into account when it decides whether to make an order imposing a sanction or whether to grant relief from a sanction imposed by the rules or any practice direction.

D PRESERVATION OF TRIAL DATE

37.08 The general approach that will be adopted where there has been a breach of case management directions that may impinge on the date or window fixed for the trial of a claim is set out in PD 28, para 5.4 (fast track) and PD 29, para 7.4 (multi-track). These provisions apply on case management hearings and applications to extend time (see 37.20). Since *Mitchell v News Group Newspapers Ltd* [2014] 1 WLR 795 it is doubtful that they apply in applications for relief from sanctions. According to PD 28 and PD 29:

(a) The court will not allow a failure to comply with directions to lead to the postponement of the trial unless the circumstances of the case are exceptional. The need to show exceptional circumstances only applies where the postponement of the trial is sought on account of a failure to comply with case management directions, not when the need to postpone arises through circumstances outside the control of the parties (*Collins v Gordon* [2008] EWCA Civ 110).

(b) If practicable to do so, the court will exercise its powers in a manner that enables the case to come on for trial on the date or within the period previously set.

(c) In particular the court will assess what steps each party should take to prepare the case for trial, direct that those steps are taken in the shortest possible time, and impose a sanction for non-compliance. Such a sanction may, for example, deprive a party of the right to raise or contest an issue or to rely on evidence to which the direction relates.

(d) Where it appears that one or more issues are or can be made ready for trial at the time fixed while others cannot, the court may direct that the trial will proceed on the issues that are or will then be ready, and order that no costs will be allowed for any later trial of the remaining issues or that those costs will be paid by the party in default.

(e) Where the court has no option but to postpone the trial it will do so for the shortest possible time and will give directions for the taking of the necessary steps in the meantime as rapidly as possible.

(f) Litigants and lawyers must be in no doubt that the court will regard the postponement of a trial as an order of last resort. The court may exercise its power to require a party as well as the party's legal representative to attend court at a hearing where such an order is to be sought.

E APPLICATION FOR SANCTIONS

37.09 Hearings where the court has to decide whether to impose a sanction can arise in a number of different ways. These include applications brought by the innocent party specifically for this purpose using the on-notice procedure described in Chapter 23, applications by the defaulting party to extend the time for complying with the relevant requirement, case management conferences and pre-trial reviews, and the trial itself. Powers available to the court include ordering a party to pay certain costs forthwith or debarring a party in default from adducing evidence in a particular form or from particular witnesses. Alternatively, the court may impose sanctions that limit or deprive a party, if successful, of interest on any money claim, or which increase the amount of interest payable by the party in default. At the top of the range, CPR, r 3.4(2)(c) gives the court the power to strike out part or the whole of a party's statement of case for failing to comply with a rule, practice direction, or court order, with judgment for the innocent party.

An applicant seeking the imposition of a sanction has the burden of proof, whereas on an **37.10** application for relief from sanctions (see 37.22ff) after non-compliance with a rule imposing a sanction for non-compliance or with an unless order, the onus is on the defaulting party (*Malekout v Medical Sickness Annuity and Life Assurance Society Ltd* (2003) LTL 20/10/03). Before imposing a sanction the court must consider the effect of making the order on the overall fairness of the proceedings, and the wider interests of justice (see 4.25) as reflected in the overriding objective (*Global Torch Ltd v Apex Global Management Ltd (No 2)* [2014] 1 WLR 4495 at [16]). Proportionality of the proposed sanction has to be considered at this stage when the sanction is imposed, whereas on an application for relief from sanctions the court has to assume the sanction is proportionate (*Walsham Chalet Park Ltd v Tallington Lakes Ltd* [2014] EWCA Civ 1607). While recognizing these differences, the Court of Appeal in *Abdulle v Commissioner of Police of the Metropolis* [2016] 1 WLR 898 said it is not wrong for the judge to consider an application for a sanction by reference to the three-stage test in *Denton v TH White Ltd* [2014] 1 WLR 3926 (see 37.26).

Dependent on the nature of the default and its consequences on the innocent party, the **37.11** management of the case, and its more general impact on the civil justice system, the court may deal with the default in a number of different ways:

(a) Minor or trivial breaches may be dealt with by forgiving the default, together with an adverse costs order in respect of any interim application needed to bring the matter before the court (*Colliers International Property Consultants v Colliers Jordan Lee Jafaar Bhd* [2008] 2 Lloyd's Rep 368).

(b) If the breach is more serious the court may make it plain it requires compliance by stating a revised deadline is 'final', usually combined with an adverse costs order. Breach of a final order usually results in a sanction being imposed on a further application to the court (*Sports Network Ltd v Calzaghe* [2008] EWHC 2566 (QB)).

(c) Alternatively, the court may make an 'unless' order with a stated sanction in default, usually combined with an adverse costs order. Breach of an unless order results in the immediate imposition of the stated sanction (see 37.17).

(d) In the further alternative, the court may impose an immediate sanction, or refuse to grant relief from a sanction imposed by the CPR.

(e) Where both sides are in breach, it may be difficult to justify imposing a sanction purely on the claimant, provided it is reasonably possible to have a fair trial notwithstanding the breach (*Hateley v Morris* [2004] 1 BCLC 582; *Chartwell Estate Agents Ltd v Fergies Properties SA* [2014] EWCA Civ 506). It may be appropriate to impose sanctions on both sides.

Like all other orders, those containing final and unless orders must specify the time within **37.12** which the step under consideration must be taken by reference to a calendar date and a specific time, typically 4 p.m. on a specific Friday (CPR, r 2.9: see 41.12). Also like all other orders, unless orders take effect on the day they are pronounced (immediately: see 41.01), and have to be complied with even if there is a delay in sealing the formal order (*Rahamim v Reich* (2009) LTL 10/2/09).

37.13 A defaulting party who thinks the sanction imposed, such as a unless order with striking out as a consequence of further default, is too onerous should appeal the order imposing the sanction rather than seeking relief from the sanction after further non-compliance (*Fred Perry (Holdings) Ltd v Brands Plaza Trading Ltd* [2012] FSR 28). By not appealing the original unless order the court dealing with any application for relief from sanctions treats the sanction as having been properly imposed and as complying with the overriding objective (*Mitchell v News Group Newspapers Ltd* [2014] 1 WLR 795 at [45]). Where the sanction is the payment of costs, the only route is to appeal (CPR, r 3.8(2)).

37.14 It may be possible to apply to vary or revoke the original order under CPR, r 3.1(7). However, there are restricted grounds for doing so, such as a material change of circumstances (see 23.64). Where an order to vary or revoke is combined with an application for relief from sanctions, the proper course is for the court to consider the application under r 3.1(7) first, and only to move on to the application for relief from sanctions if that is unsuccessful (*Mitchell v News Group Newspapers Ltd* at [45]).

F UNLESS ORDERS

37.15 A court dealing with a procedural default may make an order in the form of an unless provision. This is to the effect that, if the terms of the order are not complied with by the time specified in the order, stated consequences will follow. Paragraph 8.2 of PD 40B lays down formulae for drafting unless orders. These are in the following forms (to be adapted as necessary):

(a) 'Unless the claimant serves his list of documents by 4.00 p.m. on Friday 16 November 2018 his claim will be struck out and judgment entered for the defendant.' This is the preferred form.

(b) 'Unless the claimant serves his list of documents within 14 days of service of this order . . . '. This should be used where the defaulting party did not attend the hearing where the order was made.

37.16 The test on expiry of an unless order is whether there has been complete compliance with the terms of the order, subject only to *de minimis* exceptions (*Jani-King (GB) Ltd v Prodger* (2007) LTL 10/4/07). There is a reluctance, however, to be drawn into disputes over what may appear to be a poor attempt at performance at the interim stage rather than leaving the matter to trial (*Rahamim v Reich* (2009) LTL 10/2/09).

G NON-COMPLIANCE WITH AN UNLESS ORDER

37.17 If a party fails to comply with a rule, practice direction, or court order imposing any sanction, the sanction will take effect unless the defaulting party applies for and obtains relief from the sanction (CPR, r 3.8(1)). Therefore unless orders in the form that a claim 'shall' or 'will' be struck out or dismissed mean that on expiry of the time limit the claim is struck out or dismissed automatically, and no further order from the court is necessary (PD 3A, para 1.9).

37.18 Where the court has made an order providing that a statement of case shall be struck out if a party does not comply with the order, r 3.5 sets out the procedure for obtaining judgment on non-compliance with the order. A number of different situations are dealt with:

(a) Where the party in default is the claimant and the order provides for the striking out of the whole of the particulars of claim, the defendant may enter judgment with costs by filing a request (there is no prescribed form) stating that the right to enter judgment has arisen because the court's order has not been complied with (r 3.5(2)(a) and (3)).

(b) Where the party in default is the defendant and the order provides for the striking out of the whole of the defence, and the claim is limited to one of the following forms of relief, namely, a specified sum of money, damages, and/or delivery of goods with the alternative of paying their value, the claimant may enter judgment with costs by filing a request (again there is no prescribed form) stating that the right to enter judgment has arisen because the court's order has not been complied with (r 3.5(2)(b) and (3)).

(c) Where neither (a) nor (b) applies, such as where the order provided for striking out only part of a statement of case, or where the defendant is in default and the claimant has claimed equitable relief, the party seeking to enter judgment for non-compliance with the order must make an application in accordance with Part 23 (r 3.5(4)). This means that an application notice must be issued for a hearing on notice.

As mentioned at 37.17, the sanction embodied in an unless order takes effect without the **37.19** need for any further order if there is a material failure to comply (r 3.8(1)). In *Marcan Shipping (London) Ltd v Kefalas* [2007] 1 WLR 1864 it was held that, if the innocent party applies for judgment under r 3.5, the court's function is limited to deciding what order should properly be made to reflect the sanction which has already taken effect.

H EXTENDING TIME AND CORRECTING ERRORS

Extending time

The court has a general power to extend and abridge time (CPR, r 3.1(2)(a)). It can extend **37.20** time on its own initiative under rr 3.1(2)(a) and 3.3, and can do so even where the extension relates to an unless order (*Keen Phillips v Field* [2007] 1 WLR 686). A party who will be unable to comply with an order or direction in time (or who is already in breach), and who has not been able to agree an extension with the other side (see 37.04–37.06), may make an application under this rule asking the court to extend time for compliance. There is a fundamental difference between applying for an extension of time before a time limit has expired, and seeking relief from a sanction after the event (*Robert v Momentum Services Ltd* [2003] 1 WLR 1577 and this remains the case even after *Mitchell v News Group Newspapers Ltd* [2014] 1 WLR 795, see *Hallam Estates Ltd v Baker* [2014] EWCA Civ 661). In simple time applications under r 3.1(2)(a) the court applies the overriding objective, with the principal considerations being the reasons for the delay, whether the delay imperils any hearing dates or otherwise disrupts the proceedings, and whether there is any prejudice caused to the other side.

Remedying irregularity

On other occasions, a default may arise through defective performance. For example, it **37.21** may be that the wrong form was used, or that it was sent to the wrong address (but still came to the attention of the other side), or that the document used was not completed correctly or fully. These are errors of procedure. An example is *Bank of Ireland v Philip Bank Partnership* [2014] EWHC 284 (TCC), where a costs budget was served without a full statement of truth. By r 3.10 such errors do not invalidate the step purportedly taken, unless the court so orders. The court may make an order invalidating a step if it was so badly defective that the other side were misled, or where the defects are so great that it would not be right to regard the purported performance as performance at all. Further, by r 3.10(b) the court may make an order to remedy any error of procedure. In

Phillips v Symes (No 3) [2008] 1 WLR 180, purported service in Switzerland was defective because the English-language version of the claim form had been removed by the Swiss court from the package which was served. It was held that service had taken place, albeit irregularly. In the absence of any prejudice, it was said that the court could and should exercise its power to rectify the error of procedure using r 3.10(b). A defaulting party should consider seeking such an order where there is an objection made regarding defective performance.

I RELIEF FROM SANCTIONS AND SETTING ASIDE

37.22 There are two mechanisms for seeking to retrieve the position once a sanction comes into effect:

(a) Where judgment has been entered under CPR, r 3.5 (see 37.18) following the striking out of a statement of case for breach of an unless order, the defaulting party may apply to set aside the judgment under r 3.6.

(b) A party in breach of any other rule, practice direction, or order imposing a sanction for non-compliance may apply for relief from the sanction (CPR, r 3.8(1)).

In both types of application the court applies the principles on seeking relief from sanctions in r 3.9 (rr 3.6(4) and 3.8(1)).

37.23 Rule 3.9 provides:

> On an application for relief from any sanction imposed for a failure to comply with any rule, practice direction or court order, the court will consider all the circumstances, so as to enable it to deal justly with the application, including the need—
>
> (a) for litigation to be conducted efficiently and at proportionate cost; and
> (b) to enforce compliance with rules, practice directions, and orders.

37.24 Before it was replaced on 1 April 2013, r 3.9 listed nine factors that the court had to consider before granting relief from sanctions. It became notorious that rather than promoting compliance with orders and directions, the approach to r 3.9 by the Court of Appeal was far too indulgent and gave insufficient protection to innocent parties. Consequently, most authorities on r 3.9 before 2013 cannot be relied upon for guidance. To mark a fundamental change in approach the Jackson Reforms replaced r 3.9 and also added r 1.1(2)(f) to the effect that dealing with cases justly and at proportionate cost includes enforcing compliance with rules, practice directions, and orders.

37.25 In *Mitchell v News Group Newspapers Ltd* [2014] 1 WLR 795 the claimant filed its costs budget which estimated his costs at £500,000 on the day before the first case management conference instead of seven days in advance as required by the relevant rule at the time. The master imposed an immediate sanction of limiting the claimant to his court fees, the sanction laid down by r 3.14. Although the delay was relatively short (six days), it was a substantial breach because the court needs costs budgets well in advance of a case management hearing in order to carry out effective costs management. It was also serious, because the master had to stand out a number of important cases in order to deal with the problems caused by this particular default. The defaulting party could not keep to the deadline due to pressure of work from other cases. This was regarded as a bad reason: the solicitor should not have taken on the work if they could not comply with the requirements of the rules. In all the circumstances the court decided against granting relief. *Mitchell v News Group Newspapers Ltd* instituted a robust approach to non-compliance, and was intended to send a clear message to the profession that rules and orders were made to be complied with.

The principles governing applications for relief from sanctions were restated by *Denton v* **37.26** *TH White Ltd* [2014] 1 WLR 3926 as follows:

(a) the first stage is to identify and assess the seriousness or significance of the breach. The relevant breach comprises the original obligation (from the CPR or court directions) as extended by any unless order (so, where there is an unless order usually there will be two successive breaches of the same obligation, see *British Gas Trading Ltd v Oak Cash & Carry Ltd* [2016] 1 WLR 4530). At this stage the court only considers the breach in question, not any previous history of non-compliance. If the breach is not serious or significant, relief will usually be granted and it will usually be unnecessary for the court to spend much time on stages two and three;

(b) the second stage is to consider the reasons why the default occurred; and

(c) the third stage is to consider all the circumstances of the case. The two factors set out in r 3.9(1)(a) and (b) (that litigation be conducted efficiently and at proportionate cost, and the need to enforce compliance with rules, practice directions, and orders) are to be given 'particular weight'.

At stage one, non-payment of court fees is always serious (the *Decadent* appeal in *Denton* **37.27** *v TH White Ltd* at [62]), as is being late with costs budgets (*Mitchell v News Group Newspapers Ltd*). While being just 45 minutes late with a costs budget was regarded as trivial in the *Utilise* appeal in *Denton v TH White Ltd* (at [76]), being a day late with the costs budget in *Lakhani v Mahmud* [2017] 1 WLR 3482 was regarded as serious and justified refusing relief from the sanction in r 3.14. Being late with the exchange of evidence will be a significant breach if it results in the vacation of the trial (the *Denton* appeal in *Denton v TH White Ltd* at [54])

Regarding the second stage, a good reason for non-compliance is most likely to arise from **37.28** circumstances outside the control of the party in default (*Mitchell v News Group Newspapers Ltd* [2014] 1 WLR 795 at [43], citing S Sime and D French, *Blackstone's Guide to the Civil Justice Reforms 2013* (Oxford University Press, 2013), at paras 5.85–5.91 and A Zuckerman, 'The Revised CPR 3.9: A Coded Message Demanding Articulation' [2013] CJQ 123 at 136–7). Examples given by the Master of the Rolls included cases where the party or its solicitor suffered a debilitating illness or was involved in an accident. There may also be a good reason if later developments in the claim show that the period for compliance originally imposed was unreasonable. While these are no more than examples (*Denton v TH White Ltd* [2014] 1 WLR 3926 at [30]), most other reasons are regarded as bad ones. Bad reasons include pressure of other work (*Mitchell v News Group Newspapers Ltd*).

At the third stage the court must take into account the seriousness and significance of the **37.29** breach, and any explanation given (stages one and two), as well as giving particular weight to the two factors from r 3.9(1)(a) and (b). The more serious or significant the breach, the less likely it is that relief will be granted, unless there is a good reason for it. Other factors will vary from case to case. Whether the application for relief was made promptly is a factor, as is any history of non-compliance with other court orders. The *Decadent* appeal in *Denton v TH White Ltd* shows that there may be a clear case for relief even if stages one and two are decided against the party in default.

A rider to the *Denton* principles was added by the Supreme Court in *Global Torch Ltd* **37.30** *v Apex Global Management ltd (No 2)* [2014] 1 WLR 4495. While generally the merits of the substantive claim are irrelevant on an application for relief from sanctions, there is probably an exception where the defaulting party's claim is so strong that the other side's case has no real prospects of success. This is the test for entering summary judgment in r 24.2. Where the defaulting party has an unanswerable case the theory is that the defaulting party is not susceptible to the argument that he must face a trial, so ought not to be penalized for not preparing for trial.

37.31 Tactical opposition to an application for relief from sanctions will itself be penalized by the court (*Denton v TH White Ltd* [2014] 1 WLR 3926 at [41] to [43]). Where it is obvious that relief will be granted by the court, the innocent party should consent to relief being granted without the need for a hearing. Heavy costs sanctions under r 44.11 should be imposed on parties who do take tactical advantage of mistakes by opponents, which might include indemnity basis costs and/or freeing the winning party from the operation of r 3.18 (see 16.31) in relation to its costs budget.

37.32 Refusal of relief from sanctions is effectively a ruling that it is now too late for the defaulting party to comply. Subsequent 'compliance' is not, without additional facts, a material change of circumstances justifying reconsideration of the refusal (*Thevarajah v Riordan* [2016] 1 WLR 76 at [21]).

J IMPLIED SANCTIONS DOCTRINE

37.33 The implied sanctions doctrine is that where a party seeks a discretionary indulgence from the court in circumstances where, if the court refuses the application, the applicant will suffer adverse consequences, the applicant is in effect seeking relief from those adverse consequences, so is making an implied application for relief from sanctions. Under the doctrine this means that the court should apply the principles in CPR, r 3.9, and only grant the application if the applicant satisfies the criteria laid down in *Denton v TH White Ltd* [2014] 1 WLR 3926 (in addition to any requirements laid down for the relevant application).

37.34 Early decisions on the doctrine, such as *Sayers v Clarke Walker* [2002] 1 WLR 3095, were mainly applications to extend the time for appealing (see 50.28). If permission to appeal out of time is refused the implied sanction is that the appeal cannot be brought. While strictly r 3.9 does not apply to applications to extend time for appealing, it was held in *R (Hysaj) v Secretary of State for the Home Department* [2015] 1 WLR 2472 that the implied sanctions doctrine was too well established to be overturned, with the effect that the principles in r 3.9 are applied by analogy. In *Salford Estates (No 2) Ltd v Altomart Ltd* [2015] 1 WLR 1825 it was held that applications to extend time for serving respondents' notices in appeals are also governed by the implied sanctions doctrine.

37.35 It seems now to be established that the implied sanctions doctrine applies to applications to set aside default judgments (see 13.38) and applications under r 39.3(5) to set aside judgments entered at trial in the absence of a party (see 39.65). After some controversy, this seems to have been settled by *Gentry v Miller* [2016] 1 WLR 2696.

37.36 More far reaching, if it is correct, is *Elliott v Stobart Group Ltd* [2015] EWCA Civ 449. The defendant, who was acting person, breached two orders to serve a medical report, as well as breaking an agreed extension for the report. None of these were in 'unless order' format. The Court of Appeal at [43] held that the case was to be treated as one, by implication, where there was an order that imposed a sanction for non-compliance. This may be justified by the particular wording of the order, which made clear the consequences of non-compliance (at [37]), but there is a serious error in the court's reasoning at [35]. It is possible that this decision, combined with *Gentry v Miller*, may be developed into a general principle that the implied sanctions doctrine applies whenever an application depends on a discretion being exercised in favour of the applicant.

KEY POINTS SUMMARY

- Sanctions are imposed in order to ensure parties adhere to the directions timetable imposed by the court. **37.37**
- In deciding what to do when faced with a breach of directions or the requirements of the CPR or practice directions, the court applies the overriding objective and also bears in mind the right to a fair trial under the European Convention on Human Rights, art 6(1).
- The court seeks to impose a proportionate sanction which fits the crime.
- Often the court will give a defaulting party a last chance to comply by imposing an 'unless order', which will result in some draconian sanction applying automatically if there is a further breach.
- A party who is likely to fall into default should apply for a 'time order' under CPR, r 3.1(2)(a) extending the time for compliance.
- After a sanction has come into effect, a defaulting party can apply for relief from the sanction under CPR, r 3.9.
- Applications for relief from sanctions are approached by applying the three-stage test in *Denton* (serious or significant breach; reason for breach; all the circumstances of the case).

38

LISTING AND PRE-TRIAL REVIEWS

A LISTING FOR TRIAL . . . . .38.01   D ADJOURNMENTS 38.09
B PRE-TRIAL REVIEWS 38.07
C LISTING IN THE ROYAL COURTS OF
    JUSTICE 38.08

A LISTING FOR TRIAL

38.01 Claims that are not compromised and which do not end through striking out or summary or default judgment, have to be determined by the court at trial. Listing is the process whereby the court gives a date for the trial. Two main methods are used:

(a) Giving a fixed trial date. This is often given many months before the date allocated.
(b) Giving a trial window of a defined period, usually between one and three weeks, during which the trial will start. If this method is used, the parties find out the actual date for the trial only shortly before it starts: it is not unknown for less than 24 hours' notice to be given, although the courts usually aim to give as much notice as possible.

Listing on the different tracks

38.02 In small claims track cases, a date for the hearing is usually fixed when the court gives standard directions at about the time the case is allocated to this track (see 27.04).

38.03 In fast track claims there is a commitment to have trials heard within 30 weeks of allocation (see 28.11). Fixtures and trial windows are used as may be appropriate, and are usually given as part of the directions laid down on allocation. The detailed procedure on listing for trial in fast track claims was described at 28.17.

38.04 In multi-track claims there is a requirement that the trial date or window must be set by the court as soon as practicable (CPR, r 29.2(2): see 29.19). This may be at the first case management conference, but will often be at some later stage. The detailed procedure was described at 29.21–29.25.

38.05 In the Admiralty and Commercial Courts most cases are given fixed trial dates after the pre-trial timetable is set at the case management conference (*Commercial Court Guide*, para D16.1).

Pre-trial checklists

38.06 Pre-trial checklists are used in fast track and multi-track claims unless the court considers they are not needed (CPR, rr 28.5 and 29.6). Deadlines are fixed by directions, which typically require pre-trial checklists to be filed shortly after the exchange of evidence has been completed and

Form 38.1 Form N170 Pre-trial checklist

Listing questionnaire
(Pre-trial checklist)

Click here to clear all fields	**Name of court** COUNTY COURT AT CHELMSFORD

To be completed by, or on behalf of,

NIGEL JAMES STANIFORTH

Claim No.	CYJ2645
Last date for filing with court office	
Date(s) fixed for trial or trial period	

who is [1st][2nd][3rd][ ][Claimant][Defendant]
[Part 20 claimant][Part 20 defendant] in this claim

This form must be **completed** and **returned** to the court no later than the date given above. If not, your statement of case may be struck out or some other sanction imposed.

If the claim has settled, or settles before the trial date, you must let the court know immediately.

Legal representatives only: If no costs management order has been made. You must **attach** estimates of costs incurred to date, and of your likely overall costs. In substantial cases, these should be provided in compliance with CPR.

For multi-track claims only, you must also **attach** a proposed timetable for the trial itself.

A Confirmation of compliance with directions

1. I confirm that I have complied with those directions already given which require action by me. ☑ Yes ☐ No

   If you are unable to give confirmation, state which directions you have still to comply with and the date by which this will be done.

Directions	Date

2. I believe that additional directions are necessary before the trial takes place. ☑ Yes ☐ No

   If Yes, you should attach an application and a draft order.

   *Include in your application all directions needed to enable the claim **to be tried on the date, or within the trial period, already fixed.** These should include any issues relating to experts and their evidence, and any orders needed in respect of directions still requiring action by any other party.*

3. Have you agreed the additional directions you are seeking with the other party(ies)? ☐ Yes ☐ No

B Witnesses

1. How many witnesses (including yourself) will be giving evidence on your behalf at the trial? *(Do not include experts - see Section C)* `2`

Continued over ⤵

N170 Listing questionnaire (Pre-trial checklist) (05.14) © Crown copyright 2014 1 of 3

Form 38.1 *continued*

Witnesses continued

2. If the trial date is not yet fixed, are there any days within the trial period you or your witnesses would wish to avoid if possible? *(Do not include experts - see Section C)*

Please give details

Name of witness	Dates to be avoided, if posible	Reason
Mrs L Winter	See attached list	Holidays

Please specify any special facilities or arrangements needed at court for the party or any witness (e.g. witness with a disability).

3. Will you be providing an interpreter for any of your witnesses?   ☐ Yes ☑ No

C Experts

You are reminded that you may not use an expert's report or have your expert give oral evidence unless the court has given permission. If you do not have permission, you must make an application (see section A2 above)

1. Please give the information requested for your expert(s)

Name	Field of expertise	Joint expert?	Is report agreed?	Has permission been given for oral evidence?
Mr S Long	Orthopaedic	☑ Yes ☐ No	☑ Yes ☐ No	☐ Yes ☑ No
Miss J Pearson	Neurology	☐ Yes ☑ No	☐ Yes ☑ No	☐ Yes ☑ No
		☐ Yes ☐ No	☐ Yes ☐ No	☐ Yes ☐ No

2. Has there been discussion between experts?   ☐ Yes ☑ No

3. Have the experts signed a joint statement?   ☐ Yes ☑ No

4. If your expert is giving oral evidence and the trial date is not yet fixed, is there any day within the trial period which the expert would wish to avoid, if possible?   ☑ Yes ☐ No

If Yes, please give details

Name	Dates to be avoided, if possible	Reason
Miss J Pearson	See attached list	Professional engagements

Form 38.1 *continued*

D Legal representation

1. Who will be presenting your case at the trial?   ☐ You   ☐ Solicitor   ☑ Counsel

2. If the trial date is not yet fixed, is there any day within the trial period that the person presenting your case would wish to avoid, if possible?   ☑ Yes   ☐ No

    If Yes, please give details

Name	Dates to be avoided, if posible	Reason
Miss Helen Myers	See attached list	Professional engagements

E The trial

1. Has the estimate of the time needed for trial changed?   ☑ Yes   ☐ No

    If Yes, say how long you estimate the whole trial will take, including both parties' cross-examination and closing arguments   2 days   0 hours   0 minutes

2. If different from original estimate have you agreed with the other party(ies) that this is now the **total** time needed?   ☑ Yes   ☐ No

3. Is the timetable for trial you have attached agreed with the other party(ies)?   ☑ Yes   ☐ No

Fast track cases only
The court will normally give you 3 weeks notice of the date fixed for a fast track trial unless, in exceptional circumstances, the court directs that shorter notice will be given.

Would you be prepared to accept shorter notice of the date fixed for trial?   ☐ Yes   ☐ No

F Document and fee checklist

Tick as appropriate

I attach to this questionnaire -

☑ An application and fee for additional directions   ☑ A proposed timetable for trial

☑ A draft order   ☑ An estimate of costs

☑ Listing fee **or** quote your Fee Account no. [   ]

Signature	Your name and full postal address		
	Headley & Co 52 Higham Road Kettering Northants	*If applicable*	
[Legal Representative for the] [1st][2nd][3rd][ ] [Claimant][Defendant][Part 20 claimant]		Telephone no.	01562 891744
		Fax no.	01562 891767
		DX no.	9945 Kettering 2
	Postcode N N 1 6 2 C H	Your ref.	4332/PDL
Date [ ]/[ ]/[ ]	E-mail		

3 of 3

before any pre-trial review. The claimant is required to pay the hearing fee with its checklist. An example is given in form 38.1. These forms are used by the court to check:

(a) that directions have indeed been complied with;
(b) whether any complications have arisen;
(c) whether any further directions should be given; and
(d) whether the trial date or window can be kept.

B PRE-TRIAL REVIEWS

38.07   Pre-trial reviews were discussed at 29.26–29.33, and are mainly used in multi-track cases. They tend to be conducted by the trial judge, and are usually held some weeks before the intended start of the trial. Their main purpose is to set a trial timetable (see 28.20 and 29.32) and to ensure that everything is prepared so the trial can proceed at the set date without any problems or delays.

C LISTING IN THE ROYAL COURTS OF JUSTICE

38.08   In non-specialist cases in the Queen's Bench and Chancery Divisions proceeding in the Royal Courts of Justice and Rolls Building in London, a direction will be given as early as possible (often the first case management conference) with a view to fixing the trial or trial window. It will often direct that the trial is not to begin before a specified date, or that it will be held within a specified period. In the Queen's Bench Division the court will set a date for a listing hearing at which the claimant must bring any case summary, the particulars of claim, and any orders relevant to listing, and all parties must have details of the dates of availability of their witnesses, experts, and counsel. The Listing Officer will try to provide the earliest firm trial date or trial window consistent with the case management directions (*Queen's Bench Guide*, paras 9.4.5–9.4.8 and *Chancery Guide*, paras 21.6–21.8).

D ADJOURNMENTS

38.09   There is a general power to adjourn hearings (CPR, r 3.1(2))(b)). Adjournments are usually granted where the need to adjourn arises through events outside the control of the parties, such as witnesses being unavailable or other practical impossibility in meeting a trial date. A rigorous approach is taken in scrutinizing medical evidence in support of an application to adjourn (*Mohun-Smith v TBO Investments Ltd* [2016] 1 WLR 2919). In *Bates v Croydon London Borough Council* (2001) LTL 23/1/01, an adjournment should have been given as the appellant was awaiting a determination of an application for legal aid, and she had been served with the respondents' witness statements and other documents very shortly before the hearing. However, where the need to adjourn is caused by a failure to prepare for the trial, usually the court will refuse to adjourn. This is emphasized by PD 28, para 5.4 (fast track) and PD 29, para 7.4 (multi-track), which require exceptional circumstances before the court will vacate a trial date on account of a failure to comply with directions (see 37.08). Not applying to adjourn until the day of the trial where a party has known for many weeks that it is in difficulties may be a sufficient reason to refuse an adjournment (*National Westminster Bank plc v Aaronson* (2004) LTL 9/3/04).

39

TRIAL

A WITNESSES 39.03
B TRIAL DOCUMENTATION 39.11
C TRIAL LOCATION 39.18
D ALLOCATION TO JUDICIARY 39.19
E IMPARTIALITY OF JUDGE 39.21
F PUBLIC OR PRIVATE HEARING 39.26
G RIGHTS OF AUDIENCE AND THE
   RIGHT TO CONDUCT LITIGATION 39.29

H MCKENZIE FRIENDS 39.32
I CONDUCT OF THE TRIAL 39.35
J PRELIMINARY ISSUES 39.54
K TRIAL BY JURY 39.61
L NON-ATTENDANCE AT TRIAL 39.65
   Key points summary 39.67

Trials are primarily intended finally to determine the dispute between the parties by a judgment of the court. Most of the procedures described in this book are designed to ensure that both sides are fully prepared in advance of the hearing so that justice can be done between both sides efficiently and without wasting costs. Nevertheless, only a tiny fraction of the claims commenced reach trial. Many of the procedures laid down by the CPR are also intended to encourage the parties to resolve their differences by settling. Further, the expense of the trial itself is a great incentive to settling, and a great many cases are compromised in the run-up to the trial, or even at the door of the court. **39.01**

A number of things must be done in the period leading up to a trial. These include warning the witnesses and ensuring that any reluctant witnesses are served with witness summonses. Trial bundles need to be prepared. Counsel may need to be briefed, and skeleton arguments, case summaries, and reading lists prepared. The rules give the courts a great deal of flexibility regarding how they will deal with trials. The court can lay down trial timetables prescribing how the time available for the trial will be used, and allocating specified, limited times for examination-in-chief, cross-examination, and so on. Another power available to the court is to direct that one or more issues should be dealt with before the others as preliminary issues. Most civil claims are heard by judges sitting alone, but deceit, malicious prosecution, and false imprisonment claims may be tried by juries. **39.02**

A WITNESSES

Witness summonses

Reluctant witnesses may be compelled to attend trial by serving them with a witness summons. An example of such a summons is shown in form 39.1. A witness summons may require the named witness simply to attend to give oral evidence, or to produce specified documents, or both. A witness summons to produce documents is not a form of disclosure in the sense of disclosure between parties, and is limited to the production of documents relevant to the substantive issues in the claim. Consequently, a witness cannot be summoned to produce **39.03**

Form 39.1 Witness summons

Print form   Reset form

Witness Summons

Name of court	COUNTY COURT AT CHELMSFORD
Case no.	CYJ2645
Applicant's name or serial no.	LAURA ROBINSON
Respondent's name and ref.	NIGEL JAMES STANIFORTH
Date issued	
Solicitor's fee account no.	

To

Jennifer Edwards
48 Jesmond Road,
Chelmsford,
Essex
CM2 9SL

You are summoned to attend at *(court address)*

London House, New London Road, Chelmsford, Essex, CM2 0DR

on [ ] of [ ] at [ ] (am)(pm)

(and each following day of the hearing until the court tells you that you are no longer required.)

☑ to give evidence in respect of the above case

☑ to produce the following document(s) *(give details)*

Police Accident Report for accident involving Nigel Staniforth and Laura Robinson

The sum of £ [ ] is paid or offered to you with this summons. This is to cover your travelling expenses to and from court and includes an amount by way of compensation for loss of time.

This summons was issued on the application of the applicant (respondent) or the applicant's (respondent's) solicitor whose name, address and reference number is:

Smallwood & Co, 4 Market Place, Chelmsford, Essex CM1 4AR

Do not ignore this summons

If you were offered money for travel expenses and compensation for loss of time, at the time it was served on you, you must –

- attend court on the date and time shown and/or produce documents as required by the summons; and
- take an oath or affirm as required for the purposes of answering questions about your evidence or the documents you have been asked to produce.

Disobedience of a witness summons is a contempt of court and you may be fined or imprisoned for contempt. You may also be liable to pay any wasted costs that arise because of your non-compliance.

If you wish to set aside or vary this witness summons, you may make an application to the court that issued it.

Certificate of service

Case no.	CYJ2645
Serial no.	

I certify that the summons of which this is a true copy was served by posting to

(the witness)

on [   ] at the address stated on the summons in accordance with the request

of the applicant or his/her solicitor.

I enclosed a payable order for £ [   ] for the witness's expenses and compensation for loss of time.

Signed _____

       Officer of the Court

---

train of inquiry documents: *Macmillan Inc v Bishopsgate Investment Trust plc* [1993] 1 WLR 1372. The documents to be produced must be sufficiently described, although classes of documents may be described compendiously: *Panayiotou v Sony Music Entertainment (UK) Ltd* [1994] Ch 142. A witness summons may require the witness to produce documents either at the trial or on such other date as the court may direct (CPR, r 34.2(4)(b)), which may be some time before the trial so as to enable the parties to take stock after receipt of the documents.

39.04 Issuing a witness summons is purely administrative. The form must be completed, a fee is paid, and the form is sealed by the court. Unless the court gives permission, a witness summons will be binding on the witness only if it is served at least seven days before the trial (r 34.5). A person served with a witness summons must also be offered a sum of money (known as conduct money) to cover travelling expenses to and from the court and compensation for loss of time (r 34.7).

39.05 The court may set aside or vary a witness summons (CPR, r 34.3(4)), and may do so if it appears that the person summoned is unable to give relevant evidence, or if there is some other strong reason for not requiring his or her attendance at the trial. A judge acting in his judicial capacity, even if able to give relevant evidence, is not a compellable witness: *Warren v Warren* [1997] QB 488.

Evidence by deposition

39.06 Where it appears to be necessary in the interests of justice to do so, the court may order a witness's evidence to be given by deposition (CPR, r 34.8). This is discussed at 32.33–32.35. A party intending to use a deposition at trial must give other parties notice of that intention at least 21 days in advance of trial (r 34.11).

Letters of request

39.07 The evidence of witnesses already outside the jurisdiction may be obtained by the High Court on its own behalf or on behalf of the County Court (CPR, rr 34.13–34.24) by:

(a) the issue of letters of request to the judicial authorities of the country in question. The evidence may be given either orally or in answer to written questions. Where the witness is in an EU State (other than Denmark), the request must comply with the requirements of Council Regulation (EC) No 1206/2001; or

(b) examination before the British consular authority in the relevant country.

39.08 It was held in *Panayiotou v Sony Music Entertainment (UK) Ltd* [1994] Ch 142 that a letter of request may be confined to the production of documents in the possession of the witness outside the jurisdiction. The documents that may be required to be produced have to be identified, and must be restricted to documents which could have been the subject of a witness summons. In other words, this is not a procedure for obtaining disclosure of documents against the witness, but for obtaining admissible evidence on the issues in the claim.

Video links

39.09 The court has power under CPR, r 32.3, to allow a party to adduce the evidence of a witness by a live video link. This facility is regarded as being readily available to all litigants. In *Polanski v Condé Nast Publications Ltd* [2005] 1 WLR 637 a video-conferencing order was made to enable a fugitive to give evidence from outside the country without the risk of being extradited to the United States. Practical guidance is given by PD 32, Annex 3. A party obtaining permission to adduce evidence in this way will have to make the necessary arrangements.

Adjourning to bedside

39.10 The court has inherent power to adjourn trial to the bedside of an infirm witness: *St Edmundsbury and Ipswich Diocesan Board of Finance v Clark* [1973] Ch 323.

B TRIAL DOCUMENTATION

Trial bundles

39.11 All the documents likely to be referred to at fast track and multi-track trials should be placed into paginated files called trial bundles. Identical bundles should be made available for each of the parties, the judge, and a further set for use by the witnesses while giving evidence. This assists in ensuring that everyone is considering the same document at any one time, and avoids delays during the trial when documents are referred to. Poorly prepared bundles are perhaps the greatest source of complaint from judges.

39.12 Trial bundles should be filed by the claimant not more than seven and not less than three days before the start of the trial (CPR, r 39.5(2)). The responsibility for preparation of the trial bundles rests with the legal representative of the claimant. Paragraph 3 of PD 39A lays down detailed rules for trial bundles. Unless the court otherwise orders, the trial bundle should include:

(a) the claim form and all statements of case;
(b) a case summary and/or a chronology where appropriate;
(c) requests for further information and responses to the requests;
(d) all witness statements to be relied on as evidence;
(e) any witness summaries;
(f) any notices of intention to rely on hearsay evidence under r 33.2;
(g) any notices of intention to rely on evidence (eg a plan, photograph, etc.) under r 33.6 which is not:
    (i) contained in a witness statement, affidavit, or expert's report,
    (ii) being given orally at trial,
    (iii) hearsay evidence under r 33.2;

(h) any medical reports and responses to them;

(i) any experts' reports and responses to them;

(j) any order giving directions as to the conduct of the trial; and

(k) any other necessary documents.

The trial bundle should normally be contained in ring-binders or lever arch files. It should be **39.13** paginated continuously throughout, and indexed with a description of each document and the page number. If any document is illegible, a typed copy should be provided and given an 'A' number. The contents of the bundles should be agreed if possible. If there is any disagreement, a summary of the points in dispute should be included. Bundles exceeding 100 pages should have numbered dividers. Where a number of files are needed, each file should be numbered or distinguishable by different colours. If there is a lot of documentation a core bundle should also be prepared containing the most essential documents, and it should be cross-referenced to the supplementary documents in the other files. Identical bundles with the same colour-coded files have to be supplied to all the parties plus the bundle for the court and a further one for the use of the witnesses at the trial. See 34.20 on the admissibility of documents in agreed bundles.

Reading lists

In all QBD and ChD claims where trial bundles must be lodged, the claimant or applicant **39.14** must at the same time lodge:

(a) a reading list for the judge who will conduct the hearing;

(b) an estimated length of reading time; and

(c) an estimated length for the hearing.

This must be signed by all the advocates who will appear at the hearing. Each advocate's **39.15** name, business address, and telephone number must appear below his or her signature. In the event of disagreement about any of these matters, separate reading lists and estimates must be signed by the appropriate advocates. See *Practice Direction (RCJ: Reading Lists and Time Estimates)* [2000] 1 WLR 208. In addition to the trial bundles the trial judge has a discretion about what other material to read by way of pre-trial preparation, and may read material containing inadmissible evidence: *Barings plc v Coopers and Lybrand* [2001] CPLR 451.

Case summaries

In a case of any size it is essential that a case summary should be prepared. This should **39.16** be a short, non-contentious, summary of the issues in the case and of relevant procedural matters. If possible it should be agreed by all parties.

Skeleton arguments and authorities

Skeleton arguments are compulsory for High Court trials, and sometimes are required by **39.17** directions in the County Court. Trial skeletons are similar in concept to those used for interim applications (see 23.38–23.45) concisely summarizing the submissions to be made in relation to the issues raised and citing the authorities to be relied upon. They should be filed two days before the trial (QBD) or with the trial bundles (ChD). It is often useful to provide a short chronology of the important events.

C TRIAL LOCATION

Normally trials will take place at the court where the case has been proceeding, but it **39.18** may be transferred to another court for trial if this is appropriate having regard to the convenience of the parties and the availability of court resources (PD 28, para 8.1, for the fast track; PD 29, para 10.1, for cases on the multi-track). Multi-track cases will generally have been transferred to Civil Trial Centres when allocated to the multi-track (if commenced in a feeder court), but they may be allowed to proceed elsewhere if that is appropriate given the needs of the parties and the availability of court resources.

D ALLOCATION TO JUDICIARY

39.19 District Judges can deal with all small claims and fast track cases, so effectively their trial jurisdiction is £25,000 (PD 2B, para 11.1). District Judges may also hear most Part 8 claims automatically treated as allocated to the multi-track, certain landlord and tenant cases, assessments of damages, and cases allocated to a District Judge with the permission of the Designated Civil Judge (para 11.1). Injunction and committal applications may be heard by a District Judge if the claim has been allocated to the fast or small claims tracks; or if the value is below £25,000 (in cases that have not been allocated at the time of the application).

39.20 Most multi-track cases will be tried by High Court judges and, in the County Court, by Circuit Judges and Recorders.

E IMPARTIALITY OF JUDGE

39.21 It has long been established that a judge must not sit in his or her own cause. The rule laid down in *Dimes v Proprietors of Grand Junction Canal* (1852) 3 HL Cas 759 by Lord Campbell is now interpreted as not being confined to a claim in which the judge is a party, but applies also to a claim in which the outcome could, realistically, affect an interest of the judge. In *R v Bow Street Metropolitan Stipendiary Magistrate, ex p Pinochet Ugarte (No 2)* [2000] 1 AC 119 the House of Lords held that the principle that a judge is automatically disqualified from hearing a matter in his or her own cause is not limited to cases where the judge has a pecuniary interest in the outcome, but applies also to cases where the judge's decision would lead to the promotion of a cause in which the judge was involved together with one of the parties. The automatic disqualification rule is subject to the *de minimis* principle, in that some supposed financial interests are so small they can be ignored: *Locabail (UK) Ltd v Bayfield Properties Ltd* [2000] QB 451.

39.22 Under the European Convention on Human Rights, art 6(1), litigants are entitled to a fair hearing before an impartial tribunal, so a judge will also be unable to sit if there is an appearance of bias. According to *Porter v Magill* [2002] 2 AC 357 and *Taylor v Lawrence* [2003] QB 528, the court must first ascertain all the circumstances which have a bearing on the suggestion that the judge is biased. The court must then ask whether those circumstances would lead a fair-minded and informed observer to conclude that there was a real possibility that the judge was biased. Where the judge's explanation was not accepted by the party making the suggestion of bias (or apparent bias), that also had to be considered from the viewpoint of the fair-minded observer.

39.23 Guidance on situations where there may be a real danger of bias was given by the Court of Appeal in *Locabail (UK) Ltd v Bayfield Properties Ltd*, which is of particular relevance to cases dealt with by solicitor and barrister deputy judges. The Court of Appeal could not conceive of circumstances in which an objection could be soundly based on the religion, ethnic or national origin, gender, age, class, means, or sexual orientation of the judge. Nor, at least ordinarily, could there be a valid objection based on the judge's social, educational, service, or employment background, nor that of any member of his or her family. Nor could an objection be based on previous political associations, membership of social, sporting, or charitable bodies, or Masonic associations; previous judicial decisions; extra-curial utterances, whether in textbooks, lectures, speeches, articles, interviews, reports, or responses to consultation papers; previous receipt of instructions to act for or against any party, solicitor, or advocate engaged in the current case; or membership of the same Inn, circuit, local Law Society, or chambers.

By contrast, there might be a real danger of bias if there was personal friendship or ani- **39.24** mosity between the judge and anyone other than the lawyers involved in the present case; or if the judge was closely acquainted with a witness whose credibility was in issue; or if the judge had ruled against the credibility of a witness in a previous case in outspoken terms such as to cast doubt on whether the judge could deal with the witness in the current case with an open mind (but not if the judge had commented adversely on a party or witness in a previous case in temperate terms); or if the judge had expressed views on a matter also in issue in the present case in such extreme terms as to throw into doubt his or her ability to try the case objectively. If there is any doubt, it should be exercised in favour of refusing to sit. Judges are obliged to mention any possible conflict when they become aware of its existence. Wherever possible this is done in advance of the commencement of the trial, and any objection based on apparent bias must be made when it arises, rather than awaiting the result of the hearing (*Steadman-Byrne v Amjad* [2007] 1 WLR 2484).

Where proceedings are abandoned because of the appearance of bias on the part of a **39.25** member of the court, the Lord Chancellor is not liable for any of the costs incurred at the wasted hearing: *Re Medicaments and Related Classes of Goods (No 4)* [2002] 1 WLR 269.

F PUBLIC OR PRIVATE HEARING

Under the European Convention on Human Rights, art 6(1), parties have a right to a public **39.26** hearing. The general rule therefore is that trials will be conducted in public (CPR, r 39.2(1)). The general rule does not, however, impose an obligation to make special arrangements for accommodating members of the public. By way of exception to the general rule, r 39.2(3) provides that a hearing may be conducted in private if:

(a) publicity would defeat the object of the hearing;
(b) it involves matters relating to national security;
(c) it involves confidential information (including information relating to personal financial matters (r 39.2(3)(c)) or privileged materials (*Eurasian Natural Resources Corpn Ltd v Dechert LLP* [2016] 1 WLR 5027)) and publicity would damage that confidentiality;
(d) a private hearing is necessary to protect the interests of any child or patient;
(e) it is a hearing of an application made without notice and it would be unjust to any respondent for there to be a public hearing;
(f) it involves uncontentious matters arising in the administration of trusts or in the administration of a deceased's estate; or
(g) the court considers a private hearing to be necessary, in the interests of justice.

Further, the court may order that the identity of any party or witness must not be disclosed **39.27** if it considers non-disclosure strictly necessary in order to protect the interests of that party or witness. Anonymity orders are exceptional, and potentially raise competing claims under the European Convention on Human Rights, arts 8 (the need for privacy) and 10 (freedom of expression), which have to be balanced against each other (*Re Guardian News and Media Ltd* [2010] 2 AC 697).

Proceedings under the Prevention of Terrorism Act 2005 are often held in private (CPR, **39.28** r 76.22). As there will often be 'closed material' (see the Justice and Security Act 2013 and

CPR, r 76.28 and Part 82) in cases under this Act, the Attorney-General may appoint a 'special advocate' to represent the interests of the relevant party (rr 76.23 and 82.9–82.15). *Secretary of State for the Home Department v AHK* [2009] 1 WLR 2049 deals with the discretion to appoint a special advocate in these cases.

G RIGHTS OF AUDIENCE AND THE RIGHT TO CONDUCT LITIGATION

39.29   Rights of audience and the right to conduct litigation are reserved legal activities within the meaning of the Legal Services Act 2007 (s 12 and Sch 2). A person is only entitled to carry on these activities if they are a regulated person authorized to do so by an approved regulator or if they are exempt in relation to the relevant activity (ss 13 and 176). Approved regulators include the Law Society, the General Council of the Bar, the Institute of Legal Executives, the Council for Licensed Conveyancers, and the Association of Law Costs Draftsmen (Sch 4). These provisions ensure that persons with general rights of audience or to conduct litigation have to comply with the regulatory requirements of their approved regulator (s 176(1)). Any such person has a duty to the court to act with independence and in the interests of justice (s 188(2)).

39.30   This means the following persons have rights of audience:

(a) litigants in person (who are exempt, Sch 3, para 1(6));
(b) counsel (all courts);
(c) solicitors (all solicitors have rights of audience in the County Court. To exercise rights of audience in the High Court a solicitor needs a Law Society higher rights of audience qualification);
(d) members of the Institute of Legal Executives (County Court, for members with ILEX civil proceedings certificate);
(e) members of the Association of Law Costs Draftsmen (costs proceedings, with certification by the Association);
(f) persons given express permission by the court in relation to the relevant proceedings (who are exempt, Sch 3, para 1(2)); and
(g) persons given an express right of audience by statute (an example being the right given to local authority officers to present rent and possession claims on behalf of their employers under the County Courts Act 1984, s 60).

39.31   Rule 39.6 of the CPR provides that a company or corporation may appear at a hearing through a duly authorized employee provided the court gives permission. Paragraph 5.3 of PD 39A says that permission should usually be given unless there is some particular and sufficient reason why it should be withheld. Permission should generally be sought on an occasion prior to the hearing, but may be granted at the hearing itself.

H MCKENZIE FRIENDS

39.32   A McKenzie friend ('MF', from *McKenzie v McKenzie* [1971] P 33), is an unqualified person who assists a litigant who would otherwise be acting in person. Most MFs assist litigants who are individuals, but the court has inherent jurisdiction to permit a MF to assist a company (*Bank St Petersburg PJSC v Arkhangelsky (No 2)* [2016] 1 WLR 1081).

39.33   The primary function of a MF is to provide moral support for a litigant at a hearing. A MF is not permitted to conduct litigation or act as an advocate without the court's permission. *Practice Note (McKenzie Friends: Civil and Family Courts)* [2010] 1 WLR 1881 sets out guidance based on the statutory provisions governing rights of audience in the Legal Services Act 2007, and various decisions of the courts. Litigants in person ordinarily have a right to receive reasonable assistance from a MF if they wish, but the court retains the power to refuse to permit such assistance. The Practice Note says a MF may:

(a) provide moral support for the litigant;
(b) take notes;
(c) help with case papers; and
(d) quietly give advice on any aspect of the conduct of the case. The litigant is permitted to communicate any information, including filed evidence, to the MF for these purposes.

Limitations on what MFs are permitted to do set out in the guidance are: **39.34**

(a) a MF has no right to address the court, or examine witnesses. Any person doing these is an advocate, and requires the grant of a right of audience. Permission is granted on a case-by-case basis, but the court will be slow to grant this permission because persons exercising rights of audience must be properly trained and subject to professional discipline. An application that a MF be permitted a right of audience must be made at the start of the hearing (*Clarkson v Gilbert* [2000] 2 FLR 839). An important factor is whether a right of audience is required to ensure the litigant receives a fair hearing (*Re N (A Child) (McKenzie Friend: Rights of Audience)* [2008] 1 WLR 2743); and
(b) a MF may not act as the litigant's agent in relation to the proceedings, nor manage the litigant's case outside court, such as by signing court documents.

I CONDUCT OF THE TRIAL

Before the hearing the court should be provided with a written statement of the name and **39.35** professional address of each advocate, his or her qualification as an advocate, and the party he or she acts for (PD 39A, para 5). This is usually done by advocates completing a slip provided by the court immediately before the hearing.

The rules give the courts a great deal of flexibility regarding how they will deal with trials. **39.36** As previously discussed, the court can lay down trial timetables prescribing how the time available for the trial will be used, and allocating specified, limited times for examination-in-chief, cross-examination, and so on. The trial will then follow the timetable previously laid down, or laid down by the trial judge at the start, or will follow the traditional sequence of events.

Generally it will be the claimant who begins. However, it will be the defendant if the **39.37** defendant has admitted all the issues on which the burden of proof rests on the claimant, so that the only live issues have to be proved by the defendant.

Opening speech

The trial judge will generally have read the papers in the trial bundle before the trial. It will **39.38** often be the case that in those circumstances there is no need for an opening speech, which may be dispensed with (PD 28, para 8.2, for the fast track; PD 29, para 10.2, for cases on the multi-track). If an opening speech is allowed, counsel for the claimant will usually describe the nature of the claim, and will identify the issues to be tried by reference to the statements of case and/or the statement of issues. Some of the documentary evidence may be referred to. It sometimes happens that the judge will rise during the course of the opening to read some of the documents.

Claimant's case

39.39 After the claimant's opening speech, evidence will be called on behalf of the claimant. Broadly, evidence adduced at trial will be real evidence (ie physical items), contemporaneous documentary evidence, views of the site, and the evidence of witnesses.

39.40 The judge has a discretion to inspect the *locus in quo* if there are compelling reasons to do so, outweighing the time and expense of a view. Inspections should generally be conducted in the presence of the parties.

39.41 There are occasions when evidence is adduced in a deposition, by affidavit, or in the form of hearsay statements. It is rather more usual for evidence from witnesses to be produced by calling the witnesses to give evidence from the witness box. Witnesses are sometimes asked to leave the court until they are called so they are not influenced by the evidence given by other witnesses, but they remain in court in the large majority of cases. Subject to any trial directions they may be called in any order.

39.42 When a witness is called they are sworn or affirm in a manner they consider binding (Oaths Act 1978). Traditionally they would give their evidence in answer to non-leading questions put to them by counsel for the party calling them. However, under the CPR witness statements of witnesses called at trial will stand as the evidence-in-chief unless the court otherwise orders (r 32.5(2)). Technically, it is possible to augment the evidence contained in the exchanged statements only if, by virtue of r 32.5(3) and (4), the court considers there is good reason not to confine the witness to the contents of his or her witness statement, and for the purpose of either:

(a) amplifying the witness statement; or
(b) giving evidence in relation to new matters which have arisen since the witness statement was served on the other parties.

39.43 The CPR, r 32.5(5), provides that where the party who has disclosed a witness statement does not use it at trial, 'any other party may put the witness statement in as hearsay'. In *McPhilemy v Times Newspapers Ltd* [2000] CPLR 335, the party who disclosed a witness statement decided against calling the witness. The opposite side then attempted to put the statement into evidence for the purpose of proving that its contents were untrue. Permission was refused because of the general rule of evidence that a party is not allowed to adduce evidence that his own witnesses (in this case the witness who made the witness statement) are not to be believed on their oaths.

39.44 After being examined-in-chief, each witness may be cross-examined by counsel for the defendant. Where there is more than one defendant, they cross-examine in the order they appear on the court record. Cross-examination may be conducted using leading questions (ie questions which suggest the required answer).

39.45 A witness who has been cross-examined may be re-examined by counsel for the claimant on matters covered in cross-examination. Leading questions are not allowed.

39.46 Exhibits which are handed in and proved during the course of the trial will be recorded in an exhibit list and kept in the custody of the court until the conclusion of the trial, unless the judge directs otherwise (PD 39A, para 7). At the conclusion of the trial the parties have the responsibility for taking away and preserving the exhibits pending any possible appeal.

Submissions of no case to answer

39.47 At the conclusion of the case for the claimant, the defendant may make a submission of no case to answer. This is made on the basis that on the evidence adduced by the claimant the claim cannot succeed. A submission of no case to answer should rarely, if ever, be entertained in cases tried by a judge sitting alone (*Benham Ltd v Kythira Investments Ltd* (2003) LTL 15/12/03). As the judge is the trier of both law and fact, it is embarrassing for the judge to be asked to rule on the merits of the claim while the evidence is still incomplete. Further, if the judge's ruling were to be reversed on appeal, there would be the added cost of having a retrial.

It is therefore the general rule that defendants seeking to make a submission of no case **39.48** to answer will be put to an election as to whether they will call any evidence. It is only in exceptional cases that they will not be put to this election: *Boyce v Wyatt Engineering* (2001) LTL 1/5/01. If they are put to their election, and decide to call no evidence, they can make a submission of no case to answer, which will be decided on the basis of whether the claimant's case has been established by the evidence on the balance of probabilities, and judgment will be entered for whichever party succeeds on the submission. In cases where the defendant is not put to an election, the submission is considered on the basis of whether the claimant's case has no real prospect of success: *Miller v Cawley* (2002) *The Times*, 6 September 2002. In such a case, if the submission is unsuccessful the defendant is allowed to call its evidence and the trial continues in the normal way.

Defence case

Where the defence decides to call evidence, it may be allowed to make an opening speech **39.49** (though this is now rather unusual). It then calls its evidence in the same way as the claimant. Where there is more than one defendant, they present their evidence in the order they appear on the record.

Closing speeches

Where the defence has called evidence, the defence closing speech is made before that of **39.50** the claimant. Speeches usually deal with how the evidence that has been adduced and the inferences that can be drawn from that evidence support the case for the party in question on the factual issues involved. Counsel also argue any legal points that arise, sometimes making use of skeleton arguments. The time limits imposed by trial timetables may have the practical effect of forcing advocates to make even greater use of skeleton arguments, so as to ensure they are able to cover the required ground within the time limited by the court.

Role of the judge

During the course of the trial the judge may put questions to the witnesses, particularly if **39.51** matters remain obscure after counsel's questions. Judges should be careful to avoid interrupting the flow of counsel's questions, particularly during cross-examination: *Jones v National Coal Board* [1957] 2 QB 55. The judge will have to rule on any applications and any objections to the admissibility of evidence or questions during the course of the trial. After hearing the evidence the judge must decide where the truth lies, decide any points of law, and give judgment. The claimant has the burden of proof on a balance of probabilities. If the party with the burden of proof fails to discharge that burden, the fact is treated as not having happened. If the burden of proof is discharged, the court treats the fact as having happened. There is no halfway house between the two (*Re B (Children) (Care Proceedings: Standard of Proof)* [2009] 1 AC 11). Inherent probabilities have to be taken into account as a factor 'to whatever extent is appropriate in the particular case' (Lord Nicholls of Birkenhead in *Re H (Minors) (Sexual Abuse: Standard of Proof)* [1996] AC 563 at 583), but do not alter the balance of probabilities test.

39.52 Judgment is often given immediately, but in complicated cases may be reserved. The court will always record judgments given at trial, both in the High Court and County Court. Often the evidence will also have been recorded (PD 39A, para 6.1). Unofficial tape recording without permission (which will rarely be given) is a contempt of court. Transcripts can be obtained on payment of authorized charges. After judgment is given the court will deal with the question of costs, the form of the judgment, and any application for permission to appeal.

Reopening a hearing

39.53 Normally, once the parties have completed their evidence they are not allowed to seek to put more evidence before the court. However, there is not a complete ban. A distinction may be drawn between:

(a) requests to reopen a hearing before the judge delivers judgment. In this situation the application should probably be dealt with in accordance with the overriding objection of dealing with the case justly and at proportionate cost; and

(b) requests to reopen a hearing after judgment has been delivered, but before the judgment is drawn up (see 41.37) where the court will have regard to the *Ladd v Marshall* [1954] 1 WLR 1489 (see 50.68) principles, but with more flexibility than in appeals (*Navitaire Inc v Easyjet Airline Co Ltd* [2006] RPC 4).

J PRELIMINARY ISSUES

39.54 As a general rule, it is in the interests of the parties and the administration of justice that all issues arising in a dispute are tried at the same time. However, particularly in complex actions, costs and time can sometimes be saved if decisive, or potentially decisive, issues can be identified and ordered to be tried before or separately from the main trial.

39.55 There are three related types of order that can be made:

(a) for the trial of a preliminary issue on a point of law;

(b) for the separate trial of preliminary issues or questions of fact; and

(c) for separate trials of liability and quantum.

Procedure for trial of preliminary issues

39.56 Orders for the trial of preliminary issues are made either on the application of a party or by the court of its own initiative. It is rare for the court to make such an order without the concurrence of at least one of the parties. It is not possible to make such an order by consent. Normally the application is made at the allocation or listing stage, or on a case management hearing, although it is not unknown for an application to be made to the trial judge at the beginning of a trial.

39.57 Where an order for the preliminary trial of an issue of law or fact is made, the court must formulate the issue to be tried. It is important that the issue is defined with precision so as to avoid future difficulties of interpretation. If it is impossible to define the issue, no order should be made: *Allen v Gulf Oil Refining Ltd* [1981] AC 101. If the issue is one of law, the court must further order the issue to be tried either:

(a) on the statements of case;

(b) on a case stated; or

(c) on an agreed statement of facts.

In *Keays v Murdoch Magazines (UK) Ltd* [1991] 1 WLR 1184, an issue as to whether **39.58** words were capable of a defamatory meaning was ordered to be tried on the pleadings in conjunction with the copy of the magazine in which the offending article appeared.

Practice

Factors to be taken into account when deciding whether to order the determination of a **39.59** preliminary issue identified in *Steele v Steele* (2001) *The Times*, 5 June 2001, include:

(a) Whether the determination of the preliminary issue will dispose of the whole case or at least one aspect of the case.

(b) Whether the determination of the preliminary issue will significantly cut down the cost and the time involved in pre-trial preparation and in connection with the trial itself.

(c) If the preliminary issue is an issue of law, the amount of effort involved in identifying the relevant facts for the purposes of the preliminary issue.

(d) If the preliminary issue is an issue of law, whether it can be determined on agreed facts. If there are substantial disputes of fact it is unlikely to be safe to determine the legal issue until the facts are found.

(e) The risk that an order will increase the costs or delay the trial, and the prospects that such an order may assist in settling the dispute.

Issues raised in personal injuries cases as to the claimant's 'date of knowledge' under the **39.60** Limitation Act 1980, s 14, may be suitable for trial as preliminary issues. In *Keays v Murdoch Magazines (UK) Ltd* [1991] 1 WLR 1184, the issue whether the words published were capable of bearing a defamatory meaning was determined as a preliminary issue.

K TRIAL BY JURY

Jurisdiction

There is a right to trial by jury in actions involving claims in deceit, malicious prosecution, **39.61** and false imprisonment. This right extends to claims in the County Court (CCA 1984, s 66) and the QBD of the High Court (SCA 1981, s 69), but not to claims in the ChD. The right to trial by jury is subject to the court otherwise being of the opinion that the trial requires prolonged examination of documents or accounts, or any scientific or local investigation which cannot conveniently be made by a jury. A request for trial by jury should be made within 28 days of service of the defence (CPR, r 26.11(1)).

The right to trial by jury in defamation claims was removed by the Defamation Act 2013, **39.62** s 11. There is a theoretical discretion to allow trial by jury in defamation and even in other cases, but the courts are extremely reluctant to exercise it: *Williams v Beesley* [1973] 1 WLR 1295.

Jury procedure

Juries are eight strong in the County Court and 12 strong in the High Court. Jurors are **39.63** selected from the jury panel by ballot. They may be challenged and asked to stand down only for cause, such as proven bias. After inquiring, the trial judge should discharge any juror who will suffer inconvenience or hardship by having to serve for the estimated length of the trial (*Practice Direction (Juries: Length of Trial)* [1981] 1 WLR 1129). During the course of a High Court trial, a juror may be discharged on the ground of evident necessity.

39.64 Questions of law are for the judge, and questions of fact are decided by the jury in the light of the judge's summing-up. The jury should not deliberate until they are all together in the jury room. Verdicts should normally be unanimous, but if a jury cannot agree majority verdicts of 7:1 in the County Court and 11:1, 10:2, 10:1, and 9:1 in the High Court may be accepted.

L NON-ATTENDANCE AT TRIAL

39.65 A trial may proceed despite the non-attendance of any of the parties, and the court may simply strike out the claim or defence, and any counterclaim or defence to counterclaim (CPR, r 39.3(1)). The court has a power to restore the proceedings (or any part of the proceedings) that may have been struck out due to non-attendance (r 39.3(2)), and may set aside any judgment entered in such circumstances (r 39.3(3)). Applications to set aside or restore must be supported by evidence (r 39.3(4)). Orders to restore or set aside may, by r 39.3(5) be granted only if the applicant:

(a) acted promptly (meaning 'with alacrity') on finding out that the court had exercised its power to strike out or enter judgment or otherwise make an order against the applicant; and

(b) had a good excuse for not attending—claimants, in particular, are expected to keep in contact with their solicitors, and so have limited grounds for saying they were unaware of a hearing date: *Neufville v Papamichael* (1999) LTL 23/11/99; and

(c) has a reasonable prospect of success at a reconvened trial.

39.66 Divergent approaches have been adopted by differently constituted courts. *Mohun-Smith v TBO Investments Ltd* [2016] 1 WLR 2919 held that it was wrong to apply too rigorous an approach to the first two conditions (applying promptly and the reasons for non-attendance), and that once the three conditions are satisfied, the court would require very unusual circumstances to refuse to set aside. Conversely, *Gentry v Miller* [2016] 1 WLR 2696 held that after considering the three r 39.3(5) conditions, the court must apply the *Denton* principles (see 37.26ff) in accordance with the implied sanctions doctrine.

KEY POINTS SUMMARY

39.67 In the period leading up to trial, the following matters should be dealt with:

- Contacting witnesses to ensure they are available.
- Obtaining witness summonses where appropriate. This may be because a witness is reluctant to attend (although calling a reluctant witness is always very risky) or because the witness needs a witness summons to show to an employer.
- Briefing trial counsel.
- Considering whether there should be a pre-trial conference with counsel, the client, and any experts.
- Agreeing and compiling trial bundles (this is often a very onerous task).
- Counsel drafting skeleton arguments and reading lists for the judge.
- Drawing up chronologies and *dramatis personae*.
- Counsel preparing speeches, examination-in-chief, and cross-examination of witnesses. Depending on the nature of the case, this can be very time-intensive.
- In fast track trials, drawing up schedules of costs for the summary assessment.
- Lodging lists or bundles of authorities.

40

REFERENCES TO THE COURT OF JUSTICE OF THE EUROPEAN UNION

A QUESTIONS WHICH MAY BE
REFERRED 40.02

B MANDATORY REFERENCES 40.05

C DISCRETIONARY REFERENCES........40.07

D PROCEDURE IN ENGLAND 40.19

E PROCEDURE IN THE COURT OF
JUSTICE OF THE EUROPEAN UNION....40.25

F COSTS..........................40.28

An English court faced with a question of EU law may sometimes decide it itself, or may **40.01** refer it to the Court of Justice of the European Union ('CJEU', previously known as the European Court of Justice 'ECJ') in Luxembourg for a preliminary ruling. If a reference is made, the English proceedings will be stayed pending the ruling of the CJEU. Once it is made, the ruling is binding on the English court, but it is only a preliminary ruling, in that the English court is left to apply the ruling to the facts of the case and to give judgment. The general policy is that EU law should be applied consistently in all Member States.

A QUESTIONS WHICH MAY BE REFERRED

References to the CJEU may be made under the Treaty on the Functioning of the European **40.02** Union, art 267 (the 'EU Treaty').

It provides in its first paragraph: **40.03**

> The Court of Justice of the European Union shall have jurisdiction to give preliminary rulings concerning:
> (a) the interpretation of the Treaties;
> (b) the validity and interpretation of acts of the institutions, bodies, offices or agencies of the Union.

This includes questions on the amending Treaties and Treaties of Accession, and questions **40.04** on Regulations, Directives, and Decisions of the Council or Commission. Although the CJEU can give rulings on the interpretation of the recast Judgments Regulation (see Chapter 11), it cannot do so on the modified version of the Brussels Convention which governs allocation of jurisdiction within the UK: *Kleinwort Benson Ltd v Glasgow City Council* (Case C-346/93) [1996] QB 57.

B MANDATORY REFERENCES

Article 267 of the EU Treaty provides: **40.05**

> Where any such question is raised in a case pending before a court or tribunal of a Member State against whose decisions there is no judicial remedy under national law, that court or tribunal shall bring the matter before the Court.

40.06   Accordingly, references are mandatory in courts of last instance. In England, this is generally the Supreme Court, unless by statute or rule some lower court is the final court of appeal. However, even in the Supreme Court there must be a 'question' that needs to be referred. If a point is covered by considerable and consistent authority from the CJEU, such that its answer is obvious, there is no 'question' within the meaning of art 267 (*per* Lord Diplock in *Garland v British Rail Engineering Ltd* [1983] 2 AC 751 at 771; *Srl Cilfit v Ministry of Health* (Case 283/81) [1982] ECR 3415). If it is not necessary to decide either whether EU law applied or the scope of its application to the present case, the reference procedure is not available even in the Supreme Court: *R v Secretary of State for Health, ex p Imperial Tobacco Ltd* [2001] 1 WLR 127.

C DISCRETIONARY REFERENCES

40.07   Making a reference is discretionary for courts below the Supreme Court, and in relation to interim decisions (*Kernkraftwerke Lippe-Ems GmbH v Hauptzollamt Osnabrück* (Case C-5/14) [2016] Ch 181). The EU Treaty, art 267 provides:

> Where such a question is raised before any court or tribunal of a Member State, that court or tribunal may, if it considers that a decision on the question is necessary to enable it to give judgment, request the Court to give a ruling thereon.

40.08   Two questions arise in such cases:

(a) whether a decision on a question of EU law is necessary to enable the court to give judgment; and

(b) if so, whether the court should in the exercise of its discretion order that a reference be made.

40.09   Guidelines on both questions were given by the Court of Appeal in *HP Bulmer Ltd v J Bollinger SA* [1974] Ch 401 by Lord Denning MR at 422–5.

Guidelines for discretionary references

40.10   In *HP Bulmer Ltd v J Bollinger SA* [1974] Ch 401 Lord Denning MR laid down four guidelines as to whether a decision from the CJEU is necessary. They are no more than guidelines, and cannot be considered as binding: *Lord Bethell v SABENA* [1983] 3 CMLR 1.

Whether the point will be conclusive

40.11   Article 267 provides that the court must consider whether 'a decision on the question is necessary to enable it to give judgment'. Lord Denning's view was that the point must be such that, whichever way it is decided, it will be conclusive of the case. This is probably too onerous. Ormrod LJ in *Polydor Ltd v Harlequin Record Shops Ltd* [1982] CMLR 413 said it was sufficient if the point was 'reasonably necessary', and Bingham J in *Customs and Excise Commissioners v ApS Samex* [1983] 1 All ER 1042 said that the question must be substantially, if not quite totally, determinative of the litigation.

Previous ruling

40.12   As Lord Denning said in *HP Bulmer Ltd v J Bollinger SA*:

> In some cases . . . it may be found that the same point—or substantially the same point—has already been decided by the European Court in a previous case. In that event it is not necessary for the English court to decide it. It can follow the previous decision without troubling the European Court.

40.13   This is so even if the point has been decided differently by a national superior court and the CJEU. In such cases the national lower court should follow the previous decision of the

CJEU rather than the decision of the higher national court (*Elchinov v Natsionalna zdrav-noosiguritelna kasa* (Case C-173/09) [2011] PTSR 1308). This is subject to the proviso that, with changing social and economic factors, it may be appropriate to make another reference to the CJEU, because the CJEU is not bound by its earlier decisions.

Acte claire

Lord Denning MR went on to say in *HP Bulmer Ltd v J Bollinger SA*:   **40.14**

> In other cases the English court may consider the point is reasonably clear and free from doubt. In that event there is no need to interpret the Treaty but only to apply it.

A point may be *acte claire* after considering the text, together with decisions of the CJEU and relevant *travaux préparatoires* (*Lucasfilm Ltd v Ainsworth* [2010] Ch 503 at [114], [129]).

This should be read in the light of Lord Diplock's comment in *R v Henn* [1981] AC 850 at 906   **40.15** that the court should not be 'too ready to hold that because the meaning of the English text (which is one of [several official languages of the community each] of equal authority) seems plain no question of interpretation can be involved'. Where a point of EU law has been ruled upon by a domestic court whose decision binds the court in the instant case, a discretionary reference to the CJEU should only be made if there has been some development at the CJEU which indicates the domestic decision should be reviewed (*McCall v Poulton* [2009] PIQR P8).

Deciding the facts first

In general, it is best to decide the facts before making a reference, because it should then   **40.16** be clear whether the question of EU law is necessary, and it enables the CJEU to take into account all the relevant facts when making its ruling.

Factors relevant to the discretion

General guidance has been provided by the CJEU on when it is appropriate to refer mat-   **40.17** ters, and the following factors were identified by Lord Denning MR in *HP Bulmer Ltd v J Bollinger SA* [1974] Ch 401 as being relevant in the exercise of the court's discretion:

(a) delay in obtaining a ruling from the CJEU. Delays have been reduced in recent years;
(b) the importance of not overloading the CJEU;
(c) expense to the parties;
(d) the wishes of the parties. Although clearly relevant, the court can nevertheless make a reference even if both parties object, and, also, there is no such thing as a reference by consent. Ultimately the decision is that of the judge;
(e) difficulty and importance. Simple points should be decided by the English court;
(f) questions involving the comparison of texts in the different languages of the Member States are best decided by the CJEU: *Customs and Excise Commissioners v ApS Samex* [1983] 1 All ER 1042;
(g) questions requiring a panoramic view of the EU and its institutions, the functioning of the common market, or a broad view of the orderly development of the EU should be decided by the CJEU: *Customs and Excise Commissioners v ApS Samex*; and
(h) whether the application for a reference is made in bad faith so as to delay judgment being given: *Customs and Excise Commissioners v ApS Samex*.

Questioning the validity of EU acts

Where a national court intends to question the validity of an act of the institutions, bodies,   **40.18** offices, or agencies of the EU, it must refer the question to the CJEU: *Foto-Frost v Hauptzollamt Lübeck-Ost* (Case 314/85) [1987] ECR 4199. Where the national court has serious doubts about the validity of an EU act on which a national measure is based, the national court may, in an exceptional case, suspend or grant interim relief in respect of the national measure, but it must refer the question of validity to the CJEU: *Zuckerfabrik Süderdithmarschen AG v Hauptzollamt Itzehoe* (Joined Cases C-143/88 and C-92/89) [1991] ECR I-415.

D PROCEDURE IN ENGLAND

40.19   An order referring a question to the CJEU must be made by a judge, the Court of Appeal, or the Supreme Court. It cannot be made by consent, or by a Master or District Judge. It may be made by the court on its own initiative or on the application of any party. Although it can be made at any stage (CPR, r 68.2(1)), it is usual for a reference to be made at trial after the facts have been found. There are special procedures for granting anonymity and for expedited and urgent preliminary rulings (r 68.3 and the European Court Procedure Rules 2012, Official Journal of the European Union, L 265/1, arts 95 and 105–118). Once final judgment has been given the court is *functus officio* and has no power at that stage to order a reference: *Chiron Corporation v Murex Diagnostics Ltd (No 8)* [1995] FSR 309.

40.20   Questions referred for preliminary rulings must concern only the interpretation or validity of a provision of EU law, since the CJEU does not have jurisdiction to interpret national law or to assess its validity. The reference must be set out in a schedule to the order, and must be a self-contained document in a form that can be sent to the CJEU without the order or any separate judgment of the court (r 68.2(4)). The questions should be drafted in a general form, and not in a specific form tied to the facts of the case. They must be drafted as carefully and succinctly as possible, because they will be translated into a number of European languages as part of the referral process (PD 68, para 1.5). A reference exceeding 20 pages will be summarized for the purposes of translation, and it is only the translated summary that is circulated. In addition to the text of the questions referred to the CJEU, the European Court Procedure Rules 2012, art 94, provides that the request for a preliminary ruling must contain:

(a) a summary of the subject matter of the dispute and the relevant findings of fact as determined by the referring court or tribunal, or, at least, an account of the facts on which the questions are based;

(b) the tenor of any national provisions applicable in the case and, where appropriate, the relevant national case law;

(c) a statement of the reasons which prompted the referring court or tribunal to inquire about the interpretation or validity of certain provisions of EU law, and the relationship between those provisions and the national legislation applicable to the main proceedings.

40.21   The EU law provisions relevant to the reference should be identified as accurately as possible, and should include, if need be, a summary of the arguments of the parties to the main proceedings (Recommendations to national courts and tribunals in relation to preliminary ruling proceedings, para 23). The referring court may include a brief statement of its view on the answer to the questions being referred (para 24). The questions themselves must be in a clearly identified section of the reference, preferably at the beginning or the end (para 26). The request must also contain a statement of the grounds for making the request, which should provide the necessary background for a proper understanding of the implications of the case.

40.22   Often the applicant will prepare a draft, or the court may direct one of the parties to do so, but the order will be settled finally by the court (PD 68, para 1.1). The Senior Master will send a copy of the reference to the CJEU (r 68.4(2)) at the Registry of the CJEU in Luxembourg. County Court references are sent to the Senior Master by a court officer for onward transmission to the CJEU.

The CJEU does not encourage national courts to send additional documents in support of a **40.23** reference. If there is a need for supporting documents, they should be listed in the reference itself so that their existence is known to the judges of the CJEU. Where this is necessary, the parties should prepare a bundle of supporting documents to be sent direct to the Registrar of the CJEU (PD 68, para 2.2).

Unless the court orders otherwise, the English proceedings will be stayed pending the rul- **40.24** ing of the CJEU (CPR, r 68.5). If the reference is made by a court other than the Supreme Court, a domestic appeal against the decision to make the reference can be made (*R (Horvath) v Secretary of State for the Environment, Food and Rural Affairs* [2007] NPC 83).

E PROCEDURE IN THE COURT OF JUSTICE OF THE EUROPEAN UNION

The EU Treaty, art 263, provides that the CJEU may review the legality of acts adopted by **40.25** the European Union. Such proceedings may be brought by a Member State, the Council, or the Commission, but may also be brought by a natural or legal person if the Regulation or Decision under review is of direct and individual concern to them. This is usually interpreted as meaning that the applicant, if not a State or the Council or Commission, must be affected by the measure by reason of attributes peculiar to the applicant or a factual situation which differentiates the applicant from all other persons and distinguishes him individually (*Plaumann & Co v Commission of the European Economic Community* (Case 25/62) [1963] ECR 95). In *Union de Pequeños Agricultores v Council of the European Union* (Case C-50/00P) [2003] QB 893 it was held that the CJEU did not have jurisdiction to examine in an individual case whether national procedural rules permitted a challenge to the legality of EU measures. In *Jégo-Quéré et Cie SA v Commission of the European Communities* (Case T-177/01) [2003] QB 854 it was held that where there was no other satisfactory means of address, *Plaumann & Co v Commission of the European Economic Community* would not be followed, and that a person would be regarded as individually concerned if an EU measure affected his legal position in a definite and immediate manner by restricting his rights or imposing obligations on him.

The Registrar of the CJEU notifies the parties, Member States, and the Commission of **40.26** any reference filed. The first stage is written observations. There is then a hearing, where interested parties can present oral argument. The case is then adjourned, during which the Advocate-General delivers an opinion. The European Court Registry stays in contact with the national court until judgment of the CJEU is given, and sends various documents to the national court, including the written observations, the report of the hearing, the opinion of the Advocate-General, and the final judgment.

The ruling binds the domestic court on the interpretation of the EU provision in question **40.27** (European Court Procedure Rules 2012, art 91), but it is for the referring court to apply the relevant provision of EU law, as interpreted by the CJEU, to the facts of the case. The CJEU will exceed its jurisdiction if it disagrees with the findings of fact of the referring court (*Arsenal Football Club plc v Reed* [2003] 3 All ER 865).

F COSTS

The costs of the parties in seeking a ruling from the CJEU are always reserved to the **40.28** domestic court. No order for costs is made in respect of the involvement of Member States or the Commission.

41

JUDGMENTS AND ORDERS

A SETTLEMENTS .41.02

B ORDERS MADE AT HEARINGS 41.08

C FORM OF JUDGMENTS AND
   ORDERS 41.11

D GENERAL RULES RELATING TO DRAWING
   UP ORDERS AND JUDGMENTS 41.37

E REGISTER OF JUDGMENTS 41.49

   Key points summary 41.51

41.01 Although there is likely to be a delay between judgment being pronounced and the judgment being sealed and served, CPR, r 40.7(1) provides that judgment in fact takes effect from the day it was given. After a judgment or order has been pronounced by the court, the next step is to have it drawn up. In *Holtby v Hodgson* (1889) 24 QBD 103 Lord Esher MR said, at 107, 'pronouncing judgment is not entering judgment; something has to be done which will be a record'. The distinction between judgments and orders is that a judgment is the final decision which disposes of a claim (subject to appeal), whereas an order is an interim decision. However, there is no practical difference between the two, and both are enforceable in the same way.

A SETTLEMENTS

41.02 It is very common for parties to agree terms of settlement rather than having their dispute determined by the court. In fact it is rare for claims to proceed all the way to trial for a final determination, given the delays inherent in litigation, the expense of trials, and the financial pressures often experienced by litigants. It is also very common for parties to agree interim orders and directions. This is usually done where the matters in question are uncontentious or where there is no real defence to the order sought being made.

41.03 Where a settlement has been agreed, the parties must decide how to record it. An important consideration in this regard is how the agreement can be enforced in the event of either party failing to abide by its terms.

41.04 The simplest form of judgment provides for immediate payment of the sum agreed together with costs (often on the standard basis, to be the subject of a detailed assessment if not agreed). Enforcement proceedings can be taken on such a judgment on the same day as it is entered. Agreements are not always this simple. Five further ways of recording agreed terms were discussed by Slade J in *Green v Rozen* [1955] 1 WLR 741 (in the context of an agreement reached at the door of the court):

(a) Where a claim is settled on terms as to the payment of money, judgment may be entered for the agreed sum, subject to a stay of execution pending payment of stated instalments. If the instalments fall into arrears, the stay will be lifted, and the judgment creditor can immediately take enforcement proceedings.

(b) A consent order may be drawn up embodying the undertakings of both parties in a series of numbered paragraphs. If any of the terms are not complied with, enforcement may be possible immediately or on application to the court depending on the nature of the term in question.

(c) The agreement may be recorded in a Tomlin order. A Tomlin order has the effect of staying the claim save for the purpose of carrying the terms set out in a schedule to the order into effect. See 41.18ff.

(d) A consent order may be drawn up staying all further proceedings upon the agreed terms. If the agreement is reached immediately before the hearing its terms will usually be endorsed on counsel's briefs and the court will be asked to make a consent order in those terms. Unlike with Tomlin orders, the courts are very unwilling to remove the stay imposed by such orders, so enforcement can usually be effected only by bringing fresh proceedings for breach of the contract embodied in the compromise (*Rofa Sport Management AG v DHL International (UK) Ltd* [1989] 1 WLR 902).

(e) The court may be informed merely that the case has been settled upon terms endorsed on counsel's briefs. This is the most informal way of compromising a claim. Its effect is to supersede the existing claim with the compromise. Any breach can only be enforced by issuing fresh proceedings.

A sixth method was the subject of *Atkinson v Castan* (1991) *The Times*, 17 April 1991, **41.05** where a consent order made 'no order' save as to costs, but set out the agreed terms in recitals. It was held that the claimants were entitled to enforce the terms stated in the recitals without the need to bring a fresh claim.

Where a case is settled in advance of a hearing, each party has a responsibility to inform **41.06** the court so that the time set aside for the hearing can be reallocated to other litigants. Any order giving effect to the settlement should be filed with the listing officer (PD 39A, para 4.2). Often agreements to settle are not reduced into formal orders, although this is desirable, and will be essential if, for example, the parties agree that costs should be assessed by the court. The settlement is itself a contract, so is binding even if it is not made into a formal order of the court.

Settlements agreed after proceedings have been issued should deal with the costs of the **41.07** parties and with the future status of the claim. Options on the latter include entering final judgment, dismissing the claim, granting a stay, or discontinuing or withdrawing it. Care should be taken to ensure that the wording used reflects the parties' intentions, especially as regards any previous interim costs orders. It should be kept in mind that if a claim is discontinued, the claimant is required to pay the defendant's costs unless specific provision is made to the contrary, and that the claimant is not necessarily barred from commencing fresh proceedings in respect of the same claim (see 30.44, 30.46).

B ORDERS MADE AT HEARINGS

Counsel are under a duty to take notes of the court's judgment, and must endorse a note **41.08** of the court's decision on the backsheet of their briefs. Instructing solicitors may use this as the basis for drawing up the court's order, so accuracy in noting is of great importance. If the orders are at all complex, counsel for both sides will often consult each other immediately after the hearing to ensure that both sides are clear on what the court has ordered. Counsel's endorsement of the order is not protected by legal professional privilege.

41.09 In addition, in interim applications the Master, District Judge, or judge will:

(a) initial the relevant paragraphs of the application notice or draft minutes of the order; or
(b) initial together with making amendments; or
(c) endorse the order on the affidavit, witness statement, or application notice in abbreviated form or longhand.

41.10 Judgments in Queen's Bench Division trials are certified by the court associate.

C FORM OF JUDGMENTS AND ORDERS

41.11 The heading of a judgment or order is the same as that for the claim, except that the name of the judge, Master, or District Judge, if any, is included above the names of the parties. Certain consent orders do not need to be approved by a judicial officer. There then follow any recitals. These are followed by the body of the order, which may be short or may be complex. Undertakings tend to be set out in schedules to orders. The terms of the orders must accurately reflect the pronouncement made by the court. Often it is necessary to amplify the court's words, or to put them in imperative form. To simplify this task and to ensure consistency, in both the High Court and the County Court there are many prescribed forms for judgments and orders. There are also model form orders contained in some of the practice directions, such as those for freezing injunctions and search orders in PD 25A. These must be used where applicable, with such variations as the circumstances of the case may require. Where a party has asked for permission to appeal (see 50.13ff), the order must state whether an appeal lies from the judgment, identify the appeal court (with an indication of the appropriate Division if the appeal court is the High Court), and state whether permission to appeal was granted (CPR, r 40.2(4)).

Time limits

41.12 Where an order imposes a time limit for doing any act, the date for compliance must be expressed as a calendar date, and must include the time of day by which the act must be done (CPR, r 2.9(1)). Orders may be made subject to conditions, and may, at the court's discretion, specify the consequences of failing to comply (r 3.1(3)).

Injunction orders and penal notice

41.13 Injunction orders, undertakings given in applications for injunctions, and penal notices are considered at 42.84–42.90.

Consent orders

41.14 Many orders are made 'by consent'. A true consent order is based on a contract between the parties. As such, the contract is arrived at by bargaining between the parties, perhaps in correspondence, and the consent order is simply evidence of that contract: *Wentworth v Bullen* (1840) 9 B & C 840. To be a true consent order there must be consideration passing from each side. If this is the case, then, unlike other orders, it will be set aside only on grounds, such as fraud or mistake, which would justify the setting-aside of a contract: *Purcell v FC Trigell Ltd* [1971] 1 QB 358.

41.15 However, there is a distinction between a real contract and a simple submission to an order (*Pannone LLP v Aardvark Digital Ltd* [2011] 1 WLR 2275). In *Siebe Gorman and Co Ltd v Pneupac Ltd* [1982] 1 WLR 185, Lord Denning MR said at 189:

It should be clearly understood by the profession that, when an order is expressed to be made 'by consent', it is ambiguous . . . One meaning is this: the words 'by consent' may evidence a real contract between the parties. In such a case the court will only interfere with such an order on the same grounds as it would with any other contract. The other meaning is this: the words 'by consent' may mean 'the parties hereto not objecting'. In such a case there is no real contract between the parties. The order can be altered or varied by the court in the same circumstances as any other order that is made by the court without the consent of the parties.

A further distinction relates to family proceedings. In these the legal effect of a consent **41.16** order derives from the order, not the agreement of the parties. Where a family law consent order has been obtained by fraud, misrepresentation, mistake, or as a result of non-disclosure, there will not be a valid consent, which might be a good reason for setting aside the order (*Sharland v Sharland* [2016] AC 871).

Consent judgments and orders must be expressed as being 'by consent' (CPR, r 40.6(7)(b)) **41.17** and must be signed by the legal representatives for each party (or by the litigants in person where this is allowed: see 41.40–41.42). Paragraph 3.4 of PD 40B provides that the signatures of the legal representatives may be those of the solicitors or counsel acting for the parties.

Tomlin orders

Tomlin orders are so named after Tomlin J who, in *Practice Note* [1927] WN 290 set out **41.18** standard wording for orders staying proceedings on terms set out in a schedule. The modern form of Tomlin order (HM Courts and Tribunals Service Guidance, 23 September 2016) says:

AND the parties having agreed to the terms set out in [the attached schedule] [a confidential schedule/agreement dated . . ., copies of which are held by the parties' solicitors]

IT IS BY CONSENT ORDERED that:

(1) all further proceedings in this claim be stayed except for the purpose of carrying the terms of the agreement into effect AND for that purpose the parties have permission to apply [without the need to issue fresh proceedings].

(2) [any provision in respect of costs].

Tomlin orders are used where complex terms are agreed, or where the terms of a compromise **41.19** go beyond the boundaries of the claim (eg *EF Phillips and Sons Ltd v Clarke* [1970] Ch 322), or where it is sought to avoid publicity of the agreement. Where secrecy is desired the parties should use the separate confidential schedule or agreement format; where the terms are merely complex or go beyond the boundaries of the claim the attached (non-confidential) schedule format can be used. The court does not accept confidential schedules for filing.

By PD 40B, para 3.5, any direction for the payment of money out of court or for the pay- **41.20** ment and assessment of costs must be contained in the body of the Tomlin order and not the schedule. The reason is that these two forms of direction require action on the part of the court, and must therefore be included in the public part of the order and not concealed in the schedule. If the amount of costs has been agreed this can be included in the schedule.

Terms in the public part of a Tomlin order can be varied under CPR, r 3.1(7), if there is a mate- **41.21** rial change of circumstances. Terms in the schedule can only be varied in the circumstances allowed by the law of contract, such as fraud, misrepresentation, and mistake (*Community Care North East v Durham County Council* [2012] 1 WLR 338). In the event of the scheduled terms being breached, enforcement is a two-stage process. First, the claim must be restored under the 'liberty to apply' clause, and an order obtained to compel compliance with the term breached. Secondly, if that order is itself breached, enforcement can follow in the usual way.

Money judgments and payment by instalments

41.22 A judgment for the payment of money (including costs) must be complied with within 14 days of the judgment, unless the court specifies some other date for compliance (CPR, r 40.11). It may, for example, instead of requiring immediate payment, impose an order for payment by instalments. A judgment for payment by instalments must state the total amount of the judgment, the amount of each instalment, the number of instalments and the date on which each is to be paid, and to whom the instalments should be paid (PD 40B, para 12).

Counterclaims

41.23 The court has power to give separate judgments when dealing with cases where there are claims and counterclaims. It also has power to order a set-off between the two claims, and simply enter judgment for the balance (CPR, r 40.13(2)). Where it does so, it retains power to make separate costs orders in respect of the claims and counterclaims (r 40.13(3)).

State benefits recoupment

41.24 In personal injuries cases where some or all of the damages are subject to recovery under the Social Security (Recovery of Benefits) Act 1997, the judgment should include a preamble setting out the amounts awarded under each head of damage, and the amount by which it has been reduced in accordance with the Act (PD 40B, para 5.1). The judgment should then provide for entry of judgment and payment of the balance. There are slightly different requirements under para 5.1A where there has been a deductible lump sum payment within s 1A.

Provisional damages

41.25 At common law an award of damages had to be by way of a single sum in compensation. This did not always produce a just result in personal injuries cases involving a risk of the claimant suffering some future deterioration related to the original injury. Although the court would increase the damages awarded to take into account the risk of the future deterioration, the uplift would be only a fraction of the true loss if it occurred, and the claimant would be overcompensated if it did not occur. To remedy this shortcoming, the courts have been given power to award provisional damages by the SCA 1981, s 32A, and the CCA 1984, s 51.

41.26 These sections provide that an award of provisional damages may be made in an:

> ... action for damages for personal injuries in which there is proved or admitted to be a chance that at some definite or indefinite time in the future the injured person will, as a result of the act or omission which gave rise to the cause of action, develop some serious disease or suffer some serious deterioration in his physical or mental condition.

41.27 A provisional damages award has two elements:

(a) immediate damages in respect of the existing injuries, calculated on the assumption that the claimant will not develop the future disease or that the future deterioration will not be suffered; and

(b) an entitlement to return to court to apply for further damages if the disease develops or the deterioration is suffered.

Conditions for awarding provisional damages

There are four conditions: **41.28**

(a) The particulars of claim must include a claim for provisional damages (CPR, r 41.2(1)(a)).
(b) The future disease or deterioration must be to the claimant's physical or mental condition.
(c) The future disease or deterioration must be 'serious'. According to Scott Baker J in *Willson v Ministry of Defence* [1991] 1 All ER 638, this connotes something beyond the ordinary or commonly experienced consequences of the injury in question. It is relevant to consider the effect on the particular claimant, for example a hand injury will be more serious to a concert pianist than to most other claimants. One matter particularly considered in *Willson v Ministry of Defence* was whether possible future osteoarthritis could be the subject of a provisional damages award. An increased risk of the onset of osteoarthritis is a common factor where an accident victim has suffered fractured bones. As such, it is not beyond the ordinary, and Scott Baker J took the view that even if the future risk of osteoarthritis involved a possible need for surgery or a change in employment it would not be 'serious'.
(d) There must be a 'chance' that the future deterioration 'will' be suffered. If this is not admitted by the defendant, it must be proved on the balance of probabilities. The 'chance' that must be proved is one that is measurable as opposed to being fanciful. In *Patterson v Ministry of Defence* [1987] CLY 1194, Simon Brown J found that the claimant had about a 5 per cent risk of developing further pleural thickening, and decided there was a 'plain' chance of that happening for the purposes of making a provisional damages award.

Discretion to award provisional damages

Once these conditions have been established, the court has a discretion whether to make **41.29** a provisional damages award as opposed to a conventional lump sum award. The most important factors are usually the desirability of putting an end to litigation and the possibility of doing better justice by reserving the claimant's right to return to court for further damages. Provisional damages are more appropriate where the risk of the future deterioration is high and the nature of the possible future deterioration is very serious (eg a future risk of severe epilepsy). Provisional damages are also more likely to be awarded if the claimant can point to some clear-cut future event that will trigger the entitlement to return to court for further damages.

Provisional damages orders

A model form of provisional damages judgment is set out in PD 41A. The order: **41.30**

(a) must specify the disease or type of deterioration in respect of which an application may be made for further damages at a future date;
(b) must specify the period within which that application may be made. The period for applying for further damages may be extended; and
(c) may be made in respect of more than one disease or type of deterioration, and may, in respect of each disease or type of deterioration, specify a different period for applying for further damages.

Applying for further damages

If the deterioration occurs, an application for further damages should be made within **41.31** the period specified in the order (as extended from time to time). Only one application for further damages can be made in respect of each disease or deterioration specified in the order. The claimant must give 28 days' notice of the intention to ask for further damages. Within 21 days of the expiry of the 28 days' notice the claimant has to apply to the court for directions. In other respects, the rules relating to applying for interim payments (described in Chapter 25) apply on the application for further damages (CPR, r 41.3(6)).

Periodic payments

41.32 By virtue of an agreement between the Inland Revenue and the Association of British Insurers in 1987, periodic payments made under certain settlements and orders are deemed to be instalments of antecedent debts. The result is that the payments are capital and not income and therefore are not taxable. This tax advantage is obtained by using the whole or a part of the lump sum which would otherwise be available to purchase an annuity. There are four types of annuity which qualify under the scheme:

(a) a basic-term annuity, which runs for a fixed number of years;
(b) an index-linked (ie one which rises with inflation) fixed-term annuity;
(c) an annuity for life or for a minimum number of years (which survives for the claimant's beneficiaries); and
(d) an index-linked life or minimum-term annuity.

41.33 Annuities are bought from life offices. A life office will quote a price of an annuity if given certain details about the claimant (age, sex, medical reports, level of income required, etc.). A quotation will normally remain open for only a limited time. The basic idea is that the tax advantage should be shared between the parties, so that the claimant obtains a more favourable result which will provide more income than that obtainable under a lump sum award, and the defendant will pay less for the annuity than the conventional award. An award in the form of periodic payments can be made where both parties agree, or may be ordered by the court if it awards damages for future pecuniary loss in respect of personal injuries (Damages Act 1996, s 2, as substituted by the Courts Act 2003, s 100). A periodic payments award can only be made if the court is satisfied the continuity of payments under the order is reasonably secure (s 2(3)). It is generally thought that structuring is viable only where damages run into six figures.

41.34 A periodic payments award must specify the annual amount of the award, how each payment is to be made and at what intervals, and the amounts of the main heads of loss (CPR, r 41.8(1)). There are further requirements where the court orders the award to continue after death for the benefit of the claimant's dependants, where the award is to increase or decrease, and where there is an award for substantial capital purchases (r 41.8(2)–(4), supplemented by PD 41B, para 2). Variations may be permitted pursuant to the Damages (Variation of Periodical Payments) Order 2005 (SI 2005/841).

41.35 Where a claim which includes damages for future pecuniary loss is settled on behalf of a claimant under a disability, court approval is required (see 19.16), and the rules in PD 21, paras 6.3–6.9 relating to periodic payments must be complied with.

Fundamentally dishonest personal injury claims

41.36 The Criminal Justice and Courts Act 2015, s 57, provides that the court must dismiss a claim for damages for personal injuries, even if the court finds that the claimant is entitled to damages in respect of the claim, if the court is satisfied on the balance of probabilities that the claimant has been fundamentally dishonest in relation to the primary claim or a related claim (s 57(2)). This includes a duty to dismiss any element of the personal injury claim in respect of which the claimant has not been dishonest (s 57(3)). Damages that would have been awarded must still be recorded in the court's order (s 57(4)), and these are deducted from any costs the claimant is ordered to pay to the defendant (s 57(5)).

D GENERAL RULES RELATING TO DRAWING UP ORDERS AND JUDGMENTS

Rules 40.2(2) and 40.3(1) of the CPR provide that all judgments and orders have to be **41.37** drawn up and sealed by the court, unless it dispenses with the need to do so. Normally the court will take responsibility for drawing up, but:

(a) in the QBD, TCC, and Commercial Court, orders are drawn up by the parties; or
(b) the court may order a party to draw up an order; or
(c) a party may, with the permission of the court, agree to draw up an order; or
(d) the court may direct a party to draw up the order subject to checking by the court before it is sealed; or
(e) the court may direct the parties to file an agreed statement of the terms of the order before the court itself draws up the order; or
(f) the order may be entered administratively by consent, in which event the parties will submit a drawn-up version of their agreement for entry.

Every judgment or order (apart from judgments on admissions, default judgments, and **41.38** consent judgments) must state the name and judicial title of the judge who made it (r 40.2(1)).

A party who is required to draw up a judgment is allowed seven days to file the relevant **41.39** document, together with sufficient copies for all relevant parties, failing which any other party may draw it up and file it for sealing (CPR, rr 40.3(3) and 40.4(1)). Once an order has been drawn up the court will serve sealed copies on the applicant and respondent, and also on any other person the court may order to be served (rr 6.21(2), 40.4(2)). The court is given a specific power by r 40.5 to order service on a litigant as well as the litigant's solicitor.

Entering administrative consent orders

In order to save time and costs, CPR, r 40.6 allows certain types of consent orders to be **41.40** entered by a purely administrative process without the need for obtaining the approval of a judge. However, this process may not be used if any of the parties is a litigant in person (r 40.6(2)(b)).

The types of orders covered are: **41.41**

(a) judgments or orders for the payment of money;
(b) judgments or orders for the delivery-up of goods (other than specific delivery);
(c) orders to dismiss the whole or part of the proceedings;
(d) orders for stays on agreed terms which dispose of the proceedings, including Tomlin orders;
(e) orders setting aside default judgments;
(f) orders for the discharge from liability of any party; and
(g) orders for the payment, waiver, or assessment of costs.

The consent order has to be drawn up in the agreed terms, has to bear the words 'By Con- **41.42** sent', and has to be signed by the solicitors or counsel acting for each of the parties. In cases where terms are annexed in a schedule, provisions dealing with the payment of money out of court and for the payment and assessment of costs should be contained in the body of the order rather than in the schedule (PD 40B, para 3.5).

Consent orders approved by the court

41.43 If an order is agreed between the parties, but includes a provision going beyond the types of orders referred to in 41.41, or if one of the parties is a litigant in person, it will have to be approved by a judge (often a District Judge or Master). The name of the judge will not be known, so the draft will have to include a space for the judge's name and judicial title to be inserted (PD 23A, para 10.3). If all the parties write to the court expressing their consent, the court will treat that as sufficient signing of the consent order (PD 23A, para 10.2). The court will not necessarily make the order in accordance with the agreement between the parties, as the court retains ultimate control, particularly over case management matters. However, it will always take the terms agreed between the parties into account in whatever order it decides to make (see, eg, PD 28, para 3.8).

41.44 In cases where the court's approval must be sought, either party may make the application for approval, and the application may be dealt with without a hearing (CPR, r 40.6(5), (6)).

Chancery Division orders

41.45 Most Chancery Division orders are drawn up by the court, although the court may direct or permit a party to draw them up, and in cases where the terms of an order are agreed between the parties, the agreed statement of the terms of the order will usually be adopted as the order of the court. The *Chancery Guide*, paras 16.36–16.39, also contains a number of detailed provisions relating to consent orders in the Chancery Division.

Redacted judgments

41.46 Judgments delivered giving reasons for the court's decision are usually given in open court and include all details relevant to the reasoning process used by the judge. There are cases where some of the details in the case are highly sensitive. If such details are protected by public interest immunity the relevant government minister may issue a certificate (see 31.71), which will usually result in the protected information being removed ('redacted') from the judgment that is made public. Cogent reasons are required before the court will go behind a ministerial certificate.

Reconsideration of judgments

41.47 The court may reconsider a judgment after it has been pronounced provided this is done before it is drawn up. During this period factual errors can be corrected: *Spice Girls Ltd v Aprilia World Service BV (No 3)* (2000) *The Times*, 12 September 2000. Reconsideration should be sought only in exceptional circumstances (*Stewart v Engel* [2000] 1 WLR 2268). It would be a misuse of the jurisdiction to argue that a judge should reconsider an issue which was in dispute and already argued: that would be to subvert the appeal process: *Companie Noga d'Importation et d'Exportation SA v Abacha* [2001] 3 All ER 513.

Slip rule and appeals

41.48 Subject to the slip rule, once the judgment has been drawn up the judge is *functus officio*, which operates as a bar to further alterations by the judge (*Earl of Malmesbury v Strutt* *and Parker* (2007) 42 EG 294 (CS)). The slip rule (CPR, r 40.2(1)) gives the court power to correct any accidental slip or omission in any judgment. While the slip rule cannot be used to correct matters of substance, it can be used for the purpose of giving effect to the intention of the court (*Swindale v Forder* [2007] 1 FLR 1905). It cannot be used to enable the court to have second or additional thoughts (*Bristol-Myers Squibb Co v Baker Norton Pharmaceuticals Inc (No 2)* [2001] RPC 913), nor where the court and parties never had the point in mind (*Smithkline Beecham plc v Apotex Europe Ltd* [2006] 1 WLR 872). If the error is obvious the court may deal with the application without notice (PD 40B, para 4.3). Opposed applications will normally be listed before the judge who gave the judgment or made the order (para 4.4). Otherwise, a dissatisfied party is limited to its rights on appeal (see Chapter 50).

E REGISTER OF JUDGMENTS

A register of High Court and County Court money judgments is operated by Registry Trust Ltd under powers given by the Courts Act 2003, s 98. Courts provide periodic returns containing details of unsatisfied judgments to Registry Trust Ltd, a not-for-profit company, and the register kept by the company is open to inspection on payment of prescribed fees. The information is regularly used by financial institutions for credit scoring purposes. See <http://www.registry-trust.org.uk>. **41.49**

Tomlin orders are not regarded as money judgments (even if one of the terms provides for the payment of money) and so are not registrable, nor are exempt judgments. Judgments in family proceedings and judgments after contested hearings prior to enforcement are exempt from registration. When a registered judgment has been paid, there is provision for the court to send a certificate of satisfaction to Registry Trust Ltd, after which a note to that effect is entered on the register. Entries are cancelled after six years. **41.50**

KEY POINTS SUMMARY

- Drawing up judgments is a matter of producing an accurate record of the court's decision which can be enforced if not complied with by the relevant parties. **41.51**

- In the QBD, TCC, and Commercial Court drawing up is usually done by the parties. Elsewhere, it is generally done by the court.

- The general format of orders is discussed at 41.11ff.

- Orders with time limits (see 41.12), consent orders (see 41.14–41.17), Tomlin orders (see 41.18–41.21), and 'unless orders' (see 37.15) are particularly important in practice.

42

INTERIM INJUNCTIONS

A JUDGES ABLE TO GRANT
 INJUNCTIONS .42.05
B PRE-ACTION APPLICATIONS FOR
 INTERIM INJUNCTIONS. 42.06
C APPLICATIONS DURING
 PROCEEDINGS 42.18
D PRINCIPLES .42.25
E DEFENCES 42.83

F THE ORDER. .42.84
G UNDERTAKINGS 42.87
H INQUIRY AS TO DAMAGES 42.92
I DISCHARGE. .42.94
J BREACH. 42.95
K EFFECT OF NOT APPLYING FOR
 INTERIM RELIEF 42.97
 Key points summary 42.98

42.01 Interim injunctions are temporary orders made with the purpose of regulating the position between the parties to an action pending trial. An interim injunction is a serious imposition on a respondent, and should be restricted to appropriate cases. Such an order is particularly useful where there is evidence that the respondent's alleged wrongdoing will cause irreparable damage to the applicant's interests in the period between issue of process and trial.

42.02 Interim injunctions should be distinguished from perpetual injunctions, which are final orders, usually made at trial (but see 42.77–42.78), and which continue with no limitation of time. Further distinctions are:

(a) Injunctions made without notice. These are a form of interim injunction, usually made in circumstances of urgency, which are expressed to continue in force for a limited period, usually a few days, sufficient for the application to be renewed on a hearing with notice being given to the respondent.

(b) Mandatory injunctions require the other side to do specified acts (eg to deliver up documents or to demolish a wall), whereas prohibitory injunctions require the other side to refrain from doing specified acts (eg publishing a libel or breaching a confidence). It is the substance of the order (rather than its wording) which makes it mandatory or prohibitory. Both types of injunction can be granted on an interim basis, but the courts are more wary of granting mandatory orders (see 42.81).

(c) Where the other side has not yet committed a civil wrong, but has threatened to do so in the future, it is possible to obtain an interim injunction on a *quia timet* basis.

42.03 Interim injunctions can be applied for even in claims allocated to the small claims track (CPR, r 27.2(1)).

42.04 Any party to proceedings can apply for an interim injunction, and can do so whether or not a claim for the injunction was included in that party's originating process or statement of case (CPR, r 25.1(4)).

A JUDGES ABLE TO GRANT INJUNCTIONS

Given the serious nature of injunctions and the consequences of breach, interim injunctions **42.05** are as a matter of practice usually made to a judge rather than a Master or District Judge. There are several exceptions and restrictions. The detailed rules are to be found in PD 25A, paras 1.1–1.4, together with PD 2B. For example, search orders must be sought from High Court judges, and at the other end of the scale, County Court District Judges can grant injunctions in cases where they have trial jurisdiction (small claims and fast track cases).

B PRE-ACTION APPLICATIONS FOR INTERIM INJUNCTIONS

Rule 25.2(1) of the CPR empowers the court to grant an interim injunction before a claim **42.06** form has been issued. By CPR, r 25.2(2), an interim injunction can be obtained prior to issue of proceedings provided:

(a) no rule or practice direction prohibits the granting of the order;
(b) the matter is urgent or it is otherwise desirable to make the order in the interests of justice;
(c) in the less common circumstance in which the applicant is an intended defendant, the defendant has obtained the court's permission to make the application. The defendant cannot without this permission apply for an interim remedy prior to the filing of an acknowledgment of service or defence (which can only happen after issue).

Urgent cases

A case is 'urgent' where there is a true impossibility in giving the requisite three clear days' **42.07** notice or in arranging for the issue of process. An 'impossibility' resulting from delay on the part of the claimant will not suffice: *Bates v Lord Hailsham of St Marylebone* [1972] 1 WLR 1373. There has to be a very good reason for departing from the general rule that notice must be given (*Moat Housing Group-South Ltd v Harris* [2006] QB 606), such as an element of threat or damage that requires the immediate intervention of the court (*Mayne Pharma (USA) Inc v Teva UK Ltd* (2004) LTL 3/12/04). The relief sought must be limited to that which is necessary and proportionate given the fact the application is made without notice (*Moat Housing Group-South Ltd v Harris*).

Where a case is urgent, the usual procedural requirements are relaxed in so far as is neces- **42.08** sary to do justice between the parties. For example:

(a) The application may be made before issue of process.
(b) The application may be made without notice. However, it is still incumbent on the applicant to give the other side such notice as is possible, such as by telephone or by fax unless secrecy is essential (eg on applications for search orders and freezing injunctions). A defendant who is notified in this way may decide to attend the hearing, a situation which is known as an 'opposed hearing without notice'.
(c) Informal evidence may be relied on. This may be in the form of a draft witness statement, correspondence, or even simply facts related to the court by counsel on instructions. The applicant is usually required to undertake to put the oral facts and evidence into formal witness statements so there can be no confusion at any later stage (*Attorney-General v British Broadcasting Corporation* [2007] EWCA Civ 280).
(d) Although very much a last resort, the court may make an order without a draft having been prepared by counsel on behalf of the applicant.

Procedure on pre-action applications

42.09   There is a special form for applying for injunctions (form N16A), although PD 4 permits the use of the general application notice (form N244). It must include the title of the proposed claim, the full name of the applicant, and, as the applicant is not yet a party, the applicant's address for service. It should contain a request for a hearing or ask that the application be dealt with without a hearing (PD 23A, para 2.1). Paragraph 2.1 of PD 25A provides that an application notice for an interim injunction should:

(a) state the order sought; and
(b) give the date, time, and place of the hearing.

42.10   Many pre-action applications for injunctions are made in cases of real urgency, and the court may in such cases exercise its power in CPR, r 23.3(2)(b), to dispense with the requirement for an application notice. If the court dispenses with the application notice, it will usually do so only for the purposes of the initial hearing. Paragraph 5.1(4) of PD 25A provides that in these circumstances the court will, unless it orders otherwise, require an undertaking from the applicant to file an application notice and pay the appropriate fee on the same or the next working day.

42.11   An application for an interim remedy must be supported by evidence, unless the court orders otherwise (CPR, r 25.3(2)). The evidence required is discussed further in 42.21–42.23.

42.12   The application should be made in the court in which the substantive proceedings are likely to be issued unless 'there is good reason to make the application to a different court' (CPR, r 23.2(4)).

42.13   Especially where the terms of the injunction sought are complex, it is good practice to attach a draft of the order to the application notice and to provide it on computer disk or digital storage device (PD 25A, para 2.4). Disks are not required in the Commercial Court, because orders there are drawn up by the parties (*Commercial Court Guide*, para F1.3).

Arrangements for pre-action injunction hearings

42.14   Pre-action interim injunction applications will almost always be considered at a hearing but without full (or any) notice to the respondent. If they arise during or shortly before the ordinary times when the court is sitting, the hearing will take place in court as soon as the circumstances permit. This means that generally such applications are heard before other matters that are listed, either as soon as the court sits in the morning or immediately after lunch. Sometimes urgent applications arise during the course of the morning or afternoon in circumstances where it is not possible to wait to the beginning of the next session. If the case is sufficiently urgent the court will invariably interrupt whatever it is doing at a convenient moment so that it can hear the urgent application.

42.15   On other occasions the need for a pre-action interim injunction may arise at a time when it is not possible to wait until the next occasion when the court will be sitting. If the application is of extreme urgency it may be dealt with by telephone (PD 25A, para 4.2). If the problem has arisen outside office hours, the applicant should telephone either the High Court asking to be put in touch with the clerk to the appropriate duty judge (or the appropriate area Circuit Judge where known), or the urgent court business officer of the appropriate circuit, who will contact the local judge.

42.16   If the facilities are available, a draft of the order sought will usually be required to be sent by fax to the duty judge who will be dealing with the application. Telephone hearings are available only if the applicant is acting by solicitors or counsel (PD 25A, para 4.5(5)).

Pre-action orders

If a pre-action order is granted, the court may give directions requiring a claim to be commenced (CPR, r 25.2(3)). As the application will invariably have been made without notice to the respondent, a number of undertakings will usually be built into the order to protect the respondent (see 42.89). The order must contain a statement of the right to apply under r 23.10 to set aside or vary the order within seven days after it is served. Where possible the claim form should be served with the injunction order (PD 25A, para 4.4(2)). **42.17**

C APPLICATIONS DURING PROCEEDINGS

Procedure

Applications for interim injunctions after proceedings have been issued are made by issuing an application notice (in form N16A or N244) supported by written evidence. The applicant will generally also need to provide an electronic draft order in Word format and a skeleton argument. **42.18**

Where the court is to serve the application, sufficient copies should be provided for the court and each respondent (PD 25A, para 2.3). Service should be effected as soon as possible, and in any event not less than three clear days before the hearing. **42.19**

Respondents to applications made on notice should disclose their evidence in reply in sufficient time in advance of the hearing to avoid an adjournment. If little more than the minimum three clear days' notice has been given by the applicant, the court may be prepared to give directions as to the service of evidence on the first hearing, but it may well impose sanctions if it considers the need to give directions was caused by the default of either party. **42.20**

Evidence in support of an application for an interim injunction

An application for an interim injunction must be supported by evidence unless the court orders otherwise (CPR, r 25.3(2)). The evidence must cover the substantive issues and also, if the application is without notice, explain why notice has not been given (r 25.3(3); PD 25A, para 3.4). The evidence should also address the relevant principles for granting injunctive relief (see later). **42.21**

Paragraph 3.3 of PD 25A states that unless the court or an Act requires evidence by affidavit, evidence is to be: **42.22**

(a) by witness statement;
(b) set out in the application, provided it is verified by a statement of truth; or
(c) set out in a statement of case, provided it is verified by a statement of truth.

Paragraph 3.3 of PD 25A provides that 'the evidence must set out the facts on which the applicant relies for the claim being made against the respondent, including all material facts of which the court should be made aware'. This provision is not restricted to applications without notice. It appears to import at least some of the concepts of the duty of full and frank disclosure. The 'material facts of which the court should be made aware' are likely to be more wide-ranging in an application made without notice than in one made with the required three clear days' notice. Nevertheless, this paragraph of the practice direction may be intended to make parties address adverse facts in their evidence, even where the application is on notice and the respondent has a clear ability to file evidence and make representations at the hearing. **42.23**

Hearing of interim injunction applications

42.24 Normally the hearing of an application for an interim injunction will be listed in the usual way for disposal in public (CPR, r 39.2). There are exceptional circumstances in which the hearing will be in private, such as where the hearing involves confidential information, or the interests of children or protected parties.

D PRINCIPLES

Just and convenient

42.25 As with all forms of equitable relief, the granting of interim injunctions is a matter within the discretion of the court. The fundamental principle is contained in the SCA 1981, s 37(1) (which also applies in the County Court by virtue of CCA 1984, s 38), which provides:

> The High Court may by order (whether interlocutory or final) grant an injunction or appoint a receiver in all cases in which it appears to the court to be just and convenient to do so.

Substantive cause of action

42.26 Injunctions are only remedies, so can usually be granted only if the applicant has a substantive cause of action. As stated by Lord Diplock in *The Siskina* [1979] AC 210:

> A right to obtain an [interim] injunction is not a cause of action. It cannot stand on its own. It is dependent upon there being a pre-existing cause of action against the defendant arising out of an invasion, actual or threatened by him, of a legal or equitable right of the [claimant] for the enforcement of which the defendant is amenable to the jurisdiction of the court. The right to obtain an [interim] injunction is merely ancillary and incidental to the pre-existing cause of action.

42.27 In *The Siskina* the claimant had a cause of action against the defendant, but it was actionable only in a foreign country. It was therefore held that the English courts had no jurisdiction to grant an interim injunction to protect the applicant's position. The actual result in *The Siskina* has been reversed by the CJJA 1982, s 25 (see 11.62). The underlying principle was restated by Lord Brandon of Oakbrook in *South Carolina Insurance Co v Assurantie Maatschappij 'De Zeven Provincien' NV* [1987] AC 24, where, in relation to domestic proceedings, he said the court has a discretion to grant injunctions in only two situations:

(a) where a party has invaded or threatened to invade a legal or equitable right of another party; or

(b) where a party has behaved or threatened to behave in an unconscionable manner.

Injunctions in support of the criminal law

42.28 The High Court has jurisdiction to grant injunctions in support of the criminal law. In *Attorney-General v Chaudry* [1971] 1 WLR 1614 Lord Denning MR said:

> There are many statutes which provide penalties for breach of them—penalties which are enforceable by means of a fine—or even imprisonment—but this has never stood in the way of the High Court granting an injunction. Many a time people have found it profitable to pay a fine and go on breaking the law. In all such cases the High Court has been ready to grant an injunction . . .
>
> Whenever Parliament has enacted a law and given a particular remedy for the breach of it, such remedy being in an inferior court, nevertheless the High Court always has reserve power

to enforce the law so enacted by way of an injunction or declaration or other suitable remedy. The High Court has jurisdiction to ensure obedience to the law whenever it is just and convenient so to do.

The *American Cyanamid* guidelines

In *American Cyanamid Co v Ethicon Ltd* [1975] AC 396 Lord Diplock laid down guidelines on how the court's discretion to grant interim injunctions should be exercised in the usual types of cases. Although these guidelines are of great authority, they must not be read as if they were statutory provisions, and in practice they are applied with some degree of flexibility. However, it is common for judges to give reasoned judgments in interim injunction cases following the sequence of steps set out by Lord Diplock (eg *Rottenberg v Monjack* [1993] BCLC 374). The court must also be careful to apply the overriding objective, and to grant an injunction only if it is 'just and convenient'. **42.29**

The underlying purpose of the guidelines is to enable the court to make an order that will do justice between the parties, whichever way the decision goes at trial, while interfering with the parties' freedom of action to the minimum extent necessary (*Polaroid Corporation v Eastman Kodak Co* [1977] RPC 379 *per* Buckley LJ at 395). **42.30**

Serious question to be tried

Before *American Cyanamid Co v Ethicon Ltd*, the courts would grant an interim injunction only if the applicant could establish a *prima facie* case on the merits. Consequently, the courts needed to consider the respective merits of the parties' cases in some detail. This encouraged the filing of detailed written evidence supported by voluminous exhibits, and resulted in lengthy interim hearings. As Lord Diplock said at 407: **42.31**

> It is no part of the court's function at this stage of the litigation to try to resolve conflicts of evidence on affidavits as to facts on which the claims of either party may ultimately depend nor to decide difficult questions of law which call for detailed argument and mature consideration.

Therefore, the court needs to be satisfied only that there is a serious question to be tried on the merits. The result is that the court is required to investigate the merits to a limited extent only. All that needs to be shown is that the claimant's cause of action has substance and reality. Beyond that, it does not matter if the claimant's chance of winning is 90 per cent or 20 per cent: *Mothercare Ltd v Robson Books Ltd* [1979] FSR 466 *per* Megarry V-C at 474; *Alfred Dunhill Ltd v Sunoptic SA* [1979] FSR 337 *per* Megaw LJ at 373. **42.32**

This is not a difficult hurdle to surmount. In *Porter v National Union of Journalists* [1980] IRLR 404, the issue was whether a strike instruction by the union affected a majority of its members. If it did, the union's rule book required a ballot. Neither party adduced accurate figures of the total numbers in the union, nor of the numbers affected by the strike instruction. It was held there was a serious question to be tried. **42.33**

On the other hand, if there is no serious question to be tried on the substantive claim, for example if the claim is hopeless, the injunction must be refused (*National Commercial Bank Jamaica Ltd v Olint Corporation Ltd* [2009] 1 WLR 1405). *Morning Star Co-operative Society Ltd v Express Newspapers Ltd* [1979] FSR 113 should be regarded as not having passed this hurdle. At the time of the case, the *Daily Star* newspaper was about to be launched. The claimant alleged that it was going to be passed off as the established *Morning Star* newspaper. Apart from the fact that they were both newspapers and had the word 'Star' in their names, they were different in about every other respect. As Foster J commented, 'only a moron in a hurry would be misled' into thinking that the *Daily Star* was the *Morning Star*, so the claimant had failed to show a serious issue to be tried on the alleged cause of action. **42.34**

Adequacy of damages to the applicant

42.35 If there is a serious question to be tried on the merits of the substantive claim, the court should then consider whether the applicant will be adequately compensated by an award of damages at trial. The test was stated in the following way by Lord Diplock in *American Cyanamid Co v Ethicon Ltd* at 408:

> If damages in the measure recoverable at common law would be an adequate remedy and the defendant would be in a financial position to pay them, no [interim] injunction should normally be granted.

42.36 Damages will often be an adequate remedy for the claimant in claims for breach of contract, but the position regarding claims in respect of contracts of employment is not completely free from doubt: see *Powell v Brent London Borough Council* [1988] ICR 176. However, damages will be inadequate if:

(a) The defendant is unlikely to be able to pay the sum likely to be awarded at trial.
(b) The wrong is irreparable, for example loss of the right to vote.
(c) The damage is non-pecuniary, for example libel, nuisance, trade secrets.
(d) There is no available market. In *Howard E Perry and Co Ltd v British Railways Board* [1980] 1 WLR 1375 the defendant refused to allow the claimant to remove a consignment of steel during a steelworkers' dispute. As steel was otherwise unobtainable at the time, damages were not an adequate remedy.
(e) Damages would be difficult to assess. Examples are loss of goodwill (*Foseco International Ltd v Fordath Ltd* [1975] FSR 507), disruption of business (*Evans Marshall and Co Ltd v Bertola SA* [1973] 1 WLR 349), and where the defendant's conduct has the effect of killing off a business before it is established (*Mitchelstown Co-operative Society Ltd v Société des Produits Nestlé SA* [1989] FSR 345).
(f) Liquidated damages provided by a term of a contract are lower than the probable actual loss suffered through a breach of contract (*Bath and North East Somerset District Council v Mowlem plc* [2015] 1 WLR 785).

42.37 As where the claimant fails to show a serious question to be tried, if damages would be an adequate remedy that is the end of the matter and the injunction must be refused.

Applicant's undertaking in damages being adequate protection

42.38 Subject to some limited exceptions, an undertaking in damages is always required when an interim injunction is granted. By the undertaking the claimant is required to compensate the defendant or any other person served with the order for any loss caused by the injunction if it later appears that the injunction was wrongly granted. The normal form of undertaking just gives protection to the defendant. There is an extended undertaking which also protects third parties, and the court should consider whether this extended version should be used (PD 25A, para 5.2). Its purpose is to provide a safeguard for the defendant or other person who may be unjustifiably prevented from doing something it was entitled to do. As stated in *Wakefield v Duke of Buccleugh* (1865) 12 LT 628, this assists the court ' . . . in doing that which was its great object, viz. abstaining from expressing any opinion on the merits of the case until the hearing'.

42.39 In *American Cyanamid Co v Ethicon Ltd* Lord Diplock said at 408:

> If damages in the measure recoverable under such an undertaking would be an adequate remedy and the [claimant] would be in a financial position to pay them, there would be no reason upon this ground to refuse an [interim] injunction. It is where there is doubt as to the adequacy of the respective remedies in damages available to either party or to both, that the question of balance of convenience arises.

The way it was put by Lord Hoffmann in *National Commercial Bank Jamaica Ltd v Olint* **42.40**
Corporation Ltd [2009] 1 WLR 1405 was that if there is a serious issue to be tried, and
the claimant could be prejudiced by the acts or omissions of the defendant pending trial,
and the claimant's undertaking in damages would provide the defendant with an adequate
remedy if it transpires that his freedom of action should not have been restrained, an
interim injunction should ordinarily be granted. If despite this the court goes on to consider the balance of convenience, the fact that the defendant is adequately protected will
be a substantial factor in favour of granting the injunction: see *Bunn v British Broadcasting Corporation* [1998] 3 All ER 552. If the undertaking does not adequately protect the
defendant, although that is a reason for refusing the injunction, normally the court will
go on to consider the balance of convenience. Even a freezing injunction has been granted
in favour of a legally aided claimant (who obviously could not give a valuable undertaking in damages) where otherwise it was a proper case for granting the injunction: *Allen v
Jambo Holdings Ltd* [1980] 1 WLR 1252. In extreme cases, however, the court will refuse
the injunction without considering the balance of convenience. *Morning Star Co-operative
Society Ltd v Express Newspapers Ltd* was such a case, referred to at 42.34. In addition to
the weak cause of action, the claimant had assets of £170,000 and liabilities of £260,000,
so there was no realistic chance of it being able to honour the undertaking, especially as the
defendants were likely to suffer appreciable, unquantifiable, damages.

Balance of convenience

Most injunction cases are determined on the balance of convenience. In *American Cyana-* **42.41**
mid Co v Ethicon Ltd Lord Diplock said at 408:

> . . . it would be unwise to attempt even to list all the various matters which may need to be
> taken into consideration in deciding where the balance lies, let alone to suggest the relative
> weight to be attached to them. These will vary from case to case.

This is often an exercise in seeking to determine whether granting or refusing the injunction **42.42**
will cause irremediable prejudice, and to what extent (*National Commercial Bank Jamaica
Ltd v Olint Corporation Ltd* [2009] 1 WLR 1405). Among the matters the court may take
into account are:

(a) the prejudice the claimant may suffer if no injunction is granted or the defendant may
    suffer if it is;
(b) the likelihood of such prejudice actually occurring;
(c) the extent to which it may be compensated by an award of damages or enforcement of
    the undertaking in damages;
(d) the likelihood of either party being able to satisfy such an award; and
(e) the likelihood that the injunction will turn out to have been wrongly granted or
    withheld.

The claimants in *American Cyanamid Co v Ethicon Ltd* sought an interim injunction to **42.43**
prevent the defendants marketing a surgical suture alleged to be in breach of patent. The
claimants' patented suture had recently been introduced, and the claimants were expand-
ing their market. The defendants' product had not at that time been introduced. They
asserted that their product did not infringe the claimants' patent, alternatively that the patent was invalid. If the injunction had been granted no factories would have closed, but if
refused the claimants might have failed to increase their market and would effectively have
lost the benefit of their patent. Therefore, the balance favoured the claimants.

A claimant can reduce the potential injustice to the defendant by drafting the terms of the **42.44**
injunction as narrowly as is consistent with preserving the claimant's interests, or by offering undertakings to provide extra safeguards for the defendant.

42.45 Each case turns on its own facts, but matters found to be important include:

(a) being deprived of employment (*Fellowes and Son v Fisher* [1976] QB 122);

(b) damage to business through picketing (*Hubbard v Pitt* [1976] QB 142);

(c) damage to the goodwill of a business (*Associated Newspapers plc v Insert Media Ltd* [1991] 1 WLR 571);

(d) closing down the defendant's business, and the number of people who might lose their jobs (*Lawrence v Fen Tigers* [2014] AC 822. Closing a factory was described as being catastrophic in *Potters-Ballotini Ltd v Weston-Baker* [1977] RPC 202);

(e) although the fact that an injunction may result in a company being wound up is a weighty matter, in *Astor Chemicals Ltd v Synthetic Technology Ltd* [1990] BCLC 1 this was outweighed by other considerations, particularly the fact that the company wanted to continue trading on a very speculative venture while hopelessly insolvent;

(f) the number of people adversely affected by the defendant's activities (*Lawrence v Fen Tigers* [2014] AC 822);

(g) the public benefit of the defendant's activities (*Lawrence v Fen Tigers* [2014] AC 822 (sporting activities); *Roussel Uclaf v GD Searle and Co Ltd* [1977] FSR 125 (drug with life-saving qualities));

(h) disruption to third parties, such as through the suspension of a public procurement exercise (*B2NET Ltd v HM Treasury* (2010) 128 Con LR 53);

(i) the length of time to trial (the shorter, the stronger the argument for granting the injunction) (*Wake Forest University Health Sciences v Smith and Nephew plc* [2009] EWHC 45 (Pat)); and

(j) a failure by the claimant to respond to a letter from the defendant frankly stating its plans and enclosing sample containers, use of which is alleged by the claimant to amount to passing off (*Dalgety Spillers Foods Ltd v Food Brokers Ltd* [1994] FSR 504).

Status quo

42.46 In *American Cyanamid Co v Ethicon Ltd* [1975] AC 396 Lord Diplock said at 408 that, in considering the balance of convenience: 'Where other factors appear to be evenly balanced it is a counsel of prudence to take such measures as are calculated to preserve the status quo'. In *Garden Cottage Foods Ltd v Milk Marketing Board* [1984] AC 130 at 140, Lord Diplock said the relevant status quo is the state of affairs existing in the period immediately preceding the issue of the claim form or, if there is unreasonable delay between issuing the claim and issuing the application for the interim injunction, the period immediately before the application. It is clear that excessive weight must not be placed on the word 'immediately'. Lord Diplock continued: 'The duration of that period since the state of affairs last changed must be more than minimal, having regard to the total length of the relationship between the parties in respect of which the injunction is granted; otherwise the state of affairs before the last change would be the relevant status quo.' A ten-day period between the defendant commencing activities infringing the claimant's intellectual property rights and issuing the claim was ignored as minimal in *Play It Ltd v Digital Bridges Ltd* [2005] EWHC 1001 (Ch) at [38], [39]. Nevertheless, it behoves the claimant to act quickly.

Special factors

42.47 As Lord Diplock said in *American Cyanamid Co v Ethicon Ltd* at 409, 'there may be many special factors to be taken into consideration [in the balance of convenience] in the particular circumstances of individual cases'. If American Cyanamid Co had been refused interim relief, but had established its claim at trial, it was probable that it would have been commercially impracticable for it to have insisted on Ethicon's sutures then being withdrawn, as doctors would have by then become used to using Ethicon's new sutures.

Merits of the claim

In *American Cyanamid Co v Ethicon Ltd* Lord Diplock said at 409 that, as a last resort: **42.48**

> ... it may not be improper to take into account in tipping the balance the relative strength of each party's case as revealed by the affidavit evidence adduced on the hearing of the application. This, however, should be done only where it is apparent upon the facts disclosed by evidence as to which there is no credible dispute that the strength of one party's case is disproportionate to that of the other party. The court is not justified in embarking upon anything resembling a trial of the action upon conflicting affidavits in order to evaluate the strength of either party's case.

An example of a case where the merits were considered under this principle is *Cambridge* **42.49** *Nutrition Ltd v British Broadcasting Corporation* [1990] 3 All ER 523. The merits were considered, because the incompensable damage to each party did not differ widely.

There are some judges who, despite the principles already set out, in exceptional cases **42.50** weigh the respective merits of the parties' cases as disclosed in the written evidence and exhibits in deciding whether or not to grant interim injunctive relief. This approach finds expression in the judgment of Laddie J in *Series 5 Software Ltd v Clarke* [1996] 1 All ER 853. In his judgment Laddie J said the following were the guidelines to be adopted on a proper analysis of the *American Cyanamid* decision:

(a) that interim injunctions are discretionary and all the facts of the case must be considered;
(b) there are no fixed rules, and the relief must be kept flexible;
(c) the court should rarely attempt to resolve complex issues of disputed fact or law;
(d) important factors in exercising the jurisdiction to grant interim injunctions are:
  (i) the extent to which damages are likely to be an adequate remedy to either side, and the ability of the other party to pay;
  (ii) the balance of convenience;
  (iii) maintaining the status quo; and
  (iv) any clear view the court may reach about the relative strength of the parties' cases.

Exceptional cases

There are some well-settled categories of cases where the *American Cyanamid* guidelines **42.51** are not applied. The usual difference is that in these cases the courts will investigate the merits of the cause of action. How these various cases can be reconciled with *American Cyanamid Co v Ethicon Ltd* [1975] AC 396 is a question of some theoretical controversy. Suggestions are that they are examples of the 'special factors' mentioned by Lord Diplock; that the *American Cyanamid* guidelines apply only where the facts are in dispute; that *American Cyanamid* applies only where a trial is likely; and that the existence of some or all of the categories were not directly considered by Lord Diplock.

Final disposal of the claim

In *NWL Ltd v Woods* [1979] 1 WLR 1294 Lord Diplock said at 1306: **42.52**

> *American Cyanamid Co. v Ethicon Ltd* [1975] AC 396 ... was not dealing with a case in which the grant or refusal of an injunction at that stage would, in effect, dispose of the action finally in favour of whichever party was successful in the application, because there would be nothing left on which it was in the unsuccessful party's interest to proceed to trial.

Two questions arise (*Cayne v Global Natural Resources plc* [1984] 1 All ER 225; *Channel* **42.53** *Tunnel Group Ltd v Balfour Beatty Construction Ltd* [1993] AC 334):

(a) on the assumption that the injunction is refused, and taking into account the likely length of time it will take to get to trial and the probable factual situation at that time, is there any realistic possibility that the claimant will wish to proceed to trial? Assertions by claimants that they will in any event proceed to trial to recover damages may be disregarded if in reality a trial would be a meaningless gesture: *Lansing Linde Ltd v Kerr* [1991] 1 WLR 251; and

(b) on the assumption that the injunction is granted, is there any realistic prospect of the defendant insisting on going to trial to vindicate its defence and having the injunction discharged?

Where neither party has a real interest in going to trial, the interim application will finally determine the claim.

42.54 Where the interim application will finally dispose of the claim, the court has to consider the underlying merits of the claim (Lord Diplock in *NWL Ltd v Woods* at 1307). The degree to which the claimant must establish those merits varies with the circumstances. Thus, in *Cayne v Global Natural Resources plc*, the claimants, who were shareholders in the defendant company, sought injunctions, *inter alia*, to restrain the company from implementing a merger transaction without first obtaining the approval of the company in general meeting. There was no realistic prospect of a trial, because by the time the claim could be tried either the deal would have been implemented or the general meeting would have taken place. The claimants alleged that the purpose of the transaction was to maintain the directors in office. The defendants served evidence which, if true, completely destroyed the claimants' case. Instead of applying the *American Cyanamid* guidelines the court had to apply the broad principle of doing its best to avoid injustice. Eveleigh LJ said at 233:

> . . . it would be wrong to run the risk of causing an injustice to a defendant who is being denied the right to trial where the defence put forward has been substantiated by affidavits and a number of exhibits.

42.55 Accordingly, an injunction would have been granted only if the claimants' case was overwhelming on its merits. It was not, so the injunction was refused. Conversely, the case of *Lansing Linde Ltd v Kerr* concerned an application for an injunction to enforce a covenant in restraint of trade. It was not possible for the claim to be tried before the expiry of the period of the restraint; the claimants were not realistically interested in pursuing their claim for damages; so there was no prospect of a trial. Staughton LJ said that in the circumstances justice simply required 'some assessment of the merits . . . more than merely a serious issue to be tried'.

Defamation claims

42.56 Since *Bonnard v Perryman* [1891] 2 Ch 269, it has been held that interim injunctions will not generally be granted in defamation cases if the defendant intends to defend on the basis that the statement complained of is substantially true (Defamation Act 2013, s 2). In *Bestobell Paints Ltd v Bigg* [1975] FSR 421 it was held that this principle is unaltered by *American Cyanamid Co v Ethicon Ltd* [1975] AC 396, because of the overriding public interest in protecting the right to free speech. In *Greene v Associated Newspapers Ltd* [2005] QB 972, it was held that the rule in *Bonnard v Perryman* is also unaltered by the Human Rights Act 1998, s 12(3) (see 42.60) or by the Human Rights Act 1998, s 6 (which requires public authorities to act in ways compatible with the Convention: see 4.34). There are two conditions:

(a) The defendant must state in the evidence in reply that it is intended to set up the defence that the statement is substantially true.
(b) The alleged libel must not be obviously untruthful. The claimant may accordingly adduce evidence to prove the falsity of the words published. However, the burden on the claimant is a heavy one: *Holley v Smyth* [1998] QB 726.

Similar principles probably apply where the defendant intends to rely on the defences of **42.57** honest opinion (Defamation Act 2013, s 3) or public interest (s 4). This was the approach taken before the Defamation Act 2013 in *Fraser v Evans* [1969] 1 QB 349 (fair comment on a matter of public interest, now replaced with honest opinion) and *Harakas v Baltic Mercantile and Shipping Exchange Ltd* [1982] 1 WLR 958 (qualified privilege, where the injunction would be refused unless there was overwhelming evidence of malice).

Privacy and confidentiality

Related to defamation claims are proceedings to restrain newspapers from publishing **42.58** articles that invade the claimant's privacy. Activities such as family holidays and sporting activities are part of a person's private recreation time and are protected by the European Convention on Human Rights, art 8 (*Hannover v Germany* (Application No 59320/00) (2005) 40 EHRR 1). The question is whether there was a reasonable expectation of privacy. Photographs taken at a private wedding are therefore protected (*OBG Ltd v Allan* [2008] 1 AC 1). Photographs of a child taken in a public place, such as a street or on a shopping trip, may be protected, depending on a balance of relevant factors (*Murray v Express Newspapers plc* [2009] Ch 481). Evidence of harm to the child is not an essential element (*Weller v Associated Newspapers Ltd* [2016] 1 WLR 1541). Salacious details of a past personal relationship are usually regarded as private (*Donald v Ntuli* [2011] 1 WLR 294). Interim injunctions in these cases should normally be governed by *American Cyanamid*, as adapted by the Human Rights Act 1998, s 12(3) (see 42.60).

In most cases a duty of confidence arises out of a transaction or relationship between the **42.59** parties. For example, an employee may have expressly agreed to maintain an employer's confidences, or sensitive information may have been communicated in a letter marked 'private and confidential' (*Prince of Wales v Associated Newspapers Ltd* [2008] Ch 57). A duty of confidentiality expressly assumed under a contract should be given greater weight than an implied duty arising from the general principles of equity (*London Regional Transport v Mayor of London* [2003] EMLR 4).

Freedom of expression

Article 10(1) of the European Convention on Human Rights provides that everyone has **42.60** the right to freedom of expression. This right is subject to safeguards in art 10(2), which include restrictions for the protection of the reputation or rights of others. Protection of a defendant's art 10 rights has three elements under the Human Rights Act 1998. First, s 12(2) imposes an obligation on the claimant to take all practical steps to inform the respondent of any application to restrain a publication. Secondly, s 12(3) provides that no relief to restrain publication before trial which might affect the art 10(1) right is to be allowed 'unless the court is satisfied that the applicant is likely to establish that the publication should not be allowed'. In *Cream Holdings Ltd v Banerjee* [2005] 1 AC 253 it was held that s 12(3) requires a flexible approach to be taken. In most cases the applicant must establish a case which will probably succeed (the usual standard of proof at trial). In keeping with the flexible approach, there will be some exceptional cases where a lesser degree of likelihood will suffice to satisfy the test in s 12(3). Exceptional cases suggested by Lord Nicholls were where the potential adverse consequences of disclosure are particularly grave, and where a short-term injunction is needed to enable the court to give proper consideration to an application for an interim injunction. It was held in *Boehringer Ingelheim Ltd v Vetplus Ltd* [2007] FSR 29 that damage to reputation is not in itself sufficiently exceptional. Otherwise the exceptions would be so wide that s 12(3) would be rendered virtually meaningless. Thirdly, s 12(4) requires the court to have particular regard to the importance of the right to freedom of expression, and to whether the material is available to the public and whether it is in the public interest for the material to be published.

Cases raising conflicts between arts 8 and 10

42.61 Where both arts 8 and 10 are engaged, the court has to balance the competing interests in protecting private and family life and the freedom of expression (*Campbell v Mirror Group Newspapers plc* [2004] 2 AC 457). Neither article automatically outweighs the other. In *McKennitt v Ash* [2008] QB 73, Buxton LJ said there were two questions:

(a) whether the information is private in the sense that it is in principle protected by art 8. Information will lose its private character once it is in the public domain (*D v L* [2003] EWCA Civ 1169). If the information is not private, there is no case; and

(b) whether in all the circumstances the interest of the owner of the private information should yield to the right of freedom of expression conferred on the publisher by art 10. Much depends on whether there is a breach of confidence (*Prince of Wales v Associated Newspapers Ltd*). Where there is no breach of confidence, the balance between arts 8 and 10 usually involves weighing the nature and consequences of the breach of privacy against the public interest, if any, in the disclosure of the information. In cases where there is a breach of confidence, that is in itself a factor capable of justifying restrictions on freedom of expression under art 10(2). The court has to consider whether a fetter on the right of freedom of expression is in the particular circumstances necessary in a democratic society. This includes weighing the importance attached in a democratic society to upholding duties of confidence, as well as considering the nature of the information and the nature of the relationship giving rise to the duty of confidentiality.

Super injunctions

42.62 A super injunction is an interim injunction restraining the publication of confidential information which typically will:

(a) contain a clause prohibiting the publication or disclosure of the court proceedings and the fact the injunction has been granted to anyone other than the respondent's lawyers. Technically it is this clause that makes the injunction a super injunction;

(b) anonymize the claimant's name and redact all references to people or places that might reveal the claimant's identity;

(c) contain clauses sealing the court file so members of the public cannot obtain any of the court papers relating to the case; and

(d) be made on an application without notice to the respondent and at a hearing conducted in private.

42.63 Detailed guidance on the procedures to be followed in these cases is given in *Practice Guidance (Interim Non-disclosure Orders)* [2012] 1 WLR 1003. It will be a rare case that justifies such radical departures from the principle of open justice (*H v News Group Newspapers Ltd* [2011] 1 WLR 1645), and adverse publicity relating to the orders in 2011 has severely curtailed their use. A variant of the super injunction, the so-called hyper-injunction (which is said to prohibit revealing the existence of the injunction to a Member of Parliament), has probably never existed. Discussing the injunction outside Parliament with a Member of Parliament would be covered by a normal super injunction clause. Preventing a Member of Parliament mentioning the injunction in Parliament would infringe the Bill of Rights 1689, art 9, so would be unlawful.

Industrial disputes

42.64 After *American Cyanamid Co v Ethicon Ltd* [1975] AC 396, whenever an interim injunction was sought against a trade union that claimed it was acting in contemplation or furtherance of a trade dispute, the courts refused to investigate the respective merits of the case on each side, and tended to concentrate on the balance of convenience. Unions could rarely point to significant inconvenience if they were restrained from striking, whereas employers could readily identify their continuing financial losses. The result was that injunctions were invariably granted against unions involved in trade disputes despite the statutory defences. Legislation was accordingly passed to ensure the merits of the statutory defences are considered before injunctions are granted against trade unions. This legislation is now contained in the Trade Union and Labour Relations (Consolidation) Act 1992, s 221(2), which provides:

Where—
(a) an application for an interlocutory injunction is made to a court pending the trial of an action, and
(b) the party against whom it is sought claims that he acted in contemplation or furtherance of a trade dispute,

the court shall, in exercising its discretion whether or not to grant the injunction, have regard to the likelihood of that party's succeeding at the trial of the action in establishing any matter which would afford a defence to the action under section 219 (protection from certain tort liabilities) or section 220 (peaceful picketing).

Differing views have been expressed on the interpretation of this section. The approach **42.65** favoured by Lord Scarman in *NWL Ltd v Woods* [1979] 1 WLR 1294 was that the court must consider:

(a) whether the cause of action against the union discloses a serious action to be tried;
(b) the balance of convenience; and
(c) the likelihood of the union establishing the statutory defence.

Lord Fraser of Tullybelton in the same case pointed out that the word 'likelihood' is a **42.66** word of degree, and the weight to be given to establishing the trade dispute defence varies according to the degree of the likelihood.

Claims against public authorities

Smith v Inner London Education Authority [1978] 1 All ER 411 is authority for the prop- **42.67** osition that public authorities should not be restrained from exercising their statutory powers and duties unless the claimant has an extremely strong case on the merits. If the evidence indicates that the authority is exceeding the law, often upholding the rule of law will prevail over administrative inconvenience: *Bradbury v Enfield London Borough Council* [1967] 1 WLR 1311. Most cases of this nature should now be brought by proceedings for judicial review (see Chapter 49). Where interim injunctions are sought in judicial review proceedings, the *American Cyanamid* principles will be applied (*R v Ministry of Agriculture, Fisheries and Food, ex p Monsanto plc* [1999] QB 1161). The *Monsanto plc* case also considered how those principles ought to be applied in a public law case. An interim injunction may be granted to restrain the enforcement of a UK statute where there are strong grounds for finding that the statute contravenes EU law: *R v Secretary of State for Transport, ex p Factortame Ltd (No 2)* (Case C-213/89) [1991] 1 AC 603.

In considering an application to disapply national legislation by injunction pending a refer- **42.68** ence to the CJEU, the Court of Appeal in *R v HM Treasury, ex p British Telecommunications plc* [1994] 1 CMLR 621 said the following factors must be taken into account:

(a) The apparent strength of the EU right asserted. This is not to be considered in depth, as this is a matter for the CJEU. However, if the English court is almost persuaded that the applicant will succeed before the CJEU, albeit having enough doubt to refer the point to the CJEU, an injunction is far more likely to be granted than where the EU right is more speculative.

(b) The importance, in political terms, of the impugned legislation. An injunction is more likely to be granted where the legislation is obscure than where it is a major piece of legislation on which an election was fought.

(c) Other factors include whether the economic survival of the applicant depends on injunctive relief being granted, and the degree to which the applicant can be compensated in damages.

Negative covenants and covenants in restraint of trade

42.69   A perpetual injunction has been held to issue 'as of course' where it is established that the defendant is in breach of a valid express negative covenant: *Doherty v Allman* (1878) 3 App Cas 709. The same principle applies to applications for interim injunctions: *Attorney-General v Barker* [1990] 3 All ER 257.

42.70   Although covenants in restraint of trade are negative covenants, they will be valid only if reasonable in terms of the ambit of activities covered, geographical area, and period of time. In *Office Overload Ltd v Gunn* [1977] FSR 39, the defendant was the branch manager of the claimant's employment agency in Croydon. In his contract of employment he covenanted not to work for or set up a competing business in the Croydon area for one year after ceasing to work for the claimant. After giving notice the defendant immediately started competing. The claimant applied for an interim injunction. Given that to be valid a covenant has to be for a limited period of time, refusal of interim relief will usually deprive a claimant of the benefit of the covenant. Lord Denning MR accordingly said:

> Covenants in restraint of trade are in a special category . . . if they are *prima facie* valid and there is an infringement the courts will grant an injunction.

42.71   A covenant will be *prima facie* valid if:

(a) all the facts are before the court; and
(b) the covenant is reasonable in ambit, area, and duration.

42.72   Not all restraint of trade cases are exceptions to the *American Cyanamid* principles. *Office Overload Ltd v Gunn* applies to cases where there is no sustainable dispute concerning the claimant's cause of action. If there is real doubt about the claimant's case, *American Cyanamid* applies. Thus, in *Lawrence David Ltd v Ashton* [1991] 1 All ER 385, the claimant had dismissed the defendant from his employment, and there was a real issue as to whether that amounted to a repudiatory breach of the employment contract (and, if so, it could not insist on the covenant being observed). Further, the terms of the covenant were perhaps too wide. Given those two matters, the case was not an open-and-shut one in favour of the claimant, and the *American Cyanamid* guidelines were applied.

42.73   As the foundation of this exception is the effective deprivation of the employer of the benefit of the covenant due to the effluxion of time before trial, the exception does not apply if a trial can be arranged before the period of the covenant expires (eg through ordering a speedy trial): *Dairy Crest Ltd v Pigott* [1989] ICR 92. An example of what can be done with cooperation from all sides is *Symphony Group plc v Hodgson* [1994] QB 179, where the action was tried six weeks after the employee gave his notice.

42.74   If a covenant in a contract of employment against working for competitors is too wide and therefore void, the employer may still be able to obtain some injunctive relief if the employee resigns and starts working for a competitor under the principle in *Evening Standard Co Ltd v Henderson* [1987] ICR 588. In this case the Court of Appeal found that a newspaper production manager, whose contract provided that he had to give a year's notice, was in clear breach of his contract of employment when he purported to give two months' notice, after which he intended to work for a competitor. The claimant refused to accept the defendant's repudiation of his contract, and undertook to pay the defendant his full normal salary during his period of notice. Applying *American Cyanamid*, an injunction was granted restraining the defendant from working for any competitor for his contractual period of notice, thereby giving the defendant a period of 'garden leave'.

It is not always possible to obtain a 'garden leave' injunction even if the employee fails **42.75** to give the contractual period of notice. The cases fall into two categories (*Langston v Amalgamated Union of Engineering Workers (No 2)* [1974] ICR 510). In the first, the employment contract extends to an obligation to permit the employee to do the contractual work. Theatrical engagements usually fall into this category. In these cases the employer needs a provision in the employment contract entitling the employer to send the employee home on garden leave. There will be little scope for implying such a term into the contract. Without such a term, no injunction will be granted. In the second category the employment contract is confined to the employer agreeing to pay wages for the work done. In this category the employer is entitled to send the employee home on garden leave even in the absence of an express or implied term, because there is no contractual obligation to prevent this. Garden leave injunctions are therefore far more likely to be granted in this category. See *William Hill Organisation Ltd v Tucker* [1999] ICR 291.

Other decisions have shown that forcing a period of idleness on the defendant is a factor **42.76** to be taken into account in the balance of convenience against granting such an injunction (*Euro Brokers Ltd v Rabey* [1995] IRLR 206), and it may be appropriate to impose the injunction for a period shorter than the contractual period of notice where other 'defectors' are on shorter periods of notice than the defendant: *GFI Group Inc v Eaglestone* [1994] IRLR 119.

No defence

In *Official Custodian for Charities v Mackey* [1985] Ch 168 Scott J said that the *American* **42.77** *Cyanamid* principles: 'are not, in my view, applicable to a case where there is no arguable defence to the [claimant's] claim'. The court will not consider the balance of convenience, but will grant the relief claimed subject to the usual equitable considerations. Injunctions have been granted on this basis in cases of clear trespass (*Patel v WH Smith (Eziot) Ltd* [1987] 1 WLR 853) and of clear breach of contract (*Sheppard and Cooper Ltd v TSB Bank plc* [1996] 2 All ER 654). Similarly, if all that is at issue on the merits is a simple point of construction, the court will resolve it and dismiss or grant the application accordingly: *Associated British Ports v Transport and General Workers Union* [1989] 1 WLR 939 at 979.

Alternatively, where there is no defence with real prospects of success the claimant may **42.78** apply for summary judgment including a final order for an injunction, instead of applying for an interim order: *Viscount Chelsea v Muscatt* [1990] 2 EGLR 48.

Restraint of legal proceedings

American Cyanamid principles do not govern the exceptional jurisdiction of the courts to **42.79** restrain the commencement of legal proceedings. An injunction to prevent the presentation of a petition to wind up a company will be granted if the petition would be an abuse of process, for example if the petition debt is disputed on substantial grounds. An injunction may also be sought to restrain foreign proceedings to prevent 'forum shopping', if it can be established that the foreign proceedings would be vexatious or oppressive: *Société Nationale Industrielle Aérospatiale v Lee Kui Jak* [1987] AC 871.

Worldwide injunctions

42.80 In exceptional cases the courts may make injunctive orders having a worldwide effect. Such orders have been made in a number of freezing injunction cases, and also in an application to enforce a covenant of confidentiality against a former employee of the Royal House-hold: *Attorney-General v Barker* [1990] 3 All ER 257.

Interim mandatory injunctions

42.81 In *Shepherd Homes Ltd v Sandham* [1971] Ch 340 Megarry J said that an interim manda-tory injunction would only be granted if the court felt a 'high degree of assurance' about the merits of the claimant's cause of action. This formulation was approved in *Locabail International Finance Ltd v Agroexport* [1986] 1 WLR 657, where the Court of Appeal refused a mandatory injunction for the payment of money. Nevertheless, there are excep-tions (*Zockoll Group Ltd v Mercury Communications Ltd* [1998] FSR 354). In *Leisure Data v Bell* [1988] FSR 367, a dispute arose about the copyright in a computer program developed by the defendant for the claimant. The claimant was granted a mandatory injunction despite the merits being equally arguable either way. This was partly because the claimant was prepared to give wide-ranging undertakings to protect the defendant's position, and partly because the practical reality of the situation was that of the two parties only the claimant was in a position to make commercial use of the program. In *Incasep Ltd v Jones* (2001) LTL 26/1/01, the court considered an application for an interim mandatory injunction requiring a company to reinstate the claimant as an executive director pending the outcome of his unfair prejudice petition under the Companies Act 2006, s 994, apply-ing the *American Cyanamid* guidelines, but having regard to the potential injustice that such an injunction could cause.

42.82 In *National Commercial Bank Jamaica Ltd v Olint Corporation Ltd* [2009] 1 WLR 1405, Lord Hoffmann said there is no underlying difference in principle between interim applica-tions for prohibitory and mandatory injunctions. It is simply that it is more likely that there will be irremediable prejudice to the defendant if the injunction is mandatory in nature. If the injunction is likely to cause irremediable damage to the defendant, the court should be reluctant to grant the injunction unless it is satisfied that the chances that it will turn out to have been wrongly granted are low. It is for this reason that Megarry J in *Shepherd Homes Ltd v Sandham* [1971] Ch 340 said that such injunctions should be granted only if the court felt a 'high degree of assurance' that at trial it will turn out that the injunction was rightly granted.

E DEFENCES

42.83 Any of the following equitable defences and bars to relief may be raised on an application for an interim injunction:

(a) Acquiescence (see 21.66).
(b) Delay or laches. Delay is a more significant factor in interim applications than at trial: *Johnson v Wyatt* (1863) De GJ & S 18. To operate as a defence delay has to be combined with prejudice to the respondent. In *Bunn v British Broadcasting Corpora-tion* [1998] 3 All ER 552 a delay of 20 days was held to bar relief, where an applica-tion to restrain the broadcast of confidential information was made just two working days before the intended date of the broadcast. More frequently, this defence only arises where the delay is measured in months. Delay interrelates with the status quo (for which, see 42.46).

(c) Hardship. This is taken into account in the balance of convenience.

(d) Clean hands. Inequitable conduct by the claimant may be a bar to equitable relief: *Hubbard v Vosper* [1972] 2 QB 84.

(e) Equity does not act in vain. In *Attorney-General v Guardian Newspapers Ltd (No 2)* [1990] 1 AC 109 an injunction to restrain breach of confidence was refused where there had already been widespread publication.

(f) 'The court will not and ought not to make an order performance or obedience to which it cannot enforce' (*per* Astbury J in *Amber Size and Chemical Co Ltd v Menzel* [1913] 2 Ch 239). Injunctions are rarely granted against children, because they cannot be committed to prison and can rarely pay a fine (*G v Harrow London Borough Council* (2004) LTL 20/1/04).

(g) Difficulty in compliance. An injunction was refused in *Unique Pub Properties Ltd v Licensed Wholesale Co Ltd* (2003) LTL 13/10/03 as it would have imposed on the defendant a serious obligation to check information given to it by its tenants, any error constituting a breach.

(h) An injunction will be refused if its effect is to enforce an agreement for personal services (eg *Warren v Mendy* [1989] 1 WLR 853). This does not prevent the court granting an interim injunction prohibiting a ship owner from employing the vessel in a manner inconsistent with a non-demise charterparty (in which the owner provides a ship and crew) (*Lauritzencool AB v Lady Navigation Inc* [2005] 1 WLR 3686).

(i) The likelihood of damages being awarded in lieu of an injunction (*Lawrence v Fen Tigers* [2014] AC 822).

F THE ORDER

An example of an interim injunction order is shown in figure 42.1. The operative **42.84** part of the order should not be in terms wider than is necessary to do justice between the parties. It should be worded so that the defendant can know with certainty what is and what is not permitted (PD 25A, para 5.5). Where the order is made in the presence of all relevant parties (or at least at a hearing of which they had notice even if they did not attend), it may be expressed to last 'until trial or further order' (PD 25A, para 5.4).

An order which restrained, among other things, the defendant 'from otherwise infringing' **42.85** a patent lacked sufficient specificity: *Hepworth Plastics Ltd v Naylor Bros (Clayware) Ltd* [1979] FSR 521. In *EE and Brian Smith (1928) Ltd v Hodson* [2007] EWCA Civ 1210 the order was drawn too widely in that it prevented the company from fulfilling contracts already entered into, there was no sufficient definition of the information caught by the restrictions, and there was no exclusion of information in the public domain. It is usually best to avoid using legal terms of art, especially the names of torts, which often include matters of degree with the result that the defendant will often not know whether specific conduct will breach the order. The judge will have regard to the draft prepared by the claimant, and may initial the draft without amendment. Ultimately, however, the choice of wording is a matter within the discretion of the judge: *Khorasandjian v Bush* [1993] QB 727.

A penal notice must be inserted on the front page of the order warning the defendant that **42.86** breach may result in imprisonment or other penalties. The standard form of penal notice is in the following form:

> If you the within named [ ] do not comply with this Order you may be held to be in Contempt of Court and imprisoned or fined, or [in the case of a company or corporation] your assets may be seized.

Figure 42.1 High Court interim injunction

IN THE HIGH COURT OF JUSTICE   Claim No HQ18 21189

QUEEN'S BENCH DIVISION

BEFORE the Honourable Mr Justice Collier (judge in private)

Wednesday 22 November 2018

BETWEEN

CASPKEELER PRODUCTS LIMITED   <u>Claimants</u>

—and—

LOAMER TECHTRONICS LIMITED   <u>Defendants</u>

ORDER FOR AN INJUNCTION

IMPORTANT

NOTICE TO THE DEFENDANTS

(1) This Order prohibits you from doing the acts set out in this Order. You should read it carefully. You are advised to consult a Solicitor as soon as possible. You have a right to ask the Court to vary or discharge this Order.

(2) If you disobey this Order you may be found guilty of Contempt of Court and any of your directors may be sent to prison or fined or your assets may be seized.

An Application was made on 22 November 2018 by Counsel for the Claimants to the Judge and was attended by Counsel for the Defendants. The Judge heard the Application and read the witness statements listed in Schedule 1 and accepted the undertakings in Schedule 2 of this Order.

IT IS ORDERED that

THE INJUNCTION

(1) Until after final judgment in this claim the Defendants must not:

    (a) license the right to distribute the Loamer Techtron Capacitor anywhere in the world in the term of six years from 19 September 2016 granted to the Claimants Caspkeeler Products Limited under an agreement between the Claimants and the Defendants dated 19 September 2016;

    (b) sell Loamer Techtron Capacitors otherwise than through the Claimants Caspkeeler Products Limited;

    (c) assert or represent to customers that the Claimants Caspkeeler Products Limited are not the sole distributors of the Loamer Techtron Capacitor.

COSTS OF THE APPLICATION

(2) The costs of this application are to be the Claimants' costs in the case.

VARIATION OR DISCHARGE OF THIS ORDER

The Defendants may apply to the Court at any time to vary or discharge this Order, but if they wish to do so they must first inform the Claimants' Solicitors in writing at least 48 hours beforehand.

NAME AND ADDRESS OF CLAIMANTS' SOLICITORS

The Claimants' Solicitors are:

Figure 42.1 *continued*

Collins, Brown and Heath, of 7 Ingrave Road, Birmingham B5 8EP
Ref: JGB/4663, Telephone: 0121 215 8349.

INTERPRETATION OF THIS ORDER

(1) In this Order the words 'he' 'him' or 'his' include 'she' or 'her' and 'it' or 'its'.
(2) Where there are two or more Defendants then (unless the contrary appears):
    (a) references to 'the Defendant' mean both or all of them;
    (b) an Order requiring 'the Defendant' to do or not to do anything requires each
        Defendant to do or not to do it.

THE EFFECT OF THIS ORDER

(1) A Defendant who is an individual who is ordered not to do something must not do it
himself or in any other way. He must not do it through others acting on his behalf or on his
instructions or with his encouragement.
(2) A Defendant which is a corporation and which is ordered not to do something must not
do it itself or by its directors, officers, employees or agents or in any other way.

SERVICE OF THIS ORDER

This Order shall be served by the Claimants on the Defendants.

SCHEDULE 1
Witness Statements.

The Judge read the following witness statements before making this Order:

(1) Rachel Helen Radcliffe, made on 13 November 2018,
(2) Daniel Jordan Loamer, made on 15 November 2018.

SCHEDULE 2
Undertaking given to the Court by the Claimants

If the Court later finds that this Order has caused loss to the Defendants or any other party
served with or notified of this Order, and decides that the Defendants or any other party
should be compensated for that loss, the Claimants will comply with any Order the Court
may make.
All communications to the Court about this Order should be sent to Room 307, Royal
Courts of Justice, Strand, London WC2A 2LL quoting the case number. The office is open
between 10 a.m. and 4.30 p.m. Monday to Friday. The telephone number is (020) 7936
6148.

G UNDERTAKINGS

Applicant's undertaking in damages

Undertakings given by the applicant are incorporated into the form of the order. Invariably **42.87**
these include an undertaking to pay any damages which the respondent sustains as a result
of the injunction if it later transpires the injunction should not have been granted (PD 25A,

para 5.1(1)). The court should consider requiring an extended undertaking to cover also any damages sustained by other parties, or even persons who are not parties (para 5.2).

42.88 Undertakings in damages are not required where the Crown or a local authority is seeking an interim injunction to enforce the law (*Kirklees Metropolitan Borough Council v Wickes Building Supplies Ltd* [1993] AC 227; *United States Securities and Exchange Commission v Manterfield* [2010] 1 WLR 172), unless the defendant shows a strong *prima facie* case that its conduct is lawful (*F Hoffmann-La Roche & Co AG v Secretary of State for Trade and Industry* [1975] AC 295). The court has a discretion to order an interim injunction subject to a limited undertaking in damages: *RBG Resources plc v Rastogi* (2002) LTL 31/5/02. In environmental claims governed by the Aarhus Convention the court is required to have particular regard to the need for the terms of the order, including any undertaking in damages, not to be such as would make continuing with the claim prohibitively expensive for the claimant (PD 25A, para 5.3).

42.89 An applicant is occasionally required to fortify the undertaking in damages by providing security, paying money into court, or by requiring a non-party to be also bound to honour the undertaking. Such an order should only be made if there is a good arguable case that fortification is required (*Energy Venture Partners Ltd v Malabu* Oil and Gas Ltd [2015] 1 WLR 2309). That, according to *Brainbox Digital Ltd v Backbord Media GmbH* [2018] 1 WLR 1149, requires:

(a) a good arguable case that there is a sufficient level of risk that the respondent will suffer loss to require fortification;

(b) a good arguable case that the loss will be caused by granting the injunction; and

(c) an intelligent estimate of the likely amount of loss caused by the effects of the injunction that might not be covered by the applicant's usual undertaking in damages.

Without notice undertakings

42.90 A number of additional undertakings are usually required when interim injunctions are granted without notice to the respondent (PD 25A, para 5.1). These include:

(a) an undertaking by the applicant to the court to serve the respondent with the application notice, evidence in support, and any order made, as soon as practicable;

(b) a return date for a further hearing at which the other party can be present;

(c) if made before filing the application notice, an undertaking to file it and pay the appropriate fee on the same or next working day; and

(d) if made before issuing the claim form, an undertaking to issue it and pay the appropriate fee on the same or next working day, or the order will contain directions for the commencement of the claim.

Undertakings by respondents

42.91 Instead of contesting an application for an interim injunction, a defendant may give undertakings in similar terms to the injunction sought by the claimant. Such undertakings have the same force as an injunction ordered by the court, with the result that the defendant will be in contempt of court if the undertakings are broken. In some cases undertakings may be construed as having contractual effect between the parties (*Independiente Ltd v Music Trading On-Line (HK) Ltd* [2008] 1 WLR 608).

H INQUIRY AS TO DAMAGES

42.92 Where it transpires that an interim injunction should not have been granted (eg if the claimant loses at trial) the defendant or any other person served with the order may seek to enforce the undertaking in damages by applying for an order for an inquiry as to damages. This is done by using the Part 23 procedure supported by written evidence (*Euroil Ltd v Cameroon Offshore Petroleum SARL* [2014] EWHC 215 (Comm)). Excessive, inexcusable delay may result in an application for an inquiry as to damages being dismissed: *Barratt Manchester Ltd v Bolton Metropolitan Borough Council* [1998] 1 WLR 1003. An order for an inquiry is not penal and does not depend on fault on the part of the claimant.

An application for an inquiry made by a successful defendant at the end of the trial will **42.93** normally be refused only if it is unlikely that the defendant has suffered any provable loss: *McDonald's Hamburgers Ltd v Burgerking UK Ltd* [1987] FSR 112. Ordinary contractual principles are applied on causation, remoteness, and quantum, suitably adjusted to fit the situation (*Abbey Forwarding Ltd v Hone (No 3)* [2015] Ch 309). It is possible for aggravated or exemplary damages to be awarded in cases where the claimant has acted oppressively, and, in relation to inappropriate freezing injunctions, for the award to include damages for upset, stress, and loss of reputation. Inquiries are normally conducted by Masters and District Judges.

I DISCHARGE

Applications to vary or discharge injunctions are made by application notice to a judge, **42.94** often the same judge who granted the initial injunction. Grounds for such applications include:

(a) material non-disclosure if the injunction was granted without notice;
(b) the particulars of claim being inconsistent with the written evidence on an application without notice;
(c) the facts not justifying relief without giving notice;
(d) the claimant's failure to comply with the undertakings incorporated into the order;
(e) the order having an oppressive effect;
(f) unreasonable interference with the rights of innocent third parties. Affected third parties are entitled to apply for a variation of the order. All the circumstances have to be considered, and it is sometimes within the court's powers to grant an injunction to restrain a defendant from fulfilling a contract already entered into with an innocent third party. An example is where this is necessary in order to protect the claimant's trade secrets (*PSM International plc v Whitehouse* [1992] IRLR 279);
(g) material change in the circumstances;
(h) a failure to prosecute the substantive claim with due speed;
(i) if the claim is stayed other than by agreement between the parties, any interim injunction will be set aside unless the court orders that it should continue in force (CPR, r 25.10);
(j) if the claim is struck out for non-payment of the hearing fee, the interim injunction will lapse 14 days after the claim is struck out. However, if within that 14-day period the claimant applies to reinstate the claim, the injunction will remain in force until the hearing of that application (unless the court otherwise orders) (r 25.11).

J BREACH

Where a mandatory order has been breached the court may direct that the required act be **42.95** completed by any person at the expense of the disobedient party (CPR, r 70.2A). Breach of an injunction is a contempt of court punishable by imprisonment or sequestration. Contempt must be proved beyond reasonable doubt.

42.96   Clearly, the person against whom the order was made will be in contempt if he or she acts in breach of an injunction after having notice of it: *Z Ltd v A-Z and AA-LL* [1982] QB 558 *per* Eveleigh LJ. To establish a contempt by a non-party it must be demonstrated both that the non-party's acts defeated, in whole or in part, the court's purpose in granting the injunction, and that the non-party appreciated that this would be the effect: *Attorney-General v Punch Ltd* [2003] 1 AC 1046.

K EFFECT OF NOT APPLYING FOR INTERIM RELIEF

42.97   Delay in issuing proceedings after the claimant is aware of the defendant's breach, and deciding not to apply for an interim injunction to avoid giving an undertaking in damages, are matters to be taken into account in considering whether to grant a final injunction. They do not bar granting such an injunction where the claimant has made a clear objection to the defendant's conduct (*Mortimer v Bailey* (2004) LTL 29/10/04). Failing to apply for an interim injunction may also provide grounds for awarding damages in lieu of an injunction: *Jaggard v Sawyer* [1995] 1 WLR 269.

KEY POINTS SUMMARY

42.98
- Interim injunctions can be sought without notice if the case is urgent or if there is other sufficient reason. Otherwise, they are sought on notice to the respondents.

- Injunctions are remedies, so applications for interim injunctions have to be founded on a substantive cause of action.

- In the past, parties in applications for interim injunctions in important cases were often tempted into deploying most or all their evidence on the merits of the claim on the interim application. The *American Cyanamid* guidelines are principally designed to prevent this being necessary.

- The *American Cyanamid* guidelines apply to the vast bulk of applications for interim prohibitory injunctions.

- Most of the exceptions to *American Cyanamid* are aimed at the first stage of the guidance (whether there is a serious issue to be tried), and impose a higher standard on the merits (eg mandatory injunctions and interim injunctions which finally dispose of the case).

- Applicants are invariably required to undertake to compensate the defendant and sometimes any person served with the injunction if it later transpires that the injunction should not have been granted.

43

FREEZING INJUNCTIONS

A PROCEDURE 43.03
B PRINCIPLES 43.08
C THE ORDER. .43.24
D EFFECT OF THE ORDER. 43.43
E VARIATION OR DISCHARGE OF A
  FREEZING INJUNCTION. 43.44
F FREEZING INJUNCTIONS AFTER
  JUDGMENT 43.52
G PROPRIETARY CLAIMS 43.53
H WRIT *NE EXEAT REGNO*. 43.54
  Key points summary 43.55

A freezing injunction is an interim order restraining a party from removing assets located **43.01** within the jurisdiction out of the country, or from dealing with assets whether they are located within the jurisdiction or not (CPR, r 25.1(1)(f)). Usually the order will be restricted to assets not exceeding the value of the claim. Until the CPR came into force on 26 April 1999 this form of order was known as a *Mareva* injunction, taking its name from *Mareva Compania Naviera SA v International Bulkcarriers SA* [1980] 1 All ER 213.

The purpose of a freezing injunction is to prevent the injustice of a defendant's assets **43.02** being salted away so as to deprive the claimant of the fruits of any judgment that may be obtained. However, as Ackner LJ said in *AJ Bekhor and Co Ltd v Bilton* [1981] QB 923, the jurisdiction to grant freezing injunctions has not rewritten the law of insolvency, and the imposition of such an order does not give the claimant any priority or security if the defendant becomes insolvent. It is a relief *in personam* which simply prohibits certain acts in relation to the assets frozen.

A PROCEDURE

Until 22 April 2014 jurisdiction to grant freezing injunctions was broadly restricted to the **43.03** High Court (County Court Remedies Regulations 1991 (SI 1991/1222)). This restriction was removed by the County Court Remedies Regulations 2014 (SI 2014/982), with the effect that these orders can now be made in either the High Court or the County Court.

Given that a freezing injunction can be ordered only against an unscrupulous defendant **43.04** who is prepared to dissipate assets to prevent the claimant recovering on any judgment obtained, the application has to be made without informing the defendant if the injunction is to be effective. In *Oaktree Financial Services Ltd v Higham* (2004) LTL 11/5/04 one of the solicitors involved in the case wrote to the defendant unwittingly but in effect warning him of the possibility of a freezing injunction application being made. Laddie J was almost minded to refuse the injunction on this ground alone, as there was a strong prospect that any funds would have been dissipated once the defendant was put on notice.

The application is made to a judge sitting in private. Invariably, the application is made **43.05** before service of the claim form so as not to alert the defendant. A draft claim form, or its overseas equivalent, must be produced in order to identify the substantive claim against the defendant (see 43.10–43.11; *Fourie v Le Roux* [2007] 1 WLR 320). The application must be supported by an affidavit making full and frank disclosure of all material facts, including those going against the grant of the order. Applications for freezing injunctions are one of the exceptions where affidavits must be used (PD 25A, para 3.1). The affidavit must be clear and fair, and claimants should avoid the temptation to flood the court with voluminous exhibits, particularly where this will tend to obscure the real issues. In urgent cases informal evidence may be used, but in such cases the applicant will be required to confirm on affidavit all the evidence presented at the hearing (*Flightwise Travel Services Ltd v Gill* (2003) *The Times*, 5 December 2003). Counsel must produce a draft minute of the order sought. There is a standard form for the order, which is considered in 43.24ff. In urgent cases the application can be made before issue of the proceedings.

43.06 The papers must, wherever possible, be delivered to the court at least two hours before the hearing to allow the judge to read them in advance (PD 25A, para 4.3(1)). Further, even on applications without notice and especially where 'worldwide' freezing injunctions (see 43.16) are sought, counsel should consider drafting a skeleton argument indicating how the requirements for granting the order are made out: see *ALG Inc v Uganda Airlines Corporation* (1992) *The Times*, 31 July 1992. As the application is made without notice, there is the usual duty of full and frank disclosure (see 23.23–23.26). There is a duty on counsel to ensure the court's attention is drawn to unusual features of the evidence adduced, to the applicable law, and to the formalities and procedure to be observed (*Memory Corporation plc v Sidhu (No 2)* [2000] 1 WLR 1443). A failure to formulate the substantive claim against the defendant is a reason in itself to refuse relief (*Fourie v Le Roux*).

43.07 Paragraph 3 of the standard order provides for a return day for a further hearing on notice, which is normally a few days after the without-notice hearing. The respondent must be fully informed of the applicant's case well in advance of the hearing on notice, including being provided with the evidence and informed of the arguments advanced at the without-notice hearing (*Flightwise Travel Services Ltd v Gill*).

B PRINCIPLES

43.08 The jurisdiction to grant freezing injunctions derives from the SCA 1981, s 37(1). This section enables the court to grant interim injunctions on such terms and conditions as the court thinks just where it appears 'just and convenient' to do so. The requirements laid down by the courts for granting freezing injunctions are:

(a) a cause of action justiciable in England and Wales;
(b) a good arguable case;
(c) the defendant having assets within the jurisdiction; and
(d) a real risk that the defendant may dissipate those assets before judgment can be enforced.

43.09 However, because injunctions are granted where it is just and convenient, the court retains a discretion to refuse relief, and, in rare, exceptional cases, has power to stretch the usual rules if that is in the interests of justice. Unless the case is truly exceptional, these requirements must be established, and it is not sufficient to say that a freezing injunction should be granted because there is no immediate and obvious prejudice to the respondent (*Flightwise Travel Services Ltd v Gill* (2003) *The Times*, 5 December 2003).

Claim justiciable in England and Wales

The claimant must have a substantive cause of action, and there must be a basis for bring- **43.10**
ing the application in England and Wales. At one time, the focus under this heading was on
the jurisdiction issue. Freezing injunctions, like all other types of injunction, are remedies,
and depend for their existence on a substantive cause of action. It used to be the case that
if there was no means of bringing a substantive claim in England and Wales, there was no
basis for granting an injunction, freezing or otherwise (*The Siskina* [1979] AC 210). This
was changed by the CJJA 1982, s 25, as extended by the Civil Jurisdiction and Judgments
Act 1982 (Interim Relief) Order 1997 (SI 1997/302). The CJJA 1982, s 25 enables the High
Court to grant interim relief, including freezing injunctions, where proceedings have been
or are to be commenced in any overseas jurisdiction (see 11.62).

The result, as recognized by *Fourie v Le Roux* [2007] 1 WLR 320, is that jurisdiction, in **43.11**
the sense of whether the court has power to deal with the application, is no longer an issue.
Instead, the focus in relation to the first requirement is whether the claimant can identify a
cause of action against the defendant. To achieve this, the claimant is required to have formulated a claim for substantive relief against the defendant, whether that substantive claim
is to be brought in England and Wales or an overseas jurisdiction (*Fourie v Le Roux* at [35]).

Good arguable case

Regarding the merits of the substantive claim, the minimum threshold for the exercise **43.12**
of the discretion is the establishment of a 'good arguable case'. This imposes a higher
merits requirement than the 'serious issue to be tried' test used in applications for interim
injunctions applying the *American Cyanamid* principles (*Fiona Trust Holding Corporation
v Privalov* (2007) LTL 30/5/07). According to Kerr LJ in *Ninemia Maritime Corporation v Trave Schiffahrtsgesellschaft mbH & Co KG* [1983] 1 WLR 1412 (affirmed [1983]
2 Lloyd's Rep 660), the expression means 'a case which is more than barely capable of serious argument, and yet not necessarily one which the judge believes to have a better than
50 per cent chance of success'. This test will not be satisfied if the claimant does not have
the evidence to substantiate the case relied upon, or if the case is likely to be struck out, and
may not be satisfied if there is an arguable defence.

The courts have on occasion been reluctant to find there is a good arguable case where **43.13**
fraud is alleged, as in *Cheltenham and Gloucester Building Society v Ricketts* [1993]
1 WLR 1545, given the difficulty of proving this particular allegation. In *Fiona Trust Holding Corporation v Privalov* matters pointing to a good arguable case included a lack of
negotiations in allegedly fraudulent transactions, unconvincing evidence from the defendants to explain their conduct, a letter referring to 'the delicate nature of our exchanges', and
attempts to prevent outsiders finding out. An arguable set-off may be taken as reducing or
extinguishing the value of the claim. Anticipation that the defendant will be in breach of
contract in the future has been held to be insufficient to satisfy this part of the test (*Veracruz Transportation Inc v VC Shipping Co Inc* [1992] 1 Lloyd's Rep 353).

Assets

The requirement of proving that the defendant has assets within the jurisdiction stems from **43.14**
the principle that equity will not act in vain, so that if an injunction will not be effective
it will not be granted. There must be 'grounds for believing' that the defendant has assets
within the jurisdiction. 'Assets' includes money, shares, securities, insurance money, bills
of exchange, motor vehicles, ships, aircraft, trade goods, office equipment, jewellery, and

paintings. While ownership may be legal or beneficial, the defendant must own the assets in the same capacity as the defendant is or will be a party to the claim.

43.15 It is not enough to assert that the respondent is an apparently wealthy person. Nor is it enough to identify a closed bank account, or a bank account with a small credit balance (*Ras al Khaimah Investment Authority v Bestfort Development LLP* [2018] 1 WLR 1099). Where an asset apparently belongs to a non-party, but the claimant claims it is beneficially owned by the defendant, it was said by Nicholls LJ in *Allied Arab Bank Ltd v Hajjar* [1988] QB 787 that the claimant must normally pass the *Ninemia Maritime Corporation v Trave Schiffahrtsgesellschaft mbH & Co KG* [1983] 1 WLR 1412 threshold (see 43.12) on the question of proving beneficial ownership. A slightly different situation arose in *TSB Private Bank International SA v Chabra* [1992] 1 WLR 231. It was clear that the claimant had a good cause of action against the first defendant, and equally clear there was no independent cause of action against the second defendant, a company owned by the first defendant and/or his wife. As there was credible evidence that the assets apparently owned by the second defendant in fact belonged to the first defendant, Mummery J granted a freezing injunction against the second defendant on the ground that it was ancillary and incidental to the claim against the first defendant.

Worldwide freezing injunctions

43.16 Generally, freezing injunctions do not extend to assets outside the jurisdiction. A freezing injunction having extraterritorial effect can be granted only in an exceptional case. The power to grant worldwide freezing injunctions in support of domestic proceedings derives from the SCA 1981, s 37(1), not the CJJA 1982, s 25 (for which, see 11.62), or the Judgments Regulation, art 31 (*Masri v Consolidated Contractors International UK Ltd (No 2)* [2008] 1 All ER (Comm) 305 at [53]; [2009] QB 450 at [92]–[107]). Worldwide freezing injunctions are readily made against defendants within the jurisdiction where there is cogent evidence of international fraud (*Mediterranean Shipping Co v OMG International Ltd* [2008] EWHC 2150 (Comm)). A worldwide freezing injunction in aid of foreign proceedings affecting assets not located in the jurisdiction will only be granted where the respondent or the dispute has a sufficiently strong link with the jurisdiction, or if there is some other factor justifying the court's intervention despite the lack of such a link (*Mobil Cerro Negro Ltd v Petroleos de Venezuela SA* [2008] 1 Lloyd's Rep 684).

43.17 It has been held that the court can make a worldwide order in cases where the defendant has no assets in England: *Derby and Co Ltd v Weldon (Nos 3 and 4)* [1990] Ch 65. However, in *Banco Nacional de Comercio Exterior SNC v Empresa de Telecomunicationes de Cuba SA* [2007] 2 All ER (Comm) 1093 it was held to be inexpedient to grant a worldwide order because the judgment debtor was outside the jurisdiction, the original judgment was granted in Italy, any assets within the jurisdiction were covered by a domestic freezing injunction (which was granted), and granting a worldwide order would be likely to give rise to disharmony and confusion.

43.18 Worldwide freezing orders must include a *Babanaft* proviso that the order will not affect third parties outside the jurisdiction until, and to the extent that, it has been declared enforceable, or is enforced, by a foreign court. See *Babanaft International Co SA v Bassatne* [1990] Ch 13 and cl 19(2)(c) of the standard freezing injunction order. The claimant is further required to undertake not to enforce the order in a foreign court without first obtaining permission from the English court: (Sch B, para 10 of the standard freezing injunction order, and see *Dadourian Group International Inc v Simms (No 2)* [2007] 1 WLR 2967 for the principles on seeking permission).

Worldwide freezing injunctions must also include *Baltic* provisos to the effect that third **43.19**
parties served with the order may comply with what they reasonably believe to be their
civil and criminal obligations in the country where the assets are located (*Bank of China v
NBM LLC* [2002] 1 WLR 844 and cl 20 of the standard freezing injunction order).

Risk of disposal

The claimant must provide 'solid evidence' that there is a real risk that the defendant will dis- **43.20**
sipate assets if unrestrained: *Ninemia Maritime Corporation v Trave Schiffahrtsgesellschaft
mbH & Co KG* [1983] 1 WLR 1412; *Holyoake v Candy* [2017] 3 WLR 1131. In *Customs
and Excise Commissioners v Anchor Foods Ltd* [1999] 1 WLR 1139 Neuberger J said that
what is required is a good and arguable case for a risk of dissipation. This was found to be so
where the defendant proposed to dispose of its entire business at a price which had been inde-
pendently verified by a partner in a leading accountancy firm, because the purchaser was a
company controlled by the same people who controlled the defendant and there was contrary
valuation evidence (also from very eminent experts) indicating that the price was too low.

At one time it was thought that freezing injunctions could be granted only against foreign **43.21**
defendants. The SCA 1981, s 37(3), now provides that the jurisdiction to grant these orders
'shall be exercisable in cases where [the defendant] is, as well as in cases where he is not,
domiciled, resident or present within [the] jurisdiction'.

Factors relevant to the question of risk of dissipation include: **43.22**

(a) whether the respondent is a reputable individual or organization, accustomed to paying
its debts (*Barclay-Johnson v Yuill* [1980] 1 WLR 1259);
(b) whether the defendant has substantial assets within the jurisdiction;
(c) whether the defendant is domiciled or incorporated in a tax haven or country with tax
company law;
(d) whether English judgments are enforceable in the country where the defendant's assets
are situated: *Montecchi v Shimco (UK) Ltd* [1979] 1 WLR 1180. This is a particularly important factor where the assets are in an EU Member State due to the ease of
enforcement under the Judgments Regulation (for which, see Chapter 48);
(e) whether the evidence supporting the substantive cause of action discloses dishonesty or
a suspicion of dishonesty on the part of the defendant. This is not enough of itself: it is
still necessary to consider all the circumstances (*Thane Investments Ltd v Tomlinson
(No 1)* [2003] EWCA Civ 1272);
(f) whether there is evidence that the defendant has been dishonest, outside the actual
cause of action. This includes matters such as contrivances designed to generate an
appearance of wealth;
(g) past incidents of debt default by the defendant, although it is not essential for the claimant to have such evidence: *Third Chandris Shipping Corporation v Unimarine SA*;
(h) evidence that the defendant has already taken steps to remove or dissipate its assets:
Aiglon Ltd v Gau Shan Co Ltd [1993] 1 Lloyd's Rep 164.

Discretion

In its discretion, the court can refuse a freezing injunction even if the usual requirements **43.23**
are made out. In *Rasu Maritima SA v Perusahaan Pertambangan Minyak Dan Gas Bumi
Negara* [1978] QB 644 the Court of Appeal refused to grant an order partly because the
'cleanliness' of the claimant's hands was open to question, and partly in the exercise of its
discretion. The assets frozen were parts for a fertilizer plant, and were valued at $12 mil-
lion in the hands of the defendants, but were worth only $0.35 million as scrap. This was

regarded as only a 'drop in the ocean' in comparison with the size of the claim. In *Sions v Price* (1988) *The Independent*, 19 December 1988, an order was refused where the claim was £2,000. Freezing injunctions are only to be used in substantial cases.

C THE ORDER

Undertakings

43.24 The following undertakings by the claimant must be given to the court and incorporated into the order:

    (a) as with other interim injunctions, to pay damages to the defendant (and sometimes other persons affected by the injunction) if it transpires that the order should not have been granted (see 42.87);

    (b) to notify the defendant forthwith of the terms of the order, often by telex or fax, and to serve the defendant with the affidavit and exhibits in support. This is a consequence of applying without notice;

    (c) to pay the reasonable costs and expenses incurred by third parties in complying with the order; and

    (d) to indemnify third parties in respect of any liability incurred in complying with the order.

43.25 As with ordinary interim injunctions (see 42.88), financial undertakings (items (a) and (c) at 43.24) are not normally required if the freezing injunction is granted to a public body acting pursuant to a public duty (*Financial Services Authority v Sinaloa Gold plc* [2013] 2 AC 28).

43.26 In urgent cases, the following further undertakings may be required:

    (a) to issue a claim form as soon as practicable in the terms of the draft used on the application; and

    (b) to swear and file affidavits deposing to the facts relied on before the judge.

43.27 Under the SCA 1981, s 37(2), interim injunctions can be granted on such terms and conditions as the court thinks fit. A little latitude is permissible. So, in *Allen v Jambo Holdings Ltd* [1980] 1 WLR 1252 the Court of Appeal continued a freezing injunction in favour of a publicly funded claimant who could not give a valuable undertaking in damages. The case was unusual in that the defendants had sworn an affidavit blatantly exaggerating the effects of the order and had been less than forthcoming on a number of points. Also, in any event, the defendants could have obtained the release of their frozen aeroplane by providing security.

Assets covered by the order

43.28 Considered in relation to the assets they cover, freezing injunctions can be divided into three types:

    (a) general orders, which cover all the defendant's assets;

    (b) maximum-sum orders, which cover the defendant's assets up to the highest amount, together with interest and costs, for which there is a good arguable case. If the claim is unliquidated, the maximum sum is calculated by reference to the sum the claimant is likely to recover; and

    (c) orders attaching to specific assets, such as a ship, a cargo, or an aeroplane.

Often, orders attaching to specific assets are combined with either general or maximum-sum orders. The choice between general and maximum-sum orders was considered in *Z Ltd v A-Z and AA-LL* [1982] QB 558. Maximum-sum orders are the norm. A general order is likely to provoke an application for a variation down to a maximum-sum order. One drawback with maximum-sum orders is that banks will not necessarily know whether they can honour transactions on the defendant's accounts as they will not know the total value of the defendant's assets covered by the order at any particular time. Where such practical difficulties result in a larger sum being 'frozen' than the sum stated in the order, the claimant may be held liable on its undertakings in damages. General orders may accordingly be used where the defendant's assets are not fully known by the claimant, and are also appropriate in fraud cases where the amount of the claim may be unknown. **43.29**

The standard form of order does not cover assets held by a defendant on trust, although an extended form of order may be made to cover such assets: *Federal Bank of the Middle East Ltd v Hadkinson* [2000] 1 WLR 1695. While the standard-form freezing injunction does not directly cover assets of companies wholly owned by the defendant, disposal of assets by such companies will affect the value of the defendant's shares in such companies, and so disposals by the companies will be covered by the freezing injunction (*Lakatamia Shipping Co Ltd v Su* [2015] 1 WLR 291). **43.30**

Bank accounts

Bank accounts are one of the most common assets covered by freezing injunctions. The following points should be noted: **43.31**

(a) A joint account will not be affected by a freezing injunction unless it is specifically covered by the wording of the order: *SCF Finance Co Ltd v Masri* [1985] 1 WLR 876.

(b) If the defendant has an account containing money over which the claimant asserts a proprietary interest, mixed with the defendant's own money and/or money held by the defendant on behalf of a third party, the court has jurisdiction to freeze the entire account: *Chief Constable of Kent v V* [1983] QB 34.

(c) The claimant must give the fullest possible details (bank, branch, account name, and number) in the affidavit in support. If it is necessary to ask the bank to search for an account, the number of branches involved should be as limited as possible. The claimant will be required to pay the costs of such searches immediately, which may or may not be recoverable from the defendant as costs of the action.

(d) The bank should honour transactions entered into before the order is made. The bank must also honour cheques backed by guarantee cards and irrevocable letters of credit: see, for example, *Cretanor Maritime Co Ltd v Irish Marine Management Ltd* [1978] 1 WLR 966, and *Lewis and Peat (Produce) Ltd v Almatu Properties Ltd* (1992) *The Times*, 14 May 1992. Cheque cards should be recalled once the order has been served on the bank.

(e) A freezing injunction can apply to the *proceeds* of a letter of credit when received: *Z Ltd v A-Z and AA-LL* [1982] QB 558.

(f) A provision must be incorporated into the order to allow any bank served with the order to exercise any right of set-off it may have in respect of facilities given to the defendant before the order: *Oceanica Castelana Armadora SA v Mineral-importexport* [1983] 1 WLR 1294 and cl 17 of the standard order.

A bank does not owe a duty of care in negligence to the claimant, even after receiving notice of a freezing injunction (*Customs and Excise Commissioners v Barclays Bank plc* [2007] 1 AC 181). **43.32**

Port authorities

43.33 Where a freezing injunction affects a ship in harbour, the claimant will be required to undertake to reimburse the port authority for lost income, and a proviso will be incorporated into the order giving the port authority a discretion to move the ship for operational reasons: *Clipper Maritime Co Ltd v Mineral Import-Export* [1981] 1 WLR 1262.

Land

43.34 Freezing injunctions can be granted over land, although it may be difficult to prove that there is a 'risk of disposal'. An order, if granted, would not be made for the purpose of enforcing a judgment, so would not be registrable as a land charge: *Stockler v Fourways Estates Ltd* [1984] 1 WLR 25.

Living expenses

43.35 A freezing injunction must allow an individual defendant to use a reasonable sum each week or month to pay his or her ordinary living expenses (cl 11 of the standard order). As decided in *PCW (Underwriting Agencies) Ltd v Dixon* [1983] 2 All ER 158, a defendant is not dissipating his assets by living as he has always lived. It is a misuse of the jurisdiction to grant freezing injunctions to seek to apply pressure on the defendant (perhaps with a view to obtaining a favourable settlement) by unreasonably limiting the money available for ordinary living expenses. Spending in excess of the living expenses clause is not a breach of the injunction if it is funded by borrowing from another source: *Cantor Index Ltd v Lister* (2001) LTL 22/1/01. Living expenses money must not, however, be spent on extraordinary items, such as expensive motor cars (*TDK Tape Distributor (UK) Ltd v Videochoice Ltd* [1986] 1 WLR 141).

Trade debts

43.36 A freezing injunction must allow a defendant who is engaged in trade to pay any legitimate trade debts as they would be paid in the ordinary course of the defendant's business (cl 11 of the standard order). These are payments that are consistent with the way the defendant's business has been carried on in the past (*Abbey Forwarding Ltd v Hone* [2010] EWHC 1532 (Ch)). The philosophy behind this is that a freezing injunction is not intended to confer priority over other trade creditors. A defendant should be allowed to pay a trade debt, if the defendant is acting in good faith and in the ordinary course of business, even if the debt is not strictly enforceable: *Iraqi Ministry of Defence v Arcepey Shipping Co SA* [1981] QB 65. Whether the defendant should use assets not covered by the order where such are available depends ultimately on the defendant's motive (*Campbell Mussels v Thompson* (1984) 81 LS Gaz 2140, interpreting *A v C (No 2)* [1981] QB 961).

Costs of defending

43.37 A freezing injunction should normally also allow the defendant to pay the ordinary costs of the present claim if no other funds are available (cl 11 of the standard order). The permission to use money to pay reasonable legal costs (or living expenses or trade debts) does no more than to permit the expenditure without the defendant being in contempt of court. Thus, where the underlying cause of action asserts a proprietary claim against the defendant, the permission to use money to pay reasonable legal expenses is no guarantee that the recipients of that money will escape a later claim in constructive trust for knowing receipt should the claim be established: *United Mizrahi Bank Ltd v Doherty* [1998] 1 WLR 435.

Ancillary orders

The court has power under CPR, r 25.1(1)(g), to make ancillary orders for disclosure and **43.38** answers to requests for further information to ensure the effectiveness of the main freezing injunction. Orders requiring disclosure of the nature and whereabouts of all the defendant's assets within the jurisdiction are a standard requirement in freezing injunctions, and are generally required if the injunctions are to be effective: *Motorola Credit Corporation v Uzan* [2002] 2 All ER (Comm) 945 and cll 9 and 10 of the standard order. Defendants should be given a realistic time for compliance (*Oystertec plc v Davidson* (2004) LTL 7/4/04, where four working days was regarded as extremely short). In addition, the defendant's bank may be ordered, even if not a party, to give disclosure of documents relating to the defendant's bank account: *A v C* [1981] QB 956.

It is only in exceptional circumstances that cross-examination will be ordered on an **43.39** affidavit of assets sworn pursuant to a freezing order. However, where the claimant has justifiable concerns about whether the defendant has made a full disclosure as required by the order, the court may order the defendant to be cross-examined: *Den Norske Bank ASA v Antonatos* [1999] QB 271. The purpose of the cross-examination is solely to discover what assets the defendant has, with a view to freezing them, and so will be unnecessary if sufficient assets are known to meet the value of the claim: *Great Future International Ltd v Sealand Housing Corporation* [2001] CPLR 293. The examination will be conducted by a Master or District Judge unless the judge making the order otherwise directs (PD 2B, para 7).

Duration

A freezing order made without notice will remain in force for a limited period until the **43.40** 'return date', which will be fixed by the judge when the order is granted. So far as practicable, any application to discharge or vary the order should be dealt with on the return date. Clause 13 of the standard form of freezing order in PD 25A enables the defendant or any third party notified of the order to apply to the court at any time (ie less than the usual three clear days' notice), but must first notify the claimant's legal representatives. The standard form also says, at cl 5, that the order will continue 'until further order'. This is a reference to an order which expressly or impliedly discharges the freezing order. A freezing order does not therefore lapse when final judgment is entered against the defendant: *Cantor Index Ltd v Lister* (2001) LTL 22/11/01.

Standard-form orders

The standard-form freezing injunction order for domestic freezing injunctions and world- **43.41** wide freezing injunctions can be found in the annex to PD 25A. This form should always be used, with only such modifications as are essential to fit the circumstances of the case. Any substantial variation should be brought to the attention of the judge at the hearing. Wherever possible, a draft of the order sought should be filed with the application notice, with a copy on a digital storage device (PD 25A, para 2.4).

Notification Injunction

A slightly less draconian form of order is what is called a notification injunction. This **43.42** restrains the defendant from dealing with any of its property (usually above a stated value) without first giving the claimant's solicitors advance notice (typically seven days' notice) of any proposed transaction. Although it is less onerous than a traditional freezing injunction, the test for granting a notification injunction is the traditional freezing injunction test (*Holyoake v Candy* [2017] 3 WLR 1131). They exist to cater for cases where on balance a full freezing injunction might not be granted.

D EFFECT OF THE ORDER

43.43 A defendant or anyone else with notice of a freezing injunction will be in contempt of court if they dispose or assist in the disposal or dissipation of enjoined assets: *Z Ltd v A-Z and AA-LL* [1982] QB 558 at 572 *per* Lord Denning MR. A freezing injunction covering unspecified assets has an ambulatory effect (*Cretanor Maritime Co Ltd v Irish Marine Management Ltd* [1978] 1 WLR 966 *per* Buckley LJ). Assets acquired by the defendant after the order is granted will be covered by it, up to the maximum sum (if any) stated in the order: *TDK Tape Distributor (UK) Ltd v Videochoice Ltd* [1986] 1 WLR 141.

E VARIATION OR DISCHARGE OF A FREEZING INJUNCTION

Procedure on application to vary or discharge

43.44 Applications to vary or discharge freezing injunctions are made to a judge, either pursuant to the liberty to apply provision in the order itself, or on the claimant's application to renew the order on the return date. The application will be made in accordance with CPR, Part 23 (see Chapter 23).

43.45 A non-party who is affected by the terms of a freezing injunction can apply for a variation without intervening provided they have a clear interest (*Cretanor Maritime Co Ltd v Irish Marine Management Ltd* [1978] 1 WLR 966). If they are successful the non-party should be entitled to its costs on the indemnity basis (*Project Development Co Ltd SA v KMK Securities Ltd* [1982] 1 WLR 1470).

Grounds for variation

43.46 Variations of freezing injunctions may be allowed where the original order is more onerous to the defendant than is necessary, or if it imposes unnecessary obligations on a non-party. Examples are failures to include necessary provisos, such as for ordinary living expenses, paying trade debts, allowing banks the usual set-off, or making a general order when a maximum-sum order is appropriate. Hardship to third parties may also give grounds for a variation. In *Camdex International Ltd v Bank of Zambia (No 2)* [1997] 1 WLR 632 a freezing injunction had caught a large quantity of banknotes for issue in Zambia. It was varied to allow the release of the banknotes, to prevent serious damage being inflicted on the general population of the country.

Grounds for discharge

Case unsuitable for freezing injunction

43.47 A freezing injunction may be discharged on the ground that one of the usual requirements has not been made out. This may be on the basis, for example, that the claimant does not have a good arguable case, as in *Cheltenham and Gloucester Building Society v Ricketts* [1993] 1 WLR 1545. Alternatively, what may have appeared to be a good arguable case on the application without notice may be wiped out by an arguable defence or set-off. It may be that evidence concerning the defendant's financial status, business history, or links with this country (or other countries where an English judgment would be enforceable) will persuade the court that there is no real risk of the defendant dissipating the enjoined assets in order to frustrate any judgment the claimant may obtain. Further, a change in the management of a company defendant may remove the risk of dissipation and merit a freezing injunction being discharged: *Capital Cameras Ltd v Harold Lines Ltd* [1991] 1 WLR 54.

Security

A freezing injunction should be discharged where the defendant provides sufficient security **43.48** for the claim. Security can be provided by bond or guarantee, or by paying money into court. The standard security provision in a freezing injunction only gives 'security' against the risk of dissipation of assets. It does not provide security against the defendant's other creditors (*Technocrats International Inc v Fredic Ltd* [2005] 1 BCLC 467). Giving security can be to the advantage of the defendant, since it may be that the order has frozen an asset worth more to the defendant than the cost of the security being offered, and in any event it is often important for defendants for freezing injunctions to be discharged, as such orders carry a significant financial stigma and usually result in banking facilities being withdrawn.

Material non-disclosure

A consequence of freezing injunction applications being made without notice is that a **43.49** claimant applying for a freezing injunction is under a duty to give full and frank disclosure of any defence or other facts going against the grant of the relief sought. This duty is discussed at 23.23–23.26.

Unfair conduct

In *Negocios Del Mar SA v Doric Shipping Corporation SA* [1979] 1 Lloyd's Rep 331 the **43.50** claimants had agreed to buy a ship from the defendants. Before paying the agreed price, they discovered it was damaged. So they obtained a freezing injunction, which they served immediately on the exchange of the ship for the price. The effect was that the proceeds of the sale were immediately frozen in the hands of the sellers. This type of application is often called a 'trap application', and the circumstances are material facts which have to be disclosed under the duty of full and frank disclosure. On appeal, this was regarded as being unfair conduct on the part of the claimants, and the injunction was discharged.

Delay in the substantive proceedings

A failure to press on with the substantive claim may provide grounds for discharging a **43.51** freezing injunction. It was stated by Glidewell LJ in *Lloyds Bowmaker Ltd v Britannia Arrow Holdings plc* [1988] 1 WLR 1337 that:

> . . . a [claimant] who succeeds in obtaining a *Mareva* injunction is in my view under an obligation to press on with his action as rapidly as he can so that if he should fail to establish liability in the defendant the disadvantage which the injunction imposes upon the defendant will be lessened so far as possible.

F FREEZING INJUNCTIONS AFTER JUDGMENT

In *Orwell Steel (Erection and Fabrication) Ltd v Asphalt and Tarmac (UK) Ltd* [1984] 1 **43.52** WLR 1097 it was held that a freezing injunction may be granted in aid of the execution of a judgment debt. Provided the judgment is enforceable in England and Wales, the requirements that the claimant must have a cause of action justiciable in England and Wales and a good arguable case are satisfied by the judgment itself. Consequently, the only requirements are that the defendant has assets within the jurisdiction and there is a real risk of those assets being dissipated before judgment can be enforced. Undertakings in damages are required in the same way as in freezing injunctions before trial (*Banco Nacional de Comercio Exterior SNC v Empresa de Telecommunicationes de Cuba SA* [2007] 2 All ER (Comm) 1093) unless the exception mentioned in 43.25 applies.

G PROPRIETARY CLAIMS

43.53 Unlike a claim for damages, an equitable tracing claim is a claim of a proprietary character. The only interim protection that can be sought in a damages claim is a freezing injunction. Freezing injunctions operate in person, and freeze assets which belong to the defendant in order to prevent dissipation of those assets with the aim of ensuring the effectiveness of any eventual judgment. On the other hand, the assets covered by a proprietary claim are alleged to belong to the claimant. Rather than seeking a freezing injunction under CPR, r 25.1(1)(f), the claimant in a proprietary claim may seek an order for the detention, custody, or preservation of the property which is the subject of the claim under r 25.1(1)(c)(i). This is not a freezing injunction at all (*Fourie v Le Roux* [2007] 1 WLR 320). The key questions on such an application are whether there is sufficient evidence to establish that the property belongs to the claimant, and whether it is just to make the order. A proprietary claim may also be protected by an ordinary interim injunction, which will be granted on the usual *American Cyanamid Co v Ethicon Ltd* [1975] AC 396 principles (for which, see Chapter 42): *Polly Peck International plc v Nadir (No 2)* [1992] 4 All ER 769.

H WRIT *NE EXEAT REGNO*

43.54 The writ *ne exeat regno* prevents a person from leaving the jurisdiction. It originated in the 13th century as a prerogative writ, but was subsequently adapted by equity as a means of coercing a defendant to give bail on pain of arrest in cases where the defendant owed a debt that was equitable (so that the defendant was not liable under the old procedure of arrest on mesne process). It may be granted where the defendant may leave the jurisdiction to the damage of a claimant to whom the defendant is indebted until he or she gives security for the debt. A good deal of caution is applied before the writ will be issued: *Allied Arab Bank Ltd v Hajjar* [1988] QB 787.

KEY POINTS SUMMARY

43.55
- Freezing injunctions are prohibitory injunctions preventing dishonest defendants from dissipating their assets to frustrate any judgment that might be obtained.
- There are exacting requirements on the application (see 43.08ff).
- The order operates against the defendant personally, and does not give the claimant any advantages in any insolvency.
- It is recognized that freezing injunctions could have a draconian effect, and numerous safeguards for the defendant and persons holding the defendant's assets are built into the standard order.
- Alerting the defendant could well result in the defendant taking steps to hide its assets, so freezing injunctions are invariably sought without notice, and the applicant is under a duty of full and frank disclosure.

44

SEARCH ORDERS

A PROCEDURE 44.04
B PRINCIPLES .44.08
C REAL RISK OF DESTRUCTION 44.12
D FORM OF THE ORDER 44.15
E PRACTICE ON EXECUTION OF
   SEARCH ORDERS 44.17

F PRIVILEGE 44.28
G DISCHARGE AND VARIATION OF
   SEARCH ORDERS 44.30
H AFTER EXECUTION 44.33
I COLLATERAL USE 44.36
   Key points summary 44.37

A search order is a bundle of interim orders which require the respondent to admit anoth-   **44.01**
er party to premises for the purpose of preserving evidence which might otherwise be
destroyed or concealed by the respondent (CPR, r 25.1(1)(h)). The potential oppression
inherent in the order is recognized by the courts, and a search order is regarded as at the
extremity of the court's powers. Statutory authority for the jurisdiction is given by the
Civil Procedure Act 1997, s 7. Prior to the introduction of the CPR this form of order was
commonly known as an *Anton Piller* order, taking its name from *Anton Piller KG v Manufacturing Processes Ltd* [1976] Ch 55.

A search order is both injunctive and mandatory in nature. It requires the intended defendant   **44.02**
to allow a named supervising solicitor from an independent firm, a partner from the claimant's own solicitors, and a limited number of additional people to enter on to the defendant's
premises, and any vehicles in the defendant's control in the vicinity of those premises, so that
they can search for, inspect, take photocopies of, and remove specified items and documents.
The specified items and documents are those likely to be probative in the proceedings. The
order will also often require the intended defendant to deliver up relevant documents not
located at the premises searched, and to verify information on affidavit.

Although the jurisdiction to make search orders may be invoked in any type of claim, it is   **44.03**
most frequently encountered in claims for infringement of intellectual property rights in
the entertainment industry. A search order can also be made in aid of execution, to find evidence of a judgment debtor's assets, and for this purpose can be made against non-parties
(*Abela v Baardarani (No 2)* [2018] 1 WLR 89).

A PROCEDURE

Search orders are, by virtue of the County Court Remedies Regulations 2014 (SI 2014/982),   **44.04**
available:

(a) in the High Court, which is the usual venue. Intellectual property claims, which form
    the bulk of the cases where this type of application is likely to be made, are assigned to
    the Chancery Division; and

(b) in the County Court, provided the judge dealing with the application is a High Court or Court of Appeal judge. Otherwise the application must be made in the High Court (*Schmidt v Wong* [2006] 1 WLR 561).

44.05 Search orders are obtainable only against defendants who are likely to destroy relevant evidence if an application on notice were to be made (see 44.12–44.14). Consequently, secrecy is essential, so the application will be made without notice and the court will sit in private. Many applications are also urgent, and many are made before proceedings are issued. The general procedure for applications for interim injunctions applies, for which see 42.06–42.24. Essentially, the claimant must:

(a) have issued a claim form in respect of the substantive cause of action, unless the application is too urgent to wait for this to be done;

(b) issue an application notice;

(c) provide affidavit evidence in support (witness statements are not acceptable: PD 25A, para 3.1);

(d) provide a draft order, together with a copy on disk; and

(e) provide a skeleton argument in support.

44.06 As the application is made without notice, the claimant has the usual duty of full and frank disclosure. The courts have insisted that this is especially important in applications for search orders, and the claimant should err on the side of excessive disclosure. The affidavit must state the name and experience of the proposed supervising solicitor, and give the name and address of his or her firm. The proposed supervising solicitor must be someone experienced in the operation of search orders (PD 25A, para 7.2) and must not be a member or employee of the claimant's solicitors (para 7.6). The affidavit must disclose in very full terms the reason for seeking the order, including the probability that relevant material will disappear if the order is not made (para 7.3).

44.07 It is very common to combine applications for search orders with other forms of urgent interim relief. It is not unknown, to use the old terminology, to 'pile *Piller* upon *Mareva*' in fraud and pirating claims.

B PRINCIPLES

44.08 Ormrod LJ in *Anton Piller KG v Manufacturing Processes Ltd* [1976] Ch 55 laid down the following preconditions for granting search orders:

(a) There must be an extremely strong *prima facie* case on the merits. It is worth contrasting this with the requirement to merely show a good arguable case in applications for freezing orders.

(b) The defendant's activities must be proved to result in very serious potential or actual harm to the claimant's interests.

(c) There must be clear evidence that incriminating documents or materials are in the defendant's possession.

(d) There must be a real possibility that such items may be destroyed before any applications on notice can be made. This is considered at 44.12–44.14.

44.09 In the early 1980s it was thought that these conditions had been relaxed by *Yousif v Salama* [1980] 1 WLR 1540 and *Dunlop Holdings Ltd v Staravia Ltd* [1982] Com LR 3. In the former it was inferred that there was a real risk of the defendant disobeying any orders made on applications on notice from evidence that he had forged a signature on a cheque. In the latter, Oliver LJ said:

. . . it has certainly become customary to infer the probability of disappearance or destruction of evidence where it is clearly established on the evidence before the court that the defendant is engaged in a nefarious activity which renders it likely that he is an untrustworthy person. It is seldom that one can get cogent or actual evidence of a threat to destroy material or documents.

Since *Booker McConnell plc v Plascow* [1985] RPC 425 there has been a marked change in **44.10** judicial attitude, and nowadays the courts insist on strict compliance with the principles enunciated by Ormrod LJ in *Anton Piller KG v Manufacturing Processes Ltd*. The order is regarded as a serious stigma on the defendant's commercial reputation, and will often result in banks refusing further credit or even calling in loans. The order itself often allows the claimant's representatives to remove the defendant's stock-in-trade, and the net result is often to drive the defendant out of business. Accordingly, the order is regarded as a remedy of last resort, and should be made only 'when there is no alternative' (*per* Ormrod LJ in *Anton Piller KG v Manufacturing Processes Ltd*). As Dillon LJ explained in *Booker McConnell plc v Plascow*:

. . . the courts have always proceeded, justifiably, on the basis that the overwhelming majority of people in this country will comply with the court's order, and that defendants will therefore comply with orders to, eg, produce and deliver up documents without it being necessary to empower the [claimants'] solicitors to search the defendant's premises.

Putting the matter slightly differently, Hoffmann J in *Lock International plc v Beswick* **44.11** [1989] 1 WLR 1268 said at 1281: 'there must be *proportionality* between the perceived threat to the [claimant's] rights and the remedy granted'. Before embarking on an application for a search order, it is therefore necessary to consider whether some less draconian measure, such as applying on notice for negative injunctions or for an order that the documents be delivered up to the defendant's solicitor, or even awaiting disclosure in the usual way, would adequately protect the claimant.

C REAL RISK OF DESTRUCTION

A search order will not be made unless there is a 'real possibility' that material evidence **44.12** will be destroyed if the defendant is given notice of an application for disclosure (*Anton Piller KG v Manufacturing Processes Ltd* [1976] Ch 55). This formula has been adopted in numerous cases since 1976. It is possible that the CPR have made a slight alteration in this requirement. Paragraph 7.3(2) of PD 25A referring to the evidence needed in support of an application for a search order, says it must cover 'the probability' that relevant material would disappear if the order were not made. There is a slight difference between a 'real possibility' and a 'probability', in that the latter expression means that the risk of destruction has to be proved on the balance of probabilities, whereas the earlier expression can be satisfied by evidence coming a little distance short of establishing the risk on the balance of probabilities. However, it is doubtful that para 7.3(2), which is a provision dealing with the evidence required in support of an application, can have been intended to alter the established conditions for the remedy.

The requirement to show that there is a real risk that the defendant will destroy vital evi- **44.13** dence lies at the heart of the jurisdiction to grant search orders. Sometimes it is possible to infer this risk from the nature of the defendant's alleged conduct, for instance in video pirating claims and commercial fraud actions. Even in these cases, however, the claimant is still obliged to give full and frank disclosure of anything known about the defendant, including past responsible conduct or other matters which tend to show the defendant would obey the court's orders.

Outside the area of actions based directly on dishonesty, it will be rare for the claimant to **44.14** have evidence of a real risk of destruction. An example is *Lock International plc v Beswick*

[1989] 1 WLR 1268, where the claimant alleged that the defendants, who were former employees now competing with the claimant, were making use of its trade secrets and confidential information. A search order was executed, and the defendants successfully applied to discharge the order. Hoffmann J said the claimant's evidence:

> . . . came nowhere near [establishing] . . . a 'grave danger' or 'real possibility' that the defendants might destroy evidence . . . these defendants were no fly-by-night video pirates. They were former long-service employees with families and mortgages, who had openly said that they were entering into competition and whom the [claimant] knew to be financed by highly respectable institutions.

D FORM OF THE ORDER

44.15 A model form of search order is provided in the annex to PD 25A. This form should always be used, with only such modifications as are essential to fit the circumstances of the case. Any substantial variation from the form should be brought to the attention of the judge at the hearing.

44.16 The main provision is cl 6, which provides that the defendant 'must permit [certain people] to enter' the defendant's premises. The rest of cll 1–21 are designed to give effect to the basic purpose of the order, which is to allow the claimant to enter the defendant's premises and to take documents which might be disclosable in the proceedings or otherwise relevant, while providing suitable safeguards for the defendant. These include the appointment of an independent supervising solicitor to ensure that the order is not misused by the claimant. Clause 22 may be used to set out prohibitory injunctions ancillary to the main part of the order. Schedule B sets out the items that may be seized, and must extend no further than the minimum necessary to preserve the evidence which might otherwise be concealed or destroyed: *Columbia Picture Industries Inc v Robinson* [1987] Ch 38.

E PRACTICE ON EXECUTION OF SEARCH ORDERS

Service of the order

44.17 Since *Universal Thermosensors Ltd v Hibben* [1992] 1 WLR 840, execution of search orders has been effected by supervising solicitors who are independent of the claimant's usual solicitors. Before this case there was mounting concern about the execution of search orders by enthusiastic but inexperienced persons. Execution by a solicitor related to the claimant or by one of the claimant's directors was deprecated in *Manor Electronics Ltd v Dickson* [1988] RPC 618.

44.18 The order must be served personally by the supervising solicitor, unless the court otherwise orders. Together with the order there must be served an application notice for a hearing on notice in respect of the search order. The affidavits in support and any exhibits capable of being copied must be served at the same time as the order (PD 25A, para 7.4(1)). Confidential exhibits need not be served, but they must be made available for inspection by the defendant in the presence of the claimant's solicitors while the order is being executed. Copies of confidential exhibits may be retained by the defendant's solicitors on their undertaking not to permit the defendant to see them except in their presence, nor to allow the defendant to make or take away any note or record of them (para 7.4(2)). Unless the court otherwise orders, service may be effected only between 9.30 a.m. and 5.30 p.m., Monday to Friday (para 7.4(6)). The reason for this is that the defendant is entitled to seek legal advice, and this will be effective only if the order is executed during office hours. It is recognized that mistakes (on both sides) are less likely to occur if these orders are executed during office hours (*Adam Phones Ltd v Goldschmidt* [1999] 4 All ER 486).

Planning is essential for effective execution. If several addresses are included in the order, **44.19** it is important that execution is simultaneous. To reduce its oppressive effect the order will limit the number of persons who can assist with its execution at each address specified. Further, if the defendant is a woman living alone, a woman must accompany those executing the order (para 7.4(5)). The police will be informed beforehand if there is any prospect of a breach of the peace.

Gaining access

A search order is not a search warrant, and does not authorize the use of force to gain **44.20** access. In cases where the defendant has committed both a civil wrong against the claimant and a criminal offence, a search order must not be executed at the same time as a police search warrant. Clause 6 of the standard search order is a mandatory order that the defendant 'must permit' access to the supervising solicitor. Before entering the supervising solicitor must explain the terms and effect of the order in everyday language. The supervising solicitor must inform the defendant that legal advice may be sought before entry is permitted and of the defendant's right to apply to vary or discharge the order, and that the defendant may be entitled to avail himself of legal professional privilege and the privilege against self-incrimination. A solicitor who negligently failed to explain the effect of the order to the defendant in a fair and accurate manner was held to be in contempt of court in *VDU Installations Ltd v Integrated Computer Systems and Cybernetics Ltd* [1989] FSR 378. The right to seek legal advice means that the obligation to give permission for entry arises only after a reasonable period of time has elapsed for legal advice to be obtained: *Bhimji v Chatwani* [1991] 1 WLR 989. Thereafter, the defendant must give permission, or else will be in contempt of court. Even if there are grounds for seeking an order for the immediate discharge of the search order, while it subsists it is an order of the court and must be obeyed: *Wardle Fabrics Ltd v G Myristis Ltd* [1984] FSR 263. However, if entry is refused and the order is successfully discharged shortly thereafter, that will give the court grounds for imposing no penalty on an application to commit for contempt of court. Matters to be taken into account include whether an application to discharge is merely a device to delay the search, and whether the defendant has interfered with the evidence during the delay: *Bhimji v Chatwani*.

Search and removal

There is a heavy duty on the solicitors to comply strictly with the terms of the order as to **44.21** the premises which can be searched and the items which can be removed. The defendant's premises must not be searched, and no items may be removed, except in the presence of the defendant or a person who appears to be a responsible employee of the defendant (PD 25A, para 7.5(2)). If any of the items covered by the order exist only in computer-readable form, the defendant must immediately give the claimant's solicitors effective access, including any necessary passwords, and arrange for the material to be printed out. The claimant must take all reasonable steps to ensure that no damage is done to the defendant's computer system, and must ensure that the person searching the defendant's system has sufficient expertise to avoid causing damage (para 7.5(8)–(10)). Items seized must be recorded by the supervising solicitor in a list, and must be retained by the claimant's solicitors for the minimum time necessary to take copies and in any case for no more than two days, after which they must be returned to their owner (para 7.5(3) and (6)). Nothing should be removed until the defendant has had a reasonable opportunity to check it against the list (para 7.5(7)). Where ownership of the material seized is in dispute, the claimant's solicitors should place it in the custody of the defendant's solicitors pending trial on the defendant's solicitors undertaking to retain it in safekeeping and to produce it to the court when required (para 7.5(4)). It may be appropriate for the order to require the claimant to insure the materials seized (para 7.5(5)).

44.22 Execution of a search order in an excessive or oppressive manner will render the claimant liable under the undertaking in damages. Seizing documents not specified in the order may be penalized by an award of aggravated damages. An award of £10,000 against the claimant was made on this ground in *Columbia Picture Industries Inc v Robinson* [1987] Ch 38.

44.23 It is important that neither the claimant nor the claimant's employees are allowed to conduct searches for documents belonging to a trade competitor. Safeguards must be built into the order to protect the confidentiality of the defendant's trade secrets.

Additional powers and duties of the supervising solicitor

44.24 It may become apparent that it is impracticable to comply fully with the requirement that the defendant be allowed to check the claimant's list of materials before anything is removed from the premises, or the conditions for accessing material stored on computer. If the supervising solicitor is satisfied that compliance is impracticable, he or she may permit the search to proceed and for items to be removed without full compliance (PD 25A, para 7.5(13)).

44.25 Once the search has been completed, the supervising solicitor must provide the claimant's solicitors with a report on the carrying out of the order. The claimant's solicitors must then serve a copy on the defendant and file a copy with the court (PD 25A, para 7.5(11) and (12)).

Non-compliance by the defendant

44.26 In *Alliance and Leicester Building Society v Ghahremani* (1992) 142 NLJ 313 a search order was executed at the premises of a firm of solicitors. The order required the defendant solicitor to disclose 'documents' of various categories. There was evidence that the defendant erased information stored on computer while the order was being executed. Hoffmann J held that the word 'document' in the order was, in the light of the earlier decision of *Derby and Co Ltd v Weldon (No 9)* [1991] 1 WLR 652, wide enough to include information stored on computer, and that the defendant was guilty of contempt of court. It is probable that if the defendant had not been a lawyer the court would have held that the wording was insufficiently clear to found an application for committal. It is for this reason that the standard search order contains specific provision in cl 17 for printing out information stored on computer. In addition to being a contempt of court, 'the refusal to comply may be the most damning evidence against the defendant at the subsequent trial' (*per* Ormrod LJ in *Anton Piller KG v Manufacturing Processes Ltd* [1976] Ch 55).

44.27 On the other hand, a petty breach of a search order in circumstances where the defendant had honestly tried to obey it should be ignored by the parties. Under the CPR, given the emphasis on proportionality, an application to commit for no more than a technicality is likely to be dismissed with costs: *Adam Phones Ltd v Goldschmidt* [1999] 4 All ER 486.

F PRIVILEGE

44.28 Legal professional privilege and the privilege against self-incrimination were discussed at 31.37ff. The operation of the privilege against self-incrimination threatened to destroy the utility of search orders in intellectual property piracy claims, but this was averted by the passing of the SCA 1981, s 72, and the other statutory provisions discussed at 31.43ff. These statutory provisions are wide-ranging, but do not completely remove the privilege against self-incrimination.

In cases of disputed privilege, the usual procedure is for the defendant to ask the supervis- **44.29** ing solicitor to assess whether the materials are privileged. If they are, they will be excluded from the search. If the supervising solicitor feels they may be privileged, the supervising solicitor excludes them from the search, but retains them pending further order from the court (cl 11 of the standard order).

G DISCHARGE AND VARIATION OF SEARCH ORDERS

Applications to discharge or vary search orders are largely governed by the principles **44.30** already discussed in relation to freezing injunctions at 43.44–43.51. However, if a search order has been executed, there is a strong argument that it is an unjustified waste of costs and of the court's time to seek its discharge before trial. Doing so was said by Browne-Wilkinson V-C in *Dormeuil Frères SA v Nicolian International (Textiles) Ltd* [1988] 1 WLR 1362 to be little more than an empty gesture, and that the right course was normally to adjourn an application to set aside the order to be dealt with at trial. In *Tate Access Floors Inc v Boswell* [1991] Ch 512 it was recognized there is a conflict between the public interest in ensuring that applications made without notice are made in good faith, and the public interest in ensuring that the courts are not clogged up with long interim hearings. The Vice-Chancellor suggested the solution may be that the circumstances in which an order without notice was obtained should be investigated at the pre-trial stage only if it is clear there has been a material non-disclosure or where the nature of the alleged non-disclosure is so serious as to demand immediate investigation. Where a search order has been executed at the defendant's home, the court should allow the defendant a hearing on an application to discharge the search order unless there is not even a *prima facie* case of abuse (*Indicil Salus Ltd v Chandrasekaran* (2006) LTL 16/2/06).

The court has a discretion to exclude documents seized under a search order which is **44.31** subsequently discharged (CPR, r 32.1). The discretion is exercised in accordance with the overriding objective. Key factors are the importance of the documents, and the reasons why the search order was discharged.

One of the defendants in *Coca-Cola Co v Gilbey* [1995] 4 All ER 711 argued that he **44.32** should not be required to disclose the identities of other persons involved with him in a highly organized passing-off operation, and other information, as required by a search order, on the ground that doing so might expose him and his family to physical violence from those other persons. It was held that, although violence or threats of violence would be legitimate grounds if put forward by innocent parties, when put forward by actual participants, public policy and the interests of the victim carried more weight, and disclosure was ordered forthwith.

H AFTER EXECUTION

After executing the order, the supervising solicitor is required to compile a report of what **44.33** happened (see 44.24–44.25). The report is served on the defendant. Clause 3 of the standard search order provides that there will be a further hearing on notice to the defendants on a specified date (called the return date), which is usually a few days after the date of the original order. The applicant's solicitors are required (Sch D, para 1(iii)) to provide the supervising solicitor with an application notice for hearing on the return date, which is served with the search order.

44.34　On the return date the court will consider the supervising solicitor's report and the defendant may apply to discharge the order. Once a search order has been executed, there is an enhanced duty on the claimant to prosecute the main claim without delay. In *Hytrac Conveyors Ltd v Conveyors International Ltd* [1983] 1 WLR 44, the claimant delayed for ten weeks after obtaining a search order without serving a statement of claim. The claim was dismissed, Lawton LJ saying that claimants 'must not use [search] orders as a means of finding out what sort of charges they could make'.

44.35　If the application was made in the High Court, but is otherwise more suitable for the County Court, after the application for the search order has been disposed of the claim will be transferred down to the County Court (County Court Remedies Regulations 2014 (SI 2014/982), reg 5). The application is not treated as disposed of until any application to set the order aside has been heard, or until the expiry of 28 days during which no such application is made.

I COLLATERAL USE

44.36　As with other forms of disclosure (see 31.88–31.90), the claimant gives an undertaking not to use items seized under a search order for any collateral purposes (Sch C, para 4, to the standard search order). The court may sanction a relaxation of this undertaking in a proper case. The leading case is *Crest Homes plc v Marks* [1987] AC 829. In 1984 the claimant brought a claim against the defendant seeking injunctions to restrain breach of copyright in certain house designs. In the course of those proceedings a search order was obtained and executed. In 1985 the claimant commenced a second copyright claim against the defendant in relation to another house design, and obtained and executed a second search order. Some of the documents seized under the second search order were alleged by the claimant to show the defendant had not given full disclosure under the first search order. The claimant therefore sought to use those documents in contempt proceedings in relation to the first search order. The House of Lords held that, although there were technically two separate claims, in substance they were a single set of proceedings. As the defendant would suffer no injustice by lifting the implied undertaking, permission was given to allow the claimant to use the documents in the contempt proceedings.

KEY POINTS SUMMARY

44.37
- Search orders are principally, but not exclusively, used in intellectual property claims against defendants who are likely to destroy incriminating evidence rather than disclose it voluntarily under standard disclosure.

- There are exacting requirements: see 44.08–44.14.

- A search order is a bundle of interim orders which require the defendant to permit entry to the claimant's solicitors for the purpose of searching for and taking away relevant evidence.

- It is recognized that these orders can be draconian, and various safeguards are built into the standard-form orders, including requirements that there should be an experienced supervising solicitor present during the search, and that the search should take place during office hours so that the defendant can obtain legal advice.

45

NORWICH PHARMACAL AND RELATED DISCLOSURE ORDERS

A *NORWICH PHARMACAL* ORDERS 45.02

B MERE WITNESS RULE..............45.13

C *BANKERS TRUST* ORDERS 45.14

D DISCLOSURE BEFORE
PROCEEDINGS START..............45.18

E DISCLOSURE BY NON-PARTIES 45.27

F DISCLOSURE OF MEDIATION
EVIDENCE.......................45.34

G INSPECTION OF PROPERTY DURING
PROCEEDINGS 45.35

H INTERIM DELIVERY-UP OF GOODS.....45.39

Key points summary 45.41

General disclosure of documents was considered in Chapter 31. Search orders, whereby the **45.01** court makes mandatory orders requiring the defendant to give access to premises for the purpose of enabling the claimant to take documents which might otherwise be destroyed, were discussed in Chapter 44. This chapter considers a number of other special forms of disclosure orders, the best known of which is the *Norwich Pharmacal* order.

A *NORWICH PHARMACAL* ORDERS

Principles

There are situations where proceedings cannot be brought because the identity of the true **45.02** defendant is unknown. By reviving the 19th-century Chancery procedure of the bill of discovery, the House of Lords in *Norwich Pharmacal Co v Customs and Excise Commissioners* [1974] AC 133 provided a possible means of discovering the identity of an unknown wrongdoer. Norwich Pharmacal owned the patent for a chemical used for immunizing poultry. It was aware that importers were infringing their patent, and knew that the Commissioners knew the identities of the importers. Proceedings were brought against the Commissioners to compel them to divulge the names of the importers. Lord Reid laid down the principle at 175:

> . . . that if through no fault of his own a person gets mixed up in the tortious acts of others so as to facilitate their wrongdoing he may incur no personal liability but he comes under a duty to assist the person who has been wronged by giving him full information and disclosing the identity of the wrongdoers. I do not think that it matters whether he became so mixed up by voluntary action on his part or because it was his duty to do what he did. It may be that if this causes him expense the person seeking the information ought to reimburse him. But justice requires that he should co-operate in righting the wrong if he unwittingly facilitated its perpetration.

Although *Norwich Pharmacal* had no substantive cause of action against the Commis- **45.03** sioners, the Commissioners had unwittingly facilitated the infringement by allowing the infringing goods into the country, so were ordered to disclose the identities of the importers. The *Norwich Pharmacal* jurisdiction is not restricted to claims in tort, but is of general application, and applies to claims in breach of confidence and breach of contract (*Ashworth Hospital Authority v MGN Ltd* [2002] 1 WLR 2033).

45.04   Provision of the documents or information must be necessary (*Ashworth Hospital Authority v MGN Ltd* at [57]). This is not intended to lay down a stringent test. Authorities such as *Mitsui and Co Ltd v Nexen Petroleum UK Ltd* [2005] 3 All ER 511, which said that *Norwich Pharmacal* orders are remedies of last resort, or that they can only be made if the evidence is the final piece in the jigsaw, were deprecated in *R (Mohamed) v Secretary of State for Foreign and Commonwealth Affairs (No 1)* [2009] 1 WLR 2579 (unaffected by the appeal, [2011] QB 218). Rather, the court must consider all the circumstances, including the resources of the applicant, the urgency of the need for the information, and any public interest in satisfying the applicant's need for the information. There is no obligation to give standard disclosure of documents under a *Norwich Pharmacal* order (*Arab Monetary Fund v Hashim (No 5)* [1992] 2 All ER 911).

45.05   An order will not be made for the mere gratification of curiosity. Where the claimant genuinely intends to bring proceedings against the wrongdoer, this condition is clearly satisfied. In *British Steel Corporation v Granada Television Ltd* [1981] AC 1096 Lord Wilberforce said he would have been prepared to grant relief where the claimant intended to seek redress 'by court proceedings or otherwise'. Other forms of redress might include dismissal from employment and deprivation of pension rights (*Ashworth Hospital Authority v MGN Ltd* [2002] 1 WLR 2033).

45.06   A defendant who is a tortfeasor, and not simply a person who has innocently become 'mixed up' in some wrongdoing, is *a fortiori* under a *Norwich Pharmacal* duty to assist the claimant by disclosing the identities of other persons involved in the wrongdoing (*British Steel Corporation v Granada Television Ltd*). In *X Ltd v Morgan-Grampian (Publishers) Ltd* [1991] 1 AC 1 the House of Lords held that, where the claimant sought disclosure of the name of an unknown tortfeasor from a defendant against whom there existed a substantive cause of action related to that against the unknown party, the defendant was amenable to the full scope of the court's powers to order disclosure in the course of the proceedings. Such orders are commonly included in freezing injunctions and search orders.

45.07   Being part of the equitable jurisdiction of the court, *Norwich Pharmacal* relief is discretionary, and may be refused even if someone has got 'mixed up' in some wrongdoing so as to 'facilitate' its commission. Also, it will not override a respondent's right to assert privilege, public interest immunity, or state immunity (*Koo Golden East Mongolia v Bank of Nova Scotia* [2008] QB 717). Further, the *Norwich Pharmacal* jurisdiction does not apply to any area governed by statute. On this ground it was held in *R (Omar) v Secretary of State for Foreign and Commonwealth Affairs* [2014] QB 112 that *Norwich Pharmacal* orders are not available for use in foreign criminal proceedings, because this area is covered by the Crime (International Co-operation) Act 2003.

Journalists' sources

45.08   Section 10 of the Contempt of Court Act 1981 gives a general protection to journalists' sources of information, and was enacted to give effect to the strong public interest in preserving the right to information. Section 10 provides:

> No court may require a person to disclose, nor is any person guilty of contempt of court for refusing to disclose, the source of information contained in a publication for which he is responsible, unless it be established to the satisfaction of the court that disclosure is necessary in the interests of justice or national security or for the prevention of disorder or crime.

Section 10 applies despite any proprietary claim by the claimant for delivery-up of sto- **45.09** len documents if the documents could lead to identifying the 'source' (*Secretary of State for Defence v Guardian Newspapers Ltd* [1985] AC 339). It also applies despite non-publication of the information as long as the information was provided with a view to publication (*X Ltd v Morgan-Grampian (Publishers) Ltd* [1991] 1 AC 1). In *Totalise plc v Motley Fool Ltd* (2001) *The Times*, 15 March 2001, a website operator was ordered to disclose the identity of a website user who, it was alleged, had posted defamatory comments on the defendant's website. It was held that the Contempt of Court Act 1981, s 10, had no application to the facts because the defendant took no responsibility for items posted on their website, since the section applied to information 'contained in a publication for which he is responsible'. The interrelation between the Contempt of Court Act 1981, s 10, and the European Convention on Human Rights, art 10 (freedom of expression), was considered in *Ashworth Hospital Authority v MGN Ltd* [2002] 1 WLR 2033, where it was concluded that the section's aims coincided with those of art 10.

The two exceptions to the section most likely to arise in *Norwich Pharmacal* applications are **45.10** disclosure in the interests of justice and to prevent crime. The meaning of the phrase 'interests of justice' in the section is 'that persons should be enabled to exercise important legal rights and to protect themselves from serious legal wrongs whether or not resort to legal proceedings in a court of law will be necessary to attain these objectives' (*per* Lord Bridge of Harwich in *X Ltd v Morgan-Grampian (Publishers) Ltd*). Prevention of crime includes, according to Lord Oliver of Aylmerton in *Re an Inquiry under the Company Securities (Insider Dealing) Act 1985* [1988] AC 660, 'the detection and prosecution of crimes which are shown to have been committed and where detection and prosecution could sensibly be said to act as a practical deterrent to future criminal conduct of a similar type'. This may be the case where documents are stolen and later used as the basis of a journalistic article.

Thus, where a *Norwich Pharmacal* order is sought against a journalist, the claimant must first **45.11** satisfy the court that one of the exceptions applies. It is to be noted that the section requires such disclosure to be 'necessary'. The court must then weigh the importance of achieving justice or preventing crime in the circumstances of the case against the importance of protecting the source of the information. Factors to be taken into account include the degree of confidentiality attaching to the information, the manner in which the information was obtained, the public interest in concealing journalists' sources, and whether the information brings to light iniquity on the part of the claimant. According to Lord Bridge in *X Ltd v Morgan-Grampian (Publishers) Ltd*, disclosure should be ordered only if the balance is clearly on the side of disclosure, since otherwise the courts would be undermining the clear policy stated in the section.

Procedure

As a *Norwich Pharmacal* order is a form of substantive relief (*AB Bank Ltd v Abu Dhabi Com-* **45.12** *mercial Bank PJSC* [2017] 1 WLR 810), a claim must first be commenced against the facilitator by issuing a claim form. An interim application is then made, supported by evidence by witness statement or affidavit. *Norwich Pharmacal* orders are only available against facilitators within the jurisdiction, and there is no power to order service outside the jurisdiction (*AB Bank Ltd v Abu Dhabi Commercial Bank PJSC*). As previously mentioned, if the defendant is also a wrongdoer a *Norwich Pharmacal* order can be incorporated into freezing injunctions and search orders. In urgent cases where delay may result in substantial irreparable harm it is possible for the application to be made without notice, as happened in *Loose v Williamson* [1978] 1 WLR 639. If an order is made against an innocent party, the claimant is usually required to pay that person's costs, but may be able to recover them from the true defendant in either the same or a subsequent claim (*SmithKline and French Laboratories Ltd v RD Harbottle (Mercantile) Ltd* [1980] RPC 363).

B MERE WITNESS RULE

45.13 A person who has become mixed up in a tort in such a way as to facilitate its commission, against whom it is possible to obtain a *Norwich Pharmacal* order, must be distinguished from a mere witness. Although mere witnesses may be compelled by witness summons to give evidence at trial, they cannot generally be compelled to assist a party before then. The fact that a person knows the identity of a tortfeasor does not make that person a facilitator. Thus, in *Ricci v Chow* [1987] 1 WLR 1658 the claimant alleged that a journal published by the Seychellois National Movement defamed him. The defendant was the secretary of the Movement, knew the identities of the alleged tortfeasors, but had nothing to do with the publication of the journal. The *Norwich Pharmacal* order was refused. Also of interest is *Harrington v Polytechnic of North London* [1984] 1 WLR 1293. The claimant was a student who was prevented from attending the polytechnic by student pickets. Photographs were taken of the pickets, and the claimant sought an order compelling the lecturers to identify the pickets. It was held that the lecturers were mere witnesses when acting in their private capacity, but as employees of the polytechnic they could be compelled to provide the information as the polytechnic had become mixed up in and facilitated the wrongdoing.

C *BANKERS TRUST* ORDERS

45.14 By an extension of the *Norwich Pharmacal* principle, an order can be made for disclosure in aid of a tracing claim to find what has been done with the misapplied money. The purpose is to prevent equity being invoked in vain by the subject matter of proceedings disappearing by the time the case reaches trial. The order takes its name from *Bankers Trust Co v Shapira* [1980] 1 WLR 1274. It is an order requiring a third party, often a bank, to disclose information and documents relating to the financial affairs of the defendant.

Principles

45.15 *Bankers Trust* orders are granted only in urgent cases. If there is no urgency, the information should be sought under the Bankers' Books Evidence Act 1879. Otherwise, the preconditions to the granting of a *Bankers Trust* order are:

(a) there must be good reason to believe that the third party either holds or has held property belonging to the claimant; and

(b) the potential advantage to the claimant in obtaining the order has to be balanced against the detriment against the third party in terms of costs, invasion of privacy, and breach of obligations of confidentiality to others.

45.16 Although any documents produced by the third party in compliance with the order will be protected by an implied undertaking not to use them for any collateral purpose (see 31.88), it was held in *Omar v Omar* [1995] 1 WLR 1428 that documents obtained under such an order in a tracing claim could be used for the purpose of mounting personal claims against the individual responsible for the original breach of trust or theft.

Procedure

45.17 *Bankers Trust* orders are often included in freezing injunctions. Third parties subject to such orders are joined to the claim as additional defendants. The claimant is required to give an undertaking in damages, and must undertake to pay all expenses incurred by the third party in complying with the order. If granted, the third party is required to file and serve written evidence stating whether the property has ever been in its possession and what has become of it.

D DISCLOSURE BEFORE PROCEEDINGS START

Under the SCA 1981, s 33(2), and the equivalent County Court provision in CCA 1984, **45.18**
s 52, a person who appears to the court to be likely to be a party to proceedings and to be
likely to have or to have had in his possession, custody, or power any documents which
are relevant to an issue arising or likely to arise out of that claim, can be ordered to disclose those documents before the substantive proceedings are started. The purpose of these
provisions is to bring forward the time when disclosure takes place to the pre-action stage,
mainly with the intention of promoting early settlement if possible, or to enable a potential
litigant to make a better informed decision on whether to litigate at all, or to prepare their
statement of case, where important information is held by the other side. The jurisdiction
under these provisions ends once proceedings are commenced (*Personal Management Solutions Ltd v Gee 7 Group Ltd* [2016] 1 WLR 2132).

Ordering disclosure before proceedings

There is a two-stage approach that must be followed by a court dealing with an applica- **45.19**
tion for pre-action disclosure (*Black v Sumitomo Corporation* [2002] 1 WLR 1562). At the
first stage it considers whether the jurisdictional requirements, which are mainly in CPR,
r 31.16(3), are satisfied. If they are, the court proceeds to the second stage, where it exercises its discretion whether to make the order. The jurisdictional requirements are:

(a) The applicant must appear likely to be a party to future proceedings (CPR, r 31.16(3)(b)).
    This means court proceedings, not arbitration (*Travelers Insurance Co Ltd v Countryside
    Surveyors Ltd* [2011] 1 All ER (Comm) 631).
(b) The defendant must appear to be a likely party (r 31.16(3)(a)).
(c) It must appear likely that relevant documents are or have been in the defendant's pos-
    session, custody, or power (SCA 1981, s 33(2)).
(d) If proceedings had started, the respondent's duty by way of standard disclosure, set out
    in r 31.6, would extend to the documents or classes of documents of which the appli-
    cant seeks disclosure (r 31.16(3)(c)).
(e) Disclosure before proceedings must be desirable (r 31.16(3)(d)) in order:
    (i)   to dispose fairly of the anticipated proceedings;
    (ii) to assist the dispute to be resolved without proceedings; or
    (iii) to save costs.

There were conflicting authorities on the required strength of the substantive claim. The **45.20**
problem arose from the use of the word 'likely' in conditions (a) and (b). In *Black v Sumitomo Corporation* [2002] 1 WLR 1562 Rix LJ held that this word is intended to convey
the idea that the applicant and the respondent to the application must be likely to be
parties if subsequent proceedings are in fact issued. This should have been the end of the
issue, but the judgments then went on to discuss whether 'likely' was to be interpreted as
requiring proof on the balance of probabilities, or if it only meant that proceedings 'may
well' be issued, with the conclusion that it was the latter. Other authorities, such as *Rose
v Lynx Express Ltd* [2004] 1 BCLC 455, have used language such as 'prima facie case',
'arguable case', or 'a real prospect of success'. After reviewing these authorities, needing to
establish a case on the merits at the first stage was rejected by the Court of Appeal in *Smith
v Secretary of State for Energy and Climate Change* [2014] 1 WLR 2283 (a decision which
was approved and applied by *Jet Airways (India) Ltd v Barloworld Handling Ltd* [2014]
EWCA Civ 1311). None of the jurisdictional requirements in r 31.16 expressly refer to the
merits of the potential claim, and there is no basis for implying any such requirement at
the first stage.

45.21 Under the fifth of the jurisdictional requirements, the court has to undertake a balancing exercise to determine whether pre-action disclosure is 'desirable' in one of the three ways set out in r 31.16(3)(d): *Bermuda International Securities Ltd v KPMG* [2001] CPLR 252. Pre-action disclosure of medical records in non-clinical dispute cases is rarely 'desirable' as the issues will rarely be clear at this stage and there is the potential for disclosure of irrelevant but embarrassing information (*OCS Group Ltd v Wells* [2009] 1 WLR 1895). If the applicant already has sufficient material to plead a claim, it is unlikely to be 'desirable' to order pre-action disclosure (*First Gulf Bank v Wachovia Bank National Association* (2005) LTL 15/12/05).

45.22 At the second stage the court will consider factors such as the degree to which the documents sought are likely to support the proposed claim, whether they are merely 'train-of-inquiry' documents, together with the cost and difficulty of complying (*Black v Sumitomo Corporation* [2002] 1 WLR 1562). The merits of the substantive claim may be relevant as a discretionary factor at the second stage. Rather than talking about 'real prospect of success' or whether there is an 'arguable' claim, the court should consider whether the applicant has shown some reason to believe he has suffered some compensatable injury. If not, or if any claim is only speculative, an application may be refused in the exercise of the court's discretion.

Procedure

45.23 The procedure on applications for pre-action disclosure is laid down in CPR, r 31.16. An ordinary application notice must be issued, supported by written evidence which must address the five requirements set out earlier, and any discretionary factors. These applications are intended to be disposed of swiftly and economically, and without elaborate arguments (*Smith v Secretary of State for Energy and Climate Change* [2014] 1 WLR 2283).

Orders for disclosure before proceedings start

45.24 It is provided in CPR, r 31.16(4) and (5), that:

(4) An order under this rule must—
  (a) specify the documents or the classes of documents which the respondent must disclose; and
  (b) require him, when making disclosure, to specify any of those documents—
    (i) which are no longer in his control; or
    (ii) in respect of which he claims a right or duty to withhold inspection.

(5) Such an order may—
  (a) require the respondent to indicate what has happened to any documents which are no longer in his control; and
  (b) specify the time and place for disclosure and inspection.

Directions to commence substantive proceedings

45.25 Where the court grants an interim remedy before a claim has been commenced, it should give directions requiring a claim to be commenced (CPR, r 25.2(3)). A special rule, however, applies to applications for pre-action disclosure, with r 25.2(4) providing that the court need not direct that a claim be commenced where a pre-action disclosure order is made. The reason for the distinction is that pre-action disclosure orders may result in the claimant deciding not to bring substantive proceedings at all, as recognized in *Dunning v United Liverpool Hospitals, Board of Governors* [1973] 1 WLR 586, and it would not make sense to require the claimant to bring a substantive claim in such circumstances.

Costs of pre-action disclosure

The person against whom a pre-action disclosure order is made will usually be awarded his **45.26** costs of the application and of complying with any order made against the applicant (CPR, r 46.1(2)). However, these costs are usually recoverable as damages against the defendant to the substantive claim. The usual rule on costs may be departed from, however, having regard to whether the respondent has acted reasonably and whether the respondent has complied with the terms of any relevant pre-action protocol (r 46.1(3)). As the starting point is that the applicant must pay the respondent's costs, it is not usually unreasonable for a respondent to resist the application (*SES Contracting Ltd v UK Coal plc* (2007) 33 EG 90 (CS)). It might be right to depart from the normal rule if the application is resisted in an unreasonable way, such as by using written evidence not backed up by contemporaneous documents (*SES Contracting Ltd v UK Coal plc*).

E DISCLOSURE BY NON-PARTIES

Jurisdiction

The court has, under SCA 1981, s 34(2) and CCA 1984, s 53(2): **45.27**

> ... power to order a person who is not a party to the proceedings and who appears to the court to be likely to have in his possession, custody or power any documents which are relevant to an issue arising out of the said claim—
>
> (a) to disclose whether those documents are in his possession, custody or power; and
> (b) to produce such of those documents ... as may be specified in the order.

These provisions are similar to s 33(2), but under the present provisions the application is **45.28** made after issue of proceedings and is made against a non-party, whereas under s 33(2) the application is made before issue in order to find out if proceedings are worth commencing and is made against the likely defendant.

There are three conditions which must be satisfied before the court can exercise its discretion **45.29** whether to make the order:

(a) it must appear that there are likely to be relevant documents in the respondent's possession, custody, or power;
(b) the documents of which disclosure is sought are likely to support the case of the applicant or adversely affect the case of one of the other parties to the proceedings (CPR, r 31.17(3)(a)); and
(c) disclosure is necessary in order to dispose fairly of the claim or to save costs (r 31.17(3)(b)).

Disclosure against non-parties will therefore be granted only where the documents sought **45.30** are likely to be relevant (as opposed to disclosable under standard disclosure): see *American Home Products Corporation v Novartis Pharmaceuticals UK Ltd* (2001) LTL 13/2/01. 'Likely' should be given the same meaning as in pre-action disclosure: see 45.20. The court should primarily consider relevance in the context of the statements of case, and should not embark on determining disputes of substance as to whether the documents are relevant: *Clark v Ardington Electrical Services* (2001) LTL 4/4/01.

Where the documents are likely to be relevant, it is then necessary to consider whether the **45.31** court should refuse the order in its discretion, or impose some limit on disclosure, such as by ordering disclosure of documents only between stated dates. For example, it will require a very exceptional case to justify ordering the disclosure of a non-party's confidential medical documents (*A v X and B* (2004) LTL 6/4/04). Further, the court will not make an order if it is not satisfied that the documents sought in fact exist, so in *Re Howglen Ltd* [2001] 1 All ER 376 an application was made in general terms for documents against a non-party bank for bank records and interview notes. An order was made limited to the notes of three interviews identified in the evidence in support.

Procedure

45.32 An application for disclosure against a non-party can be made at any time after substantive proceedings have been issued. It is made by application notice, and must be supported by written evidence (CPR, r 31.17(2)).

The order

45.33 It is provided in CPR, r 31.17(4) and (5) that:

(4) An order under this rule must—
  (a) specify the documents or the classes of documents which the respondent must disclose; and
  (b) require the respondent, when making disclosure, to specify any of those documents—
    (i) which are no longer in his control; or
    (ii) in respect of which he claims a right or duty to withhold inspection.

(5) Such an order may—
  (a) require the respondent to indicate what has happened to any documents which are no longer in his control; and
  (b) specify the time and place for disclosure and inspection

F DISCLOSURE OF MEDIATION EVIDENCE

45.34 Evidence of what was said or written in connection with a reference to mediation will generally be protected from use in legal proceedings because it will be confidential and also because it will almost certainly be protected by without prejudice privilege (see 31.57). This can be inconvenient, particularly where the events in a mediation are relevant to questions (eg costs) that have to be decided in litigation. As an exception to the general rule, mediation evidence arising out of a cross-border mediation may be adduced under the Mediation Directive (Directive 2008/52/EC). A mediation will qualify as being cross-border where at least one of the parties is domiciled or habitually resident in a different Member State from that of another party (art 2). In these cases it is possible, by applying under CPR, r 78.26, to obtain orders for the disclosure and inspection of mediation evidence that is in the control of the mediator provided:

(a) all parties to the mediation agree to the disclosure or inspection; or
(b) disclosure or inspection is necessary for overriding considerations of public policy; or
(c) disclosure or inspection of the mediation settlement is necessary to implement or enforce the mediation settlement agreement.

G INSPECTION OF PROPERTY DURING PROCEEDINGS

45.35 It commonly happens in litigation that an expert instructed on behalf of one party will need to inspect property in the possession of another party. It may be that in a personal injury claim the claimant's engineering expert needs to inspect the machinery alleged to have caused the claimant's injuries, or that in a professional negligence claim against a surveyor the defendant's expert surveyor needs to inspect the claimant's house. Among the general interim remedies available to the court set out in CPR, r 25.1, are powers to make orders:

(a) for the detention, custody, or preservation of relevant property;
(b) for the inspection of relevant property;
(c) for the taking of a sample of relevant property; and
(d) for the carrying out of an experiment on or with relevant property.

These orders can be combined with an order: **45.36**

(e) authorizing a person to enter any land or building in the possession of a party to the proceedings for the purposes of carrying out an order under (a)–(d).

For these purposes, 'relevant property' means property (including land) which is the subject **45.37** of a claim or as to which any question may arise on a claim. Orders for inspection are commonly sought at the allocation stage. They can be asked for in a covering letter sent with the completed directions questionnaire (the letter should be disclosed to the other parties at the same time), or in draft consent directions filed with the directions questionnaire. Otherwise, such orders may be made on the case management conference or on an application issued for the purpose at any time after proceedings have been issued. No written evidence is required.

The main restriction on such application is that the rule is limited to physical things. It **45.38** appears, therefore, that an order under the rule cannot extend to methods of manufacture or working (*Tudor Accumulator Co Ltd v China Mutual Steam Navigation Co Ltd* [1930] WN 200). However, in *Ash v Buxted Poultry Ltd* (1989) *The Times*, 29 November 1989 it was held that the court has inherent jurisdiction to make an order allowing the claimant to make a video film of the defendant's manufacturing process.

H INTERIM DELIVERY-UP OF GOODS

Under the Torts (Interference with Goods) Act 1977, s 4(2), the courts have power to make **45.39** orders for the delivery-up of any goods which are, or may become, the subject matter of proceedings for wrongful interference, or as to which any question may arise in such proceedings. Applications under the 1977 Act are among the general interim remedies available under CPR, r 25.1, and are made by application notice, usually on notice, supported by written evidence. In urgent cases (for which, see 42.07–42.08) the application may be made without notice and even before the issue of process. A number of guidelines for the exercise of this jurisdiction were laid down by the Court of Appeal in *CBS United Kingdom Ltd v Lambert* [1983] Ch 37:

(a) there must be clear evidence that the defendant intends to dispose of the goods in order to prevent the claimant recovering them through an order of the court;
(b) there must be some evidence that the defendant acquired the goods wrongfully; and
(c) the order must not act oppressively on the defendant. Usually the court will need to balance the need to protect the claimant against the defendant's grounds for retaining the goods.

An order made under this section should clearly identify the goods to be delivered up, and **45.40** may provide for delivery to the claimant or to a person appointed by the court. In *CBS United Kingdom Ltd v Lambert* it was said that the order should authorize the claimant to enter the defendant's land but only with the defendant's permission, and must make adequate provision for the safe custody of the goods. As an alternative to ordering delivery-up, the court may make orders for the preservation and detention of the goods.

Table 45.1 Comparison of various disclosure orders

Order	Type of case	Respondent	Stage	Procedure
Search, order	Real possibility of defendant destroying vital evidence	Defendant	On issue	Without notice to judge
Norwich Pharmacal identity of tortfeasor	Unknown defendant	Facilitator	Pre-action	Claim form and application
Bankers Trust whereabouts of stolen funds	Tracing claim	Recipient	Pre-action	Without notice
SCA 1981, s 33(2), pre-action disclosure	General application	Likely defendant	Pre-action	Application notice
SCA 1981, s 34(2), disclosure against non-party	General application	Non-party	After issue	Application notice
Torts (Interference with Goods) Act 1977, s 4, delivery-up	Wrongful interference	Defendant	After issue (unless urgent)	Application notice

KEY POINTS SUMMARY

45.41
- *Norwich Pharmacal* orders are primarily used for finding the identity of an unknown potential defendant.

- They can only be sought against a person who facilitated and got 'mixed up' in the wrong-doing. *Norwich Pharmacal* orders therefore cannot be made against 'mere witnesses'.

- Pre-action disclosure orders bring forward the time when disclosure of documents takes place to the period before a claim is issued. The procedure can be useful where an intending claimant needs more information so they can plead an adequate claim.

- Pre-action disclosure is only ordered if exacting requirements are satisfied (see 45.19–45.22). These include jurisdictional requirements such as the applicant being likely to be a party to a subsequent claim, and pre-action disclosure being 'desirable' for fairly dealing with the claim or for saving costs, and a second stage when the court exercises its discretion.

- Disclosure against non-parties enables the court to order a witness to produce documents in advance of the trial, thereby avoiding adjournments when documents are produced at the last minute at trial.

- An overview of different disclosure and inspection procedures can be seen in table 45.1.

46

COSTS

A COSTS ORDERS: GENERAL
  PRINCIPLES 46.04
B COSTS FOLLOW THE EVENT 46.14
C RANGE OF POSSIBLE COSTS
  ORDERS 46.33
D INTERIM COSTS ORDERS 46.35
E INFORMING THE CLIENT 46.42
F INDEMNITY PRINCIPLE 46.43
G BASIS OF QUANTIFICATION 46.46
H PROPORTIONALITY 46.49
I SUMMARY ASSESSMENT 46.52

J DETAILED ASSESSMENT 46.58
K FAST TRACK FIXED COSTS 46.61
L FIXED AND SCALE COSTS 46.65
M COSTS AND TRACK ALLOCATION 46.66
N PUBLICLY FUNDED LITIGANTS 46.68
O *PRO BONO* COSTS ORDERS 46.70
P COSTS AGAINST NON-PARTIES 46.71
Q WASTED COSTS ORDERS 46.74
  Key points summary 46.80

Legal costs will be incurred on behalf of a litigant from the time a solicitor is first retained **46.01** until the solicitor's retainer is terminated, perhaps after enforcement of any judgment that is obtained. The client (or the Legal Aid Agency if the client is publicly funded) bears the primary responsibility for paying its own solicitor's bill. The bill comprises the solicitor's remuneration for the work done on the case, together with counsel's and any experts' fees, court fees, and any other charges, expenses, and disbursements. Solicitors' costs are divided into contentious and non-contentious costs, the distinction being that contentious costs relate to costs 'in and for the purpose of proceedings' (Solicitors Act 1974, s 87(1)). Proceedings before tribunals and inquiries are regarded as being non-contentious. *Bilkus v Stockler Brunton* [2010] 1 WLR 2526 says contentious costs includes work done for future proceedings, but the traditional view is that such work counts as non-contentious costs unless proceedings are actually started. This chapter is mainly concerned with the rules relating to contentious costs.

Although each client is primarily responsible for its own solicitor's costs, it is usual **46.02** for the successful party in a claim to be awarded an order for costs against the unsuccessful party. Costs shifting in this way is compliant with the European Convention on Human Rights, First Protocol, art 1, because it may act as a disincentive to unnecessary litigation (*Hoare v United Kingdom* (2011) 53 EHRR SE1). Orders for costs are invariably made after each interim hearing (for the costs of the interim application), the trial (for the costs of the whole proceedings other than any interim costs orders), and any appeal or enforcement proceedings. There are different bases for assessing, on the one hand, the costs payable by a client to its own solicitor, and, on the other hand, the costs recoverable by a successful litigant from an unsuccessful litigant. The result is that even a successful litigant usually has to pay something to its own solicitor, and an unsuccessful litigant has to pay both its own solicitor's costs and a substantial proportion of the other side's costs.

46.03　Sir Rupert Jackson has conducted a thorough *Review of Civil Litigation Costs* (December 2009) with the aim of improving access to justice and controlling costs. That *Review* contained 109 recommendations, many of which were implemented with effect from 1 April 2013. A *Supplemental Report on Fixed Recoverable Costs* (2017) recommended extending the cases covered by fixed costs, together with an 'intermediate track' for certain claims up to £100,000 which can be tried in three days or less.

A COSTS ORDERS: GENERAL PRINCIPLES

46.04　The two main principles when it comes to deciding which party should pay the costs of an application or of the whole proceedings are:

(a) the costs payable by one party to another are in the discretion of the court (SCA 1981, s 51; CPR, r 44.2(1)); and

(b) the general rule is that the unsuccessful party will be ordered to pay the costs of the successful party (r 44.2(2), sometimes referred to as 'costs follow the event'). It is incumbent on a judge to give reasons for departing from the usual rule that costs follow the event: *Aspin v Metric Group Ltd* (2007) LTL 25/9/07.

46.05　The starting point on final costs orders is that the winner should be awarded the whole of his costs of the proceedings, even if there are issues on which he had been unsuccessful (*Actavis Ltd v Merck and Co Inc* (2007) LTL 7/8/07). This is a strong principle, and despite the fact that costs orders are discretionary (SCA 1981, s 51; CPR, r 44.2(1)), an appeal court will intervene where a judge fails to give the principle sufficient weight (*Adamson v Halifax plc* [2003] 1 WLR 60). A claimant who wins on primary liability should normally recover the whole of its costs even if there is a finding of contributory negligence (*Krysia Maritime Inc v Intership Ltd* [2009] 1 All ER (Comm) 292). In a suitable case the principle that costs follow the event will give way to other considerations, such as partial success, or past failure to comply with protocols or directions. Merely failing to recover as much as had been claimed does not give grounds for reducing the winner's costs (*Hall v Stone* (2007) *The Times*, 1 February 2008).

46.06　The discretion granted by the SCA 1981, s 51(1), is very wide, and the courts are opposed to limitations being imposed on it by implication or rigid rules of practice (*Bankamerica Finance Ltd v Nock* [1988] AC 1002). However, like any other discretion, it must of course be exercised judicially and for reasons connected with the case (*Donald Campbell and Co Ltd v Pollock* [1927] AC 732, and the speech of Viscount Cave LC).

46.07　In exercising its discretion on costs the court is required to have regard to all the circumstances, and in particular to the following matters (CPR, r 44.2(4) and (5)):

(a) the conduct of all the parties, which includes:
   (i) their conduct before as well as during the proceedings, and the extent to which they followed any applicable pre-action protocol;
   (ii) the extent to which it was reasonable for the parties to raise, pursue, or contest each of the allegations or issues;
   (iii) the manner in which the parties pursued or defended the claim or particular allegations or issues;
   (iv) whether the successful party exaggerated the value of the claim;
(b) whether a party was only partly successful; and
(c) any admissible offer to settle.

Factor (a)(i) is one of the methods by which pre-action protocols will be enforced, albeit **46.08** indirectly (see 5.23). Factors (a)(ii) and (b) require the court to take into account the extent to which the overall winner was in fact successful on the various issues, heads of claim, etc., raised in the case, when dealing with costs. This is intended to support the aspects of the overriding objective relating to identifying the real issues in the case, and only pursuing those issues to trial (CPR, r 1.4(2)(b) and (c)). In *Winter v Winter* (2000) LTL 10/11/00, the claimant had litigated over two issues, abandoned one a few days before trial, and won at trial on the remaining issue. It was held that the trial judge was plainly wrong to award the claimant the entire costs of the claim, as that failed to reflect the fact that one of the main issues had been abandoned. Generally, when a party is partially successful, the trial judge should award one party a percentage of its costs rather than awarding costs on different issues to different parties, because a percentage order avoids a great deal of complication on assessment of costs (*English v Emery Reimbold and Strick Ltd* [2002] 1 WLR 2409). In *Carver v Hammersmith & Queen Charlotte's Health Authority* (2000) LTL 31/7/00, Nelson J held that the appropriate way on the facts for dealing with a claimant who won, but had to abandon a number of issues, and who had been guilty of delay, was to deprive her of 15 per cent of her costs. Each case obviously turns on its own facts.

Factor (a)(iii), which covers unreasonable conduct, has always been relevant on costs, **46.09** but could also be used against parties who fail to conduct litigation in accordance with the overriding objective, such as those who are unreasonably uncooperative (r 1.4(2)(a)). Exaggeration of the value of a claim (factor (a)(iv)) is usually engaged in cases of deliberate conduct, such as pretending that an injury is far more serious than it really is, or alleging it is of a continuing nature despite making a recovery. Overvaluing a genuine claim does not amount to exaggeration in the absence of an element of blameworthiness (*Morton v Portal Ltd* [2010] EWHC 1804 (QB)).

Nominal damages and minimal damages

A claimant who has claimed substantial damages but has recovered only nominal damages **46.10** will normally be ordered to pay the defendant's costs: *Texaco Ltd v Arco Technology Inc* (1989) *The Times*, 13 October 1989. Likewise, a claimant who wins on liability, but who is only awarded a tiny amount in damages, may be the losing party for the purposes of costs (*Marcus v Medway Primary Care Trust* [2011] EWCA Civ 750). In this case the claim was for £525,000, but judgment was only for £2,000. The defendant was awarded 75 per cent of its costs.

Failure to consider or participate in ADR

In *Dunnett v Railtrack plc* [2002] 1 WLR 2434 the successful respondent in an appeal to **46.11** the Court of Appeal had refused to submit to ADR on the ground that doing so would necessarily involve paying sums over and above those previously offered to the appellant. This was regarded as a misunderstanding of the purpose of ADR (for which, see Chapter 10). To reflect this, instead of the respondent being awarded costs of the appeal, no order was made as to costs. Taking an unreasonable stance in a mediation is treated in the same way as unreasonably refusing to mediate at all (*Earl of Malmesbury v Strutt and Parker* [2008] 118 Con LR 68). In *Leicester Circuits Ltd v Coates Industries plc* [2003] EWCA Civ 333 a successful appellant was deprived of costs on the ground that it had unreasonably withdrawn from mediation shortly before the trial. On the other hand, a 10–15 per cent reduction in the costs order was regarded as a proportionate response to failing to consider negotiating in *Straker v Tudor Rose* [2007] EWCA Civ 368.

46.12 The burden is on the unsuccessful party in an application to disallow a successful party's costs for unreasonably refusing to use ADR procedures (*Halsey v Milton Keynes General NHS Trust* [2004] 1 WLR 3002). Factors relevant to the question of whether a refusal to agree to ADR is unreasonable are set out at 10.15. There is no presumption that costs will be awarded against a party who does not use ADR. Each case depends on its own facts. A defendant who refused to negotiate after receiving a Part 36 offer from a claimant was held not to have acted unreasonably in *Daniels v Commissioner of Police for the Metropolis* [2005] EWCA Civ 1312. The result at trial in this case (dismissal of the claim) rather established the reasonableness of the defendant's stance. Otherwise, defendants with meritorious defences would in effect be compelled to negotiate or else be penalized in costs.

Claims wrongly commenced in the High Court

46.13 Where a claim has been commenced in the High Court which should have been commenced in the County Court, the court must take that error into account when quantifying costs (SCA 1981, s 51(8)). Usually this will result in a reduction in the costs which would otherwise be allowed, but such reduction must not be in excess of 25 per cent.

B COSTS FOLLOW THE EVENT

46.14 The main rule that costs follow the event was considered at 46.04. There now follows a discussion of how this principle is applied in a number of different situations.

Situations in which costs do not follow the event

46.15 The following are situations where costs orders usually do not follow the event.

(a) The costs of any application to extend time are borne by the party making the application.

(b) A party failing to make admissions of fact or in relation to documents after service of a notice to admit facts or documents, or after service of a list of documents, is usually responsible for paying the costs of proving those matters.

(c) In claims under the Slander of Women Act 1891, costs must not exceed the damages awarded, unless the court is satisfied that there were reasonable grounds for bringing the claim.

(d) If successive claims are brought against persons jointly or otherwise liable for the same damage, costs will be ordered in favour of the claimant in the first claim only unless there were reasonable grounds for bringing the later claims (Civil Liability (Contribution) Act 1978, s 4).

Multiple parties

Multiple defendants

46.16 Where a claimant succeeds against joint tortfeasors, costs will be ordered against each defendant, and the claimant can then recover costs against any one (or more) of the defendants. Any defendant paying such costs can then seek a contribution from the others under the Civil Liability (Contribution) Act 1978. If successful defendants are separately represented, the claimant should be liable for any additional costs only if the separate representation was reasonable.

An example of what can happen where joint defendants are successful is *Korner v H Korner* **46.17**
and Co Ltd [1951] Ch 10. Eight defendants were jointly represented, and seven of them
were successful in the proceedings. It was held that generally the defence costs should be
regarded as incurred by each defendant equally, which would in this case have resulted in
the claimant paying seven-eighths of the total defence costs. However, as different defences
had been delivered for each defendant, each successful defendant was awarded one-eighth
of the general costs of the proceedings, together with such costs and counsel's fees as were
attributable to their own defence.

Bullock *and* Sanderson *orders*

Where a claimant claims against two defendants in the alternative in circumstances where it **46.18**
was reasonable to join both defendants, and succeeds against one only, the court has a discretion to make a *Bullock* or *Sanderson* order (*Bankamerica Finance Ltd v Nock* [1988] AC
1002). These orders take their names from *Bullock v London General Omnibus Co* [1907] 1
KB 264 and *Sanderson v Blyth Theatre Co* [1903] 2 KB 533. In deciding whether to make one
of these orders, the court must look at all the facts the claimant knew or could reasonably have
discovered as at the date the defendants were joined and consider whether the joinder was
reasonable. If it was not reasonable to join the two defendants, costs should follow the event.

For the purposes of exposition, assume that the claim of the claimant ('C') against the first **46.19**
defendant ('D1') is dismissed, but that C obtains judgment against the second defendant
('D2'). In a *Bullock* order, C is ordered to pay D1's costs, and D2 is ordered to pay C's costs
and is also ordered to reimburse (for the costs paid to D1). The difference between a *Bullock* order and the usual rule that costs follow the event is that if costs followed the event C
would not be reimbursed by D2 for the costs C had to pay D1. In a *Sanderson* order, D2 has
to pay C's costs, and D2 also has to pay D1's costs direct. C has no liability to pay D1's costs.

Provided all parties are solvent, the eventual effect of *Bullock* and *Sanderson* orders is the **46.20**
same. However, the *Bullock* form is more usual because it most closely follows the rule
that costs follow the event. Traditionally, the *Sanderson* form has been said to be appropriate where C is either publicly funded or insolvent, because in those circumstances only
a *Sanderson* order adequately protects the successful D1. Despite the traditional view, a
Sanderson order was upheld by the House of Lords in *Bankamerica Finance Ltd v Nock*
where D2, not C, was insolvent, the judge having decided to make a *Sanderson* order
because it tended to spread the hardship caused by irrecoverable costs most fairly between
C and D1, the successful defendant.

Multiple claimants

Problems are not so likely to be caused through having different judgments in respect of **46.21**
different claimants because proceedings with joint claimants are allowed to continue only
if the claimants are jointly represented. It is implicit in this that there must be a large degree
of identity of interest between the joint claimants, so split judgments must be very rare.

Multiple issues

Counterclaims

Where a claimant succeeds on a claim and defeats a counterclaim, or a defendant defeats **46.22**
a claim and succeeds on a counterclaim, the principle that costs follow the event simply
means that the successful party is entitled to the costs of the proceedings. Where one party
succeeds on the claim, but the other party succeeds on the counterclaim, the court may
award one party the costs of the claim, and the other party the costs of the counterclaim.
These costs orders may be set off against each other (CPR, r 44.12).

46.23 In *Medway Oil and Storage Co Ltd v Continental Contractors Ltd* [1929] AC 88 the House of Lords decided that an award of costs of the claim to one party, and the costs of the counterclaim to the other party, entitled the party who won on the claim to all its costs of the proceedings save those costs exclusively referable to the counterclaim. Under this principle there is no apportionment of costs, but items of costs common to both the claim and counterclaim, such as counsel's brief fee, may be divided between the claim and counterclaim. This approach is nowadays regarded as too technical, and it is more common to make a simple percentage costs order (*English v Emery Reimbold and Strick Ltd* [2002] 1 WLR 2409).

Additional claims under Part 20

46.24 Where a claimant succeeds in a claim against a defendant, and the defendant successfully claims an indemnity from a third party, the third party should be ordered to pay all the defendant's costs, including the costs the defendant will have been ordered to pay the claimant: *Jablochkoff Co v McMurdo* [1884] WN 84. In such a case, if the defendant proves to be insolvent, the claimant will be unable to recover its costs from the third party, because it has no direct order against the third party. Therefore, it may, in a proper case, be appropriate to make an order akin to a *Sanderson* order requiring the third party to pay the claimant's costs directly: *Edginton v Clark* [1964] 1 QB 367. If a claimant succeeds against a defendant who succeeds against a third party, but the court considers that the defendant has defended the claim for reasons which provided no benefit to the third party, the third party will be ordered to pay the costs of the additional claim only: *Blore v Ashby* (1889) 42 ChD 682.

46.25 Where a claimant loses to a defendant who therefore loses against a third party, the claimant should be ordered to pay the defendant's costs of the whole proceedings, including the additional claim, but only if it was reasonable for the defendant to have brought the additional claim.

Litigants under a disability

46.26 Costs payable to a person under a disability are assessed in the usual way. In many cases there is no need for any further detailed assessment of solicitor and own client costs because solicitors often waive the right to claim further costs when acting for persons under a disability (PD 46, para 2.1). A litigation friend who has incurred additional costs or expenses on behalf of a child or protected person can apply at the end of the case for these to be paid out of any money recovered in the claim (CPR, r 21.12; PD 21, para 11).

46.27 Costs payable by a person under a disability have to be assessed by a detailed assessment (r 46.4). An order for costs can be made against the litigation friend acting for a claimant who is a person under disability by virtue of the undertaking to pay the costs that may be ordered against the person under disability required by r 21.4(3)(c). A successful party seeking such an order must apply promptly after judgment.

Trustees and personal representatives

46.28 Trustees and personal representatives are, in so far as costs are not recovered from another party, entitled to recover their costs on the indemnity basis out of the fund (*Grender v Dresden* [2009] EWHC 500 (Ch)). The court may, however, order otherwise and may do so where the party otherwise entitled to the costs has acted unreasonably. A trustee or personal representative who has acted substantially for his or her own benefit is likely to be treated like any other party. This may be the case where the proceedings are adversarial in nature (*Shovelar v Lane* [2012] 1 WLR 637).

Contractual right to costs

46.29 Leases and other forms of contract sometimes have express terms that one party to the contract will pay the other's costs if the parties become involved in litigation. Costs orders in these cases tend to be made having regard to the contractual term on costs, as recognized by CPR, r 44.5. A costs order will usually be made in accordance with contractual terms even in claims on the small claims track, which is usually a no-costs regime (*Chaplair Ltd v Kumari* [2015] EWCA Civ 798).

Mortgagees

46.30 It is an established principle that a mortgagee is entitled to add any properly incurred costs, charges, or expenses to the secured debt (and see PD 44, paras 7.1–7.3). Many mortgages make express provision for this, but even if they do not such a term will be implied: *Cottrell v Stratton* (1872) LR 8 Ch App 295. A court may disallow any costs, charges, or expenses which were not 'properly incurred', unless the mortgage makes express provision to alter this (although a mortgage deed that purported to entitle the mortgagee to add improperly incurred costs might be open to question on public policy grounds: *Gomba Holdings (UK) Ltd v Minories Finance Ltd (No 2)* [1993] Ch 171).

Costs after an appeal

46.31 A court dealing with a successful appeal can make orders relating to the costs of the proceedings giving rise to the appeal as well as the appeal itself (CPR, r 44.10(4)). The appeal court may order the losing party to pay the costs 'here and below', or may make different orders relating to the proceedings at the two levels, or may leave the costs order of the court below undisturbed while making whatever order may be appropriate for the costs of the appeal. It may be appropriate to deprive a party of its costs if the decision on the appeal turned on points not raised below, or on points not raised in the notice of appeal, or where the appeal is only partly successful, or where the court's time has been wasted.

Set-off of costs orders

46.32 As mentioned at 46.22, costs orders against different parties can be set off against each other (CPR, r 44.12). Where one costs order is summarily assessed, and the competing costs order is directed to be subject to a detailed assessment (see 46.50–46.53), the court may preserve the set-off by varying the time for payment of the summarily assessed costs.

C RANGE OF POSSIBLE COSTS ORDERS

46.33 Under CPR, r 44.2(6), there are seven possible variations from the main rule that the unsuccessful party should pay the whole of the successful party's costs. These variations are that a party must pay:

(a) only a proportion of another party's costs;
(b) a specified amount in respect of the other side's costs;
(c) costs from or until a certain day only;
(d) costs incurred before proceedings have begun;
(e) costs relating only to certain steps taken in the proceedings;

(f) costs relating only to a certain distinct part of the proceedings, although an order of this type can only be made if an order in either of the forms set out at (a) or (c) would not be practicable (r 44.2(7)); or

(g) interest on costs from or until a certain date, including a date before judgment.

46.34 Where it is the losing party that is guilty of the misconduct, the court has various powers that may be exercised which include:

(a) Ordering costs to be paid on the indemnity basis rather than the standard basis (see 46.46). The discretion to award indemnity-basis costs has to be exercised judicially, taking into account the circumstances of the case, and having regard to the matters set out in r 44.2: *Reid Minty v Taylor* [2002] 1 WLR 2800. In most cases of adversarial litigation indemnity-basis costs will not be justified unless there are reasons to disapprove of the way the case has been conducted, but indemnity costs may be justified if the litigation has been conducted in an unreasonable manner even if that falls short of conduct which lacks moral probity or conduct deserving moral condemnation. Such conduct would have to be unreasonable to a high degree to justify an order for indemnity-basis costs: *Kiam v MGN Ltd (No 2)* [2002] 1 WLR 2810.

(b) Ordering payment of interim costs forthwith, rather than requiring the party obtaining the costs order to wait until after trial for payment (r 44.2(1)(c)). Note that an order stating the amount payable in respect of costs (eg a summary assessment) must be complied with within 14 days (r 44.7).

(c) Ordering payment of interest on costs from or until a certain date, including a date before judgment (r 44.2(6)(g)). The normal rule is that Judgments Act 1838 rate interest (currently 8 per cent a year simple interest) is payable on costs arising from court orders and judgments from the date of the judgment on liability.

(d) Ordering interest on costs at a rate different from the Judgments Act 1838 rate (eg PD Pre-action conduct, para 4.6(5), which allows the court to impose interest on costs at a rate up to 10 per cent above base rate in cases where a protocol has been breached leading to proceedings being commenced which might otherwise have been avoided).

D INTERIM COSTS ORDERS

46.35 At the end of almost every interim application, and when almost any interim application is disposed of by consent, an order will be made or agreed declaring which party should pay the costs of that application. Costs of interim applications are in the discretion of the court, but the discretion is usually (but not always) exercised in favour of the party who was successful in the application. Success may be established either by winning a contested application, or by showing that the need to make the application arose through the default of the other party. Other types of application are essentially of a case management nature, so there is no 'winner', and in these applications the costs are usually treated as part of the general costs of the claim. To cater for these various possibilities (and situations where neither party is entirely successful) the courts can resort to a wide selection of different interim costs orders.

46.36 If an order makes no reference to costs, the general rule is that none are payable in respect of the proceedings to which the order relates (CPR, r 44.10(1)). There are exceptions for:

(a) trustees and personal representatives, who are entitled to their costs from the relevant fund;

(b) landlords and mortgagees, who may be able to recover their costs under the terms of the relevant agreement; and

(c) orders which are silent on costs made on applications without notice, which mean 'applicant's costs in the case' (r 44.10(2)).

Paragraph 4.2 of PD 44 sets out in tabular form the meanings of commonly used interim **46.37** costs orders: see table 46.1.

Method of assessment of interim costs

Where an interim hearing takes no more than a day, and where the costs order awards the **46.38** costs of the interim hearing to one of the parties in any event, the court will usually immediately make a summary assessment of those costs (PD 44, para 9.7). Otherwise, an order

Table 46.1 The meanings of common interim costs orders

Term	Effect
Costs/costs in any event	The party in whose favour the order is made is entitled to the costs in respect of the part of the proceedings to which the order relates whatever other costs orders are made in the proceedings.
Costs in the case/costs in the application	The party in whose favour the court makes an order for costs at the end of the proceedings is entitled to his costs of the part of the proceedings to which the order relates.
Costs reserved	The decision about costs is deferred to a later occasion, but if no later order is made the costs will be costs in the case. Costs reserved may be appropriate for interim applications without notice, and after a split trial on liability (where the judge has a wide discretion on whether to reserve costs to the remedies hearing: see *Shepherds Investments Ltd v Walters* [2007] EWCA Civ 292).
Claimant's/defendant's costs in case/application	If the party in whose favour the costs order is made is awarded costs at the end of the proceedings, that party is entitled to his costs of the part of the proceedings to which the order relates. If any other party is awarded costs at the end of the proceedings, the party in whose favour the costs order is made is not liable to pay the costs of any other party in respect of the part of the proceedings to which the order relates.
Costs thrown away	Where, eg, a judgment or order is set aside, the party in whose favour the costs order is made is entitled to the costs which have been incurred as a consequence. This includes the costs of— (a) preparing for and attending any hearing at which the judgment or order which has been set aside was made; (b) preparing for and attending any hearing to set aside the judgment or order in question; (c) preparing for and attending any hearing at which the court orders the proceedings or the part in question to be adjourned; and (d) any steps taken to enforce a judgment or order which has subsequently been set aside.
Costs of and caused by	Where, eg, the court makes this order on an application to amend a statement of case, the party in whose favour the costs order is made is entitled to the costs of preparing for and attending the application and the costs of any consequential amendment to his own statement of case.
Costs here and below	The party in whose favour the costs order is made is entitled not only to his costs of the proceedings in which the court makes the order but also to his costs of the proceedings in any lower court. In the case of an appeal from a Divisional Court the party is not entitled to any costs incurred in any court below the Divisional Court.
No order as to costs/each party to pay his own costs	Each party is to bear his own costs of the application, subject to the exceptions referred to at 46.36.

for costs made at an interim hearing is treated as requiring a detailed assessment (PD 44, para 8.2). Detailed assessments generally take place after the proceedings are concluded.

Representation by counsel

46.39 Paragraph 5.1 of PD 44 provides that the court may state an opinion as to whether the hearing was fit for counsel. It will generally do so where the paying party asks for the court to express a view, where more than one counsel attended for a party, or where the judge thinks the hearing was not fit for counsel.

Amendment

46.40 The costs of and arising from any amendment to a statement of case are, unless the court orders otherwise, borne by the party making the amendment (see notes to PD 19A).

46.41 An order for payment of the costs of an amendment will also require payment of the costs of making consequential amendments to other documents. It is possible to ask for a less onerous costs order where, for example, the need to amend cannot be characterized as being the fault of the party seeking permission. Another point is that if permission is sought at a very late stage to make amendments having a fundamental effect on the way the case is set out, particularly where the other side are prejudiced, such as by being unable to make an effective Part 36 offer, the court may impose very stringent costs terms when granting permission to amend. Thus in *Beoco Ltd v Alfa Laval Co Ltd* [1995] QB 137 permission to amend was granted on terms that the claimant paid the defendant's costs up to the date of the amendment, and 85 per cent of the defendant's costs thereafter.

E INFORMING THE CLIENT

46.42 Where a costs order is made against a legally represented client who is not present in court when the order is made, the solicitor representing the client is under a duty to inform the client of the costs liability within seven days of the order being made (CPR, r 44.8). The 'client' may be the Lord Chancellor, or an insurer, or trade union who has instructed the solicitor (PD 44, para 10.1). At the same time as informing the client about the order, the solicitor should explain why it was made. The court has the power to order the solicitor to produce evidence that reasonable steps were taken to comply with the duty to notify the client (PD 44, para 10.3).

F INDEMNITY PRINCIPLE

46.43 The 'indemnity principle' is that a party cannot be liable to pay more to the other side in costs than the winner is liable to pay its own lawyers. Thus, if the lawyers representing the successful party have intimated that their client need 'not worry' about paying their fees, there is a prospect that the court will hold the loser has no liability in costs: *British Waterways Board v Norman* (1993) 26 HLR 232.

46.44 If the arrangement between the solicitor and the client amounts to an unlawful agreement to conduct litigation (see 2.10), the client will not be entitled to seek an order for costs even if successful (*Hughes v Kingston upon Hull City Council* [1999] QB 1193; *Awwad v Geraghty and Co* [2000] 1 All ER 608). In *Bailey v IBC Vehicles Ltd* [1998] 3 All ER 570 it was held that the court has the power to order disclosure of documents and the provision of information to check whether the indemnity principle has been infringed, but went on to say that the jurisdiction to do so should not be over-enthusiastically deployed.

Solicitors are under a duty to provide the best information possible about the cost of a matter **46.45** (SRA Code of Conduct 2011), which must include the charging arrangements between them and their client, how the client should pay, and likely payments and liabilities to others. This is usually done in a client care letter (see figure 2.1). Where there is a dispute as to the receiving party's liability to pay its own solicitors, that letter, or any other written arrangement affecting the costs payable between solicitor and client, must be filed with the court as part of any detailed assessment (PD 47, para 13.2(i)). Further, the bill of costs used in any detailed assessment must set out a short but adequate explanation of any agreement or arrangement between the solicitor and client which affects the costs claimed against the paying party.

G BASIS OF QUANTIFICATION

There are two bases of assessment of costs: the standard basis and the indemnity basis. **46.46** As its name suggests, the standard basis is the one usually applied in costs orders between the parties in litigation. The indemnity basis is used when a client is paying its own solicitor, and also when a trustee's costs are payable out of the trust fund. It can also be used between competing parties in litigation as a penalty for misconduct, or as a result of a claimant recovering more at trial than the amount offered in a Part 36 offer. Costs orders should identify the intended basis of quantification.

On an assessment on the standard basis, which is the least generous basis, r 44.3(1), (2) of **46.47** the CPR provides that the court will:

(a) only allow costs which have been reasonably incurred and which are reasonable in amount;
(b) only allow costs which are proportionate to the matters in issue;
(c) disallow or reduce costs which are disproportionate within the meaning set out in r 44.3(5) (see 46.50) even if they were reasonably or necessarily incurred; and
(d) resolve any doubt which it may have about whether costs were reasonably and proportionately incurred or were reasonable and proportionate in amount in favour of the paying party.

On an assessment on the indemnity basis, again, costs will only be allowed if reasonably **46.48** incurred and if they are reasonable in amount, but there is no reference to proportionality, and any doubt whether costs were reasonably incurred or were reasonable in amount is resolved in favour of the receiving party (r 44.3(1), (3)).

H PROPORTIONALITY

One of the main aims of the CPR is to provide a system of civil justice which is reasonably **46.49** affordable. Allied to this is the goal of making the costs of litigation more predictable, so that clients will have a fairly clear idea of the likely cost of proceedings they might become involved in at as early a stage as possible. A combination of measures seeks to achieve these objectives. These are:

(a) Solicitors are under a duty to give their clients the best information possible about the overall costs both at the outset and as the case progresses (SRA Code of Conduct 2011, Outcome 1.13).
(b) Encouraging use of CFAs and DBAs (see Chapter 2). Litigants who take advantage of CFAs and DBAs will know that, provided they keep to the agreement they reach with

their solicitors, they will not have to pay anything towards their own lawyers' costs. By taking out ATE insurance they may also be able to obtain protection against having to pay the costs of the other side.

(c) Costs recoverable from the losing party in small claims track cases are limited to the court fees paid by the successful party, a nominal fixed sum to cover the claimant's solicitor's costs of issuing the claim, and limited witness expenses and experts' fees (CPR, r 27.14, see Chapter 27).

(d) There is a system of fixed costs in CPR, Part 45 (see 46.61–46.65). This covers a number of situations, including fast track RTA and EL/PL claims.

(e) Judicial case management of cases, with the aim of focusing case preparation on the real issues in the case, and ensuring litigation progresses to trial without undue delay (see Chapter 15).

(f) Costs budgeting and costs management in multi-track claims, which are used to inform the court when making case management decisions with a view to ensuring litigation is conducted at proportionate cost (see Chapter 16).

(g) A limit on recoverable costs may be imposed by making a costs capping order (see Chapter 17).

46.50   Underpinning most of these measures is the definition of proportionality used in assessing costs. This is set out in CPR, r 44.3(5), which provides that costs incurred are proportionate if they bear a reasonable relationship to:

(a) the sums in issue in the proceedings;
(b) the value of any non-monetary relief in issue in the proceedings;
(c) the complexity of the litigation;
(d) any additional work generated by the conduct of the paying party; and
(e) any wider factors involved in the proceedings, such as reputation or public importance.

46.51   In *Walker Construction (UK) Ltd v Quayside Homes Ltd* [2014] EWCA Civ 93 the defendant won, and was awarded £10,885 on its counterclaim. The Court of Appeal held it was plainly wrong and disproportionate to award the defendant the entirety of its costs amounting to £345,000. A more controversial decision is *Willis v MRJ Rundell & Associates Ltd* [2013] EWHC 2923 (TCC), where the combined costs budgets totalled £1.6 million in a claim with a value of £1.1 million. Coulson J held that on that basis alone the costs budgets were disproportionate, and he refused to approve them.

I SUMMARY ASSESSMENT

46.52   Summary assessment of costs involves the court determining the amount payable by way of costs immediately at the end of a hearing, usually on a relatively rough-and-ready basis. They are used for hearings and appeals lasting no more than a day, and for assessing costs in fast track claims (PD 44, para 9.2).

46.53   Summary assessment will be unnecessary in cases where the parties have agreed the amount of costs (PD 44, para 9.4). The court must not make a summary assessment of the costs of a publicly funded party (para 9.8). Nor may it make a summary assessment of the costs of a party under a disability, unless that party's solicitor has waived the right to further costs (para 9.9(1)). Paragraphs 9.8 and 9.9(1) do not prevent the court making a summary assessment of any interim costs which it decides are payable by an assisted party or a party under a disability (paras 9.8 and 9.9(2)), although the court should not make such costs payable immediately (in the case of an assisted paying party) unless it also makes a determination under LASPO 2012, s 26(1) (see 2.46).

Statement of costs

To assist the judge in making a summary assessment of costs, each party is required by PD **46.54** 44, para 9.5, to file and serve a signed statement of their costs in form N260. This must be served and filed not less than 24 hours before an interim hearing, and not less than two days before a fast track trial. It must set out:

(a) the number of hours claimed;
(b) the hourly rate claimed;
(c) the grade of fee earner;
(d) the amount and nature of disbursements;
(e) the legal representative's costs for attending or appearing at the hearing;
(f) counsel's fees; and
(g) VAT on the costs.

Any failure to file or serve a statement of costs, without reasonable excuse, will be taken **46.55** into account in deciding the costs order to be made on the application (PD 44, para 9.6). In *Wheeler v Chief Constable of Gloucestershire Constabulary* [2013] EWCA Civ 1791 a failure to file a statement of costs resulted in the court ordering a detailed assessment. The failure was penalized by ordering the successful party to pay the costs of the detailed assessment.

Conducting a summary assessment

On a summary assessment of costs the court must focus on the detailed breakdown of costs **46.56** actually incurred by the party in question as shown on its statement of costs on an item-by-item basis (*Morgan v Spirit Group Ltd* [2011] PIQR P9). The court is entitled to draw on its general experience of costs in comparable cases, and it may be helpful to draw on that experience in deciding whether the sum provisionally assessed by the court based on the figures in the statement of costs is reasonable and proportionate. The court can call for whatever evidence is available at the time in deciding on the figure to be specified, such as looking at counsel's brief to see the brief fee, as well as hearing the advocates on the work involved in the matter.

Payment of summarily assessed costs

Summarily assessed costs are generally payable within 14 days of the date of the order **46.57** (CPR, r 44.7(1)(a)). The court retains a discretion to decide when such costs are to be paid (r 44.7(1)(c)), but any application for an extension of time in which to pay such costs should be supported by evidence: *Pepin v Watts* [2001] CPLR 9.

J DETAILED ASSESSMENT

A detailed assessment of costs involves leaving the quantification of costs to a costs judge, **46.58** who will consider the amount to be allowed at an assessment hearing at some stage in the future after the parties have been given the opportunity of setting out the amount claimed and points of dispute in writing. Detailed assessments are carried out mainly by District Judges in the County Court, and there is a special office, called the Senior Courts Costs Office, for the High Court. Generally the court has a discretion to decide whether to make a summary assessment or to order a detailed assessment if the costs cannot be agreed. However, where money is claimed by, or ordered or agreed to be paid to, or for the benefit of a child or protected party, the court in general must order a detailed assessment of the costs payable by the claimant to his solicitor (CPR, r 46.4). Any assessment of the costs of a publicly funded party must be by way of a detailed assessment (PD 44, para 9.8, and the effect of the Civil Legal Aid (Remuneration) Regulations 2013 (SI 2013/422)).

Procedure on detailed assessment

46.59 Detailed assessment proceedings must be commenced within three months of the judgment, order, award, or other determination giving rise to the right to costs (CPR, r 47.7). This is done by serving on the paying party a notice of commencement in form N252, together with the bill of costs and, if required by PD 47, a breakdown of the costs claimed for each phase of the proceedings in Precedent Q (r 47.6(1)). In multi-track claims the bill of costs should be in spreadsheet format allowing for automatic recalculation of figures if input data is changed. The paying party may dispute any item in the bill by serving the receiving party with points of dispute. These must be served within 21 days after service of the notice of commencement (r 47.9). If the paying party fails to serve points of dispute within the permitted time, the receiving party may, on filing a request, obtain a default costs certificate (rr 47.9(4) and 47.11). The receiving party has the right, but is not obliged, to serve a reply to any points of dispute. Any reply should be served on the party who served the points of dispute within 21 days after service (r 47.13). Hearings are relatively informal, with the points in dispute being taken in turn and both sides making submissions and the costs officer making rulings on each point in turn. There is a shortened provisional assessment procedure for bills of costs not exceeding £75,000 (r 47.15).

Interim payment on account of costs

46.60 A detailed assessment can take several months to complete. To prevent a successful party being kept out of its money for a protracted period, CPR, r 44.2(8) says that where the court orders a detailed assessment it will order the paying party to pay a reasonable sum on account of costs unless there is a good reason not to do so.

K FAST TRACK FIXED COSTS

46.61 There are two systems of fixed costs on the fast track. One covers the whole of the costs incurred on the case, and applies only to personal injury claims that leave the RTA and EL/PL protocols (see Chapter 9 and 9.44). The second, in CPR, Part 45, Section VI, applies to all other fast track cases, but only imposes fixed costs on the trial, not the whole of the proceedings. Fixed trial costs apply only if there has been an actual allocation to the fast track (PD 45, para 4.2), and do not apply to disposal hearings (for which, see 13.23). Fast track fixed advocates' costs are set out in table 46.2.

46.62 For a successful claimant the value of the claim is the amount of the judgment excluding interest, costs, and any reduction for contributory negligence, whereas for a successful defendant it is the amount of the claim specified on the claim form (or the maximum amount that could have been recovered on the pleaded case) (r 45.38(3)). If there is a counterclaim with a greater value than the claim, and the claimant succeeds on the claim and defeats the counterclaim, the relevant amount is the value of the counterclaim (r 45.38(6)). There are

Table 46.2 Fixed fast track trial costs

Value of claim	Non-PI	RTA	EL/PL
No more than £3,000	£485	£500	£500
£3,000 to £10,000	£690	£710	£710
£10,000 to £15,000	£1,035	£1,070	£1,070
£15,000 to £25,000	£1,650	£1,705	£1,705
Attendance by solicitor with counsel	£345	N/A	N/A
Non-monetary relief	£690	N/A	N/A

detailed rules dealing with cases where there are several claimants or several defendants, including whether more than one party can be awarded fast track trial costs, which are set out in r 45.40. For claims for non-monetary remedies the value of the claim is deemed to be in the £3,000 to £10,000 category unless the court orders otherwise (r 45.38(4)).

The solicitor's attendance fee is only available in non-personal injury claims. It will be **46.63** payable only if the court awards fast track trial costs and if the court considers that it was necessary for a legal representative to attend to assist counsel (r 45.39(2)).

A successful party may, by r 45.39(7), be awarded less than the quoted fixed fast track trial costs **46.64** for unreasonable or improper behaviour during the trial, and the losing party may be ordered to pay an additional amount if it is guilty of behaving improperly during the trial (r 45.39(8)).

L FIXED AND SCALE COSTS

There is a system of fixed and scale costs in certain types of proceedings as set out in CPR, **46.65** Part 45. Fixed costs in fast track claims were discussed at 46.61. There are also modest fixed costs set by rr 45.1–45.8 for taking certain common steps in proceedings. These include the costs of issuing a claim, entry of judgment in default, and for enforcing a judgment. The fixed costs in rr 45.1–45.8 apply unless the court orders otherwise (r 45.1(1)), and tend to be used only in simple cases. In the Intellectual Property Enterprise Court there are scale costs which are set out in PD 45, Section IV, specifying the maximum amounts that will be awarded for each stage of the claim.

M COSTS AND TRACK ALLOCATION

Once a claim is allocated to either of the small claims or fast tracks the costs rules relating **46.66** to that track will apply to work done before as well as after allocation (CPR, r 46.11(2)), with the exception that any costs orders made before a claim is allocated to one of these two tracks are not affected by any subsequent allocation (r 46.13(1)). Where a small claims case is reallocated to another track, the fast track or multi-track costs rules apply only from the date of reallocation (r 27.15).

In cases which conclude without being allocated to a track, the court may restrict the **46.67** recoverable costs to those that would have been allowed on the track to which the claim would have been allocated if allocation had taken place (r 46.13(3)).

N PUBLICLY FUNDED LITIGANTS

Successful publicly funded party

If a publicly funded party succeeds, the court will make an order for costs on exactly the same **46.68** principles as apply in unassisted cases, and the amounts to be allowed must be determined as if the publicly funded party were not legally aided (Civil Legal Aid (Costs) Regulations 2013 (SI 2013/611), reg 21). The recovered costs are used to pay the publicly funded costs. Any damages or property recovered or preserved in the proceedings will be subject to the first charge under LASPO 2012, s 25, in respect of any shortfall between the solicitor's charges and costs recovered from the other side and contributions paid by the assisted person (see 2.38).

Costs against a publicly funded party

An unsuccessful assisted person is protected from the usual costs consequences by LASPO **46.69** 2012, s 26 (see 2.46). It is also possible for a successful unassisted party to obtain a costs order against the Lord Chancellor (see 2.47), but the criteria for doing so are very restrictive, and such orders are uncommon.

O *PRO BONO* COSTS ORDERS

46.70 Section 194 of the Legal Services Act 2007 allows the court to order any person to make a payment to the charity prescribed under the Act in respect of legal representation of a party which was provided free of charge. By CPR, r 46.7, such an order will be for fixed costs under Part 45 where Part 45 would otherwise apply. Where Part 45 does not apply the costs are assessed on the same basis as if the legal services had not been provided free of charge.

P COSTS AGAINST NON-PARTIES

46.71 In *Aiden Shipping Co Ltd v Interbulk Ltd* [1986] AC 965 the House of Lords decided that the SCA 1981, s 51, confers a sufficiently wide discretion on the court on the question of costs to allow it to award costs against non-parties. Such orders are always exceptional (*Re Land and Property Trust Co plc* [1991] 1 WLR 601). The essential policy is that the need to protect the successful party by granting an effective costs order has to yield to the right of access to the courts to litigate the dispute in the first place (*Hamilton v Al Fayed (No 2)* [2003] QB 1175 and the European Convention on Human Rights, art 6(1)). It is in the public interest that funding for litigation should be available, provided the essential motivation is to enable a party to litigate what the funders perceive to be a genuine case. Consequently, a pure funder of litigation should not ordinarily be liable to a non-party costs order, and it is only if there is something exceptional in the circumstances that such an order can be justified. Even if there is some exceptional feature present, an order will also be refused if there is no causation (*Hamilton v Al Fayed*).

46.72 Such orders may possibly be made against an outsider who was funding the litigation on behalf of the unsuccessful party (*Singh v Observer Ltd* [1989] 2 All ER 751, doubted in *Symphony Group plc v Hodgson* [1994] QB 179); against directors of a company who improperly cause the other side to incur costs in a winding-up petition (*Re a Company (No 004055 of 1991)* [1991] 1 WLR 1003); and where the non-party has been found, under the law concerning maintenance and champerty, to have maintained the action (*McFarlane v EE Caledonia Ltd (No 2)* [1995] 1 WLR 366). Such an order may also be made in the case of wanton and officious intermeddling with litigation falling short of champerty in the strict sense: *Nordstern Allgemeine Versicherungs AG v Internav Ltd* [1999] 2 Lloyd's Rep 139. A non-party costs orders is unlikely to be made against a liquidator funding litigation in the name of the company: *Eastglen Ltd v Grafton* [1996] 2 BCLC 279. It is also unlikely to be made against a solicitor who fails to arrange ATE insurance, even though that will often mean the other side are unlikely to be successful in recovering their costs from the solicitor's client (*Heron v TNT (UK) Ltd* [2014] 1 WLR 1277).

46.73 By extension of the jurisdiction, a costs order can be made in favour of a non-party who has funded litigation (*J v Oyston* [2002] CPLR 563, where an order was made in favour of the Solicitors' Indemnity Fund Ltd).

Q WASTED COSTS ORDERS

46.74 Under the SCA 1981, s 51(6), legal representatives may be made personally liable for any wasted costs. This provision is intended to arm the courts with an effective remedy where loss and expense have been caused by the unjustifiable conduct of litigation by either side's lawyers. Wasted costs orders can be made against the legal representatives for the other side or against the legal representatives acting for the applicant: *Medcalf v Mardell* [2003] 1 AC 120. Applications can be made against legal or other representatives exercising rights of audience and rights to conduct litigation (s 51(13)). Applications against counsel are not restricted to their conduct in court, but extend to counsel's involvement in advising, drafting, and settling documents in relation to proceedings: *Brown v Bennett* [2002] 2 All ER 273. Wasted costs may simply be disallowed or an order may be made that the legal representative responsible must pay the whole or a part of them.

Nature of wasted costs

The wasted costs powers against lawyers and other parties are compensatory in nature. **46.75** Therefore, in *Ridehalgh v Horsefield* [1994] Ch 205 the Court of Appeal held that a wasted costs order can be made only if three conditions are satisfied:

(a) The applicant must satisfy the court that the lawyer has acted improperly, unreasonably, or negligently (SCA 1981, s 51(7)). 'Improper' conduct covers any substantial breach of the relevant codes of professional conduct for solicitors and barristers such as making unsupported allegations of fraud contrary to the Code of Conduct of the Bar of England and Wales (*Medcalf v Mardell* [2003] 1 AC 120). It also includes conduct which would be regarded as improper according to the consensus of professional opinion. 'Unreasonable' conduct includes anything that is designed to harass the other side or is otherwise vexatious. The acid test is whether there is a reasonable explanation for the conduct. 'Negligence' in this context does not have the same meaning as in the well-known tort, but simply means a failure to act with the competence reasonably expected from ordinary members of the profession.
(b) The conduct complained of caused the applicant to incur unnecessary costs.
(c) In all the circumstances of the case it must be just to order the lawyer to compensate the applicant for the whole or part of the wasted costs.

Conduct justifying a wasted costs order may include failing to attend an appointment, **46.76** failing to comply with the court's orders, negligent mispleading of the case, inefficient presentation of the case at trial through being ill-prepared, and pressing on with a claim after it has become hopeless (eg through failing to read the materials disclosed by the other side on disclosure). A solicitor is not entitled to abdicate all responsibility for a case by instructing counsel, but the more specialist the area the more reasonable it is to follow counsel's advice. Thus in *R v Horsham District Council, ex p Wenman* [1995] 1 WLR 680 a solicitor was absolved from liability when acting on counsel's advice in judicial review proceedings. Acting for a client in a weak case does not justify a wasted costs order, but such an order may be made if the claim is hopeless and a breach of the lawyer's duty to the court or involves conduct approximating to an abuse of process (*Patel v Air India Ltd* [2010] EWCA Civ 443).

Where legal professional privilege is not waived by the client, the court should be slow to **46.77** draw adverse inferences on the quality of advice given, and where there is room for doubt, assumptions and inferences should be made in favour of the legal representatives: *Brown v Bennett* [2002] 2 All ER 273. Consequently, a wasted costs order in such cases should not be made unless, proceeding with extreme care, the court is satisfied that there is nothing the practitioner could say, if unconstrained, to resist the order, and provided also that it is fair in all the circumstances to make the order: *Medcalf v Mardell*.

Procedure on wasted costs applications

46.78 Applications for wasted costs orders should generally be made after trial, as interim applications would deprive the other side of the advisers of their choice (*Filmlab Systems International Ltd v Pennington* [1995] 1 WLR 673; PD 46, para 5.2). Wasted costs orders can be made on an application by a party made under Part 23, or by the court on its own initiative (PD 46, paras 5.3 and 5.4). On an application by a party, the legal representative against whom the order is sought must be given written notice, at least three days before the hearing, of what he or she is alleged to have done or failed to do and of the costs sought (PD 46, para 5.9). The court is required to give the legal representative a reasonable opportunity to attend a hearing to give reasons why the order should not be made (CPR, r 46.8(2)). The court will give directions to ensure that the issues are dealt with in a way that is fair and as simple and summary as the circumstances permit (PD 46, para 5.6). The court may also direct that notice be given to the legal representative's client.

46.79 Wasted costs applications will generally be considered in two stages (PD 46, para 5.7):

(a) At the first stage the applicant has to adduce evidence which, if unanswered, would be likely to lead to a wasted costs order, and the court must be satisfied that the wasted costs application appears to be justified having regard to the likely costs involved.

(b) At the second stage the court will give the legal representative an opportunity of putting forward his or her case, and will make a wasted costs order only if (PD 46, para 5.5):
    (i) the legal representative has acted improperly, unreasonably, or negligently;
    (ii) the legal representative's conduct has caused another party to incur unnecessary costs; and
    (iii) it is just in all the circumstances to order the legal representative to compensate that party for the whole or part of those costs.

If the court makes an order, it must specify the amount to be paid or disallowed. There is also an obligation on the court to inform the relevant professional regulator and the Director of Legal Aid Casework (SCA 1981, s 51(7A)).

KEY POINTS SUMMARY

46.80 • Costs orders are always discretionary.

• Costs usually follow the event, in that the winner usually is awarded costs against the loser.

• These principles apply to interim costs orders as well as costs orders made at trial.

• The different formulae used in interim costs orders described in table 46.1 are designed to give effect to the principle that costs follow the event.

• Likewise, the detailed rules on *Bullock* orders, counterclaims, additional claims, etc. are designed to give effect to the principle that costs follow the event when the court is faced by situations at trial where there is no clear-cut winner.

• A court may depart from the costs follow the event principle where (broadly) there has been unreasonable conduct by the winner (CPR, r 44.2, described at 46.04–46.09).

• Different types of untoward conduct may result in costs orders being made against non-parties (see 46.71) or wasted costs orders being made against the lawyers (see 46.74).

• Special provision is made for litigants who are publicly funded (see 46.68) and claimants in personal injuries claims (see Chapter 47), in particular protecting them against the usual effects of costs following the event.

47

QUALIFIED ONE-WAY COSTS SHIFTING

A CASES WHERE QOCS APPLIES........47.04   C LOSS OF QOCS PROTECTION 47.14
B EFFECT OF QOCS ....47.07   Key points summary 47.21

Qualified one-way costs shifting ('QOCS') was introduced on 1 April 2013, and provides **47.01** costs protection to claimants in personal injuries claims. 'Costs shifting' is a formal expression describing the usual rule that costs follow the event (see 46.04) or that costs are otherwise paid by one side to the other. The costs incurred by the successful party are 'shifted' to the losing party under the usual costs order. QOCS adjusts this traditional position by saying that the usual costs order should only be enforceable in favour of the claimant. This means that if the claimant wins, the defendant should be ordered to pay the claimant's costs in the usual way. However, if the claimant loses, under QOCS while the claimant remains liable to pay its own lawyers' costs, and may be ordered to pay the successful defendant's costs, the claimant will be protected against actually having to pay those costs to the defendant.

Under QOCS a claimant therefore has a valuable protection against paying the defend- **47.02** ant's costs. As a result, there should be no need for a claimant who will have the benefit of QOCS to take out ATE insurance (see 2.08), because normally the claimant will not be required to pay the defendant's costs even if they lose.

QOCS is 'qualified' one-way costs shifting, because this protection to the claimant is not abso- **47.03** lute. To avoid abuse, perhaps with some claimants indulging in costs inflating practices secure in knowing they will never be brought to account, there are exceptions built into the QOCS scheme for different types of misbehaviour. Further, there is no protection against the enforcement of adverse costs orders against damages and interest recovered in the proceedings.

A CASES WHERE QOCS APPLIES

By CPR, r 44.13(1) the provisions on QOCS apply in favour of the claimant in proceedings **47.04** which include a claim for damages:

(a) for personal injuries;
(b) under the Fatal Accidents Act 1976; or
(c) which arises out of death or personal injury and survives for the benefit of an estate by virtue of s 1(1) of the Law Reform (Miscellaneous Provisions) Act 1934.

In this chapter these will collectively be referred to as claims for personal injuries. In addition to typical personal injuries claims in negligence, QOCS also applies to claims against the MIB pursuant to secondary legislation (*Howe v Motor Insurers' Bureau (No 2)* [2018] 1 WLR 923).

47.05 There is an extended definition of 'claimant' for the purposes of the rules on QOCS in r 44.13(2). A person bringing a claim for personal injuries is a claimant, as is an estate on behalf of which such a claim is brought, and also a person making a counterclaim or an additional claim. This is intended to mean that it does not matter whether the personal injuries claim is brought as an original claimant or in a defence and counterclaim or in an additional claim, such as a third party claim, under Part 20. QOCS only applies in favour of a personal injuries claimant. In *Wagenaar v Weekend Travel Ltd* [2015] 1 WLR 1968 the claimant sued the defendant for damages for personal injuries, and the defendant brought in a third party under Part 20 to seek an indemnity or contribution. At trial the claim and third party claim were defeated. QOCS protected the claimant, but not the defendant on the Part 20 claim, who was not itself bringing a claim for personal injuries.

47.06 QOCS does not apply to proceedings in which the claimant has entered into a pre-commencement funding arrangement as defined by r 48.2 (r 44.17). This means that if the claimant, for example, entered into a CFA before 1 April 2013, QOCS will not apply. Also excluded are applications for pre-commencement disclosure pursuant to the Senior Courts Act 1981, s 33 or the County Courts Act 1984, s 52 (these procedures are discussed in Chapter 45).

B EFFECT OF QOCS

47.07 One-way costs shifting is achieved by CPR, r 44.14(1) which provides:

> Subject to rules 44.15 and 44.16, orders for costs made against a claimant may be enforced without the permission of the court but only to the extent that the aggregate amount in money terms of such orders does not exceed the aggregate amount in money terms of any orders for damages and interest made in favour of the claimant.

Claimant loses the case

47.08 If the claimant loses the case with no award of damages, the effect of CPR, r 44.14(1) is that no costs will be payable by the claimant, because the aggregate amount referred to in the rule is nil. The form taken by r 44.14(1) is not to prevent an adverse costs order being made against the unsuccessful claimant, but to say that any costs order that is made is not enforceable against the claimant. It is therefore rather like the costs protection granted to legally aided parties (see 2.46). Under r 44.14(1) all the court has to do is to make a normal adverse costs order against the unsuccessful claimant. The order may but need not say that it may not be enforced without the court's permission. Rule 44.14(1) then applies to the effect that (as nothing has been recovered in the litigation) nothing is payable by the claimant towards the defendant's costs.

Claimant partially successful

47.09 In cases where the claimant is partially successful, CPR, r 44.14(1) operates in a slightly different way. First, the court will have to decide what costs order to make given the respective degrees of success of the parties and the other factors set out in r 44.2 (see 46.07). If the court makes a full or partial costs award in favour of the claimant, r 44.14 has no application. However, if the court makes an adverse costs order against the claimant (whether a full costs order in favour of the defendant, or a percentage costs order in favour of the defendant), r 44.14(1) applies to restrict the amount of costs that the defendant can recover from the claimant to the aggregate amount in money terms of any orders for damages and interest made in favour of the claimant. In such a case QOCS does not provide full costs protection for the claimant, because the money award may be eaten up by the costs order in favour of the defendant, but the claimant is protected in the sense that taking into account such sums as they were awarded in the case, they will not have to pay anything beyond that to the defendant under the defendant's costs order.

Judgment not as advantageous as Part 36 offer

The wording of CPR, r 44.14(1) means the defendant can enforce a split costs order made **47.10** under r 36.17(3) where the defendant has made a Part 36 offer, and the claimant has failed to achieve a judgment more advantageous than that offer (see 36.32). Assuming the claimant with the benefit of QOCS has succeeded on liability and obtained a money award, r 36.17(3) says that unless the court considers it unjust to do so, it will award costs to the claimant up to the end of the relevant period (as defined by r 36.3(g)), and the defendant its costs thereafter.

The two costs orders can be set off against each other under r 44.12. The effect, especially **47.11** if the Part 36 offer was made in the early stages of the claim, is that there is often a net costs liability due from the claimant to the defendant under the usual r 36.17(3) order. By virtue of r 44.14(1), that net costs liability can be enforced without permission against the awards in favour of the claimant for damages and interest, up to the extent of reducing those figures to zero.

Interim costs orders against claimants

QOCS protection also applies to interim costs orders. By CPR, r 44.14(2) an order for **47.12** costs made against a claimant may only be enforced after the proceedings have been concluded and the costs have been assessed or agreed.

Credit scoring

By CPR, r 44.14(3) an order for costs which is enforced only to the extent permitted by **47.13** r 44.14(1) shall not be treated as an unsatisfied or outstanding judgment for the purposes of any court record (see 41.49).

C LOSS OF QOCS PROTECTION

Striking out

As mentioned at 47.03, the protection given by QOCS is not absolute. The CPR, r 44.15 **47.14** provides:

> Orders for costs made against the claimant may be enforced to the full extent of such orders without the permission of the court where the proceedings have been struck out on the grounds that—
> (a) the claimant has disclosed no reasonable grounds for bringing the proceedings;
> (b) the proceedings are an abuse of the court's process; or
> (c) the conduct of—
>   (i) the claimant; or
>   (ii) a person acting on the claimant's behalf and with the claimant's knowledge of such conduct,
>
> is likely to obstruct the just disposal of the proceedings.

47.15 The expressions used in r 44.15 are the same as the terms used in r 3.4(2)(a) and (b) (see 30.04). It means that costs protection will be lost under r 44.15 if a case is struck out under r 3.4(2)(a) or (b) for any of the reasons discussed at 30.13–30.36. It is only if the claim is struck out under r 3.4 that QOCS protection is lost under r 44.15. Several of the situations covered by the striking-out cases discussed at 30.13–30.36, such as the limitation cases, and cases where there may be doubts over whether the defendant owed the claimant a duty of care, could be taken either as strike-out applications or as preliminary issues (see 39.54). A claimant who loses such a point as a preliminary issue will not lose QOCS protection under r 44.15, but automatically loses QOCS protection if the point was taken in a striking-out application.

Fraudulent claims

47.16 The second problem with CPR, r 44.15 is that it only applies if the claim has actually been struck out. Many fraudulent claims will not come within r 44.15 because it is extremely difficult to strike out a claim on the basis it is fraudulent. The nature of such an allegation means it is rarely going to be a suitable issue to decide on an interim application, and so it will usually be left to be determined at trial (*Summers v Fairclough Homes Ltd* [2012] 1 WLR 2004).

Fundamentally dishonest claim

47.17 While there are examples of actual striking-out orders being made in fraudulent claims (in which event costs protection under QOCS is lost automatically under CPR, r 44.15), this is unusual. Most cases of alleged fraud will therefore be considered under r 44.16(1), which gives the court a power to grant permission to enforce an adverse costs order against a claimant in a personal injuries claim where the court decides the claim was fundamentally dishonest on the balance of probabilities. 'Fundamentally dishonest' means dishonesty going to the root of the whole case or to a substantial part of it. Adequate warning that this will be raised must be given to the claimant, but there is no requirement to set out the allegation in the defence (*Howlett v Davis* [2018] 1 WLR 948). A decision on fundamental dishonesty will usually be made at trial (PD 44, para 12.4(a)). Under the Criminal Justice and Courts Act 2015, s 57, a fundamentally dishonest claim will be dismissed (see 41.36).

Allegations of fraud in settled and discontinued claims

47.18 Unless there are exceptional circumstances, the court will not inquire into whether a claim was fundamentally dishonest if the proceedings have been settled (PD 44, para 12.4(b)).

47.19 Where a personal injuries claim has been discontinued, the effect of CPR, r 44.14(1) is that generally the claimant has costs protection under QOCS which overrides the usual costs position in discontinued claims as set out in r 38.6. However, the court may in such a case inquire into whether the claim was fundamentally dishonest under r 44.16(1), and can do so even if the notice of discontinuance has not been set aside (PD 44, para 12.4(c)).

Proceedings for the financial benefit of another

47.20 The court may grant permission to enforce a costs order against a claimant who would otherwise have costs protection under QOCS if the proceedings include a claim which is made for the financial benefit of another person (CPR, r 44.16(2)). Examples are subrogated claims and claims for credit hire (PD 44, para 12.2), but do not include the provision of personal services rendered gratuitously for things like personal care, domestic assistance, etc.

(para 12.3). In such a case the court may also make a non-party costs order against that other person (r 44.16(3), for which see 46.71), and in fact usually will do so (PD 44, para 12.5).

KEY POINTS SUMMARY

- QOCS applies in favour of claimants in personal injuries claims.

47.21

- In cases where QOCS applies the court should make a normal party and party costs order.
- Under QOCS any costs order against the claimant is not normally enforceable.
- QOCS protection will be lost if the claim is struck out.
- The court has the power to remove QOCS protection if it finds the claim was, on the balance of probabilities, fundamentally dishonest.

48

ENFORCEMENT

A ENFORCEMENT OF MONEY
   JUDGMENTS 48.02
B ENFORCEMENT OF JUDGMENTS
   FOR THE DELIVERY OF GOODS 48.42
C ENFORCEMENT OF JUDGMENTS
   FOR THE POSSESSION OF LAND 48.44

D RECEIVERS BY WAY OF EQUITABLE
   EXECUTION 48.47
E CONTEMPT OF COURT. 48.50
F ENFORCEMENT OF FOREIGN
   JUDGMENTS 48.58
   Key points summary 48.61

48.01 Entering judgment does not provide a litigant with the remedy sought in the proceedings. Parties occasionally refuse to comply with the judgments and orders of the court. Public confidence in the legal system would be eroded if the court were without powers to enforce compliance. In fact, a range of enforcement procedures is available, each being designed to deal with different situations. Where a number of procedures are available, a judgment creditor can choose whichever one seems likely to be the most effective, and can use more than one method of enforcement either at the same time or one after another (CPR, r 70.2(2)(b); but see 48.31 for an exception). Largely, the procedures are similar in both the High Court and the County Court. The major exception is that attachment of earnings orders (see 48.25) are generally available only in the County Court. High Court enforcement is carried out by enforcement officers authorized under the Courts Act 2003, whereas County Court enforcement is carried out by enforcement agents authorized under the Tribunals, Courts and Enforcement Act 2007, ss 63 and 64 and the Certification of Enforcement Agents Regulations 2014 (SI 2014/421).

A ENFORCEMENT OF MONEY JUDGMENTS

General provisions

Transfers

48.02 A case may need to be transferred before enforcement proceedings are taken:

(a) A County Court claim will have to be transferred to the High Court if:
   (i) (other than judgments arising from regulated agreements under the Consumer Credit Act 1974) enforcement by taking control of goods is sought of a judgment exceeding £5,000 (High Court and County Courts Jurisdiction Order 1991 (SI 1991/724), art 8(1)(a)); or
   (ii) enforcement of a charging order by sale is sought where the amount owing exceeds £350,000 (CCA 1984, s 23(c) and County Court Jurisdiction Order 2014 (SI 2014/503), art 3).
(b) A High Court claim will have to be transferred to the County Court if:
   (i) enforcement by taking control of goods is sought of a judgment for under £600 (High Court and County Courts Jurisdiction Order 1991, art 8(1)(b));

(ii) a charging order is sought where the judgment debt is under £5,000 (Charging Orders Act 1979, s 1(2) and County Court Jurisdiction Order 2014 (SI 2014/503), art 3); or

(iii) an attachment of earnings order is sought (Attachment of Earnings Act 1971, s 1).

(c) County Court enforcement must be made at the County Court hearing centre serving the address where the judgment debtor resides or carries on business (CPR, rr 71.2, 72.3; CCR, ord 28, r 1, and PD 70, para 9.1) where the judgment creditor wishes to apply for:

(i) information from a debtor in a County Court money claim;

(ii) a third party debt order in a County Court money claim; or

(iii) a judgment summons.

(d) County Court charging order applications (other than for charges over funds in court) and attachment of earnings applications are made to the County Court Money Claims Centre (CPR, rr 73.3(2) and 89.3).

Stay of execution

A judgment debtor who is unable to pay a money judgment or order, or who alleges that **48.03** there are special circumstances that render it inexpedient to enforce the judgment, may apply for a stay of execution (CPR, r 83.7). A stay may be for whatever period and on whatever terms the court thinks fit (Tribunals, Courts and Enforcement Act 2007, s 70(1)). There is a similar power to stay execution on non-money judgments and orders on the ground that events have occurred since the date of the judgment or order (r 40.8A). It is also possible for either side to apply to vary the date of payment, or to convert a judgment into an order to pay by instalments (r 40.9A). Applications under these provisions must be supported by written evidence substantiating the grounds relied on, and usually have to include a full statement of the debtor's means. Often the result of a successful application will be a stay of execution pending payment of the judgment by instalments.

Obtaining information from debtors

Where little is known about a judgment debtor's finances, an application can be made to **48.04** obtain information from the judgment debtor. This requires the debtor to attend court to be questioned to establish the debtor's financial status, including amounts, names, addresses, account numbers, and policy numbers. A 'debtor' for these purposes includes a director of a debtor company (*Masri v Consolidated Contractors International (UK) Ltd (No 4)* [2009] Bus LR 246), but it is not possible to use Part 71 against a director who is outside the jurisdiction (*Masri v Consolidated Contractors International Co SAL* [2010] 1 AC 90). There is a prescribed form for the application notice (form N316), which must state the debtor's name and address, identify the judgment, and state the amount presently owing under the judgment (PD 71, para 1.2). If the creditor wishes the debtor to be questioned before a judge (which will be allowed only if there are compelling reasons: para 2.2) or to produce specific documents (eg bank statements and other financial material), these matters must be stated in the application notice (para 1.2).

If the application complies with these requirements it will be dealt with by a court officer **48.05** without a hearing (CPR, r 71.2), who will make an order requiring the debtor to attend court, produce documents, and answer questions. That order has to be served personally not less than 14 days before the hearing (r 71.3), with service usually being effected by the creditor rather than the court (PD 71, para 3). Once served, the debtor has seven days to ask the judgment creditor for a reasonable sum to cover the debtor's travelling expenses to court, which must be paid (r 71.4). The judgment creditor must swear an affidavit (a witness statement being insufficient) giving details of service of the order, any request for and payment of travelling expenses, and how much of the judgment remains unpaid. This affidavit must be filed two days before the hearing or produced at the hearing (r 71.5). At the hearing the court officer will ask a set of standard questions as set out in the appendices to PD 71. The judgment creditor may ask questions, or may request the court officer to ask additional, written questions (PD 71, para 4.2). If the hearing takes place before a judge, the questioning is conducted by the creditor or the creditor's legal representative (para 5.1).

48.06 If the debtor fails to attend or otherwise fails to comply, the court usually makes a suspended committal order, which gives the debtor a second chance to comply (PD 71, para 7.1). If the debtor again fails to comply, a committal order can be made by the judge (CPR, r 71.8).

Enforcement by taking control of goods

48.07 Enforcement by taking control of goods involves an enforcement officer (High Court) or enforcement agent (County Court) taking control of the judgment debtor's goods and sell- ing them to recover the sum owed under a judgment debt (Tribunals, Courts and Enforce- ment Act 2007, s 62(1)). It is commenced by issuing a writ of control (High Court) or warrant of control (County Court). Enforcement by taking control of goods is not avail- able if the judgment is payable by instalments, and the instalments are up to date (CPR, r 83.15(10)). Nor is it available where the debtor is a child under 16 (Taking Control of Goods Regulations 2013 (SI 2013/1894), reg 10).

48.08 A writ or warrant of control is normally issued simply by filing a request for its issue, producing the judgment (High Court only) (CPR, rr 83.9, 83.15), and paying the court fee. However, permission to issue the writ or warrant is required in a number of situations, such as where six years or more have passed since the date of the judgment, or where any of the parties have died since the date of the judgment (r 83.2).

48.09 It sometimes happens that more than one creditor will seek to enforce by taking control of the debtor's goods at about the same time. The priority of a writ of control is determined by reference to the time it is received by the enforcement officer, whereas the priority of a warrant of control is determined by reference to the date it is issued (CPR, r 83.4(5)).

Notice of enforcement

48.10 Before taking control of the debtor's goods the enforcement agent must give the judg- ment debtor notice of enforcement in the prescribed form. This must be served on the debtor at the address where they usually live or carry on business (Taking Control of Goods Regulations 2013, reg 8) at least seven clear days before the enforcement agent takes control of the goods (reg 6). This gives the debtor a chance to pay off the judgment before their goods are seized.

Seizing goods

48.11 A writ or warrant of control is valid for a period of 12 months, but the court can order it to be extended for a further 12 months (reg 9). Enforcement by this method can be effected on any day of the week (reg 12), but only between the hours of 6 a.m. and 9 p.m. (reg 13), unless the court orders otherwise. Entry must be through a door or other usual means of access, such as through a loading bay (reg 20). Normally force should not be used to gain entry, but reasonable force may be used if this is necessary where enforcement is at premises where the debtor usually lives or carries on a trade or business (and some other situations) (Tribunals, Courts and Enforcement Act 2007, Sch 12, paras 14–19A).

48.12 Unless the goods seized are goods on the highway (typically a car or van), the enforcement officer or agent may not take control of goods whose aggregate value is more than the amount outstanding (Tribunals, Courts and Enforcement Act 2007, Sch 12, para 12). It is only goods that belong to the debtor (para 10) and which are in the place where the debtor usually lives or carries on business (paras 9(a) and 14(6)) that may be seized. Exempt goods may not be seized (para 11). Exempt goods are defined by the Taking Control of Goods Regulations 2013, regs 4 and 5. They include:

(a) items or equipment used personally by the debtor in his employment, business, trade, profession, study, or education, up to a value of £1,350;
(b) clothing, bedding, furniture, household equipment, items, and provisions as are reasonably required to satisfy the basic domestic needs of the debtor and every member of the debtor's household;
(c) assistance dogs and vehicles with disabled persons badges;
(d) goods which happen to be the debtor's home, such as a houseboat.

Taking control of goods involves doing one of the following (Tribunals, Courts and Enforcement Act 2007, Sch 12, para 13): **48.13**

(a) securing the goods on the premises. This may be by locking them in a cupboard or outbuilding, or immobilizing them;
(b) securing them on the highway;
(c) removing them and securing them elsewhere. Unless there are exceptional circumstances, they must be secured within a reasonable distance from where they were seized. The debtor must be provided with an inventory of the removed goods as soon as reasonably practicable (para 34), and the enforcement officer or agent has a duty to take reasonable care of the removed goods (para 35); or
(d) entering into a controlled goods agreement.

Controlled goods agreement

Under a controlled goods agreement the debtor is permitted to retain custody of the goods, but acknowledges that the enforcement agent is taking control of them, and agrees not to remove or dispose of them, or permit anyone else to do so, before the debt is paid (para 13(4)). It can be entered into between the enforcement agent and the debtor, or an adult authorized to do so by the debtor, or someone with apparent authority if the premises are used for a trade or business (Taking Control of Goods Regulations 2013, reg 14). The agreement must be in writing, and comply with the requirements in reg 15. Subject to the court authorizing shorter notice, the enforcement agent has to give the debtor two days' advance notice in writing of any intention to re-enter the premises (usually because the enforcement agent now intends to remove the seized goods) (regs 23–27 and Tribunals, Courts and Enforcement Act 2007, Sch 12, para 16). **48.14**

Sale

Often, the threat of sale is sufficient incentive to persuade the debtor to pay. On payment the execution is superseded and the goods are released (Tribunals, Courts and Enforcement Act 2007, Sch 12, para 6(3)(a)). Otherwise, the enforcement agent must make or obtain a valuation of the controlled goods (para 36), and must sell or dispose of them for the best price that can reasonably be obtained (para 37). The debtor must be given seven clear days' notice in writing of the arrangement for sale (para 40). Unless the court orders otherwise, the goods will be sold by public auction (para 41). The auction must be publicly advertised and must be conducted by a qualified auctioneer or on an online auction or internet auction site (Taking Control of Goods Regulations 2013, reg 43). After the sale the debtor is given a detailed account in writing of the sale, and the proceeds are used to pay the amount outstanding on the judgment (Tribunals, Courts and Enforcement Act 2007, Sch 12, para 50). Purchasers of the goods acquire good title (para 51). **48.15**

Administration orders

48.16 By virtue of the CCA 1984, s 112, the County Court has power, of its own initiative or on the application of either the debtor or the creditor, in respect of a debtor who is unable to pay his or her debts, to make an administration order in respect of the debtor's estate. Such an order has the immediate effect of restricting creditors named in the order from joining in bankruptcy petitions against the debtor. The order will usually provide for the debtor to make specified payments by instalments, with periodic dividends being paid to the named creditors.

Third party debt orders

48.17 A third party debt order has the effect of transforming a debt payable by a third party to the debtor into an obligation to pay the debt to the judgment creditor. This is a particularly effective method of enforcement where the third party is a responsible body, such as a bank or building society. It is not restricted to such bodies. For this purpose, evidence that the judgment debtor had an account which in the past was in credit is sufficient, at least for the purposes of obtaining an interim order (*Alawiye v Mahmood* [2007] 1 WLR 79). Enforcement by this method is a two-stage process. First, the creditor makes an application without notice for an interim third party debt order. Secondly, there is a hearing on notice for a final order.

Procedure

48.18 The first stage is commenced by a without-notice application (CPR, r 72.3) verified by a statement of truth in form N349 containing the information prescribed by PD 72, para 1.2. The required information includes details of the judgment debtor, the judgment, and the third party debt. Speculative applications will be rejected, and orders will be made only if there is evidence substantiating the belief that the debtor has (say) an account with a specific bank or building society (PD 72, para 1.3). The application is considered without a hearing by a judge (r 72.4(1)), who may make an interim third party debt order directing the third party not to make any payment which reduces the amount he owes the judgment debtor to less than the amount specified in the order. The judge will also fix a hearing to consider making the order final.

48.19 An interim order must be served on the third party who owes money to the judgment debtor not less than 21 days before the date fixed for the hearing to consider making the order final (r 72.5(1)(a)), and is binding on the third party when it is served on him (r 72.4(4)). If the third party is a bank or building society it must carry out a search to identify all accounts held by the judgment debtor, and must disclose to the court and the judgment creditor the account numbers, whether they are in credit, and, if so, whether the balance is sufficient to cover the amount specified in the interim order or the amount in the account if insufficient (r 72.6(1), (2)). Unless the court orders otherwise, an interim third party debt order only affects bank or building society accounts in the sole name of the judgment debtor (PD 72, para 3.1), and the bank or building society is not required by r 72.6 to retain money in, or disclose information relating to, joint accounts (para 3.2). Any third party who is not a bank or building society has seven days after service to notify the court and the judgment creditor in writing if he claims not to owe any money to the judgment debtor or to owe less than the amount specified in the interim order (r 72.6(4)).

48.20 The interim order must also be served on the judgment debtor. This needs to be done not less than seven days after service on the third party, and not less than seven days before the date fixed for the hearing (r 72.5(1)(b)). Where service is effected by the judgment creditor a certificate of service must be filed not less than two days before the hearing, or must be produced at the hearing (r 72.5(2)). A judgment debtor who is an individual and who is suffering hardship in meeting ordinary living expenses as a result of the interim order may apply for a hardship payment order permitting one or more payments out of the account (r 72.7).

The second stage is when the court considers whether to make a final third party debt **48.21** order on the date fixed when the interim order was made. A judgment debtor or third party objecting to the final order, or who knows or believes someone else has a claim to the money, must file and serve written evidence stating the grounds of any objection or details of the other claim not less than three days before the hearing (r 72.8). If the court is notified that another person has a claim to the money it will serve notice of the application and the hearing on that person (r 72.8(5)). At the hearing the court may make a final third party debt order, discharge the interim order, decide any issues, or direct a trial of any issues (r 72.8(6)).

Attachable money

It is possible to obtain a third party debt order only over a 'debt due or accruing due' to the **48.22** judgment debtor. Examples are money in a bank account, trade debts, judgment debts, and rent due to a landlord. Conversely, claims for damages, matrimonial maintenance orders, and salary not presently payable are not attachable. Nor is money in a joint bank account (*Hirschon v Evans* [1938] 2 KB 801).

Effect of the orders

Once served, an interim order binds the third party to freeze any debts due to the judgment **48.23** debtor up to the amount of the judgment debt and fixed costs (r 72.4(3)). A final third party debt order is enforceable as an order to pay money. By r 72.9(2) the third party is discharged as against the judgment debtor to the extent of the amount paid under the order.

Discretion

A third party debt order may be refused if it would be inequitable to grant it. This may **48.24** be so if there is a possibility of the third party having to pay twice over, such as where the third party would remain liable before a foreign court: *Société Eram Shipping Co Ltd v Compagnie Internationale de Navigation* [2004] 1 AC 260. The insolvency of the judgment debtor is a sufficient reason for refusing to make an order, because its effect may be to prefer the judgment creditor over the general body of creditors: *Roberts Petroleum Ltd v Bernard Kenny Ltd* [1983] 2 AC 192.

Attachment of earnings

Where a judgment debtor is employed, but has no other substantial assets, the most effec- **48.25** tive method of enforcement is by obtaining an attachment of earnings order. Such an order can be made, unless the application is by the debtor, only if the debtor has failed to make one or more payments as required by the relevant adjudication (Attachment of Earnings Act 1971, s 3(3)). The Attachment of Earnings Act 1971, s 6(1), provides:

> An attachment of earnings order shall be an order directed to a person who appears to the court to have the debtor in his employment and shall operate as an instruction to that person—
> (a) to make periodical deductions from the debtor's earnings . . . and
> (b) at such times as the order may require, or as the court may allow, to pay the amounts deducted to the collecting officer of the court, as specified in the order.

As mentioned at 48.02, the High Court has no jurisdiction to make attachment of earnings **48.26** orders, and High Court claims need to be transferred to the County Court Money Claims Centre. Magistrates' courts have some jurisdiction to make these orders, such as to enforce payment of arrears of council tax.

Earnings attachable

48.27   An attachment of earnings order may be made in respect of wages, salaries, fees, bonuses, commission, and overtime payable under a contract of service, including occupational pensions and statutory sick pay. An order cannot be made in respect of self-employed income, nor State pensions, benefits, or allowances (Attachment of Earnings Act 1971, s 24).

Procedure

48.28   An application for an attachment of earnings order is made by filing a request in a standard form certifying the amount of money remaining due under the judgment, and paying the fee. The court then notifies the debtor of a hearing date at least 21 days in advance, enclosing a reply form concerning the debtor's means. The reply form should be completed by the debtor and filed at court within eight days after service. A copy of the reply form is sent to the judgment creditor. The reply form is considered by an administrative officer of the court, who may make an attachment of earnings order if there is sufficient information to do so (CPR, r 89.7(1)). If either party objects, or if the court officer decides not to make an order, the application is referred to the District Judge.

48.29   At the hearing the District Judge confirms that the debtor is not unemployed or self-employed. Provided the debtor is employed, the District Judge will consider the debtor's income and regular outgoings, and will fix:

(a) The debtor's protected earnings rate. This is the amount the debtor is considered to need to maintain his or her family, each week or month, and any deductions made under the order will not reduce the debtor's income below this level.
(b) The debtor's normal deduction rate. This is the amount, subject to the protected earnings rate, which is deducted from the debtor's earnings each week or month.

48.30   Normally, the order will then be served on the debtor's employer, who will make the deductions specified and pay the money deducted to the court. Alternatively, the court may make a suspended attachment of earnings order, which will be served on the employer only if the debtor fails to pay agreed instalments promptly. A debtor with several creditors may be ordered to file a list of creditors with a view to making an administration order (see 48.16) or a consolidated attachment of earnings order.

Supplementary points

48.31   While an attachment of earnings order is in force, permission of the court is required before a warrant of control will be issued for the judgment debt (Attachment of Earnings Act 1971, s 8(2)(b)). Also, during the currency of the order the debtor is under a duty (enforceable by imprisonment or a fine: s 23) to notify the court of any change in his or her employment (s 15).

Charging orders

48.32   A charging order is defined by the Charging Orders Act 1979, s 1(1), as an order 'imposing on any such property as may be specified in the order a charge for securing the payment of any money due or to become due under [a] judgment or order'. A charging order therefore *secures* a judgment debt: it does not of itself produce any money. By s 3(4) a charge imposed by a charging order has the same effect, and is enforceable in the same way, 'as an equitable charge created by the debtor by writing under his hand'. Once obtained and registered at the Land Registry, a charging order can give a measure of long-term security, which is necessary if there is no immediate prospect of recovery by other methods. It was held in *Ezekiel v Orakpo* (1994) *The Times*, 8 November 1994 that a charging order extends to cover the judgment debt, interest, and costs even if it does not expressly say so. Exceptionally, it may be possible to enforce the charge by bringing sale proceedings (see 48.38), or the charge may result in the judgment being paid if the charged property is sold by the judgment debtor and the purchaser wishes (as is usual) to purchase it clear of encumbrances.

Chargeable property

Section 2 of the Charging Orders Act 1979 specifies the property which may be charged: **48.33**

(1) Subject to subsection (3) below, a charge may be imposed by a charging order only on—
  (a) any interest held by the debtor beneficially—
    (i) in any asset of a kind mentioned in subsection (2) below, or
    (ii) under any trust; or
  (b) any interest held by a person as trustee of a trust ('the trust'), if the interest is in such an asset or is an interest under another trust and—
    (i) the judgment or order in respect of which a charge is to be imposed was made against that person as trustee of the trust, or
    (ii) the whole beneficial interest under the trust is held by the debtor unencumbered and for his own benefit, or
    (iii) in a case where there are two or more debtors all of whom are liable to the creditor for the same debt, they together hold the whole beneficial interest under the trust unencumbered and for their own benefit.

(2) The assets referred to in subsection (1) above are—
  (a) land,
  (b) securities of any of the following kinds—
    (i)   government stock,
    (ii) stock of any body (other than a building society) incorporated within England and Wales,
    (iii) stock of any body incorporated outside England and Wales or of any State or territory outside the United Kingdom, being stock registered in a register kept at any place within England and Wales,
    (iv) units of any unit trust in respect of which a register of the unit holders is kept at any place within England and Wales, or
  (c) funds in court.

(3) In any case where a charge is imposed by a charging order on any interest in an asset of a kind mentioned in paragraph (b) or (c) of subsection (2) above, the court making the order may provide for the charge to extend to any interest or dividend payable in respect of the asset.

Procedure

Like third party debt orders (see 48.17), applications for charging orders follow a two- **48.34**
stage procedure. The first stage is to apply for an interim charging order by issuing an application notice in form N379 verified by a statement of truth (CPR, r 73.3(5)) containing the information prescribed by PD 73, para 1.2. The required information includes details of the judgment debtor, the judgment, and details of the property which it is intended to charge. The application is considered without a hearing (by a court officer at the County Court Money Claims Centre, by a Master in the High Court), who will consider making an interim order and (in the High Court) will fix a hearing to consider making a final charging order (r 73.6(3)). If the interim order relates to registered land, it is usual to protect it by entering a unilateral or agreed notice under the Land Registration Act 2002, ss 32 and 34.

48.35 There are slightly different procedures thereafter in County Court Money Claims Centre and High Court cases. In the High Court, at least 21 days before the final hearing (which is the second stage) the judgment debtor, such other creditors as the court may direct, and certain other specified persons must be served with the interim charging order, application notice, and any supporting documents (r 73.7(5)). Service of an interim charging order effectively prevents dealings with the assets charged pending the final hearing (r 73.8). If service is effected by the judgment creditor, a certificate of service must be filed at least two days before the final hearing or produced at the hearing (r 73.7(6)). Any person objecting to the order being made final must file and serve written evidence setting out the grounds of the objection not less than seven days before the hearing (r 73.10A(2)). At the hearing the court may make a final charging order, discharge the interim order, decide any issues, or direct a trial of any issues (r 73.10A(3)). There is no obligation to quantify the judgment debtor's beneficial interest in jointly owned property even at the final charging order stage (*Walton v Allman* [2016] 1 WLR 2053). This can await any application for an order for sale.

48.36 Particular matters laid down in the Charging Orders Act 1979, s 1(5), that the court must consider in deciding whether to make a charging order, are:

(a) the personal circumstances of the debtor; and

(b) whether any other creditor of the debtor would be likely to be unduly prejudiced by the making of the order. Something exceptional is required on this ground, and the mere fact other creditors may receive nothing if the charging order is made is not an exceptional circumstance (*British Arab Commercial Bank plc v Alsosaibi* [2011] EWHC 2444 (Comm)).

48.37 If a final charging order is made it is usual to register it under the Land Registration Act 2002. This is probably not strictly necessary if the interim order was registered, because there is only one charging order, which is continued by the final order.

Sale proceedings

48.38 Proceedings for the sale of charged property are commenced by issuing separate proceedings under CPR, Part 8, supported by written evidence (CPR, r 73.10C). The written evidence gives details of the charging order, the property charged, verifies the debtor's title to the property charged, identifies prior encumbrances, certifies the amount outstanding on the judgment, and estimates the price which would be obtained on sale (PD 73, para 4.3). It is usual to apply for an order that the debtor vacate the premises as well, so that a sale can be made with vacant possession. A sale order may be refused, or postponed to give the judgment debtor a final chance to pay, if the judgment debt is very small compared to the value of the property (*Packman Lucas Ltd v Mentmore Towers Ltd* [2010] BLR 465).

48.39 Where the charged property is owned by more than one person, instead of using r 73.10C, any application for an order for sale has to be made under the Trusts of Land and Appointment of Trustees Act 1996, s 14 (PD 73, para 4.5). Where it is residential property, the court has to balance the rights of the creditor under Protocol 1, art 1, and the rights of the debtor and his family under the European Convention on Human Rights, art 8 (*National Westminster Bank plc v Rushmer* [2010] 2 FLR 362).

Insolvency

48.40 Often a failure to pay a judgment debt is evidence that the judgment debtor is insolvent. Consequently, it may be more apt to bring bankruptcy or winding-up proceedings than to apply for enforcement. A brief guide to the procedure on winding-up petitions can be found at 8.15ff.

Judgment summonses

A judgment summons is a procedure for punishing a defaulting judgment debtor who **48.41** could pay, but has chosen not to, with a period in prison (Debtors Act 1869, s 5). The punitive nature of the provision was stressed in *Woodley v Woodley* (1993) *The Times*, 15 March 1993. Since the Administration of Justice Act 1970, s 11, came into force, judgment summonses have been available only for enforcing matrimonial maintenance orders and arrears of some taxes.

B ENFORCEMENT OF JUDGMENTS FOR THE DELIVERY OF GOODS

Enforcement of judgments for the delivery of goods is by means of warrants (or, in the High **48.42** Court, writs) of delivery. There are two types, corresponding with the forms of relief stated in the Torts (Interference with Goods) Act 1977, s 3. The first is known as a warrant (or writ) of specific delivery (CPR, r 83.23). It requires the enforcement officer or enforcement agent to seize the goods specified in the judgment with no alternative of recovering their value. The second is known as a warrant (or writ) of delivery. It requires the enforcement officer or enforcement agent to seize either the goods specified in the judgment or their value.

Like enforcement by taking control of goods (see 48.07), issue is simply a matter of the **48.43** creditor filing a request accompanied by the judgment (High Court), and paying the court fee. Before enforcement is levied the debtor must be served with a written warning of the warrant at least seven days in advance (CPR, r 83.24).

C ENFORCEMENT OF JUDGMENTS FOR THE POSSESSION OF LAND

Procedure

Permission is required to issue a warrant of possession (CPR, r 83.13(2)), unless the claim **48.44** was against trespassers (r 83.13(3)). Permission will not be granted unless every person in actual possession of the land is given sufficient advance notice to be able to apply for any relief to which they might be entitled (r 83.13(8) and *Gupta v Partridge* [2018] 1 WLR 1). The police are often informed of the time when possession will be enforced, as entry may be gained by force if necessary. The claimant will also usually need to attend to change the locks and make the premises secure after possession is obtained.

When enforcing the warrant or writ, the enforcement officer or enforcement agent is **48.45** required to turn out everyone on the premises, even if they are not parties: *R v Wandsworth County Court, ex p Wandsworth London Borough Council* [1975] 1 WLR 1314. However, there is a divergence of practice regarding goods in the premises. In the High Court, these too must be removed by the enforcement officer, but in the County Court this is unnecessary (CCA 1984, s 111(1)).

Warrants and writs of restitution

It sometimes happens that persons ejected when a warrant or writ of possession is enforced **48.46** regain entry at some later date. Such persons may be removed a second time under a warrant (County Court) or writ (High Court) of restitution. These are a species of warrant (or writ) in aid of a primary warrant (or writ). Permission is required for the issue of such warrants or writs (CPR, r 83.26(8)). The application is made without notice by application notice supported by written evidence giving details of the wrongful re-entry. The court looks for a plain and sufficient nexus between the original recovery of possession and the need to effect further recovery of the same land: *Wiltshire County Council v Frazer (No 2)* [1986] 1 WLR 109.

D RECEIVERS BY WAY OF EQUITABLE EXECUTION

Nature of receivership

48.47 A receivership order has the effect of appointing some responsible person to receive rents, profits, and moneys receivable in respect of the judgment debtor's interest in certain property, and to apply that income in specified ways, including payment of a judgment debt. According to *Maclaine Watson and Co Ltd v International Tin Council* [1988] Ch 1, such an order can only be made where:

(a) it is impossible to enforce using any of the other methods of enforcement; and
(b) the appointment of a receiver will be effective.

48.48 On the question whether the appointment of a receiver will be effective, the SCA 1981, s 37(1), provides that an appointment can be made only if it is just and convenient. Under PD 69, para 5, the court must have regard to the amount claimed by the judgment creditor, the amount likely to be obtained by the receiver, and the probable costs of the appointment. It may be appropriate to appoint a receiver where the judgment debtor has some valuable right not in the nature of a debt (and hence not amenable to a third party debt order). A receiver might also be appointed to receive rents from a number of tenants who are suing their landlord for failing to maintain the premises, and to apply the money in effecting necessary repairs: *Hart v Emelkirk Ltd* [1983] 1 WLR 1289.

Procedure

48.49 An application for the appointment of a receiver may be made without notice, but is made by issuing an application notice supported by written evidence (CPR, r 69.3). The evidence needs to address the circumstances making the appointment of a receiver desirable, and must also address the suitability of the person nominated to act as the receiver. There are further detailed requirements in PD 69, para 4. If an order is made it is usually served on the receiver and all the parties to the proceedings, and the court may direct that it be served on other interested persons (r 69.4). The receiver may be required to provide security to cover his liability for any acts and omissions as a receiver (r 69.5 and PD 69, para 7). Once appointed a receiver will be remunerated (often out of the income of the property managed by the receiver), and the receiver will be required to provide accounts for his dealings with the property (r 69.8 and PD 69, para 10). Once the receiver's duties are completed the receiver or any party may apply for the receiver to be discharged (r 69.10).

E CONTEMPT OF COURT

48.50 Contempt of court consists of interfering with the administration of the law: see *Attorney-General v Leveller Magazine Ltd* [1979] AC 440 *per* Lord Edmund-Davies at 459. It can take many forms, but the most common are:

(a) disobedience by the contemner of an order requiring him or her to take or refrain from taking specified action;

(b) assisting another to breach such an order;

(c) taking action which impedes or interferes with the course of justice; and

(d) making a false statement of truth.

Proceedings for contempt are essentially punitive in character, although they also have the **48.51** purpose of securing compliance with the court's orders. The main punishments for contempt are imprisonment (for up to two years: Contempt of Court Act 1981, s 14(1)), fines, and sequestration, although the court can order the taking of security, award damages, or deliver a strong reprimand. Given the nature of the punishments for contempt, the courts have insisted on the establishment of *mens rea* and proof to the criminal standard (so the court is sure).

Committal for breach of an order

Formalities

Committal for breach of a court order or undertaking normally arises in relation to injunc- **48.52** tions, although it is possible for other orders and judgments to be couched in a form rendering breach a contempt of court. The order must contain a penal notice prominently displayed on its front warning that disobedience will be a contempt of court punishable by imprisonment, a fine, or sequestration of assets (CPR, r 81.9). Unless the court dispenses with service under r 81.8, it is necessary to have served the order personally on the defendant (rr 81.5 and 81.6).

Procedure on application

Applications to commit a contemner to prison are made by a Part 8 claim form or, if made **48.53** in existing proceedings, by application notice (CPR rr 81.14 and 81.18). The claim form or application notice must include a prominent notice stating the possible consequences of the court making a committal order and of the respondent not attending the hearing (PD 81, paras 12(4) and 13.2(4) and Annex 3). A detailed statement of the applicant's grounds for bringing the committal application is required, together with an affidavit (not a witness statement) setting out the facts and exhibiting all documents relied upon.

The claim form or application notice must be served personally on the respondent, who has **48.54** 14 days to file an acknowledgment of service and to file and serve evidence (r 81.14(3)). A respondent who intends to attend the hearing must give seven days' notice in writing to the court and other parties, and must provide a written summary of the submissions the respondent intends to make (r 81.14(5)).

The hearing has to be before a judge (PD 81, para 10.2). Unless the court otherwise **48.55** orders, the applicant is restricted to the grounds and evidence filed with the claim form or application notice (r 81.28(1)). The court has power to order any person, other than the respondent, to give evidence at the hearing. A respondent may give oral evidence at the hearing despite not filing any written evidence (r 81.28(2)). A respondent who gives evidence may be cross-examined.

Purging contempt

A contemner does not necessarily serve the entire term of imprisonment imposed by the **48.56** judge. An application for discharge may be made on the ground that the contempt has been purged or that the contemner desires to purge the contempt. The main consideration is whether the contemner has been sufficiently punished for the contempt, although the court will also be concerned with whether the contemner is likely to obey the court's order in the future, and whether the contemner has shown suitable remorse: *Enfield London Borough Council v Mahoney* [1983] 1 WLR 749.

Sequestration

48.57 Applications for permission to issue writs of sequestration are made by issuing an application notice supported by affidavit evidence, and are heard by a judge (CPR, rr 81.19–81.27 and 83.2A). If the contempt is proved and sequestration is ordered, four sequestrators are appointed to enter the contemner's lands, and to seize the contemner's personal property, and to hold the same until the contempt is purged. Third parties are under a duty not knowingly to take any action which will obstruct compliance by the sequestrators with the terms of the writ of sequestration: see the judgment of Donaldson P in *Eckman v Midland Bank Ltd* [1973] QB 519. Sequestration was used in a number of well-publicized trade union cases in the 1980s to enforce compliance with injunctions.

F ENFORCEMENT OF FOREIGN JUDGMENTS

48.58 At common law a foreign judgment can be enforced in this country by bringing an English action claiming the amount of the judgment as a debt. In theory, the foreign judgment gives rise to an implied contract to pay, which can be enforced in England: *Grant v Easton* (1883) 13 QBD 302. However, English proceedings can be commenced only if the English courts have jurisdiction (see Chapter 11), and although it may be possible to obtain summary judgment on such a claim, a number of defences can be raised (eg that the foreign court lacked jurisdiction, fraud, that the judgment is contrary to public policy, that the foreign proceedings were in breach of an agreement as to the settling of the dispute, or that the judgment is for the enforcement of a foreign penal law).

48.59 The UK is party to international conventions providing for the direct enforcement of foreign judgments which have been incorporated into English law by the following provisions:

(a) The Administration of Justice Act 1920, by which an application can be made by issuing a Part 8 claim form for the registration of a judgment of a superior court of a Commonwealth country in the High Court within 12 months of the date of the judgment in question. The court has a discretion whether to register the judgment, and the defendant can make use of most of the defences available at common law.

(b) The Foreign Judgments (Reciprocal Enforcement) Act 1933, by which an application can be made by issuing a Part 8 claim form for the registration of judgments of recognized courts and tribunals of States with which the UK has entered into reciprocal enforcement arrangements, provided the application is made within six years of the judgment. This Act considerably increased the circumstances in which foreign judgments can be registered, but enforcement is subject to a wide range of defences similar to those available at common law.

(c) The Judgments Regulation (the Lugano Convention and the Hague Convention 2005 are similar), by which a judgment of a court of another EU Member State may be registered in the courts of this country. When registered, such a judgment has the same force and effect as if the judgment had been given in this country. Applications for registration are made without notice supported by an affidavit or witness statement stating whether the judgment provides for payment of money or interest, the grounds on which the applicant has a right to enforce the judgment, and the amount unsatisfied on the judgment, and giving an address for service within the jurisdiction. The written evidence must exhibit the judgment or a certified copy, evidence of service, legal aid documents from the State in which the judgment was given, and translations. Articles 34 and 35 of the Judgments Regulation set out a number of defences to registration, such as recognition being contrary to public policy, the defendant not having been duly served with the document instituting the foreign proceedings, and the judgment being irreconcilable with another judgment. Recognition of a Dutch judgment which had been obtained in manifest contravention of the European Convention on Human Rights, art 6(1) was refused as being contrary to public policy under what is now art 34(1) in *Maronier v Larmer* [2003] QB 620. However, art 36 provides that there cannot, under any circumstances, be a review of the substance of such a judgment.

(d) European Enforcement Orders. Certification and enforcement of European Enforcement Orders is governed by Council Regulation (EC) No 805/2004 (the 'EEO Regulation'). The EEO Regulation is annexed to PD 74B, and the procedure for enforcement under the EEO Regulation is dealt with by CPR, rr 74.27–74.33.

Detailed provisions dealing with the registration in the Queen's Bench Division of foreign **48.60** judgments can be found in CPR, Part 74.

KEY POINTS SUMMARY

- A judgment creditor can ask for the court's assistance in discovering the assets available for **48.61** enforcement by applying to obtain information from the judgment debtor.

- A money judgment can be enforced by writ or warrant of control against the judgment debtor's goods, by third party debt order against a bank (etc.) account, by attachment of earnings against the judgment debtor's salary, or can be secured by obtaining a charging order.

- Each type of non-money judgment has its own enforcement procedure (land, goods, injunctions).

- Most enforcement procedures are dealt with administratively by the court.

- Exceptions are third party debt orders, charging orders, and committal, which all require court orders.

- Third party debt orders and charging orders have a two-stage process. Interim orders are sought without notice, and final orders are sought at a final hearing.

- Various additional formalities apply to applications to commit for contempt, such as penal notices, personal service, the use of affidavits, and proof to the criminal standard.

49

JUDICIAL REVIEW

A PARTIES. 49.03
B *LOCUS STANDI* 49.07
C PUBLIC LAW 49.08
D REMEDIES IN JUDICIAL REVIEW 49.14
E JUDICIAL REVIEW PRE-ACTION
   PROTOCOL 49.22
F APPLYING FOR PERMISSION TO
   PROCEED 49.24
G SUBSTANTIVE HEARING 49.38
H CONVERSION TO A COMMON
   LAW CLAIM. 49.46
I CONSENT ORDERS 49.47
   Key points summary 49.48

49.01 'Judicial review, as the words imply, is not an appeal from a decision, but a review of the manner in which the decision was made.' So said Lord Brightman in *Chief Constable of the North Wales Police v Evans* [1982] 1 WLR 1155. In the same case, Lord Hailsham of St Marylebone LC said that the purpose of judicial review is to ensure that an individual is given fair treatment by a wide range of authorities, whether judicial, quasi-judicial, or administrative, to which the individual has been subject. It is no part of that purpose to substitute the opinion of the judiciary or of individual judges for that of the authority constituted by law to decide the matters in question.

49.02 Most applications for judicial review must be brought in the Administrative Court Office of the QBD in the High Court (CCA 1984, s 38(3)). Judicial review challenges of planning decisions, highways, compulsory purchase orders, and EU environmental legislation, etc. are brought in the Planning Court (CPR, rr 54.21–54.24). The law governing when judicial review will lie is a subject in its own right, and reference should be made to specialist books on the subject.

A PARTIES

49.03 Judicial review proceedings are not brought by or at the instigation of the Crown, whose only involvement is as a nominal party: *R (Ben-Abdelaziz) v Haringey London Borough Council* [2001] 1 WLR 1485. They are therefore not brought by or at the instigation of a public authority within the meaning of the Human Rights Act 1998, s 22(4), and consequently do not give rise to a right to claim damages against a public authority under s 7(1) of the Act.

49.04 In general, judicial review will lie against any body charged with the performance of a public duty. Examples are government ministers and government departments, local authorities, police authorities, prison governors, and even disciplinary bodies exercising statutory powers (see, eg, *R v General Medical Council, ex p Gee* [1987] 1 WLR 564). In *R v Criminal Injuries Compensation Board, ex p Lain* [1967] 2 QB 864, Lord Parker CJ said that private and domestic tribunals have always been outside the scope of judicial review. A former requirement that the body being reviewed should have a duty to act judicially was removed by the House of Lords in *O'Reilly v Mackman* [1983] 2 AC 237. In *Council of Civil Service Unions v Minister for the Civil Service* [1985] AC 374 the House of Lords extended the possibility of judicial review to a person exercising a purely prerogative power.

Subject to exceptions, judicial review lies against inferior courts and tribunals. Inferior **49.05** courts include magistrates' courts, the County Court, election courts, coroners' courts, and (on matters unconnected to trial on indictment) the Crown Court. It is only in rare situations that judicial review will lie against a decision of the County Court, because the proper remedy is to seek to appeal rather than to seek a judicial review (*R (Sivasubramaniam) v Wandsworth County Court* [2003] 1 WLR 475). A distinction is drawn between cases where the judge has simply got it wrong, or even extremely wrong, on the law, or the facts, or both (where judicial review is not available) and cases where the judicial process itself had been frustrated or corrupted (where it is) (*Strickson v Preston County Court* [2007] EWCA Civ 1132). The superior courts (the Crown Court, in matters connected with trials on indictment, the High Court, Court of Appeal, and Supreme Court) are not subject to judicial review.

While the Upper Tribunal is amenable to judicial review, applications for judicial review from **49.06** decisions of the Upper Tribunal refusing permission to appeal to itself are subject to restrictions set out in CPR, r 54.7A. These include a 16-day time limit for bringing the claim for judicial review from the date of the notice of the decision to refuse permission to appeal (r 54.7A(3)). This is because there is already a two-stage appeal process to the Upper Tribunal from decisions of First-tier Tribunals.

B LOCUS STANDI

A claimant seeking judicial review must have 'a sufficient interest in the matter to which **49.07** the application relates' (SCA 1981, s 31(3)). The essential idea is to exclude busybodies. A direct or personal interest in the decision should suffice. Whether a general interest is sufficient is a mixed question of law and fact. It depends on the relationship between the claimant and the complaint, with the court needing to consider the relevant duties of the authority concerned, the complaint made, and the relief sought (*Inland Revenue Commissioners v National Federation of Self-Employed and Small Businesses Ltd* [1982] AC 617). In that case it was held that a group of taxpayers did not have standing to impugn the Inland Revenue Commissioners' dealings with other taxpayers. In *R v Inspectorate of Pollution, ex p Greenpeace Ltd* [1994] 1 WLR 570, Otton J said that the court had to take into account the nature of the claimant, the extent of the claimant's interest in the issues raised, and the nature of the relief sought. On the latter point, if a mandatory order is sought the court is more likely to hold that the claimant has no standing than if the primary relief is a quashing order. In this decision Greenpeace Ltd, an environmental interest group of international standing, was held to have *locus standi* in relation to an issue involving the discharge of radioactive waste. In *R v Secretary of State for Employment, ex p Equal Opportunities Commission* [1995] 1 AC 1 the EOC was held to have *locus standi* in judicial review proceedings relating to sex discrimination.

C PUBLIC LAW

Decision susceptible to judicial review

The subject matter of an application for judicial review is either a decision or a refusal by **49.08** the defendant to make a decision. According to Lord Diplock in *Council of Civil Service Unions v Minister for the Civil Service* [1985] AC 374 a decision must affect some other person either by altering rights which are enforceable in private law or by depriving that other person of some benefit or advantage. A government department's circular dealing with contraception advice was held to be a 'decision' in *Gillick v West Norfolk and Wisbech Area Health Authority* [1986] AC 112. However, a claimant wishing to apply for judicial review of government policy or of a statutory provision cannot manufacture a decision by engaging in correspondence with the appropriate government department, and then relying on the department's reply as a 'decision' (*R v Secretary of State for Employment, ex p Equal Opportunities Commission* [1995] 1 AC 1).

Issues of public law

49.09 Generally, a claimant complaining of an infringement of public law rights must proceed by way of judicial review rather than by ordinary claim. In *O'Reilly v Mackman* [1983] 2 AC 237 Lord Diplock said at 285:

> . . . it would in my view as a general rule be contrary to public policy, and as such an abuse of the process of the court, to permit a person seeking to establish that a decision of a public authority infringed rights to which he was entitled to protection under public law to proceed by way of an ordinary action and by this means to evade the provisions [governing judicial review] for the protection of such authorities.

49.10 Lord Bridge of Harwich in *Cocks v Thanet District Council* [1983] 2 AC 286 identified the various protections given by the rules governing judicial review as:

> . . . the need to obtain [permission] to apply on the basis of [written] evidence which makes frank disclosure of all relevant facts known to the applicant; the court's discretionary control of both [disclosure of documents] and cross-examination; the capacity of the court to act with the utmost speed when necessary; and the avoidance of the temptation for the court to substitute its own decision of fact for that of the [authority].

49.11 As recognized in *Mercury Communications Ltd v Director General of Telecommunications* [1996] 1 WLR 48, the precise limits of what is known as 'public law' and 'private law' have not been fully worked out, so there is often scope for argument whether the *O'Reilly v Mackman* principle applies to any individual case. In *O'Reilly v Mackman* the claimants were prison inmates who commenced common law claims complaining of a loss of remission. These claims were struck out, because the claimants had no right to remission in private law. Their claims raised questions of public law, so should have been brought by way of judicial review. Since the introduction of the CPR, whether a claim should be struck out depends on whether in all the relevant circumstances, including any delay in commencing the proceedings, there has been an abuse of the process of the court (*P v Home Office* [2017] 1 WLR 3189 at [41]).

49.12 There are exceptions to this general rule. In *O'Reilly v Mackman*, Lord Diplock expressly referred to two of them:

(a) where the invalidity of the decision arises as a collateral issue in a claim for the infringement of the claimant's rights under private law, for example where the validity of a planning authority's enforcement notice is an issue in a claim by the claimant against its solicitors for professional negligence;

(b) where none of the parties objects to the matter being brought by a common law claim.

49.13 Later decisions of the House of Lords provide further exceptions to the general rule:

(a) where the claim has been framed in tort without raising any issue of public law as a live issue (*Davy v Spelthorne Borough Council* [1984] AC 262);

(b) where the validity of an authority's decision is raised by way of defence (*Wandsworth London Borough Council v Winder* [1985] AC 461);

(c) where a claim, although involving a challenge to a public law decision, is dominated by a consideration of the claimant's private law rights (*Roy v Kensington and Chelsea and Westminster Family Practitioner Committee* [1992] 1 AC 624).

D REMEDIES IN JUDICIAL REVIEW

There are six remedies available on applications for judicial review. The first three (see **49.14** 49.15–49.18) are the old prerogative remedies. Generally, the various forms of relief may be claimed either in the alternative or in addition to each other, provided they arise out of, or relate to, or are connected with, the same matter.

Quashing order

Quashing orders used to be known as orders of *certiorari*. A quashing order is an order **49.15** quashing the decision of an inferior court, tribunal, or public authority. It will often also remit the matter with a direction for the lower court, tribunal, or authority to reach a decision consistent with the findings of the High Court (SCA 1981, s 31(5)(a)). While remitting back is the usual outcome, the High Court has the alternative power under s 31(5)(b) and (5A) to substitute its own decision provided:

(a) the decision quashed was made by a court or tribunal (so this is not available where the decision was that of an authority);

(b) the decision was quashed for an error of law; and

(c) without the error, there would have been only one decision that the lower court or tribunal could have reached.

Where permission is sought to apply for a quashing order in respect of a judgment or order **49.16** which is subject to appeal, the QBD may adjourn the application for permission until the appeal is determined or the time for appealing has expired. If permission to apply is granted, the judge may, under CPR, r 54.10(2), impose a stay of the impugned proceedings.

Mandatory orders

Mandatory orders used to be known as *mandamus*. A mandatory order is an order requir- **49.17** ing an inferior court, tribunal, or public authority to carry out its duties. It is the appropriate order where the body in question is guilty of wrongful inaction, which includes a refusal to exercise a discretion. Disobedience is a contempt of court (*R v Poplar Borough Council, ex p London County Council (No 2)* [1922] 1 KB 95). The remedy does not lie against the Crown (*R v Powell* (1841) 1 QB 352).

Prohibitory order

Prohibitory orders used to be known as prohibitions. A prohibitory order is an order **49.18** restraining an inferior court, tribunal, or public authority from acting outside its jurisdiction. In *R v Electricity Commissioners, ex p London Electricity Joint Committee Co (1920) Ltd* [1924] 1 KB 171, Atkin LJ said:

> I can see no difference in principle between [a quashing order] and [a prohibitory order], except that the latter may be invoked at an earlier stage. If the proceedings establish that the body complained of is exceeding its jurisdiction by entertaining matters which would result in

its final decision being subject to being brought up and [a quashing order made], I think that [a prohibitory order may be made] to restrain it from so exceeding its jurisdiction.

Declaration

49.19   A declaration is a decision of the court on a question of law or rights. It is a discretionary remedy. The question involved must be a real rather than a theoretical question, and it must be raised between parties with a true interest in having it resolved (*Russian Commercial and Industrial Bank v British Bank for Foreign Trade Ltd* [1921] 2 AC 438). The declaration is a particularly useful remedy in administrative law as it can be granted against the Crown (*Dyson v Attorney-General* [1912] 1 Ch 158).

Injunction

49.20   An injunction is a mandatory or prohibitory order designed to regulate the future relationship between the parties. It will be granted where it is just and convenient (SCA 1981, s 37). Injunctions cannot be ordered against the Crown under English law (Crown Proceedings Act 1947, s 21(2)), but may be granted against the Crown or an officer of the Crown if it is necessary to protect rights deriving from EU law (*R v Secretary of State for Transport, ex p Factortame Ltd (No 2)* (Case C-213/89) [1991] 1 AC 603, ECJ and HL). An interim injunction can be granted in pending judicial review proceedings, the court applying much the same rules as apply in other cases (see Chapter 42; *R v Advertising Standards Authority Ltd, ex p Vernons Organisation Ltd* [1992] 1 WLR 1289).

Money awards

49.21   An award of damages, restitution, or the recovery of a sum due may be made on an application for judicial review, but only in conjunction with the other remedies available in judicial review claims (CPR, r 54.3(2)). Money may be awarded if the court is satisfied that, if the claim had been made in ordinary proceedings, the claimant could have been awarded such a remedy.

E   JUDICIAL REVIEW PRE-ACTION PROTOCOL

49.22   Persons intending to apply for judicial review should generally comply with the judicial review pre-action protocol before issuing proceedings. Compliance with the protocol will not be appropriate where the defendant has no legal power to change the decision being challenged, or if the application is very urgent, such as the failure of a local housing authority to secure interim accommodation for a homeless claimant. Even in very urgent cases, it is good practice to alert the defendant by telephone and to e-mail a draft of the claim form. Compliance with the protocol does not affect the time limit in CPR, r 54.5 (see 49.26).

49.23   Under the protocol the intending claimant should send a letter before claim to the defendant seeking to establish whether litigation can be avoided and identifying the issues (para 14). A template for this letter is set out at Annex A to the protocol. Defendants should normally reply within 14 days (para 20), and a template for the letter of response is set out in Annex B. Where it is not possible to reply within this time, an interim reply should be sent proposing a reasonable extension (para 21). The response should say in clear and unambiguous terms whether the claim is conceded in full, in part, or is disputed (para 22). Where appropriate it should contain a new decision, fuller reasons for the decision, or address any points of dispute (para 23). It should also enclose any documents requested by the claimant or explain why they are not being provided.

F APPLYING FOR PERMISSION TO PROCEED

There are two stages in an application for judicial review. These are, first, an application for **49.24** permission to proceed with the application for judicial review, and if permission is granted, secondly, the substantive hearing. The purpose of the requirement of obtaining permission is to filter out frivolous and hopeless applications with the minimum waste of court time.

If it becomes clear that the paperwork is incorrect, the court may be prepared to allow it to **49.25** be amended. In *R (Burkett) v Hammersmith and Fulham London Borough Council* [2002] 1 WLR 1593 the House of Lords allowed an application to be amended from a review of a planning resolution to a review of a planning permission. In public law the emphasis should be on substance rather than form.

Time limit for filing the claim form

The claim form initiating an application for judicial review must be filed promptly, and **49.26** in any event not later than three months after the grounds to make the claim arose (CPR, r 54.5(1)). This time period may not be extended by agreement between the parties (r 54.5(2)). An extension of time may be granted by the court under r 3.1(2)(a) if there is a good reason or a reasonable explanation for the delay. A fair balance has to be struck between the interests of the respective parties and the public interest (*R (Gerber) v Wiltshire Council* [2016] 1 WLR 2593 at [46]).

It follows from this wording that an application may be refused for delay even if it is made **49.27** within three months if it has not been made promptly: *R v Independent Television Commission, ex p TV NI Ltd* (1991) *The Times,* 30 December 1991. The additional requirement of promptness probably does not apply to cases based on rights conferred by EU Directives, because of the need in these cases for time limits to be certain (*R (Buglife) v Medway Council* [2011] Env LR 27). The point is not free from doubt as it was avoided by the Court of Appeal in *R (Macrae) v Hertfordshire District Council* (2012) LTL 9/3/12. The court has a discretion to refuse an application for permission if there has been delay, where it considers that granting the relief sought would be likely to cause substantial hardship to, or substantially prejudice the rights of, any person (including the general public), or if it would be detrimental to good administration (SCA 1981, s 31(6); *R v Stratford-on-Avon District Council, ex p Jackson* [1985] 1 WLR 1319). In considering whether the application is likely to be detrimental to good administration, the court may take into account the effect of the application in relation to other potential applicants: *R v Dairy Produce Quota Tribunal for England and Wales, ex p Caswell* [1989] 1 WLR 1089. There is no requirement for a causal connection between prejudice and the delay. What is required is a connection between prejudice and the grant of the relief sought: *R v Secretary of State for Health, ex p Furneaux* [1994] 2 All ER 652.

An extension beyond three months can only be granted by the court, applying the overriding **49.28** objective. Shorter time limits apply for certain categories of case, such as the six-week time limit for judicial review of planning decisions in CPR, r 54.5(5).

Issuing the claim form

A claim for judicial review is made using form N461, the judicial review claim form. It **49.29** has some similarities with Part 8 claims (see Chapter 8). By virtue of CPR, r 54.6, PD 16, para 15, and PD 54A, a judicial review claim form must state:

(a) the name and address of any person the claimant considers to be an interested person. Where the claim for judicial review relates to proceedings in a court or tribunal, all other parties to those proceedings must be named as interested persons (PD 54A, para 5.1);

(b) that the claimant is requesting permission to proceed with a claim for judicial review;

(c) any remedy (including any interim remedy) that is being claimed, and any relief sought under the Human Rights Act 1998 (PD 16, para 15.1(2));

(d) where the claimant is seeking to raise any issue under the Human Rights Act 1998, or seeks a remedy available under that Act, precise details of the Convention right alleged to have been infringed and details of the infringement;

(e) where the relief sought includes a declaration of incompatibility under the Human Rights Act 1998, s 4, precise details of the legislative provision and the alleged incompatibility;

(f) where a claim under the Human Rights Act 1998 is founded on a finding of unlawfulness by another court or tribunal, details of the finding; and

(g) where a claim under the Human Rights Act 1998 is founded on a judicial act which is alleged to have infringed a Convention right as provided by the Human Rights Act 1998, s 9, details of the judicial act and of the lower court or tribunal.

49.30 Paragraph 5.6 of PD 54A provides that a judicial review claim form must include, or be accompanied by, the following:

(a) a detailed statement of the claimant's grounds for bringing the claim for judicial review;

(b) a statement of the facts relied upon;

(c) any application to extend the time limit for filing the claim form; and

(d) any application for directions.

When the Criminal Justice and Courts Act 2015, s 85, comes into force, there will also be an obligation on the claimant to provide the court with information about the financing of the application (SCA 1981, s 31(3)(b)). This will be used when the court is considering who should pay the costs, and to what extent (Criminal Justice and Courts Act 2015, s 86).

49.31 Paragraph 5.7 of PD 54A provides that a judicial review claim form must be accompanied by:

(a) any written evidence in support of the claim or any application to extend time;

(b) a copy of any order that the claimant seeks to have quashed;

(c) where the claim relates to the decision of a lower court or tribunal, an approved copy of the reasons for that decision;

(d) copies of any documents relied upon by the claimant;

(e) copies of any relevant statutory material; and

(f) a list of the essential documents for advance reading by the court, with page references for the passages relied upon.

49.32 Two copies of a paginated and indexed bundle containing all the documents required under PD 54A, paras 5.6 and 5.7 must be filed when the claim is issued (para 5.9 and CPR, r 54.6(2)).

Service of the claim form

49.33 The judicial review claim form and the other documentation described at 49.30–49.32 (CPR, r 54.6(2)) must be served on the defendant and the other interested parties within seven days after the date of issue (r 54.7). The usual rules on service apply; see Chapter 6.

Acknowledgment of service

49.34 Any person served with the claim form who wishes to take part in the judicial review proceedings must file an acknowledgment of service on form N462 within 21 days after service (CPR, r 54.8(2)(a)). The acknowledgment must also be served on the claimant and any other interested parties within seven days after it is filed (r 54.8(2)(b)). Acknowledgments used in judicial review proceedings must set out a summary of the grounds on which the claim is contested, include a summary of any grounds for arguing that the outcome would not have been substantially different for the claimant (see 49.44), and give the names and addresses of any other persons whom the person filing it considers to be interested persons (r 54.8(4)). A person who fails to file an acknowledgment of service is not allowed to take part in any hearing to decide whether permission should be granted, unless the court allows him to do so (r 54.9(1)).

Considering whether to grant permission

Generally, the papers are considered by a judge without a hearing. Permission should be **49.35** granted if, on the material available and without going into the matter in depth, there is an arguable case for granting the relief claimed (*Inland Revenue Commissioners v National Federation of Self-Employed and Small Businesses Ltd* [1982] AC 617 *per* Lord Diplock). Permission may be refused where a successful application for judicial review would bring no practical benefit (*R (O) v Secretary of State for the Home Department* [2016] UKSC 19 at [50]). The judge's order, and the reasons for the decision, are then served on the claimant, defendant, and any other person who filed an acknowledgment of service (CPR, r 54.11). This is the most convenient and least costly way of proceeding. Alternatively, the claimant can ask for the question of permission to be considered at a hearing, in which event neither the defendant nor any interested party is expected to attend unless the court directs otherwise (PD 54, para 8.5). A hearing, which may be before a Divisional Court, is more likely in cases where the court needs to determine whether it is highly unlikely that the outcome for the claimant would not have been substantially different had the conduct complained of not occurred (r 54.11A, and see 49.44).

Reconsideration

Where an application for permission to proceed is refused on the papers, the claimant may **49.36** file a request for the decision to be reconsidered at a hearing (CPR, r 54.12(3)). The application must be made within seven days of service of the refusal of permission. The claimant, defendant, and any other person who filed an acknowledgment will be given at least two days' notice of the hearing date. Neither the defendant nor any other interested person is expected to attend the hearing, unless the court otherwise directs (PD 54A, para 8.5), and if they do attend, the court will not generally make an order for costs against the claimant.

Appeal against refusal of permission

An appeal against the refusal of permission to apply for judicial review may be made to the **49.37** Court of Appeal (CPR, r 52.15(1)). An application for permission to appeal must be made within seven days of the High Court's refusal of permission to apply for judicial review (r 52.15(2)).

G SUBSTANTIVE HEARING

Following permission to apply for judicial review

Where permission is granted, the court will give reasons, and may also give case manage- **49.38** ment directions (CPR, r 54.10). These may include provisions about serving the claim form and evidence on other persons, and may include a direction for the proceedings to be heard by a Divisional Court. Where a claim is made under the Human Rights Act 1998, a direction may be made for giving notice to the Crown or for joining the Crown as a party (see 4.58–4.59 and PD 54A, para 8.2). Once permission is granted, other parties are not allowed to apply to have the permission set aside (CPR, r 54.13).

Contesting the claim

49.39 Assuming that permission to proceed is granted, a defendant or any other person served with the claim form who wishes to contest the claim (or support it on additional grounds) must file and serve detailed grounds and any written evidence relied upon within 35 days after service of the order giving permission (CPR, r 54.14). A party relying on any documents not already filed must file a paginated bundle of those additional documents with his detailed grounds (PD 54A, para 10.1). Claimants and their legal advisers are under an obligation to reconsider the merits of their claim in the light of the written evidence served by the other parties.

Interveners

49.40 Any person may apply for permission to file evidence or to be able to make representations at the hearing (CPR, r 54.17). Any such application should be made promptly. If permission is granted, it may be given subject to conditions, and the court may make case management directions (PD 54A, para 13.2). A person will only be joined if they are directly affected by the main claim. They are not permitted to advance a different claim from the one advanced by the claimant (*R (McVey) v Secretary of State for Health* [2010] EWHC 1225 (Admin)). Unless there are exceptional circumstances the claimant and defendant should not be ordered to pay an intervener's costs, but an intervener who has behaved unreasonably may be ordered to pay costs (Criminal Justice and Courts Act 2015, s 87).

Interim orders

49.41 The usual position in judicial review claims is that there will be no oral evidence, and any disputes of fact are resolved in favour of the defendant (*R v Board of Visitors of Hull Prison, ex p St Germain (No 2)* [1979] 1 WLR 1401). Nevertheless, it is possible to apply for orders for disclosure of documents, further information under Part 18, and for permission to cross-examine any person who has given written evidence as well as for interim injunctions to restrain the body under review. Disclosure is not required except under an express court order (PD 54A, para 12.1). Disclosure is more likely to be ordered in cases where proportionality issues arise, but even in these cases will be carefully limited: *Tweed v Parades Commission* [2007] 1 AC 650. Disclosure, further information, and cross-examination will not be allowed where the claimant is seeking to fish for the existence of some mistake by the decision maker: *R v Independent Television Commission, ex p TSW Broadcasting Ltd* (1992) *The Times*, 30 March 1992. Indeed, cross-examination of deponents will be granted only where the interests of justice so require: *O'Reilly v Mackman* [1983] 2 AC 237 *per* Lord Diplock.

Skeleton arguments

49.42 The claimant must file and serve a skeleton argument not less than 21 working days before the hearing date (or warned date) (PD 54A, para 15.1). Other parties must file and serve their skeleton arguments not less than 14 working days before the hearing or warned date (para 15.2). The claimant's skeleton argument must be accompanied by a paginated and indexed bundle of all relevant documentation (para 16.1). Skeleton arguments (see 23.40) must contain:

(a) a time estimate for the complete hearing, including delivery of judgment;
(b) a list of issues;
(c) a list of the legal points to be taken (together with relevant authorities and page references for passages relied upon);
(d) a chronology (with page references to the bundle of documents);
(e) a list of the essential documents for advance reading by the judge; and
(f) a list of the persons referred to.

The hearing

Hearings are conducted in public, subject to the usual principles justifying a hearing in private (see 39.27). Normal judicial review hearings are conducted on the basis of written material and legal submissions to the court. There are rare cases where the court will order witnesses to attend for cross-examination (*R (Wilkinson) v Responsible Medical Officer Broadmoor Hospital* [2002] 1 WLR 419). In the usual case where there is no cross-examination the facts stated in the defendant's evidence have to be assumed to be correct (*R (McVey) v Secretary of State for Health* [2010] EWHC 437 (Admin)). In addition to the materials before the decision maker, it was held in *R v Secretary of State for the Environment, ex p Powis* [1981] 1 WLR 584 that the court will consider the following categories of fresh evidence: **49.43**

(a) evidence bearing on any question of fact as to whether the decision maker had jurisdiction;
(b) evidence on whether any procedural requirements were observed; and
(c) evidence to prove misconduct—examples are bias on the part of the decision maker, and fraud or perjury by a party.

The court is not bound by the decision to grant permission, and considers whether the claimant has standing, whether the grounds for seeking review are made out, and whether, in its discretion, it ought to grant relief. Under the Criminal Justice and Courts Act 2015, s 84, relief must be refused if it appears to the court to be highly likely that the outcome for the claimant would not have been substantially different if the conduct complained of had not occurred (SCA 1981, s 31(2A)), unless there are reasons of exceptional public interest (s 31(2B)).   **49.44**

The position where the decision-making authority has expressed more than one reason for a decision and the claimant successfully impugns one or some of them was considered in *R v Broadcasting Complaints Commission, ex p Owen* [1985] QB 1153. May LJ said that where the reasons can be disentangled, and the court is satisfied that, despite one reason being bad in law, the same decision would have been reached for the valid reasons, then, as a matter of discretion, the High Court would not intervene by way of judicial review.   **49.45**

H CONVERSION TO A COMMON LAW CLAIM

The court has power (under CPR, r 54.20) to order judicial review proceedings to continue as proceedings brought under CPR, Part 7. This power may be exercised where the relief claimed is a declaration, an injunction, or damages, and the court considers that such relief should not be granted on an application for judicial review, but might be granted in an ordinary claim.   **49.46**

I CONSENT ORDERS

49.47 Where the parties to an application for judicial review agree terms for disposing of the application, it is possible to obtain an order from the court to put that agreement into effect without the need for attending at a hearing. The procedure is laid down in PD 54A, para 17 and *Practice Direction (Administrative Court: Uncontested Proceedings)* [2008] 1 WLR 1377. A document setting out the terms of the proposed order and containing a short statement of the matters relied on as justifying the making of the order, quoting the authorities and statutory provisions relied on, should be signed by all of the parties. The original of this document, together with two copies, should be handed in to the Administrative Court Office, which will submit the document to a judge. If the judge is satisfied that an order can be made, the proceedings will be listed for hearing and the order will be pronounced in a public hearing without the parties needing to attend. If the judge is not satisfied that it would be proper to make the proposed order, the proceedings will be listed for hearing in the usual way.

KEY POINTS SUMMARY

49.48
- Judicial review lies against public bodies, and must be brought by a person with a sufficient interest.

- The six public law remedies are described at 49.14–49.21.

- Before commencing judicial review proceedings, a claimant should comply with the judicial review pre-action protocol.

- Judicial review proceedings must be started promptly, and in any event not later than three months from the events complained of.

- Permission must be sought to proceed with a claim for judicial review.

- Defendants must be served with the judicial review claim form, and unless they acknowledge service they cannot appear at the permission hearing unless the court allows them to attend.

50

APPEALS

A ROUTES OF APPEAL 50.06
B PERMISSION TO APPEAL 50.13
C TIME FOR APPEALING 50.27
D PROCEDURE ON APPEALING 50.31
E RESPONDENT'S NOTICE 50.40
F APPLICATIONS WITHIN APPEALS 50.46
G STAY 50.48

H STRIKING OUT APPEAL
   NOTICES AND SETTING ASIDE OR
   IMPOSING CONDITIONS 50.50
I HEARING OF APPEALS 50.52
J APPEAL COURT'S POWERS 50.66
K APPEALS BY WAY OF CASE STATED 50.74
L APPEALS TO THE SUPREME COURT 50.78
   Key points summary 50.82

From time to time decisions are made in error, and the system of appeals is designed to **50.01** ensure that these are corrected. Of course, a decision is not necessarily 'wrong' just because it is not the result hoped for by the client. There is a strong public interest in regarding judicial decisions as final and binding, and an open-ended appeals system would undermine this by encouraging unsuccessful litigants to have 'another bite at the cherry'. Striking a balance between encouraging finality and correcting mistakes is not easy, and explains some of the complications that arise in the area of appeals.

Lawyers appearing at a hearing, whether it is an interim matter or a trial, will invariably **50.02** hold a formal or informal conference with their clients immediately afterwards. Whatever the result, most clients ask, or are concerned about, whether the decision can be appealed. The lawyer must be able to give sound advice on this topic. Indeed, the question of an appeal will often have to be addressed by the lawyer before the judge rises at the end of the hearing, because permission to appeal must often be sought from the court appealed from. In these cases the lawyer asks for permission to appeal at the end of the hearing after the question of costs has been decided.

Careful thought must be given before embarking on an appeal. Lord Donaldson of **50.03** Lymington MR once said:

> The question which the adviser may ask himself is whether, looking at the matter objectively, there are sufficient grounds for believing not only that the case should have been decided differently, but that in all the circumstances it can be demonstrated to the satisfaction of the Court of Appeal that there are grounds for reversing the judge's findings. In considering this question the adviser must never forget the financial risk which an appellant undertakes of having not only to pay his own costs of the appeal, but those of his opponent and, for this purpose, the adviser has two clients if the litigant is [publicly funded]. Nor must he underrate the effect upon his client of the emotional and other consequences of a continued state of uncertainty pending an appeal. In a word, one of the most important duties of a professional legal adviser is to save his clients from themselves and always to remember that, whilst it may well be reasonable to institute or to defend particular proceedings at first instance, a wholly new and different situation arises once the claim has been fully investigated by the court and a decision given.

50.04   There are a number of salient points that need to be addressed:

(a) The court to which any appeal will lie. This is considered at 50.06ff.

(b) The period within which the appeal must be commenced. This is usually 21 days from the decision of the lower court; see 50.27ff.

(c) The grounds on which appeals may be allowed. Generally, it is necessary to show that the decision in the lower court was wrong, or that it was unjust because of a serious procedural or other irregularity. This is considered further at 50.57–50.65.

50.05   This chapter considers the structure of non-family civil appeals. For family appeals, see specialist works on family law and PD 52A, Table 3.

A ROUTES OF APPEAL

Basic civil appeals structure

50.06   The basic civil appeals structure is by the Access to Justice Act 1999 (Destination of Appeals) Order 2016 (SI 2016/917) (the 'Destination of Appeals Order') and PD 52A, Table 1 as follows:

(a) County Court District Judges may be appealed to the County Court Circuit Judge;

(b) High Court Masters and District Judges, and Insolvency and Companies Court Judges may be appealed to a High Court judge;

(c) County Court Circuit Judges may be appealed to a High Court judge;

(d) High Court judges may be appealed to the Court of Appeal; and

(e) the Court of Appeal may be appealed to the Supreme Court.

50.07   These basic routes of appeal also apply in relation to deputy judges and their equivalents, such as Recorders sitting as County Court Circuit Judges. Specialist areas often have their own rules for appeals. For example, appeal routes in insolvency proceedings are laid down in the Insolvency (England and Wales) Rules 2016 (SI 2016/1024), r 12.59, and for family proceedings by the Family Procedure Rules 2010 (SI 2010/2995) and PD 30A to those rules.

Destination of second appeals

50.08   By way of exception, appeals are made to the Court of Appeal rather than to a High Court judge if the lower court's decision was itself an appeal (in other words, the current appeal is a second appeal: see Destination of Appeals Order, art 6). Thus, where an interim application is first dealt with by a Master or District Judge, a first appeal will be to the Circuit Judge (for County Court claims) or High Court judge (for High Court claims). A second appeal based on the same application, which will be an appeal either from the Circuit Judge or High Court judge, is, by virtue of the exception, always to the Court of Appeal.

50.09   In *Southern & District Finance plc v Turner* (2003) LTL 7/11/03 a County Court District Judge dismissed an application to set aside a possession order. Eight months later the defendant brought an appeal against that decision, but omitted to seek permission to appeal out of time (see 50.28). The Circuit Judge dismissed the appeal on the ground that no permission to extend time for appealing had been included in the appellant's notice. An appeal from the Circuit Judge's refusal to consider extending time (whether this was on the basis of the judge deciding he had no jurisdiction to extend time, or a decision not to extend time) was held to be a first appeal, not a second appeal coming within art 6, so should have been taken to a High Court judge in accordance with the basic routes of appeal.

Appeal centres in High Court appeals

County Court and District Registry appeals to a High Court judge must be brought in the **50.10**
District Registry for an appeal centre on the Circuit in which the lower court is situated
(PD 52B, para 2.1). Lists of appeal centres can be seen in PD 52B, Tables A and B.

Leapfrog appeals to the Court of Appeal

If the normal route for a first appeal from a decision of a District Judge or Master would **50.11**
be to a Circuit Judge or to a High Court judge, either the lower court or the appeal court
may order the appeal to be transferred to the Court of Appeal. This may be done if it is
considered that the appeal will raise an important point of principle or practice or there
is some other compelling reason for the Court of Appeal to hear it (CPR, r 52.23(1)). This
power is not available to the judge in the lower court if permission to appeal (see 50.13)
is refused, because if permission is refused there is no appeal (*7E Communications Ltd v
Vertex Antennentechnik GmbH* [2007] 1 WLR 2175). The Master of the Rolls has a similar power to divert appeals to the Court of Appeal (Access to Justice Act 1999, s 57(1)).

Leapfrog appeals to the Supreme Court

Very exceptionally, a direct appeal from the decision of a High Court judge to the Supreme **50.12**
Court is possible under the Administration of Justice Act 1969, ss 12, 13, and 15. Leapfrog
appeals to the Supreme Court can also be made from the Upper Tribunal, Employment
Appeal Tribunal, and the Special Immigration Appeals Commission (see Criminal Justice
and Courts Act 2015, ss 63–66 and the legislation amended by these provisions). There
are exacting conditions for bringing leapfrog appeals, which vary slightly depending on
the lower court, and there are alternative conditions for leapfrog appeals from the High
Court. The original High Court conditions are that:

(a) the appeal must involve a point of law of general public importance;
(b) the point of law must either relate to the construction of an Act of Parliament or
    statutory instrument, or else be a point on which the judge at first instance is bound
    by a decision of the Court of Appeal, or of the House of Lords or Supreme Court;
(c) all parties must consent;
(d) the trial judge must certify, either immediately at the end of the trial or within the next
    14 days, that the case is a suitable one for a direct appeal to the Supreme Court; and
(e) the Supreme Court must grant permission to bring the appeal. An application for per-
    mission must be made within one month of the date of the judge's certificate.

B PERMISSION TO APPEAL

Requirement for permission to appeal

Rule 52.3(1) of the CPR provides that an appellant or respondent requires permission to **50.13**
appeal:

(a) where the appeal is from a decision of a judge in the County Court or the High Court,
    except where the appeal is against:
    (i) a committal order (but only if the appellant is the contemnor: *Poole Borough
         Council v Hambridge* [2007] EWCA Civ 990; and only if the penalty is immediate
         or suspended committal to prison: *Masri v Consolidated International Co SAL*
         [2012] 1 WLR 223);

    (ii) a refusal to grant *habeas corpus*; or

    (iii) a secure accommodation order made under the Children Act 1989, s 25; or

(b) as provided by PD 52A–52E.

Exceptions

50.14 The exceptions set out in CPR, r 52.3(1)(a) are cases where the liberty of the subject is in issue, and in these three cases appeals may be brought as of right. Nor is permission required for appeals from decisions of authorized officers in detailed assessment proceedings to a costs judge or District Judge (rr 47.21 and 52.1(2)).

Initial oral application for permission to appeal

50.15 Generally, permission to appeal may be sought either from the lower court at the hearing at which the decision to be appealed was made or from the appeal court (CPR, r 52.3(2)). Applications for permission to appeal sought from the lower court are made orally at the end of the hearing, usually as the last item of business after costs have been determined, or at an adjourned hearing when the judgment is handed down (*Monroe v Hopkins (No 2)* [2017] 1 WLR 3587).

Renewed application for permission to appeal

50.16 Where the lower court refuses an application for permission to appeal, a further application for permission to appeal may be made to the appeal court (CPR, r 52.3(3)). Renewed applications for permission to appeal are made to the appeal court in writing in the appellant's notice (r 52.3(2)(b)). How renewed permission applications are dealt with by the appeal court differs depending on whether or not the appeal court is the Court of Appeal.

Renewed application for permission to appeal to the County Court or High Court

50.17 Appellants bringing appeals from County Court District Judges to the County Court Circuit Judge, and from Circuit Judges to the High Court, have three opportunities to obtain permission to appeal. Their initial application is made orally to the judge in the court below (see 50.15). They can then seek permission from the appeal court on the papers without a hearing, unless the court otherwise directs (CPR, r 52.4(1)). The renewed application is made in the appeal notice (r 52.3(2)(b)). If permission is granted, the parties are notified in writing. If permission is refused, the appellant can within seven days of being served with the notice that permission has been refused request the decision to be reconsidered at an oral hearing (r 52.4(2) and (6)).

Renewed application for permission to appeal to the Court of Appeal

50.18 Appellants bringing appeals to the Court of Appeal have two opportunities to obtain permission to appeal. Their initial application is made orally to the judge in the court below (see 50.15). They can then seek permission from the Court of Appeal. The renewed application is made in the appeal notice (CPR, r 52.3(2)(b)). The Lord Justice of Appeal considering the application for permission to appeal will determine the application on the papers without an oral hearing (r 52.5(1)) unless they come to the view that the application cannot be fairly determined without an oral hearing (r 52.5(2)). Where this is the case the Lord Justice of Appeal will themselves deal with the oral hearing, which must be listed no later than 14 days after the direction for an oral hearing (r 52.5(3)). The direction for an oral hearing of the permission application may identify any issues on which the appellant should specifically focus its submissions (r 52.5(4)(a)).

The court will notify the respondent of any oral hearing, but the respondent is not expected **50.19** to attend unless the court so directs (PD 52C, para 16(1)). Such a direction may be made when listing the application for permission for an oral hearing, and the court may direct the respondent to serve and file written submissions (r 52.5(4)(b)). Where the respondent is directed to attend, the appellant must supply the respondent with copies of the appellant's skeleton argument and any documents to which the appellant intends to refer (PD 52C, para 16(2)). The respondent then has 14 days to file and serve a brief statement, not exceeding 3 pages, of any reasons why permission to appeal should be refused (para 19(1)).

Test for granting permission on first appeals

Rule 52.6(1) of the CPR provides that permission to appeal on a first appeal may be given **50.20** only where either:

(a) the court considers that the appeal would have a real prospect of success; or
(b) there is some other compelling reason why the appeal should be heard.

Permission to appeal should be granted if there is an arguable case that the decision of the **50.21** lower court was plainly wrong or unjust through a serious irregularity (*Re W (Children) (Permission to Appeal)* [2007] Fam Law 897). Lord Woolf MR said in *Swain v Hillman* [2001] 1 All ER 91, that a 'real' prospect of success means that the prospects of success must be realistic rather than fanciful. There is some reluctance in giving permission to appeal against case management decisions, such as disclosure orders and orders dealing with the timetable of the claim. In these cases the court will also consider whether the issue is of sufficient significance to justify the costs of an appeal; the procedural consequences of an appeal (eg losing a trial date); and whether it would be more convenient to determine the point at or after trial (PD 52A, para 4.6).

Second appeals to the Court of Appeal

As discussed at 50.15–50.19, generally permission to appeal may be sought from either the **50.22** lower court or the appeal court. Second appeals are in a different category. Rule 52.7(1) of the CPR provides that permission is required from the Court of Appeal (and cannot be given by the lower court) for any appeal to the Court of Appeal from a decision of the County Court or the High Court which was itself made on appeal. By r 52.7(2) the Court of Appeal will not give permission unless it considers that:

(a) the appeal would have a real prospect of success and raise an important point of principle or practice; or
(b) there is some other compelling reason for the Court of Appeal to hear it.

Limiting the issues on granting permission

By CPR, r 52.6(2), an order giving permission to appeal may limit the issues to be heard **50.23** and be made subject to conditions. If a court confines its permission to some issues only, it should expressly refuse permission on any remaining issues (PD 52C, para 18).

No appeal against grant or refusal of permission

There is no appeal from a decision of a court to allow or refuse permission to appeal (Access **50.24** to Justice Act 1999, s 54(4)). This subsection specifically says this ban does not affect the above processes for renewal and reconsideration of permission, which are therefore the extent to which an appellant can seek permission to appeal. The ban in s 54(4) prevents the Court of Appeal from reviewing a High Court judge's refusal of permission to appeal from the decision of a costs judge, and there is no residual inherent jurisdiction to hear such an appeal: *Riniker v University College London* [2001] 1 WLR 13.

Practice in refusing permission

50.25 Short reasons are usually all that is given on a refusal of permission. Just because they are short does not mean they infringe the requirement for a reasoned decision in the European Convention on Human Rights, art 6: *Hyams v Plender* [2001] 1 WLR 32 at [17].

50.26 A judge faced with an application for permission to appeal made out of time may come to the conclusion both that the appeal is weak on the merits and that time should not be extended. By reason of the Access to Justice Act 1999, s 54(4), refusing permission to appeal will result in an end to the appeal process. Taking the easier course of refusing permission to extend time will not, as the appellant can apply for permission to appeal the refusal of the extension, which can be renewed to the Court of Appeal. This difference should be kept in mind when deciding which course to take: *Foenander v Bond Lewis & Co* [2002] 1 WLR 525.

C TIME FOR APPEALING

General rule

50.27 An appellant must normally initiate an appeal or seek permission to appeal no later than 21 days from the date of the decision of the lower court (CPR, r 52.12(2)(b)). However, the lower court may direct some other period for filing a notice of appeal (r 52.12(2)(a)). Judgments and orders take effect from the date on which they are given or made, or such other date as the court may specify (r 40.7(1)). Delays in formally drawing up the order do not, therefore, delay time running for the purposes of appeals.

Extending time for appealing

50.28 Rule 3.1(2)(a) of the CPR provides that the court may extend or shorten the time for compliance with any rule, practice direction, or court order (even if an application for extension is made after the time for compliance has expired). This includes the time for bringing an appeal. By r 52.15(1), an application to vary the time limit for filing an appellant's notice must be made to the appeal court. The parties may not (by r 52.15(2)) agree between themselves to extend any date or time limit for the purposes of appealing.

50.29 Permission to extend time for appealing is sought by including an application for more time in the appellant's notice (PD 52B, para 3.2; PD 52C, para 4). The notice should state the reason for the delay and the steps taken prior to the application being made. Applications to extend the time for appealing engage the implied sanctions doctrine (see 37.34), and so are considered by applying the three-stage test in *Denton v TH White Ltd* [2014] 3924 for applications under r 3.9 (see 37.26).

50.30 Where an extension is sought the respondent has the right to be heard on the question whether an extension of time should be allowed. However, a respondent who unreasonably opposes an extension of time runs the risk of being ordered to pay the appellant's costs of the application to extend time (PD 52C, para 4(3)(b), and see 37.31 on uncooperative behaviour).

D PROCEDURE ON APPEALING

Appellant's notice

An appellant must file the appellant's notice at the appeal court within such period as **50.31** may be directed by the lower court or, where the court makes no such direction, 21 days after the date of the decision of the lower court that the appellant wishes to appeal (CPR, r 52.12(2)). It must be served on each respondent as soon as practicable, and in any event within seven days of being filed (r 52.12(3)).

An appellant's notice must be in form N161. The grounds of the appeal must identify as **50.32** concisely as possible why the decision was wrong or unjust (PD 52C, para 5(1); *Perotti v Collyer-Bristow* [2004] 4 All ER 53 at [37] and [40]). To do this, specific incidents, directions, or findings made by the court below must be identified which are alleged to be wrong or unjust through serious procedural or other irregularity. Each ground should be stated as an appeal on a point of law or against a finding of fact. An appellant seeking, for the first time, to rely on any issue or to seek any remedy under the Human Rights Act 1998 must include information complying with PD 16, para 15.1 in the appellant's notice. The notice may also need to include an application for permission to appeal, for permission to appeal out of time, and may include applications for interim remedies in the course of the appeal (PD 52B, para 4.3).

By CPR, r 52.21(5), a party may not rely at the hearing of the appeal on a matter not con- **50.33** tained in its appeal notice unless the appeal court gives permission.

Appeal bundle

Appeal bundles must contain the documents listed in PD 52B, para 6.4 (general appeals) **50.34** or PD 52C, para 27 (appeals to the Court of Appeal). These include a sealed copy of the appellant's notice, a copy of the appellant's skeleton argument, relevant statements of case, a transcript of the judgment of the lower court, and other documents which the parties consider to be relevant to the appeal. Appeal bundles in the County Court and High Court have to be filed within 35 days of the filing of the appellant's notice. Core and supplementary bundles are used in the Court of Appeal, and must be filed no less than 42 days before the appeal hearing.

Skeleton argument

Skeleton arguments are obligatory in appeals to the Court of Appeal (PD 52C, paras 3, 9, **50.35** and 13), and should be served on each respondent at the same time as service of the appellant's notice (para 7.1A). Two additional copies must be brought to the hearing for the use of law reporters. In appeals to the County Court and High Court they should be used where the complexity of the issues justifies their use, or if they would assist the court in respects not readily apparent from the papers (PD 52B, para 8.3). For general guidance, see 23.40.

Small claims appeals

There are simplified rules for appeals from small claims track cases. There is a simplified **50.36** appellant's notice (form N164), and obtaining a transcript of the judgment is not obligatory (PD 52B, para 6.2).

Service on the respondent

50.37 By CPR, r 52.12(3), unless the appeal court orders otherwise, an appellant's notice must be served on each respondent as soon as practicable, and in any event not later than seven days after it is filed. A respondent need not take any action when served with an appellant's notice, but is encouraged to file and serve a brief written statement of any reasons why permission should be refused (PD 52C, para 19(1)). Costs will not normally be allowed to a respondent either for its brief written statement or for attendance at any permission hearing unless specifically directed to do so (PD 52B, para 8.1; PD 52C, para 20).

After the permission stage

50.38 The court notifies the parties of the decision and its reasons on the question of permission to appeal. The appeal court may make orders for the case management of the appeal (PD 52B, para 5.1), and such directions prevail over the provisions of the relevant practice directions (PD 52C, para 2). For appeals to the Court of Appeal there are detailed procedures laid down in PD 52C. In these cases the Civil Appeals Office sends the parties a listing window notification, which is a letter giving notice of the window within which the appeal is likely to be heard.

50.39 In accordance with the usual sequence of events, once permission to appeal is granted:

(a) the respondent files and serves a respondent's notice (if any, see 50.40) and respondent's skeleton argument;

(b) the appellant serves a proposed appeal bundle index on the respondent;

(c) the appellant must complete and file an appeal questionnaire with a time estimate for the appeal;

(d) the appellant serves its skeleton argument on the respondent;

(e) the parties agree the appeal bundle;

(f) if the respondent has not filed a respondent's notice at step (a), the respondent now files and serves its skeleton argument;

(g) thereafter a hearing window will be set by the court, and final versions of the appeal bundle, replacement skeleton arguments with cross-references to pages in the appeal bundle, and bundles of authorities, are filed.

E RESPONDENT'S NOTICE

Need for a respondent's notice

50.40 In any appeal a respondent *may* file and serve a respondent's notice (CPR, r 52.13(1)). A respondent's notice *must* be filed by a respondent who:

(a) is asking the appeal court for permission to appeal; or

(b) wishes to ask the appeal court to uphold the order of the lower court for reasons different from or additional to those given by the lower court (r 52.13(2)).

50.41 Respondents accordingly fall into three broad categories:

(a) Those who simply wish to uphold the decision of the court below for the same reasons as given by the judge below. Such a respondent need not serve a respondent's notice.

(b) Those who wish to uphold the decision of the court below for reasons different from or additional to those given by the lower court. Such a respondent is not appealing as such, so there is no question of seeking permission to cross-appeal. However, a respondent's notice is required for the purpose of setting out the different or additional reasons (PD 52C, para 8(3)).

(c) Those who wish to ask the appeal court to vary the order of the lower court are cross-appealing, and permission to appeal must be sought on the same basis as for an appellant (PD 52C, para 8(2)). A respondent's notice is required for setting out the grounds on which it is to be argued that the order of the court below should be varied.

Form of respondent's notice

A respondent's notice is similar to an appellant's notice (see 50.31–50.33) and must be in form N162. Together with appellants' notices they are called 'appeal notices' in the CPR (r 52.1(3)(f)). Where the respondent seeks permission from the appeal court it must be requested in the respondent's notice (r 52.13(3)). **50.42**

Filing and serving a respondent's notice

A respondent's notice must be filed within such period as may be directed by the lower court or, where the court makes no such direction, 14 days, after the date in CPR, r 52.13(5) (r 52.13(4)). Rule 52.13(5) provides: **50.43**

The date referred to in paragraph (4) is—

(a) the date the respondent is served with the appellant's notice where—
   (i) permission to appeal was given by the lower court; or
   (ii) permission to appeal is not required;
(b) the date the respondent is served with notification that the appeal court has given the appellant permission to appeal; or
(c) the date the respondent is served with notification that the application for permission to appeal and the appeal itself are to be heard together.

Unless the appeal court orders otherwise a respondent's notice must be served on the appellant and any other respondent as soon as practicable, and in any event not later than seven days, after it is filed (r 52.13(6)). **50.44**

Respondent's skeleton argument

A respondent who proposes to address arguments to the court must provide it with a skeleton argument. It should conform to the principles applicable to the appellant's skeletons, but should also seek to answer the arguments in the appellant's skeleton. It may be included in the respondent's notice, or may be lodged and served within 14 days of filing the notice (PD 52C, para 9). **50.45**

F APPLICATIONS WITHIN APPEALS

Notice of an application made to the appeal court for a remedy incidental to the appeal (eg an application for security for costs) may be included in the appeal notice or by an ordinary application notice under CPR, Part 23 (PD 52B, para 4.3). **50.46**

An appeal notice may be amended with permission (CPR, r 52.17). This probably engages the implied sanctions doctrine (*Lighting and Lamps UK Ltd v Clarke* (2016) LTL 4/3/2016, and see 37.33). Such an application will normally be dealt with at the hearing of the appeal, unless that course would cause unnecessary expense or delay, in which case **50.47** a request should be made for the application to amend to be heard in advance (PD 52C, para 30(3)).

G STAY

50.48 By CPR, r 52.16, an appeal shall not operate as a stay of any order or decision of the lower court unless:

(a) the appeal court or the lower court orders otherwise; or
(b) the appeal is from the Immigration and Asylum Chamber of the Upper Tribunal.

50.49 While it is said the court has an unfettered discretion to impose a stay of execution if the justice of the case so demands (*BMW AG v Commissioners of HM Revenue and Customs* [2008] EWCA Civ 1028), this tends to be approached by weighing up the risks involved in either granting or refusing the stay.

H STRIKING OUT APPEAL NOTICES AND SETTING ASIDE OR IMPOSING CONDITIONS

50.50 An appeal court may strike out the whole or part of an appeal notice, set aside permission to appeal in whole or in part, or impose or vary conditions upon which an appeal may be brought (CPR, r 52.18(1)). It is recognized that the power to strike out an appeal notice 'is one that is just as capable of abuse as is the power to put in hopeless notices of appeal': *Burgess v Stafford Hotel Ltd* [1990] 1 WLR 1215, *per* Glidewell LJ. Rule 52.18(2) therefore provides that the court will exercise its powers under r 52.18(1) only where there is a compelling reason for doing so. There may be a compelling reason where the appeal is being brought to secure some collateral advantage, or where the application will achieve a substantial saving of time. A party who was present at the hearing at which permission was given may not subsequently apply for an order that the court exercise its powers to set aside permission or to impose conditions (r 52.18(3)).

50.51 A condition requiring an appellant to pay the costs whether they won or lost was held to be excessive in *King v Daltray* [2003] EWCA Civ 808, substituting an order that there be no order as to costs. A condition requiring a payment into court may be varied on the ground that the appeal will be stifled because the appellant cannot afford to pay. It is for the appellant to establish, on the balance of probabilities, that it cannot raise the proposed payment (*Goldtrail Travel Ltd v Onur Air Tasimacilik AS* [2017] 1 WLR 3014).

I HEARING OF APPEALS

Composition of the court

50.52 Substantive appeals to the Court of Appeal from interim orders, the County Court, and Masters' and District Judges' final orders are generally heard by two-judge courts; otherwise appeals to the Court of Appeal are heard by three-judge courts (SCA 1981, s 54). Where a two-judge court is equally divided, either party may apply for a rehearing before a three-judge court.

50.53 For other appeals from first instance decisions, the appeal court will generally consist of the judge sitting alone. Occasionally a judge will sit with assessors, such as some appeals on costs issues. The Supreme Court generally sits in five-member courts.

Last-minute settlements

Solicitors and counsel have a duty to inform the court as soon as it is known that an appeal **50.54** which has been listed for hearing will not proceed, so that judges can avoid unnecessary preparation. Even if a case settles very late in the day steps must taken through the Royal Courts of Justice switchboard to notify the appeal court judges' clerks (*Tasyurdu v Immigration Appeal Tribunal* [2003] CPLR 343).

The hearing

Normally it is unnecessary for the advocate for the appellant to open the appeal, as the **50.55** judges normally do fairly extensive pre-reading. In most cases the judges will have pre-read the appeal bundle and skeleton arguments, and usually will have read the core authorities bundle (if there is one). The judge (or presiding judge in a multi-member court) usually indicates the extent of the pre-reading that has been done. In appeals to the Court of Appeal, if it is felt that it would be helpful for the appellant's advocate to open the appeal, the presiding judge will notify the advocates in advance. The intention is that court time is spent dealing with the substance of the arguments, and time should not be wasted in extensive reading from documents.

Rehearing or review

By CPR, r 52.21(1), every appeal is, with limited exceptions, heard by way of a review **50.56** of the decision below. An appeal from an interim application will generally involve consideration of all the material before the court below. It is nevertheless technically a review (*McFaddens Solicitors v Chandrasekaran* [2007] EWCA Civ 220). The exceptional nature of holding a rehearing rather than a review on an appeal was stressed in *Secretary of State for Trade and Industry v Lewis* (2001) *The Times*, 16 August 2001. The power to conduct an appeal by way of rehearing is to be exercised in rare cases where that is necessary in order for justice to be done. The fair trial requirements of the European Convention on Human Rights, art 6, do not compel the court to conduct rehearings in appeals from without-notice decisions (*Dyson Ltd v Registrar of Trademarks* (2003) *The Times*, 23 May 2003).

Grounds for allowing an appeal

An appeal can only be brought on a point taken in the court below (*Gover v Propertycare* **50.57** *Ltd* [2006] ICR 1073), unless a sufficient reason, such as a recent legal development, is established to depart from this rule (*Thorne v Lass Salt Garvin* [2009] EWHC 100 (QB)). Appeals will be successful (CPR, r 52.21(3)) only if the decision below was either:

(a) wrong (which means 'unsustainable': see *Abrahams v Lenton* [2003] EWHC 1104 (QB)); or
(b) unjust because of a serious procedural or other irregularity in the proceedings in the lower court.

An insubstantial point, or a point that does not affect the overall decision, even if a techni- **50.58** cal error, does not render a decision wrong (*Orford v Rasmi Electronics Ltd* (2004) LTL 4/8/04). The strength of the other evidence at trial may mean that, despite an error, the decision below was not wrong (*Daly v Sheikh* (2004) LTL 13/2/04). A party can appeal against a decision of a lower court, but not against the reasons for a decision given in his favour (*Compagnie Noga d'Importation et d'Exportation SA v Australia and New Zealand Banking Group Ltd* [2003] 1 WLR 307).

Questions of fact

50.59 The trial judge sees the demeanour of witnesses, and can assess their intelligence and credibility in a way that an appeal court cannot, even with the benefit of a transcript. Nevertheless the parties are entitled to appeal on questions of fact if the decision was plainly wrong. This will be the case where the decision cannot reasonably be explained or justified, and so is one which no reasonable judge could have reached (*Henderson v Foxworth Investments Ltd* [2014] 1 WLR 2600).

Discretionary and case management decisions

50.60 The most important statement on the role of an appellate court in an appeal from a discretionary decision is that of Lord Diplock in *Hadmor Productions Ltd v Hamilton* [1983] 1 AC 191. This was an appeal in respect of an interim injunction, but his Lordship's comments are equally applicable to appeals from any discretionary decision. His Lordship said:

> Upon an appeal from the judge's grant or refusal of an [interim] injunction the function of an appellate court, whether it be the Court of Appeal or your Lordships' House, is not to exercise an independent discretion of its own. It must defer to the judge's exercise of his discretion and must not interfere with it merely upon the ground that the members of the appellate court would have exercised the discretion differently. The function of the appellate court is initially one of review only. It may set aside the judge's exercise of his discretion on the ground that it is based upon a misunderstanding of the law or of the evidence before him or upon an inference that particular facts existed or did not exist, which, although it was one that might legitimately have been drawn upon the evidence that was before the judge, can be demonstrated to be wrong by further evidence that has become available by the time of the appeal; or upon the ground that there has been a change of circumstances after the judge made his order that would have justified his acceding to an application to vary it. Since reasons given by judges for granting or refusing [interim] injunctions may sometimes be sketchy, there may also be occasional cases where even though no erroneous assumption of law or fact can be identified the judge's decision to grant or refuse the injunction is so aberrant that it must be set aside upon the ground that no reasonable judge regardful of his duty to act judicially could have reached it. It is only if and after the appellate court has reached the conclusion that the judge's exercise of his discretion must be set aside for one or other of these reasons, that it becomes entitled to exercise an original discretion of its own.

50.61 An appeal against a case management direction can only succeed if it was one the judge could not properly have given (*Global Torch Ltd v Apex Global Management Ltd (No 2)* [2014] 1 WLR 4495 at [13]). The way it was put by Lord Fraser of Tullybelton in *G v G (Minors: Custody Appeal)* [1985] 1 WLR 647 is that the appeal court:

> . . . should only interfere when it considers that the judge of first instance has not merely preferred an imperfect solution which is different from an alternative imperfect solution which the Court of Appeal might or would have adopted, but has exceeded the generous ambit within which a reasonable disagreement is possible.

Inferences

50.62 Rule 52.21(4) of the CPR provides that the appeal court may draw any inference of fact which it considers justified on the evidence. This includes inferences to be drawn from the facts found by the judge in the lower court and inferences to be drawn from the documents: *The Mouna* [1991] 2 Lloyd's Rep 221.

Errors of law and principle

Pure errors of law and applying the wrong principles do not require any explanation. **50.63**

Substantial procedural irregularities

Procedural irregularities include misdirections to the jury (in jury trials), and the improper **50.64** admission or non-admission of evidence. Frequent or intemperate interventions may give grounds for an appeal. Sending a letter to the judge without providing a copy to the other side is a serious procedural irregularity (*National Westminster Bank plc v Rushmer* [2010] 2 FLR 362). An appeal may be based on excessive delay in delivering judgment. A lapse of 12 months in delivering judgment after trial would be excessive (*Cobham v Frett* [2001] 1 WLR 1775), as would a delay of three or four weeks in relation to an interim injunction (*EE and Brian Smith (1928) Ltd v Hodson* [2007] EWCA Civ 1210). It is only if there are errors possibly attributable to the delay that an appeal should be allowed on this ground: *Cobham v Frett*. By CPR, r 52.21(3), this is a valid ground for appeal only if the irregularity was a serious one, and the irregularity caused an unjust decision in the lower court: *Tanfern Ltd v Cameron-MacDonald* [2000] 1 WLR 1311.

Inadequate reasons

The definition of issues, marshalling of evidence, and giving of reasons are the building **50.65** blocks of the reasoned judicial process. A failure to make findings on the secondary issues on which counsel had relied justified setting aside a judgment in *Glicksman v Redbridge Healthcare NHS Trust* (2001) LTL 12/7/01. Whether reasons are inadequate has to be considered by looking at the judgment in the light of the evidence and submissions at the hearing (*English v Emery Reimbold and Strick Ltd* [2002] 1 WLR 2409). There is no obligation to deal with every argument advanced by the parties, provided the basis of the decision is sufficiently clear (*Hague Plant Ltd v Hague* [2014] EWCA Civ 1609 at [4]). Appellants relying on inadequate reasons must raise this with the judge in the lower court, who is permitted to provide supplementary reasons (which may remove the ground of complaint). An appeal court dealing with such an appeal may remit the case back to the lower court for additional reasons, which again may result in the point disappearing.

J APPEAL COURT'S POWERS

General powers vested in the appeal court

By CPR, r 52.20(1), in relation to an appeal the appeal court has all the powers of the **50.66** lower court. In particular, by r 52.20(2), the appeal court has power:

(a) to affirm, set aside, or vary any order or judgment made or given by the lower court;
(b) to refer any claim or issue for determination by the lower court;
(c) to order a new trial or hearing, although this is a matter of last resort: *White v White* (2001) LTL 21/6/01. When making such an order the appeal court must make it clear on the face of its order whether the rehearing should be at appeal court level, or remitted back to the lower court (*Fowler de Pledge v Smith* (2003) *The Times*, 27 May 2003);
(d) to make orders for the payment of interest; and
(e) to make a costs order.

By r 52.20(3), in an appeal from a claim tried with a jury the Court of Appeal may, instead **50.67** of ordering a new trial, make an order for damages or vary the award made by the jury.

Fresh evidence

50.68 By CPR, r 52.21(2), unless it orders otherwise, the appeal court will not receive oral evidence or any evidence which was not before the lower court. Under the old rules a restrictive approach was taken to the introduction of fresh evidence on appeals, the guiding principles being laid down in *Ladd v Marshall* [1954] 1 WLR 1489. The rule in *Ladd v Marshall* applied to appeals from trials and final determinations, and reflected the policy of requiring parties to advance their entire case at trial, and not deliberately leaving over points for the purpose of appeals (and thereby obtaining a 'second bite at the cherry'). It has never applied to interim appeals, where fresh evidence may be adduced if there has been a change of circumstances (*Anglo Irish Asset Finance plc v Flood* [2011] EWCA Civ 799). Since the introduction of the CPR, strong grounds have to be shown before fresh evidence will be admitted in final appeals, and the *Ladd v Marshall* principles will be looked at with considerable care, but not as strict rules: *Hertfordshire Investments Ltd v Bubb* [2000] 1 WLR 2318. Under *Ladd v Marshall* fresh evidence would only be allowed on an appeal if the evidence:

(a) could not have been obtained with reasonable diligence for use at the hearing in the lower court;

(b) would probably have an important influence on the result; and

(c) was apparently credible.

50.69 Applications for permission to adduce fresh evidence can be made to the Master of the Court of Appeal, but they are often directed to be listed for hearing at the same time as the appeal (*Practice Direction (Court of Appeal: Procedure)* [1995] 1 WLR 1191). A fresh evidence bundle should be prepared in order to keep material that may be disallowed separate from the main appeal bundles.

Handed-down judgments

50.70 Below the Court of Appeal, it is usual for the court to give judgment immediately after the arguments, although occasionally judgment will be reserved. Reserving judgment is rather more common in the Court of Appeal, where written judgments are sent out to the advocates two working days before being pronounced in court (PD 40E). This is to enable the parties' legal advisers to consider the judgment and any consequential orders they should seek. It is an abuse of process for advocates to lodge detailed commentaries on draft judgments (*R (Edwards) v Environment Agency* [2008] 1 WLR 1587). Judgments are released in this way on the condition that they are to be kept confidential until they are pronounced in court.

Reopening appeals

50.71 Confirming the decision in *Taylor v Lawrence* [2003] QB 528, CPR, r 52.30 enables the Court of Appeal and the High Court to reopen an appeal (or application for permission to appeal, PD 52A, para 7.1) in exceptional circumstances. The jurisdiction is based on the court's inherent jurisdiction, so there is no such power to reopen an appeal to a Circuit Judge in the County Court (r 52.30(3)). An appeal may be reopened (r 52.30(1)) if:

(a) it is necessary to do so to avoid real injustice (eg where new facts come to light after the court makes its decision, as in *Taylor v Lawrence*);

(b) the circumstances are exceptional and make it appropriate to reopen the appeal; and

(c) there is no alternative effective remedy (so if the injustice could be remedied by a readily available further appeal, the court will not reopen the present appeal).

Costs

Under CPR, r 52.20(2)(e), the appeal court has power to make costs orders in relation to the appeal hearing and for the proceedings in the lower court. Costs may be summarily assessed (see 46.52) if the hearing lasts no more than one day (PD 44, para 9.2(b)). Any statement of costs must show the amount claimed for the skeleton argument separately from the brief fee (PD 52A, para 5.3). **50.72**

Non-disclosure of Part 36 offers

The fact that a Part 36 offer has been made must not be disclosed to any judge of the appeal court who is to hear and finally determine an appeal or application for permission to appeal until all questions (other than costs) have been determined, unless the Part 36 offer is relevant to the substance of the appeal (CPR, r 52.22). **50.73**

K APPEALS BY WAY OF CASE STATED

Appeals to the High Court by way of case stated may be brought on questions of law or jurisdiction. Such appeals may be brought from any of the inferior courts, so can be brought from the County Courts as well as the magistrates' courts, and from certain tribunals and under certain statutes. This section will only consider such appeals from the magistrates' courts. **50.74**

The appellant must apply in writing to the justices within 21 days after the relevant decision to state a case for the opinion of the High Court (Magistrates' Courts Act 1980, s 111). If the justices are of the opinion that an application to state a case is frivolous, they may refuse to do so (s 111(5)). Such a refusal may be reviewed and a mandatory order may be granted. The procedure for drafting the case is governed by the Criminal Procedure Rules. Within 21 days after receiving a request, the magistrates' clerk must send a draft case to the parties for comments. After receiving comments, the case may be amended, and is then signed by two justices or their clerk. The case stated must state the facts found by the magistrates and the question or questions of law or jurisdiction on which the opinion of the High Court is sought. Unless one of the questions is whether there was evidence on which the magistrates could have come to their decision, the case must not contain a statement of the evidence: see *Bracegirdle v Oxley* [1947] KB 349. **50.75**

The appellant must file an appellant's notice at the appeal court within ten days of receiving the case, together with the following documents: **50.76**

(a) the stated case;
(b) a copy of the judgment, order, or decision in respect of which the case has been stated; and
(c) where the lower court's decision was itself a decision on an appeal, a copy of the judgment, order, or decision of the original court (PD 52E, para 2.3).

The appellant's notice and the accompanying documents must be served on all respondents within four days after they are filed at the appeal court (para 2.4). **50.77**

L APPEALS TO THE SUPREME COURT

Appeals from the Court of Appeal

An appeal from the Court of Appeal generally lies to the Supreme Court. Permission must be obtained either from the Court of Appeal or from the Supreme Court. The Court of Appeal can deal with an application for permission to appeal by written submissions, and **50.78** will apply the same criteria as those applied by the Supreme Court (*Henry Boot Construction Ltd v Alstom Combined Cycles Ltd* [2005] 1 WLR 3850). If permission is refused by the Court of Appeal, an application for permission to appeal may be made to the Supreme Court on form SC001, which is a combined notice of appeal and application for permission to appeal (Supreme Court Rules 2009 (SI 2009/1603) ('SCR'), r 10(1); PD 3 Supreme Court, para 3.1.2). The application must be served on every respondent and any intervener in the court below before it is filed (SCR, r 12). Filing in the Registry of the Supreme Court must be in accordance with r 7, and effected within 28 days of the date of the order of the court below (r 11(1)). This period runs from the date of the substantive order appealed from, not from the date on which the order is sealed or the date of any subsequent procedural order (eg an order refusing permission to appeal) (PD 2 Supreme Court, para 2.1.12(a)).

50.79 Applications for permission to appeal are considered on paper without a hearing by a panel of justices (SCR, r 16(1)). Permission to appeal is granted for applications that, in the opinion of the appeal panel, raise an arguable point of law of general public importance which ought to be considered by the Supreme Court at that time, bearing in mind that the matter will already have been the subject of judicial decision and may have already been reviewed on appeal (PD 3 Supreme Court, para 3.3.3). There is great reluctance to entertain appeals to the Supreme Court on points of procedure, which are regarded as primarily within the province of the Court of Appeal (*Roberts v Gill and Co* [2011] 1 AC 240).

50.80 Where permission to appeal is granted by the Supreme Court, the application for permission to appeal will stand as the notice of appeal and the grounds of appeal are limited to those on which permission has been granted (SCR, r 18(1)). The appellant must, within 14 days of the grant of permission to appeal, file notice under r 18(1)(c) that he intends to proceed with the appeal. When the notice is filed, the application for permission to appeal will be resealed and the appellant must then serve a copy on each respondent, and on any intervener. After service, the appellant must file the original notice of appeal and three copies (r 18(2); PD 4 Supreme Court, para 4.1.1), together with a certificate of service.

50.81 There are detailed rules on the documents that have to be filed. They include the orders of the courts below, all the documents relevant to the arguments on the appeal, and bundles of authorities. The Supreme Court has a president, deputy president, and ten justices of the Supreme Court. It sits with at least three justices, but always with an uneven number of justices. Judgment is usually delivered in open court, but may be promulgated by the Registrar (SCR, r 28).

KEY POINTS SUMMARY

50.82
- Appeals are always exceptional.
- With limited exceptions (mostly related to the liberty of the person), permission is always required for civil appeals.
- Permission should be granted if the appeal has a real prospect of success.
- An appellant's notice must be filed within 21 days of the decision under appeal.
- There are strict routes of appeal, and special rules for second appeals.
- The basic test at the appeal hearing is whether the decision of the court below is wrong. A wide ambit is given to discretionary decisions, which is why many interim orders and costs orders are very difficult to appeal.
- Fresh evidence is rarely allowed on appeals from final decisions, and applications to adduce fresh evidence are guided by the *Ladd v Marshall* principles.

APPENDIX 1

Additional Chapter

An additional chapter to accompany this text can be found on the Online Resource Centre: **www.oxfordtextbooks.co.uk/orc/apacivil21e/**.

INTRODUCTION: THE JACKSON REFORMS

Taken from *Blackstone's Guide to the Civil Justice Reforms 2013* by Stuart Sime and Derek French, this introductory chapter provides a concise overview of Sir Rupert Jackson's *Review of Civil Litigation Costs*, often referred to as 'The Jackson Reforms'.

The chapter examines the central aims and concerns of the *Final Report*, which was published on 14 January 2010, and outlines its overall goals and recommendations. It leads the reader through the reforms aimed at ensuring costs payable in a case are proportionate and facilitating access to the court system with a range of funding options, supporting the Civil Procedure Rules, through to the end goal of enabling practitioners and the courts to deliver the best possible service to civil litigants at the lowest possible cost.

The key recommendations made by Lord Justice Jackson are outlined, covering party cost orders, protection of vulnerable parties against adverse cost orders through qualified one-way costs shifting, that success fees should no longer be recoverable from the losing party, and the new proportionality test for the costs that may be recovered from the losing party. The aftermath of the report, and the effects of the subsequent Civil Procedure (Amendment) Rules 2013, are also discussed.

INDEX

A

Aarhus Convention
  costs capping
        orders, 194–5
  interim injunctions, 478
Abuse of process
  commentaries on draft
        judgments, 572
  duplication of
        proceedings, 337
  interim injunctions, 473
  limitations
    cases outside the
        Limitation Act, 232
    relitigation, 247
  striking out
    collateral attacks, 331
    CPR provisions, 330
    general examples, 330–1
    relitigation, 331–2
  use of without prejudice
        documents, 356
  wasted costs, 527
  winding-up petitions, 96
Accrual of cause of action
  contractual claims, 236–8
  contribution claims, 241
  conversion, 239
  defective products, 241
  fatal accidents, 240–1
  general claims in
        tort, 238–9
  general rules, 235
  mortgage shortfalls, 236
  personal injury
        claims, 239–40
  statutory debts, 236
  title to land, 235–6
  trespass and libel, 239
Acknowledgments, 244
Acknowledgments of service
  see also **Default judgments**
  applications for permission
        for judicial
        review, 555
  forms and content, 133–4
  Part 8 Claims to determine
        quantum, 107–8
  part of response pack, 69
  partnerships, 210
  time limit for filing, 132

Acquiescence, 247–8, 474
Active case management
  alternative dispute
        resolution, 115–16
  cases generally, 35–6
  increasing use of
        technology, 36
  interim applications, 36
  provisions of CPR, 35
**Additional claims (Part
      20)** *see* **Part 20 claims**
Adjournments
  see also **Stays**
  amendments to
        pleadings, 251–2
  avoidance through
        exchange of
        evidence, 8, 367, 461
  general powers, 428
  non-attendance at
        CMCs, 319
Adjudication, 111–12
Administration orders
  amendment to parties
        after expiry of
        limitations, 256–7
  enforcement of
        judgments, 538
Administrative Court
  damages for breach of
        human rights, 46
  general organization, 24
  human rights
        claims, 46–7
  judicial review, 548, 558
  jurisdiction, 30
  specialist claim forms, 62,
        65
Admiralty Court
  composition and
        administration, 23–4
  issue of claim forms, 6
  jurisdiction, 30
  responding to claims, 136
Admissibility
  expert evidence
    established field of
        expertise, 386–7
    five preconditions, 385
    independence and
        impartiality, 387

  issues requiring
        expertise, 386
    non-expert evidence, 388
    qualifications and
        experience, 367
    ultimate issue
        rule, 387–8
  hearsay
    CEA 1995, 373–5
    failure to serve hearsay
        notice, 376
    general rule, 372–3
    preservation of former
        common law
        exceptions, 375
  trial bundles, 315, 384
Admissions
  authenticity of disclosed
        documents, 362
  forms and content, 132–3
  notices to admit
    facts, 381–3
    costs, 381–3
    form and contents, 382
    purpose, 381
    uses, 381
  overview, 379–80
  part of response
        pack, 70–1
  permission to
        withdraw, 380–1
  pre-action admissions of
        liability, 380
  summary judgments, 288
  time limit for filing, 132
Affidavits
  false affidavits, 371
  form and contents, 364–5,
        370
  overview, 364
  persons qualified to take
        affidavit, 370
  persons under
        disability, 370–1
  proof, 383
Affirmations
  affidavits
        distinguished, 370
  application notices, 365
  depositions, 365
  form and contents, 364–5

Affirmations (*Cont.*)
overview, 364
statement of truth, 150–1, 365
After the event litigation insurance (ATE) insurance
consideration at first interview with solicitor, 4
exclusions, 13
general principles, 13
Alternative dispute resolution (ADR)
active case management, 115–16
adjudicative and non-adjudicative processes compared, 111–12
advantages, 1
advantages and disadvantages, 112–14
contract terms for references, 114–15
costs
failure to consider or participate, 513–14
overview, 114
sanctions, 116–17
stays at case management stage, 177
Alternative service, 77–8
Amendments
alternative to striking out, 330
by consent, 249
interim costs orders, 520
notice of appeal, 567–8
overview, 249
with permission
adding defendants, 253
after expiry of limitations, 254–9
changes to parties, 252–3
costs, 252
general principles, 250–2
merits of case, 252
procedure, 259–60
procedure
after permission granted, 259–60
applying for permission, 259

making
amendments, 259
at summary judgment hearings, 289
without permission, 249–50
American Cyanamid **guidelines,** 463–74
Appeals
advantages of arbitration, 113
applications for permission for judicial review, 555
basic civil appeals structure, 560
case-stated appeals, 573
costs after, 518
court powers
costs, 573
fresh evidence, 572
general powers vested in the appeal court, 571
handed-down judgments, 572
non-disclosure of Pt 36 offers, 573
reopening appeals, 572
general jurisdiction, 22
grounds for allowing
errors of law, 571
inadequate reasons, 571
inferences, 570
judicial discretion, 570
overview, 569
procedural irregularities, 571
questions of fact, 570
hearings
judiciary, 568
last-minute settlements, 569
procedure, 569
High Court appeal centres, 561
incidental remedies, 567–8
judicial review distinguished, 548
leapfrog appeals
to the High Court, 561
to Supreme Court, 561
overview, 559–60
Part 36 offers and payments, 413
permission

amendments, 567–8
application procedure, 562–3
exceptions, 562
grounds for appeal to Court of Appeal, 563
grounds for first appeal, 563
limiting issues to be heard, 563
refusals, 563–4
requirement for permission to appeal, 561–2
procedure, 565–6
renewal of process, 88
respondent's notice, 566–7
second appeals, 560
security for costs, 301–2
setting aside, 568
slip rule, 456–7
stays, 568
striking out, 568
to Supreme Court, 573–4
time limits
extensions of time, 564
general rule, 564
Arbitration
adjudicative and non-adjudicative processes compared, 111–12
case management, 174
contract terms for references, 114–15
costs, 114
Assessment of costs
basis of quantification, 521
detailed assessment, 523–4
general procedure after trial, 9
interim costs orders, 519–20
proportionality, 521–2
summary assessment, 522–3
Assignment of claims
amendments after expiry of limitations, 254
appropriate parties, 218–19
security for costs, 299
Assumed jurisdiction
contractual claims, 126
forum non conveniens, 126–7

general interpretation, 125
grounds for granting
permission, 125
principles governing
permission, 124
procedure for seeking
permission, 127
proper parties, 125–6
recast Judgments
Regulation, 120
tort claims, 126

**Attachment of
earnings,** 539–40

Attorney-General
amendments to
proceedings, 256
intervention, 217
proceedings brought in
name of, 212
proceedings for
false witness
statements, 369
'special advocate', 456
vexatious litigants, 214

Authorities
with notice interim
applications, 271–2
trial bundles, 433

B

Bankers Trust **orders**
aid of tracing, 504
principles for
granting, 504
procedure, 504

Bankruptcy
amendment to parties
after expiry of
limitations, 256
description of
parties, 208–9
enforcement of money
judgments, 543

Barristers
see also **Legal profession;
Solicitors**
business structures, 2
duties to LAA, 20
duty of confidentiality, 5
endorsement of orders on
brief, 449–50
general duties, 2
interim costs orders, 520
solicitors distinguished, 2
specialist advice, 4

Beddoe **orders,** 192–3

**Before the event litigation
expenses insurance
(BTE),** 4

Benefits
recoupment in
judgments, 452
reduction of interim
payments, 295

Best evidence rule, 383

Budgets
approval of budgets, 188
case management, 188
costs management, 185
discussion reports, 187
failure to file, 187
formats, 185–7
judicial control, 189
Part 36 offers and
payments, 412

Bullock **orders,** 515

Bundles of documents *see*
trial bundles under
Documents

Business and property courts
Administrative Court, 30
Admiralty Court, 30
Commercial Court, 29–30
Companies Court, 30
electronic filing, 264
Financial List, 30–1
organization of High
Court, 24, 29
Patents Court, 30
Technology and
Construction Court
(TCC), 29

**Business document
certificates,** 377

C

Calderbank **offers**
format and effect, 400
pre-action offers, 57
without prejudice
communications, 57

Cargo claims
freezing injunctions, 486
jurisdiction, 30
limitations, 232
renewal of process, 87
summary judgments, 287

Case management
see also **Costs
management; Track
allocation**
active case management

alternative dispute
resolution, 115–16
cases generally, 35–6
increasing use of
technology, 36
interim applications, 36
provisions of CPR, 35
appeals, 570
control of witness
statements, 368
costs budgets, 188
directions questionnaires
failure to comply with
notice, 164–73
filing, 164
forms and
content, 164–72
docketing, 163
fast track cases, 310–11,
311, 312
human rights
incompatibility, 45
judicial review, 555–6
litigants in person, 214
multi-track
cases, 319–22
overview, 162–3
overview of track
allocation, 181
Part 20 claims, 229–30
Part 8 Claims, 90
procedural judges, 163,
312
sanctions *see* **Sanctions**
specialist claims, 173–4
stays
for ADR, 177
general power, 336
settlements, 177
transfers of
proceedings, 178
trials
pilot schemes to reduce
costs, 181–2
pre-trial
checklists, 179–80
Royal Courts of Justice
or Rolls Building, 178
triggered by filing of
defence, 160

Case management conferences
menu option
disclosure, 347
multi-track cases, 320–1

Case-stated appeals, 573

Case summaries
see also **Skeleton arguments**
case management, 172
fast track cases, 315
general requirements, 429
importance, 433
inclusion in trial bundles, 432
listing in RCJ, 428
multi-track cases, 319, 320
Causes of action
accrual for purpose of limitations
contractual claims, 236–8
contribution claims, 241
conversion, 239
defective products, 241
fatal accidents, 240–1
general claims in tort, 238–9
general rules, 235
mortgage shortfalls, 236
personal injury claims, 239–40
statutory debts, 236
title to land, 235–6
trespass and libel, 239
amendment to parties after expiry of limitations, 257–9
'fishing' requests, 201
freezing injunctions, 130
interim injunctions, 462
joinder, 214–15
lis pendens, 128
Part 20 claims, 221
particulars of claim, 7, 64
permission to serve out of jurisdiction, 127
persons under disability, 205
statements of case, 149, 151–3
Certificates of service
form and contents, 81–2
requirement to file, 80
Champerty, 14
Chancery Division
allocation of business between divisions, 28
composition and administration, 23
consent orders, 456

docketing, 163
issue of claim forms, 65
Charging orders, 540–2
Cheques
effect of freezing injunctions on bank accounts, 487
search orders, 494
summary judgments, 285–8
Children
see also **Persons under disability**
costs management, 184
default judgments, 140
road traffic claims for personal injuries under £25.000
child settlements, 108–9
fixed costs, 103
Civil Procedure Rules
active case management, 35
disapplication in small claims track, 306
interpretation
general approach, 36
human rights, 38
natural meaning, 37
new procedural code, 36–7
overriding objective, 37
precedent, 38
overriding objective, 34–5
Part 20 claims, 222
power to review, 84–5
responding to claims, 132
sanctions, 414–15
setting aside default judgments, 143
Claim forms
applications for permission for judicial review, 553–4
filing at court, 82–3
form and contents, 59–62
High Court endorsements, 62
issue of proceedings, 65–6
overview, 6
particulars of claim, 62
sealing by court, 59, 65
service
addresses for service, 74–5
companies, 75

deemed date of service, 78–9
dispensing with service, 78
hierarchy of service methods, 68–74
importance, 66
methods of effecting service, 75–8
period of validity, 67–8
relevant documents, 68–73
specialist claims, 62–5
Clients
client care letter, 10–11
disclosure responsibilities, 342
duty to inform client of costs liability, 520
waiver of privilege, 356
Closing speeches, 439
Code of Conduct of the Bar, 3
Collateral attacks, 331
Collateral use
disclosure, 362
experts' reports, 398
responses to requests for further information, 202
search orders, 500
witness statements, 369
Commencement of proceedings
see also **Issue of proceedings; Pre-action protocols; Renewal of process**
choice of court, 6
claim forms
form and contents, 59–62
High Court endorsements, 62
particulars of claim, 62
specialist claims, 62–5
issue of claim forms, 6
overview, 59
Part 8 Claims
applicability, 89–90
issue and service, 90
overview, 89
particulars of claim, 62
petitions

forms and content, 91
scope, 91
recast Judgments
Regulation, 124
scope of solicitors
authority, 4
winding-up petitions, 94
in wrong court, 28
Commercial arbitration
adjudicative and non-
adjudicative processes
compared, 111–12
costs, 114
Community Legal Service *see*
Legal aid
Community mediation
adjudicative and non-
adjudicative processes
compared, 112
costs, 114
Companies
see also **Winding-up**
petitions
Chancery Division
jurisdiction, 28
description of parties, 210
exclusion from legal
aid, 18
in liquidation, 211
overseas
companies, 210–11
representation, 210
rights of audience and
representation, 436
security for costs
exercise of
discretion, 304
necessary condition, 301
service of claims, 75
Companies Court
composition and
administration, 23–4
jurisdiction, 30
Concurrent claims
service on foreign
defendant, 119
stays, 337
Concurrent evidence, 397
Conditional fee agreements
(CFAs)
consideration at first
interview with
solicitor, 4
development of law, 14
'no win, no fee' basis, 15

success fees, 15
Conditional orders
relationship with interim
payments, 293
security for costs, 300
summary judgments, 279,
288–9
Confidentiality
see also **Privacy (Art 8)**
application of Art 8, 43
Bankers Trust
orders, 504
collateral use of
documents, 362
interim injunctions, 469,
470
journalistic sources, 503
lawyers duties, 5
legal professional
privilege, 355
opposing lawyers, 355
private hearings, 435
public interest
immunity, 359
search orders, 498
worldwide injunctions, 474
Consent
agreed directions
fast track cases, 314
multi-track
cases, 317–17, 324
agreed proposals for menu
option disclosure, 347
amendments, 249
interim payments, 291
orders
administrative consent
orders, 455–6
approval by court, 456
Chancery Division
rules, 456
child settlement
applications, 108
contribution claims, 241
judicial review, 558
Part 8 Claims, 207
real contract and
simple submission
distinguished, 450–1
stays on settlement, 336
Tomlin orders, 451
Consolidation of claims, 217
Contempt of court
affidavits in support, 365
collateral use, 362, 500

committal for breach of an
order, 545
disclosure statements, 349
false affidavits, 371
false witness
statements, 367, 369
freezing injunctions, 490
interfering with the
administration of the
law, 544–5
interim injunctions, 475,
479–80
mandatory orders, 551
privilege against self-
incrimination, 351,
351–2
search orders, 497, 498
sequestration
orders, 546
statement of truth, 151
tape recording of
trials, 440
undertakings, 478
Contractual claims
assumed jurisdiction, 126
costs, 517
example of defence, 156–7
recast Judgments
Regulation, 122–3
summary judgments, 284
Contractual method of service
prescribed hierarchy for
service, 68
procedure for service, 77
Contribution claims
accrual of cause of
action, 241
limitation periods, 232
Part 20 claims
applicable
situations, 223
distinguished, 222
notices, 228
procedure, 228
security for costs, 299
Corporations, 211
Correspondence
overriding objective
to ensure
cooperation, 40
pre-action
correspondence, 5–6
pre-action protocols
cases not covered, 49
general requirements, 48

Correspondence (*Cont.*)
　personal injury
　　claims, 52–3
　professional
　　negligence, 49–51
　published protocols and
　　their scope, 48–9
　scope of solicitor's
　　authority, 4
Costs *see also* **Funding**
　advantages of ADR, 1
　alternative dispute
　　resolution
　　advantages of ADR, 113
　　disadvantages of
　　　ADR, 113
　　failure to consider or
　　　participate, 513–14
　　overview, 114
　　sanctions, 116–17
　amendments with
　　permission, 252
　appeals, 573
　assessment of costs *see*
　　Assessment of costs
　Calderbank offers, 400
　consideration at first
　　interview with
　　solicitor, 3–4
　controlling the costs of
　　disclosure, 338
　costs capping orders *see*
　　Costs capping orders
　costs management *see*
　　Costs management
　effect of track
　　allocation, 525
　fixed costs
　　costs management, 184
　　fast track cases, 524–5
　　road traffic claims for
　　　personal injuries under
　　　£25.000, 103, 109
　　scale costs in certain
　　　proceedings, 525
　　small claims track, 308
　follow the event
　　exceptions, 514–17
　　main rule, 514
　group litigation orders, 219
　indemnity principle, 520–1
　interim applications, 276
　interim orders
　　range of possible
　　　orders, 518–20

notices to admit
　facts, 381–3
orders
　duty to inform client of
　　liability, 520
　failure to comply
　　with pre-action
　　protocol, 55
　general
　　principles, 512–14
　impact of costs
　　management, 189–90
　interim costs
　　orders, 518–20
　legally aided
　　litigants, 525–6
　against Lord
　　Chancellor, 20
　non-parties, 526
　pro bono costs
　　orders, 526
　against publicly funded
　　litigants, 20
　range of possible
　　orders, 517–18
　setting aside default
　　judgments, 145–6
　wasted costs
　　orders, 526–8
overriding
　objective, 39–40
overview, 511–12
Part 36 offers and
　payments
　failure to file costs
　　budget, 412
　misjudged failure to
　　accept, 410–11
　offers by claimants, 411
　offers by
　　defendants, 411
　unjust to apply usual
　　rule, 412
pilot schemes to reduce trial
　costs, 181–2
pre-action
　disclosure, 505–7
qualified one-way costs
　shifting *see* **Qualified
　one-way costs shifting**
references to CJEU, 447
security for costs *see*
　Security for costs
small claims track, 308–9
Costs capping orders

Aarhus Convention
　cases, 194–5
　cost limitation orders, 195
　form and contents, 192
　general rules
　　application
　　　procedure, 191–2
　　nature of orders, 191
　　requirements for making
　　　order, 192
　judicial review, 194
　protective costs
　　orders, 193–4
Costs management
　see also **Case management**
　applicable cases, 184–5
　budgets
　　approval of
　　　budgets, 188
　　case management, 188
　　general rules, 185–7
　　judicial control, 189
　essential elements, 184
　impact on costs
　　orders, 189–90
　orders
　　approval of budgets, 188
　　nature of orders, 187
　overview, 183–4
Counsel *see* **Barristers**
Counterclaims
　see also **Set-offs**
　costs, 515–16
　effect on interim
　　payments, 293–4
　forms of judgment, 452
　general principles, 157–8
　interim payments, 294
　Part 20 claims
　　applicable
　　　situations, 222–3
　　distinguished, 221
　part of response
　　pack, 72–3
　recast Judgments
　　Regulation, 124
　reply and defence to
　　counterclaims, 159
　subsequent statements of
　　case, 159
　summary judgments, 285
County Court
　application of CPR, 33–4
　applications for permission
　　to appeal, 563

basic civil appeals
structure, 560
commencement of
proceedings, 6
composition and
administration, 23
general jurisdiction, 22
issue of claim forms, 65–6
jurisdiction
inherent jurisdiction, 34
money claims, 28
overview, 25–7
personal injury
claims, 27–8
jury trials, 441
registration of money
judgments, 457
second appeals, 560
Court guides, 33
Court of Appeal
applications for permission
to appeal
grounds, 563
procedure, 563
basic civil appeals
structure, 560
composition and
administration, 23–4
references to CJEU, 446
second appeals, 560
**Court of Justice of European
Union** *see* **References
to CJEU**
Courts
allocation for trial, 433–4
Business and Property
Courts
Administrative Court, 30
Admiralty Court, 30
Commercial
Court, 29–30
Companies Court, 30
electronic filing, 264
Financial List, 30–1
organization of High
Court, 24, 29
Patents Court, 30
Technology and
Construction Court
(TCC), 29
composition and
administration
County Court, 23
High Court, 23–4
magistrates' courts, 22

County Court *see* **County
Court**
Court of Appeal *see* **Court
of Appeal**
distribution of business
between
judiciary, 24–5
general jurisdiction, 22
High Court *see* **High Court**
interim applications, 262
issue of claim forms, 65
jurisdiction
commencement in wrong
court, 28
County Court, 25–7
High Court, 25, 27
magistrates' courts, 25
money claims, 28
personal injury
claims, 27–8
specialist courts *see*
Specialist courts
Supreme Court *see*
Supreme Court
Covenants, 472–3
Credibility notices, 377
Cross-claims
interim
payments, 294
Part 20 claims, 221–2
Part 36 offers and
payments, 406
set-offs, 158–9
summary
judgments, 285–7
track allocation, 176
Cross-examination
hearsay, 376–7
interim applications, 366
at trial, 369

D
Damages
American Cyanamid
guidelines
adequacy of
damages, 464
applicant's
undertaking, 464–5
amount to be decided
default
judgments, 141–2
track allocation, 173
costs, 513
default judgments, 141–2
disposal hearings

assessment of
damages, 143
relevant orders, 142
track allocation, 142
failure to comply with pre-
action protocol, 55–6
human rights claims, 46
human rights claims against
Crown, 45
Part 36 offers and
payments, 410–11
provisional damages
awards, 452–4
remedy following judicial
review, 552
undertakings
discharge, 479
general principles, 477–8
inquiry as to
damages, 478–9
**Damages-based agreements
(DBAs)**
consideration at first
interview with
solicitor, 4
general principles, 16
**Declarations of
incompatibility**
applicability, 40
effect, 46
notice to Crown, 45
transfers of proceedings, 45
Defamation claims
excluded from public
funding, 18
interim injunctions, 468–9
limitation periods
accrual of cause of
action, 239
extensions of time, 244
statutory provisions, 232
Default judgments
see also **Summary
judgments**
damages
amount to be
decided, 141–2
disposal hearings, 142–3
entering judgment
delivery of
goods, 139–40
money claims, 139–40,
140–1
non-money claims, 140
time limit, 137–8

Default judgments (*Cont.*)
  time limits, 146
  excluded cases, 138–9
  final judgments, 141–2
  overview, 137
  Part 20 claims, 229
  service outside
     jurisdiction, 131
  setting aside
    Civil Procedure
     Rules, 143
    on conditions, 145–6
    consequential
     orders, 146
    defendants outside
     jurisdiction, 145
    discretionary
     procedure, 143–4
    good reasons, 144–5
    relief from
     sanctions, 145
    as of right, 143
  track allocation for
    damages, 173
Defences
  see also **Counterclaims;**
    Set-offs
  answer to particulars of
    claim, 155–6
  effect on interim
    payments, 293–4
  example of contractual
    claim, 156–7
  extensions of time, 134
  forms and content, 133
  general principles, 154–5
  interim injunctions, 474–5
  part of response
    pack, 72–3
  reply and defence to
    counterclaims, 159
  response to statement of
    claim, 8
  summary judgments
    cases with no real
     prospect of
     success, 282
    defences with real
     prospect of
     success, 282–3
    partial defences, 285
    weak defences, 283
  time limit for filing, 132
  timing of summary
    judgment, 278

  trigger for case
    management, 160
Delay
  see also **Laches**
  advantages of ADR, 1, 112
  defence to interim
    injunction, 474
  discretion to award security
    for costs, 303
  growing concern over
    access to justice, 1
  interim applications, 263–4
  overriding objective, 39–40
  setting aside default
    judgments, 145
Delivery of goods
  default judgments, 139–40
  enforcement of
    judgments, 543
  interim orders, 509
  limitations, 237
  unless orders, 419
Depositions, 365, 371
Destroyed documents, 350
Directions
  accompaniment to track
    allocation, 8
  disclosure
    menu option
     disclosure, 347–8
    standard disclosure, 345
  experts
    disclosure of
     reports, 389–92
    single joint
     experts, 391–2
  fast track cases
    agreed directions, 314
    disclosure, 311
    expert evidence, 311–12
    listing directions, 313
    listing for trial, 312–13
    overview, 310–11
    pre-trial checklists, 312
    witness statements, 311
  group litigation orders, 219
  multi-track cases
    agreed
     directions, 317–17
    case management
     conferences, 320–1
    directions at other
     hearings, 324–5
    pre-trial review
     directions, 324

  Part 8 Claims to determine
    quantum, 108
  petitions, 91
  questionnaires
    failure to comply with
     notice, 164–73
    filing, 164
    forms and
     content, 164–72
    sanctions, 415–16
  small claims track
    special directions, 307
    standard directions, 307
  summary judgments, 290
  at track allocation
    stage, 176–7
  witness statements, 368
Disability *see* **Persons under**
  disability
Discharge *see* **Variation or**
  discharge of orders
Disclosure, 500
  admissions of
    authenticity, 362
  clients' responsibilities, 342
  collateral use, 362
  documents mentioned
    in statement of
    case, 361
  duty to search, 348–9
  experts' reports
    directions, 389–92
    failure to disclose, 393
  general principles, 8
  inspection of
    documents, 359–60
  lawyers'
    responsibilities, 341
  lists of documents
    'disclosure
     statements', 349
    form and contents, 349
    lost and destroyed
     documents, 350
    standard
     disclosure, 339–41
  menu option disclosure
    agreed proposals, 347
    applicability, 345
    case management
     conferences, 347
    directions, 347–8
    form of report, 346
    'key of the warehouse'
     orders, 320–1

train of inquiry
documents, 320–1
non-disclosure of interim
payments at
trial, 295–6
orders
advance disclosure, 8–9
alternative paths, 342–3
Bankers Trust orders *see*
Bankers Trust orders
failure to disclose, 360
mediation evidence, 508
non-parties, 507–8
Norwich Pharmacal
orders *see Norwich*
Pharmacal **orders**
objections to disclosure or
inspection, 360
before proceedings
start, 505–7
specific disclosure or
inspection, 360–1
overview, 338
Part 36 offers and
payments, 413
partnership names, 210
privilege
effect on disclosure, 350
legal professional
privilege, 352–5
mistaken disclosure
of privileged
documents, 358
objections to
disclosure, 360
secondary evidence, 357–8
against self-
incrimination, 350–2
waiver of
privilege, 356–7
'without prejudice'
communications,
355–6
public interest immunity
controlling the costs of
disclosure, 338
general principles, 358
Ministerial
certificates, 358–9
Norwich Pharmacal
orders, 502
objections to
disclosure, 368
other confidential
information, 359

redacted judgments, 456
standard disclosure
'control' defined, 344–5
directions to limit, 345
'document; defined, 344
electronic
documents, 344
form of list, 339–41
relevant
documents, 343–4
timing, 342
without notice interim
applications
freezing
injunctions, 265–6
general duty, 265
Discontinuance
see also **Stays; Striking out**
after settlement, 449
fraud, 532
general principles, 334–5
personal injury claims under
£25000, 110
pre-trial checklists, 312,
322
stays to enforce compliance
with orders, 337
time-barred cases, 231
Disposal hearings
assessment of damages, 143
relevant orders, 142
track allocation, 142
Docketing, 25, 163
Document exchange (DX)
prescribed hierarchy for
service, 68
procedure for service, 76
Documents
see also **Disclosure**
consideration at first
interview with
solicitor, 3
description of parties, 203–
4
filing of documents at
court, 82–3
inspection of
documents, 359–60
legal professional
privilege, 354
lists of documents *see* **Lists**
of documents
with notice interim
applications, 270
proof, 383–4

in support of statements of
case, 150
trial bundles
appeals, 565
case management, 172
case summaries, 433
Commercial Court, 174
default judgments, 143
Electronic Working Pilot
Scheme, 83
fast track cases, 315–16
form and contents, 432–3
interim applications, 262,
270
proof, 384
reading lists, 433
skeleton arguments, 433
Due diligence, 3
E
Early neutral evaluation
(ENA), 111
Electronic documents
directions for
disclosure, 348
inspection, 360
lawyers' responsibilities to
advise, 341
menu option disclosure, 345
standard disclosure, 344
Electronic service
prescribed hierarchy for
service, 68
procedure for
service, 76–7
Electronic Working Pilot
Scheme, 83
Employers' liability and public
liability
pre-action protocol for
claims under £25,000
fixed costs, 109
limitations, 109
scope, 100
when protocol ceases to
apply, 109–10
pre-action protocols
for claims under
£25,000, 109–10
Enforcement
see also **Sanctions**
advantages of ADR, 112
case management
sanctions, 414–15
application
procedure, 416–18

Enforcement (*Cont.*)
Civil Procedure
Rules, 414–15
directions, 415–16
extensions of
time, 419–20
implied sanctions
doctrine, 422–3
pre-action
protocols, 414
preservation of trial
date, 416
relief and setting
aside, 419–20
unless orders, 418
contempt of court
affidavits in support, 365
collateral use, 362, 500
committal for breach of
an order, 545
disclosure
statements, 349
false affidavits, 371
false witness
statements, 367, 369
freezing injunctions, 490
interfering with the
administration of the
law, 544–5
interim injunctions, 475,
480
mandatory orders, 551
privilege against self-
incrimination, 351
search orders, 497, 498
sequestration
orders, 546
statement of truth, 151
tape recording of
trials, 440
undertakings, 478
disadvantages of ADR, 113
foreign judgments, 546–7
freezing injunctions after
judgment, 491–2
human rights claims
available remedies, 46
speedy determination of
claims, 46–7
judgments
limitation periods, 232,
243–4
against partners, 210
judgments for possession of
land, 543–4

money judgments
administration
orders, 538
attachment of
earnings, 539–40
charging orders, 540–2
general
provisions, 534–5
insolvency, 543
obtaining information
from debtors, 535–6
taking control of
goods, 536–7
third party debt
orders, 538–9
overview, 534
pre-action interim
applications, 263
qualified one-way costs
shifting, 530
receivership
nature of
receivership, 544
procedure, 544
remedies following judicial
review
damages, 552
injunctions, 552
mandatory orders, 551
prohibitory
orders, 551–2
quashing orders, 551
security for costs, 301
sequestration writs, 546
stays to enforce compliance
with orders, 337
Equality of arms
fair trial (Art 6), 42
overriding objective, 39
striking out, 329
Errors and mistakes
amendments after expiry of
limitations, 255
application of
CPR, 33–4
calculation of limitation
periods, 242–3
case management
sanctions, 419–20
commencement in wrong
court, 28
costs where proceedings
wrongly commenced
in High Court, 514
describing parties, 203

disadvantages of
arbitration, 113
grounds for
appeal, 571
irregular service, 80–2
mistaken disclosure
of privileged
documents, 358
Part 8 Claims, 90
slip rule, 456–7
EU law
Aarhus Convention
costs capping
orders, 194–5
interim injunctions, 478
direct claims against
insurers, 204
European Small Claims
Procedure, 306
inter-relation between
assumed jurisdiction
and the jurisdiction
conventions, 118–19
recast Judgments
Regulation
co-defendants, 123–4
commencement of
proceedings, 124
contractual
disputes, 122–3
counterclaims, 124
determination of
international
jurisdiction, 121
disputing jurisdiction
upon receipt of
claim, 135
domicile, 121–2
exclusive
jurisdiction, 120
Part 20 claims, 124
scope, 121
tort claims, 123
trusts, 123
references to CJEU
costs, 447
discretionary
references, 444–6
mandatory
references, 443–4
procedure in
CJEU, 447
procedure in
England, 446–7
relevant questions, 443

service may be effected at the lawyer's business address, 69

skeleton arguments, 272

stays in pending proceedings, 336

European Court of Justice *see* **References to CJEU**

Evidence *see* also **Disclosure**

consideration at first interview with solicitor, 3

disclosure *see* **Disclosure**

experts *see* **Experts**

fresh evidence on appeal, 572

hearsay *see* **Hearsay**

interim hearings, 275

interim injunctions, 461

interim payments, 294–5

judicial review hearings interveners, 556 procedure, 557

medical evidence road traffic claims for personal injuries under £25.000, 104

multi-track cases case management conferences, 321–2

with notice interim applications, 267, 270

notices to admit facts costs, 381–3 form and contents, 382 purpose, 381 uses, 381

Part 8 Claims, 90

petitions, 91

real evidence, 373

search orders *see* **Search orders**

solicitor's duty to preserve, 4

trial procedure claimant's case, 438 defence case, 439 no case submissions, 438–9 reopening hearings, 440

use of statements of case at trial, 161

witness statements *see* **Witness statements**

Exchange of experts' reports, 390

Expert determination (ED), 111

Experts

admissibility of evidence established field of expertise, 386–7 five preconditions, 385 independence and impartiality, 387 issues requiring expertise, 386 non-expert evidence, 388 qualifications and experience, 367 ultimate issue rule, 387–8

advance disclosure of evidence, 9

after the event litigation insurance (ATE) insurance, 13

appointment under pre-action protocols, 53–5

control of evidence by court, 388

examination of subject matter handwriting comparisons, 394 medical examinations, 395–6

fast track cases evidence, 311–12 questions to experts, 312

immunity from suit, 398

inspection of property, 508–9

multi-track cases, 320–1

reports disclosure, 389–92 failure to disclose, 393 form and contents, 392–3 privilege, 388–9 supporting documentation, 393 use after trial, 398

at trial concurrent evidence, 397 conflicts with other evidence, 397 general principles, 396

single joint experts, 396–7

without prejudice discussions, 393

written questions to, 393–4

Extensions of time

appeals, 564

case management sanctions, 419–20

limitations defamation, 244 judicial review, 244 personal injury claims, 244–7

F

Fair trial (Art 6), 42

appeals, 569

application to civil litigation, 42–3

interim hearings, 274

principles for fair hearing, 41–2

public or private hearings, 435–6

rights established for the parties, 42

security for costs, 297

Family Division

allocation of business between divisions, 28

composition and administration, 23

Family law

assumed jurisdiction, 121

Fast track cases

see also **Multi-track cases; Small claims cases**

agreed directions, 314

allocation directions disclosure, 311 expert evidence, 311–12 listing for trial, 312–13 overview, 310–11 pre-trial checklists, 312 questions to experts, 312 witness statements, 311

disclosure alternative paths, 342–3 limits on standard disclosure, 345 timing, 342

fixed costs, 524–5

listing for trial, 424 case summaries, 315

Fast track cases (*Cont.*)
court requirements,
314–15
trial bundles, 315
trial timetable, 315
overview, 310
rules based on financial
value, 175
standard timetable, 313
varying timetable, 314
Fatal accidents
see also **Personal injury
claims**
interim payments, 292
limitation periods
accrual of cause of
action, 240–1
statutory provisions, 232
limitations
date of knowledge, 241
general claims in
tort, 238
Part 36 offers and
payments, 408
particulars of claim, 151
qualified one-way costs
shifting, 529
Filing of documents at court
case management
conferences, 319
claim forms
generally, 82–3
costs budgets, 187
directions
questionnaires, 164
interim applications
with notice
applications, 267
without notice
applications, 264
Part 8 Claims, 90
pre-trial checklists
case management, 179–80
fast track cases, 312
multi-track cases, 322–3
respondent's notice of
appeal, 567
responding to claims, 132
Financial List, 30–1
'Fishing' requests, 201
Fixed costs
fast track cases, 524–5
road traffic claims for
personal injuries under
£25.000, 103, 106

scale costs in certain
proceedings, 525
small claims track, 308
Foreign judgments, 546–7
Forfeiture
concurrent jurisdiction, 26
summary judgments, 290
Forum non conveniens, 126–7,
129–30, 212, 337
Fraud
application of new
procedural code, 37
calculation of limitation
periods, 242
cheque rule, 286
summary judgments
inappropriate, 284
**Freedom of expression (Art
10)**
interim injunctions, 44–5,
469–70
scope of protection, 44
Freezing injunctions
after judgment, 491–2
ancillary orders, 489
assets covered by order
bank accounts, 487
land, 488
types of assets, 486–7
defendant's requirements
costs of defending, 488
living expenses, 488
trade debts, 488
defined, 481
duration, 489
effect of order, 490
interim applications
full and frank
disclosure, 265–6
pre-action
applications, 263
levels of judiciary, 24
notification
injunctions, 489–90
principles for granting
arguable case, 483
assets within the
jurisdiction, 483–4
claim justiciable
in England and
Wales, 483
judicial
discretion, 485–6
overview, 482
risk of disposal, 485

procedure, 481–2
proprietary claims, 492
reimbursement of port
authorities, 488
required undertakings
incorporated in
order, 486
standard-form orders, 489
varying or discharge, 490–
1
worldwide
injunctions, 484–5
Funding *see also* **Costs**
champerty and
maintenance, 14
conditional fee agreements
(CFAs)
development of law, 14
'no win, no fee' basis, 15
success fees, 15
consideration at first
interview with
solicitor, 3–4
damages-based agreements
(DBAs)
general principles, 16
duty to advise, 10–11
irrecoverable costs of
setting up, 20
legal aid
costs against publicly
funded litigants, 20
costs orders against Lord
Chancellor, 20
criteria for funding, 18
duties to LAA, 20
excluded claims, 18
excluded parties, 18
financial eligibility, 18
payment of moneys
recovered direct to
LAA, 19
prospects of success
criterion, 18–19
range of services
covered, 17–18
revocation or
discharge, 20
role of Legal Aid
Agency, 17
statutory charges, 19
legal expenses insurance
after the event litigation
insurance (ATE)
insurance, 13

before the event litigation
expenses insurance
(BTE), 4
taking on new
instructions, 13
payments on account, 10
professional duties, 10
retainers, 11–13
third parties, 16–17
Further information *see*
**Requests for further
information**

G

Government
departments, 211
Group litigation orders, 219

H

Handed-down
judgments, 572
Handwriting
comparisons, 394
Hearings
see also **Fair trial (Art
6); Trials**
appeals
last-minute
settlements, 569
procedure, 569
disposal hearings
assessment of
damages, 143
relevant orders, 142
track allocation, 142
interim hearings
non-attendance, 275
procedure, 275–6
written evidence, 275
interim injunctions, 462
judicial review
case management, 555–6
contested
claims, 556
interim orders, 556
interveners, 556
procedure, 557
skeleton
arguments, 556–7
multi-track cases
case management
conferences, 320–1
directions at other
hearings, 324–5
listing hearings, 323
non-payment of hearing
fees, 180

with notice interim
applications, 273–4
petitions, 91
small claims track
determination without
hearing, 308
final hearings, 308
summary judgments
amendments at
hearing, 289
fixed by the court of its
own initiative, 278
winding-up petitions, 97
without notice interim
applications, 264–5
Hearsay
admissibility
CEA 1995, 373–5
preservation of former
common law
exceptions, 375
advance disclosure, 9
general rule, 372–3
notice procedure
advance notice, 375–6
business document
certificates, 377
credibility notices, 377
cross-examination,
376–7
failure to serve hearsay
notice, 376
form of notices, 376
overview, 372
real evidence
distinguished, 373
at trial
assessing the weight of
evidence, 378
credibility, 377–8
general principles, 377
High Court
allocation between
divisions, 28
appeal centres, 561
application of CPR, 33–4
applications for permission
to appeal, 563
basic civil appeals
structure, 560
Business and Property
Courts
Administrative Court, 30
Admiralty Court, 30
Commercial
Court, 29–30

Companies Court, 30
electronic filing, 264
Financial List, 30–1
general organization, 24,
29
Patents Court, 30
Technology and
Construction Court
(TCC), 29
case-stated appeals, 573
Chancery Division
allocation of business
between divisions, 28
composition and
administration, 23
consent orders, 456
docketing, 163
issue of claim forms, 65
commencement of
proceedings, 6
composition and
administration, 23–4
costs where proceedings
wrongly
commenced, 514
endorsement of claim
forms, 62
Family Division
allocation of business
between divisions, 28
composition and
administration, 23
issue of claim forms, 65
jurisdiction
allocation between
divisions, 28
concurrent
jurisdiction, 25
exclusive jurisdiction, 27
inherent jurisdiction, 34
money claims, 28
overview, 22
leapfrog appeals, 561
Queen's Bench Division
allocation of business
between divisions, 28
certification of
judgments, 450
composition and
administration, 23
docketing, 25
issue of claim forms, 65
jury trials, 441
registration of money
judgments, 457
second appeals, 560

'Hot-tubbing', 397
Human rights
declarations of
incompatibility
applicability, 40
effect, 46
notice to Crown, 45
transfers of
proceedings, 45
fair trial (Art 6) *see* **Fair trial (Art 6)**
freedom of expression (Art 10), *see* **Freedom of expression (Art 10)**
importance, 32
incorporation under HRA 1998, 40
interpretation of CPR, 38
judicial review, 556
levels of judiciary, 24
limitation periods, 232
particulars of claim, 153
pleadings, 41
privacy (Art 8) *see* **Privacy (Art 8)**
raising points in practice
advance notice of
authorities relied
upon, 46
Art 5 claims, 46
available remedies, 46
interventions, 45
jurisdiction, 45
speedy determination of
claims, 46–7
statements of case, 45
transfers of
proceedings, 45
right to respect for private
and family life *see*
Privacy (Art 8)

I

Immunity from suit
experts, 398
human rights
compatibility, 43
Impartiality *see* **Independence and impartiality**
Indemnity principle, 14, 520–1
Independence and impartiality
experts, 387
fair trial (Art 6), 41–2
judiciary, 434–5
Industrial disputes, 470–1

Inequality of arms *see*
Equality of arms
Initial instructions
first interview, 3–4
written instructions, 4
Injunctions
classification of
proceedings, 1
freezing injunctions *see*
Freezing injunctions
interim injunctions *see*
Interim injunctions
notification
injunctions, 489–90
remedy following judicial
review, 552
restraint of foreign
proceedings, 130
restraint of winding-up, 96
Insolvency
see also **Winding-up petitions**
amendment to parties
after expiry of
limitations, 256
companies in
liquidation, 211
description of
parties, 208–9
enforcement of money
judgments, 543
Inspection of documents
documents mentioned in
statement of case, 361
general principles, 359–60
orders
objections to disclosure
or inspection, 360
specific disclosure or
inspection, 360–1
Insurance
legal expenses insurance
after the event litigation
insurance (ATE)
insurance, 13
taking on new
instructions, 13
notification of RTA
claims, 56
parties to direct action
claim, 204–5
road traffic claims for
personal injuries under
£25.000
commencement of
process, 101–3

response by defendant's
insurers, 103
Intellectual property claims
assumed jurisdiction, 121
privilege against self-
incrimination, 351–2
Interest on damages
failure to comply
with pre-action
protocol, 55
Part 36 offers and
payments
misjudged failure to
accept, 410–11
unjust to apply usual
rule, 412
Interim applications *see also*
Interim orders
active case management, 36
after striking out, 327
costs, 276
judicial review, 556
jurisdiction
appropriate court, 262
appropriate judges, 262
non-attendance, 275
with notice
authorities, 271–2
chronologies and lists of
relevant persons, 272
documents, 270
draft orders, 272
evidence in support, 267,
270
filing of documents at
court, 267
form of
application, 268–9
hearings, 273–4
service, 272–3
skeleton arguments, 271
overview, 261–2
pre-action remedies, 263
procedure, 275–6
procedure generally, 24
service outside
jurisdiction, 130–1
timing
overriding
objective, 263–4
pre-action
applications, 262
without notice
full and frank
disclosure, 265–6
hearings, 264–5

orders without
notice, 266
procedure, 264
witnesses
cross-examination, 366
disclosure of
statements, 366
written evidence, 275
Interim injunctions
contempt of court, 479–80
damages
undertakings in
damages, 477–9
defences, 474–5
effect of failure to apply for
interim relief, 480
evidence in support, 461
form and contents of
order, 475–7
freedom of expression (Art
10), 44–5
hearings, 462
overview *see* **Injunctions**
pre-action
procedures, 459–61
principles for granting
American Cyanamid
guidelines, 463–74
cause of action, 462
just and convenient, 462
in support of criminal
law, 462–3
procedure, 461
referral to judge, 459
Interim orders *see also*
Interim applications
costs
qualified one-way costs
shifting, 531
range of possible
orders, 518–20
delivery-up of goods, 509
draft orders, 272
judicial review, 556
made on the court's own
initiative, 274
overview, 261–2
pre-action
applications, 263
varying or revoking, 276
without notice
applications, 264–5
Interim payments, *see also*
**Part 36 offers and
payments**

amount to be ordered
certificate of recoverable
benefits, 295
evidence of need, 294–5
proportion of total
award, 294
costs, 524
defined, 291
discretionary
procedure, 294
effect of counterclaims and
defence, 293–4
instalment payments, 295
multiple defendants, 292–3
necessary conditions, 292
non-disclosure at
trial, 295–6
overview, 291
Part 36 offers and
payments, 406
procedure, 291–2
relationship with summary
judgments, 293
road traffic claims for
personal injuries under
£25.000, 104
standard of proof, 293
subsequent
applications, 295
varying or discharge, 296
Interpretation of CPR
general approach, 36
human rights, 38
natural meaning, 37
new procedural
code, 36–7
overriding objective, 37
precedent, 38
Issue of proceedings
see also **Commencement of
proceedings**
applications for permission
for judicial
review, 553–4
claim forms
overview, 6
procedure, 65–6
filing of documents at
court, 82–3
Part 8 Claims, 90
petitions, 91
sealing of claim form, 59,
65

J

Jackson reforms

after the event litigation
insurance (ATE)
insurance, 13
conditional fee agreements
(CFAs), 14
costs management, 183–4
docketing, 163
indemnity principle, 14
interim applications, 262
Online Resource Centre,
App 1
Part 36 offers and
payments, 411
personal injury claims, 99
promoting administration
of justice, 38
relief from sanctions, 420
Joinder
criteria for
decision, 214–15
separate trials, 215
statutory provisions, 214
Journalists' sources, 502–3
Judgements
reasoned decisions
fair trial (Art 6), 42
relevance of ECtHR, 41
Judgments *see also* **Orders**
certification
in QBD, 450
counterclaims, 452
drawing up, 455–7
effective date, 448
enforcement
limitation periods, 232,
243–4
against partners, 210
foreign judgments, 546–7
format and contents, 450
handed-down
judgments, 572
money claims, 452
personal injury claims
dishonest
claims, 454–5
periodic payments
awards, 454
provisional
damages, 452–4
recoupment of
benefits, 452
registration of money
judgments, 457
summary judgments *see*
Summary judgments

Judicial review
consent orders, 558
conversion to common law
claim, 556
costs capping orders, 194
defined, 548
extension of
limitations, 244
fair trial (Art 6), 42
limitation periods, 232
permission to proceed
acknowledgments of
service, 554–5
appeals against
refusal, 555
grounds for
granting, 555
issue of claim
forms, 553–4
reconsideration, 555
service of claim
forms, 554
time limits, 553
two-stage
application, 553
potential defendants,
548–9
pre-action protocol, 552
remedies
damages, 552
injunctions, 552
mandatory orders, 551
prohibitory orders,
551–2
quashing orders, 551
standing, 549
subject matter of
applications
overview, 549–50
public law issues, 550–1
substantive hearings
case management, 555–6
contested claims, 556
interim orders, 556
interveners, 556
procedure, 557
skeleton
arguments, 556–7
Judiciary
allocation for trial, 434
appeal hearings, 568
capacity to hear interim
applications, 261
County Court, 23
distribution of business
between, 24–5

High Court, 23–4
impartiality, 434–5
interim injunctions, 459
magistrates' courts, 22
procedural judges, 163,
312
role at trial, 439–40
sources of law, 33
Jurisdiction
Administrative Court, 30
Admiralty Court, 30
advantages of
arbitration, 113
commencement in wrong
court, 28
Commercial Court, 29–30
Companies Court, 30
County Court
inherent jurisdiction, 34
money claims, 28
overview, 25–7
court system as a whole, 22
disputing jurisdiction upon
receipt of claim, 134–
5
Financial List, 30–1
freezing injunctions *see*
Freezing injunctions
High Court
allocation between
divisions, 28
concurrent
jurisdiction, 25
exclusive jurisdiction, 27
inherent jurisdiction, 34
money claims, 28
overview, 22
human rights claims, 45
human rights remedies, 46
interim applications
appropriate court, 262
appropriate judges, 262
jury trials, 441
magistrates' courts, 25
money claims, 28
Patents Court, 30
personal injury claims, 27–
8
recast Judgments
Regulation
co-defendants, 123–4
commencement of
proceedings, 124
contractual
disputes, 122–3
counterclaims, 124

determination of
international
jurisdiction, 121
disputing jurisdiction
upon receipt of
claim, 135
domicile, 121–2
exclusive
jurisdiction, 120
Part 20 claims, 124
scope, 121
tort claims, 123
trusts, 123
security for costs, 300–1
service outside
assumed
jurisdiction, 124–7
cases outside general
rules, 120–1
default judgments, 131
foreign defendants within
jurisdiction, 119
interim relief, 130–1
preventing
conflicts, 128–30
recast Judgments
Regulation, 121–4
service abroad, 127–8
submission to
jurisdiction, 119–20
setting aside default
judgments, 145
specific disclosure
or specific
inspection, 360–1
Technology and
Construction Court
(TCC), 29
writs *ne exeat regno*, 492
Jury trials
jurisdiction, 441
procedure, 441–2
Justice
growing concern over
access to justice, 1

L
Laches, 247–8, 474
Land claims
assumed jurisdiction, 120
enforcement of
judgments, 543–4
freezing injunctions, 488
limitation periods
accrual of cause of
action, 235–6

statutory provisions, 232
particulars of claim, 153
Latent damage, 243
Leapfrog appeals, 561
Legal aid
consideration at first
interview with
solicitor, 3–4
costs against publicly
funded litigants, 20
costs orders against Lord
Chancellor, 20
costs orders against
parties, 525–6
criteria for funding, 18
excluded claims, 18
excluded parties, 18
financial eligibility, 18
payment of moneys
recovered direct to
LAA, 19
prospects of success
criterion, 18–19
range of services
covered, 17–18
revocation or discharge, 20
role of Legal Aid
Agency, 17
statutory charges, 19
Legal expenses insurance
after the event litigation
insurance (ATE)
insurance, 13
before the event litigation
expenses insurance
(BTE), 4
taking on new
instructions, 13
Legal profession
see also **Barristers;**
Solicitors
advice on Part 36
offers, 412–13
business structures, 2
lawyers duties, 2
privilege
communications
connected with
litigation, 354–5
connection with
general duty of
confidentiality, 5
Counsel's endorsement of
orders, 449
experts' reports, 388,
389, 396

first interview with
solicitor, 3
initial instructions, 3
legal advice
privilege, 353–4
overview, 352–3
public interest immunity
distinguished, 358
search orders, 497–9,
498–9
waiver, 356–7
waiver by client, 356
wasted costs, 527
witness statements, 368
rights of audience, 436
split between solicitors and
barristers, 2
wasted costs orders
general principles, 526–8
non-attendance at
CMCs, 319
non-disclosure, 296
transfers of
proceedings, 25
Limitations
see also **Time limits**
accrual of cause of action
contractual
claims, 236–8
contribution claims, 241
conversion, 239
defective products, 241
fatal accidents, 240–1
general claims in
tort, 238–9
general rules, 235
mortgage shortfalls, 236
personal injury
claims, 239–40
statutory debts, 236
title to land, 235–6
trespass and libel, 239
acknowledgments and
part-payments, 244
acquiescence, 247–8
amendments with
permission
adding defendants close
to expiry, 253
after expiry of
limitations, 254–9
calculation of time periods
concealment, 242
fraud, 242
general rules, 241
latent damage, 243

mistake, 242–3
persons under
disability, 242
compliance with pre-action
protocols, 55
cross-border
mediation, 244
effect of issue of claim, 6
extensions of time
defamation, 244
judicial review, 244
personal injury
claims, 244–7
fair trial (Art 6), 43
fatal accidents
date of knowledge, 241
general claims in
tort, 238
international law rules, 235
laches, 247–8
overview, 231
Part 20 claims, 228
problems in personal
injuries claims, 234
problems in trusts and
equity claims, 233–4
road traffic claims for
personal injuries under
£25.000, 109
special cases cases, 232–5
time periods, 231–2
Lis pendens, 128, 336
Listing for trial
adjournments, 428
on the different
tracks, 424
fast track cases
case summaries, 315
court requirements,
314–15
directions, 312–13
trial bundles, 315
trial timetable, 315
form and content of
questionnaire, 425–7
general procedure, 9
multi-track cases
fixing the trial date, 322
listing hearings, 323
overview, 424
pre-trial checklists, 424–8
pre-trial reviews, 428
Royal Courts of
Justice, 428
sanctions to preserve trial
date, 416

Lists of documents
'disclosure statements', 349
form and contents, 348–9
lost and destroyed
documents, 350
standard disclosure,
339–41
Litigants in person
rights of audience, 436
rules of procedure, 213–14
Litigation friends
certificate of
suitability, 206
child settlement
applications, 108, 207
children attaining 18, 207
costs, 516
general principles, 205
investment of funds, 208
protected parties, 207
Litigation funding
consideration at first
interview with
solicitor, 4
general principles, 16–17
Locus standi
judicial review, 549
winding-up petitions, 93
Lord Chancellor
approval of Practice
Directions, 33
costs orders against, 20,
46, 69
notice of claims against
judiciary, 45
notice of costs liability, 520
Losses
consideration at first
interview with
solicitor, 3
human rights claims, 46
schedule attached to
particulars of
claim, 154
**Lost and destroyed
documents**, 350

M

Magistrates' courts
composition and
administration, 22
general jurisdiction, 22
jurisdiction, 25
Maintenance
litigation funding, 14
Mandatory orders, 551

McKenzie friends
litigants in person, 213
rights of audience and
representation, 436–7
Mediation
adjudicative and non-
adjudicative processes
compared, 111–12
advantages for international
disputes, 113
contract terms for
references, 114–15
costs, 114
cross-border
mediation, 244
disclosure orders, 508
Small Claims Mediation
Service
form of ADR, 116
track allocation, 173
Medical evidence
road traffic claims for
personal injuries under
£25.000, 104
Menu option disclosure
agreed proposals, 347
applicability, 345
case management
conferences, 347
directions, 347–8
form of report, 346
train of inquiry
documents, 320–1
Mere witness rule, 504
Mistakes *see* **Errors and
mistakes**
Modes of address
County Court, 23
High Court, 24
magistrates' courts, 22
Money claims
default judgments
final judgments, 141–2
general rule, 139–40
permission
required, 140–1
enforcement of judgments
administration
orders, 538
attachment of
earnings, 539–40
charging orders, 540–2
general provisions, 5
34–5
insolvency, 543

obtaining information
from debtors, 535–6
taking control of
goods, 536–7
third party debt
orders, 538–9
issue of claim forms
County Court, 65–6
online claims, 66
judgments and payments by
instalments, 452
Part 36 offers and
payments, 406
registration of
judgments, 457
transfers of
proceedings, 135–6
Money laundering
consideration at first
interview with
solicitor, 3
privilege against self-
incrimination, 352
Motor Insurers Bureau, 56–7,
100
Multi-track cases
see also **Fast track cases;
Small claims
cases**
agreed directions, 317–19
case management
conferences, 319–22
costs management, 184–5
directions at other
hearings, 324–5
disclosure
alternative paths, 342–3
menu option
disclosure, 345
timing, 342
listing for trial
CPR requirements, 424
fixing the trial date, 322
listing hearings, 323
overview, 317
Part 8 Claims, 90
pre-trial checklists, 322–3
pre-trial reviews, 323–4
procedural judges, 163
rules based on financial
value, 175
variation of timetable, 325
Multiple parties
costs, 514–15
disadvantages of ADR, 113

interim payments, 292–3
joinder
  criteria for
    decision, 214–15
  separate trials, 215
  statutory provisions, 214
misjudged failure to accept
  Pt 36 offer, 411
renewal of process, 87
representative
  proceedings, 215–16
response to requests
  for further
  information, 200

N

Ne exeat regno **writs,** 492
Negligence claims
accrual of cause of
  action, 238
particulars of claim, 151–4
pre-action protocol, 49–51
summary judgments, 284
Negotiation, 111
No case submissions, 438–9
Nominal claimants, 301
Non-attendance
interim hearings, 275
small claims hearings, 308
at trial, 442
Non-disclosure *see* **Disclosure**
Non-parties
amendment to parties
  after expiry of
  limitations, 258
costs orders against, 526
disclosure orders, 342,
  507–8
intervention, 216–17
Part 20 claims, 229
Part 20 claims
  distinguished, 222
winding-up petitions, 96
witness summonses, 383
Norwich Pharmacal **orders**
Bankers Trust orders *see*
  Bankers Trust **orders**
mere witness rule, 504
overview of related
  orders, 510
principles for
  granting, 501–2
procedure, 503
protection for journalists'
  sources, 502–3
specialized procedures, 342

Notification injunctions,
  489–90

O

Offers to settle
Calderbank offers
  format and effect, 400
  pre-action offers, 57
  without prejudice
    communications, 57
overview, 399–400
Part 36 offers and
  payments *see* **Part 36
  offers and payments**
Online claims, 66
Opening speeches, 437
Orders *see also* **Judgments**
conditional orders
  relationship with interim
    payments, 293
  security for costs, 300
  summary
    judgments, 279,
    288–9
consent orders
  administrative consent
    orders, 455–6
  approval by court, 456
  Chancery Division
    rules, 456
  child settlement
    applications, 108
  contribution claims, 241
  judicial review, 558
  Part 8 Claims, 207
  real contract and
    simple submission
    distinguished, 450–1
  stays on settlement, 336
  Tomlin orders, 451
costs
  duty to inform client of
    liability, 520
  failure to comply
    with pre-action
    protocol, 55
  general principles,
    512–14
  impact of costs
    management, 189–90
  interim costs
    orders, 518–20
  legally aided
    litigants, 525–6
  against Lord
    Chancellor, 20, 46.69

non-parties, 526
pro bono costs
  orders, 526
against publicly funded
  litigants, 20
range of possible
  orders, 517–18
setting aside default
  judgments, 145–6
wasted costs
  orders, 526–8
costs capping orders
  Aarhus Convention
    cases, 194–5
  Beddoe orders, 192–3
  cost limitation
    orders, 195
  form and contents, 192
  general rules, 191–2
  judicial review, 194
  protective costs
    orders, 193–4
costs management
  approval of budgets, 188
  nature of orders, 187
disclosure
  alternative paths, 342–3
  Bankers Trust orders *see*
    Bankers Trust **orders**
  failure to disclose, 360
  'key of the warehouse'
    orders, 320–1
  mediation evidence, 508
  non-parties, 507–8
  Norwich Pharmacal
    orders *see* *Norwich
    Pharmacal* **orders**
  objections to disclosure
    or inspection, 360
  before proceedings
    start, 505–7
  specialized
    procedures, 342
  specific disclosure or
    inspection, 360–1
  train of inquiry
    documents, 320–1
drawing up, 455–7
format and contents, 450
freezing injunctions *see*
  Freezing injunctions
group litigation orders, 219
injunctions *see* **Injunctions**
inspection of
  property, 508–9

Orders *see also* **Judgments**
    (*Cont.*)
  interim applications
    delivery-up of
      goods, 509
    draft orders, 272
    judicial review, 556
    made on the court's own
      initiative, 274
    overview, 261–2
    pre-action
      applications, 263
    varying or revoking, 276
    without notice
      applications, 264–5
  interim injunctions *see*
    Interim injunctions
  interim payments, *see*
    Interim payments
  made at hearings, 449–50
  response to requests
    for further
    information, 200–1
  search orders *see* **Search
    orders**
  security for costs *see*
    Security for costs
  setting aside default
    judgments
    consequential
      orders, 146
    costs, 145–6
  striking out *see* **Striking
    out**
  summary judgments, 279
    conditional orders, 279,
      288–9
    equitable relief, 290
  time limits, 450
  Tomlin orders, 451
  for trial of preliminary
    issues
    overview, 440
    practice, 441
    procedure, 440–1
  winding-up orders, 97–8
Originating processes *see* **Part
  8 Claims**
Overriding objective
  active case management
    cases generally, 35–6
    increasing use of
      technology, 36
    interim applications, 36
    provisions of CPR, 35
  application in practice

    ensuring cooperation
      between parties, 40
    ensuring parties are on
      equal footing, 39
    first rule in the CPR, 38
    good use of the court's
      resources, 40
    justice as primary
      concern, 38–9
    proportionality, 39
    saving expense, 39–40
  case management, 162
  early interim
    applications, 263–4
  importance, 32
  interpretation of CPR, 37
  provisions of CPR, 34–5
  small claims track, 306

P

Part 20 claims
  alternative procedures
    distinguished, 221–2
  applicable situations
    Civil Procedure
      Rules, 222
    contributions, 223
    counterclaims, 222–3
    discretionary cases,
      225–6
    indemnities, 223–4
    related questions, 224–5
    'some other remedy', 224
  case management, 229–30
  contributions
    notices, 228
    procedure, 228
  costs, 516
  default judgments, 229
  limitations, 228
  nature of claim, 221
  non-parties, 229
  recast Judgments
    Regulation, 124
  relation to main claim, 230
  statements of case
    example, 227–8
    particulars of claim, 226
    prescribed forms, 226
    subsequent statements of
      case, 226
**Part 36 offers and
  payments**, 401–5
  acceptance
    late acceptance, 408
    notice, 407

    part claims, 408
    permission, 408–9
    stays, 407
    time for payment, 407
    during trial, 408
  appeal court powers, 573
  appeals, 413
  defence of tender before
    claim, 406–7
  failure to comply
    with pre-action
    protocol, 56
  form and contents, 401–5
  formalities
    effect of defects, 406
    statutory
      requirements, 400
  legal advice on offers,
    412–13
  misjudged failure to accept
    damages, costs, and
      interest, 410–11
    multiple defendants, 411
  misjudged failure to accept
    Pt 36 offer
    offers by claimants, 411
    offers by
      defendants, 411
    unjust to apply usual
      rule, 412
  money claims, 406
  non-disclosure to
    judge, 413
  Part 36 offers and
    payments
    failure to file costs
      budget, 412
  personal injury claims, 406
  pre-action procedures,
    57–8
  qualified one-way costs
    shifting, 531
  rejection, 409
  service, 407
  solicitor's duty to advise, 4
  terms
    clarification, 407
    requirement to state, 406
  timing, 400
  withdrawal and amendment
    effect, 410
    timing, 409
Part 7 claims
  conversion of
    judicial review
    proceedings, 557

costs management, 184
default judgments
    excluded cases, 138–9
    time limit, 137–8
    general use for disputed
        claims, 89, 90
    personal injury claims
        under £25000
        amendment of Part
            8 claims, 90, 102,
            107–8, 108
        cases dropping out of
            RTA protocol, 110
        fixed costs, 109
    statements of case, 147
Part 8 Claims
    applicability, 89–90
    assessment of damages for
        small PI claims
        acknowledgments of
            service, 107–8
    directions, 108
    overview of
        procedure, 106–7
    transfers of
        proceedings, 108
    withdrawal of admissions
        and offers, 108
    case management, 90
    costs management, 184–5
    evidence in support, 90
    issue and service, 90
    overview, 89
    unavailability of default
        judgments, 138
Part-payments, 244
Particulars of claim
    see also **Statements of case**
    details of claimant's
        case, 7
    formal written statement of
        claim, 62
    forms and content, 151–4
    Part 20 claims, 226
    service, 68
Parties
    amendments with
        permission
        adding defendants, 253
        after expiry of
            limitations, 255–7
        changes to parties,
            252–3
    assignment of claims,
        218–19
    bankruptcy, 208–9

bodies suing in own
    names, 211–12
companies, 210
consolidation of
    claims, 217
deceased parties, 209
descriptions
    according to
        proceedings, 203
    heading of statements of
        case and other court
        documents, 203–4
errors and mistakes, 203
foreign parties, 212
group litigation orders, 219
individuals, 204
insurers, 204–5
intervention by non-
    parties, 216–17
joinder
    criteria for
        decision, 214–15
    separate trials, 215
    statutory provisions, 214
litigants in person, 213–14
multiple parties
    disadvantages of
        ADR, 113
    renewal of process, 87
    response to requests
        for further
        information, 200
in name of Attorney-
    General, 212
notice of track
    allocation, 176
overriding objective, 39
partnerships, 209
persons under
    disability, 205–8
persons unknown
    Part 8 Claims, 216
    proceedings against, 213
representative
    proceedings, 215–16
rights established by fair
    trial (Art 6), 42
stakeholder claims
    application
        procedure, 217–18
    controlled and executed
        goods, 218
    defined, 217
trusts, 208
unincorporated
    associations, 212

vexatious litigants, 214
    against whom security for
        costs is ordered, 299
Partnerships
    acknowledgments of
        service, 210
    description of parties, 209
    disclosure of partners
        names, 210
    enforcement of
        judgments, 210
    service of documents, 210
Patents Court, 30
Payments, *see* **Interim
    payments**, *see* **Part 36
    offers and payments**
Performance bonds, 287–8
**Periodic payments
    awards**, 454
Permission
    acceptance of Part 36
        offers, 408–9
    amendments with
        adding defendants, 253
        after expiry of
            limitations, 254–9
        changes to parties,
            252–3
        costs, 252
        general principles, 250–2
        merits of case, 252
        procedure, 259–60
    amendments without,
        249–50
    appeals
        amendments, 567–8
        application
            procedure, 562–3
        exceptions, 562
        grounds for appeal to
            Court of Appeal, 563
        grounds for first
            appeal, 563
        limiting issues to be
            heard, 563
        refusals, 563–4
        requirement for
            permission to
            appeal, 561–2
    assumed jurisdiction rules
        grounds for granting
            permission, 125
        principles governing
            permission, 124
        procedure for seeking
            permission, 127

Permission (*Cont.*)
  default judgments, 140–1
  discontinuance of
    claim, 334
  group litigation orders, 219
  judicial review
    acknowledgments of
      service, 554–5
    appeals against
      refusal, 555
    grounds for
      granting, 555
    issue of claim
      forms, 553–4
    reconsideration, 555
    service of claim
      forms, 554
    time limits, 553
    two-stage
      application, 553
  Part 20 claims
    contribution notices, 228
    non-parties, 229
  sequestration writs, 546
  withdrawal of
    admissions, 380–1
Personal injury claims
  see also **Fatal accidents**
  under £25,000
    child settlements, 108–9
    claim notification, 101
    commencement of
      process, 101–3
    CRU certificates, 103
    excluded cases, 100–1
    failure to
      compromise, 106
    fixed costs, 103, 109
    interim payments, 104
    limitations, 109
    litigants in person, 104
    medical evidence, 104
    overview, 99–100
    Part 8 Claims
      to determine
        quantum, 106–8
    payments, 106
    response by defendant's
      insurers, 103
    RTA pre-action
      protocol, 101
    settlement
      negotiations, 105–6
    settlement packs, 105
    valuing claim, 100

  when protocol ceases to
    apply, 109–10
  amendment to parties
    after expiry of
      limitations, 257
  commencement of
    proceedings, 6
  excluded from public
    funding, 18
  interim payments
    certificate of recoverable
      benefits, 295
  judgments
    dishonest claims, 454–5
    periodic payments
      awards, 454
    provisional
      damages, 452–4
    recoupment of
      benefits, 452
  jurisdiction, 27–8
  limitation periods
    accrual of cause of
      action, 239–40
    extensions of time,
      244–7
    problems in personal
      injuries claims, 234
    statutory provisions, 232
  medical
    examinations, 395–6
  Part 36 offers and
    payments, 406
  particulars of claim, 151–4
  pre-action protocol, 52–3
  privacy (Art 8), 44
  qualified one-way costs
    shifting
    see also **Qualified one-
      way costs shifting**
  standard disclosure, 344
Personal service
  prescribed hierarchy for
    service, 68
  procedure, 76
Persons under disability
  affidavits, 370–1
  costs
    orders against, 516
    summary
      assessment, 522
    third party
      indemnities, 516
  default judgments, 140
  defined, 205

  discontinuance, 334
  instructions to medical
    expert, 54
  interim payments, 291
  limitations, 242, 245
  litigation friends, 205–6
  periodic payments, 454
  track allocation, 27
Persons unknown
  Part 8 Claims, 216
  proceedings against, 213
Petitions
  forms and content, 91
  hearings, 91
  scope, 91
  unavailability of default
    judgments, 138
  winding-up petitions
    advertisement, 96
    certificates of
      compliance, 96
    commencement of
      proceedings, 94
    disputed claims, 96
    forms and content, 94–5
    hearings, 97
    other creditors, 96
    service, 95–6
    statutory demands, 92–3
    statutory provisions, 91
    winding-up orders, 97–8
Points of law
  appeals
    grounds for
      permission, 574
    leapfrog appeals to the
      Supreme Court, 561
    procedure, 565
  statements of case, 149
  summary judgments, 282,
    284
Possession of land *see* **Land
  claims**
Postal service
  prescribed hierarchy for
    service, 68
  procedure, 76
Practice directions, 33
Pre-action correspondence,
  5–6
Pre-action procedures
  admissions of liability, 380
  disclosure orders, 342,
    505–7
  interim applications, 263

interim injunctions, 459–61

Part 36 offers and payments, 57–8

Pre-action protocols

appointment of experts, 53–5

cases not covered protocols, 49

difficulties with limitations, 55

disclosure of experts' reports, 389

general requirements, 48

judicial review, 552

personal injury claims, 52–3

professional negligence, 49–51

published protocols and their scope, 48–9

road traffic claims

Motor Insurers Bureau, 56–7

notification of insurers, 56

road traffic claims for personal injuries under £25.000

child settlements, 108–9

claim notification, 101

commencement of process, 101–3

CRU certificates, 103

excluded cases, 100–1

failure to compromise, 106

fixed costs, 103, 109

interim payments, 104

limitations, 109

litigants in person, 104

medical evidence, 104

Part 8 Claims

to determine quantum, 106–8

payments, 106

response by defendant's insurers, 103

settlement negotiations, 105–6

settlement packs, 105

valuing claim, 100

when protocol ceases to apply, 109–10

sanctions, 55–6, 414

Pre-trial checklists

case management, 179–80

discontinuance, 312, 322

fast track cases, 312

listing for trial, 424–8

multi-track cases, 322–3

Pre-trial reviews

listing for trial, 428

multi-track cases, 323–4

Precedent, 38

Preliminary issues orders

overview, 440

practice, 441

procedure, 440–1

Privacy (Art 8)

see also **Confidentiality**

interim injunctions, 469, 470

scope of protection, 43–4

Private hearings

advantages of ADR, 112

general rule, 435–6

Privilege

see also **Public interest immunity**

effect on disclosure, 350

experts' reports, 388–9

legal professional privilege

communications connected with litigation, 354–5

connection with general duty of confidentiality, 5

Counsel's endorsement of orders, 449

experts' reports, 388, 389, 396

first interview with solicitor, 3

initial instructions, 3

legal advice privilege, 353–4

overview, 352–3

public interest immunity distinguished, 358

search orders, 497–9, 498–9

waiver, 356–7

waiver by client, 356

wasted costs, 527

witness statements, 368

mistake in allowing inspection, 358

objections to disclosure, 360

search orders, 498–9

secondary evidence, 357–8

against self-incrimination

common law rule, 350–1

limitations on rule, 351–2

search orders, 498–9

waiver of privilege, 356–7

'without prejudice' privilege

alternative dispute resolution, 116

Calderbank offers, 400

discussion between experts, 394

general principles, 355–6

mediation evidence, 508

Part 36 offers, 399

pre-action Part 36 offers, 57

response to letter before action, 51

withdrawn Part 36 offers, 410

Pro bono **costs orders,** 526

Procedural judges, 163, 312

Professional negligence

accrual of cause of action, 238

pre-action protocol, 49–51

Prohibitory orders, 551–2

Proof

see also **Evidence**

documents, 383–4

impecuniosity justifying security for costs, 301

interim payments, 293

notices to admit facts

costs, 381–3

form and contents, 382

purpose, 381

uses, 381

summary judgments, 282

Proportionality

assessment of costs, 521–2

case management, 162

costs capping orders, 192

interim applications, 262

overriding objective, 39

small claims track, 306

Protected parties *see* **Persons under disability**

Protective costs orders (PCOs), 193–4

Protocols *see* Pre-action
  protocols
Provisional damages
  awards, 452–4
Public funding *see* Legal aid
Public interest immunity
  see also Privilege
  controlling the costs of
    disclosure, 338
  general principles, 358
  Ministerial
    certificates, 358–9
  Norwich Pharmacal
    orders, 456
  objections to
    disclosure, 360
  other confidential
    information, 359
  redacted judgments, 456
Public liability *see* Employers'
  liability and public
  liability

Q
Qualified one-way costs
  shifting
  applicable cases, 529–30
  effects
    claimant loses case, 530
    claimant partially
      successful, 530–1
    credit scoring, 531
    failure to equal Part 36
      offer, 531
    interim costs orders, 531
  loss of protection
    fraudulent claims, 532
    proceedings for the
      financial benefit of
      another, 532–3
    striking out, 531–2
  overview, 529
Quashing orders, 551
Quasi-governmental public
  bodies, 211–12
Queen's Bench Division
  allocation of business
    between divisions, 28
  certification of
    judgments, 450
  composition and
    administration, 23
  docketing, 25
  issue of claim forms, 65
  jury trials, 441
Questionnaires

directions questionnaires
  failure to comply with
    notice, 164–73
  filing, 164
  forms and
    content, 164–72
  listing for trial, 322

R
Reading lists
  time for lodging, 271
  trial bundles, 433
Real evidence, 373
Reasoned decisions, 42
  fair trial (Art 6), 42
Recast Judgments Regulation
  co-defendants, 123–4
  commencement of
    proceedings, 124
  contractual disputes, 122–3
  counterclaims, 124
  determination of
    international
    jurisdiction, 121
  disputing jurisdiction upon
    receipt of c
    laim, 135
  domicile, 121–2
  exclusive jurisdiction, 120
  Part 20 claims, 124
  scope, 121
  tort claims, 123
  trusts, 123
Receivership
  nature of receivership, 544
  procedure, 544
Reconsidered judgments, 456
Redacted judgments, 456
References to CJEU
  costs, 447
  discretionary
    references, 444–6
  mandatory
    references, 443–4
  procedure in CJEU, 447
  procedure in
    England, 446–7
  relevant questions, 443
Remedies *see* Enforcement
Renewal of process
  appeals, 88
  applications
    after expiry of validity
      period, 86
    during period of
      validity, 85–6

without notice
  applications, 87
  cargo claims, 87
  multiple defendants, 87
  overview, 84
  power to review, 84–5
  during stay, 87
Reply and defence to
  counterclaims, 159
Representative proceedings
  rules of procedure, 215–16
  unincorporated bodies, 212
Requests for further
  information
  example, 199–200
  form and contents, 197–8
  multiple parties, 200
  objecting to request, 200
  orders, 200–1
  overview, 196
  responses on form
    provided, 198
  scope of response, 200,
    201–2
Rescission
  equitable remedy, 114
  summary judgments, 290
Responding to claims
  see also Default judgments
  acknowledgments of
    service, 133–4
  Admiralty Court, 136
  admissions, 132–3
  appeals, 566–7
  Commercial Court, 136
  defences, 133
  disputing service or
    jurisdiction, 134–5
  failure to respond or enter
    default judgment, 146
  overview, 132
  service outside
    jurisdiction, 128
  Technology and
    Construction Court
    (TCC), 136
  time limits, 132
  transfers of
    proceedings, 135–6
Retainers
  client care letter, 10–11
  discussion at first
    interview, 4
  example
    arrangement, 11–13

expert witnesses, 391
termination, 511
Right to respect for private and family life *see* **Privacy (Art 8)**
Rights of audience
general rules, 436
McKenzie friends, 436–7
Road traffic claims
particulars of claim, 151–4
pre-action protocol for claims under £25,000
child settlements, 108–9
claim notification, 101
commencement of process, 101–3
CRU certificates, 103
excluded cases, 100–1
failure to compromise, 106
fixed costs, 103, 109
interim payments, 104
limitations, 109
litigants in person, 104
medical evidence, 104
Part 8 Claims to determine quantum, 106–8
payments, 106
response by defendant's insurers, 103
settlement negotiations, 105–6
settlement packs, 105
valuing claim, 100
when protocol ceases to apply, 109–10
pre-action protocols
Motor Insurers Bureau, 56–7
notification of insurers, 56
Rolls Building, 24, 83, 177, 181
case management, 178
listing, 428
multi-track cases, 317
pilot schemes to reduce costs, 181–2
Royal Courts of Justice, 24, 163, 178, 569
case management, 178
listing, 428
multi-track cases, 317
pilot schemes to reduce costs, 181–2

Rules *see* **Civil Procedure Rules**

S
Sanctions
see also **Default judgments**
alternative dispute resolution, 116–17
application procedure, 416–18
Civil Procedure Rules, 414–15
directions, 415–16
extensions of time, 419–20
failure to comply with directions notice, 164–73
failure to file costs budgets, 187
implied sanctions doctrine, 422–3
non-payment of hearing fees, 180
pre-action protocols, 55–6, 414
preservation of trial date, 416
relief and setting aside, 419–20
unless orders, 418
disclosure, 360
failure to file statement of truth, 418
general principles, 418
implied sanctions doctrine, 422
non-compliance, 418–19
setting aside judgment, 420–1
varying directions timetable, 314
without notice applications, 264
Sanderson **orders**, 515
Scott schedule, 147, 160
Search orders
collateral use, 500
form of order, 496
levels of judiciary, 24
meaning and scope, 493
post-execution reports, 499–500
practice on execution, 496–8
pre-action applications, 263

principles for granting overview, 494–5
real risk of destruction of evidence, 495–6
privilege, 498–9
procedure, 493–4
specialized procedures, 342
variation or discharge, 499
Security for costs
alternatives to orders, 305
appeals, 301–2, 567
applicable parties, 299
appropriate amount, 304–5
exercise of discretion
delay, 303
impecunious companies, 304
pre-CPR cases, 302
prospect of success at trial, 302–3
stifling of genuine claim, 303
form of application, 297–9
necessary conditions
claimant trying to avoid enforcement, 301
impecunious companies, 301
nominal claimants, 301
overview, 299–300
residence outside jurisdiction, 300–1
overview, 297
procedure, 297–9
repayment after trial, 305
residence outside jurisdiction, 303–4
Self-incrimination privilege
common law rule, 350–1
limitations on rule, 351–2
search orders, 498–9
Sequestration writs, 546
Service
appeals
notice of appeal, 566
respondent's notice, 567
applications for permission for judicial review, 554
certificates of service
form and contents, 81–2
requirement to file, 80
claim forms and 'response pack'
addresses for service, 74–5

Service (*Cont.*)
companies, 75
deemed date of
service, 78–9
dispensing with
service, 78
hierarchy of service
methods, 68–74
importance, 66
methods of effecting
service, 75–8
overview, 6
period of validity, 67–8
relevant
documents, 68–73
disputing service upon
receipt of
claim, 134–5
documents other than claim
forms
available methods of
service, 79
deemed date of
service, 79–80
irregular service, 80–2
with notice interim
applications, 272–3
outside jurisdiction
assumed
jurisdiction, 124–7
cases outside general
rules, 120–1
default judgments, 131
foreign defendants within
jurisdiction, 119
interim relief, 130–1
preventing
conflicts, 128–30
recast Judgments
Regulation, 121–4
service abroad, 127–8
submission to
jurisdiction, 119–20
overseas companies, 210–11
Part 36 offers and
payments, 407
Part 8 Claims
claim forms, 90
evidence in support, 90
partnerships, 210
persons under
disability, 207
renewal of process *see*
Renewal of process
search orders, 496–7

winding-up petitions, 95–6
Set-offs
see also **Counterclaims**
costs orders, 518
general principles, 158–9
interim payments, 294
summary judgments, 285
Setting aside
appeals, 568
default judgments
Civil Procedure
Rules, 143
on conditions, 145–6
defendants outside
jurisdiction, 145
discretionary
procedure, 143–4
good reasons, 144–5
relief from
sanctions, 145
as of right, 143
non-attendance at small
claims hearings, 308
notice of
discontinuance, 335
relief from
sanctions, 419–20
Settlements
appeals, 569
bar to later
proceedings, 332–3
overview, 448–9
persons under
disability, 207–8
road traffic claims for
personal injuries under
£25,000
child settlements, 108–9
payments, 106
settlement
negotiations, 105–6
settlement packs, 105–6
stays at case management
stage, 177
Single joint experts
reports, 390–1
at trial, 396–7
Skeleton arguments
see also **Case summaries**
appeals
applicant's, 565
respondent's, 567
judicial review, 556–7
with notice interim
applications, 271

trial bundles, 433
Slip rule, 456–7
Small claims cases
see also **Fast track cases;**
Multi-track cases
Small Claims Mediation
Service
form of ADR, 116
track allocation, 173
Small claims track
appeals, 565
costs, 308–9
directions
special directions, 307
standard directions, 307
disapplication of some CPR
rules, 306
hearings
determination without
hearing, 308
final hearings, 308
interim payments, 291
listing for trial, 424
non-attendance, 308
proportionality, 306
rules based on financial
value, 174–5
Solicitors
see also **Barristers; Legal**
profession
barristers distinguished, 2
business structures, 2
champerty and
maintenance, 14
disclosure
responsibilities, 341
duties to LAA, 20
duty of confidentiality, 5
duty to inform client of
costs liability, 520
funding
duty to advise, 10–11
payments on account, 10
professional duties, 10
retainers, 11–13
general duties, 2
initial instructions
first interview, 3–4
written instructions, 4
overriding objective
to ensure
cooperation, 40
pre-action
correspondence, 5–6
search orders

post-execution
reports, 499–500
supervision, 493
**Solicitors regulation Authority
(SRA)**
consideration of fee
arrangements, 3
duty to advise on
funding, 10–11
lawyers duties, 2
Sources of law
court guides, 33
judiciary, 33
practice directions, 33
statutory sources, 32–3
'Special advocates', 436
Specialist courts
Administrative Court
damages for breach of
human rights, 46
general organization, 24
human rights
claims, 46–7
judicial review, 548, 558
jurisdiction, 30
specialist claim
forms, 62, 65
Admiralty Court
composition and
administration, 23–4
issue of claim forms, 6
jurisdiction, 30
responding to
claims, 136
business and property
courts
Administrative Court, 30
Admiralty Court, 30
Commercial
Court, 29–30
Companies Court, 30
electronic filing, 264
organization of High
Court, 24, 29
Patents Court, 30
Technology and
Construction Court
(TCC), 29
Circuit Commercial Court
case management, 174
default judgments, 138
general organization, 29
jurisdiction, 30
Commercial Court
composition and
administration, 23–4

default judgments, 138
docketing, 25
issue of claim forms, 6
jurisdiction, 29–30
responding to
claims, 136
security for costs, 305
specialist claim
forms, 62–5
time limit for response to
claim, 6
trial bundles, 174
Companies Court
composition and
administration, 23–4
jurisdiction, 30
Patents Court, 30
Technology and
Construction Court
(TCC)
case management, 173–4
composition and
administration, 23–4
issue of claim forms, 6
jurisdiction, 29
responding to
claims, 136
specialist claim
forms, 62
Specific performance
costs, 308
County Court
jurisdiction, 27
equitable remedies, 247
summary judgments, 290
Stakeholder claims
application
procedure, 217–18
controlled and executed
goods, 218
defined, 217
Standard disclosure
'control' defined, 344–5
directions to limit, 345
'document' defined, 344
electronic
documents, 344
form of list, 339–41
relevant documents, 343–4
Standing
judicial review, 549
winding-up petitions, 93
Statements of case
see also **Defences;
Particulars of claim**
after reply, 159

description of
parties, 203–4
disclosure of documents
mentioned in, 361
dispensing with, 159
factual contentions, 6–7
filing at court, 82–3
forms and content
content, 148–50
final endorsements, 150
headings, 148
physical form, 148
statement of
truth, 150–1
supporting
documentation, 150
human rights claims, 41,
45
overview, 147–8
Part 20 claims
example, 227–8
particulars of claim, 226
prescribed forms, 226
subsequent statements of
case, 226
requests for further
information
collateral use, 202
example, 199–200
form and
contents, 197–8
multiple parties, 200
objecting to request, 200
orders, 200–1
overview, 196
responses on form
provided, 198
scope of response, 200,
201–2
Scott schedule, 147, 160
use at trial, 161
Statutory charges, 19
Statutory demands
compliance, 93
forms and content, 92–3
Stays
see also **Adjournments;
Discontinuance;
Striking out**
acceptance of Part 36
offers, 407
appeals, 568
case management
for ADR, 177
general power, 336
settlements, 177

Stays (*Cont.*)
commencement of second
claim, 327
effect on renewal of
process, 87
enforcement of money
judgments, 535
enforcement of orders, 337
failure to comply
with pre-action
protocol, 55
failure to respond or enter
default judgment, 146
forum non
conveniens, 129–30
pending proceedings, 336
to protect concurrent
claims, 337
on settlement, 336
summary judgments, 279,
289
Striking out
see also **Discontinuance;**
Sanctions; Stays
abuse of process
collateral attacks, 331
CPR provisions, 330
general examples, 330–1
relitigation, 331–2
appeals, 568
application procedure
by court officials, 328
by parties, 327–8
consequential
orders, 333–4
failure to disclose
sustainable claim or
defence, 329–30
general principles, 328–9
main rule
commencement of
second claim, 327
CPR provisions, 327
no subsequent interim
applications, 327
non-payment of hearing
fees, 180
obstructions of
justice, 333–4
overview, 326
Part 20 claims, 230
qualified one-way costs
shifting, 531–2
settlements as bar to later
proceedings, 332–3

summary judgments, 279
winding-up petitions, 96
Submission to jurisdiction
filing acknowledgment of
service, 134–5
recast Judgments
Regulation, 119–20
Summary judgments
see also **Default judgments**
admissions, 288
allegations of reprehensible
conduct, 284
amendments at
hearing, 289
applications
form of notice, 280–1
timing of, 277–8
avoidance of mini-
trials, 283–4
burden of proof, 282
cases with no real prospect
of success, 282
cheque rule, 285–8
complex claims, 284
conditional
orders, 288–9
contractual claims, 284
counterclaims, 285
defences with real prospect
of success, 282–3
defendant's
application, 278
directions, 290
excluded claims, 278–9
fair trial (Art 6), 43
hearings, 278
negligence claims, 284
orders, 279
overview, 277
Part 20 claims, 230
partial defences, 285
points of law, 284
procedure, 279
refusal if compelling reason
for trial, 289–90
relationship with interim
payments, 293
set-offs, 285
statutory
considerations, 282
stays, 289
weak defences, 283
Super injunctions, 470
Supreme Court
appeals to, 573–4

failure to apply new
procedural code, 37
leapfrog appeals, 561
references to CJEU, 446
rules of precedent, 38, 41

T
Technology and Construction
Court (TCC)
case management, 173–4
composition and
administration, 23–4
issue of claim forms, 6
jurisdiction, 29
responding to claims, 136
specialist claim forms, 62
Tender before claim, 406–7,
413
Third parties
additional claims under
Pt 20
alternative procedures
distinguished, 221–2
applicable
situations, 222–6
nature of claim, 221
costs, 516
enforcement of money
judgments, 538–9
funding
consideration at first
interview with
solicitor, 4
general principles, 16–17
interveners in judicial
review, 556
Time limits
see also **Limitations;**
Pre-action protocols
appeals
extensions of time, 564
general rule, 564
applications for permission
for judicial
review, 553
disputing service or
jurisdiction, 134
entering default
judgments, 137–8
expressed by date, 450
extensions of time
defences, 134
fair trial (Art 6), 43
limitation periods, 231–2
responding to
claims, 132

response to claim, 6
service of claim forms, 67–8
Tomlin orders, 451, 455, 457
Track allocation
see also **Case management;
Fast track cases;
Multi-track cases;
Small claims cases**
changing tracks, 178–9
claims with no financial
value, 176
directions, 176–7
discretionary factors, 176
disposal hearings, 142
effect on costs, 525
fast track cases *see* **Fast
track cases**
general procedure, 8
multi-track cases *see* **Multi-
track cases**
non-payment of hearing
fees, 180
notice to parties, 176
overview, 162
overview of case
management, 181
Part 8 Claims, 90
particular situations, 173
provisional track
allocation, 164
rules based on financial
value
fast track cases, 175
multi-track cases, 175
primary rules, 174
small claims
track, 174–5
small claims track *see*
Small claims track
timing, 173
timing of summary
judgment, 278
Trade unions, 211
**Train of inquiry
documents**, 320–1
Transfers of proceedings
case management, 178
changing tracks, 178–9
commencement in wrong
court, 28
enforcement of money
judgments, 534–5
group litigation
orders, 219
human rights claims, 45

money claims, 135–6
Part 8 Claims to determine
quantum, 108
track allocation, 173
Trials
see also **Fair trial (Art
6); Hearings**
acceptance of Part 36
offers, 408
allocation of judiciary, 434
case management
pilot schemes to reduce
costs, 181–2
pre-trial checklists, 179–
80
Royal Courts of Justice
or Rolls Building, 178
conduct and procedure
claimant's case, 438
closing speeches, 439
defence case, 439
no case
submissions, 438–9
opening speeches, 437
reopening hearings, 440
role of judge, 439–40
court allocation, 433–4
expert witnesses
concurrent evidence, 397
conflicts with other
evidence, 397
general principles, 396
single joint
experts, 396–7
general procedure, 9
hearsay evidence
assessing the weight of
evidence, 378
credibility, 377–8
general principles, 377
by jury
jurisdiction, 441
procedure, 441–2
listing for trial *see* **Listing
for trial**
non-attendance, 442
non-disclosure of interim
payments, 295–6
overview, 429
of preliminary issues
overview, 440
practice, 441
procedure, 440–1
public or private
hearings, 435–6

rights of audience
general rules, 436
McKenzie f
riends, 436–7
sanctions to preserve trial
date, 416
separate trials for multiple
parties, 215
trial bundles *see* trial
bundles under
Documents
use of statements of
case, 161
witness statements
as evidence-in-chief at
trial, 369
exchange of witness
statements, 368
witness summonses
mere witness rule, 504
non-parties, 383
reluctant witnesses,
428–31
Tribunals
fair trial (Art 6), 41–2
general jurisdiction, 22
relevance of ECtHR
judgments, 41
Trusts
Beddoe orders, 192–3
costs, 516
description of
parties, 208
limitation periods
problems in trusts and
equity claims, 233–4
statutory provisions, 232
Part 8 Claims
against persons
unknown, 216
recast Judgments
Regulation, 123

U
Ultimate issue rule, 387–8
**Unincorporated
associations**, 212
Unless orders
case management
sanctions, 418
disclosure, 360
failure to file statement of
truth, 418
implied sanctions
doctrine, 422
non-compliance, 418–19

Unless orders (*Cont.*)
setting aside
judgment, 420–1
varying directions
timetable, 314
without notice
applications, 264

V

**Variation or discharge of
orders**
freezing injunctions, 490–1
interim payments, 296
legal aid funding, 20
search orders, 499
Vexatious litigants, 214

W

Waiver of privilege, 356–7
Wasted costs orders
experts, 398
general principles, 526–8
non-attendance at
CMCs, 319
non-disclosure, 296
transfers of proceedings, 25
Winding-up petitions
advertisement, 96
certificates of
compliance, 96
commencement of
proceedings, 94
disputed claims, 96
enforcement of money
judgments, 543
forms and content, 94–5
hearings, 97
other creditors, 96
service, 95–6
statutory demands
compliance, 93
forms and content, 92–3
winding-up orders, 97–8
With notice applications
interim applications
authorities, 271–2
chronologies and lists of
relevant persons, 272

documents, 270
draft orders, 272
evidence in support, 267,
270
filing of documents at
court, 267
form of
application, 268–9
hearings, 273–4
service, 272–3
skeleton arguments, 271
interim injunctions, 461
super injunctions, 470
undertakings in
damages, 478
Without notice applications
interim applications
full and frank
disclosure, 265–6
hearings, 264–5
orders without
notice, 266
procedure, 264
renewal of process, 87
'Without prejudice' privilege
alternative dispute
resolution, 116
discussion between
experts, 394
general principles, 355–6
mediation evidence, 508
offers to settle
Calderbank offers, 400
Part 36 offers, 399
withdrawn Part 36
offers, 410
pre-action Part 36
offers, 57
response to letter before
action, 51
Witness statements
case management to
control, 368
collateral use, 369
consideration at first
interview with
solicitor, 3

cross-examination
at trial, 369
as evidence-in-chief at
trial, 369
example, 366
exchange of trial
statements, 368
failure to comply with
directions, 368
false witness
statements, 369
fast track
cases, 311
filing at court, 82–3
format, 365–7
interim applications
cross-examination, 366
disclosure in, 366
legal professional
privilege, 368
opposition to winding-up
petitions, 96
overview, 364
proof, 383
Witness summaries, 361, 364,
369, 371, 432
Witnesses
see also **Evidence**
consideration at first
interview with
solicitor, 3
cross-examination
hearsay, 376–7
interim applications,
366
at trial, 369
experts *see* **Experts**
general procedure at
trial, 9
summonses to attend trial
mere witness
rule, 504
non-parties, 383
reluctant witnesses,
428–31
Worldwide injunctions, 474,
484–5